Business Studies 1

Volume I

D1419294

PEARSON CUSTOM PUBLISHING

Business Studies 1
Volume I

Compiled from:

Fundamentals Of Strategy
First Edition
by Gerry Johnson, Richard Whittington And Kevan Scholes

Fundamentals Of Strategy
Second Edition
by Gerry Johnson, Richard Whittington And Kevan Scholes

Managerial Economics: An Analysis Of Business Issues
Third Edition
by Howard Davies and Pun-Lee Lam

Essentials Of Marketing
Fifth Edition
by Jim Blythe

Marketing: An Introduction
Second Edition
by Gary Armstrong, Philip Kotler, Michael Harker and Ross Brennan

Operations And Process Management:
Principles And Practice For Strategic Impact
Third Edition
by Nigel Slack, Alistair Brandon-Jones,
Robert Johnston and Alan Betts

Introduction to Management Science
Eleventh Edition, Global Edition
by Bernard W. Taylor III

PEARSON

Harlow, England • London • New York • Boston • San Francisco • Toronto • Sydney • Auckland • Singapore • Hong Kong
Tokyo • Seoul • Taipei • New Delhi • Cape Town • Sao Paulo • Mexico City • Madrid • Amsterdam • Munich • Paris • Milan

Pearson Education Limited
Edinburgh Gate
Harlow
Essex CM20 2JE

And associated companies throughout the world

Visit us on the World Wide Web at:
www.pearsoned.co.uk

This Custom Book Edition © Pearson Education Limited 2014

Compiled from:

Fundamentals Of Strategy, First Edition
by Gerry Johnson, Richard Whittington And Kevan Scholes
ISBN 978 0 273 71310 4
© Pearson Education Limited 2009

Fundamentals Of Strategy, Second Edition
by Gerry Johnson, Richard Whittington And Kevan Scholes
ISBN 978 0 273 75725 2
© Pearson Education Limited 2009, 2012

Managerial Economics: An Analysis Of Business Issues, Third Edition
by Howard Davies and Pun-Lee Lam
ISBN 978 0 273 64628 0
© Howard Davies 1991
© Howard Davies and Pun-Lee Lam 2001

Essentials Of Marketing, Fifth Edition
by Jim Blythe
ISBN 978 0 273 75768 9
© Financial Times Professional Limited 1998
© Pearson Education Limited 2001, 2012

Marketing: An Introduction, Second Edition
by Gary Armstrong, Philip Kotler, Michael Harker and Ross Brennan
ISBN 978 0 273 76260 7
© Pearson Education Limited 2009, 2012

Operations And Process Management: Principles And Practice For Strategic Impact
Third Edition
by Nigel Slack, Alistair Brandon-Jones, Robert Johnston and Alan Betts
ISBN 978 0 273 75187 8
© Pearson Education Limited 2006, 2009, 2012

Introduction to Management Science, Eleventh Edition, Global Edition
by Bernard W. Taylor III
ISBN 978 0 273 76640 7
© Pearson Education Limited 2013

ISBN 978 1 78376 393 1

Printed and bound in Great Britain by Clays Ltd, Bungay, Suffolk

Contents

Section 3: Marketing   195

Section 4: Operations Management   433

Section 5: Management Science   613

Introduction

Welcome to Business Studies 1.

We have pleasure in introducing you to these two volumes of our revised customised text that have been designed exclusively for this course, in collaboration with Pearson Education UK. The readings and teaching materials contained herein bring together in one text essential reading tailored specifically to the goals, design and content of the course.

The modular design of Business Studies 1 covers the chief functional areas of the discipline, with the aim of providing a basic grounding in all aspects of business, including the key management specialisms. This will provide you with an informed basis from which to select options for more specialist study in subsequent years, in line with your own specific interests, aptitudes and career intentions. One problem with a course so designed is that no single textbook can simultaneously attain the required breadth of content, and the depth of treatment demanded by the individual specialist modules. Prior to the introduction of the customised text, we recommended a key textbook for each module, an approach that proved costly and inconvenient for students. This initiative considerably eased these pressures by integrating into one affordable text key readings from different specialist textbooks, as well as allowing incorporation of teaching and lecturing material from individual course contributors. The separate course booklet (the "Yellow Book") provides guidance on how the contents of this customised text relate to the individual modules and lectures.

Please note that the chapters we have selected for inclusion in this revised edition will contain references to other relevant chapters from the underlying works that have not been included in this custom edition. The Main Library stocks copies of all the underlying works, so that such cross-referencing provides a pathway for further reading. The yellow course-booklet also specifies some additional reading for specific topics. Moreover, there are web resources for each of the chapters from the underlying works. Students can access the link to these via WebCT (Learn 9 from September 2012).

As a means of directing students efficiently to relevant literature, we are confident that this initiative continues to represent a considerable advance in terms of costs and convenience especially in courses such as this, which seek to create a learning experience that combines breadth and depth of study.

The University of Edinburgh
Business School

Section 1:

Strategy

1

INTRODUCING STRATEGY

Learning outcomes

After reading this chapter you should be able to:

- Explain what 'strategy' is about.

- Summarise the strategy of an organisation in a 'strategy statement'.

- Identify key issues for an organisation's strategy according to the *Exploring Strategy* model.

- Distinguish between *corporate*, *business* and *operational* strategies.

PEARSON
mystrategylab

MyStrategyLab is designed to help you make the most of your studies. Visit www.mystrategylab.com to discover a wide range of resources specific to this chapter, including:

- A personalised **Study plan** that will help you understand core concepts.

- **Audio** and **video clips** that put the spotlight on strategy in the real world.

- **Online glossaries** and **flashcards** that provide helpful reminders when you're looking for some quick revision.

See p. xiv for further details.

1.1 INTRODUCTION

Strategy is about key issues for the long-term future of organisations. For example, how should Google – originally a search company – manage its expansion into the mobile phone industry? Should universities concentrate their resources on research excellence or teaching quality or try to combine both? How should a small video games producer relate to dominant console providers such as Nintendo and Sony? What should a rock band do to secure revenues in the face of declining CD sales?

All these are strategy questions. Naturally, they concern entrepreneurs and senior managers at the top of their organisations. But these questions matter more widely. Middle managers also have to understand the strategic direction of their organisations, both to know how to get top management support for their initiatives and to explain their organisation's strategy to the people they are responsible for. Anybody looking for a management-track job needs to be ready to discuss strategy with their potential employer. Indeed, anybody taking a job should first be confident that their new employer's strategy is actually viable. There are even specialist career opportunities in strategy, for example as a strategy consultant or as an in-house strategic planner, often key roles for fast-track young managers.

This book takes a broad approach to strategy, looking at both the economics of strategy and the people side of managing strategy in practice. The book is also relevant to any kind of organisation responsible for its own direction into the future. Thus the book refers to large private-sector multinationals and small entrepreneurial start-ups; to public-sector organisations such as schools and hospitals; and to not-for-profits such as charities or sports clubs. Strategy matters to almost all organisations, and to everybody working in them.

1.2 WHAT IS STRATEGY?[1]

KEY CONCEPT

Strategy

In this book, **strategy is the long-term direction of an organisation**. Thus the long-term direction of Nokia is from mobile phones to mobile computing. The long-term direction of Disney is from cartoons to diversified entertainment. This section examines the practical implication of this definition of strategy; distinguishes between different levels of strategy; and explains how to summarise an organisation's strategy in a 'strategy statement'.

1.2.1 Defining strategy

Defining strategy as the long-term direction of an organisation implies a more comprehensive view than some influential definitions. Figure 1.1 shows the strategy definitions of three leading strategy theorists: Alfred Chandler and Michael Porter, both from the Harvard Business School, and Henry Mintzberg, from McGill University, Canada. Each points to important but distinct elements of strategy. Chandler emphasises a logical flow from the determination of goals and objectives to the allocation of resources. Porter focuses on deliberate choices, difference and competition. On the other hand, Mintzberg uses the word 'pattern' to allow for the fact that strategies do not always follow a deliberately chosen and logical plan, but can emerge in more

Figure 1.1 Definitions of strategy

'the determination of the long-run goals and objectives of an enterprise and the adoption of courses of action and the allocation of resource necessary for carrying out these goals'

Alfred D. Chandler

'Competitive strategy is about being different. It means deliberately choosing a different set of activities to deliver a unique mix of value'

Michael Porter

'a pattern in a stream of decisions'

Henry Mintzberg

'the long-term direction of an organisation'

Exploring Strategy

Sources: A.D. Chandler, *Strategy and Structure: Chapters in the History of American Enterprise*, MIT Press, 1963, p. 13; M.E. Porter, 'What is strategy?', *Harvard Business Review*, 1966, November–December, p. 60; H. Mintzberg, *Tracking Strategy: Toward a General Theory*, Oxford University Press, 2007, p. 3.

ad hoc ways. Sometimes strategies reflect a series of incremental decisions that only cohere into a recognisable pattern – or 'strategy' – after some time.

All of these strategy definitions incorporate important elements of strategy. However, this book's definition of strategy as 'the long-term direction of an organisation' has two advantages. First, the long-term direction of an organisation can include both deliberate, logical strategy and more incremental, emergent patterns of strategy. Second, long-term direction can include both strategies that emphasise difference and competition, and strategies that recognise the roles of cooperation and even imitation.

The three elements of this strategy definition – the long term, direction and organisation – can each be explored further. The strategy of News Corporation,* owner of social networking company MySpace, illustrates important points (see Illustration 1.1):

- *The long term*. Strategies are typically measured over years, for some organisations a decade or more. The importance of a long-term perspective on strategy is emphasised by the 'three horizons' framework in Figure 1.2. **The three horizons framework suggests that every organisation should think of itself as comprising three types of business or activity, defined by their 'horizons' in terms of years.** *Horizon 1* businesses are basically the current core activities. In the case of News Corporation, Horizon 1 businesses include the original print newspapers. Horizon 1 businesses need defending and extending, but the expectation is

---

* The enquiries into News Corporation's involvement in telephone 'hacking' and its associated governance implications were just under way as this edition of the book was going to press.

ILLUSTRATION 1.1

MySpace becomes part of a bigger network

Social networking site MySpace presents opportunities and challenges for the global media conglomerate News Corporation.

The social networking site MySpace was founded in California in 2003 by MBA graduate Chris DeWolfe and rock musician Tom Anderson. From the first, the networking site was strong on music, and helped launch the careers of the Arctic Monkeys and Lily Allen. By 2005, it had 22 million members, with more page views than Google. That was the point when the multinational media conglomerate News Corporation bought it for $580m (€406m).

News Corporation started in Australia in the newspaper business, acquiring the *Times* newspaper group in the United Kingdom and the *Wall Street Journal* in the United States. It also diversified into television (for example Fox News and BSkyB) and film, including 20th Century Fox, responsible for the hit film *Avatar*. Its chairman is Rupert Murdoch, whose family owns a controlling interest: Rupert Murdoch's son James is expected to succeed him at the top.

In 2005, with media audiences increasingly moving to the internet, Rupert Murdoch declared his ambition to create 'a leading and profitable internet presence'. The acquisition of MySpace seemed a good fit. Chris DeWolfe and Tom Anderson were retained at the head of MySpace, but within a new division providing oversight for all News Corporation's internet interests. Ross Levinsohn, long-time News Corporation insider and head of the new division, told the *Financial Times*: 'The MySpace guys were really freaked out that we were going to come in and turn it into Fox News. One of the things we said was: "We're going to leave it alone"'.

Some adjustments had to be made. Tom Anderson told *Fortune* magazine: 'Before, I could do whatever I wanted. Now it takes more time to get people to agree on things. All the budget reviews and processes. That can be a pain. But it's not stopping us.' News Corporation was able to fund a more robust technology platform to cope with the thousands of new users MySpace was getting each day. In 2006, MySpace signed a three-year advertising contract with Google worth $900m, which

paid for the original acquisition with money left over. Executives summed up MySpace's distinctive positioning by saying: 'Your mom uses Facebook'.

But business then got tougher. Facebook overtook MySpace in terms of unique visitors in 2008. News Corporation executives complained about the excessive new initiatives at MySpace and the failure to prioritise: DeWolfe and Anderson were even considering launching their own film studio. Then Rupert Murdoch announced a target of $1bn in advertising revenues for 2008, without consulting DeWolfe. MySpace missed the target by about 10 per cent. The push from News Corporation to increase advertisements on MySpace, and a reluctance to remove pages with advertising from the site, began to make MySpace increasingly less attractive for users.

During 2009, MySpace's share of the social networking market fell to 30 per cent, from a peak of 66 per cent. The company missed the online traffic targets set by the Google contract. Losses were expected to be around $100m. In March, Chris DeWolfe was removed as Chief Executive of MySpace. The new Chief Executive was Alan Van Natta, from Facebook. Van Natta told the *Financial Times* that MySpace was no longer competing with Facebook: 'we're very focused on a different space . . . MySpace can foster discovery [of music, films and TV] in a way that others can't'.

Sources: M. Garnham, 'The rise and fall of MySpace', *Financial Times*, 4 December 2009; P. Sellers, 'MySpace Cowboys', *Fortune*, 29 August 2006; S. Rosenbusch, 'News Corp's Place in MySpace', *Business Week*, 19 July 2005.

Questions

1 How valuable is MySpace's distinctive position in the social networking market?

2 How should News Corporation have managed MySpace?

Figure 1.2 Three horizons for strategy

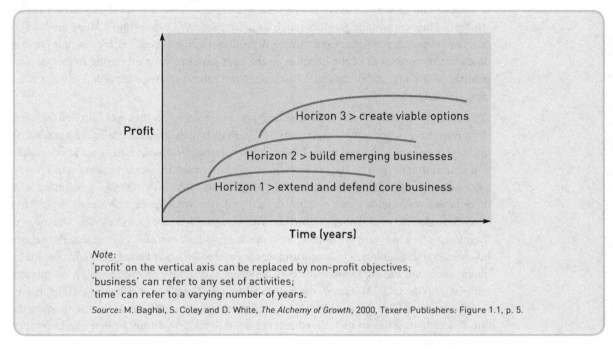

Note:
'profit' on the vertical axis can be replaced by non-profit objectives;
'business' can refer to any set of activities;
'time' can refer to a varying number of years.
Source: M. Baghai, S. Coley and D. White, *The Alchemy of Growth*, 2000, Texere Publishers: Figure 1.1, p. 5.

that in the long term they will likely be flat or declining in terms of profits (or whatever else the organisation values). *Horizon 2* businesses are emerging activities that should provide new sources of profit. In News Corporation, those include the various internet initiatives, principally MySpace. Finally, there are *Horizon 3* possibilities, for which nothing is sure. These are typically risky Research & Development (R&B) projects, start-up ventures, test-market pilots or similar, some of which may fuel growth in the future even if most are likely to fail. For a fast-moving internet organisation like MySpace, *Horizon 3* might only be a couple of years from the present time. In a pharmaceutical company, where the R&D and regulatory processes for a new drug take many years, *Horizon 3* might be a decade ahead. While timescales might differ, the basic point about the 'three horizons' framework is that managers need to avoid focusing on the short-term issues of their existing activities. Strategy involves pushing out Horizon 1 as far as possible, at the same time as looking to Horizons 2 and 3.

● *Strategic direction.* Over the years, strategies follow some kind of long-term direction or trajectory. The strategic direction of News Corporation is from print to internet media, as represented by MySpace. Sometimes a strategic direction only emerges as a coherent pattern over time. Typically, however, managers and entrepreneurs try to set the direction of their strategy according to long-term *objectives*. In private-sector businesses, the objective guiding strategic direction is usually maximising profits for shareholders. Thus Rupert Murdoch's acquisition of MySpace was driven by the objective to create a leading and profitable presence on the internet. However, profits do not always set strategic direction. First, public-sector and charity organisations may set their strategic direction according to other objectives: for example, a sports club's objective may be to move up from one league to a higher one. Second, even in the private sector, profit is not always the sole criterion for strategy. Thus controlling families (such as perhaps News Corporation's Murdoch family) may sometimes sacrifice the maximisation of profits for family objectives, for example passing down the management of the business to the next generation or exercising influence over political affairs and public opinion. The objectives behind strategic direction always need close scrutiny.

- *Organisation*. In this book, organisations are not treated as discrete, unified entities. Organisations involve complex relationships, both internally and externally. This is because organisations typically have many internal and external *stakeholders*, in other words people and groups that depend on the organisation and upon which the organisation itself depends. Internally, organisations are filled with people, typically with diverse, competing and more or less reasonable views of what should be done. At MySpace, the News Corporation executives clashed over strategic direction with MySpace founder Chris DeWolfe. In strategy, therefore, it is always important to look *inside* organisations and to consider the people involved and their different interests and views. Externally, organisations are surrounded by important relationships, for example with suppliers, customers, alliance partners, regulators and shareholders. For MySpace, the relationship with Google was critical. Strategy, therefore, is also crucially concerned with an organisation's external *boundaries*: in other words, questions about what to include within the organisation and how to manage important relationships with what is kept outside.

Because strategy typically involves managing people, relationships and resources, the subject is sometimes called 'strategic management'. This book takes the view that managing is always important in strategy. Good strategy involves understanding the managerial context and consequences of strategy, not just the strategic decisions themselves.

1.2.2 Levels of strategy

Inside an organisation, strategies can exist at three main levels. Again they can be illustrated by reference to MySpace and News Corporation (Illustration 1.1):

- **Corporate-level strategy is concerned with the overall scope of an organisation and how value is added to the constituent businesses of the organisational whole.** Corporate-level strategy issues include geographical scope, diversity of products or services, acquisitions of new businesses, and how resources are allocated between the different elements of the organisation. For News Corporation, diversifying from print journalism into television and social networking are corporate-level strategies. Being clear about corporate-level strategy is important: determining the range of businesses to include is the *basis* of other strategic decisions.

- **Business-level strategy is about how the individual businesses should compete in their particular markets** (for this reason, business-level strategy is often called 'competitive strategy'). These individual businesses might be stand-alone businesses, for instance entrepreneurial start-ups, or 'business units' within a larger corporation (as MySpace and Fox are inside

News Corporation). Business-level strategy typically concerns issues such as innovation, appropriate scale and response to competitors' moves. In the public sector, the equivalent of business-level strategy is decisions about how units (such as individual hospitals or schools) should provide best-value services. Where the businesses are units within a larger organisation, business-level strategies should clearly fit with corporate-level strategy.

- **Operational strategies are concerned with how the components of an organisation deliver effectively the corporate- and business-level strategies in terms of resources, processes and people.** For example, MySpace engineers had to keep developing enough processing capacity to cope with the strategy of rapid growth. In most businesses, successful business strategies depend to a large extent on decisions that are taken, or activities that occur, at the operational level. Operational decisions need, therefore, to be closely linked to business-level strategy. They are vital to successful strategy implementation.

This need to link the corporate, business and operational levels underlines the importance of *integration* in strategy. Each level needs to be aligned with the others.

1.2.3 Strategy statements

David Collis and Michael Rukstad[2] at the Harvard Business School argue that all entrepreneurs and managers should be able to summarise their organisation's strategy with a 'strategy statement'. **Strategy statements should have three main themes: the fundamental *goals* that the organisation seeks, which typically draw on the organisation's stated mission, vision and objectives; the *scope* or domain of the organisation's activities; and the particular *advantages* or capabilities it has to deliver all of these.** These various contributing elements of a strategy statement are explained as follows, with examples in Illustration 1.2:

- *Mission.* This relates to goals, and refers to the overriding purpose of the organisation. It is sometimes described in terms of the apparently simple but challenging question: '*What business are we in?*' The mission statement helps keep managers focused on what is central to their strategy.

- *Vision.* This too relates to goals, and refers to the desired future state of the organisation. It is an aspiration which can help mobilise the energy and passion of organisational members. The vision statement, therefore, should answer the question: '*What do we want to achieve?*'

- *Objectives.* These are more precise and, ideally, quantifiable statements of the organisation's goals over some period of time. Objectives might refer to profitability or market share targets for a private company, or to examination results in a school. Objectives introduce discipline to strategy. The question here is: '*What do we have to achieve in the coming period?*'

- *Scope.* An organisation's scope or domain refers to three dimensions: customers or clients; geographical location; and extent of internal activities ('vertical integration'). For a university, scope questions are twofold: first, which academic departments to have (a business school, an engineering department and so on); second, which activities to do internally themselves (vertically integrate) and which to externalise to subcontractors (for example, whether to manage campus restaurants in-house or to subcontract them).

ILLUSTRATION 1.2

Strategy statements

Both Nokia, the Finnish telecommunications giant, and University College Cork, based in the West of Ireland, publish a good deal about their strategies.

Nokia vision and strategy

Our vision is a world where everyone can be connected. Our promise is to help people feel close to what is important to them.

The businesses of Nokia

- Compelling consumer solutions with devices and services
- Strong infrastructure business with Siemens Networks

Our competitive advantage is based on scale, brand and services

- Scale-based assets and capabilities
- Leading brand
- Build further competitive advantage by differentiating our offering through services

Our business strategy

- Maximize Nokia's lifetime value to consumer
- Best mobile devices everywhere
  - Take share and drive value across price brands and geographies
  - Enhance and capture market growth in emerging markets
- Context-enriched services
  - Take share of the internet services market by delivering winning solutions
  - Take share of business mobility market

University College Cork (UCC), Strategic Plan 2009–2012

University College Cork (UCC) . . . is sited in Ireland's second city . . . UCC's motto *'Where Finbarr taught let Munster learn'* binds us to the sixth-century monastery and place of learning established by St. Finbarr . . . UCC was established in 1845 as one of three Queen's Colleges . . . The campus today is home to over 18,000 students including 2,000 international students from

93 countries. . . . A third of our staff are from overseas. Our strategic alliances with world-ranking universities in Asia, Europe and North America ensure that we learn from and contribute to the best standards of teaching, learning and research.

Vision

To be a world-class university that links the region to the globe.

Mission

In an environment which gives parity of esteem to teaching, learning and research and where students are our highest priority, the University's central roles are to create, preserve and communicate knowledge and to enhance intellectual, cultural, social and economic life locally, regionally and globally.

Targets by 2012 (selected from 'Teaching, Learning and the Student Experience')

- Achieve a first year retention rate of 93 per cent or greater
- Increase the proportion of students at postgraduate level from 19 per cent to 30 per cent
- Increase flexible/part-time provision to 15 per cent of undergraduate entrants

Sources: www.nokia.com; www.ucc.ie.

Questions

1 Construct short strategy statements covering the goals, scope and advantage of Nokia and University College Cork. How much do the different contexts matter?

2 Construct a strategy statement for your own organisation (university or employer). What implications might this statement have for your particular course or department?

- *Advantage*. This part of a strategy statement describes how the organisation will achieve the objectives it has set for itself in its chosen domain. In competitive environments, this refers to the *competitive* advantage: for example, how a particular company or sports club will achieve goals in the face of competition from other companies or clubs. In order to achieve a particular goal, the organisation needs to be better than others seeking the same goal. In the public sector, advantage might refer simply to the organisation's capability in general. But even public-sector organisations frequently need to show that their capabilities are not only adequate, but superior to other rival departments or perhaps to private-sector contractors.

Collis and Rukstad suggest that strategy statements covering goals, scope and advantage should be no more than 35 words long. Shortness keeps such statements focused on the essentials and makes them easy to remember and communicate. Thus for News Corporation, a strategy statement might be: 'to build a leading and profitable presence in both old and new media, drawing on competitive advantages in terms of the scale, diversity and international range of our businesses'. The strategy statement of American financial advisory firm Edward Jones is more specific: 'to grow to 17,000 financial advisers by 2012 by offering trusted and convenient face-to-face financial advice to conservative individual investors through a national network of one-financial adviser offices'. Of course, such strategy statements are not always fulfilled. Circumstances may change in unexpected ways. In the meantime, however, they can provide a useful guide both to managers in their decision-making and to employees and others who need to understand the direction in which the organisation is going. The ability to give a clear strategy statement is a good test of managerial competence in an organisation.

As such, strategy statements are relevant to a wide range of organisations. For example, a small entrepreneurial start-up will need a strategy statement to persuade investors and lenders of its viability. Public-sector organisations need strategy statements not only for themselves, but to reassure external clients, funders and regulators that their priorities are the right ones. Voluntary organisations need to communicate persuasive strategy statements in order to inspire volunteers and donors. Thus organisations of all kinds frequently publish materials relevant to such strategy statements on their websites or annual reports. Illustration 1.2 provides published materials on the strategies of two very different organisations: the technology giant Nokia from the private sector and the medium-sized University College Cork from the public sector.

(1.3) THE *EXPLORING STRATEGY* MODEL

This book is structured around a three-part model that encompasses issues of economics and people equally. The *Exploring Strategy* Model includes understanding *the strategic position of an organisation; assessing strategic choices for the future; and managing strategy in action*. Figure 1.3 shows these elements as overlapping circles, each closely interlinked with the others. However, because this book is about the *fundamentals* of strategy, it concentrates on the first two elements of position and choice. There is less emphasis on the management issues of strategy in action: on these, the book focuses just on key issues such as managing strategic change and putting in structures and systems to deliver the chosen strategy. Other issues to do

Figure 1.3 The *Exploring Strategy* Model

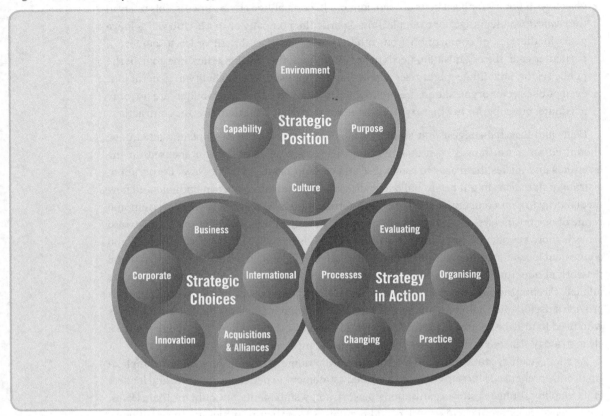

with strategy in action – such as strategic planning and the practice of strategy – are covered more fully in *Exploring Strategy*.[3]

It is important to understand why the *Exploring Strategy* Model is drawn as interlinked circles. Figure 1.3 could have shown the model's three elements in a linear sequence – first understanding the strategic position, then making strategic choices and finally turning strategy into action. Indeed, this logical sequence is implicit in the definition of strategy given by Alfred Chandler (Figure 1.1) and many other textbooks on strategy. However, as Henry Mintzberg recognises, in practice the elements of strategy do not always follow this linear sequence. Choices often have to be made before the position is fully understood. Sometimes too, a proper understanding of the strategic position can only be built from the experience of trying a strategy out in action. The real-world feedback that comes from launching a new product is often far better at uncovering the true strategic position than remote analysis carried out in a strategic planning department at head office.

The interconnected circles of Figure 1.3 are designed to emphasise this potentially non-linear nature of strategy. Position, choices and action should be seen as closely related, and in practice none has priority over another. It is only for structural convenience that this book follows a sequence with its subject matter; the book is not meant to suggest that the process of strategy must follow a logical path of distinct steps. The three circles are overlapping and non-linear, just as strategy often is in real life. Strategy rarely occurs in tidy ways and it is better not to expect it to do so.

However, the *Exploring Strategy* Model does provide a comprehensive and integrated framework for analysing an organisation's position, considering the choices it has and putting strategies into action. Each of the chapters can be seen as asking fundamental strategy questions and providing the essential concepts and techniques to help answer them. Working systematically through questions and answers provides the basis for persuasive strategy recommendations.

1.3.1 Strategic position

The **strategic position** is concerned with the impact on strategy of the external environment, the organisation's strategic capability (resources and competences), the organisation's goals and the organisation's culture. Understanding these four factors is central for evaluating future strategy. These issues, and the fundamental questions associated with them, are covered in Chapters 2–4 of this book:

Strategic
position

- *Environment*. Organisations operate in a complex political, economic, social and technological world. These environments vary widely in terms of their dynamism and attractiveness. The fundamental question here relates to the *opportunities* and *threats* available to the organisation in this complex and changing environment. Chapter 2 provides key frameworks to help in focusing on priority issues in the face of environmental complexity and dynamism.

- *Strategic capability*. Each organisation has its own strategic capabilities, made up of its *resources* (e.g. machines and buildings) and *competences* (e.g. technical and managerial skills). The fundamental question on capability regards the organisation's *strengths* and *weaknesses* (for example, where is it at a competitive advantage or disadvantage?). Are the organisation's capabilities adequate to the challenges of its environment and the demands of its goals? Chapter 3 provides tools and concepts for analysing such capabilities.

- *Strategic purpose*. Although sometimes unclear or contested, most organisations claim for themselves a particular purpose, as encapsulated in their *vision*, *mission* and *objectives*. The strategic purpose is a key criterion against which strategies must be evaluated. This strategic purpose is influenced by both the *governance structure* of the organisation and its *culture*. The third fundamental question therefore is: what is the organisation's strategic purpose; what does it seek to achieve?

Applying the *Exploring Strategy* Model to the positioning of News Corporation (Illustration 1.1) raises the following issues. News Corporation was threatened by an environmental shift from print to the internet. It also lacked the capabilities to develop a social networking business on its own. The company was determined to grow its internet business fast, setting demanding objectives that MySpace struggled to meet. Finally, there appeared to be culture clashes between the traditional family-owned conglomerate and the young entrepreneurial start-up.

1.3.2 Strategic choices

Strategic choices involve the options for strategy in terms of both the *directions* in which strategy might move and the *methods* by which strategy might be pursued. For instance, an organisation might have a range of strategic directions open to it: the organisation could diversify into new products; it could enter new international markets; or it could transform its existing products and markets through radical innovation. These various directions could be pursued by different methods: the organisation could acquire a business already active in the product or market area; it could form alliances with relevant organisations that might help its new strategy; or it could try to pursue its strategies on its own. Typical strategic choices, and the related fundamental questions, are covered in Chapters 5 to 9 of this book, as follows:

- *Business strategy*. There are strategic choices in terms of how the organisation seeks to compete at the individual *business level*. Typically these choices involve strategies based on *cost* (for example, economies of scale) or *differentiation* (for example, superior quality). Crucial is deciding how to win against competitors (for this reason, business strategy is sometimes called 'competitive strategy'). The fundamental question here, then, is how should the business unit compete? Key dilemmas for business-level strategy, and ways of resolving them, are discussed in Chapter 5.

- *Corporate strategy and diversification*. The highest level of an organisation is typically concerned with corporate-level strategy, focused on questions of portfolio scope. The fundamental question in corporate-level strategy is therefore which businesses to include in the portfolio. This relates to the appropriate degree of *diversification*, in other words the spread of products and markets. Corporate-level strategy is also concerned both with the relationship between the various businesses that make up the corporate portfolio of the business and with how the corporate 'parent' (owner) adds value to the individual businesses. Chapter 6 provides tools for assessing diversification strategies and the appropriate relationships within the corporate portfolio.

- *International strategy*. Internationalisation is a form of diversification, but into new geographical markets. It is often at least as challenging as product or service diversification. Here the fundamental question is: where internationally should the organisation compete? Chapter 7 examines how to prioritise various international options and identifies key methods for pursuing them: export, licensing, direct investment and acquisition.

- *Innovation strategies*. Most existing organisations have to innovate constantly simply to survive. Entrepreneurship, the creation of a new enterprise, is an act of innovation too. A fundamental question, therefore, is whether the organisation is innovating appropriately. Chapter 8 considers key choices about innovation and entrepreneurship, and helps in selecting between them.

- *Mergers, acquisitions and alliances*. Organisations have to make choices about methods for pursuing their strategies. Many organisations prefer to grow 'organically', in other words by building new businesses with their own resources. Other organisations might develop through mergers and acquisitions or strategic alliances with other organisations.

The fundamental question here, then, is whether to buy another company, ally or to go it alone. How to choose between these alternative methods is discussed in Chapter 9.

Again, issues of strategic choice are live in the case of News Corporation and MySpace (Illustration 1.1). The *Exploring Strategy* Model asks the following kinds of questions here. Should MySpace compete against Facebook by emphasising its music strengths? Should a newspaper company diversify into the new social networking market and, if it does, is an acquisition the best method? How should News Corporation add value to its entrepreneurial new business? And should MySpace be allowed to continue to innovate in its old, loosely disciplined style?

1.3.3 Strategy in action

Strategy in action is concerned with how chosen strategies are actually put into practice. Chapter 10 covers three key issues for strategy in action:

- *Structuring* an organisation to support successful performance. A key question here is who is in charge and who is accountable.

- *Systems* are required to control the way in which *strategy is implemented*. The issue here is how to ensure that strategies are implemented according to plan.

- Managing *strategic change* is typically an important part of putting strategy into action. How should change be led?

Strategy in action issues loom large in the MySpace case (Illustration 1.1). For example, should the new business have been integrated into a larger division within News Corporation? Was it appropriate to impose big company systems on a new social networking company? Chapter 10 is an introduction to such important issues of strategy in action. There is also the question of *evaluating* the strategy behind the MySpace acquisition: Appendix 1 to this book provides a guide to evaluating strategic options, which should be useful for checking recommendations on case analyses or assignments generally. All these issues, and related ones to do with strategic planning and practice, are dealt with more extensively in Johnson, Whittington and Scholes' *Exploring Strategy.*

1.4 STRATEGY DEVELOPMENT PROCESSES

The previous section introduced strategic position, strategic choices and strategy in action. However, strategies do not always develop in a logical sequence of analysis, choice and action. There are two broad explanations of strategy development:

- The *rational–analytic view* of strategy development is the conventional explanation. Here strategies are developed through rational and analytical processes, led typically by top managers. There is a linear sequence. First, the strategic position is analysed; then options are weighed up and choices are made; finally, structures, processes and change procedures are put in place to allow effective implementation. Often formal strategic planning systems are important to the analysis and formulation of the strategy. In this view, strategies are *intended*, in other words the product of deliberate choices. This rational–analytical view is associated with theorists such as Alfred Chandler and Michael Porter, in Figure 1.1.

- The *emergent strategy* view is the alternative broad explanation of how strategies develop. In this view, strategies often do not develop as intended or planned, but tend to emerge in organisations over time as a result of ad hoc, incremental or even accidental actions. Good ideas and opportunities often come from practical experience at the bottom of the organisation, rather than from top management and formal strategic plans. Even the best laid plans may need to be abandoned as new opportunities arise or the organisation learns from the marketplace. This is a view associated with Henry Mintzberg, referenced in Figure 1.1.

The two views are not mutually exclusive. Intended strategies can often succeed, especially in stable markets where there are few surprises. Moreover, an organisation's key stakeholders – employees, owners, customers, regulators and so on – will typically want to see evidence of deliberate strategy-making: it is rarely acceptable to say that everything is simply emergent. The tools and concepts throughout the book are particularly helpful in this deliberate strategy-making. But it is wise to be open as well to the possibilities of emergence. Inflexible plans can hinder learning and prevent the seizing of opportunities. Moreover, strategic choices do not always come about as a result of simple rational analysis: *cultural and political processes* in organisations can also drive changes in strategy, as will become apparent in the discussions in Chapter 4.

This book allows for *both* the rational–analytical view and the emergent view. Indeed, the interconnected circles of the *Exploring Strategy* Model in Figure 1.3 deliberately underline the possibly non-linear aspects of strategy. It is not just a matter of putting strategic choices into action in a logical sequence leading from strategy formulation to strategy implementation. Strategy in action often creates the strategic choices in the first place, as new opportunities and constraints are discovered in practice. Implementation can lead to formulation as well.[4]

SUMMARY

- Strategy is the long-term direction of an organisation. A 'strategy statement' should cover the *goals* of an organisation, the *scope* of the organisation's activities and the *advantages* or *capabilities* the organisation brings to these goals and activities.

- *Corporate-level strategy* is concerned with an organisation's overall scope; *business-level strategy* is concerned with how to compete; and *operational strategy* is concerned with how resources, processes and people deliver corporate- and business-level strategies.

- The *Exploring Strategy* Model has three major elements: understanding the *strategic position*, making *strategic choices* for the future and managing *strategy in action*.

RECOMMENDED KEY READINGS

It is always useful to read around a topic. As well as the specific references below, we particularly highlight:

- Three accessible introductory articles on the nature of strategy are M. Porter, 'What is strategy?', *Harvard Business Review*, November–December 1996, pp. 61–78; F. Fréry, 'The fundamental dimensions of strategy', *MIT Sloan Management Review*, vol. 48, no. 1 (2006), pp. 71–75; and D. Collis and M. Rukstad, 'Can you say what your strategy is?', *Harvard Business Review*, April 2008, pp. 63–73.

- For contemporary developments in strategy practice, business newspapers such as the *Financial Times*, *Les Echos* and the *Wall Street Journal* and business magazines such as *Business Week*, *The Economist*, *L'Expansion* and *Manager-Magazin*. See also the websites of the leading strategy consulting firms: www.mckinsey.com; www.bcg.com; www.bain.com.

REFERENCES

1. The question 'What is strategy?' is discussed in R. Whittington, *What is Strategy – and Does it Matter?*, International Thomson, 1993/2000 and M.E. Porter, 'What is strategy?', *Harvard Business Review*, November–December 1996, pp. 61–78.
2. D. Collis and M. Rukstad, 'Can you say what your strategy is?', *Harvard Business Review*, April 2008, pp. 63–73.
3. G. Johnson, R. Whittington and K. Scholes, *Exploring Strategy*, 9th edition, Pearson, 2010.
4. The classic discussion of the roles of rational strategy formulation and strategy implementation is in H. Mintzberg, 'The design school: reconsidering the basic premises of strategic management', *Strategic Management Journal*, vol. 11 (1991), pp. 171–95 and H.I. Ansoff, 'Critique of Henry Mintzberg's The Design School', *Strategic Management Journal*, vol. 11 (1991), pp. 449–61.

CASE EXAMPLE

Glastonbury – from hippy weekend to international festival

Steve Henderson, Leeds Metropolitan University

Glastonbury Festival has become a worldwide attraction for music fans and artists alike. In 2009, Bruce Springsteen was added to the long list of acts (from Paul McCartney to Oasis) that have appeared at the festival. It started in 1970 when 1,500 hippy revellers gathered on a farm near Glastonbury Tor to be plied with free milk and entertainment from a makeshift stage. Now, Glastonbury is a major international festival that attracts over 150,000 attenders. Without any knowledge of the line-up, the tickets for the 2010 Festival sold out in days.

In those early days, the Festival was developed by local farmer, Michael Eavis, whose passion for music and social principles led to a weekend of music as a means of raising funds for good causes. It was a social mission rooted in the hippy counter-culture of the 1960s and events such as Woodstock. Today, the Glastonbury Festival attender finds that those early days of hippy idealism are a long way off. The scale of the organisation demands strong management to support the achievement of the festival's social aims.

At first, the statutory requirements for an event held on private land were minimal. Jovial policemen looked over hedges while recreational drugs were sold from tables near the festival entrance as if this was just a slightly unusual village fête. Needless to say, the festival began to attract the attention of a number of different groups, especially as legislation around the running of events tightened. Eavis struggled with local residents who hated the invasion of their privacy; with hippy activist groups who felt that their contribution in helping at the festival gave them a sense of ownership; with drug dealers carrying on their activities on the fringes of the festival; and fans climbing over the fences to get free access.

The festival's continued expansion has resulted in a festival with over ten stages covering jazz, dance, classical, world music and other genres. Added to this, there is comedy, poetry, circus, theatre and children's entertainment alongside more esoteric street theatre

Source: Getty Images.

performances. Much of this is organised into specific grassy field areas where, for example, the Dance Village uses a number of tents dedicated to different types of dance music. Indeed, such is the range of entertainment on offer that some attenders spend the whole weekend at the festival without seeing a single live music act. Though the Eavis family remain involved with the main programme, much of the other entertainment is now managed by others. Reflecting this shift towards more diverse entertainment, the name of the festival was changed from Glastonbury Fayre (reflecting the ancient cultural heritage of the area) to the Glastonbury Festival for Contemporary Performing Arts.

In some years, the festival is forced to take a year off to allow the farmland to recover from the trampling of thousands of pairs of feet. Not only is this wise on an agricultural front but also gives the local residents a rest from the annual invasion of festival goers. Despite this, the festival has met with a number of controversies such as when a large number of gatecrashers spoilt the fun in 2000. This caused the festival to be fined due to exceeding the licensed attendance and excessive noise after the event. Furthermore, health and safety laws now require the event management to have a 'duty of care' to everyone on the festival site. To address these health and safety concerns, support was sought from Melvin Benn who ran festivals for the Mean Fiddler organisation. With a steel fence erected around the perimeter, Melvin Benn helped re-establish the festival in 2002 after a year off.

Ownership of the festival remained with the Eavis family but Melvin Benn was appointed Managing Director. However, concerns arose in 2006 when his employer, Mean Fiddler, was taken over by major music promoters, Live Nation and MCD Productions. In a worrying move, Live Nation announced that they would entice a number of major artists to appear on the weekend normally used by Glastonbury at a new UK festival called Wireless. Based in London, this seemed set to offer a city-based alternative to Glastonbury. At much the same time, Live Nation announced that they would launch their own online ticket agency to support the sales of their music events. This shift in power between the major music promoters indicated not only their interest in the ownership of key events but their desire to control income streams.

Elsewhere in the world of live entertainment, the success of Glastonbury had not gone unnoticed and the festival market showed considerable growth. Some of the other festivals tried to capitalise on features that Glastonbury could not offer. For example, Glastonbury was famous for its wet weather with pictures of damp revellers and collapsed tents being commonplace. Live Nation's city-based Wireless festival offered the opportunity to sleep under a roof at home or hotel, as opposed to risking the weather outdoors. Alternatively, Benicassim in southern Spain offered a festival with an excellent chance of sunshine and top acts for the price of a low cost airline ticket. Other festivals noted that Glastonbury attenders enjoyed the wider entertainment at the event. In doing this, they realised that many festival goers were attracted by the whole social experience. So, sidestepping major acts and their related high fees, smaller festivals were created for just a few thousand attenders. These offered entertainment in various formats, often in a family-friendly atmosphere. Sometimes described as boutique festivals, Freddie Fellowes, organiser of the Secret Garden Party, describes this type of festival as a chance 'to be playful, to break down barriers between people and create an environment where you have perfect freedom and perfect nourishment, intellectually and visually'. Festival Republic, the rebranded Mean Fiddler, created a boutique festival on a larger scale with their Latitude festival. Similarly, Rob da Bank, a BBC DJ, put together Bestival on the Isle of Wight where the attenders are encouraged to join in the fun by appearing in fancy dress. Quite clearly, audiences are now being presented with a wide range of festivals to consider for their leisure time entertainment.

Many of these festivals attract sponsors with some becoming prominent by acquiring naming rights on the festival. Others have low profile arrangements involving so-called 'contra' deals as opposed to sponsorship payments. For example, Glastonbury has official cider suppliers who typically boost their brand by giving the festival a preferential deal on their products in exchange for publicity. Though these commercial relationships are sometimes spurned by the smaller festivals that see the branding as an intrusion on their fun environment, larger festivals often need such relationships to survive. In order to attract sponsors, large festivals are turning to radio and television broadcasters as a means to expand the audience and offer wider exposure for the sponsor. Indeed, in 2009, the BBC sent over 400 staff members down to Glastonbury for broadcasting aimed at satisfying the interest of the armchair viewer/listener.

With such huge demand for their talents, artists can have a lucrative summer moving between festivals. Similarly, audiences can make lengthy treks to their favourite festivals. For some, this has caused environmental concerns with Glastonbury's rural location, poor transport links and large audience being cited as a specific problem. On the other hand, artists are not only finding that the festivals offer a good source of income but that private parties and corporate entertainment have emerged as alternative, often greater, income opportunities. One newspaper claimed that George Michael pocketed more than £1.5m (~€1.65m; ~$2.25m) to entertain revellers at the British billionaire retailer Sir Philip Green's 55th birthday party in the Maldives. Hence, for many artists, the summer has become a case of 'cherry picking' their favourite festivals or seeking out the most lucrative opportunities.

Over time, the shift from small, homespun event to corporate-controlled festival has provided awkward situations for Michael Eavis – from the difficulties with establishment figures who felt the event was out of control to the demands of counter-cultural groups such as the travelling hippies. However, along the way, the festival has maintained its aim of supporting charities like CND and, later, Greenpeace, Oxfam and a number of local charities. In the mind of the audience, this helps position the festival as a fun event with a social conscience. The continued expansion and shift in management of the festival has freed Michael Eavis to be the figurehead for the event and to pursue the original social mission of the festival.

Given this growing and increasingly competitive market, there is much to consider for the festivals involved. In recent years, Glastonbury has sold all its tickets and made donations to its favoured causes, confirming the financial viability of its current business model. Indeed, the festival's iconic status has traditionally meant that it is a rite of passage for many young music fans. Yet, in 2008, Eavis publicly registered concern over the age of the Glastonbury audience suggesting that selling tickets by phone would help attract a younger audience. Maybe Eavis was concerned by comments such as those in *The Times* newspaper that cruelly declared Glastonbury as suited to the 'the hip-op generation' and questioned whether young people thought it was 'cool' to go to the same music events as their parents. On the other hand, their parents belong to the 'baby boomer' generation that grew up with popular music and festivals like Glastonbury. So, there is no real surprise that they would enjoy this eclectic event. Whatever disturbed Eavis, he announced that Jay-Z, an American rap artist, was to headline in order to help attract a younger audience. With sales slower compared with previous sell-out years, he later stated 'We're not trying to get rid of anybody. The older people are fantastic, but we do need young people coming in as well.' Then, reflecting on the 2008 festival in 2009, Michael Eavis displayed concerns over the future of the festival saying 'Last year I thought that maybe we'd got to the end and we'd have to bite the bullet and fold it all up. A lot of the bands were saying Glastonbury had become too big, too muddy and too horrible.'

With such an established festival as Glastonbury, one would expect the management might be looking to leverage its brand with, for example, further events. Yet, the comments of Michael Eavis suggest not only a lack of clarity about the target audience but also concern over whether it can persist. Furthermore, Eavis seems nervous about the festival's appeal to artists who have lots of opportunities to make appearances over the summer. Audiences and artists are the two key factors that underpin financial success at these events, as successful festival promoters are well aware.

Sources: The history of Glastonbury is charted on its website (http://www.glastonburyfestivals.co.uk/history) while ownership and finances are available through Companies House.

Most of the background to the festival and related market has been drawn from online news resources such as the BBC, Times Online and the *Guardian*, or industry magazines such as *Music Week*.

More information on UK Festivals is available from Mintel.

Questions

1 Sticking to the 35-word limit suggested by Collis and Rukstad in section 1.2.3, what strategy statement would you propose for the Glastonbury Festival?

2 Carry out a 'three horizons' analysis (section 1.2.1) of the Glastonbury Festival, in terms of both existing activities and possible future ones. How might this analysis affect their future strategic direction?

3 Using the headings of environment, strategic capability and strategic purpose seen in section 1.3.1, identify key positioning issues for the Glastonbury Festival and consider their relative importance.

4 Following on from the previous question and making use of section 1.3.2, what alternative strategies do you see for the Glastonbury Festival?

5 Converting good strategic thinking into action can be a challenge: examine how the Glastonbury Festival has achieved this by considering the elements seen in section 1.3.3.

2

THE ENVIRONMENT

Learning outcomes

After reading this chapter, you should be able to:

- Analyse the broad macro-environment of organisations in terms of political, economic, social, technological, environmental ('green') and legal factors (*PESTEL*).

- Identify key drivers in this macro-environment and use these key drivers to construct alternative *scenarios* with regard to environmental change.

- Use *Porter's five forces* analysis in order to define the attractiveness of industries and sectors and to identify their potential for change.

- Identify successful *strategic groups*, valuable *market segments* and attractive '*Blue Oceans*' within industries.

- Use these various concepts and techniques in order to recognise *threats* and *opportunities* in the marketplace.

PEARSON mystrategylab

MyStrategyLab is designed to help you make the most of your studies. Visit **www.mystrategylab.com** to discover a wide range of resources specific to this chapter, including:

- A personalised **Study plan** that will help you understand core concepts.
- **Audio** and **video clips** that put the spotlight on strategy in the real world.
- **Online glossaries** and **flashcards** that provide helpful reminders when you're looking for some quick revision.

See p. xiv for further details.

(2.1) INTRODUCTION

The environment is what gives organisations their means of survival. It creates opportunities and it presents threats. For example, the success of Apple's iPhone created rich market opportunities for the writers of mobile phone apps. On the other hand, the rise of the free online news content has severely threatened the survival of many traditional newspapers, who can no longer count on customers paying for their daily print editions. Although the future can never be predicted perfectly, it is clearly important that entrepreneurs and managers try to analyse their environments as carefully as they can in order to anticipate and – if possible – influence environmental change.

This chapter therefore provides frameworks for analysing changing and complex environments. These frameworks are organised in a series of 'layers' briefly introduced here and summarised in Figure 2.1.

● *The macro-environment* is the highest-level layer. This consists of broad environmental factors that impact to a greater or lesser extent on almost all organisations. Here, the PESTEL framework can be used to identify how future issues in the *political, economic, social, technological, environmental ('green') and legal* environments might affect organisations. This PESTEL analysis

Figure 2.1 Layers of the business environment

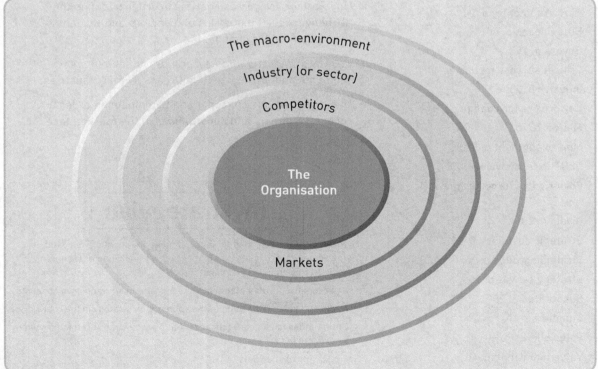

provides the broad 'data' from which to identify *key drivers of change*. These key drivers can be used to construct *scenarios* of alternative possible futures.

● *Industry, or sector,* forms the next layer within this broad general environment. This is made up of organisations producing the same products or services. Here the *five forces* framework is particularly useful in understanding the attractiveness of particular industries or sectors and potential threats from outside the present set of competitors.

● *Competitors and markets* are the most immediate layer surrounding organisations. Here the concept of *strategic groups* can help identify different kinds of competitors. Similarly, in the marketplace, customers' expectations are not all the same. They have a range of different requirements the importance of which can be understood through the *concepts of market segments* and *critical success factors*.

This chapter works through these three layers in turn, starting with the macro-environment.

2.2 THE MACRO-ENVIRONMENT

The three concepts in this section – PESTEL, key drivers and scenarios – are interrelated tools for analysing the broad macro-environment of an organisation. *PESTEL* provides a wide overview; *key drivers* help focus on what is most important; and *scenarios* build on key drivers to explore different ways in which the macro-environment might change.

2.2.1 The PESTEL framework

The **PESTEL framework** categorises environmental influences into six main types: **political, economic, social, technological, environmental and legal.** Thus PESTEL provides a comprehensive list of influences on the possible success or failure of particular strategies.[1] In particular, Politics highlights the role of governments; Economics refers to macro-economic factors such as exchange rates, business cycles and differential economic growth rates around the world; Social influences include changing cultures and demographics, for example ageing populations in many Western societies; Technological influences refer to innovations such as the internet, nano-technology or the rise of new composite materials; Environmental stands specifically for 'green' issues, such as pollution and waste; and finally Legal embraces legislative constraints or changes, such as health and safety legislation or restrictions on company mergers and acquisitions. Illustration 2.1 provides examples of PESTEL factors for the airline industry.

KEY CONCEPT

PESTEL framework

For managers, it is important to analyse how these factors are changing, drawing out implications for their organisations. Many of these factors are linked together. For example, technology developments may simultaneously change economic factors (for example, creating new jobs), social factors (facilitating more leisure) and environmental factors (reducing pollution). As can be imagined, analysing these factors and their interrelationships can produce long and complex lists.

Rather than getting overwhelmed by a multitude of details, it is necessary to step back eventually to identify the key drivers for change. **Key drivers for change** are the environmental

ILLUSTRATION 2.1

PESTEL analysis of the airline industry

Environmental influences on organisations can be summarised within six categories. For the airline industry, an initial list of influences under the six PESTEL analysis categories might include the following:

Political

- Government support for national carriers
- Security controls
- Restrictions on migration

Economic

- National growth rates
- Fuel prices

Social

- Rise in travel by elderly
- Student international study exchanges

Technological

- Fuel-efficient engines and airframes
- Security check technologies
- Teleconferencing for business

Environmental

- Noise pollution controls
- Energy consumption controls
- Land for growing airports

Legal

- Restrictions on mergers
- Preferential airport rights for some carriers

Questions

1 What additional environmental influences would you add to this initial list for the airline industry?

2 From your more comprehensive list, which of these influences would you highlight as likely to be the 'key drivers for change' for airlines in the coming five years?

factors likely to have a high impact on the success or failure of strategy. Typical key drivers will vary by industry or sector. Thus a retailer may be primarily concerned with social changes driving customer tastes and behaviour, for example forces encouraging out-of-town shopping, and economic changes, for example rates of economic growth and employment. Identifying key drivers for change helps managers to focus on the PESTEL factors that are most important and which must be addressed as the highest priority. Many other changes will depend on these key drivers anyway (for example, an ageing population will drive changes in retail clothing markets). Without a clear sense of the key drivers for change, managers will not be able to take the decisions that allow for effective action.

2.2.2 Building scenarios

When the business environment has high levels of *uncertainty* arising from either complexity or rapid change (or both), it is impossible to develop a single view of how environmental influences might affect an organisation's strategies – indeed it would be dangerous to do so. Scenario analyses are carried out to allow for different possibilities and help prevent managers from closing their minds about alternatives. Thus scenarios offer plausible alternative views of how the business environment might develop in the future, based on key drivers for change about which there is a high level of uncertainty.[2] Scenarios typically build on PESTEL analyses and key drivers for change, but do not offer a single forecast of how the environment will change. The point is not to predict, but to encourage managers to be alert to a range of possible futures.

Illustration 2.2 shows an example of scenario planning for the global financial system to 2020. Rather than incorporating a multitude of factors, the authors focus on two key drivers which (i) have high potential impact and (ii) are uncertain: geo-economic power shifts and international coordination on financial policy. Both of these drivers may produce very different futures, which can be combined to create four internally consistent scenarios for the next decade. The authors do not predict that one will prevail over the others, nor do they allocate relative probabilities. Prediction would close managers' minds to alternatives, while probabilities would imply a spurious kind of accuracy.

Scenario analyses can be carried out as follows:[3]

- *Identifying the scope* is an important first step. Scope refers to the subject of the scenario analysis and the time span. For example, scenario analyses can be carried out for a whole industry globally, or for particular geographical regions and markets. They can be for a decade or so (as in Illustration 2.2) or for just three to five years ahead.

- *Identifying key drivers for change* comes next. Here PESTEL analysis can be used to uncover issues likely to have a major impact upon the future of the industry, region or market.

- *Selecting opposing key drivers* is crucial in order to generate a range of different but plausible scenarios. Typically scenario analyses select from the various key drivers for change two key drivers which both have high uncertainty and have the potential for producing significantly divergent or opposing outcomes. In the oil industry, for example, political stability in the oil-producing regions is one major uncertainty; another is the capacity to develop major new oilfields, thanks to new extraction technologies or oilfield discoveries.

- *Developing scenario 'stories'*: as in films, scenarios are basically stories. Having selected opposing key drivers for change, it is necessary to knit together plausible 'stories' that incorporate both key drivers and other factors into a coherent whole. Thus in Illustration 2.2, the Fragmented protectionism scenario brings together in a consistent way failure to achieve international coordination and a slow rate of geo-economic shift: nationalistic protectionist measures in the West would prevent coordination at the same time as delaying the rise of the Asian economies. But completing the 'story' of Fragmented protectionism would also

ILLUSTRATION 2.2

Scenarios for the global financial system, 2020

Founded in 1971, the World Economic Forum (www.weforum.org) is a not-for-profit organisation based in Geneva and dedicated to developing new thinking amongst political, business and society leaders from countries worldwide. Participants at its famous annual Davos meetings have included German Chancellor Angela Merkel, Microsoft founder Bill Gates and South African President Nelson Mandela. As the world wrestled with the financial crisis of 2008–09, the World Economic Forum proposed to the 2009 Davos meeting four long-range scenarios for how the global financial system might develop to 2025. These scenarios were developed through eight separate workshops involving over 250 financial executives, regulators, policy-makers and senior academics.

The scenarios were based on two key drivers, each governed by a great deal of uncertainty. The first key driver was the pace of geo-economic power shifts, in particular from the traditional centres of economic power in the United States and Europe to the emerging ones in Asia and elsewhere. The second key driver was the degree of international coordination of financial policy, referring to issues such as banking regulation and currency policies. It was the upsides and downsides of these key drivers that defined the following four scenarios.

Re-engineered Western-centrism proposes a world in which the power-shift from the West is reasonably slow and policy-makers manage to coordinate a stable financial framework in which to navigate change. This is a comforting scenario for many Western companies. The *Rebalanced multilateralism* scenario envisages a more rapid shift from the West, but none the less policy-makers are able to coordinate change. For most Western companies, this is challenging but manageable, with Asia continuing to value their participation. More limiting is the *Financial regionalism* scenario. Here policy-makers are unable to find global agreement and the world splits into three major blocs, an American one, a European one and an increasingly powerful Asian one. Western companies are obliged to adopt very different strategies and structures for each of the three main blocs. The final scenario of *Fragmented protectionism* is daunting. Here nationalistic protectionism slows the shift from the West, but also reduces economic growth and leads to the collapse of the integrated Eurozone. All kinds of international business suffer from volatility, conflict and controls.

The World Economic Forum made no forecast about which scenario was more probable. But in presenting the alternatives, it aimed to get policy-makers to see the need for serious action, at the same time as warning business leaders that 'business as usual' was not a likely prospect.

Source: http://www.weforum.org/pdf/scenarios/TheFutureoftheGlobalFinancialSystem.pdf.

	Slow geo-economic shift	Rapid geo-economic shift
Harmonised financial coordination	Re-engineered Western-centrism	Rebalanced multilateralism
Discordant financial coordination	Fragmented protectionism	Financial regionalism

Question

Over which of the two drivers – the geo-economic power shift and policy coordination – do companies have the most influence? How should they exercise this influence?

involve incorporating other consistent factors: for example, slow economic growth resulting from barriers to trade; possible military conflicts due to lack of international cooperation; and illiberal domestic politics associated with nationalism.

- *Identifying impacts* of alternative scenarios on organisations is the final key stage of scenario building. Fragmented protectionism would obviously have a very negative impact for most multinational corporations. Rebalanced multilateralism on the other hand would favour multinationals, especially those from the rising Asian economies. It would be important for an organisation to carry out *robustness checks* in the face of each plausible scenario and develop *contingency plans* in case they happen.

2.3 INDUSTRIES AND SECTORS

The previous section looked at how forces in the macro-environment might influence the success or failure of an organisation's strategies. But the impact of these general factors tends to surface in the more immediate environment through changes in the competitive forces surrounding organisations. An important aspect of this for most organisations will be competition within their industry, sector or market. **An industry is a group of firms producing products and services that are essentially the same.**[4] Examples are the automobile industry and the airline industry. Industries are also often described as 'sectors', especially in public services (for example, the health sector or the education sector). Industries and sectors are often made up of several specific markets. **A market is a group of customers for specific products or services that are essentially the same (for example, a particular geographical market).** Thus the automobile industry has markets in North America, Europe and Asia, for example.

This section concentrates on industry analysis, starting with Michael Porter's *five forces framework* and then introducing techniques for analysing the *dynamics* of industries. However, while the following section will address markets in more detail, this section will refer to markets and most of the concepts apply similarly to markets and industries.

2.3.1 Competitive forces – the five forces framework

Porter's five forces framework helps identify the attractiveness of an industry in terms of five competitive forces: the threat of entry, the threat of substitutes, the power of buyers, the power of suppliers and the extent of rivalry between competitors. These five forces together constitute an industry's 'structure' (see Figure 2.2), which is typically fairly stable. For Porter, an attractive industry structure is one that offers good profit potential. His essential message is that where the five forces are high, industries are not attractive to compete in. There will be too much competition, and too much pressure, to allow reasonable profits.

Porter's five forces framework

Although initially developed with businesses in mind, the five forces framework is relevant to most organisations. It can provide a useful starting point for strategic analysis even where profit criteria may not apply. In the public sector, it is important to understand how powerful suppliers can push up costs; amongst charities, it is important to avoid excessive rivalry within the same market. Moreover, once the degree of industry attractiveness has been understood,

Figure 2.2 The five forces framework

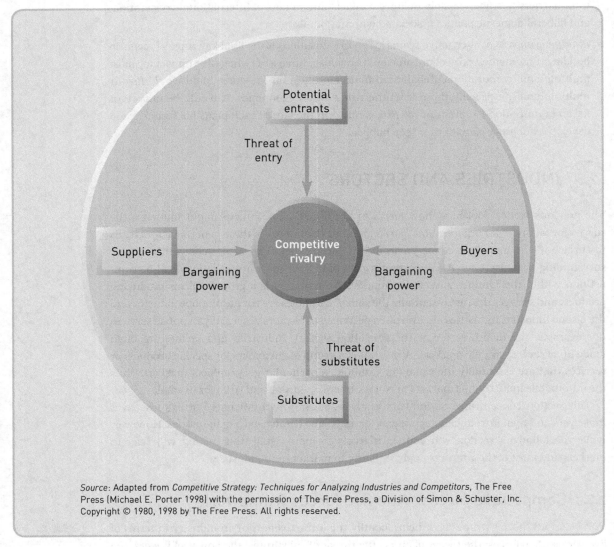

the five forces can help set an agenda for action on the various critical issues that they identify: for example, what should be done to control excessive rivalry in a particular industry? The rest of this section introduces each of the five forces in more detail. Illustration 2.3 on the evolving steel industry provides examples.

The threat of entry

How easy it is to enter the industry obviously influences the degree of competition. The greater the threat of entry, the worse it is for incumbents (existing competitors) in an industry. An attractive industry has high barriers to entry in order to reduce the threat of new competitors.

ILLUSTRATION 2.3

The consolidating steel industry

Five forces analysis helps understand the changing attractiveness of an industry.

For a long time, the steel industry was seen as a static and unprofitable one. Producers were nationally-based, often state-owned and frequently unprofitable – the early 2000s saw 50 independent steel producers going into bankruptcy in the United States alone. But recent years have seen a turnaround. During 2006, Mittal Steel paid $35bn (~€24.5bn) to buy European steel giant Arcelor, creating the world's largest steel company. The following year, Indian conglomerate Tata bought Anglo-Dutch steel company Corus for $13bn. These high prices indicated considerable confidence in the prospects of a better industry structure.

New entrants

In the last two decades, two powerful groups have entered world steel markets. First, after a period of privatisation and reorganisation, Russia had become the world's second largest steel exporting country (behind Japan) in 2009, led by giants such as Severstal and Evraz. China too had become a major force. Between the early 1990s and 2009, Chinese producers have increased their capacity six times. Although Chinese share of world capacity reached over 40 per cent in 2009, most of this was directed at the domestic market. China was the word's fourth largest steel exporter in 2009.

Substitutes

Steel is a nineteenth-century technology, increasingly substituted for by other materials such as aluminium in cars, plastics and aluminium in packaging and ceramics and composites in many high-tech applications. Steel's own technological advances sometimes work to reduce need: thus steel cans have become about one-third thinner over the last few decades.

Buyer power

The major buyers of steel are the global car manufacturers. Car manufacturers are sophisticated users, often leading in the technological development of their materials. In North America at least, the decline of the once dominant 'Big Three' – General Motors, Ford and Chrysler – has meant many new domestic buyers, with companies such as Toyota, Nissan, Honda and BMW establishing local production plants. Another important user of steel is the metal packaging industry. Leading can producers such as Crown Holdings, which makes one-third of all food cans produced in North America and Europe, buy in large volumes, coordinating purchases around the world.

Supplier power

The key raw material for steel producers is iron ore. The big three ore producers – Vale, Rio Tinto and BHP Billiton – control about 70 per cent of the market for internationally traded ore. Iron ore prices had multiplied four times between 2005 and 2008, and, despite the recession, were still twice the 2005 level in 2010.

Competitive rivalry

The industry has traditionally been very fragmented: in 2000, the world's top five producers accounted for only 14 per cent of production. Companies such as Nucor in the US, Thyssen-Krupp in Germany as well as Mittal and Tata responded by buying up weaker players internationally. By 2009, the top five producers accounted for 20 per cent of world production. New steel giant ArcelorMittal alone accounted for about 10 per cent of world production, with one-fifth of the European Union market. None the less, despite a cyclical peak in 2008 and a slump in 2009, the world steel price was basically the same in 2010 as in 2005.

Questions

1 In recent years, which of the five forces has become more positive for steel producers, which less so?

2 Explain the acquisition strategies of players such as Mittal, Tata and Nucor.

3 In the future, what might change to make the steel industry less or more attractive?

Barriers to entry are the factors that need to be overcome by new entrants if they are to compete in an industry. Typical barriers are as follows:

- *Scale and experience.* In some industries, *economies of scale* are extremely important: for example, in the production of automobiles or the advertising of fast-moving consumer goods. Once incumbents have reached large-scale production, it will be very expensive for new entrants to match them and until they reach a similar volume they will have higher unit costs. This scale effect is increased where there are high *investment requirements* for entry, for example research costs in pharmaceuticals or capital equipment costs in automobiles. Barriers to entry also come from *experience curve* effects that give incumbents a cost advantage because they have learnt how to do things more efficiently than an inexperienced new entrant could possibly do (see section 5.2.1). Until the new entrant has built up equivalent experience over time, it will tend to produce at higher cost.

- *Access to supply or distribution channels.* In many industries manufacturers have had control over supply and/or distribution channels. Sometimes this has been through direct ownership (vertical integration), sometimes just through customer or supplier loyalty. In some industries this barrier has been overcome by new entrants who have bypassed retail distributors and sold directly to consumers through e-commerce (for example, Dell Computers and Amazon).

- *Expected retaliation.* If an organisation considering entering an industry believes that the retaliation of an existing firm will be so great as to prevent entry, or mean that entry would be too costly, this is also a barrier. Retaliation could take the form of a price war or a marketing blitz. Just the knowledge that incumbents are prepared to retaliate is often sufficiently discouraging to act as a barrier. Thus the history of fierce retaliation in the Atlantic airline market helps deter potential new entrants.

- *Legislation or government action.* Legal restraints on new entry vary from patent protection (e.g. pharmaceuticals), to regulation of markets (e.g. pension selling), through to direct government action (e.g. tariffs). Of course, organisations are vulnerable to new entrants if governments remove such protection, as has happened with deregulation of the airline industry.

- *Differentiation.* Differentiation means providing a product or service with higher perceived value than the competition; its importance will be discussed more fully in section 5.2.2. Cars are differentiated, for example, by quality and branding. Steel, by contrast, is by-and-large a commodity, undifferentiated and therefore sold by the ton. Steel buyers will simply buy the cheapest. Differentiation reduces the threat of entry because of increasing customer loyalty.

The threat of substitutes

Substitutes are products or services that offer a similar benefit to an industry's products or services, but by a different process. For example, aluminium is a substitute for steel in automobiles; trains are a substitute for cars; television and videogames are substitutes for each other. Managers often focus on competitors in their own industry, and neglect the threat posed by substitutes. Substitutes can reduce demand for a particular type of product as customers switch to alternatives – even to the extent that this type of product or service becomes obsolete. However, there does not have to be much actual switching for the substitute threat to have an effect. The simple risk of substitution puts a cap on the prices that can be charged in an industry. Thus, although Eurostar has no direct competitors in terms of train services from Paris to London, the prices it can charge are ultimately limited by the cost of flights between the two cities.

There are two important points to bear in mind about substitutes:

- *The price/performance ratio* is critical to substitution threats. A substitute is still an effective threat even if more expensive, so long as it offers performance advantages that customers value. Thus aluminium is more expensive than steel, but its relative lightness and its resistance to corrosion give it an advantage in some automobile manufacturing applications. It is the ratio of price to performance that matters, rather than simple price.

- *Extra-industry effects* are the core of the substitution concept. Substitutes come from outside the incumbents' industry and should not be confused with competitors' threats from within the industry. The value of the substitution concept is to force managers to look outside their own industry to consider more distant threats and constraints. The higher the threat of substitution, the less attractive the industry is likely to be.

The power of buyers

Buyers **are the organisation's immediate customers, not necessarily the ultimate consumers.** If buyers are powerful, then they can demand cheap prices or insist on costly improvements in products or services.

Buyer power is likely to be high when some of the following conditions prevail:

- *Concentrated buyers.* Where a few large customers account for the majority of sales, buyer power is increased. This is the case with items such as milk in the grocery sector in many European countries, where just a few retailers dominate the market. If a product or service accounts for a high percentage of the buyers' total purchases, their power is also likely to increase as they are more likely to 'shop around' to get the best price and therefore 'squeeze' suppliers than they would be for more trivial purchases.

- *Low switching costs.* Where buyers can easily switch between one supplier and another, they have a strong negotiating position and can squeeze suppliers who are desperate for their business. Switching costs are typically low for weakly differentiated commodities such as steel.

- *Buyer competition threat.* If the buyer has the capability to supply itself, or if it has the possibility of acquiring such a capability, it tends to be powerful. In negotiation with its suppliers, it can raise the threat of doing the suppliers' job themselves. This is called *backward vertical integration* (see section 6.4.1), moving back to sources of supply, and might occur if satisfactory prices or quality from suppliers cannot be obtained. For example, some steel companies have gained power over their iron ore suppliers as they have acquired iron ore sources for themselves.

It is very important that *buyers* are distinguished from *ultimate consumers*. Thus for companies like Procter & Gamble or Unilever (makers of shampoo, washing powders and so on), their buyers are retailers such as Carrefour or Tesco, not ordinary consumers (see discussion of the 'strategic customer' in 2.4.2). Carrefour and Tesco have much more negotiating power than an ordinary consumer would have. The high buying power of such supermarkets has become a major source of pressure for the companies supplying them.

The power of suppliers

Suppliers are those who supply the organisation with what it needs to produce the product or service. As well as fuel, raw materials and equipment, this can include labour and sources of finance. The factors increasing supplier power are the converse to those for buyer power. Thus *supplier power* is likely to be high where there are:

- *Concentrated suppliers.* Where just a few producers dominate supply, suppliers have more power over buyers. The iron ore industry is now concentrated in the hands of three main producers, leaving the steel companies, still relatively fragmented, in a weak negotiating position for this essential raw material.

- *High switching cost.* If it is expensive or disruptive to move from one supplier to another, then the buyer becomes relatively dependent and correspondingly weak. Microsoft is a powerful supplier because of the high switching costs of moving from one operating system to another. Buyers are prepared to pay a premium to avoid the trouble, and Microsoft knows it.

- *Supplier competition threat.* Suppliers have increased power where they are able to cut out buyers who are acting as middlemen. Thus airlines have been able to negotiate tough contracts with travel agencies as the rise of online booking has allowed them to create a direct route to customers. This is called *forward vertical integration*, moving up closer to the ultimate customer.

Most organisations have many suppliers, so it is necessary to concentrate the analysis on the most important ones or types. If their power is high, suppliers can capture all their buyers' own potential profits simply by raising their prices. Star football players supply their labour at astronomical cost, with the result that even the leading football clubs – their 'buyers' – struggle to make money.

Competitive rivalry

These wider competitive forces (the four arrows in the model in Figure 2.2) all impinge on the direct competitive rivalry between an organisation and its most immediate rivals. Thus low barriers to entry increase the number of rivals; powerful buyers with low switching costs force their suppliers to high rivalry in order to offer the best deals. The more competitive rivalry there is, the worse it is for incumbents within the industry.

Competitive rivals are organisations with similar products and services aimed at the same customer group (i.e. not substitutes). In the European airline industry, Air France and British Airways are rivals; trains are a substitute. As well as the influence of the four previous forces, there are a number of additional factors directly affecting the degree of competitive rivalry in an industry or sector:

- *Competitor balance*. Where competitors are of roughly equal size there is the danger of intensely rivalrous behaviour as one competitor attempts to gain dominance over others, through aggressive price cuts for example. Conversely, less rivalrous industries tend to have one or two dominant organisations, with the smaller players reluctant to challenge the larger ones directly (for example, by focusing on niches to avoid the 'attention' of the dominant companies).

- *Industry growth rate*. In situations of strong growth, an organisation can grow with the market, but in situations of low growth or decline, any growth is likely to be at the expense of a rival, and meet with fierce resistance. Low growth markets are therefore often associated with price competition and low profitability. The *industry life cycle* influences growth rates, and hence competitive conditions: see section 2.3.2.

- *High fixed costs*. Industries with high fixed costs, perhaps because requiring high investments in capital equipment or initial research, tend to be highly rivalrous. Companies will seek to spread their costs (i.e. reduce unit costs) by increasing their volumes: to do so, they typically cut their prices, prompting competitors to do the same and thereby triggering price wars in which everyone in the industry suffers. Similarly, if extra capacity can only be added in large increments (as in many manufacturing sectors, for example a chemical or glass factory), the competitor making such an addition is likely to create short-term over-capacity in the industry, leading to increased competition to use capacity.

- *High exit barriers*. The existence of high barriers to exit – in other words, closure or disinvestment – tends to increase rivalry, especially in declining industries. Excess capacity persists and consequently incumbents fight to maintain market share. Exit barriers might be high for a variety of reasons: for example, high redundancy costs or high investment in specific assets such as plant and equipment that others would not buy.

- *Low differentiation*. In a commodity market, where products or services are poorly differentiated, rivalry is increased because there is little to stop customers switching between competitors and the only way to compete is on price.

Some analysts add a 'sixth force' to Porter's five forces, organisations supplying complementary products and services. For example, suppliers of microprocessors (such as Intel) and suppliers of software (such as Microsoft) are *complementors* to each other in the sense that the value of one of their products depends on the effectiveness of the other (good software needs good microprocessors). The profitability of an industry can be affected by the effectiveness of complementors. For example, personal computer makers depend on Microsoft to drive demand for their products. Better software may increase the market for more advanced computers.

2.3.2 The dynamics of industry structure

Industry structure analysis can easily become too static: after all, structure implies stablility.[5] However, scenario analysis raises the issue of how competitive forces may change *over time*.

ILLUSTRATION 2.4

Chugging and the structure of the charity sector

Industry structure contributes to inefficiency and aggression in the United Kingdom's charity sector.

The charity sector has become controversial in the United Kingdom. The aggressive fund-raising of some charities is epitomised by workers soliciting donations from shoppers on a commission basis. Such is their perceived aggression that these charity workers are known as 'chuggers', compared with the violent street-crime of 'muggers'.

In 2008, there were 189,000 charities registered in England and Wales, 95 per cent having annual incomes of less than £500,000. However, about 80 per cent of all charity income is raised by the largest twenty charities, headed by Cancer Research UK (2008 income, £355m (~€390m; ~$532m)). According to *Charity Market Monitor*, in 2008, the top 300 charities averaged a 0.9 per cent increase in income, but the largest 10 managed income growth of 2.3 per cent (excluding impact of mergers).

The United Kingdom government introduced the 2006 Charities Act with the specific intention of assisting mergers between independent charities. This had followed a report of the Charity Commission, the regulator for charities in England and Wales, that had commented on the charity sector thus:

Some people believe that there are too many charities competing for too few funds and that a significant amount of charitable resource could be saved if more charities pooled their resources and worked together . . .

The majority of charities are relatively small, local organisations that rely entirely on the unpaid help of their trustees and other volunteers. They may have similar purposes to many other charities but they are all serving different communities. The nature of these charities suggests that there are less likely to be significant areas of overlap . . . It is the much larger, professionally run, charities which, because of their size, tend to face charges of duplication, waste and over-aggressive fund-raising. Whilst there are some clear advantages to be had from a healthy plurality of charities, which are constantly refreshed by new charities pursuing new activities, there are also big benefits of public confidence and support

to be had from showing collaborative, as opposed to over-competitive, instincts.

Local authorities in particular were frustrated by duplication and waste, as they increasingly commission local charities to deliver services. With respect to small charities, local authority budgets are relatively large. One charity sector chief executive, Caroline Shaw, told *Charity Times* as she pursued more cooperation between local charities:

'Without a doubt there is increased competition when it comes to [local authority] commissioning . . . Our driving force has really been to try to create a more effective service for front line organisations; to offer more projects, more diverse services, more effective services. There's a huge amount [of charities] all fighting for funding. I really think that people should be looking at working more closely together.'

During 2008, more than 230 charity mergers were registered with the Charity Commission. As the recession began to put pressure on charitable donations throughout the sector, early 2009 saw the merger of two well-established charities helping the elderly in the United Kingom, Help the Aged and Age Concern. The new charity, Age UK, has a combined income of around £160 million, including £47 million a year raised through fundraising, and over 520 charity shops.

Sources: 'RS 4a – Collaborative working and mergers: Summary', http://www.charity-commission.gov.uk/publications/rs4a.asp; *Charity Times*, 'Strength in Numbers', August 2007; *Charity Market Monitor*, 2009.

Questions

1 Which of Porter's five forces are creating problems for the United Kingdom's charity sector?

2 What type of industry structure might the charity industry be moving towards? What would be the benefits and disadvantages of that structure?

The key drivers for change are likely to alter industry structures and scenario analyses are useful for analysing possible impacts. An illustration of changing industry structure, and the competitive implications of this, is provided by Illustration 2.4 on the UK charity sector. This section examines two additional approaches to understanding change in industry structure: the *industry life cycle* concept and *comparative five forces analyses*.

The industry life cycle

The power of the five forces typically varies with the stages of the industry life cycle. The industry life cycle concept proposes that industries start small in their development stage, then go through a period of rapid growth (the equivalent to 'adolescence' in the human life cycle), culminating in a period of 'shake-out'. The final two stages are first a period of slow or even zero growth ('maturity'), and then the final stage of decline ('old age'). Each of these stages has implications for the five forces.[6]

The *development stage* is an experimental one, typically with few players, little direct rivalry and highly differentiated products. The five forces are likely to be weak, therefore, though profits may actually be scarce because of high investment requirements. The next stage is one of high *growth*, with rivalry low as there is plenty of market opportunity for everybody. Buyers may be keen to secure supplies of the booming new product and may also lack sophistication about what they are buying, so diminishing their power. One downside of the growth stage is that barriers to entry may be low, as existing competitors have not built up much scale, experience or customer loyalty. Another potential downside is the power of suppliers if there is a shortage of components or materials that fast-growing businesses need for expansion. The *shake-out stage* begins as the growth rate starts to decline, so that increased rivalry forces the weakest of the new entrants out of the business. In the *maturity stage*, barriers to entry tend to increase, as control over distribution is established and economies of scale and experience curve benefits come into play. Products or service tend to standardise. Buyers may become more powerful as they become less avid for the industry's products or services and more confident in switching between suppliers. Market share is typically crucial at the maturity stage, providing leverage against buyers and competitive advantage in terms of cost. Finally, the *decline stage* can be a period of extreme rivalry, especially where there are high exit barriers, as falling sales force remaining competitors into dog-eat-dog competition. Figure 2.3 summarises some of the conditions that can be expected at different stages in the life cycle.

It is important to avoid putting too much faith in the inevitability of life-cycle stages. One stage does not follow predictably after another: industries vary widely in the length of their growth stages, and others can rapidly 'de-mature' through radical innovation. The telephony industry, based for nearly a century on fixed-line telephones, de-matured rapidly with the introduction of mobile and internet telephony. Anita McGahan of Toronto University warns of the 'maturity mindset', which can leave many managers complacent and slow to respond to new competition.[7] Managing in mature industries is not necessarily just about waiting for decline. However, even if the various stages are not inevitable, the life-cycle concept does remind managers that conditions are likely to change over time. Especially in fast-moving industries, five forces analyses need to be reviewed quite regularly.

Figure 2.3 The industry life cycle

Development	Growth	Shake-out	Maturity	Decline

Market size

| *Low rivalry:* High differentiation Innovation key | *Low rivalry:* High growth and weak buyers, but low entry barriers Growth ability key | *Increasing rivalry:* Slower growth and some exits Managerial and financial strength key | *Stronger buyers:* Low growth and standard products, but higher entry barriers Market share and cost key | *Extreme rivalry:* Typically many exits and price competition Cost and commitment key |

Typical five forces

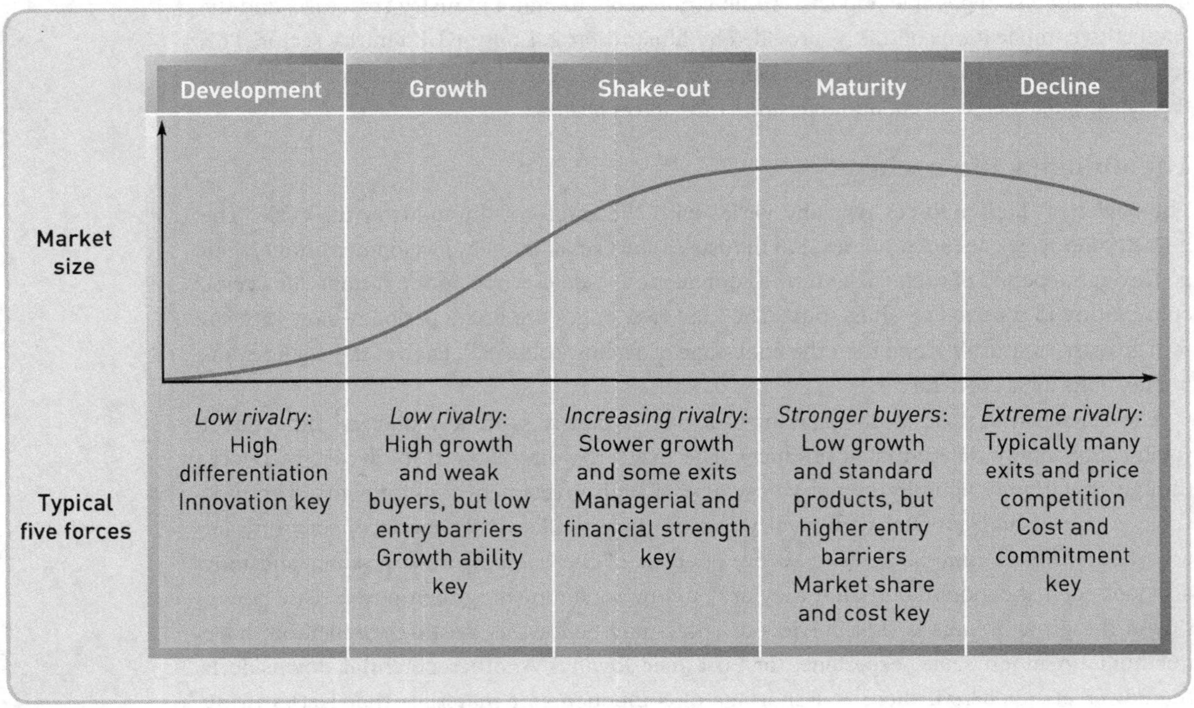

Comparative industry structure analyses

The industry life cycle underlines the need to make industry structure analysis dynamic. One effective means of doing this is to compare the five forces over time in a simple 'radar plot'.

Figure 2.4 provides a framework for summarising the power of each of the five forces on five axes. Power diminishes as the axes go outwards. Where the forces are low, the total area enclosed by the lines between the axes is large; where the forces are high, the total area enclosed by the lines is small. The larger the enclosed area, therefore, the greater is the profit potential. In Figure 2.4, the industry at Time 0 (represented by the light blue lines) has relatively low rivalry (just a few competitors) and faces low substitution threats. The threat of entry is moderate, but both buyer power and supplier power are relatively high. Overall, this looks like only a moderately attractive industry to invest in.

However, given the dynamic nature of industries, managers need to look forward – here five years represented by the green lines in Figure 2.4. Managers are predicting, in this case, some rise in the threat of substitutes (perhaps new technologies will be developed). On the other hand, they predict a falling entry threat, while both buyer power and supplier power will be easing. Rivalry will reduce still further. This looks like a classic case of an industry in which a few players emerge with overall dominance. The area enclosed by the green lines is large, suggesting a relatively attractive industry. For a firm confident of becoming one of the dominant players, this might be an industry well worth investing in.

Figure 2.4 Comparative industry structure analysis

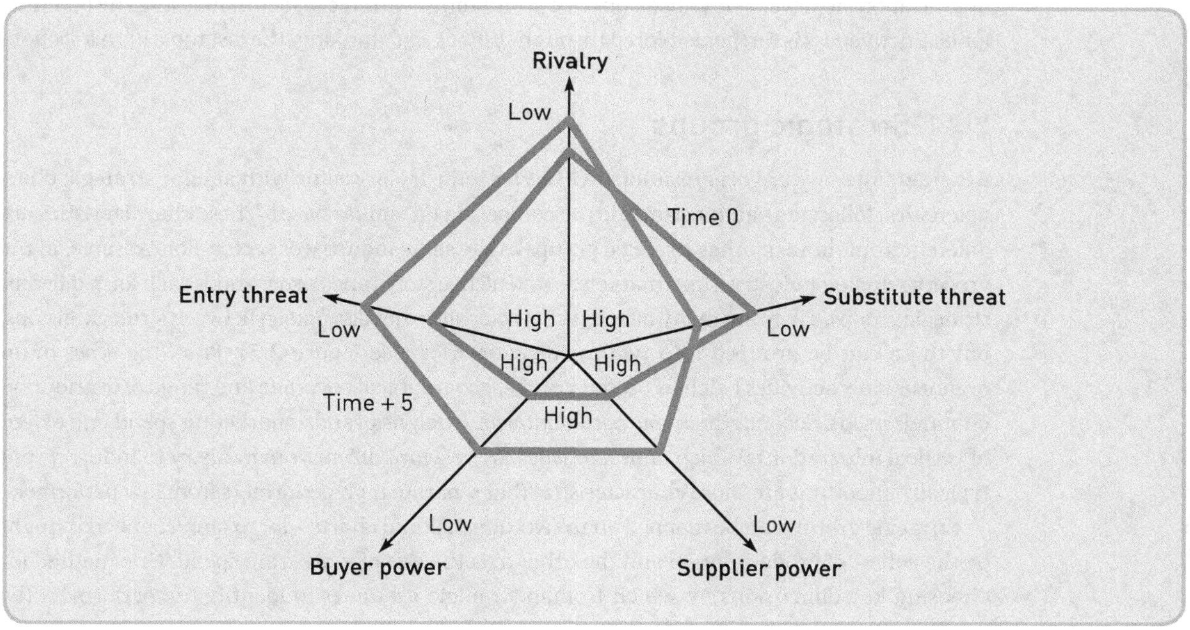

Comparing the five forces over time on a radar plot thus helps to give industry structure analysis a dynamic aspect. Similar plots can be made to aid diversification decisions (see Chapter 6), where possible new industries to enter can be compared in terms of attractiveness. The lines are only approximate, of course, because they aggregate the many individual elements that make up each of the forces into a simple composite measure. Notice too that if one of the forces is very adverse, then this might nullify positive assessments on the other four axes: for example, an industry with low rivalry, low substitution, low entry barriers and low supplier power might still be unattractive if powerful buyers were able to demand highly discounted prices. With these warnings in mind, such radar plots can none the less be both a useful device for initial analysis and an effective summary of a final, more refined analysis.

(2.4) COMPETITORS AND MARKETS

An industry or sector analysis may be at too high a level to provide a detailed understanding of competition. The five forces can impact differently on different kinds of players in an indistry. Thus Hyundai and Porsche may be in the same broad industry (automobiles), but they are positioned differently: they are protected by different barriers to entry and competitive moves by one are unlikely to affect the other. It is often useful to disaggregate. Many industries contain a range of companies, each of which has different capabilities and competes on different bases. These competitor differences are captured by the concept of *strategic groups*. Customers too can differ significantly and these can be captured by distinguishing between different *market segments*.

Thinking in terms of different strategic groups and market segments provides opportunities for organisations to develop highly distinctive positionings within broader industries. The potential for distinctiveness is further explored through '*Blue Ocean*' thinking, the last topic in this section.

2.4.1 Strategic groups[8]

Strategic groups are organisations within an industry or sector with similar strategic characteristics, following similar strategies or competing on similar bases. These characteristics are different from those in other strategic groups in the same industry or sector. For example, in the grocery retailing industry, supermarkets, convenience stores and corner shops each form different strategic groups. There are many different characteristics that distinguish between strategic groups, but these can be grouped into two major categories (see Figure 2.5). First, the *scope* of an organisation's activities (such as product range, geographical coverage and range of distribution channels used). Second, the *resource commitment* (such as brands, marketing spend and extent of vertical integration). Which characteristics are relevant differs from industry to industry, but typically important are those characteristics that separate high performers from low performers.

Strategic groups can be mapped on to two-dimensional charts – for example, one axis might be the extent of product range and the other axis the size of marketing spend. One method for choosing key dimensions by which to map strategic groups is to identify top performers (by

Figure 2.5 Some characteristics for identifying strategic groups

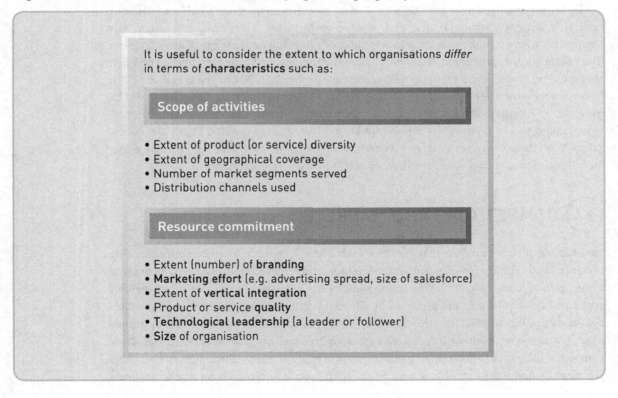

growth or profitability) in an industry and to compare them with low performers. Characteristics that are shared by top performers, but not by low performers, are likely to be particularly relevant for mapping strategic groups. For example, the most profitable firms in an industry might all be narrow in terms of product range, and lavish in terms of marketing spend, while the less profitable firms might be more widely spread in terms of products and restrained in their marketing. Here the two dimensions for mapping would be product range and marketing spend. A potential recommendation for the less profitable firms would be to cut back their product range and boost their marketing.

Figure 2.6 shows strategic groups amongst Indian pharmaceutical companies, with research and development intensity (R&D spend as a percentage of sales) and overseas focus (exports and patents registered overseas) defining the axes of the map. These two axes do explain a good deal of the variation in profitability between groups. The most profitable group is the Emergent Globals (11.3 per cent average return on sales), those with high R&D intensity and high overseas focus. On the other hand, the Exploiter group spends little on R&D and is focused on domestic markets, and only enjoys 2.0 per cent average return on sales.

Figure 2.6 Strategic groups in the Indian pharmaceutical industry

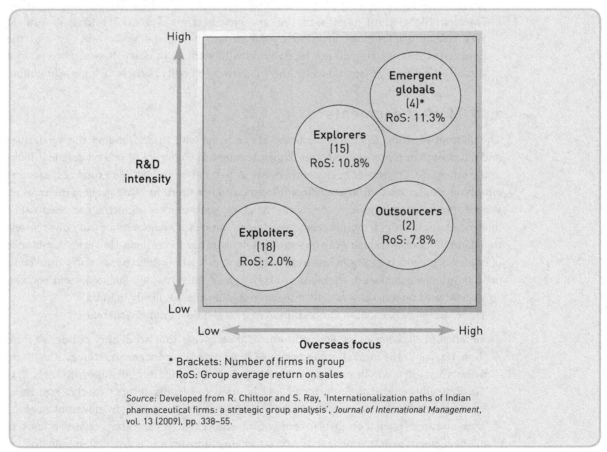

* Brackets: Number of firms in group
RoS: Group average return on sales

Source: Developed from R. Chittoor and S. Ray, 'Internationalization paths of Indian pharmaceutical firms: a strategic group analysis', *Journal of International Management*, vol. 13 (2009), pp. 338–55.

This strategic group concept is useful in at least three ways:

- *Understanding competition.* Managers can focus on their direct competitors within their particular strategic group, rather than the whole industry. They can also establish the dimensions that distinguish them most from other groups, and which might be the basis for relative success or failure. These dimensions can then become the focus of their action.

- *Analysis of strategic opportunities.* Strategic group maps can identify the most attractive 'strategic spaces' within an industry. Some spaces on the map may be 'white spaces', relatively under-occupied. In the Indian pharmaceutical industry, the white space is high R&D investment combined with focus on domestic markets. Such white spaces might be unexploited opportunities. On the other hand, they could turn out to be 'black holes', impossible to exploit and likely to damage any entrant. A strategic group map is only the first stage of the analysis. Strategic spaces need to tested carefully.

- *Analysis of mobility barriers.* Of course, moving across the map to take advantage of opportunities is not costless. Often it will require difficult decisions and rare resources. Strategic groups are therefore characterised by 'mobility barriers', obstacles to movement from one strategic group to another. These are similar to barriers to entry in five forces analysis. Although movement from the Exploiter group in Indian pharmaceuticals to the Emergent Global group might seem very attractive in terms of profits, it is likely to demand very substantial financial investment and strong managerial skills. Mobility into the Emergent Global group will not be easy. As with barriers to entry, it is good to be in a successful strategic group into which there are strong mobility barriers, to impede imitation.

2.4.2 Market segments

The concept of strategic groups discussed above helps with understanding the similarities and differences in terms of competitor characteristics. The concept of market segment looks at the other side, differences in customer needs. A **market segment**[9] **is a group of customers who have similar needs that are different from customer needs in other parts of the market.** Where these customer groups are relatively small, such market segments are often called 'niches'. Dominance of a market segment or niche can be very valuable, for the same reasons that dominance of an industry can be valuable following five forces logic. However, dominance of market segments is typically less secure than that of a whole industry, as entry from competitors in adjacent market segments is likely to be relatively easy. For long-term success, strategies based on market segments must keep customer needs firmly in mind.

Three issues are particularly important in market segment analysis, therefore:

- *Variation in customer needs.* Focusing on customer needs that are highly distinctive from those typical in the market is one means of building a secure segment strategy. Customer needs vary for a whole variety of reasons – some of which are identified in Table 2.1. Theoretically, any of these factors could be used to identify distinct market segments. However, the crucial bases of segmentation vary according to market. In industrial markets, segmentation is often thought of in terms of industrial classification of buyers: steel producers might segment by automobile industry, packaging industry and construction industry, for example. On the other hand, segmentation by buyer behaviour (for example, direct buying

Table 2.1 Some bases of market segmentation

Type of factor	Consumer markets	Industrial/organisational markets
Characteristics of people/organisations	Age, sex, race Income Family size Life-cycle stage Location Lifestyle	Industry Location Size Technology Profitability Management
Purchase/use situation	Size of purchase Brand loyalty Purpose of use Purchasing behaviour Importance of purchase Choice criteria	Application Importance of purchase Volume Frequency of purchase Purchasing procedure Choice criteria Distribution channel
Users' needs and preferences for product characteristics	Product similarity Price preference Brand preferences Desired features Quality	Performance requirements Assistance from suppliers Brand preferences Desired features Quality Service requirements

versus those users who buy through third parties such as contractors) or purchase value (for example, high-value bulk purchasers versus frequent low-value purchasers) might be more appropriate. Being able to serve a highly distinctive segment that other organisations find difficult to serve is often the basis for a secure long-term strategy.

- *Specialisation.* Within a market segment, this can also be an important basis for a successful segmentation strategy and is sometimes called a 'niche strategy'. Organisations that have built up most experience in servicing a particular market segment should not only have lower costs in so doing, but also have built relationships which may be difficult for others to break down. Experience and relationships are likely to protect a dominant position in a particular segment. However, precisely because customers value different things in different segments, specialised producers may find it very difficult to compete on a broader basis. For example, a small local brewery competing against the big brands on the basis of its ability to satisfy distinctive local tastes is unlikely to find it easy to serve other segments where tastes are different, scale requirements are larger and distribution channels are more complex.

- *Strategic customers.* It is crucial to understand whose needs matter. The **strategic customer is the person(s) at whom the strategy is primarily addressed because they have the most influence over which goods or services are purchased.** As above, for a food manufacturer, it is the retailers' needs that matter most directly, not simply the ultimate consumers of the food. It is retailers who pay the manufacturer and decide what to stock. Retailers care about price and quality because consumers do, so the manufacturer must take these needs into account, but retailers also care about delivery convenience and reliability. For a food manufacturer, therefore, the strategic customer is the retailer: the retailer's needs, not just the ultimate consumers' needs, should shape strategy. In the public sector, the strategic customer is very often the agency that controls the funds or authorises use, rather than the user of the service. In public health care, therefore, it is hospitals, not patients, that are the strategic customers of pharmaceutical companies.

2.4.3 Blue Ocean thinking

The more differentiated views of competitors and customers embodied in strategic groups and market segments can be taken a step further by 'Blue Ocean' thinking. As developed by W. Chan Kim and Renée Mauborgne at INSEAD, **Blue Oceans are new market spaces where competition is minimised.**[10] Blue Oceans contrast with 'Red Oceans', where industries are already well defined and rivalry is intense. Blue Oceans evoke wide empty seas. Red Oceans are associated with bloody competition and 'red ink', in other words financial losses.

Blue Ocean thinking therefore encourages entrepreneurs and managers to be different by finding or creating market spaces that are not currently being served. Strategy here is about finding *strategic gaps*, opportunities in the environment that are not being fully exploited by competitors. The strategy canvas is one framework that can effectively assist this kind of Blue Ocean thinking. A **strategy canvas compares competitors according to their performance on key success factors in order to develop strategies based on creating new market spaces.** Figure 2.7 shows a strategy canvas for three engineering components companies, highlighting the following three features:

- **Critical success factors** (CSFs) **are those factors that are either particularly valued by customers or which provide a significant advantage in terms of cost.** Critical success factors are therefore likely to be an important source of competitive advantage or disadvantage. Figure 2.7 identifies five established critical success factors in this engineering components market (cost, after-sales service, delivery reliability, technical quality and testing facilities). Note there is also a new sixth critical success factor, design advisory services, which will be discussed under the third subhead, value innovation.

- **Value curves are a graphic depiction of how customers perceive competitors' relative performance across the critical success factors.** In Figure 2.7, companies A and B perform well on cost, service, reliability and quality, but less well on testing. They do not offer any design advice. Company C has a radically different value curve, characteristic of a 'value innovator'.

- **Value innovation is the creation of new market space by excelling on established critical success factors on which competitors are performing badly and/or by creating new critical success factors representing previously unrecognised customer wants.** Thus in Figure 2.7, company C is a value innovator in both senses. First, it excels on the established customer need of offering testing facilities for customers' products using its components. Second, it offers a new and valued design service advising customers on how to integrate their components in order for them to create better products.

Company C's strategy exemplifies two critical principles in Blue Ocean thinking: *focus* and *divergence*. First, Company C focuses its efforts on just two factors, testing and design services, while maintaining only adequate performance on the other critical success factors where its

Figure 2.7 Strategy canvas for electrical components companies

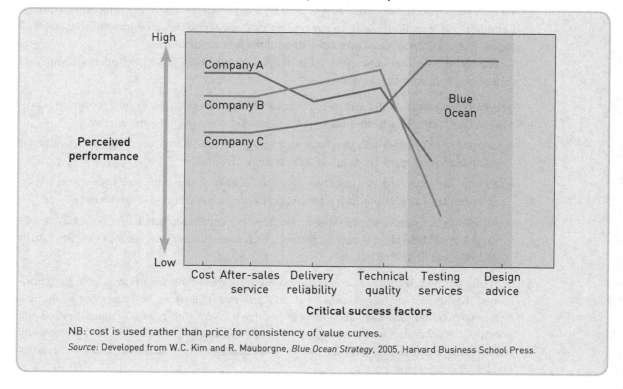

NB: cost is used rather than price for consistency of value curves.

Source: Developed from W.C. Kim and R. Mauborgne, *Blue Ocean Strategy*, 2005, Harvard Business School Press.

competitors are already high performers. Second, it has created a value curve that significantly diverges from its competitors' value curves, creating a substantial strategic gap, or Blue Ocean, in the areas of testing and design services. This is shrewd. For Company C, beating Companies A and B in the areas where they are performing well anyway would require major investment and likely provide little advantage given that customers are already highly satisfied. Challenging A and B on cost, after-sales service, delivery or quality would be a Red Ocean strategy. Far better is to concentrate on where a large gap can be created between competitors. Company C faces little competition for those customers who really value testing and design services, and consequently can charge good prices for them.

(2.5) OPPORTUNITIES AND THREATS

The concepts and frameworks discussed above should be helpful in understanding the factors in the macro-, industry and competitor/market environments of an organisation. However, the critical issue is the *implications* that are drawn from this understanding in guiding strategic decisions and choices. The crucial next stage, therefore, is to draw from the environmental analysis specific strategic opportunities and threats for the organisation. Identifying these opportunities and threats is extremely valuable when thinking about strategic choices for the future (the subject of Chapters 5 to 9). Opportunities and threats forms one half of the Strengths, Weaknesses, Opportunities and Threats (SWOT) analyses that shape many companies' strategy formulation (see section 3.4.3). In responding strategically to the environment, the goal is to reduce identified threats and take advantage of the best opportunities.

The techniques and concepts in this chapter should help in identifying environmental threats and opportunities, for instance:

- a *PESTEL analysis* of the macro-environment might reveal threats and opportunities presented by technological change, or shifts in market demographics and similar;
- identification of *key drivers for change* can help generate different scenarios for managerial discussion, some more threatening, others more favourable;
- a *Porter five forces analysis* might for example identify a rise or fall in barriers to entry, or opportunities to reduce industry rivalry, perhaps by acquisition of competitors;
- *Blue Ocean* thinking might reveal where companies can create new market spaces; alternatively it could help identify success factors which new entrants might attack in order to turn 'Blue Oceans' into 'Red Oceans'.

While all these techniques and concepts are important tools for understanding environments, it is important to recognise that any analysis is likely to be somewhat subjective. Entrepreneurs and managers often have particular blinkers with regard to what they see and prioritise.[11] Techniques and concepts can be helpful in challenging existing assumptions and encouraging broader perspectives, but they are unlikely to overcome human subjectivity and biases completely.

SUMMARY

- Environmental influences can be thought of as layers around an organisation, with the outer layer making up the *macro-environment*, the middle layer making up the *industry or sector* and the inner layer *strategic groups* and *market segments*.

- The macro-environment can be analysed in terms of the *PESTEL factors*, from which *key drivers of change* can be identified. Alternative *scenarios* about the future can be constructed according to how the key drivers develop.

- Industries and sectors can be analysed in terms of the *Porter five forces* – barriers to entry, substitutes, buyer power, supplier power and rivalry. Together, these determine industry or sector attractiveness.

- Industries and sectors are dynamic, and their changes can be analysed in terms of the *industry life cycle* and *comparative five forces radar plots*.

- In the inner layer of the environment, *strategic group* analysis, *market segment* analysis and the *strategy canvas* can help identify strategic gaps or opportunities.

- *Blue Ocean* strategies characterised by low rivalry are likely to be better opportunities than *Red Ocean* strategies with many rivals.

VIDEO CASE

Visit *MyStrategyLab* and watch the *Hiscox* case study.

1 Describe recent environmental changes in the insurance industry in terms of Porter's five forces. What else needs to be factored into an environmental analysis?

2 Assess Hiscox's strategic position in this environmental context.

RECOMMENDED KEY READINGS

- There is a good summary of industry analysis in M.E. Porter, 'The five competitive forces that shape strategy', *Harvard Business Review*, vol. 86, no. 1 (2008), pp. 58–77.

- For approaches to how environments change, see K. van der Heijden, *Scenarios: The Art of Strategic Conversation*, 2nd edition, Wiley, 2005, and the work of Michael Porter's colleague, A. McGahan, *How Industries Evolve*, Harvard Business School Press, 2004.

REFERENCES

1. PESTEL is an extension of PEST (Politics, Economics, Social and Technology) analysis, taking more account of environmental ('green') and legal issues.
2. For a discussion of scenario planning in practice, see K. van der Heijden, *Scenarios: The Art of Strategic Conversation*, 2nd edition, Wiley, 2005. For how scenario planning fits with other forms of environmental analysis such as PESTEL, see G. Burt, G. Wright, R. Bradfield and K. van der Heijden, 'The role of scenario planning in exploring the environment in view of the limitations of PEST and its derivatives', *International Studies of Management and Organization*, vol. 36, no. 3 (2006), pp. 50–76.
3. Based on P. Schoemaker, 'Scenario planning: a tool for strategic thinking'. *Sloan Management Review*, vol. 36 (1995), pp. 25–34.
4. See M.E. Porter, *Competitive Strategy: Techniques for Analysing Industries and Competitors*, Free Press, 1980, p. 5.
5. There is a good discussion of the static nature of the Porter model, and other limitations, in M. Grundy, 'Rethinking and reinventing Michael Porter's five forces model', *Strategic Change*, vol. 15 (2006), pp. 213–29.
6. An overview of the industry life cycle is A. McGahan, 'How industries evolve', *Business Strategy Review*, vol. 11, no. 3 (2000), pp. 1–16.
7. A. McGahan, 'How industries evolve', *Business Strategy Review*, vol. 11, no. 3 (2000), pp. 1–16.
8. For an example of strategic group analysis, see G. Leask and D. Parker, 'Strategic groups, competitive groups and performance in the UK pharmaceutical industry', *Strategic Management Journal*, vol. 28, no. 7 (2007), pp. 723–45.
9. A useful discussion of segmentation in relation to competitive strategy is provided in M.E. Porter, *Competitive Advantage*, Free Press, 1985, Chapter 7.
10. W.C. Kim and R. Mauborgne, 'How strategy shapes structure', *Harvard Business Review*, September 2009, pp. 73–80.
11. P. Schoemaker and G. Day, 'How to make sense of weak signals', *Sloan Management Review*, vol. 50, no. 3 (2009), pp. 81–89.

CASE EXAMPLE

Global forces and the Western European brewing industry

Mike Blee and Richard Whittington

This case is centred on the European brewing industry in Western Europe and examines how the increasingly competitive pressure of operating within global markets is causing consolidation through acquisitions, alliances and closures within the industry. This has resulted in the growth of the brewers' reliance upon super-brands.

In the early years of the 21st century, European brewers faced a surprising paradox. The traditional centre of the beer industry worldwide and home to the world's largest brewing companies, Europe, was turning off beer. Beer consumption was falling in the largest markets of Germany and the United Kingdom, while burgeoning in emerging markets around the world. In 2008, Europe's largest market, Germany, ranked only 5th in the world, behind China, the United States, Brazil and Russia. China, with 12 per cent annual growth between 2003 and 2008, had become the largest single market by volume, alone accounting for 23 per cent of world consumption (Euromonitor, 2010).

Table 1 details the overall decline of European beer consumption. Decline in traditional key markets is due to several factors. Governments are campaigning strongly against drunken driving, affecting the propensity to drink beer in restaurants, pubs and bars. There is increasing awareness of the effects of alcohol on health and fitness. Particularly in the United Kingdom, there is growing hostility to so-called 'binge drinking', excessive alcohol consumption in pubs and clubs. Wines have also become increasingly popular in Northern European markets. However, beer consumption per capita varies widely between countries, being four times higher in Germany than in Italy, for example. Some traditionally low consumption European markets have been showing good growth.

The drive against drunken driving and binge drinking has helped shift sales from the 'on-trade' (beer consumed on the premises, as in pubs or restaurants) to the off-trade (retail). Worldwide, the off-trade increased from 63 per cent of volume in 2000 to 67 per

Source: Picturesbyrob/Alamy.

Table 1 European beer consumption by country and year (000 hectolitres)

Country	1980	2000	2003	2007
Austria	7651	8762	8979	9100
Belgium	12945	10064	9935	9137
Denmark	6698	5452	5181	4840
Finland	2738	4024	4179	4073
France	23745	21420	21168	18781
Germany‡	89820	103105	97107	91000
Greece	N/A	4288	3905	4600
Ireland	4174	5594	5315	5193
Italy	9539	16289	17452	17766
Luxembourg	417	472	373	429
Netherlands	12213	13129	12771	12910
Norway*	7651	2327	2270	2670
Portugal	3534	6453	6008	6200
Spain	20065	29151	33451	35658
Sweden	3935	5011	4969	4900
Switzerland*	4433	4194	4334	4489
UK	65490	57007	60302	51300

* Non-EU countries; ‡ 1980 excludes GDR. Figures adjusted.

Source: Based on information from www.Brewersofeurope.org.

cent in 2008. The off-trade is increasingly dominated by large supermarket chains such as Tesco or Carrefour, who often use cut-price offers on beer in order to lure people into their shops. More than one-fifth of beer volume is now sold through supermarkets. German retailers such as Aldi and Lidl have had considerable success with their own 'private-label' (rather than brewery-branded) beers. Pubs have suffered: in the United Kingdom, an estimated 50 pubs closed per week during the recessionary year 2009. However, although on-trade volumes are falling in Europe, the sales values are generally rising, as brewers intro-duce higher-priced premium products such as non-alcoholic beers, extra cold lagers or fruit-flavoured beers. On the other hand, a good deal of this increas-ing demand for premium products is being satisfied by the import of apparently exotic beers from overseas (see Table 2).

Brewers' main purchasing costs are packaging (accounting for around half of non-labour costs), raw material such as barley, and energy. The European packaging industry is highly concentrated, dominated by international companies such as Crown in cans and

Owens-Illinois in glass bottles. In the United Kingdom, for example, there are just three can makers: Ball Packaging Europe, Crown Bevcan and REXAM.

Acquisition, licensing and strategic alliances have all occurred as the leading brewers battle to control the market. There are global pressures for consolidation due to over-capacity within the industry, the need to contain costs and benefits of leveraging strong brands. For example, in 2004, Belgian brewer Interbrew merged with Am Bev, the Brazilian brewery group, to create the largest brewer in the world, InBev. In 2008, the new InBev bought the second largest brewer, the American Anheuser-Busch, giving it nearly 20 per cent of the world market. In 2002, South African Breweries acquired the Miller Group (USA) and Pilsner Urquell in the Czech Republic, becoming SABMiller. SABMiller in turn bought Dutch specialist Grolsch in 2007. Smaller players in the fast-growing Chinese and Latin American markets are being snapped up by the large international brewers too: in 2010, Dutch Heineken bought Mexico's second largest brewery, FEMSA. On the other hand, medium-sized Australian brewer Fosters has withdrawn from the European market. The European Commission fined Heineken and Kronen-bourg in 2004 for price-fixing in France, and Heineken, Grolsch and Bavaria in 2007 for a price-fixing cartel in the Dutch market.

Table 3 lists the world's top ten brewing companies, which accounted for about 60 per cent of world beer volumes in 2009. However, there remain many specialist, regional and microbreweries, for example Greene King (see below). Germany, with its pub-brewing tradition (the Brauhaus), still has 1319 separate breweries owned by 583 separate brewing companies. None the less, market concentration has increased in Western Europe: in 2000, the top two players (Heineken and Interbrew) had 19.3 per cent of the market; in 2009, the top two players, Heineken and Carlsberg, held 28.5 per cent of the Western European market, with A-B InBev account-ing for a further 10.6 per cent.

Three brewing companies

The European market contains many very different kinds of competitor: this section introduces the world's largest brewer and two outliers.

Table 2 Imports of beer by country

Country	Imports 2002 (% of consumption*)	Imports 2008 (% of consumption)
Austria	5.1	6.6
Belgium	4.74	12.8
Denmark	2.6	10.5
Finland	2.3	10.1
France	23	31.4
Germany	3.1	7.6
Greece	4.1	6.5
Ireland	NA	16.8
Italy	27.2	33.5
Luxembourg	NA	43.1
Netherlands	3.2	18.6
Norway	5.4	3.7
Portugal	1.1	0.6
Spain	11.7	8.6
Sweden	NA	23.4
Switzerland	15.4	17.6
United Kingdom	10.9	17.7

Note: Import figures do not include beers brewed under licence in home country; also countries vary in measuring per cent of consumption.

Source: Based on information from www.Brewersofeurope.org.

Table 3 The world's top ten brewery companies by volume: 2000 and 2009

2000		2009	
Company	Share global volume %	Company	Share global volume %
Anheuser-Busch (US)	8.8	A-B InBev (Belgium)	19.5
AmBev (Brazil)	4.6	SABMiller (UK)	9.5
Heineken (Dutch)	4.3	Heineken (Dutch)	6.9
Interbrew (Belgium)	4.0	Carlsberg (Danish)	5.9
Miller (US)	3.6	China Resources (China)	4.5
SAB (South Africa)	3.3	Tsingtao (China)	3.1
Modelo (Mexico)	2.7	Modelo (Mexico)	2.9
Coors (US)	2.0	Molson Coors (US)	2.8
Asahi (Japan)	2.0	Beijing Yanjing (China)	2.5
Kirin (Japan)	1.9	FEMSA (Mexico)	2.3

Source: Euromonitor International, 2010.

Anheuser-Busch InBev (Belgium)

A-B InBev has roots going back to 1366, but has transformed itself in the last decade with a series of spectacular mergers. First, InBev was created in 2004 from the merger of Belgian InterBrew and Brazilian AmBev. As well as making it the second largest brewing company in the world, this merger gave it a significant position in the Latin American soft drinks market. Then in 2008 InBev acquired the leading American brewer Anheuser-Busch for $52bn (~€36.4bn), making the company indisputably the world leader. The company now has nearly 300 brands, led by such well-known international beers as Beck's, Budweiser and Stella Artois. The company has nearly 50 per cent share of the US market, and owns 50 per cent of Mexico's leading brewer, Modelo, famous for its global Corona brand. In 2008, the new A-N InBev had four of the top ten selling beers in the world, and a number one or number two position in over 20 national markets. However, the company has been reducing its stake in the Chinese market in order to raise funds to pay for the Anheuser-Busch acquisition and to meet local monopoly authority concerns. It also sold its Central and Eastern beer operations in 2009.

The company is frank about its strategy: to transform itself from the biggest brewing company in the world to the best. It aims to do this by building strong global brands and increasing efficiency. Efficiency gains will come from more central coordination of purchasing, including media and IT; from the optimisation of its inherited network of breweries; and from the sharing of best practice across sites internationally.

A-B InBev is now emphasising organic growth and improved margins from its existing business. Its declared intention is to be 'The Best Beer Company in a Better World'.

Greene King (United Kingdom)

Established in 1799, Greene King is now the largest domestic British brewer, owner of famous brands such as Abbot, IPA and Old Speckled Hen. It has expanded through a series of acquisitions including Ruddles (1995), Morland (1999) and Hardys and Hansons (2006). Acquisition is typically followed by the closure of the acquired brewery, the termination of minor brands and the transfer of major brand production to its main brewery in Bury St Edmunds. This strategy has led to critics calling the company 'Greedy King'. IPA is the UK's top cask ale, with over 20 per cent of the on-trade market, and Old Speckled Hen is the top premium UK ale with more than one-eighth of the multiple retailer market. Greene King is unusual among contemporary breweries in operating many of its own pubs, having added to its original chain several acquisitions (notably Laurels with 432 pubs and Belhaven with 271). Greene King now operates nearly 2000 pubs across the United Kingdom, with a particularly dominant position in its home region of East Anglia. The company is also active in restaurants. Business is effectively confined to the UK market. In 2009, Greene King raised £207m (~€228m; ~$310m) on the financial markets in order to fund further acquisitions. Greene King explains its success formula in brewing thus: 'The Brewing Company's continued out-performance is driven by a consistent, focused strategy: most importantly, we brew high quality beer from an efficient, single-site brewery; [and] we have a focused brand portfolio, minimising the complexity and cost of a multibrand strategy.'

Tsingtao (China)

Tsingtao Brewery was founded in 1903 by German settlers in China. After state ownership under Communism, Tsingtao was privatised in the early 1990s and listed on the Hong Kong Stock Exchange in 1993. In 2009, the Japanese Asahi Breweries held 19.9 per cent of the shares, purchased from A-B InBev (which also sold the remainder of its original stake – 7 per cent – to a Chinese private investor). Tsingtao has 13 per cent market share of its home market but has long had an export orientation, accounting for more than 50 per cent of China's beer exports. Tsingtao Beer was introduced to the United States in 1972 and is the Chinese brand-leader in the US market. A bottle of Tsingtao appeared in the 1982 science fiction film *Blade Runner*. Tsingtao set up its European office in 1992 and its beer is now sold in 62 countries. The company has described its ambition thus: 'to promote the continuous growth of the sales volume and income to step forward (sic) the target of becoming an international great company'.

Sources: Ernst & Young, The Contribution Made by Beer to the European Economy, 2009; Euromonitor International, Global Alcoholic Drinks: Beer – Opportunities in Niche Categories, April, 2009; Euromonitor, Strategies for Growth in an Increasingly Consolidated Global Beer Market, February 2010.

Questions

1 Using the data from the case (and any other sources available), carry out for the Western European brewing industry (i) a PESTEL analysis and (ii) a five forces analysis. What do you conclude?

2 For the three breweries outlined above (or breweries of your own choice) explain:

   a how these trends will impact differently on these different companies; and

   b the relative strengths and weaknesses of each company.

3

STRATEGIC CAPABILITIES

Learning outcomes

After reading this chapter you should be able to:

● Identify what comprises *strategic capabilities* in terms of organisational *resources* and *competences* and how these relate to the strategies of organisations.

● Analyse how strategic capabilities might provide sustainable competitive advantage on the basis of their *value*, *rarity*, *inimitability and non-substitutability (VRIN)*.

● Diagnose strategic capability by means of *value chain analysis*, *activity mapping* and *SWOT analysis*.

---

mystrategylab
PEARSON

MyStrategyLab is designed to help you make the most of your studies. Visit **www.mystrategylab.com** to discover a wide range of resources specific to this chapter, including:

● A personalised **Study plan** that will help you understand core concepts.

● **Audio** and **video clips** that put the spotlight on strategy in the real world.

● **Online glossaries** and **flashcards** that provide helpful reminders when you're looking for some quick revision.

See p. xiv for further details.

(3.1) INTRODUCTION

Chapter 2 outlined how the external environment of an organisation can create both strategic opportunities and threats. However, manufacturers of saloon cars compete within the same market and within the same technological environment, but with markedly different success. BMW has been relatively successful consistently. Ford and Chrysler have found it more difficult to maintain their competitive position. And others, such as Rover in the UK, have gone out of business. It is not so much variations in the environment which explain these differences in performance, but the differences in their *strategic capabilities* in terms of the *resources and competences* they have or have tried to develop. It is the strategic importance of such capabilities that is the focus of this chapter.

The key issues posed by the chapter are summarised in Figure 3.1. Underlying these are two key concepts. The first is that organisations are not identical, but have different capabilities. The second is that it can be difficult for one organisation to obtain or copy the capabilities of another. For example, competitors cannot readily obtain or access a successful business's experience built up over decades of success. The implication for managers is that they need to understand how their organisations are different from their rivals in ways that may be the basis of achieving competitive advantage and superior performance. These concepts underlie what has become known as the **resource-based view** (RBV) of strategy[1] (though it might more appropriately be labelled the 'capabilities view'): **that the competitive advantage and superior performance of an organisation is explained by the distinctiveness of its capabilities.** RBV has become very influential in strategy and this chapter draws on it a good deal. It should be borne in mind, however, that there are different treatments of the topic. So, whilst the terminology and concepts employed here align with RBV, readers will find different terminology used elsewhere.

Figure 3.1 Strategic capabilities: the key issues

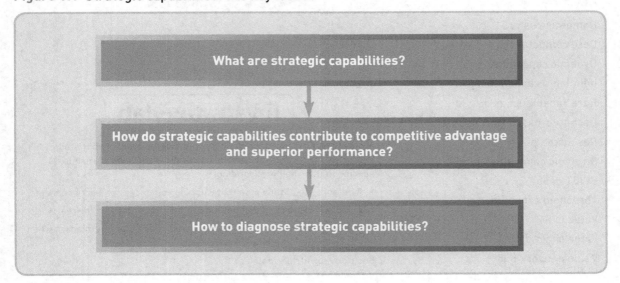

The chapter has four further sections:

- Section 3.2 discusses the foundations of *strategic capability*; in particular what is meant by *resources, competences* and the related concept of *dynamic capabilities*. It also draws a distinction between *threshold capabilities* required to be able to compete in a market and *distinctive capabilities* that may be a basis for achieving competitive advantage and superior performance.

- Section 3.3 explains the ways in which distinctive capabilities may contribute to the *developing and sustaining of competitive advantage* (in a public-sector context the equivalent concern might be how some organisations sustain relative superior performance over time). In particular, the importance of the *Value, Rarity, Inimitability* and *Non-substitutability (VRIN)* of capabilities is explained.

- Finally section 3.4 moves on to consider different ways in which strategic capability might be analysed. These include *value chain analysis* and *activity system mapping*. The section concludes by explaining the use of *SWOT* analysis as a basis for pulling together the insights from the analyses of the environment (explained in Chapter 2) and of strategic capabilities in this chapter.

FOUNDATIONS OF STRATEGIC CAPABILITY

Given that different writers, managers and consultants use different terms and concepts it is important to understand how concepts relating to strategic capabilities are used in this book. Here strategic capabilities means **the capabilities of an organisation that contribute to its long-term survival or competitive advantage**. What follows in the rest of this section is an explanation of the components of such capabilities and the characteristics of those components.

3.2.1 Resources and competences

There are two components of strategic capability: resources and competences. Resources **are the assets that organisations have or can call upon** (e.g. from partners or suppliers); competences **are the ways those assets are used or deployed effectively**. A shorthand way of thinking of this is that resources are 'what we *have*' and competences are 'what we *do well*'. Other terms are common. For example, Gary Hamel and C.K. Prahalad refer to *core competences* and many writers use the term *intangible assets* as an umbrella term to include intangible resources such as brands and business systems as well as competences.

Typically, all strategic capabilities have elements of both resources and competences as Table 3.1 shows. Resources are certainly important, but how an organisation employs and deploys its resources matters at least as much. There would be no point in having state-of-the-art equipment if it were not used effectively. The efficiency and effectiveness of physical or financial resources, or the people in an organisation, depend, not just on their existence, but on the systems and processes by which they are managed, the relationships and cooperation between people, their adaptability, their innovatory capacity, the relationship with customers and suppliers and the experience and learning about what works well and what does not.

Table 3.1 Components of strategic capabilities

Strategic capability		
Resources: what we have, e.g.		Competences: what we do well, e.g.
Machines, buildings, raw materials, products, patents, data bases, computer systems	Physical	Ways of achieving utilisation of plant, efficiency, productivity, flexibility, marketing
Balance sheet, cash flow, suppliers of funds	Financial	Ability to raise funds and manage cash flows, debtors, creditors etc.
Managers, employees, partners, suppliers, customers	Human	How people gain and use experience, skills, knowledge, build relationships, motivate others and innovate

Long-term survival and competitive advantage

3.2.2 Dynamic capabilities[2]

If they are to provide a basis for long-term success, strategic capabilities cannot be static; they need to change. University of Berkeley economist David Teece has introduced the concept of **dynamic capabilities**, by which he means **an organisation's ability to renew and recreate its strategic capabilities to meet the needs of changing environments**. He argues that the capabilities that are necessary for efficient operations:

> maintaining incentive alignment, owning tangible assets, controlling costs, maintaining quality, optimizing inventories – are necessary but . . . are unlikely to be sufficient for sustaining superior performance.[3]

Moreover he acknowledges the further danger that capabilities that were the basis of competitive success may over time be imitated by competitors, become common practice in an industry or become redundant as its environment changes. Harvard's Dorothy Leonard-Barton also warns of the danger that, despite a changing environment, such capabilities can become 'rigidities'.[4] So, the important lesson is that if capabilities are to be effective over time they need to change; they cannot be static.

Dynamic capabilities may take the form of relatively formal organisational systems, such as recruitment and management development processes, or major strategic moves, such as acquisitions or alliances, by which new skills are learned and developed. For example, Stanford's Kathy Eisenhardt[5] has shown that successful acquisition processes can bring in new knowledge to organisations. However, this depends on high-quality pre- and post-acquisition understanding of how the acquisition can be integrated into the new organisation so as to capture synergies and bases of learning from that acquisition. As Teece acknowledges, then, dynamic capabilities are likely to have foundations in less formal, behavioural aspects of organisations, such as the way in which decisions get taken, personal relationships, and entrepreneurial and intuitive skills.

3.2.3 Threshold and distinctive capabilities

A distinction also needs to be made between strategic capabilities that are at a threshold level and those that might help the organisation achieve competitive advantage and superior performance. Table 3.2 summarises these distinctions.

Threshold capabilities **are those needed for an organisation to meet the necessary require-ments to compete in a given market and achieve parity with competitors in that market.** Without such capabilities the organisation could not survive over time. Indeed, many start-up businesses find this to be the case. They simply do not have or cannot obtain the resources or competences needed to compete with established competitors. Identifying threshold require-ments is, however, also important for established businesses. By the end of the first decade of the 21st century, BP faced declining oil output in countries such as the US, the UK and Russia. BP's board regarded securing new sources of supply as a major challenge. There could also be changing *threshold resources* required to meet minimum customer requirements: for example, the increasing demands by modern multiple retailers of their suppliers mean that those suppliers have to possess a quite sophisticated IT infrastructure simply to stand a chance of meeting retailer requirements. Or they could be the *threshold competences* required to deploy resources so as to meet customers' requirements and support particular strategies. Retailers do not simply expect suppliers to have the required IT infrastructure, but to be able to use it effectively so as to guarantee the required level of service.

While threshold capabilities are important, they do not of themselves create competitive advantage or the basis for superior performance. These are dependent on an organisation having distinctive or unique capabilities that are of value to customers and which competitors find difficult to imitate. This could be because the organisation has *distinctive resources* that critically underpin competitive advantage and that others cannot imitate or obtain – a long-established brand, for example. Or it could be that an organisation achieves competitive advantage because it has *distinctive competences* – ways of doing things that are unique to that organisation and effectively utilised so as to be valuable to customers and difficult for competitors to obtain or imitate. Gary Hamel and C.K. Prahalad[6] argue that the distinctive competences that are especially important are likely to be: 'a bundle of constituent skills and technologies

Table 3.2 **Threshold and distinctive capabilities**

	Resources	Competences
Threshold capabilities Required to be able to compete in a market	Threshold resources	Threshold competences
Distinctive capabilities Required to achieve competitive advantage	Distinctive resources	Distinctive competences

Core competences

rather than a single, discrete skill or technology'. They use the term **core competences** to emphasise **the linked set of skills, activities and resources that, together, deliver customer value, differentiate a business from its competitors and, potentially, can be extended and developed.** Core competences may extend and develop as markets change or new opportunities arise. There are, then, also similarities here to Teece's conceptualisation of dynamic capabilities.

Bringing these concepts together, a supplier that achieves competitive advantage in a grocery retail market might have done so on the basis of a distinctive resource such as a powerful brand, but also by distinctive competences such as the building of excellent relations with retailers. However, it is likely that what will be most difficult for competitors to match and will therefore be the basis of competitive advantage will be the multiple and linked ways of providing products, high levels of service and building relationships – its core competence.

Illustration 3.1 shows how executives in the medical technology business of Sandvik explain the importance of its resources and capabilities.

Section 3.3 that follows discusses in more depth the role played by distinctive resources and competences in contributing to long-term, sustainable competitive advantage. Section 3.4 then explores further the importance of linkages of activities.

3.3 'VRIN': STRATEGIC CAPABILITIES AS A BASIS FOR COMPETITIVE ADVANTAGE

How, then, does a strategist consider on what bases organisational capabilities might be the foundation for sustainable competitive advantage and superior economic performance? As argued above, this is unlikely if the organisation is no different from its rivals and therefore has nothing that provides a basis for earning greater profits. Threshold capabilities may achieve parity with competitors, but not advantage over those competitors. Jay Barney, a leading proponent of RBV proposes four key criteria by which capabilities can be assessed in terms of their providing a basis for achieving such competitive advantage: Value, Rarity, Inimitability and Non-substitutability – or **VRIN**.[7]

3.3.1 V – value of strategic capabilities

Strategic capabilities are of value when they provide potential competitive advantage in a market at a cost that allows an organisation to realise acceptable levels of return (in the case of the private sector). There are four components here:

- *Taking advantage of opportunities and neutralising threats.* The most fundamental question is whether the capabilities provide the potential to address the opportunities and threats that arise in the organisation's environment.

- *Value.* It may seem an obvious point to make that capabilities need to be of value both to customers and to the well being of the organisation itself. In practice this can be overlooked or poorly understood. For example, managers may seek to build on capabilities that *they* may see as valuable but which do not meet customers' critical success factors (see section 2.4.3).

ILLUSTRATION 3.1

Sandvik's strategic capabilities

Strategic capabilities are central to the search for competitive advantage.

Swedish-based global industrial group, Sandvik, manufactures products for companies operating in a wide range of industries including medical technology. In a 2009 press release, it announced it had:

> invested in a technologically advanced direct metal laser sintering machine (DMLS) in order to provide rapid production capabilities to its customers, unique amongst contract manufacturers.
>
> Sandvik is now significantly reducing the time required to cost-effectively develop working prototypes, which means its customers can bring new innovations to market far more quickly than was previously possible. Sandvik is also exploiting the powder-based technique used by the DMLS machine to manufacture to almost any design, thereby removing limitations previously imposed on design teams within medical device OEMs (original equipment manufacturers). In an industry where innovation and speed to market are crucial differentiators, these benefits represent a real commercial advantage to OEMs.
>
> Through this investment and the enhanced capabilities it brings, Sandvik has further strengthened its position as a strategic partner to medical technology companies, helping them improve their competitiveness.

Tord Lendau, President of Sandvik MedTech, explained:

> Medical device OEMs operate in a highly competitive market. We want to leverage Sandvik's long experience within powder metallurgy to deliver real value to OEMs and so must continuously introduce new manufacturing techniques, which is why we have made this significant investment . . . Medical device manufacturers can now capitalise on enhanced capabilities and improve the speed to market of their new designs and innovations.

The press release continued:

> The new capabilities provided by the DMLS machine are ideal for the production of working prototypes of medical devices and for complex custom-made instruments.

It quoted John Reynolds, a special projects manager at Sandvik:

> Prototyping is an important stage in the creation of a new device, since it provides the opportunity to explore the design and make the necessary adjustments prior to full production. However, most rapid prototyping processes do not produce a working model, while those that do are time consuming and more expensive . . . By using the DMLS machine we can bring to bear rapid production techniques that enable us to quickly and cost-effectively manufacture a working prototype. This means our customers can present a working model to their customers in a fraction of the time it would take with conventional manufacturing techniques and bring the final design to market far quicker . . . We can also now manufacture almost any design the OEM can create, irrespective of the complexity of the geometry. This means our customers' design teams are not constrained by the manufacturing limitations previously typical in the industry. They have the flexibility to respond with precision to the individual preferences of any one surgeon or the specific needs of a patient.

The press release concluded:

> By enhancing its capabilities through this significant investment and combining it with its materials and manufacturing expertise, Sandvik is helping OEMs achieve real competitive advantage in a challenging market.

Source: www.smt.sandvik.com/sandvik. © AB Sandvik Materials Technology.

Questions

1 Categorise Sandvik's range of capabilities in terms of section 3.2. and Tables 3.1 and 3.2.

2 Assess the bases of Sandvik's strategic capabilities using the VRIN criteria (section 3.3).

3 Which are the key strategic capabilities which provide, or could provide, Sandvik with sustainable competitive advantage?

Or they may see a distinctive capability as of value simply because it is distinctive. Having capabilities that are different from other organisations is not, of itself, a basis for competitive advantage. So the discussion in sections 3.3.2 and 3.3.3 and the lessons it draws are important here.

- *Providing potential competitive advantage.* The capabilities do, nonetheless, need to be capable of delivering a product or service that competitors do not currently have or do not currently emphasise.

- *Cost.* The product or service needs to be provided at a cost that still allows the organisation to make the returns expected of it (e.g. by investors). The danger is that the cost of developing the capabilities to deliver what customers especially value is such that products or services are not profitable.

Managers should therefore consider carefully which of their organisation's activities are especially important in providing such value and which are of less value. Value chain analysis and activity mapping explained in sections 3.4.1 and 3.4.2 can help here.

3.3.2 R – rarity

If competitors have similar capabilities, they can respond quickly to the strategic initiative of a rival. This has happened in competition between car manufacturers as they have sought to add more accessories and gadgets to cars. As soon as it becomes evident that these are valued by customers, they are introduced widely by competitors who typically have access to the same technology. **Rare capabilities**, on the other hand, **are those possessed uniquely by one organisation or by a few others.** Here competitive advantage might be longer-lasting. For example, a company may have patented products or services that give it advantage. Service organisations may have rare resources in the form of intellectual capital – perhaps particularly talented individuals. Some libraries have unique collections of books unavailable elsewhere; a company may have a powerful brand; or retail stores may have prime locations. In terms of competences, organisations may have unique skills developed over time or have built special relationships with customers or suppliers not widely possessed by competitors. However, there are two important points to bear in mind about the extent to which rarity might provide competitive advantage:

- *Meeting customer need.* Again rarity, of itself, is of little value unless the resources or capabilities lead to outputs in the form of products or services that meet customer needs and are therefore of value to them.

- *Sustainability.* Rarity could be temporary. For example, uniquely talented individuals may be an advantage but can also be a risk. In 2009, and again in 2011, the financial press reported increasing concerns about Apple, given the health of its CEO Steve Jobs, with headlines such as: 'Can Apple survive without Steve Jobs?'[8] Moreover, it may be dangerous to assume that resources and capabilities that are rare will remain so. If an organisation is successful on the basis of something distinctive, then competitors will very likely seek to imitate or obtain that distinctiveness. So it may be necessary to consider other bases of sustainability.

3.3.3 I – inimitability

It should be clear by now that the search for strategic capability that provides sustainable competitive advantage is not straightforward. Having capabilities that are valuable to customers and relatively rare is important, but this may not be enough. Sustainable competitive advantage also involves identifying inimitable capabilities – **those that competitors find difficult to imitate or obtain.**

At the risk of over-generalisation, it is unusual for competitive advantage to be explainable by differences in the tangible resources of organisations, since over time these can usually be acquired or imitated. Advantage is more likely to be determined by the way in which resources are deployed and managed in terms of an organisation's activities; in other words on the basis of competences.[9] For example, it is unlikely an IT system will improve an organisation's competitive standing of itself, not least because competitors can probably buy something very similar in the open market. On the other hand, the capabilities to manage, develop and deploy such a system to the benefit of customers may be much more difficult to imitate. This is likely to be so if two conditions are met.

- *Superior performance.* The capabilities lead to levels of performance of product or service that are significantly better than competitors'.
- *Linked competences.* If the capability integrates activities, skills and knowledge both inside and outside the organisation in distinct and mutually compatible ways. It is, then, the *linkages* of the activities that go to make up capabilities that can be especially significant.

There are four reasons that may make capabilities particularly difficult for competitors to imitate.

Complexity

The capabilities of an organisation may be difficult to imitate because they are complex. This may be for two main reasons.

- *Internal linkages.* There may be linked activities and processes that, together, deliver customer value. The discussion of activity systems in section 3.4.2 below explains this in more detail and shows how such linked sets of activities might be mapped so that they can be better understood.
- *External linkages.* Organisations can make it difficult for others to imitate or obtain their bases of competitive advantage by developing activities together with the customer such that the customer becomes dependent on them. For example, an industrial lubricants business moved away from just selling its products to customers by coming to an agreement with them to manage the applications of lubricants within the customers' sites against agreed targets on cost savings. The more efficient the use of lubricants, the more both parties benefited. Similarly software businesses can achieve advantage by developing computer programs that are distinctively beneficial to specific customer needs.

Causal ambiguity[10]

Another reason why capabilities might be difficult to imitate is that competitors find it difficult to discern the causes and effects underpinning an organisation's advantage. This is called *causal ambiguity*. This might be for at least two reasons. First, because the capability itself is difficult to discern or comprehend, perhaps because it is based on tacit knowledge based on people's experience. For example, the know-how of the buyers in a successful fashion retailer may be evident in the sales achieved for the ranges they buy, but it may be very difficult for a competitor to see just what that know-how is. Second, because competitors may not be able to discern which activities and processes are dependent on which others to form linkages that create core competences. The expertise of the fashion buyers is unlikely to be lodged in the one individual or even one function. It is likely that there will be a network of suppliers, intelligence networks to understand the market and links with designers.

Culture and history

Competences may become embedded in an organisation's culture. So coordination between various activities occurs 'naturally' because people know their part in the wider picture or it is simply 'taken for granted' that activities are done in particular ways. We see this in high-performing groups or sports teams that work together to combine specialist skills, but also in how some firms integrate different activities in their business to deliver excellent customer service.

Change

The concept of dynamic capabilities is relevant here. If an organisation builds a basis of competitive advantage on resources or capabilities that change as the dynamics of a market or the needs of customers change, they will be more difficult for competitors to imitate. Indeed, arguably, organisations that wish to be market leaders, to innovate and create new markets, must do so on the basis of dynamic capabilities. They are, in effect, continually seeking to stay ahead of their competitors by evolving new bases for doing so.

3.3.4 N – non-substitutability[11]

Providing value to customers and possessing competences that are rare and difficult to imitate may mean that it is very difficult for organisations to copy them. However, the organisation may still be at risk from substitution. Substitution could take two different forms:

- *Product or service substitution*. As already discussed in Chapter 2 in relation to the five forces model of competition, a product or service as a whole might be a victim of substitution. For example, increasingly e-mail systems have substituted for postal systems. No matter how complex and culturally embedded were the competences of the postal service, it could not avoid this sort of substitution.

- *Competence substitution*. Substitution might, however, not be at the product or service level but at the competence level. For example, task-based industries have often suffered because of an over-reliance on the competences of skilled craft workers who have been replaced by expert systems and mechanisation.

In summary and from a resource-based view of organisations, managers need to consider whether their organisation has strategic capabilities to achieve and sustain competitive

Figure 3.2 VRIN

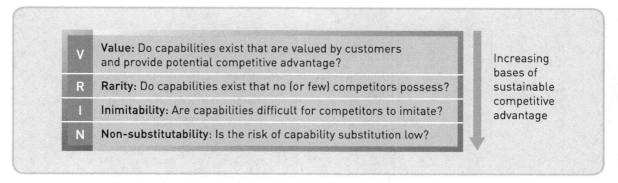

advantage – to do so they need to consider how and to what extent it has capabilities which are (i) valuable to buyers, (ii) rare, (iii) inimitable and (iv) non-substitutable.

As Figure 3.2 shows, there is an additive effect here. Strategic capabilities provide sustainable bases of competitive advantage the more they meet all four criteria. If such capabilities for competitive advantage do not exist, then managers need to consider if they can be developed.

(3.4) DIAGNOSING STRATEGIC CAPABILITIES

So far, this chapter has been concerned with explaining concepts associated with the strategic significance of organisations' resources and capabilities. This section now explains ways in which strategic capabilities can be understood and diagnosed.

3.4.1 The value chain and value network

The **value chain describes the categories of activities within an organisation which, together, create a product or service.** Most organisations are also part of a wider **value network, the set of inter-organisational links and relationships that are necessary to create a product or service.** Both are useful in understanding the strategic position of an organisation.

Value chain and value network

The value chain

If organisations are to achieve competitive advantage by delivering value to customers, managers need to understand which of the activities their organisation undertakes are especially important in creating that value and which are not. It can, then, be used to model the value system of an organisation. The important point is that the concept of the value chain invites the strategist to think of an organisation in terms of sets of activities. There are different frameworks for considering these categories: Figure 3.3 is a representation of a value chain as developed by Michael Porter.[12]

Primary activities are directly concerned with the creation or delivery of a product or service, for example, for a manufacturing business.

Figure 3.3 **The value chain within an organisation**

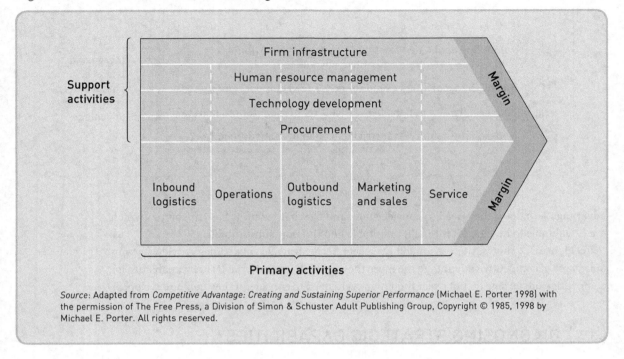

- *Inbound logistics* are activities concerned with receiving, storing and distributing inputs to the product or service including materials handling, stock control, transport etc.

- *Operations* transform these inputs into the final product or service: machining, packaging, assembly, testing etc.

- *Outbound logistics* collect, store and distribute the product to customers; for example, warehousing, materials handling, distribution.

- *Marketing and sales* provide the means whereby consumers or users are made aware of the product or service and are able to purchase it. This includes sales administration, advertising and selling.

- *Service* includes those activities that enhance or maintain the value of a product or service, such as installation, repair, training and spares.

Each of these groups of primary activities is linked to *support activities* which help to improve the effectiveness or efficiency of primary activities.

- *Procurement*. Processes that occur in many parts of the organisation for acquiring the various resource inputs to the primary activities. These can be vitally important in achieving scale advantages. So, for example, many large consumer goods companies with multiple businesses none the less procure advertising centrally.

- *Technology development*. All value activities have a 'technology', even if it is just know-how. Technologies may be concerned directly with a product (e.g. R&D, product design) or with processes (e.g. process development) or with a particular resource (e.g. raw materials improvements).

- *Human resource management.* This transcends all primary activities and is concerned with recruiting, managing, training, developing and rewarding people within the organisation.
- *Infrastructure.* The formal systems of planning, finance, quality control, information management and the structure of an organisation.

The value chain can be used to understand the strategic position of an organisation in three ways.

- As a *generic description of activities* it can help managers understand if there is a cluster of activities providing benefit to customers located within particular areas of the value chain. Perhaps a business is especially good at outbound logistics linked to its marketing and sales operation and supported by its technology development. It might be less good in terms of its operations and its inbound logistics.
- In *analysing the competitive position of the organisation* using the VRIN criteria as follows:

  V Which value-creating activities are especially significant for an organisation in meeting customer needs and could they be usefully developed further?

  R To what extent and how does an organisation have bases of value creation that are *rare*? Or conversely are all elements of their value chain common to their competitors?

  I What aspects of value creation are difficult for others to *imitate*, perhaps because they are *embedded* in the activity systems of the organisation (see section 3.4.2 below)?

  N What aspects of the value chain are or are not vulnerable to substitution?

- To *analyse the cost and value of activities*[13] of an organisation. This could involve considering the following steps:

  - *Relative importance of activity costs internally.* Does the significance of the costs align with the strategic significance of the activities? Which activities most add value to the final product or service (and in turn to the customer) and which do not? For example, organisations that have undertaken such analyses often find that central services have grown to the extent that they are a disproportionate cost to internal sets of activities and to the customer.

  - *Relative importance of activities externally.* How does value and the cost of a set of activities compare with the similar activities of competitors? For example, although they are both global oil businesses, BP and Shell are different in terms of the significance of their value chain activities. BP has historically outperformed Shell in terms of exploration; but the reverse is the case with regard to refining and marketing.

  - *Where and how can costs be reduced?* For example, can costs be reduced in some areas without affecting the value created for customers? Can some activities be outsourced, for example, those that are relatively free-standing and do not add value significantly? Can cost savings be made by increasing economies of scale or scope; for example, through central procurement or consolidating currently fragmented activities (e.g. manufacturing units)?

The value network

A single organisation rarely undertakes in-house all of the value activities from design through to the delivery of the final product or service to the final consumer. There is usually specialisation of roles so, as Figure 3.4 shows, any one organisation is part of a wider *value network*. There are questions that arise here that also build on an understanding of the value chain.

● *What are the activities and cost/price structures of the value network?* Just as costs can be analysed across the internal value chain, they can also be analysed across the value network: Illustration 3.2 shows how value network analysis was used by Ugandan fish farmers as a way of identifying what they should focus on in developing a more profitable business model.

● The *'make or buy'* or *outsourcing* decision for a particular activity is critical given some of the above questions. Increasingly, outsourcing is becoming common as a means of lowering costs. Of course, the more an organisation outsources, the more its ability to influence the performance of other organisations in the value network may become a critically important capability in itself and even a source of competitive advantage. For example, the quality of a cooker or a television when it reaches the final purchaser is not only influenced by the

ILLUSTRATION 3.2

A value chain for Ugandan chilled fish fillet exports

Even small enterprises can be part of an international value chain. Analysing it can provide strategic benefits.

A fish factory in Uganda barely made any profit. Fish were caught from small motorboats owned by poor fishermen from local villages. Just before they set out they would collect ice and plastic fish boxes from the agents who bought the catch on their return. The boxes were imported, along with tackle and boat parts. All supplies had to be paid for in cash in advance by the agents. Sometimes ice and supplies were not available in time. Fish landed with insufficient ice achieved half of the price of iced fish, and sometimes could not be sold to the agents at all. The fish factory had always processed the fillets in the same way – disposing of the waste back into the lake. Once a week, some foreign traders would come and buy the better fillets; they didn't say who they sold them to, and sometimes they didn't buy very much.

By mapping the value chain it was clear that there were opportunities for capturing more value along the chain and reducing losses. Together with outside specialists, the fish factory and the fishing community developed a strategy to improve their capabilities, as indicated in the figure, until they became a flourishing international business, The Lake Victoria Fish Company, with regular air-freight exports around the world. You can see more of their current operations at http://www.ufpea.co.ug/, and find out more about the type of analytical process applied at www.justreturn.ch.

[The approximate costs and prices given represent the situation before improvements were implemented.]

Questions

1 Draw up a value chain for another business in terms of the activities within its component parts.

2 Estimate the relative costs and/or assets associated with these activities.

3 What are the strategic implications of your analysis?

Figure 3.4 **The value network**

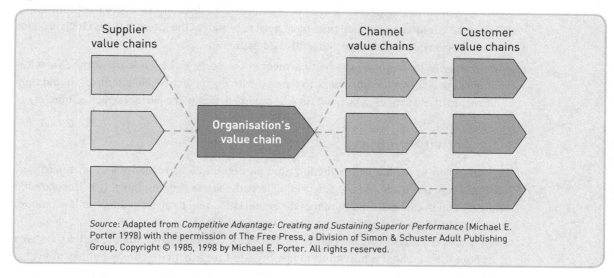

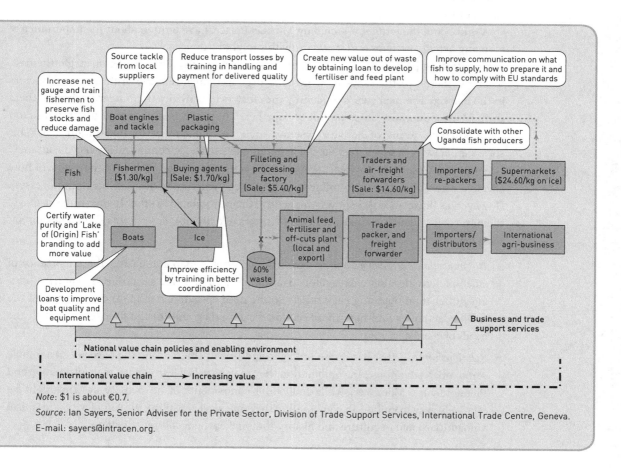

Note: $1 is about €0.7.

Source: Ian Sayers, Senior Adviser for the Private Sector, Division of Trade Support Services, International Trade Centre, Geneva. E-mail: sayers@intracen.org.

activities undertaken within the manufacturing company itself, but also by the quality of components from suppliers and the performance of the distributors. There is, of course, the converse question: which activities most need to be part of the internal value chain because they are central to achieving competitive advantage?.

- *Partnering.* Who might be the best partners in the parts of the value network? And what kind of *relationships* are important to develop with each partner? For example, should they be regarded as suppliers or should they be regarded as alliance partners (see section 9.4),

3.4.2 Activity systems

The discussion so far highlights the fact that all organisations comprise sets of capabilities, but that these are likely to be configured differently across organisations. It is this variable configuration of capabilities that makes an organisation and its strategy more or less unique. So for the strategist, understanding this matters a good deal.

Value chain analysis can help with this, but so too can understanding the activity systems of an organisation. So it is important to identify what these activities are, why they are valuable to customers, how the various activities fit together and how they differ from those of competitors.

A number of the writers,[14] including Michael Porter, have written about the importance of mapping activity systems and shown how this might be done.

The starting point is to identify what Porter refers to as 'higher order strategic themes'. In effect, these are the ways in which the organisation meets the critical success factors in the market. The next step is to identify the clusters of activities that underpin each of these themes and how these do or do not fit together. The result is a picture of the organisation represented in terms of activity systems such as that shown in Illustration 3.3. This shows an activity systems map for the Scandinavian strategic communications consultancy, Geelmuyden.Kiese.[15] At the heart of its success is its knowledge, built over the years, of how effective communications can influence 'the power dynamics of decision making processes'. However, as Illustration 3.3 shows, this central theme is related to other higher-order strategic themes, each of which is underpinned by clusters of activities. Four points should be emphasised here:

- *The importance of linkages and fit.* An activity systems map emphasises the importance of different activities that create value to customers pulling in the same direction and supporting rather than opposing each other. So the need is to understand (a) the fit between the various activities and how these reinforce each other and (b) the fit externally with the needs of clients.

- *Relationship to VRIN.* It is these linkages and this fit that can be the bases of sustainable competitive advantage. In combination they may be *valuable* to clients, truly distinctive and therefore *rare.* Moreover, while individual components of an activity system might be relatively easy to imitate, in combination they may well constitute the complexity and causal ambiguity rooted in culture and history that makes them *difficult to imitate.*

- *Disaggregation.*[16] Useful as an activity map is, the danger is that, in seeking to explain capabilities underpinning their strategy, managers may identify capabilities at too abstract a level. If the strategic benefits of activity systems are to be understood, greater disaggregation is likely to be needed. For example, managers may talk of 'innovation' or 'putting the customer first' as a basis for 'good service'. These terms are, however, generic descriptors of activities that exist at an even more operational level than those shown in the activity map. If an activity map is to be useful for the purposes of managing activities then managers need to identify specific activities at an operating level that are manageable. To take an example from Illustration 3.3, there is the recognition that the mentoring of junior staff by partners is important; but the map itself does not show specifically how this is done.

- *Superfluous activities.* Just as in value chain analysis, but at a more detailed level, the question can be asked: are there activities that are not required in order to pursue a particular strategy? Or how do activities contribute to value creation? If activities do not do this, why are they being pursued by the organisation? Whether Ryanair used activity mapping or not, they have systematically identified and done away with many activities that other airlines commonly have. They are also continually seeking further activities that can be eliminated or outsourced to reduce cost.

3.4.3 SWOT[17]

It can be helpful to summarise the key issues arising from an analysis of the business environment and the capabilities of an organisation to gain an overall picture of its strategic position. **SWOT summarises the strengths, weaknesses, opportunities and threats likely to impact on strategy development** that arise from such analyses. This can also be useful as a basis against which to generate strategic options and assess future courses of action.

The aim is to identify the extent to which strengths and weaknesses are relevant to, or capable of dealing with, the changes taking place in the business environment. Illustration 3.4 takes the example of a pharmaceuticals firm (Pharmcare). It assumes that key environmental impacts have been identified from analyses explained in Chapter 2 and that major strengths and weaknesses have been identified using the analytic tools explained in this chapter. A scoring mechanism (+5 to −5) is used as a means of getting managers to assess the interrelationship between the environmental impacts and the strengths and weaknesses of the firm. A positive (+) denotes that the strength of the company would help it take advantage of, or counteract, a problem arising from an environmental change or that a weakness would be offset by that change. A negative (−) score denotes that the strength would be reduced or that a weakness would prevent the organisation from overcoming problems associated with that change.

Pharmcare's share price had been declining because investors were concerned that its strong market position was under threat. This had not been improved by a merger that was proving problematic. The pharmaceutical market was changing, with new ways of doing business, driven by new technology, the quest to provide medicines at lower cost and politicians seeking ways to cope with soaring healthcare costs and an ever more informed patient. But was Pharmcare keeping pace? The strategic review of the firm's position (Illustration 3.4(a))

ILLUSTRATION 3.3

Activity systems at Geelmuyden.Kiese

The strategic capabilities of an organisation can be understood and analysed in terms of linked activities (an activity system)

Geelmuyden.Kiese is a Scandinavian strategic communications consultancy – an extension of what has traditionally been known as public relations services (PR). Their clients include organisations in the financial, oil, energy, pharmaceuticals and healthcare sectors. These clients typically approach Geelmuyden.Kiese when they have a problem, the solution for which critically depends on effective external or internal communication. In this context, Geelmuyden.Kiese's services include facilitation of contacts with public agencies, officials and government, investor relations, media relations, communication campaigns for new product launches, crisis management and in-company communication on key strategic issues.

At the heart of the company's success is the knowledge they have built up since their founding in 1989 of the dynamics of decision-making processes, often within influential bodies such as government and, linked to this, 'how effective communication may move power within those decision making processes'. This knowledge is underpinned by some key aspects in the way in which they do business, summarised here and shown as an activity system opposite.

- They seek to *work at a strategic level* with their clients, prioritising those clients where such work is especially valued. Here they employ their own in-house methodology, developed on the basis of their years of experience, and systematically review the assignments they undertake both internally and on the basis of client surveys.

- They take a clear stance on *integrity of communication*. They always advise openness of communication rather than suppression of information and only deal with clients who will accept such principles. They also take a stance on this approach often in controversial and high profile issues in the public domain.

- Staff are given high degrees of *freedom*, but with some absolute criteria of *responsibility*. In this regard there are strict rules for handling clients' confidential information and strict sanctions if such rules are broken.

- *Recruitment* is based on ensuring that such responsibility can be achieved. It is largely on the basis of values of openness, integrity but also humour. The emphasis tends to be on recruiting junior personnel and developing them. Geelmuyden.Kiese has learned that this is a better way of delivering its services than recruiting established 'high profile' consultants. Combined with its mentoring system for competence development of junior staff, they therefore believe that it offers the *best learning opportunities* inScandinavia for young communications consultants.

- Geelmuyden.Kiese also offers *strong financial incentives* for top performance within the firm. Such performance includes rewards for the development of junior personnel, but is also based on the internal evaluation of leadership qualities and performance.

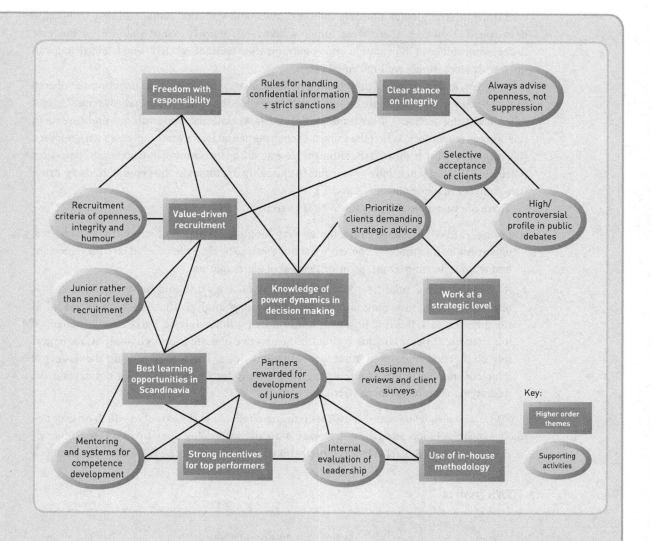

Questions

1 Assuming Geelmuyden.Kiese managers are correct that they have capabilities that provide competitive advantage:

   a What would competitors find difficult to imitate and why?

   b Are there any activities that could be done away with without threatening that advantage?

2 If disaggregation (see section 3.4.2) is important, suggest what even more specific activites underpinning those in the activity map that might be important.

confirmed its strengths of a flexible salesforce, well-known brand name and new healthcare department. However, there were major weaknesses, namely relative failure on low-cost drugs, competence in information and communication technology (ICT) and a failure to get to grips with increasingly well-informed users.

However, in the context of this chapter, if this analysis is to be useful, it must be remembered that the exercise is not absolute but relative to its competitors. So SWOT analysis is most useful when it is comparative – if it examines strengths, weaknesses, opportunities and threats in relation to competitors. When the impact of environmental forces on competitors was analysed (Illustration 3.4(b)), it showed that Pharmcare was still outperforming its traditional competitor (Company W), but potentially vulnerable to changing dynamics in the general industry structure courtesy of niche players (X and Y).

There are two main dangers in a SWOT exercise:

- *Listing.* A SWOT exercise can generate very long lists of apparent strengths, weaknesses, opportunities and threats, whereas what matters is to be clear about what is really important and what is less important. So prioritisation of issues matters.

- *A summary, not a substitute.* SWOT analysis is an engaging and fairly simple tool. It is also useful in summarising and consolidating other analysis that has been explained in Chapters 2 and 3. It is not, however, a substitute for that analysis. There are two dangers if it is used on its own. The first is that, in the absence of more thorough analysis, managers rely on preconceived, often inherited and biased views. The second is again the danger of a lack of specificity. Identifying very general strengths, for example, does not explain the underlying reasons for those strengths.

SWOT can also help focus discussion on future choices and the extent to which an organisation is capable of supporting these strategies. A useful way of doing this is to use a TOWS matrix[18] as shown in Figure 3.5. This builds directly on the information in a SWOT exercise. Each box

Figure 3.5 The TOWS matrix

		Internal factors	
		Strengths (S)	**Weaknesses (W)**
External factors	**Opportunities (O)**	**SO Strategic options** Generate options here that use srengths to take advantage of opportunities	**WO Strategic options** Generate options here that take advantage of opportunities by overcoming weaknesses
	Threats (T)	**ST Strategic options** Generate options here that use srengths to avoid threats	**WT Strategic options** Generate options here that minimise weaknesses and avoid threats

ILLUSTRATION 3.4

SWOT analysis of Pharmcare

A SWOT analysis explores the relationship between the environmental influences and the strategic capabilities of an organisation compared with its competitors.

(a) SWOT analysis for Pharmcare

	Environmental change (opportunities and threats)					
	Healthcare rationing	Complex and changing buying structures	Increased integration of healthcare	Informed patients	+	−
Strengths						
Flexible salesforce	+3	+5	+2	+2	12	0
Economies of scale	0	0	+3	+3	+6	0
Strong brand name	+2	+1	0	−1	3	−1
Healthcare education department	+4	+3	+4	+5	+16	0
Weaknesses						
Limited competences in biotechnology and genetics	0	0	−4	−3	0	−7
Ever lower R&D productivity	−3	−2	−1	−2	0	−8
Weak ICT competences	−2	−2	−5	−5	0	−14
Over-reliance on leading product	−1	−1	−3	−1	0	−6
Environmental impact scores	+9	+9	+9	+10		
	−6	−5	−13	−12		

(b) Competitor SWOT analyses

	Environmental change (opportunities and threats)				
	Healthcare rationing	Complex and changing buying structures	Increased integration of healthcare	Informed and passionate patients	Overall impact
Pharmcare *Big global player suffering fall in share price, low research productivity and post-mega-merger bureaucracy*	−3 Struggling to prove cost-effectiveness of new drugs to new regulators of healthcare rationing	+6 Well-known brand, a flexible salesforce combined with a new healthcare education department creates positive synergy	−3 Weak ICT and lack of integration following mergers means sales, research and admin. are all underperforming	−2 Have yet to get into the groove of patient power fuelled by the internet	−2 Declining performance over time worsened after merger
Company W *Big pharma with patchy response to change, losing ground in new areas of competition*	−4 Focus is on old-style promotional selling rather than helping doctors control costs through drugs	−4 Traditional salesforce not helped by marketing which can be unaccommodating of national differences	+0 Alliances with equipment manufacturers, but little work done across alliance to show dual use of drugs and new surgical techniques	+4 New recruits in the ICT department have worked cross-functionally to involve patients like never before	−4 Needs to modernise across the whole company
Organisation X *Partnership between a charity managed by people with venture capital experience and top hospital geneticists*	+3 Potentially able to deliver rapid advances in genetic-based illnesses	+2 Able possibly to bypass these with innovative cost effective drug(s)	+2 Innovative drugs can help integrate health care through enabling patients to stay at home	+3 Patients will fight for advances in treatment areas where little recent progress has been made	+10 Could be the basis of a new business model for drug discovery – but all to prove as yet
Company Y Only develops drugs for less common diseases	+3 Partnering with big pharma allows the development of drugs discovered by big pharma but not economical for them to develop	0 Focus on small market segments so not as vulnerable to overall market structure, but innovative approach might be risky	+2 Innovative use of web to show why products still worthwhile developing even for less common illnesses	+1 Toll-free call centres for sufferers of less common illnesses. Company, like patients, is passionate about its mission	+6 Novel approach can be considered either risky or a winner, or both!

Questions

1 What does the SWOT analysis tell us about the competitive position of Pharmcare with the industry as a whole?

2 How readily do you think executives of Pharmcare identify the strengths and weaknesses of competitors?

3 Identify the benefits and dangers (other than those identified in the text) of a SWOT analysis such as that in the illustration.

Prepared by Jill Shepherd, Segal Graduate School of Business, Simon Fraser University, Vancouver, Canada.

of the TOWS matrix can be used to identify options that address a different combination of the internal factors (strengths and weaknesses) and the external factors (opportunities and threats). For example, the top left-hand box prompts a consideration of options that use the strengths of the organisation to take advantage of opportunities in the business environment. An example for Pharmcare might be the re-training of the sales force to deal with changes in pharmaceuticals buying. The bottom right-hand box prompts options that minimise weaknesses and also avoid threats; for Pharmcare this might include the need to develop their ICT systems to service better more informed patients. Quite likely this would also help take advantage of opportunities arising from changes in the buying structure of the industry (top right). The bottom left box suggests the need to use strengths to avoid threats, perhaps by building on the success of their healthcare education department to also better service informed patients.

SUMMARY

- *The competitive advantage* of an organisation is likely to be based on the strategic *capabilities* it has that are valuable to customers and that its rivals do not have or have difficulty in obtaining. Strategic capabilities comprise both *resources* and *competences*.

- The concept of *dynamic capabilities* highlights that strategic capabilities need to change as the market and environmental context of an organisation changes.

- Sustainability of competitive advantage is likely to depend on an organisation's capabilities being of at least *threshold value* in a market but also being *valuable*, relatively *rare*, *inimitable* and *non-substitutable*.

- Ways of *diagnosing organisational capabilities* include:

- Analysing an organisation's *value chain* and *value network* as a basis for understanding how value to a customer is created and can be developed.

  - *Activity mapping* as a means of identifying more detailed activities which underpin strategic capabilities.

  - *SWOT analysis* as a way of drawing together an understanding of the strengths, weaknesses, opportunities and threats an organisation faces.

VIDEO CASE

Visit *MyStrategyLab* and watch the *Maersk* case study.

1 What are the strategic capabilities that Maersk claim provide them with competitive advantage in the global freight market?

2 Drawing on VRIN, suggest on what bases might these be sustainable over time.

RECOMMENDED KEY READINGS

- For an understanding of the resource-based view of the firm, an early and much cited paper is by Jay Barney: 'Firm resources and sustained competitive advantage', *Journal of Management*, vol. 17 (1991), pp. 99–120.

- Michael Porter explains how mapping activity systems can be important in considering competitive strategy in his article 'What is strategy?' (*Harvard Business Review*, November–December 1996, pp. 61–78).

- For a critical discussion of the use and misuse of SWOT analysis see T. Hill and R. Westbrook, 'SWOT analysis: it's time for a product recall', *Long Range Planning*, vol. 30, no. 1 (1997), pp. 46–52.

REFERENCES

1. The concept of resource-based strategies was introduced by B. Wernerfelt, 'A resource-based view of the firm', *Strategic Management Journal*, vol. 5, no. 2 (1984), pp. 171–80. A much cited paper is by Jay Barney: 'Firm resources and sustained competitive advantage', *Journal of Management*, vol. 17, no. 1 (1991), pp. 99–120.

2. For summary papers on dynamic capabilities see C.L. Wang and P.K. Ahmed, 'Dynamic capabilities: a review and research agenda', *International Journal of Management Reviews*, vol. 9, no. 1 (2007), pp. 31–52, and V. Ambrosini and C. Bowman, 'What are dynamic capabilities and are they a useful construct in strategic management?', *International Journal of Management Reviews*, vol. 11, no. 1 (2009), pp. 29–49.

3. David Teece has written about dynamic capabilities; see D. Teece, Explicating dynamic capabilities: the nature and microfoundations of (sustainable) enterprise performance, *Strategic Management Journal*, vol. 28 (2007), pp. 1319–50, pp. 1320–21.

4. D. Leonard-Barton, 'Core capabilities and core rigidities: a paradox in managing new product development', *Strategic Management Journal*, vol. 13 (1992), pp. 111–25.

5. K.M. Eisenhardt and J.A. Martin, 'Dynamic capabilities: what are they?', *Strategic Management Journal*, vol. 21, no. 10/11 (2000), pp. 1105–21.

6. Gary Hamel and C.K. Prahalad were the academics who promoted the idea of core competences. For example, G. Hamel and C.K. Prahalad, 'The core competence of the corporation', *Harvard Business Review*, vol. 68, no. 3 (1990), pp. 79–91.

7. The VRIN criteria were originally introduced by Jay Barney in his 1991 paper (see 1 above).

8. 'Can Apple survive without Steve Jobs', *Sunday Times*, 18 January 2009.

9. This is borne out in a meta-study of research on RBV by S.L. Newbert, 'Empirical, research on the Resource Based View of the firm: an assessment and suggestions for future research, *Strategic Management Journal*, vol. 28, (2007), pp. 121–46.

10. The seminal paper on causal ambiguity is S. Lippman and R. Rumelt, 'Uncertain imitability: an analysis of inter-firm differences in efficiency under competition', *Bell Journal of Economics*, vol. 13 (1982), pp. 418–38.

11. The importance of non-substitutability and ways of identifying possible bases of substitution are discussed in M.A. Peteraf and M.E. Bergen, 'Scanning dynamic competitive landscapes: a market and resource based framework', *Strategic Management Journal*, vol. 24, no. 10 (2003), pp. 1027–42.

12. An extensive discussion of the value chain concept and its application can be found in M.E. Porter, *Competitive Advantage*, Free Press, 1985.

13. For an extended example of value chain analysis see Andrew Shepherd, 'Understanding and using value chain analysis', in V. Ambrosini (ed.), *Exploring Techniques of Analysis and Evaluation in Strategic Management*, Prentice Hall, 1998.

14. See M. Porter, 'What is strategy?', *Harvard Business Review*, November–December 1996, pp. 61–78; and N. Siggelkow, 'Evolution towards fit', *Administrative Science Quarterly*, vol. 47, no. 1 (2002), pp. 125–59.

15. We are grateful for this example based on the doctoral dissertation of Bjorn Haugstad, 'Strategy as the intentional structuration of practice, translation of formal strategies into strategies in practice', submitted to the Saïd Business School, University of Oxford in 2009.

16. 'Disaggregation' is a term used by D. Collis and C. Montgomery, 'Competing on resources', *Harvard Business Review*, July–August 2008, pp. 140–50.

17. The idea of SWOT as a commonsense checklist has been used for many years: for example, S. Tilles, 'Making strategy explicit', in I. Ansoff (ed.), *Business Strategy*, Penguin, 1968. For a critical discussion of the (mis)use of SWOT, see T. Hill and R. Westbrook, 'SWOT analysis: it's time for a product recall', *Long Range Planning*, vol. 30, no. 1 (1997), pp. 46–52.

18. See H. Weihrich, 'The TOWS matrix – a tool for situational analysis', *Long Range Planning*, April 1982, pp. 54–66.

CASE EXAMPLE

'Inside Dyson': a distinctive company?

Jill Shepherd, Segal Graduate School of Business, Simon Fraser University, Vancouver, Canada

Dyson is a private company, famous for its distinctive vacuum cleaners. It is not listed on a stock market and James Dyson, its founder and master inventor, has accumulated a personal fortune of over £1bn (~€1.1bn; ~$1.5bn). He is the sole owner of the company and is one of the few people to appear on Top Rich lists who has made money from his own inventions.

In 2005 the profit of the company reached £100m despite selling fewer vacuum cleaners than competitor Hoover. In terms of value rather than units sold, Dyson sells more in the US than Hoover, a company it sued for patent infringement winning around $5 (~€3.5) million. It is a global company, distributing its products in 45 countries including competitive markets such as China, the USA and Japan, as well as in its home market of the UK.

The company is built upon innovative products that are marketed as robust, presented well in bright colours and often in advertisements featuring James Dyson himself. From bag-less vacuum cleaners to energy-efficient and time-efficient hand-dryers for public places, to desk fans with no blades; all of the products are distinctive. His latest idea involves space saving kitchen appliances and even whole kitchens. All elements of the kitchens will be cubes with controls sliding into the main body so that the cubes fit and stack together into bigger cubes.

It hasn't all been straightforward success though, Dyson was about to launch a vacuum that could pick up water and dust. Customers were suspicious that such '3 in 1' products would not work and were not at all positive about wetting their carpets no matter how attractive the product design. Similarly a purple and silver washing machine with two rotating drums did not sell well and was also withdrawn.

Sir James Dyson

Dyson promote a story of their own heritage that suggests that the way the company works today is a

Source: Getty Images.

function of the early career development path of its leader. Dyson studied in art schools, rebelling against his family's tradition of reading Classics at Cambridge University. At art school he sought to apply engineering to functional problems in a way that respected design as an art. His first commercially successful vacuum product used cyclone technology. But from the beginning, he had problems convincing manufacturers both that the technology could be transferred to vacuum cleaners and could be patented. His confident answer was to set up his own firm: adopting unconventional routes and taking risks are still embedded within the organisational culture of Dyson.

Though, by 2010, the company was run by CEO Martin McCourt, James Dyson's own image and personal brand remained central to the firm's promotion. Apart from featuring in many of their adverts, he was highly visible beyond corporate boundaries. He appears to enjoy promoting engineering and design. He finances yearly design awards, collaborated with fashion designer Issey Miyake in an engineering themed fashion show and attempted to fund a Dyson School of Design Innovation. This latter endeavour was abandoned when the UK government put too many hurdles in its way thus limiting Dyson's own independence.

Engineering and design

Investment in R&D at Dyson quadrupled between 2004 and 2009. Dyson HQ is in a rural part of the west of England and is home to 350 engineers and scientists as well as the usual company personnel. It is also linked to 20 specialist laboratories all close by. Their large testing facility in Malaysia operates continually with over 120 testing stations. The operation in the UK employs 1200 varied people: some experienced, some freshly qualified, some with 'way out' ideas. James Dyson has said:

> 'We want people who are creative and courageous – unconditioned fresh-thinkers. We don't strap people into a suit and plonk them behind a desk, we like to give people the chance to make a difference.'

Success revolves around engineering ideas that are fine-tuned, not always on computer screens, but in the hands of engineers who make 100s, even 1000s of prototypes. Special computerised technology helps the engineers develop prototypes but they also use plasticine, cardboard or whatever material they wish to make prototypes in an almost child-like fashion. The engineers will tell you that the journey from prototype to prototype is an iterative journey of failures that creates new ideas. In walkabouts and feedbacks, they are encouraged to fiddle, to 'take the road less travelled' and to be 'less than sensible'. The same engineers report that, whilst competitors may have good robust engineering, they are not as inventive in terms of initial ideas and do not have the persistence

and patience to make wacky ideas work in robust terms.

There is a clear corporate-level commitment to product development with half of all profit being channelled into the creation of new ideas supported by their mantra of *thinking, testing, breaking, questioning*. It is product engineering that takes centre stage on the company website and generally in all company communications. This company is obvious in its desire to promote the idea that a Dyson product means new, different, a radical change: a Dyson product whether vacuum or washing machine *is* an innovation and the bright colours help these clever products stand out from the crowd. For example, the Dyson air multiplier™ performs the same function as a conventional air fan but in a radically different way. Conventional fans cause buffering of the air as the blades interrupt its flow. The multiplier™ 'amplifies surrounding air, giving an uninterrupted stream of flow of smooth air'. When you look at its sleek design you wonder whether it is a function of the innovation in engineering or design or the blurring of the two. Either way, design is deeply embedded in engineering and of all the capabilities at Dyson engineering is king.

Unlike Apple, another design great, who designs then subcontracts all manufacturing, Dyson believe the combination of design engineering and manufacturing is crucial in developing the most inimitable competences that can be protected through patents. Dyson believes in patents to protect its differentiated products, but this does not mean competitors do not try to imitate. Within Dyson's vacuums there is 'patented Ball technology for improved manoeuvrability'. The Miele equivalent has 'unique swivel head technology'. Hoover USA has Wind Tunnel vacuums available in 'fresh colours'. Dyson's colours are usually bright and it does launch exclusive editions based on novel colours. Dyson's hand-blade hand dryer wipes water off your hands in seconds using less energy rather than evaporating water as in standard hand dryers. The competitor product from US specialists in hand drying, the Xlerator, also claims to dry hands in seconds and with far less energy than standard hand dryers. The Dyson desk fan has 11 patent separate applications and involved every discipline within the company.

Global working

James Dyson was heavily criticised in the UK press for taking the managerial decision to place the manufacturing part of his vacuum value chain in Malaysia and later that of his hand dryers in Nanjing in China. He needed, he said, to follow competitors to lower cost manufacturing as margins were being eaten away. One hundred jobs were lost in the UK in the first move and several hundred in the second. Later, with manufacturing costs down and profits up, more engineers were hired in the UK. James Dyson says the decision to move to Malaysia was not an easy one for him. It was not solely based on cost but also his belief that he needed to have a testing facility nearer to suppliers and those were all in the East. In contrast, Miele and Excel Dryer Corporation keep their manufacturing in their home countries.

Dyson claims to be helping national competitiveness by pulling the UK up the value chain as global competition heats up. China claims contracts like Dyson's help pull China up the manufacturing value chain too towards ever more complex products of the highest quality. Dyson himself appears to view China as a major market. He has made choices to reflect that, such as launching his hand dryers there by offering them free to the Sofitel Hotel in Nanjing. As the costs of making things seem to be an ever decreasing part of the price a consumer pays, perhaps design and development are the future.

Dyson's secrecy of success

Undoubtedly a success story, it is a firm that prefers to keep its secret of success just that – secret. So much is evident, for example in their UK HQ. Access to the building and then subsequent areas is via thumb print and even then some areas are out of bounds. They have even developed their own sound-absorbing panels to ensure that conversations can be kept secret.

Postscript: In March 2010 James Dyson stood down as chairman, although he maintained his role as 'chief inventor'.

Questions

1 Using frameworks from the chapter, analyse the strategic capabilities of Dyson.

2 To what extent do you think any of the capabilities can be imitated by competitors?

3 Which of Dyson's distinctive capabilities may, over time, become threshold capabilities?

4 Bearing in mind your answers to questions 1 and 2, how crucial is Sir James Dyson to the future of of the company? What might be the effect of his completely leaving or selling the company?

Dyson and its competitors

Company	Location of headquarters	Product range	Manufacturing locations	Relative company size (1 largest, 5 smallest) based on approximate global turnover	Distribution	Distinctive capabilities?
Dyson	UK	Vacuums, fan, hand dryers, moving into integrated kitchens and robotic vacuums following the success of iRobots	Asia	4	Own online and through retail outlets	Engineering design
Electrolux	Sweden	Range of vacuums, washing machines, fridges and ovens and a robotic vacuum	Not known	2	Retail outlets	Emphasis on energy-saving products Brand licensing of over 50 brands
Hoover (Techtronic Floor Care Technology Limited)	USA and Hong Kong for (TTI)	Vacuums and for TTI Floor Care power tools, outdoor power equipment, floor care appliances, solar-powered lighting and electronic measuring products In USA Hoover range includes patented and trade-marked 'Wind Tunnel' with no loss of suction	Not known, possibly various around Asia	1	Vacuums sold through retail outlets and own online shop in the USA	Possibly the sheer scale of its global operations rather than any particular capability gives it the edge?
Hoover Limited	UK (Italy)	Vacuums and a wide range of domestic appliances			Hoovers sold in retail outlets and online accessories only	
Miele	Germany	Domestic appliances from microwaves to wine storage	Germany ('90% of value creation within Germany')	3	Only through stores including Miele stores, Miele specialists and Miele studios Online stores also	Engineering that results in highly reliable and robust products
Excel Dryer Corporation	USA	A range of hand dryers	USA (products very much advertised as 'Made in USA')	5	Can be bought direct or through licensed distributors Sees end users (e.g. restaurants), distributors, architects and government as customers	Transformation possibly, given the choice by new owner in 1997 to collaborate with a partner – Invent Resources – that produced the Xlerator product and changed the financial profile of the company

Business-Level Strategy

LEARNING OUTCOMES

After reading this chapter you should be able to:

→ Explain bases of achieving competitive advantage in terms of 'routes' on the strategy clock.

→ Assess the extent to which these are likely to provide sustainable competitive advantage.

→ Explain the relationship between competition and collaboration.

Photo: © BAA Ltd. www.baa.com/photolibrary

6.1   INTRODUCTION

This chapter is about a fundamental strategic choice: what competitive strategy to adopt in order to gain competitive advantage in a market at the business unit level. For example, faced with increasing competition from low price airlines, should British Airways seek to compete on price or maintain and improve their strategy of differentiation? Exhibit 6.1 shows the main themes that provide the structure for the rest of the chapter:

- First, *bases of competitive strategy* are considered. These include price-based strategies, differentiation strategies, hybrid and focus strategies.
- Section 6.3 considers *ways of sustaining competitive advantage* over time.
- The final section (6.4) considers the question of when *collaborative strategies* may be advantageous rather than direct competition.

Exhibit 6.1   **Business level strategies**

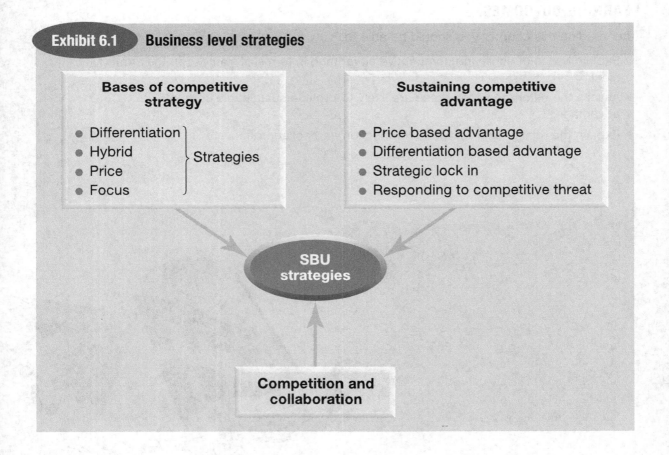

| 6.2 | **BASES OF COMPETITIVE ADVANTAGE: THE 'STRATEGY CLOCK'** |

Competitive strategy is concerned with the basis on which a business unit might achieve competitive advantage in its market

Strategy clock

This section reviews different ways of thinking about **competitive strategy**, the bases on which a business unit might achieve competitive advantage in its market. For public service organisations, the equivalent concern is the bases on which the organisation chooses to achieve superior quality of services in competition with others for funding, i.e. how it provides 'best value'.

This book employs 'market-facing' generic strategies similar to those used by Bowman and D'Aveni.[1] These are based on the principle that competitive advantage is achieved by providing customers with what they want, or need, better or more effectively than competitors. Building on this proposition, Michael Porter's[2] categories of differentiation and focus alongside price can be represented in the strategy clock (see Exhibit 6.2) – as discussed in the sections below.

In a competitive situation, customers make choices on the basis of their perception of value-for-money, the combination of price and perceived product/service benefits. The 'strategy clock' represents different positions in a market where customers (or potential customers) have different 'requirements' in terms of value-for-money. These positions also represent a set of generic strategies for achieving competitive advantage. Illustration 6.1 shows examples of different competitive strategies followed by firms in terms of these different positions on the strategy clock. The discussion of each of these strategies that follows also acknowledges the importance of an organisation's costs – particularly relative to competitors. But it will be seen that cost is a strategic consideration for all strategies on the clock – not just those where the lead edge is low price.

Since these strategies are 'market-facing' it is important to understand the critical success factors for each position on the clock. Customers at positions 1 and 2 are primarily concerned with price, but only if the product/service benefits meet their threshold requirements. This usually means that customers emphasise functionality over service or aspects such as design or packaging. In contrast, customers at position 5 require a customised product or service for which they are prepared to pay a price premium. The volume of demand in a market is unlikely to be evenly spread across the positions on the clock. In commodity-like markets demand is substantially weighted towards positions 1 and 2. Many public services are of this type too. Other markets have significant demand in positions 4 and 5. Historically professional services were of this type. However, markets change over time. Commodity-like markets develop value-added niches which grow as disposable incomes rise. For example, this has occurred in the drinks market with premium and speciality beers. And customised markets may become more commodity-like particularly where IT can demystify and routinise the professional content of the product – as in financial services.

The strategy clock: competitive strategy options

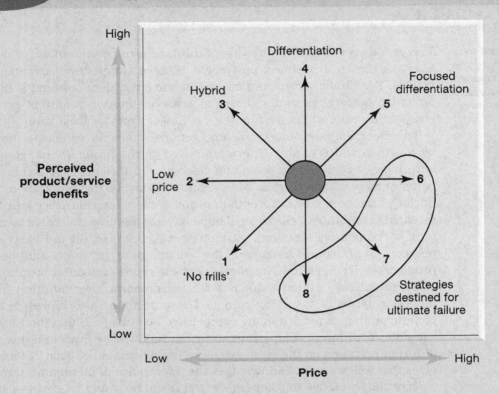

	Needs/risks	
1 'No frills'	Likely to be segment specific	
2 Low price	Risk of price war and low margins; need to be cost leader	
3 Hybrid	Low cost base and reinvestment in low price and differentiation	
4 Differentiation (a) Without price premium	Perceived added value by user, yielding market share benefits	Differentiation
(b) With price premium	Perceive added value sufficient to bear price premium	
5 Focused differentiation	Perceived added value to a particular segment, warranting price premium	
6 Increased price/standard value	Higher margins if competitors do not follow; risk of losing market share	Likely failure
7 Increased price/low value	Only feasible in monopoly situation	
8 Low value/standard price	Loss of market share	

Note: The strategy clock is adapted from the work of Cliff Bowman (see D. Faulkner and C. Bowman, *The Essence of Competitive Strategy*, Prentice Hall, 1995). However, Bowman uses the dimension 'Perceived Use Value'.

Illustration 6.1

Competitive strategies on the strategy clock

The competitive strategies of UK grocery retailers have shifted in the last three decades.

The supermarket retail revolution in the UK began in the late 1960s and 1970s as, initially, Sainsbury's began to open up supermarkets. Since the dominant form of retailing at that time was the corner grocery shop, Sainsbury's supermarkets were, in effect, a hybrid strategy: very clearly differentiated in terms of the physical layout and size of the stores as well as the quality of the merchandise, but also lower priced than many of the corner shop competitors.

As more and more retailers opened up supermarkets a pattern emerged. Sainsbury's was the dominant differentiated supermarket retailer. Tesco grew as a 'pile it high, sell it cheap' no frills operator. Competing in between as lower priced, but also lower quality than Sainsbury's, were a number of other supermarket retailers.

The mid-1990s saw a major change. Under the leadership of Ian Maclaurin, Tesco made a dramatic shift in strategy. It significantly increased the size and number of its stores, dropped the 'pile it high, sell it cheap' stance and began offering a much wider range of merchandise. Still not perceived as equal to Sainsbury's on quality, it none the less grew its market share at the expense of the other retailers and began to challenge Sainsbury's dominance. However the big breakthrough came for Tesco when it also shifted to higher-quality merchandise but still at perceived lower prices than Sainsbury's. In effect it was now adopting a hybrid strategy. In so doing it gained massive market share. By early 2007 this stood at over 30 per cent of the retail grocery market in the UK. In turn Sainsbury's had seen its share eroded to just 16 per cent, as it sought to find a way to resurrect its differentiated image of quality in the face of this competition.

In the meantime, other competitive strategy positions had consolidated. The low-price strategy was being followed by Asda (Wal-Mart) which also had a 16 per cent share of the market and Morrison's (with 11 per cent). In the no-frills segment was Netto, Lidl and Aldi, all retail formats that arrived in the 1990s from European neighbours and with a combined share of around 6 per cent.

The strategy of differentiation no longer really existed in a pure form. The closest was Waitrose (almost 4 per cent) emphasising a higher-quality image, but targeting a more select, upper-middle-class, market in selected locations. The focused differentiated stance remained the domain of the specialists: delicatessens and, of course in a London context, Harrods Food Hall.

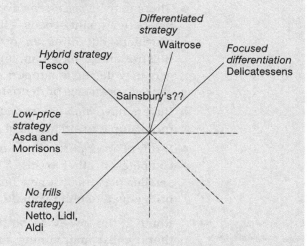

Questions

1 Who is 'stuck in the middle' here? Why?

2 Is a differentiated strategy or a low-price strategy defensible if there is a successful hybrid strategy, similar to that being followed by Tesco?

3 What might prevent other competitors following the Tesco strategy and competing successfully with them? (That is, does Tesco have strategic capabilities that provide sustainable competitive advantage?)

4 For another market of your choice, map out the strategic positions of the competitors in that market in terms of the strategy clock.

(Tesco is the case example in Chapter 9.)

So the strategy clock can help managers understand the changing requirements of their markets and the choices they can make about positioning and competitive advantage. Each position on the clock will now be discussed.

6.2.1 Price-based strategies (routes 1 and 2)

A 'no frills' strategy combines a low price, low perceived product/service benefits and a focus on a price-sensitive market segment

Route 1 is the **'no frills' strategy**, which combines a low price with low perceived product/service benefits and a focus on a price-sensitive market segment. These segments might exist because of the following:

- The existence of *commodity markets*. These are markets where customers do not value or discern differences in the offering of different suppliers, so price becomes the key competitive issue. Basic foodstuffs – particularly in developing economies – are an example.

- There may be *price-sensitive customers*, who cannot afford, or choose not, to buy better-quality goods. This market segment may be unattractive to major providers but offer an opportunity to others (Aldi, Lidl and Netto in Illustration 6.1 for example). In the public services funders with tight budgets may decide to support only basic-level provision (for example, in subsidised spectacles or dentistry).

- Buyers have *high power and/or low switching costs* so there is little choice – for example in situations of tendering for government contracts.

- It offers an opportunity to *avoid major competitors*: Where major providers compete on other bases, a low-price segment may be an opportunity for smaller players or a new entrant to carve out a niche or to use route 1 as a bridgehead to build volume before moving on to other strategies.

A low-price strategy seeks to achieve a lower price than competitors whilst trying to maintain similar perceived product or service benefits to those offered by competitors

Route 2, the **low-price strategy**, seeks to achieve a lower price than competitors whilst maintaining similar perceived product or service benefits to those offered by competitors. Increasingly this has been the competitive strategy chosen by Asda (owned by Wal-mart) and Morrisons in the UK supermarket sector (see Illustration 6.1). In the public sector, since the 'price' of a service to the provider of funds (usually government) is the unit costs of the organisation receiving the budget, the equivalent is year-on-year efficiency gains achieved without loss of perceived benefits.

Competitive advantage through a low-price strategy might be achieved by focusing on a market segment that is unattractive to competitors and so avoiding competitive pressures eroding price. However, a more common and more challenging situation is where there is competition on the basis of price, for example in the public sector and in commodity-like markets. There are two pitfalls when competing on price:

- *Margin reductions for all*. Although tactical advantage might be gained by reducing price this is likely to be followed by competitors, squeezing profit margins for everyone.

- An *inability to reinvest*. Low margins reduce the resources available to develop products or services and result in a loss of perceived benefit of the product.

So, in the long run, both a 'no frills' strategy and a low-price strategy cannot be pursued without a *low-cost base*. However, low cost in itself is not a basis for advantage. Managers often pursue low-cost that does not give them competitive advantage. The challenge is how costs can be reduced in ways which others cannot match such that a low-price strategy might give sustainable advantage. This is difficult but possible ways are discussed in section 6.3.1 below. Illustration 6.2 also shows how easyJet has sought to reduce costs to pursue its 'no frills' strategy.

6.2.2 (Broad) differentiation strategies (route 4)

A **differentiation strategy** seeks to provide products or services benefits that are different from those of competitors and that are widely valued by buyers

The next option is a broad **differentiation strategy** providing products or services that offer benefits different from those of competitors and that are widely valued by buyers.[3] The aim is to achieve competitive advantage by offering better products or services at the same price or enhancing margins by pricing slightly higher. In public services, the equivalent is the achievement of a 'centre of excellence' status, attracting higher funding from government (for example, universities try to show that they are better at research or teaching than other universities).

The success of a differentiation approach is likely to be dependent on two key factors:

- *Identifying and understanding the strategic customer*. The concept of the strategic customer is helpful because it focuses consideration on who the strategy is targeting. However, this is not always straightforward, as discussed in section 2.4.3. For example, for a newspaper business, is the customer the reader of the newspaper, the advertiser, or both? They are likely to have different needs and be looking for different benefits. For a branded food manufacturer is it the end consumer or the retailer? It may be important that public sector organisations offer perceived benefits, but to whom? Is it the service user or the provider of funds? However *what is valued* by the strategic customer can also be dangerously taken for granted by managers, a reminder of the importance of identifying critical success factors (section 2.4.4).

- *Identifying key competitors*. Who is the organisation competing against? For example, in the brewing industry there are now just a few major global competitors, but there are also many local or regional brewers. Players in each strategic group (see section 2.4.1) need to decide who they regard as competitors and, given that, which bases of differentiation might be considered. Heineken appear to have decided that it is the other global competitors – Carlsberg and Anheuser Busch for example. SABMiller built their global reach on the basis of acquiring and developing national brands and competing

Illustration 6.2

easyJet's 'no frills' strategy

Multiple bases for keeping costs down can provide a basis for a successful 'no frills' strategy.

Launched in 1995, easyJet was seen as the brash young upstart of the European airline industry and widely tipped to fail. But by the mid-2000s this Luton-based airline had done more than survive. From a starting point of six hired aircraft working one route, by 2006 it had 122 aircraft flying 262 routes to 74 airports and carrying over 33 million passengers per annum and impressive financial results: £129m profit on £1,619m revenue (≈ €187m on ≈ €2,348m).

The principles of its strategy and its business model were laid down in annual reports year by year. For example, in 2006:

- The internet is used to reduce distribution costs . . . now over 95% of all seats are sold online, making easyJet one of Europe's biggest internet retailers;
- Maximizing the utilization of substantial assets. We fly our aircraft intensively, with swift turnaround times each time we land. This gives us a very low unit cost;
- Ticket-less travel. Passengers receive booking details via an email rather than paper. This helps to significantly reduce the cost of issuing, distributing, processing and reconciling millions of transactions each year;
- No 'free lunch'. We eliminate unnecessary services, which are complex to manage such as free catering, pre-assigned seats, interline connections and cargo services. This allows us to keep our total costs of production low;
- Efficient use of airports. easyJet flies to main destination airports throughout Europe, but gains efficiencies compared to traditional carriers with rapid turnaround times, and progressive landing charge agreements with airports. [It might have added here that since it does not operate a hub system, passengers have to check in and offload their luggage at each stage. This means that aircraft are not held up whilst luggage is transferred between flights.]

It might also have added that other factors contributed to low costs:

- A focus on the Airbus A319 aircraft, and the retirement of 'old generation' Boeing 737 aircraft, meant 'a young fleet of modern aircraft secured at very competitive rates' benefiting maintenance costs. And, since an increasing proportion of these were owned by easyJet, financing costs were being reduced.
- A persistent focus on reducing ground handling costs.
- In the face of rising fuel costs, hedging on future buying of fuel.

In addition to all the factors above the 2006 annual report stated that easyJet's customer proposition is defined by

low cost with care and convenience. . . . We fly to main European destinations from convenient local airports and provide friendly onboard service. People are a key point of difference at easyJet and are integral to our success. This allows us to attract the widest range of customers to use our services – both business and leisure.

Source: easyJet annual report 2006.

Questions

1 Read sections 6.2.1 and 6.3.1 and identify the bases of easyJet's 'no frills' strategy.

2 How easy would it be for larger airlines such as BA to imitate the strategy?

3 On what bases could other low-price airlines compete with easyJet?

on the basis of local tastes and traditions, but have more recently also acquired Miller to compete globally.

The competitor analysis explained in section 2.4.4 (and Exhibit 2.7) can help in both of these regards.

- The *difficulty of imitation*. The success of a strategy of differentiation must depend on how easily it can be imitated by competitors. This highlights the importance of non-imitable strategic capabilities discussed in section 3.4.3.

- The extent of *vulnerability to price based competition*. In some markets customers are more price sensitive than others. So it may be that bases of differentiation are just not sufficient in the face of lower prices. Managers often complain, for example, that customers do not seem to value the superior levels of service they offer. Or, to take the example of UK grocery retailing (see Illustration 6.1), Sainsbury could once claim to be the broad differentiator on the basis of quality but customers now perceive that Tesco is comparable and seen to offer lower prices.

6.2.3 The hybrid strategy (route 3)

A **hybrid strategy** seeks simultaneously to achieve differentiation and a price lower than that of competitors

A **hybrid strategy** seeks simultaneously to achieve differentiation and low price relative to competitors. The success of this strategy depends on the ability to deliver enhanced benefits to customers together with low prices whilst achieving sufficient margins for reinvestment to maintain and develop bases of differentiation. It is, in effect the strategy Tesco is seeking to follow. It might be argued that, if differentiation can be achieved, there should be no need to have a lower price, since it should be possible to obtain prices at least equal to competition, if not higher. Indeed, there is a good deal of debate as to whether a hybrid strategy can be a successful competitive strategy rather than a suboptimal compromise between low price and differentiation. If it is the latter very likely it will be ineffective. However, the hybrid strategy could be advantageous when:

- Much *greater volumes* can be achieved than competitors so that margins may still be better because of a low cost base, much as Tesco is achieving given its market share in the UK.

- *Cost reductions are available outside its differentiated activities*. For example IKEA concentrates on building differentiation on the basis of its marketing, product range, logistics and store operations but low customer expectations on service levels allow cost reduction because customers are prepared to transport and build its products.

- Used as an *entry strategy* in a market with established competitors. For example, in developing a global strategy a business may target a poorly run operation in a competitor's portfolio of businesses in a geographical area of the world and enter that market with a superior product at a lower price to establish a foothold from which it can move further.

6.2.4 Focused differentiation (route 5)

A **focused differentiation** strategy provides high perceived product/service benefits, typically justifying a substantial price premium, usually to a selected market segment (or niche). These could be premium products and heavily branded, for example. Manufacturers of premium beers, single malt whiskies and wines from particular chateaux all seek to convince customers who value or see themselves as discerning of quality that their product is sufficiently differentiated from competitors' to justify significantly higher prices. In the public services centres of excellence (such as a specialist museum) achieve levels of funding significantly higher than more generalist providers. However, focused differentiation raises some important issues:

A focused differentiation strategy seeks to provide high perceived product/service benefits justifying a substantial price premium, usually to a selected market segment (niche)

- A *choice* may have to be made between a focus strategy (position 5) and broad differentiation (position 4). A firm following a strategy of international growth may have to choose between building competitive advantage on the basis of a common global product and brand (route 4) or tailoring their offering to specific markets (route 5).

- *Tensions between a focus strategy and other strategies.* For example broad-based car manufacturers, such as Ford, acquired premier marques, such as Jaguar and Aston Martin, but learned that trying to manage these in the same way as mass market cars was not possible. By 2007 Ford had divested Aston Martin and were seeking to divest others. Such tensions limit the degree of diversity of strategic positioning that an organisation can sustain, an important issue for corporate-level strategy discussed in Chapter 7.

- *Possible conflict with stakeholder expectations.* For example, a public library service might be more cost-efficient if it concentrated its development efforts on IT-based online information services. However, this would very likely conflict with its purpose of social inclusion since it would exclude people who were not IT literate.

- *Dynamics of growth for new ventures.* New ventures often start in very focused ways – offering innovative products or services to meet particular needs. It may, however, be difficult to find ways to grow such new ventures. Moving from route 5 to route 4 means a lowering of price and therefore cost, whilst maintaining differentiation features.

- *Market changes may erode differences between segments*, leaving the organisation open to much wider competition. Customers may become unwilling to pay a price premium as the features of 'regular' offerings improve. Or the market may be further segmented by even more differentiated offerings from competitors. For example, 'up-market' restaurants have been hit by rising standards elsewhere and by the advent of 'niche' restaurants that specialise in particular types of food.

6.3   SUSTAINING COMPETITIVE ADVANTAGE

Organisations that try to achieve competitive advantage hope to preserve it over time and much of what is written about competitive strategy takes the need for sustainability as a central expectation. This section builds on the discussion in section 3.2 relating to strategic capability to consider how sustainability might be possible.

6.3.1   Sustaining price-based advantage

An organisation pursuing competitive advantage through low prices might be able to sustain this in a number of ways:

- *Operating with lower margins* may be possible for a firm either because it has much greater sales volume than competitors or can cross-subsidise a business unit from elsewhere in its portfolio (see section 7.5 for further discussion of portfolio strategies).

- *A unique cost structure.* Some firms may have unique access to low-cost distribution channels, be able to obtain raw materials at lower prices than competitors or be located in an area where labour cost is low.

- *Organisationally specific capabilities* may exist for a firm such that it is able to drive down cost throughout its value chain. Indeed Porter defines cost leadership as '*the* low-cost producer in its industry . . . [who] must find and exploit all sources of cost advantage'.[4] (see section 3.3 and Exhibit 3.3).

Of course, if either of these last two approaches is to be followed it matters that the operational areas of low cost do truly deliver cost advantages to support real price advantages over competition. It is also important that competitors find these advantages difficult to imitate as discussed in Chapter 3. This requires a mindset where innovation in cost reduction is regarded as essential to survival. An example of this is RyanAir in the low price 'no frills' airline sector who, in 2006, declared it was their ambition to be able to eventually offer passengers flights for free.

- *Focusing on market segments* where low price is particularly valued by customers but other features are not. An example is the success of dedicated producers of own-brand grocery products for supermarkets. They can hold prices low because they avoid the high overhead and marketing costs of major branded manufacturers. However, they can only do so provided they focus on that product and market segment.

There are however dangers with trying to pursue low-price strategies:

- *Competitors may be able to do the same.* There is no point in trying to achieve advantage through low price on the basis of cost reduction if competitors can do it too.

Illustration 6.3

The strategy battle in the wine industry: Australia vs. France

The benefits of successful differentiation may be difficult to sustain.

For centuries French wines were regarded as superior. Building on the Appellation d'Origine Contrôlée (AOC) system, with its separate label requirements and controls for nearly 450 wine-growing regions, the emphasis was on the distinct regionality of the wines and the chateau-based branding. In the AOC system the individual wine-grower is a custodian of the *terroir* and its traditions. The quality of the wines and the distinct local differences are down to the differences in soil and climate as well as the skills of the growers, often on the basis of decades of local experience.

However, by 2001 the traditional dominance of French wines in the UK seemed to have ended, with sales of Australian wine outstripping them for the first time. This went hand in hand with huge growth in wine consumption as it became more widely available in supermarkets, where Australian wine was especially succesful. The success of Australian wines with retailers was for several reasons. The quality was consistent, compared with French wines that could differ by year and location. Whilst the French had always highlighted the importance of the local area of origin of the wine, in effect Australia 'branded' the country as a wine region and then concentrated on the variety of grape – a Shiraz or a Chardonnay, for example. This avoided the confusing details of the location of vineyards and the names of chateaux that many customers found difficult about French wines. The New World approach to the production of wine in terms of style, quality and taste was also based around consumer demand, not local production conditions. Grapes were sourced from wherever necessary to create a reliable product. French wines could be unpredictable – charming to the connoisseur, but infuriating to the dinner-party host, who expects to get what he or she paid for.

Between 1994 and 2003 France lost 84,000 growers. There was so much concern that in 2001, the French government appointed a committee to study the problem. The committee's proposals were that France should both improve the quality of its appellation wine and also create an entirely new range of quality, generic wines, so-called 'vins de cepage'

(wines based on a grape variety). A company called OVS planned to market the Chamarré brand – French for 'bursting with colours', to sell between £5 and £7 (€7.25 and €10.15), the price range where New World wines have made the biggest inroads. OVS President Pascal Renaudat, who has had 20 years in the wine business, explained:

We have to simplify our product and reject an arrogant approach that was perhaps natural to us. It is important to produce wine that corresponds to what people want to drink and at a good price. . . . This is not wine for connoisseurs. It is for pleasure.

'It's time to get rid of the stuffy pretentiousness that surrounds French wine,' said Renaud Rosari, Chamarré's master wine-maker. 'Chamarré is about bringing our wines to life for the consumers – the brand is lively, uncomplicated and approachable and means consistently high quality wines, with the fresh easy drinking style customers are looking for.'

There was qualified optimism: Jamie Goode of wineanorak.com saw it as a brave commercial decision. However: 'The trouble is that everybody is doing it. . . . Access to market is key. You need to get into the supermarkets, but you need to have a strong brand with which to negotiate or else they will savage you on price.'

Sources: Adapted from *Financial Times*, 11 February and 3/4 March (2001); *Independent*, 4 August (2003); *Sunday Times*, 5 February (2006); Guardian Unlimited, 7 February (2006).

Questions

1 Explain the high and distinct reputation of French wines of the past in terms of the bases of sustainable differentiation explained in sections 3.4 and 6.3.2.

2 What were the reasons for the success of Australian wines? Are these as sustainable?

3 What competitive strategy is Chamarré adopting to respond to the challenge of Australian (and other 'New World') wines?

- Customers start to *associate low price with low product/service benefits* and an intended route 2 strategy slips to route 1 by default.

- Cost reductions may result in an *inability to pursue a differentiation strategy*. For example, outsourcing IT systems for reasons of cost efficiency may mean that no one takes a strategic view of how competitive advantage might be achieved through IT.

6.3.2 Sustaining differentiation-based advantage

There is little point in striving to be different if competitors can imitate readily; there is a need for sustainability of the basis of advantage. For example, many firms that try to gain advantage through launching new products or services find them copied rapidly by competitors. Illustration 6.3 shows how wine producers in France and Australia have been seeking bases of differentiation over each other over the years.

Ways of attempting to sustain advantage through differentiation include the following:

- *Create difficulties of imitation*. Section 3.4.3 discussed the factors that can make strategies difficult to imitate.

- *Imperfect mobility* such that the capabilities that sustain differentiation cannot be *traded*. For example, a pharmaceutical firm may gain great benefits from having top research scientists, or a football club from its star players, but they may be poached by competitors: they are tradable. On the other hand, some bases of advantage are very difficult to trade. For example:

  - *Intangible assets* such as brand, image, or reputation that are intangible or competences rooted in an organisation's culture are difficult for a competitor to imitate or obtain. Indeed even if the competitor acquires the company to gain these, they may not readily transfer given new ownership.

  - There may be *switching costs*. The actual or perceived cost for a buyer of changing the source of supply of a product or service may be high. Or the buyer might be dependent on the supplier for particular components, services or skills. Or the benefits of switching may simply not be worth the cost or risk.

  - *Co-specialisation*. If one organisation's resources or competences are intimately linked with the buyers' operations. For example, a whole element of the value chain for one organisation, perhaps distribution or manufacturing, may be undertaken by another.

- A *lower cost position* than competitors can allow an organisation to sustain better margins that can be reinvested to achieve and maintain differentiation. For example, Kellogg's or Mars may well be the lowest cost in their markets, but they reinvest their profits into branding and product and service differentiation not low prices.

6.3.3 **Strategic lock-in**

Strategic lock-in is where an organisation achieves a proprietary position in its industry; it becomes an industry standard

Another approach to sustainability, whether for price based or differentiation strategies is the creation of **strategic lock in**.[5] This is where an organisation achieves a proprietary position in its industry; it becomes an industry standard. For example, Microsoft became an industry standard. Many argue that technically the Apple Macintosh had a better operating system, but Microsoft Windows became the industry standard by working to ensure that the 'architecture' of the industry was built around them. Other businesses had to conform or relate to that standard in order to prosper.

The achievement of lock-in is likely to be dependent on:

- *Size or market dominance*. It is unlikely that others will seek to conform to such standards unless they perceive the organisation that promotes it as dominant in its market.
- *First mover dominance*. Such standards are likely to be set *early in life cycles of markets*. In the volatility of growth markets it is more likely that the single-minded pursuit of lock-in by the *first movers* will be successful than when the market is mature. For example Sky, with the financial support of the News Corporation, was able to undercut competitors and invest heavily in technology and fast market share growth, sustaining substantial losses over many years, in order to achieve dominance.
- *Self-reinforcing commitment*. When one or more firms support the standard more come on board, then others are obliged to, and so on.
- *Insistence on the preservation* of the lock-in position. Insistence on conformity to the standard is strict so rivals will be seen off fiercely. This can of course lead to problems, as Microsoft found in the American courts when it was deemed to be operating against the interests of the market.

6.3.4 **Responding to competitive threat**[6]

The preservation of competitive advantage in the face of competitors who attack by targeting customers on the basis of a different competitive strategy can be a serious threat. One of the most common is low price competitors entering markets dominated by firms that have built a strong position through differentiation. For example low price airlines have taken substantial share from most of the leading airlines throughout the world. An equivalent situation in the public sector arises given the insistence by funding providers on year-on-year 'efficiency gains'. It is an opportunity for new entrants to undercut existing service providers, or indeed it may be that those providers find themselves being forced to undercut themselves.

Exhibit 6.3 suggests the series of questions that might be asked and the appropriate responses and there are some general guidelines. First, *if a strategy*

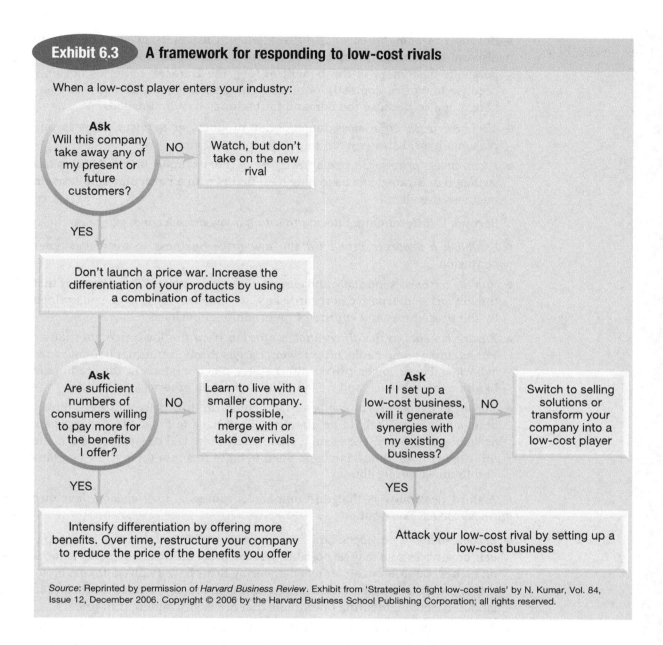

Exhibit 6.3 — **A framework for responding to low-cost rivals**

When a low-cost player enters your industry:

Ask Will this company take away any of my present or future customers? — NO → Watch, but don't take on the new rival

YES ↓

Don't launch a price war. Increase the differentiation of your products by using a combination of tactics

↓

Ask Are sufficient numbers of consumers willing to pay more for the benefits I offer? — NO → Learn to live with a smaller company. If possible, merge with or take over rivals → **Ask** If I set up a low-cost business, will it generate synergies with my existing business? — NO → Switch to selling solutions or transform your company into a low-cost player

YES ↓ (left)   YES ↓ (right)

Intensify differentiation by offering more benefits. Over time, restructure your company to reduce the price of the benefits you offer

Attack your low-cost rival by setting up a low-cost business

of differentiation is retained as the basis of retaliation (or in the public sector if the decision is to maintain a 'centre of excellence' status):

● *Build multiple bases of differentiation.* There is more likelihood of highlighting relative benefits if they are multiple: for example, Bang and Olufsen's design of hi-fi systems linked to product innovation and their relationships with retailers to ensure they present their products distinctly in stores.

- *Ensure a meaningful basis of differentiation*. Customers need to be able to discern a meaningful benefit. For example Gillette has found it difficult to persuade customers of the benefit of long life Duracell batteries not only because low price competitors offer multipacks of cheap batteries to compete, but also because the demand for batteries has diminished.

- *Minimise price differences* for superior products or services. This is one reason a hybrid strategy can be so effective of course.

- *Focus on less price sensitive market segments*. For example, British Airways has switched its strategic focus to long haul flights with a particular emphasis on business travellers.

Second, if differentiators decide to *set up a low price business*:

- *Establish a separate brand* for the low price business to avoid customer confusion.

- *Run the business separately* and *ensure it is well resourced*: The danger is that the low price alternative is regarded as 'second class' or is over-constrained by the procedures and culture of the traditional business.

- *Ensure benefits to the differentiated offering* from the low price alternative. For example some banks offer lower charges through Internet banking subsidiaries. These lower priced alternatives reach customers the traditional bank might not reach and raise funds they would otherwise not have.

- *Allow the businesses to compete*. Launching the low price business purely defensively is unlikely to be effective. They have to be allowed to compete as viable separate SBUs; as such, quite likely there will be substitution of one offering with another. Managers need to build this into their strategic plans and financial projections.

A third possibility is that differentiated businesses may *change their own business model*. For example:

- *Become solutions providers*. Low-price entrants are likely to focus on basic products or services so it may be possible to reconstruct the business model to focus on higher-value services. Many engineering firms have realised, for example, the higher-value potential of design and consultancy services rather than labour-based engineering operations that are easily undercut in price.

- *Become a low-price provider*. The most radical response would be to abandon the reliance on differentiation and learn to compete head on with the low-price competitor.[7] Perhaps not surprisingly, there is not much evidence of the success of such a response, not least because it would mean competing on the basis of competences better understood by the incumbent.

6.4 COMPETITION AND COLLABORATION[8]

So far the emphasis has been on competition and competitive advantage. However, advantage may not always be achieved by competing. Collaboration between organisations may be a way of achieving advantage or avoiding competition. Collaboration between potential competitors or between buyers and sellers is likely to be advantageous when the combined costs of purchase and buying transactions (such as negotiating and contracting) are lower through collaboration than the cost of operating alone. Collaboration also helps build switching costs. This can be shown by returning to the five forces framework from section 2.3.1 (also see Exhibit 6.4):

● *Collaboration to increase selling power.* In the aerospace industry component manufacturers might seek to build close links with customers. Achieving accredited supplier status can be tough, but may significantly increase seller power once achieved. It may also help in research and development activities, in reducing stock and in joint planning to design new products.

● *Collaboration to increase buying power.* Historically, the power and profitability of pharmaceutical companies were aided by the fragmented nature of their buyers – individual doctors and hospitals. But many governments have promoted, or required, collaboration between buyers of pharmaceuticals

Exhibit 6.4 **Competition and collaboration**

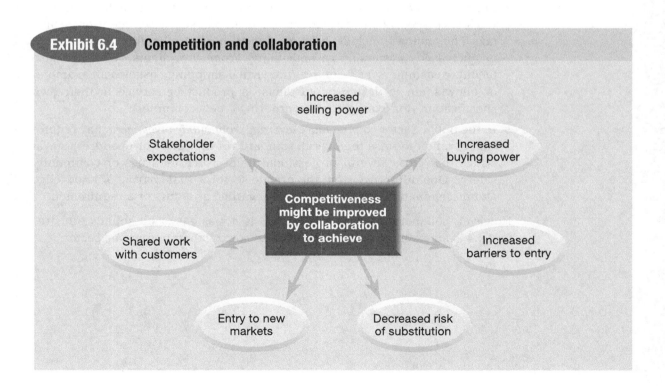

and centralised government drug-specifying agencies, the result of which has been more coordinated buying power.

- *Collaboration to build barriers to entry or avoid substitution.* Faced with threatened entry or substitute products, firms in an industry may collaborate to invest in research and development or marketing. Trade associations may promote an industry's generic features such as safety standards or technical specifications to speed up innovation and pre-empt the possibility of substitution.

- *Collaboration to gain entry and competitive power.* Organisations seeking to develop beyond their traditional boundaries (for example, geographical expansion) may collaborate with others to gain entry into new arenas. Gaining local market knowledge may also require collaboration with local operators. Indeed, in some parts of the world, governments require entrants to collaborate in such ways. Collaboration may also help in developing required infrastructure such as distribution channels, information systems or research and development activities. It may also be needed because buyers may prefer to do business with local rather than expatriate managers. Especially in hi-tech and hypercompetitive situations there is increasing disintegration (or 'unbundling') of value chains because there is innovatory competition at each stage of that chain. In such circumstances there also is likely to be increasing need for co-operative strategies between such competitors to offer coherent solutions for customers.[9]

- *Collaboration to share work with customers.* An important trend in public services is *co-production* with clients, for example, self-assessment of income tax. The motives include cost efficiency, quality/reliability improvement or increased 'ownership/responsibility' from the clients. Websites also facilitate customers' self-service (the virtual shopping basket is an example) or allow them to design or customise a product or service to their own specification (for example, when ordering a new computer).

- In the public sector *gaining more leverage from public investment* may require collaboration to raise the overall standards of the sector or to address social issues that cross several professional fields (such as drugs or community safety). One difference from the private sector is that sharing of knowledge and dissemination of best practice is regarded as a duty or a requirement.

However, collaborating with competitors is not as easy as it sounds. Illustration 6.4 is an example of public/private sector collaboration in one sector.

Illustration 6.4

Business–university collaboration in the creative and cultural industries

Public/private sector collaboration may bring benefits to both parties.

In 2003 the UK government set up a committee (The Lambert Committee) to report on business–university collaboration in the UK and to propose how it might be improved. The first stage was to seek ideas from a wide range of stakeholders. The following is an extract from the Arts and Humanities Research Council (AHRC), which supported work that was fundamental to a range of creative and cultural industries:

We are in the early stages of exploring a range of partnerships and possible strategic interventions (see below). In collaboration with the Department for Culture, Media and Sports (DCMS) and others, a Creative Industries/Higher Education Forum has been established. This group will seek to bring together the supply and demand side of this relationship to foster stronger links and new activities.

Creative and cultural industries: a role for creative clusters

Many universities have developed links with businesses in the creative and cultural industries. . . . However, many of the companies in the creative industries are small (SMEs). . . . An organic development in recent years has been the creation of a number of 'creative clusters' bringing together local or regional HEIs with business for the generation of new ideas, products and processes. Examples exist from around the country, including Scotland, Sheffield, London, Bristol, Nottingham. Such creative clusters supported by business enterprise and support services could provide the basis for supporting small-scale individual entrepreneurship.

Working with Regional Development Agencies (RDAs)

Both the Research Councils and RDAs are channels to their respective communities, and work has already commenced on identifying ways in which jointly they can be both a catalyst for new ideas and a facilitator of knowledge transfer. Such activities might cover individual projects, jointly-sponsored schemes, and facilitation of sector clusters, such as creative clusters.

Embedding practitioners and professionals in HEIs

Many traditional models of the relationship between HEIs and business describe a linear process in which knowledge is passed to industry. However, it can be argued that, increasingly, knowledge transfer is not a process, but an interaction based on access to people, information, data and infrastructure. In the creative and performing arts the concept of portfolio careers is not uncommon. Individuals can hold part-time research or teaching positions alongside other forms of employment or self-employment, including artistic performance. In addition, it is not uncommon for businesses and other non-private sector organisations to provide visiting professorships or lectureships.

Widening the definition of knowledge transfer in a knowledge economy

Increasingly a large number of people are trading their knowledge, expertise and experience through non-conventional employment means. However, in looking for evidence of knowledge transfer from academia to business the focus tends to be on the numbers of patents, spin-outs and companies created. These are undoubtedly important indicators to industrial performance, but a wider evidence base looking at employment patterns and self-employment would give a wider perspective.

Charting this new landscape

It is the role of bodies such as the AHRC to provide an environment that enables the ideas and creativity of the academic community to be unlocked and developed. Working with analogous bodies in other sectors, such as the RDAs, the aspiration is to find ways to improve the links out from academia to the wider society and economy.

Source: AHRC Response from the AHRC to the Lambert Review of Business–University Collaboration, http://www.ahrc.ac.uk.

Questions

1 Look at section 6.4 and then identify the potential benefits from business–university collaboration to a number of the important stakeholders.

2 What are the risks of collaboration to each of these stakeholders (as against 'going it alone')?

SUMMARY

- Competitive strategy is concerned with seeking competitive advantage in markets at the business level, or in the public services, providing best value services.
- Different bases of competitive strategy include:
  - A *'no frills'* strategy, combining low price and low perceived added value.
  - A *low-price* strategy providing lower price than competitors at similar added value of product or service to competitors.
  - A *differentiation* strategy, which seeks to provide products or services which are unique or different from competitors.
  - A *hybrid* strategy, which seeks simultaneously to achieve differentiation and prices lower than competitors.
  - A *focused differentiation* strategy, which seeks to provide high perceived value justifying a substantial price premium.
- Managers need to consider the bases upon which price based or differentiation strategies can be sustained based on strategic capabilities, developing durable relationships with customers or the ability to achieve a 'lock-in' position so becoming the 'industry standard' recognised by suppliers and buyers.
- Strategies of collaboration may offer alternatives to competitive strategies or may run in parallel.

Recommended key readings

- The foundations of the discussions of generic competitive strategies are to be found in the writings of Michael Porter, which include *Competitive Strategy* (1980) and *Competitive Advantage* (1985), both published by Free Press. Both are recommended for readers who wish to understand the background to discussions in sections 6.3 and 6.4 of this chapter on competitive strategy and competitive advantage.
- There is a lively debate about whether sustainable competitive advantage is possible. Two papers offering different evidence on this are R.W. Wiggins and T.W. Ruefli, 'Schumpeter's Ghost: Is Hypercompetition Making the Best of Times Shorter?', *Strategic Management Journal*, vol. 26 (2005), 887–911, which argues there is no evidence for sustainable competitive advantage; and G. McNamara, P.M. Vaaler and C. Devers, 'Same as it Ever Was: the Search for Evidence of Increasing Hypercompetition', *Strategic Management Journal*, vol. 24 (2003), 261–278, which argues that it is.

References

1. See D. Faulkner and C. Bowman, *The Essence of Competitive Strategy*, Prentice Hall, 1995. A similar framework is also used by Richard D'Aveni, *Hypercompetitive Rivalries: Competing in highly dynamic environments*, Free Press, 1995.

2. M. Porter, *Competitive Advantage*, Free Press, 1985.

3. B. Sharp and J. Dawes, 'What is differentiation and how does it work?', *Journal of Marketing Management*, vol. 17, no. 7/8 (2001), pp. 739–759 reviews the relationship between differentiation and profitability.

4. These quotes concerning Porter's three competitive strategies are taken from his book *Competitive Advantage*, Free Press, 1985, pp. 12–15.

5. The Delta Model is explained and illustrated more fully in A.C. Hax and D.L. Wilde II, 'The Delta Model', *Sloan Management Review*, vol. 40, no. 2 (1999), pp. 11–28.

6. This section is based on research by N. Kumar, 'Strategies to Fight Low Cost Rivals', *Harvard Business Review*, vol. 84, no. 12 (2006), 104–113.

7. For a discussion of how to compete in such circumstances, see A. Rao, M. Bergen and S. Davis, 'How to fight a price war', *Harvard Business Review*, vol. 78, no. 2 (2000), pp. 107–115.

8. Useful books on collaborative strategies are Y. Doz and G. Hamel, *Alliance Advantage: The art of creating value through partnering*, Harvard Business School Press, 1998; *Creating Collaborative Advantage*, ed. Chris Huxham, Sage Publications, 1996 and D. Faulkner, *Strategic Alliances: Co-operating to compete*, McGraw-Hill, 1995.

9. This case for cooperation in hi-tech industries is argued and illustrated by V. Kapur, J. Peters and S. Berman, 'High Tech 2005: the Horizontal, Hypercompetitive Future', *Strategy and Leadership*, vol. 31, no. 2 (2003).

Madonna: still the reigning queen of pop?

Phyl Johnson, Strategy Explorers

The music industry has always been the backdrop for one-hit wonders and brief careers. Pop stars who have remained at the top for decades are very few. Madonna is one such phenomenon; the question is, after over 25 years at the top, how much longer can it last?

Described by *Billboard Magazine* as the smartest business woman in show business, Madonna, Louise Ciccone, began her music career in 1983 with the hit single 'Holiday' and in 2005–2006 once again enjoyed chart success for her album 'Confessions on a Dance Floor'. In the meantime she had consistent chart success with her singles and albums, multiple sell-out world tours, major roles in six films, picked up 18 music awards, been the style icon behind a range of products from Pepsi and Max Factor to the Gap and H&M, and became a worldwide best-selling children's author.

The foundation of Madonna's business success was her ability to sustain her reign as the 'queen of pop' since 1983. Along with many others, Phil Quattro, the President of Warner Brothers, has argued that 'she always manages to land on the cusp of what we call contemporary music, every established artist faces the dilemma of maintaining their importance and relevance, Madonna never fails to be relevant.' Madonna's chameleon-like ability to change persona, change her music genre with it and yet still achieve major record sales has been the hallmark of her success.

Madonna's early poppy style was targeted at young 'wannabe' girls. The image that she portrayed through hits such as 'Holiday' and 'Lucky Star' in 1983 was picked up by Macy's, the US-based department store. It produced a range of *Madonna lookalike* clothes that mothers were happy to purchase for their daughters. One year later in 1984, Madonna then underwent her first image change and, in doing so, offered the first hint of the smart cookie behind the media image. In the video for her hit 'Material Girl', she deliberately mirrored the glamour-based, sexual pussycat image of Marilyn Monroe whilst simultaneously mocking both the growing materialism of the late 1980s and the men fawning

Photo: Roland weihrauch/DPA/PA Photos

after her. Media analysts Sam and Diana Kirschner commented that with this kind of packaging, Madonna allowed the record companies to keep hold of a saleable 'Marilyn image' for a new cohort of fans, but also allowed her original fan base of now growing up wannabe girls to take the more critical message from the music. The theme of courting controversy but staying marketable enough has been recurrent throughout her career, if not slightly toned down in later years.

Madonna's subsequent image changes were more dramatic. First she took on the Catholic Church in her

1989 video 'Like a Prayer' where, as a red-dressed 'sinner', she kissed a black saint easily interpreted as a Jesus figure. Her image had become increasingly sexual whilst also holding on to a critical social theme: for example, her pointed illustration of white-only imagery in the Catholic Church. At this point in her career, Madonna took full control of her image in the $60m (€48m; £33m) deal with Time-Warner that created her record company Maverick. In 1991, she published a coffee-table soft-porn book entitled *Sex* that exclusively featured pictures of herself in erotic poses. Her image and music also reflected this erotic theme. In her 'Girlie' tour, her singles 'Erotica' and 'Justify my Love' and her fly-on-the-wall movie 'In bed with Madonna' she played out scenes of sadomasochistic and lesbian fantasies. Although allegedly a period of her career she would rather forget, Madonna more than survived it. In fact, she gained a whole new demography of fans who not only respected her artistic courage, but also did not miss the fact that Madonna was consistent in her message: her sexuality was her own and not in need of a male gaze. She used the media's love affair with her, and the *cause célèbre* status gained from having MTV ban the video for 'Justify my Love', to promote the message that women's sexuality and freedom is just as important and acceptable as men's.

Changing gear in 1996, Madonna finally took centre stage in the lead role in the film *Evita* that she had chased for over five years. She beat other heavyweight contenders for the role including Meryl Streep and Elaine Page, both with more acceptable pasts than Madonna. Yet she achieved the image transition from erotica to saint-like persona of Eva Peron and won critical acclaim to boot. Another vote of confidence from the 'establishment' came from Max Factor, who in 1999 signed her up to front its relaunch campaign that was crafted around a glamour theme. Procter and Gamble (owners of the Max Factor make-up range) argued that they saw Madonna as 'the closest thing the 90s has to an old-style Hollywood star . . . she is a real woman'.

With many pre-release leaks, Madonna's keenly awaited album 'Ray of Light' was released in 1998. Radio stations worldwide were desperate to get hold of the album being billed as her most successful musical voyage to date. In a smart move, Madonna had teamed up with techno pioneer William Orbit to write and produce the album. It was a huge success, taking

Madonna into the super-trendy techno sphere, not the natural environment for a pop star from the early 1980s. Madonna took up an 'earth mother/spiritual' image and spawned a trend for all things Eastern in fashion and music. This phase may have produced more than just an image as it is the time in Madonna's life which locates the beginning of her continued faith in the Kabbalah tradition of Eastern spiritual worship.

By 2001, her next persona was unveiled with the release of her album 'Music'. Here her style had moved on again to 'acid rock'. With her marriage to British movie director Guy Ritchie, the ultimate 'American Pie' had become a fully fledged Brit babe earning the endearing nick name of 'Madge' in the British press.

By 2003 some commentators were suggesting that an interesting turn of events hinted that perhaps 'the cutting-edge' Madonna, 'the fearless', was starting to think about *being part of* rather than *beating* the establishment when she launched her new Che-Guevara-inspired image. Instead of maximising the potential of this image in terms of its political and social symbolism during the Second Gulf War, in April 2003 she withdrew her militaristic image and video for the album 'American Life'. That action timed with the publication of her children's book *The English Roses*, based on the themes of compassion and friendship, which sparked questions in the press around the theme 'has Madonna gone soft?'.

By late 2003 she had wiped the military image from the West's collective memory with a glitzy high-profile ad campaign for the Gap, the clothing retailer in which she danced around accompanied by rapper Missy Elliot to a retrospective remix of her 1980s' track 'Get into the Groove'. Here Madonna was keeping the 'thirty-somethings', who remembered the track from first time around, happy. They could purchase jeans for themselves and their newly teenage daughters whilst also purchasing the re-released CD (on sale in store) for them to share and a copy of *The English Roses* (also promoted in the Gap stores) for perhaps the youngest member of the family.

Late 2005 saw the release of the 'Confessions on a Dance Floor' album that was marketed as her comeback album after her lowest-selling 'American Life'. It and the linked tour achieved one of the highest-selling peaks of her career. The album broke a world record for solo-female artists when it debuted at number one in 41 countries. By February 2007 it had sold 8 million copies.

Releases	Year	Image	Target audience
Lucky Star	1982	Trashy pop	Young wannabe girls, dovetailing from fading disco to emerging 'club scene'
Like a Virgin *Like a Prayer*	1984	Originally a Marilyn glamour image, then became a saint and sinner	More grown-up rebellious fan base, more critical female audience and male worshippers
Vogue *Erotica* *Bedtime Stories*	1990 1992 1994	Erotic porn star, sadomasochistic, sexual control, more Minelli in *Cabaret* than Monroe	Peculiar mix of target audiences: gay club scene, 1990s' women taking control of their own lives, also pure male titillation
Something to Remember Evita	1995	Softer image, ballads preparing for glamour image of *Evita* film role	Broadest audience target, picking up potential film audiences as well as regular fan base. Most conventional image. Max Factor later used this mixture of Marilyn and Eva Peron to market its glamour image
Ray of Light	1998	Earth mother, Eastern mysticism, dance music fusion	Clubbing generation of the 1990s, new cohort of fans plus original fan base of now 30-somethings desperately staying trendy
Music	2000	Acid rock, tongue in cheek Miss USA/cow girl, cool Britannia	Managing to hit the changing club scene and 30-something Brits
American Life	2003	Militaristic image Che Guevara Anti-consumerism of American dream	Unclear audience reliant on existing base
Confessions on a Dance Floor	2005	Retro-1980s' disco imagery, high-motion dance–pop sound	Strong gay–icon audience, pop–disco audience, dance-based audience

Here Madonna focused on the high-selling principal of *remix*, choosing samples of the gay–iconic disco favourites of Abba and Giorgio Moroder to be at the heart of her symbolic reinvention of herself from artist to DJ. By cross-marketing the album image with Dolce & Gabbana in its men's fashion shows, Madonna cashed in on her regaining the dance–pop crown. Will this, her latest album, stand the musical test of time? Who knows? But for now it seems to have more than met the moment.

Sources: 'Bennett takes the reins at Maverick', *Billboard Magazine*, 7 August (1999); 'Warner Bros expects Madonna to light up international markets', *Billboard Magazine*, 21 February (1998); 'Maverick builds on early success', *Billboard Magazine*, 12 November (1994); A. Jardine 'Max Factor strikes gold with Madonna', *Marketing*, vol. 29 (1999), pp. 14–15; S. Kirschner and D. Kirschner, 'MTV, adolescence and Madonna: a discourse analysis', in *Perspectives on Psychology & the Media*, American Psychological Association, Washington, DC, 1997; 'Warner to buy out maverick co-founder', *Los Angeles Times*, 2 March (1999); 'Why Madonna is back in Vogue', *New Statesman*, 18 September (2000); 'Madonna & Microsoft', *Financial Times*, 28 November (2000).

Questions

1 Describe and explain the strategy being followed by Madonna in terms of the explanation of competitive strategy given in Chapter 6.

2 Why has she experienced sustained success over the past two decades?

3 What might threaten the sustainability of her success?

7.2 STRATEGIC DIRECTIONS

KEY CONCEPT

Strategic directions (Ansoff)

The Ansoff product/market growth matrix[1] provides a simple way of generating four basic alternative directions for strategic development: see Exhibit 7.2. An organisation typically starts in box A, the top left-hand one, with its existing products and existing markets. According to the matrix, the organisation basically has a choice between *penetrating* still further within its existing sphere (staying in box A); moving rightwards by *developing new products* for its existing markets (box B); moving downwards by bringing its *existing products into new markets* (box C); or taking the most radical step of full *diversification*, with altogether new markets and new products (box D).

The Ansoff matrix explicitly considers growth options. Growth is rarely a good end in itself. Public sector organisations are often accused of growing out-of-control bureaucracies; similarly, some private-sector managers are accused of empire-building at the expense of shareholders. This chapter therefore adds *consolidation* as a fifth option. Consolidation involves protecting existing products and existing markets and therefore belongs in box A. The rest of this section considers the five strategic directions in more detail.

Exhibit 7.2   **Strategic directions (Ansoff matrix)**

	Products	
Markets	**Existing**	**New**
Existing	**A** **Market penetration** **Consolidation**	**B** **Product development**
New	**C** **Market development**	**D** **Diversification**

Source: Adapted from H.I. Ansoff, *Corporate Strategy*, Penguin, 1988, Chapter 6. (The Ansoff matrix was later developed – see reference 1.)

7.2.1 Market penetration

Market penetration is
where an organisation
gains market share

Further **market penetration**, by which the organisation takes increased share of its existing markets with its existing product range, is on the face of it the most obvious strategic direction. It builds on existing strategic capabilities and does not require the organisation to venture into uncharted territory. The organisation's scope is exactly the same. Moreover, greater market share implies increased power *vis-à-vis* buyers and suppliers (in terms of the five forces), greater economies of scale and experience curve benefits.

However, organisations seeking greater market penetration may face two constraints:

- *Retaliation from competitors*. In terms of the five forces (Section 2.3), increasing market penetration is likely to exacerbate industry rivalry as other competitors in the market defend their share. Increased rivalry might involve price wars or expensive marketing battles, which may cost more than any market share gains are actually worth. The dangers of provoking fierce retaliation are greater in low-growth markets, as any gains in volume will be much more at the expense of other players. Where retaliation is a danger, organisations seeking market penetration need strategic capabilities that give a clear competitive advantage. In low growth or declining markets, it can be more effective simply to acquire competitors. Some companies have grown quickly in this way. For example, in the steel industry the Indian company LNM (Mittal) moved rapidly in the 2000s to become the largest steel producer in the world by acquiring struggling steel companies around the world. Acquisitions can actually reduce rivalry, by taking out independent players and consolidating them under one umbrella: see also the consolidation strategy in 7.2.2 below.

- *Legal constraints*. Greater market penetration can raise concerns from official competition regulators concerning excessive market power. Most countries have regulators with the powers to restrain powerful companies or prevent mergers and acquisitions that would create such excessive power. In the UK, the Competition Commission can investigate any merger or acquisition that would account for more than 25 per cent of the national market, and either halt the deal or propose measures that would reduce market power. The European Commission has an overview of the whole European market and can similarly intervene. For example, when Gaz de France and Suez, two utility companies with dominant positions in France and Belgium, decided to merge in 2006, the European Commission insisted that the two companies reduced their power by divesting some of their subsidiaries and opening up their networks to competition.[2]

7.2.2 Consolidation

Consolidation is where organisations focus defensively on their current markets with current products

Consolidation is where organisations focus defensively on their current markets with current products. Formally, this strategy occupies the same box in the Ansoff matrix as market penetration, but is not orientated to growth. Consolidation can take two forms:

- *Defending market share*. When facing aggressive competitors bent on increasing their market share, organisations have to work hard and often creatively to protect what they already have. Although market share should rarely be an end in itself, it is important to ensure that it is sufficient to sustain the business in the long term. For example, turnover has to be high enough to spread essential fixed costs such as R&D. In defending market share, differentiation strategies in order to build customer loyalty and switching costs are often effective.

- *Downsizing or divestment*. Especially when the size of the market as a whole is declining, reducing the size of the business through closing capacity is often unavoidable. An alternative is divesting (selling) some activities to other businesses. Sometimes downsizing can be dictated by the needs of shareholders, for instance an entrepreneur wishing to simplify their business as they approach retirement. Divesting or closing peripheral businesses can also make it easier to sell the core business to a potential purchaser.

The term consolidation is sometimes also used to describe strategies of *buying up rivals* in a fragmented industry, particularly one in decline. By acquiring weaker competitors, and closing capacity, the consolidating company can gain market power and increase overall efficiency. As this form of consolidation increases market share, it could be seen as a kind of market penetration, but here the motivation is essentially defensive.

Although both consolidation and market penetration strategies are by no means static ones, their limitations often propel managers to consider alternative strategic directions.

7.2.3 Product development

Product development is where organisations deliver modified or new products to existing markets

Product development is where organisations deliver modified or new products (or services) to existing markets. This is a limited extension of organizational scope. In practice, even market penetration will probably require some product development, but here product development implies greater degrees of innovation. For Sony, such product development would include moving the Walkman portable music system from audio tapes, through CDs to MP3-based systems. Effectively the same markets are involved, but the technologies are radically different. In the case of the Walkman, Sony probably had little choice but to make these significant product developments. However, product development can be an expensive and high-risk activity for at least two reasons:

- *New strategic capabilities*. Product development typically involves mastering new technologies that may be unfamiliar to the organisation. For example, many banks entered online banking at the beginning of this century, but suffered many setbacks with technologies so radically different to their traditional high street branch means of delivering banking services. Success frequently depended on a willingness to acquire new technological and marketing capabilities, often with the help of specialised information technology and e-commerce consultancy firms.[3] Thus product development typically involves heavy investments and high risk of project failures.

- *Project management risk*. Even within fairly familiar domains, product development projects are typically subject to the risk of delays and increased costs due to project complexity and changing project specifications over time. A famous recent case was the €11bn (£7.6bn) Airbus A380 double-decker airline project, which suffered two years of delays in the mid-2000s because of wiring problems. Airbus had managed several new aircraft developments before, but the high degrees of customisation required by each airline customer, and incompatibilities in computer-aided design software, led to greater complexity than the company's project management staff could handle.

7.2.4 Market development

If product development is risky and expensive, an alternative strategy is market development. **Market development** involves offering existing products to new markets. Again, the extension of scope is limited. Typically, of course, this may entail some product development as well, if only in terms of packaging or service. Market development might take three forms:

> Market development is where existing products are offered in new markets

- *New segments*. For example in the public services, a college might offer its educational services to older students than its traditional intake, perhaps via evening courses.

- *New users*. Here an example would be aluminium, whose original users packaging and cutlery manufacture are now supplemented by users in aerospace and automobiles.

- *New geographies*. The prime example of this is internationalisation, but the spread of a small retailer into new towns would also be a case.

In all cases, it is essential that market development strategies are based on products or services that meet the *critical success factors* of the new market (see Section 2.4.4). Strategies based on simply off-loading traditional products or services in new markets are likely to fail. Moreover, market development faces similar problems as product development. In terms of strategic capabilities, market developers often lack the right marketing skills and brands to make progress in a market with unfamiliar customers. On the management side, the challenge is coordinating between different segments, users and geographies, which might all have different needs. International market development strategy is considered in Chapter 8.

For a description of the various strategic directions considered by chief executive Mattias Döpfner for the German publisher Axel Springer see Illustration 7.1.

Illustration 7.1

Strategic directions for Axel Springer

This German publishing company has many opportunities, and the money to pursue them.

In 2007, Mathias Döpfner, Chairman and Chief Executive of Axel Springer publishers, had about €2bn (£1.5bn) to invest in new opportunities. The previous year, the competition authorities had prohibited his full takeover of Germany's largest television broadcaster, ProSiebenSat.1. Now Döpfner was looking for alternative directions.

Founded in 1946 by Axel Springer himself, the company was in 2007 already Germany's largest publisher of newspapers and magazines, with more than 10,000 employees and over 150 titles. Famous print titles included *Die Welt*, the *Berliner Morgenpost*, *Bild* and *Hörzu*. Outside Germany, Axel Springer was strongest in Eastern Europe. The company also had a scattering of mostly small investments in German radio and television companies, most notably a continuing 12 per cent stake in ProSiebenSat.1. Axel Springer described its strategic objectives as market leadership in the German-language core business, internationalisaton and digitalisation of the core business.

Further digitalisation of the core newspaper and magazine business was clearly important and would require substantial funding. There were also opportunities for the launch of new print magazine titles in the German market. But Döpfner was considering acquisition opportunities: 'it goes without saying,' he told the *Financial Times*, 'that whenever a large international media company comes on to the market (i.e. is up for sale), we will examine it very closely – whether in print, TV or the online sector'.

Döpfner mentioned several specific kinds of acquisition opportunity. For example, he was still interested in buying a large European television broadcaster, even if it would probably have to be outside Germany. He was also attracted by the possibility of buying undervalued assets in the old media (namely, print), and turning them around in the style of a private equity investor: 'I would love to buy businesses in need of restructuring, where we can add value by introducing our management and sector expertise'. However, Döpfner reassured his shareholders by affirming that he felt no need 'to do a big thing in order to do a big thing'. He was also considering what to do with the 12 per cent minority stake in ProSiebenSat.1.

Main source: *Financial Times Deutschland*, 2 April (2007).

Questions

1 Referring to Exhibit 7.1, classify the various strategic directions considered by Mattias Döpfner for Axel Springer.

2 Using the Ansoff matrix, what other options could Döpfner pursue?

7.2.5 Diversification

Diversification is defined as a strategy that takes an organisation away from both its existing markets and its existing products

Diversification is strictly a strategy that takes the organisation away from both its existing markets and its existing products (i.e. box D in Exhibit 7.2). In this sense, it radically increases the organisation's scope. In fact, much diversification is not as extreme as implied by the closed boxes of the Ansoff growth matrix. Box D tends to imply unrelated or conglomerate diversification (see section 7.3.2), but a good deal of diversification in practice involves building on relationships with existing markets or products. Frequently too market penetration and product development entail some diversifying adjustment of products or markets. Diversification is a matter of degree.

Nonetheless, the Ansoff matrix does make clear that the further the organisation moves from its starting point of existing products and existing markets, the more it has to learn to do. Diversification is just one direction for developing the organisation, and needs to be considered alongside its alternatives. The drivers of diversification, its various forms and the ways it is managed are the main topics of this chapter.

7.3 REASONS FOR DIVERSIFICATION

In terms of the Ansoff matrix, diversification is the most radical strategic direction.[4] Diversification might be chosen for a variety of reasons, some more value-creating than others. Three potentially value-creating reasons for diversification are as follows.

Synergy refers to the benefits that are gained where activities or assets complement each other so that their combined effect is greater than the sum of the parts

- *Efficiency gains* can be made by applying the organisation's existing resources or capabilities to new markets and products or services. These are often described as *economies of scope*, by contrast to economies of scale.[5] If an organisation has underutilised resources or competences that it cannot effectively close or sell to other potential users, it can make sense to use these resources or competences by diversification into a new activity. In other words, there are economies to be gained by extending the scope of the organisation's activities. For example, many universities have large resources in terms of halls of residence, which they must have for their students but which are underutilised out of term-time. These halls of residence are more efficiently used if the universities expand the scope of their activities into conferencing and tourism during vacation periods. Economies of scope may apply to both *tangible* resources, such as halls of residence, and *intangible* resources and competences, such as brands or staff skills. Sometimes these scope advantages are referred to as the benefits of **synergy**,[6] by which is meant that activities or assets are more effective together than apart (the famous 2 + 2 = 5 equation). Thus a film company and a music publisher would be synergistic if they were worth more together than separately. Illustration 7.2 shows how a French company, Zodiac, has diversified following this approach.

Illustration 7.2

Zodiac: inflatable diversifications

An organisation may seek the benefits of synergies by building a portfolio of businesses through related diversification.

The Zodiac company was founded near Paris, France, in 1896 by Maurice Mallet just after his first hot-air balloon ascent. For 40 years, Zodiac manufactured only dirigible airships. In 1937, the German Zeppelin *Hindenburg* crashed near New York, which abruptly stopped the development of the market for airships. Because of the extinction of its traditional activity, Zodiac decided to leverage its technical expertise and moved from dirigibles to inflatable boats. This diversification proved to be very successful: in 2004, with over 1 million units sold in 50 years, the Zodiac rubber dinghy (priced at approximately €10,000 (£7,000)) was extremely popular worldwide.

However, because of increasing competition, especially from Italian manufacturers, Zodiac diversified its business interests. In 1978, it took over Aerazur, a company specialising in parachutes, but also in life vests and inflatable life rafts. These products had strong market and technical synergies with rubber boats and their main customers were aircraft manufacturers. Zodiac confirmed this move to a new market in 1987 by the takeover of Air Cruisers, a manufacturer of inflatable escape slides for aircraft. As a consequence, Zodiac became a key supplier to Boeing, McDonnell Douglas and Airbus. Zodiac strengthened this position through the takeover of the two leading manufacturers of aircraft seats: Sicma Aero Seats from France and Weber Aircraft from the USA. In 1997, Zodiac also took over, for €150m, MAG Aerospace, the world leader for aircraft vacuum waste systems. Finally, in 1999, Zodiac took over Intertechnique, a leading player in active components for aircraft (fuel circulation, hydraulics, oxygen and life support, electrical power, flight-deck controls and displays, systems monitoring, etc.). By combining these competences with its traditional expertise in inflatable products, Zodiac launched a new business unit: airbags for the automobile industry.

In parallel to these diversifications, Zodiac strengthened its position in inflatable boats by the takeover of several competitors: Bombard-L'Angevinière in 1980, Sevylor in 1981, Hurricane and Metzeler in 1987.

Finally, Zodiac developed a swimming-pool business. The first product line, back in 1981, was based on inflatable structure technology, and Zodiac later moved – again through takeovers – to rigid above-ground pools, modular in-ground pools, pool cleaners and water purification systems, inflatable beach gear and air mattresses.

In 2003, total sales of the Zodiac group reached €1.48bn with a net profit of €115m. Zodiac was a very international company, with a strong presence in the USA. It was listed on the Paris Stock Exchange and rumours of takeovers from powerful US groups were frequent. However, the family of the founder, institutional investors, the management and the employees together held 55 per cent of the stocks.

Far above the marine and the leisure businesses, aircraft products accounted for almost 75 per cent of the total turnover of the group. Zodiac held a 40 per cent market share of the world market for some airline equipment: for instance, the electrical power systems of the new Airbus A380 were Zodiac products. In 2004, Zodiac even reached Mars: NASA Mars probes *Spirit* and *Opportunity* were equipped with Zodiac equipment, developed by its US subsidiary Pioneer Aerospace.

Prepared by Frédéric Fréry, ESCP-EAP European School of Management.

Questions

1 What were the bases of the synergies underlying each of Zodiac's diversifications?

2 What are the advantages and potential dangers of such a basis of diversification?

- *Stretching corporate parenting capabilities* into new markets and products or services can be another source of gain. In a sense, this extends the point above about applying existing competences in new areas. However, this point highlights corporate parenting skills that can otherwise easily be neglected. At the corporate parent level, managers may develop a competence at managing a range of different products and services which can be applied even to businesses which do not share resources at the operationing unit level. Prahalad and Bettis have described this set of corporate parenting skills as the 'dominant general management logic', or 'dominant logic' for short.[7] Thus the French conglomerate LVMH includes a wide range of businesses – from champagne, through fashion and perfumes, to financial media – that share very few operational resources or competences. LVMH creates value for these specialised companies by adding parenting skills – for instance, the support of classic brands and the nurturing of highly creative people – that are relevant to all these individual businesses (see section 7.4.1).

- *Increasing market power* can result from having a diverse range of businesses. With many businesses, an organisation can afford to cross-subsidise one business from the surpluses earned by another, in a way that competitors may not be able to. This can give an organisation a competitive advantage for the subsidised business, and the long-run effect may be to drive out other competitors, leaving the organisation with a monopoly from which good profits can then be earned. This was the fear behind the European Commission's refusal to allow General Electric's $43bn (£24bn; €37bn) bid for electronic controls company Honeywell in 2001. General Electric might have bundled its jet engines with Honeywell's aviation electronics in a cheaper package than rival jet engine manufacturers could possibly match. As aircraft manufacturers and airlines increasingly chose the cheaper overall package, rivals could have been driven out of business. General Electric would then have the market power to put up its prices without threat from competition.

There are several other reasons that are often given for diversification, but which are less obviously value-creating and sometimes serve managerial interests more than shareholders' interests.

- *Responding to market decline* is one common but doubtful reason for diversification. It is arguable that Microsoft's diversification into electronic games such as the Xbox – whose launch cost $500m (£280m; €415m) in marketing alone – is a response to slowing growth in its core software businesses. Shareholders might have preferred the Xbox money to have been handed back to shareholders, leaving Sony and Nintendo to make games, while Microsoft gracefully declined. Microsoft itself defends its various diversifications as a necessary response to convergence in electronic and computer media.

- *Spreading risk* across a range of businesses is another common justification for diversification. However, conventional finance theory is very sceptical about risk-spreading by business diversification. It argues that investors can diversify more effectively themselves by investing in a diverse portfolio of quite different companies. While managers might like the security of a diverse range of businesses, investors do not need each of the companies they invest in to be diversified as well – they would prefer managers to concentrate on managing their core business as well as they can. On the other hand, for private businesses, where the owners have a large proportion of their assets tied up in the business, it can make sense to diversify risk across a number of distinct activities, so that if one part is in trouble, the whole business is not pulled down.

- *The expectations of powerful stakeholders*, including top managers, can sometimes drive inappropriate diversification. Under pressure from Wall Street analysts to deliver continued revenue growth, in the late 1990s the US energy company Enron diversified beyond its original interest in energy trading into trading commodities such as petrochemicals, aluminium and even bandwidth.[8] By satisfying the analysts in the short term, this strategy boosted the share price and allowed top management to stay in place. However, it soon transpired that very little of this diversification had been profitable, and in 2001 Enron collapsed in the largest bankruptcy in history.

In order to decide whether or not such reasons make sense and help organisational performance, it is important to be clear about different forms of diversification, in particular the degree of relatedness (or unrelatedness) of business units in a portfolio. The next sections consider related and unrelated diversification.

7.3.1 Related diversification

Related diversification is corporate development beyond current products and markets, but within the capabilities or value network of the organisation

Vertical integration is backward or forward integration into adjacent activities in the value network

Backward integration is development into activities concerned with the inputs into the company's current business

Related diversification can be defined as corporate development beyond current products and markets, but within the capabilities or the value network of the organisation (see section 3.4). For example, Procter and Gamble and Unilever are diversified corporations, but virtually all of their interests are in fast-moving consumer goods distributed through retailers. Their various businesses benefit therefore from shared capabilities in research and development, consumer marketing, building relationships with powerful retailers and global brand development.

The value network provides one way of thinking about different forms of related diversification is shown in Exhibit 7.3:

- **Vertical integration** describes either backward or forward integration into adjacent activities in the value network. **Backward integration** refers to development into activities concerned with the inputs into the company's current business (i.e. they are further back in the value network). For example, the acquisition by a car manufacturer of a component supplier would be

Exhibit 7.3 Related diversification options for a manufacturer

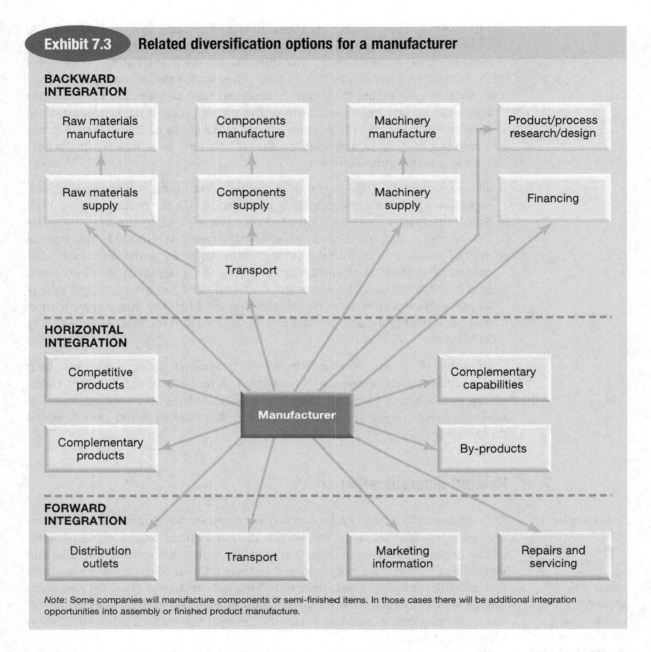

Note: Some companies will manufacture components or semi-finished items. In those cases there will be additional integration opportunities into assembly or finished product manufacture.

Forward integration is development into activities which are concerned with a company's outputs

Horizontal integration is development into activities which are complementary to present activities

related diversification through backward integration. **Forward integration** refers to development into activities which are concerned with a company's outputs (i.e. are further forward in the value system): for a car manufacturer, this might be distribution, repairs and servicing.

● **Horizontal integration** is development into activities which are complementary or adjacent to present activities. For example, Internet search company Google has spread horizontally into news, images and maps, amongst other services (another example is Zodiac – see Illustration 7.2).

It is important to recognise that capabilities and value links are distinct. A link through the value network does not necessarily imply the existence of capabilities. For example, in the late 1990s some car manufacturers began to integrate forward into repairs and servicing following a value network logic. The car manufacturers thought they could create value by using forward links to ensure a better overall customer experience with their cars. However, the manufacturers rapidly realised that these new businesses involved quite different capabilities: not manufacturing in large factories, but service in many scattered small units. In the end, the absence of relevant capabilities outweighed the potential from the value-network links, and the car manufacturers generally withdrew from these forward integration initiatives. Synergies are often harder to identify and more costly to extract in practice than managers like to admit.[9]

It is also important to recognise that relationships have potential disadvantages. Related diversification can be problematic for at least two reasons:

- *corporate-level time and cost* as top managers try to ensure that the benefits of relatedness are achieved through sharing or transfer across business units;

- *business unit complexity*, as business unit managers attend to the needs of other business units, perhaps sharing resources or adjusting marketing strategies, rather than focusing exclusively on the needs of their own unit.

In summary, a simple statement such as 'relatedness matters' has to be questioned.[10] Whilst there is evidence that it may have positive effects on performance (see 7.3.3), each individual diversification decision needs careful thought about just what relatedness means and what gives rise to performance benefits.

7.3.2 Unrelated diversification

Unrelated diversification is the development of products or services beyond the current capabilities and value network

If related diversification involves development within current capabilities or the current value network, **unrelated diversification** is the development of products or services beyond the current capabilities or value network. Unrelated diversification is often described as a *conglomerate* strategy. Because there are no obvious economies of scope between the different businesses, but there is an obvious cost of the headquarters, unrelated diversified companies' share prices often suffer from what is called the 'conglomerate discount' – in other words, a lower valuation than the individual constituent businesses would have if they stood alone. In 2003, the French conglomerate Vivendi-Universal, with interests spreading from utilities to mobile telephony and media, was trading at an estimated discount of 15–20 per cent. Naturally, shareholders were pressurising management to break the conglomerate up into its more highly valued parts.

However, the case against conglomerates can be exaggerated and there are certainly potential advantages to unrelated diversification in some conditions:

- *Exploiting dominant logics*, rather than concrete operational relationships, can be a source of conglomerate value creation. As at Berkshire Hathaway (see Illustration 7.3), a skilled investor such as Warren Buffett, the so-called Oracle of Omaha and one of the richest men in the world, may be able to add value to diverse businesses within his dominant logic.[11] Berkshire Hathaway includes businesses in different areas of manufacturing, insurance, distribution and retailing, but Buffett focuses on mature businesses that he can understand and whose managers he can trust. During the e-business boom of the late 1990s, Buffett deliberately avoided buying high-technology businesses because he knew they were outside his dominant logic.

- *Countries with underdeveloped markets* can be fertile ground for conglomerates. Where external capital and labour markets do not yet work well, conglomerates offer a substitute mechanism for allocating and developing capital or managerial talent within their own organisational boundaries. For example, Korean conglomerates (the chaebol) were successful in the rapid growth phase of the Korean economy partly because they were able to mobilise investment and develop managers in a way that standalone companies in South Korea traditionally were unable to. Also, the strong cultural cohesion amongst managers in these chaebol reduced the coordination and monitoring costs that would be necessary in a Western conglomerate, where managers would be trusted less.[12] The same may be true today in other fast growing economies that still have underdeveloped capital and labour markets.

It is important also to recognise that the distinction between related and unrelated diversification is often a matter of degree. As in the case of Berkshire Hathaway, although there are very few operational relationships between the constituent businesses, there is a relationship in terms of similar parenting requirements. As in the case of the car manufacturers diversifying forwards into apparently related businesses such as repairs and servicing, operational relationships can turn out to be much less valuable than at first they appear. The boundary between related and unrelated diversification is blurred and it is easy to exaggerate relatedness.

7.3.3 Diversification and performance

Because most large corporations today are diversified, but also because diversification can sometimes be in management's self-interest, many scholars and policy-makers have been concerned to establish whether diversified companies really perform better than undiversified companies. After all, it would be deeply troubling if large corporations were diversifying simply to spread risk for managers, to save managerial jobs in declining businesses or to preserve the image of growth, as in the case of Enron.

Berkshire Hathaway Inc.

A portfolio manager may seek to manage a highly diverse set of business units on behalf of its shareholders.

Berkshire Hathaway's Chairman is Warren Buffett, one of the world's richest men, and Charles Munger is Vice Chairman. The businesses in the portfolio are highly diverse. There are insurance businesses, including GEICO, the sixth largest automobile insurer in the USA, manufacturers of carpets, building products, clothing and footwear. There are service businesses (the training of aircraft and ship operators), retailers of home furnishings and fine jewellery, a daily and Sunday newspaper and the largest direct seller of housewear products in the USA.

The annual report of Berkshire Hathaway (2002) provides an insight into its rationale and management. Warren Buffett explains how he and his vice chairman run the business.

Charlie Munger and I think of our shareholders as owner-partners and of ourselves as managing partners. (Because of the size of our shareholdings we are also, for better or worse, controlling partners.) We do not view the company itself as the ultimate owner of our business assets but instead view the company as a conduit through which our shareholders own the assets. . . . Our long term economic goal . . . is to maximise Berkshire's average annual rate of gain in intrinsic business value on a per-share basis. We do not measure the economic significance or performance of Berkshire by its size; we measure by per-share progress.

Our preference would be to reach our goal by directly owning a diversified group of businesses that generate cash and consistently earn above average returns on capital. Our second choice is to own parts of similar businesses, attained primarily through purchases of marketable common stocks by our insurance subsidiaries. . . . Charlie and I are interested only in acquisitions that we believe will raise the per-share intrinsic value of Berkshire's stock.

Regardless of price we have no interest at all in selling any good businesses that Berkshire owns. We are also very reluctant to sell sub-par businesses as long as we expect them to generate at least some cash and as long as we feel good about their managers and labour relations. . . . Gin rummy managerial behaviour (discard your least promising business at each turn) is not our style. We would rather have our overall results penalised a bit than engaged in that kind of behaviour.

Buffett then explains how they manage their subsidiary businesses:

. . . we delegate almost to the point of abdication: though Berkshire has about 45,000 employees, only 12 of these are at headquarters. . . . Charlie and I mainly attend to capital allocation and the care and feeding of our key managers. Most of these managers are happiest when they are left alone to run their businesses and that is customarily just how we leave them. That puts them in charge of all operating decisions and of despatching the excess cash they generate to headquarters. By sending it to us, they don't get diverted by the various enticements that would come their way were they responsible for deploying the cash their businesses throw off. Further more, Charlie and I are exposed to a much wider range of possibilities for investing these funds than any of our managers could find in his/her own industry.

Source: Berkshire Hathaway Annual Report, 2002.

Questions

1 Berkshire Hathaway's businesses are very diverse, but exclude high-technology businesses. Why might that be, given the group's parenting style?

2 Using the checklist explained in section 7.4, suggest how and in what ways Berkshire Hathaway may or may not add value to its shareholders.

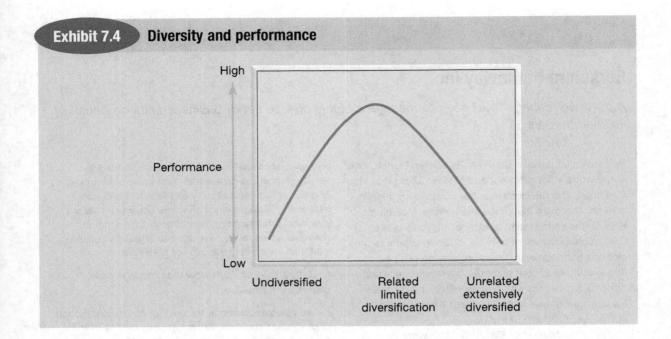

Exhibit 7.4   **Diversity and performance**

Research studies of diversification have generally found some performance benefits, with *related diversifiers* outperforming both firms that remain *specialised* and those which have *unrelated* diversified strategies.[13] In other words, the diversification–performance relationship tends to follow an inverted (or upside down) U-shape, as in Exhibit 7.4. The implication is that some diversification is good – but not too much.

However, these performance studies produce statistical averages. Some related diversification strategies fail – as in the case of the vertically-integrating car manufacturers – while some conglomerates succeed – as in the case of Berkshire Hathaway. The case against unrelated diversification is not solid, and effective dominant logics or particular national contexts can play in its favour. The conclusion from the performance studies is that, although on average related diversification pays better than unrelated, any diversification strategy needs rigorous questioning on its particular merits.

Strategy Methods and Evaluation

LEARNING OUTCOMES

After reading this chapter you should be able to:

→ Identify the *methods* by which strategies can be pursued: *organic development, mergers and acquisitions and strategic alliances.*

→ Employ three *success criteria* for evaluating strategic options: *suitability, acceptability and feasibility.*

→ Use a range of different *techniques for evaluating strategic options.*

9.1   INTRODUCTION

Chapter 6 offered a range of choices about how to position the organisation in relation to competitors. Within this generalised choice about the basis of competitive strategy there are more specific choices to be made about the strategic direction of the organisation; in particular which markets and which products are most appropriate. These choices were set out in Chapter 7 and developed further in Chapter 8 in the context of international strategy. However, there is a third level of choice concerned with the *methods by which competitive strategy and strategic direction can be pursued*. This is the theme of section 9.2, the first half of this chapter.

Bearing in mind that the use of the concepts and tools introduced in Chapters 2 to 5 of the book will also have generated ideas about strategies that might be followed, the strategist may well need to consider many possible options. The second half of this chapter therefore discusses the *success criteria* by which they can be assessed and, building on these criteria, explains some of the *techniques for evaluating strategic options*.

Exhibit 9.1 summarises the overall structure of the chapter.

Exhibit 9.1   Strategy methods and evaluation: chapter structure

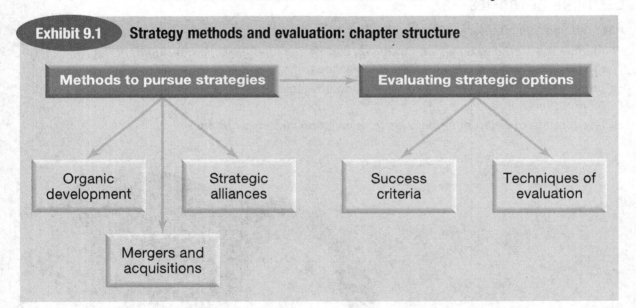

9.2   METHODS OF PURSUING STRATEGIES

A strategic method is the *means* by which a strategy can be pursued

Any of the strategy directions discussed in Chapters 6 to 8 may be undertaken in different ways or by different **strategic methods**: the *means* by which a strategy can be pursued. These methods can be divided into three types: organic development, acquisition (or disposal) and alliances.

9.2.1 Organic development[1]

Organic development or internal development is where strategies are developed by building on and developing an organisation's own capabilities. For many organisations organic development has been the primary method of strategy development, and there are some compelling reasons why this should be so:

Organic development is where strategies are developed by building on and developing an organisation's own capabilities

- *Highly technical products* in terms of design or method of manufacture lend themselves to organic development since the process of development may be the best way of acquiring the necessary capabilities to compete successfully. These competences may of course in turn spawn new products and create new market opportunities.

- *Knowledge and capability development* may be enhanced by organic development. For example, a business may feel that the direct involvement gained from having its own sales force rather than using sales agents gains greater market knowledge and therefore competitive advantage over other rivals more distant from their customers.

- *Spreading investment over time*. The final cost of developing new activities internally may be greater than that of acquiring other companies. However spreading these costs over time may be a more favourable option than major expenditure at a point in time required for an acquisition. This is a strong motive for organic development in small companies or many public services that may not have the resources for major one-off investments.

- *Minimising disruption*. The slower rate of change of organic development may also minimise the disruption to other activities and avoid the political and cultural problems of acquisition integration that can occur (see section 9.2.2).

- *The nature of markets* may dictate organic development. In many instances organisations breaking new ground may not be in a position to develop by acquisition or joint development, since they are the only ones in the field. Or there may be few opportunities for acquisitions, as for example, for foreign companies attempting to enter Japan.

KEY CONCEPT
www.pearsoned.co.uk/ios

Alliances, mergers and acquisitions

9.2.2 Mergers and acquisitions

An acquisition is where an organisation takes ownership of another organisation

A merger is a mutually agreed decision for joint ownership between organisations.

An **acquisition** is where an organisation takes ownership of another organisation, whereas a **merger** implies a mutually agreed decision for joint ownership between organisations. In practice, few acquistions are hostile and few mergers are the joining of equals. So both acquisitions and mergers typically involve the managers of one organisation exerting strategic influence over the other. Global activity in mergers is dominated by North America and Western Europe whereas it is much less common in other economies, for example, Japan. This reflects the influence of the differences in governance systems that exist (see section 4.2).

Motives for acquisitions and mergers

There are different motives for developing through acquisition or merger. A major reason can be the need to keep up with a changing *environment*:

- *Speed of entry*. Products or markets may be changing so rapidly that acquisition becomes the only way of successfully entering the market, since the process of internal development is too slow.

- The *competitive situation* may influence a company to prefer acquisition. In static markets and where market shares of companies are steady it can be difficult for a new company to enter the market, since its presence may create excess capacity. If entry is by acquisition the risk of competitive reaction may be reduced.

- *Consolidation opportunities*. Where there are low levels of industry concentration, there may be an opportunity for improving the balance between supply and demand by acquiring companies and shutting down excess capacity. In many countries, *deregulation* of public utilities has also created a level of fragmentation that was regarded as suboptimal. This was then an opportunity for acquisitive organisations to rationalise provision and/or seek to gain other benefits, for example, through the creation of 'multi-utility' companies offering electricity, gas, telecommunications and other services to customers.

- *Financial markets* may provide conditions that motivate acquisitions. If the share value or price/earnings (P/E) ratio of a company is high, it may see the opportunity to acquire a firm with a low share value or P/E ratio. Indeed, this is a major stimulus for the more opportunistic acquisitive companies. An extreme example is asset stripping, where the main motive is short-term gain by buying up undervalued assets and disposing of them piecemeal.

There may also be *capability considerations*:

- *Exploitation of strategic capabilities* can motivate acquisitions, for example, through buying companies overseas in order to leverage marketing or R&D skills internationally.

- *Cost efficiency* is a commonly stated reason for acquisitions typically by merging units so as to rationalise resources (for example, head office services or production facilities) or gain scale advantages.

- *Obtaining new capabilities* may also be achieved through acquisitions, or at least be a motive for acquisition. For example, a company may be acquired for its R&D expertise, or its knowledge of particular business processes or markets.

Acquisition can also be driven by the *stakeholder expectations*:

- *Institutional shareholder expectations* may be for continuing growth and acquisitions may be a quick way to deliver this growth. There are considerable dangers, however, that acquisitive growth may result in value destruction rather than creation – for some of the reasons discussed in Chapter 7.

- *Managerial ambition* may motivate acquisitions because they speed the growth of the company. In turn, this might enhance their self-importance, provide better career paths and greater monetary rewards.

- *Speculative motives* of some stakeholders may stimulate acquisitions that bring a short-term boost to share value. Other stakeholders are usually wary of such speculation since their short-term gain can destroy longer-term prospects.

Acquisitions and financial performance

Acquisitions are not an easy or guaranteed route to improving financial performance. As many as 70 per cent of acquisitions end up with lower returns to shareholders of both organisations. The most common mistake is in paying too much for a company – possibly through lack of experience in acquisitions, or poor financial advice (for example, from the investment bank involved). In addition the managers of the acquiring company may be over-optimistic about the benefits of the acquisition. An acquisition will probably include poor resources and competences as well as those which were the reason for the purchase; or it may be that the capabilities of the merging organisations are not compatible. This was the case, for example, in the 2004 acquisition in the UK of the Safeway supermarket chain by its competitor Morrisons. Amongst the problems was that Morrisons spent a year trying to integrate the IT systems of the two companies before abandoning the attempt. Indeed for this reason acquirers may attempt to buy products or processes rather than whole companies if possible. At the very best it may take the acquiring company considerable time to gain financial benefit from acquisitions.

Making acquisitions work

The implementation agenda following an acquisition or merger will vary depending on its purpose. Nonetheless there are four frequently occurring issues that account for success or failure of an acquisition/merger.

- *Adding value.* The acquirer may find difficulty in adding value to the acquired business (the parenting issue as discussed in section 7.4).

- *Gaining the commitment of middle managers* responsible for the operations and customer relations in the acquired business is important in order to avoid internal uncertainties and maintain customer confidence. Linked to this, deciding which executives to retain in the acquired business needs to be done quickly.

- *Expected synergies may not be realised,* either because they do not exist to the extent expected or because it proves difficult to integrate the activities of the acquired business. For example where the motive was the transfer of competences or knowledge it may be difficult to identify what these are (see section 3.4.3).

● *Problems of cultural fit.* This can arise because the acquiring business finds that 'everyday' but embedded aspects of culture (for example, organisation routines) differ in ways that prove difficult to overcome but are not readily identifiable before the acquisition. This can be particularly problematic with cross-country acquisitions.

9.2.3 Strategic alliances

A strategic alliance is where two or more organisations share resources and activities to pursue a strategy

KEY CONCEPT

Alliances, mergers and acquisitions

A **strategic alliance** is where two or more organisations share resources and activities to pursue a strategy. They vary from simple two-partner alliances co-producing a product to one with multiple partners providing complex products and solutions. By the turn of the century the top 500 global companies had an average of 60 alliances each. This kind of joint development of new strategies has become increasingly popular. This is because organisations cannot always cope with increasingly complex environments or strategies (such as globalis-ation) from internal resources and competences alone. They may need to obtain materials, skills, innovation, finance or access to markets but recognise that these may be as readily available through cooperation as through ownership. However about half of all alliances fail[2] so careful thought is needed as to reasons for success and failure.

Motives for alliances

A frequent reason for alliances is to obtain resources that an organisation needs but does not itself possess. For example banks need to gain access to the payment systems that allow credit cards to be used in retail outlets (for example, Visa or Mastercard) and to the automated teller machines (ATMs) to allow cash withdrawals. These resources do not, however, confer competitive advantage on members of the alliance; nor are they intended to do so – they are threshold requirements for modern banking. Such arrangements are '*infra-structure alliances*' that involve the sharing or pooling of resources and mech-anism of cooperation, but which are not seeking to gain competitive advantage.[3] Here, however, we are concerned with *strategic alliances* that do seek to gain such advantage.

Motives for such alliances are of three main types:

● The need for *critical mass*, which alliances can achieve by forming partner-ships with either competitors or providers of complementary products. This can lead to cost reduction and improved customer offering.

● *Co-specialisation* – allowing each partner to concentrate on activities that best match their capabilities: for example to enter new geographical markets where an organisation needs local knowledge and expertise in distribution, marketing and customer support. Similarly alliances with organisations in other parts of the value chain (for example, suppliers or distributors) are common.

- *Learning* from partners and developing competences that may be more widely exploited elsewhere. For example, first steps into e-business may be achieved with a partner that has expertise in website development. However, the longer-term intention might be to bring those activities in-house. Organisations may also enter alliances as a means of *experimentation* since it allows them to break out of a sole reliance on the exploitation of their own resources and capabilities. Indeed they may use alliances as a basis for developing strategic options different from those being developed in house organically.[4]

Types of alliance

There are different types of strategic alliance. Some may be formalised inter-organisational relationships. At the other extreme, there are loose arrangements of cooperation and informal networking between organisations, with no shareholding or ownership involved:

- *Joint ventures* are relatively formalised alliances and may take different forms themselves. Here organisations remain independent but set up a newly created organisation jointly owned by the parents. Joint ventures are a favoured means of collaborative ventures in China for example. Local firms provide labour and entry to markets; Western companies provide technology, management expertise and finance.

- *Consortia* may involve two or more organisations in a joint venture arrangement typically more focused on a particular venture or project. Examples include large civil engineering projects, or major aerospace undertakings, such as the European Airbus. They might also exist between public sector organisations where services (such as public transport) cross administrative boundaries.

- *Networks* are less formal arrangements where organisations gain mutual advantage by working in collaboration without relying on cross ownership arrangements and formal contracts. Carlos Jarillo suggests that characteristic of such network arrangements are a reliance on coordination through mutual adaptation of working relationships, mutual trust (see below) and, typically, a 'hub organisation' that may have promoted the network and maintains a proactive attitude to it.[5] Such networked arrangements may exist between competitors in highly competitive industries where some form of sharing is nonetheless beneficial: for example, in the Formula 1 industry, where state of the art know-how tends to flow between firms.

Other alliance arrangements exist usually of a contractual nature and are unlikely to involve ownership:

- *Franchising* involves the franchise holder undertaking specific activities such as manufacturing, distribution or selling, whilst the franchiser is responsible for the brand name, marketing and probably training. Perhaps the best-known examples are Coca-Cola and McDonald's.

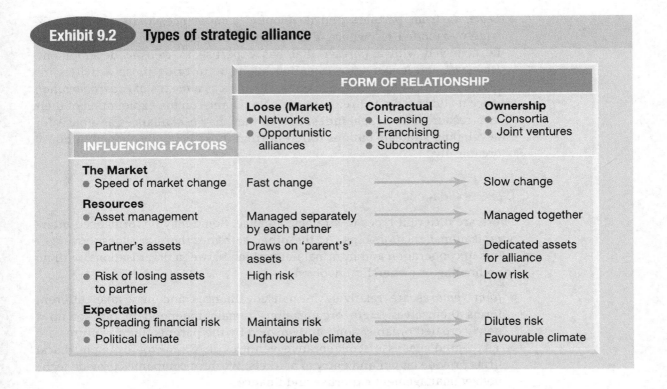

Exhibit 9.2   Types of strategic alliance

INFLUENCING FACTORS	FORM OF RELATIONSHIP		
	Loose (Market) ● Networks ● Opportunistic alliances	**Contractual** ● Licensing ● Franchising ● Subcontracting	**Ownership** ● Consortia ● Joint ventures
The Market ● Speed of market change	Fast change ⟶		Slow change
Resources ● Asset management	Managed separately by each partner ⟶		Managed together
● Partner's assets	Draws on 'parent's' assets ⟶		Dedicated assets for alliance
● Risk of losing assets to partner	High risk ⟶		Low risk
Expectations ● Spreading financial risk	Maintains risk ⟶		Dilutes risk
● Political climate	Unfavourable climate ⟶		Favourable climate

- *Licensing* is common in science-based industries where, for example, the right to manufacture a patented product is granted for a fee.
- With *subcontracting*, a company chooses to subcontract particular services or part of a process: for example, increasingly in public services responsibility for waste removal, cleaning and IT services may be subcontracted (or 'outsourced') to private companies.

Exhibit 9.2 shows three important factors that can influence types of alliance:

- *Speed of market change* will require strategic moves to be made quickly. So less formal and flexible network arrangements may be more appropriate than a joint venture, which could take too long to establish.
- *The management of resources and capabilities*. If a strategy requires separate, dedicated, resources then a joint venture will be appropriate. In contrast, if the strategic purpose and operations of the alliance can be supported by the current resources of the partners this favours a looser contractual relationship or network.
- The *expectations and motives* of alliance partners will play a part. For example if alliance partners see the alliance as a means of spreading their financial risk, this will favour more formal arrangements such as joint ventures.

Ingredients of successful alliances[6]

Although organisations may establish an alliance for one or more of the reasons outlined above, the benefits of alliances tend to evolve. It may, for example, be established to address a particularly complex technological opportunity, but yield new and unexpected opportunities. The success of alliances is therefore dependent on how they are managed and the way in which the partners foster the evolving nature of the partnership. Given this, success factors fall under three broad headings:

- *Strategic purpose.* A clear strategic purpose is likely to be helpful at the outset of an alliance. However alliance members will, quite likely, have differing if compatible reasons for being part of the alliance. As an alliance develops it is likely that their expectations and perceived benefits will evolve – not least because they are often built to cope with dynamic or complex environments. If the expectations of alliance members start to diverge the alliance may eventually disintegrate. If the evolving expectations remain compatible or converge then it is likely the alliance will continue. It is also possible that convergance could give rise to more formalised ownership arrangements such as a merger of the alliance partners.

- *Alliance expectations and benefits.* Similarly, given that the expectations of alliance partners may vary, managing those expectations as the alliance evolves is vital. At the most basic level, expectations cannot be met without a willingness to exchange information, including performance information that would not normally be shared between organisations. However, beyond this, given that many alliances are about learning and experimentation, the acceptance of these as benefits of themselves by alliance members may be important. If one of the partners does not buy into such benefits and attempts to impose a 'static' strategy on the alliance this may well lead to problems.[7] There are also indications that alliances that develop knowledge-based products and services (as distinct from physical product) tend to bind alliance partners more closely together since they are likely to be mutually dependent on shared tacit knowledge in the development of such products and services.[8]

- *Managing alliance relationships.* Senior management support for an alliance is important since alliances require a wider range of relationships to be built and sustained. This can create cultural and political hurdles that senior managers must help to overcome. In turn, strong interpersonal relationships to achieve *compatibility at the operational level* is also needed. In cross-country partnerships this includes the need to transcend national cultural differences. Consistently, however, research shows that *trust* is the most important ingredient of success and a major reason for failure if it is absent. But trust has two separate elements. Trust can be *competence based* in the sense that each partner is confident that the other has the resources and competences to fulfil their part in the alliance. Trust is also *character based* and concerns whether partners trust each other's motives and are compatible in terms of attitudes to integrity, openness, discretion and consistency of behaviour. Overall the message is that it is the quality of the relationships in an alliance that are of prime importance; indeed to a greater extent than the physical resources in an alliance.

A consistent message that recurs, then, is that whilst it may be very helpful to ensure that an alliance has clear *goals, governance and organisational arrangements* concerning activities that cross or connect the partners, it is also important to keep the alliance *flexible*, such that it can *evolve and change*.

Section 2:

Managerial Economics

2 Business objectives and basic models of the firm

This chapter considers a number of basic models of the firm, each one based upon different assumptions about its objective. The neo-classical model is developed first and then the chapter goes on to examine some of the criticisms that have been directed at that model, and some of the alternatives that have been put forward in its place.

The neo-classical economic model of the firm

There are many different models of the firm, embodying many different assumptions, which could be described as 'economic' models. However, there is one particular version that forms the mainstream orthodox treatment of the firm, to be found in every introductory textbook and explained in more depth by Kreps (1990, chs 7 and 19). That is the 'neo-classical model of the firm'. This model centres around three basic sets of assumptions concerning the aim of the firm, and the cost and demand conditions facing it.

The assumption of profit maximisation

The first component of the neo-classical model of the firm is the assumption that the objective of the firm is to maximise profits, defined as the difference between the firm's revenues and its costs. In that form the assumption is too vaguely specified, because it makes no reference to the period of time over which profits are to be maximised. That may be resolved in one of two ways. The simplest is to see the model as a one-period or short-run model, where the firm's assumed aim is to make as much profit as possible in the short run. The short run is defined by economists as the period in which the firm is restricted to a given set of plant and equipment, and has some fixed costs which cannot be avoided even by ceasing production.

A slightly more complex version, which establishes a multi-period setting for the model, is to assume that the objective of the firm is to maximise the wealth of its shareholders, which in turn is equal to the discounted value of the expected future net cash flows into the firm. In that case, the firm can be seen as facing two interrelated kinds of decision. First, it has to take long-run or *investment decisions* on the level of capacity and the type of plant it wishes to install. Second, it has to decide upon the most profitable use of that set of plant and equipment. These short-run, *capacity utilisation*, decisions are essentially the same as those facing the firm maximising profits in the short run, and the same analysis applies.

If the profits made in each period are independent of each other, the single-period and multi-period models will be consistent with each other. However, there is a more difficult problem if the profits made in the current period could have an influence on the profits made in the future, because in that case it is possible that shareholders' wealth could be maximised by sacrificing profits in the current period. For instance, if a firm has a monopoly position, the maximum profit possible in the current period may be very large. However, if the firm uses its monopoly power to make that maximum profit, other firms may be attracted into the industry, or it might draw the attention of the anti-trust authorities. In either case, it is possible that the maximisation of shareholders' wealth will be better achieved by not taking the maximum profit available in the short run. The simple neo-classical model of the firm does not consider such complications, and it is best to interpret it as being concerned with the maximisation of short-run or single-period profits.

The assumption of profit maximisation gives the basic model of the firm a number of characteristics that distinguish it from other models. In the first place, it identifies a model that is *holistic* in the sense that, however large and complex, the firm is seen as an entity that can have objectives of its own and that can be said to take decisions. This is in marked contrast to the 'behavioural' model of the firm, where it is argued that 'only people can have objectives, organisations cannot'.

The second characteristic of the model, which also stems from the assumption of profit maximisation, is that it is an *optimising* model, where the firm is seen as attempting to achieve the best possible performance, rather than simply seeking 'feasible' performance which meets some set of minimum criteria. Again, this is in contrast to the behavioural model and to many quantitative techniques in operational research or operations management which seek to identify feasible rather than optimal solutions to problems.

Costs and output

The second component of the textbook model of the firm concerns the nature of the firm's production and the behaviour of costs, considered in more detail in Chapter 9. The firm is assumed to produce a single, perfectly divisible, standardised product for which the cost of production is known with *certainty*. In the short run, when some costs are fixed, the average cost curve will be U-shaped, as shown in Figure 2.1.

Cost per unit falls over the range A to B, as the fixed costs are spread over a larger number of units, but begins to rise beyond B as the principle of diminishing returns leads to increasing variable costs per unit.

As the textbook model is concerned with the short-run situation, it is short-run cost curves that are most relevant, and which are shown in the diagrams. The model depicts a firm that is attempting to maximise its profit with respect to a particular set of plant and equipment which has a particular short-run cost curve. If we also wish to consider long-run decisions then attention needs to

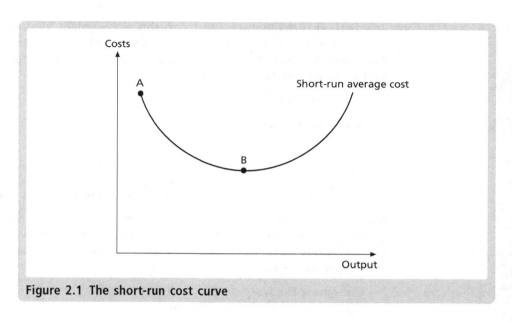

Figure 2.1 The short-run cost curve

be paid to the behaviour of costs in the long run, considered in more detail in Chapter 9.

Demand conditions

The third component of the orthodox model of the firm is the assumption that the firm has certain knowledge of the volume of output that can be sold at each price. These 'demand conditions' are considered in more detail in Chapters 6 to 8. For the purposes of this chapter it is sufficient to note that demand depends upon two sets of factors. First, it depends upon the behaviour of consumers, which determines the total demand for the product. Second, it depends upon the structure of the industry in which the firm is operating, and the behaviour of rival sellers. The simplest example to consider is that of the monopolist, where there is only one supplier of the product in question. In that case, consumer demand for the product can only be met by the single firm and there is no distinction between the total demand for the product and the demand for the individual firm. There is only one demand curve, which serves for both the firm and the industry. The precise shape of that curve depends upon the nature of the product in question, the number of consumers in the market concerned and their incomes, wealth and tastes. However, as the analysis in Chapters 6 and 7 shows, it can generally be assumed that the demand curve will slope downwards from left to right, indicating that more of the product can be sold at lower prices.

Equilibrium in the profit-maximising monopoly model

Having assumed profit maximisation and certain knowledge of cost and demand conditions, it is possible to move on to the second stage of model-building, which is to draw out the implications, or predictions, that follow from the assumptions.

The method of reasoning used to do this is essentially that of the mathematician. It is assumed that the problem has been solved, and then the conditions that must therefore hold are examined. The mathematical formulation of the model can be simply set out as follows:

Maximise $(q)

$(q) = R(q) − C(q)   where

> $(q) = profit
> R(q) = total revenue
> C(q) = total costs
> q = units of output produced and sold

Translated into words, this simply means 'maximise profit where profit is equal to revenue minus costs, and where costs and revenue each depend upon the amount of output that is sold'. Elementary calculus shows that if profit is maximised, the following conditions must hold:

Condition 1: d$/dq = dR/dq − dC/dq = 0
        or dR/dq = dC/dq

Condition 2: $d^2R/dq^2 > d^2C/dq^2$

Restating these equations verbally, profit will be a maximum if the firm produces the level of output such that marginal revenue (dR/dq) equals marginal cost (dC/dq) and when the slope of the marginal cost curve exceeds the slope of the marginal revenue curve. This rather formal presentation of the model can be expanded upon using a diagrammatic version, shown in Figure 2.2.

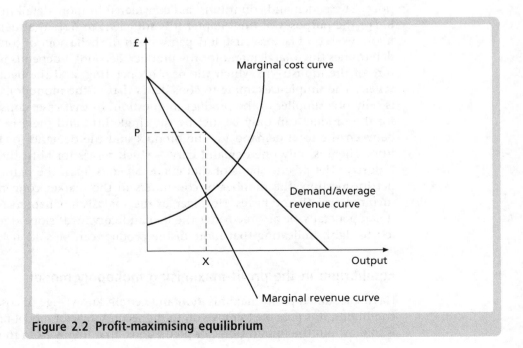

Figure 2.2 Profit-maximising equilibrium

In Figure 2.2, the profit-maximising level of output is X and the profit-maximising price is P. The reason for that is easily explained without resort to mathematics. The decision that the firm is facing concerns the level of output that should be produced and sold using the set of plant and equipment that has been installed. (The simple model always assumes that sales volume and output are equal, taking no account of the possibility of producing to stock or selling from stock.) It will pay the firm to produce any unit of output for which the extra revenue earned (marginal revenue) exceeds the extra cost (marginal cost). At level of output X all such units are being produced. If output is increased further, the additional units produced will add more to costs than to the revenues, and the level of profit will fall.

The diagram and the equations set out above identify the profit-maximising equilibrium for the firm. In the short run, under the assumptions made, the firm will produce the indicated level of output and sell it at the indicated price. If cost and demand conditions remain the same, the firm has no incentive to alter its price or output, and the firm is said to be in equilibrium.

Applications of the simple model

The model that has been developed above may be used in a number of ways. Its purpose in mainstream economic theory is essentially to predict how a firm will respond to changes in its environment. If some aspect of the environment changes, the model indicates the ways in which the firm will respond in order to move to a new equilibrium. For instance, if demand increases, both price and output will increase. If costs rise, price will rise but output will fall. Table 2.1 shows the comparative static properties of the profit-maximising model.

In addition to these 'positive' uses of the model, it may be used (with caution) for 'normative' purposes, providing prescriptions telling managers what they 'ought to do' in certain circumstances. For instance, a direct implication of the model is that a firm seeking maximum profit should produce every unit of output for which the marginal revenue exceeds marginal cost. If it is not doing so, then it is not maximising. That point may be presented as a prescription, and it is often extended in the management accounting literature into the very similar finding that firms should always agree to accept business that brings in greater *incremental revenue* than *incremental cost*. (The difference between the two is that *marginal* revenue and cost refers to the changes in total revenue and total cost when *one*

Table 2.1 The comparative static properties of the profit-maximising model

Change	Impact of the change on:	
	Price	Output
Demand increase	Increases	Increases
Demand fall	Falls	Falls
Increase in variable cost	Increases	Falls
Lump sum tax or change in fixed costs	No effect	No effect

more unit of output is produced and sold – or the rates of change of revenue and cost with output – while *incremental* revenue and cost refers to the change in total revenue and cost associated with an increase in output of any size, usually a batch or an order.)

Such prescriptions are valid, provided that the firm is attempting to maximise profit and the assumptions of the model are completely fulfilled. If they are not, however, it could be inappropriate to adopt the prescriptions without further thought.

Profits in the long run: the maximisation of shareholders' wealth

The profit-maximising model set out above is concerned with capacity utilisation and the short run. The firm has some fixed costs, arising from a given set of plant and equipment, and is concerned to make as much profit as possible, given the constraints set by that equipment. However, the firm also has to take investment decisions, which are concerned with the long run, in which no costs are fixed and when the firm is free to choose whichever set of plant and equipment it prefers.

When considering these long-run decisions it is not sufficient to characterise the firm's objective as 'profit maximisation' because profit is defined as revenue minus opportunity cost in a single period, without reference to the pattern of returns over time. It might be argued very simplistically that long-run profit maximisation consists of maximising the simple sum of profits over a number of short periods, but that would leave the unanswered question 'over how long should profits be added up?'. More significantly, such a simple addition would give the same weighting to returns occurring at different times, thereby ignoring the time-value of money (see Chapter 17 for a fuller explanation).

In order to avoid this difficulty, the long-run objective of the profit-maximising firm is said to be the maximisation of shareholders' wealth, which is achieved by maximising the value of the firm. This in turn is measured by the *present value* of the stream of expected future net cash flows accruing to the firm. The restatement of the firm's profit objective in this way allows the short run and the long run to be properly integrated. In the long run, as shown on Chapter 17, the firm decides upon the set of capital equipment to purchase by using investment appraisal techniques based upon the calculation of present values. However, these calculations themselves require estimates of the revenues and costs that are associated with each investment project, on the assumption that the equipment, once purchased, will be used to secure maximum profit. Choosing a set of capital equipment in the long run therefore requires the solution of the questions concerning revenues, costs and profits in the short run.

If the profits earned in each period, or each short run, are independent of each other, then the maximisation of profit in each period will lead to the maximisation of shareholders' wealth. However, as noted earlier in this chapter, if profits in one period depend upon profits in another, there may be a conflict between the two objectives. A firm with a monopoly position might make maximum profit in the short run by exploiting that position to the full, but in doing so it might attract entry to the industry, or anti-trust action from government, which would reduce profit in future periods. Maximising shareholders' wealth could require the sacrifice of immediate profits in order to protect their value in the longer term, depending upon the shape of the time-stream of profits, and the *discount rate* used to calculate present values. As the long-run objective, formulated in present value terms, takes account of the relative weighting to be given to profits accruing at different times, it should be given priority if such a conflict between objectives arises.

Managerial discretion models of the firm

'Managerial' criticisms of the profit-maximising model

The textbook model of the profit-maximising firm has been criticised on a number of different grounds. Perhaps the best known of these centres around the claim that it is unrealistic to assume that firms aim for maximum profits in a modern economy where ownership and control of firms lie with different groups of individuals. The pioneering work of Berle and Means (1932) in the United States demonstrated that the modern corporation was not simply a larger version of the owner-managed firm, but that ownership and control had become separated. Control lay in the hands of professional managers while ownership rested with shareholders. If the interests of shareholders and managers differ, if shareholders have relatively limited information about the performance of the firms they own, and if shareholders take relatively little interest in the firms' operations (provided that a satisfactory dividend is paid), then managers may have a good deal of 'discretion' to pursue their own objectives. This will be particularly true where firms have some degree of monopoly power and do not need to compete keenly in order to make a satisfactory level of profit. It has been suggested, therefore, that in such markets firms do not pursue profit as their major objective.

The suggestion that profit is not the objective of modern corporations has led to the search for alternative models based upon different assumptions about the firm's objective. There are many such models, but the classic examples are:

- the sales revenue maximising model, developed by Baumol (1958)
- the managerial utility maximising model (O. Williamson 1963)
- J. Williamson's integrative model (1966).

Baumol's sales revenue maximising model

Baumol's model stems from his observation that the salaries of managers, their status and other rewards often appear to be more closely linked to the size of the companies in which they work, measured by sales revenue, than to their profitability. In that case, managers may be more concerned to increase size than to increase profits, and the firm's objective will be to maximise sales revenue rather than profits.

If the assumption of profit maximisation is replaced by that of sales revenue maximisation, then a different model results. In many respects, it shares

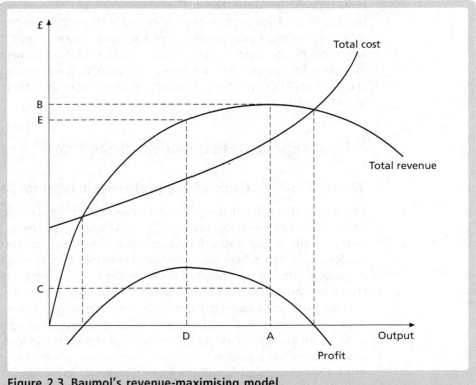

Figure 2.3 Baumol's revenue-maximising model

fundamental characteristics with the standard model, as it is also an optimising model in which a single product firm aims for a single objective, having perfect information about its cost and demand conditions. Nevertheless, the details are different, as illustrated in Figure 2.3, which sets out the basic version of the model, using total revenue, total cost and profit curves.

In Figure 2.3 the firm will choose to produce level of output A, giving total revenue B and profit C. Note that this implies a higher level of output, and therefore a lower price, than the equivalent profit-maximiser, who would produce output D and earn revenue E.

A straightforward revenue-maximiser will always produce more and charge less than a profit-maximising firm facing the same cost and demand conditions for the following reason:

● for revenue maximisation, marginal revenue = 0
● for profit maximisation, marginal revenue = marginal cost
● as marginal cost must be greater than 0, then for a profit-maximiser marginal revenue must be greater than 0
● therefore marginal revenue for a profit-maximiser must be greater than marginal revenue for a revenue-maximiser
● as marginal revenue slopes downwards to the right, equilibrium output must be higher for a revenue-maximiser than for the profit-maximiser.

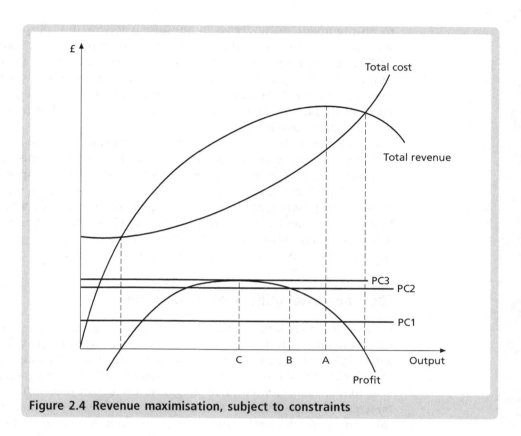

Figure 2.4 Revenue maximisation, subject to constraints

In the example shown in Figure 2.3 the sales-maximiser also makes some profit. However, this may not be enough to satisfy the shareholders, and in many cases maximising revenue may imply making losses. As a result the simple revenue-maximising model is implausible, and the model needs to be amended to include a profit constraint. Instead of simply assuming that the firm aims for maximum revenue, without regard to the implications for profit, it is assumed that the objective is the maximisation of sales revenue, subject to meeting a minimum profit constraint. This version is shown in Figure 2.4.

As the figure shows, there are three possible cases in this amended version of the model. The first is where the profit constraint is as shown by the line PC1. In this case the constraint does not 'bite'. At the level of output that maximises revenue, enough profit is made to satisfy the shareholders. The second case is where the profit constraint is as indicated by PC2. At the revenue-maximising level of output, insufficient profit is made to satisfy the shareholders. Hence, output is reduced until that constraint is met, at level of output B. The third case is where the minimum profit required to satisfy the shareholders is equal to the maximum profit that can be made, in which case the firm has to reduce its output to C.

In this third case, the firm behaves in exactly the same way with respect to its output and price as a profit-maximiser, despite the fact that it has set itself a different objective. This is an important point, which takes the analysis back to an argument made above in the discussion on the purpose of models. If shareholders insist upon the maximum level of profit being earned, then the profit-maximising model will provide accurate predictions of the behaviour of a firm whose management prefers to maximise sales revenue. If the purpose of the model is to predict the firm's behaviour, the fact that managers see their aim as maximising sales revenue, and not profit, is irrelevant. The firm behaves 'as if' it were a profit-maximiser.

The revenue-maximising model can be compared to the profit-maximising model with respect to its comparative static properties, which reveals both similarities and differences. If demand increases, both types of firm respond in the same way, with an increase in output and price. On the other hand, it has been shown above for a profit-maximiser that if fixed costs increase, or a lump-sum tax is imposed, price and output will not change. However, for a revenue-maximiser whose profit constraint is already biting, a lump-sum tax will reduce profits and will force the firm to lower its output and raise its price.

The managerial utility maximising model

In Baumol's sales revenue maximising model, managers' interests are tied to a single variable, with the addition of a profit constraint. Oliver Williamson's managerial utility maximising model takes account of a wider range of variables by introducing the concept of 'expense preferences', beginning with the assumption that managers attempt to maximise their own utility. The term 'expense preference' simply means that managers get satisfaction from using some of the firm's potential profits for unnecessary spending on items from which they personally benefit. Williamson identifies three major types of expense from which managers derive utility. These are:

1. *The amount that managers can spend on staff, over and above those needed to run the firm's operations (S).* This variable captures the power, prestige, status and satisfaction that managers experience from having control over larger numbers of people.
2. *Additions to managers' salaries and benefits in the form of 'perks' (M).* These include unnecessarily luxurious company cars, extravagant entertainment and clothing allowances, club subscriptions, palatial offices and similar items of expenditure. Such items may also be thought of as 'managerial slack' or 'X-inefficiency' (see below). They appear as costs to the firm, but are not necessary for the efficient conduct of its activities and are in effect coming out of profits.
3. *Discretionary profits (D).* These are after-tax profits over and above the minimum required to satisfy the shareholders. They are therefore available to the managers as a source of finance for 'pet projects' and allow the managers to invest in developing the firm in directions that suit them, enhancing their power, status and satisfaction.

Clearly there are conflicts and trade-offs between the different objectives in this model, and it is considerably more complex than those considered thus far. The detailed workings of the model require mathematics that go beyond the requirements of this text. Nevertheless, the main outlines are reasonably accessible. The basic form of the model is as follows:

$U = f(S, M, D)$ – managerial utility (U) depends upon the levels of S, M and D available to the managers

In common with the theory of consumer behaviour (see Chapter 6) it is assumed that the *principle of diminishing marginal utility* applies, so that additional increments to each of S, M and D yield smaller increments of utility to the management.

If R = revenue, C = costs and T = taxes, then:

Actual profit = $R - C - S$

Reported profit = $R - C - S - M$

If the minimum post-tax profit required by the shareholders is Z, then:

$D = R - C - S - M - T - Z$

The solution to the model requires the use of calculus in order to maximise the utility function (see the Illustration to this chapter on page 27 for an outline of the working). However, it is possible to set out a simplified version. If managerial utility is to be maximised, the last pound spent on S, M and D must yield the same marginal utility, i.e.:

$MU_S = MU_M = MU_D(1 - t)$ where t is the rate of tax on profits

This can be used to examine some of the comparative static properties of the model. If demand declines, then at every level of output D will decline. On the assumption of diminishing marginal utility, MU_D will rise, so that the equilibrium condition is no longer fulfilled. To regain equilibrium the available profits will be redistributed towards D and away from S and M. The level of output will fall. Similarly for a rise in fixed costs, or a lump-sum tax.

If the tax on profits increases, then $MU_D(1 - t)$ will fall and there will be a shift towards S and M, accompanied by increasing output.

The complexity of the Williamson model can make it difficult to examine in every detail. However, it does have an interesting application in explaining how take-overs are often followed very quickly by increases in reported profits. If the new management team exhibits a weaker preference for S and M, both of which entail unnecessary costs, they will prune these in line with their own preferences and will be able to report higher profits very quickly without too much difficulty and before altering any of the fundamentals of the business.

As in the case of the Baumol model, it should always be remembered that the logic of the utility-maximising model depends upon the management team having the discretion to earn less than maximum profits. If the minimum profit required by the shareholders is equal to the maximum possible, the managers will not have the discretion to indulge their taste for 'perks' and unnecessary staff.

J. Williamson's integrative model

Both of the models outlined above have been based around a single objective function. J. Williamson's integrative model goes one step further by combining single-period profit and sales maximisation with growth maximisation and the maximisation of the present value of future sales. All of these are shown in Figure 2.5.

The lower part of the diagram in Figure 2.5 shows total cost, revenue and profit in a single period, along with the profit constraint required in the Baumol model. The upper quadrant shows the relationship between the rate of growth and current sales revenue. Growth of sales revenue is assumed to be directly related to profits, so that growth is maximised when profits are maximised and growth is zero when profits are zero. A single-period profit-maximiser and a sales growth-maximiser will therefore both produce level of output Q_1. A single-period revenue-maximiser, subjected to the externally imposed profit constraint PC_{ext} will produce a higher level of output Q_2.

A firm that aims to maximise the present value of future sales will seek the combination of current revenue and growth rate that gives such a maximum. That can be found in Figure 2.5 by constructing 'iso-present-value' curves joining all points that have the same present value. As present value increases with both the growth rate and the current sales value, the maintenance of a constant present value requires that a higher growth rate be combined with a lower current

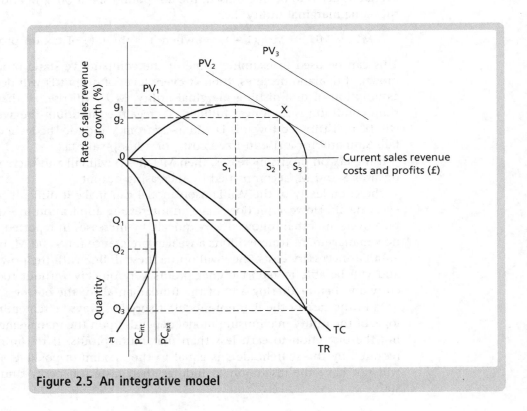

Figure 2.5 An integrative model

value of sales and vice versa. The 'iso-present-value' lines must therefore be negatively sloped as shown in the diagram by the lines PV_1 to PV_3. Higher present values are given by lines that are further away from the origin and the present value of sales is maximised at point X. That must lie to the right of the profit-maximising position, by virtue of the downward slope of the 'iso-present-value' lines, so that a firm that aims to maximise the present value of sales will always choose a level of output that exceeds that of the profit-maximiser. If the firm is to achieve its maximisation target it must grow at rate g_2, which requires the level of current profit given by the profit constraint PC_{int}, which is an internally imposed profit constraint set by the management in recognition of the need to achieve growth rate g_2.

In the diagram shown, the internally generated profit constraint is lower than that imposed externally. Maximising the present value of sales requires an output level greater than Q_2 and there is a conflict between the firm's desire for a higher level of sales and the need to meet the profit constraint. The outcome of that conflict depends upon the extent to which the managers of the firm have the discretion to pursue their own objectives when they conflict with others.

The behavioural approach to the firm

'Behavioural' criticisms of models of the firm

The 'managerial' models of the firm stem from criticism of the profit-maximising assumption, on the grounds that when ownership and control are separate, and many firms compete in relatively comfortable market structures, managers are able to direct the resources of companies towards their own ends. In many other respects the managerial models share similar characteristics with the orthodox textbook model of the firm. They are 'holistic' in the sense that the firm behaves as if it were a single entity, being capable of having objectives, even if those objectives are held by a group of managers and differ from those of the shareholders. The firm is seen as taking and implementing decisions. The models outlined above are all optimising models and it is also assumed that the firm has certain knowledge of the cost and demand conditions facing it. In effect the managerial models differ from the orthodox only in that they begin with a different assumption with respect to the firm's objective.

A more radical attack on the orthodox model of the firm, which also implies criticism of the managerial models, has been made by a group of theorists referred to as the 'behavioural school', building on seminal work by Simon (1959) and Cyert and March (1963). In this approach attention focuses on behaviour within the firm, which is not seen as a single entity but as a set of shifting coalitions among individuals, each of which has their own set of objectives. The fundamental argument is that organisations cannot have objectives, only people can, and that to perceive a firm as having an objective is an example of 'reification', confusing an abstract concept with a real entity.

In addition to rejecting the notion that a firm can have objectives, the behavioural theorists also reject the assumption that those taking decisions are perfectly informed. The assumption of certainty is abandoned and emphasis is placed on the idea that most organisations are so complex that the individuals within them have only limited information with respect to both internal and external developments.

The behavioural alternative

The behavioural model of the firm is therefore very different from either the orthodox model or the managerial models. It is not a 'holistic' model because the firm is not seen as a single entity with a single purpose. It is not an optimising model where the firm achieves the best possible performance with respect to its objective, and it is not based upon the assumption of certainty. In place of these features of the other models, it contains a number of key elements.

First, the 'firm' hardly exists, consisting of a group of individuals who form coalitions and alliances among themselves based upon common interests or characteristics, departmental loyalties or personal affinity. As a result the firm has multiple objectives which are in conflict with each other and which cannot be reconciled through a concept like the utility function, which gives a weight to each objective and allows an overall 'score' to be achieved. The accountants in a firm may wish to keep the level of stocks down in order to reduce the costs of holding them. At the same time the sales force may wish to hold a high level of stocks in order to be able to meet orders quickly. The research department may wish to employ a large number of qualified scientists, while the marketing department would prefer to spend more on advertising. Longer established employees may wish to avoid interruptions to their routine while newly employed executives may be anxious for change. Each individual will themselves have multiple objectives, arising from their personal histories, preferences and position within the firm and these multiple sets of objectives cannot be reduced to any simple overall statement that explains what the organisation as a whole is attempting to achieve.

The second major feature of the behavioural model, which distinguishes it from those outlined above, is that decision-makers exhibit 'satisficing' behaviour rather than 'optimising' behaviour. Neither the firm nor its component coalitions, nor individuals, are seen as attempting to maximise or minimise anything. Instead, each person or group has a 'satisficing' level for each of its objectives. If these levels are reached, they will not seek for more, in the short term at least, but if they are not met, action will be taken in order to remedy the problem. An important consequence of satisficing behaviour is that firms acting in this way will not keep costs down to a minimum. Instead they will exhibit 'organisational slack', incurring higher costs than are absolutely necessary.

A third feature of the behavioural model is that action within the firm takes the form of 'problem-oriented search using rules-of-thumb'. If one of the multiple objectives is not met, so that someone within the firm is dissatisfied, a search will take place for a means of meeting that objective. However, the search will be fairly narrow, relating solely to the objective that is not being met, and the firm will use rules-of-thumb to attempt to put the problem right. These rules of thumb are not arrived at through any detailed analysis, but are a function of the past experience of the firm and the people within it. For instance, if revenue falls, the firm may automatically raise its price, because that has been tried in the past and appeared to be successful.

Fourth, the aspirations of the individuals within the firm, which determine the levels of each objective with which they will be satisfied, change over time as a result of 'organisational learning'. If a firm succeeds in meeting all of its objectives for a period of time then eventually the individuals and groups will raise their aspiration levels, demanding more of whatever it is they care about. Eventually a situation will be reached where not everyone achieves 'satisficing' levels with respect to all of their objectives, at which point a problem-oriented search will take place to seek a solution to the problem. If one is found, the process of gradually increasing aspirations can continue. On the other hand, if a solution is not found despite a number of searches, aspiration levels with respect to the particular variable concerned will have to be reduced.

Clearly, the behavioural model is very different to the others that have been considered, and describes a number of very familiar features of organisational life. In many respects it is descriptively more realistic than either the orthodox or the managerial models and is attractive for that reason. However, it also has to be recognised that it has relatively limited value in addressing the questions with which managerial economics is concerned. If we consider the positive question of 'how do firms respond to changes in their environment?', the model offers little assistance because it focuses entirely within the firm. If we consider the normative question 'can we identify the decision rules that firms should follow in order to meet their objectives?', that question is not addressed either by the behavioural model. On the other hand, a firm that conforms well to the description set out by the behavioural theorists could behave in exactly the same way with respect to price and output decisions as the profit-maximising firm, or the firm described by one of the managerial models. If the shareholders are a powerful group within the firm and will only be satisfied with maximum profit, and if employees and managers are concerned for the firm's survival, the process of organisational learning may lead the firm towards profit maximisation. For the purposes of managerial economics, then, the behavioural model is of relatively limited usefulness.

The concept of X-inefficiency

A useful concept that links the behavioural model and the managerial utility model is that of *X-inefficiency*. In the standard, neo-classical, profit-maximising model it is assumed that the firm incurs the minimum cost achievable for the level of output being produced, given the set of plant and equipment that has been installed. In terms of the diagram, the firm is on its cost curve. Such a firm may be described as being 'X-efficient' or 'operationally efficient'. However, this may not be the case. A firm that is maximising managerial utility, for instance, will tend to spend more on staff and on 'perks' for the management than is necessary, in which case it may be said to be 'X-inefficient'. In terms of a diagram, it will be above its cost curve, as shown in Figure 2.6.

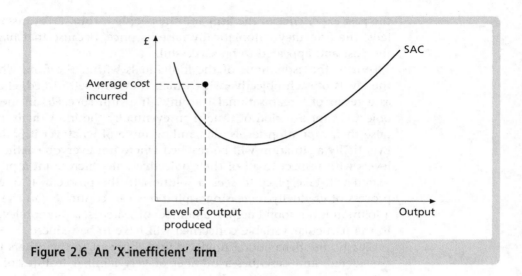

Figure 2.6 An 'X-inefficient' firm

Similarly, a firm that conforms to the behavioural model will incur higher costs than are strictly necessary and be X-inefficient, or have 'organisational slack'. Leibenstein (1966) emphasised the importance of X-inefficiency and considered the factors that are likely to encourage or discourage it. That analysis draws together a number of issues already considered above.

First, the degree of X-inefficiency will be partly determined by factors that are internal to the firm. If contracts between *principals* (the owners) and *agents* (managers and workers) are not efficient, then workers and managers will not be motivated to keep costs down, and the firm will be X-inefficient. If larger firms are more difficult to control, with a greater degree of bureaucratic rigidity, then they will also tend to be more X-inefficient.

The second set of factors that determine the degree of X-inefficiency is to be found in the external environment in which the firm operates. If the firm is forced by its environment to aim for maximum profit, it must eliminate X-inefficiency. On the other hand, if the management has the discretion to avoid profit maximisation, it will allow its costs to rise above the level that is strictly necessary. The environmental factors that lead to X-inefficiency are therefore the converse of the factors that force the firm to aim for maximum profits. If shareholdings are diffused among a large number of relatively ill-informed small shareholders, there may be little pressure from that direction. If the threat of take-over is limited, perhaps because the firm is too large to be under serious threat, or because anti-trust legislation prevents take-over, then the likelihood of X-inefficiency is correspondingly higher.

Similarly, the degree of X-inefficiency will tend to be higher as the market structure in which the firm operates is less competitive. If there are a small number of competitive rivals who are able to avoid direct competition with each other, and they are protected by barriers to entry into the industry, then there will be few penalties for slackness and X-inefficiency is correspondingly more likely to result.

In defence of the profit-maximising model

The methodological defence

The models described above have their origins in dissatisfaction with the profit-maximising model, arising from the claim that in practice firms do not attempt to maximise profits. The world is an uncertain place, where ownership and control are separate, where firms may not have a unified purpose and where they have a degree of monopoly power that cushions them from the need to maintain profits at their maximum level.

These issues are examined in more detail in Chapter 4, which deals with the relationship between ownership and control in the modern corporation. At this point, however, it is worth noting that supporters of the profit-maximising model may put forward a methodological argument in its defence. As explained in Chapter 1, the descriptive realism of an assumption is not necessarily a valid criterion on which to judge a model. If the purpose of the model is to predict, rather than to describe, then the criteria for evaluation are quite clear. First, the model must yield predictions, which is true for the profit-maximising model. Second, those predictions should be testable against the data, which is a test the model also passes. Third, the predictions should be supported by the data, which its supporters would claim is also the case. If this proposition is accepted, then the basic arguments of the managerial and behavioural schools are ill founded, because the realism of the profit-maximising assumption is irrelevant. It has been shown in Baumol's model, for instance, that a revenue-maximising firm will produce the same output and sell it at the same price as a profit-maximiser if the profit constraint is tight enough. It has also been shown that a firm that behaves as described by the behavioural model will make the same price and output decisions as a profit-maximiser if shareholders are powerful enough to insist on their right to the highest return on their investment. In both of these cases it would be descriptively inaccurate to describe the firm's objective as profit, but the profit-maximising model will predict behaviour very well.

Illustration   ## Using calculus to solve Williamson's utility-maximising model

The Williamson model is relatively complex but an outline of its solution illustrates how economic models can be constructed and used. The basic problem is as follows, following Moschandreas (1994, pp. 320–1):

Maximise managerial utility = $U = f(S, M, D)$

Subject to $\Pi_r = \Pi_{min} + T$

Where: S = spending on staff; M = spending on managerial perquisites; D = discretionary investment spending; Π = total profit; Π_r = reported profit; Π_{min} = minimum profit required by shareholders; T = taxes, which are equal to the tax rate 't' multiplied by reported profit, i.e. $T = t\Pi_r$.

$\Pi = R(q) - C(q) - S$

▶

Where: R = total revenue; C = total cost of production and sales; q = output.

$$\Pi_r = \rho\Pi = \rho(R(q) - C(q) - S)$$

Where: ρ = the proportion of profit that is reported.

$$M = (1 - \rho)\Pi \text{ and:}$$

$$D = \Pi_r - \Pi_{min} - T$$

It follows from these equations that:

$$M = (1 - \rho)(R(q) - C(q) - S), \text{ and:}$$

$$D = \rho(R(q) - C(q) - S) - \Pi_{min} - t\rho(R - C - S), \text{ which can be written as:}$$

$$D = \rho(1 - t)(R(q) - C(q) - S) - \Pi_{min}$$

This definition of D implies that the constraint can be ignored. Hence the problem becomes one of simple maximisation, as follows:

Maximise $U = f[S, (1 - \rho)(R(q) - C(q) - S), \rho(1 - t)(R(q) - C(q) - S) - \Pi_{min}]$

Define $\delta U/\delta S = U_S$; $\delta U/\delta M = U_M$; $\delta U/\delta D = U_D$

The decision variables are output (q), staff spending (S) and the proportion of profit to be reported (ρ). The first-order conditions for a maximum are then:

$$\delta U/\delta q = U_M(1 - \rho)(dR/dq - dC/dq) + U_D\rho(1 - t)(dR/dq - dC/dq) = 0$$

$$\delta U/\delta S = U_S + U_M(1 - \rho)(dR/dS - 1) + U_D\rho(1 - t)(dR/dS - 1) = 0$$

$$\delta U/\delta\rho = U_M(-1)(R(q) - C(q) - S) + U_D(1 - t)(R(q) - C(q) - S) = 0$$

For the first of these conditions to hold $dR/dq = dC/dq$, so that production decisions are made in the usual way.

From the second condition:

$$dR/dS = 1 - [U_S/(U_M(1 - \rho) + U_D\rho(1 - t)]$$

Since U_S, U_M, U_D, $1 - \rho$, and $1 - t$ are all positive, $dR/dS < 1$ and spending on staff is carried beyond the profit-maximising level.

From the third condition:

$$(R(q) - C(q) - S)[-U_M + U_D(1 - t)] = 0$$

Therefore, if $R(q) > C(q) + S$ (and there is some profit) then:

$$U_M/U_D = 1 - t$$

U_M and U_D are the rates of change of utility with M and D, and their ratio is referred to as the 'marginal rate of substitution' (MRS). It indicates the rate at which a utility maximiser will exchange M for D. If the tax rate is higher so the MRS is lower, indicating that the proportion of profits that will be absorbed as managerial perquisites will be higher and the amount of discretionary investment will be lower.

Derivation of the full set of comparative static results for Williamson's model is beyond a text at this level but the exposition here should be enough to illustrate the general approach.

References and further reading

W. Baumol, 'On the Theory of Oligopoly', *Economica*, N.S. 25, 1958, pp. 187–98.

A.A. Berle and G. Means, *The Modern Corporation and Private Property*, New York, Macmillan, 1932.

R. Cyert and J. March, *Behavioural Theories of the Firm*, Englewood Cliffs, NJ, Prentice Hall, 1963.

D. Kreps, *A Course in Microeconomic Theory*, Princeton, Princeton University Press, 1990.

H. Leibenstein, 'Allocative Efficiency vs X-Efficiency', *American Economic Review*, vol. 56, 1966, pp. 392–415.

M. Moschandreas, *Business Economics*, London, Thomson, 1994.

H. Simon, 'Theories of Decision-Making in Economics and Behavioural Science', *American Economic Review*, vol. 49, June 1959, pp. 253–83.

J. Williamson, 'Profit, Growth and Sales Maximisation', *Economica*, vol. 34, February 1966, pp. 1–16.

O. Williamson, 'Managerial Discretion and Business Behaviour', *American Economic Review*, vol. 53, December 1963, pp. 147–62.

Self-test questions

1. In which of the following models will the firm incur higher costs than are necessary?

   (a) Baumol's revenue-maximising model
   (b) Williamson's managerial utility model
   (c) the behavioural model

2. Which of the following concepts are compatible with the behavioural model of the firm?

   (a) optimising
   (b) satisficing
   (c) certainty
   (d) aspiration levels
   (e) rules of thumb

3. If fixed costs rise, what will happen to the level of output in each of the following models?

   (a) profit-maximising
   (b) revenue-maximising, with a profit constraint
   (c) managerial utility maximising

4. Which firm would you expect to have the highest share price?

   (a) a profit-maximiser
   (b) a revenue-maximiser
   (c) a managerial utility maximiser

Essay question

Explain the relationship between the neo-classical theory of the firm and the concept of X-inefficiency.

3 The nature of the firm

In Chapter 2 it was taken for granted that firms exist and carry out some set of production and marketing functions. No attention was paid to why they exist or to the factors that differentiate the activities that take place *within* firms from those that take place *between* firms. This chapter turns to that issue, setting out a conceptual framework that has proved to be very powerful in the analysis of a wide range of business decisions.

Why do firms exist?

In a market economy most economic analysis is concerned with the fundamental question of how the allocation of resources is brought about by market forces. The analysis of supply and demand, for instance, explains the way in which prices act as a coordinating mechanism, answering the basic economic questions of 'what should be produced and how much?', 'how should it be produced?' and 'who gets it?' The answers to such questions are not provided by a central decision-maker, or by a single firm, but by the price mechanism, acting as a decentralised system of social organisation. However, not all resource allocation is carried out in this way, as when a foreman or a manager in a firm orders a subordinate to move from one task to another. Coase (1937) quotes Robertson (1923) to the effect that there are 'islands of conscious power in this ocean of unconscious co-operation'. Outside the firm it is the price mechanism that coordinates the use of resources. Inside the firm, market transactions are replaced by the directives of the management. The essence of the firm, then, is that it is the super-session of the market mechanism. To put the same point in a slightly different way, the firm is 'the system of relationships which comes into existence when the direction of resources is dependent on an entrepreneur' (Coase 1937).

Having established this starting point it is possible to consider the question 'why do firms exist?' Why is the market so often superseded and what are the factors that determine this super-session?

Some simple explanations

A number of simple ideas offer themselves. The first is that individuals might prefer to be directed by other people, rather than simply taking part in abstract market transactions. Coase dismissed that explanation, although some organisational psychologists might disagree. The second possibility is that some individuals may desire to exercise power over others, and would therefore be willing to pay others more than they would receive in a straightforward market transaction. That, too, can be dismissed as unlikely because it implies that those who exercise authority in firms would have to pay for the privilege, rather than being paid more than those they direct.

If these very simple explanations for the existence of the firm are rejected, a number of others may be considered. Knight (1921) argued that because there is uncertainty, some person must take the responsibility for forecasting market conditions and deciding on output and price. But the income resulting from those decisions is very uncertain and most people prefer to work for fixed or at least agreed incomes. Hence entrepreneurs take responsibility for forecasting. They accept the risks involved and pay other workers fixed wages, in return for the right to any profits. In return for the fixed wages, workers agree to accept the orders of the entrepreneur. The problem with this explanation is that a person with superior forecasting ability need not necessarily set up their own firm in order to profit from that ability. They could sell their forecasts to others. Furthermore, the entrepreneur does not need to coordinate the workers directly. The entrepreneur could simply have a contract with independent workers, guaranteeing them payment in return for the completion of certain tasks. Therefore the existence of uncertainty in itself does not require firms to be set up. Forecasters could forecast, selling that information to entrepreneurs who then set up contracts with independent workers to carry out assigned tasks.

Another approach to explaining the emergence of the firm was put forward by Alchian and Demsetz (1972). They argued that the fundamental problem lies in the 'team' nature of production, whereby many goods and services are produced by a group of people working jointly. Because it is not possible for one worker to measure the contribution of the others to the joint output, it is difficult for the team as a whole to detect whether an individual worker is shirking. If a worker does shirk, that person reaps all of the benefit from the shirking but the costs, in terms of lower output, are spread across the whole team. Hence there is a problem of *moral hazard* and an incentive to shirk in team production, which applies to all workers. Team production tends to be less efficient than it could be and that inefficiency creates an incentive for the workers to seek a solution. One possibility would be for them to appoint a monitor or overseer to observe the individual members and punish them if they do not make their best efforts. However, if the monitor is simply another worker, receiving a fixed payment in return for an unobservable level of effort, that person faces the same incentive to shirk and the problem is not solved. What would be effective (assuming that the monitor can actually gauge the effort of the other workers) is an arrangement whereby the monitor is the *residual claimant*. Ordinary workers receive a fixed level of payment and the monitor has the right to receive whatever remains of the revenue after the wages and other expenses have been paid. In that case the monitor has a clear incentive to increase output by preventing shirking and the problem is solved. If the right to the residual income can be bought and sold, then competition among rival monitors will guarantee that the monitor who can extract the largest output will own the rights, and the result will be an efficient one from society's overall point of view.

The Alchian and Demsetz explanation for the emergence of the firm is a useful one, drawing attention to the importance of asymmetric information, the moral hazard that it causes, the role of property rights and the tendency to efficiency under the right institutional conditions. However, those issues are not exclusive to the team production situation and a more general analytical framework has come to dominate explanations for why firms emerge.

Transaction cost analysis

One of the most powerful conceptual frameworks to become popular in the 1980s and 1990s has been 'transaction cost analysis' (TCA). TCA is a set of concepts and propositions that was first put forward by Ronald Coase in 1937 and has since been further developed by a number of authors, most notably Williamson (1975, 1986, 1996). While TCA has its origins in economics, it has formed the basis for studies in a wide range of other disciplines including business strategy, contract law, corporate finance, international business, marketing, political science and sociology (see Rindfleisch and Heide 1997 for an overview presented from a marketing perspective). Hence it deserves careful attention.

The 'Coasian' analysis

The key question being addressed is 'why do firms exist in market economies?' Coase suggested that the most obvious answer is that using the market involves transaction costs that might be avoided by using the firm. A transaction takes place whenever a good or a service passes from one party to another. The *direct costs* involved in making that transaction between independent parties include those that arise in respect of:

- locating buyers and sellers
- acquiring information about their availability, quality, reliability and prices
- negotiating, re-negotiating and concluding contracts
- coordinating the agreed actions of the parties
- monitoring performance with respect to fulfilment of contracts
- taking action to correct any failure to perform.

In addition to those direct costs, there are also the *opportunity costs* that arise if transacting between independent parties leads to more efficient courses of action not being taken (Masten *et al.* 1991). For instance, it may be efficient for a new piece of equipment to be purchased but that may not happen if the two parties cannot agree. Similarly, the parties to a transaction may be inappropriate for each other's requirements, they may fail to adapt properly to a changing environment or they may have to waste resources in adjusting their activities.

If two independent parties are to transact, they need to establish an agreement, a contract, which sets out the obligations of the buyer and seller. However, such contracts cannot be complete – they cannot specify what both parties will do in every possible future circumstance – because there may be thousands of such circumstances. If transaction costs are to be kept as low as possible, it would be preferable to establish long-term contracts, rather than a series of short-term contracts. However, the longer the period of the contract, the more uncertain are the purchaser's precise requirements. As a result, it will be desirable to establish a form of contract where the supplier is under an obligation to provide goods or services within certain limits, with the details left until a later date, to be decided by the buyer as their requirements become more clearly defined. Once such incomplete contracts are established, resources are directed by the authority exerted by the buyer and *a firm has come into existence.*

Another general reason for preferring internalised transactions to external ones is that internal transactions are less accessible to governments and other regulatory bodies, so that it may be profitable in some situations to internalise transactions in order to avoid taxes or controls on output.

To sum up thus far, the notion of the firm as super-session of the market mechanism leads naturally to the existence of transaction costs as the major reason for the existence of the firm. Having established that proposition, Coase went on to provide a pioneering analysis of the factors that determine the boundaries of the firm.

If there were no disadvantages to market transactions there would be no firms and all transactions would take place between individuals through markets. At the other extreme, if internalised transactions were always superior to market transactions the economy would consist of a single firm, in effect becoming centrally planned. (It can be helpful to appreciate that a firm is essentially a planned economy and a planned economy is a single firm.) As the reality lies in between these two extremes the question that remains is 'what factors determine the optimal balance between the two different types of transaction, and hence the boundaries of firms?' Coase suggested that at small firm sizes internal transactions are generally superior. However, as size or scope increases, so does the cost of organising the extra transactions until it becomes cheaper to organise the marginal transaction through the market or through the establishment of another firm. In this way the analysis of firm size and scope becomes amenable to the economist's standard marginalist tool kit.

A second factor that will set a limit to firm size will be 'managerial diseconomies of scale', whereby management makes less and less effective use of resources as the number of transactions to be handled increases. Finally, a limit might be set on firm size if larger firms have to pay more for resources than smaller firms. (It has been noted in Chapter 2, when explaining Baumol's model, that the salaries of executives may be directly correlated with firm size, with larger firms offering larger salaries. It is difficult to argue wholly convincingly that the executives of larger firms are necessarily superior to those in small or medium-sized companies.)

As a further step in the analysis, Coase identified three other factors that could cause the cost of organising additional transactions to arise. The first is an increase in the physical or geographical space over which transactions are organised. If this is the case, then any technological development that reduces the cost of organising across distance will tend to increase the size of the firm. The second factor identified is the dissimilarity of the transactions involved, an issue that is relevant to the development of the conglomerate, highly diversified, firm. The third factor is the probability of changes in the environment and in prices. If prices change rapidly then the cost of organising a transaction within the firm may rise more rapidly than the costs of organising through markets.

Coase pitched his analysis at a very general level, rather than concerning itself directly with business decisions. Nevertheless, it is easy to see that it may be applicable in more detail to a number of different choices facing the firm, particularly with respect to the level of vertical integration, the degree of diversification and the choice of overseas operation. Vertical integration is considered below, while diversification and 'multinationalisation' are considered in Chapters 4 and 5. Before turning to those issues it is useful to develop the TCA framework in more detail.

Williamson's analysis

The most powerful extension and development of TCA has been that of Williamson (1975, 1986, 1996), which sets out a general framework within which to analyse the forms that different types of transaction may take. Almost all of the studies using TCA have drawn on Williamson's version of the analysis in the attempt to explain a wide variety of phenomena (Rindfleisch and Heide 1997).

Williamson's analysis is difficult and often expressed in rather convoluted prose. It has also been extended and developed by others who express the same central ideas in slightly different ways (Milgrom and Roberts 1992, Acs and Gerlowski 1996, Besanko *et al.* 1996). However, its essence lies in bringing together two sets of concepts. The first consists of those factors that determine the cost of organising an 'arm's length' transaction between two independent parties. The second consists of a set of 'governance structures' or 'types of contracting' that are the mechanisms available for the control and coordination of the transaction. These two sets of variables are matched to show which governance structures are best suited to which set of transactional circumstances. For the purposes of prediction it is then assumed that efficiency prevails (at least in the long run) and that firms choose the type of governance structure that is best suited to the type of transaction being undertaken.

The characteristics of a transaction

A transaction takes place whenever a good or a service passes from one party to another. In the TCA framework, the relative cost of organising a transaction through different forms of governance is determined by four characteristics. These are as follows:

1. The extent to which *complete contracts* are possible (the term 'contract' refers to any agreement between parties, not only those that are formally written down).
2. The extent to which there is a threat of *opportunism* on the part of transactors.
3. The degree of *asset specificity* or *idiosyncratic investment* involved in a transaction.
4. The *frequency* with which the transaction is repeated.

These ideas require further examination in order to understand the ways in which they influence the choice of governance structure. A *complete contract* is one in which every possible future contingency is specified and the actions to be taken by both parties to the contract are also specified for every one of those contingencies. This is almost always impossible for four reasons. First, there is the existence of *uncertainty and/or complexity* with respect to the transaction. These make it difficult and expensive to identify the terms that would constitute a complete contract. Second, human beings exhibit *bounded rationality*. They do not have full information about everything, language is imprecise and there are limits to human beings' capacity to process information. Hence people are 'intendedly rational but only limitedly so'. Third, there are often *measurement problems* – difficulties in specifying and measuring the performance that is required of contractors. Fourth, there is often *asymmetric information*. That simply means that the parties to the transaction have access to different information. The differences may take the form of either 'hidden information' or 'hidden action', which lead to the problems of *adverse selection* or *moral hazard* respectively. 'Hidden information' is where at least one party to the contract has information not available to the other. 'Hidden action' is where at least one party takes actions relevant to the performance of the contract that are not observable by the other.

The difficulties associated with writing complete contracts are so fundamental that such contracts almost never exist. There is always a possibility that unforeseen events will take place and the parties will need to reach agreement on how to adapt to the new circumstances. That introduces increased negotiation costs and raises the possibility that one party might lose because of the behaviour of the other.

The difficulty of writing complete contracts would not create problems for the parties to a transaction if it were absolutely certain that they would all treat each other reasonably when unforeseen events take place. In that case the contract could state that all parties promise not to take advantage of each other in the event of unforeseen circumstances, or such a promise could be made implicitly as part of a 'gentlemen's agreement'. Whenever something happens that is not covered by the contract, the parties meet and re-negotiate, with both sides being open and truthful about everything that is relevant. However, TCA assumes that there is an additional problem, which is the threat of *opportunism*.

Opportunism is defined as 'self-interest-seeking with guile' (Williamson 1985, p. 47) and it includes lying, cheating, hiding information and breaking agreements. Opportunistic behaviour can take place both before and after a contract is agreed – it may be *ex ante* opportunism or *ex post*.

Ex ante opportunism arises when the different parties have access to different information at the time when they are negotiating the contract. For instance, each party will be better informed about their own valuation of a product or service than will their potential trading partner. As a result there will often be attempts at *strategic misrepresentation*. A buyer will try to pretend that they place a lower valuation on their potential purchase, while a seller will try to pretend that it costs more to produce than it really does.

Opportunism may also be *ex post* – it may take place after the contract has been agreed. In that situation there are two forms of behaviour that can make transacting difficult. These are *reneging* and *hold-up*. Reneging is where one of the parties to the contract does not honour it. Hold-up is where one of the parties takes advantage of the other's vulnerability, created by commitments made to meeting the contract, in order to seize a larger share of the available profits.

The combination of incomplete contracts and opportunism increases the cost of transacting between independent parties. However, it would not be important if markets were competitive and the contracting parties had nothing to lose by shifting to an alternative supplier or customer. If something went wrong with a transaction, and a mutually agreeable conclusion could not be reached, both parties could deal with someone else. Perhaps the most important characteristic of a transaction, therefore, is the extent to which it involves *idiosyncratic investment* or *asset specificity*.

Idiosyncratic investment is investment in assets whose value arises from their use in a transaction with a particular partner and whose value will be at least partly lost if the transaction does not take place. Asset specificity is the name given to the characteristic that such assets have and may be thought of as the 'value that is lost when the asset is used outside the specific setting or relationship' (Milgrom and Roberts 1992, p. 135).

Asset specificity may arise in at least five different forms. *Site specificity* is where the assets involved in a transaction are located side by side in order to reduce transport costs or achieve operating efficiencies. Steel mills make steel plates, rods and bars and they are located next to the blast furnaces that make the steel in order to conserve the energy costs of heating the materials to melting point. Factories making cans for drinks are located next to can-filling drinks plants in order to economise on inventory and transportation costs. *Physical or intellectual asset specificity* is where the assets are tailor-made for a particular usage and cannot be cheaply reconfigured for alternative uses. The jigs and fixtures used to make car bodies, for instance, and the engineering knowledge involved, are specific to a particular make and model of car. *Dedicated asset specificity* is where a firm makes an investment in general-purpose plant and equipment in order to fulfil the needs of a particular customer. In that case, the assets are not physically configured in a special way to suit the customer but they cannot be used for other customers because no such customers are currently available. *Human capital specificity* arises when individual staff members develop knowledge, skills and capabilities that have value when dealing with one particular transacting partner but which are lost if the firm deals with someone else. Finally, *brand-name specificity* arises when the value of an asset is heavily dependent upon its being using in conjunction with a particular brand name. Actors who work in a well-known soap opera will receive higher pay and other opportunities as a result of their association with that brand name and hence the value of their acting skills are brand-name specific.

Whichever form it takes, asset specificity brings about what Williamson (1985) called a 'fundamental transformation'. Before the specific investments are made, the parties to the transaction are in a 'large numbers' situation. They are free to choose among many different buyers or sellers in order to make their transaction. However, after the investment has been made they find themselves in a 'small numbers' or *bilateral monopoly* situation where they must deal with one specific exchange partner or lose the value of the idiosyncratic investments that have been made. If that partner should renege on the contract, or try to hold up the investor, the asset-specific investments will be lost. The presence of asset specificity means that opportunistic behaviour can be damaging and it makes the investor vulnerable to the actions of the other party. That vulnerability might be reduced if the investor in specific assets spends on additional monitoring of the other party's behaviour and on enforcing the contract through legal or non-legal means (a private army perhaps). However, these are all additional transaction costs that make it less attractive to deal with an independent other party.

The fourth characteristic of a transaction that needs to be taken into account is its *frequency* – the number of times it is expected to take place. If a transaction is 'one-off' it will not be efficient to devote significant resources to its coordination and control. On the other hand, if it is expected to take place many times over many years, the cost of making special arrangements for its management may be justified.

Alternative governance structures

The factors that create difficulties for transacting between independent parties through markets and contracts are the factors that make internalised transacting more attractive. Therefore it is the combination of incomplete contracts, opportunistic behaviour, asset specificity and high frequency that make coordination through managerial authority more efficient than coordination through a market. In the simplest interpretation of Williamson's analysis only two alternatives – markets and hierarchies – are considered. However, a more complete approach to the issue identifies four types of 'governance structure' which encompass a richer range of alternatives.

The first type of governance structure is *classical contracting*. In this case the identity of the two parties to the contract is irrelevant. All future contingencies are accounted for and the transaction is 'self-liquidating'. When it has been completed, neither party has any remaining obligations. This type of governance structure corresponds to the spot-market transaction in economic theory and is the way in which most personal retail transactions are governed. If a customer buys a pound of sausages or a bottle of water from a shop, that is an example of classical contracting. The contract is not written down. Neither party is concerned with the identity of the other party, the law of contract (and consumer protection legislation) takes account of any future contingencies and the transaction is completely finished when the water or sausages and the payment change hands.

The second type of governance is *neo-classical contracting*. This is used when it is not possible to account for all future possible contingencies, and therefore the agreement between two parties is recognised to be incomplete. Because of that incompleteness the contract provides some form of arbitration which allows the transaction to be completed even if there is disagreement. Contracts for large construction projects are an example of this kind of contracting. It is recognised that in the course of construction, unanticipated changes will need to be made

Table 3.1 Idiosyncratic investment, frequency and governance structures

Frequency	Extent of idiosyncratic investment		
	Low	Medium	High
Occasional	Classical contracting	Neo-classical contracting	Neo-classical contracting
Recurrent	Classical contracting	Obligational contracting	Unified governance

Source: Based on Williamson (1986).

to the design and construction of the road, bridge or building. Mechanisms are in place for the amendment of the contract and some form of arbitration is agreed to in case of conflict over the best way in which to proceed.

The third type of governance mechanism is *relational contracting*, which is even further from the classical concept of the discrete one-off transaction. Relational contracting involves links between the parties that have greater duration and complexity, where the original agreement between the parties may cease to become a point of reference, and where the relationship itself becomes the focus. The relationship may become 'a mini-society with a vast array of norms beyond those centred on the exchange and its immediate processes' (Williamson 1986). To put it more simply, the parties to a relational contract 'make it up as they go along'. Contracts of employment are an example of relational contracting. Within the general category of relational contracting, Williamson identified two variants. The first is *obligational contracting* where the transaction takes place between two independent organisations. The second is *unified governance* where the transactions are internalised within the hierarchy of a single firm.

The most appropriate form of governance for a particular transaction depends upon the four characteristics outlined above: the extent to which a complete contract can be written; the threat of opportunistic behaviour; the degree of asset specificity; and the frequency of the transaction. In so far as complete contracts never exist, there is always significant uncertainty and opportunistic behaviour is assumed to be the norm, it is asset specificity and frequency that are the most important determinants of the mode of governance to be selected. Table 3.1 shows the relationship as predicted by Williamson (1986).

As Table 3.1 shows, transactions will take place within a firm, through unified governance, when the level of idiosyncratic investment is high and when transactions take place frequently. When there is very little asset specificity, classical contracting is most appropriate and there are situations between these extremes where other forms of governance, like long-term contracts, joint ventures or strategic alliances, are the most appropriate format.

Viewed from the TCA perspective the firm may be seen as 'a set of transactions co-ordinated by managerial authority'. Alternatively it might be seen as 'a conscious, wilful effort to organise economic activity that consists of a collection of contracts when more than one party is involved' (Acs and Gerlowski 1996, p. 2). These two interpretations are only slightly different. The personnel of a firm are joined to it by contracts of employment which are relational contracts. Such contracts are incomplete, they allow the senior managers of the firm to direct those below them in the hierarchy, subject to certain limitations, and they are enforced internally by the exercise of authority. Therefore within the firm transactions are coordinated by authority, not by the market or (in detail) by the contract.

Transaction costs and the vertical boundaries of the firm

One of the most important business decisions to which TCA has been applied is the level of vertical integration, defined as the extent to which different stages of production take place within the same firm. In this case, the transactions that are internalised link the flow of output between different stages of production, from the extraction and processing of raw materials at one extreme to retail supply at the other.

It is important to recognise that all firms are vertically integrated to some extent because most stages of production can be sub-divided into increasingly smaller stages. A firm that was totally 'disintegrated' vertically would carry out a single indivisible operation and contract with independent parties for everything else. The question is not whether a firm will be vertically integrated, but what level of integration will be optimal, and what factors will encourage more or less integration to take place.

The most obvious advantages of coordinating vertically through internal transactions relate to technical economies in production, where close coordination between different stages of production can reduce costs. Bain (1968) argued that unless such technical relations are involved, there are unlikely to be substantial cost savings. The most common example used here is vertical integration in the steel industry where the direct transfer of hot metal from blast furnace to rolling mill saves considerable quantities of energy. This is a useful example, because it also shows that the fundamental issue is not technological, but lies in the disadvantages of classical or neo-classical contracting.

In principle, it would be possible for one firm to specialise in the production of molten steel, and another in the use of that steel to make sheets, rods and bars. However, to be technically efficient, the two plants would need to be located side by side in which case they would only be able to transact with each other. That would involve a very high level of site-specific investment by both parties and it would introduce the 'small numbers' problem. In order to protect their investments they would need to negotiate, draft, monitor and enforce a very detailed contract between two independent firms, which could substitute for the internal organisation of the flows of hot metal from one stage of the process to another. The provision of such a contract would be so difficult, expensive and risky that internal organisation – unified governance – is the preferred mechanism. The employees working in both the blast furnace and the rolling mill have contracts of employment which require them to follow the instructions of the same group of managers. When something unexpected happens, that group of managers can instruct workers in both facilities without having to re-negotiate a contract.

Vertical integration in the motor-car industry

TCA is expressed in rather abstract terms and it can be difficult to measure variables like asset specificity, frequency, uncertainty and the threat of opportunism. It is useful therefore to examine some examples of its application. The motor industry provides a number of classic cases.

The first example involves the relationship between General Motors and Fisher Body (Klein *et al.* 1978). In the 1920s General Motors (GM) assembled vehicles using bodies purchased from Fisher Body, which was an independent company. As motor-car technology developed, wooden bodies were replaced by metal and GM realised that, to be technically efficient, car bodies should be produced next to the assembly plant. The senior management therefore requested that Fisher Body build a new body plant adjacent to a new GM plant. However, that would involve a very high level of idiosyncratic investment in assets that were both site-specific and physical and intellectual asset-specific. If the Fisher Body plant were not used to make bodies for GM it would lose almost all of its value, partly because bodies could not be shipped to car assembly firms in other places and partly because the bodies being made were specifically designed to fit GM cars. Fisher Body executives were not prepared to meet GM's request, fearing that once they had made the investment they would be vulnerable to any demands that GM might later make – *ex post* opportunism. GM solved the problem by purchasing Fisher Body and building the body plant where it was required.

In the GM/Fisher Body case vertical integration involved two major aspects of the production process – body manufacture and vehicle assembly. Monteverde and Teece (1982) extended the analysis, noting that vehicle assembly involves bringing together thousands of components, some of which are purchased from independent suppliers and some of which are produced in-house. They hypothesised that the key determinant of the make/buy choice for components lies in the level of 'applications engineering' effort required to develop each component for use in a particular model of vehicle. Spending on such development generates specialised, non-patentable know-how that is highly specific to the particular transaction involved – there is intellectual asset and human capital specificity. It may also lead to the development of customised equipment and fixtures, adding an element of physical capital specificity. There is therefore a risk that supplier or buyer will behave opportunistically by demanding better terms at the last moment, knowing that the other party to the transaction cannot simply take their business elsewhere. In that situation (frequent transactions, high level of idiosyncratic investment), economising requires that the transactions be organised through unified governance. On the other hand, if a component does not require a high level of engineering effort specific to the vehicle manufacturer's products, there is no asset specificity, no 'small numbers' problem, and it is more efficient to source the product on the open market from independent suppliers who compete with each other.

Monteverde and Teece found a way to measure the applications engineering cost associated with 133 different motor-car components used by GM and Ford and their hypothesis was supported in that components involving higher costs were more likely to be produced in-house.

While the Monteverde and Teece study showed that TCA has significant explanatory power, its findings also showed a need for caution. The two companies studied were very different, with GM choosing in-house production of many components which were bought in by Ford. Acs and Gerlowski (1996, pp. 160–2) point out that in the early 1990s Chrysler was even less vertically integrated than Ford, having taken a deliberate decision to give outside suppliers a larger role in the vehicle production process, from design and component production to assembly. If different firms embody different capabilities, built up over decades of experience, those differences may outweigh transactional considerations. If those capabilities include the skills needed to build good relationships with suppliers so that opportunism is less of a threat, the balance of advantage between internalised and arm's length transactions may shift.

This last point draws attention back to the fact that it is the combination of incomplete contracts, asset specificity and opportunism that makes arm's length transacting difficult. Most analyses have taken opportunism for granted, making it an assumption (Rindfleisch and Heide 1997). If contracts are always incomplete, that identifies asset specificity as the main determinant of the firm/arm's length contract decision. However, it may be inappropriate, or unnecessarily cynical, to assume that behaviour is always opportunistic. Business reputation is important to firms, because a reputation for fair dealing may help in acquiring custom. It can therefore be a powerful mechanism for preventing opportunism. That tendency is often reinforced through informal and social connections between executives, and in some cases by formal systems of experience ratings where firms pool their knowledge of dealings with suppliers and customers (Leff 1970). Even when complete contracts cannot be written or enforced, and there are valuable specific assets at risk, market transactions between independent firms may still be possible through 'obligational contracting' if the parties in question place a high value on their reputation. In industries where this effect is strong, vertical integration need not proceed as far as would otherwise be the case, because long-term relationships between firms substitute for common ownership and acceptance of the same supervisory authority.

The problems of vertical integration

TCA makes it clear that the transacting problems that arise when dealing with independent parties provide an explanation for the internalisation of many transactions, leading to vertical integration. The ability of a firm's managers to use their authority to direct employees (within the limits of their employment contracts) avoids the costs of negotiation and re-negotiation and the risk of losing value in specific assets. However, it should also be noted that internal transactions suffer from their own limitations so that the optimal choice of governance mode depends on balancing the costs and benefits of the alternatives. Williamson (1975, 1986) also extended Coase's analysis on this issue, pointing to some of the limits to internal transactions in the context of vertical integration.

The first of these is the tendency for internal sources of supply to distort procurement decisions. If a supplying division is set up within a firm, the interests of the managers responsible for that division may militate against the use of outside sources of supply, even if they should become more efficient and cost effective. It may also be difficult to make proper comparisons between the cost of purchasing a product and the cost of making it in-house because of the problems and potential arbitrariness involved in allocating overhead costs to individual products. One of the unusual features of the firm/market distinction is that it is often easier to measure the cost of a product produced by someone else and purchased on the market than to measure the cost of producing it in-house.

Even if managers have guaranteed employment there will often be loss of status attaching to association with a 'failed' operation, and they may resist attempts to close down inefficient parts of the firm. There may also be a more general resistance to change stemming from the bureaucratic nature of many organisations, and the horse-trading that takes place as managers form shifting alliances with each other in support of their own 'pet projects'. This weakness of internal organisation is closely related to the 'persistence' phenomenon, whereby existing activities in organisations tend to be continued even in preference to demonstrably superior new projects. It also involves the wasteful expenditure of resources on what Milgrom and Roberts (1992) refer to as 'influence activities' where managers spend their time on office politics, trying to influence the alloca-tion of the firm's resources in their favour.

Another weakness of internal organisation lies in the distortion of communica-tions between managers, who may tend to tell their supervisors or subordinates what they hope to hear, rather than the truth. If information about the firm's operations were easily checked, this tendency could be curbed through internal audit procedures. However, in many cases information is too deeply embedded in the details of operations for supervisors to be able to check its truthfulness at reasonable cost. In that case there are important information asymmetries within the firm, as well as between firms, and they may lead to inefficiencies.

Limitations of the TCA approach

The TCA approach is a flexible framework expressed at a rather abstract level, and not a set of fixed propositions. Its power lies in the fact that it can be interpreted and extended in many different directions in order to explain many different organisational phenomena. At the same time, a number of important criticisms may be noted. Most fundamentally, the central constructs that make up TCA are not directly observable, which raises fundamental problems when trying to carry out empirical research (Godfrey and Hill 1995). Milgrom and Roberts (1992, pp. 33–4) note that transaction costs can often not be identified separately from other categories of cost and that efficiency does not necessarily require that transaction costs be minimised. They also point out that there may be many different efficient solutions to a transactional problem so that the assumption of efficiency may not be a strong enough criterion for prediction. For instance, in a situation of high asset specificity, unified governance is said to be most effi-cient. That basic insight underpins most of the studies carried out using the TCA framework. But its validity hangs on the assumption that there is a significant threat of opportunism. If some method can be found to reduce opportunism then another form of governance could also be efficient.

This last point leads to two further criticisms. The first is that the TCA framework assumes that opportunism is universal when a whole body of literature suggests that it may be avoided. As John (1984) put it, 'refusals to honour agreements and misrepresentation of intentions cannot be taken for granted'. Ghoshal and Moran (1996) go so far as to suggest that the assumption of opportunism, and teaching TCA to students, is bad for business practice because it encourages managers to take opportunism for granted. There are mechanisms, like reputation and prior cooperation, that can reduce opportunism and rational managers will use those mechanisms. There is a very substantial literature on trust, showing that it provides an important 'cement' for many business relationships. It has also been pointed out that in many Asian cultures business transactions are based almost entirely around personal trust, with formal written agreements playing a very limited role (Whitley 1992).

TCA's adherents could argue that the assumption of opportunism is not so strong, and it may be relaxed. However, in that case TCA becomes so flexible that it leads very easily to *ex post* rationalisation. Almost any outcome can be explained in TCA terms after it has been observed, but it is more doubtful whether the prediction could have been made in advance. For instance, if Fisher Body had agreed to build the plant for GM, the decision could have been explained in TCA terms as evidence that GM and Fisher Body managers had found ways to limit the threat of opportunism, and thereby made the specific investments much less vulnerable to hold-up. When Fisher Body did not build the plant, the case is explained by maintaining the assumption of opportunism.

Finally, most economists are comfortable with the assumption that efficiency will generally be achieved in the long run. However, others are not and it should be recognised that TCA depends upon that assumption for its predictive power (though not for its prescriptions).

Illustration   A diversity of applications

A useful way to illustrate the range of issues that have been addressed using transaction cost analysis is to provide diverse examples.

1. Geographical differences in the same industry: power stations and coal mines in the United States

Joskow (1988) examined the relationships between coal mines and coal-burning electricity plants in the continental United States. In the west of the country, the quality and composition of the coal varies a great deal from mine to mine. Hence the power stations that use that coal must be designed specifically for a particular type of coal. There is *physical asset specificity*. In the east of the country, coal is very homogenous. In the west, transport costs for coal are higher than in the east so that coal mines and power stations must be closer together in order to be efficient. There is a greater degree of *site specificity* in the west. The governance structures for the transaction of coal from mines to power stations reflect these differences. In the west there are many 'mine-mouth' power stations where the two facilities are located next door to each other, and these are vertically integrated. Where power stations and coal mines are not vertically integrated, supply contracts are for longer terms and are more complex in the west than in the east. The spot market for coal (classical contracting) is important in the east but not in the west.

Joskow's findings are consistent with TCA in terms of the general pattern of differences between the east and the west. However, it is also instructive to consider why there is not more vertical integration in the west, where long-run contracts are frequently used. Given the described pattern of asset specificity, and the huge expense associated with both power stations and mines, it seems surprising that contracts between independent firms are used at all. The reason given is that coal is not the only source of energy for power stations and the relative cost of different energy sources may fluctuate. Hence the electricity companies might want to switch to a different type of fuel at some time in the future if coal becomes relatively expensive. In TCA terms that means that the degree of asset specificity might become less in future as the value of the power station depends less upon its being used in conjunction with the coal mine. That explanation is satisfying but it also amounts to saying that in many cases asset specificity is too high in the short term for spot markets and short-term contracts but too low in the long term for vertical integration. As the boundaries between 'too high' and 'too low' and between 'short term' and 'long term' are not specified, it is difficult to argue convincingly that TCA would have predicted the observed pattern in advance. Once the pattern is observed it can be seen to have elements consistent with the theory. Whether the theory really passes the test of providing testable predictions in advance of observing the phenomenon is questionable.

2. Differences across similar industries world-wide: tin and aluminium

In the aluminium industry there is almost always vertical integration between the bauxite mines that produce the ore and the refineries that use it to produce the metal itself (Hennart 1988). In the tin industry, mining for tin ore and refining are carried out by independent companies (Hennart 1986). The explanation is essentially the same as that for the east/west differences in the US coal industry. Bauxite varies very significantly in its composition from one mine to another. Hence the plants that process the ore exhibit a high degree of *physical asset specificity*. They cannot function without the ore from their co-specialised mine and the ore from that mine cannot be processed elsewhere without very significant additional expense. Tin ore does not vary very much from one source to another. Neither mines nor processing plants are subject to significant asset specificity. Hence there is no 'small numbers' problem. Mines and processing plants compete for each other's business and transactions are organised on the basis of spot transactions or short-term contracts. Longer-term contracts or vertical integration is not required.

3. The choice between joint ventures and wholly owned subsidiaries

Joint ventures (JVs) are firms that are formed by a contract between two or more parent companies. They are often referred to as 'hybrid' forms of governance because they combine obligational contracting between the parents with unified governance

▶

inside the JV itself. A number of authors, including Hennart (1988, 1991), Erramilli and Rao (1993) and Hu and Chen (1993), have used the TCA framework to explain how firms choose between shared (JV) versus full control (subsidiary) forms of operation. The details of the methods used vary widely, and the chains of reasoning that link the theory with the hypotheses tested are often rather long. However, overall the results suggest that TCA can explain the choice made in many cases.

4. The information content of technology transfers

Davies (1993) used a TCA approach to compare the information content of technology transfers carried out through licensing agreements between independent companies with the information content of in-house internalised transactions. Evidence from machine tool companies in Britain, Germany and the US showed that licensing agreements tended to involve older technology and more limited packages of assistance. Licensed transfers tended to be limited to engineering knowledge, involving the 'one-off' provision of designs and drawings for complete machine tools. Internalised transfers more frequently provided for the transfer of 'team' knowledge involving marketing and management as well as engineering, and of components. Overall, the type of information and assistance provided under licensing agreements involved less important knowledge assets – reducing the risks arising from opportunism – and less physical and human capital specificity. Internalised transfers were used for strategically important knowledge and for more complex knowledge whose transfer required the development of specific skills.

5. Applications in marketing

There have been enough applications of TCA in the marketing field to justify a review in the discipline's leading journal (Rindfleisch and Heide 1997). Topics include: the choice between a direct sales force and manufacturer's representatives (Anderson 1985); manufacturer and distributor commitment to their relationship (Anderson and Weitz 1992); single or multiple vendors in the distribution of semiconductor devices (Dutta and John 1995); outsourcing of the warehousing function (Maltz 1994); perceptions of opportunism, contractual safeguards and the performance of strategic alliances (Parkhe 1993).

The application of TCA in marketing provides an illustration of the framework's flexibility. Most of the studies examined begin with reference to Williamson (1975, 1986) and make use of the same set of concepts – the TCA paradigm. At the same time, however, the relationships among the concepts are often specified in very different ways from those in the original. In particular the assumption of opportunism is often questioned and the threat of such behaviour treated as an endogenous or dependent variable.

References and further reading

Z. Acs and D. Gerlowski, *Managerial Economics and Organization*, New Jersey, Prentice Hall, 1996.

A. Alchian and R. Demsetz, 'Production, Information Costs and Economic Organization', *American Economic Review*, vol. LXII, no. 5, 1972, pp. 777–95.

E. Anderson, 'The Salesperson as Outside Agent or Employee: A Transaction Cost Analysis', *Marketing Science*, vol. 4, Summer 1985, pp. 234–54.

E. Anderson and B. Weitz, 'The Use of Pledges to Build and Sustain Commitment in Distribution Channels', *Journal of Marketing Research*, vol. 29, February 1992, pp. 18–34.

J.S. Bain, *Industrial Organization*, New York, Wiley, 1968.

D. Besanko, D. Dranove and M. Shanley, *Economics of Strategy*, New York, Wiley, 1996.

R.H. Coase, 'The Nature of the Firm', *Economica*, vol. 4, 1937, pp. 386–405.

H. Davies, 'The Information Content of Technology Transfers', *Technovation*, vol. 13, no. 2, 1993, pp. 93–100.

S. Dutta and G. John, 'Combining Lab Experiments and Industry Data in Transaction Cost Analysis: The Case of Competition as a Safeguard', *Journal of Law, Economics and Organization*, vol. 11, no. 1, 1995, pp. 87–111.

M.K. Erramilli and C.P. Rao, 'Service Firms' International Entry Mode Choice: A Modified Transaction-Cost Approach', *Journal of Marketing*, vol. 57, July 1993, pp. 19–38.

S. Ghoshal and P. Moran, 'Bad for Practice: A Critique of the Transaction Cost Theory', *Academy of Management Review*, vol. 21, no. 1, January 1996, pp. 13–48.

P. Godfrey and C. Hill, 'The Problem of Unobservables in Strategic Management Research', *Strategic Management Journal*, vol. 16, no. 7, October 1995, pp. 519–34.

J-F. Hennart, 'The Tin Industry', in M. Casson and Associates, *Multinationals and World Trade*, London, George Allen & Unwin, 1986.

J-F. Hennart, 'A Transaction Costs Theory of Equity Joint Ventures', *Strategic Management Journal*, vol. 9, 1988, pp. 361–74.

J-F. Hennart, 'Transaction Costs Theory of Joint Ventures: An Empirical Study of Japanese Subsidiaries in the United States', *Management Science*, vol. 4, April 1991, pp. 483–97.

M. Hu and H. Chen, 'Foreign Ownership in Chinese Joint Ventures: A Transaction Cost Approach', *Journal of Business Research*, vol. 26, Fall 1993, pp. 149–60.

G. John, 'An Empirical Examination of Some Antecedents of Opportunism in a Marketing Channel', *Journal of Marketing Research*, vol. 21, August 1984, pp. 278–89.

P. Joskow, 'Asset Specificity and the Structure of Vertical Relationships: Empirical Evidence', *Journal of Law, Economics and Organization*, vol. 4, no. 1, 1988, pp. 95–117.

B. Klein, R. Crawford and A. Alchian, 'Vertical Integration, Appropriable Rents and the Competitive Contracting Process', *Journal of Law and Economics*, vol. 21, 1978, pp. 297–326.

F. Knight, *Risk, Uncertainty and Profit*, Boston, Houghton Mifflin, 1921.

A. Leff, 'Contract as a Thing', *American University Law Review*, 1970.

A. Maltz, 'Outsourcing the Warehousing Function: Economic and Strategic Considerations', *Logistics and Transportation Review*, vol. 30, September 1994, pp. 245–65.

S. Masten, J. Meehan and E. Snyder, 'The Costs of Organization', *Journal of Law, Economics and Organization*, vol. 7, Spring 1991, pp. 1–25.

P. Milgrom and J. Roberts, *Economics, Organization and Management*, New Jersey, Prentice Hall, 1992.

K. Monteverde and D. Teece, 'Supplier Switching Costs and Vertical Integration in the Automobile Industry', *Bell Journal of Economics*, vol. 13, Spring 1982, pp. 206–13.

A. Parkhe, 'Strategic Alliance Structuring: A Game Theoretic and Transaction Cost Examination of Interfirm Cooperation', *Academy of Management Journal*, vol. 36, August 1993, pp. 794–829.

A. Rindfleisch and J. Heide, 'Transaction Cost Analysis: Past, Present and Future Applications', *Journal of Marketing*, vol. 61, October 1997, pp. 30–54.

D.H. Robertson, *The Control of Industry*, London, Nisbet, 1923.

R. Whitley, *Business Systems in East Asia: Markets, Firms and Societies*, London, Sage, 1992.

O. Williamson, *Markets and Hierarchies*, New York, Free Press, 1975.

O. Williamson, *The Economic Institutions of Capitalism*, London, Collier Macmillan, 1985.

O. Williamson, *Economic Organization*, Brighton, Wheatsheaf, 1986.

O. Williamson, *The Mechanisms of Governance*, New York, Oxford University Press, 1996.

Self-test questions

1. Give an example of each of the following transactions:

   (a) an infrequent transaction, involving no idiosyncratic investment
   (b) a frequent transaction involving a high level of idiosyncratic investment
   (c) an infrequent transaction involving a high level of idiosyncratic investment
   (d) an infrequent transaction involving some idiosyncratic investment

2. For each of the transactions in Question 1, identify the most appropriate form of governance structure.

3. Give an example for each of the five different types of asset specificity.

4. Which of the following components would you expect a motor-car assembler to produce in-house?

   (a) engines
   (b) electric motors for windows and windscreen wipers
   (c) wheels
   (d) bodies
   (e) light bulbs

Essay questions

Book publishers usually have their books printed by independent firms. Newspaper publishers usually print their paper themselves. Consider how transaction cost analysis might explain that difference.

4 Ownership and control, diversification and mergers

Chapter 3 has examined why firms exist, focusing on the idea that the firm is the super-session of the market, or a set of transactions that are coordinated by managerial authority, within a set of contracts. It has also explained the major factors that determine the extent of vertical integration. In this chapter attention shifts to three related questions:

1. To what extent do firms seek maximum profit when ownership and control are in the hands of different people?
2. What factors determine the extent to which a firm diversifies across different industries?
3. How and why do mergers and take-overs take place?

Do firms really try to maximise profits?

The traditional model of the firm, which underpins our understanding of the market economy, assumes that the aim of the firm is to maximise profits or shareholder value. However, it has been pointed out in Chapter 2 that the assumption of profit maximisation may be unrealistic in a world where ownership and control are in the hands of different groups of people. At the same time, it is possible to identify counter-arguments to suggest that the basic assumption is in fact more realistic than its critics might suggest. This part of the chapter assesses that debate.

Do shareholders always seek maximum profits?

Most of the debate on ownership, control and profit maximisation in the joint stock company assumes that shareholders unambiguously prefer higher profits. In that case the question 'do firms try to maximise profits?' can be re-stated as 'do senior managers behave in ways that are consistent with shareholders' interests?' However, there are situations where a shareholder may not prefer maximum profit, as Kreps (1990, p. 727) and Milgrom and Roberts (1992, p. 40) point out. For instance, if the firm has some degree of market power and a shareholder is also a customer, the shareholder may lose more from being charged higher profit-maximising prices than they gain from the enhanced value of their shareholding. This will be particularly marked if the shareholding in the firm is small but the purchases made from it are large. If a shareholder is also a supplier to a firm, they may prefer that the firm does not use that market power to maximise profits because that may entail bidding down the price paid for the supplies. If the shareholder has a diversified portfolio of shares, maximising the profit made by one firm may reduce the value of the others.

Even if a shareholder faces none of these conflicts, buying nothing from the firm, selling nothing to it and owning shares in no other firms, they may still face a penalty for profit maximisation. If the shareholder consumes a product that is complementary to an input that the firm uses, and the drive for profit leads the firm to force the price of that input downwards, demand for the input from other sources will rise, increasing demand for the complement and forcing the shareholder to pay a higher price for it!

This last example may seem rather far-fetched, given that the effects involved, and the consequent loss, are likely to be quite small. However, it illustrates the central point that, *if a firm can influence prices* and its shareholders are affected by those prices, they may prefer to sacrifice some profit and hence will not seek to maximise.

There is another reason why shareholders may not seek profit maximisation. In the long term, profit maximisation requires maximising the present value of the stream of profits made into the future. However, the valuation of that stream depends upon the relative weighting given to the future by each individual shareholder. If different shareholders have different weightings (some value income in the future more or less than others) they will give different valuations to the alternatives facing the firm and will not be able to agree on which is the maximising alternative.

Both of these conflicts disappear if the firm is a price-taker, operating in a competitive market where it cannot influence prices, and if markets are complete in the sense that a full set of competitive product, financial and insurance markets are in place. In that situation the only connection between the firm's behaviour and shareholders' well-being lies in the profits earned and hence shareholders will want to maximise those. The problem of placing different valuations on the future is also solved as there will be a market-determined 'overall' weighting of the future relative to the present, represented by the interest rate. Rational shareholders will seek to maximise profits using that weighting and those who place more value on income in the future will invest their share of the profits, while those who prefer income immediately can use financial markets to borrow.

In the discussion that follows it is generally assumed that shareholders seek profits, even though there are doubts on that issue. That is the starting point for most economic analysis and it is useful to appreciate that when economists say 'we assume' they do not mean 'we believe this to be true'. An assumption is a working hypothesis or a logical starting point which simplifies the world and allows models yielding predictions to be made. The logic is 'if shareholders do aim to maximise the value of the firm, what are the problems they face when direct control is in the hands of a separate group of managers?'

Links between ownership and control

It has been pointed out in Chapter 2 that 'managerial discretion' models of the firm, like Baumol's revenue-maximiser and Williamson's utility-maximiser, had their inspiration in the pioneering work of Berle and Means (1932) in the United States. Their key finding was that in large public corporations shareholdings were highly dispersed, with large numbers of small shareholders. As that type of shareholder has relatively little invested, they are unlikely to spend much effort monitoring the running of the company. Furthermore, their dispersion would make it difficult for them to coordinate any action against the managers. Berle and Means therefore drew the conclusion that shareholders in such firms would not be able to exert control over the managers. 'Management-controlled' firms were defined as those in which no single shareholder held more than 20 per cent and on that criterion 58 per cent of the assets of America's 200 largest firms were management controlled in 1929. An updating of that calculation for 1963 showed a rising trend, to 85 per cent (Larner 1966).

Clearly, the set of people who own a public corporation is not the same as the set of people who manage it. However, that separation between ownership and control, and the dispersed nature of shareholdings, are not enough to demonstrate that managers are able to run the company in their own interests, without regard to shareholders' objectives, for a number of reasons.

First of all, although shareholders and managers are not the same set of people, there is considerable overlap between the two. In most firms the CEO, the directors and other senior executives own shares in the company. If a large part of their income arises from the return on those shares they will have a powerful incentive to aim for maximum profit. Studies have differed on the extent to which this is the case. Cosh and Hughes (1987) reported that in the United States 33 per cent of executive directors and 21 per cent of all directors had holdings in their own companies worth more than one million pounds, the implication being that they would be motivated towards profit. Certainly, the personal wealth of many high-profile CEOs of major companies arises from their ownership of shares in the firms they manage, the granting of options to purchase stock at predetermined prices and profit-related bonuses. On the other hand, Jensen and Murphy (1990) calculated that for CEOs in the United States the additional personal wealth arising from an increase in shareholder value of $1,000 was only $3.25 which they concluded was not sufficient to align CEOs' interests with those of shareholders. Wherever the balance lies, there is a very important group of individuals who are both shareholders and senior managers, bridging the gap between ownership and control.

The concentration of ownership

Berle and Means classified firms as 'management controlled' if no single shareholder held more than 20 per cent of the voting stock. But the extent to which shareholders can exert control need not depend solely on that figure. Cubbin and Leech (1983) argued that the power of a coalition of the largest shareholders increases as it holds a larger proportion of the shares and as the remaining shares are more widely dispersed across other, smaller, shareholders. In that case it could be possible for a very small group of shareholders, each holding a relatively small proportion of the total stock, to exert effective control. The costs of forming a coalition among a small number of shareholders would not be large and many more firms would therefore be subject to effective shareholder control. Leech and Leahy (1991) applied this idea to a large sample of UK companies and concluded that in 54 per cent of cases a coalition of three shareholders or fewer could potentially wield control. Even more dramatically, they found that the patterns of shareholding were such that in only one case would a coalition need to have more than ten members in order to have control.

The influence of institutional shareholders

The argument that managers do not seek maximum profit is also based in part on the idea that shareholders are not well informed about the activities of the firms they own, and exhibit only minor concern about their performance. They are seen as being disinclined to criticise or displace the incumbent management, provided that a moderate level of dividend is paid.

In so far as shareholders are private individuals, with small shareholdings and limited time to spend monitoring their performance, this is a valid argument. However, ownership of shares is not typically spread across private individuals alone, but is frequently concentrated in the hands of financial institutions like pension funds, investment trusts, insurance companies and other similar organisations. Table 4.1 shows the figures for a number of OECD countries at the end of 1996.

As the figures show, the financial sector holds very significant proportions of corporate equity, especially in the United Kingdom, the United States and Japan. Whether this puts managers under pressure to seek shareholder value depends upon the behaviour of those institutions. It could be argued that they depend

Table 4.1 The ownership of listed corporate equity by category of shareholder – per cent at the end of 1996

	United States	Japan	Germany	France	United Kingdom	Sweden	Australia
Financial sector, of which:	46	42	30	30	68	30	37
Banks	6	15	10	7	1	1	3
Insurance companies and pension funds	28	12	12	9	50	14	25
Investment funds	12	–	8	11	8	15	–
Other financial institutions	1	15	–	3	9	–	9
Non-financial enterprises	–	27	42	19	1	11	11
Public authorities	–	1	4	2	1	8	–
Households	49	20	15	23	21	19	20
Rest of the world	5	11	9	25	9	32	32
Total	100	100	100	100	100	100	100

Source: Thompson (1998).

upon the financial performance of the firms in which they have invested in order to attract funds and to survive and make profits themselves. In that case they will be motivated to employ professional managers to monitor their investments and to use industry analysts (usually employed by their stockbrokers) to scrutinise the performance of the firms in which they have invested. Institutional shareholders are powerful and have the potential to be well informed about the firms in which they own shares. As a result they may exert considerable pressure on managers to aim for maximum profit, removing the discretion they must have if the managerial models are to apply.

The validity of this argument depends upon the actual behaviour of the financial institutions. Cosh and Hughes (1987) found that while institutional shareholders had great potential power, very few of them were prepared to use it. They believed that attempts to intervene in the running of companies they owned would be expensive and not very effective. There may be a number of reasons for that apparent lack of interest. If the financial institutions themselves are under little competitive pressure they may make only limited efforts to monitor and control the firms in which they own shares. A financial institution may become 'locked into' a firm in which it has a major financial stake, being afraid to make public any doubts it has about the firm's policies and performance for fear of seeing a fall in the share price and a weakening of the performance of its own investment portfolio.

The balance of the argument is not completely clear. However, it does appear that a significant change took place from the late 1980s onwards. Liberalisation and de-regulation of the financial services industry led to much greater competition in that sector, which in turn forced the financial institutions to pay much greater attention to the performance of the companies they own (Thompson 1998).

One interesting aspect of the debate over the role of institutional shareholders concerns the differences between the American and British systems, on the one hand, and the Japanese and German on the other. The US and UK systems may be described as 'outsider' or 'market-oriented' systems (Berglof 1990, Thompson 1998). In that type of system institutional shareholders play a limited role in monitoring and influencing the managers of the firms they own. Instead, they simply observe the share price and sell the shares of firms they think are underperforming. In Hirschman's (1970) terminology, they exert pressure by 'exit' rather than 'voice'. That contrasts with the German and Japanese approaches which are 'insider' or 'bank-oriented' systems. In Germany and Japan the banks have 'obligational' contracts with the firms they own. They are not simply concerned at arm's length with the share prices of those firms. Instead they have direct representation on the boards of the companies they own, they buy and sell shares less frequently and they are part of the 'insider' group whose 'voice' controls those firms.

The consensus judgement on the merits of the two approaches has shifted over time with the relative performance of the economies they serve. In the 1960s and 1970s it was often argued that German and Japanese financial institutions took a longer-term view of the companies in which they invested, because of their closer involvement. As a result they were more prepared to support spending on research and development and expensive entry into new markets overseas, which was seen as an advantage. The American and British systems were criticised for encouraging 'short-termism' among senior managers who were required to keep constant vigilance over their share prices which were in turn determined by short-sighted participants in the stock market. However, in the last two decades of the twentieth century both the Japanese and the German 'miracles' ground to a halt. It became clear in Japan that the cosy 'insider' relationships between banks and companies had allowed both sectors to become inefficient and mismanaged, to the point where the Japanese financial sector might easily collapse altogether. The Asian financial crisis of 1997 further emphasised the dangers of 'insider' systems, from Japan to Thailand, South Korea, Indonesia and the Philippines. Comparison with the stellar performance of the US and (to a lesser extent) the UK economy convinced the world that 'outsider' systems based on markets were a superior approach to corporate governance.

The 'market for corporate control'

Shareholders may use 'voice' to exert direct pressure on the management of a company if they believe it to be earning less profit than it could, or they could use 'exit' – selling shares in a company if they think that it is poorly managed. The existence of a market for voting shares – the market for corporate control – therefore provides a source of pressure on managers through the working of share prices.

Share prices are determined fundamentally by the amount that investors are willing to pay for them. For rational profit-seeking investors this will be equal to the present value of future profits. If a company's management is considered by the market to be using the firm's resources to make less than maximum profit, the share price will be lower than it would be if the management were more efficient. The firm and its assets will therefore be under-valued. The company will present an attractive target to 'take-over raiders', who may seek to buy up the undervalued shares, shake up or dispose of the existing management, and use the firm's resources more effectively in order to produce higher profits and a capital gain through an increase in the share price.

This form of discipline may work in two different ways. The most obvious one is where take-overs actually take place and lazy managers are displaced or disciplined by new owners with a greater concern for profits. Alternatively (see Holl 1977) the threat of possible take-over may be enough in itself to act as a disciplinary force. In either case, the ability of managers to exercise discretion over the ways in which the firm's resources are used is severely restricted.

John Thompson, Head of the Financial Affairs Division of the Organization for Economic Co-operation and Development (OECD), has argued that one of the most important structural changes in the world's economy in the 1980s and 1990s has been the emergence of increasingly efficient markets for corporate control which give shareholders a much greater ability to influence the senior managers of publicly held companies (Thompson 1998).

However, as Kreps (1990, p. 725) points out, the effectiveness of this mechanism depends upon whether under-performing firms really are threatened with take-over and whether the senior managers of 'victim' firms suffer enough loss of wealth or prestige to motivate them to avoid it through diligence and effort.

There are a number of factors that may limit the effectiveness of the take-over mechanism as a means of exerting discipline over managers (Shleifer and Vishny 1988). First, there are always information asymmetries so that a firm whose value is perceived by the market to be low may not be badly run at all. It may be well run and facing real difficulties of which the market is not aware. Rational market participants will understand this and be unsure whether a take-over is worthwhile. Second, it should be recognised that take-over will only take place if the 'raider' stands to benefit and this is not as clear as the simple analysis suggests.

In the simple analysis a victim firm is under-valued, relative to the price it would command when properly run. The raider buys it at the low price and makes a large profit when the management is improved. But consider the position of a shareholder in the victim firm. If they know that shares in a firm will be worth £50 after a take-over is successful, they will not be willing to sell their shares for less than that amount. The raider will be forced to offer that amount in order to get control. However, a take-over bid involves significant costs and therefore there will be no profit for the raider, who will therefore not bid for the firm. On this logic the threat of take-overs cannot act as an effective disciplinary mechanism.

The senior management of a raiding firm could benefit from a take-over if they accumulated a holding in the victim firm at lower prices before the take-over bid is made. In that case they could afford to pay other shareholders the full value of their shares and then benefit from the capital appreciation in their own holdings. However, the pre-bid acquisition would have to go unnoticed by the market or the raiders would be unable to purchase at the lower price. That in turn implies that the pre-bid holding would have to be quite small and the post-merger gains would therefore need to be very large in order to compensate for the cost of implementing the take-over.

There are other reasons for suspecting that the effectiveness of the take-over mechanism is limited. The managers of companies at risk of being taken over may use a variety of stratagems to defend themselves (Ricketts 1994, pp. 256–9). They may persuade their shareholders to change the company constitution so that large majority votes are needed for the approval of mergers or changes in the board of directors – *supermajority amendments*. They might issue categories of stock that carry the right to dividends but no voting rights. They might adopt a *poison pill* defence whereby existing shareholders are given the right to sell their shares to the company at high prices after a change in ownership takes place, giving the incumbent an impossible burden if the take-over should succeed. They might agree to a *green-mail* arrangement where the raider is offered a high price for the shares it has already purchased in return for abandoning the bid, or they may award themselves *golden parachutes* in the form of large severance payments following take-over. If the parachutes were very large, they would have the same effect as a poison pill, but their more usual effect would simply be to undermine the incentive properties of take-over.

Taken overall, it is clear that there are limits to the effectiveness of take-over as a mechanism for forcing senior managers to aim for maximum profit. It would be wrong to dismiss it entirely but naïve to presume that it operates with full force.

Managerial labour markets

If shareholder pressure and the market for corporate control do not force senior managers to aim for maximum profit, another possibility is that they are disciplined by managerial labour markets – the arrangements that determine whether they can find jobs and the returns they receive in those jobs (Fama 1980). If top managers' earnings are dependent upon their reputations for effectiveness, and those reputations are determined by their track records, they may be under adequate pressure to perform well. Managers' wages fall when they are associated with failure and rise when they are associated with success. In that case, there is an external pressure on managers to perform and hence they will not shirk.

The difficulty with this idea (Ricketts 1994, p. 239) is that the selection of senior managers is determined by a company's existing senior management. If those managers are not disciplined by some other mechanism to seek out the best interest of the shareholders, there is no reason to assume that they will pick the best performer. When shareholders are unable to observe their abilities, incumbent managers might even prefer to appoint incompetent new colleagues in order to make themselves appear more able.

The idea that external labour markets might exert firm discipline over senior managers is credible if managers are constantly moving from job to job, if they believe that other managers can observe any shirking and will punish them for it because they, in turn, believe that they themselves will be punished if they do not. However, such beliefs would essentially be based on 'thin air' and the proposition is not convincing. A more persuasive argument refers back to the take-over mechanisms examined above. If senior managers are aware that the market contains at least some external observers who are capable of identifying under-performance, and that those observers have an incentive to act on that information by taking the firm over and influencing appointments, then managerial labour markets may discipline managers.

Principal/agent theory

The difficulties that arise in respect of shareholders' ability to exert control over managers may be described as an example of the principal/agent problem. This arises whenever one economic actor (the principal) engages another (the agent) to carry out a task on their behalf in a situation where perfect information is not free and monitoring is costly. As the principal (the shareholders) cannot observe the level of effort that the agent (the manager) puts into the job, there is an incentive for the agent to shirk. The problem is that of *moral hazard*, defined as 'an ex post contracting situation and a source of transaction costs that occurs when one party's actions are imperfectly observable and when the incentives of the parties are imperfectly aligned' (Acs and Gerlowski 1996, p. 446). Moral hazard is a general problem whose solution lies in designing the relationship between principal and agent in a way that aligns their incentives. There are two basic ways with which it may be dealt.

The first approach to solving the moral hazard problem is *monitoring*. The principal spends more time, effort and resources in observing the agent's behaviour and punishing the agent for shirking. As noted in Chapter 3, a major difficulty with that approach is that the principal has limited time available and if the principal hires someone else as the monitor, that person is simply another agent with the same incentive to shirk. In the shareholder/manager situation, the chief executive officer (CEO) may be seen as the monitor hired to control the other managers and workers. The problem that the shareholders then face is how to monitor the monitor. By giving the CEO a share in the residual rights, through profit-related bonuses or share options, the shareholders avoid the difficulty of observing the CEO's effort. Provided that they can observe performance (profit), they can align the CEO's incentives with the objectives of the shareholders.

Ownership of shares and the granting of profit-linked bonuses and options are therefore examples of *incentive contracts*, which are the alternative to monitoring. The threat of take-over or managerial labour markets may act as another form of incentive contract whereby the CEO seeks maximum profit because they will lose their job or suffer reduced pay if they do not perform well. However, questions have been raised above concerning whether the incentives arising in these ways are actually sufficient to motivate CEOs to seek maximum profit.

Profit-maximisers or not?

The sections above have tried to establish whether managers have the discretion to use the resources of the firm in their own interests, or whether they are under sufficient pressure to put the shareholders' interests before their own. The conclusion must be mixed. On the one hand there are a variety of mechanisms that prevent managers from simply doing as they please. Indeed, if they were able to do whatever they like it is unlikely that the market economy would have proven so successful. On the other hand, both theoretical analysis and the evidence makes it unreasonable to believe that managers are tied completely to the service of their shareholders.

Overall, it seems reasonable to conclude that in many large firms the senior managers have significant room for discretion, especially in the short to medium term. However, if they use that discretion to generate excessive slack and to sacrifice significant proportions of the potential profits, there are sufficient sources of discipline to bring retribution in the longer term.

We must doubt the descriptive realism of the profit-maximisation assumption. However, that does nothing to reduce its value as the starting point for positive models of the firm. Nor does it prevent analysts from developing useful prescriptions based on the fundamental logic of the profit-maximising model. If the aim of the firm is to maximise profit, how should it behave?

New directions in the debate on ownership and control: did Berle and Means get it wrong?

Before moving on to examine diversification and mergers it is useful to consider a number of studies that have recently returned the ownership and control debate back to its beginnings. Berle and Means (1932) established a picture of the modern corporation as 'widely held', that is to say having ownership and the right to vote on major issues spread across a large number of shareholders. That image of the large firm has dominated thinking for two generations and focused attention on the issues that arise when ownership is dispersed and control is in the hands of managers. However, increased interest in the question of corporate governance (Shleifer and Vishny 1997) and the experience of the Asian financial crisis have shed doubt on the empirical validity of that image. A recent study by La Porta *et al.* (1999) examined the twenty largest firms in the world's twenty-seven richest economies. First, following Grossman and Hart (1986), they distinguished between the voting rights held by shareholders and their rights to the cash flows generated. They then focused on voting rights and attempted to distinguish between firms that are *widely held*, as in the Berle and Means image, and those that have *ultimate owners* or *controlling shareholders*. In common with Berle and Means's original approach, they used 20 per cent ownership as the cut-off point for defining a corporation as having a controlling shareholder, so that any corporation having a shareholder holding more than 20 per cent of the voting rights is said to have an ultimate owner. However, this analysis went further than Berle and Means by paying careful attention to the patterns of cross-holdings and pyramid structures whereby an ultimate owner may have both *direct voting rights* (through shares registered in their own name) and *indirect voting rights* (through shares held by entities that the ultimate owner controls). The results showed that for the twenty-seven countries as a whole, only 36 per cent of the largest firms were widely held. Thirty per cent were family controlled, 18 per cent were state controlled and the remaining 15 per cent were controlled by other types of ultimate owner, including widely held industrial or financial firms.

While the overall figures cast a general doubt on the conventional wisdom held since Berle and Means (1932), the results for individual countries show very significant variation from place to place. The proportion of widely held firms ranged from 100 per cent in the United Kingdom, 90 per cent in Japan and 80 per cent in the United States down to zero in Argentina and Mexico. Family-controlled firms ranged from 100 per cent in Mexico and 70 per cent in Hong Kong to 5 per cent in Australia and Japan. La Porta *et al.* (1999) suggest that a major reason for these differences lies in the extent to which the law in different countries provides for *anti-director rights*. Such rights are defined as 'high' when: shareholders can mail proxy votes to the firm; shareholders are not required to deposit their shares prior to a General Meeting; proportional representation of minority shareholders is allowed; an oppressed minorities mechanism is in place; less than 10 per cent ownership is needed for a shareholder to be entitled to call an Extraordinary Shareholders' Meeting; shareholders have pre-emptive rights that can only be waived by a vote of the shareholders.

If anti-director rights are high (as in rich common-law countries) there is good legal protection of minority shareholders and hence controlling shareholders will be less worried about being expropriated in case of a take-over. They will therefore be more willing to reduce their voting rights by selling shares. Certainly the data presented by La Porta *et al.* (1999) support that view overall because the proportion of widely held large companies was 48 per cent in countries with 'high' anti-director rights and only 27 per cent where anti-director rights were low. On the other hand, there were very wide variations within the two categories, with no large firms being widely held in Argentina and only 10 per cent and 15 per cent being widely held in Hong Kong and Singapore respectively, despite all three countries having a high level of anti-director rights.

Another interesting feature of these results lies in the relative importance of the family in comparison with financial institutions. While family-controlled firms made up 30 per cent of the large firms examined, only 5 per cent were controlled by widely held financial institutions. Even in the United States, where the Berle and Means image remains most applicable, 20 per cent of large publicly traded firms were family controlled. Furthermore, in these family firms typically there were no other large shareholders having sufficient voting rights to exercise restraint over the family. As La Porta *et al.* (1999, p. 505) conclude: 'Family control of firms appears to be common, significant and typically unchallenged by other equity holders.' This rediscovery of the family firm as a powerful force in most major economies has led to further work in a number of directions. Claessens *et al.* (2000) examine the situation in East Asia, providing results for nearly 3,000 corporations in nine countries. Perhaps unsurprisingly, they also find that family control is extensive, with the largest ten families in Indonesia, the Philippines and Thailand controlling half of the corporate assets in the sample. In Hong Kong and Korea the top ten families control about one-third of the corporate sector.

A major concern in East Asia, and by extension in other economies where family control is substantial, concerns the impact of 'crony capitalism' on the efficiency of the economy and on its development. When a small number of families control such a large part of the economy they have both the means and the motivation to lobby government for preferential treatment like import controls, award of public contracts and government financing, which reduce the efficiency of the economy. They may also inhibit the development of legal structures that protect other shareholders and hence reduce the efficiency of the country's investment allocation mechanisms.

These concerns over 'crony capitalism' are by no means restricted to East Asia because in western Europe as a whole, family control is actually more pronounced than in East Asia. However, as Faccio *et al.* (forthcoming) have shown, the controlling shareholders in East Asia seem to be much more able and willing to use their position to expropriate the corporation's assets. In Europe, family-held firms pay higher dividends than such firms in East Asia, suggesting that European capital markets recognise the danger of expropriation and force firms to issue higher dividends, taking the assets out of the hands of the insiders. In East Asia these mechanisms are weaker, especially in the case of loosely held groups where the linked shareholdings exceed 10 per cent but not 20 per cent. In such groups it is almost impossible to trace related transactions. That gives the controlling shareholders the ability to extract high returns for themselves from projects that yield negative returns for the corporation.

This analysis echoes the original Berle and Means concern, but in a different way. The original finding was that corporations are widely held and that, as a result, the shareholders could lose when the managers expropriated their assets in the form of unnecessary slack, over-large workforces and unnecessary perquisites for themselves. The owner-controlled firm was seen as one in which agency problems were less severe and hence efficiency was more likely to be achieved. In the new view, the Berle and Means stereotype is only typical for the United Kingdom, the United States and Japan because many corporations elsewhere are not widely held. However, these owner/family-controlled firms represent a different type of problem because the insider shareholders may be able to use their position to expropriate the assets of the others. In the better developed legal and financial systems of western Europe this effect seems to be controlled by the law's ability to protect minority shareholders and the market's ability to force insiders to pay dividends to outsiders in compensation for their vulnerability. In countries where the institutional framework is less well developed, shareholders outside the family are much more open to expropriation.

The extent of diversification

In the elementary model of the firm, the business produces a single product. However, virtually all firms in all industries are multi-product and the question is not whether to be diversified, but how far the diversification should be taken. Companies may be diversified along a very narrow spectrum of closely related activities, or they may be 'broad-spectrum diversified' or 'conglomerate', encompassing a range of activities that bear little technological or marketing connection with each other.

There are a number of factors that are important in determining the most efficient degree of diversification.

Economies of scope

Economies of scope are examined in more detail in Chapter 9. The term is used to refer to a situation where it is cheaper to combine two or more product lines in one firm, rather than producing them separately.

The key feature of economies of scope is that they are linked to the existence of inputs that are 'sharable' in the sense that, once purchased or hired for the production of one product, they are also available at little or no additional cost for the production of others. Generators for electric power and the cables and equipment needed to distribute the power are an example as they can be used for different products at the same time. Other examples are factory buildings, human capital like managerial skill or inputs like sheep and cattle which produce joint outputs (mutton and wool, beef and hides). The range of such sharable inputs is quite broad, and could extend as far as marketing skills which can be used for a variety of products, or to the ownership of distribution channels down which a variety of goods could be sent. If such sharable inputs exist there will be economies of scope. Wherever such economies exist it is to be expected that the multi-product firm will be the norm, because any firm that is not producing an appropriate range of products will be at a cost disadvantage relative to those who do.

Economies of scope undoubtedly exist and provide the rationale for diversification in many cases. However, if diversification is to be fully explained in this way, it might be expected that the different businesses involved would share either similar production technologies or similar markets. In fact, Nathanson and Cassano (1982) found that was not the case for many diversified US firms and hence it seems unlikely that the extent of diversification in practice can be fully explained in these terms.

The exploitation of specific assets

A slightly different interpretation of the economies of scope issue concerns the possession and development of specific assets that may be exploitable in a number of different activities, thereby linking different technologies and different markets. Companies may have 'core' skills or 'key capabilities' that provide the foundation for a move into a wider range of activities. Hence there may be economies of scope even if there are no shared technologies or markets in the narrow sense. Penrose (1959) noted that as firms grow, some of their assets are constantly regenerated in changing forms, which allow them to carry out new activities. Prahalad and Bettis (1986) suggested that senior managers may subscribe to a 'dominant general management logic' which allows them (or so they believe) to allocate resources well across a variety of unrelated activities.

One example of a core skill that might lead to diversification concerns research and development activity (R&D). If a firm carries out R&D successfully then it may produce new discoveries in products or processes that can be exploited outside the firm's current range of products and markets. Some of the early empirical evidence (Gort 1969) showed a distinct relationship between the level of R&D in firms and industries and the extent of diversification.

This again raises the issue that was considered in detail in Chapter 3 – the choice between an internalised transaction that takes place within the hierarchy of the firm and a transaction between independent firms, coordinated by contract. If arm's length transactions in knowledge or capabilities were superior to internalised transactions, firms having those capabilities would not become more diversified. Instead, they would sell or license their innovation or capabilities to others. If a technology is easily identified and protected, if it can be cheaply transferred to a licensee, and if competition pushes the licence fee high enough, then licensing will be preferred (Davies 1977, 1993). In that case, the ownership of technological assets will not lead to greater diversification on the part of the innovating firm. On the other hand, if it is expensive to transfer the know-how from one firm to another, and if the technological advantage is difficult to protect, the cost of an arm's length transaction will be high. As a result it will be more profitable to use the technology in-house and diversification will take place.

The general argument here is that diversification is required if a firm has any kind of specialised resource that can be used in a variety of activities at the same time and which cannot be transacted at arm's length. As with economies of scope, it is clear that at least some of the diversification that is observed in practice can be explained in this way. However, the obvious difficulty is that it can be almost impossible to verify with any certainty that some types of resource exist at all, or have real value. Pilkington's clearly expanded into diverse markets and products on the basis of their core skills in glass (Edwards and Townsend 1967). On the other hand, a group of senior managers may deem themselves to possess a particularly effective 'dominant logic' and proceed to diversify in order to use it, when in fact they possess nothing more than an inflated notion of their own abilities.

The reduction of risk and uncertainty

The issues considered above concern diversification into activities that have some connection with the firm's existing operations, either through the structure of costs, the firm's core skills, or its R&D activity. However, with the possible exception of the 'dominant logic', none of these factors is sufficient to explain the existence of the true conglomerate firm composed of a completely disparate set of activities.

One possible explanation for the existence of unrelated conglomerate firms lies in the reduction of risk and uncertainty. If the firm is viewed as a financial asset, then it is easily shown that the risk associated with it can be reduced by grouping together a number of different activities. This can happen in two ways. First, the average risk will be reduced as activities are 'pooled'. Second, risk can be reduced most effectively by combining activities whose returns are negatively correlated with each other. As a result, the diversified firm may be a more attractive prospect to suppliers of capital.

The problem with this argument is that an investor could achieve the same result, or better, by investing in a diversified portfolio of shares, or a unit trust, rather than in a diversified firm. In fact, if investors are rational and dislike risk they will already have done so. Hence a diversified firm will have no additional attraction for investors.

This last proposition is only valid when capital markets are perfect, and investors well informed. Investors might therefore rate the diversification skills of managers with inside information more highly than their own or those of investment managers. Williamson (1985), for instance, has argued that the top managers of multi-divisional conglomerates have access to better and more detailed information on investment opportunities within the firm than does the external capital market.

It might be true that the managers of a diversified firm have advantages over the capital market in respect of their knowledge on how resources should be allocated within the firm. However, as the first part of this chapter and the discussion of vertical integration in Chapter 3 have made clear, they may not use that knowledge to the benefit of the shareholders. Much of the evidence suggests that the managers of diversified firms practise a kind of 'corporate socialism' (Scharfstein 1998), shifting funds towards poorly performing divisions which 'need' them. Many diversified firms tolerate losses for much longer than specialised firms would allow (Berger and Ofek 1995). They over-invest in industries that have poor investment prospects and they under-invest where prospects are good (Lamont 1997). That tendency is particularly marked in firms whose business is spread across a range of sectors that have widely divergent investment prospects (Rajan *et al.* 1998). Berlin (1999) concludes that in diversified firms the internal capital market is not an efficient mechanism for the allocation of resources because their head offices tend to buy the cooperation of the weaker business units by shifting funds in their direction, something that the external capital market would not do.

Trends in diversification and the relationship with firm performance

The sections above have shown that some degree of diversification is necessary for efficiency but that the extent to which it is taken in practice may not be optimal. Palich *et al.* (2000) reviewed more than fifty studies of the diversification–performance linkage and confirmed a curvilinear relationship whereby performance improved as firms shifted from single-business strategies to 'related diversification' but then decreased as they diversified further into unrelated industries.

This section examines how corporate attitudes to diversification have shifted over time, partly in response to changes in the balance of power between managers and shareholders, and partly in response to its perceived performance consequences.

In the 1960s and 1970s companies generally became more diversified. However, while the typical purchaser acquired a firm that was performing better than the average for its industry, the merged firm usually suffered from deteriorating performance (Ravenscraft and Scherer 1987). It also became clear in the 1980s and 1990s that there was a 'diversification discount' whereby stock markets valued a diversified firm at approximately 15 per cent less than the sum of its component parts (Berger and Ofek 1995). It appeared in many cases that diversifying firms had not understood the markets into which they were moving, or their skills were not useful in their new settings.

As might be expected in a relatively efficient market system, stockholders and the market for corporate control responded to the diversification discount by forcing managers to restructure towards greater focus (Berger and Ofek 1997). Firms either divested themselves of earlier diversified acquisitions or they were taken over by corporate raiders who then sold off, spun off or liquidated the less related activities (Kaplan and Weisbach 1992). Stock markets responded favourably to asset sales and divestitures which reduced the degree of diversification (Berlin 1999) and, as a result, the trend towards diversification was reversed (Comment and Jarrell 1995), with the possible exception of the very largest firms in the United States (Montgomery 1994).

The evidence that the diversification of the 1960s and 1970s failed so comprehensively, when viewed with hindsight, naturally raises the question of 'why did it happen in the first place?' Two possible answers offer themselves. The first is that the economy has changed in some way so that diversification was efficient in the earlier period but became less so later. That possibility is supported by the fact that the diversification discount was not apparent in the United States during the first half of the 1970s. As financial markets were considerably less developed and considerably less competitive in the earlier period, it could be argued that internal capital markets did then have advantages over external markets. It was therefore efficient to diversify at that time but became less so as financial markets were de-regulated and liberalised in the 1980s and 1990s. That explanation is plausible, although Berlin (1999) suggests that more concrete evidence is needed before it could be regarded as wholly convincing.

The other explanation for the shift is that diversification was instigated by managers, against the interest of the shareholders, but that over time shareholders increasingly asserted their influence and replaced the diversifying management teams with new teams more intent on serving shareholder interests. Certainly Berger and Ofek (1997) found that firms that had re-focused between 1983 and 1994 were more likely to have replaced their senior managers in the preceding year. Firms whose managers hold higher proportions of the company's stock are usually more focused because in that case the managers are also shareholders and therefore more likely to seek the maximisation of shareholder value (Denis *et al.* 1997).

These alternative explanations for the shift away from conglomerates and back towards focus share a common foundation in the idea that financial markets have become significantly more efficient over the last twenty years. The consequences of the 'Big Bang' in the City of London, de-regulation, liberalisation, globalisation and increased competition extend far beyond the financial sector into the systems that monitor and control the behaviour of senior managers in non-financial corporations.

Mergers and take-overs

Firms may diversify or integrate vertically through two different routes. The first is through *internal development* and the second is through *merger* or *acquisition*. An examination of the forces that lead mergers to take place, and an analysis of their consequences, provide some additional insight into the issues that have been discussed in the earlier sections of this chapter.

Alternative forms of merger

A merger may be defined as the process by which a firm acquires resources that are already organised by another firm. If this process is uncontested, it is referred to as a merger. If the incumbent managers of the 'victim' contest the process, then it is usually referred to as a 'take-over'. In practice the distinction between mergers and take-overs is often blurred. Three types of merger may be distinguished. These are:

1. *Horizontal mergers*, between potential competitors.
2. *Vertical mergers*, between firms at different stages of the production process.
3. *Conglomerate mergers*, between firms in unrelated activities.

Mergers in a perfect world: synergy or the acquisition of market power

The simplest way to begin is to consider the situation where all managers are efficient; the market value of every firm is an accurate reflection of expected future earnings; there is no uncertainty; managers are constrained to act in the interests of shareholders; and every investor uses the same discount rate in the evaluation of future returns.

In this situation, every investor will place the same value on every company and no one will be willing to pay more for a firm than anyone else. Mergers will then only take place if the merged firm has a higher value than the sum of its parts. This could arise for two basic reasons, which are as follows.

Synergy

Synergy is a blanket term covering the general idea that 'two plus two may be greater than four'. In times of merger booms there are often rather vague claims made for the existence of synergistic effects, which amount to wishful thinking or *ex post* rationalisation. Nevertheless the effects could be real and could arise through a number of different mechanisms, many of which have been outlined in Chapter 3 and earlier sections of this chapter.

One source of synergy could be under-exploited economies of scope in production, marketing or distribution. Similarly, if there are under-exploited economies of scale, a merger may allow the combined firm to produce at lower unit cost. One of the most important sources of such scale economies is indivisible resources. If a firm has an indivisible and under-utilised management team, distribution network or set of plant and equipment, it may be able to reduce costs by applying these resources to a larger set of merged activities.

Synergy may also arise if transaction costs are reduced by replacing market transactions with internalised transactions, if there are economies in raising finance, or if the merged firm has enhanced debt capacity. If any of these factors are present, there will be real synergistic effects arising from merger and the value of the merged firm will exceed the value of its pre-merger components.

Increased market power

A horizontal merger, or a vertical merger, may give the combined firm more market power, allowing an element of monopoly profit to be made and enhancing the value of the merged firm above that of its pre-merger components. If restrictive collusive agreements between firms are outlawed, for instance, as under the UK restrictive practices legislation, mergers may take place in order to allow the same collusive arrangement to continue within a single firm. Of course, such mergers might also fall foul of the competition legislation.

In the perfect world described, mergers would only take place if synergy or market power effects really exist. Indeed, in such a perfect world all the mergers that increase the value of the firm will already have taken place so that new mergers will only arise if technologies, markets or institutions change to create hitherto unavailable opportunities. A first possible explanation for merger activity, then, is that some change in the environment has altered the most efficient configuration of the firm in such a way that the integration of previously separate organisations has become more efficient.

Mergers as the transfer of resources to more efficient managers

It has been noted above that if the market for corporate control works efficiently, the value of a firm's shares will reflect the future profits that the firm is expected to earn. If some managers are more efficient than others, companies run by them will have higher expected profits and higher valuations. Conversely, firms run by less competent or X-inefficient managers will have relatively low valuations and relatively low share prices.

In this situation a strong management team will place a higher value than the market on the assets of a firm being run by a poor management team, the presumption being that the stronger team would be able to use the same assets to make a higher level of profit. As a result, the market for corporate control will ensure that mergers are a means by which the economy's resources are concentrated in the hands of more efficient managers (Manne 1965). More efficient managers scan the market for less efficiently run firms which may be taken over, to the benefit of the shareholders.

In this view, mergers are an important mechanism for the improvement of efficiency. However, the limitations of the market for corporate control have been examined above and the implied improvement in post-merger performance is difficult to find empirically, as explained below.

Mergers as a result of stock market manipulation

In the absence of well-informed investors it is possible that mergers could take place as part of a ploy by merger promoters. In the early American merger booms, for instance, the practice of 'stock watering' was common. That involved a merger promoter planting rumours that there would be substantial gains to be had from a merger. If the rumours were believed, investors would place an unrealistically high price on the stock of a merged firm, at least until the market recognised the fallacy, by which time the merger promoter had realised a substantial profit and sold any holdings. Koutsoyannis (1982, p. 244) outlines a more sophisticated version of this technique, known as 'bootstrapping'. If a firm has a high price/earnings (P/E) ratio and acquires a firm with a lower P/E ratio by swapping shares, then if investors can be persuaded that the combined operation should be valued at the higher ratio, the share price of the combined firm will rise. It is likely, of course, that the acquired firm had a lower P/E ratio because it had more limited prospects and that eventually the higher P/E ratio will be seen by the market to have been unrealistic. However, in the short term, substantial speculative profits could be made.

Mergers as a result of valuation discrepancies

Discrepancies in valuation may arise because managers have different levels of ability and better managers value the same set of assets more highly. However, differences in the valuation of the same firm by different investors could arise in other ways. In times of economic disturbance, for instance, with rapid technological progress, shifting demand patterns and widely fluctuating share prices, there will often be genuine opportunities to exploit new synergies or sources of market power. However, in such uncertain conditions, different groups of investors may also develop different expectations about the value of the same business. Hence mergers may take place for that reason, independently of poor managers, synergies or market power. Gort (1969) suggested that this effect could account for the existence of merger 'booms'. In periods of enhanced uncertainty valuation discrepancies emerge more often and merger activity tends to be concentrated in such periods.

The performance consequences of mergers

If mergers take place in order to exploit new opportunities for synergy, to increase market power, or to strengthen management, it should be expected that the performance of merged firms will improve. However, the empirical evidence provides very limited support for that proposition. In the United States more than 35,000 corporate acquisitions were completed between 1976 and 1990 (Jensen 1993) without any clear pattern of performance improvement emerging. In some cases companies did perform better and Healy *et al.* (1992) found improvements in productivity and cash flows in a sample of the fifty largest US mergers. However, if a general pattern is to be found it is that acquisitions have a neutral to negative effect on the shareholder value of acquirors (Bradley *et al.* 1988, Berkovitch and Narayan 1993). In many cases the shareholders of the acquired firm do gain, because the 'raider' pays a premium over the market price for the 'victim'. However, those gains are not part of an overall increase in the value of the company, simply a shift in wealth from the shareholders of the acquiring firm to the shareholders of the so-called 'victim'.

These results for the United States echo earlier studies in the United Kingdom. Singh (1971) found that at least half of the firms involved in a sample of British mergers experienced decreases in profitability after the merger. Newbould (1970) showed that in many cases firms considering a merger carried out little or no analysis of their 'victim' in the pre-merger stage, and only about half of the studies even attempted to secure synergistic gains post-merger. On balance there is little evidence that mergers consistently lead to significant improvements in corporate performance.

Are mergers really for managers?

If the shareholders of the acquiring firm do not gain from a merger it is natural to consider whether the managers gain and whether mergers are another example of managerial discretion. It has been noted above that a conglomerate merger may reduce the level of risk, but that it is a relatively inefficient way of doing so for an investor, who could simply buy a more highly diversified portfolio of shares. For the managers, however, who are restricted to working in one firm at a time, the risk attached to their employment arises from the volatility of that single firm's activities. From their point of view, risk reduction through in-house diversification may be very attractive, providing for a quieter life. Mergers may also take place because firm size, or growth, is an important element in the managers' objective function, giving them status, prestige and higher benefits. In that case, it is the needs and interests of managers that determine merger activity, not those of the shareholders or the economy as a whole.

This idea that mergers are for managers has been taken further by Roll (1986) and Hayward and Hambrick (1997). They argue that many mergers take place because the CEOs of the acquiring companies suffer from *hubris*, which may be defined as 'exaggerated pride or self-confidence, often resulting in retribution'. Furthermore, because they exaggerate their own ability to improve the performance of the acquired companies, such CEOs tend to pay too much for the companies they buy and hence actually cause the poor performance that so often follows. Hayward and Hambrick (1997) test a model in which CEOs' hubris is increased by three factors: the recent success of the organisation they head; positive media coverage of the CEO; and the CEO's self-importance as measured by the size of the compensation package relative to other top executives. Each of these factors increases the premium paid for an acquired company, defined as the ratio of the price offered to the pre-bid price of the firm. That premium is then negatively related to the performance of the merged firm, post acquisition. Statistical tests of the model support all of the implied hypotheses. The premiums paid were higher when the acquiring firm had performed well recently, when the CEO had been praised by the media, and when the CEO was very highly paid relative to other executives. Higher premiums were also associated with lower shareholder returns in the period following the merger.

Clearly, the Hayward and Hambrick (1997) study points to significant managerial discretion in the acquisition process and links back to the discussion above on ownership and control. Some of the more detailed results are also interesting in that context. For instance, the study also tried to measure the extent to which the board of directors exerted vigilance over the CEO, using proxy variables. If the CEO was chairman of the board, that was interpreted as indicating a lower level of board vigilance, as was a higher proportion of internal board members. Both of those variables had a powerful 'interaction effect' on the size of the premiums paid. In other words, the positive effect of CEO hubris on acquisition premiums was stronger when the board of directors exerted less vigilance and weaker when the board had more control.

| Illustration 1 | ## The impact of hostile take-overs on managerial turnover in the United Kingdom |

One of the mechanisms that may reduce managerial discretion and force top executives to seek maximum profits is the hostile take-over. A number of analysts have argued that while friendly take-overs are usually motivated by perceived synergies between the merging companies, hostile take-overs (those that are opposed by the incumbent management) are motivated by under-performance and followed by replacement of the poorly performing managers and restructuring of the firm's assets. Dahya and Powell (1998) examined this issue using a sample of ninety-two successful take-overs in the United Kingdom, thirty-eight of which were classified as 'hostile'. The results showed that target firms as a whole reported negative growth in profitability in the twelve months preceding the announcement of the bid. Those firms that were subjected to hostile take-overs reported the most dramatic decline in profitability, at 22 per cent over the preceding twelve months, compared with 13 per cent for the firms involved in friendly take-overs. The hypothesis that firms subject to hostile take-overs have been performing badly (and worse than those in friendly take-overs) is therefore supported. For the sample as a whole, 47 per cent experienced a change in the top executive category following the take-over bid compared with 16.5 per cent and 17.5 per cent three years and two years before the bid. Interestingly enough, 26 per cent saw top executive departures in the year preceding the bid, which is significantly more than the preceding years but significantly less than after the take-overs took place. It would appear that signs of trouble and the possibility of a bid lead some top executives to leave before the take-over actually materialises. For the firms involved in hostile take-overs the proportions that experienced top executive departures in the year before the bid and in the year after the take-over were much higher than for the firms involved in friendly take-overs.

Overall, these results show that hostile take-overs do involve firms that are under-performing due to poor management and they are accompanied by a relatively high degree of 'top management disciplining'. If that interpretation is correct, it suggests that the hostile take-over mechanism is an effective means by which management teams are changed and redirected towards the search for shareholder value.

| Illustration 2 | ## Incumbent British insiders resist US-style pressure for change in Hong Kong, but for how long? |

The Jardine group of companies has its origins in one of the British 'hongs' – major trading companies established in Hong Kong in the nineteenth century. Control of the company, which was established by William Jardine, a Scot, passed into the hands of the Keswick family in 1874. Having built the original business and profits around trade (most notoriously in opium) the company grew to become a well-respected pillar of the Hong Kong colonial establishment. Its generally upper-class British managers were known as 'Jardine Johnnies', newly recruited management trainees as 'cadets' and the company's place of influence in business, politics and expatriate social life was assured. By the 1970s the firm had become a major conglomerate whose activities included supermarkets, prestigious hotels, property,

▶

distribution franchises and financial services and it enjoyed a reputation as a well-run company with a solid portfolio of valuable assets.

This picture of corporate strength began to change in the 1980s. In the first year of that decade local tycoon Y-K. Pao was able to seize control of Wharf Holdings, a major Jardine company. Shortly afterwards, Hong Kong 'Superman' Li Ka-shing, noted for the brilliance of his deal-making, bought a minority share in Jardine Matheson, perhaps as part of a take-over attempt, and then sold it back to the company at a higher price in what amounted to a 'green-mail' arrangement.

Faced with these threats to their control, and a further 'attack' from local tycoons, the Jardine management, dominated by the Keswick family, took a number of steps. First, they moved the domicile of the company to Bermuda where the authorities obligingly passed 'one of the most astonishing pieces of companies legislation ever written in a British legal jurisdiction' (Pritchard 2000). The Jardine Matheson Holdings Consolidation and Amendment Act 1988 contained a number of provisions designed to block a hostile take-over, including the 'chain principle' that forces a bidder for a Jardine subsidiary to bid for the rest of the group also.

Second, the Jardine management put in place a cross-shareholding structure which effectively sealed the Keswick family's control. Under the cross-shareholding arrangement the company is organised around two major entities – Jardine Matheson Holdings (JMH) and Jardine Strategic Holdings (JSH). JMH owns 61 per cent of JSH while JSH owns 40 per cent of JMH. The Keswick family and the Weatherall family are estimated to hold around 5 per cent each (Pritchard 2000) while a management remuneration trust, with trustees appointed by the company, holds a similar amount, and stock options allocated to staff carry voting rights. Under this arrangement, resolutions supported by board members are bound to succeed, and those put forward by minority shareholders are bound to fail.

A third step to protect the company from take-over was taken in 1994/5 when the group de-listed in Hong Kong in order to ensure that it would not be subject to the city's take-over code after the hand-over to China in 1997.

While the Jardine management was constructing these defences against a hostile take-over, the business performance of the group was increasingly poor. Alone among the major corporations in Hong Kong, the company failed to make any strategic alliances with powerful interests from the Chinese mainland. Indeed, Henry Keswick described the Chinese regime to the British Parliament as 'Marxist–Leninist, thuggish, oppressive'. In an era when huge corporate growth and profits were to be had in Hong Kong port operations, telecommunications and residential property, the group took no advantage of those opportunities. An expansion into Asia was disastrously timed, coming just before the crisis in 1997, and a series of acquisitions – property in Britain, stock-broking in the United States, sugar in Hawaii, cars in Arabia (van der Kamp 2000) – proved to have been poor decisions.

As a result of this poor performance, the share price languished at a level in mid-2000 below that of 1973. With a sum-of-the-parts valuation as high as US$40 billion, but a market value of only US$11 billion, the group clearly represented a poor reward to shareholders and a potential opportunity for anyone who found the key to unlocking the potential value. This led to a dramatic sequence of events in 2000. In March of that year Alasdair Morrison, group managing director and 'taipan', was ousted, supposedly at one hour's notice. The reason for that coup against a 'Jardine Johnny' of almost thirty years' standing was apparently that he had challenged the authority of the Keswick family by suggesting an unravelling of the cross-shareholding operation (Porter 2000). Morrison was replaced as taipan by Percy Weatherall, Henry Keswick's nephew, whose appointment had been regarded as unlikely just a few months earlier on the grounds that it would be an 'unacceptable throwback to the days of nepotism' (Pritchard 2000).

While the hold of the controlling insiders seemed to be as firm as ever, the challenge to them began to gain pace. An American investor, Brandes Investment Partners of San Diego, led by managing partner Brent Woods and owning 8 per cent of JMH and 2 per cent of JSH, put six resolutions to the boards calling for the dissolution of the cross-holding. As anticipated, those resolutions were rejected, with a 75.7 per cent majority. Brandes represented 80 to 90 per cent of the independent shareholders and Woods made the case that such shareholders had no voice in decision-making and were unable to receive full value for their shares.

Although the insiders comfortably won the vote in June 2000 there were a number of signs that their position was becoming exposed. It was argued by Woods that Jardine's overlapping directors were placing themselves in a difficult personal position, practically and legally, because of the potential conflict of interest and because they were effectively voting for themselves. It has been suggested that directors of both JMH and JSH could be personally vulnerable to class-action law suits brought by shareholders for breach of fiduciary duty and that action might be brought in the United States where JMH has American Depositary Receipt shares. In addition to the pressure being brought to bear by Brandes, the opposition to Jardine's management has been joined by Brierley Investments of Singapore, whose managing director Greg Terry was a former Jardine's director involved in crafting the legal defences and hence is well informed about any possible weaknesses they might have.

In the face of this pressure, a number of the 'insider' directors were said to be wavering, either from fear of their own position or because they no longer felt able to support the anachronistic governance structure of the company. A number of well-known investment 'gurus', including Mark Mobius of Templeton Investments, began taking an interest in the issue and in the background Li Ka-shing remained a quiet observer.

It was not clear in the summer of 2000 whether the Jardine insiders would lose their grip on the company. However, the case is a useful illustration of the way in which managers owning relatively small proportions of a company can ignore shareholder value for a significant period of time by crafting safeguards for themselves. At the same time it also shows how the resulting unrealised opportunity for profit leads to very powerful long-term pressures, tending to force shareholder value back into the forefront of managers' minds.

Another fascinating aspect of the case concerns the strategy being followed by Li Ka-shing. The most obvious interpretation of his position is that he will return to make another attack on the company if its defences begin to unravel. On the other hand, some observers of the Hong Kong business scene note that Jardine represents the only competition to Li's companies in a number of fields. As Hong Kong legislators become more concerned about the high degree of monopoly power that is being exercised over some market sectors, it may suit Mr Li to have at least some competition, especially one whose senior managers are more focused on defending themselves against merger than on competing effectively.

References and further reading

Z. Acs and D. Gerlowski, *Managerial Economics and Organization*, New Jersey, Prentice Hall, 1996.

P. Berger and E. Ofek, 'Diversification's Effect on Firm Value', *Journal of Financial Economics*, vol. 37, 1995, pp. 39–65.

P. Berger and E. Ofek, 'Bustup Takeovers of Value-destroying Diversified Firms', *Journal of Finance*, vol. 51, September 1996, pp. 1175–200.

P. Berger and E. Ofek, 'Causes and Effects of Corporate Re-focusing Programs', Working Paper, New York University, August 1997.

E. Berglof, 'Capital Structure as a Mechanism of Control: A Comparison of Financial Systems', in M. Aoki *et al.* (eds) *The Firm as a Nexus of Treaties*, New York, Sage, 1990.

E. Berkovitch and M. Narayan, 'Motives for Take-overs: An Empirical Investigation', *Journal of Financial and Quantitative Analysis*, vol. 28, 1993, pp. 347–62.

A. Berle and G. Means, *The Modern Corporation and Private Property*, New York, Harcourt, Brace and World, 1932 (rev. edn 1967).

M. Berlin, 'Jack of All Trades? Product Diversification in Nonfinancial Firms', *Business Review – Federal Reserve Bank of Philadelphia*, May/June 1999, pp. 15–29.

S. Bhagat, A. Shleifer and R. Vishny, 'Hostile Take-overs in the 1980s: The Return to Corporate Specialization', *Brookings Papers on Economic Activity: Microeconomics*, 1990, pp. 1–72.

A. Bhide, 'Reversing Corporate Diversification', *Journal of Applied Corporate Finance*, vol. 3, 1990, pp. 70–81.

S. Claessens, S. Djankov and L. Lang, 'The Separation of Ownership and Control in East Asian Corporations', *Journal of Financial Economics*, October 2000.

R. Comment and G. Jarrell, 'Corporate Focus and Stock Returns', *Journal of Financial Economics*, vol. 37, 1995, pp. 67–87.

A. Cosh and A. Hughes, 'The Anatomy of Corporate Control: Directors, Shareholders and Executive Remuneration in Giant US and UK Corporations', *Cambridge Journal of Economics*, vol. 11, 1987, pp. 285–313.

J. Cubbin and D. Leech, 'The Effect of Shareholding Dispersion on the Degree of Control of British Companies: Theory and Measurement', *Economic Journal*, vol. 93, no. 2, 1983, pp. 351–69.

J. Dahya and R. Powell, 'Ownership, Managerial Turnover and Take-overs: Further UK Evidence on the Market for Corporate Control', *Multinational Finance Journal*, March 1988, pp. 63–85.

H. Davies, 'Technology Transfer Through Commercial Transactions', *Journal of Industrial Economics*, vol. 26, 1977, pp. 161–75.

H. Davies, 'The Information Content of Technology Transfers: A Transactions Cost Analysis of the Machine Tool Industry', *Technovation*, vol. 13, No. 2, March 1993, pp. 99–107.

D. Denis, D. Denis and A. Sarin,' 'Agency Problems, Equity Ownership and Corporate Diversification', *Journal of Finance*, vol. 52, March 1997, pp. 1350–60.

R. Edwards and H. Townsend, *Business Enterprise*, London, Macmillan, 1967.

M. Faccio, L. Lang and L. Young, 'Dividends and Expropriation', *American Economic Review*, forthcoming, 2001.

E. Fama, 'Agency Problems and the Theory of the Firm', *Journal of Political Economy*, vol. 88, 1980, pp. 288–307.

R. Fox, 'Agency Theory: A New Perspective', *Management Accounting*, 1984.

M. Gort, 'An Economic Disturbance Theory of Mergers', *Quarterly Journal of Economics*, vol. 83, November 1969, pp. 624–42.

S. Grossman and O. Hart, 'One Share – One Vote and the Market for Corporate Control', *Journal of Financial Economics*, vol. 20, 1986, pp. 175–202.

M. Hayward and D. Hambrick, 'Explaining the Premium Paid for Large Acquisitions: Evidence of CEO Hubris', *Administrative Science Quarterly*, vol. 42, no. 1, March 1997, pp. 103–27.

P. Healy, K. Palepu and R. Ruback, 'Does Corporate Performance Improve After Mergers?', *Journal of Financial Economics*, vol. 31, no. 2, April 1992, pp. 135–77.

A. Hirschman, *Exit, Voice and Loyalty: Responses to Decline in Firms, Organizations and States*, Cambridge, MA, Harvard University Press, 1970.

P. Holl, 'Control Type and the Market for Corporate Control in Large US Corporations', *Journal of Industrial Economics*, vol. 23, no. 4, 1977, pp. 257–72.

M. Jensen, 'The Modern Industrial Revolution, Exit and the Failure of Internal Control Systems', *Journal of Finance*, vol. 48, 1993, pp. 53–80.

M. Jensen and K. Murphy, 'CEO Incentives', *Harvard Business Review*, vol. 68, no. 3, 1990.

S. Kaplan and M. Weisbach, 'The Success of Acquisitions: Evidence from Divestitures', *Journal of Finance*, vol. 47, March 1992, pp. 107–38.

J. Kose and E. Ofek, 'Asset Sales and Increase in Focus', *Journal of Financial Economics*, vol. 37, 1995, pp. 105–26

A. Koutsoyannis, *Non-price Decisions*, London, Macmillan, 1982.

D. Kreps, *A Course in Micro-economic Theory*, Princeton, Princeton University Press, 1990.

R. La Porta, F. Lopez-de-Silanes and A. Shleifer, 'Corporate Ownership Around the World', *Journal of Finance*, vol. 54, no. 2, April 1999, pp. 471–517.

O. Lamont, 'Cash Flow and Investment: Evidence from Internal Capital Markets', *Journal of Finance*, vol. 52, March 1997, pp. 83–109.

R. Larner, 'Ownership and Control in the 200 Largest Non-financial Corporations, 1929 and 1963', *American Economic Review*, vol. 56, 1966, p. 777.

D. Leech and J. Leahy, 'Ownership Structure, Control Type Classifications and the Performance of Large British Companies', *Economic Journal*, vol. 101, no. 409, 1991, pp. 1418–37.

W. Lewellen, 'A Pure Financial Rationale for the Conglomerate Merger', *Journal of Finance, Papers and Proceedings*, vol. 26, 1971, pp. 521–37.

H. Manne, 'Mergers and the Market for Corporate Control', *Journal of Political Economy*, vol. 73, April 1965, pp. 110–20.

P. Milgrom and J. Roberts, *Economics, Organization and Management*, New Jersey, Prentice Hall, 1992.

C. Montgomery, 'Corporate Diversification', *Journal of Economic Perspectives*, vol. 8, Summer 1994, pp. 163–78.

D. Nathanson and J. Cassano, 'What Happens to Profits When a Company Diversifies?', *Wharton Magazine*, Summer 1982, pp. 19–26.

G. Newbould, *Management and Merger Activity*, Liverpool, Guthstead, 1970.

L. Palich, L. Cardinal and C. Miller, 'Curvilinearity in the Diversification–Performance Linkage: An Examination Over Three Decades of Research', *Strategic Management Journal*, February 2000, pp. 155–74.

E. Penrose, *The Theory of the Growth of the Firm*, Oxford, Blackwell, 1959.

B. Porter, 'Jardine's Taipan Removed "After Challenging the Keswick Family" ', *South China Morning Post*, 23 March 2000.

C. Prahalad and R. Bettis, 'The Dominant Logic: A New Linkage Between Diversity and Performance', *Strategic Management Journal*, vol. 7, 1986, pp. 485–501.

S. Pritchard, 'Jardine's Chief May Find Hong Uncomfortably Exposed', *South China Morning Post*, 1 March 2000.

S. Pritchard, 'Venerable Hong Has Rarely Looked Cheaper', *South China Morning Post*, 24 March 2000.

S. Pritchard, 'Last Lair of a Taipan', *South China Morning Post*, 16 May 2000.

R. Rajan, H. Servaes and L. Zingales, 'The Cost of Diversity: The Diversification Discount and Inefficient Investment', Working Paper, University of Chicago, June 1998.

D. Ravenscraft and F. Scherer, *Mergers, Sell-offs and Economic Efficiency*, Brookings Institution, Washington DC, 1987.

M. Ricketts, *The Economics of Business Enterprise*, 2nd edn, Hemel Hempstead, Wheatsheaf, 1994.

R. Roll, 'The Hubris Hypothesis of Corporate Take-overs', *Journal of Business*, vol. 59, 1986, pp. 197–216.

D. Scharfstein, 'The Dark Side of Internal Capital Markets II: Evidence From Diversified Conglomerates', Working Paper 6532, National Bureau of Economic Research, January 1998.

A. Shleifer and R. Vishny, 'Value Maximization and the Acquisition Process', *Journal of Economic Perspectives*, vol. 2, no. 1, 1988, pp. 7–20.

A. Shleifer and R. Vishny, 'Take-overs in the '60s and '80s: Evidence and Implications', *Strategic Management Journal*, vol. 12, 1991, pp. 51–9.

A. Shleifer and R. Vishny, 'A Survey of Corporate Governance', *Journal of Finance*, vol. 52, 1997, pp. 737–83.

H-H. Shin and R. Stulz, 'Are Internal Capital Markets Efficient?', *Quarterly Journal of Economics*, vol. 112, May 1998, pp. 531–52.

A. Singh, *Takeovers*, Cambridge, Cambridge University Press, 1971.

J.K. Thompson, 'Shareholder Value and the Market in Corporate Control in OECD Countries', *Financial Market Trends*, no. 69, February 1998, pp. 15–38.

J. van der Kamp, 'Jardines Learns An Old Trick', *South China Morning Post*, 7 August 2000.

O. Williamson, *Economic Organization*, Brighton, Wheatsheaf, 1985.

Self-test questions

1. Explain whether each of the following will make firms *more likely* or *less likely* to adopt profit maximisation as their objective.

   (a) an anti-trust policy which forbids take-overs
   (b) powerful, well-informed shareholders
   (c) an efficient stock market
   (d) oligopolistic market conditions
   (e) stock option schemes for managers

2. Give *two* reasons that a shareholder might prefer lower profits to higher profits.

3. Describe the difference between an 'outsider' or 'market-based' financial system and an 'insider' system.

4. List *three* characteristics of a company that may lead it to pay a premium when it takes over another company.

Essay question

Discuss the view that the liberalisation of the financial sector has significantly reduced managerial discretion and improved the effectiveness of the market for corporate control.

Section 3:

Marketing

1

WHAT DO MARKETERS DO?

Objectives

After reading this chapter you should be able to:

- Describe the main roles marketers have
- Explain the responsibilities of various types of marketing manager
- Explain the core concepts of marketing
- Explain how marketing activities fit in with other business disciplines
- Describe the development of the marketing concept.

INTRODUCTION

This chapter is an introduction to the basic concepts of marketing, seen in terms of the roles that marketers carry out in their day-to-day jobs. Although marketers have many different job titles, what they have in common is the same orientation towards running the organisation; marketing is concerned with ensuring the closest possible fit between what the organisation does and what its customers need and want.

VIDEO CASE
www.pearsoned.co.uk/blythe

Electrolux

Electrolux is a long-established Swedish electrical goods manufacturer. The company prides itself on producing innovative products based on finding solutions for consumers. Often the company finds itself producing items that people were not aware they needed, but it does not seek to innovate for innovation's sake.

Understanding customers is therefore paramount for Electrolux. Aware that customers are the driving force of everything the company does, Electrolux know that they will only succeed in a cluttered market if they are able to offer real advantages that other manufacturers cannot match. Company representatives observe how people relate to their appliances and are aware of macro-trends in the market – for example, the move towards open-plan kitchen and dining areas, so that appliances are on show for guests and family.

Monitoring what competitors are doing is also important. The company watches what all the main competitors are doing, not for the purpose of copying them, but in order to find gaps in the market – areas where competitors are not meeting customer need.

Hans Stråbirg, President of the Electrolux Group

Watch the video clip, then try to answer the following questions. The answers are on the companion website.

Questions

1 How does Electrolux manage exchange?

2 What is the role of customer need in the Electrolux strategy?

3 How would a brand manager for Electrolux try to go about his or her job?

ABOUT MARKETING

Marketing is the term given to those activities which occur at the interface between the organisation and its customers. It comes from the original concept of a market-place, where buyers and sellers would come together to conduct transactions (or exchanges) for their mutual benefit. The aim of marketing as a discipline is to ensure that customers will conduct exchanges with the marketer's organisation rather than with the other 'stallholders'. To do this effectively, marketers must provide those customers with what they want to buy, at prices which represent value for money.

This basic concept of managing exchange leads us on to the most important concept in marketing, that of customer centrality. Marketing, above all else, uses the customer (who is often also the consumer) and his or her needs as the starting point for all decisions. Of all the building blocks of marketing, in both theory and practice, this is far and away the most important: it is also often difficult to do because it involves thinking like someone else.

The two most widely used definitions of marketing are these:

Marketing is the management process which identifies, anticipates, and supplies customer requirements efficiently and profitably. (UK Chartered Institute of Marketing)

Marketing is the process of planning and executing the conception, pricing, promotion and distribution of ideas, goods and services to create exchange and satisfy individual and organisational objectives. (American Marketing Association 2004)

Both of these definitions have been criticised. The Chartered Institute of Marketing (CIM) definition has been criticised because it takes profit as being the only outcome of marketing, whereas marketing approaches and techniques are widely used by organisations such as charities and government departments that do not have profit as their goal. The American Marketing Association (AMA) definition has also been criticised for failing to take account of the increasing role of marketing in a broader social context, and for appearing to regard consumers as being passive in the process. The same criticism could equally be applied to the CIM definition. Interestingly, neither definition includes the word 'consumer'. This may be because there are many customers who buy the product, but do not themselves consume it (for example, a grocery supermarket buyer might buy thousands of cans of beans, but dislike beans himself). Equally, someone can be a consumer without actually making the buying decision – an example would be a child whose parents make most of the decisions about food, clothing, entertainment and so forth on behalf of the child.

To the non-marketer, marketing often carries negative connotations; there is a popular view that marketing is about persuading people to buy things they do not want, or about cheating people. In fact, marketing practitioners have the responsibility for ensuring that the customer has to come first in the firm's thinking, whereas other professionals might be more concerned with getting the balance sheet to look right or getting the production line running smoothly. Marketers are well aware that the average customer will not keep coming back to a firm that does not provide good products and services at an acceptable price, and without customers there is no business.

Competition in many markets is fierce. If there is room for four companies in a given market, there will be five companies, each trying to maximise their market share; the customer is king in that situation, and firms that ignore the customer's needs will go out of business. Marketers therefore focus their attention entirely on the customer, and put the customer at the centre of the business.

THE DEVELOPMENT OF THE MARKETING CONCEPT

The marketing concept is a fairly recent one, and has been preceded by other business philosophies. These philosophies have not necessarily come about in the straight progression implied by the following section: although at different times there may have been a general way in which business was conducted, there have certainly been considerable overlaps between the different philosophies, and many firms have not been part of this general trend.

Production orientation

During the nineteenth century it was often thought that people would buy anything, provided it was cheap enough. This belief had some truth in it, since the invention of the steam engine allowed very much cheaper mass-produced items to be made. If an item was on sale at around one-tenth the price of the hand-made equivalent, most customers were prepared to accept poorer quality or an article that didn't exactly fit their needs. The prevailing attitude among manufacturers was that getting production right was all that mattered; this is called production orientation. This paradigm usually prevails in market conditions under which demand greatly exceeds supply, and is therefore somewhat rare in the twenty-first century (although it does exist in some markets, for example in some Communist countries).

With rising affluence people are not prepared to accept standardised products, and global markets allow manufacturers to reap the benefits of mass production despite providing more specialised products; therefore the extra cost of having something that fits one's needs more exactly is not high enough to make much difference.

Product orientation

Because different people have different needs some manufacturers thought that an ideal product could be made, one that all (or most) customers would want. Engineers and designers developed comprehensively equipped products, with more and 'better' features, in an attempt to please everybody. This philosophy is known as product orientation.

Product orientation tends to lead to ever-more complex products at ever-increasing prices; customers are being asked to pay for features that they may not need, or that may even be regarded as drawbacks.

Sales orientation

As manufacturing capacity increases, supply will tend to outstrip demand. In this scenario, some manufacturers take the view that a 'born salesman' can sell anything to anybody and therefore enough salesmen could get rid of the surplus products, provided they are determined enough and don't take no for an answer. This is called sales orientation, and relies on the premise that the customers can be fooled, the customer will not mind being fooled and will let you do it again later, and that if there are problems with the product these can be glossed over by a fast-talking sales representative. Up until the early 1950s, therefore, personal selling and advertising were regarded as the most important (often the only) marketing activities.

Sales orientation takes the view that customers will not ordinarily buy enough of the firm's products to meet the firm's needs, and therefore they will need to be persuaded to buy more. Sales orientation is therefore concerned with the needs of the seller, not with the needs of the buyer (Levitt 1960). Essentially, what these businesses try to do is to produce a product with given characteristics, then change the consumers to fit it. This is, of course, extremely difficult to do in practice.

Selling orientation and the practice of selling are two different things – modern salespeople are usually concerned with establishing long-term relationships with customers who will come back and buy more (Singh and Koshy 2011). This is an important distinction that is often missed by marketing theorists; there is more on this later in the book (Chapter 9). In the meantime, though, selling skills are a necessary factor in successful marketing (Wachner *et al.* 2009, Troilo *et al.* 2009).

Customer orientation

Modern marketers take the view that the customers are intelligent enough to know what they need, can recognise value for money when they see it, and will not buy again from the firm if they do not get value for money. This is the basis of the *marketing concept.*

Putting the customer at the centre of all the organisation's activities is more easily said than done. The marketing concept affects all areas of the business, from production (where the engineers and designers have to produce items that meet customers' needs) through to after-sales services (where customer complaints need to be taken seriously). The marketing concept is hard to implement because, unlike the sales orientation approach which seeks to change the customers' behaviour to fit the organisation's aims, the marketing concept seeks to change the organisation's behaviour to fit one or more groups of customers who have similar needs. This means that marketers often meet resistance from within their own organisations.

At this point, it may be useful to remind ourselves of the distinction between customers and consumers. Customers are the people who buy the product; consumers are those who consume it. Customers could therefore be professional buyers who are purchasing supplies for a company, or possibly a parent buying toys for a child. The customer might also be the consumer, of course, but the consumer could equally be the recipient of a gift or the user of a service which is paid for by others.

Critical thinking

Many companies say that they are customer (or consumer) orientated, but how true is this? Do companies seriously expect us to believe that the customers come first when they reserve the best parking space for the managing director? Or that the customer comes first when they raise their prices? Or that the customer comes first when the offices close at weekends?

In fact, would it be fairer to say that we always consider the customer's needs, since this is the best way of getting their money off them?

Societal marketing

Societal marketing holds that marketers should take some responsibility for the needs of society at large, and for the sustainability of their production activities. This orientation moves the focus away from the immediate exchanges between an organisation and its customers, and even away from the relationship between the organisation and its consumers, and towards the long-term effects on society at large. This need not conflict with the immediate needs of the organisation's consumers: for example, Body Shop operates a highly successful consumer-orientated business while still promising (and delivering) low environmental impact.

Kotler *et al.* (2001) say that products can be classified according to their immediate satisfaction and their long-run consumer benefits. Figure 1.1 illustrates this. In the diagram, a product which has high long-term benefits and is also highly satisfying is classified as a desirable product. For example, a natural fruit juice which is high in vitamins and also tastes good might fit this category. A product which has long-term benefits but which is not immediately satisfying, for example a household smoke alarm, is a salutary product. Products which are bad for consumers in the long run, but which are immediately satisfying (such as alcohol, cigarettes and confectionery) are called pleasing products: research shows that people believe that 'unhealthy' foods taste better (Raghunathan *et al.* 2006). Finally, products which are neither good for consumers nor satisfying are called deficient products; examples might include ineffective slimming products, or exercise equipment which is poorly designed and causes injury. In theory, firms should aim to produce desirable products – but consumers often choose the pleasing products instead; for example, eating unhealthy foods when they feel unhappy (Garg *et al.* 2006).

Figure 1.1 Societal classification of new products

		Immediate satisfaction: Low	Immediate satisfaction: High
Long-run consumer benefits	High	**Salutary products**	**Desirable products**
	Low	**Deficient products**	**Pleasing products**

Source: Kotler, P., Armstrong, G., Saunders, J. and Wong, V., 2001, *Principles of Marketing*. Pearson Education Limited © 2001.

The societal marketing concept includes the marketing concept in that it recognises the needs of individual consumers, but it goes further in that it aims to improve the well-being of the wider society in which the firm operates. This means that the organisation takes on responsibility for good citizenship, rather than expecting consumers to understand or take account of the wider implications of their consumption behaviour. The problem is that firms need to balance three factors: customer needs, company profits (or other objectives) and the needs of society as a whole. Since competing companies may not be so concerned about society at large, it is not clear how societal marketing will contribute to creating competitive advantage; it is very clear how customer orientation helps firms to compete, however.

Ultimately, consumer orientation and societal marketing both seek to ensure that the organisation (whether a business or a non-profit organisation) should be looking to create greater value for customers, and thus meet the competition better (or even create competition in new markets).

Relationship marketing

During the 1990s, marketing thinking moved towards the **relationship marketing** concept. Traditional marketing has tended to concentrate on the single transaction with a short-term focus. Relationship marketing focuses on the 'lifetime' value of the customer. For example, a motor manufacturer might have one model aimed at young drivers, another aimed at families with children, and another aimed at middle-aged motorists. Each segment might be treated as a separate and unique entity. Under a relationship marketing paradigm, the organisation recognises that the young motorist will pass through each lifestyle stage in turn, and is then a customer for a different model each time. Relationship marketing aims to determine who will be (or could be) the most loyal customer throughout his or her life: marketers are responsible for establishing and maintaining these relationships.

In practice, relationship marketing has met with its greatest success in the business-to-business world. Companies which sell to other companies have generally been most proactive in establishing long-term cooperative relationships; for example, aircraft engine manufacturers such as Rolls-Royce and Pratt & Whitney need to establish close relationships with aircraft manufacturers such as Airbus Industrie and Boeing, since the designs of airframes and engines need to be coordinated. The ability to adapt the designs to meet the needs of the other company has obvious advantages in terms of cost savings and (eventually) greater profits, but it also has an advantage from the supplier's viewpoint in that close cooperation makes it harder for competitors to enter the market. Customers that have committed to a shared design process are unlikely to want to start the process all over again with another supplier. Creating this kind of loyalty has a significant effect on future revenues (Andreassen 1995).

The key elements in relationship marketing are the creation of customer loyalty (Ravald and Gronroos 1996), the establishment of a mutually rewarding connection, and a willingness to adapt behaviour to maintain the relationship (Takala and Uusitalo 1996).

Critical thinking

Do we really want to have a relationship with the companies which supply our needs? Of course politeness is one thing – but we aren't going to go on a long walking holiday with our bank, are we? Maybe the relationship is a bit one-sided: the company wants to lock us in to a long-term deal, and offers us all kinds of incentives to do so, whereas actually we would rather be free to choose between firms. We soon learn that threatening to leave means we get freebies, so the more they try to hang on to us, the more we take advantage!

Hardly the basis for a long-term relationship, is it?

There is more on relationship marketing throughout the book: it has become, like the Internet, central to marketing practice in recent years.

MARKETING AND OTHER BUSINESS DISCIPLINES

As the marketing concept has evolved from production orientation through to customer orientation, the role marketing occupies relative to other business functions has also evolved. Under a production-orientated regime, marketing usually occupies a departmental role; the marketing role is contained within a marketing department which carries out the communications functions of the firm.

Figure 1.2 shows the evolution of marketing's role within the organisation.

Figure 1.2 Evolution of marketing's role

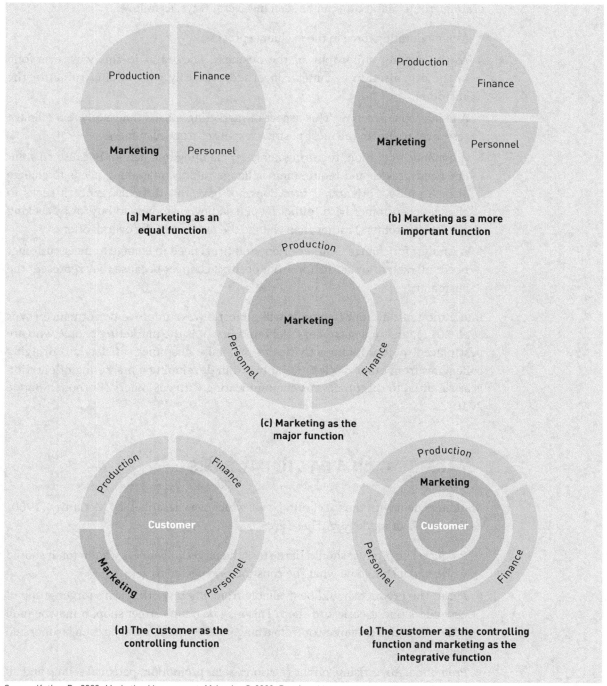

(a) Marketing as an equal function

(b) Marketing as a more important function

(c) Marketing as the major function

(d) The customer as the controlling function

(e) The customer as the controlling function and marketing as the integrative function

Source: Kotler, P., 2003, *Marketing Management*, 11th edn, © 2003. Reprinted by permission of Pearson Education Inc., Upper Saddle River, NJ.

If customers are central to the organisation's thinking, marketers act as the moderating group. Marketing can be seen in several ways, as follows:

- As a moderating force in the exchange process.
- As the driving philosophy of the business. Looked at in this way, everyone in the organisation becomes concerned primarily with adding value for the customer.
- A managerial function. This aspect of marketing means that marketers manage resources to obtain the most positive responses from customers.
- A dynamic operation, requiring analysis, planning and action. Because customers' needs, tastes and requirements change rapidly, marketing needs to change also. A product-orientated firm does not have this difficulty, since it seeks to change its customer base (either by persuading customers to buy, or by seeking out new customers) rather than change the product or the overall offer.
- A catalyst for change. Market-orientated firms need to change to meet customer need: marketers are at the forefront of these changes because they represent the customer.

Integration of different functions will almost always improve performance (Lyus *et al.* 2011), and in a customer-orientated firm it is the marketing people who are best placed to coordinate activities to maximise customer satisfaction. Bringing colleagues from other disciplines on board in developing a marketing orientation is as essential to this process as communicating with customers (Korhonen-Sande 2010).

MARKETING ON A DAY-TO-DAY BASIS

Marketers deal with the **marketing mix**, which was described by McCarthy (1960) as the four Ps of marketing. These are:

- *Product.* The product should fit the task the target consumers want it for, it should work, and it should be what the consumers expected to get.
- *Place.* The product should be available from wherever the firm's target group of customers find it easiest to shop. This may be a high street shop, it may be mail order through a catalogue or from a magazine coupon, or it may even be doorstep delivery.
- *Promotion.* Advertising, public relations, sales promotion, personal selling and all the other communications tools should put across the organisation's message in a way that fits what the particular group of consumers and customers would like to hear, whether it be informative or appealing to the emotions.

- *Price.* The product should always be seen as representing good value for money. This does not necessarily mean that it should be the cheapest available; one of the main tenets of the marketing concept is that customers are usually prepared to pay a little more for something that really works well for them.

The 4-P model has been useful when applied to the manufacture and marketing of physical products, but with the increase in services provision the model does not provide a full enough picture. In 1981 Booms and Bitner proposed a 7-P framework to include the following additional factors:

- *People.* Virtually all services are reliant on people to perform them, very often dealing directly with the consumer; for example, the waiters in restaurants form a crucial part of the total experience for the consumers. In effect, the waiter is part of the product the consumer is buying.
- *Process.* Since services are usually carried out with the consumer present, the process by which the service is delivered is, again, part of what the consumer is paying for. For example, there is a great deal of difference between a silver-service meal in an upmarket restaurant and a hamburger bought from a fast-food outlet. A consumer seeking a fast process will prefer the fast-food place, whereas a consumer seeking an evening out might prefer the slower process of the restaurant.
- *Physical evidence.* Almost all services contain some physical elements; for example, a restaurant meal is a physical thing, even if the bulk of the bill goes towards providing the intangible elements of the service (the decor, the atmosphere, the waiters, even the dishwashers). Likewise, a hairdressing salon provides a completed hairdo, and even an insurance company provides glossy documentation for the policies it issues.

In fact, virtually all products combine a physical product with a service element. In some cases, the service element is the main factor in distinguishing one product from another, especially in business-to-business markets (Raddats and Easingwood 2010).

Each of the above elements of the marketing mix will be dealt with in greater detail throughout the book, but it is important to recognise that the elements need to be combined as a mix. Like a recipe, one ingredient of the mix will not substitute for another, and each ingredient must be added in the right quantities at the right time if the mix is to prove successful in achieving consumer satisfaction. Each organisation will tend to have its own approach to the mix, and therefore no two firms will follow exactly the same marketing approach. This is one of the features that distinguishes marketing from the other business disciplines such as accountancy or company law. The marketing mix concept is also useful as a way of thinking about marketing, but in practice many marketing activities do not fall neatly within the boxes: there is considerable overlap. For example, a money-off special offer overlaps between pricing and sales promotion.

To illustrate how the marketing concept is implemented in practice, the next section looks at some of the jobs that marketers have.

MARKETING JOBS

In a sense, everybody in the organisation is responsible to some extent for ensuring that the consumers' needs are met. Clearly, though, some individuals will have greater responsibility than others for this; some of the job titles that marketers hold are shown in Table 1.1.

In market-orientated companies it is the customer who has the major say in what happens, and it is the marketing team that works within the company to ensure

Table 1.1 Marketing job titles and descriptions

Job title	Job description
Brand manager	Responsible for all the decisions concerning a particular brand. This concept was originally introduced at Mars; brand managers compete with each other as well as with other firms for market share in the chocolate bar market, even though they are all working for the same firm. This tends to result in greater efforts and greater corporate share all round.
Product manager	Responsible for all the decisions around a group of similar products within a firm. For example, a biscuit manufacturer might have one product manager in charge of chocolate-covered snack biscuits, and another in charge of savoury biscuits for cheese.
Sales manager	Responsible for controlling, training and motivating the salesforce and the sales back-up team. Sales managers often also have a role in credit control, since they are in the best position to know the individual customers and can give an opinion on the customer's creditworthiness or (as a last resort) on the least damaging way to get the customer to pay up.
Salesperson	Finds out what each customer needs, and tries to arrange for it to be delivered. Salespeople do this by selecting from the range of products that the company has on offer, and explaining those products in terms of how they will meet the client's needs.
Advertising manager	Controls media purchases, deals with advertising agencies, generally handles the flow of information to the company's customers and consumers.
Public relations manager	Monitors the company's public image and applies corrective measures if the company is acquiring a bad reputation. Organises events and activities that will put the company in a good light, and tries to ensure that the company behaves responsibly towards its wider publics.
Market research manager	Collects evidence about what it is that consumers really need, and what they would really like to buy. Sometimes this also includes monitoring competitors' activity so that the company can take action early to counteract it.
Webmaster	Controls the design and maintenance of the corporate website, including regular updates to reflect changes in the product range, and arranges the design of new promotions (for example, online games and viral marketing activities).

that everything is geared to the customer's (and consumer's) needs. Not all companies are market-orientated in the sense of putting customer satisfaction at the core of everything the business does; even some marketing managers see marketing as being purely a departmental responsibility rather than an organisational one (Hooley *et al.* 1990). In fact, everyone within the firm has some responsibility for ensuring customer satisfaction; those who have direct contact with the firm's customers have a particular role to play (for example, secretaries, delivery drivers, receptionists, telephonists and credit controllers).

The marketing orientation is adopted because it works better than any other orientation; customers are more likely to spend money on goods and services that meet their needs than on those that do not. In other words, looking after customers is good for business, and organisations which adopt a customer orientation are more likely to meet their objectives than those which do not. This applies even in non-profit organisations; charities, government departments and other organisations that offer benefits to 'customers' also function more effectively if they put their customers at the centre of everything they do (Modi and Mishra 2010).

KEY CONCEPTS IN MARKETING

Apart from customer centrality, there are several more key concepts which are the running themes of any marketing course or career. These will be dealt with in more detail later in the book, but they are as follows:

- *Managing exchange.* This goes further than promoting exchange through clever advertising and sales techniques: it also means ensuring that goods are where they should be when they should be, and ensuring that the products themselves are worthy of exchange. Viewing marketing as the management of the exchange process gives clear guidance to people working within the firm.

- *Segmentation and targeting.* This is the idea that people can be grouped according to their needs (i.e. there are groups of potential customers who are looking for the same type of product) and that we can, and should, devote our limited resources to meeting the needs of a few groups rather than trying to please everybody.

- *Positioning.* As marketers, we often seek to create an appropriate attitude towards our brands, and the firms for whom we work. This perception needs to be accurate, at least for our target customers, otherwise they will be disappointed and will not do business with us again. The position our brand occupies in the minds of the target group is therefore critical, and in this context the brand is the focusing device for all our planning – it is the lens through which our customers see us.

DEFINITIONS OF SOME MARKETING TERMS

Customers are the people or firms who buy products; *consumers* actually use the product, or consume it. Frequently customers are also consumers, so the terms might be used interchangeably, but often the person who buys a product is not the one who ultimately consumes it.

A need is a perceived lack of something. This implies that the individual not only does not have a particular item, but also is aware of not having it. This definition has nothing to do with necessity; human beings are complex, and have needs which go far beyond mere survival. In wealthy western countries, for example, most people eat for pleasure rather than from a fear that they might die without eating – the need for enjoyment comes long before there is a necessity for food.

A want, on the other hand, is a specific satisfier for a need. An individual might need food (hunger being awareness of the lack of food) and want (for example) a curry rather than a sandwich.

Wants become demands when the potential customer also has the means to pay for the product. Some marketers have made their fortunes from finding ways for people to pay for the products, rather than from merely producing the product. The demand for a given product is therefore a function of need, want and ability to pay.

A product is a bundle of benefits. This is a consumer-orientated view, because consumers will buy a product only if they feel it will be of benefit. Diners in a restaurant are not merely buying a full stomach; they are buying a pleasant evening out. Customers in a bar are not buying fizzy water with alcohol and flavourings in it; they are buying a social life. Here a distinction should be made between *physical goods* and *services*. For marketers, both of these are products, since they may well offer the same benefits to the consumer. An afternoon at a football match or a case of beer might serve the same morale-raising function for some men. Services and physical goods are difficult to distinguish between, because most services have a physical good attached to them and most physical goods have a service element attached to them. The usual definition of services says that they are mainly intangible, that production usually happens at the same time as consumption, that they are highly perishable, and that services cannot be owned (in the sense that there is no second-hand market for them).

Publics are any organisations or individuals that have actual or potential influence on the marketing organisation. This is an important definition for public relations practitioners, because they have the task of monitoring and adjusting the firm's activities relative to all the firm's publics, which can include government departments, competitors, outside pressure groups, employees, the local community and so forth.

Markets are all the actual and potential buyers of the firm's products. Few firms can capture 100% of the market for their products; marketers more commonly aim for whichever portions of the market the firm can best serve. The remainder of the customers would go to the competition, or just be people who never hear of the product and therefore do not buy it. Even giant firms such as Coca-Cola have less than half of the market for their product category. For this reason, marketers usually break down the overall market into *segments* (groups of customers with similar needs and characteristics) or even *niches* (very specific need and product categories).

Price is the amount of money for which a product is sold. *Value* is what the product is worth to the customer or consumer. The value is always higher than the price, or no business would result, but individual customers will make a judgement as to whether the product is good value or poor value. If the product is poor value, the customer will try to find alternatives; if the product is good value, the customer will remain loyal. The decision about value for money is, of course, subjective; what one customer considers a great bargain, another customer might see as a waste of good money.

MEETING MARKETING RESISTANCE

Most organisations still tend to see marketing as one function of the business, rather than seeing it as the whole purpose of the business. Marketing departments are frequently seen as vehicles for selling the company's products by whatever means present themselves, and marketers are often seen as wizards who can manipulate consumers into buying things they do not really want or need. This means that many marketers find that they meet resistance from within the firm when they try to introduce marketing thinking.

This is at least in part due to the fact that the practice of marketing is difficult. Adopting a marketing stance means trying to think like somebody else, and to anticipate somebody else's needs. It means trying to find out what people really need, and develop products that they will actually want. It means bending all the company's activities towards the customer. Inevitably there will be people within the firm who would rather not have to deal with these issues, and would have a quieter life if it were not for customers.

Table 1.2 shows some typical arguments encountered within firms, together with responses that the marketer could use.

Overcoming this type of resistance is not always easy because of the following factors:

- Lack of a leadership which is committed to the marketing concept.
- Lack of a suitable organisational infrastructure. For example, information about customers and consumers is a great deal more difficult to communicate throughout the firm if the firm's information technology systems are inadequate.
- Autocratic leadership style from senior management. In companies where the top managers believe that only their own ideas are right, the idea of changing the corporate direction to meet customer need better is less likely to take root.

Table 1.2 Reasons not to adopt a marketing philosophy

Source	Argument	Response
Production people	This is what we make efficiently. It's a good, well made product, and it's up to you to find people to sell it to.	You might like the product, but the customers may have other ideas. What we need to do is not just 'keep the punters happy' but *delight* our customers and ensure their loyalty in future.
Accountants and financial directors	The only sensible way to price is allocate all the costs, then add on our profit margin. That way we know for sure we can't lose money! Also, how about cutting out the middle man by selling direct to the retailers?	If you use cost-plus pricing, you will almost certainly either price the product lower than the consumers are prepared to pay, in which case you are giving away some of your profit, or you'll price it too high and nobody will buy the product. And that way you'll *really* lose some money! And cutting out the wholesalers means we'd have to deliver odd little amounts to every corner shop in the country, which would make our transport costs shoot up. Not to mention that the retailers won't take us seriously – we need the wholesalers' contacts!
Legal department	We have no legal obligation to do more than return people's money if things go wrong. Why go to the expense of sending somebody round to apologise?	With no customers, we have no business. We have all our eggs in one basket; we can't afford to upset any of them.
Board of Directors	Business is not so good, so everybody's budgets are being cut, including the marketing department. Sorry, you'll just have to manage with less.	If you cut the marketing budget, you cut the amount of business coming in. Our competition will seize the advantage, and we'll lose our customer base and market share – and we won't have the money coming in to get it back again, either.
Front-line staff	I'm paid to drive a truck, not chat up the customers. They're getting the stuff they've paid for, what more do they want?	Giving the customer good service means they're pleased to see you next time you call. It pays dividends directly to you because your job is more pleasant, but also it helps business and keeps you in a job.
Salesforce	You're paying me commission to get the sale, so getting the sale is all I'm interested in.	You can get sales once by deceit, but what happens when you go back? How much more could you sell if your customers know you're a good guy to do business with? And apart from all that, if you're doing your best for the customers, you can sleep at nights. Collaboration between sales and marketing is known to improve overall business performance (Le Meunier-Fitzhugh and Piercy 2007).

- Inherent mistrust of marketing by some individuals in positions of power.
- A preference for a production or sales focus (as seen in Table 1.2).
- A transactional approach to business, in which making each sale is seen as the appropriate focus rather than thinking in terms of encouraging customers to return.

In an ideal corporate situation, marketing would be seen as the coordinating function for every department. The marketing function would be supplying information about the customer base, there would be common control systems in place to ensure that each department contributes primarily to customer satisfaction, the business strategy would be based around customer need, and goals for the organisation would be realistic and aimed at customer satisfaction. In practice, most firms have some way to go in reaching this ideal.

QUOTATIONS ABOUT MARKETING

For companies to be successful, the management must put the customer first. Here are some quotations that illustrate this.

> Probably the most important management fundamental that is being ignored today is staying close to the customer to satisfy his needs and anticipate his wants. In too many companies the customer has become a bloody nuisance whose unpredictable behaviour damages carefully-made strategic plans, whose activities mess up computer operations, and who stubbornly insists that purchased products should work.
>
> (Lew Young, Editor-in-Chief of *Business Week*)

> Marketing is so basic that it cannot be considered a separate function . . . It is the whole business seen from the point of view of its final result, that is, from the customer's point of view.
>
> (Peter F. Drucker, 1973)

> There is only one boss – the customer. And he can fire everybody in the company from the chairman on down, simply by spending his money somewhere else.
>
> (Sam Walton, American founder of Wal-Mart Stores, the largest retail chain in the world)

And finally, Tom Watson of IBM was once at a meeting where customer complaints were being discussed. The complaints were categorised as engineering complaints, delivery complaints, servicing complaints, etc., perhaps ten categories in all. Finally Watson went to the front of the room, swept all the paper into one heap, and said 'There aren't any categories of problem here. There's just one problem. Some of us aren't paying enough attention to our customers.' And with that he swept out, leaving the executives wondering whether they would still have jobs in the morning. IBM salespeople are told to act at all times as if they were on the customer's payroll – which of course they are.

CASE STUDY 1 Waitrose

Waitrose is a UK supermarket chain operating mainly in England, with a few branches in Wales and Scotland. It is an unusual company because it is in fact a partnership between its employees. As part of the John Lewis Partnership, the chain is owned by the people who work there – which, as one might imagine, gives them a much greater commitment to the firm and its customers than might be the case elsewhere. Waitrose operates differently from other supermarket chains in other ways, too. For one thing, the stores do not compete on price. They do not claim to be cheaper than anywhere else, but they do claim to provide much higher quality products and a much better customer service: Waitrose customers are happy to pay a small premium to obtain these very important benefits.

For example, Waitrose staff will pack customers' groceries at the checkout and carry the bag to the customers' cars if necessary. Staff will accompany customers round the store if necessary, so that they can find products easily. A subsidiary, Waitrose Entertaining, will help plan and cater for important events such as weddings, birthdays and christenings, supplying canapés, buffets, drinks and glasses. Or, if you prefer, Waitrose will lend you glasses, fish kettles, and other items free of charge. Customers only pay for breakages, and there is no obligation to make any purchase at all (although few people would be cheeky enough to borrow without buying anything).

Another unique service is the Quick Check scan-as-you-shop system. Customers can, if they wish, use a hand-held scanner while they shop, packing the goods as they go. At the checkout, the customer simply downloads the scanner information and pays for the goods, without having to queue for a checkout operator or pack and repack the goods. This is a great saving in time for many people, but it also reduces the number of times that goods are packed and repacked, which helps to ensure that the goods reach the customer's home undamaged.

Customers can also order by telephone or on the Internet for home delivery, or even (unusually) visit the store in person, do the shopping, and leave the goods to be delivered later. The customer doesn't even need to go to the checkout for this service – he or she simply leaves the trolley at the customer service desk and goes home. Waitrose staff will scan the goods, pack them and arrange delivery. This service is obviously useful to people who are disabled, or who use public transport, or who perhaps walked to the store and have too much shopping to carry home.

Waitrose's only concession to the fixation on price that many customers have is to say that they offer 'Quality food, honestly priced'. The company's aim is to offer the convenience of a supermarket with the expertise of a small shop – no small feat, but possible, given modern communications technology.

Waitrose has certainly made a considerable success of the enterprise. The company has won several awards for customer service, and has been awarded the Royal Warrant, which makes them the official grocers to Her Majesty the Queen (and, incidentally, Prince Charles, the Prince of Wales). They were formerly grocers to Her Majesty the Queen Mother as well.

In 2011 Waitrose won the prestigious Customer Satisfaction Award from the Institute of Customer Service. Attention to customer needs, attention to the quality of the products on offer and, most especially, attention to the service being given to customers has been the foundation of Waitrose's success. No doubt there are other supermarkets which are bigger, and no doubt there are chains which are cheaper, but Waitrose has a solid base of customers who appreciate being treated as the most important element in the company's success.

Questions

1 Why shouldn't Waitrose compete on price as well?

2 Why does the company offer to lend people glasses and other equipment rather than steer them towards the company's catering side?

3 How might relationship marketing help the company?

4 Why might staff, who own the firm after all, pay so much attention to customer service?

5 Why is the Royal Warrant important to a firm like Waitrose?

SUMMARY

This chapter has been about the terms and concepts of marketing. Here are some key points from the chapter:

- Marketing is about understanding what the consumer needs and wants, and seeing that the company provides it.
- A need is a perceived lack; a want is a specific satisfier.
- Customers buy things; consumers use them.
- Price is what something costs; value is what it is worth.
- A product is a bundle of benefits; it is only worth what it will do for the consumer.
- Consumer (or customer) orientation is used because it is the most profitable in the long run.

CHAPTER QUESTIONS

1 In a situation where supply exceeds demand, which orientation would you expect most firms to have?

2 Why might a consumer feel that paying £150 for a pair of designer jeans represents good value for money?

3 What needs are met by buying fashionable clothes?

4 What needs might a mother meet by buying a child sweets?

5 Why should marketers always refer back to the consumer when making decisions?

Further reading

The Marketing Book **edited by Michael Baker** (London, Heinemann/Chartered Institute of Marketing, 1991) contains a very good chapter by Michael Baker himself on the history of the marketing concept.

*Marketing: Concepts and Strategies,*4th edn by S. Dibb, L. Simkin, W. Pride and O.C. Ferrell (London, Houghton Mifflin, 2000) contains a realistic and interesting appendix on careers in marketing.

Principles of Marketing, 3rd edn by Frances Brassington and Stephen Pettitt (Harlow, Financial Times Prentice Hall, 2002) has a good overview of marketing's relationship with other business disciplines in Chapter 1.

References

Andreassen, T.W.: 'Small, high-cost countries' strategy for attracting MNCs' global invest-ments', *International Journal of Public Sector Management*, **8** (3) (1995), pp. 110–18.

Booms, B.H. and Bitner, M.J.: 'Marketing strategies and organisation structures for serv-ice firms', in *Marketing of Services*, J. Donnelly and W.R. George, eds (Chicago, IL, American Marketing Association, 1981).

Drucker, P.F.: *Management: Tasks, Responsibilities, Practices* (New York, Harper & Row, 1973).

Garg, N., Wansink, B. and Inman, J.J.: 'The influence of incidental affect on consumers' food intake', *Journal of Marketing*, **71** (1) (2006), pp. 194–206.

Hooley, G.J., Lynch, James E., Shepherd, Jenny *et al.*: 'The marketing concept: putting theory into practice', *European Journal of Marketing*, **24** (9) (1990), pp. 7–23.

Korhonen-Sande, S.:'Micro-foundations of market orientation: influencing non-marketing manag-ers' customer information processing', *Industrial Marketing Management*, **39** (4) (2010), pp. 661–71.

Kotler, P., Armstrong, G., Saunders, J. and Wong, V.: *Principles of Marketing* (Harlow, Financial Times Prentice Hall, 2001).

Le Meunier-Fitzhugh, K. and Piercy, N.F. 'Exploring collaboration between sales and market-ing', *European Journal of Marketing*, **41** (7/8) (2007), pp. 939–55.

Levitt, T.: 'Marketing myopia', *Harvard Business Review* (July–August 1960), pp. 45–56.

Lyus, D., Rogers, B. and Simms, C.: 'The role of sales and marketing integration in improv-ing strategic responsiveness to market change', *Journal of Database Marketing and Customer Strategy Management*, **18** (1) (2011), pp. 39–49.

McCarthy, E.J.: *Basic Marketing: A Managerial Approach*, 9th edn (Homewood, IL, Irwin, 1987; 1st edition 1960).

Modi, P. and Mishra, D.: 'Conceptualising market orientation in non-profit organizations: defini-tion, performance, and preliminary construction of a scale', *Journal of Marketing Management*, **26** (5 & 6) (2010), pp. 548–69.

Raddats, C. and Easingwood, C.: 'Services growth options for B2B product-centric businesses', *Industrial Marketing Management*, **39** (8) (2010), pp. 1334–45.

Raghunathan, R., Naylor, R.W. and Hoyer, W.D.: 'The unhealthy = tasty intuition and its effects on taste inference, food enjoyment, and choice of food products', *Journal of Marketing*, **70** (4) (2006), pp. 170–84.

Ravald, A. and Gronroos, C.: 'The value concept and relationship marketing', *European Journal of Marketing*, **30** (2) (1996), pp. 10–30.

Singh, R. and Koshy, A.: 'Does salesperson's customer orientation create value in B2B relation-ships? Empirical evidence from India', *Industrial Marketing Management*, **40** (1) (2011), pp. 78–85.

Takala, T. and Uusitalo, O.: 'An alternative view of relationship marketing: a framework for ethi-cal analysis', *European Journal of Marketing*, **30** (2) (1996), pp. 45–60.

Troilo, G., DeLuca, L.M. and Guenzi, P.: 'Dispersion of influence between marketing and sales: its effects on superior customer value and market performance', *Industrial Marketing Management*, **38** (8) (2009), pp. 872–82.

Wachner, T., Plouffe, C.R. and Gregoire, Y.: 'SOCO's impact on individual sales performance; the integration of selling skills as a missing link', *Industrial Marketing Management*, **38** (1) (2009), pp. 32–44.

CONSUMER AND BUYER BEHAVIOUR

Objectives

After reading this chapter you should be able to:

- Explain how consumers make purchasing decisions
- Describe the differences between the ways in which professional buyers work and the ways consumers make decisions
- Explain how consumers develop a perceptual map of the product alternatives
- Develop ways of dealing with customer complaints.

INTRODUCTION

This chapter is about how buyers think and behave when making purchasing decisions. Buyers fall into two categories: *consumers*, who are buying for their own and for their family's consumption, and *industrial buyers*, who are buying for business use. In each case, the marketer is concerned with both the practical needs of the buyer or the buyer's organisation, and the emotional or personal needs of the individual.

Royal Enfield

Royal Enfield is an Indian-based manufacturer of motorcycles. The original Royal Enfield company was British, but the Indian side of the business was taken over after Indian independence in the late 1940s. The technology is basically unchanged since the 1950s, so the main appeal to a British customer base is that of nostalgia. This is different from the appeal in India, where the brand is regarded as an upmarket, large motorcycle. This has dramatic implications for the company's promotional policy.

Different policies have to be adopted for different countries in Europe: the bike's appeal cannot be solely based on price, even though it is a relatively cheap bike in Europe. Within Europe, the biggest markets are the UK and Germany, both well established biking nations, and Europe now accounts for 10% of sales. The company is well aware that it is competing with leisure products – nobody buys a Royal Enfield to commute. Typical buyers are likely to be men in their fifties who had motorbikes when they were young, and are reassured by the Enfield's old-fashioned appearance and basic technology.

The basic platform for Royal Enfield in the UK is the concept of 'true motorcycling'. The fun aspects are emphasised, and the 'back to one's youth' feel is foremost.

Ashish Joshi, Director, Royal Enfield Motorcycles Europe

Watch the video clip, then try to answer the following questions. The answers are on the companion website.

Questions

1 How does perception affect Royal Enfield's marketing?

2 What are the main drivers for Royal Enfield consumers in the UK?

3 What is the role of sociology theory in Royal Enfield's success in the UK as compared to India?

CONSUMER BEHAVIOUR

The consumer decision-making process follows the stages shown in Figure 3.1.

Problem recognition

Problem recognition arises when the consumer realises that there is a need for some item. This can come about through assortment depletion (where the consumer's stock of goods has been used up or worn out) or assortment extension (which is where the consumer feels the need to add some new item to the assortment of possessions). At this point the consumer has only decided to seek a solution to a problem, perhaps by buying a category of product. The needs felt can be categorised as either utilitarian (concerned with the functional attributes of the product) or hedonic (concerned with the pleasurable or aesthetic aspects of the product) (Holbrook and Hirschmann 1982). The current view is that there is a balance between the two types of need in most decisions (Engel *et al.* 1995).

An internal stimulus, or drive, comes about because there is a gap between the actual and desired states. For example, becoming hungry leads to a drive to find food; the hungrier the individual becomes, the greater the drive becomes, but once the hunger has been satisfied the individual can move on to satisfying other needs. For marketers, the actual state of the individual is usually not susceptible to influence, so much marketing activity is directed at influencing the desired state (e.g. 'Don't you deserve a better car?'). Thus drives are generated by encouraging a revision of the desired state. The higher the drive level (i.e. the greater the gap between actual and desired states), the more open the individual is to considering new ways

Figure 3.1 Consumer decision-making

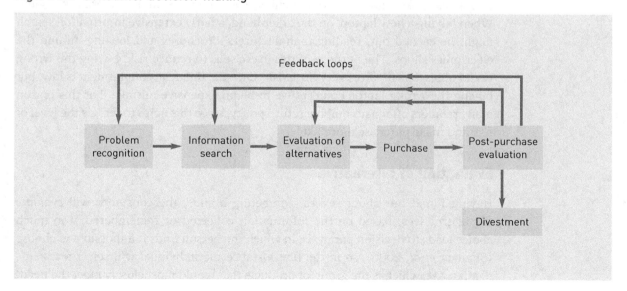

of satisfying the need – in simple terms, a starving man will try almost any kind of food.

It is, of course, stimulating and enjoyable to allow gaps to develop between the desired and actual states: working up a thirst before going for a drink makes the experience more pleasurable, for example. Each individual has an optimal stimulation level (OSL), which is the point at which the drive is enjoyable and challenging, without being uncomfortable. OSL is subjective; research shows that those with high OSLs like novelty and risk-taking, whereas those with low OSLs prefer the tried and tested. Those with high OSLs also tend to be younger (Raju 1980).

Drives lead on to motivation, which is the reason why people take action. The level of motivation will depend on the desirability of the end goal, and the ease of achieving the end goal; motivations are subjective, so it is difficult to infer motivation from behaviour. Few actions take place as a result of a single motivation, and sometimes a motivation may not even be apparent to the individual experiencing it; in other words, some motivations operate below the conscious level.

Information search

Having become motivated to seek a solution to the need problem, consumers engage in two forms of information search.

- The internal search involves remembering previous experiences of the product category and thinking about what he/she has heard about the product category
- The external search involves shopping around, reading manufacturers' literature and advertisements, and perhaps talking to friends about the proposed purchase.

For most purchases, the internal search is probably sufficient. For example, a consumer who needs to buy biscuits will easily remember what his or her favourite brand tastes like, and will also remember where they are on the supermarket shelf. When buying a new laptop, on the other hand, a fairly extensive information search might be carried out, reading manufacturers' brochures and looking around the electronics shops. The purpose of this exercise is to reduce risk; buying the wrong brand of biscuits involves very little risk, since the financial commitment is low, but buying the wrong laptop could prove to be an expensive mistake. For this reason many retailers offer a no-quibble return policy, since this helps to reduce the level of risk and make purchase more likely.

Evaluation of alternatives

Having found out about several competing brands, the consumer will *evaluate* the alternatives, based on the information collected or remembered. Too much choice leads to decision paralysis, in which the person finds it impossible to choose (Shankar *et al.* 2006), so in the first instance the individual will select a consideration set, which is the group of products that would most closely meet the need.

Typically a consumer will use **cut-offs** to establish a consideration set: these are the minimum and maximum acceptable values for the product characteristics. For example, a consumer will typically have a clear idea of the acceptable price range for the product. (This price range might have a minimum as well as a maximum; the individual may not want something that is perceived as being cheap and nasty.) **Signals** are important when making choices; a particular price tag, a brand name, even the retailer will have some effect on the consumer's perception of the product. Price is frequently used as an indicator of quality, for example, but this can be reduced in the presence of other signals. The purpose is to reduce confusion, which comes from three sources: similarity, information overload and ambiguity. Confusion and information overload leads to decision postponement, and also to loyalty behaviour – sticking with the tried and tested rather than risking a mistake with something new (Walsh *et al.* 2007, Wang 2006).

Occasionally the use of cut-offs eliminates all the possibilities from the consideration set, in which case the consumer will have to revise the rules. This can result in the creation of a hierarchy of rules. For marketers, the challenge is often to ensure that the product becomes a 'member' of the consideration set.

The decision-making process appears lengthy and complex as stated here, yet most of us make several purchasing decisions in a day without going through a lengthy decision-making process. This is because most of us use **heuristics**, or decision-making rules, for most purchases. These are simple 'if ... then' rules that reduce risk by using previous experience as a guide. For example, an international traveller in a strange city might have a heuristic of eating only in restaurants that are full of local people, on the grounds that the inhabitants of the city would know which are the best restaurants. Heuristics divide into three categories:

- *Search heuristics*, which are concerned with rules for finding out information
- *Evaluation heuristics*, which are about judging product offerings
- *Choice heuristics*, which are about evaluation of alternatives.

The decision-making process may contain a number of **interrupts** – points at which the search is temporarily suspended. Interrupts come in four categories:

- **Environmental stimuli**, which include in-store promotions (perhaps eye-catching posters for other products)
- **Affective states**, which include physiological needs (the sudden need to go to the toilet or to have a coffee)
- *Unexpected information*; for example, a change of layout in the shop or some change in the product attributes
- *Conflicts*, which occur when the consumer realises that the original decision-making plan cannot be followed, or an alternative plan appears that is not consistent with the original plan.

For example, an approach–approach conflict occurs when a second product is presented that would probably do the job just as well. This means that the consumer has to make a comparison, and the search pattern is temporarily suspended. An approach–avoidance conflict might arise when the consumer finds out that the product is much more expensive than expected; an avoidance–avoidance conflict might arise when the two alternatives are equally distasteful (an example might be the reluctance to spend money on new shoes while at the same time not wanting to be embarrassed by wearing old ones).

The effect of the interrupt will depend on the consumer's interpretation of the event. Sometimes the interrupt activates a new end goal (for example, a long shopping trip might be transformed into a search for somewhere to sit down and have a coffee), or perhaps a new choice heuristic might be activated (for example, meeting a friend who recommends a brand). Sometimes the interrupt is serious enough for the search to be abandoned altogether; here the strength of the interrupt is important. Clearly a sudden desire for a cup of tea will not permanently interrupt a search process, but the news that one has lost one's job very well might.

In most cases, consumers will resume the interrupted problem-solving process once the stimulus has been absorbed and accepted or rejected.

Purchase

The actual *purchase* comes next; the consumer will locate the required brand, and perhaps choose a retailer he or she has faith in, and will also select an appropriate payment method.

Post-purchase evaluation

Post-purchase evaluation refers to the way the consumer decides whether the product purchase has been a success or not. This process usually involves a comparison between what the consumer was expecting to get and what was actually purchased, although sometimes new information obtained after the purchase will also colour the consumer's thinking (Oliver 1980). In some cases, particularly in the virtual environment, the value obtained from the product can be manipulated by consumers after purchase; this means that the interpretation of value is subject to change (Harwood and Garry 2010).

Before the purchase, the consumer will have formed expectations of the product's capabilities in terms of:

- Equitable performance (what can be reasonably expected given the cost and effort of obtaining the product)
- Ideal performance (what the consumer hopes the product will do)
- Expected performance (which is what the product probably will do).

Sometimes this evaluation leads to post-purchase dissonance, when the product has not lived up to expectations, and sometimes to post-purchase consonance, when the product is as expected or better. In either event, the consumer will feed back this information into memory to inform the internal search for next time.

One of the more interesting aspects of dissonance is that there is evidence to show that a small discrepancy between expectation and outcome may provoke a bigger change in attitude than a large discrepancy. This is because a small discrepancy may force the consumer to confront the purchase behaviour without offering a ready explanation for it; for example, a general feeling of being unhappy with a new car might crystallise around its poor acceleration (a major problem), and the consumer might simply shrug and accept this as part of the deal. On the other hand, if the only immediately identifiable problem is that the car's ashtray is poorly positioned, this may lead the owner to look for other faults with the car (and, of course, find them).

Consumers will usually act to reduce post-purchase dissonance. There are four general approaches to doing this:

1 Ignore the dissonant information and concentrate on the positive aspects of the product.
2 Distort the dissonant information (perhaps by telling oneself that the product was, after all, the cheap version).
3 Play down the importance of the issue.
4 Change one's behaviour.

From a marketing viewpoint, it is generally better to ensure that the consumer has accurate information about the product beforehand so as to avoid post-purchase dissonance, but if it occurs then marketers need to reduce it in some way. People differ in their propensity to complain – complaints are more likely if the consumer is involved with the product and also acts on impulse; they are less likely if the consumer self-monitors, i.e. is very aware of his or her behaviour (Sharma *et al.* 2010b). Consumers express dissatisfaction in one of three ways:

● **Voice responses**, in which the customer comes back and complains. Older people in particular are often reluctant to take this route, which may mean that the supplier is unaware of dissatisfaction among customers (Grougiou and Pettigrew 2009). The possibility of a repeated violation of trust appears to be more important in voice responses than the magnitude of the violation (Sijun and Huff 2007), which has implications for complaint-handling
● **Private responses**, in which the consumer complains to friends. In some cultures this is more likely than voice responses (Ngai *et al.* 2007)
● **Third-party responses**, which may include complaints to consumer organisations, trade associations and TV consumer programmes, or even legal action (Singh 1988).

The most effective way of reducing post-purchase dissonance is to provide a product that meets the customer's expectations. This is partly a function for the manufacturer, but is also a problem for the retailer to address since it should be possible to ensure that the consumer's needs are fully understood before a recommendation about a product is made. As a fall-back position, though, every effort should be made to encourage the consumer to complain if things do not come up to expectations. This is why waiters always ask if the meal is all right, and why shops frequently have no-quibble money-back guarantees. Ferry companies and airlines provide customer comment slips, and some marketers even make follow-up telephone calls to consumers to check that the product is meeting expectations. There is more on these techniques in Chapter 5.

In business-to-business markets, where buyer–seller relationships are often long term, negative incidents can give rise to shifts in the relationship. Analysing these negative events can be very useful in assessing the relationship and making adjustments where necessary, so complaint handling serves an extremely useful function in relationship marketing (Strandvik and Holmlund 2008).

Research shows that the perceptions of employees about the shared values of the firm, and especially their view of how fair the firm is in its dealings, are reflected in the way in which they deal with customer complaints. This in turn is reflected in the ways in which customers perceive the complaint-handling process (Maxham and Netemeyer 2003).

It is important that dissatisfied customers are allowed to voice their complaint fully, and that the appropriate compensation is negotiated in the light of:

- The strength of the complaint
- The degree of blame attaching to the supplier, from the consumer's viewpoint
- The legal and moral relationship between the supplier and the consumer.

A consistent failure to solve problems raised by post-purchase dissonance will, ultimately, lead to irreparable damage to the firm's reputation. In the last analysis, it is almost always cheaper to keep an existing customer than it is to attract a new one, and therefore it makes sense for suppliers to give customers every chance to express problems with the service or product provision. Customer retention is, according to one research exercise, associated with complaint-handling procedures – and nothing else (Ang and Buttle 2006).

Critical thinking

It sounds as if we are going back to the idea that the customer is always right. What about people who deliberately find fault with everything, in the hope of winning some concession from the company? What about simple misunderstandings, where someone has bought a product and then decided it wasn't what they wanted after all? And what about the people who buy a new item of clothing, wear it to go out for the evening, then bring it back the next day?

Surely we aren't expected to put up with fraud, lies and stupidity! Or is that a small price to pay for looking after the genuine cases – after all, the customers may not always be right, but they are always the customers!

Divestment

Finally, the divestment stage refers to the way the individual disposes of the product after use. This could be as simple as throwing an empty food container into the bin, or it could be as complex as the trade-in of a second-hand car. This stage is of increasing importance to marketers, both in terms of green marketing (the environmental issues raised) and in terms of the possibility of making sales of new products (for example, on trade-in deals). There is more on divestment in Chapter 12, in relation to the environmental impact of the disposal of packaging and used products.

This model of the decision-making process appears somewhat long and involved, but in practice most purchasing decisions are habitual, and the process is carried out quickly and virtually automatically. Table 3.1 shows a comparison of a non-habitual purchase and a habitual purchase, showing how each stage in the decision-making model is carried out.

Table 3.1 Habitual *v* non-habitual purchase behaviour

Stage in the process	New DVD player	Can of tuna
Problem recognition	The old DVD player doesn't have a facility for recording DVDs, and for some reason it suddenly skips to another part of the movie.	We used the last can yesterday, and we're going to the supermarket tonight.
Information search	Ask a few friends, see what they've got. Go online to a comparison site. Visit some local electronics stores (predominantly an external search).	Remember the brand that we like (predominantly an internal search).
Evaluation of alternatives	Discuss the options with one's husband or wife. Perhaps ask a knowledgeable friend for advice.	Find the right one on the shelves. Perhaps look at a premium brand and compare it with the store's own brand.
Purchase	Return to the store or the website and make the purchase. Perhaps use a credit card to spread the cost.	Put the can in the basket and run it through the checkout with everything else. Possibly (if we're desperate for tuna) buy it from the corner shop.
Post-purchase evaluation	Try playing a movie. Judge the ease of use of the equipment and the quality of playback. Decide on aspects such as reliability as time goes on. File the information away, or pass it on to friends as necessary.	Eat the tuna. Was it up to the usual standard? If so, no further action. If not, perhaps go back to the shop and complain, or perhaps buy a different brand in future.
Divestment	When the DVD player becomes obsolete, sell it on eBay, give it to a friend or simply throw it away.	Throw the empty can into the bin or take it for recycling.

PERCEPTION

Human senses constantly feed information into the brain; the amount of stimulation this involves would seriously overload the individual's system if the information were not filtered in some way. People therefore quickly learn to abstract information from the environment; the noise from a railway line near a friend's home might seem obvious to you, but your host is probably unaware of it. In effect, the brain is automatically selecting what is relevant and what is not, and for this reason the information being used by the brain does not provide a complete view of the world.

The gaps in the world view thus created are filled in by the individual's imagination and experience. The cognitive map of the world is affected by the following factors:

- *Subjectivity:* the existing world view of the individual
- *Categorisation:* the pigeon-holing of information. This usually happens through a 'chunking' process, whereby information is grouped into associated items. For example, a particular tune might make someone recall a special evening out from some years ago
- *Selectivity:* the degree to which the individual's brain has selected from the environment. This is also a subjective phenomenon; some people are more selective than others
- *Expectation:* the process of interpreting later information in a specific way. For example, look at this series of letters and numbers:

$$\mathcal{A} \; \mathcal{B} \; C \; \mathcal{D} \; \mathcal{E} \; \mathcal{F} \; \mathcal{G} \; \mathcal{H} \; \mathcal{I}$$
$$10 \quad 11 \quad 12 \quad 13 \quad 14 \quad 15 \quad 16$$

In fact, the number 13 appears in both series, but would be interpreted as a B in the series of letters because that is what the brain is being led to expect

- *Past experience:* this leads us to interpret information in the light of existing knowledge. This is also known as the **law of primacy**. The sound of sea birds might make us think of a day at the beach, but could in fact be part of an advertisement's soundtrack.

In practice, people develop a model of how the world works and make decisions based on the model. Since each individual's model differs slightly from every other individual's model, it is sometimes difficult for marketers to know how to approach a given person.

One of the problems for marketers is that the perception the consumers have of marketing communications may not be what was intended. For example, fast-paced advertisements on television attract people's attention involuntarily, but have little effect on people's voluntary attention, so the message is often lost. Furthermore, a fast pace focuses attention on the style of the advertisement at the expense of its message (Bolls *et al.* 2003). Likewise, people often 'straighten up' gay imagery in TV shows or advertising if they find it embarrassing – in other words, they reinterpret the imagery to find a different explanation (Borgerson *et al.* 2006).

INFLUENCES ON THE BUYING DECISION

The main influences on the buying decision are of three types:

- *Personal factors* are features of the consumer that affect the decision process
- *Psychological factors* are elements of the consumer's mental processes
- *Social factors* are those influences from friends and family that affect decision-making.

Personal factors are shown in Table 3.2.

Involvement can be a major factor in consumer decision-making. Consumers often form emotional attachments to products, and most people would be familiar with the feeling of having fallen in love with a product – even when the product itself is hopelessly impractical. Involvement can also operate at a cognitive level, though; the outcome of the purchase may have important practical consequences for the consumer. For example, a rock climber may feel highly involved in the purchase of a climbing rope, since the consequences of an error could be fatal. Whether this is a manifestation of a logical thought process regarding the risk to life and limb or whether it is an emotional process regarding a feeling of confidence about the product would be hard to determine. People also become involved with companies and become champions for them (Bhattacharya and Sen 2003). Customers are often swayed by their relationship with the people who work for the firms they buy

Table 3.2 Personal factors in the buying decision

Personal factor	Explanation
Demographic factors	Individual characteristics such as age, gender, ethnic origin, income, family life cycle and occupation. These are often used as the bases for segmentation (see Chapter 4).
Situational factors	Changes in the consumer's circumstances. For example, a pay rise might lead the consumer to think about buying a new car; conversely, being made redundant might cause the consumer to cancel an order for a new kitchen.
Level of involvement	Involvement concerns the degree of importance the consumer attaches to the product and purchasing decision. For example, one consumer may feel that buying the right brand of coffee is absolutely essential to the success of a dinner party, where another consumer might not feel that this matters at all. Involvement is about the emotional attachment the consumer has for the product.

from; research shows that the relationship with the dealer is more important than the price when buying a new car (Odekerken-Schroder *et al.* 2003).

Involvement can be extremely complex: a study carried out with members of a major art gallery in the UK found six characteristics of involvement in total. These were: (1) centrality and pleasure, (2) desire to learn, (3) escapism, both spiritual and creative, (4) sense of belonging and prestige, (5) physical involvement, and (6) drivers of involvement (Slater and Armstrong 2010). Obviously, people who have joined an art gallery, as opposed to simply visiting one, will have much higher involvement than most.

Psychological factors in the decision-making process are as shown in Table 3.3. Consumers' attitudes to products can be complex. They vary according to:

- **Valence** – whether the attitude is positive, negative or neutral
- **Extremity** – the strength of the attitude
- **Resistance** – the degree to which the attitude can be changed by outside influences
- **Persistence** – the degree to which the attitude erodes over time
- **Confidence** – the level at which the consumer believes the attitude is correct.

Table 3.3 Psychological factors in the buying decision

Psychological factor	Explanation
Perception	This is the way people build up a view of the world. Essentially, this process of selection or analysis means that each person has an incomplete picture of the world; the brain therefore fills in the gaps by a process of synthesis using hearsay, previous experience, imagination, etc. Marketers are able to fill some of the gaps through the communication process, but will come up against the problem of breaking through the selection and analysis process.
Motives	The internal force that encourages someone towards a particular course of action. Motivation is a vector; it has both intensity and direction.
Ability and knowledge	A consumer who is, for example, a beginner at playing the violin is unlikely to spend thousands of pounds on a Stradivarius. Ability therefore affects some buying decisions. Likewise, pre-existing knowledge of a product category or brand will also affect the way the consumer approaches the decision. Pre-existing knowledge is difficult for a marketer to break down; it is much better to try to add to the consumer's knowledge wherever possible.
Attitude	Attitude has three components: cognition, which is to do with conscious thought processes; affect, which is about the consumer's emotional attachment to the product; and conation, which is about planned courses of behaviour. For example, 'I love my Volkswagen (affect) because it's never let me down (cognition). I'll definitely buy another (conation)'. Conations are only intended actions – they do not always lead to action, since other factors might interrupt the process.
Personality	The traits and behaviours that make each person unique. Personalities change very slowly, if at all, and can be regarded as constant for the purposes of marketing. Typically marketers aim for specific personality types, such as the gregarious, the competitive, the outgoing or the sporty.

People who are particularly knowledgeable ('savvy' consumers) are usually competent in the use of technology, good at interpersonal networking both in person and online, marketing-literate, empowered by their own consumer effectiveness and know what to expect from firms (Macdonald and Uncles 2007). These personal characteristics make them efficient and effective at getting what they want from firms.

It should be noted that the conation component of attitude (see Table 3.3) is not necessarily consistent with subsequent behaviour; a consumer's intentions about future behaviour do not always materialise, if only because of the existence of interrupts. For example, an individual with a grievance against a bank may intend to move his/her account to a different bank, but find that the difficulties of switching the account would create too much paperwork to be worthwhile.

The traditional view of attitude is that affect towards an object is mediated by cognition; Zajonc and Markus (1985) challenged this view and asserted that affect can arise without prior cognition. In other words, it is possible to develop a 'gut feeling' about something without conscious evaluation.

Attitude contains elements of belief (knowledge of attributes) and opinion (statements about a product), but is neither. Belief is neutral, in that it does not imply attraction or repulsion, whereas attitude has direction; and, unlike opinion, attitudes do not need to be stated.

From the marketer's viewpoint, attitudes are important since they often precede behaviour. Clearly a positive attitude towards a firm and its products is more likely to lead to purchase of the firm's products than a negative attitude. There is, however, some evidence to show that people often behave first, then form attitudes afterwards (Fishbein 1972) and therefore some car manufacturers find that it is worthwhile to give special deals to car rental companies and driving schools so that consumers can try the vehicles before forming their attitudes. Trial is considerably more powerful than advertising in forming attitudes (Smith and Swinyard 1983).

Social factors

Social factors influence consumers through:

- **Normative compliance** – the pressure exerted on the individual to conform and comply
- **Value-expressive influence** – the need for psychological association with a particular group
- **Informational influence** – the need to seek information from a group about the product category being considered.

Of the three, normative compliance is probably the most powerful; this works because the individual finds that acting in one way leads to the approval of friends or family, whereas acting in a different way leads to the disapproval of friends and family. This process favours a particular type of behaviour as a result. Good moral behaviour is probably the result of normative compliance.

Peer-group pressure is an example of normative compliance. The individual's peer group (a group of equals) will expect a particular type of behaviour, including (probably) some purchase behaviour. For example, most cigarette smokers began to smoke as a result of pressure from their friends when they were young teenagers. The desire to be a fully accepted member of the group is far stronger than any health warnings.

The main source of these pressures is reference groups. These are the groups of friends, colleagues, relatives and others whose opinions the individual values. Table 3.4 gives a list of types of reference group. The groups are not mutually exclusive; a formal group can also be a secondary group, and so forth. Some researchers go so far as to identify reference groups as tribes, especially when the group

Table 3.4 Reference group influences

Reference group	Explanation
Primary groups	The people we see most often. Family, friends, close colleagues. A primary group is small enough to allow face-to-face contact on a regular, perhaps daily, basis. These groups have the strongest influence.
Secondary groups	People we see occasionally and with whom we have a shared interest; for example, the members of a golf club or a trade association. These groups sometimes have formal rules that members must adhere to in their business dealings or hobbies, and may also have informal traditions (e.g. particular clothing or equipment) that influence buying decisions.
Aspirational groups	The groups to which we wish we belonged. These groups can be very powerful in influencing behaviour because the individual has a strong drive towards joining; this is the source of value-expressive influences. These groups can be particularly influential in fashion purchases.
Dissociative groups	The groups with which the individual does not want to be associated. This makes the individual behave in ways opposite to those of the group; for example, somebody who does not wish to be thought of as a football hooligan might avoid going to football matches altogether.
Formal groups	Groups with a known, recorded membership list. Often these groups have fixed rules; a professional body will lay down a code of conduct, for example.
Informal groups	Less structured, and based on friendship. There are no formalities to joining; one merely has to fit in with the group's joint ideals.
Automatic groups	The groups we belong to by virtue of age, race, culture or education. These are groups that we do not join voluntarily, but they do influence our behaviour; for example, a woman of 45 will not choose clothes that make her look like 'mutton dressed as lamb'. Likewise, expatriates often find that they miss food from home or seek out culture-specific goods of other types.

focuses around a specific object such as a celebrity or a brand. In some cases, groups may arise through social networking sites, and thus be virtual groups: often these have tribal characteristics, since the networking site may be established around a celebrity, a brand or a specific hobby such as aviation or support for a sports team. Such tribes can become creative, and usually offer their members a strong feeling of belonging (Hamilton and Hewer 2010).

Roles

The roles we play are also important in decision-making. Each of us plays many different roles in the course of our lives (in fact, in the course of a day) and we buy products to aid us accordingly (Goffman 1969). Somebody who is to be best man at a wedding will choose a suitable suit, either to buy or to hire, to avoid looking ridiculous or otherwise spoiling the day. In terms of longer-lasting roles, the role of Father will dictate purchasing behaviour on behalf of children; the role of Lover may dictate buying flowers or wearing perfume; the role of Friend might mean buying a gift or a round of drinks; the role of Daughter might mean buying a Mother's Day present. In some immigrant families, parental roles involve negotiating cultural boundaries as well (Lindridge and Hogg 2006).

Family roles influence decision-making far beyond the normative compliance effects. Frequently, different members of the family take over the role of buyer for specific product categories; the husband may make the main decisions about the car and its accessories and servicing, while the wife makes the main decisions about the decor of the home. Recent research shows that some convenience foods can empower mothers to take control of their 'caretaker' role within the family, provided that marketers can remove the guilt feelings many women feel about using convenience foods (Carrigan and Szmigin 2006). Older children may decide on food, choosing the healthy or environmentally friendly alternatives, and often help their parents to learn about new products (Ekstrom 2007).

In terms of its functions as a reference group, the family differs from other groups in the following respects:

- Face-to-face contact on a daily basis
- *Shared consumption* of such items as food, housing, car, TV sets and other household durables
- *Subordination of individual needs* to the common welfare. There is never a solution that will suit everybody
- *Purchasing agents* will be designated to carry out the purchasing of some items. As the number of working parents grows, pre-teens and young teens are taking an ever-increasing role in family shopping.

Conflict resolution within the family decision-making unit is usually more important than it would be for an individual, since there are more people involved. Whereas an individual might have difficulty in choosing between two equally attractive holiday destinations, discussions about family holidays are inevitably much more difficult since each family member will have his or her own favourite idea on a holiday destination or activity. There is likely to be a degree of negotiation, and even small children quickly develop skills in negotiating, justifying the benefits of a particular choice, forming coalitions with other family members and compromising where necessary (Thomson *et al*. 2007).

Culture can have a marked effect: African cultures tend to be male-dominated, whereas European and North American cultures show a more egalitarian pattern of decision-making (Green *et al*. 1983). This may be because decision-making becomes more egalitarian when both partners earn money outside the home (Filiatrault and Brent Ritchie 1980).

Decision-making stage also affects the roles of the family in the decision; problem recognition may come from any family member, whereas information search and product evaluation may be undertaken by different members. For example, the father may notice that the teenage son needs new football boots, the son might ask around for types, and the mother might decide which type falls within the family's budget.

Four kinds of marital role specialisation have been identified:

- *Wife dominant*, where the wife has most say in the decision
- *Husband dominant*, where the husband plays the major role
- *Syncratic or democratic*, where the decision is arrived at jointly
- *Autonomic,* where the decision is made entirely independently of the partner (Davies and Rigaux 1974).

Marketers need to know which type of specialisation is most likely to occur in the target market, since this will affect the style and content of promotional messages; for example, some advertising in the UK has tended to portray men as being incompetent at household tasks, despite evidence that men are taking a more active role in housework (Dwek 1996).

In most industrialised countries the family is undergoing considerable changes because of the rising divorce rate and the increasing propensity for couples to live together without marrying. In the above role specialisations, the terms 'husband' and 'wife' apply equally to unmarried partners.

Children have an increasing role in purchasing decisions: 'pester power' often results in increased family purchases of particular brands of chocolate, pizza, burgers and snack foods (Dwek 1995). Consequently, marketers often try to reach children aged between 5 and 12 through the use of sponsorship of teaching materials, free samples and sponsorship of prizes in schools (Burke 1995). Some recent research indicates that children are well aware of the possible responses parents might make, and view this kind of activity as a game; children tend to regard this as good-natured rather than as a conflict (Lawlor and Prothero 2011).

Children sometimes have greater influence on the family purchasing decisions than do the parents themselves, for the following reasons:

- Often they do the shopping since both parents are out at work
- They watch more TV than do their parents, so they are more knowledgeable about products. Often older children (and female children) are more aware of these issues than are their parents (Nancarrow *et al.* 2011)
- They tend to be more attuned to consumer issues, and have the time to shop around for (for example) environmentally friendly products
- Parents are often concerned about the image the child presents; poor families, in particular, go to great lengths to ensure that their children are not embarrassed by poverty (Hamilton and Catterall 2006).

Purchasing behaviour is also affected by people's identity – in other words, their view of themselves. The more closely the purchasing behaviour fits with the person's identity, the more likely it is to occur; this is particularly important in non-profit marketing such as charitable donations or participation in voluntary work, where the exchange involves individuals and is often based on social exchanges (Arnett *et al.* 2003). For some women, buying things for a new baby reinforces their own role as mother; research shows that purchase of a pram carries a public signal meaning, a private signal meaning, an experiential meaning and a role embrace. Each of these aspects contributes to the mother's self-image (Thomsen and Sorensen 2006).

Interestingly, consumption behaviour has a role in binding families closer together. Apart from the obvious aspects of sharing some items, such as household equipment and family cars, older family members often pass down heirlooms to younger members. These goods are valued far beyond their usefulness or monetary value since they provide a link with older family members, helping to create and nurture a family identity (Curasi 2011).

IMPULSE BUYING

Impulse purchases are not based on any plan, and usually happen as the result of a sudden confrontation with a stimulus.

Pure impulse is based on the novelty of the product. Seeing something new may prompt the consumer to buy it just to try it. Reminder impulse acts when the consumer suddenly realises that something has been left off the shopping list. Suggestion impulse arises when confronted with a product that meets a previously unfelt need, and planned impulse occurs when the consumer has gone out to meet a specific need, but is prepared to be swayed by what is on special offer.

For example, someone may be on a shopping trip to buy a new jacket for a weekend dinner party. In the shop he notices a rack of bow ties, and buys one because he has never owned one before (pure impulse). Next he remembers that he has not got a suitable summer shirt, so he picks one up from the counter (reminder impulse), and near it he sees a rack of cotton trousers which are on offer (suggestion impulse). Finally, he sees a safari jacket which, although it is not the style he was thinking of, is actually ideal for the job so he buys it (planned impulse). Most shoppers are familiar with these situations, and, indeed, they commonly occur when browsing in supermarkets.

The purchase process itself is an important part of the benefits that consumers get from consumption; research has shown that satisfaction with the process relates to the desire to participate in future purchases (Tanner 1996). Typically, impulse buyers are also variety seekers; impulse buying often results from the desire to do something stimulating and interesting as an antidote to boredom (Sharma *et al.* 2010a).

Impulse buying has perhaps been made easier by the Internet. There is certainly evidence that people often act on impulse when browsing the websites of charities (Bennett 2009), and it seems likely that the ease of purchase on the Internet will foster impulsive behaviour.

INDUSTRIAL BUYER BEHAVIOUR

Industrial buyers differ from consumers in that they are (at least theoretically) more formalised in their buying behaviour. The major areas where organisational buying differs from consumer buying are as follows:

- Bigger order values in terms of finance and quantity
- Reciprocity; the firms may buy each other's products as part of a negotiated deal
- Fewer buyers, because there are fewer firms than there are individuals
- More people in the decision process
- Fewer sales in terms of the number of deals
- More complex techniques exist for buying and for negotiating.

Organisational buyers are buying to meet the organisation's needs, but it should also be remembered that they have their personal needs. These might be a need for *prestige*, a need for *career security,* for *friendship and social needs,* and other personal factors such as the satisfaction of driving a hard bargain, or the buyer's personality, attitudes and beliefs (Powers 1991). The astute marketer, and particularly the astute salesperson, will not ignore these personal needs of the buyers.

Critical thinking

Are professional buyers really so easily swayed by their personal needs? After all, they have their careers to think about – surely that implies a certain amount of care about how they behave, and showing favouritism to one supplier over another almost smacks of corruption!

Of course, we are all human – and we each bring our humanity to our working day, so maybe we shouldn't expect buyers to be any different from the rest of us.

Table 3.5 Industrial buyers' methods

Method	Explanation
Description	Managers within the organisation lay down exactly what is required and the buyer is given the brief of finding the best supplier. The buyer might, for example, be asked to find a supplier of steel bolts. He or she will then ask manufacturers to quote prices, and will make a judgement based on price and delivery reliability.
Inspection	This is commonly carried out for variable goods, such as second-hand plant and equipment. Car dealers will usually inspect the cars before buying, for example.
Sampling	Commonly used for agricultural products. A buyer might sample, say, wool from an Australian sheep-station and fix a price for it on the basis of its quality. Often these decisions will be made by reference to a very small sample, perhaps only a few strands of wool.
Negotiation	Typically used for one-off or greenfield purchase situations. This involves the greatest input in terms of both the buyer's skills and the salesperson's time, and it is likely that a number of people from the buying organisation will be involved.

Regarding the organisation's needs, however, the chief considerations of most buyers appear to revolve around quality, delivery, service and price (Green and Wind 1968). This often means that buyers will be working to a set of *specifications* about the products, and will probably use some or all of the formal techniques shown in Table 3.5.

The industrial purchase task might be a *new task,* in which case the buyer will need to adopt extensive problem-solving behaviour. The vendor has the opportunity of establishing a relationship which might last for many years, however. New-task situations will often involve the greatest amount of negotiation, since there is little (if any) previous experience to draw on.

Straight re-buy tasks are routine; the buyer is simply placing an order for the same products in the same quantities as last time. This requires very little thought or negotiation on the part of either buyer or seller. Often these deals are conducted over the telephone rather than spending time and money on a face-to-face meeting.

Modified re-buy involves some change in the purchase order; for example, a larger order value or a different delivery schedule. Sometimes the re-buy can be modified by the salesperson, for example by suggesting that the buyer orders a slightly larger value of goods than usual or by altering the delivery schedule in some way. In circumstances where the two firms have an ongoing relationship, buyers will often track the performance of their suppliers over a long period of time; buying firms that monitor their suppliers effectively can gain real competitive advantage, because they can control their supply of inputs much better (Bharadwaj 2004). Unfortunately, most firms appear reluctant to develop their suppliers (Wagner 2006).

Often the demand for industrial products will be dictated by factors outside the buying organisation's control. For example, derived demand occurs because the buyers are using the products either for resale or in making other products. The demand is therefore dictated by the demand for the end product. Frequently the demand for a component will be *inelastic*; for example, the price of wheel nuts will not affect the demand for them much, since they form only a tiny proportion of the price of a car, and also the car cannot be made without them. Joint demand occurs because the demand for one type of product dictates the demand for another. For instance, if the demand for guitars rises, so will the demand for guitar strings in the following months.

Fluctuating demand is more extreme in industrial markets because a small reduction in consumer demand for a product will lead to de-stocking by retailers and wholesalers, which causes a big reduction in demand from the manufacturers. A rise in consumer demand is likely to lead to re-stocking, which causes a bigger than expected rise in demand from the producers. In this way the fluctuations in demand for industrial products are more extreme than for consumer products.

Decision-making units

Industrial buying decisions are rarely made in isolation. Usually several people are involved in the process at different stages.

Gatekeepers such as secretaries and receptionists control the flow of information to the decision-makers. Often they will act as a barrier to salespeople, and see their role as being primarily to prevent interruptions to the decision-maker's work pattern.

Influencers are those individuals who 'have the ear' of the decision-makers. They could be people within the firm whom the decision-maker trusts, or they could be golf partners, spouses or even children.

Users are those who will actually use the product. For example, if the organisation is contemplating the purchase of a new computer system, the finance department and the IT department will clearly want to have some say in the decision.

Deciders are the ones who make the real decision. These are usually the hardest to influence, since they are usually the more senior people in the decision-making unit and are surrounded by gatekeepers. They are also sometimes hard to identify. They are not necessarily buyers, but they do hold the real power in the buying decision.

Buyers are the ones given the task of actually going through the process of buying. The buyers may be given a very specific brief by the decider, and may have very little room to negotiate except on areas such as price and delivery schedules.

Sometimes they are merely there to handle the mechanical aspects of getting tenders from possible suppliers.

Each of these people has an independent existence outside the organisation; each will bring their own personal needs and aspirations to their role. In some cases this will be a job-related need (for example, career progression or the need to appear professional); in other cases the individual may have personal needs, such as a need to exercise power or the hedonic need to drive a hard bargain. The need to impress others within the firm can be extremely powerful.

From the viewpoint of the industrial marketer, it is essential to get to the deciders in some way rather than wait for the buyers to make the first contact by issuing a tender. The reason for this is that a tender will usually be very specific, and the buyers will then be deciding on the basis of price. The only way to get the order in those circumstances is to be the cheapest, and this inevitably results in reduced profits. If the seller has managed to approach the decision-maker beforehand, the seller can persuade the decision-maker to include certain essential aspects of the product in the tender, and thus ensure that the tender contains specifications that are difficult or impossible for the competition to meet.

Webster and Wind (1972) theorised that four main forces determine organisational buyer behaviour: environmental forces (such as the state of the economy), organisational forces (for example, the size of the organisation and therefore its buying power), group forces (internal politics and the relative power of group members) and individual forces (the personality and preferences of the decision-maker). These forces combine in complex ways to influence the final decision.

This means that the role of the salesperson is crucial in industrial markets. Salespeople are able to identify potential customers and approach them with a solution for their specific problem; even in cases where the buyer is going to invite tenders from other firms, the salesperson can often ensure that the tender is drawn up in a way that excludes the competition. Salespeople, and in particular key-account salespeople, are crucially important in relationship marketing, since they negotiate the terms of the relationship and are the human face of the supplying corporation.

In the end, organisations do not make purchases. Individuals make purchases on behalf of organisations, and therefore salespeople are always dealing with human beings who have their own needs, failings, attitudes and blind spots. Purchasing decisions are not made entirely rationally; often the personal relationship between the representatives of the buying and selling companies has the biggest role in the purchase. Buyers will naturally prefer to deal with someone they know and trust (see the section on personal selling in Chapter 9).

CASE STUDY 3 Choosing a holiday

Forty years ago the majority of holidays were package deals. Ever since Butlins invented the all-inclusive holiday in the 1930s, there has been a demand for the kind of holiday where everything is arranged in advance, there are no surprises and no challenges, and the holidaymaker can simply enjoy the experience without having any stressful situations to deal with.

During the 1950s and 1960s, the air-inclusive package holiday grew in popularity. People could travel to foreign countries (mainly Spain, France and Italy in those days) and have everything organised for them, including the flight and the hotel, without having to speak the language or deal with travel arrangements. Also, such holidays were relatively cheap because they got around the stringent international flight restrictions that were then in force – scheduled flights were all operated by national flag-carrying airlines and were expensive, whereas chartered aircraft were exempt from the international agreements restricting destinations and charges.

However, as time went by several changes occurred in the marketplace. First, there were some high-profile bankruptcies of tour operators, with holidaymakers left stranded abroad, often with their hotels unpaid and the proprietors demanding money. This led to the establishment of a compensation and licensing system funded by the industry, which put costs up. Second, the European Union agreed an 'open skies' policy which did away with the old treaties and allowed low-cost airlines to start operations. Third, the Internet made it easy for people to book their own flights, transfers, hotels and so forth. Fourth, increased travel meant increased confidence among consumers, so that people felt happy to organise their own holidays. Fifth, an increasing mood of independent thinking, born from increasing wealth and universal education, meant people did not want to be regimented on holiday, or even be forced to stay in the same hotel for 2 weeks. Sixth, the wider availability of information about foreign countries (gleaned from television or from independent travel guides such as *Rough Guides* or *Lonely Planet*) encouraged people to travel 'off the beaten track' more. Finally, increased wealth meant that people were more prepared to take a risk, knowing that most problems could be overcome with a big cheque book.

Choosing a holiday has therefore become less a matter of selecting from a fixed menu of destinations, hotels and tour options, and more a process of deciding where one wants to go and what one wants to do there and then putting together the various elements of flight, hotels, local transport, tour bookings and so forth. This makes the decision process more complex, but at the same time it is more engaging and interesting for the person planning the trip – and the Internet makes the whole process relatively straightforward anyway, since airline websites offer hotels and car hire.

Whatever the reasons, holiday choices are much wider than they used to be, and holiday companies are struggling to keep up with the changed environment. Many former package tour operators now sell flights and hotels separately for those who prefer to make their own arrangements, and many more have found the new conditions too tough and have closed down. The new consumer empowerment may have proved too much for some firms, but it has transformed holiday choices forever.

Questions

1 What influence might family roles have on the buying process for a holiday?

2 How has demographic change affected the holiday market?

3 How might people evaluate the alternatives?

4 How might someone establish a consideration set when booking an independent holiday?

5 How has the information search become modified over the past 40 years, as far as holiday booking is concerned?

SUMMARY

In this chapter we have looked at how people behave when faced with buying decisions. We have looked at the decision-making process both for consumers and for organisational buyers, and at the influences and pressures on each group.

Here are the key points from this chapter:

- Consumers buy because they recognise either assortment depletion or assortment extension needs
- Complaints should be encouraged, because they give the opportunity to cure post-purchase dissonance and create loyal customers
- Individuals belong to several reference groups and are also influenced by groups to which they do not belong such as aspirational groups and dissociative groups
- Normative compliance is probably the most powerful factor in attitude formation and decision-making
- The family is probably the most powerful reference group
- Industrial buying is complex because of the number of people involved, and because of greater formality in the process
- Gatekeepers, users, influencers, deciders and buyers are all involved in organisational decision-making. They each have personal agendas, and none of them should be ignored if the deal is to go through
- The route to success in industrial marketing is to make sure the tender has something in it that the competition cannot match.

CHAPTER QUESTIONS

1 How do family members influence each other's buying behaviour?

2 What are the main differences between industrial buyers and consumers?

3 What is the difference between assortment depletion and assortment extension?

4 How can the use of choice heuristics reduce post-purchase dissonance?

5 How can a marketer use interrupts to influence consumer behaviour?

Further reading

Consumer Behavior: A European Perspective 4th edition by Michael R. Solomon, Gary Bamossy, Soren Askegaard, and Margaret K. Hogg (Harlow, FT Prentice Hall, 2009). This is a very comprehensive text adapted from an American book, covering all aspects of consumer behaviour.

Business Marketing Management: A Global Perspective by Jim Blythe and Alan Zimmerman (London, Thomson, 2005). This book provides an in-depth view of business-to-business marketing, taking a global perspective. It covers all aspects of marketing to other businesses, including buyer behaviour and strategic issues.

References

Ang, Lawrence and Buttle, Francis: 'Customer retention management processes', *European Journal of Marketing*, **40** (1/2) (2006), pp. 83–9.

Arnett, Dennis B., German, Steve D. and Hunt, Shelby D.: 'The identity salience model of relationship marketing success: the case of non-profit marketing', *Journal of Marketing*, **67** (April 2003), pp. 89–105.

Bennett, Roger: 'Impulsive donation decisions during online browsing of charity websites', *Journal of Consumer Behaviour*, **8** (2 and 3) (Mar–Jun 2009), pp. 116–34.

Bharadwaj, Neeraj: 'Investigating the decision criteria used in electronic components procurement', *Industrial Marketing Management*, **33** (4) (2004), pp. 317–23.

Bhattacharya, C.B. and Sen, Sankar: 'Consumer-company identification: a framework for understanding consumers' relationships with companies', *Journal of Marketing*, **67** (2) (April 2003), pp. 76–88.

Bolls, Paul D., Muehling, Darrel D. and Yoon, Kak: 'The effects of television commercial pacing on viewers' attention and memory', *Journal of Marketing Communications*, **9** (1) (March 2003), pp. 17–28.

Borgerson, Janet, Schroeder, Jonathan, Blomberg, Britta and Thorssen, Erica: 'The gay family in the ad: consumer responses to non-traditional families in marketing communication', *Journal of Marketing Management*, **22** (9) (2006), pp. 955–78.

Burke, J.: 'Food firms pester pupils for sales', *Sunday Times* (11 June 1995).

Carrigan, Marylyn and Szmigin, Isabelle: '"Mothers of invention": maternal empowerment and convenience consumption', *European Journal of Marketing*, **40** (9/10) (2006), pp. 1122–42.

Curasi, Carolyn F.: 'Intergenerational possession transfers and identity maintenance', *Journal of Consumer Behaviour*, **10** (2) (Mar/April 2011), pp. 111–18.

Davies, Harry L. and Rigaux, Benny P.: 'Perception of marital roles in decision processes', *Journal of Consumer Research*, **1** (June 1974), pp. 5–14.

Dwek, R.: 'In front of the children', *The Grocer*, **2** (December 1995), pp. 45–9.

Dwek, R.: 'Man trouble', *Marketing Business* (February 1996), p. 18.

Ekstrom, Karin M.: 'Parental consumer learning, or keeping up with the children', *Journal of Consumer Behaviour*, **6** (4) (2007), pp. 203–17.

Engel, James F., Blackwell, Roger D. and Miniard, Paul W.: *Consumer Behaviour*, 8th edn (Fort Worth, TX, Dryden Press, 1995).

Filiatrault, Pierre and Brent Ritchie, J.R.: 'Joint purchasing decisions; a comparison of influence structure in family and couple decision-making units', *Journal of Consumer Research*, **7** (September 1980), pp. 131–40.

Fishbein, Martin: 'The search for attitudinal-behavioural consistency', in Joel E. Cohen (ed.) *Behavioural Science Foundations of Consumer Behaviour* (New York, Free Press, 1972), pp. 257–67.

Goffman, Erving: *The Presentation of Self in Everyday Life* (Harmondsworth, Penguin, 1969).

Green, P., Robinson, P. and Wind, Y.: 'The determinants of vendor selection: the evaluation function approach', *Journal of Purchasing* (August 1968).

Green, Robert T., Leonardi, Jean-Paul, Chandon, Jean-Louis, Cunningham, Isabella C.M., Verhage, Bronis and Strazzieri, Alain: 'Societal development and family purchasing roles; a cross-national study', *Journal of Consumer Research*, **9** (March 1983), pp. 436–42.

Grougiou, Vassiliki, and Pettigrew, Simone: 'Seniors' attitudes to voicing complaints: a qualitative study', *Journal of Marketing Management*, **25** (9/10) (2009), pp. 987–1001.

Hamilton, Cathy and Catterall, Miriam: 'Consuming love in poor families: children's influence on consumption decisions', *Journal of Marketing Management*, **22** (9/10) (2006), pp. 1031–82.

Hamilton, Kathy, and Hewer, Paul: 'Tribal mattering spaces: social-networking sites, celebrity affiliations, and tribal innovations', *Journal of Marketing Management*, **26** (3 and 4) (2010), pp. 271–9.

Harwood, Tracy, and Garry, Tony: 'It's Mine! Participation and ownership within virtual co-creation environments', *Journal of Marketing Management*, **26** (3 and 4) (2010), pp. 290–301.

Holbrook, Morris P. and Hirschmann, Elizabeth C.: 'The experiential aspects of consumption; consumer fantasies, feelings and fun', *Journal of Consumer Research*, **9** (September 1982), pp. 132–40.

Lawlor, Margaret-Anne, and Prothero, Andrea: 'Pester power – a battle of wills between children and their parents', *Journal of Marketing Management*, **27** (5 and 6) (2011), pp. 561–81.

Lindridge, Andrew M. and Hogg, Margaret K.: 'Parental gate-keeping in diasporic Indian families: examining the intersection of culture, gender and consumption', *Journal of Marketing Management*, **22** (9/10) (2006), pp. 979–1008.

Macdonald, Emma K. and Uncles, Mark D.: 'Consumer savvy: conceptualization and measurement', *Journal of Marketing Management*, **23** (5/6) (2007), pp. 497–517.

Maxham, James G. III and Netemeyer, Richard G.: 'Firms reap what they sow: the effect of shared values and perceived organizational justice on customers' evaluation of complaint handling', *Journal of Marketing*, **67** (1) (January 2003), pp. 46–62.

Nancarrow, Clive, Tinson, Julie and Brace, Ian: 'Profiling key purchase influencers: those perceived as consumer savvy', *Journal of Consumer Behaviour*, **10** (2) (2011), pp. 102–10.

Ngai, Eric W.T., Heung, Vincent C., Wong, Y.H. and Chan, Fanny K.Y.: 'Consumer complaint behaviour of Asians and non-Asians about hotel services: an empirical analysis', *European Journal of Marketing*, **41** (11/12) (2007), pp. 1375–91.

Odekerken-Schroder, Gaby, Ouwersloot, Hans, Lemmink, Jos and Semeijn, Janjaap: 'Consumers' trade-off between relationship, service, package and price: an empirical study in the car industry', *European Journal of Marketing*, **37** (1) (2003), pp. 219–42.

Oliver, Richard L.: 'A cognitive model of the antecedents and consequences of satisfaction decisions', *Journal of Marketing Research*, **17** (November 1980), pp. 460–9.

Powers, T.L.: *Modern Business Marketing: A Strategic Planning Approach to Business and Industrial Markets* (St Paul, MN, West, 1991).

Raju, P.S.: 'Optimum stimulation level; its relationship to personality, demographics, and exploratory behaviour', *Journal of Consumer Research*, **7** (December 1980), pp. 272–82.

Shankar, Avi, Cherrier, Helene and Canniford, Robin: 'Consumer empowerment: a Foucauldian interpretation', *European Journal of Marketing*, **40** (9/10) (2006), pp. 1013–30.

Sharma, Piyush, Sivakumaran, Bharadwaj and Marshall, Roger: 'Exploring impulse buying and variety seeking by retail shoppers: towards a common conceptual framework', *Journal of Marketing Management*, **26** (5 and 6) (2010a), pp. 473–94.

Sharma, Piyush, Marshall, Roger, Reday, Peter Alan and Na, Woonbang: 'Complainers vs non-complainers: a multinational investigation of individual and situational influences on customer complaint behavior', *Journal of Marketing Management*, **26** (1 and 2) (2010b), pp. 163–80.

Sijun, Wang and Huff, Leonard C.: 'Exploring buyers' response to sellers' violation of trust', *European Journal of Marketing*, **41** (9/10) (2007), pp. 1033–52.

Singh, Jagdip: 'Consumer complaint intentions and behaviour: definitions and taxonomical issues', *Journal of Marketing*, **52** (January 1988), pp. 93–107.

Slater, Alex and Armstrong, Kate: 'Involvement, Tate, and me', *Journal of Marketing Management*, **26** (7&8) (2010), pp. 727–48.

Smith, Robert E. and Swinyard, William R.: 'Attitude-behaviour consistency; the impact of product trial versus advertising', *Journal of Marketing Research*, **20** (August 1983).

Strandvik, Tore and Holmlund, Maria: 'How to diagnose business-to-business relationships by mapping negative incidents', *Journal of Marketing Management*, **24** (3/4) (2008), pp. 351–81.

Tanner, J.F.: 'Buyer perceptions of the purchase process and its effect on customer satisfaction', *Industrial Marketing Management*, **25** (2) (March 1996), pp. 125–33.

Thomsen, Thyra Uth and Sorensen, Elin Brandi: 'The first four-wheeled status symbol: pram consumption as a vehicle for the construction of motherhood identity', *Journal of Marketing Management*, **22** (9/10) (2006), pp. 907–27.

Thomson, Elizabeth S., Laing, Angus W. and McKee, Lorna: 'Family purchase decision making: exploring child influence behavior', *Journal of Consumer Behaviour*, **6** (4) (2007), pp. 182–202.

Wagner, Stephan M.: 'Supplier development practices: an exploratory study', *European Journal of Marketing*, **40** (5/6) (2006), pp. 554–71.

Walsh, Gianfranco, Hennig-Thurau, Thorsten and Mitchell, Vincent-Wayne: 'Consumer confusion proneness: scale development, validation and application', *Journal of Marketing Management*, **23** (7/8) (2007), pp. 697–721.

Wang, Shih-Lun Alex: 'The effects of audience knowledge on message processing of editorial content', *Journal of Marketing Communications*, **12** (4) (2006), pp. 281–96.

Webster, F.E. and Wind, Y.: *Organisational Buying Behaviour* (Englewood Cliffs, NJ, Prentice Hall, 1972).

Zajonc, Robert B. and Markus, Hazel: 'Must all affect be mediated by cognition?' *Journal of Consumer Research*, **12** (December 1985), pp. 363–4.

4

SEGMENTATION, TARGETING AND POSITIONING

Objectives

After reading this chapter you should be able to:

- Describe the main methods of segmenting markets
- Explain how segmentation aids profitability
- Decide whether a given segment is sufficiently profitable to be worth targeting
- Explain the purpose of segmentation
- Develop ways of assessing the economic viability of segments
- Explain the growth of segmented markets
- Establish strategies for dealing with segmented markets
- Describe perceptual mapping
- Describe the main issues surrounding the positioning of brands.

INTRODUCTION

The segmentation concept was first developed by Smith (1957) and is concerned with grouping consumers in terms of their needs. The aim of segmentation is to identify a group of people who have a need or needs that can be met by a single product, in order to concentrate the marketing firm's efforts most effectively and economically. For example, if a manufacturer produces a standardised product by a mass production method, the firm would need to be sure that there are sufficient people with a need for the product to make the exercise worthwhile.

The assumptions underlying segmentation are:

- Not all buyers are alike
- Sub-groups of people with similar behaviour, backgrounds, values and needs can be identified
- The sub-groups will be smaller and more homogeneous than the market as a whole
- It is easier to satisfy a small group of similar customers than to try to satisfy large groups of dissimilar customers (Zikmund and D'Amico 1995).

Continued on p. 76

Birmingham

Marketing a whole city may seem like a tall order, but all cities need to attract industry, tourists and even residents, or it will die. The marketers involved are in a unique position because they do not own the brand – the brand is owned and developed by the people who live in the city.

Identifying appropriate market segments is far from easy: a city the size of Birmingham contains within it virtually all segments of both consumer and business markets. The aim of Birmingham's positioning is to place the city as a youthful, lively city, on the basis that nobody believes that they are old.

Repositioning Birmingham as an exciting city to visit means building on what was essentially an industrial past – removing the image of a grimy industrial town and replacing it with a vibrant city where many events happen is a challenge that the marketers seek to meet.

The marketers monitor the league tables published by tourism organisations, and carry out their own research to determine how many people visit, how much they spend, how long they stay and whether they intend to return. Monitoring the market is essential for future decision-making about promotion activities.

Neil Rami, Managing Director

Watch the video clip, then try to answer the following questions. The answers are on the companion website.

Questions

1 What segmentation bases are most appropriate for Birmingham?
2 What positioning problems are apparent for the city?
3 How should Birmingham target potential visitors?

Targeting is concerned with choosing at which segments to aim. Segmentation is essentially about dividing up the market; targeting is about the practicalities of doing business within the market. The two are clearly closely linked, since the segmentation process will usually provide information as to which segments are likely to prove most profitable or will help the firm to achieve its strategic objectives in other ways.

Positioning is concerned with the brand's relationship with other brands aimed at the same segment. Positioning is about the place the brand occupies in the minds of potential customers, relative to other brands.

REASONS FOR SEGMENTING MARKETS

Each consumer is an individual with individual needs and wants. On the face of it, this creates a major problem for marketers, since it would clearly be impossible to tailor-make or customise each product to the exact requirements of each individual.

Before the Industrial Revolution most products were individually made. This proved to be expensive and essentially inefficient once mass production techniques had come into being. Unfortunately, mass production (taken to the extreme) means a reduction in the available choice of product, since the best way to keep production costs low is to have long production runs, which means standardising the product. Every adaptation costs money in terms of retooling and repackaging the product. In some economies, particularly those in parts of Eastern Europe and in the Third World, there is not sufficient wealth or investment in industry to allow for the production of many different types of product. These economies still rely heavily on mass production and mass marketing.

Mass marketing (or undifferentiated marketing) in which a standard product is produced for all consumers will only be effective if the consumers concerned have little choice and do not already own a product that meets the main needs. For example, in 1930s Germany few families owned cars. Hitler promised the German people that every family would own a car, so Porsche was commissioned to develop the Volkswagen (literally 'people's car') as a basic vehicle which could be cheaply produced for the mass market. The car had few refinements: it even lacked a fuel gauge.

This approach is less effective in economies where most consumers already own the core benefits of the product. Once car ownership was widespread and the core benefit of personal transportation was owned by most families, consumers demanded choices in features and design of their vehicles. Segmentation deals with finding out how many people are likely to want each benefit, roughly how much they will be willing to pay for it, and where they would like to buy it from. In this way, the firm approaching a segmented market is able to offer more functional benefits and more attention to *hedonic needs*, i.e. the products are more fun (see Chapter 3).

To make these adaptations worthwhile, marketers need to be reasonably sure that there is a large enough market for the product to be viable economically. On the other hand, concentrating on a smaller segment means that economies can be made in the supplier's communications activities; rather than advertise to a mass market, for example, the marketer would be better off concentrating resources on producing an advertisement that is tailored to the target segment – an ad, in other words, designed for the ideal customer and no other.

The reason for this is that we are surrounded by advertising messages. Consequently, people learn to avoid advertisements, and particularly to avoid ones that are clearly never going to be of any interest. At the same time, consumers will go out of their way to find out about products they have some interest in, often by reading special interest magazines. Therefore an advertisement that is tailored to a specific group of consumers and that appears in a medium that those consumers use is likely to be far more effective than an untargeted advertisement in a general interest medium.

Companies that aim for small segments usually have much greater credibility with consumers, and can learn to provide exactly what most pleases those consumers. In recent years, the Internet has provided opportunities for companies to relate to customers as individuals, and to be able to use interactive communications as a method of developing a 'segment of one' (Bailey *et al.* 2009).

Overall, the main purpose of segmenting is to enable the company to concentrate its efforts on pleasing one group of people with similar needs, rather than trying to please everybody and probably ending up pleasing nobody. Table 4.1 shows the advantages of segmenting the market.

Table 4.1 Advantages of segmentation

Advantage	Explanation
Customer analysis	By segmenting, the firm can get to understand its best customers better.
Competitor analysis	It is much easier to recognise and combat competition when concentrating on one small part of the overall market.
Effective resource allocation	Companies' scarce resources can be concentrated more effectively on a few consumers, rather than spread thinly across the masses.
Strategic marketing planning	Planning becomes easier once the firm has a clear picture of its best customers.
Expanding the market	Good segmentation can increase the overall size of the market by bringing in new customers who fit the profile of the typical customer, but were previously unaware of the product.

It is useful to remember that segmentation is not only concerned with choosing the right customers – it also means deciding which customers cannot be served effectively. Sometimes this is because the firm lacks the resources and sometimes it is because some groups of customers are more trouble than they are worth. Rejecting some customers is called demarketing (Kotler and Levy 1971), and research conducted by Medway *et al.* (2011) showed that marketers responsible for managing places (for example, ancient monuments) use demarketing as a way of controlling sustainability of the place as well as controlling such factors as seasonality and crisis prevention.

SEGMENTATION VARIABLES

A segment must fulfil the following requirements if it is to be successfully exploited:

- *It must be measurable, or definable.* In other words, there must be some way of identifying the members of the segment and knowing how many of them there are.
- *It must be accessible.* This means it must be possible to communicate with the segment as a group, and to get the product to them as a group.
- *It must be substantial,* i.e. big enough to be worth aiming for.
- *It must be congruent,* that is to say the members must have a close agreement on their needs.
- *It must be stable.* The nature and membership of the segment must be reasonably constant.

The three key criteria are accessibility, substance and measurability (Kotler 1991), but it is important also to look at the causes underlying the segmentation (Engel *et al.* 1995). This enables the marketers to anticipate changes more easily and sometimes to verify that the segmentation base is correctly defined.

There are many bases for segmenting, but the following are the main ones:

- *Geographic.* Where the consumers live, the climate, the topology, etc. For example, cars in Brazil almost always have air conditioning but may not have heaters; cars in Sweden have headlights that stay on constantly because of the poor quality of the light for much of the year. Geographic segmentation is very commonly used in international marketing, but is equally useful within single nations.
- *Psychographic.* Based on the personality type of the individuals in the segment. For example, the home insurance market might segment into those who are afraid of crime, those who are afraid of natural disasters and those who are afraid of accidental damage to their property.
- *Behavioural.* This approach examines the benefits, usage situation, extent of use and loyalty. For example, the car market might segment into business users and private users. The private market might segment further to encompass those

who use their cars primarily for commuting, those who use their cars for hobbies such as surfing or camping and those who use the car for domestic duties such as shopping or taking children to school. The business market might segment into 'prestige' users such as managing directors and senior executives, or high mileage users such as salespeople.

- *Demographic.* Concerned with the structure of the population in terms of ages, lifestyles and economic factors. For example, the housing market can be divided into first-time buyers, families with children, older retired people and elderly people in sheltered accommodation; equally, the market could be segmented according to lifestyle, with some accommodation appealing to young professionals, some appealing to country lovers, and so forth.

Geographic segmentation

Geographic segmentation may be carried out for a number of reasons.

- The nature of the product may be such that it applies only to people living within a specific area or type of area. Clothing manufacturers know that they will sell more heavy-weather clothing in cold coastal areas than in warm inland areas.
- If the company's resources are limited, the firm may start out in a small area and later roll out the product nationally.
- It might be that the product itself does not travel well. This is true of sheet glass, wedding cakes and most personal services such as hairdressing.

Markets may be segmented geographically according to the type of housing in the area. Firms that supply products specifically aimed at elderly people may wish to locate (or at least concentrate their marketing efforts) in retirement areas. Products aimed at young people might be heavily marketed in university towns, and so forth.

Psychographic segmentation

Psychographic segmentation classifies consumers according to their personalities. Psychographic segmentation remains problematical because of the difficulties of measuring consumers' psychological traits on a large scale. This type of segmentation can therefore fail on the grounds of accessibility. For example, researchers might find out that there is a group of people who relate the brand of coffee that they buy to their self-esteem. The problem then is that there is no obvious medium in which to advertise this feature of the coffee – if there were a magazine called *Coffee Makes Me Feel Good* there would be no problem.

In recent years, the Internet has increased the number of possibilities for allowing people to self-define into segments: our coffee-drinkers might have a website dedicated to them, at relatively little cost, where they might be able to exchange views and ideas. Segmentation can therefore be conducted in reverse by seeing who visits the website.

Behavioural segmentation

Behavioural segmentation can be a useful and reliable way of segmenting. At its most obvious, if the firm is marketing to anglers they are not interested in how old the anglers are, what their views are on strong drink or where they live. All the firm cares about is that they go fishing and might therefore be customers for a new type of rod. Accessing the segment would be easily undertaken by advertising in angling magazines or by developing an attractive website (for example, one which offers useful tips on angling). At a deeper level the firm might be interested in such issues as where they buy their fishing tackle, how much they usually spend on a rod, what kind of fish they are after, and so forth, but this information is easily obtained through questionnaire-type surveys, or by running an online forum. *Lifestyle* analysis has been widely used for the past 30 years or so, and seeks to segment markets according to how consumers spend their time, what their beliefs are about themselves and about specific issues, and the relative importance of their various possessions (e.g. cars, clothes, homes). The attraction of this approach is that it takes account of a wide range of characteristics of the segment, encompassing some psychographic features and some behavioural features (Plummer 1974).

Demographic segmentation

Demographic segmentation is the most commonly used method of segmenting markets, probably because it is easy to pick up the relevant information from government statistics. Demographics is the study of how people differ in terms of factors such as age, occupation, salary and lifestyle stage.

Typically, demographic segmentation revolves around age. While this is relevant in many cases, it is often difficult to see the difference between, say, a 20-year-old's buying pattern and a 30-year-old's buying pattern. Equally, it cannot be said with much reliability that all 10-year-olds share the same tastes. There are undoubtedly 10-year-olds who would not want to visit Disneyland or Luna Park and 10-year-olds who would prefer duck á l'orange to a hamburger. Age is, of course, relevant but it should be included as part of a range of measures, not relied upon on its own.

Critical thinking

Can we really be pigeonholed this easily? Surely our behaviour cannot be entirely governed by our age, or our gender, or our religious beliefs! As we grow older, or change our jobs, or have children, or become better educated, do our basic likes and dislikes really change?

If you like chips, you like chips, and no amount of lottery wins will make you suddenly like caviar instead. But then again – how are our tastes determined in the first place? By our upbringing, our friends, our experiences – and these are governed by our age, our gender, our religious beliefs, our education, etc. etc.

Maybe we CAN be pigeonholed that easily!

As we saw in Chapter 2, demographic variables are shifting over time, as the birth rate falls and the average age of the population rises. In addition, the number of single-person households is rising as people marry later and divorce rates increase; in 2001, single-person households represented 30% of UK households (Office for National Statistics 2003). The implications of this one change for marketers are far-reaching. Here are some of the possibilities:

- Increase in sales of individual packs of food
- Increase in sales of recipe products and ready meals
- Decrease in sales of gardening equipment and children's items
- Increase in sales of mating-game items
- Decrease in family-sized cars, packs of breakfast cereal, cleaning products, etc.

In Australia, immigration from South-East Asia is causing major changes in eating habits, religious observances and the linguistic structure of the country. In some cases, marketing activities have themselves contributed to a cross-fertilisation of cultural behaviour, so that individuals from one ethnic group behave in ways more usually associated with another group. This culture swapping means that ethnic and racial segmentation is no longer possible in most cases (Jamal 2003, Lindridge 2010).

Overall, demographic change means that new segments are emerging, some of which offer greater opportunities to marketers than do the segments they replace. Marketers need to monitor these changes in the demography if they are to remain able to segment the market effectively.

Not all segmentation variables will be appropriate to all markets. A pizza company might segment a market geographically (locating in a town centre) but would not segment by religion; the situation would be reversed for a wholesale kosher butcher. This is despite the fact that both firms are in the food business. Single-variable segmentation is based on only one variable; for example, size of firm. This is the simplest way to segment, but is also the most inaccurate and would rarely be used in practice. To achieve multivariable segmentation, several characteristics are taken into account. The more characteristics that are used, the greater the accuracy and effectiveness, but the smaller the resulting markets.

In practice, segmentation is difficult to apply. Many managers have difficulty in interpreting segmentation solutions presented to them by researchers; some even confess to a lack of understanding of segmentation theory (Dolnicar and Lazarevski 2009).

SEGMENTING INDUSTRIAL MARKETS

Industrial or organisational markets can be, and are, segmented by marketers according to the following criteria:

- *Geographic location.* Probably the commonest method, since most organisational markets are serviced by salespeople, and geographical segmentation enables the salesperson to make best use of drive time. Often firms in the same industry will locate near each other, perhaps because of availability of raw materials, or for traditional reasons to do with availability of local skilled workers.

- *Type of organisation.* IBM segments its market according to the industry the customer is in. This means that some IBM salespeople specialise in banking, others in insurance, others perhaps in local government applications of the equipment.
- *Client company size.* Many companies have separate salesforces to deal with large accounts, and often such salespeople need to use special techniques for dealing at this level.
- *Product use.* Oil companies have separate strategies (and sometimes separate subsidiaries) for marketing household central heating oil, for the plastics industry, for petrochemicals and for automotive sales.
- Usage rate. Customers who use large quantities of a given product will expect (and get) different treatment from customers who buy only in small quantities. This is partly because their needs are different, and partly because the supplier will tend to value the large buyer over the small buyer.

Bonoma and Shapiro (1984) suggest a nested approach to organisational market segmentation. This approach entails starting with broad characteristics such as the type of industry and the size of the organisations in it, then narrowing the segment by working through operating variables (processes, product types, etc.), then looking at the purchasing approach of the organisations, followed by situational factors such as delivery lead times and order size, and finally looking at the individual types of buyer in each firm.

For example, a glass manufacturer might begin by segmenting according to type of industry (window glass for construction, toughened glass for cars or bottles and jars for food packaging). Within the food packaging market the industry might break down further to pickles and sauces, wines and beers, and soft drinks. The wine and beer bottle market may further break down into major brewers and bottlers who buy in large quantities, and small privately owned vineyards who buy on a once-a-year basis. Some of the brewers may buy by tender, some may prefer to use a regular supplier and some may have special requirements in terms of bottle shape or design.

As in consumer markets, it is not necessarily the case that buyers act from wholly rational motives (see Chapter 3), so it would be unreasonable not to include the buyers' personal characteristics in the segmentation plan somewhere. This is likely to be the province of the salesforce since they are dealing with the buyers on a day-to-day basis.

SEGMENTATION EFFECTIVENESS

If a segment is correctly identified, it should be possible for the marketer to meet the needs of the segment members much more effectively than their competitors can. The firm will be able to provide specialist products that are more nearly right for the consumers in the segment, and will be able to communicate better with them. From the consumer's viewpoint, this is worth paying an extra premium for. Rather than

Figure 4.1 Segmentation trade-offs

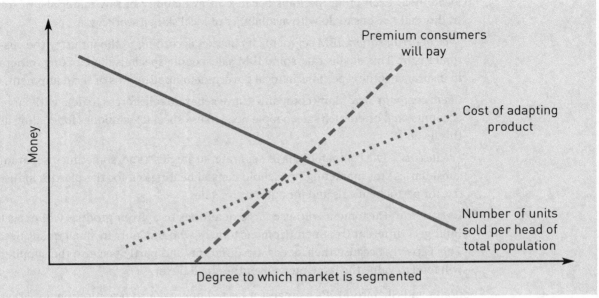

putting up with a product that does not quite fit the bill, the consumer will pay a little more for something that more closely approaches the ideal.

The segment will be profitable as long as the **premium** that the consumer will pay is greater than the cost to the manufacturer of making the modifications. There is therefore a trade-off; the finer-tuned the segmentation, the smaller the market but the greater the premium the target consumers will be prepared to pay. This is illustrated in Figure 4.1.

As the segmentation becomes narrower, fewer units will be sold, so the number of items sold as compared with the population at large will drop. This is partly offset by higher prices, but the profitability of the segment will begin only where the premium line and the cost line diverge. Where the costs of adaptation are higher than the premium, it is not worthwhile to make the adaptations; where the premium is higher than the cost, it may be worthwhile but the firm must still take account of the reduction in unit sales overall.

GLOBAL SEGMENTATION

Although cultural variance (and differences in consumer behaviour) are still major issues for international marketers (Hofstede 1994), transnational segments are still identifiable. The main bases for segmentation are:

- By country
- By individual characteristics (in much the same way as segmentation is handled within one's own country).

Countries can be grouped according to economic development criteria, by cultural variables or by a combination of factors, such as economic, political and R&D factors (Lee 1990). One of the best known studies is that of Hofstede (1980) in which countries were classified according to power distance (the degree to which power is centralised), individualism (the degree to which people act independently of others), uncertainty avoidance (the degree to which people are prepared to take risks) and masculinity (the degree of male domination). The success rate of country classification as a practical route to segmentation is doubtful, however; variations between individuals within a country are usually much greater than those between countries. It should also be remembered that Hofstede's original research was carried out in the 1960s, when travel, tourism and migration were all at much lower levels; the findings may therefore be a great deal less relevant now than they were then.

Transnational consumer segmentation looks at lifestyles, behaviour and situation-specific behaviour. An example of lifestyle segmentation is the transnational teenage market; there is also evidence of an 'elite' market (Hassan and Katsanis 1991). It is usually the wealthier members of a society that can travel abroad and become exposed to ideas from other cultures. An example of situation-specific segmentation is the attitudes to gift-giving, which seem to be common to many cultures (Beatty *et al.* 1991). More recent research has found transnational segments for dairy products, although the researchers found that some of the marketing communications needed to be adapted to address some aspects of the product, even when the consumers showed similar characteristics (Moskowitz *et al.* 2008).

The main difficulty with seeking transnational consumer segments lies in generating adequate research within the target countries.

TARGETING

Having divided the market into segments, managers must decide which segment will be the best to target, given the firm's overall objectives. Normally managers would choose the most profitable segment, but equally a firm may decide to aim for a particular segment of the market that is currently neglected, on the grounds that competitors are less likely to enter the market. The process of selecting a segment to aim for is called targeting. There are three basic strategic options open to marketers.

1 Concentrated marketing (single segment). This is also known as niche marketing; Pickfords heavy haulage and MTV follow this approach. The niche marketer concentrates on being the very best within a single tiny segment.

2 Differentiated marketing (multisegmented) means concentrating on two or more segments, offering a differentiated marketing mix for each. Holiday Inn aims to attract business travellers during the week but aims for the leisure market at the weekend and promotes to families. At the weekend, the hotels often have events for children and special room rates for families.

3 **Undifferentiated marketing** is about using a 'scattergun' approach. The producers who do this are usually offering a basic product that would be used by almost all age groups and lifestyles. For example, the market for petrol is largely undifferentiated. Although oil producers occasionally try to differentiate their products by the use of various additives and detergents, the use of petrol is much the same for everybody, and there would not appear to be any relationship between segmentation variables and petrol use. It would be difficult to imagine any real adaptation to the product that would meet people's needs sufficiently well to merit a premium price. Such examples of undifferentiated products are increasingly rare; even the producers of such basic commodities as salt and flour have made great strides forward in differentiating their products (i.e. meeting consumers' needs better).

The decision regarding which strategy to adopt will rest on the following three factors:

● The company's *resources*
● The product's features and benefits
● The characteristics of the segment(s).

Clearly, if resources are limited the company will tend to adopt a concentrated marketing approach. This approach is taken by Titleist, the golf supply company. Titleist supplies everything the golfer needs, from clubs to golfing clothes, rather than diversifying into a general sporting products market. This enables the firm to become very close to its market, and to understand the needs of golfers (and intermediaries such as club professionals) better than any other firm.

A higher level of resourcing coupled with a range of segments to approach will lead to a differentiated approach, and a simple made-for-everybody type product will lead to an undifferentiated approach. Table 4.2 shows this in action.

Table 4.2 Resourcing and degree of differentiation

		Type of product	
		High-differentiation consumers	Low-differentiation consumers
High-resource company	Mass market	Differentiated	Undifferentiated
	Specialist market	Differentiated	Concentrated
Low-resource company	Mass market	Concentrated	Differentiated (perhaps geographically)
	Specialist market	Concentrated	Concentrated

Table 4.3 Targeting decisions

Segment size	Profit per unit sold	Number of competitors	Strategic decision rationale
Large	Large	Large	A large market with large profits will attract competitors; prices will fall rapidly, and so will profits.
Large	Small	Large	This is a mature market. A new entrant would have to have something special to dominate the market: perhaps a much reduced cost base.
Small	Large	Large	A small segment with a high profit per unit and a large number of competitors can be captured entirely by a penetration pricing strategy.
Large	Large	Small	If the segment is both large and profitable, competitors will certainly enter the market. A skimming policy is best for this market; as competitors enter, it will be possible to reduce prices to compete effectively.
Large	Small	Small	This is a mature market, but should be low risk; the lack of competition means that it should be easy to capture a share, and the low profit margin will discourage others from entering.
Small	Small	Large	This is a dying market. Really not worth entering at all.
Small	Large	Small	This is a niche market. It should be possible to capture all of this market.
Small	Small	Small	This is clearly not a very profitable segment at all. Unless the firm has something very new to bring to the segment, this is probably not worth targeting.

Companies with a small resource base are often unable to make their voices heard in mass markets simply because they cannot afford the level of promotional spend. They therefore need to segment narrowly, perhaps by starting out in a small area of the country (geographical segmentation) and gradually spreading nationwide as resources become available.

Table 4.3 shows the decision matrix for choosing a segment to target. The marketing strategy should be tailored to fit the intended audience – this means that each of the seven Ps, and every element of the promotion mix, needs to be built around the segment.

Accurate targeting is best achieved by carrying out detailed market research into the needs and wants of the target group (see Chapter 5). In this way the company is able to decide what to offer the target audience to improve on the competitors' offering. Note that three factors are being taken into account here. First, what do the

Table 4.4 Market coverage strategies

Strategy	Explanation	Example
Product/market concentration	Niche marketing; the company takes over one small part of the market	Tie Rack, Sock Shop
Product specialisation	Firm produces a full line of a specific product type	Campbell's Soup
Market specialisation	Firm produces everything that a specific group of consumers needs	Titleist golf clubs, golf balls, tees, caddies
Selective specialisation	Firm enters selective niches that do not relate closely to each other, but are profitable	British Telecom sells telephone services to consumers and industry, but also owns satellite time, which it sells to TV broadcasters and others
Full coverage	Firm enters every possible segment of its potential market	Mitsubishi Industries, which produces everything from musical instruments to supertankers

consumers in the target segment need? Second, what is already available to them? Third, what can the firm offer that would be better than what is currently available? There is a danger in that companies can sometimes hinder their future targeting by placing too much emphasis on currently successful target market responses. This is especially prevalent in online and database marketing, where managers can end up focusing only on those people who were contacted in the first place; sometimes there are people in the target market who, for one reason or another, were not targeted in the particular mailing (Rhee and McIntyre 2009). This results in what is known as selection bias.

The five basic strategies of market coverage were outlined by Derek F. Abell in 1980. They are shown in Table 4.4.

Choosing the right market and then targeting it accurately are possibly the most important activities a marketer carries out. Choosing the wrong segment to target or, worse, not attempting to segment the market at all, leads to lost opportunities and wasted effort. Most firms find that Pareto's Law applies, and the firm obtains 80% of its profits from 20% of its customers – choosing the right group therefore becomes absolutely crucial to success.

Accessing the target market is another issue that deserves attention. For a segment to be viable, it needs to be accessible via some communications medium or another; the segment may comprise people who read a particular magazine or watch a particular TV station. If there is no way to reach the segment, it cannot become a target market. In some cases the segment is defined by the medium; for example, *Cosmopolitan* readers represent a group of independently minded women with career aspirations, usually with high disposable incomes or aspirations in that direction, and interests that are more likely to run to business issues than to knitting patterns. These women represent a valuable market segment in their own right, but can probably only be easily identified as a group because they read *Cosmopolitan*.

POSITIONING

Positioning has been defined as: 'The place a product occupies in a given market, as perceived by the relevant group of customers; that group of customers is known as the target segment of the market' (Wind 1984). Usually positioning refers to the place the product occupies in the consumer's perceptual map of the market: for instance, as a high-quality item or as a reliable one or perhaps as a cheap version. The product is positioned in the perceptual map alongside similar offerings; this is a result of the categorisation and chunking processes (see Chapter 3).

Consumers build up a position for a product based on what they expect and believe to be the most pertinent features of the product class. Marketers therefore need to find out first what the pertinent features of the products are in the target consumers' perceptions. The marketer can then adjust the mix of features and benefits, and the communications mix, to give the product its most effective position relative to the other brands in the market. Sometimes the positioning process is led by consumers, sometimes by marketers.

Research shows that consumers use a relatively short list of factors in determining the position of a product (Blankson and Kalafatis 2004). These are as follows.

- *Top-of-the-range.* This refers to the product which consumers believe to be the most expensive or 'the best'. In the UK, this is often called 'the Rolls-Royce of...' whichever product type is under discussion.
- *Service.* The service levels which surround the product can be an important factor.
- *Value for money.* This is the degree to which the product's benefits represent a fair exchange for the price being asked.
- *Reliability.* Products are often positioned as being more (or less) reliable than their competitors.
- *Attractiveness.* This can refer to factors other than appearance, but implies factors other than the purely practical, performance-related factors.
- *Country of origin.* Some countries have a reputation for producing the best examples of some categories of product. For example, German engineering is highly regarded whereas the French are known for their food and wine. Some countries have a correspondingly poor reputation, of course, and this can be difficult to overcome (Martin *et al.* 2011). Firms can use self-focused mental imagery to develop a better image for these countries' products.
- *Brand name.* Branding is a key issue in positioning, as it identifies the product and conveys an impression of its quality (see Chapter 6).

- *Selectivity.* The degree to which the consumer can distinguish between brands and select from the range is a factor in positioning.

Ultimately, product positioning depends on the attitudes of the particular target market, so the marketer must either take these attitudes as they are and tailor the product to fit those attitudes or they must seek to change the attitudes of the market. Usually it is easier and cheaper to change the product than it is to change the consumers, but sometimes the market's attitudes to the product are so negative that the manufacturer feels constrained to reposition the product. For example, Skoda cars had to fight hard to throw off the negative connotations of the vehicle's Eastern European origins. Not wishing to be classed with Ladas, Yugos and Polski Fiats and thus share the perception of poor workmanship and unreliability, Skoda made great efforts to emphasise Volkswagen's takeover of the company and to position the car next to VW in the consumer's mind.

Skoda has pointed out that, under the auspices of VW ownership, the company's quality control and engineering procedures have been greatly improved. Skoda was, in any case, the jewel in the crown of Eastern European car manufacture, so the firm has been able to demonstrate that the cars are made to a high standard.

To determine the product's position, research is carried out with the target group of consumers, and a perceptual map such as the one in Figure 4.2 will be produced.

From Figure 4.2 it can be seen that Brand B has the image of being both high price and high quality: this is probably the Rolls-Royce of the products (top-of-the-range factor). Brand D is perceived as being low price but low quality: this would be a cheap, everyday brand. Brand A has a problem: although tending towards a high

Figure 4.2 Perceptual mapping

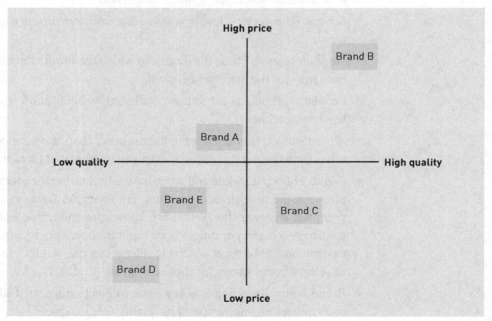

price, this product is perceived as being below-average quality. Sales are likely to be low, or will take place only when the consumer has no other choice available. Brand C, on the other hand, enjoys a low price and good quality, so is probably the top-selling brand (value-for-money factor).

It should be noted that these positions are based on average responses from consumers in the target groups. They are not objective, nor are they based on the firm's view of the quality of its products. For this reason, they can sometimes be changed by promotional efforts. Far more commonly, though, the firm will need to do something more practical about changing the product or changing its price to make the necessary changes.

In Figure 4.2, the products have been mapped against only two dimensions, but it is perfectly possible (perhaps even advisable) to map the product against more dimensions. This can be done on a computer using multidimensional mapping software.

One of the most useful tactical aspects of positioning maps is that they can be used to identify gaps in the market. Using Figure 4.2 as an example, there is clearly a gap next to Brand A and below Brand B for a medium-to-high quality product at a medium-to-high price. Currently this market seems to be dominated by lower-priced brands; a brand entering this market would need to be perceived as higher quality than Brand C, but at a lower price than Brand B.

SALES FORECASTING

Having segmented the market, targeted the appropriate segments and decided on a positioning strategy, the firm is in a better position to forecast the expected sales of the product.

Two overall strategic approaches to sales forecasting exist: break-down and build-up.

The break-down approach begins with the overall market for the product category and seeks to predict what the firm's share of that market will be. For example, a bank may have access to government economic forecasts which can be used to calculate the total loans market for the following year. The bank forecasters will know what the bank's share of the market was in previous years and can use this information to make a reasonable estimate of what the bank's total lending will be in the ensuing year.

The build-up method, on the other hand, begins with the market segments (and even individual consumers) and builds up to a total market share. The bank in the above example might begin with an estimate of how many home loans it might make (based on market research) and how many business loans, how many car loans, and so forth. By adding these figures together, an overall estimate of the total sales for the following year is arrived at.

Sales forecasts help to determine the viability of a segment, and also help the firm to plan its budgets and indeed virtually all of its other activities. Forecasting the future is always difficult; many firms rely on **executive judgement**, using the skill and experience of its senior people in deciding whether a product is a winner or not. Unfortunately, this approach can fail because the executives will favour a product that they would buy as private consumers, rather than a product that the target market segment would buy.

Through a **customer survey** firms are able to ask potential customers how much of a given product they are likely to buy within the next 12 months or so. These intent-to-buy studies work best for existing product categories; for a radically new product it is much more difficult, since only the most innovative of consumers will be able to say with any certainty that they would be prepared to buy the product early in its launch. The main drawback with this method is that customers may intend to purchase, but change their minds during the course of the year, perhaps owing to a competitor's actions. On the other hand, some customers who say in the survey that they will not buy may well do so if their circumstances change.

Other firms may use a **salesforce survey**, asking the salesforce how much of a given product they might expect to sell over the next 12 months. This has the advantage that the salespeople, unlike senior management, are usually close to the customer and are able to make judgements based on this. Also, salespeople will be wary about making rash forecasts that they might later be held to. On the other hand, salespeople generally like to be consulted about their own targets and quotas. A variation on the salesforce survey is the **distributor survey**, where the company's distributors are asked how much they expect to sell over a specific period. Since the distributors will be giving the total sales in the product category (e.g. supermarkets might be asked how much mineral water they expect to sell in the next 12 months), the company will then have to make a judgement regarding the amount of market share they might reasonably expect to capture.

The **Delphi technique** involves taking in the managers' and salespeople's forecasts, combining them centrally, then sending the aggregate forecast back to the individuals concerned for revision. This approach has proved popular with firms because it tends to produce a consensus of opinion to which all those concerned can adhere. A problem with using Delphi might be that individuals will only make forecasts that they are quite sure are achievable: in other words, they might underestimate the possible sales rather than risk being unable to hit targets.

Time-series analysis uses the company's past sales records to predict what will happen in the future. Although this can be quite accurate, it does not take account of the unexpected – a sudden entry by a competitor, a change in legislation or a change in the company's fortunes through takeover or merger. Few forecasting methods can take account of these factors, of course, and ultimately the company has to plan in some way. Time-series forecasters usually perform four types of analysis, as shown in Table 4.5 (Marino 1986). Having carried out each of these analyses, the forecaster is able to combine the results to develop the sales forecast.

Time-series analysis works best for well established products with fairly stable purchasing patterns. It is not suitable for new products or for products with erratic demand cycles.

Table 4.5 Time-series analysis

Type of analysis	Description
Trend analysis	Focuses on aggregate sales data collected over a long period to determine whether sales are rising, falling or staying level
Cycle analysis	Here the forecaster examines the sales figures from a number of years to see whether there is a cyclical pattern; perhaps a response to the economic boom-and-bust cycle. This method has been largely discredited for most markets, since the cycles do not follow a regular pattern
Seasonal analysis	Sales figures are analysed on a monthly or even weekly basis to see whether there is a seasonal cycle operating
Random factor analysis	In any analysis there will be figures that do not fit the pattern; random factor analysis seeks to attribute explanations for these abnormal findings. For example, a spell of unseasonal weather might have affected one month's figures

For new products, a **test marketing** exercise might be carried out. This involves making the product available in one geographical area for a period of time, and monitoring the actual sales of the product in the area. The key to success with test marketing lies in ensuring that the area chosen is an accurate representation of the country as a whole; if not, the predicted sales on national roll-out will not be as expected. The major drawback of test marketing is that it allows the firm's competitors to see the product and possibly develop their own version before the product goes national. For this reason, test marketing exercises are usually short.

CASE STUDY 4 Selling Ford

Ford Motor Company is probably one of the best known vehicle manufacturers in the world. The company is the fifth largest car manufacturer in the world and is the company that originally invented mass production in 1903. At first, all the cars were identical: Henry Ford, the company's founder, famously said that 'Any customer can have a car painted any colour that he wants so long as it is black'. However, it quickly became apparent that people were making changes to the cars – altering the engines to gain more power, cutting off the bodywork to make truck versions, altering the seating to gain more space, and so forth. This represented a possible loss of revenue to the company, so Ford decided to produce different models for different markets.

Today, that approach has become standard. Originally, Ford built different models in each national market (e.g. the Taunus in Germany, the Anglia and Cortina in Britain and, of course, entirely separate (and larger) cars for the US market). Eventually, Ford tried to create 'world' models but, with the exception of the Focus, these did not always do well – the Mondeo, which sold extremely well in Europe, did not do well in the US (marketed as the Contour) or in Australia, where it met with strong competition from the Falcon. Most of the 'world cars' have been developed in Europe, and therefore tend to suit European conditions.

Ford produce a full range of vehicles for each global market, however. Some are large family models (such as the Mondeo and the Galaxy), some are small economical cars (such as the Fiesta and the Ka) and some are luxury models (Ford owns Lincoln and has owned Volvo, Jaguar and Land Rover). Furthermore, the company produces light vans such as the Transit, sometimes called 'the people's van' because it is used by so many small enterprises and is hired by so many people for the purpose of moving furniture, collecting large items or going on camping trips.

Ford keeps a very careful eye on how the market is developing. With this in mind, the company has developed a number of vehicles designed to run on alternative fuels. In Brazil, the company has for many years offered cars which run on pure alcohol or on an alcohol petrol mix, since these fuels have been available there for many years. However, the company has added hybrid vehicles to the range and expects to be producing fully electrically powered vehicles during the next decade or so. The problem is the availability of charging stations for such vehicles; currently, they are too few and far between for the project to be viable.

In all, Ford offers an extremely wide range, aiming to fill every segment of its market. In this, they do moderately well; the problem lies in identifying the right segments.

Questions

1 How might Ford segment the market behaviourally?

2 What have been the problems with geographical segmentation?

3 How might Ford segment demographically?

4 How can global markets be targeted?

5 How is Ford positioning its brands?

SUMMARY

This chapter has been about ways of dividing markets up into manageable portions. Here are the key points from this chapter:

- There are few, if any, mass markets left untouched
- If most consumers already own the core benefits of a product, the market must be segmented if success is to follow, since there is otherwise no reason for consumers to switch brands
- Segments must be measurable, accessible, substantial and congruent
- The profitability of a segment is calculated as the number of people in the segment multiplied by the premium they are willing to pay

- The narrower the segment the fewer the customers, but the greater the satisfaction and the greater the premium they are willing to pay (provided the segment has been correctly identified)

- There are many ways to segment a market – in fact, as many ways as there are groups with congruent needs

- Targeting is concerned with selecting an appropriate segment or segments, and approaching it in a consistent and effective way

- Some segments are defined by the media used to target them

- Sales forecasting is difficult, but can most easily be accomplished where the product is a fairly standard item

- Forecasting is likely to be self-fulfilling if all the interested parties are involved in the process.

CHAPTER QUESTIONS

1 What might be the segmentation bases for the home computer market?

2 What sales forecasting approaches would be most suitable for the launch of a new family car?

3 When should an industrial market be segmented geographically?

4 When should a consumer market be segmented geographically?

5 How might a TV company assess the viability of a new drama series?

Further reading

Unlike consumer behaviour or marketing communications, there are relatively few texts that cover segmentation in any great detail.

Consumer Behaviour and Marketing Strategy, 8th edn, by J. Paul Peter and Jerry C. Olson (Chicago, IL, Irwin, 2007) has a good section on segmenting consumer markets in Chapter 16.

References

Abell, Derek F.: *Defining the Business: The Starting Point of Strategic Planning* (Englewood Cliffs, NJ, Prentice Hall, 1980).

Bailey, Christine, Baines, Paul, R., Wilson, Hugh and Clark, Moira: 'Segmentation and customer insight in contemporary services marketing practice: why grouping customers is no longer enough', *Journal of Marketing Management*, **25** (3 and 4) (2009), pp. 227–52.

Beatty, S.E., Kahle, L. and Homer, P.: 'Personal values and gift-giving behaviours: a study across cultures', *Journal of Business Research*, **22** (1991), pp. 149–57.

Blankson, Charles and Kalafatis, Stavros P.: 'The development and validation of a scale measuring consumer/customer derived generic typology of positioning strategies', *Journal of Marketing Management*, (1) **20** (February 2004), pp. 5–43.

Bonoma, T.V. and Shapiro, B.P.: 'How to segment industrial markets', *Harvard Business Review* (May/June 1984), pp. 104–10.

Dolnicar, Sara and Lazarevski, Katie: 'Methodological reasons for the theory/practice divide in market segmentation', *Journal of Marketing Management*, **25** (3 and 4) (2009), pp. 357–73.

Engel, J.F., Blackwell, R.D. and Miniard, P.W.: *Consumer Behaviour*, 8th edn (Fort Worth, TX, Dryden Press, 1995).

Hassan, S.S. and Katsanis, L.P.: 'Identification of global consumer segments: a behavioural framework', *Journal of International Consumer Marketing*, **3** (2) (1991), pp. 11–28.

Hofstede, G.: 'Management scientists are human', *Management Science*, **40** (1) (1994), pp. 4–13.

Hofstede, G.: *Culture's Consequences: International Differences in Work-Related Values* (Beverly Hills, Sage, 1980).

Jamal, Ahmed: 'Marketing in a multicultural world: the interplay of marketing, ethnicity and consumption', *European Journal of Marketing*, **37** (1) (2003), pp. 1599–620.

Kotler, P.: *Marketing Management*, 7th edn (Englewood Cliffs, NJ, Prentice Hall, 1991).

Kotler, Philip and Levy, Sidney: 'Demarketing, Yes, Demarketing', *Harvard Business Review*, (Nov–Dec 1971), pp. 71–80.

Lee, C.: 'Determinants of national innovativeness and international market segmentation', *International Marketing Review*, **7** (5) (1990), pp. 39–49.

Lindridge, Andrew: 'Are we fooling ourselves when we talk about ethnic homogeneity? The case of religion and ethnic subdividions among Indians living in Britain', *Journal of Marketing Management*, **26** (5 and 6) (2010), pp. 441–72.

Marino, Kenneth E.: *Forecasting Sales and Planning Profits* (Chicago, IL, Probus Publishing, 1986), p. 155.

Martin, Brett A.S., Lee, Michael, Shyue, Wai and Lacey, Charlotte: 'Countering negative country of origin effects using imagery processing', *Journal of Consumer Behaviour*, Mar/Apr, **10** (2) (2011), pp. 80–92.

Medway, Dominic, Warnaby, Gary and Dhami, Sheetal: 'Demarketing places: rationales and strategies', *Journal of Marketing Management*, **27** (1 and 2) (2011), pp. 124–42.

Moskowitz, Howard R., Beckley, Jacqueline H., Luckow, Tracy and Paulus, Klaus: 'Cross-national segmentation for a food product: defining them and a strategy for finding them in the absence of "mineable" databases', *Journal of Database Marketing & Customer Strategy Management*, June, **15** (3) (2008), pp. 191–206.

Office for National Statistics: Census 2001, www.statistics.gov.uk/cci/nugget.cisp?id=350, 2003.

Plummer, Joseph T.: 'The concept and application of life style segmentation', *Journal of Marketing* (January 1974), pp. 33–7.

Rhee, Eddie and McIntyre, Shelby: 'How current targeting can hinder targeting in the future and what to do about it', *Journal of Database Marketing and Customer Strategy Management*, Mar, **16** (1) (2009), pp. 15–28.

Smith, W.R.: 'Product differentiation and market segmentation as alternative marketing strategies', *Journal of Marketing* (21 July 1957).

Wind, Yoram: 'Going to market: new twists for some old tricks', *Wharton Magazine*, **4** (1984).

Zikmund, William G. and D'Amico, Michael: *Effective Marketing: Creating and Keeping Customers* (St Paul, MN, West, 1995), p. 232.

PRODUCTS, BRANDING
AND PACKAGING

Objectives

After reading this chapter you should be able to:

- Describe the stages that a product goes through from introduction to obsolescence
- Assess products in a given range and decide which ones are worth keeping and which should be dropped from the range
- Decide on an appropriate policy for developing and introducing new products to the market
- Identify some of the risks inherent in new product development
- Understand what a marketer means by 'product'.

INTRODUCTION

This chapter is about developing new products and about product policy. The success of an organisation will depend, ultimately, on what bundles of benefits it offers to consumers; the decisions about what the firm should be offering need to be made in the light of the consumer's needs and wants.

There is a strong positive relationship between a firm's innovative activities and its ability to survive and prosper (Hart 1993), so many companies place a strong emphasis on developing new products to replace those which become obsolete or which are superseded by competitors' offerings.

Acme Whistles

Normally, whistles are not things that we think about a great deal. Yet a great many whistles are sold each day – some for sporting events, some for emergency purposes (whistles on lifejackets, for example) and some just for fun – no carnival would be complete without dancers blowing whistles!

Acme Whistles are the world leaders in making whistles. The company prides itself on the reliability of its products – each whistle is individually tested before it leaves the factory (by using an air line – the days of the company's founder blowing every whistle before it left are long gone). New products are developed at the rate of two a year – even whistles eventually date, since every product has its life cycle. New product development (NPD) also keeps the company ahead of its competitors. The company aims to develop patentable whistles as a way of protecting its intellectual property from competitors.

The company is well aware of the needs of its customers. For business-to-business customers, who may be adding the whistles to an existing product such as a fire safety kit, the company emphasises the reliability of the whistle, since this will reduce returns of faulty products. For consumer markets, the company produces a range of specialist whistles, such as the *Titanic* Mate's Whistle, a replica of the whistles the company made for the crew of the *Titanic*. Overall, the company has a surprisingly wide range of whistles!

Simon Topman, Managing Director

Watch the video clip, then try to answer the following questions. The answers are on the companion website.

Questions

1 What is the significance of the company's brand?

2 What type of NPD strategy does Acme have?

3 Why does the company aim to produce two patentable new products a year?

DEFINING PRODUCTS

Marketers define a *product* as being a *bundle of benefits*. This means that the product is more than just the sum of its physical characteristics; it includes fringe elements such as the brand image, the way the product is packed and delivered, even the colour of the box it comes in. **Primary characteristics** are those core benefits of the product that it has in common with its competitors; **auxiliary characteristics** are the features and benefits that are unique to the product. For instance, consider the contrast between a pizza from a delivery service and a pizza from the supermarket freezer. The primary characteristics of each are the same: a dough base with tomato sauce and cheese on top, with other ingredients included. The primary benefit is that each provides a tasty and filling meal; it is the auxiliary characteristics that make the difference.

Apart from the differences in flavour, ingredients and so forth, the delivery service is more expensive (perhaps double the price of the supermarket version). The supermarket pizza can be kept in the freezer and heated when needed, and can even be 'customised' by adding extra cheese or other ingredients. On the other hand, the delivery service pizza includes the service element of delivery, and is already heated and ready to eat. Clearly the benefits are different and therefore a marketer would say that the products are different.

Marketers need to be aware of the ways in which the needs and wants of consumers are changing so that the benefits offered by the product range can be tailored to fit those needs and wants. This is the function of market research (see Chapter 5), but it is important to make good use of the information gathered to see which new products might be developed or which old products might be adapted, and also to see which products are nearing the end of their useful lives.

CLASSIFYING PRODUCTS

Products bought to satisfy personal and family needs are **consumer products**; products bought for the purposes of resale or to be used to make other products are **industrial products**. As in any other question of marketing, the subdivision of these broad categories into smaller, more convenient, categories is carried out by reference to the consumer or the customer. In the case of consumer goods, the classification will be as shown in Table 6.1.

Likewise, industrial products can be categorised according to the use the purchasers intend to make of them. Table 6.2 illustrates this. In some ways, industrial buying has parallels with consumer buying behaviour (see Chapter 3), so parallels can also be drawn with the types of product purchased. First, the company must

Table 6.1 Classification of consumer products

Classification	Explanation
Convenience products	*Cheap, frequently purchased items that do not require much thought or planning.* The consumer typically buys the same brand or goes to the same shop. Examples are newspapers, basic groceries and soft drinks. Normally, convenience products would be distributed through many retail outlets and the onus is on the producer to promote the products because the retailer will not expend much effort on such low-priced items.
Shopping products	*Products people shop around for.* Usually infrequently purchased items such as computers, cars, hi-fi systems or household appliances. From the manufacturer's viewpoint, such products require few retail outlets, but will require much more personal selling on the part of the retailer. Hence there is usually a high degree of cooperation between manufacturer and retailer in marketing the products.
Speciality products	*People plan the purchase of these products with great care, know exactly what they want and will accept no substitutes.* Here the consumer's efforts bend towards finding an outlet that can supply exactly the item needed: this accentuates the exclusivity of the product, so some marketers deliberately limit the number of outlets that are franchised to sell the products. An example of this is the American hair-product manufacturer Redken, which appoints a limited number of hair salons to carry its products.
Unsought products	*These products are not bought; they are sold.* Examples are life insurance, fitted kitchens and encyclopaedias. While most people would recognise the need for these items, it is rare for consumers to go out looking for them; far more commonly the products are sold either by salespeople or are bought as the result of a sudden change of circumstances (for example, most mortgage lenders require house buyers to take out life insurance).

develop a clear view of what the customer is buying. Levitt (1986) has suggested the following hierarchy of levels:

1 *Core or generic.* This is the basic physical product, or the minimum features that the customer would expect it to have. For example, a microwave oven would be expected to have a timer and a space inside to put the food, and would be expected to heat things up effectively.

2 *Expected.* This is the generic product plus some extra features that the customer would reasonably expect to see. In the microwave example, the customer would expect there to be an instruction book, a guarantee and some kind of servicing network in case of breakdowns.

3 *Augmented.* These are the factors that differentiate the product. For the microwave, this could be a sensor to say when the food is cooked, a defrost facility, free delivery or an after-sales call to check the product is functioning well. These are the features that make the customer buy one brand rather than another.

Table 6.2 Categorisation of industrial products

Categorisation	Explanation
Raw materials	*Basic products that will be transformed entirely into something else.* These are usually bought in large quantities and usually have a standardised quality range and prices; this makes it hard for the producer to differentiate the product from those of the competitors.
Major equipment	*The capital machinery and tools used for running the buyer's business.* These are equivalent to shopping goods; the purchasers spend considerable time and effort in choosing which to buy, and therefore there is considerable emphasis on personal selling and on product differentiation. After-sales service is also crucial to success in this market.
Accessory equipment	*Equipment used for the peripheral needs of the firm.* Examples are office equipment and health and safety equipment. Often these are distributed through many outlets and are more standardised than the major equipment items. This means there is more competition, but also a bigger market for such items as fire extinguishers or PCs.
Component parts	*Manufactured items which will be assembled into the finished product.* These are usually bought by negotiation or tender; often the purchaser has the most power in the relationship, as with car manufacturers.
Process materials	Rather more advanced than raw materials, process materials might be the special alloys used in aircraft construction, or specially tailored plastics. From a marketing viewpoint, process materials are similar to component parts, but with more opportunity for differentiation.
Consumable supplies	*Materials that are used by the purchasers but that do not become part of the finished product:* for example, industrial cleansing products. Consumable supplies are used for maintenance, repair and operation, so they are sometimes called MRO items.
Industrial services	*The intangible products used by firms:* for example, industrial cleaning services, accountancy and legal services, and some maintenance services. Some firms provide these for themselves; for others it is cheaper to buy in the services as needed (for instance, a ten-person light engineering firm would not need a full-time lawyer on the staff).

4 *Potential.* This is all the possible features and benefits that could be wanted by customers. It is unlikely that any product could have all the necessary features (and it would be too expensive to buy anyway), but this list still needs to be developed so that the company can produce different models of the product for different customer needs. If a microwave oven manufacturer knows who the end buyer of the microwave is, it would be possible to keep the customer informed of new models coming onto the market in, say, three years' time when the old microwave is beginning to show signs of wear. The idea behind this is to encourage the customer to remain loyal to the original manufacturer.

From the consumer's viewpoint, some of those benefits are essential requirements, others are less important but still good to have, while others are not really relevant. Each consumer will have a different view as to which benefit belongs to which category.

MANAGING THE PRODUCT RANGE

The **product life cycle (PLC)** is a useful concept to describe how products progress from introduction through to obsolescence. The theory is that products, like living things, have a natural life cycle beginning with introduction, going through a growth phase, reaching maturity, then going into decline and finally becoming obsolete. Figure 6.1 illustrates this in graphical form.

In the introduction phase, the product's sales grow slowly and the profit will be small or negative because of heavy promotion costs and production inefficiencies. If the product is very new, there will also be the need to persuade retailers and others to stock it.

In the growth stage, there will be a rapid increase in sales as the product becomes better known. At this stage profits begin to grow, but competition will also be entering the market so the producer may now need to think about adapting the product to meet the competitive threat.

In the maturity phase the product is well known and well established; at this point the promotional spend eases off and production economies of scale become established. By this time competitors will almost certainly have entered the market, so the firm will need to develop a new version of the product.

In the decline phase, the product is losing market share and profitability rapidly. At this stage the marketer must decide whether it is worthwhile supporting the product for a little longer or whether it should be allowed to disappear; supporting a product for which there is little natural demand is very unprofitable, but sometimes products can be revived and relaunched, perhaps in a different market.

The assumption is that all products exhibit this life cycle, but the timescale will vary from one product to the next. Some products, for example computer games,

Figure 6.1 Product life cycle

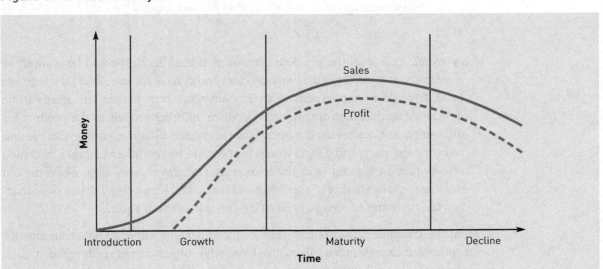

may go through the entire life cycle in a matter of months. Others, like pitta bread, have a life cycle measured in thousands of years, and may never become obsolete.

The PLC concept is a useful way of looking at product development but, like many simple theories, it has a number of flaws:

- The theory assumes that changes in consumer preference go only one way, and that there is no swing back to an earlier preference. Some clothing fashions return after a few years and some styles of music enjoy periodic revivals; also, some traditional products can suddenly become popular again, often following advertising campaigns based on nostalgia.

- The model assumes that nobody does anything to revive the product when it begins to decline or be superseded by other products. Most marketers would look at their declining products and decide whether a revival is possible, or worthwhile.

- The model looks at only one product, whereas most marketing managers have to balance the demands of many differing products and decide which ones are most likely to yield the best return on investment.

Note here that the PLC concept is useful to describe what is happening, but is not much use for predicting what is going to happen, since it is virtually impossible to tell how long the maturity phase will continue. This makes it difficult to use as a decision-making device; marketers are not easily able to tell which part of the PLC the product currently occupies. A temporary fall-off in sales might be caused by extraneous factors such as a recession or new competitive activity, without actually heralding the beginning of the decline phase.

Most firms produce several different products at the same time, and it is possible to superimpose the PLC diagrams for each product onto the graph to give a composite view of what is happening to the firm's product portfolio. This will give a long-term overview, but the problems of prediction still remain; for many managers, a 'snapshot' of what is happening now is more useful. The Boston Consulting Group (BCG) developed a matrix for decision-making in these circumstances. The original BCG matrix is as shown in Figure 6.2.

Stars are products with rapid growth and a dominant share of the market. Usually, the costs of fighting off the competition and maintaining growth mean that the product is actually absorbing more money than it is generating, but eventually it is hoped that it will be the market leader and the profits will begin to come back in. The problem lies in judging whether the market is going to continue to grow or whether it will go down as quickly as it went up. It may be difficult to judge whether a Star is going to justify all the money that is being poured in to maintain its growth and market share, but a firm that does not do this will end up just with Dogs. Even the most successful Star will eventually decline as it moves through the life cycle.

Cash Cows are the former Stars. They have a dominant share of the market but are now in the maturity phase of the life cycle and consequently have low growth. A Cash Cow is generating cash, and can be 'milked' of it to finance the Stars. These are the products that have steady year-in year-out sales and generate much of the

Figure 6.2 Boston Consulting Group matrix

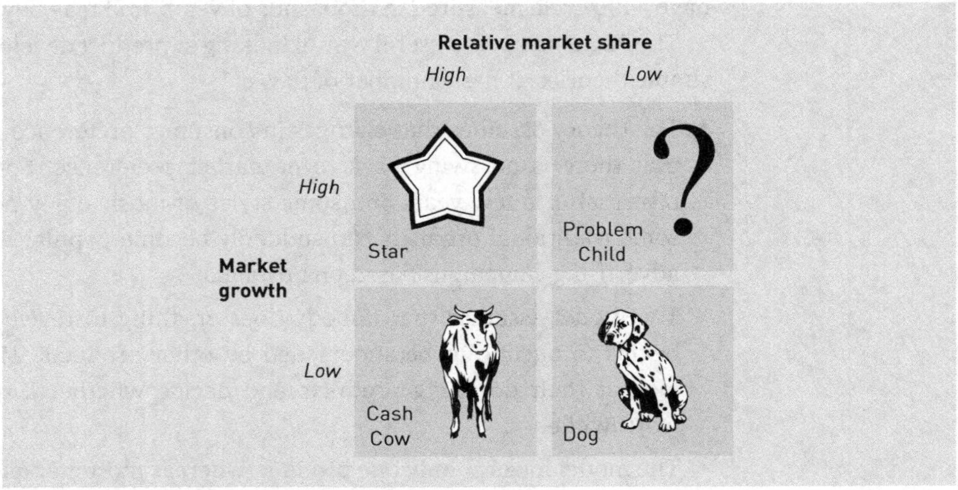

Source: Reprinted by permission of the Boston Consulting Group

firm's profits: examples might be the Big Mac hamburger, Coca-Cola and the Ford Mondeo.

Dogs have a low market share and low growth prospects. The argument here is not whether the product is profitable; it almost always is. The argument is about whether the firm could use its resources to make something that would be more profitable, and this is also almost always the case.

The **Problem Child** (also sometimes shown as a question mark) has a small share of a growth market and causes the marketer the most headaches since it is necessary to work out a way of building market share to turn the product into a Star. This means finding out why the share is so low and developing strategies to increase market share rapidly. The Problem Child could be backed with an even bigger promotion campaign or it could possibly be adapted in some way to fit the market better. Market research plays a crucial role in making these decisions; finding out how to adapt a product is a difficult area of research, but the potential rewards are huge, and adapting the product to meet people's needs better is almost always cheaper than increasing the advertising spend.

The policy decisions that arise from this view of the firm's product portfolio lie in the following areas:

- Which products should be dropped from the range entirely? This question not only hinges on how profitable the product itself is; sales of one product often indirectly generate sales of another, more profitable, product. For example, Black and Decker sell electric saws cheaply, but make their profit on sales of replacement saw blades.

- Which products should be backed with promotion campaigns? Backing the wrong product can be extremely expensive; advertising campaigns have no second-hand value, so if it does not work the money is lost forever.

- Which products could be adapted to fit the market better, and in what ways? This very much hinges on the market research findings and on customer feedback.
- Which new products could be introduced and at what cost?

Like the PLC, the BCG matrix is a simple model that helps marketers to approach strategic product decisions; again, like the PLC, it has a number of flaws. It is based on the following assumptions:

- Market share can be gained by investment in marketing. This is not always the case; some products will have lost their markets altogether (perhaps through environmental changes) and cannot be revived, no matter how much is invested.
- Market share gains will always generate cash surpluses. However, if market share is gained by drastic price cutting, cash may actually be lost.
- Cash surpluses will be generated when the product is in the maturity stage of the life cycle. This is not necessarily so; mature products may well be operating on such small margins because of competitive pressure that the profit generated is low.
- The best opportunity to build a dominant market position is during the growth phase. In most cases this would be true, but this does not take account of competition. A competitor's product might be growing even faster.

Barksdale and Harris (1982) proposed two additions to the BCG matrix. **War Horses** have high market share but the market has negative growth; the problem for management is to decide whether the product is in an irreversible decline or whether it can be revived, perhaps by repositioning into another market. **Dodos** have a low share of a negative growth market and are probably best discontinued (Figure 6.3).

The BCG matrix has proved a useful tool for analysing product portfolio decisions, but it is really only a snapshot of the current position with the products it describes. Since most markets are to a greater or lesser extent dynamic, the matrix should be used with a certain degree of caution.

Critical thinking

The BCG matrix is all very well, but how do we decide whether a market is 'high growth' or 'low growth?' Is 5% per annum high growth? It would be in the car industry – but not in mobile telephones. Likewise, what is a high market share? 5%? 50%? 2%? Any of these might be regarded as a respectable share in some markets.

Maybe we are back to executive judgement as the key factor in decisions – or maybe the BCG matrix just helps to focus our thinking!

The size of the product portfolio and the complexity of the products within it can have further effects on the firm's management. For example, it has been shown that manufacturing a wide range of products with many options makes it difficult for

Figure 6.3 Expanded Boston Consulting Group matrix

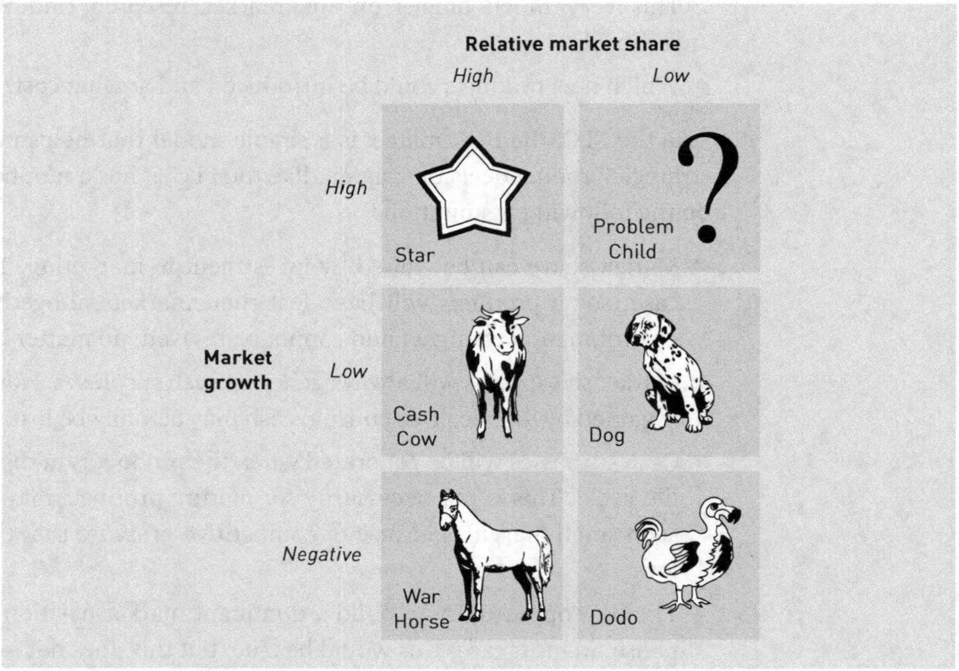

Source: Barksdale and Harris, 1982

the firm to use just-in-time purchasing techniques and complicates the firm's supply activities (Benwell 1996).

DEVELOPING BETTER PRODUCTS

There is often debate within firms as to what constitutes a 'better' product. For marketers, the definition must be 'a product that more closely meets our customers' needs than does the product it supersedes'. Engineers, accountants and managers may have differing definitions; there is, however, general agreement that firms must introduce new products if they are not to be left with a range of obsolete, dying products. New product development (NPD) is therefore a crucial area of marketing activity and a great deal has been published on the subject.

New product development

Venture teams or *project teams* develop new products or projects. Typically a venture team will be an interdisciplinary group, perhaps comprising engineers, research scientists, finance experts and marketers. Among other considerations, marketers need to take an overview of the product range to see how the proposed new products match up with existing products. Sometimes a new product can lead to cannibalism of old product lines (in other words, the company ends up competing with itself). Sometimes it can be more effective to carry out a product modification (in terms of quality, function or style) rather than develop a new product from scratch.

The task of creating new products is, of course, more art than science; however, customer orientation does appear to make firms more innovative (Tajeddini *et al.* 2006). It is therefore difficult to generalise about the process, but a frequently quoted model of the NPD process was given by Cooper and Kleinschmidt (1988) and follows this sequence:

1 *New product strategy.* The firm examines its current portfolio, opportunities and threats and decides what kind of new product would best fit in with future strategy.
2 *Idea generation.* Specific ideas for the product are expressed, perhaps through a brainstorming session of the venture team.
3 *Screening and evaluation.* The ideas are checked for feasibility and marketability.
4 *Concept testing.* Having selected the ideas which show promise, discussions take place with customers, production engineers and anyone else who may have something to contribute, to develop the ideas further.
5 *Business analysis.* The feasibility of the product is estimated in terms of its potential profitability, effects on sales of other products, possible competitive responses and so forth.
6 *Technical development.* The engineering aspects of the product are investigated and a prototype is developed. The final design of the product needs to reflect the results of the concept testing stage.
7 *Market testing.* Formal market research is carried out to assess the product's viability in the market.
8 *Commercialisation.* Assuming the market research is positive about the product, the firm puts it into production.

All of these stages are likely to be covered in one form or other, but in many cases the methods used are likely to be subjective or carried out ineffectively. This can often be a source of problems following the launch; for example, a proper market appraisal may not be carried out because the venture team fall in love with the project and champion it through the process. *Product champions* within firms often perform a valuable function in ensuring that the new product actually comes into existence rather than being sidelined by the routine tasks of making existing products; this is sometimes encouraged by firms, but is believed by some researchers to be a sign of a failed management who have abdicated their responsibility for keeping the firm up to date (Johne and Snelson 1990).

There are six broad types of innovation strategy:

1 *Offensive.* Pride in being the first. This is very much the strategy of firms such as Sony and 3M.
2 *Defensive.* 'Me-toos', copies of other companies' products, but slightly better.
3 *Imitative.* Straight copies of other companies' products.

4 *Dependent*. Led by bigger companies, perhaps customers or suppliers. For example, Microsoft produces new computer software, so it is dependent on new technology developed by computer chip manufacturers.

5 *Traditional*. Not really innovative at all; the firm is merely resurrecting old-fashioned designs.

6 *Opportunist*. Selling and marketing of inventions.

Launch decisions might revolve around areas such as test marketing (see Chapter 5); if the firm *test markets* the product (i.e. launches the product in a small geographical area to see whether it will be successful), this may save money on promotion but loses the advantage of surprise. On the other hand, if the firm goes for a national launch, this means committing large amounts of money and mistakes are much harder to correct afterwards. The process of launching in one area at a time is called *roll-out*. The promotion policy will be affected by the customer category the firm is aiming for: innovators, early adopters, early majority, late majority or laggards.

Whether to go ahead or not with a new product is a decision which revolves around five dimensions (Carbonell-Foulquie *et al.* 2004). These are as follows:

1 *Strategic fit*. The degree to which the new product fits in with the company's overall marketing strategy.

2 *Technical feasibility*. Whether an effective product can be made economically.

3 *Customer acceptance*. Whether customers like the product.

4 *Market opportunity*. The level of competition the firm might be expected to face and the current state of the external environment.

5 *Financial performance*. Whether the product will prove sufficiently profitable to be worth launching.

Of these, customer acceptance should be the most important consideration throughout the NPD process.

Success and failure in NPD

NPD is extremely risky; eight out of ten new products eventually fail (i.e. do not recover their development costs) and the remaining two out of ten thus have to fund all the others (Clancy and Shulman 1991). Great effort has been expended on trying to find better ways of forecasting a product's prospects in the market, with only limited results.

First of all, though, it is necessary to define what a new product is, and the researchers Calentone and Cooper (1981) have identified nine categories of new product, as shown in Table 6.3. The clusters were identified according to whether the product was new to the firm or new to the world, and whether there was a production or marketing *synergy* with the firm's existing products.

Success rates for each cluster were as laid out in Table 6.4. Data were obtained on 102 successes and 93 failures. Some 177 firms were surveyed, and there were 103 usable replies.

Table 6.3 New product clusters

Clusters	Description
Cluster 1 **The Better Mousetrap with No Synergy**	This is a product that, while being an improvement over existing offerings, does not fit in with the firm's existing product lines.
Cluster 2 **The Innovative Mousetrap that Really Wasn't Better**	This might be a product that, while being technically excellent, has no real advantage for the consumer over existing products.
Cluster 3 **The Close-to-Home Me-Too Product**	A copy of a competitor's offering. Not likely to be perceived as new by consumers.
Cluster 4 **The Innovative High-Tech Product**	A truly new-to-the-world product.
Cluster 5 **The Me-Too Product with No Technical/ Production Synergy**	A copy of a competitor's product, but with no real connection with existing product lines.
Cluster 6 **The Old But Simple Money-Saver**	Not a new product at all, except to the firm producing it.
Cluster 7 **The Synergistic Product that was New to the Firm**	A product that fits the product line, but is new.
Cluster 8 **The Innovative Superior Product with No Synergy**	A product that does not fit the existing product line, but is new.
Cluster 9 **The Synergistic Close-to-Home Product**	A product line extension; perhaps a minor improvement over the firm's existing products.

Clusters 9, 8 and 6 were the most successful by far, perhaps indicating that the safest course is not to be too innovative. In recent years, many new products have been introduced which are reproductions of old designs: the Chrysler PT, Volkswagen Beetle and Mini Cooper are all examples from the motor industry, and there are many household appliances which have been designed with a 'retro' image. These products rely on the following factors for their success (Brown *et al.* 2003):

- *Allegory*. This is the brand 'story', the history of the original product
- *Aura*. This is the 'essence' of the brand, the mystique surrounding it
- *Arcadia*. This is the idealised community in which such products might be used. Based on nostalgia, Arcadia is the place people would like to return to (for example, the 1960s, when they owned their first VW Beetle)

Table 6.4 Success rates of new products

Cluster	Success ratio	% successes	% of cases
9 The Synergistic Close-to-Home Product	1.39	72	12.82
8 The Innovative Superior Product with No Synergy	1.35	70	10.26
6 The Old But Simple Money-Saver	1.35	70	10.26
7 The Synergistic Product that was New to the Firm	1.2	67	10.76
4 The Innovative High-Tech Product	1.23	64	14.35
3 The Close-to-Home Me-Too Product	1.08	56	8.20
1 The Better Mousetrap with No Synergy	0.69	36	7.17
5 The Me-Too Product with No Technical/Production Synergy	0.27	14	10.26
2 The Innovative Mousetrap that Really Wasn't Better	0.00	0	10.26

Source: Calentone and Cooper, 1981

- *Antinomy*. This is brand paradox. New technology is viewed as unstoppable and overpowering, yet at the same time is responsible for people's desire to return to a simpler, less high-tech past.

Although not all products in Cluster 6 are retro, the advent of a significant interest in retro styling has certainly changed the success rate of such products.

Cluster 8 contains the truly innovative, new-to-the-world product, but until it is actually launched it may be difficult to distinguish from Cluster 2, the Innovative Mousetrap that Really Wasn't Better. This category had no successes at all.

What the above research does not show is the degree to which new products are successful. The innovative, new-to-the-world product may carry the highest risks, but potentially it also carries the highest rewards if successful. The evidence is, therefore, that the safest route is to produce 'me-too' products (minor adaptations of existing market leaders), but that the much riskier route of producing real innovations (e.g. the Nintendo Wii) is the only way to become a world-leading company. Producing retro products may well be a useful strategy, combining the success factors of both approaches.

The research also does not consider what a firm might use as a measure of success. Is it profitability? Or is it market share? This will depend on the firm's overall strategy, which may or may not put profitability first. Research shows that the most commonly used measures of success in NPD are customer acceptance, customer satisfaction, product performance and quality (Huang *et al*. 2004).

Another aspect not addressed by the Calentone and Cooper research is that of the consumer's view of new products. Although a given product may be new to the firm, and may even involve a radical rethink of the company's production and marketing methods, consumers may not see the product as being significantly different from what is already available. If consumers do not see any advantage in using the new product, they will not buy it; this re-emphasises the importance of good market research and analysis.

Calentone and Cooper's research was borne out by research published in 2006, in which the authors found that incremental innovations (those which are a small improvement on existing products) carry the least risk for firms who are first to bring them to market. Discontinuous innovation (truly new-to-the-world products) carry the greatest risk for firms first into the market and for firms which follow later; in other words, being first to market only carries risks, not rewards (Min *et al*. 2006).

Overall, NPD is concerned with replacing the firm's existing product range with fresh products that come even closer to meeting customer needs. Firms that do not innovate will, eventually, lose market share to firms that do, since the competitor firms will be offering better products. This places a heavy premium on NPD. Having said that, new products do not sell themselves – unsurprisingly, firms which provide high levels of marketing and technological support for their new products experience greater financial rewards from their innovations (Sorescu *et al*. 2003). It is therefore no surprise that firms with a strong market orientation are more likely to be successful in launching new-to-the-world products (Augusto and Coelho 2009), nor that firms with strong customer relationship management also find it easier to innovate (Battor and Battor 2010).

DIFFUSION OF INNOVATION

New products are not immediately adopted by all consumers. Some consumers are driven to buy new products almost as soon as they become available, whereas others prefer to wait until the product has been around for a while before risking their hard-earned money on it. Innovations therefore take time to filter through the population: this process is called diffusion and is determined partly by the nature of consumers and partly by the nature of the innovation itself.

Everett M. Rogers (1962) classified consumers as follows:

- **Innovators**: those who like to be first to own the latest products. These consumers predominate at the beginning of the PLC
- **Early adopters**: those who are open to new ideas, but like to wait a while after initial launch. These consumers predominate during the growth phase of the PLC
- **Early majority**: those who buy once the product is thoroughly tried and tested. These consumers predominate in the early part of the maturity phase of the PLC
- **Late majority**: those who are suspicious of new things and wait until most other people already have one. These consumers predominate in the latter part of the maturity phase of the PLC
- **Laggards**: those who adopt new products only when it becomes absolutely necessary to do so. These consumers predominate in the decline phase of the PLC.

The process of diffusion of innovation is carried out through reference-group influence (see Chapter 3). Theories concerning the mechanisms for this have developed over the past 100 years, the three most important ones being trickle-down theory, two-step flow theory and multistage interaction theory.

Trickle-down theory says that the wealthy classes obtain information about new products and the poorer classes then imitate their 'betters' (Veblen 1899). This theory has been largely discredited in wealthy countries because new ideas are disseminated overnight by the mass media and copied by chain stores within days; for example, the dress worn by Kate Middleton when she married Prince William in 2011 was copied almost immediately by Chinese dressmakers in Suzhou (Moore 2011).

Critical thinking

Perhaps nowadays we don't blindly copy the doings of the aristocracy, or even the upper middle class, but does that mean we are entirely uninfluenced by our betters? We seem to have developed a new aristocracy, largely composed of entertainers such as footballers and singers, who set the fashions for us in many ways.

Even without celebrity endorsement, where such people are paid to say they use a particular brand of perfume or a particular set of golf clubs, we watch avidly to see what they are wearing, buying and doing. So maybe Veblen was stating a universal truth, back in 1899!

Two-step flow theory is similar, but this time it is 'influentials' rather than wealthy people who are the start of the adoption process (Lazarsfield *et al.* 1948). This has considerable basis in truth, but may be less true now than it was in the 1940s, when the theory was first developed; access to TV and other information media has proliferated, and information about innovation is disseminated much faster.

The multistage interaction model (Engel *et al.* 1995) recognises this and allows for the influence of the mass media. In this model the influentials emphasise or facilitate the information flow (perhaps by making recommendations to friends or acting as advisers). A more recent concept is that of the market maven: a maven is someone who knows a great deal about a product category (for example, someone who knows a lot about computer software) and is willing to share the knowledge. Mavens usually have confidence in their ability to acquire knowledge, and confidence that people will respond positively to their offers of help. Mavens are usually very strong influencers and are therefore an important group from a marketer's viewpoint (Clark *et al.* 2008).

Whether people are innovators, late adopters, laggards, etc. may depend on the degree to which they like to differentiate themselves from others. There is a conflict between wanting to be different and wanting to fit in with others, so adoption may relate to the individual's perception of the size of the group that uses the product already. If someone likes to be different, he or she might be attracted to a small group of users and would thus tend to be an innovator (Timmor and Katz-Navon 2008). On the other hand, the actual usefulness of the product is often decided by referring to internal factors, with little reference to social factors (Munnukka and Jarvi 2011).

Consumers often need considerable persuasion to change from their old product to a new one. This is because there is always a cost of some sort. For example, somebody buying a new car will lose money on trading in the old car (a *switching cost*), or perhaps somebody buying a new computer will also have to spend money on new software and spend time learning how to operate the new equipment (an *innovation cost*).

On the other hand there is strong evidence that newness as such is an important factor in the consumer's decision-making process (Haines 1966). In other words, people like new things, but there is a cost attached. Provided the new product offers real additional benefits over the old one (i.e. fits the consumer's needs better than the old product), the product will be adopted.

Consumers must first become aware of the new product, and then become persuaded that there is a real advantage in switching from their existing solution. A useful model of this adoption process is as follows:

- *Awareness.* This will often come about as a result of promotional activities by the firm.
- *Trial.* For a low-price item (e.g. a packet of biscuits) this may mean that the consumer will actually buy the product before trying it; for a major purchase, such as a car, the consumer will usually need to have a test-drive. Increasingly, supermarkets hold tasting sessions to allow customers to try new products.
- *Adoption.* This is the point at which the consumer decides to buy the product or make it part of the weekly shopping list.

Rogers (1962) identified the following perceived attributes of innovative products, by which consumers apparently judge the product during the decision-making process:

- **Relative advantage**. The degree to which the innovation is perceived as better than the idea it supersedes.

- **Compatibility**. Consistency with existing values, past experiences and needs of potential adopters.
- **Complexity**. Ideas that are easily understood are adopted more quickly.
- **Trialability**. Degree to which a product can be experimented with.
- **Observability**. The degree to which the results of an innovation are visible to others.

In some cases, the actual usefulness of the product is determined in part by the number of people who already own it. This is particularly true of innovations in communications technology: e-mail is of no use unless a large number of people use it, and the recent growth in social networking sites is only possible if a lot of people join the sites (Wang and Lo 2008).

Apart from the issue of adopting a product as it stands, there is the concept of reinvention. Sometimes users find new ways to use the product (not envisaged by the designers) and sometimes this leads to the creation of whole new markets. For example, in the 1930s it was discovered that baking soda is good for removing stale smells from refrigerators, a fact that was quickly seized on by baking soda manufacturers. Deodorising fridges is now a major part of the market for baking soda.

BRANDING

Many products are so similar to other manufacturers' products that consumers are entirely indifferent as to which one they will buy. For example, petrol is much the same whether it is sold by Shell, Esso, BP, Statoil, Elf or Repsol: such products are called commodity products because they are homogeneous commodities rather than distinct products with different benefits from the others on offer.

At first sight, water would come into the category of a commodity product. Yet any supermarket has a range of bottled waters, each with its own formulation and brand name, and each with its loyal consumers. In these cases the original commodity product (water) has been converted into a brand. Branding is a process of adding value to the product by use of its packaging, brand name, promotion and position in the minds of the consumers. Even non-profit-making firms are more successful if they are brand-oriented (Napoli 2006).

DeChernatony and McDonald (1998) offer the following definition of brand:

A successful brand is an identifiable product, service, person or place, augmented in such a way that the buyer or user perceives relevant, unique added values which match their needs most closely. Furthermore, its success results from being able to sustain those added values in the face of competition.

This definition emphasises the increased value that accrues to the consumer by buying the established brand rather than a generic or commodity product. The values that are added may be in the area of reassurance of the brand's quality, they may be in the area of status (where the brand's image carries over to the consumer) or they may be in the area of convenience (making search behaviour easier).

Figure 6.4 Commodity products *v* branded products

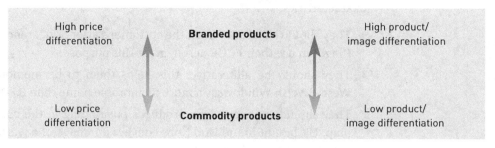

Figure 6.4 shows the relationship between commodity products and branded products in terms of image and price. Commodity products tend to be undifferentiated in price (for example, petrol tends to be much the same price in petrol stations within a given geographical area; a differential of even 10% would be very noticeable). They also tend to have a low degree of differentiation in the product characteristics and the image. Branded goods, on the other hand, score high on both factors; since they command a premium price, this is likely to lead to an increased profit, which strengthens the case for developing a strong brand.

Brand names

When a new product has been developed, the producer will usually give it a *brand name*. A brand name is a term, symbol or design that distinguishes one seller's product from its competitors. The strategic considerations for brand naming are as follows:

- *Marketing objectives.* The brand name should fit the overall marketing objectives of the firm: for example, a firm intending to enter the youth market will need to develop brand names that appeal to a young audience.
- *Brand audit.* An estimate of the internal and external forces such as critical success factor (also known as the unique selling proposition).
- *Brand objectives.* As with the marketing objectives, the overall intentions about the brand need to be specified.
- *Brand strategy alternatives.* The other ways of achieving the brand's objectives and the other factors involved in its success have a bearing on the choice of brand name.

Brand names can be protected in most countries by *registration*, but there is some protection for brands in that it is illegal to try to 'pass off' a product as being a branded one when it is not. For example, using a very similar brand name to a famous brand, or even using similar package design, could be regarded as passing off. This is a civil offence, not a criminal one, so it is up to the offended brand owner to take legal action.

Ries (1995) suggests that brand names should have some, or all, of the following characteristics:

- They should shock, i.e. catch the customer's attention. French Connection United Kingdom use their FCUK acronym for this purpose.
- They should be alliterative: this helps them to be memorable. For example, West'n'Welsh Windows is a more memorable name than BJ Double Glazing.
- They should connect to the product's positioning in the consumer's perceptual map. UK biscuit brand Hob Nobs conveys an image of a warm kitchen (the hob) with friendliness (hob-nobbing).
- They should link to a visual image: again, this helps the memorability. Timberland outdoor clothing conjures a visual image of mountain country.
- They should communicate something about the product or be capable of being used to communicate about the product. Duracell conveys the main advantage of the batteries – they are durable. Brand names in French are often perceived as being more hedonic (Salciuviene *et al.* 2010).
- They should encourage the development of a nickname (for example, Bud for Budweiser Beer).
- They should be telephone- and directory-friendly. Words often seem muffled on the telephone, so that 'Bud' becomes 'Mud'.

Brands and semiotics

Semiotics is the study of meaning, and is concerned with the symbolism conveyed by objects and words. Semiotics refers to systems of signs; the most obvious system is words, but other systems exist. For example, a film would use the sign systems of the spoken word, the gestures of the actors, the music of the soundtrack and the conventions of movie direction and production to generate an overall meaning. The overall meaning is generated as a result of an interaction between the sign system and the observer or reader; the viewer interprets the information in the light of existing knowledge and attitudes, later including it in an overall perceptual map of reality (see Chapter 3).

Brands are important symbols, often using more than one sign system to create meaning; the brand name, the logo, the colour and the design of the packaging all contribute. In terms of semiotics, brands have four levels:

1 *A utilitarian sign.* This is about the practical aspects of the product and includes meanings of reliability, effectiveness, fitness for purpose and so forth.
2 *A commercial sign.* This is about the exchange values of the product, perhaps conveying meanings about value for money or cost-effectiveness.
3 *A socio-cultural sign.* This is about the social effects of buying (or not buying) the product, with meanings about membership of aspirational groups or about

the fitness of the product for filling social roles. Research shows that even young children are affected by this – having the right brand of snack in the lunch-box was found to be extremely important for 8- to 11-year-olds (Roper and La Niece 2009).

4 *A sign about the mythical values of the product.* Myths are heroic stories about the product, many of which have little basis in fact; for example, the Harley Davidson motorcycle brand has a strong mythical value due (in part) to its starring role in the film *Easy Rider.*

Myths provide a conceptual framework through which the contradictions of life can be resolved, and brands can build on this. For example, modern industrial life is, presumably, the antithesis of frontier adventure. Yet the Harley Davidson, a product of twentieth-century industry, was used to represent the (probably mythical) freedom and adventure of the American West. Most powerful brands have at least some mythical connotations – in the United Kingdom, the Hovis bread brand has mythical connotations centred around corner bakery shops at the turn of the century; in Malaysia and Singapore Tiger Balm carries mythical connotations about ancient Chinese apothecaries; in Australia Vegemite carries mythical connotations about Australian family life that its main competitor, Promite, has never tapped into.

The association of different values with the brand name can be extremely useful when researching the acceptability of a brand's image. The importance that consumers place on these values can be researched using focus groups, with a subsequent analysis of the key signs contained within the brand, and consumers can be segmented according to their responsiveness to the particular signs contained within the brand and their relevance to the consumer's own internal values.

Research carried out by Gordon and Valentin (1996) into retail buying behaviour showed that different retail outlets convey different meanings to consumers in terms of a continuum from planned, routine shopping through to impulse buying. Each store type met the needs differently and conveyed different meanings in terms of appropriateness of behaviour. Convenience stores conveyed an image of disorder and feelings of guilt and confusion (perhaps associated with having forgotten to buy some items in the course of the regular weekly shop). Supermarkets represented planned shopping and conveyed an image of efficient domestic management and functionality. Petrol stations carried a dual meaning of planned purchase (for petrol) and impulse buying (in the shop). Business travellers seeking a break from work and pleasure travellers seeking to enhance the 'holiday' feeling both indulged in impulsive behaviour motivated by the need for a treat. Finally, off-licences legitimated the purchase of alcohol, allowing shoppers to buy drinks without the uneasy feeling that other shoppers might disapprove. Off-licences also provided an environment in which people felt able to experiment with new purchases.

These signs are relevant not only for the retailers themselves in terms of their own branding, but also for branded-goods manufacturers who need to decide which outlets are most appropriate for their brands and where in the store the brand should be located. For example, snack foods and chocolate are successfully sold in petrol stations, where travellers are often looking for a treat to break up a boring journey.

STRATEGIC ISSUES IN BRANDING

Adding value to the product by branding involves a great deal more than merely giving the product a catchy name. Branding is the culmination of a range of activities across the whole marketing mix, leading to a brand image that conveys a whole set of messages to the consumer (and, more importantly, to the consumer's friends and family) about quality, price, expected performance and status. For example, the Porsche brand name conveys an image of engineering excellence, reliability, sporty styling, high speed and high prices, and of wealth and success on the part of the owner. People do not buy Porsches simply as a means of transport.

Because branding involves all the elements of the marketing mix, it cannot be regarded simply as a tactical tool designed to differentiate the product on the supermarket shelves. Instead, it must be regarded as the focus for the marketing effort, as a way of directing the thought processes of the management towards producing consumer satisfaction. The brand acts as a common point of contact between the producer and the consumer, as shown in Figure 6.5.

As the figure shows, the consumer benefits from the brand in terms of knowing what the quality will be, knowing what the expected performance will be, gaining some self-image values (for example, a prestigious product conveys prestige to the consumer by association – conversely, a low-price product might enhance a consumer's sense of frugality and ability to find good value for money).

In many cases the core product has very little to differentiate it from other products, and the brand is really the only differentiating feature. A famous example is the rivalry between Pepsi Cola and Coca-Cola; in blind taste tests, most people prefer the flavour of Pepsi, but Coca-Cola outsells Pepsi in virtually every market. This apparent discrepancy can only be explained by the brand image which Coca-Cola has, and in taste tests where consumers are able to see the can the drink comes out of, Coca-Cola is the preferred brand.

Despite the apparently artificial nature of differentiation by branding, the benefits to the consumer are very real; experiments show that branded analgesics work better than generic analgesics at relieving pain, even though the chemical formula is identical. This is because of the psychosomatic power of the brand. Someone driving a prestige car gains very real benefits in terms of the respect and envy of others, even if the performance of the car is no better than that of its cheaper rival.

Brands can be looked at in a number of different ways. Table 6.5 shows eight different strategic functions of brands.

Branding clearly has advantages for the manufacturer and the retailer, since it helps to differentiate the product from the competitor's product. Economies of scale and scope are attributed to branding, and a brand with high sales will generate

Figure 6.5 Brands as a contact point

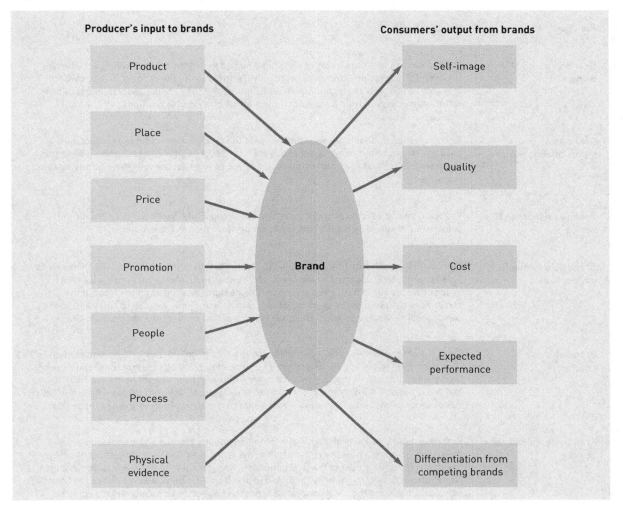

production economies. A successful brand also creates a *barrier to entry*, so that competitors find it harder to enter the market (Demsetz 1982). Brands also allow firms to compete other than on price, which clearly has advantages since the firm does not have to cut its profit margins to compete.

Furthermore, brands that are held in high esteem tend to be more consistent in their sales, riding over the ups and downs of the marketplace (Png and Reitman 1995). Not all brands are priced at a premium; many brands are competitively priced to take advantage of consistent sales.

Branding has advantages for the consumer; it is easy to recognise the product and easy to identify with it. Messages about the formulation and benefits are clearly conveyed, and in most cases the use of a particular brand says something about the consumer (for example, wearing designer clothes) (Bagwell and Bernheim 1996). Because most purchases involve only limited problem-solving behaviour, branding

Table 6.5 Strategic functions of brands

Function	Explanation
Brand as a sign of ownership	Brands were at one time a way of showing who had instigated the marketing activities for the brand. This was an attempt to protect the formulation of the product in cases where intellectual property protection was insufficient, and also to ensure that customers knew whether they were buying a manufacturer's brand or a retailer's brand.
Brand as a differentiating device	A strong brand undoubtedly does differentiate the product from similar products, but having a strong brand name is not enough. The product itself also needs to be different in some way; the brand image is the communicating device that conveys the difference to the consumer.
Brand as a functional device	Branding can be used to communicate functional capability. In other words, the brand conveys an image of its quality and expected performance to the consumer.
Brand as a symbolic device	The symbolism of some brands enables the consumer to say something about themselves. This is particularly apparent in the 'designer' clothes industry – a very ordinary T-shirt acquires added value because the name of the designer is printed on the front. If the consumers believe that the brand's value lies in its communication ability they will spend considerable time and effort in choosing the brand that conveys the appropriate image.
Brand as a risk reducer	Every purchase involves a degree of risk; the product might not perform as expected and if it fails to do so then the vendor might not be prepared to put matters right. Buying a strongly branded product offers the consumer a degree of reassurance about both the product and the producer. Astute marketers find out what types of risk are of most concern to the customers or consumers and develop a brand presentation which addresses those risks.
Brand as a shorthand device	Brands are used as a way of 'tagging' information about a product in the consumers' memories. This is particularly relevant when the brand is extended to other product categories, since the consumer's view of the parent brand is transferred to the new brand. For example, Virgin has successfully extended the brand image from CDs to retailing to airlines to financial services, all offering the same innovative approach and serving similar market segments.
Brand as a legal device	Brands give a certain amount of legal protection to the producer, since pack design and name can be protected where (often) the formulation of the product cannot. Strong branding offers some protection for the firm's intellectual property.
Brand as a strategic device	The assets constituting the brand can be identified and managed so that the brand maintains and builds on the added value that it represents.

helps to reduce the decision-making time and also the effort of evaluating competing products: brands do not necessarily need to have unique features for this to happen (Romaniuk and Gaillard 2007). Consumers who either do not want to spend time on an extended information search or do not have the expertise to do so can use the brand as an implicit guarantee of quality. These positive feelings about the brand are called consumer brand equity and can be affected by all aspects of the brand, including country of origin (Pappu *et al*. 2006).

In business-to-business markets, buyers may be prepared to pay a premium for a known brand, based on the following dimensions (Persson 2010):

1 *Brand familiarity.*

2 *Product solution.* This is the extent to which the product is known to provide a solution to the buyer's problems.

3 *Service associations.* This is the degree to which the buyer can see that there will be good after-sales services.

4 *Distribution associations.* This is the degree to which the deliveries will be reliable and effective.

5 *Relationship associations.* This is the degree to which the buyer has good working relationships with the supplier.

6 *Company associations.* These are the factors surrounding the supplying company's reputation.

Information storage and retrieval in humans are carried out by a process of 'chunking', or collecting information in substantial quantities and storing them under a single 'file name' (Buschke 1976). In effect, the brand name provides an informational chunk; the individual is able to summon up a huge amount of information from memory using the brand name as the trigger.

From a strategic viewpoint, the brand image provides a focus for the creative energies of the marketing team. Koestler (1964) suggested that creativity involves the bringing together of hitherto unrelated, yet familiar, objects to generate a creative insight. The difficulty for marketers is that product and brand development is often a team process and, as such, the team needs to keep a firm picture of what the product is intended to convey – the 'personality' of the product – if they are to maintain consistency in their creative activities. One way of doing this is to use a metaphor for the product. For example, the Honda Accord developers used the metaphor 'Rugby player in a dinner suit' to achieve product coherence across the team, even though the entire creative team consisted of hundreds of people, from automotive stylists through to ad designers (Clark and Fujimoto 1990).

Brand planning is important but time-consuming; often the job is given to a brand manager, many of whom are young and inexperienced. Developing the brand is a process of integrating a number of strands of business activity, so a clear idea of the brand image is essential, as is a long-term view. To see branding as merely being about design or advertising or naming is inadequate and short-sighted; successful brands are those that act as a lens through which the consumer sees the corporation and the product. Constant evaluation of the image seen through the lens is essential if the brand is to retain its status.

Occasionally products need to be rebranded, sometimes because of a bad association (for example, after the Zeebrugge ferry disaster the company rebranded itself from Townsend Thoresen to P&O Ferries), but more commonly because of a structural change in the firm, perhaps caused by a merger or a takeover (Muzellec and Lambkin 2006). Within the European Union, rebranding has often occurred in recent years to develop a Europe-wide identity (as in the case of Jif cleaners, which became Cif). Such rebranding needs to be handled carefully, and invariably involves added promotional expenditure to establish the new brand.

EXTENDING THE BRAND

A brand extension is another product in the company's range that uses a similar brand name. For example, Cherry Coke is a brand extension of the original Coca-Cola. Overall, family branding is where one brand name is used for a range of products, such as Heinz 57 Varieties, and line family branding is where a smaller group of brands carries a single identity.

In each case the aim is to convey a message of quality to the consumer by borrowing from the established reputation of the parent brand, and to appeal to the target market, who are already familiar with the parent brand. Properly carried out, the establishment of a brand is a long-term project, which can be expensive; this leads to an emphasis by some firms on brand extensions that are intended to maximise the return on the investment made in establishing the brand. In some cases, brands have been extended to the breaking point; relatively few brands (Virgin being one example) can be extended apparently indefinitely, and even as well-established a brand as Levi Strauss jeans could not extend itself to smart suits (the company's attempt to do so in the early 1980s turned to disaster). The most important driver for brand extension success is the fit between the present brand and the extension product (Volckner and Sattler 2006); Virgin's ability to extend relies on the brand's image as being original and fresh-thinking, coupled with a combination of solidity and practicality. Even so, the bad publicity which surrounded Virgin Trains at the beginning of the century is thought to have damaged the brand and the company has been forced to make major investments in their rolling stock to recover some of the lost ground.

Having a strong brand associated with a new product does affect consumer perceptions significantly; people will generally have a higher perception of a new product if it is associated with a well-known and trusted brand (Besharat 2010). Conversely, people will often look for other ways of confirming the quality of an unbranded item, and will even be prepared to pay a premium for such confirmation (Ubilava *et al*. 2011).

A more recent development has been compositioning, in which products are grouped under a brand name to create a composite value greater than that of the components (Ruttenberg *et al*. 1995). Joint marketing and distribution alliances come under this heading. The products concerned do not necessarily come from the same producer and may not even be in the same general category; for example, Disneyland has 'official airlines' or 'official ferry companies' to transport visitors to its theme parks. A further extension of this concept is brand architecture (Uncles *et al*. 1995), which is concerned with setting up 'partner' brands and creating a balance between branding at the product level and corporate or banner levels.

Within the international arena, firms have the opportunity to extend the brand across international frontiers. This raises fundamental strategic issues; for example, should the brand be globalised, with the firm offering a standard package throughout the world (as does Coca-Cola), or should the brand be adapted for each market (as does Heinz)? Some firms brand globally, but advertise locally (Sandler and Shani 1992), while others organise task groups to handle the brand on a global scale (Raffee and Kreutzer 1989).

RETAILERS' OWN-BRANDS

Retailer power has grown considerably over the past 30 years, with a proliferation of own-brand products. In the past, the retailer's own-brand products were usually of poorer quality than manufacturers' brands, but they are now often of equal or even superior quality. These brands now account for up to 60% of the sales in some major retail stores such as Tesco and Sainsbury in the United Kingdom, and Carrefour in France (slogan: *'Carrefour – c'est aussi une marque'*, which translates as 'Carrefour – it's also a brand') (Hankinson and Cowking 1997). For manufacturers this creates a problem of response; should the manufacturer try to invest in the firm's brands more heavily to overcome the retailer's brand, or should he or she capitulate entirely and produce on behalf of the retailer (Quelch and Harding 1995). Often manufacturers will become suppliers of retailer-brand products which compete with their own branded goods. Reasons for doing this are as follows:

- *Economies of scale.* The manufacturer may be able to buy raw materials in greater quantities or may be able to invest in more efficient production methods if the throughput of product is increased.
- *Utilise excess capacity.* Seasonality or production synergies may make production of own-brand products attractive in some cases.
- *Base for expansion.* Supplying a retailer with own-brand goods may lead to other opportunities to supply the retailer with other products in future.
- *No promotion costs.* The retailer bears all the investment in the brand (which is, of course, a brand extension of the retailer's trading name in any case).
- *No choice.* Some retailers (the UK's Marks & Spencer being an example) only trade in their own brands. Manufacturers who wish to trade with these retailers have no choice but to produce under the retailer's brand name.
- *To shut out the competition.* If the manufacturer does not produce goods under the retailer's brand name, another manufacturer will and will thus gain ground.

Manufacturers with very strong branding often refuse to produce own-brand goods, Kellogg's breakfast cereals being a notable example. If the brand is strong enough this allows the firm to promote on an 'accept no substitutes' platform.

In the past, own-brand products were cheap versions of the leading brands, but in more and more cases the retailers now have enough financial strength to fund the development of entirely new versions of products, some of which are superior to the proprietary brands and have achieved substantial market shares.

In many cases this is achieved by producing 'lookalike' branding, where the product looks very similar to the brand leader. In the United Kingdom this led to the formation of the British Producers and Brand Owners Group, which lobbied Parliament to regulate the visual and physical simulation of successful brands. In fact, research showed that few, if any, consumers accidentally pick up the wrong brand (Balabanis and Craven 1997), but some confusion is engendered. Retailers (perhaps disingenuously) claim that using similar packaging helps consumers identify products, whereas manufacturers claim that lookalikes give the impression that the products are identical. In other words, the confusion arises not at the level of picking up the wrong pack, but at the more subtle level of forming inaccurate beliefs about the lookalike's attributes based on the attributes of the leading brand (Foxman *et al.* 1992).

A further argument advanced by retailers is that strong manufacturers' brands have created generic product categories of their own – 'Gold Blend-type' instant coffees, for example. The retailers argue that products with similar quality and specifications should look as similar as possible to the brand that first created those values – an argument that is particularly annoying to manufacturers who have invested large sums of money in creating those brand values in the first place.

PACKAGING

Packaging of the product is equally part of the product, since the packaging can itself convey benefits. In fact, recent research shows that attractive packaging triggers areas of the brain which are normally associated with rewards, while unattractive packaging triggers activity in a different part of the brain, one which is usually associated with processing things such as unfair offers or disgusting pictures (Stoll *et al.* 2008).

The main purpose of packaging is to protect the contents from the outside environment and vice versa, but packaging also carries out the following functions:

- Informs customers
- Meets legal information requirements
- Sometimes aids the use of the product (e.g. ring pulls on drinks cans make it easier to open the can).

Packaging decisions might include such areas as tamper resistance (paper strips around caps to prevent bottles being opened while on supermarket shelves) and *customer usage* (e.g. the resealable nipples on mineral water bottles, making it easier to drink the water while participating in sports such as running or cycling). The protection of the environment has become important to consumers in recent years, so much packaging is either recyclable or biodegradable. Customer acceptability is of obvious importance; packaging must be hygienic and convenient for the consumer. Within the United Kingdom there has been a growing trend to develop packaging designs that can be legally protected under the 1994 Trade Marks Act; the purpose of this is to prevent imitators from making close copies of the packaging. In some cases the package design has been made expensive to copy, requiring retooling for unusual pack shapes, or expensive printing processes (Gander 1996). 'Me-too' packaging has become particularly common among supermarket own-brand versions of popular products, and there has been some debate about the ethics of this. In some countries these close copies infringe copyright or patent laws (Davies 1995).

Colour can also be important; for example, Heinz's use of a turquoise label for their baked beans tin emphasises the orange colour of the beans when the can is opened. Even the proportions of the package make a difference; the ratio of the sides of the package affect perception (Raghubir and Greenleaf 2006).

In recent years, because of the huge upsurge in world trade, it has also become necessary to consider the legal requirements of labelling, which differ from one country to the next; nutritional information may have to be in a different form for each country (for example, in the United States food has to be labelled with the amount of fat it contains expressed as a percentage of a 2000-calorie daily intake). In recent years there has been a requirement in many countries to label foods which contain genetically modified crops; this has created a major problem for global food corporations, since they may source ingredients from many places, as well as market-finished products globally (D'Souza *et al.* 2008).

Packaging can often be used for promotion of other products in the manufacturer's range (via recipe instructions, for example) or for joint promotions with non-competing companies. Interestingly, corporate brands on packaging seem to have little impact on the desirability of the product, whereas brand category dominance has a significant effect (LaForet 2011).

CASE STUDY 6 G24 Innovations

Global warming, dwindling resources and rising fuel costs have certainly raised interest in alternative energy sources in recent years. Solar power in particular has received a lot of interest – solar cells are not noisy like wind turbines, they are less obtrusive and they can often be used to power small appliances in locations away from mains power sources.

Into this market has stepped G24 Innovations. G24i is a company based in South Wales, founded by two Americans, Ed Stevenson and Bob Hertzberg. The technology they are applying is really futuristic; the company has acquired the rights to organic inks (developed by Michael Graetzel, a Swiss chemist) which generate electricity when exposed to sunlight. This means that the company can manufacture flexible solar panels – so flexible that they can be sewn onto the tops of shoulder bags and bicycle panniers.

The solar generators are manufactured as a continuous strip, kilometres long, which can be cut to any shape. The strips are not as flexible as cloth, but are certainly flexible enough to be moulded around unusual shapes, unlike traditional solar panels which are rigid and fairly thick.

Obviously the power generated in this way is very small, but it means that a customer can charge up a mobile telephone from a panel on a shoulder bag or recharge bicycle lights from a pannier's top. Hertzberg, a former politician from California, says that standby power is their 'killer app' – the application that will fuel the company's growth. Having electronic devices on standby uses up a surprising amount of power – around 8% of total power consumption – but using a solar panel to provide the standby power removes the problem. Hertzberg and Stevenson say that their solar panels have the potential to generate enough power to replace the giant Drax power station in Yorkshire, England. Drax, according to Stevenson and Hertzberg, is the biggest single source of pollution in Western Europe.

So far the company has produced a limited range of products using the technology. Solar-powered handbags and panniers are probably at the 'gimmick' end of the market, being a startling way of demonstrating the technology, but developments such as solar-powered computer keyboards and mice have real potential. Although the organic inks are less efficient than traditional rigid solar panels, they have the advantage (not being rigid) that they can easily be manufactured in a range of shapes and thus be incorporated into many products. Using ordinary room lighting, they can generate enough power to run a wireless keyboard or mouse.

This capability has led Texas Instruments to sign a one-year partnership agreement with G24i: Texas Instruments say that G24i's products are the most efficient for harvesting room light to power small equipment. G24i hopes to seal deals with other major electronics manufacturers to integrate the technology into their products and has several deals in the pipeline.

Other applications include products where using mains power or even batteries would be inconvenient; for example, smoke detectors. With one of G24i's solar strips wrapped round its base, there is no need to check and replace the batteries in a smoke detector. Electric clocks might be another example, or wireless doorbells – the possibilities are endless.

The company's production line is based in Cardiff, South Wales, but the founders continue to live in California, where they are well placed to negotiate with the industry. Day-to-day management of the company is handled by a UK-based team of executives, some of whom are American.

Clearly, there are many possible applications for solar-power units and the company is active in seeking out ways of exploiting the technology. However, in some ways this is a product in search of a market – the advantages over conventional solar panels are relatively few and must outweigh the increased efficiency of a conventional panel if the product is to sell. So far, the founders have burned through $120m and have a deal to raise another $40m – as Hertzberg said in an interview with *The Times*, 'We never thought it would be this expensive but the thing is, this stuff is really hard to get right' (*The Times*, 17 July 2011).

Questions

1 What type of innovation is this?

2 What type of innovation strategy do G24i appear to be following?

3 Currently the company does not have a product brand. How might branding help the company?

4 At what stage in the product life cycle are the solar panels?

5 In Calentone and Cooper's definitions, what type of product is this?

SUMMARY

This chapter has been about those decisions that are closest to the product. The main issues revolve around managing the product portfolio to ensure that the firm continues to offer relevant products to meet the needs of consumers, knowing when to drop a product from the mix and knowing when to introduce a new product.

Branding is concerned with communicating the unique selling proposition of the product to the consumers and is the focus of all the firm's marketing activities relating to the product. The brand is the 'personality' of the product, communicating subtle messages about quality and performance.

Here are the key points from this chapter:

- The product life cycle is a useful description, but not much help in prediction
- Products in the Star stage will cost more money to maintain than they bring in, but are an investment for the future
- Dogs may still be profitable, but are probably a poor use of resources and could be replaced by more profitable products
- War Horses and Dodos will eventually disappear unless they can be repositioned into new, growing markets
- Most products will decline and must be replaced eventually
- The safe route in NPD is the me-too; the high-growth route is innovation
- A product is a bundle of benefits, not merely the sum of its physical characteristics.

CHAPTER QUESTIONS

1 What are the stages of new product development?

2 Why should firms innovate?

3 How might a firm use reinvention when repositioning a product?

4 From the BCG matrix, which products would probably be bought by the late majority of adopters?

5 What disadvantages might family-line branding have over individual branding?

Further reading

Innovation Management and New Product Development by Paul Trott (Harlow, FT Prentice Hall, 2011) provides a detailed account of the new product development process and the management of the adoption process by customers.

Services Marketing: Concepts, Strategies and Cases by K. Douglas Hoffman and John E.G. Bateson (South Western Educational Publishing, 2010) has an excellent overview of service product marketing.

Building Strong Brands by David A. Aaker (Pocket Books, 2010) gives a good, practitioner-orientated guide to developing brands.

References

Augusto, Mario, and Coelho, Filipe: 'Market orientation and new-to-the-world products: exploring the moderating effects of innovativeness, competitive strength, and environmental forces'. *Industrial Marketing Management*, **38** (1) (2009), pp. 94–108.

Bagwell, L.S. and Bernheim, B.D.: 'Veblen effects in a theory of conspicuous consumption', *The American Economic Review*, **86** (1996), pp. 349–73.

Balabanis, G. and Craven, S.: 'Consumer confusion from own-brand lookalikes: an exploratory survey', *Journal of Marketing Management*, **13** (4) (May 1997), pp. 299–313.

Barksdale, H.C. and Harris, C.E.: 'Portfolio analysis and the PLC', *Long Range Planning*, **15** (6) (1982), pp. 74–83.

Battor, Moustafa, and Battor, Mohamed: 'The impact of customer relationship management capability on innovation and performance advantages: testing a mediated model', *Journal of Marketing Management*, **26** (9/10) (2010), pp. 842–57.

Benwell, M.: 'Scheduling stocks and storage space in a volatile market', *Logistics Information Management*, **9** (4) (1996), pp. 18–23.

Besharat, Ali: 'How co-branding versus brand extensions drive consumers' evaluations of new products: a brand equity approach', *Industrial Marketing Management*, **39** (8) (2010), pp. 1240–9.

Brown, Stephen, Sherry, John F. and Kozinetts, Robert V.: 'Teaching old brands new tricks: retro branding and the revival of brand meaning', *Journal of Marketing*, **67** (3) (July 2003), pp. 19–33.

Buschke, H.: 'Learning is organised by chunking', *Journal of Verbal Learning and Verbal Behaviour*, **15** (1976), pp. 313–24.

Calentone, Roger J. and Cooper, Robert G.: 'New product scenarios: prospects for success', *American Journal of Marketing*, **45** (Spring 1981), pp. 48–60.

Carbonell-Foulquie, Pilar, Munuera-Aleman, Jose L. and Rodriguez-Escudero, Ana I.: 'Criteria employed for go/no-go decisions when developing successful highly innovative products', *Industrial Marketing Management*, **33** (4) (April 2004), pp. 307–16.

Clancy, Kevin J. and Shulman, Robert S.: *The Marketing Revolution* (New York, Harper Business, 1991), p. 6.

Clark, K. and Fujimoto, T.: 'The power of product integrity', *Business Review* (November/December 1990), pp. 107–18.

Clark, Ronald A., Goldsmith, Ronald L. and Goldsmith, Elizabeth B.: 'Market mavenism and consumer self-confidence', *Journal of Consumer Behaviour*, (May/Jun) **7** (3) (2008), pp. 239–48.

Cooper, R.G. and Kleinschmidt, E.J.: 'An investigation into the new product process: steps, deficiencies and impact', *Journal of Product Innovation Management*, (June 1988), pp. 71–85.

Davies, I.: 'Look-alikes; fair or unfair competition?' *Journal of Brand Management* (October 1995), pp. 104–20.

DeChernatony, L. and McDonald, M.: *Creating Powerful Brands*, 2nd edn (Oxford, Butterworth Heinemann, 1998).

Demsetz, H.: 'Barriers to entry', *American Economic Review*, **72** (1982), pp. 47–57.

D'Souza, Clare, Rugimbana, Robert, Quazi, Ali and Nanere, Marthin G.: 'Investing in consumer confidence through genetically modified labeling: an evaluation of compliance options and their marketing challenges for Australian firms', *Journal of Marketing Management*, **24** (5/6) (2008), pp. 621–35.

Engel, James F., Blackwell, Roger D. and Miniard, Paul W.: *Consumer Behaviour*, 8th edn (Fort Worth, TX, Dryden Press, 1995).

Foxman, E.R., Berger, P.W. and Cote, J.A.: 'Consumer brand confusion: a conceptual framework', *Psychology and Marketing*, **19** (1992), pp. 123–41.

Gander, P.: 'Patently obvious', *Marketing Week* (28 June 1996), pp. 51–5.

Gordon, W. and Valentin, V.: 'Buying the brand at point of choice', *Journal of Brand Management*, **4** (1) (1996), pp. 35–44.

Haines, George H.: 'A study of why people purchase new products', *Proceedings of the American Marketing Association* (1966), pp. 685–97.

Hankinson, G. and Cowking, P.: 'Branding in practice: the profile and role of brand managers in the UK', *Journal of Marketing Management*, **13** (4) (May 1997), pp. 239–64.

Hart, Susan: 'Dimensions of success in new product development; an exploratory investigation', *Journal of Marketing Management*, **9** (1) (January 1993), pp. 23–42.

Huang, Xueli, Soutar, Geoffrey N. and Brown, Alan: 'Measuring new product success: an empirical investigation of Australian SMEs', *Industrial Marketing Management*, **33** (2) (February 2004), pp. 101–23.

Johne, A. and Snelson, P.: *Successful Product Development: Management Practices in American and British Firms* (Oxford, Basil Blackwell, 1990).

Koestler, A.: *The Act of Creation* (London, Pan Books Ltd, 1964).

LaForet, Sylvie: 'Brand names on packaging and their impact on purchase preference', *Journal of Consumer Behaviour*, (Jan/Feb) **10** (1) (2011), pp. 18–30.

Lazarsfield, Paul F., Bertelson Bernard R. and Gaudet, Hazel: *The People's Choice* (New York, Columbia University Press, 1948).

Levitt, T.: *The Marketing Imagination* (New York, The Free Press, 1986).

Min, Sungwook, Kauwani, Manohar U. and Robinson, William T.: 'Market pioneer and early follower survival risks: a contingency analysis of really new vs. incrementally new products', *Journal of Marketing*, **70** (1) (2006), pp. 15–33.

Moore, Malcolm: 'Royal wedding: Chinese tailors rush to copy Kate Middleton's dress', *Daily Telegraph,* 30 April 2011.

Munnukka, Juha, and Jarvi, Pentti: 'The value drivers of high-tech consumer products', *Journal of Marketing Management*, **27** (5/6) (2011), pp. 582–601.

Muzellec, Laurent and Lambkin, Mary: 'Corporate rebranding: destroying, transferring or creating brand equity?' *European Journal of Marketing*, **40** (7/8) (2006), pp. 803–24.

Napoli, Julie: 'The impact of non-profit brand orientation on organizational performance', *Journal of Marketing Management*, **22** (7/8) (2006), pp. 673–94.

Pappu, Ravi, Quester, Pascale and Cooksey, Ray W.: 'Consumer-based brand equity and country of origin relationships', *European Journal of Marketing*, **40** (5/6) (2006), pp. 696–717.

Persson, Niklas: 'An exploratory investigation of the elements of B2B brand image and its relationship to price premium', *Industrial Marketing Management,* **39** (8) (2010), pp. 1269–77.

Png, J.P. and Reitman, D.: 'Why are some products branded and others not?' *Journal of Law and Economics*, **38** (1995), pp. 207–24.

Quelch, J. and Harding, D.: 'Brands versus private labels: fighting to win', *Harvard Business Review* (January–February 1995), pp. 99–109.

Raffee, H. and Kreutzer, R.: 'Organisational dimensions of global marketing', *European Journal of Marketing*, **23** (5) (1989), pp. 43–57.

Raghubir, Priya and Greenleaf, Eric A.: 'Ratios in proportion: what should the shape of the package be?' *Journal of Marketing*, **70** (2) (2006), pp. 95–107.

Ries, A.: 'What's in a name?' *Sales and Marketing Management* (October 1995), pp. 36–7.

Rogers, Everett M.: *Diffusion of Innovations* (New York, Macmillan, 1962).

Romaniuk, Jenni and Gaillard, Elise: 'The relationship between unique brand associations, brand usage and brand performance: analysis across eight categories', *Journal of Marketing Management,* **23** (3/4) (2007), pp. 267–84.

Roper, Stuart, and LaNiece, Caroline: 'The importance of brands in the lunch-box choices of low-income British schoolchildren', *Journal of Consumer Behaviour,* (Mar-Jun), **8** (2/3) (2009), pp. 84–9.

Ruttenberg, A., Kavizky, A. and Oren, H.: 'Compositioning – the paradigm-shift beyond positioning', *Journal of Brand Management* (December 1995), pp. 169–79.

Salciuviene, Laura, Ghauri, Pervez N., Streder, Ruth Salomea, and De Mattod, Claudio: 'Do brand names in a foreign language lead to different brand perceptions?' *Journal of Marketing Management,* **26** (11/12) (2010), pp. 1037–56.

Sandler, D. and Shani, D.: 'Brand globally but advertise locally? An empirical investigation', *Marketing Review* (1992), pp. 18–31.

Sorescu, Alina B., Chandy, Rajesh K. and Prabhu, Jaideep C.: 'Sources and financial consequences of radical innovation: insights from pharmaceuticals', *Journal of Marketing*, **67** (4) (October 2003), pp. 82–102.

Stoll, Marco, Baecke, Sebastian, and Kenning, Peter: 'What they see is what they get? An fMRI study on neural correlates of attractive packaging', *Journal of Consumer Behaviour,* (Jul–Oct) **7** (4/5) (2008), pp. 342–59.

Tajeddini, Kayhan, Trueman, Myfanwy and Larsen, Gretchen: 'Examining the effect of marketing orientation on innovativeness', *Journal of Marketing Management,* **22** (5/6) (2006), pp. 529–51.

Timmor, Yaron, and Katz-Navon, Tal: 'Being the same and different: a model explaining new product adoption', *Journal of Consumer Behaviour,* (May/Jun) **7** (3) (2008), pp.249–62.

Ubilava, David, Foster, Kenneth A., Lusk, Jayson L. and Nilsson, Tomas: 'Differences in consumer preferences when facing branded versus non-branded choices', *Journal of Consumer Behaviour,* (Mar/Apr) **10** (2) (2011), pp. 61–70.

Uncles, M., Cocks, M. and Macrae, C.: 'Brand architecture: reconfiguring organisations for effective brand management', *Journal of Brand Management* (October 1995), pp. 81–92.

Veblen, T.: *The Theory of the Leisure Class* (New York, Macmillan, 1899).

Volckner, Franziska and Sattler, Henrik: 'Drivers of brand extension success', *Journal of Marketing*, **70** (2) (2006), pp. 18–34.

Wang, Chih-Chien, Lo, Shao-Kang, and Fang, Wenchang: 'Extemding the technology acceptance model to mobile telecommunication innovation: the existence of network externalities', *Journal of Consumer Behaviour,* **7** (2) (2008), pp. 101–10.

7

PRICING STRATEGIES

Objectives

After reading this chapter you should be able to:

- Explain the advantages and disadvantages of different pricing methods
- Calculate prices using different approaches
- Choose the correct pricing strategy to fit a firm's overall objectives
- Explain some of the economic theories underlying the marketer's view of price and value.

INTRODUCTION

Pricing may not be exciting, but it is one of the most important issues for marketers; it is crucial not only to the profit that is to be made, but also to the quantity of the products that will be sold. It touches on all the other elements of the marketing mix because it clarifies the offer of exchange being made – it is the signal to the customer of what we expect in exchange for what we are offering. This chapter examines the different ways of pricing that are used and offers some ideas on how to choose a pricing strategy.

Tata

Tata is India's largest industrial company, generating more than 3% of the country's gross national product. The company's motor division manufactures trucks, buses, scooters and three-wheel motor rickshaws. India is a large country, but most people are poor – in fact, too poor to own cars at all.

Tata's promise was to build a car for 1 lakh rupees (a lakh is 100,000). This price equates to around £1500, a price which the company thought was realistic for many Indians (although still out of reach of the poorest, many of whom would struggle to afford a bicycle).

Most major car manufacturers thought that this target was entirely unrealistic, given the cost of raw materials: even with the low wage structure of India, producing even a very small car for £1500 seemed out of the question. No matter how basic, the task seemed impossible.

The Tata Nano was eventually unveiled and, true to his promise, Ratan Tata, the company's chairman, put the car on the market for 1 lakh. The car has a 600 cc engine, continuous transmission (no gearbox or clutch), no passenger mirror, no radio and only one windscreen wiper. The car meets all safety standards for India, but might need adapting for Europe or the United States – but it is still a remarkable feat of engineering.

Ratan Tata, Chairman

Watch the video clip, then try to answer the following questions. The answers are on the companion website.

Questions

1 What type of pricing is Tata using for the Nano?

2 What should be the company's pricing policy for Europe?

3 Should the car meet the European safety standards?

4 What are the drawbacks of charging such a low price?

ECONOMIC THEORIES OF PRICING AND VALUE

Classical economists assumed that prices would automatically be set by the laws of *supply and demand*. Figure 7.1 shows how this works.

As prices rise, more suppliers find it profitable to enter the market, but the demand for the product falls because fewer customers think the product is worth the money. Conversely, as prices fall there is more demand, but fewer suppliers feel it is worthwhile supplying the product so less is produced. Eventually a state of equilibrium is reached where the quantity produced is equal to the quantity consumed, and at that point the price will be fixed.

Unfortunately, this neat model has a number of drawbacks.

- The model assumes that customers know where they can buy the cheapest products (i.e. it assumes perfect knowledge of the market)
- Second, it assumes that all the suppliers are producing identical products, which is rarely the case
- Third, it assumes that price is the only issue that affects customer behaviour, which is clearly not true
- Fourth, it assumes that customers always behave completely rationally, which, again, is substantially not the case
- Fifth, there is an assumption that people will always buy more of a product if it is cheaper. This is not true of such products as wedding rings or artificial limbs
- Finally, the model assumes that the suppliers are in perfect competition – that none of them has the power to 'rig' the market and set the prices (see Chapter 2).

Figure 7.1 Supply and demand

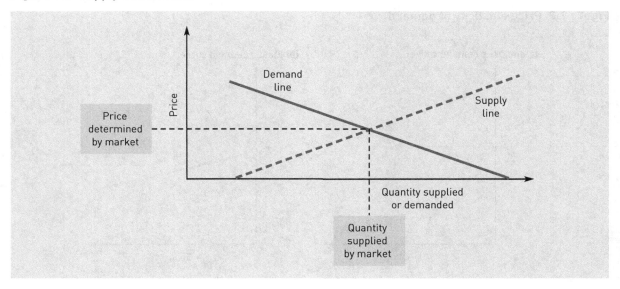

The model does, at least, take account of customers, and it was the pioneer economist Adam Smith who first said that 'the customer is king' (Smith 1776). Unfortunately, the shortcomings of the model mean that it has little practical use, no matter how helpful it is in understanding a principle. Economists have therefore added considerably to the theory.

Elasticity of demand

This concept states that different product categories will show different degrees of sensitivity to price change.

Figure 7.2(a) shows a product where the quantity sold is affected only slightly by price fluctuations, i.e. the demand is inelastic. An example of this is salt. Figure 7.2(b) shows a product where even a small difference in price leads to a very substantial shift in the quantity demanded, i.e. the demand is elastic. An example of this is borrowed money, e.g. mortgages, where even a small rise in interest rates appears to affect the propensity to borrow. Although these examples relate to consumers, the same is true for suppliers; in some cases suppliers can react very quickly to changes in the quantities demanded (for example, banking), whereas in other cases the suppliers need long lead times to change the production levels (for instance, farming).

The price elasticity of demand concept implies that there is no basis for defining products as necessities or luxuries. If a necessity is defined as something without which life cannot be sustained, then its demand curve would be entirely inelastic; whatever the price was, people would have to pay it. In practice, no such product exists.

Economic choice

Economists have demonstrated that there can never be enough resources in the world to satisfy everybody's wants, and therefore resources have to be allocated in

Figure 7.2 Price elasticity of demand

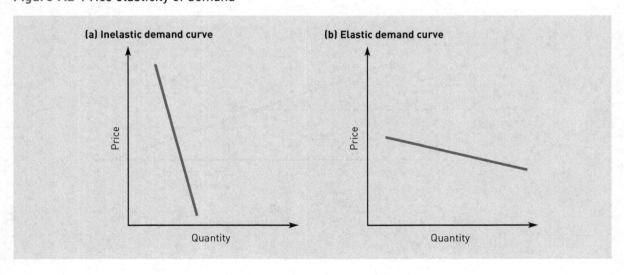

some way (which will probably mean an equality of dissatisfaction). Resources used for one purpose cannot, of course, be used for another; this is the concept of the economic choice.

For example, a clothing manufacturer has only a certain number of machinists who work a certain number of hours. This means that it may be possible to produce either 8000 shirts with the available resources or 4000 pairs of trousers. If the manufacturer has two orders, one for each type of product, he or she will have to choose which order to supply and disappoint the other customer.

From the customer's viewpoint, the economic choice means having to choose between going to the cinema or going to the pub; there may not be the time or the money to do both. Because of this, customers may also take into account the price of activities other than those the prospective supplier is providing; the pub, for example, may not be aware that the cinema is competition, and that a fall in the price of going to the cinema may affect the takings over the bar. In the UK in recent years, pubs have been closing down at an unprecedented rate, largely owing to the availability of cheap alcoholic drinks from supermarkets; many pubs have failed to recognise this as competition and counter it effectively.

Although the economists' view of pricing offers some interesting insights, there is little practical value in the theories offered because they do not take account of the consumer decision-making process (see Chapter 3). Consumers are not always rational; marketers are aware of this.

Critical thinking

Are we really that illogical when we buy things? It's a rather bleak comment on human beings – after all, we are the most intelligent creature so far discovered! If we don't use our brains to decide how to spend our hard-earned money, doesn't that imply that we don't use our brains much for anything else?

Of course, maybe we do think about things sometimes. If it's an important purchase or if we are short of money, we might make more effort – but who bothers to spend time thinking about the price of a bar of chocolate? Apart, of course, from marketers!

PRICING AND MARKET ORIENTATION

As in any other question of marketing, pricing is dependent on how customers will react to the prices set. Customers do not usually buy the cheapest products; they buy those that represent good value for money. If this were not so, the most popular cars in Britain would be cheap Eastern European models, rather than Nissans and Fords. Typically, customers will assess the promises the supplier has made about what the product is and will do, and will measure this against the price being asked (Zeithaml 1988).

This leaves the marketer with a problem. Marketers need to decide what price will be regarded by customers as good value for money, while still allowing the company to make a profit.

The main methods of pricing used by firms are cost-based, customer-based and competition-based.

Cost-based pricing

Cost-based methods are the least customer-orientated; two still used are **cost-plus pricing** and **mark-up pricing**.

Cost-plus pricing

Cost-plus pricing is commonly advocated by accountants and engineers, since it is simple to use and appears to guarantee that the company meets a predetermined profit target. The method works by calculating the cost of manufacturing the product, including distributed overhead costs and research and development costs, then adding on a fixed percentage profit to this figure to arrive at the price. Such a calculation might look like Table 7.1.

A variant of cost-plus pricing is absorption costing, which works by calculating the costs of each unit of production, including an allowance for overheads within the unit price. This allows the firm to calculate a break-even point at which further sales will be profitable.

On the face of it, this type of pricing seems logical and straightforward; unfortunately, it does not take account of how customers will react to the prices quoted. If customers take the view that the price does not represent value for money, they will not buy the product and the result will be that the company will have made 20,000 units of a product for which there will be no sales. Conversely, if customers take the view that the price is incredibly good value for money, the company may not have enough stocks on hand to meet demand and competitors will be able to enter the market easily (not to mention that the company could have charged more for the product and therefore made more money).

Table 7.1 Cost-plus pricing

Item	Cost per unit
Labour costs	£2.52
Raw materials	£4.32
Electricity	£0.27
Tooling costs (assuming production run of 20,000 units)	£1.78
Overheads	£3.43
Total production cost per unit	£12.32
Plus profit of 20%	£2.46
Net price	**£14.78**

Some government contracts are awarded on a cost-plus basis, but experience in the United States has shown that allowing cost-plus contracts to be granted will often result in the supplier inflating the costs to make an extra profit.

Mark-up pricing

Mark-up pricing is similar to cost-plus pricing, and is the method used by most retailers. Typically, a retailer will buy in stock and add on a fixed percentage to the bought-in price (a mark-up) to arrive at the shelf price. The level will vary from retailer to retailer, depending on the type of product; in some cases the mark-up will be 100% or more, in others it will be near zero (if the retailer feels that stocking the product will stimulate other sales). Usually there is a standard mark-up for each product category.

Here the difference needs to be shown between a mark-up and a margin. Mark-up is calculated on the price the retailer pays for the product; margin is calculated on the price the retailer sells for. This means that a 100% mark-up equals a 50% margin; a 25% mark-up equals a 20% margin (Table 7.2).

Retailers use this method because of the number of lines the shop may be carrying. For a hypermarket, this could be up to 20,000 separate lines, and it would clearly be impossible to carry out market research with the customers for every line. The buyers therefore use their training and knowledge of their customer base to determine which lines to stock and (to some extent) rely on the manufacturers to carry out formal market research and determine the recommended retail prices.

This method is identical to the cost-plus method except for two factors; first, the retailer is usually in close contact with the customers and can therefore develop a good 'feel' for what customers will be prepared to pay; second, retailers have ways of disposing of unsold stock. In some cases, this will mean discounting the stock back to cost and selling it in the January sales; in other cases, the retailer will have a sale-or-return agreement with the manufacturer so that unsold stock can be returned for credit. This is becoming increasingly common with major retailers such as Toys 'R' Us who have sufficient 'clout' in the market to enforce such agreements. In a sense, therefore, the retailer is carrying out market research by test-marketing the product; if the customers do not accept the product at the price offered, the retailer can drop the price to a point that will represent value for money or can return it to the manufacturer for credit.

Table 7.2 Mark-up *v* margin

Bought-in price	£4.00
Mark-up at 25% of £4.00	£1.00
Price on the shelf	£5.00
Margin of 20% of £5.00	£1.00
Bought-in price	£4.00

Customer-based pricing methods

The various approaches to *customer-based pricing* do not necessarily mean offering products at the lowest possible price, but they do take account of customer needs and wants.

Customary pricing

Customary pricing is customer-orientated in that it provides the customer with the product for the same price at which it has always been offered. An example is the price of a call from a coin-operated telephone box. Telephone companies need only reduce the time allowed for the call as costs rise. For some countries (e.g. Australia) this is problematical since local calls are allowed unlimited time, but for most European countries this is not the case.

The reason for using customary pricing is to avoid having to reset the call-boxes too often. Similar methods exist for taxis, some children's sweets and gas or electricity pre-payment meters. If this method were to be used for most products there would be a steady reduction in the firm's profits as the costs caught up with the selling price, so the method is not practical for every firm.

Demand pricing

Demand pricing is the most market-orientated method of pricing. Here, the marketer begins by assessing what the demand will be for the product at different price levels. This is usually done by asking the customers what they might expect to pay for the product and seeing how many choose each price level. This will lead to the development of the kind of chart shown in Table 7.3.

As the price rises, fewer customers are prepared to buy the product, as fewer will still see the product as good value for money. In the example given in Table 7.3, the fall-off is not linear, i.e. the number of units sold falls dramatically once the price goes above £5. This kind of calculation could be used to determine the stages of a skimming policy (see below) or it could be used to calculate the appropriate launch price of a product.

For demand pricing, the next stage is to calculate the costs of producing the product in the given quantities. Usually the cost of producing each item falls as more are made (i.e. if we make 50,000 units, each unit costs less than would be the case if

Table 7.3 Demand pricing

Price per unit	Number of customers who said they would buy at this price
£3 to £4	30,000
£4 to £5	25,000
£5 to £6	15,000
£6 to £7	5000

Table 7.4 Costings for demand pricing

Number of units	Unit cost (labour and materials)	Tooling-up and fixed costs	Net cost per unit
30,000	£1.20	£4000	£1.33
25,000	£1.32	£4000	£1.48
15,000	£1.54	£4000	£1.81
5000	£1.97	£4000	£2.77

we made only 1000 units). Given the costs of production, it is possible to select the price that will lead to a maximisation of profits. This is because there is a trade-off between quantity produced and quantity sold; as the firm lowers the selling price, the amount sold increases but the income generated decreases.

The calculations can become complex, but the end result is that the product is sold at a price that customers will accept and that will meet the company's profit targets. Table 7.4 shows an example of costings to match up with the above figures. The tooling-up cost is the amount it will cost the company to prepare for producing the item. This will be the same whether 1000 or 30,000 units are made.

Table 7.5 shows how much profit could be made at each price level. The price at which the product is sold will depend on the firm's overall objectives; these may not necessarily be to maximise profit on this one product, since the firm may have other products in the range or other long-term objectives that preclude maximising profits at present.

Based on these figures, *the most profitable* price will be £4.50. Other ways of calculating the price could easily lead to making a lower profit from this product. For instance, the price that would generate *the highest profit per unit* would be £6.50, but at this price they would sell only 5000 units and make £18,650. The price that would generate *the highest sales* would be £3.50, but this would (in effect) lose the firm almost £10,000 in terms of foregone profit.

A further useful concept is that of *contribution*. Contribution is calculated as the difference between the cost of manufacture and the price for which the product is sold – in other words, it does not take account of overheads. Sometimes a product

Table 7.5 Profitability at different price bands

Number of units sold	Net profit per unit	Total profit for production run	Percentage profit per unit
30,000	£2.17	£65,100	62
25,000	£3.02	£75,500	67
15,000	£3.61	£54,150	66
5000	£3.73	£18,650	57

is worth producing because it makes a significant extra contribution to the firm's profits without actually adding to the overheads. It is not difficult to imagine a situation where a product carries a low profit margin and is therefore unable to support a share of the overheads, but is still worth producing (perhaps because it supports sales of something else or is bought by our most loyal customers). A calculation which included an overall share of the overheads might not give a fair picture, since the contribution would be additional to existing turnover.

Demand pricing works by knowing what the customers are prepared to pay and what they will see as value for money.

Product-line pricing

Product-line pricing means setting prices within linked product groups. Often sales of one product will be directly linked to the sales of another, so that it is possible to sell one item at a low price to make a greater profit on the other one. Gillette sells its razors at a very low price, with the aim of making up the profit on sales of the blades. In the long run, this is a good strategy because it overcomes the initial resistance of consumers towards buying something untried, but allows the firm to show high profits for years to come (incidentally, this approach was first used by King C. Gillette, the inventor of the disposable safety razor blade).

Polaroid chose to sell its instant cameras very cheaply (almost for cost price) for the US market and to take their profit from selling the films for a much higher price. For Europe, the firm chose to sell both films and cameras for a medium level price and profit from sales of both. Eventually this led Kodak to enter the market with its own instant camera, but this was withdrawn from sale in the face of lawsuits from Polaroid for patent infringement.

Skimming

Skimming is the practice of starting out with a high price for a product, then reducing it progressively as sales level off. It relies on two main factors: first, that not all customers have the same perception of value for money and, second, that the company has a technological lead over the opposition which can be maintained for long enough to satisfy the market.

Skimming is usually carried out by firms which have developed a technically advanced product. Initially the firm will charge a high price for the product, and at this point only those who are prepared to pay a premium price for it will buy. Profit may not be high, because the number of units sold will be low and therefore the cost of production per unit will be high. Once the most innovative customers have bought and the competition is beginning to enter the market, the firm can drop the price and 'skim' the next layer of the market, at which point profits will begin to rise. Eventually, the product will be sold at a price that allows the firm only a minimum profit, at which point only replacement sales or sales to late adopters will be made.

The advantage of this method is that the cost of developing the product is returned fairly quickly, so that the product can later be sold near the marginal cost of production. This means that the competitors have difficulty entering the market at all, since their own development costs will have to be recovered in some other way.

Skimming is commonly used in consumer electronics markets. This is because firms frequently establish a technological lead over the competitors and can sometimes even protect their products by taking out patents, which take some time for competitors to overcome. An example of this is the MP3 player, which sold at a premium price when it was first launched. As competitors entered the market with cloned products, the price dropped dramatically. Research shows that customers are aware of skimming in electronics markets and are delaying purchases of new electronic devices until the prices drop. This may affect the way firms view skimming in the future.

Skimming requires careful judgement of what is happening in the marketplace, in terms both of observing customer behaviour and of observing competitive response. Market research is therefore basic to the success of a skimming policy, and very careful monitoring of sales is needed to know when to cut the price again.

Critical thinking

Skimming seems like a bit of a cheat. The firm makes the product for a low price, then sells it at a high price, knowing that the price is going to fall later. Isn't this a bit like cheating the first few customers by overcharging them?

Or maybe they are enjoying the fun of being the first to own the product and the firm is making them pay for the privilege. It seems an expensive bit of fun to have, though – and anyway, people know about skimming.

On the other hand, of course, firms are not in business for the fun of it. They are entitled to make a profit, and of course recover the rather expensive research and development costs they incur in producing new products for us!

Psychological pricing

Psychological pricing relies on emotional responses from the consumer. Higher prices are often used as an indicator of quality (Erickson and Johansson 1985), so some firms will use prestige pricing. This applies in many service industries, because consumers are often buying a promise; a service that does not have a high enough quality cannot be exchanged afterwards. Consumers' expectations of high-priced restaurants and hairdressers are clearly higher in terms of the quality of service provision; cutting prices in those industries does not necessarily lead to an increase in business. Interestingly, there is evidence that the price–quality relationship was affected considerably in Germany by the introduction of the euro. Prices previously expressed in Deutschmarks appeared higher than the new price in euros because there were approximately two euros to the Deutschmark – people's perception was that the price had 'halved' which lowered their expectations of quality (Molz and Gielnik 2006).

Odd–even pricing is the practice of ending prices with an odd number, for example £3.99 or $5.95 rather than £4 or $6. It appears that consumers tend to categorise these prices as '£3 and a bit' or '$5 and change' and thus perceive the price as being lower. The effect may also be due to an association with discounted or sale prices; researchers report that '99' endings on prices increase sales by around 8% (Schindler and Kirby 1997). Paradoxically, some recent research shows that people are more likely to try a new product for the first time if the price is a round number (Bray and Harris 2006).

This apparent discrepancy may be due to cultural differences. Research has shown that odd–even pricing does not necessarily work in all cultures (Suri *et al.* 2004). In Poland, for example, the effects are negligible. Odd–even pricing also has effects on perceptions of discounts during sales. Rounding the price to (say) £5 from £4.99 leads people to overvalue the size of the discount, which increases the perception of value for money (Gueguen and Legoherel 2004). Thus the positive effect on sales of using a 99-ending can be negated by the effect when the product is on offer in a sale.

Another effect of discounting can arise when retailers set upper or lower purchase requirements on discounted prices. A retailer offering a discount for buying more of a product (for example, 10% off for buying at least three items) leads people to want to buy more of the product than they had intended, whereas with a discount which has an upper limit (10% off, limited to two items per customer), people tend to want to buy less of the product than they had intended (Yoon and Vargas 2011). This response seems almost perverse, but it certainly shows which type of discount a retailer should use.

Second-market discounting

Second-market discounting is common in some service industries and in international markets. The brand is sold at one price in one market and at a lower price in another; for example, museums offer discounts to students, some restaurants offer discounts to elderly people on week-nights, and so forth. Often these discounts are offered to even out the loading on the firm; week-night discounts fill the restaurant on what would otherwise be a quiet night, so the firm makes more efficient use of the premises and staff.

In international markets, products might be discounted to meet local competition. For example, Honda motorcycles are up against strong local competition in India from Royal Enfield, so the price of their basic 100-cc motorcycle is around Rs39,000 (about £600). A similar Honda motorcycle in the UK costs around £2000. The specifications of the motorcycles do differ somewhat, and the import duty structures are different – however, it is difficult to see any difference that would account for a £1400 price differential.

Competitor-based pricing

Competitor-based pricing recognises the influence of competition in the marketplace. Strategically, the marketer must decide how close the competition is in providing for the consumers' needs; if the products are close, then prices will need to be similar to those of the competition. A meet-the-competition strategy has the advantage of avoiding price wars and stimulating competition in other areas of marketing, thus maintaining profitability. An **undercut-the-competition strategy** is often the main plank in the firm's marketing strategy; it is particularly common among retailers, who have relatively little control over product features and benefits and often have little control over the promotion of the products they stock. Some multinational firms (particularly in electronics) have the capacity to undercut rivals since they are able to manufacture in low-wage areas of the world or are large enough to use widespread automation. There is a danger of starting price wars when using an undercutting policy (see penetration pricing below). Undercutting (and consequent price wars) may be becoming more common (Mitchell 1996).

Firms with large market shares often have enough control over their distribution systems and the production capacity within their industries to become **price leaders**. Typically, such firms can make price adjustments without starting price wars and can raise prices without losing substantial market share (see Chapter 2 for monopolistic competition) (Rich 1982). Sometimes these price leaders become sensitive to the price and profit needs of their competitors, in effect supporting them, because they do not wish to attract the attention of monopoly regulators by destroying the competition. Deliberate price fixing (managers colluding to set industry prices) is illegal in most countries.

Penetration pricing

Penetration pricing is used when the firm wants to capture a large part of the market quickly. It relies on the assumption that a lower price will be perceived as offering better value for money (which is, of course, often the case).

For penetration pricing to work, the company must have carried out thorough research to find out what the competitors are charging for the nearest similar product. The new product is then sold at a substantially lower price, even if this cuts profits below an acceptable level; the intention is to capture the market quickly before the competitors can react with even lower prices. The danger with this pricing method is that competitors may be able to sustain a price war for a long period and will eventually bankrupt the incoming firm. It is usually safer to compete on some other aspect of the offering, such as quality or delivery.

Predatory pricing

In some cases, prices are pitched below the cost of production. The purpose of this is to bankrupt the competition so that the new entrant can take over entirely; this practice is called **predatory pricing** and (at least in international markets) is illegal. Predatory pricing was successfully used by Japanese car manufacturers when entering European markets in the 1970s, and is commonly used by large firms who are entering new markets. For the strategy to be successful, it is necessary for the market to be dominated by firms that cannot sustain a long price war. It is worth doing if the company has no other competitive edge, but does have sufficient financial reserves to hold out for a long time. Naturally, this method is customer-orientated since it can work only by providing the customers with very much better value for money than they have been used to. The company will eventually raise prices again to recoup the lost profits once the market presence has been established, however.

The ultimate in predatory pricing is dumping. This is the practice of selling goods at prices below the cost of manufacture and was at one time commonly practised by Communist countries desperate for hard currency. Dumping is illegal under international trade rules, but is difficult to prove, and by the time the victim countries have been able to prove their case and have the practice stopped, it is usually too late.

Competitor-based pricing is still customer-orientated to an extent, since it takes as its starting point the prices that customers are currently prepared to pay.

SETTING PRICES

Price setting follows eight stages, as shown in Table 7.6.

Price setting can be complex if it is difficult to identify the closest competitors, but it should be borne in mind that no product is entirely without competition; there is almost always another way in which customers can meet the need supplied by the product. Also, different customers have different needs and therefore will have differing views on what constitutes value for money – this is why markets need to be segmented carefully to ensure that the right price is being charged in each segment. As in any question of marketing, it is wise to begin with the customer.

Table 7.6 Eight stages of price setting

Stage	Explanation
Development of pricing objectives	The pricing objectives derive from the organisation's overall objectives; does the firm seek to maximise market share or maximise profits?
Assessment of the target market's ability to purchase and evaluation of price	Buyers tend to be more sensitive to food prices in supermarkets than to drinks prices in clubs. Also, a buyer's income and availability of credit directly affect the ability to buy the product at all.
Determination of demand	For most products demand falls as price rises. This is not necessarily a straight-line relationship, nor is the line necessarily at 45 degrees; for some products even a small price rise results in a sharp fall in demand (e.g. petrol), whereas for other products (e.g. salt) even a large price rise hardly affects demand at all.
Analysis of demand, cost and profit relationships	The firm needs to analyse the costs of producing the item against the price that the market will bear, taking into account the profit needed. The cost calculation will include both the fixed costs and the unit costs for making a given quantity of the product; this quantity will be determined by the market and will relate to the selling price.

continued

Table 7.6 continued

Stage	Explanation
Evaluation of competitors' prices	This will involve a survey of the prices currently being charged, but will also have to consider the possible entry of new competitors. Prices may be pitched higher than those of competitors to give an impression of exclusivity or higher quality; this is common in the perfume market and in services such as restaurants and hairdressing.
Selection of a pricing policy	The pricing policy needs to be chosen from the list given in the early part of the chapter.
Development of a pricing method	Here the producer develops a simple mechanism for determining prices in the future. The simplest method is to use cost-plus or mark-up pricing; these do not take account of customers, however, so something a little more sophisticated should be used if possible.
Determining a specific price	If the previous steps have been carried out in a thorough manner, determining the actual price should be a simple matter.

Source: Adapted from Dibb *et al*. 1994.

CASE STUDY 7 Grey markets

A grey market is one in which goods are sold which, although not illegal, are distributed through channels the manufacturer did not intend, usually for lower prices. Grey markets have grown up because of differential pricing – the practice of pricing the same goods at different prices for different markets.

In 2002, Levi Strauss obtained an injunction against Tesco's supermarket in the UK preventing them from establishing a grey market for jeans. Tesco's had been importing Levi's jeans from Eastern Europe, where they were being sold at lower prices than could be obtained in the UK. Levi claimed that Tesco's were damaging their brand image by such drastic undercutting, and the judge agreed – meaning that Tesco's had to withdraw the product. This was, according to Tesco's spokespeople, a sad day for consumers.

A similar market was created for the Apple iPhone. Apple launched the phone in New York, amid a blaze of publicity, and planned on rolling out the launch across the world in easy stages. The aim was to ensure that the production could match the demand. This time, though, the price went up: middle-men bought up thousands of the phones and sold them at premium prices in other countries.

Sometimes the grey market is created because the manufacturer knows that the product cannot sell for the same price in markets where the incomes and wealth levels are very different. At other times, the market comes about because of limited supplies of the product. In still other cases, the market comes about because of rights restrictions. This is the case in the broadcasting market. For example, Sky Digital is a satellite service which is only available to subscribers in the UK and Ireland for copyright reasons. In countries where there is a large expatriate population of British and Irish people, cards for decoding Sky are widely used, even though this breaches Sky's agreements with its suppliers of programmes. Sky has the technology to disable the cards and does not condone their use, but it is extremely difficult to catch the people using the cards. Equally, Canadians who wish to access some American satellite services can buy 'bootleg' decoders.

The problem for producers is serious. A carefully laid strategic plan can be completely undermined by the grey marketers – and in some cases profits can be eaten away dramatically as products cannot be sold at the intended price. On the other hand, for consumers the grey market seems to be fairer. After all, why should someone have to pay more for goods simply because he or she lives in a particular place? Or be unable to buy something that other people are able to buy?

Questions

1 How might companies counteract the grey market?
2 What makes grey markets attractive to firms?
3 Why might consumers find that the grey market is not as beneficial as it at first appears?
4 What might be the role of governments in controlling grey markets?
5 What are the dangers for broadcasters should they simply ignore the grey market?

SUMMARY

Value for money is a subjective concept; each person has a differing view of what represents value for money, and this means that different market segments will have differing views on whether a given price is appropriate. Marketing is about encouraging trade so that customers and manufacturers can maximise the satisfaction gained from their activities; to this end, marketers always try to make exchanges easier and pleasanter for customers.

Here are the key points from this chapter:

- Prices, ultimately, are fixed by market forces, not by suppliers alone. Therefore suppliers would be ill-advised to ignore the customer
- There is no objective difference between necessities and luxuries; the distinction lies only in the mind of the customer
- Customers cannot spend the same money twice, so they are forced to make economic choices. A decision to do one thing implies a decision not to do another
- Customers have a broad and sometimes surprising range of choices when seeking to maximise utility
- Pricing can be cost-based, competition-based or customer-based; ultimately, though, consumers have the last word because they can simply spend their money elsewhere.

CHAPTER QUESTIONS

1 What is the difference between margin and mark-up?

2 When should a skimming policy be used?

3 How can penetration pricing be used in international markets?

4 Why should a firm be wary of cost-plus pricing?

5 How does customary pricing benefit the supplier?

Further reading

For a fairly readable text on the economic aspects of pricing, **Richard Lipsey and Alec Chrystal's** *Economics*, **12th edn** (Oxford, Oxford University Press, 2011) is worth looking at.

Len Rogers' *Pricing for Profit* (Oxford, Basil Blackwell, 1990) is a practitioner-style book which contains a very comprehensive 'how-to' guide to pricing.

References

Bray, Jeffrey Paul and Harris, Christine: 'The effect of 9-ending prices on retail sales: a quantitative UK-based field study', *Journal of Marketing Management*, **22** (5/6) (2006), pp. 601–7.

Dibb, S., Simkin, L., Pride, W. and Ferrell, O.C.: *Marketing; Concepts and Strategies*, 2nd edn (London, Houghton Mifflin, 1994).

Erickson, G.M. and Johansson, J.K.: 'The role of price in multi-attribute product evaluation', *Journal of Consumer Research*, **12** (1985), pp. 195–9.

Gueguen, Nicolas and Legoherel, Patrick: 'Numerical encoding and odd-ending prices: The effect of a contrast in discount perception', *European Journal of Marketing,* **38** (1) (2004), pp. 194–208.

Mitchell, A.: 'The price is right', *Marketing Business,* **50** (May 1996), pp. 32–4.

Molz, Gunter and Gielnik, Michael: 'Does the introduction of the Euro have an effect on subjective hypotheses about the price-quality relationship?' *Journal of Consumer Behaviour*, **5** (3) (2006), pp. 204–10.

Rich, Stuart A.: 'Price leaders: large, strong, but cautious about conspiracy', *Marketing News* (25 June 1982), p. 11.

Schindler, R.M. and Kirby, P.N.: 'Patterns of right-most digits used in advertised prices: implications for nine-ending effects', *Journal of Consumer Research* (September 1997), pp. 192–201.

Smith, Adam: *An Inquiry into The Wealth of Nations* (1776).

Suri, Rajneesh, Anderson, Rolph E. and Kotlov, Vassili: 'The use of 9-ending prices: contrasting the USA with Poland', *European Journal of Marketing*, **38** (1) (2004), pp. 56–72.

Yoon, Sukki, and Vargas, Patrick: 'More leads to "Want more" but "No less" leads to "Want less": Consumers' counterfactual thinking when faced with quantity restriction discounts', *Journal of Consumer Behaviour*, **10** (2) (2011), pp. 93–101.

Zeithaml, Valerie A.: 'Consumer perceptions of price, quality and value', *Journal of Marketing*, **52** (July 1988), pp. 2–22.

8

DISTRIBUTION

Objectives

After reading this chapter you should be able to:

- Understand the role of distribution as providing an integral part of the product's benefits
- Explain the way agents, wholesalers and retailers work in the distribution system
- Choose the best distribution channel for a given market segment and product
- Explain some of the challenges facing retailers
- Know what to expect of different types of wholesaler
- Understand the difference between logistics and distribution.

INTRODUCTION

Producing something that consumers would like to buy is only part of the story; people can only buy products that are available and easily obtained. In terms of the seven Ps, distribution is the means by which place is determined. Marketers therefore spend considerable effort on finding the right channels of distribution and on ensuring that the products reach consumers in the most efficient way.

In business-to-business marketing, distribution is often the real key to success. Business buyers may buy through agents or wholesalers rather than direct from producers, so that tapping into a good distribution network is the most important step a company can take.

Friday's

Friday's is a family business in the egg-producing business. Although the company produces foods other than eggs, fresh egg production and selling is the core of the business. The company has grown from a small chicken farm: it produces 4 billion eggs a year, which is about 6% of the UK market. Sixty per cent of the eggs are produced intensively, but free-range and barn eggs are also sold. Most of the eggs are

sold under the supermarkets' own brands: the company is happy to help the supermarkets to brand the eggs appropriately. About 40% of the free-range eggs produced in Europe are produced in the UK.

Eggs are labelled with the Red Lion mark, which indicates that the eggs are British and the chickens are vaccinated against diseases such as salmonella. The lion mark was originally used in the 1950s and 1960s but fell out of use. Consumer confidence was shaken in the 1980s by a salmonella scare, but the brand has now been re-established via a series of TV advertisements.

Friday's is a price taker rather than a price maker: either the supermarkets set the price or prices are set by supply and demand. Feed prices create a problem for producers – consumers have already moved away from organic eggs due to the cost and clearly supermarkets are driven by what consumers are prepared (or able) to pay.

Distribution is a problem with such a fragile and perishable commodity. Friday's seek to minimise the distance from farm to retailer, and are the only egg producer able to deliver local eggs in the south east of Britain.

David Friday, Managing Director

Watch the video clip, then try to answer the following questions. The answers are on the companion website.

Questions

1 What are the main logistical problems for Friday's?

2 Why do Friday's distribute mainly through supermarkets?

3 Why does the company produce a mix of free-range and intensively farmed eggs?

LOGISTICS v DISTRIBUTION

Physical distribution is concerned with the ways organisations position physical products at a point where it is most convenient for consumers to buy them. *Logistics* takes a wider view; originally based on military terminology, logistics is concerned with the process of moving raw materials through the production and distribution processes to the point at which the finished product is needed. This involves strategic decision-making about warehouse location, materials management, stock levels and information systems. Logistics is the area in which purchasing and marketing overlap.

In some ways the physical distribution of a product is part of the bundle of benefits that make up that product. For example, a jacket bought online offers convenience benefits which a chain-store jacket does not. Conversely, the chain-store purchase may include hedonic benefits (the fun of shopping around, the excitement of finding a real bargain), which the Internet retailer does not supply. Even when the actual jacket is identical, the benefits derived from the distribution method are different.

The purpose of any physical distribution method is to get the product from its point of production to the consumer efficiently and effectively. The product must arrive in good condition and fit the consumer's need for convenience, or cheapness, or choice, or whatever else the particular target market thinks is important. Thus, from a marketing viewpoint, the subject of distribution covers such areas as transportation methods, wholesaling, high street retailing, direct mail marketing and even farm-gate shops.

Physical distribution is to do with transportation methods; **distribution strategy** decisions are about which outlets should be used for the product.

Transportation methods

Transportation methods vary according to speed, cost and ability to handle the type of product concerned. As a general rule, the quicker the method the more expensive it is, but in some cases it may be cheaper to use a faster method because the firm's capital is tied up for less time. The same applies to perishable items.

The transportation method chosen for a particular product will depend on the factors listed in Table 8.1. In all these cases, there will be trade-offs involved. Greater customer service will almost always be more expensive; greater reliability may increase transit time, as will greater traceability because in most cases the product will need to be checked on and off the transport method chosen. As with any other aspect of marketing activity, the customer's overall needs must be taken into account, and the relative importance of those needs must be judged with some accuracy if the firm is to remain competitive.

Distribution channels

Transportation method is also affected by the **channel of distribution**, or marketing channel. Figure 8.1 shows some of the possible channels of distribution that a consumer product might go through.

Table 8.1 Choosing a transportation method

Factor	Explanation and examples
The physical characteristics of the product	If the product is fragile (e.g. sheet glass), distribution channels need to be short and handling minimised. For perishable goods (e.g. fruit), it may be cheaper to use standby airfreight than to ship by sea, because there will be less spoilage en route.
The methods used by the competition	It is often possible to gain a significant competitive edge by using a method which is out of the ordinary. For example, most inner-city courier companies use motorbikes to deliver urgent documents, but a few use bicycles. In heavy traffic bicycles are often quicker and can sometimes use routes that are not open to powered vehicles, so deliveries are quicker.
The costs of the various channels available	The cheapest is not always the best; for example, computer chips are light, but costly, and therefore it is cheaper to use airfreight than to tie up the company's capital in lengthy surface transportation.
The reliability of the channel	Emergency medical supplies must have 100% reliable transportation, as must cash deliveries.
The transit time	This also applies to fruit and computer chips.
Security	Highly valuable items may not be easily distributed through retailers. Direct delivery may work much better.
Traceability	The ease with which a shipment can be located or redirected. For example, oil tankers can be diverted to deliver to different refineries at relatively short notice. This allows the oil companies to meet demand in different countries.
The level of customer service required	Customers may need the product to be delivered in exact timings (for example, in just-in-time manufacturing). The Meals on Wheels service is another example; it is essential that deliveries are 100% reliable.

Source: Adapted from *The Management of Business Logistics*, 4th edn, by Coyle, Bardi and Langley. © 1988 South-Western, a part of Cengage Learning, Inc. Reproduced by permission. www.cengage.com/permissions

Products are rarely delivered directly from producer to consumer, but instead pass through the hands of wholesalers, agents, factors or other middle men. For example, it is hardly likely to be very efficient for a tuna importer to deliver directly to every small grocery business in the country. (It would be even less efficient to deliver to each consumer.) The importer will probably employ an agent (who will be working for several manufacturers) to take orders from wholesalers. The importer will bulk-deliver the tuna to the wholesalers, who will then break the delivery down to send out to the retailers. The wholesaler will either deliver to the retailers along with the products of many other importers and manufacturers or will offer a cash-and-carry service so that the retailers can make all their supply purchases in one trip. The net result is a great saving in time since the trucks are not going perhaps hundreds of miles with one case of tuna on board.

Figure 8.1 Channels of distribution

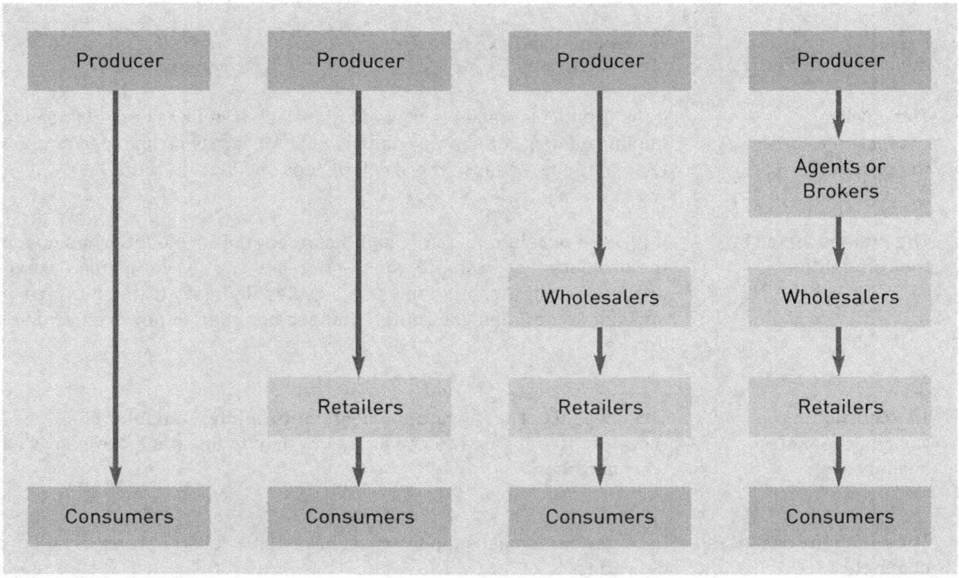

Source: Dibb *et al.* 1998

In fact, food frequently passes through lengthy and complex distribution systems. Each intermediary in the process performs a useful function, increasing the efficiency of the exchanges. Table 8.2 shows some of the functions carried out by intermediaries.

Table 8.2 Functions of channel members

Function	Explanation
Sorting out	Separating out heterogeneous deliveries into homogeneous ones. For example, sorting a tomato crop into those suitable for retail sale and those suitable only for juice production.
Accumulation	Aggregating small production batches into amounts big enough to be worth shipping. Forwarding agents will arrange for small exporters to share a container, for example.
Allocation	Breaking down large shipments into smaller amounts. A wholesaler receiving a truckload of baked beans will sell them on a case at a time. This is also called bulk breaking.
Assorting	Combining collections of products that will appeal to groups of buyers. For example, clothes shops stock clothes from many manufacturers; food cash-and-carry wholesalers will specialise in all the products needed by caterers and grocers, including shop signs and plastic knives and forks.

'Cutting out the middle man' is popularly supposed to be a way of buying things cheaper. In fact, for most products where agents and wholesalers are used, the savings made by greater efficiency more than cover the cost of the extra mark-up on the product. This means that cutting out the middle man is more likely to increase the cost of the product.

Critical thinking

If cutting out the middle man is such a bad idea, why do companies often advertise it as if it's an advantage? And if it reduces efficiency, why have so many developed interactive websites so that people can order online?

Is it actually cheaper to order online (taking account of delivery costs) or is it more about convenience? And how convenient is it, in fact, when one may have to visit several websites to buy items which are available in one convenient retail store – why not just stop on the way home from work and browse?

Perhaps it depends on one's personal circumstances!

Direct producer-to-consumer channels are typical of personal services such as hairdressing, where use of intermediaries would be impossible, and of major capital purchases such as houses or home improvements. This is because these products cannot be broken down into smaller units, or assorted, or accumulated. There is therefore no function for the middle men to fulfil.

If the distribution network is efficiently managed, goods come down the channel and information goes up. Retailers can feed back information about what consumers need, either *formally* (by carrying out a monitoring exercise and passing the information to the manufacturer or wholesaler) or *informally* (since retailers order only what is selling, producers can infer what is required by the consumers). A good salesperson will also act as an information channel and will find out from the retailers what they think consumers want, as well as convey information from the manufacturers to the retailer.

Major manufacturers often have several distribution channels, catering for different market segments. Food processing firms will usually have separate channels for caterers and for retailers, car manufacturers may deal directly with large fleet operators rather than operating through their retail dealer network and electronics manufacturers may have one channel for consumer products and another for defence products.

Table 8.3 shows the functions of some of the members of a channel of distribution.

Table 8.3 Categories of channel members

Channel member	Function
Agents	Agents usually act purely as a sales arm for the manufacturer, without actually buying the products. The agent never takes title to the goods; agency sales representatives call on major retailers and on wholesalers on behalf of a number of manufacturers, and take orders and arrange delivery. This saves the manufacturer the cost of operating a large salesforce to carry perhaps only a small product range.
Wholesalers	Wholesalers actually buy the goods from the manufacturers, often through an agent, then sell the goods on to the retailers or sometimes the final consumers.
Retailers	A retailer is any organisation that offers goods directly to consumers. This includes mail order companies, door-to-door salespeople and e-commerce organisations selling over the Internet.

WHOLESALERS

Wholesalers carry out the following functions:

- Negotiate with suppliers
- Some promotional activities: advertising, sales promotion, publicity, providing a salesforce
- Warehousing, storage and product handling
- Transport of local and sometimes long-distance shipments
- Inventory control
- Credit checking and credit control
- Pricing and collection of pricing information, particularly about competitors
- Channel of information up and down the distribution network, again particularly with regard to competitors' activities.

All of these functions would have to be carried out by each manufacturer individually if the wholesaler did not exist; by carrying them out on behalf of many manufacturers the wholesaler achieves economies of scale which more than cover the profit taken.

The wholesaler also provides services to the retailers, as follows:

- Information gathering and dissemination
- One-stop shopping for a wide range of products from a wide range of manufacturers

- Facilities for buying relatively small quantities
- Fast deliveries – often cash-and-carry
- Flexible ordering – can vary amounts as demand fluctuates.

Again, from the retailer's viewpoint it is much more convenient and cheaper to use a wholesaler. Only if the retailer is big enough to order economic quantities direct from the manufacturer will it be worthwhile to do so. For example, few hairdressers are big enough to order everything direct from the manufacturers, so a large part of a salon's stock-in-trade is bought from wholesalers.

There are many different types of wholesalers:

- **Merchant wholesalers** buy in goods and sell directly to the retailers, usually delivering the goods and having a salesforce calling on retailers in their area.
- **Full-service merchant wholesalers** provide a very wide range of marketing services for retailers, including shop design, sales promotion deals, advertising (sometimes nationally), coupon redemption, own-brand products and so forth. A good example is Spar, the grocery wholesaler, which supplies corner shops throughout the UK and parts of the rest of Europe. The shops carry the Spar logo and stock Spar's own-brand products, but each shop is individually owned and managed.
- **General-merchandise wholesalers** carry a wide product mix, but little depth, dealing mainly with small grocery shops and general stores. They operate as a one-stop shop for these retailers. Cash-and-carry warehouses are a good example.
- **Limited-line wholesalers** offer only a limited range of products, but stock them in depth. They are often found in industrial markets, selling specialist equipment (such as materials handling equipment) and offering expertise in the field.
- **Speciality line wholesalers** carry a very narrow range, for example concentrating on only one type of food (e.g. tea). They are typically found dealing in goods that require special knowledge of the buying, handling or marketing of the product category.
- **Rack jobbers** own and maintain their own stands or displays in retail outlets. Typical products might be cosmetics, tights or greetings cards. The retailer pays only for the goods sold, and usually does not take title to the goods – this can be a big saving in terms of capital and, since the rack jobber undertakes to check the stock and restock where necessary, the retailer also saves time.
- **Limited-service wholesalers** take title to goods, but often do not actually take delivery, store inventory or monitor demand. A typical example might be a coal wholesaler, who buys from a producer and arranges for the coal to be delivered direct to coal merchants, without the coal first being delivered to the wholesaler.
- **Cash-and-carry wholesalers** offer a way for wholesalers to supply small retailers at minimum cost. The cash-and-carry wholesaler operates like a giant supermarket; retailers call, select the cases of goods needed and pay at a

checkout, using their own transport to take the goods back to their shops. This is an extremely flexible and efficient system for both parties.

- **Drop shippers** (or *desk jobbers*) obtain orders from retailers and pass them on to manufacturers, buying the goods from the manufacturer and selling to the retailer without ever actually seeing the goods. The drop shipper provides the salesforce and takes on the credit risk on behalf of the manufacturer, but does not have the storage costs or the overheads of a merchant wholesaler.

- *Mail order wholesalers* use catalogues to sell to retailers and industrial users. This avoids the use of an expensive salesforce and works best for dealing with retailers in remote areas. Goods are despatched through the post or by commercial carriers; these wholesalers take title to the products.

To summarise, wholesalers perform a wide variety of functions, all aimed at making the exchange of goods easier and more efficient. This leaves the manufacturer free to concentrate resources on improving production efficiencies and the physical product offering, and retailers to concentrate on providing the most effective service for the consumer.

RETAILERS

Retailers deal with any sales that are for the customer's own use, or for the use of family and friends. In other words, any purchases that are not for business needs are the domain of the retailer.

Therefore, a retailer is not necessarily a high street shop or a market trader; mail order catalogues, TV phone-in lines, online retailers such as Amazon and even door-to-door salesmen are all retailers. Tupper Corporation (which sells Tupperware on the party plan) is as much a retailer as Aldi, Makro or Coles, even though the product is sold in the customer's own home.

Traditionally most retail outlets have been in city centres or suburban high streets. Partly this was for convenience, so that shoppers had a central area to visit for all their shopping requirements, and partly it was due to planning regulations which zoned most retail shops in traditional retail areas, away from industrial parks and housing estates.

More recently, out-of-town hypermarkets and shopping parks have been growing up. This is in response to the following factors:

- Greater car ownership means an increase in **outshopping** (shopping outside the area where the consumer lives)

- High city-centre rents and property taxes make out-of-town sites more attractive for retailers

- Town planners have used retail parks as a way of regenerating decaying industrial sites on the edges of towns.

Such out-of-town sites have not necessarily damaged all town-centre retailers, although there has been a shift in the composition of city-centre retail districts. For example, food retailers have largely gone from central sites in major cities, except for delicatessens and speciality food outlets. In the United Kingdom, supermarket chain Tesco has begun to reverse this trend, with the establishment of Tesco Metro stores in city centres. These stores carry a limited range of products, usually in smaller pack sizes, and aim at office workers shopping in their lunch hours or convenience shopping.

Here are some descriptions of different types of retail outlet:

- **Convenience stores**, or corner shops, offer a range of grocery and household items. These local shops often open until late at night. They are usually family-run, often belong to a trading group such as Spar, Circle K or 7-Eleven, and cater for last-minute and emergency purchases. In recent years, the Circle K and 7-Eleven franchises have expanded internationally from the United States and are making inroads into the late-night shopping market. Convenience stores have been under threat from supermarkets as later opening has become more common, and as the laws on Sunday trading in many countries have been relaxed.

- **Supermarkets** are large self-service shops which rely on selling at low prices. Typically they are well laid-out, bright, professionally run shops carrying a wide range of goods.

- **Hypermarkets** are even bigger supermarkets, usually in an out-of-town or edge-of-town location. A typical hypermarket would carry perhaps 20,000 lines. The true hypermarket sells everything from food to TV sets.

- **Department stores** are located in city centres and sell everything; each department has its own buyers and functions as a separate profit centre. Examples are Harrods of London, El Corte Ingles in Spain and Clery's in Dublin. Within department stores, some functions are given over to **concessionaires**, who pay a rental per square foot plus a percentage of turnover to set up a store-within-a-store. Miss Selfridge, Brides and Principles all operate in this way within department stores. The trend is towards allowing more concessionaires and around 70% of Debenham's floor space is allocated this way.

- **Variety stores** offer a more limited range of goods, perhaps specialising in clothes (e.g. Primark) or in books and stationery (e.g. WH Smith).

- **Discounters** (sometimes called baby sharks) are grocery outlets offering a minimum range of goods at very low prices. Often the decor is basic, the displays almost non-existent and the general ambience one of pile-it-high-and-sell-it-cheap. German retailers Lidl and Aldi are examples of this approach; such stores typically carry only 700 lines or so.

- **Niche marketers** stock a very limited range of products, but in great depth. Examples are Sock Shop and Tie Rack. They frequently occupy tiny shops (even kiosks at railway stations) but offer every possible type of product within their very narrow spectrum. Niche marketers were the success story of the 1980s but declined somewhat during the 1990s.

- **Discount sheds** are out-of-town DIY and hardware stores. They are usually businesses requiring large display areas, but with per-square-metre turnovers and profits that do not justify city-centre rents. Service levels are minimal, the stores are cheaply constructed and basic in terms of decor and ambience, and everything is geared towards minimising the overhead.

- **Catalogue showrooms** have minimal or non-existent displays and are really an extension of the mail order catalogue. Customers buy in the same way as they would by mail order, by filling in a form, and the goods are brought out from a warehouse at the rear of the store. These outlets usually have sophisticated electronic inventory control.

- **Non-store retailing** includes door-to-door selling, vending machines, telemarketing (selling goods by telephone), mail order and catalogue retailing. **Telemarketing** may be inbound or outbound; inbound means that customers telephone the retailer to place an order, whereas outbound means the retailer telephones potential customers to ask them to buy. Outbound telemarketing has grown in the UK in recent years; it is often used to make appointments for sales representatives to call, for products such as fitted kitchens or double glazing, and is also used for direct selling of some items which are then delivered by mail. In general, it is unpopular with customers and in both the USA and the UK systems have been set up to allow people to be removed from the lists of telesales companies. In the UK, the system is the Telephone Preference Service (TPS); firms that continue to call after someone has registered with the TPS can be fined, although in practice this is rare. The TPS has no power to prevent people being telephoned from outside the UK, nor does it have any power to curb companies with whom the person has an existing relationship; for example, the individual's bank or electricity supply company.

E-commerce refers to retailing over the Internet. In its early days, e-commerce was dominated by business-to-business marketing, but dot.com firms such as Amazon.com, Lastminute.com and Priceline.com quickly made inroads into consumer markets. The growth of such firms is limited mainly by the growth in Internet users; as more people go online, the potential market increases and is likely to do so for the foreseeable future. The other main limiting factor is the degree to which people enjoy the process of shopping – factors such as a social experience outside the home, the pleasure of bargaining, diversion and sensory stimulation are all likely to ensure that people will continue to enjoy visiting traditional retail stores. Traditional retailers have not been slow to respond to the perceived threat, however; many retailers now offer an Internet service, with free delivery. The Internet is more likely to be used when the customer has high levels of experience with the product and the Internet, and a low perceived risk; conventional retailers or call centres are more likely to be used when the customer has low experience levels and high perceived risk (Rhee 2010).

Because consumer needs change rapidly, there are fashions in retailing (the rise and fall of niche marketing demonstrates this). Being responsive to consumer needs is, of course, important to all marketers, but retailers are at the 'sharp end' of this process and need to be able to adapt quickly to changing trends. The following factors have been identified as being crucial to retail success:

- *Location.* Being where the consumer can easily find the shop – in other words, where the customers would expect such a shop to be. A shoe shop would typically be in a high street or city-centre location, whereas a furniture warehouse would typically be out of town.

- *Buying the right goods in the right quantities* to be able to supply what the consumer wants to buy.

- *Offering the right level of service.* If the service level is less than the customer expects, he/she will be dissatisfied and will shop elsewhere. If the service level is too high, the costs increase and the customer may become suspicious that the prices are higher than they need be. Discount stores are expected to have low service levels and consumers respond to that by believing that the prices are therefore lower.

- *Store image.* If the shop and its goods are upmarket, so must be the image in the consumer's mind. As with any other aspect of the product, the benefits must be as expected or post-purchase dissonance will follow. Trust in the store extends to trust in the store's own-brand goods (see Chapter 6); conversely, mistrust will reduce intention to buy the retailer's own brands (LaForet 2008).

- *Atmospherics.* These are the physical elements of the shop design that encourage purchase. Use of the right colours, lighting, piped music and even odours can greatly affect purchasing behaviour (Bitner 1992). For example, playing slow-tempo music to a supermarket queue makes people feel more relaxed and satisfied and also makes the waiting time seem shorter; however, music played when the supermarket is overcrowded can make people irritable (Oakes and North 2008).

- *Product mix.* The retailer must decide which products will appeal to his/her customers. Sometimes this results in the shop moving away from its original product range into totally unrelated areas.

Recent trends in retail include the greater use of EPOS (electronic point-of-sale) equipment and laser scanners to speed checkout queues through (and, incidentally, to save staffing costs), and the increasing use of loyalty cards. These cards give the customer extra discounts based on the amount spent at the store over a given period. The initial intention is to encourage customers to buy at the same store all the time to obtain the discounts, and in this sense the cards are really just another sales promotion. This type of loyalty programme, involving economic benefits, does have a positive effect on customer retention. The schemes also tend to help in terms of increasing the retailer's share of the customers (Verhoef 2003).

There is a further possibility inherent in EPOS technology, however. It is now possible to keep a record of each customer's buying habits and to establish the purchasing pattern, based on the EPOS records. Theoretically, this would mean that customers could be reminded at the checkout that they are running low on certain items, since the supermarket computer would know how frequently those items are usually bought. The phrase Domesday marketing has been coined by Professor Martin Evans to describe this; whether it could be seen as a useful service for consumers or as an unwarranted invasion of privacy remains a topic for discussion (Evans 1994). Loyal customers tend to be attracted to store brands during promotional periods, presumably because they trust the store (Rajagopal 2008).

EPOS systems in the UK were redesigned in 2004 to allow for the introduction of chip-and-pin credit cards, which require customers to enter a personal identity number (PIN) rather than sign a receipt. These have been used in France and Spain for many years to reduce credit card fraud and reduce time spent at the checkouts, and UK cards can now be used in those countries.

Perception is important in the retail environment. Store atmospherics have already been mentioned, but people also like to be able to touch products, open the boxes and see what they are buying. This can cause problems, since people will tend to open the box to examine the product but then take an unopened box to the checkout. The opened box will probably not sell until it is the last one, since people tend to believe that the product is contaminated and no longer new if other people have handled it. This phenomenon is known as shop soiling, but is explained by anthropologists in terms of magic; the 'contaminated' product has had part of the essence of the other shopper transferred to it (Argo *et al.* 2006).

SELECTING CHANNELS

Choosing a channel involves a number of considerations. These are as follows:

- Whether to use a single channel, or several channels
- Location of customers
- Compatibility of the channels with the firm
- Nature of the goods
- Geographic, environmental and terrain decisions
- Storage and distribution issues
- Import and export costs.

Above all, of course, the firm must begin by considering the customers' needs. Having said that, the needs of channel members will also be involved, since they are unlikely to cooperate if their needs are not considered.

Using a single channel clearly provides the channel members with the security of knowing that they will not be competing with other firms carrying the same product line. Some retailers insist on being given exclusive rights to the products they carry, so that they can make 'price promises' without fear of consumers actually being able to buy the identical product anywhere else, whether at a lower price or not. On the other hand, the needs of consumers are best met by having the product widely available.

Location of customers influences the channel as well as the physical distribution. Some channels might be unavailable in some countries – for example, distribution via the Internet is not viable in many African countries because few people are online and the road infrastructure makes delivery difficult.

Channels need to be compatible with the firm's capability and size; small manufacturers can become overwhelmed by dealing with large retailers, for example.

The nature of the goods determines which type of retailer would be best. Sometimes firms have obtained a competitive advantage by using unusual routes to market – jewellery firms have distributed through hairdressing salons, for example.

Geographic and environmental (in the sense of business environment) considerations can render some routes unviable. For example, mail order in the United States became popular with people living in remote regions during the nineteenth century (a geographical consideration). Such people were unable to reach major stores easily and local stores were unable to carry all the products people might need. Mail order grew in Germany for a different reason; at one time, the business environment required retail stores to close at 5 pm and prohibited weekend opening except for one Saturday a month. This meant that most working people had serious difficulty in getting to shops, and mail order became a favourite way of buying almost everything.

Storage and distribution costs, particularly for overseas markets, may mean that a wholesaler becomes necessary simply because of the need to make few large deliveries rather than many small ones. Likewise, if storage is expensive, an on-demand service such as that supplied by motor factors to small garages might be necessary.

Import and export costs, especially duties and tariffs, might mean that a local agent (or even a local assembly plant) might need to be used. Shipping costs are likely to make it more efficient to fill a shipping container rather than send small quantities at a time, but the nature of the product needs to be considered – perishable or expensive products might need to be sent immediately, rather than waiting until there are enough to fill a container.

MANAGING DISTRIBUTION CHANNELS

Channels can be led by any of the channel members, whether they are producers, wholesalers or retailers, provided that the member concerned has channel power. This power comes from seven sources, as shown in Table 8.4 (Michman and Sibley 1980).

Channel cooperation is an essential part of the effective functioning of channels. Since each member relies on every other member for the free exchange of goods

Table 8.4 Sources of channel power

Economic sources of power	Non-economic sources of power	Other factors
Control of resources. The degree to which the channel member has the power to direct goods, services or finance within the channel	Reward power. The ability to provide financial benefits or otherwise favour channel members	Level of power. This derives from the economic and non-economic sources of power
Size of company. The bigger the firm compared with other channel members, the greater the overall economic power	Expert power. This arises when the leader has special expertise which the other channel members need	Dependency of other channel members
Referent power emerges when channel members try to emulate the leader		Willingness to lead. Clearly some firms with potential for channel leadership prefer not to have the responsibility or are unable to exercise the potential for other reasons
Legitimate power arises from a superior–subordinate relationship. For example, if a retailer holds a substantial shareholding in a wholesaler, it has legitimate power over the wholesaler		
Coercive power exists when one channel member has the power to punish another		

down the channel, it is in the members' interests to look after each other to some extent. Channel cooperation can be improved in the following ways:

- The channel members can agree on target markets, so that each member can best direct effort towards meeting the common goal.
- The tasks each member should carry out can be defined. This avoids duplication of effort or giving the final consumer conflicting messages.

A further development is co-marketing, which implies a partnership between manufacturers, intermediaries and retailers. This level of cooperation involves pooling of market information and full agreement on strategic issues (Marx 1995).

Channel conflict arises because each member wants to maximise its own profits or power. Conflicts also arise because of frustrated expectations; each member expects the other members to act in particular ways, and sometimes these expectations are unfulfilled. For example, a retailer may expect a wholesaler to maintain large enough stocks to cover an unexpected rise in demand for a given product, whereas the wholesaler may expect the manufacturers to be able to increase production rapidly to cover such eventualities.

An example of channel conflict occurred when EuroDisney (now Disneyland Paris) first opened. The company bypassed travel agents and tried to market directly to the public via TV commercials. Unfortunately, this did not work because European audiences were not used to the idea of booking directly (and also were not as familiar with the Disney concept as American audiences), so few bookings resulted. At the same time Disney alienated the travel agents and has had to expend considerable time and money in wooing them back again. This is a general problem for companies seeking to use multiple channels of distribution; if the company decides to deal direct with the public via its website or uses several different routes, existing channel members may feel that the relationship is being undermined. This does not mean that using multiple channels is impossible; it simply means that marketers need to be cautious not to damage the interests of existing channel members. In general, there is unlikely to be a problem if the new channels approach a segment of the market which the existing channels do not reach.

Channel management can be carried out by cooperation and negotiation (often with one member leading the discussions) or it can be carried out by the most powerful member laying down rules that weaker members have to follow. Table 8.5 shows some of the methods which can be used to control channels. Most attempts to control distribution by the use of power are likely to be looked on unfavourably by the courts, but of course the abuse of power would have to be fairly extreme before a channel member would be likely to sue.

Critical thinking

If controlling the channel is regarded as unfair, how about buyers who specify particular ways in which potential suppliers can approach them? Is it unreasonable to ask for salespeople to call on a particular day or only by appointment? Clearly not. But then, would it be unreasonable to expect suppliers to draw up detailed reports on their ability to meet delivery schedules and quality standards? Hmmm . . . Perhaps. Would it be unreasonable to expect suppliers to provide copies of their accounts and allow the customer's auditors to check on the supplier's financial stability and probity? Well, maybe not. Would it be reasonable to use knowledge of a supplier's financial difficulties to force through lower prices? Maybe, maybe not.

Business isn't exactly a coffee morning, but there are ethical and practical issues at stake. Knowing where to draw the line might not be so easy.

Sometimes the simplest way to control a distribution channel is to buy out the channel members. Buying out members across a given level (for example, a wholesaler buying out other wholesalers to build a national network) is called **horizontal integration**; buying out members above or below in the distribution chain (for example, a retailer buying out a wholesaler) is **vertical integration**. An example of extreme vertical integration is the major oil companies, which extract crude oil, refine it, ship it and ultimately sell it retail through petrol stations. At the extremes,

Table 8.5 Channel management techniques

Technique	Explanation	Legal position
Refusal to deal	One member refuses to do business with one or more other members; for example, hairdressing wholesalers sometimes refuse to supply mobile hairdressers on the grounds that this is unfair competition for salons.	In most countries suppliers do not have to supply anybody with whom they do not wish to deal. However, grounds may exist for a lawsuit if the refusal to deal is a punishment for not going along with an anti-competitive ruling by a supplier or is an attempt to prevent the channel member from dealing with a third party with whom the manufacturer is in dispute.
Tying contracts	The supplier (sometimes a franchiser) demands that the channel member carries other products as well as the main one. If the franchiser insists that all the products are carried, this is called *full-line forcing*.	Most of these contracts are illegal, but are accepted if the supplier alone can supply goods of a given quality or if the purchaser is free to carry competing products as well. Sometimes they are accepted when a company has just entered the market.
Exclusive dealing	A manufacturer might prevent a wholesaler from carrying competitors' products or a retailer might insist that no other retailer be supplied with the same products. This is often used by retailers to ensure that their 'price guarantees' can be honoured – obviously consumers will not be able to find the same product at a lower price locally if the retailer has prevented the manufacturer from supplying anybody else.	Usually these are legal provided they do not result in a monopoly position in a local area; in other words, provided the consumer has access to similar products, there will not be a problem.
Restricted sales territories	Intermediaries are prevented from selling outside a given area. The intermediaries are often in favour of this idea because it prevents competition within their own area.	Courts have conflicting views about this practice. On the one hand, these deals can help weaker distributors and can also increase competition where local dealers carry different brands; on the other hand, there is clearly a restraint of trade involved.

this type of integration may attract the attention of government monopoly regulation agencies, since the integration may cause a restriction of competition.

Producers need to ensure that the distributors of their products are of the right type. The image of a retailer can damage (or enhance) the image of the products sold (and vice versa). Producers need not necessarily sell through the most prestigious retailer, and in fact this would be counter-productive for many cheap, everyday items. Likewise, a prestigious product should not be sold through a down-market retail outlet.

In the long run, establishing good relationships between channel members will improve overall profitability for all members. As the relationship between members of the distribution channel becomes closer, power and conflict still remain important, but they are expressed in other ways and the negotiations for their resolution change in nature (Gadde 2004).

EFFICIENT CONSUMER RESPONSE

Efficient consumer response (ECR) seeks to integrate the activities of manufacturers and retailers using computer technology; the expected result is a more responsive stocking system for the retailer, which in turn benefits the manufacturer. Some of the features of ECR are as follows:

- *Continuous replenishment* under which the supplier plans production using data generated by the retailer.

- *Cross-docking* attempts to coordinate the arrival of suppliers' and retailers' trucks at the distribution centres so that goods move from one truck to the other without going into stock. Although transport efficiency falls because a supermarket truck collecting (say) greengrocery might have to wait for several suppliers' trucks to arrive, the overall speed of delivery of products improves, which can be crucial when dealing with fresh foods.

- *Roll-cage sequencing* allows storage of products by category at the warehouse; although this adds to the labour time at the warehouse, it greatly reduces labour time at the retail store.

The main problem with ECR is that it relies on complete cooperation between supplier and retailer. In any channel of distribution where the power base is unequal, this is less likely to happen; despite the overall savings for the channel as a whole, self-interest on the part of channel members may lead to less than perfect cooperation.

CASE STUDY 8 Davies Turner

Davies Turner is a freight-forwarding company based in London and Manchester. It is the largest freight-forwarding company in Britain, sending goods all over the world via land, sea and air. The company was founded in 1870 by Alfred Davies, in partnership with his father in law; their major innovation was to combine a number of shipments into one bill of lading, thus saving a great deal of the administrative charges imposed by shipping companies.

This idea of consolidating shipments grew; in the 1890s the company developed the idea of re-useable lift vans, the precursor to modern containers. By 1914, the company had its own fleet of motorised trucks, giving them a major advantage over other companies who were still using horse-drawn wagons for road freight. In 1950, when London's Heathrow Airport opened, Davies Turner developed an air freight division; in 1960 the company operated the first TIR services to the Continent, using trailers which had been sealed by Customs officers and which were transported on the first roll-on-roll-off ferries.

The company now has over 750 employees and a turnover of £145m per annum. It offers a complete freight service – everything from grouping small shipments into one large shipment through to booking the lorries, ships, aircraft space and warehouse space to accommodate shipments. The company will organise all the necessary paperwork and clearances, will track shipments (and, in fact, has a page on the website where customers can track their own shipments) and will arrange insurance. For air freight, Davies Turner has its own in-house security X-ray equipment so that all freight leaving the warehouses is acceptable to the airlines without delaying the shipment.

Davies Turner operates a fleet of vehicles for local collections and deliveries, but relies heavily on its relationships with local freight companies throughout the world as well as with shipping companies and airlines. Davies Turner is in the business of organising the logistics – not in the business of actually running a shipping line or a fleet of heavy goods vehicles. As a result, the company can offer a specialist service which covers almost any kind of freight, almost anywhere, whether it is fresh fruit or fashion garments, heavy machinery or ladies' watches, vehicle parts or excess luggage. The measure of the company's versatility lies in its specialist departments – there is a department dedicated to shipping live fish and reptiles, one dedicated to fine wine, one dedicated to fashion, and so forth.

Broadly, Davies Turner will move anything, anywhere, by any means. A truly versatile company!

Questions

1 Why is there the need to be so versatile?

2 What is the advantage of working through other companies rather than owning one's own transport fleet?

3 Why would a major company use Davies Turner rather than having its own department for freight-forwarding?

4 Why is there the need for someone to handle the paperwork?

5 What might be the drawbacks of using Davies Turner from the viewpoint of a manufacturer?

SUMMARY

This chapter has been about getting the goods to the consumer in the most efficient and effective way possible.

Here are the key points from this chapter:

- Distribution forms part of the product because it has benefits attached to it
- The faster the transport, the more expensive in upfront costs but the greater the savings in terms of wastage and in capital tied up
- Transport methods must consider the needs of the end user of the product
- Cutting out the middle man is likely to increase costs in the long run, not decrease them
- Retailing includes every transaction in which the purchase is to be used by the buyer personally or for family use
- Retailing is not necessarily confined to high street shops.

CHAPTER QUESTIONS

1 Under what circumstances might air freight be cheaper than surface transport?

2 How might wholesalers improve the strength of their position with retailers?

3 Why might a wholesaler be prepared to accept a restricted-territory sales agreement?

4 When should a manufacturer consider dealing direct with retailers?

5 When should a manufacturer consider dealing direct with the public?

Further reading

Marketing Channels: A Management View, 8th edn, by **Bert Rosenbloom** (South-Western, 2012). A readable text, with a practically orientated view of how to deal with distribution issues.

Logistics and Supply Chain Management by **Martin Christopher** (Harlow, FT Prentice Hall 2010) gives a good readable overview of logistics problems, though not really from a marketing perspective as such.

References

Argo, Jennifer J., Dahl, Darren W. and Morales, Andrea C.: 'Consumer contamination: how consumers react to products touched by others', *Journal of Marketing*, **70** (2) (2006), pp. 81–94.

Bitner, Mary Jo: 'Servicescapes: the impact of physical surroundings on customers and employees', *Journal of Marketing* (April 1992), pp. 57–71.

Coyle, J., Bardi, E. and Langley C.: *The Management of Business Logistics* (St Paul, MN, West, 1988).

Dibb, S., Simkin, L., Pride, W. and Ferrell, O.C.: *Marketing: Concepts and Strategies* (London, Houghton Mifflin, 1998).

Evans, Martin: 'Domesday marketing', *Journal of Marketing Management*, **10** (5) (1994), pp. 409–31.

Gadde, Lars-Erik: 'Activity co-ordination and resource combining in distribution networks: implications for relationship involvement and the relationship atmosphere', *Journal of Marketing Management*, **20** (1) (2004), pp. 157–84.

LaForet, Sylvie: 'Retail brand extension – perceived fit, risks and trust', *Journal of Consumer Behaviour*, (May/Jun) **7** (3) (2008), pp. 189–209.

Marx, W.: 'The co-marketing revolution', *Industry Week* (2 October 1995), pp. 77–9.

Michman, R.D. and Sibley, S.D.: *Marketing Channels and Strategies*, 2nd edn (Worthington, OH, Publishing Horizons Inc., 1980).

Oakes, Steve, and North, Adrian C.: 'Using music to influence cognitive and affective responses in queues of low and high crowd density', *Journal of Marketing Management*, **24** (5/6), pp. 589–602.

Rajagopal: 'Point-of-sales promotions and buying stimulation in retail stores', *Journal of Database Marketing and Customer Strategy Management*, (Dec) **15** (4) (2008), pp. 249–66.

Rhee, Eddie: 'Multi-channel management in direct marketing retailing: Traditional call centre versus Internet channel', *Journal of Database Marketing and Customer Strategy Management*, (June) **17** (2) (2010), pp. 70–7.

Verhoef, Peter C.: 'Understanding the effect of customer relationship management efforts on customer retention and customer share development', *Journal of Marketing*, **67** (4) (October 2003), pp. 30–45.

9

MARKETING COMMUNICATIONS AND PROMOTIONAL TOOLS

Objectives

After reading this chapter you should be able to

- Explain how marketing communications operate
- Plan a promotional campaign
- Explain how the elements of the promotional mix fit together to create a total package
- Select suitable promotional tools for achieving a given objective
- Understand what public relations (PR) will do for you and what it will not do
- Explain the main pitfalls of defensive PR
- Plan a media event
- Understand the problems facing a PR executive or agent
- Formulate a suitable PR policy for a given set of circumstances
- Formulate a brief for an advertising agency
- Explain the main criteria for writing advertising copy
- Understand what personal selling is intended to achieve for the firm
- Outline the main features of sales management
- Explain the role of word-of-mouth communication
- Explain how sponsorship helps in building a positive corporate image.

INTRODUCTION

This chapter is about communicating the organisation's messages to the public. The tools of communication (advertising, personal selling, PR and sales promotions) are the most visible aspects of marketing, so non-marketers tend to think they represent the whole of marketing.

Communication requires the active participation of both the sender and the receiver, so the messages not only have to contain the information the organisation wishes to convey but must also be sufficiently interesting to the consumers (or the organisation's other publics) for them to pay attention to it.

VIDEO CASE
www.pearsoned.co.uk/blythe

Voluntary Service Overseas

VSO is a voluntary organisation which sends skilled volunteers overseas to help with projects in the Third World. The volunteers are usually people with significant experience in industry or education who are prepared to work for up to two years in another country. Volunteers are paid at local rates. Often this is well below their previous salaries, but the typical volunteer is someone who has had a successful career and now wants to put something back.

Volunteers find the whole process very rewarding – but the professionals still need to be recruited and there are many needs that volunteers have. VSO, like most charities, has a relatively small budget for marketing, so the organisation has to get the most from its funding by careful targeting. Professional needs are very diverse – some go for the experience of living abroad, some get a warm glow of satisfaction, some go for the professional challenge, but clearly none of them do it for the money!

Obviously VSO needs cash donations as well as volunteers; the volunteers still need to be sent overseas, and even at Third World rates they still need to be paid.

Vicky Starnes, Head of Marketing

Watch the video clip, then try to answer the following questions. The answers are on the companion website.

Questions

1 Which communications tools are most appropriate for VSO?

2 What is the role of public relations in VSO's work?

3 How might VSO use database marketing?

MARKETING COMMUNICATIONS THEORY

Communication is one of the most human of activities. The exchange of thoughts that characterises communication is carried out by conversation (still the most popular form of entertainment in the world), by the written word (letters, books, magazines and newspapers) and by pictures (cartoons, television and film).

Communication has been defined as a transactional process between two or more parties whereby meaning is exchanged through the intentional use of **symbols** (Engel *et al.* 1994). The key elements here are that the communication is intentional (a deliberate effort is made to bring about a response), it is a transaction (the participants are all involved in the process) and it is symbolic (words, pictures, music and other sensory stimulants are used to convey thoughts). Since human beings are not telepathic, all communication needs the original concepts to be translated into symbols that convey the required meaning.

This means that the individual or firm issuing the communication must first reduce the concepts to a set of symbols which can be passed on to the recipient of the message; the recipient must decode the symbols to get the original message. Thus the participants in the process must share a common view of what the symbols involved actually mean. In fact, the parties must share a common field of experience. This is illustrated in Figure 9.1.

The sender's field of experience must overlap with the receiver's field of experience, at least to the extent of having a common language. The overlap is likely to be much more complex and subtle in most marketing communications; **advertisements** typically use references from popular culture such as TV shows, from proverbs and common sayings, and will often make puns or use half-statements which the audience is able to complete because it is aware of the cultural referents involved. This is why foreign TV adverts often seem unintentionally humorous or even incomprehensible.

Figure 9.1 Model of the communication process

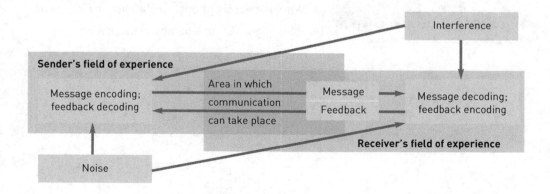

Figure 9.2 Redundancy in communication

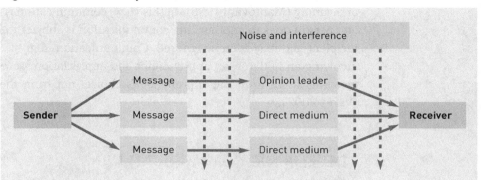

Noise is the surrounding distraction present during the communications process and varies from children playing during the commercial break through to arresting headlines in a magazine. Interference is deliberate attempts to distract the audience's attention with intelligent communications. For example, a car driver may be distracted away from a radio ad by another car cutting in (noise) or by seeing an interesting billboard (interference). For most marketing purposes, the difference is academic.

The above model is essentially a one-step model of communication. This is rather oversimplified; communications do not necessarily occur in a single step in this way. In most cases, the message reaches the receiver via several routes. Sending the same message by more than one route is called redundancy, and is a good way of ensuring that the message gets through. Figure 9.2 shows this diagrammatically.

In the diagram, the sender sends almost identical messages via different routes. The effect of noise and interference is to distort the message, and the opinion leader will moderate the message, but by using three different routes the meaning of the message is more likely to get through. This is the rationale behind the integration of marketing communications.

Critical thinking

When messages are sent by different routes, the medium must surely affect the message. After all, a news story written for a tabloid newspaper comes across very differently from the same story printed in a respectable broadsheet. And that's a comparison between two newspapers! How different the story would be if it were to be broadcast on TV or read over the radio!

Yet we're being asked to believe that an advertisement can be designed which will convey the same message, even though it is sent through several different media. How is that going to be accomplished?

An alternative view of communication is that it is concerned with the co-creation of meaning (Mantovani 1996). In this view, communication is not something which one person does to another; the communication is subject to interpretation by the recipient and may even be ignored. Communication might be better thought of as involving an initiator, an apprehender and appreciation; acceptance of a common meaning arises from the apprehender's choice, not from the initiator's intention (Varey 2002).

DEVELOPING COMMUNICATIONS

Developing effective marketing communications follows a six-stage process, as follows:

1 *Identify the target audience.* In other words, decide who the message should get to.
2 *Determine the response sought.* What would the marketer like members of the audience to do after they get the message?
3 *Choose the message.* Write the copy, or produce an appropriate image.
4 *Choose the channel.* Decide which newspaper, TV station or radio station the audience uses.
5 *Select the source's attributes.* Decide what it is about the product or company that needs to be communicated.
6 *Collect feedback.* For example, carry out market research to find out how successful the message was.

Communication is always expensive; full-page advertisements in Sunday colour supplements can cost upwards of £11,000 per insertion; a 30-second TV ad at peak time can cost £30,000 per station. It is therefore worthwhile spending time and effort in ensuring that the message is comprehensible by the target audience. Communications often follow the AIDA approach:

Attention

Interest

Desire

Action.

This implies that marketers must first get the customer's *attention*. Clearly, if the receiver is not 'switched on' the message will not get through. Second, the marketer must make the message *interesting*, or the receiver will not pay attention to it. This should, if the message is good, lead to a *desire* for the product on the part of the receiver, who will then take *action*. Although this is a simplistic model in some ways, it is a useful guide to promotional planning; however, it is very difficult to get all four of these elements into one communication. For this reason, marketers usually use a mixture of approaches for different elements, called the **promotional mix**.

THE PROMOTIONAL MIX

The basic promotional mix consists of advertising, **sales promotion**, **personal selling** and **public relations (PR)**. When the concept of the promotional mix was first developed, these were the only elements available to marketers, but in the past 40 years more promotional methods have appeared which do not easily fit within these four categories. For example, a logo on a T-shirt might be considered as advertising or as public relations. For the purposes of this book, however, the original four components are still considered to be the main tools available to marketers.

The important word here is 'mix'. The promotional mix is like a recipe, in which the ingredients must be added at the right times and in the right quantities for the promotion to be effective. Figure 9.3 shows how the mix operates. Messages from the company about its products and itself are transmitted via the elements of the promotional mix to the consumers, employees, pressure groups and other publics. Because each of these groups is receiving the messages from more than one transmitter, the elements of the mix also feed into each other so that the messages do not conflict.

The elements of the promotional mix are not interchangeable, any more than ingredients in a recipe are interchangeable; a task that calls for personal selling cannot be carried out by advertising, nor can public relations tasks be carried out by using sales promotions. Promotion is all about getting the message across to the customer (and the consumer) in the most effective way, and the choice of method will depend on the message, the receiver and the desired effect.

Figure 9.3 The promotional mix

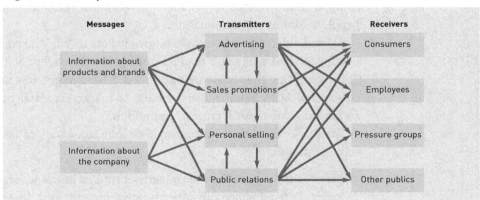

MANAGING ADVERTISING

Advertising is defined as 'a paid message inserted in a medium'. This definition can be broken down as follows:

- *Paid:* news about a company or its products is not necessarily advertising; sometimes a medium (television, radio, newspaper or magazine) will carry a message about a company in the form of a news item, but this is not advertising unless the space is paid for.
- *Message:* there must be some kind of communication intention in an advertisement, however obscure.
- *In a medium:* the message must appear in a newspaper, magazine, billboard or broadcast medium. Leaflets through doors, company names printed on T-shirts and telephone selling are not necessarily advertising (but they are promotion).

Most advertising works below the conscious level. People are often familiar with a brand name and even know a lot about the product without being able to remember where they saw the product advertised. Advertising is a *non-personal* communication in that it has to speak to a large number of people, so the message has to be clear for the whole of the target audience to understand. Research by Farris and Buzzell (1979) indicated that the proportion of promotional spending devoted to advertising is higher under the following conditions:

- The product is standardised rather than produced to order
- There are many end users (for example, most households)
- The typical purchase amount is small
- Sales are made through channel intermediaries (such as retail shops) rather than direct to users.

For example, a company selling detergents will spend the largest proportion of its promotional budget on advertising, probably on TV and in the press, whereas a company selling cars will spend a relatively higher proportion of its money on salespeople's salaries and commission.

TV and video remote controls allow viewers to 'zap' the commercial breaks, and newspaper and magazine readers quickly become adept at flipping past the ads. This means that the consumer's attention is hard to get. It is not usually possible to cover all of AIDA in one advertisement, so marketers usually spread the communication load over several types of promotion.

For this reason, there are many different categories of ad campaign. Here are some examples:

- Teaser campaigns. Here the advertiser runs an initial advertisement that is meaningless in itself. Once the advertisement has run for a few weeks, the advertiser runs a second ad which explains the first one. The first ad is intended to attract attention by being mysterious. An example is the campaign run by modu, the mobile phone brand, in January 2008. A video was placed on YouTube showing people going about their normal day's activities, making calls, driving, preparing for work in the morning, and so forth without any explanation of what modu is or does. The video clip was engaging and entertaining, but the product was not featured – just the brand name at the end of the clip. Eventually the actual nature of the product was revealed, during February of that year.

- **Lifestyle campaigns**. These associate the product with a desirable lifestyle. Many perfume ads have taken this approach, showing women leading interesting or exciting lives. Lifestyle campaigns are mainly about positioning the product in the consumer's mind and linking it to an aspirational group (see Chapter 3).

- **Rational campaigns** appeal to the consumer's cognition. These advertisements are heavy on facts and seek to persuade by rational argument. Often an authoritative figure (a doctor, dentist or scientist) appears in the ad to lend greater weight to the arguments. Typically, this style is used for medicated shampoos, acne creams and over-the-counter medicines.

Advertising is mainly about getting the consumer's attention and arousing interest (the A and I of AIDA). To stimulate desire and action, marketers often link a special offer (sales promotion) to the advertisement.

Advertising is always culturally based. This means that an advertisement shown in one country, or aimed at a particular audience, is unlikely to work for consumers in other countries, or for a different audience. Research into standardisation of advertising shows that relatively few firms use an entirely standardised approach (Harris 1996). Of 38 multinational companies surveyed, 26 said that they used standard advertisements, but only four of these were completely standardised; the others varied from limited standardisation (perhaps only a corporate logo in common) through limited standardisation of the key executional elements to standard execution with some modifications. Even though the sample of firms is relatively small, it appears likely that the majority of multinationals would adapt their approaches to fit the markets they are targeting.

Advertising can often be over-used because firms place greater faith in it than is perhaps justified. There is an underlying assumption that a bigger advertising spend will inevitably lead to a greater sales volume. Table 9.1 contains a checklist for making decisions about advertising.

Of course, the checklist in Table 9.1 should also include a monitoring and review procedure to ensure that the advertising has achieved its objectives.

Advertising can be used for the following purposes:

- *To help the salesforce to open sales.* For example, an advertisement may contain a reply coupon for a brochure, which the salesperson can follow up.

- *To stimulate demand for the product category.* This is used by institutions, or firms that have a large market share; for example, the UK Meat and Livestock Commission advertises British meat on behalf of farmers and butchers.

Table 9.1 Advertising decision-making checklist

Question	Explanation
Does the product possess unique, important features?	Homogeneous products such as salt, petrol and cigarettes require considerably more advertising effort than differentiated products such as cars or holiday resorts. The product must not only be different, but the consumers must believe that those differences are important.
Are hidden qualities important to buyers?	If the product can be judged by looking at it or trying it out, advertising has less of a role to play than if there are features that are not apparent to the naked eye. For instance, the Pentium computer chip has been successfully advertised because it would not be immediately apparent to a computer purchaser that the machine has one.
Is the general demand trend for the product favourable?	If the product category is in decline, advertising will be less effective than if the category is generally increasing its sales.
Is the market potential for the product adequate?	Advertising will work only when there are enough actual or potential users of the product in the market. This is because advertising is a mass medium; much of the spend is wasted on advertising to people who will not be interested anyway.
Is the competitive environment favourable?	A small firm would have great difficulty competing with a large firm in terms of getting the message through. Advertising will not be sufficient when competing against a company with a large market share and correspondingly large budget.
Are general economic conditions favourable for marketing the product?	It is much easier to promote in times of rising prosperity, particularly for durable goods such as videos, cars, computers and household appliances. Such products are difficult to advertise successfully during a recession.
Is the organisation able and willing to spend the money required to launch an advertising campaign?	As a rule of thumb, if the organisation seeks to achieve a 20% market share, it must be willing to spend at least 20% of the total advertising spend of the industry on capturing that market. In other words, if the industry as a whole spends £5 million per annum on advertising, the company must be prepared to commit at least £1 million to the campaign.
Does the firm possess sufficient marketing expertise to market the product?	The company will need to coordinate all its activities, not just expect the advertisements to produce business. Not all firms possess this capability.

Source: Adapted from Patti 1977.

- *To promote specific brands.* This accounts for most advertising activity.
- *To counteract competitors' promotional activities.* Often used to counteract a possible loss in market share owing to a new competitor entering the market.
- *To suggest new ways to use the product.* Knorr hired chef Marco Pierre White to demonstrate the use of their stock cubes as an 'instant marinade' for chicken, mixing the cube with olive oil rather than water.
- *To remind consumers about the product.* For example, advertisements for traditional Christmas foods are run during December.

- *To reinforce consumers' good feelings about the product.* For example, chocolate advertising typically emphasises the 'reward' and 'pleasure' aspects of eating chocolate.
- *To support the value of the company's shares.* There is evidence that advertising expenditure helps reduce the risk of a fall in share values (McAlister *et al.* 2007).

Advertising can also be used to improve awareness of the company itself. This type of advertising is called institutional advertising and is commonly carried out by very large firms such as BP or Ford. It is almost a public relations activity, but the media space is paid for. Most advertising is product advertising, which means that the products are the main part of the advertisement.

Since advertising is a paid-for medium, there will be a budgetary constraint on the management as well as a creative constraint. The advertising manager must therefore carry out the planning functions shown in Table 9.2.

Table 9.2 Advertising planning functions

Planning function	Explanation
Setting the budget	This can be done in four ways. First, the objective and task approach involves setting *objectives*, and setting aside an appropriate amount of money to achieve the objectives. This method is difficult to apply because it is difficult to assess how much will be needed to achieve the objective. Second, the *percentage of sales* approach sets the budget as a percentage of sales. This is based on the false idea that sales create advertising and usually results in less being spent on advertising when sales fall, thus reducing sales further. Third, the *competition matching approach* means that the company spends the same as the competition; this means that the firm is allowing its budgets to be set by its enemies. Fourth, there is the *arbitrary* approach whereby a senior executive (usually a finance director) simply says how much can be allowed within the firm's overall budgets. This does not take account of how the firm is to achieve the objectives.
Identifying the target	Deciding to whom the ad is to be directed. It is better to approach a small segment of the market than try to use a 'scattergun' approach on everybody (see Chapter 4).
Media planning	This is about deciding where the ads are going to appear. There are two main decision areas: the reach (number of potential consumers the ad reaches) and the frequency (number of times each consumer sees the ad) of coverage. The decision is frequently made on the basis of cost per thousand readers/viewers, but this does not take into account the impact of the ad or the degree to which people are able to skip past it.
Defining the objectives	Deciding what the ads are supposed to achieve. It is essential here to give the advertising agency a clear brief: 'We want to raise awareness of the product to 50% of the adult population' is a measurable objective. 'We want to increase sales as much as possible' is not measurable, so there is no way of knowing whether it has been achieved.
Creating the advertising platform	Deciding the basic issues and selling points that the advertising must convey. This clarifies the advertising agency briefing or at least clarifies the thinking on producing the advertising materials.

Following on from the planning stage, the advertisements themselves will need to be produced. Some firms do this themselves, but most large firms will use specialist advertising agencies. Ad agencies are paid via discounts from the media so, provided that the advertising budget is big enough to interest an agency, their services cost the advertiser nothing. Typical agency discount is 15%.

Producing advertisements

Advertisements contain three key elements: the brand itself, the pictorial element and the text. The pictorial element is superior for capturing attention, regardless of the size of the ad or the picture. The text element captures attention proportional to its size and the brand element transfers attention to the other elements (Pieters and Wedel 2004).

When writing advertising copy the primary rule is to keep it short and simple. This is because people will not normally read a lengthy advertisement. Equally, the headline of the advertisement is important because people frequently read only the headline, quickly skipping on as they realise it is an advertisement. Declining literacy skills also play a role – many people are actually unable to read and understand a long and complicated message.

For example, Figures 9.4 and 9.5 show two fictitious advertisements for a surfboard. The first is written factually, the second is written as an advertisement. The first ad clearly contains more information and is really much more use to the consumer, but the second ad is much more likely to be read and acted upon because it has a more lively execution format. What the copywriter wants the consumers to do is go to the surfboard retailer and look at the SurfKing (this could be linked with

Figure 9.4 Factual advertisement for a surfboard

SurfKing Surfboards are hand-made from the finest materials at our factory in Edinburgh.

They are used by some of the world's top surfers, and use the latest technology to ensure the maximum surfing pleasure.

They are available from all leading surf shops, or can be ordered direct from our mail office.

Please allow 14 days for delivery.

Figure 9.5 Simpler advertisement for a surfboard

a sales promotion). There is no need to tell the readers everything in one advertisement. A surprising number of advertisements are written in the first style because the advertisers are trying to communicate everything about the product to the consumer without having first ensured that people will read the advertisement.

Artwork should be eye-catching and relevant to the purpose. It is usually a good idea to include a picture of the product where this is possible, since it aids recognition when the consumer sees the product on the supermarket shelf. Much artwork is available off-the-shelf for smaller businesses, either from computer clipart folders or from books of non-copyright artwork.

Memory is stimulated by emotion-arousing advertisements, but it appears that women are more affected by this factor than are men (Baird *et al.* 2007). The reasons for this are obscure. Creating annoying or irritating copy or using several variants of a slogan also helps to fix an advertisement in people's memories as well as helping in matching the slogan to the brand (Rosengren and Dahlen 2006).

Assessing advertising effectiveness

Four elements appear to be important in the effectiveness of advertising:

- Awareness
- Liking
- Interest
- Enjoyment.

There is a high correlation between brand loyalty and **brand awareness** (Stapel 1990); likeability appears to be the single best predictor of sales effectiveness since likeability scales predict 97% of sales successes (Biel 1989), interest clearly relates to likeability (Stapel 1991) and enjoyment appears to be a good indicator in advertising pre-tests (Brown 1991). People's responses to advertising can be positive or negative; recent research shows that people who complain about advertising fall into four groups, as follows (Volkov *et al.* 2006):

1 *Advertising aficionados*. These people believe that, in general, advertising is a good thing, paints a fair picture and is a good source of information.

2 *Consumer activist*. These people are on a mission to protect other people and will complain to the manufacturer or through the press.

3 *Advertising moral guardians*. These people believe advertising is creating a materialist society and that it appeals to people's baser instincts.

4 *Advertising seeker*. This type of person watches a lot of TV advertising and enjoys it as entertainment.

Clearly, people will complain about advertising which offends them; in the UK, such complaints are regulated by the Advertising Standards Authority (see Chapter 12).

It is worthwhile making some efforts to find out whether the advertising has been effective in achieving the objectives laid down. This is much easier if clear objectives were set in the first place, of course, and if the advertising agency was given a clear brief.

Advertising effectiveness can be assessed by market research, by returned coupons and (sometimes) by increased sales. The last method is somewhat risky, however, since there may be many other factors that could have increased the sales of the product. Table 9.3 shows some common techniques for evaluating advertising effectiveness.

Table 9.3 Advertising effectiveness

Technique	Description and explanation
Pre-tests	These are evaluations of the advertising before it is released. Pre-tests are sometimes carried out using focus groups (see Chapter 5).
Coupon returns or enquiries	The advertiser counts up the number of enquiries received during each phase of an advertising campaign. This allows the marketing management to judge which advertisements are working best, provided the coupons have an identifying code on them.
Post-campaign tests (post-tests)	The particular testing method used will depend largely on the objectives of the campaign. Communications objectives (product awareness, attitude change, brand awareness) might be determined through surveys; sales objectives might be measured according to changes in sales that can be attributed to the campaign. This is difficult to do because of other factors (changes in economic conditions, for example) that might distort the findings.
Recognition tests and recall tests	In recognition tests, consumers are shown the advertisement and asked if they recognise it. They are then asked how much of it they actually recall. In an unaided recall test the consumer is asked which advertisements he or she remembers seeing recently; in an aided recall test the consumer is shown a group of advertisements (without being told which is the one the researcher is interested in) and is asked which ones he or she has seen recently.

Obviously, it is important to distinguish between remembering the advertisement and remembering the product. Research shows that humour in advertising frequently results in people remembering the advert but failing to remember the product (Hansen *et al.* 2009).

SALES PROMOTION

Sales promotions are short-term activities designed to generate a temporary increase in sales of the products.

Sales promotion has many guises, from money-off promotions to free travel opportunities. The purpose of sales promotion is to create a temporary increase in sales by bringing purchasing decisions forward and adding some immediacy to the decision-making process. Sales promotions have four characteristics, as follows (D'Astous and Landreville 2003):

1 *Attractiveness*. This is the degree to which the customer perceives the promotion as being desirable.

2 *Fit to product category*. A promotion which has no relationship with the product is less likely to appeal to customers.

3 *Reception delay*. If the promotional gift or discount will not arrive for some time, it is less attractive.

4 *Value*. High-value promotions work better than low-value ones, but it is the value as perceived by the customer which is important.

These characteristics interact with each other, so that an unattractive offer may still work if it is a good fit with the product category (for example).

Table 9.4 shows some of the techniques of sales promotion, and when they should be used to greatest effect.

Sales promotion will often be useful for low-value items and is most effective when used as part of an integrated promotion campaign. This is because advertising and PR build sales in the long term, whereas sales promotion and personal selling tend to be better for making quick increases in sales. The combination of the two leads to the **ratchet effect**: sales get a quick boost from sales promotions, then build gradually over the life of an ad campaign (Moran 1978).

Care needs to be taken with sales promotions. First, a sales promotion that is repeated too often can become part of the consumer's expectations; for example, UK furniture retailer Court's had a near-permanent 'sale' on, with large discounts: eventually, customers would not buy anything unless it was heavily discounted and eventually the company went bankrupt.

Second, brand switching as a result of a sales promotion is usually temporary, so it is unlikely that long-term business will be built by a short-term sales promotion.

Third, the promotion will benefit consumers who would have bought the product anyway, so a proportion of the spend will have been effectively wasted (though this

Table 9.4 Sales promotion techniques

Sales promotion technique	When to use to best effect
Free 'taster' samples in supermarkets	When a new product has been launched on the market. This technique works by allowing the consumer to experience the product first-hand and also places the consumer under a small obligation to buy the product. The technique is effective but expensive (Rajagopal 2008).
Money-off vouchers in press advertisements	This has the advantage that the company can check the effectiveness of the advertising by checking which vouchers came from which publications. It tends to lead to short-term brand switching; when the offer ends, consumers frequently revert to their usual brand.
Two-for-the-price-of-one	May encourage short-term brand switching. Appeals to the price-sensitive consumer, who will switch to the next cheap offer next time. Can be useful for rewarding and encouraging existing customers.
Piggy-backing with another product; e.g. putting a free jar of coffee whitener onto a jar of instant coffee	Good for encouraging purchasers of the coffee to try the whitener. Can be very successful in building brand penetration, since the consumer's loyalty is to the coffee, not to the whitener. Will not usually encourage brand switching between the 'free sample' brand and its competitors. Can also use vouchers on the backs of labels of other products (see co-marketing in Chapter 8).
Instant-lottery or scratchcards	Commonly used in petrol stations. The intention is to develop a habit among motorists of stopping at the particular petrol station. In the United Kingdom, for legal reasons, these promotions cannot require a purchase to be made or be linked to spending a specific amount, but few people would have the courage to ask for a card without buying anything.
Free gift with each purchase	Often used for children's cereals. Can be good for encouraging brand switching and is more likely to lead to permanent adoption of the brand because consumers do not usually switch brands when buying for children. This is because the children are not price-sensitive and will want their favourite brand.

is true of most promotional tools). Good targeting can help overcome this, but care should be taken that existing customers do not feel that they have been unfairly dealt with because they did not receive the promotional offer.

Fourth, discounting on price can seriously damage brand values because the product becomes perceived as being cut-price. Since price is widely used as a signal for quality, the potential for damage is obvious.

Sales promotions can be carried out from manufacturer to intermediary (*trade promotions*), from retailer to consumer (*retailer promotions*) or direct from the manufacturer to the consumer (*manufacturer promotions*).

Trade promotions can be used for the following purposes:

- *To increase stock levels.* The more stock the intermediary holds, the more commitment there will be to selling the stock and the less space there is for competitors' stock. (See push strategies in Chapter 10.)

- *To gain more or better shelf space.* The more eye-catching the position of the product in the retail shop, the more likely it is to sell.

- *To launch a new product.* New products always carry an element of risk for retailers as well as manufacturers (see Chapter 6). This means that the manufacturer may need to give the retailer an extra incentive to stock the product at all.

- *To even out fluctuating sales.* Seasonal offers may be used to encourage retailers to stock the products during slack periods. For example, the toy industry sells 80% of its production over the Christmas period, so it is common for firms to offer extra incentives to retailers to stock up during the rest of the year.

- *To counter the competition.* Aggressive sales promotion can sometimes force a competitor off the retailer's shelves, or at least cause the retailer to drive a harder bargain with a competitor.

Retailer promotions are used for the following purposes:

- *To increase store traffic.* Almost any kind of sales promotion will increase the number of people who come into the shop, but retailers commonly have special events or seasonal sales.

- *To increase frequency and amount of purchase.* This is probably the commonest use of sales promotions; examples are two-for-one offers, buy-one-get-discount-off-another-product, and so forth.

- *To increase store loyalty.* Loyalty cards are the main example of this (although these have other uses – see Chapter 8). Using the loyalty card enables the customer to build up points, which can be redeemed against products.

- *To increase own-brand sales.* Most large retailers have their own brands, which often have larger profit margins than the equivalent national brands. Own-brands sometimes suffer from a perception of lower quality, and therefore increased sales promotion effort may need to be made. In fact, own-brands help to increase sales of manufacturers' brands but, since heavy own-brand consumers contribute less to the retailer's overall profits (because they spend less overall, being bargain hunters), retailers might do better to encourage sales of manufacturers' brands as a way of encouraging bigger-spending customers (Ailawadi and Bari 2004).

- *To even out busy periods.* Seasonal sales are the obvious examples, but some retailers also promote at busy times to ensure a larger share of the market.

Manufacturer promotions are carried out for the following reasons:

- *To encourage trial.* When launching a new product the manufacturer may send out free samples to households or may give away samples with an existing product. (See Chapter 10 for pull strategies.)

- *To expand usage.* Sales promotion can be used to encourage reinvention of the product for other uses (see Chapter 6).

- To attract new customers.

- *Trade up.* Sales promotions can encourage customers to buy the larger pack or more expensive version of the product.

- *Load up.* Encouraging customers to stock up on a product (perhaps to collect coupons) effectively blocks out the competition for a period.

- To generate a mailing list for direct marketing purposes (for example, by running an on-pack competition).

- *To enhance brand values* by (for example) running some type of **self-liquidating offer**. For example, a promotion offering a discounted wristwatch that carries the brand logo might encourage sales of the product as well as ensuring that the brand remains in the forefront of the consumer's attention.

Often, the gains made from sales promotions are only temporary, but in many cases this is acceptable since a temporary shift in demand is all that is required to meet the firm's immediate need. Also, much sales promotion activity is carried out with the intention of spoiling a competitor's campaign; using sales promotion to respond to a competitive threat, particularly by offering a price incentive, can be very fast and effective.

MANAGING PERSONAL SELLING

Selling is probably the most powerful marketing tool the firm has. A salesperson sitting in front of a prospect, discussing the customer's needs and explaining directly how the product will benefit him or her, is more likely to get the business than any advertising, PR or sales promotion technique available. Unfortunately, selling is also the most expensive promotional tool for the firm; on average, a sales representative on the road will cost a firm around £60,000 p.a. and will probably call on only 1600 prospects or so in that time, at best. Selling is therefore used only for high-order-value or highly technical products that need a lengthy decision-making procedure.

Some retail shop assistants are trained in selling techniques, in particular in shops where the customer needs advice, such as electrical goods outlets or shoe shops. In these cases the retailer may spend considerable time and effort in training salespeople both in the technicalities of the product range and in selling techniques. Selling is learned – there is no such thing as a 'born' salesperson, although (as is true of any skill) some people have a greater aptitude for selling than do others.

Salespeople fall into four categories:

- **Order takers**, who collect orders for goods from customers who have already decided to buy

- **Order getters**, who find solutions for new and existing customers and persuade them to buy

- **Missionaries**, who seek out new customers and prepare them to buy

- Support staff such as technical salespeople who demonstrate technical products and persuade users to adopt them.

What the firm expects of its salespeople is that they will close business by persuading customers to buy the firm's products rather than a competitor's products. The firm wants its salespeople to be able to explain the benefits of the products in terms of the customer's needs, then ask for the order – in some industries (though by no means the majority), this results in a better than 50% success rate, which is, of course, vastly greater than the best advertising responses.

Salespeople have a bad reputation, largely undeserved, for being pushy and manipulative. In practice, successful salespeople know that they are as much there to help the customer as to help the firm achieve its sales objectives. It is a common saying among salespeople that it is easier to get another company than it is to get new customers, so salespeople find it pays to look after the customer's interests. Many salespeople regard themselves as managers of the firm's relationships with the customers; however, some will inevitably develop inappropriate attitudes to their role and may need some careful management or retraining (Davies *et al.* 2010).

Good salespeople begin by finding out the customer's needs, and go on to decide which of the company's products will best meet those needs. The next stage is to give an explanation of the product's benefits to the customer, connecting these to the customer's needs. Finally, the salesperson closes the deal by asking for the order. The process is the same as that conducted by marketers generally, except that the salesperson is dealing on a one-to-one basis rather than with a mass market. In this sense, selling can be seen as micro-marketing.

This means that the customer can 'pick the brains' of the salesperson, who presumably has superior knowledge of the products that are available. This can cut a lot of the effort out of the search for the most suitable product and the salesperson can also help people through the decision-making barrier. Experienced salespeople often say that the hardest part of the job is to get a decision, not necessarily to get a sale.

The salesperson therefore combines knowledge of the product (obtained beforehand) with knowledge of the customer's needs (obtained during the presentation) and knowledge of sales techniques (which are aids to decision-making) to help the customer arrive at a decision.

MANAGING THE SALESFORCE

Possibly the most expensive marketing tool the company has, the salesforce is in some ways the hardest to control. This is because it is composed of independently minded people who each have their own ideas on how the job should be done, and who are working away from the office and out of sight of the sales managers.

Sales managers are responsible for recruitment, training, motivation, controlling and evaluating salesforce activities, and managing sales territories.

Recruitment

Recruitment is complicated by the fact that there is no generally applicable set of personality traits that go to make up the ideal salesperson. This is because the sales task varies greatly from one firm to another, and the sales manager will need to draw up a specific set of desirable traits for the task in hand. This will involve analysing the company's successful salespeople and also the less successful ones to find out what the differences are between them.

Some companies take the view that almost anybody can be trained to sell, and therefore the selection procedures are somewhat limited, or even non-existent; other companies are extremely selective and subject potential recruits to a rigorous selection procedure. Sources of potential recruits are advertising, employment agencies, recommendations from existing sales staff, colleges and universities, and internal appointments from other departments.

Training

Training can be long or short, depending on the product and the market. Table 9.5 illustrates the dimensions of the problem. The role the salesperson is required to take on will also affect the length of training: *missionary salespeople* will take longer to train than order takers, and *closers* will take longer than *telephone canvassers*.

Typically, training falls into two sections: *classroom training*, in which the recruits are taught about the company and the products and may be given some grounding in sales techniques; and *field training*, which is an ongoing training programme carried out in front of real customers in the field. Field training is often the province of the sales managers, but classroom training can be carried out by other company personnel (in some cases, in larger firms, there will be specialists who do nothing else but train salespeople).

Table 9.5 Factors relating to length of training of sales staff

Factors indicating long training	Factors indicating short training
Complex, technical products	Simple products
Industrial markets with professional buyers	Household, consumer markets
High order values (from the customer's viewpoint)	Low order values
High recruitment costs	Low recruitment costs
Inexperienced recruits – for example, recruited direct from university	Experienced recruits from the same industry

People tend to learn best by performing the task, so most sales training programmes involve substantial field training, either by sending out rookies (trainees) with experienced salespeople or by the 'in-at-the-deep-end' approach of sending rookies out on their own fairly early in their careers. The latter method is indicated if there are plenty of possible customers for the product; the view is that a few mistakes (lost sales) will not matter. In industrial selling, though, it is often the case that there are very few possible customers and therefore the loss of even one or two could be serious. In these circumstances it would be better to give rookies a long period of working alongside more experienced salespeople.

Sales team learning is impacted by their perceptions of the organisation's readiness to change. Salespeople working for an organisation which has demonstrated the ability to adapt to new conditions are more willing to spend time learning new techniques and new products than they would be in organisations which rarely move with the times (Ranganjaran *et al.* 2004).

Ultimately, of course, salespeople will lose more sales than they get. In most industries, fewer than half the presentations given result in a sale; a typical proportion would be one in three.

Payment

Payment for salespeople traditionally has a commission element, but it is perfectly feasible to use a *straight salary* method, or a *commission-only* method. Although it is commonly supposed that a commission-only salesperson will be highly motivated to work hard, since otherwise he or she will not earn any money, this is not necessarily the case. Salespeople who are paid solely by commission will sometimes decide that they have earned enough for this month and will give themselves a holiday; the company has very little moral power to compel them to work since there is no basic salary being paid. Conversely, a salesperson who is paid a salary only may feel obligated to work to justify the salary.

Herzberg (1966) said that the payment method must be seen to be fair if demotivation is to be avoided; the payment method is not in itself a good motivator. Salespeople are out on the road for most of their working lives and do not see what other salespeople are doing – whether they are competent at the job, whether they are getting some kind of unfair advantage, even whether they are working at all. In these circumstances a commission system does at least reassure the salesperson that extra effort brings extra rewards. Table 9.6 shows the trade-offs between commission-only and salary-only; of course, most firms have a mixture of salary and commission.

Salespeople tend to judge whether their pay is fair or not by looking at factors other than the actual money (Ramaswamy and Singh 2003). They tend to look at such factors as the fairness of their supervision, trust between themselves and the sales manager, and interactional fairness (negotiation and explanation). This is perhaps not surprising; the implication is that people only become concerned about their salary levels if they feel they are being unfairly dealt with or are unhappy in the job.

Table 9.6 Trade-offs in salespeople's pay packages

Mainly salary	Mainly commission
Where order values are high	Where order values are low
Where the sales cycle is long	Where the sales cycle is short
Where staff turnover is low	Where staff turnover is high
Where sales staff are carefully selected against narrow criteria	Where selection criteria for staff are broad
For new staff or staff who have to develop new territories	For situations where aggressive selling is indicated (e.g. selling unsought goods)
Where sales territories are seriously unequal in terms of sales potential	Where sales territories are substantially the same

Motivation

Motivation, perhaps surprisingly, tends to come from sources other than payment. The classic view of motivation was proposed by Abraham Maslow (1954). Maslow's Hierarchy of Need theory postulates that people will fulfil the needs at the lower end of a pyramid (survival needs and security needs) before they move on to addressing needs at the upper end (such as belonging needs, esteem needs and self-actualisation needs). Thus, once a salesperson has assured his or her basic survival needs, these cease to be motivators; the individual will then be moving on to esteem needs or belonging needs. For this reason sales managers usually have a battery of motivational devices for which salespeople can aim.

For rookies (new salespeople), the award of a company tie might address the need to belong; for more senior salespeople, membership of a Millionaire's Club (salespeople who have sold more than a million pounds' worth of product) might address esteem needs. Many sales managers offer prizes for salespeople's spouses or partners. This can be a powerful incentive since salespeople often work unusual hours and thus have disrupted home lives; the spouse or partner is sometimes neglected in favour of the job, so a prize aimed at them can help assuage the salesperson's natural feelings of guilt.

There is some evidence to suggest that salespeople perform better if they are allowed to manage themselves within a team environment. Control of teamwork facilitates performance on the team level; performance at the individual level is influenced more by control of selling skills (Lambe *et al.* 2009).

Sales territory management

Sales territory management involves ensuring that the salesforce have a reasonably equal chance of making sales. Clearly a home-improvement salesperson in a major city will have an easier task than one in a rural area, simply because of the shorter distances between prospects; such a salesperson would spend more time in presentations and less time driving. On the other hand, the city salesperson would probably face more competition and might also have to cover poorer homes who would be less likely to spend much money on improvements.

Territories can be divided *geographically* or by *industry*; IBM divides territories by industry, for example, so that salespeople get to know the problems and needs of the specific industry for which they have responsibility. IBM salespeople might be given responsibility for banks, insurance companies or local government departments. This sometimes means that salespeople have greater distances to travel to present IBM products, but are more able to make sensible recommendations and give useful advice. Geographical territories are more common, since they minimise travel time and maximise selling time.

It is virtually impossible to create exactly equal territories. Thus it is important to discuss decisions with salespeople to ensure that people feel they are being treated fairly. For example, some salespeople may be quite happy to accept a rural territory because they like to live and work in the country, even if it means earning less.

MANAGING PR

PR, or public relations, is about creating favourable images of the company or organisation in the minds of consumers. PR officers and marketers often have differing viewpoints: PR people tend to see their role as being about image-building with everybody who has anything at all to do with the firm, whereas marketers are concerned mainly with customers and consumers. There is therefore a lack of fit between the information-processing requirements of marketers and PR people (Cornelissen and Harris 2004).

PR is defined as 'the planned and sustained effort to establish and maintain goodwill and mutual understanding between an organisation and its publics: customers, employees, shareholders, trade bodies, suppliers, Government officials, and society in general' (Institute of Public Relations 1984). PR managers have the task of coordinating all the activities that make up the public face of the organisation, and will have some or all of the following activities to handle:

- Organising press conferences
- Staff training workshops
- Events such as annual dinners
- Handling incoming criticisms or complaints

- Grooming senior management for the press or for TV appearances
- Internal marketing; setting the organisation's culture towards a customer orientation.

The basic routes by which PR operates are word-of-mouth, press and TV news stories, and personal recommendation. The aim is to put the firm and its products into people's minds and conversations in a positive way. PR is not advertising; advertising is aimed at generating specific behaviour (usually a purchase), whereas PR is aimed at creating a good impression.

Here are some examples of good PR activities:

- A press release saying that a company has developed a way of recycling garbage from landfills to produce plastics
- The company sponsors a major charitable or sporting event (e.g. the London Marathon or a famine-relief project)
- An announcement that one of the firm's senior executives has been seconded to a major government job-creation programme
- Body Shop requires all their franchise operations to run projects to benefit their local communities. This gives a positive image of the company to the community and also gives the staff pride in working for a caring firm. Such initiatives are not always exportable, however; McDonald's ran into difficulties in Norway when they tried to establish a Ronald McDonald house, with strong resistance from political parties, academics and others (Bronn 2006)
- McDonald's counters the negative publicity from environmental pressure groups by running litter patrols outside the restaurants.

These examples have in common that they are newsworthy and interesting, that they put the companies concerned in a good light, and that they encourage people to talk about the companies in a positive way.

Public relations and staff

PR is largely concerned with creating favourable impressions in people's minds. It is rarely, if ever, connected with directly bringing in business, and in this respect it differs from the other tools in the promotional mix. Although most of the time and for most activities PR will be the responsibility of a press agent or PR officer, PR is the responsibility of everybody who comes into contact with people outside the organisation. This will include the 'front-liners', the people whose day-to-day work brings them into contact with outsiders. For example:

- Receptionists
- Telephonists
- Truck drivers
- Warehouse staff
- Serving staff in the canteen.

This is apart from the marketing staff, such as salespeople, who come into contact with outsiders. In a sense, everybody in the organisation must take some responsibility for PR since everybody in the organisation goes home after work (and discusses their company with their friends).

In this context, a bad approach to PR (but one that is all too common) is to hire somebody with a nice smile and a friendly voice to sit by the telephone to handle complaints and smooth over any problems that arise. This is a *fire-fighting* or reactive approach.

A good PR approach is to make all the staff feel positive about the company. This is done by ensuring that everybody knows what the organisation is doing, what the policies are and what the company's overall aims are, in simple language. Most people would like to think that they are working for a good, responsible, successful organisation; it is part of the job of PR to ensure that this is communicated to staff. This is sometimes done by using a slogan or company motto to sum up the company's main aim. Some examples are given in Table 9.7.

Internal PR uses staff newsletters, staff training programmes and staff social events to convey a positive image. Intranet-enabled PR can include e-mailing staff about corporate developments, forums and blogs to encourage discussion of issues of interest, and there is also the capacity for direct contact with senior management. Such systems can be abused, but in most cases they are a force for good in helping to develop the corporate culture.

Because most of the front-liners are working away from the company's headquarters, the PR process has to be handled by persuasion, not by command. It would be impossible for the PR staff to be everywhere at once, following people around to ensure that they say and do the 'right' things.

Table 9.7 Examples of company slogans

Example	Explanation
We're Number Two, So We Try Harder (Avis)	This communicates to staff that the company is among the biggest, but that their efforts to 'try harder' are recognised and appreciated. It also conveys a valuable image to the customers. This slogan has become so well-known that Avis have now reduced it to 'We try harder'.
Créateur des Automobiles (Renault)	The literal translation of this French phrase, Creator of Automobiles, may not mean much, but the French phrase conveys an image of care and artistry – the cars are created, not manufactured.
Putting the Community First (Barnet Council)	Like many local government organisations, Barnet wants to reassure residents that they come first in its thinking. This slogan emphasises the community and implies that there is neighbourliness and solidarity within Barnet.

PR has a role in conciliation and internal arbitration, although much of this will be handled by human resources departments. Because internal conflict can lead to bad feeling towards the organisation, part of the PR role is to provide a clear lead in terms of corporate culture.

Public relations and the press

Usually, PR communicates through the news media. Newspapers and magazines earn their money mainly through paid advertising, but they attract readers by having stimulating articles about topics of interest to the readership.

Press releases

PR often involves creating a news story or event that brings the product or company to the public attention. A news story is more likely to be read than an advertisement and is also more likely to be believed. A press release differs from advertising in that the message is not paid for directly; the newspaper or magazine prints the story as news, and of course is able to slant the story in any way it wishes. PR people are often ex-journalists who have some contacts with the news media, and who know how to create a story that will be printed in the way the company wants it to be done. Newspaper editors are wary of thinly disguised advertisements and will only print items that are really newsworthy.

Good press releases can be much more effective than advertising for the following reasons:

- The press coverage is free, so there is better use of the promotional budget
- The message carries greater credibility because it is in the editorial part of the paper
- The message is more likely to be read, because while readers tend to skip past the advertisements, their purpose in buying the paper is to read the news stories.

Table 9.8 shows the criteria under which the press stories must be produced if they are to be published.

The news media will, of course, reserve the right to alter stories, add to them, comment on them or otherwise change them around to suit their own purposes. For example, a press agent's great little story on the launch of Britain's most powerful sports car may become part of an article on dangerous driving. There is really very little the firm can do about this.

For this reason, a large part of the PR manager's job lies in cultivating good relationships with the media. Sometimes this will involve business entertaining, but more often it will involve making the journalists' lives as easy as possible. A well written press release will often be inserted in the paper exactly as it stands, because the editorial staff are too busy to waste time rewriting something that is already perfectly acceptable.

The journals and newspapers gain as well. Normally editors have to pay for editorial, either paying freelance writers to produce articles or paying the salaries of journalists to come up with interesting stories. A good press release can go in with

Table 9.8 Criteria for successful press releases

Criterion	Example
Stories must be newsworthy, i.e. of interest to the reader	Articles about your new lower prices are not newsworthy; articles about opening a new factory creating 200 jobs are.
Stories must not be merely thinly disguised advertisements	A story saying your new car is the best on the market at only £7999 will not go in. A story saying your new car won the East African Safari Rally probably would.
Stories must fit the editorial style of the magazine or paper to which they are being sent	An article sent to the *Financial Times* about your sponsored fishing competition will not be printed; an article about the company's takeover of a competitor will.

little or no editing, and no legwork on the part of journalists, so it fills space with minimal cost to the paper.

Media events

Often companies will lay on a media event, a launch ceremony for a new product or to announce some change in company policy. Usually this will involve inviting journalists from the appropriate media, providing a free lunch with plenty of free drinks and inviting questions about the new development in a formal press conference. This kind of event has only a limited success, however, unless the groundwork for it has been very thoroughly laid.

Journalists tend to be suspicious of media events, sometimes feeling that the organisers are trying to buy them off with a buffet and a glass of wine. This means they may not respond positively to the message the PR people are trying to convey, and may write a critical article rather than the positive one that was hoped for.

To minimise the chance of this happening, media events should follow these basic rules:

- Do not call a media event or press conference unless you are announcing something that the press will find interesting
- Check that there are no negative connotations in what you are announcing
- Ensure that you have some of the company's senior executives there to talk to the press, not just the PR people
- Only invite journalists with whom you feel you have a good working relationship
- Do not be too lavish with the refreshments
- Ensure that your senior executives (in fact, anybody who is going to speak to the press) have had some training in doing this. This is particularly important for TV
- Be prepared to answer all questions truthfully. Journalists are trained to spot lies and evasions.

Journalists much prefer to be able to talk directly to genuine corporate executives rather than being allowed only to talk to the PR department; however, care should be exercised in ensuring that the executives spoken to are able to handle this type of questioning. It is also a good idea to have a press office that can handle queries from journalists promptly, honestly and enthusiastically and can arrange interviews with senior personnel if necessary.

PR and the Internet

It goes without saying that a good, interactive website is an essential component for effective PR. Most people considering doing business with a company will want to check the website first, if only to find out what the company can offer. Since people will probably check several websites, the PR people need to ensure that the company's website presents a fair but positive image of the company.

A good corporate website will include the following features:

- *Company history.* The background to the company's foundation and development is an important factor for people in deciding how solid the firm is
- *Mission or vision statement.* This tells prospective customers what the company is all about; in other words, its guiding philosophy
- *Profiles of senior management.* This puts a human face on the company. For example, Waterstone's bookshop website has a section where senior managers talk about their favourite books
- *Any sponsorship or charitable activities undertaken by the firm.* Apart from the opportunity to increase the effectiveness of those activities, their inclusion on the website shows that the company takes its corporate responsibilities seriously
- *A contact point for comments about the company or its products.* This should be an e-mail address, but a telephone number should also be included since a lack of a contact point may make it seem that the company has something to hide or is not prepared to speak to its customers
- *A press page.* This should include latest press releases and contact details for the press officer or PR manager.

All of the above features should be included purely from a PR perspective. Obviously the website will also have sections aimed at increasing business; for example, product descriptions and pictures, contact details for salespeople and retailers and possibly online ordering facilities.

PR and other publics

PR involves dealing with the company's other publics, apart from the consumers. These are typically the following groups:

- Shareholders, for whom the company will produce end-of-year reports, special privileges and so forth

- Government departments, with whom the company will liaise about planned legislation or other government activities
- The workforce
- External pressure groups such as environmentalists or lobbyists.

Pressure groups can cause problems for companies by producing adverse publicity, by picketing company plants or by encouraging boycotting of company products. This can usually be dealt with most effectively by counter-publicity.

Sometimes adverse publicity from pressure groups is dealt with by advertising. For example, McDonald's was attacked by environmental groups for indirectly encouraging the destruction of rainforests for the purpose of producing cheap beef. McDonald's responded with a series of full-page press adverts proving that beef for their hamburgers comes only from sources in the countries where it is eaten and is not imported from the Third World.

Usually a journalist who is offered a story from a pressure group will respond by trying to get the other side of the story from the firm. This is partly for legal reasons, since newspapers can be sued for libel if they print stories that turn out to be untrue, but it is also because most journalists want to ensure the accuracy and fairness of their stories. This means that a firm's press office, a PR manager or even a senior executive may be asked for comment with little or no prior warning. It is therefore advisable to be as prepared as possible beforehand and to answer as fully as possible in the event of being asked questions. However, it is better to delay comment than to say something that will make matters worse.

In these circumstances, it is better to use a phrase such as 'I'm sorry, I'll have to look into that and get back to you later' than to use the standard 'No comment'. The former phrase at least gives the impression that you are trying to help, whereas 'No comment' gives the impression that you are trying to hide something.

Defensive PR

Defensive PR is about responding to attacks from outside the firm and counteracting them as they arise. The attacks might come from pressure groups, from investigative reporters or from members of parliament. The safest way to handle this type of attack is to begin by trying to understand the enemy and, to this end, the following questions should be asked:

- Are they justified in their criticism?
- What facts do they have at their disposal?
- Who are they trying to influence?
- How are they trying to do it?

If the pressure group is justified in its criticisms, it may be necessary to help them to effect the changes in the organisation to quell the criticism. Otherwise the problem will simply continue. Good PR people will always respond in some way; however, as anyone who watches investigative reporters on TV will know, the company managers and directors who flee with a hasty 'No comment' always look guilty, whereas the ones who are prepared to be interviewed always appear honest (until the reporter produces the irrefutable evidence, of course).

During such a crisis, the news media can greatly increase the negative effects on the brand image, as compared with the effects that would occur purely through consumers' direct experience (Yannopoulou *et al.* 2011).

Another aspect of defensive PR is crisis management. Some industries (for example airlines) are more prone to crises than others, but any company can be subject to bad publicity of one sort or another. A good approach to handling crises is to be prepared beforehand by establishing a crisis team who are able to speak authoritatively to the media in the event of a problem arising. The crisis team should meet regularly and should consider hypothetical cases and their responses to them. They should also ensure that they are immediately available in the event of a crisis occurring.

Proactive PR

Proactive PR means setting out deliberately to influence opinion, without waiting for an attack from outside. Here the manager will decide on the following:

- Whom to influence
- What to influence them about
- How to influence them
- How to marshal the arguments carefully to maximise the impact.

Overall, it is probably better to be proactive rather than defensive (or reactive) because that way the PR office is in control of the process and is better prepared. If the firm is planning on dumping toxic waste in a beauty spot, for example, it is better to contact Greenpeace beforehand and get its opinion rather than suffer the inevitable protests afterwards and take a chance on being able to patch up any problems.

What PR will do

Good PR will achieve the following outcomes for the firm:

- Help to build a positive image
- Counter bad publicity
- Improve employee motivation
- Improve the effectiveness of both advertising and the salesforce.

On the other hand, here are some of the things that PR will *not* do for the firm:

- Directly increase sales
- Cover up something adverse to the company
- Replace other promotional activities.

Ultimately, PR works best as part of a planned and integrated programme of promotional activities which includes advertising, sales promotion and personal selling. It works worst when used only occasionally and in isolation.

Word-of-mouth

Word-of-mouth is probably the most powerful communication medium in existence and can be used by marketers to good effect. The reasons for the power of word-of-mouth are as follows:

- It is interactive, involving a discussion between the parties. This forces the recipient to think about the communication. The problem for marketers is that the interaction takes place between parties who are not usually under the control of the firm
- It allows for feedback and confirmation of the messages
- The source, being a disinterested friend or acquaintance, carries a lot more credibility than any marketer-generated communications.

People often discuss products and services; they like to talk about their own recent purchases, to advise people considering a purchase, to show friends and family their latest acquisitions and even to discuss controversial or interesting marketing communications. The problem for marketers is that people will talk about products and companies whether the firm likes it or not, and there is very little that firms can do to control the process. Word-of-mouth communications can therefore be positive or negative, and it often appears that bad news travels twice as fast as good news, so that much word-of-mouth is negative. Interestingly, some word-of-mouth is more effective before the initiator of it has experienced the product; there is evidence that word-of-mouth is at its most active before a movie is released, rather than afterwards (Yong 2006). The richness of the message and the degree of implied or explicit advocacy of the product are key themes in the success of positive word-of-mouth (Mazzarol *et al.* 2007).

Table 9.9 shows some of the ways that marketers can increase positive word-of-mouth. Part of the problem for the marketer lies in identifying the opinion leaders in a given market. Journalists, influential individuals and organisations in industry, and some prominent TV pundits are obviously easy to identify, but among the general public it usually takes careful research to identify the people who are likely to be opinion leaders regarding a particular product. The main characteristics of influentials are shown in Table 9.10.

Much word-of-mouth communication is, unfortunately, negative. Some authorities state that dissatisfied customers tell three times as many people about the product than do satisfied customers; if true, this means that preventing negative word-of-mouth is actually a more pressing problem for marketers than is generating positive word-of-mouth. Complaint handling is therefore a key issue (see Chapter 3).

The electronic version of word-of-mouth, word-of-mouse, has become vastly more important with the advent of social networking sites. Astute marketers have tapped into this; many corporations now have pages on Facebook, and the use of free games on corporate websites has encouraged people to e-mail their friends with links to the site. There is more on social networking in Chapter 12.

Table 9.9 Ways to encourage positive word-of-mouth

Method	Explanation and examples
Press releases	A press release with a good, newsworthy story will usually stimulate discussion, particularly if it is linked to another promotion. For example, a press release announcing a sports competition for school squash players will generate word-of-mouth among squash players.
Bring-a-friend schemes	In these schemes an existing customer is invited to recruit a friend in exchange for a small reward. In some cases, the reward is given to the friend rather than to the introducer – some people feel uncomfortable about accepting a reward for 'selling' to a friend. For example, a health club might have special 'bring a friend' days when the friend is allowed to use all the facilities free for a day. This gives the member a chance to show off his or her club, and encourages the friend to join.
Awards and certificates	Trophies and certificates are sometimes displayed, and often talked about. For example, Laphroaig Whisky distillery has a Friends of Laphroaig club, in which the members (regular drinkers of the whisky) are given a square foot of land on the island of Islay and a certificate of ownership. The proud owners of this little piece of Scotland frequently mention it to their friends, especially when offering them a glass of the whisky itself. The distillers also occasionally invite the Friends of Laphroaig to nominate a friend to receive a free miniature of the whisky, on the grounds that the 'Friend' could be sure of a 'dram' when calling on the 'friend'.
T-shirts	Promotional clothing often excites comment from friends: designer labels, names of bands, names of tourist destinations and names of concert venues all provoke comment from friends and acquaintances.
Viral marketing	Some websites include games, jokes or interesting images which visitors are invited to 'e-mail to a friend'. In most cases, the web link would only be sent on to those friends the original visitor thinks might be interested in the product category. Note: this is entirely different from the unsolicited e-mails called spam which are sent out indiscriminately.

Table 9.10 Characteristics of influentials

Characteristic	Description of influential
Demographics	Wide differences according to product category. For fashions and film-going, young women dominate. For self-medication, women with children are most influential. Generally, demography shows low correlation and is not a good predictor.
Social activity	Influencers and opinion leaders are usually gregarious.
General attitudes	Generally innovative and positive towards new products.
Personality and lifestyle	Low correlation of personality with opinion leadership. Lifestyle tends to be more fashion conscious, more socially active, more independent.
Product-related	Influencers are more interested in the specific product area than are others. They are active searchers and information gatherers, especially from the mass media.

People who are knowledgeable about products and like to advise other people are called mavens. They often have a higher need for variety than opinion leaders and are often less involved with the product categories; however, both groups have high levels of satisfaction with the products they use and recommend (Stokburger-Sauer and Hoyer 2009).

Sponsorship

Sponsorship of the arts or of sporting events is an increasingly popular way of generating positive feelings about firms. Sponsorship has been defined as 'An investment, in cash or kind, in an activity in return for access to the exploitable commercial potential associated with this activity' (Meenaghan 1991).

Sponsorship in the United Kingdom grew from £4 million in 1970 (Buckley 1980) to £35 million by 1980[1] (Mintel 1990) and £400 million by 1993 (Mintel 1993). Much of this increase in expenditure came about because tobacco firms are severely restricted in what they are allowed to advertise and where they are allowed to advertise it; thus sponsorship of Formula One racing and of horse racing and cricket matches by tobacco firms became commonplace. This source of sponsorship has now ceased, because tobacco firms are no longer allowed to sponsor events; in some cases this has forced events to cut back or even disappear altogether.

Companies sponsor for a variety of different reasons, as Table 9.11 shows (Zafer Erdogan and Kitchen 1998).

Sponsorship attempts to link beliefs about the sponsoring organisation or brand and connect them to an event or organisation that is highly valued by target consumers (Zafer Erdogan and Kitchen 1998). The success of a sports team has a significant effect on fans' purchase of sponsors' products (Lings and Owen 2007), so it is worthwhile spending some time choosing the correct team to back – it is also worthwhile being loyal to a team, as audiences become increasingly aware of the

Table 9.11 Reasons for sponsorship

Objectives	% Agreement	Rank
Press coverage/exposure/opportunity	84.6	1
TV coverage/exposure/opportunity	78.5	2
Promote brand awareness	78.4	3
Promote corporate image	77.0	4
Radio coverage/exposure/opportunity	72.3	5
Increase sales	63.1	6
Enhance community relations	55.4	7
Entertain clients	43.1	8
Benefit employees	36.9	9
Match competition	30.8	10
Fad/fashion	26.2	11

sponsor's brand the longer the sponsorship continues (Mason and Cochetel 2006; Lacey *et al.* 2007). Sponsoring rival teams is a mistake; although it might seem as if the company is hedging its bets, supporters of each team resent support of the rivals, thus cancelling out any goodwill engendered by support for their own team (Davies *et al.* 2006).

Sponsorship is not adequate as a stand-alone policy. Although firms can run perfectly adequate PR campaigns without advertising, sponsorship will not work effectively unless the sponsoring firm is prepared and able to publicise the link. Some researchers estimate that two to three times the cost of sponsorship needs to be spent on advertising if the exercise is to be effective (Heffler 1994). In most cases it is necessary to spell out the reasons for the firm's sponsorship of the event to make the link clear to the audience; merely saying 'Official snack of the Triathlon' is insufficient. Since the audience is usually interested in anything about the event, it is quite possible to go into a brief explanation of the reasoning behind the sponsorship; for example, to say 'Our snack gives energy – and that's what every triathlete needs more than anything. That's why we sponsor the Triathlon.'

The evidence is that consumers do feel at least some gratitude towards the sponsors of their favourite events; whether this is gratitude *per se* or whether it is affective linking is hard to say, and the answer to that question may not be of much practical importance anyway (Crimmins and Horn 1996). There are certainly spin-offs for the internal PR of the firm; most employees like to feel that they are working for a caring organisation, and sponsorship money also (on occasion) leads to free tickets or price reductions for staff of the sponsoring organisation.

Sponsorship appears to work best when there is some existing link between the sponsoring company and the event itself. In other words, a company that manufactures fishing equipment would be more successful sponsoring a fishing competition than it would in sponsoring a painting competition. More subtly, a bank would be better off sponsoring a middle-class, 'respectable' arts event such as an opera rather than an open-air rock concert. The following criteria apply when considering sponsorship (Heffler 1994):

- The sponsorship must be economically viable; it should be cost-effective, in other words
- The event or organisation being sponsored should be consistent with the brand image and overall marketing communications plans
- It should offer a strong possibility of reaching the desired target audience
- Care should be taken if the event has been sponsored before; the audience may confuse the sponsors and you may be benefiting the earlier sponsor.

Occasionally a competitor will try to divert the audience's attention to themselves by implying that they are sponsoring the event; this is called ambushing (Bayless 1988). For example, during the 2010 World Cup it was common for firms to use World Cup events in their advertising or sales promotions without actually sponsoring anything to do with the event itself.

Another risk in sponsoring an individual (say, a sportsperson) is that there may be a negative incident such as a drugs conviction. Brand managers may respond to these events in many different ways, depending on attribution of blame, societal norms, zone of tolerance and perceived severity of the event (Westberg *et al.* 2011). If a cultural event has been sponsored for some time, ending the relationship can be difficult for the staff who have been involved in the sponsorship programme – in some cases they may try to continue with relationships established with the other organisation during the sponsorship period despite management attempts to prevent this (Ryan and Blois 2010).

Critical thinking

If it's so easy to ambush an event, why would anybody pay to be a sponsor? After all, ambushing is easy – all the firm has to do is put 'Olympic-Size Offers!' on its publicity to cash in on the Olympic Games, or 'Marathon Guarantees!' to ride piggy-back on the London Marathon.

On the other hand, maybe supporters and fans of these events can see through that kind of ploy – and react accordingly. Being exposed as a bit of a liar is hardly good for the corporate image.

Sponsorship is likely to grow in importance in the foreseeable future. More credible than advertising, it is often cheaper and has important effects on both brand and corporate image; given the restrictions being imposed on advertising, sponsorship has much to offer.

INTEGRATING THE PROMOTIONAL MIX

Communication does not necessarily create all its impact at once. A series of communications will move the recipient up a 'ladder' of effects, as shown in Figure 9.6. At the bottom of the ladder are those consumers who are completely unaware of the product in question; at the top of the ladder are those who actually purchase the product.

Given the differing nature of the consumer's involvement at each stage of the hierarchy, it is clear that no single communication method will work at every stage. Equally, not every consumer will be at the same stage at the same time; therefore it follows that several different communications approaches will need to run at once if the communications package is to work effectively.

- In the early stages of a product launch, moving consumers from *brand ignorance* to *brand awareness* will be largely the province of advertising. At first, the marketer needs to get the consumers' attention and prepare them for the more detailed information which is to follow. A teaser campaign is almost entirely concerned with creating awareness.

Figure 9.6 The hierarchy of communications effects

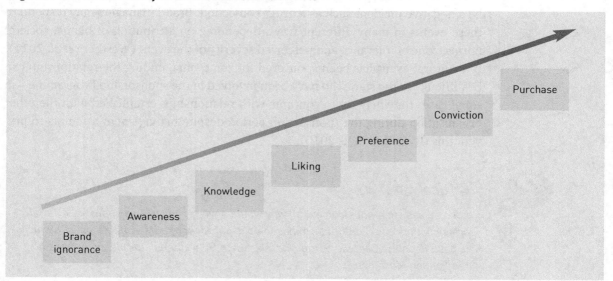

- Having made the target audience aware of the product, the next stage is to build *knowledge*. Again, mass advertising will play a major role, but if the product is complex it may be necessary to use **mailshots** or other more personal communications. This is because the emphasis is on providing information about the product: what it is, what it does, how it works and even that it works at all. In some cases an element of prior knowledge can be assumed; for example, most people would already know that fluoride is a good thing to have in toothpaste, not quite so many would know that it helps prevent tooth decay and very few would know how it works.

- *Liking* for the product might come from trying it (perhaps through a sales promotion), from reading positive news stories about it (PR) or from persuasive advertising. Liking is an attitude towards a product, and therefore has elements of affect, cognition and conation (see Chapter 3).

- *Preference* for the product implies comparison with other brands, so is very much concerned with positioning. An important point to note is that preference will come about only if the product matches up to (or exceeds) the claims made for it in the earlier advertising; if the claims made were inaccurate, unrealistic or simply misunderstood, the consumer will be disappointed and will not buy the product again. Also, preference implies that the consumer will need to have sufficient knowledge of the pros and cons of other brands; salespeople will play a role in this part of the process if the product is a high-value one, since they will often be able to point out the drawbacks of competing brands.

- **Conviction** may come about only after several trials of the product (if it is a fast-moving consumer good) or after a lengthy discussion with a salesperson if the product is a high-value or high-involvement item. **Adoption** is the final stage of the process, when the consumer builds the product into his or her daily life.

There is likely to be some 'slippage' because it is not possible to expose all the target audience to the communication at the same time. Also, some consumers will already know more than others about the product category. Marketers will need to overlap the promotional effort to give maximum coverage.

One of the problems with the hierarchy of communications effects is that it implies that the process is invariably linear. This is not necessarily the case; an individual can become aware of a product and form an instant liking for it without having detailed knowledge of the product. Equally, it is perfectly possible for a consumer to buy a product on impulse and form an opinion about it afterwards.

Having said that, the hierarchy of effects model is helpful in planning communications campaigns, since different communications methods and styles can be used according to the consumer's level on the hierarchy. For example, when a new product is introduced (or a product is introduced into a new market), few of the target audience will know anything about it.

CASE STUDY 9 British Gas

During the Industrial Revolution, the discovery of coal gas revolutionised energy distribution in towns and cities throughout Britain. The gas, extracted by heating coal, could be piped to homes and businesses to be used for lighting, cooking and heating; the residue from the manufacturing process, coke, could be burned as an almost smokeless fuel with very few harmful emissions. Initially, coal gas (or town gas, as it was commonly known) was produced by local town councils or by private companies, each operating only within its local area. This system worked well, since the technology did not exist at the time to pump the gas over long distances; making gas-tight pipework was prohibitively expensive since it had to be made of lead. However, following on from the Second World War, gas production and distribution had been so badly damaged by bombing that the local gas producers were unable to repair the damage and thus the country's entire gas industry was nationalised. The country was divided up into twelve regions, each with its own Gas Board, each under independent management.

During the 1960s the gas boards diversified, opening up high street showrooms to promote the use of gas for all household energy needs. At the same time, the other great nationalised energy business, the Electricity Board, was also promoting the use of its fuel. However, in the mid-1960s large reserves of natural gas were discovered under the North Sea and the decision was made to convert the entire country to natural gas. Over the following 10 years, new gas mains were laid throughout the country and a gas national grid was developed to move gas to where it was needed.

During the 1980s British Gas was privatised, with shares being sold largely to the general public. Following this, the energy industry was deregulated, allowing any competent company to enter the market and thus opening up real competition for the first time. This meant that British Gas had to compete directly with the electricity companies, but could sell electricity as well as gas. Deregulation led to a wide range of companies entering the market and thus to cut-throat competition; householders found that salespeople were appearing on the doorstep looking to persuade them to switch suppliers and there were many instances of sharp practice by these salespeople – forging signatures on documents was far from unknown, and many people were surprised to find themselves being telephoned by their supplier asking why they were defecting to the opposition. This kind of behaviour tended to bring the industry into disrepute and major efforts were made to clean up the marketing effort.

Nowadays, British Gas offers a wide range of services. In common with other energy suppliers, the company offers a range of energy-saving devices. It also offers a maintenance service for gas-fired central heating systems, mainly through a monthly insurance payment. The company sells central heating systems and replacement boilers, but no longer operates high street retail outlets for appliances; these are catered for more effectively through more general retailers, who are able to offer dual-fuel devices (for example, cookers with electric ovens and gas hobs) which were formerly unavailable owing to the monopoly positions of the gas and electricity suppliers.

For British Gas, the main marketing problem lies in creating a unique selling proposition. Gas is gas is gas – the specifications of the core product cannot be altered, and in any case the gas is supplied through the same grid whichever company markets it, i.e. British Gas has to pay wholesale prices for the gas it puts into the grid, and receives the retail price from its consumers – there is no way of identifying which exact molecules of gas are which once it enters the pipeline. In common with other suppliers, British Gas has to be creative in its pricing structure – offering people fixed prices for a given period, offering special tariffs for high users, and so forth. In terms of electricity supplies, there is slightly more scope; some suppliers offer sustainably sourced power from wind farms or hydroelectric dams, some specialise in nuclear power sources, and so forth – but again, the actual electrons are pretty much identical.

This being the case, British Gas relies heavily on its peripheral services and has developed a strong position in the servicing, maintenance and fitting area. Although there are many small local gas fitters who will service central heating boilers, British Gas has by far the largest share of the market. The company also has an extensive training programme, helped by the fact that UK law prevents anyone who is not a qualified gas fitter from servicing boilers or any other gas appliances. Similar rules do not as yet apply to electrical work, although there are moves to introduce such regulations. Engineers who service the boilers are in a strong position to recommend new boilers when necessary – the life of a boiler can be as short as 10–12 years, and engineers are able to recommend boilers which are more reliable or better suited to the circumstances of the householder. It is obviously in the interests of British Gas to recommend reliable boilers, since the service contracts operate on a fixed monthly subscription rather than a per-call basis.

There are clearly some threats on the horizon, however. North Sea Gas is running out; the UK is no longer self-sufficient in gas but has to rely on imports from Russia and elsewhere. Gas prices are rising rapidly, and consequently people are beginning to shift to other fuels – wood-burning stoves are gaining a new popularity since they are more environmentally sustainable and also many people are able to obtain wood at a low cost, or even free. The cost advantage gas used to have over electric heating has also been eroded, as more electricity is generated from wind farms and nuclear power. Recent changes in the tax regime for gas producers have meant that some very large gas fields have become uneconomic and have been closed. On the other hand, new gas fields may be discovered at any time.

For the time being, British Gas seems to be holding its own against competition, insecure supplies and legislative changes. Whether the company can continue to reinvent itself as the environment around it shifts is another matter.

Questions

1 How might British Gas use PR to counter the bad publicity surrounding doorstep selling?

2 How might British Gas use innovative communications methods to create a USP?

3 How might British Gas counter the threat from alternative fuels?

4 What might be the role of sales promotion for British Gas?

5 How could the personal selling process be managed better?

SUMMARY

This chapter has been about the ways companies communicate with their publics. In it, we have looked at the main promotional tools that marketers have at their disposal, and at the strengths and weaknesses of each of those tools.

Here are the key points from this chapter:

- Communications work best when there is feedback
- It is essential for the sender of the message to have a common field of experience with the receiver
- The AIDA model can rarely be achieved with one form of communication
- The promotional mix is a recipe; the ingredients are not interchangeable
- Publicity and PR are probably the most cost-effective promotional tools you have available
- The media are interested only in newsworthy items, not in thinly disguised advertisements. PR works best when used as part of an integrated programme of activities
- PR requires a long-term commitment to cultivating the media
- It is advisable to invest in training anybody who may have to deal with the press, and even more so with TV
- PR will only help publicise your good points; it will not give you what you have not got
- Advertising is not the only way to increase sales, and may not even be the best way
- Advertising needs to be planned and targeted to the right segment to avoid wasting money and effort on people who will not buy the product
- People will not read long-winded advertisements
- Artwork is more memorable than copy
- Selling is about meeting the customer's needs with a suitable product from the range
- Selling is learned, not somehow magically inborn
- Sponsorship tends to have strong positive effects on both brand and corporate images.

CHAPTER QUESTIONS

1 How can sales promotions help a company's production planning process?

2 What are the main advantages of PR over advertising?

3 'The aim of marketing must be to make selling superfluous.' Discuss.

4 Which part of the AIDA model does personal selling best achieve?

5 What is the purpose of sponsorship?

Further reading

Marketing Communications: Interactivity, Communities and Content, 5th edn by Chris Fill (Harlow, FT Prentice Hall, 2009) gives a very good, readable overview of marketing communications. Chris Fill is a Senior Examiner for the Chartered Institute of Marketing, and the book certainly covers all the necessary ground.

Marketing Communications, 3rd edn by Jim Blythe (Harlow, Financial Times Prentice Hall, 2005) offers a more in-depth look at marketing communications theory and practice than is possible in this chapter.

How I Raised Myself from Failure to Success in Selling by Frank Bettger (London, Cedar Press, 1990; 1st edn, World's Work 1947). Anecdotes of a highly successful American salesman. This book is out of print at present, but if you can find a copy in a library or second-hand bookshop it makes riveting bedtime reading. A real classic!

References

Ailawadi, Kusum L. and Harlam, Bari: 'An empirical analysis of the determinants of retail margins: the role of store brand share', *Journal of Marketing,* **68** (1) (January 2004), pp. 147–55.

Baird, Thomas R., Wahlers, Russel G. and Cooper, Crystal K.: 'Non-recognition of print advertising: emotional arousal and gender effects', *Journal of Marketing Communications,* **13** (1) (2007), pp. 39–57.

Bayless, A.: 'Ambush marketing is becoming a popular event at Olympic Games', *Wall Street Journal* (8 February 1988).

Biel, A.: 'Love the advertisement, buy the product?' *ADMAP* (October 1989).

Bronn, Peggy Simcic: 'Building corporate brands through community involvement: is it exportable? The case of the Ronald McDonald House in Norway', *Journal of Marketing Communication,* **12** (4) (2006), pp. 309–20.

Brown, G.: 'Modelling advertising awareness', *ADMAP* (April 1991).

Buckley, D.: 'Who pays the piper?' *Practice Review* (Spring 1980).

Cornelissen, Joep P. and Harris, Phil: 'Interdependencies between marketing and public relations disciplines as correlates of communication organization', *Journal of Marketing,* **20** (1) (February 2004), pp. 237–65.

Crimmins, J. and Horn, M.: 'Sponsorship: from management ego trip to marketing success', *Journal of Advertising Research,* **36** (4) (July/August 1996), pp. 11–21.

D'Astous, Alain and Landreville, Valerie: 'An experimental investigation of factors affecting consumers' perceptions of sales promotions', *European Journal of Marketing,* **37** (11) (2003), pp. 1746–61.

Davies, Fiona, Veloutsou, Cleopatra and Costa, Andrew: 'Investigating the influences of a joint sponsorship of rival teams on supporter attitudes and brand preferences', *Journal of Marketing Communications,* **12** (1) (2006), pp. 31–48.

Davies, Iain A., Ryals, Lynette J. and Holt, Sue: 'Relationship management: a sales role, or a state of mind? An investigation of functions and attitudes across a business-to-business sales force', *Industrial Marketing Management* **39** (7) (October 2010), pp. 1049–62.

Engel, James F., Warshaw, Martin R. and Kinnear, Thomas C.: *Promotional Strategy* (Chicago, Irwin, 1994).

Farris, P.W. and Buzzell, R.D.: 'Why advertising and promotional costs vary: some cross-sectional analyses', *Journal of Marketing* (Fall, 1979).

Hansen, Jochim, Strick, Madelijn, van Baaren, Rick B., Hooghuis, Mirjam and Wigboldus, Daniel H.: 'Exploring memory for product names advertised with humour', *Journal of Consumer Behaviour*, **8** (2/3) (Mar–Jun 2009), pp. 135–48.

Harris, Greg: 'International advertising: developmental and implementational issues', *Journal of Marketing Management*, **12** (1996), pp. 551–60.

Heffler, Mava: 'Making sure sponsorship meets all the parameters', *Brandweek* (May 1994), p. 16.

Herzberg, F.: *Work and Nature of Man* (London, William Collins, 1966).

Institute of Public Relations: *Public Relations Practice: Its Roles and Parameters* (London, The Institute of Public Relations, 1984).

Lacey, Russel, Sneath, Julie Z., Finney, Zachary R. and Close, Angeline G.: 'The impact of repeat attendance on event sponsorship effects', *Journal of Marketing Communications*, **13** (4) (2007), pp. 243–55.

Lambe, C. Jay, Webb, Kevin L. and Ishida, Chiharu: 'Self-managing selling teams and team performance: The complementary role of empowerment and control', *Industrial Marketing Management*, **38** (1) (January 2009), pp. 5–16.

Lings, Ian N. and Owen, Kate M.: 'Buying a sponsor's brand: the role of affective commitment to the sponsored team', *Journal of Marketing Management*, **23** (5/6) (2007), pp. 483–96.

Mantovani, G.: *New Communication Environments: From Everyday to Virtual* (London, Taylor & Francis, 1996).

Maslow, Abraham: *Motivation and Personality* (New York, Harper and Row, 1954).

Mason, Roger B. and Cochetel, Fabrice: 'Residual brand awareness following the termination of a long-term event sponsorship and the appointment of a new sponsor', *Journal of Marketing Communications*, **12** (2) (2006), pp. 125–44.

Mazzarol, Tim, Sweeney, Gillian C. and Soutar, Geoffrey N.: 'Conceptualising word-of-mouth activities, triggers and conditions: an exploratory study', *European Journal of Marketing*, **41** (11/12) (2007), pp. 1475–94.

McAlister, Leigh, Srinavasan, Raji and Kim, Minching: 'Advertising, research and development, and systematic risk of the firm', *Journal of Marketing*, **71** (1) (2007), pp. 35–45.

Meenaghan, J.A.: 'The role of sponsorship in the marketing communication mix', *International Journal of Advertising*, **10** (1) (1991), pp. 35–47.

Mintel: *Special Report on Sponsorship* (London, Mintel, 1990).

Mintel: *Special Report on Sponsorship* (London, Mintel, 1993).

Moran, W.T.: 'Insights from pricing research' in E.B. Bailey (ed.), *Pricing Practices and Strategies* (New York, The Conference Board, 1978), pp. 7 and 13.

Patti, Charles H.: 'Evaluating the role of advertising', *Journal of Advertising* (Fall, 1977), pp. 32–3.

Pieters, Rik and Wedel, Michel: 'Attention capture and transfer in advertising: brand, pictorial and text-size effects', *Journal of Marketing*, **68** (2) (April 2004), pp 36–50.

Rajagopal: 'Outsourcing salespeople in building arousal towards retail buying', *Journal of Database Marketing and Customer Strategy Management*, **15** (2) (2008), pp.106–18.

Ramaswamy, Sridhar N. and Singh, Jagdip: 'Antecedents and consequences of merit pay fairness for industrial salespeople', *Journal of Marketing*, **67** (4) (October 2003), pp. 46–66.

Ranganjaran, Deva, Chonko, Lawrence B., Jones, Eli and Roberts, James A.: 'Organisational variables, sales force perceptions of readiness for change, learning and performance among boundary-spanning teams: a conceptual framework and propositions for research', *Industrial Marketing Management*, **33** (4) (2004), pp. 289–305.

Rosengren, Sara and Dahlen, Micael: 'Brand-slogan matching in a cluttered environment', *Journal of Marketing Communication*, **12** (4) (2006), pp. 263–79.

Ryan, Annemarie and Blois, Keith: 'The emotional dimension of organizational work when cultural sponsorship relationships are dissolved', *Journal of Marketing Management*, **26** (7&8) (2010), pp. 612–34.

Stapel, J.: 'Monitoring advertising performance', *ADMAP* (July/August 1990).

Stapel, J.: 'Like the advertisement but does it interest me?' *ADMAP* (April 1991).

Stokburger-Sauer, Nicola E and Hoyer, Wayne D.: 'Consumer advisers revisited: What drives those with market mavenism and opinion leadership and why?' *Journal of Consumer Behaviour*, **8** (2/3) (Mar–Jun 2009), pp.100–15.

Varey, Richard: *Marketing Communications: A Critical Introduction* (London, Routledge, 2002).

Volkov, Michael, Harker, Michael and Harker, Debra: 'People who complain about advertising: the aficionados, guardians, activists and seekers', *Journal of Marketing Management*, **22** (3/4) (2006), pp. 379–405.

Westberg, Kate, Stavros, Constantino and Wilson, Bradley: 'The impact of degenerative episodes on the sponsorship B2B relationship: Implications for brand management', *Industrial Marketing Management*, **40** (4) (May 2011), pp. 603–11.

Yannopoulou, Natalia, Koronis, Epaminondas and Elliott, Richard: 'Media amplification of a brand crisis and its effect on brand trust', *Journal of Marketing Management*, **27** (5&6) (2011), pp. 530–46.

Yong, Liu: 'Word of mouth for movies: its dynamics and impact on box-office revenue', *Journal of Marketing*, **70** (3) (2006), pp. 74–9.

Zafer Erdogan, B. and Kitchen, P.J.: 'The interaction between advertising and sponsorship: uneasy alliance or strategic symbiosis?' *Proceedings of the 3rd Annual Conference of the Global Institute for Corporate and Marketing Communications*, Strathclyde Graduate Business School, 1998.

5

MARKET RESEARCH

Objectives

After reading this chapter you should be able to:

- Explain the difference between data and information
- Describe the research process
- Explain the difference between qualitative and quantitative research
- Explain the difference between primary and secondary research
- Develop a sampling frame for a given piece of research
- Design a suitable questionnaire
- Explain the importance of correct interview technique.

INTRODUCTION

There is considerable debate over the term 'market research'; many marketers believe that the term 'marketing research' is more appropriate. Market research is usually considered to be research into customer needs, wants and preferences; marketing research is sometimes used to describe all research carried out for the purpose of supporting marketing decisions. Whichever term is used, market research is concerned with the disciplined collection and evaluation of specific data in order to help suppliers understand their customers' needs better (Chisnall 1992).

HSBC Private Banking

The Hong Kong and Shanghai Banking Corporation started out (not surprisingly) in China, but was founded by British bankers to provide finance for the Hong Kong colonies and British business in the Far East. In the intervening 150 years the company has taken over other banks and has become a global brand. From 1998 the company rebranded all its 'local' banks in each country as HSBC – over night, the bank became a global brand.

HSBC brands itself as the world's local bank. With branches worldwide, this is no idle boast; the company prides itself on knowing its individual markets and with understanding local cultural issues.

When HSBC wanted to launch a new private bank venture in India, market research played a vital role. India is a very large market – although the country is often portrayed as poor, there are over 200 million people who would fit into the 'middle class' category, and more millionaires than there are in the UK or even the USA. Tapping into this market was the aim of HSBC Private Banking, and establishing and maintaining relationships with this wealthier group was crucial to the success of the new venture.

Using the image of a butterfly emerging from an egg, HSBC advised customers 'Assume nothing'. This striking image helped put the bank into the forefront of customers' minds.

Chris Meares, Chief Executive Officer, Group Private Banking, HSBC

Watch the video clip, then try to answer the following questions. The answers are on the companion website.

Questions

1 What is the importance of market research for HSBC Private Banking?

2 What research methods might be most appropriate for the bank?

3 How does the company's product offering benefit directly from research?

THE NEED FOR MARKET RESEARCH

Market research is the process of collecting, analysing and presenting useful information about consumers. Marketing research also encompasses more general research into markets, which includes competitive activities and also environmental issues such as government activities and economic shifts. The ability to measure marketing performance has a significant positive impact on firm performance, profitability, stock market valuation and (of course) the status of marketing within the organisation (O'Sullivan and Abela 2007).

The first question any marketer should ask before embarking on a research exercise is whether the information gained will be worth more than the cost of collecting it. Market research can represent a substantial investment in both time and money terms; in some cases it is undoubtedly cheaper simply to go ahead with the project without carrying out any research at all. For example, if the total cost of sending out a mailing is less than £10,000, but research into finding out whether or not it would be effective would cost £12,000, it is obviously better not to do the research. More subtly, if the managers feel that the risk of the mailshot failing altogether is low, they may still not run the research even if it is much cheaper. If, for example, the management estimated the risk of failure at only 10%, the value of the research would be only £1000. Therefore it might not be worthwhile carrying out research even if the cost of it were, say, £3000.

In general, however, it is not wise to embark on a major commitment (such as launching a new product) without carrying out some market research beforehand. The vast majority of new products fail (see Chapter 6), and this is usually because consumers do not think that the product is worth the money. Good market research will reduce the risk of this happening, and it has been said (wisely) that those who find research expensive should think about what ignorance would cost.

Types of research that are carried out by marketers are as follows:

- Customer research
- Promotion research
- Product research
- Distribution research
- Sales research
- Marketing environment research.

Customer research is intended to produce facts about markets and market segments; it provides information about where customers live, what they do with their time, what their motivations are, what they like to spend money on and what their spending power is, and what the trends are in the market.

Promotion research measures the success of promotions in terms of their objectives. It relies on careful planning of objectives (see Chapter 9) but can provide information about the suitability of the approach used in reaching a target audience.

Research is also useful for determining which media should be used; since promotion in general, and advertising in particular, tends to be expensive it is important that the effort is not squandered on advertising in the wrong place.

Product research is used to identify new uses for existing products or to identify needs for new products. Product research is often used to refine the design of an existing product to produce an improved 'Mark 2' version.

Distribution research is concerned with finding the best channels of distribution for a product; often it overlaps with consumer research, since the location of retail outlets will depend on where the target consumers live and on their habits. For example, many DIY products are distributed through edge-of-town outlets, which means that only those consumers with cars will be able to reach the store and buy the product. This will not matter if the product is an automotive one, but may matter if it is a product for elderly people, who may not own cars (or who may perhaps prefer not to drive).

Sales research is intended to help the sales management process by ensuring that territories are of equal size or value, that the techniques and approaches being used are effective, that the training of the salesforce is appropriate and sufficient and that salesforce motivation is appropriate (see Chapter 9).

Finally, **marketing environment research** examines aspects of the micro- and macro-environments (see Chapter 2). The purpose of the exercise is to ensure that the firm can anticipate environmental change and develop responses in advance.

Very often research can be carried out fairly quickly and cheaply, since much of the information needed will probably already exist, either in published form or within the company's own records. Often the company records contain a great deal of useful **data**, or raw facts; analysis of those facts will turn it into usable **information**. The data items themselves are worthless until there has been some kind of thoughtful analysis to convert them to information. Data mining is an important component of database marketing, in which the database drives everything the company does. Provided the entire company (from invoicing department to shipping) uses the same database, all the information about the customer can be collated to form a complete picture. This information might range from whether the customer is a good payer through to whether they prefer deliveries on Wednesdays – all the data on the customer is likely to prove useful to someone in the company at some time.

Marketing information systems are often set up to provide an automatic flow of data into the firm, with systems for regular analysis of the data. Often these systems can be set up to collect data from anywhere in the firm (for example, from salespeople's laptops) so that the firm's IT systems can collate information from several sources. There is always a trade-off involved between the value of information and the cost in time, effort and money of obtaining it; by reducing the cost element, computers have increased the possibilities for obtaining useful data and converting it into usable information. **Decision support systems** can be fully automated; an example is the electronic point-of-sale (EPOS) systems used by large retailers. These record every purchase made in the store so that the retailer can reorder stock in the correct amounts, can automatically analyse trends and can even (with the use of loyalty cards) track an individual customer's purchases over a period of time.

Decision support systems need to be user-friendly so that managers without training in data analysis can use them.

THE RESEARCH PROCESS

The purpose of the research is to collect data (and sometimes information) and process it into usable information that can be used to make management decisions. The first stage in any research process is to define the problem and set objectives. Figure 5.1 shows the research process.

After setting the objectives, the process of collecting the data can begin. Data can be collected from either primary research sources or secondary research sources. Primary sources are original research: questionnaires, interviews, experiments or product tests with consumers. Secondary research (also called *desk research*) comes from already published information in journals, newspapers, commercially published market research, government statistics, directories, yearbooks, CD-ROM databases, the Internet and other published materials. Secondary data are, in effect, second-hand data.

Normally it is sensible to begin the research process by looking at secondary sources. The reasons for this are as follows:

- It is always cheaper
- It is always quicker
- Sometimes all the necessary information for making the decision has already been published and is available
- Even when the published information is incomplete, the researchers will only have to fill in the gaps with primary research rather than gather all the information first-hand.

Figure 5.1 The market research process

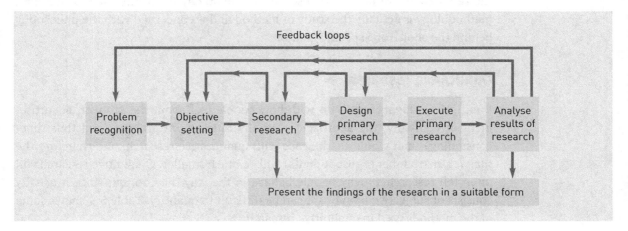

Secondary research will not necessarily tell the researchers everything they need to know. For example, if the company is planning to launch a new solar-powered mobile telephone there is unlikely to be research already available on solar-powered mobile telephones. There will probably be research on mobile telephone use and ownership, on environment-friendly consumers and on solar power, so all these sources should be examined first. This will, at the very least, help with the design of the primary research.

The other main drawbacks with secondary research are that it is often out of date and that it can be hard for the researcher to be confident of its accuracy since it is often published without giving details of the methods used in its collection. This is particularly the case with Internet sources, which are notoriously unreliable; there is nothing to stop anyone publishing anything on the Internet, whether it is true or false, and in the absence of any kind of checking there have certainly been some highly biased statements and faked 'research' published. Researchers therefore need to exercise some caution, but that certainly does not mean that secondary sources should be ignored.

Having completed the search for secondary data, it is possible to design the primary research. This will involve deciding: (a) what gaps there are, in terms of the objectives and what is known from the secondary sources; (b) who we need to approach to get the information; and (c) the methods to be used.

Deciding what we need to find out from the primary research means comparing what the secondary research says with the objectives that were originally set. Where information is lacking, the researchers need to decide how to find it out, and who would have the information.

APPROACHING RESPONDENTS

Respondents are the subjects of research – the people whose behaviour and opinion are of interest to the researchers. The *methodology* will depend on what the researchers are hoping to discover. Methodology is not the same as method; methodology is actually the study of method and is concerned with the philosophy behind the choice of a specific method.

Qualitative research

Qualitative research is to do with how people feel about the product, advertisement or company; the approach is usually much more probing (and thus time-consuming) than would be the case with quantitative research, and therefore the *sample size* (number of respondents) will be much smaller. Qualitative research will often tell researchers why people behave in the way they do, but since it usually consists of subjective opinions it can be difficult to quantify. Table 5.1 shows some of the methods used in qualitative research.

Table 5.1 Qualitative methods

Method	Explanation
Group depth interview or focus group	A group of six or eight people is recruited and invited to talk about the subject. This method tends to produce a wide range of opinion, because each member of the group will 'trigger' the other members to think of things to say. On the other hand, group pressure may mean that only the most talkative respondents' views are expressed.
Exploratory groups	A type of focus group used at the initial stages of market research to find the dimensions of the problem. Dimensions are the factors which are of interest to respondents about a particular marketing issue. Exploratory groups usually consist of a cross-section of potential consumers.
Clinical focus groups	On some issues, respondents' attitudes may be hidden below the conscious level. These groups are used in a clinical setting where the researcher can judge whether the person's true feelings are being expressed, so such groups are often video-recorded so that facial expressions and body language can be analysed.
Experiencing focus groups	These groups are homogeneous (i.e. composed of similar people), and allow the researcher to gauge the feelings of a group of actual customers for the product category under consideration. Such groups might be asked to interact with a product – for example, to feel samples of material. Experiments show that people respond better to such experiments if they are also given verbal information (D'Astous and Kamau 2010).
Teleconferencing	Teleconferencing involves a group discussion conducted over the telephone or using Skype. Similar to a focus group, this avoids the necessity of bringing people together physically and also can make people feel easier about expressing themselves. The technique is particularly useful for focus groups involving managers in industry.
Video-conferencing	Like teleconferencing, but with vision. This has the major advantage of allowing the researcher to see people's facial reactions, which often say more about a person's true feelings than do words. VOIP (Voice Over Internet Protocol) systems such as Skype have made this method very much easier.
Depth interviews	Usually carried out by highly trained interviewers or psychologists, the depth interview uses probing questions to uncover the respondent's deepest feelings.
Projective techniques	Subjects are presented with ambiguous, unstructured situations and invited to respond. Because the situation is unclear, the respondents must use their imaginations to respond, in the course of which their own true feelings will be revealed. Projective techniques are used when a direct response might be embarrassing for the respondent.
Word association	A projective technique in which the respondent is asked to say the first thing that comes to mind when the researcher says a particular word. The theory is that the respondent does not have time to censor his or her response, so that the respondent's true feelings are revealed.
Cartoon tests	Another projective technique; the respondent is shown a cartoon and asked to supply the captions for it. The respondent will actually put his or her true feelings down; since it is only a cartoon, no blame can attach to the respondent for what the characters are 'saying'.

Table 5.1 continued

Method	Explanation
Third-person techniques	This projective technique is simple to apply: the respondent is asked what he or she thinks another person ('your neighbour' or 'most people') would say or do in a given situation. The respondent would typically give their own opinion as if it were that of the third person.
Analogy	Here the respondent's personality is linked to a prospective purchase. For example, the respondent might be asked to imagine what it would be like to actually be a new BMW car. The respondent might say 'I feel powerful' or 'I feel ready for my new executive owner' (Proctor 2000). Analogies help marketers develop communications strategies targeted at specific groups of consumers.
Experimentation	Respondents are invited to do something or are shown an item and their responses are monitored. For example, Goodyear Tire and Rubber Company used a virtual shopping computer simulation to examine brand equity issues (Burke 1996).
Observation	The researcher watches the consumers and notes their behaviour. For example, a researcher might stand outside a shopping mall and count how many people go in. At one time, Fisher Price, the toy manufacturer, ran a free crèche in Chicago and gave the children prototype toys to play with to see which ones the children liked best and how they played with the toys (Stewart 1989).
Virtual focus group	Here respondents are recruited for an online chatroom to discuss the subject of interest. This technique has the great advantage that people can respond from their home or workplace, which means they can be recruited from anywhere in the world if need be. Also, they do not have to be online at the same time – the focus group can run for days or weeks if necessary. Third, a degree of anonymity can be preserved. Finally, analysis is made much easier because there is no need to prepare a transcript – the responses are already written down.

It is not unusual to carry out qualitative research before designing a quantitative study to find out the dimensions of the problem; the researcher might then carry out a questionnaire-type survey to find out how many people agree with the statements made in the qualitative study. Because of the cost and time involved, there has been a movement away from this extensive approach, however, and much more research is being done using qualitative methods only.

Quantitative research

Quantitative research methodology deals with areas that can be expressed in numbers. It will tell researchers, for example, what proportion of the population drinks tea in the mornings and what their ages and occupations are; what it will not do very easily is tell researchers why those people prefer tea to coffee.

Surveys

Most people have at some time or other been asked to participate in a survey, and this method remains the commonest method of collecting quantitative data.

Surveys can elicit facts about the respondent's behaviour and possessions, can find out opinions about issues and ideas and can sometimes elicit interpretations of the respondent's actions or opinions. Table 5.2 shows some survey techniques.

A major problem with any survey lies in ensuring that the right questions are asked and that they are asked in the right way. A typical questionnaire would ask respondents about their behaviour and attitudes and about themselves; this is important for classification purposes. Obviously the researcher will be unable to say '25% of 25–35-year-olds buy beer at least twice a week' if the questionnaire did not ask the respondents their age, but most questionnaires would need to contain much more detail about the respondents. The questions about the respondents themselves must be discreet as well as relevant, and this requires considerable skill on the part of the researcher in deciding what might or might not be relevant to the study at hand.

Questionnaire design can be a lengthy process for this reason. The criteria for writing survey questions are as follows:

- Questions need to be short, simple and unambiguous
- Questions should not be leading – in other words, they should not direct the respondent towards a particular answer
- The questionnaire's introduction should be persuasive and must qualify the respondent as belonging in the sample
- The answers must be capable of analysis, preferably by computer
- Questions must be necessary and relevant to the study
- The respondent must have the information needed to answer the question
- Respondents must be willing to answer the questions. If the questions get too personal, people will not respond
- Questions must be specific. Avoid asking two questions at once, e.g. 'Was your holiday pleasant and good value for money?' Holidays can be pleasant without being good value
- Hypothetical questions should be avoided; they require guesswork on the part of respondents and also can rarely be worded in such a way that respondents have enough information to answer.

Even experienced researchers have difficulty in writing effective questionnaires; what is a clear and obvious question to one person may have a different meaning to another, so it is usually a good idea to **pilot** all questionnaires. This means testing the first draft of the questionnaire by asking a group of typical respondents to fill it in, then analysing the results. Often (in fact, usually) this process will highlight errors in the design; these can be corrected before the finished version is used on the overall sample of respondents. If several errors are detected at the pilot stage, it may be worth considering piloting a second time; many surveys have been run only to find that there is a major ambiguity in one or more questions, invalidating the entire project.

Table 5.2 Survey techniques

Method	Explanation
Postal surveys	Questionnaires sent to respondents through the mail. Respondents fill in the answers and mail the survey back. They have the advantages of being cheap, of avoiding interviewer bias and of being capable of containing questions on a broad range of issues. They have the disadvantages of (typically) having a low response rate, of not allowing the researcher control over the respondent and of the possibility of someone other than the addressee (e.g. a secretary or assistant) filling in the replies.
Personal structured interviews	Here the researcher goes through the questions face-to-face with the respondent. This technique is more expensive than a postal survey, but gives the researcher control over the process (e.g. the order in which questions are asked and answered). The cost is high and the refusal rate (the proportion of people who refuse to participate) is also high.
Telephone surveys	Here the questionnaire is administered over the telephone. This has the advantage of being quick and cheap, with a high response rate, while still allowing the researcher to control the process. The disadvantage is that respondents sometimes suspect that they are about to be subjected to an unwanted sales pitch and the list of telephone numbers may be out of date. In the UK, people can opt out of inclusion on telephone lists by registering with the Telephone Preference Service, which means that a large number of potential respondents have been removed from the system.
Self-administered surveys (feedback cards)	This method is often used in service industries such as hotels and restaurants. Questionnaires are left for customers to fill in and put into a box or mail back. The major drawback of this method is that not all customers will fill in the survey; only those who are exceptionally pleased or exceptionally disappointed are likely to fill them in, so the management will get a distorted picture of the customer satisfaction levels. Managers would be well advised to treat any comment other than 'excellent' as a complaint.
Panels	A panel is a group of respondents who regularly respond to surveys and are usually paid for participating. Some panels are set up on a permanent basis and are often made available to researchers by commercial market research companies. Sometimes panels are used by a group of firms to carry out research which is syndicated to the group. Panels are expensive to set up, but are relatively cheap to run and have the major advantage of offering a very high response rate.
Omnibus studies	Omnibus surveys are usually carried out by commercial market research agencies who combine several studies into one questionnaire. This reduces the cost for each client and ultimately reduces effort for respondents since they will need to give their personal details only once. For an omnibus survey, respondents will be asked about several unrelated topics; the questionnaires tend to be somewhat long and arduous to complete so respondents are often rewarded with a small gift.
Online surveys	Several online survey systems exist (surveymonkey, for example). Researchers can post their questionnaires on the site, then direct respondents to it. The major advantage is that analysis can be conducted virtually instantly; the main disadvantage is ensuring that the sample is representative, though of course this is a problem with all surveys.

Critical thinking

This is all very well, but how do we know people are telling us the truth? Even if they want to, might they not misunderstand the question or have something else on their minds? People often tell lies, especially if they are confronted with something embarrassing – and in any case, almost all of us like to appear in a good light.

Furthermore, there is the widespread view that a nosy question deserves a lying answer – people might appear to be cooperating, but instead will deliberately mislead us. And if that's the case, how can any research be worthwhile?

Sampling

Sampling means choosing who to ask. It is usually not feasible or necessary to ask everybody in the target market to give an opinion on a given issue, but it is important to ask enough of the right type of people to ensure that the data we get are reasonably representative of the market as a whole. In some cases sampling can be very simple; if we want to know what were the key factors in making a purchase, we could arrange for a simple questionnaire to be taken at the point of sale – in other words ask people to provide us with their main reasons for buying while they are still in the shop.

Finding the right mix of respondents is important because the researcher is attempting to draw conclusions about the target market as a whole; for some surveys, less than 100 respondents' opinions would be solicited to draw conclusions about consumers numbering in the millions. This means that a small sampling error will be multiplied many times when the analysis takes place. In general, the bigger the sample the less likely that there will be **sampling bias**, particularly if the survey is intended to find out the opinions of a small minority of the population.

The **sampling frame** is the list of possible respondents from whom the researcher wishes to draw a **sample**. In some cases this list will be available; for example, if a researcher wants to sample the opinions of doctors, it is possible to obtain a list of names and addresses for every doctor in the country. It would then be relatively simple to construct a sample from the list. It is more likely, though, that the list the researcher wants is unavailable; for example, a list of people who have played squash in the past 3 months probably does not exist. In those circumstances the researcher would have to construct a representative sample of individuals with the required characteristics. This can be a difficult task (Mouncey 1996).

Table 5.3 shows some sampling methods.

Recently there has been a move away from probability sampling towards quota sampling and a growing use of databases for sampling (Cowan 1991). The reasons for this are that quota sampling is easier and more reliable, and databases provide a quick and easy way of sampling for postal questionnaires.

Table 5.3 Sampling methods

Sampling method	Description	Advantages	Disadvantages
Random sample or probability sample	Each individual in the population at large has an equal chance of being included in the sample.	Will give a clear cross-section of the population.	Almost impossible to achieve. Most so-called 'random' samples are seriously biased; for example, choosing names from the telephone book might seem 'random', but in fact only people with landline telephones will be included and, even then, those who are ex-directory will not be included.
Quota sample	An analysis of the population is undertaken first, often from census data. Then a quota for each category (e.g. women aged 35, men aged 20, middle-aged professionals) is drawn up and interviewers are told to fill the quota.	Will produce a clear cross-section of opinion, provided the basis for the quota is correctly set.	Often means that interviewers are rejecting respondents because they do not fit the quota, and towards the end of the day the interviewers might be spending a lot of time looking for that last 35-year-old manual worker with two children.
Stratified sample	Similar to quota sampling in that broad bands of the population are specified, but the final choice of respondent is almost taken by chance.	Less waste of respondents than quota sampling, more flexibility for interviewers and therefore cheaper.	Not as accurate as quota sampling.

Interview technique

When conducting interviews, it is all too easy for the interviewer to 'lead' the respondents into making the 'right' statements. Sometimes respondents will encourage this by asking questions themselves; good interviewers will avoid the temptation to step in and help at this point.

Some ways to avoid this are to use statements such as, 'Well, it's your opinion that's important. What do you think?' or perhaps just to give a questioning look. It is also advisable to explain to the respondents beforehand that you will not be able to help them with the answers.

In the case of a focus group or group depth interview, there is a problem in judging whether to let a particular line of conversation continue or not. What may at first appear to be an entirely irrelevant digression from the subject may eventually turn round and produce something very insightful; on the other hand, if the interview degenerates into a general chat nothing useful will arise. The moderator could ask how the topic relates to the subject of the research. This will sometimes produce a quick explanation of the relationship or otherwise a quick return to the point of discussion.

In practice, groups usually do keep to the subject at hand; digressions are few and usually short-lived.

Sources of bias

Bias is the effect whereby the results of a survey are rendered unreliable by some external force. The commonest sources are sampling bias and interviewer bias.

Sampling bias

This results from taking a sample that is not representative of the population we wish to study. It is easy to fall into the trap of thinking that the sample is representative, when in fact it has been drawn from a small population. For example, a researcher might carry out a survey in a high street, stopping every third shopper. This survey will not be representative, since it includes only those who shop on that high street on that day. A survey of this type undertaken on a Tuesday afternoon, for example, might include a higher proportion of pensioners and unemployed people than there are in the population at large. A similar survey undertaken on a Saturday afternoon might exclude most sports fans. Sample bias is common and difficult to avoid.

Interviewer bias

Interviewers naturally want to get through the questionnaire with the minimum of problems and they are also acutely aware that the respondent probably has better things to do than answer awkward or badly phrased questions. If the interviewer finds that respondents are showing a negative reaction to some questions, he or she might skip past those questions in future and 'guess' the answers or might try to 'help' respondents formulate their answers. Sadly, it has been known for some unscrupulous interviewers to fake the answers altogether if they are having difficulty in finding enough respondents to fill the quota (Kieker and Nelson 1996).

Interviewer bias can be subtle; in one-to-one open-ended interviews the interviewer's body language (facial expressions, movements, etc.) can convey a message to the respondent that leads to a specific answer being given or to some information being withheld. Likewise, people tend to answer differently when the interviewer is male rather than female or older rather than younger.

ANALYSING THE RESULTS

Analysis has three distinct stages: editing, which means discarding any inconsistent or spoiled responses; tabulating, which means totalling the various responses and cross-tabulating them; and interpreting, which means saying what the figures mean.

Qualitative data analysis

Until relatively recently the analysis of *qualitative data* was heavily reliant on the judgement of the researcher. The traditional approach has been to make transcripts of recordings made during focus groups or depth interviews and then make an overall judgement of the views expressed using quotes to support the argument. This approach has been criticised on the grounds that it lacks the rigour of quantitative methods.

With the widespread use of computers, programs have become available for the analysis of qualitative data. Programs are available to carry out the following operations:

- Find individual words or phrases. Having decided which are the key phrases or words that are significant in the study, the researcher can tell the computer to find and count such words and phrases.

- Create *indexes* to show where and in what context the words and phrases have been used. Rather like a book index, this allows the researcher to attribute phrases to types of individual.

- Attach key words or codes to segments of text. Sometimes respondents will be talking about a particular issue without using the actual words that the researcher believes are the key ones. Some programs allow the researcher to add relevant codes and key words to identify subject areas in the text.

- Connecting the categories. This allows the researcher to see whether some types of statement are associated with other types of statement; for example, whether those respondents who make politically right-wing comments also prefer powerful cars.

Table 5.4 gives some examples of computer programs for analysis of qualitative data. The list is by no means exhaustive; there are many other programs available to help in qualitative analysis and more are being developed. Such programs can only help take the tedium out of the analysis; they will not do the thinking for the researcher and a great deal of judgement is still needed in qualitative analysis (Catterall and Maclaran 1995).

Presentation of the data is not numeric. It is not appropriate to ascribe percentages to the comments made, since the sample used is small and the process of ascribing key words and codes to the data is not precise. Typically, qualitative data analysis results in a set of **matrices**, or a **network**. A matrix is the cross-tabulation of two lists, set up as rows and columns; a network is a diagram showing the relationship between concepts.

For example, a *tree* **taxonomy** is a network showing how concepts relate; it is rather like a family tree. A tree taxonomy for eating out is shown in Figure 5.2.

The final stage in qualitative analysis is to interpret the findings into something usable by managers. Again, this requires a degree of judgement on the part of

Table 5.4 Analysis tools for qualitative data

Program	Description
QSR NUD*IST	Indexes, searches and supports theorising; will handle text or non-textual records such as photographs and tape recordings. Connects categories and is good at generating taxonomies (see below).
QUALPRO	Researcher has to segment and code, then QUALPRO will find and assemble the indicated segments.
ETHNOGRAPH	Does what QUALPRO does but can also find text that has been coded two or more ways.
WEFT QDA	This is free software which can code and retrieve text, conduct simple statistical analysis and can use Boolean logic to search and code materials.

the researcher and (in common with quantitative analysis) researchers can usually only draw inferences about what is probably happening, rather than make
categorical statements about what is happening. For this reason, most market
research reports tend to be lengthy and contain details on the reasoning behind
the statements made.

Figure 5.2 Tree taxonomy for eating out

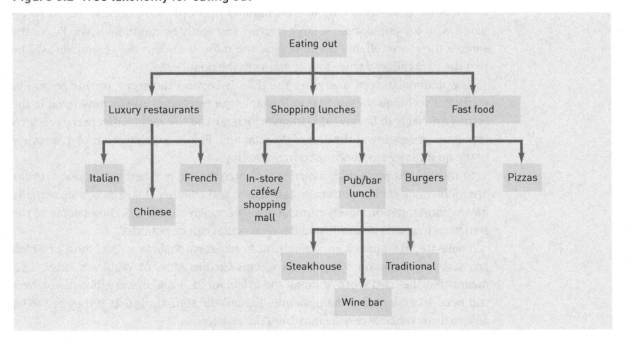

Critical thinking

If so much of this research analysis depends on judgement, what's the point? We might as well just sit down and make it up, might we not? Turning everything into numbers might seem very scientific, but what happens if the basis for the calculations starts from the wrong place?

Maybe, though, just going through the process helps to focus our thinking. Is it the formal process that is important, then, or the results?

Quantitative data analysis

Quantitative data analysis follows the editing, tabulating and interpreting format described earlier. Putting the data into tables needs to be considered at the design stage of the research; projects have been known to collapse because the questionnaire proved impossible to analyse. Normally the data would be cross-tabulated so that the researcher can identify which type of respondent gives each type of answer. For example, research into soft drink consumption might show that 40% of the respondents buy soft drinks at least four times a week and 5% buy soft drinks every day. The researcher would now need to identify which of the respondents do this and what else they have in common. Are they all young? What are their incomes? Which newspapers and magazines do they read? This enables the marketers to target that segment of the market.

One of the problems of quantitative analysis is determining how reliable the information is. Because only a small number of people have been surveyed (compared with the population at large), errors can easily be multiplied. The larger the sample the more reliable it will be and the more confident the researcher will be that the data reflect a true state of affairs in the population.

The mathematics of analysing the data is beyond the scope of this book, but statistical techniques exist that will enable the researcher to say how reliable the results are likely to be, and also to say which are the relevant factors in the research (see Further reading at the end of the chapter). Figure 5.3 shows a broad overview of the quantitative methods used in marketing.

Statistical testing should, if carried out correctly, tell us whether this year's results are following a similar pattern to last year's, and whether this relationship actually means something or merely came about by accident. Table 5.5 shows some of the statistical methods available and the results that can be obtained.

There are, of course, a great many more statistical tools available, most of which are easily available on computer programs such as SPSS or Windows Excel. This means that the hard work of doing the calculations is taken away, but researchers still need to understand the principles behind the statistical tools if they are to be able to draw sensible conclusions from the answers.

Figure 5.3 Statistical methods chart: PERT, program evaluation and review technique; CPM, critical path method

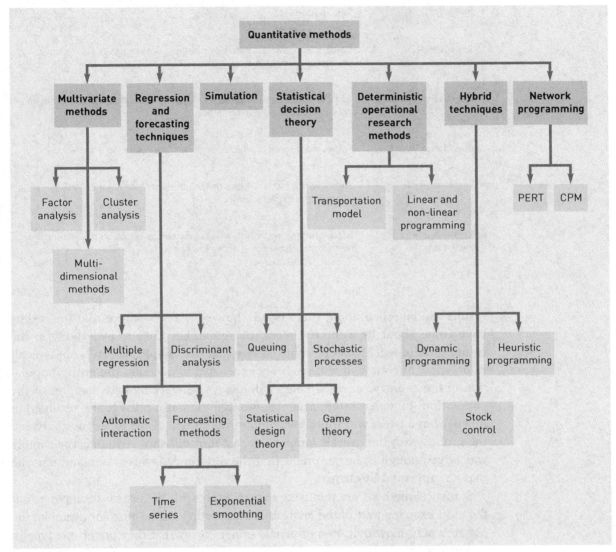

Source: Adapted from Meidan, 1987

For example, a researcher might have surveyed 100 people to find out how many of them would be prepared to buy a new brand of beer. The researcher finds that 42% of them, having tasted the beer, say that they would buy the beer and, on looking at the results for those people, it turns out that three-quarters of them are manual workers. This seems to show that manual workers are much more likely to try the beer than are white-collar workers, but it is possible that the researcher just happened to ask an unusual group of manual workers, and that most manual workers in the population at large would stay loyal to their current brand of beer.

A *t*-test might show that the results of the survey are significant at the 95% confidence interval. This means that the researcher is 95% confident that the

Table 5.5 Common statistical methods

Statistical method	Explanation
Exponential smoothing	Detects trends in the data by smoothing out the peaks and troughs. Gives more weight to recent data.
Regression analysis	Compares one set of data with another to show whether a trend in one set relates to a trend in the other.
Correlation	Shows the degree to which one set of data relates to another.
Factor analysis	Shows which factors relate to each other by relating them to a set of (theoretical) extra factors.
Significance testing, e.g. t-tests	Tests whether the results of a survey can be relied on or whether they could simply have come about by chance.

results can be relied upon; there is still, however, a 5% chance that the results have come about by a fluke. Unless the researcher talks to everybody in the country, there will always be some chance that the sample chosen is not typical; in practice, of course, it is impossibly expensive to question the entire population of the country, so researchers will always be working with samples of the population. In general, the larger the sample the more reliable the results, but this is what a t-test will show. By comparing the size of the difference between the groups with the overall sample size, a t-test will show whether the sample was large enough to be confident that the difference is a real one and not one that has appeared by chance.

Statistical methods are relatively easy to apply with the use of a computer, but the most exacting part of the analysis is interpreting the results. For example, the research may show that 40% of people under 35 say that they prefer one type of washing powder to another. This is an interesting piece of information but it still begs the question of why this should be so. Often research of this nature generates as many questions as it answers and the researchers may find themselves going back to the beginning and redesigning the research to answer a different set of questions. Usually, qualitative research is more useful than quantitative research in finding out why people behave the way they do.

Overall, market research is not a simple proposition. There are many pitfalls for the unwary, but the alternative is almost always worse; examples abound of companies who failed to carry out appropriate market research, launched their products and lost millions before their mistakes could be corrected. Because of the subjective nature of consumer behaviour, no market research is ever going to be fully accurate, but good research will always improve the marketer's 'batting average'.

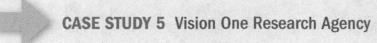

CASE STUDY 5 Vision One Research Agency

Vision One is a commercial market research agency based in Camden Town, London. The agency was founded in 1999 by Tony Lewis, whose career thus far had involved working for First Choice Holidays as market research manager and Lyons Tetley as research manager. The company's clients include major firms such as Virgin Megastores, Nikon, Austin Reed and Marks & Spencer.

Vision One offer a very wide range of services, especially considering the small size of the agency. The firm offers qualitative research, including focus groups, depth interviewing and ethnographic research (which involves observing people's behaviour in real situations). Perhaps most interestingly, Vision One can offer eye-tracking technology, which is a method of recording people's eye movements when they are confronted with stimuli. Quantitative research is carried out both through traditional pen-and-paper surveys and through web-based and e-mail surveys.

The firm has developed considerable expertise in retail market research based around its eye-tracking system. Respondents are asked to wear a lightweight headset which records their eye movements as they move around the retail store. Analysis of the recording reveals which products are most eye-catching, how long the respondent spends looking at a particular product or display stand and how the eye tracks in finding products. One of the big advantages of eye-tracking is that it includes unconscious behaviour – people are not always aware of what they find eye-catching and interesting or may not be prepared to admit to it, but the eye-tracking system will determine exactly what the respondent shows most interest in. The implications for packaging design, display lay-outs and product design are obvious, and clearly this is a very powerful tool for carrying out direct research.

Eye-tracking can also be used in a clinical environment. For example, respondents might be shown a series of advertisements while the eye-tracker is focused on them. The eye-tracker will reveal which advertisements are the most stimulating; this is a considerable advance on the old method of asking respondents which adverts they can recall or which brands they remember from the adverts.

Ultimately, eye-tracking can only be a part of the research programme – knowing what people do is one thing, knowing why they do it is quite another, and that's where a full-service agency like Vision One scores. The agency is able to use a wide range of methods to triangulate on the problem – in other words, the same research question can be analysed using several different approaches and the results compared. For Vision One, eye-tracking is only one of many tools in the box.

Questions

1 Why might it be difficult simply to ask people which products and displays they found most interesting?

2 How might companies use the information from eye-tracking to improve their packaging?

3 What other research methods could be used in conjunction with eye-tracking?

4 What are the potential pitfalls of using eye-tracking?

5 Why not use projective techniques instead?

SUMMARY

Market research is the starting point of marketing planning since it focuses on the needs of the customer and provides information that supports decisions designed to meet those needs. Without good information systems, the marketing planning and strategy activities have little hope of success and will almost always focus on the beliefs of the senior management, which may bear no relationship to the real needs of customers.

Here are the key points from this chapter:

- Data (raw facts) are useless until analysed and interpreted
- Secondary research should always be conducted before embarking on primary research
- Self-completion questionnaires need to be simple and unambiguous
- All questionnaires should be piloted at least once
- Careful training is needed to avoid interviewer bias
- Quantitative research is about the how and the what; qualitative research is about the why
- Market research is never 100% reliable.

CHAPTER QUESTIONS

1 What steps would you take to research the market for a new computer game?

2 Questionnaires can sometimes be ambiguous or ask irrelevant questions. How can these sources of error be reduced?

3 What can be done to overcome interviewer bias?

4 Under what circumstances would qualitative research be more appropriate than quantitative research?

5 What are the main drawbacks of questionnaires?

6 What type of focus group would be best suited to an investigation of working women's food shopping habits?

Further reading

Interpreting Qualitative Data: Methods for Analysing Talk, Text and Interaction by **David Silverman** (London, Sage, 2006) has a very clear, comprehensive approach to the often-difficult subject of analysing qualitative data.

Essentials of Marketing Research, **3rd edn, by Tony Proctor** (Harlow, Financial Times Prentice Hall, 2005) gives a concise yet comprehensive guide to marketing research techniques. In particular, Chapter 10 gives a straightforward guide to data analysis and the mathematical tools used by market researchers.

Contemporary Marketing Research, 8th edn, by Carl McDaniel and Roger Taylor (John Wiley and Sons, 2009) is a comprehensive American text with a wealth of examples. The explanations are clear and the examples are realistic, although the whole book is geared to a US audience.

References

Burke, R.R.: 'Virtual shopping; breakthrough in marketing research', *Harvard Business Review* (March–April, 1996), p. 120.

Catterall, M. and Maclaran, P.: 'Using a computer to code qualitative data', Proceedings of the 1995 Annual Conference of the Marketing Education Group 'Making Marketing Work', Bradford University, July 1995, pp. 133–42.

Chisnall, P.: *Marketing Research*, 4th edn (Maidenhead, McGraw-Hill, 1992).

Cowan, Charles D.: 'Using multiple sample frames to improve survey coverage, quality and costs', *Marketing Research* (December 1991), pp. 66–9.

D'Astous, Alain, and Kamau, Estelle: 'Consumer product evaluation based on tactical sensory information', *Journal of Consumer Behaviour*, **9** (3) (2010), pp. 206–13.

Kieker, P. and Nelson, J.E.: 'Do interviewers follow telephone survey instructions?' *Journal of the Market Research Society* (April 1996), pp. 161–76.

Meidan, A.: 'Quantitative methods in marketing', in M.J. Baker (ed.) *The Marketing Book* (London, Heinemann/Chartered Institute of Marketing, 1987).

Mouncey, Peter: 'With growing demands for data, will purity prove only theoretical?' *Research Plus* (May 1996), p. 9.

O'Sullivan, Don and Abela, Andrew V.: 'Marketing performance measurement ability and firm performance', *Journal of Marketing*, **71** (2) (2007), pp. 79–93.

Proctor, Tony: *Essentials of Marketing Research*, 2nd edn (Harlow, Financial Times Prentice Hall, 2000).

Stewart, Doug: 'In the cut-throat world of toy sales, child's play is serious business', *Smithsonian* (December 1989), pp. 76–8.

St Paul's Cathedral

St Paul's Cathedral is an icon of London. Built just after the Great Fire of London, it is a major tourist attraction based at the heart of London's financial district. At the same time it is a working church, with a congregation and regular religious services. Around 700,000 visitors a year visit St Paul's, about 75% of whom come from overseas, but it still needs £5.5 million a year to keep its doors open.

St Paul's, as a religious monument, is a non-profit organisation. It is primarily a place of worship, and the Dean and Chapter welcome anybody to come in, but equally the church needs contributions, so entrance charges are levied for visiting some parts of the building. This is regarded as a compromise between free access for Christian worshippers and others, and the need for finance. No one has to pay to come to a service, since this would conflict with the church's primary purpose, and some people object strongly to having to pay to go into a church.

Reconciling the needs of visitors and the needs of the church is only part of the problem – meeting the needs of people who may only be in London for a short visit while at the same time remaining competitive with other major attractions in London (of which there are many, spread out over a large city). The fact that the cathedral has been there for nearly 350 years is, paradoxically, not helpful – people can always come back next year, or in another 50 years, and the cathedral will still be there.

Canon Precentor Lucy Winkett

Watch the video clip, then try to answer the following questions. The answers are on the companion website.

Questions

1 How can St Paul's reconcile the conflict between the internal and external environments?

2 What micro-environmental factors most impact on St Paul's?

3 What macro-environmental factors most affect St Paul's?

Indian tourism

Marketing an entire country is not easy – there are too many factors to take into account. In the case of India, the Tourist Authority is dealing with an extremely diverse nation. India has everything – from beaches to ancient monuments, deserts to the highest mountains in the world, internationally famous cuisine to adventure trips in the jungle. The potential customers are also diverse; student backpackers on gap years, middle-aged tourists on world cruises, adventure seekers and sports enthusiasts, amateur historians, wildlife enthusiasts and beach-lovers all come to India. In recent years, as the Indian economy has taken off, more than 400,000 internal tourists travel to resorts and sites of interest in India every year.

Promoting this diversity led to the 2008 'Incredible India' campaign, which involved TV advertising on international cable channels such as CNN. This was coupled with poster advertising at major airports to appeal directly to regular travellers. The aim is to move Indian tourism upmarket; currently, the majority of tourists visiting India do so on a tight budget since it is one of the world's cheapest destinations. India is a very big country, well able to absorb and cater for much larger numbers of tourists; the difficulty lies in attracting wealthier tourists.

Sujata Thakur, Regional Director, Incredible India

Watch the video clip, then try to answer the following questions. The answers are on the companion website.

Questions

1 How would you measure the results of the Incredible India campaign?

2 What targets are the Tourist Authority setting – and how realistic are they?

3 How should the Tourist Authority plan for attracting a more upmarket group of tourists?

CHAPTER 15
THE GLOBAL MARKETPLACE

AFTER STUDYING THIS CHAPTER, YOU SHOULD BE ABLE TO

- discuss how the international trade system, and economic, political-legal and cultural environments affect a company's international marketing decisions
- describe three key approaches to entering international markets
- explain how companies adapt their marketing mixes for international markets
- identify the three major forms of international marketing organisation

THE WAY AHEAD
Previewing the concepts

It's difficult to find an area of marketing that doesn't contain at least some international issues. In this chapter, we'll focus on the special considerations that companies face when they market their products and brands globally. Advances in communications, transportation and other technologies have made the world a much smaller place. Today, almost every firm, large or small, faces international marketing issues. In this chapter, we will examine six major decisions marketers make in going global.

Our first story of issues and problems that arise from marketing in other countries is the example of Volkswagen and their trials and tribulations in China.

VOLKSWAGEN IN CHINA: THE PEOPLE'S CAR IN THE PEOPLE'S REPUBLIC

Wing Lam, Durham University

'China used to be an easy game. Not anymore'.[1]

No Western company entering China has experienced such a rollercoaster experience as Volkswagen (VW), the German automobile giant. When China started its economic reforms and gradually opened its door to foreign investors in the early 1980s, many foreign companies were reluctant to invest, either because of state restrictions on technology transfer or concerns about protecting patents from Chinese partners. VW was the very first and the only foreign car maker to form a joint venture with a Chinese partner in the 80s, signing a joint-venture agreement with Shanghai Automotive Industry Corp., to form the Shanghai Volkswagen Automotive Co. (SVW), and soon after another with First Automobile Works (FAW) in the northern Chinese city of Changchun in 1990 to produce Jetta, Golf, Bora and Audi branded sedans in China.[2]

When the joint-venture started in 1985, there were only a handful of domestic car makers in China, all of them state-owned. VW as the only real alternative fascinated Chinese buyers and initially proved to be very successful. Despite operating at full production capacity, waiting lists still grew creating a thriving black market in VW cars. By the mid-1990s, almost all Shanghai taxis were VW Santana cars. In 2007, VW set a new sales record of 910,491 vehicles, up 28 per cent from 2006.[3] The company expected to sell one million vehicles in China in 2008. Sounds like a complete success story? A closer examination suggests otherwise.

Despite its record sales figures, VW's market leader position in China has been steadily eroding since China joined the WTO in 2001 – this opened the market to other joint-ventures and impelled domestic manufacturers to improve themselves radically. Whilst the number of cars sold is an impressive figure, it represents a shrinking proportion of the overall market – sales are growing rapidly, but the market is growing much more rapidly. VW's once-dominant market share has gone from 59 per cent in 1998 to 26 per cent in 2004 to 18 per cent in 2007. In 2005, General Motors overtook VW to become the sales leader in China.[4]

So what went wrong?

Model as brand

Despite VW's early success in China, it failed to establish the VW brand. As a consequence, VW Santana, its very first model when the joint-venture was formed in 1985, gained more recognition than the VW corporate brand. For the majority of Chinese, Santana is a brand in its own

品味心风尚

记得在末班地铁前结束. Party!
毕竟, 你还没买Polo劲情.

Remember to end the party before the last subway train because after all, you don't have a POLO GP.

Source: Volkswagen Group.

right, many consumers failing to realise its connection with VW. A worry for VW is that the Santana is an obsolete model (as was the case in Germany two decades ago) and its popularity is declining as the domestic car-makers catch up with the technology, whilst increased purchasing power and preferences make other Western brands attractive and available. When VW began assembling cars in China in the 80s, the government was the main customer – individuals now account for more than half of China's car market.[5]

Distribution channels

Another issue facing VW China is the collaboration with its two Chinese joint-ventures, which have separate marketing, sales and distribution channels. In other words, they are not working together to develop the VW brand, but are competing against each other in the same market segments. According to VW China, the rationale behind VW's two separate distribution channels is that vehicles of FAW-Volkswagen target more success-oriented customers, whilst Shanghai VW target urban trendsetters.[6] It can be argued that the separate sales and distribution networks limit Volkswagen's ability to gather customer data, which may contribute to poor product decisions.[7] To make matters more complicated, VW's Chinese partner, Shanghai Automotive Industry Corp (SAIC), signed a joint-venture with VW China's biggest competitor, General Motors, in 1997. Even more perturbing is that SAIC launched its own cars in China in late 2006, directly competing with both VW and GM.

Many of VW's competitors, especially the new foreign and local smaller car manufacturers, have much smaller distribution networks than the well-established VW network, but they do not seem to have any problems in competing with VW. The problem is not the size or degree of cooperation/competition of the two VW joint-ventures, but their ability to gather market information and most importantly, their abilities to respond to consumers' needs.

Responding to customer needs

Shaken by the rapid decline in market share, VW has recently reorganised its China operation to place more decision-making power there. The key objective is to actively understand consumers and respond to their needs. According to the vice president of sales and marketing of Volkswagen Group China, 'VW previously segmented the market along more traditional demographic lines, such as age and income. It placed vehicles in low-, middle- and high-end price groups. In order to better respond to consumer needs, VW now divides Chinese consumers into 48 customer groups based on factors such as income and lifestyles.'[8].

Knowing consumers is one thing, responding to their needs is another. VW's previous attempt to meet customer needs included its launch of the Golf in July 2003 as a business car at RMB147,000 (€14,640). After poor sales, VW repositioned the Golf as a family car and cut its price to €13,470. Another example was its small car Gol; it was launched in May 2003 at a very low price – €7,400. The fact that it didn't have an air conditioner – a necessity in China's summer – has made it very unattractive to Chinese consumers. VW was forced to re-launch the Gol with an air conditioner and radio to meet the basic requirements of its consumers.

VW's German-centric decision making still hinders quick responses to the increasingly sophisticated Chinese consumer needs in a rapidly evolving Chinese market environment. According to one Chinese VW employee, a senior product design engineer in Shanghai, 'Our ideas are rarely respected. Every single suggestion has to go through the headquarters in Germany. It is quite obvious that a junior engineer in Germany has more power than a local engineer with over 20 years' engineering experience in VW China.' VW's rigid structure and product development procedures offers little help – for every single new design, even parts or small accessories, the local design team has to draw up a manual as thick as a phone book. The 'phone book' then needs to be sent to Germany for approval. Even a minor change suggested by a junior engineer in Germany would mean that the whole design team in China has to draw another 'phone book' from scratch. It is very common that experienced engineers have to draw over a dozen 'phone books' in order to get one new part approved. For an industry like car-making, this practice is understandable as quality and reliability are the top priorities. In fact, the Chinese staff appreciate it as good practice quality control. However, from the designers' point of view, to devote most of their time working on the 'phone books' largely kills off their creativity in respect of improving the product, never mind their motivation to respond to consumers' needs. In fact, the organisational culture of VW has little to do with customer orientation, as perceived by its employees in their product design departments. The result is obvious, the decision makers do not necessarily know the consumers' needs while those who know the consumers have little influence or are distracted by other duties and requirements.

The 'white ceiling'

VW is proud of its staff development programme for its local Chinese staff. According to the company, training for Chinese employees is one of VW's paramount goals in China. Apprenticeships and advanced training schemes for local personnel are conducted in Germany and abroad as well as in China itself.[9] Many current and former employees of VW China agree that they benefited enormously from the training offered by VW. However, things started to turn sour when the local managers hit the 'White Ceiling' – looking at any of VW China's department organisation charts shows that most managerial positions above a certain level are taken by German managers.

Frustrated by the feeling that they have little say in decision making, and little chance of promotion to a senior managerial position, a significant number of experienced local staff leave VW each year for better job prospects. Many of them stay in the same industry, working for VW's parts suppliers or most worryingly for VW, its competitors. Inadvertently, VW has become the *de facto* training school for China's car industry.[10]

The way forward

Traditionally VW China focused its marketing on promoting individual cars. For the first time in nearly twenty years, VW has recently launched a marketing campaign to build corporate brand identity.[11] Additionally, and just as importantly, the People's Car company in the People's Republic is working hard to retain its own staff by introducing sincere localisation of senior managerial posts in order to encourage creativity and innovation in China, in order to better serve another group of people, their customers.

Source: See notes 1–11 at the end of this chapter.

International trade goes back thousands of years in Europe – from the Greeks and Romans in ancient times, through the Vikings and then the Venetians to the modern day

Source: Alamy Images/Rob Bartree.

Almost all companies begin by serving their local markets. These customers are closer, more convenient to serve and are most easily understood by the firm. Managers don't immediately need to learn other languages, deal with strange and changing currencies, face another set of political and legal uncertainties, or adapt their products to different customer needs and expectations in other nations and cultures. In essence, the domestic market is relatively easy and relatively safe. Some cultures have historically been better at this than others, by virtue of possibility or necessity – Germany has long been a world leader in terms of exports, exploiting its strengths in engineering. Italy and Greece are two European nations with Mediterranean-centric trading patterns dating back 25 centuries and more, and a company in Switzerland or Luxembourg will have international markets only a few miles away. Archaeologists recently discovered coins from Damascus, Persia and Africa in Sweden – brought back by Viking traders in the ninth century AD.[12] Napoleon called England 'a nation of shopkeepers', and the financial instruments used by London-based bankers such as the Rothschilds played as much a part in his eventual downfall as did Waterloo.

Some nations have historically been less proactive international traders. Japan closed its borders to most foreign influences in the middle of the seventeenth century, only reopening them 200 years later after some gunboat diplomacy by the United States. US companies themselves have until recently existed in a mostly homogenous market with many tens of millions of customers domestically – and this has lessened the imperative to make a priority of overseas markets.

GLOBAL MARKETING IN THE TWENTY-FIRST CENTURY

Today, however, the situation is much different. The world is shrinking rapidly with the advent of faster communications, transportation and financial flows. Products developed in one country – Gucci handbags, Sony electronics, McDonald's hamburgers, BMWs – are finding enthusiastic acceptance in other countries. We would not be surprised to hear about a German businessman wearing an Italian suit meeting a French friend at a Japanese restaurant in Moscow who later returns home to drink Scotch whisky and watch Spanish football on a Korean TV.

International trade is booming. Since 1969 the number of multinational corporations in the world has grown from 7,000 to more than 63,000. Some of these multinationals are true giants. In fact, of the largest 100 'economies' in the world, only 47 are countries. The remaining 53 are multinational corporations. ExxonMobil, one of the world's largest companies, has annual revenues greater than the gross domestic product of all but the world's 20 largest countries.[13]

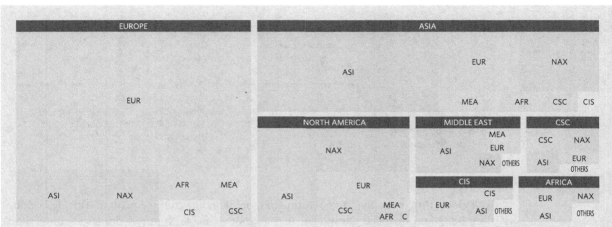

NAX: North America; CSC: Central and South America and the Caribbean; EUR: Europe; CIS: Commonwealth of Independent States; AFR: Africa; MEA: Middle East; ASI: Asia

World merchandise exports by region and destination, 2009

Source: WTO (2010), *International Trade Statistics 2010*, p. 5.

In 2010, the WTO reported that world trade had – after a decade of growth – shrunk in the face of a global recession. Despite this, the volume and value of goods traded internationally was immense. China's growth had seen it overtake Germany to become the leading exporter in the world – with the US declining to third place. Taken as a whole, Europe was responsible for 42 per cent of all global exports – three times that of the US and four times that of China – powered by the 'big 4' of Germany, France, Italy and the UK. China also became the second largest importer of goods, after the United States.[14] The destination of exports also revealed that three quarters of European trade went to another European nation. If you've been wondering why the EU causes such a fuss, that should tell you.

Many companies have long been successful at international marketing – Unilever, Coca-Cola, BMW, KPMG, Sony, Toyota, BP, Nokia, Nestlé, Royal Bank of Scotland, Boeing, McDonald's, and dozens of others have made the world their market. Michelin, the oh-so-French tyre manufacturer, now does a third of its business in the United States and Mexico; Johnson & Johnson, the maker of quintessentially all-American products like Band-Aids and Johnson's Baby Shampoo, does 42 per cent of its business abroad.[15]

But while global trade is growing, global competition is intensifying. Foreign firms are expanding aggressively into new international markets, and home markets are no longer as rich in opportunity. Few industries are now safe from foreign competition. If companies delay taking steps towards internationalising, they risk being shut out of growing markets in Western and Eastern Europe, China and the Pacific Rim, Russia and elsewhere. Firms that stay at home to play it safe might not only lose their chances to enter other markets but also risk losing their home markets.[16] Domestic companies that never thought about foreign competitors suddenly find these competitors on their own doorstep.

Ironically, although the need for companies to go abroad is greater today than in the past, so are the risks. Companies that go global may face highly unstable governments and currencies, restrictive government policies and regulations, and high trade barriers. Corruption is also an increasing problem – officials in some countries often award business not to the best bidder but to the highest briber. This isn't an issue that is likely to go away, but in this age of easy exchange and dissemination of information, it is a lot harder to keep it quiet – organisations like Transparency International challenge governments, societies and businesses on corruption related issues. Sweden's Volvo was recently fined £3.5 million for illegally bypassing UN trade restrictions in Iraq.[17]

FIGURE 15.1
Major international
marketing decisions

A **global firm** is one that, by operating in more than one country, gains marketing, production, R&D and financial advantages that are not available to purely domestic competitors. The global company sees the world as one market. It minimises the importance of national boundaries and develops 'transnational' brands. It raises capital, obtains materials and components, and manufactures and markets its goods wherever it can do the best job. For example, Otis Elevator gets its elevator door systems from France, small geared parts from Spain, electronics from Germany, and special motor drives from Japan. It uses the United States only for systems integration. 'Borders are so twentieth century,' says one global marketing expert. 'Transnationals take "stateless" to the next level.'[18]

This does not mean that small and medium-sized firms must operate in a dozen countries to succeed. These firms can practise *global niching*. But the world is becoming smaller, and every company operating in a global industry – whether large or small – must assess and establish its place in world markets.

The rapid move towards globalisation means that all companies will have to answer some basic questions: What market position should we try to establish in our country, in our economic region, and globally? Who will our global competitors be, and what are their strategies and resources? Where should we produce or source our products? What strategic alliances should we form with other firms around the world?

As shown in Figure 15.1, a company faces six major decisions in international marketing. We will discuss each decision in detail in this chapter.

LOOKING AT THE GLOBAL MARKETING ENVIRONMENT

Before deciding whether to operate internationally, a company must understand the international marketing environment. That environment has changed a great deal in the last two decades, creating both new opportunities and new problems.

The international trade system

Companies looking abroad must start by understanding the international *trade system*. When selling to another country, a firm may face restrictions on trade between nations. Foreign governments may charge *tariffs*, taxes on certain imported products designed to raise revenue or to protect domestic firms. Or they may set *quotas*, limits on the amount of foreign imports that they will accept in certain product categories. The EU currently has quotas for the import of products as varied as light bulbs, shoes and many agricultural commodities. The purpose of a quota is sometimes to conserve foreign exchange/rates but more usually to protect local industry and employment. Firms may also face *exchange controls*, which limit the amount of foreign exchange and the exchange rate against other currencies.

The company may also face *non-tariff trade barriers*, such as biases against non-domestic company bids or restrictive product standards that go against current product features:

One of the cleverest ways the Japanese have found to keep foreign manufacturers out of their domestic market is to plead 'uniqueness'. Japanese skin is different, the government argues, so foreign cosmetics companies must test their products in Japan before selling there. The Japanese say their stomachs are small and have room for only the mikan, the local tangerine, so imports of oranges are limited. Now the Japanese have come up with what may be the flakiest argument yet: their snow is different, so ski equipment should be too.[19]

At the same time, certain forces *help* trade between nations. Examples include the General Agreement on Tariffs and Trade (GATT) and various regional free trade agreements. In Europe, the biggest is, of course, the EU, although there are others, like EFTA (European Free Trade Association – members include Iceland and Norway) and CEFTA (Central European Free Trade Association – members include Croatia, Serbia and Albania).

The World Trade Organization and GATT

The GATT is a 65-year-old treaty designed to promote world trade by reducing tariffs and other international trade barriers. Since the treaty's inception in 1948, member nations (currently numbering 148) have met in eight rounds of GATT negotiations to reassess trade barriers and set new rules for international trade. The first seven rounds of negotiations reduced the average worldwide tariffs on manufactured goods from 45 per cent to just 5 per cent.[20]

The most recently completed GATT negotiations, dubbed the Uruguay Round, dragged on for seven long years before concluding in 1993. It reduced the world's remaining merchandise tariffs by 30 per cent – one concern of many economists is that the recent economic turbulence might reverse that trend. The agreement also extended GATT to cover trade in agriculture and a wide range of services, and it toughened international protection of copyrights, patents, trademarks and other intellectual property. Although the financial impact of such an agreement is difficult to measure, research suggests that cutting agriculture, manufacturing and services trade barriers by one-third would boost the world economy by $613 billion, the equivalent of adding another Australia to the world economy.[21]

Beyond reducing trade barriers and setting global standards for trade, the Uruguay Round set up the World Trade Organization (WTO) to enforce GATT rules.[22] In general, the WTO acts as an umbrella organisation, overseeing GATT, mediating global disputes and imposing trade sanctions. The previous GATT organisation never possessed such authorities. A new round of GATT negotiations, the Doha round, began in Doha, Qatar, in late 2001 and was set to conclude in January 2005. As of late 2011, this round shows no signs of coming to a conclusion and there is a significant way to go before a consensus can be established.[23]

Regional free trade zones

Certain countries have formed *free trade zones* or **economic communities**. These are groups of nations organised to work towards common goals in the regulation of international trade. One such community is the European Union (EU). Formed in 1957, the European Union set out to create a single European market by reducing barriers to the free flow of products, services, finances and labour among member countries and developing policies on trade with non-member nations. Today, the EU represents one of the world's single largest markets. Its current 27 Member States (with Turkey, Croatia and Macedonia hoping to join) contain some 500 million consumers.[24]

As a result of increased unification, European companies have grown bigger and more competitive. Perhaps an even greater concern, however, is that lower barriers *inside* Europe will create only thicker *outside* walls. Some observers envision a 'Fortress Europe' that gives favours to firms from EU countries but hinders outsiders by imposing obstacles – this is especially a concern for African nations, but also for the USA and China.

Progress towards European unification has been slow – many doubt that complete unification can or should be achieved. In recent years, 12 Member States have taken a significant step towards unification by adopting the euro as a common currency – but this project is

Economic communities: the European Union represents one of the world's largest single markets. Its current 27 Member States contain more than 493 million consumers and account for 20 per cent of the world's exports

Source: Alamy Images/BL Images Ltd.

now under pressure and it remains to be seen whether or not it can be sustained in the long term. At the macro-economic level the euro may be causing discombobulation to national governments, but the adoption of the euro has decreased much of the currency risk associated with doing business in Europe from the perspective of firms, making Member States with previously weak currencies more attractive markets.[25]

However, even with the adoption of the euro, it is unlikely that the EU will ever go against 2,000 years of tradition and become the 'United States of Europe'. A community with dozens of different languages and cultures will always have difficulty coming together and acting as a single entity. Still, although only partly successful so far, unification has made Europe a global force with which to reckon, with a combined EU annual GDP of more than $16 trillion.[26]

Following the apparent success of the EU and NAFTA, the North American Free Trade Association,[27] the Central American Free Trade Agreement (CAFTA) established a free trade zone between the United States and Costa Rica, the Dominican Republic, El Salvador, Guatemala, Honduras and Nicaragua in 2005. Talks are now under way to investigate establishing a Free Trade Area of the Americas (FTAA). This mammoth free trade zone would include 34 countries stretching from the Bering Strait to Cape Horn, with a population of 800 million and a combined gross domestic product of about $17 trillion.[28]

Other free trade areas have formed in Latin America and South America. For example, MERCOSUR links nine Latin America and South America countries and the Andean Community (CAN, for its Spanish initials) links five more. In late 2004, MERCOSUR and CAN agreed to unite, creating the South American Community of Nations (CSN), which will be modelled after the EU. Complete integration between the two trade blocs was agreed in 2008 and all tariffs between the nations are to be eliminated by 2019. With a population of more than 367 million, a combined economy of more than $2.8 trillion a year, and exports worth $181 billion, the CSN will make up the largest trading bloc after NAFTA and the EU.[29]

Although the recent trend towards free trade zones has caused great excitement and new market opportunities, some see it as a mixed blessing. For example, in Germany and France, trade unions like IG Metall and Force Ouvrière fear that EU expansion will lead to the exodus of manufacturing jobs to Eastern Europe, where wage rates are much lower. Environmentalists worry that companies that are unwilling to play by the strict rules of the EU or North America will relocate in Mexico or China, where pollution regulation is more lax.[30]

Each nation has unique features that must be understood. A nation's readiness for different products and services and its attractiveness as a market to foreign firms depend on its economic, political, legal and cultural environments.

Economic environment

The international marketer must study each country's economy. Two economic factors reflect the country's attractiveness as a market: the country's industrial structure and its income distribution.

The country's *industrial structure* shapes its product and service needs, income levels and employment levels. The four types of industrial structures are as follows:

- *Subsistence economies*: In a subsistence economy, the vast majority of people engage in simple agriculture. They consume most of their output and barter the rest for simple goods and services. They offer few market opportunities.

- *Raw material exporting economies*: These economies are rich in one or more natural resources but poor in other ways. Much of their revenue comes from exporting these resources. Examples are Chile (tin and copper), Democratic Republic of Congo (copper, cobalt and coffee) and Saudi Arabia (oil). These countries are good markets for large equipment, tools and supplies, and trucks. If there are many foreign residents or a wealthy upper class, they are also a market for luxury goods.

- *Industrialising economies*: In an industrialising economy, manufacturing accounts for 10–20 per cent of the country's economy. Examples include Egypt, India and Brazil. As manufacturing increases, the country needs more imports of raw textile materials, steel and heavy machinery, and fewer imports of finished textiles, paper products and vehicles. Industrialisation typically creates a new rich class and a small but growing middle class, both demanding new types of imported goods.

- *Industrial economies*: Industrial economies are major exporters of manufactured goods, services and investment funds. They trade goods among themselves and also export them to other types of economies for raw materials and semi-finished goods. The varied manufacturing activities of these industrial nations and their large middle class make them rich markets for all sorts of goods. Many European nations have this form of industrial structure – but some argue that a more realistic description of the most developed European nations would be 'post-industrial economies', where production of goods and products forms a minority of an economy that is dominated by services – such as the UK and Germany with their large financial services sectors.

The second economic factor is the country's *income distribution*. Industrialised nations may have low-, medium- and high-income households. In contrast, countries with subsistence economies may consist mostly of households with very low family incomes. Still other countries may have households with only either very low or very high incomes. However, even poor or developing economies may be attractive markets for all kinds of goods, including luxuries. For example, many luxury brand marketers are rushing to take advantage of China's rapidly developing consumer markets:

> More than half of China's 1.3 billion consumers can barely afford rice, let alone luxuries. According to the World Bank, more than 400 million Chinese live on less than $2 a day. For now, only some 1 per cent of China's population (about 13 million people) earns enough to even consider purchasing luxury-brand products. Yet posh brands – from Gucci and Cartier to BMW and Bentley – are descending on China in force. How can purveyors of $2,000 handbags, $20,000 watches, and $1 million limousines thrive in a developing economy? Easy, says a Cartier executive. 'Remember, even medium-sized cities in China . . . have populations larger than Switzerland's. So it doesn't matter if the percentage of people in those cities who can afford our products is very small.'
>
> Dazzled by the pace at which China's booming economy is minting millionaires and swelling the ranks of the middle class, luxury brands are rushing to stake out shop space, tout their wares, and lay the foundations of a market they hope will eventually include as many as 100 million conspicuous consumers. 'The Chinese are a natural audience for luxury goods,' notes one analyst. After decades of socialism and poverty, China's elite are suddenly 'keen to show off their newfound wealth'.

Europe's fashion houses are happy to assist. Giorgio Armani . . . hosted a star-studded fashion show to celebrate the opening of his 12,000-square-foot flagship store on Shanghai's waterfront . . . and promised 30 stores in China before the 2008 Beijing Olympics. Gucci recently opened stores in Hangzhou and Chengdu, bringing its China total to six. And it's not just clothes. Cartier, with nine stores in China and seven on the drawing board, has seen its China sales double for the past several years. Car makers, too, are racing in. BMW recently cut the ribbon on a new Chinese factory that has the capacity to produce 50,000 BMWs a year. Audi's sleek A6 has emerged as the car of choice for the Communist Party's senior ranks, despite its $230,000 price tag. Bentley, which sold 70 cars in China in 2003 – including 19 limousines priced at more than $1 million each, boasts three dealerships in China, as does Rolls-Royce.[31]

Thus, country and regional economic environments will affect an international marketer's decisions about which global markets to enter and how.

Political-legal environment

Nations differ greatly in their political-legal environments. In considering whether to do business in a given country, a company should consider factors such as the country's attitudes towards international buying, government bureaucracy, political stability and monetary regulations.

Some nations are very receptive to foreign firms; others are less accommodating. For example, India has tended to bother foreign businesses with import quotas, currency restrictions and other limitations that make operating there a challenge. In contrast, neighbouring Asian countries such as Singapore and Thailand court foreign investors and shower them with incentives and favourable operating conditions. Political stability is another issue. India's government is notoriously unstable – the country has elected ten new governments in the past 20 years, and there is a history of high-level political assassinations – increasing the risk of doing business there. Although most international marketers still find India's huge market attractive, the unstable political situation will affect how they handle business and financial matters.[32]

Companies must also consider a country's monetary regulations. Sellers want to take their profits in a currency of value to them. Ideally, the buyer can pay in the seller's currency or in other world currencies. Short of this, sellers might accept a blocked currency – its removal from the country is restricted by the buyer's government – if they can buy other goods in that country that they need themselves or can sell elsewhere for a needed currency. Besides currency limits, a changing exchange rate also creates high risks for the seller.

Most international trade involves cash transactions. Yet many nations have too little hard currency to pay for their purchases from other countries. They may want to pay with other items instead of cash, which has led to a growing practice called **countertrade**. Countertrade takes several forms. *Barter* involves the direct exchange of goods or services, as when Azerbaijan imports wheat from Romania in exchange for crude oil, and Vietnam exchanges rice for fertiliser and coconuts from the Philippines. Another form is *compensation* (or *buyback*), whereby the seller sells a plant, equipment or technology to another country and agrees to take payment in the resulting products. Thus, Japan's Fukusuke Corporation sold knitting machines and raw textile materials to Shanghai clothing manufacturer Chinatex in exchange for finished textiles produced on the machines. The most common form of countertrade is *counterpurchase*, in which the seller receives full payment in cash but agrees to spend some of the money in the other country. For example, Boeing sells aircraft to India and agrees to buy Indian coffee, rice, castor oil and other goods and sell them elsewhere.[33]

Countertrade deals can be very complex. For example, a few years ago DaimlerChrysler agreed to sell 30 trucks to Romania in exchange for 150 Romanian jeeps, which it then sold to Ecuador for bananas, which were in turn sold to a German supermarket chain for the then German currency (the Deutschmark). Through this roundabout process, DaimlerChrysler finally obtained payment in German money.

Cultural environment

Each country has its own traditions, norms and taboos. When designing global marketing strategies, companies must understand how culture affects consumer reactions in each of its world markets. In turn, they must also understand how their strategies affect local cultures.

The impact of culture on marketing strategy

The seller must examine the ways consumers in different countries think about and use certain products before planning a marketing programme. There are often surprises. For example, the average French man uses almost twice as many cosmetics and grooming aids as his wife. The Germans and the French eat more packaged, branded spaghetti than do Italians. Italian children like to eat chocolate bars between slices of bread as a snack. Women in Tanzania will not give their children eggs for fear of making them bald or impotent.

Companies that ignore such differences can make some very expensive and embarrassing mistakes. Here's an example:

> McDonald's and Coca-Cola managed to offend the entire Muslim world by putting the Saudi Arabian flag on their packaging. The flag's design includes a passage from the Koran, and Muslims feel very strongly that their Holy Writ should never be tossed in the garbage. Nike faced a similar situation in Arab countries when Muslims objected to a stylised 'Air' logo on its shoes, which resembled 'Allah' in Arabic script. Nike apologised for the mistake and pulled the shoes from distribution.[34]

Business norms and behaviour also vary from country to country. For example, Western executives often like to get right down to business and engage in fast and tough face-to-face bargaining. However, Japanese and other Asian businesspeople often find this behaviour offensive. They prefer to start with polite conversation, and they rarely say no in face-to-face conversations. As another example, South Americans like to sit or stand very close to each other when they talk business – in fact, almost nose-to-nose. Business executives need to be briefed on these kinds of factors before conducting business in another country.[35]

By the same token, companies that understand cultural nuances can use them to advantage when positioning products internationally. Consider the following examples of how European products have adapted to local conditions in the increasingly important market of China:

> A product marketed with a well-designed and localised name creates an instant connection with local consumers, yet maintains the prestige and perceptions of high quality that are frequently associated with foreign products. Carrefour, a French hypermarket chain, localised its name into '家乐福,' or 'jia le fu' when entering the Chinese market. This name literally translates as 'Happy Family'. However, the individual characters bring with them the associations of harmony, luck and prosperity – a highly desirable combination in Chinese thought.
>
> Sometimes, localising a product's appearance can also mean changing the product's physical presentation to fit in with cultural events. Häagan Dazs, the epitome of fine ice cream, localised its product appearance to capitalise on Chinese holidays, which are peak buying seasons throughout China. To fit in with the local culture, Häagan Dazs produced ice cream in the form of a Chinese moon cake. By doing so, it could both charge a premium price for the 'foreign experience', while taking advantage of a surge in sales usually enjoyed only by bakeries. To localise the content means adjusting the product to the local language, measurement system, currency and local ideals. The sophisticated international magazine on fashion, beauty, and style – *Elle* – not only localises the content into Chinese language, but it also sensitises to local cultural ideals and has adapted its content to profile Chinese models, publish more conservative editorials, and advertise beauty products that appeal to the Chinese ideals of beauty such as whitening cream for a paler complexion.[36]

Thus, understanding cultural traditions, preferences and behaviours can help companies not only to avoid embarrassing mistakes but also to take advantage of cross-cultural opportunities.

The impact of marketing strategy on cultures

Whereas marketers worry about the impact of culture on their global marketing strategies, others may worry about the impact of marketing strategies on global cultures. For example, some critics argue that 'globalisation' really means 'Americanisation'. Globalisation as a concept or topic is not one that is seen positively in all corners of the world. In France, for example, there is real concern and debate about the connection between the culture of business and the culture of society as whole – a recent survey found that only one in three French think a free market economy is the best way to develop the nation. Of course, France is home to many of the leading global brands, and French companies have operations all round the world – one third of Europe's top 100 companies are French in origin.[37]

Critics worry that the more people around the world are exposed to Western lifestyles in the food they eat, the stores they shop in and the television shows and films they watch, the more they will lose their individual cultural identities. They contend that exposure to Western values and products erodes other cultures and westernises the world – see Marketing at Work 15.1 for the story of how the Big Mac went East.

McDonald's: serving customers around the world

MARKETING AT WORK 15.1

The first McDonald's stand popped up in California in 1954, and what could be more American than burger-and-fries fast food? But as it turns out, the quintessentially all-American company now sells more burgers and fries outside the country than within. Nearly 65 per cent of McDonald's $23.5 billion of sales come from outside the United States, and its international sales are growing at close to twice the rate of domestic sales growth.

McDonald's today is a truly global enterprise. Its 32,000 restaurants serve more than 58 million people in more than 100 countries each day. Few firms have more international marketing experience than McDonald's. But going global hasn't always been easy, and McDonald's has learned many important lessons in its journeys overseas. To see how far McDonald's has come, consider its experiences in Russia, a market that's very different culturally, economically, and politically from our own.

McDonald's first set its sights on Russia (then a part of the Soviet Union) in 1976, when George Cohon, head of McDonald's in Canada, took a group of Soviet Olympics officials to a McDonald's while they visited for the

Source: Getty Images/AFP.

Montreal Olympic Games. Cohon was struck by how much the Soviets liked McDonald's hamburgers, fries, and other fare. Over the next 14 years, Cohon flew to Russia more than 100 times, first to get Soviet permission for McDonald's to provide food for the 1980 Moscow Olympics, and later to be allowed to open McDonald's restaurants in the country. He quickly learned that no one in Russia had any idea what a McDonald's was. The Soviets turned Cohon down flat on both requests.

Finally, in 1988, as Premier Mikhail Gorbachev began to open the Russian economy, Cohon forged a deal with the city of Moscow to launch the first Russian McDonald's in Moscow's Pushkin Square. But obtaining permission was only the first step. Actually opening the restaurant brought a fresh set of challenges. Thanks to Russia's large and bureaucratic government structure, McDonald's had to obtain some 200 separate signatures just to open the single location. It had difficulty finding reliable suppliers for even such basics as hamburgers and buns. So McDonald's forked over $45 million to build a facility to produce these things itself. It even brought in technical experts from Canada with special strains of disease-resistant seed to teach Russian farmers how to grow Russet Burbank potatoes for french fries, and it built its own pasteurising plant to ensure a plentiful supply of fresh milk.

When the Moscow McDonald's at Pushkin Square finally opened its doors in January 1990, it quickly won the hearts of Russian consumers. However, the company faced still more hurdles. The Pushkin Square restaurant is huge – 26 cash registers and 900 seats (compared with 40 to 50 seats in a typical McDonald's). The logistics of serving customers on such a scale was daunting, made even more difficult by the fact that few employees or customers understood the fast-food concept.

Although Western consumers were well acquainted with McDonald's, the Russians were clueless. So, in order to meet its high standards for customer satisfaction in this new market, the US fast feeder had to educate employees about the time-tested McDonald's way of doing things. It trained Russian managers at Hamburger University and subjected each of 630 new employees (most of whom didn't know a chicken McNugget from an Egg McMuffin) to 16 to 20 hours of training on such essentials as cooking meat patties, assembling Filet-O-Fish sandwiches, and giving service with a smile. Back in those days, McDonald's even had to train consumers – most Muscovites had never seen a fast-food restaurant. Customers waiting in line were shown videos telling them everything from how to order and pay at the counter, to how to put their coats over the backs of their seats, to how to handle a Big Mac.

However, the new Moscow McDonald's got off to a spectacular start. An incredible 50,000 customers swarmed the restaurant during its first day of business. And in its usual way, McDonald's began immediately to build community involvement. On opening day, it held a kick-off party for 700 Muscovite orphans and then donated all opening-day proceeds to the Moscow Children's Fund.

Today, only 20 years after opening its first restaurant there, McDonald's is thriving in Russia. The Pushkin Square location is now the busiest McDonald's in the world, and Russia is the crown jewel in McDonald's global empire. The company's 240 restaurants in 40 Russian cities each serve an average of 850,000 diners a year – twice the per-store traffic of any of the other 122 countries in which McDonald's operates.

Despite the long lines of customers, McDonald's has been careful about how rapidly it expands in Russia. In recent years, it has reined in its rapid growth strategy and focused instead on improving product and service quality and profitability. The goal is to squeeze more business out of existing restaurants and to grow slowly but profitably. One way to do that is to add new menu items to draw in consumers at different times of the day. So, as it did many years ago in the United States, McDonald's in Russia is now adding breakfast items.

Although only about 5 per cent of Russians eat breakfast outside the home, more commuters in the big cities are leaving home earlier to avoid heavy traffic. The company hopes that the new breakfast menu will encourage commuters to stop off at McDonald's on their way to work. However, when the fast-food chain added breakfast items, it stopped offering its traditional hamburger fare during the morning hours. When many customers complained of 'hamburger withdrawal', McDonald's introduced the Fresh McMuffin, an English muffin with a sausage patty topped with cheese, lettuce, tomato, and special sauce. The new sandwich became an instant hit.

To reduce the lines inside restaurants and to attract motorists, McDonald's is also introducing Russian consumers to drive-thru windows. At first, many Russians just didn't get the concept. Instead, they treated the drive-thru window as just another line, purchasing their food there, parking, and going inside to eat. Also, Russian cars often don't have cupholders, so drive-thru customers bought fewer drinks. However, as more customers get used to the concept, McDonald's is putting drive-thru and walk-up windows in about half of its new stores.

So, that's a look at McDonald's in Russia. But just as McDonald's has tweaked its formula in Russia, it also adjusts its marketing and operations to meet the special needs of local consumers in other major global markets. To be sure, McDonald's is a global brand. Its restaurants around the world employ a common global strategy – convenient food at affordable prices. And no matter where you go in the world – from Moscow to Montréal or Shanghai to Cheboygan, Michigan – you'll find those good old golden arches and a menu full of Quarter Pounders, Big Macs, fries, milkshakes, and other familiar items. But within that general strategic framework, McDonald's adapts to the subtleties of each local market. Says a McDonald's Europe executive, 'Across Europe with 40 different markets, there are 40 sets of tastes. There are also differences within each market. We are a local market but a global brand.'

In the past, US companies paid little attention to international trade. If they could pick up some extra sales through exporting, that was fine. But the big market was at home, and it teemed with opportunities. The home market was also much safer. Managers did not need to learn other languages, deal with strange and changing currencies, face political and legal uncertainties, or adapt

their products to different customer needs and expectations. Today, however, the situation is much different. Organisations of all kinds, from Coca-Cola, IBM and Google to MTV and even the NBA, have gone global.

Sources: Quotes and other information from Janet Adamy, 'Steady Diet: As Burgers Boom in Russia, McDonald's Touts Discipline', *The Wall Street Journal*, 16 October 2007, p. A1; Fern Glazer, 'NPD: QSR Chains Expanding Globally Must Also Act Locally', *Nation's Restaurant News*, 22 October 2007, p. 18; 'McDonald's Eyes Russia with 40 New Stores', www.reuters.com; and information from www.mcdonalds.com.

DECIDING WHETHER TO GO INTERNATIONAL

Not all companies need to venture into international markets to survive. Operating domestically is easier and safer. Managers don't need to learn another country's language and laws. They don't have to deal with unstable currencies, face additional political and legal uncertainties, or redesign their products to suit different customer expectations. However, companies that operate in global industries, where their strategic positions in specific markets are affected strongly by their overall global positions, must compete on a worldwide basis to succeed.

Any of several factors might draw a company into the international arena. Global competitors might attack the company's home market by offering better products or lower prices. The company might want to counter-attack these competitors in their home markets to tie up their resources. Or the company's home market might be stagnant or shrinking, and foreign markets may present higher sales and profit opportunities. Or the company's customers might be expanding abroad and require international servicing.

Before going abroad, the company must weigh several risks and answer many questions about its ability to operate globally. Can the company learn to understand the preferences and buyer behaviour of consumers in other countries? Can it offer competitively attractive products? Will it be able to adapt to other countries' business cultures and deal effectively with foreign nationals? Do the company's managers have the necessary international experience? Has management considered the impact of regulations and the political environments of other countries?

Because of the difficulties of entering international markets, most companies do not act until some situation or event thrusts them into the global arena. Someone – a domestic exporter, a foreign importer, a foreign government – may ask the company to sell abroad. Or the company may be saddled with overcapacity and need to find additional markets for its goods.

DECIDING WHICH MARKETS TO ENTER

Before going abroad, the company should try to define its international *marketing objectives and policies*. It should decide what *volume* of foreign sales it wants. Most companies start small when they go abroad. Some plan to stay small, seeing international sales as a small part of their business. Other companies have bigger plans, seeing international business as equal to or even more important than their domestic business.

The company also needs to choose *how many* countries it wants to market in. Companies must be careful not to spread themselves too thin or to expand beyond their capabilities by operating in too many countries too soon. Next, the company needs to decide on the *types* of countries to enter. A country's attractiveness depends on the product, geographical factors, income and population, political climate and other factors. The seller may prefer certain country groups or parts of the world. In recent years, many major new markets have emerged, offering both substantial opportunities and daunting challenges.

TABLE 15.1 Indicators of market potential

Demographic characteristics	Sociocultural factors
Education	Consumer lifestyles, beliefs and values
Population size and growth	Business norms and approaches
Population age composition	Social norms
	Languages
Geographic characteristics	**Political and legal factors**
Climate	National priorities
Country size	Political stability
Population density – urban, rural	Government attitudes towards global trade
Transportation structure and market accessibility	Government bureaucracy
	Monetary and trade regulations
Economic factors	
GDP size and growth	
Income distribution	
Industrial infrastructure	
Natural resources	
Financial and human resources	

After listing possible international markets, the company must carefully evaluate each one. It must consider many factors. For example, Colgate's decision to enter the Chinese market seems fairly straightforward: China's huge population makes it the world's largest toothpaste market. And given that only 20 per cent of China's rural dwellers now brush daily, this already huge market can grow even larger. Yet Colgate must still question whether market size *alone* is reason enough to invest heavily in China.

Colgate must ask some important questions: Will it be able to overcome cultural barriers and convince Chinese consumers to brush their teeth regularly? Does China provide for the needed production and distribution technologies? Can Colgate compete effectively with dozens of local competitors, a state-owned brand managed by Unilever and Procter & Gamble's Crest? Will the Chinese government remain stable and supportive? Colgate's current success in China suggests that it could answer yes to all of these questions. By aggressively pursuing promotional and educational programmes – from massive ad campaigns to visits to local schools to sponsoring oral care research – Colgate has expanded its market share from 7 per cent in 1995 to 35 per cent today. Still, the company's future in China is filled with uncertainties.[38]

Possible global markets should be ranked on several factors, including market size, market growth, cost of doing business, competitive advantage and risk level. The goal is to determine the potential of each market, using indicators such as those shown in Table 15.1. Then the marketer must decide which markets offer the greatest long-term return on investment.

DECIDING HOW TO ENTER THE MARKET

Once a company has decided to sell in a foreign country, it must determine the best mode of entry. Its choices are *exporting, joint venturing* and *direct investment*. Figure 15.2 shows three market entry strategies, along with the options each one offers. As the figure shows, each succeeding strategy involves more commitment and risk, but also more control and potential profits.

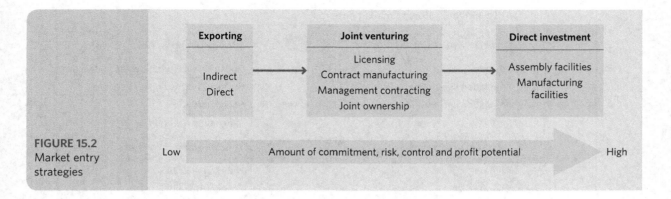

FIGURE 15.2
Market entry
strategies

Exporting

The simplest way to enter a foreign market is through **exporting**. The company may passively export its surplus production from time to time, or it may make an active commitment to expand exports to a particular market. In either case, the company produces all its goods in its home country. It may or may not modify them for the export market. Exporting involves the least change in the company's product lines, organisation, investments or mission – making it by far the simplest method to enter a foreign market.

Companies typically start with *indirect exporting*, working through independent international marketing intermediaries. Indirect exporting involves less investment because the firm does not require an overseas marketing organisation or set of contacts. It also involves less risk. International marketing intermediaries bring know-how and services to the relationship, so the seller normally makes fewer mistakes.

Sellers may eventually move into *direct exporting*, whereby they handle their own exports. The investment and risk are somewhat greater in this strategy, but so is the potential return. A company can conduct direct exporting in several ways. It can set up a domestic export department that carries out export activities. It can set up an overseas sales branch that handles sales, distribution and perhaps promotion. The sales branch gives the seller more presence and programme control in the foreign market and often serves as a display centre and customer service centre. The company can also send home-based salespeople abroad at certain times in order to find business. Finally, the company can do its exporting either through foreign-based distributors who buy and own the goods or through foreign-based agents who sell the goods on behalf of the company.

Joint venturing

A second method of entering a foreign market is **joint venturing** – joining with foreign companies to produce or market products or services. Joint venturing differs from exporting in that the company joins with a host country partner to sell or market abroad. VW did this with its Chinese partners. It differs from direct investment in that an association is formed with someone in the foreign country. There are four types of joint ventures: licensing, contract manufacturing, management contracting and joint ownership.[39]

Licensing

Licensing is a simple way for a manufacturer to enter international marketing. The company enters into an agreement with a licensee in the foreign market. For a fee or royalty, the licensee buys the right to use the company's manufacturing process, trade mark, patent, trade secret or other item of value. The company thus gains entry into the market at little risk; the licensee gains production expertise or a well-known product or name without having to start from scratch.

Coca-Cola markets internationally by licensing bottlers around the world and supplying them with the syrup needed to produce the product. In Japan, Budweiser beer flows from

Kirin breweries, and Tokyo Disneyland is owned and operated by Oriental Land Company under licence from the Walt Disney Company. GW Pharmaceuticals strikes deals with Japanese partners to produce their new drugs in the UK.

Licensing has potential disadvantages, however. The firm has less control over the licensee than it would over its own production facilities – the Danish toy company, Lego, recently took over production at its licensed partner's production facility in the Czech Republic for strategic reasons, but this company – Flextronic – will continue production in Mexico.[40] Furthermore, if the licensee is very successful, the firm has given up these profits, and if and when the contract ends it may find it has created a competitor.

Contract manufacturing

Another option is **contract manufacturing** – the company contracts with manufacturers in the foreign market to produce its product or provide its service. Boots, the large UK pharmaceutical retailer, has a division which manufactures health and beauty products for many other companies like French Connection, Toni&Guy and Soltan sunblock in the UK, France and Germany.[41] For these brands there are potential drawbacks – decreased control over the manufacturing process and loss of potential profits on manufacturing. The benefits are the chance to start faster, with less risk, and the later opportunity either to form a partnership with or to buy out the local manufacturer.

Management contracting

Under **management contracting**, the domestic firm supplies management know-how to a foreign company that supplies the capital. The domestic firm exports management services rather than products. Hilton uses this arrangement in managing hotels around the world.

Management contracting is a low-risk method of getting into a foreign market, and it yields income from the beginning. The arrangement is even more attractive if the contracting firm has an option to buy some share in the managed company later on. The arrangement is not sensible, however, if the company can put its scarce management talent to better uses or if it can make greater profits by undertaking the whole venture. Management contracting also prevents the company from setting up its own operations for a period of time.

Joint ownership

Joint ownership ventures consist of one company joining forces with foreign investors to create a local business in which they share joint ownership and control. A company may buy an interest in a local firm, or the two parties may form a new business venture. Joint ownership may be needed for economic or political reasons. The firm may lack the financial, physical or managerial resources to undertake the venture alone. Or a foreign government may require joint ownership as a condition for entry.

Inchcape is a leading car retailer, with operations in Austria, Belgium, Greece, the UK and many other countries outside Europe. Wishing to enter the growing Russian market, it went into partnership with a local organisation, the Olimp Group, several years ago. Having gained experience of this new market, it bought out Olimp and now has sole ownership of the operation.[42] Tesco now operates in many countries – in Thailand it partners with a local company called Lotus to provide stores of a similar format to the Tesco Express shops in the UK – 24-hour convenience stores.[43] Lotus provides local knowledge, contacts and familiarity, and Tesco brings its expertise in logistics and distribution, as well as the customer-centred ethos that has helped it dominate in its home market.

Direct investment

The biggest involvement in a foreign market comes through **direct investment** – the development of foreign-based assembly or manufacturing facilities. If a company has gained experience in exporting and if the foreign market is large enough, foreign production facilities offer many advantages. The firm may have lower costs in the form of cheaper labour or raw materials, foreign government investment incentives and freight savings. The firm may improve its image in the host country because it creates jobs – perhaps developing a deeper relationship with government, customers, local suppliers and distributors, allowing it to adapt its products to the local market better. Finally, the firm keeps full control over the investment and therefore can develop manufacturing and marketing policies that serve its long-term international objectives.

The main disadvantage of direct investment is that the firm faces many risks, such as restricted or devalued currencies, falling markets or government changes. In some cases, a firm has no choice but to accept these risks if it wants to operate in the host country.

MAKING CONNECTIONS Linking the concepts

Slow down here and think again about Volkswagen's global marketing issues.

- To what extent can Volkswagen standardise for the Chinese market? What marketing strategy and programme elements can be similar to those used in Europe and other parts of the Western world? Which ones must be adapted? Be specific.

- To what extent can Volkswagen standardise its products and programmes for the UK market? Which elements can be standardised and which must be adapted?

- To what extent are Volkswagen's 'globalisation' efforts contributing to 'Westernisation' of countries and cultures around the world? What are the positives and negatives of such cultural developments?

DECIDING ON THE GLOBAL MARKETING PROGRAMME

Companies that operate in one or more foreign markets must decide how much, if at all, to adapt their marketing strategies and programmes to local conditions. At one extreme are global companies that use a **standardised marketing mix**, selling largely the same products and using the same marketing approaches worldwide. At the other extreme is an **adapted marketing mix**. In this case, the producer adjusts the marketing mix elements to each target market, bearing more costs but hoping for a larger market share and return.

The question of whether to adapt or standardise the marketing strategy and programme has been much debated in recent years. On the one hand, some global marketers believe that technology is making the world a smaller place, and that consumer needs around the world are becoming more similar. This paves the way for 'global brands' and standardised global marketing. Global branding and standardisation, in turn, result in greater brand power and reduced costs from economies of scale. See Table 15.2 for the brands that have achieved world domination.

On the other hand, the marketing concept holds that marketing programmes will be more effective if tailored to the unique needs of each targeted customer group. If this concept applies within a country, it should apply even more in international markets. Despite global convergence, consumers in different countries still have widely varied cultural backgrounds. They still differ significantly in their needs and wants, spending power, product preferences and shopping patterns. Because these differences are hard to change, most marketers adapt their products, prices, channels and promotions to fit consumer desires in each country.[44]

However, global standardisation is not an all-or-nothing proposition but rather a matter of degree. Most international marketers suggest that companies should 'think globally but act locally' – that they should seek a balance between standardisation and adaptation. These marketers advocate a 'glocal' strategy in which the firm standardises certain core marketing

TABLE 15.2 Top global brands

Rank	Previous rank	Brand	Country/Region	Sector	Brand value ($m)	Change in brand value
1	1	Coca-Cola	United States	Beverages	70,452	2%
2	2	IBM	United States	Business Services	64,727	7%
3	3	Microsoft	United States	Computer Software	60,895	7%
4	7	Google	United States	Internet Services	43,557	36%
5	4	General Electric	United States	Diversified	42,808	−10%
6	6	McDonald's	United States	Restaurants	33,578	4%
7	9	Intel	United States	Electronics	32,015	4%
8	5	Nokia	Finland	Electronics	29,495	−15%
9	10	Disney	United States	Media	28,731	1%
10	11	Hewlett Packard	United States	Electronics	26,867	12%
11	8	Toyota	Japan	Automotive	26,192	−16%
12	12	Mercedes Benz	Germany	Automotive	25,179	6%
13	13	Gillette	United States	FMCG	23,298	2%
14	14	Cisco	United States	Business Services	23,219	5%
15	15	BMW	Germany	Automotive	22,322	3%
16	16	Louis Vuitton	France	Luxury	21,860	4%

Source: Adapted from Interbrand Global Brands Survey 2010, available from www.interbrand.com.

elements and localises others. The corporate level gives global strategic direction; local units focus on individual consumer differences across global markets. Simon Clift, head of marketing for global consumer goods giant Unilever, puts it this way: 'We're trying to strike a balance between being mindlessly global and hopelessly local.'[45]

McDonald's operates this way. It uses the same basic fast-food operating model in its restaurants around the world but adapts its menu to local tastes. In Korea, it sells roast pork on a bun with a garlicky soy sauce. In India, where cows are considered sacred, McDonald's serves McChicken, Filet-O-Fish, McVeggie (a vegetable burger), Pizza McPuffs, McAlooTikki (a spiced-potato burger), and the Maharaja Mac – two all-chicken patties, special sauce, lettuce, cheese, pickles and onions on a sesame-seed bun. McDonald's in France sells beer. Similarly, L'Oréal markets truly global brands – including, among others, Maybelline, Garnier, Lancôme, Kiehl's and Biotherm, as well as Ralph Lauren and Giorgio Armani Parfums, always adapting its brands to meet the cultural nuances of each local market:

How does a French company with a British CEO successfully market a Japanese version of an American lipstick in Russia? Ask L'Oréal, which sells more than $18 billion worth of cosmetics, hair-care products and fragrances each year in 150 countries, making it the world's biggest cosmetics company. L'Oréal markets its brands globally by understanding how they appeal to cultural nuances in specific local markets. For L'Oréal, that means finding local brands, sprucing them up, positioning them for a specific target market, and exporting them to new customers all over the globe. Then, to support this effort, the company spends $4 billion annually to tailor global marketing messages to local cultures.

For example, in 1996, the company bought the stodgy American make-up producer, Maybelline. To reinvigorate and globalise the brand, it moved the unit's headquarters from Tennessee to New York City and added 'New York' to the label. The resulting urban, street-smart, Big Apple image played well with the mid-price positioning of the workaday make-up brand. The makeover earned Maybelline a 20 per cent market share in its category in Western

Europe. The young urban positioning also hit the mark in Asia, where few women realise that the trendy 'New York' Maybelline brand belongs to French cosmetics giant L'Oréal. When CEO Lindsey Owens-Jones recently addressed a UNESCO conference, nobody batted an eyelid when he described L'Oréal as 'the United Nations of Beauty'.[46]

Product

Five strategies allow for adapting product and marketing communication to a global market (see Figure 15.3).[47] We first discuss the three product strategies and then turn to the two communication strategies.

Straight product extension means marketing a product in a foreign market without any change. Top management tells its marketing people, 'Take the product as is and find customers for it.' The first step, however, should be to find out whether foreign consumers use that product and what form they prefer.

Straight product extension has been successful in some cases and disastrous in others. Kellogg's cereals, Gillette razors, Heineken beer and Black & Decker tools are all sold successfully in about the same form around the world. But General Foods introduced its standard powdered Jell-O in the British market only to find that British consumers prefer a solid wafer or cake form. Likewise, Philips began to make a profit in Japan only after it reduced the size of its coffeemakers to fit into smaller Japanese kitchens and its shavers to fit smaller Japanese hands. Straight extension is tempting because it involves no additional product development costs, manufacturing changes or new promotion. But it can be costly in the long run if products fail to satisfy foreign consumers.

Product adaptation involves changing the product to meet local conditions or wants. For example, Procter & Gamble's Vidal Sassoon shampoos contain a single fragrance worldwide, but the amount of scent varies by country: more in Europe but less in Japan, where subtle scents are preferred. Gerber serves Japanese baby food that might turn the stomachs of many Western consumers – local favourites include flounder and spinach stew, cod roe spaghetti, mugwort casserole, and sardines ground up in white radish sauce. And Finnish mobile phone maker Nokia customises its mobile phones for every major market. Developers build in rudimentary voice recognition for Asia where keyboards are a problem and raise the ring volume so phones can be heard on crowded Asian streets.

Product invention consists of creating something new for a specific country market. This strategy can take two forms. It might mean maintaining or reintroducing earlier product forms that happen to be well adapted to the needs of a given country. Volkswagen continued to produce and sell its old VW Beetle model in Mexico until just recently. Or a company might create a new product to meet a need in a given country. For example, Sony added the 'U' model to its VAIO personal computer line to meet the unique needs of Japanese consumers – amongst which were a requirement for it to be small and usable while the user is standing – even though it wouldn't have much appeal in other world markets.

		PRODUCT		
		Don't change product	Adapt product	Develop new product
COMMUNICATIONS	Don't change communications	Straight extension	Product adaptation	Product invention
	Adapt communications	Communication adaptation	Dual adaptation	

FIGURE 15.3 Five global product and communications strategies

Some companies standardise their advertising around the world, adapting only to meet cultural differences. Guy Laroche uses similar ads in Europe (left) and Arab countries (right), but tones down the sensuality in the Arab version – the man is clothed and the woman barely touches him

Source: Courtesy of Bernard Matussiere.

Promotion

Companies can either adopt the same communication strategy they used in the home market or change it for each local market. Consider advertising messages. Some global companies use a standardised advertising theme around the world. Of course, even in highly standardised communications campaigns, some small changes might be required to adjust for language and minor cultural differences. For example, Guy Laroche uses virtually the same ads for its Drakkar Noir fragrances in Europe as in Arab countries. However, it subtly tones down the Arab versions to meet cultural differences in attitudes towards sensuality. (Refer to Table 15.3 for a summary of the top global advertisers.)

Colours are also changed sometimes to avoid taboos in other countries. Purple is associated with death in most of Latin America, white is a mourning colour in Japan, and green is associated with sickness in Malaysia. Even names must be changed. Kellogg's had to rename Bran Buds cereal in Sweden, where the name roughly translates as 'burned farmer'. And in the Americas, Mitsubishi changed the Japanese name of its Pajero SUV to Montero – it seems that *pajero* in Spanish is a slang term for sexual self-gratification. (See Marketing at Work 15.2 for more on language blunders in international marketing.)

TABLE 15.3 How Coca-Cola spends its advertising money globally 2011

Measured media spending in millions of US dollars			
By region	2009	2008	% chg
Africa	55.8	59.7	−6.5
Asia and Pacific	602.4	529.1	13.9
Europe	1,057.2	1,173.4	−9.9
Latin America	180.9	176.8	2.3
Middle East	126.9	103.2	23.0
Canada	12.9	10.9	18.5
Subtotal media outside the US	2,036.1	2,053.0	−0.8
US media spending	406.1	442.2	−8.2
Worldwide	$2,442.2	$2,495.2	−2.1

Source: www.adage.com.

Watch your language!

Many global companies have had difficulty crossing the language barrier, with results ranging from mild embarrassment to outright failure. Seemingly innocuous brand names and advertising phrases can take on unintended or hidden meanings when translated into other languages. Careless translations can make a marketer look downright foolish to foreign consumers.

We've all run across examples when buying products from other countries. Here's one from a firm in Taiwan attempting to instruct children on how to install a ramp on a garage for toy cars: 'Before you play with, fix waiting plate by yourself as per below diagram. But after you once fixed it, you can play with as is and no necessary to fix off again.' Many US firms also are guilty of such atrocities when marketing abroad.

The classic language blunders involve standardised brand names that do not translate well. When Coca-Cola first marketed Coke in China in the 1920s, it developed a group of Chinese characters that, when pronounced, sounded like the product name. Unfortunately, the characters actually translated to mean 'bite the wax tadpole'. Now, the characters on Chinese Coke bottles translate as 'happiness in the mouth'.

Several US car makers have had similar problems when their brand names crashed into the language barrier. Chevy's Nova translated into Spanish as *no va* – 'it doesn't go'. GM changed the name to Caribe (Spanish for Caribbean) and sales increased. Buick scrambled to rename its new LaCrosse sedan the Allure in Canada after learning that the name comes too close to a Quebecois slang word for masturbation. And Rolls-Royce avoided the name Silver Mist in German markets, where *mist* means 'manure'. Sunbeam, however, entered the German market with its Mist Stick hair-curling iron. As should have been expected, the Germans had little use for a 'manure wand'. A similar fate awaited Colgate when it introduced a toothpaste in France called Cue, the name of a notorious porno magazine.

One well-intentioned firm sold its shampoo in Brazil under the name Evitol. It soon realised it was claiming to sell a 'dandruff contraceptive'. An American company reportedly had trouble marketing pet milk in French-speaking areas. It seems that the word *pet* in French means, among other things, 'to break wind'. Similarly,

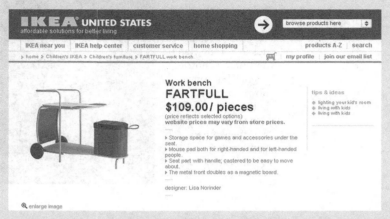

Global language barriers: some standardised brand names do not translate well globally

Source: Inter IKEA Systems BV.

IKEA marketed a children's workbench named FARTFULL (the word means 'speedy' in Swedish) – it soon discontinued the product. Hunt-Wesson introduced its Big John products in Quebec as Gros Jos before learning that it means 'big breasts' in French. Unlike FARTFULL, this gaffe had no apparent effect on sales.

Interbrand of London, the firm that created household names such as Prozac and Acura, recently developed a brand-name 'hall of shame' list, which contains these and other foreign brand names you're never likely to see inside the local Morrisons: Krapp toilet paper (Denmark), Crapsy Fruit cereal (France), Happy End toilet paper (Germany), Mukk yogurt (Italy), Zit lemonade (Germany), Poo curry powder (Argentina) and Pschitt lemonade (France).

Travellers often encounter well-intentioned advice from service firms that takes on meanings very different from those intended. The menu in one Swiss restaurant proudly stated, 'Our wines leave you nothing to hope for'. Signs in a Japanese hotel pronounced, 'You are invited to take advantage of the chambermaid'. At a laundry in Rome, it was, 'Ladies, leave your clothes here and spend the afternoon having a good time'. The brochure at a Tokyo car hire firm offered this sage advice: 'When passenger of foot heave in sight, tootle the horn. Trumpet him melodiously at first, but if he still obstacles your passage, tootle him with vigour.'

Advertising themes often lose – or gain – something in the translation. The Coors beer slogan 'get loose with Coors' in Spanish came out as 'get the runs with Coors'. Coca-Cola's 'Coke adds life' theme in Japanese translated into 'Coke brings your ancestors back from the dead'. The milk industry learned too late that its American advertising question 'Got Milk?' translated in Mexico as a more pro-vocative, 'Are you lactating?' In Chinese, the KFC slogan 'fingerlickin' good' came out as 'eat your fingers off'. And Frank Perdue's classic line, 'It takes a tough man to make a tender chicken', took on added meaning in Spanish: 'It takes an aroused man to make a chicken affectionate'. Even when the language is the same, word usage may differ from country to country. Thus, the British ad line for Electrolux vacuum cleaners – 'Nothing sucks like an Electrolux' – would capture few customers in the United States.

So, what can a company do to avoid such mistakes? One answer is to call in the experts. Brand consultancy Lexicon Branding has been dreaming up brand names for more than twenty years, including names like Dasani, Swiffer and Blackberry. David Placek, Lexicon's founder and president acknowledges that 'coming up with catchy product names is a lot harder than [you] might imagine, especially in this Global Age, when a word that might inspire admiration in one country can just as easily inspire red faces or unintended guffaws in another.'

Lexicon maintains a global network of high-quality linguists from around the world that it calls GlobalTalk –

'so we can call on them to evaluate words for language and cultural cues and miscues'. Beyond screening out the bad names, the GlobalTalk network can also help find good ones. 'We created the brand name Zima for Coors with help from the GlobalTalk network,' says Placek. 'I put out a message saying that we were looking for a name for a light alcoholic drink that would be cold, crisp, and refreshing. I got a fax in quickly from our Russian linguist saying that *zima* meant "winter" in Russian. I circled the word because I thought it was beautiful and unusual, and the client loved it. We sent it around the world to make sure that it didn't have a negative connotation anywhere, and it didn't.'

Sources: Lexicon example and quotes from 'Naming Products Is No Game', BusinessWeek Online, 9 April 2004, accessed at www.businessweekonline.com. For the above and other examples, see David A. Ricks, 'Perspectives: Translation Blunders in International Business', *Journal of Language for International Business*, 7:2, 1996, pp. 50–55; Ken Friedenreich, 'The Lingua Too Franca', *World Trade*, April 1998, p. 98; Sam Solley, 'Developing a Name to Work Worldwide', *Marketing*, 21 December 2000, p. 27; Thomas T. Sermon, 'Cutting Corners in Language Risky Business', *Marketing News*, 23 April 2001, p. 9; Martin Croft, 'Mind Your Language', *Marketing*, 19 June 2003, pp. 35–39; Mark Lasswell, 'Lost in Translation', *Business 2.0*, August 2004, pp. 68–70; 'Lost in Translation', *Hispanic*, May 2005, p. 12; and Ross Thomson, 'Lost in Translation', *Medical Marketing and Media*, March 2005, p. 82.

Other companies follow a strategy of **communication adaptation**, fully adapting their advertising messages to local markets. Kellogg's ads in the United States promote the taste and nutrition of Kellogg's cereals versus competitors' brands. In France, where consumers drink little milk and don't eat much for breakfast, Kellogg's ads must convince consumers that cereals are a tasty and healthful breakfast. In India, where many consumers eat heavy, fried breakfasts, Kellogg's advertising convinces buyers to switch to a lighter, more nutritious breakfast diet.

Similarly, Coca-Cola sells its low-calorie beverage as Diet Coke in North America, the UK, and the Middle and Far East but as Light elsewhere. According to Diet Coke's global brand manager, in Spanish-speaking countries Coke Light ads 'position the soft drink as an object of desire, rather than as a way to feel good about yourself, as Diet Coke is positioned in the US and UK'. This 'desire positioning' plays off research showing that 'Coca-Cola Light is seen in other parts of world as a vibrant brand that exudes a sexy confidence'.[48]

Media also need to be adapted internationally because media availability varies from country to country. TV advertising time is very limited in Europe, for instance, ranging from four hours a day in France to none in Scandinavian countries. Advertisers must buy time months in advance, and they have little control over airtimes. Magazines also vary in effectiveness. For example, magazines are a major medium in Italy and a minor one in Austria. Newspapers are mostly national in the UK but are only local in Spain.[49]

Price

Companies also face many problems in setting their international prices. For example, how might Black & Decker price its power tools globally? It could set a uniform price all around the world, but this amount would be too high a price in poor countries and not high enough in rich ones. It could charge what consumers in each country would bear, but this strategy ignores differences in the actual costs from country to country. Finally, the company could use a standard mark-up of its costs everywhere, but this approach might price Black & Decker out of the market in some countries where costs are high.

To deal with such issues, P&G adapts its pricing to local markets. For example, in Asia it has moved to a tiered pricing model.

When P&G first entered Asia, it used the approach that had made it so successful in the United States. It developed better products and charged slightly higher prices than competitors. It also charged nearly as much for a box of Tide or bottle of Pantene in Asia as it did in North America. But such high prices limited P&G's appeal in Asian markets, where most consumers earn just a few dollars a day. So last year P&G adopted a tiered pricing strategy to help compete against cheaper local brands while also protecting the value of its global brands. It slashed Asian production costs, streamlined distribution channels, and reshaped its product line to create more affordable prices. For example, it introduced a 320-gram bag of Tide Clean White for 23 cents, compared with 33 cents for 350 grams of Tide Triple Action. Clean White doesn't offer such benefits as stain removal and fragrance, and it contains less advanced cleaning enzymes. But it costs less to make and outperforms every other brand at the lower price level. The results of P&G's new tiered pricing have been dramatic. Using the same approach for toothpaste, P&G now sells more Crest in China than in the United States. Its Olay brand is the best-selling facial cream in China and Rejoice is the bestselling shampoo.[50]

Regardless of how companies go about pricing their products, their foreign prices probably will be higher than their domestic prices for comparable products. A Gucci handbag may sell for the equivalent of $60 in Italy and $240 in the United States. Why? Gucci faces a *price escalation* problem. It must add the cost of transportation, tariffs, importer margin, wholesaler margin and retailer margin to its factory price. Depending on these added costs, the product may have to sell for two to five times as much in another country to make the same profit. For example, a pair of Levi's jeans that sells for $30 in the United States typically fetches $63 in Tokyo and $88 in Paris. Typically, a computer that sells for $1,000 in New York may cost £1,000 in the United Kingdom – twice as much. A Ford car priced at $20,000 in the United States might sell for more than $80,000 in South Korea.

Another problem involves setting a price for goods that a company ships to its foreign subsidiaries. If the company charges a foreign subsidiary too much, it may end up paying higher tariff duties even while paying lower income taxes in that country. If the company charges its subsidiary too little, it can be charged with *dumping*. Dumping occurs when a company either charges less than its costs or less than it charges in its home market. Various governments and multi-state bodies like the EU and NAFTA watch for dumping abuses, and they often force companies to set the price charged by other competitors for the same or similar products. As examples of this, in 2007 the EU took legal steps against dumping in 35 cases and India 31 – for products as varied as cars, shoes, steel and cotton. Globally, Chinese exports were the target of 37 per cent of these actions and this issue – and the complex legal and diplomatic questions it raises – is becoming of increasing importance between China and its trading partners.[51]

Recent economic and technological forces have had an impact on global pricing. For example, in much of the EU the transition to the euro has reduced the amount of price differentiation. As consumers recognise price differentiation by country, companies are being forced to harmonise prices throughout the countries that have adopted the single currency. Consumers are willing and able to drive a few miles over a border to make a substantial saving – a real and growing issue in countries like Austria and Germany where Polish prices are often markedly lower. Companies and marketers that offer the most unique or necessary products or services will be least affected by such 'price transparency'.

For Marie-Claude Lang, a 72-year-old retired Belgian postal worker, the euro is the best thing since bottled water – or French country sausage. Always on the prowl for bargains, Ms Lang is now stalking the wide aisles of an Auchan hypermarket in Roncq, France, a 15-minute drive from her Wervick home . . . Ms Lang has been coming to France every other week for years to stock up on bottled water, milk, and yogurt. But the launch of the euro . . . has opened her eyes to many more products that she now sees cost less across the border. Today she sees that 'saucisse de campagne' is cheaper 'by about five euro cents', a savings she didn't notice when she had to calculate the difference between Belgian and French francs.[52]

The Internet will also make global price differences more obvious. When firms sell their wares over the Internet, customers can see how much products sell for in different countries. They might even be able to order a given product directly from the company location or dealer offering the lowest price. This will force companies towards more standardised international pricing.

Distribution channels

The international company must take a **whole-channel view** of the problem of distributing products to final consumers. Figure 15.4 shows the three major links between the seller and the final buyer. The first link, the *seller's headquarters organisation*, supervises the channels and is part of the channel itself. The second link, *channels between nations*, moves the products to the borders of the foreign nations. The third link, *channels within nations*, moves the products from their foreign entry point to the final consumers. Some manufacturers may think their job is done once the product leaves their hands, but they would do well to pay more attention to its handling within foreign countries.

Channels of distribution within countries vary greatly from nation to nation. First, there are the large differences in the *numbers and types of intermediaries* serving each foreign market.

International distribution: distribution channels vary greatly from nation to nation, as this photo from the streets of Beijing suggests.

Source: Press Association Images/Greg Baker/AP.

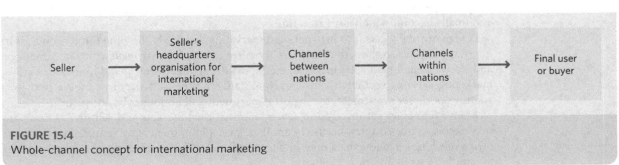

Seller → Seller's headquarters organisation for international marketing → Channels between nations → Channels within nations → Final user or buyer

FIGURE 15.4
Whole-channel concept for international marketing

For example, a European company marketing in China must operate through a frustrating maze of state-controlled wholesalers and retailers. Chinese distributors often carry competitors' products and frequently refuse to share even basic sales and marketing information with their suppliers. Hustling for sales is an alien concept to Chinese distributors, who are used to selling all they can obtain. Working with or getting around this system sometimes requires much time and investment.

When Coke first entered China, for example, customers bicycled up to bottling plants to get their soft drinks. Many shopkeepers still don't have enough electricity to run soft drink coolers. Now, Coca-Cola has set up direct-distribution channels, investing heavily in refrigerators and trucks, and upgrading wiring so that more retailers can install coolers. The company has also built an army of more than 10,000 sales representatives that makes regular visits on resellers, often on foot or bicycle, to check on stocks and record sales. 'Coke and its bottlers have been trying to map every supermarket, restaurant, barbershop, or market stall where a can of soda might be consumed,' notes an industry observer. 'Those data help Coke get closer to its customers, whether they are in large hypermarkets, Spartan noodle shops, or schools.' Still, to reach the most isolated spots in the country, Coca-Cola relies on some pretty unlikely business partners – teams of delivery donkeys. 'Massive advertising budgets can drum up demand,' says another observer, 'but if the distribution network doesn't exist properly or doesn't work, the potential of China's vast market cannot be realised.'[53]

Another difference lies in the *size and character of retail units* abroad. Whereas large-scale retail chains dominate in much of Europe, much retailing in other countries is done by many small, independent retailers. In India, millions of retailers operate tiny shops or sell in open markets. Their mark-ups are high, but the actual price is lowered through haggling. Supermarkets could offer lower prices, but supermarkets are difficult to build and open because of many economic and cultural barriers. Incomes are low, and people prefer to shop daily for small amounts rather than weekly for large amounts. They also lack storage and refrigeration to keep food for several days. Packaging is not well developed because it would add too much to the cost. These factors have kept large-scale retailing from spreading rapidly in developing countries.

A further issue is that of grey markets. These are created when manufactured products are exported from their domestic market and then resold back to a retailer in that home market by a foreign intermediary. Companies like Adidas and Levi have suffered from this as they set prices in the Far East at a much lower level than in Western Europe and North America – retailers in these nations can pay for the goods to be imported back to them and still undercut the domestic retail price charged by companies which bought from the manufacturers directly.

DECIDING ON THE GLOBAL MARKETING ORGANISATION

Companies manage their international marketing activities in at least three different ways: most companies first organise an export department, then create an international division and finally become a global organisation.

A firm normally gets into international marketing by simply shipping out its goods. If its international sales expand, the company organises an *export department* with a sales manager and a few assistants. As sales increase, the export department can expand to include various marketing services so that it can actively go after business. If the firm moves into joint ventures or direct investment, the export department will no longer be adequate.

Many companies get involved in several international markets and ventures. A company may export to one country, license to another, have a joint ownership venture in a third and own a subsidiary in a fourth. Sooner or later it will create *international divisions* or subsidiaries to handle all its international activity.

International divisions are organised in a variety of ways. An international division's corporate staff consists of marketing, manufacturing, research, finance, planning and personnel specialists. It plans for and provides services to various operating units, which can be organised in one of three ways. They can be *geographical organisations*, with country managers who are responsible for salespeople, sales branches, distributors and licensees in their respective countries. Or the operating units can be *world product groups*, each responsible for worldwide sales of different product groups. Finally, operating units can be *international subsidiaries*, each responsible for its own sales and profits.

Many firms have passed beyond the international division stage and become truly *global organisations*. They stop thinking of themselves as national marketers who sell abroad and start thinking of themselves as global marketers. The top corporate management and staff plan worldwide manufacturing facilities, marketing policies, financial flows and logistical systems. The global operating units report directly to the chief executive or executive committee of the organisation, not to the head of an international division. Executives are trained in worldwide operations, not just domestic *or* international. The company recruits management from many countries, buys components and supplies where they cost the least, and invests where the expected returns are greatest.

Moving further into the twenty-first century, major companies must become more global if they hope to compete. As foreign companies successfully invade their domestic markets, companies must move more aggressively into foreign markets. They will have to change from companies that treat their international operations as secondary, to companies that view the entire world as a single borderless market.

THE JOURNEY YOU'VE TAKEN Reviewing the concepts

It's time to stop and think back about the global marketing concepts you covered in this chapter. Companies today can no longer afford to pay attention only to their domestic market, regardless of its size. Many industries are global industries, and firms that operate globally achieve lower costs and higher brand awareness. At the same time, global marketing is risky because of variable exchange rates, unstable governments, protectionist tariffs and trade barriers, and several other factors. Given the potential gains and risks of international marketing, companies need a systematic way to make their global marketing decisions.

1   **Discuss how the international trade system, economic, political-legal and cultural environments affect a company's international marketing decisions**

A company must understand the global marketing environment, especially the international trade system. It must assess each foreign market's economic, political-legal and cultural characteristics. The company must then decide whether it wants to go abroad and consider the potential risks and benefits. It must decide on the volume of international sales it wants, how many coun-

tries it wants to market in and which specific markets it wants to enter. This decision calls for weighing the probable rate of return on investment against the level of risk.

2   **Describe three key approaches to entering international markets**

The company must decide how to enter each chosen market – whether through exporting, joint venturing or direct investment. Many companies start as exporters, move to joint ventures and finally make a direct investment in foreign markets. In exporting, the company enters a foreign market by sending and selling products through international marketing intermediaries (indirect exporting) or the company's own department, branch, or sales representative or agents (direct exporting). When establishing a joint venture, a company enters foreign markets by joining with foreign companies to produce or market a product or service. In licensing, the company enters a foreign market by contracting with a licensee in the foreign market, offering the right to use a manufacturing process, trademark, patent, trade secret or other item of value for a fee or royalty.

3 Explain how companies adapt their marketing mixes for international markets

Companies must also decide how much their products, promotion, price and channels should be adapted for each foreign market. At one extreme, global companies use a standardised marketing mix worldwide. Others use an adapted marketing mix, in which they adjust the marketing mix to each target market, bearing more costs but hoping for a larger market share and return.

4 Identify the three major forms of international marketing organisation

The company must develop an effective organisation for international marketing. Most firms start with an export department and graduate to an international division. A few become global organisations, with worldwide marketing planned and managed by the top officers of the company. Global organisations view the entire world as a single, borderless market.

NAVIGATING THE KEY TERMS

Adapted marketing mix 512
Communication adaptation 517
Contract manufacturing 511
Countertrade 504
Direct investment 511
Economic community 501

Exporting 510
Global firm 499
Joint ownership 511
Joint venturing 510
Licensing 510
Management contracting 511

Product adaptation 514
Standardised marketing mix 512
Straight product extension 514
Whole-channel view 519

NOTES AND REFERENCES

1 D. Roberts, 'GM and VW: How Not to Succeed in China', *BusinessWeek*, 5 September 2005, p. 94.

2 Volkswagen China official website: **http://www.vw.com.cn/cds/?menu_uid=551**, accessed on 8 January 2008.

3 *International Business Times*, 8 January 2008, 'VW's China Sales Reach Record' **http://www.ibtimes.com**, accessed on 18 January 2008.

4 A. Webb, 'GM Tops VW for China Sales Lead', *Automotive News*, 79(6161), 2005, p. 6; and Xinhua, China News Agency, **http://news.xinhuanet.com/english/2008-01/11/content_7401796.htm**, accessed on 24 January 2008.

5 A. Webb, 'As its Sales Plunge in China, VW Tries a New Approach', *Automotive News*, 80(6176), 2005, p. 24B.

6 Volkswagen China official website: **http://www.vw.com.cn/cds/?menu_uid=567**, accessed on 12 January 2008.

7 A. Webb, 'China Skid: Where VW Went Wrong', *Automotive News Europe*, 9(13), 2004, pp. 1–28.

8 A. Webb, 'As Its Sales Plunge in China, VW Tries a New Approach', *Automotive News*, 80(6176), 2005, p. 24B.

9 Volkswagen China official website: **http://www.vw.com.cn/cds/?menu_uid=565**, accessed on 15 January 2008.

10 Volkswagen China official website: **http://www.vw.com.cn/cds/?menu_uid=565**, accessed on 15 January 2008.

11 N. Madden, 'VW Hopes to Pull Chinese Heartstrings', *Automotive News*, 78(6103), 2004, p. 28.

12 Read the background in English: 'Swedes Find Viking-era Arab Coins' at *BBC News*, **www.bbc-co.uk/news**; and in the original Swedish at: Silverskattfran Vikingatidenfunnen, **www.raa.se**, accessed September 2011.

13 George Melloan, 'Feeling the Muscles of the Multinationals', *The Wall Street Journal*, 6 January 2004, p. A19.

14 Numbers from WTO, 'International Trade Statistics', available from **www.wto.org**, accessed September 2011.

15 See 'Compagnie Générale des Établissements Michelin', *Hoover's Company Records*, 15 July 2005, p. 41240; and 'Johnson & Johnson', *Hoover's Company Records*, 15 July 2005, p. 10824.

16 See: U. Golob and K. Podnar, 'Competitive Advantage in the Marketing of Products within the Enlarged European Union', *European Journal of Marketing*, 41(3/4), 2007, pp. 245–56; and S. Paliwoda and S. Marinova, 'The Marketing Challenges Within the Enlarged Single European Market', *European Journal of Marketing*, 41(3/4), 2007, pp. 233–44.

17 For context on this see the Transparency International pages at **www.transparency.org** and the Volvo press releases from **www.volvo.com** – search for Iraq.

18 Steve Hamm, 'Borders Are So 20th Century', *BusinessWeek*, 22 September 2003, pp. 68–73.

19 'The Unique Japanese', *Fortune*, 24 November 1986, p. 8. See also James D. Southwick, 'Addressing Market Access Barriers in Japan Through the WTO', *Law and Policy in International Business*, Spring 2000, pp. 923–76; and US Commercial Service, *Country Commercial Guide Japan, FY 2005*, ch. 5, accessed at **www.buyusa.gov**, 18 June 2005.

20 Read *'What is the WTO?'*, at **www.wto.org/**, accessed September 2011.

21 This prediction made in 'WTO Annual Report 2004', and '10 Benefits of the WTO Trading System', accessed at **www.wto.org**. We'll never know if it was true.

22 Read more about the history and future of GATT in 'Timeline: World Trade Organization' from *BBC News*, **www.bbc.co.uk/news**, accessed September 2011.

23 The complete story: 'Fearful or Cheerful? The Prospects for the World Trade Talks' in *The Economist*, **www.economist.com**, accessed September 2011.

24 'See The European Union at a Glance', at **europa.eu/about-eu/facts-figures/economy** for a top line overview of the EU economy; accessed September 2011.

25 'Overviews of European Union Activities: Economic and Monetary Affairs', accessed at europa.eu/pol/emu/, September 2011.

26 IMF Data from 'World Economic Outlook Database', **www.imf.org**, accessed September 2011.

27 Read more about NAFTA via **www.nafta.org**.

28 See Angela Greiling Keane, 'Counting on CAFTA', *Traffic World*, 8 August 2005, p. 1; Gilberto Meza, 'Is the FTAA Floundering', *Business Mexico*, February 2005, pp. 46–8; Peter Robson, 'Integrating the Americas: FTAA and Beyond', *Journal of Common Market Studies*, June 2005, p. 430; 'Rank Order GDP', *The World Factbook*, accessed at **www.cia.gov**, 18 June 2005, and 'Foreign Trade Statistics', accessed at **www.census.gov**, 18 June 2005.

29 Richard Lapper, 'South American Unity Still a Distant Dream', *Financial Times*, 9 December 2004, accessed at **www.news.ft.com**; and Mary Turck, 'South American Community of Nations', Resource Center of the Americas, accessed at **www.americas.org**, August 2005.

30 Read 'A Large Black Cloud' from *The Economist* at **www.economist.com**, accessed September 2011.

31 Adapted from information found in Clay Chandler, 'China Deluxe', *Fortune*, 26 July 2004, pp. 148–56. See also 'Selling to China's Rich and Not So Rich', *Strategic Directions*, June 2005, pp. 5–8; and Lisa Movius, 'Luxury's China Puzzle', *WWD*, 15 June 2005, p. 1. See also David Woodruff, 'Ready to Shop until They Drop', *BusinessWeek*, 22 June 1998, pp. 104–8; and James MacAonghus, 'Online Impact of a Growing Europe', *New Media Age*, 12 February 2004, p. 15.

32 See Om Malik, 'The New Land of Opportunity', *Business 2.0*, July 2004, pp. 72–9.

33 Ricky Griffin and Michael Pustay, *International Business*, 4th edn (Upper Saddle River, NJ: Prentice Hall, 2005), pp. 522–3.

34 Rebecca Piirto Heath, 'Think Globally', *Marketing Tools*, October 1996, pp. 49–54; and 'The Power of Writing', *National Geographic*, August 1999, pp. 128–9.

35 For other examples and discussion, see **www.executiveplanet.com**, December 2005; *Dun & Bradstreet's Guide to Doing Business Around the World* (Upper Saddle River, NJ: Prentice Hall, 2000); Ellen Neuborne, 'Bridging the Culture Gap', *Sales & Marketing Management*, July 2003, p. 22; Richard Pooley, 'When Cultures Collide', *Management Services*, Spring 2005, pp. 28–31; and Helen Deresky, *International Management*, 5th edn (Upper Saddle River, NJ: Prentice Hall, 2006).

36 Adapted from 'Importance of Adapting to the Chinese Market' from **www.renmenbi.com**, accessed September 2011.

37 Information from Lucy Ash, 'France Versus the World', from *BBC News* **www.bbc.co.uk/news**

38 See Jack Neff, 'Submerged', *Advertising Age*, 4 March 2002, p. 14; and Ann Chen and Vijay Vishwanath, 'Expanding in China', *Harvard Business Review*, March 2005, pp. 19–21.

39 For a good discussion of joint venturing, see James Bamford, David Ernst and David G. Fubini, 'Launching a World-Class Joint Venture', *Harvard Business Review*, February 2004, pp. 91–100.

40 See Lego at **www.lego.com** and Flextronic at **www.flextronics.com**.

41 Read more about BCM at their online home: **www.boots-manufacturing.com**

42 Visit Inchcape online at **www.inchcape.com**; some context to the story in the *Financial Times* – Stanley Pignal, 'Inchcape Takes Full Ownership in Russia', **www.ft.com**, accessed September 2011.

43 Read more about Tesco and their operations in Asia at **www.tescolotus.com**. Some context the story 'Global Tendrils' in *The Economist* at **www.economist.com**, accessed September 2011.

44 See: A. Schuh, 'Brand Strategies of Western MNCs as Drivers of Globalization in Central and Eastern Europe', *European Journal of Marketing*, 41(3/4), 2007, pp. 274–91; and T.L. Powers and J.J. Loyka, 'Market, Industry, and Company Influences on Global Product Standardization', *International Marketing Review*, 24(6), 2007, pp. 678–94.

45 For good discussions, see Laura Mazur, 'Globalization Is Still Tethered to Local Variations', *Marketing*, 22 January 2004, p. 18; Johny K. Johansson and Ilkka A. Ronkainen, 'The Brand Challenge: Are Global Brands the Right Choice for Your Company?', *Marketing Management*, March/April 2004; Douglas B. Holt, John A. Quelch and Earl L. Taylor, 'How Global Brands Compete', *Harvard Business Review*, September 2004, pp. 68–75; and Boris Sustar and Rozana Sustar, 'Managing Marketing Standardization in a Global Context', *Journal of American Academy of Business*, September 2005, pp. 302–10.

46 Quotes and other information from Richard Tomlinson, 'L'Oréal's Global Makeover', *Fortune*, 30 September 2002, p. 141; Gail Edmondson, 'The Beauty of Global Branding', *BusinessWeek*, 28 June 1999, pp. 70–5; Jeremy Joesephs, 'O-J's Powers of Seduction Hard to Resist', 25 March 2003, accessed at **www.jeremyjoesephs.com**; 'Consumer Products Brief: L'Oréal', *The Wall Street Journal*, 23 February 2004, p. 1; Vito J. Racanelli, 'Touching Up', 16 February 2004, pp. 18–19; Ross Tucker, 'L'Oréal Global Sales Rise', *WWD*, 18 February 2005, and information accessed at **www.loreal.com**, September 2005.

47 Warren J. Keegan, *Global Marketing Management*, 7th edn (Upper Saddle River, NJ: Prentice Hall, 2002), pp. 346–51. See also Phillip Kotler and Kevin Lane Keller, *Marketing Management*, 12th edn (Upper Saddle River, NJ: Prentice Hall, 2006), pp. 677–84.

48 Kate MacArthur, 'Coca-Cola Light Employs Local Edge', *Advertising Age*, 21 August 2000, pp. 18–19; and 'Case Studies: Coke Light Hottest Guy', Advantage Marketing, msn India, accessed at **http://advantage.msn.co.in**, 15 March 2004.

49 See Alicia Clegg, 'One Ad One World?', *Marketing Week*, 20 June 2002, pp. 51–2; and George E. Belch and Michael A. Belch, *Advertising and Promotion: An Integrated Marketing Communications Perspective*, 6th edn (New York, NY: McGraw-Hill, 2004), pp. 666–8.

50 Adapted from Normandy Madden and Jack Neff, 'P&G Adapts Attitude Toward Local Markets', *Advertising Age*, 23 February 2004, p. 28; and information found in 'P&G Hits No. 1 in China', *SPC Asia*, November 2004, p. 3.

51 See the Chinese side of the story by reading 'China Dissatisfied with EU Anti-Dumping Duties', **www.chinadaily.com.cn**, accessed September 2011.

52 Sarah Ellison, 'Revealing Price Disparities, the Euro Aids Bargain-Hunters', *The Wall Street Journal*, 30 January 2002, p. A15.

53 See Patrick Powers, 'Distribution in China: The End of the Beginning', *China Business Review*, July–August 2001, pp. 8–12; Drake Weisert, 'Coca-Cola in China: Quenching the Thirst of a Billion', *The China Business Review*, July–August 2001, pp. 52–5; Gabriel Kahn, 'Coke Works Harder at Being the Real Thing in Hinterland', *The Wall Street Journal*, 26 November 2002, p. B1; Leslie Chang, Chad Terhune and Betsy McKay, 'A Global Journal Report; Rural Thing – Coke's Big Gamble in Asia', *The Wall Street Journal*, 11 August 2004, p. A1; and Jo Bowman, 'Target: Managing Channels', 22 October 2004, p. S8.

Section 4:

Operations Management

1

Operations and processes

Introduction

Operations and process management is about how organisations create goods and services. Everything you wear, eat, use or read comes to you courtesy of the operations managers who organised its creation, as does every bank transaction, hospital visit and hotel stay. The people who created them may not always be called operations managers, but that is what they really are. Within the operations function of any enterprise, operations managers look after the processes that create products and services. But managers in other functions, such as Marketing, Sales and Finance, also manage processes. These processes often supply internal 'customers' with services such as marketing plans, sales forecasts, budgets, and so on. In fact, parts of all organisations are made up of processes. That is what this book is about – the tasks, issues and decisions that are necessary to manage processes effectively, both within the operations function, and in other parts of the business where effective process management is equally important. This is an introductory chapter, so we will examine some of the basic principles of operations and process management. The model that is developed to explain the subject is shown in Figure 1.1.

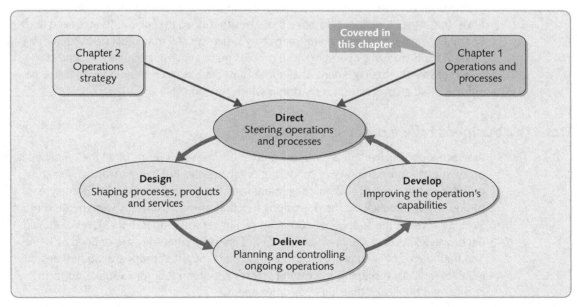

Figure 1.1 Operations and process management is about how organisations produce goods and services

EXECUTIVE SUMMARY

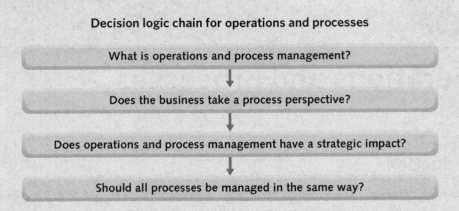

Decision logic chain for operations and processes

> What is operations and process management?
>
> ↓
>
> Does the business take a process perspective?
>
> ↓
>
> Does operations and process management have a strategic impact?
>
> ↓
>
> Should all processes be managed in the same way?

Each chapter is structured around a set of diagnostic questions. These questions suggest what you should ask in order to gain an understanding of the important issues of a topic, and, as a result, improve your decision making. An executive summary addressing these questions is provided below.

What is operations and process management?

The operations function is the part of the organisation that produces products or services. Every organisation has an operations function because every organisation produce some mixture of products and services. 'Operations' is not always called by that name, but whatever its name, it is always concerned with managing the core purpose of the business – producing some mix of products and services. Processes also produce products and services, but on a smaller scale. They are the component parts of operations. But, other functions also have processes that need managing. In fact *every* part of *any* business is concerned with managing processes. All managers have something to learn from studying operations and process management, because the subject encompasses the management of all types of operation, no matter in what sector or industry, and all processes, no matter in which function.

Does the business take a process perspective?

A 'process perspective' means understanding businesses in terms of all their individual processes. It is only one way of modelling organisations, but it is a particularly useful one. Operations and process management uses the process perspective to analyse businesses at three levels: the operations function of the business, the higher and more strategic level of the supply network, and at a lower more operational level of individual processes. Within the business, processes are only what they are defined as being. The boundaries of each process can be drawn as thought appropriate. Sometimes this involves radically reshaping the way processes are organised, for example, to form end-to-end processes that fulfil customer needs.

Does operations and process management have a strategic impact?

Operations and process management can make or break a business. When they are well managed, operations and processes can contribute to the strategic impact of the business in four ways: cost, revenue, investment and capabilities. Because the operations function has responsibility for much of a business's cost base, its first imperative is to keep costs under control. But also, through the way it provides service and quality, it should be looking to enhance the business's ability to generate revenue. Furthermore, as all failures are ultimately process failures, well-designed processes should have less chance of failing and more chance of recovering quickly from failure. Also, because operations are often the source of much investment, it should be aiming to get the best possible return on that investment. Finally, the operations function should be laying down the capabilities that will form the long-term basis for future competitiveness.

Should all processes be managed in the same way?

Not necessarily. Processes differ, particularly in what are known as the four Vs: volume, variety, variation and visibility. High-volume processes can exploit economies of scale and be systematised. High-variety processes require enough inbuilt flexibility to cope with the wide variety of activities expected of them. High-variation processes must be able to change their output levels to cope with highly variable and/or unpredictable levels of demand. High-visibility processes add value while the customer is 'present' in some way and therefore must be able to manage customers' perceptions of their activities. Generally, high volume together with low variety, variation and visibility facilitate low-cost processes, while low volume together with high levels of variety, variation and visibility all increase process costs. Yet in spite of these differences, operations managers use a common set of decisions and activities to manage them. These activities can be clustered under four groupings: directing the overall strategy of the operation; designing the operation's products, services and processes; planning and controlling process delivery; developing process performance.

What is operations and process management?

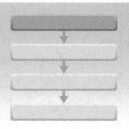

Operations and process management is the activity of managing the resources and processes that produce products and services. The core body of knowledge for the subject comes from 'operations management', which examines how the 'operations function' of a business produces products and services for external customers. We also use the shorter terms 'the operation' or 'operations', interchangeably with the 'operations function'. In some organisations an operations manager could be called by some other name, for example, a 'fleet manager' in a logistics company, an 'administrative manager' in a hospital, or a 'store manager' in a supermarket.

All business have 'operations', because all businesses produce products, services or a mixture of both. If you think that you don't have an operations function, you are wrong. If you think that your operations function is not important, you are also wrong. Look at the six businesses illustrated in Figure 1.2. There are two financial service companies, two manufacturing companies and two hotels. All of them have *operations functions* that produce the things that their customers are willing to pay for. Hotels produce accommodation services, financial services invest, store, move or sell us money and investment opportunities, and manufacturing businesses physically change the shape and the nature of materials to produce products. These businesses are from different sectors (banking, hospitality and manufacturing), but the main difference between their operations activities is not necessarily what one expects. There are often bigger differences *within* economic sectors than *between* them. All the three operations in the left-hand column provide value-for-money products and services and compete largely on cost. The three in the right-hand column provide more 'up-market' products and services that are more expensive to produce and compete on some combination of high specification and customisation. The implication of this is important. It means that the surface appearance of a business and its economic sector are less important to the way its operations should be managed than its intrinsic characteristics, such as the volume of its output, the variety of different products and services it needs to produce, and, above all, how it is trying to compete in its market.

> **OPERATIONS PRINCIPLE**
>
> *All organisations have 'operations' that produce some mix of products and services.*

> **OPERATIONS PRINCIPLE**
>
> *The economic sector of an operation is less important in determining how it should be managed than its intrinsic characteristics.*

Operations *and process* management

Within the operations shown in Figure 1.2, resources such as people, information systems, buildings and equipment will be organised into several individual 'processes'. A 'process' is an arrangement of resources that transforms inputs into outputs that satisfy (internal or external) customer needs. So, among other processes, banking operations contain account management processes, hotel operations contain room cleaning processes, furniture manufacturing operations contain assembly processes, and so on. The difference between *operations* and *processes* is one of scale, and therefore complexity. Both transform inputs into outputs, but processes are the smaller version. They are the component parts of operations, so the total operations function is made up of individual processes. But, within any business, the production of products and services is not confined to the operations function. For example, the marketing function 'produces' marketing plans and sales forecasts, the accounting function 'produces' budgets, the human resources function 'produces' development and recruitment

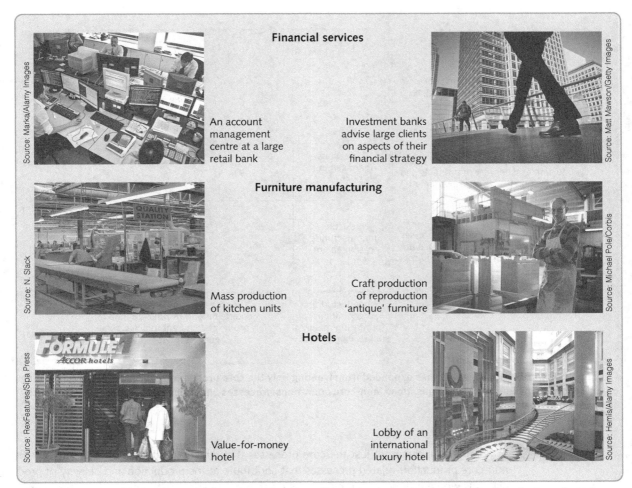

Figure 1.2 All types of business have 'operations' because all businesses produce some mix of products and services. The differences in the operations *within* a category of business are often greater than the differences *between* businesses

plans, and so on. In fact *every* part of *any* business is concerned with managing processes. So, 'operations and process management' is the term we use to encompass the management of all types of operation, no matter in what sector or industry, and all processes, no matter in which function of the business. The general truth is that processes are everywhere, and all types of manager have something to learn from studying operations and process management.

From 'production', to 'operations', to 'operations and process' management

Figure 1.3 illustrates how the scope of this subject has expanded. Originally, operations management was seen as very much associated with the manufacturing sector. In fact, it would have been called 'production' or 'manufacturing' management, and was concerned exclusively with the core business of producing physical products. Starting in the 1970s and 1980s, the term *operations management* became more common. It was used to reflect two trends. First, and most importantly, it was used to imply that many of the ideas, approaches and techniques traditionally used in the manufacturing sector could be equally applicable in the production of services. The second use of the term was to expand the scope of 'production' in manufacturing

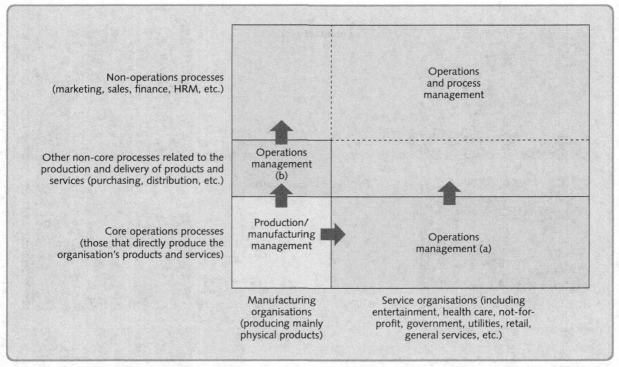

Figure 1.3 Operations management has expanded from treating only the core production processes in manufacturing organisations to include service organisations, non-core operations processes and processes in other functions such as marketing, finance and HRM

companies to include not just the core processes that directly produce products, but also the non-core production-related processes that contribute to the production and delivery of product. This would include such processes as purchasing, physical distribution, after-sales service, and so on. More recently the term *operations and process management* (or sometimes just *process management*) has been used to denote the shift in the scope of the subject to include the whole organisation. It is a far wider term than operations management because it applies to all parts of the organisation. This is very much how we treat the subject in this book. That is why it is called 'Operations and *Process* Management'. It includes the examination of the operations function in both manufacturing and service sectors and also the management of processes in non-operations functions.

Towards the beginning of all chapters we present two examples of individual businesses, or types of business, that illustrate the topic being examined in the chapter. Here we look at two businesses, one service company, and one manufacturing company, which have succeeded in large part because of their effective use of operations and process management principles.

EXAMPLE   **IKEA**[1]

It's the school holidays in an IKEA superstore in London, and parents with children in tow are crowding the isles and café area. Families push their way past the 'Anniversary Edition' of the 'Billy' bookcase (one of the firm's most popular products) proudly displayed by the entrance. Looking at the crowds it is easy to believe that IKEA is the most successful furniture retailer ever. With stores all over the world, they have managed to develop their own special way of

Source: Vario Images GmbH & Co./Alamy

Source: Jim Lai/AFP/Getty

selling furniture. Their stores' layout means customers often spend two hours in the store – far longer than in rival furniture retailers. IKEA's philosophy goes back to the original business, started in the 1950s in Sweden by Ingvar Kamprad. He built a showroom on the outskirts of Stockholm where land was cheap and simply set the furniture out as it would be in a domestic setting. Also, instead of moving the furniture from the warehouse to the showroom area, he asked customers themselves to pick the furniture up from the warehouse – still the basis of IKEA's process today.

The stores are all designed to facilitate the smooth flow of customers, from parking, moving through the store itself, to ordering and picking up goods. At the entrance to each store large noticeboards provide advice to shoppers who have not used the store before. For young children, there is a supervised children's play area, a small cinema, a parent and baby room and toilets, so parents can leave their children in the supervised play area for a time. Parents are recalled via the loudspeaker system if the child has any problems. IKEA 'allow customers to make up their minds in their own time' but 'information points' have staff who can help. All furniture carries a ticket with a code number which indicates its location in the warehouse. (For larger items customers go to the information desks for assistance.) There is also an area where smaller items are displayed, and can be picked directly. Customers then pass through the warehouse where they pick up the items viewed in the showroom. Finally, customers pay at the checkouts, where a ramped conveyor belt moves purchases up to the checkout staff. The exit area has service points, and a loading area that allows customers to bring their cars from the car park and load their purchases.

IKEA's success is founded on 'listening to its customers' and a disciplined (some would say, obsessive) elimination of waste in its processes; not just its retail processes, but also its design, distribution and administrative processes. Yet success brings its own problems and some customers became increasingly frustrated with overcrowding and long waiting times. In response, IKEA in the UK launched a programme to 'design out' the bottlenecks. The changes include:

- clearly marked in-store short cuts allowing customers who just want to visit one area to avoid having to go through all the preceding areas
- express checkout tills for customers with a bag only rather than a trolley
- extra 'help staff' at key points to help customers
- redesign of the car parks, making them easier to navigate
- dropping the ban on taking trolleys out to the car parks for loading (originally implemented to stop vehicles being damaged)
- a new warehouse system to stop popular product lines running out during the day
- more children's play areas.

IKEA spokeswoman Nicki Craddock said: *'We know people love our products but hate our shopping experience. We are being told that by customers every day, so we can't afford not to make changes. We realised a lot of people took offence at being herded like sheep on the long route around stores. Now if you know what you are looking for and just want to get in, grab it and get out, you can.'*

And the future? Martin Hansson, who runs the UK arm of IKEA, wants to see more emphasis on promoting their environmental agenda. *'We can be better at that. We're not good at showing how we handle waste and energy – it's a lost opportunity.'*

EXAMPLE ### Operations at Virgin Atlantic[2]

The airline business is particularly difficult to get right. Few businesses can cause more customer frustration and few businesses can lose their owners so much money. This is because running an airline, and also running the infrastructure on which the airlines depend, is a hugely complex business, where the difference between success and failure really is how you manage

Source: © Tristar Photos/Alamy

your operations on a day-to-day basis. In this difficult business environment, one of the most successful airlines, and one whose reputation has grown because of the way it manages its operations, is Virgin Atlantic. Part of Sir Richard Branson's Virgin Group, Virgin Atlantic Airways was founded in 1984 and is owned 51 per cent by the Virgin Group and 49 per cent by Singapore Airlines. Now, the airline flies over 5,000,000 passengers to 30 destinations worldwide with a fleet of 38 aircraft and almost 10,000 employees.

In many ways, it can be seen as being representative of the whole Virgin story – a small newcomer taking on the giant and complacent establishment while introducing better services and lower costs for passengers, yet also building a reputation for quality and innovative service development. The company's mission statement is 'to grow a profitable airline, that people love to fly and where people love to work', a commitment to service excellence that is reflected in the many awards they have won.

Virgin Atlantic's reputation includes a history of innovation in its service processes. It spent £100,000,000 installing its revolutionary new Upper Class suite that provides the longest and most comfortable flat bed and seat in airline history. It was also the first airline to offer business class passengers individual televisions. It now has one of the most advanced in-flight entertainment systems of any airline with over 300 hours of video content, 14 channels of audio, over 50 CDs, audio books and computer games on demand. The Upper Class area at London's Heathrow airport has a dedicated security channel exclusively for the use of Virgin Atlantic customers enabling business passengers to speed through the terminal moving from limousine to lounge in minutes.

Virgin Atlantic emphasise the practical steps they are taking to make their business as sustainable as possible, using the slogan 'we recycle exhaustively, especially our profits'. This refers to the pledge given by the company's chairman, Sir Richard Branson, to invest profits over the next ten years from the Virgin transport companies into projects to tackle climate change. *'We must rapidly wean ourselves off our dependence on coal and fossil fuels,'* Sir Richard said. *'The funds will be invested in schemes to develop new renewable energy technologies, through an investment unit called Virgin Fuels.'* Friends of the Earth welcomed Sir Richard's announcement, but the environmental pressure group also warned that the continued fast growth in air travel could not be maintained 'without causing climatic disaster'.

What do these two examples have in common?

All the operations managers in these two companies will be concerned with the same basic task – managing the processes that produce their products and services. And many, if not most, of the managers in each company who are called by some other title, will be concerned with managing their own processes that contribute to the success of their business. Although there will be differences between each company's operations and processes, such as the type of services they provide, the resources they use, and so on, the managers in each company will be making the same *type* of decisions, even if *what* they actually decide is different. The fact that both companies are successful because of their innovative and effective operations and processes also implies further commonality. First it means that they both understand the importance of taking a 'process perspective' in understanding their supply networks, running their operations, and managing all their individual processes. Without this they could not have sustained their strategic impact in the face of stiff market competition. Second, both businesses will expect their operations to make a contribution to their overall competitive strategy. Third, in achieving a strategic impact, they both will have come to understand the importance of managing *all* their individual processes throughout the business so that they too can all contribute to the businesses success.

DIAGNOSTIC QUESTION

Does the business take a process perspective?

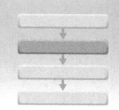

Video

If a business takes a process perspective, it understands that all parts of the business can be seen as processes, and that all processes can be managed using operations management principles. But it is also important to understand that a process perspective is not the only way of describing businesses, or any type of organisation. One could represent an organisation as a conventional 'organisational structure' that shows the reporting relationships between various departments or groups of resources. But even a little experience in any organisation shows that rarely, if ever, does this fully represent the way the organisation actually works. Alternatively one could describe an organisation through the way it makes decisions: how it balances conflicting criteria, weighs up risks, decides on actions and learns from its mistakes. On the other hand, one could describe the organisation's culture (its shared values, ideology, pattern of thinking and day-to-day rituals) or its power relationships (how it is governed, seeks consensus – or at least reconciliation – and so on. Or, and this is the significant point, one can represent the organisation as a collection of processes, interconnecting and (hopefully) all contributing to fulfilling its strategic aims. This is the perspective that we emphasise throughout this book. As we define it here, the process perspective analyses businesses as a collection of interrelated processes. Some of these processes will be within the operations function, and will contribute directly to the production of its products and services. Other processes will be in the other functions of the business, but will still need managing using similar principles to those within the operations function.

OPERATIONS PRINCIPLE

There are many valid approaches to describing organisations. The process perspective is a particularly valuable one.

None of these various perspectives gives a total picture. Each perspective adds something to our ability to understand and therefore more effectively manage a business. Nor are they mutually exclusive. A process perspective does not preclude understanding the influence of power relationships on how processes work, and so on. We use the process perspective here, not because it is the *only* useful and informative way of understanding businesses, but because it is the perspective that directly links the way we manage resources in a business with its strategic impact. Without effective process management, the best strategic plan can never become reality. The most appealing promises made to clients or customers will never be fulfilled. In addition, the process perspective has traditionally been undervalued. The subject of operations and process management has only recently come to be seen as universally applicable and, more importantly, universally valuable.

So, operations and process management is relevant to all parts of the business

If processes exist everywhere in the organisation, operations and process management will be a common responsibility of all managers irrespective of which function they are in: Each function will have its 'technical' knowledge of course. In Marketing, this includes the market expertise needed for designing and shaping marketing plans; in Finance, it includes the technical knowledge of financial reporting conventions. Yet each will also have an *operations* role that entails using its processes to produce plans, policies, reports and services. For example, the Marketing function has processes with inputs of market information, staff, computers, and so on. Its staff transform the information into outputs such as marketing plans, advertising campaigns and sales force organisation. In this sense, all functions are operations with their own collection of processes. The implications of this are very important. Because every manager in all parts of an organisation is, to some extent, an operations manager, they all should want to give good service to their customers, and they all will want to do this efficiently. So, operations management must be relevant for all functions, units and groups within the organisation. And the concepts, approaches and techniques of operations management can help to improve any process in any part of the organisation.

The 'input–transformation–output' model

Central to understanding the processes perspective is the idea that all processes transform *inputs* into *outputs*. Figure 1.4 shows the *general transformation process model* that is used to describe the nature of processes. Put simply, processes take in a set of input resources, some of which are transformed into outputs of products and/or services and some of which do the transforming.

Process inputs

Transformed resource inputs are the resources that are changed in some way within a process. They are usually materials, information or customers. For example, one process in a bank prints statements of accounts for its customers. In doing so, it is processing materials. In the bank's branches, customers are processed by giving them advice regarding their financial affairs, cashing their cheques, etc. However, behind the scenes, most of the bank's processes are concerned with processing information about its customers' financial affairs. In fact, for the bank's operations function as a whole, its information transforming processes are probably the

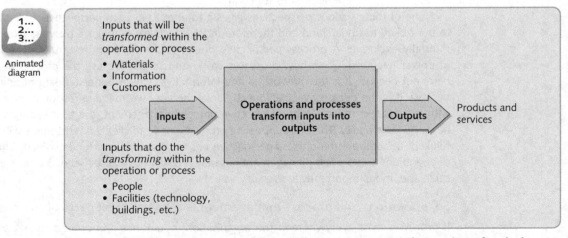

Figure 1.4 All processes are input-transformation-output systems that use 'transforming' resources to work on 'transformed' resources in order to produce products and services

most important. As customers, we may be unhappy with badly printed statements and we may even be unhappy if we are not treated appropriately in the bank. But if the bank makes errors in our financial transactions, we suffer in a far more fundamental way.

There are two types of *transforming* resource that form the 'building blocks' of all processes. They are *facilities* – the buildings, equipment, plant and process technology of the operation, and *people* – who operate, maintain, plan and manage the operation.

The exact nature of both facilities and people will differ between processes. In a five-star hotel, facilities consist mainly of buildings, furniture and fittings. In a nuclear-powered aircraft carrier, its facilities are the nuclear generator, turbines and sophisticated electronic detection equipment. Although one operation is relatively 'low-technology' and the other 'high-technology', their processes all require effective, well-maintained facilities. Staff will also differ between processes. Most staff employed in a domestic appliance assembly process may not need a very high level of technical skill, whereas most staff employed by an accounting firm in an audit process are highly skilled in their own particular 'technical' skill (accounting). Yet although skills vary, all staff have a contribution to make to the effectiveness of their operation. An assembly worker who consistently misassembles refrigerators will dissatisfy customers and increase costs just as surely as an accountant who cannot add up.

Process outputs

All processes produce products and services, and although products and services are different, the distinction can be subtle. Perhaps the most obvious difference is in their respective tangibility. Products are usually tangible (you can physically touch a television set or a newspaper), services are usually intangible (you cannot touch consultancy advice or a haircut – although you may be able to see or feel the results). Also, services may have a shorter stored life. Products can usually be stored for a time, some food products only for a few days, and some buildings for thousands of years. But the life of a service is often much shorter. For example, the service of 'accommodation in a hotel room for tonight' will 'perish' if it is not sold before tonight – accommodation in the same room tomorrow is a different service.

The three levels of analysis

Operations and process management uses the process perspective to analyse businesses at three levels. The most obvious level is that of the business itself, or more specifically, the operations function of the business. The other functions of the business could also be treated at this level, but that would be beyond the scope of this book. And, while analysing the business at the level of the operation is important, for a more comprehensive assessment we also need to analyse the contribution of operations and process management at a higher and more strategic level (the level of its supply network) and at a lower more operational level (the level of the individual processes). These three levels of operations analysis are shown in Figure 1.5.

The process perspective at the level of the operation

The operations part of a business is itself an input–transformation–output system, which transforms various inputs to produce (usually) a range of different products and services. Table 1.1 shows some operations described in terms of their main inputs, the purpose of their operations, and their outputs. Note how some of the inputs to the operation are transformed in some way while other inputs do the transforming. For example, an airline's aircraft, pilots, air crew, and ground crew are brought into the operation in order to act on passengers and cargo

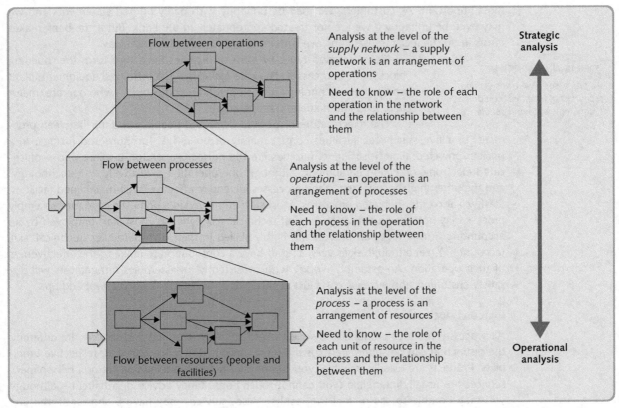

Figure 1.5 Operations and process management requires analysis at three levels: the supply network, the operation and the process

Table 1.1 Some operations described in terms of their inputs, purpose and outputs

Type of operation	What are the operation's inputs?	What does the operation do?	What are operation's outputs?
Airline	Aircraft Pilots and air crew Ground crew *Passengers* *Cargo*	Moves passengers and freight around the world	Transported passengers and freight
Department store	*Goods for sale* Staff sales Computerised registers *Customers*	Displays goods Gives sales advice Sells goods	Customers and goods 'Assembled' together
Police department	Police officers Computer systems *Information* *Public (law-abiding and criminal)*	Prevents crime Solves crime Apprehends criminals	Lawful society Public with feeling of security
Frozen food manufacturer	*Fresh food* Operators Food-processing equipment Freezers	Food preparation Freezes	Frozen food

Note: input resources that are transformed are printed in *italics*.

and change (transform) their location. Note also how in some operations customers themselves are inputs. (The airline, department store and police department are all like this.) This illustrates an important distinction between operations whose customers receive their outputs without seeing inside the operation, and those whose customers are inputs to the operation and therefore have some visibility of the operation's processes. Managing high visibility operations where the customer is inside the operation usually involves different set of requirements and skills to those whose customers never see inside the operation. (We will discuss this issue of visibility later in this chapter.)

Most operations produce both products and services

Some operations produce just products and others just services, but most operations produce a mixture of the two. Figure 1.6 shows a number of operations positioned in a spectrum from almost 'pure' goods producers to almost 'pure' service producers. Crude oil producers are concerned almost exclusively with the product which comes from their oil wells. So are aluminium smelters, but they might also produce some services such as technical advice. To an even greater extent, machine tool manufacturers produce services such as technical advice and applications engineering services as well as products. The services produced by restaurants are an essential part of what the customer is paying for. They both manufacture food and provide service. A computer systems services company may produce software 'products', but more so, it is providing an advice and customisation service to its customers. A management consultancy, although producing reports and documents, would see itself largely as a service provider. Finally, some pure services do not produce products at all. A psychotherapy clinic, for example, provides therapeutic treatment for its customers without any physical product.

> **OPERATIONS PRINCIPLE**
>
> *Most operations produce a mixture of tangible products and intangible services.*

Services and products are merging

Increasingly the distinction between services and products is both difficult to define and not particularly useful. Even the official statistics compiled by governments have difficulty in

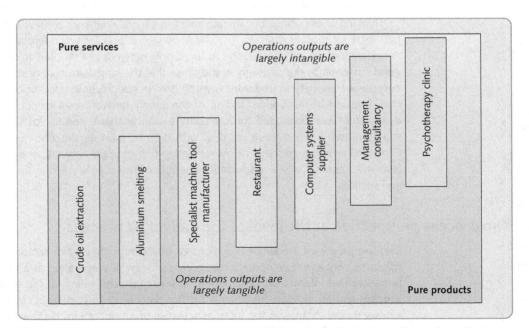

Figure 1.6 Relatively few operations produce either purely products or purely services. Most types of operation produce a mixture of goods and services

separating products and services. Software sold on a disk is classified as a product. The same software sold over the internet is a service. Some authorities see the essential purpose of all businesses, and therefore all operations, as being to 'serve customers'. Therefore, they argue, all operations are service providers who may (or may not) produce products as a means of serving their customers. Our approach in this book is close to this. We treat operations and process management as being important for all organisations. Whether they see themselves as manufacturers or service providers is very much a secondary issue.

The process perspective at the level of the supply network

Any operation can be viewed as part of a greater network of operations. It will have operations that supply it with the products and services it needs to make its own products and services, and unless it deals directly with the end consumer, it will supply customers who themselves may go on to supply their own customers. Moreover, any operation could have several suppliers, several customers and may be in competition with other operations producing similar services to those it produces itself. This collection of operations is called the supply network.

There are three important issues to understand about any operation's supply network. First, it can be complex. Operations may have a large number of customers and suppliers who themselves have large numbers of customers and suppliers. Also, the relationships between operations in the supply network can be subtle. One operation may be in direct competition with another in some markets while at the same time acting as collaborators or suppliers to each other in others. Second, theoretically the boundaries of any operation's supply chain can be very wide indeed. They could go back to the operation that digs raw material out of the ground and go forward to the ultimate reuse and/or disposal of a product. Sometimes it is necessary to do this (for example, when considering the environmental sustainability of products), but generally some kind of boundary to the network needs to be set so that more attention can be given to the most immediate operations in the network. Third, supply networks are always changing. Not only do operations sometimes lose customers and win others, or change their suppliers, they also may acquire operations that once were their customers or suppliers, or sell parts of their business, so converting them into customers or suppliers.

Thinking about operations management in a supply network context is a particularly important issue for most businesses. The overarching question for any operations manager is, 'Does my operation make a contribution to the supply network as a whole?' In other words, are we a good customer to our suppliers in the sense that the long-term cost of supply to us is reduced because we are easy to do business with? Are we good suppliers to our customers in the sense that, because of our understanding of the supply network as a whole, we understand their needs and have developed the capability to satisfy them. Because of the importance of the supply network perspective we deal with it twice more in this book; at a strategic level in Chapter 3 where we discuss the overall design of the supply network, and at a more operational level in Chapter 7 where we examine the role of the supply chain in the delivery of products and services.

The process perspective at the level of the individual process

Because processes are smaller versions of operations, they have customers and suppliers in the same way as whole operations. So we can view any operation as a network of individual processes that interact with each other, with each process being, at the same time, an internal supplier and an internal customer for other processes. This 'internal customer' concept provides a model to analyse the internal activities of an operation. If the whole operation is not working as it should, we may be able to trace the problem back along this internal network of customers and suppliers. It can also be a useful reminder to all parts of the operation that, by

Table 1.2 Some examples of processes in non-operations functions

Organisational function	Some of its processes	Outputs from its process	Customer(s) for its outputs
Marketing and sales	Planning process Forecasting process Order-taking process	Marketing plans Sales forecasts Confirmed orders	Senior management Sales staff, planners, operations Operations, finance
Finance and accounting	Budgeting process Capital approval processes Invoicing processes	Budget Capital request evaluations Invoices	Everyone Senior management, requestees External customers
Human resources management	Payroll processes Recruitment processes Training processes	Salary statements New hires Trained employees	Employees All other processes All other processes
Information technology	Systems review process Help desk process System implementation project processes	System evaluation Advice Implemented working systems and aftercare	All other processes All other processes All other processes

treating their internal customers with the same degree of care that they exercise on their external customers, the effectiveness of the whole operation can be improved. Again, remember that many of an organisation's processes are not operations processes, but are part of some other function. Table 1.2 illustrates just some of the processes that are contained within some of the more common non-operations functions, the outputs from these processes and their 'customers'.

There is an important implication of visualising each function of an organisation as being a network of processes. The diverse parts of a business are connected by the relationships between their various processes, and the organisational boundaries between each function and each part of the business is really a secondary issue. Firms are always reorganising the boundaries between processes. They frequently move responsibility for tasks between departments. The tasks and the processes change less often. Similarly, tasks and processes may move between various businesses; that is what outsourcing and the 'do or buy' decision is all about (see Chapter 3). In other words, not only can separate businesses be seen as networks of processes, whole supply networks can also. Who owns which processes and how the boundaries between them are organised are separate decisions.

OPERATIONS PRINCIPLE

Whole businesses, and even whole supply networks, can be viewed as networks of processes.

'End-to-end' business processes

Animated diagram

This separation of process boundaries and organisational boundaries also applies at a more micro level. This means that we can define what is inside a process in any way we want. The boundaries between processes, the activities that they perform, and the resources that they use, are all there because they have been designed in that way. It is common in organisations to find processes defined by the type of activity they engage in, for example, invoicing processes, product design processes, sales processes, warehousing processes, assembly processes, painting processes, etc. This can be convenient because it groups similar resources together, but it is only one way of drawing the boundaries between processes. Theoretically, in large organisations there must be an almost infinite number of ways that activities and resources could be collected together as distinct processes. One way of redefining the boundaries and responsibilities of processes is to consider the 'end-to-end' set of activities that satisfy defined

OPERATIONS PRINCIPLE

Processes are defined by how the organisation chooses to draw process boundaries.

customer needs. Think about the various ways in which a business satisfies its customers. Many different activities and resources will probably contribute to 'producing' each of its products and services. Some authorities recommend grouping the activities and resources together in an end-to-end manner to satisfy each defined customer need. This approach is closely identified with the 'business process engineering' (or re-engineering) movement (examined in Chapter 13). It calls for a radical rethink of process design that will probably involve taking activities and resources out of different functions and placing them together to meet customer needs. Remember though, designing processes around end-to-end customer needs is only one way (although often the sensible one) of designing processes.

EXAMPLE

The Programme and Video Division (PVD)

A broadcasting company has several divisions including several television and radio channels (entertainment and news), a 'general services' division that includes a specialist design workshop, and the 'Programme and Video Division' (PVD) that makes programmes and videos for a number of clients including the television and radio channels that are part of the same company. The original ideas for these programmes and videos usually come from the clients who commission them, although PVD itself does share in the creative input. The business is described at the three levels of analysis in Figure 1.7.

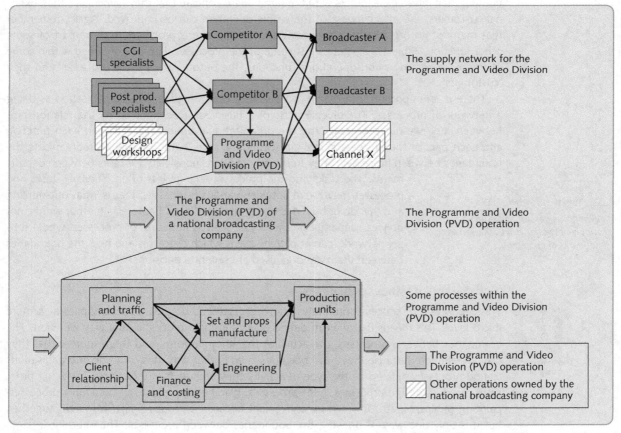

Figure 1.7 Operations and process management analysis for the Programme and Video Division (PVD) of a national broadcasting company at three levels: the supply network, the operation and individual processes

At the level of the operation – the division produces products in the form of tapes, discs and media files, but its real 'product' is the creativity and 'artistry' that is captured in the programmes. '*We provide a service,*' says the division's boss, '*that interprets the client's needs (and sometimes their ideas), and transforms them into appealing and appropriate shows. We can do this because of the skills, experience and creativity of our staff, and our state-of-the-art technology.*'

At the level of the supply network – the division has positioned itself to specialise in certain types of product, including children's programmes, wild life programmes and music videos. '*We did this so that we could develop a high level of expertise in a few relatively high margin areas. It also reduces our dependence on our own broadcasting channels. Having specialised in this way, we are better positioned to partner and do work for other programme makers who are our competitors in some other markets. Specialisation has also allowed us to outsource some activities such as computer graphic imaging (CGI) and post-production that are no longer worth keeping in-house. However, our design workshop became so successful that they were "spun out" as a division in their own right and now work for other companies as well as ourselves.*'

At the level of individual processes – many smaller processes contribute directly or indirectly to the production of programmes and videos, include the following:

- The planning and traffic department who act as the operations managers for the whole operation. They draw up schedules, allocate resources and 'project manage' each job through to completion.
- Workshops that manufacture some of the sets, scenery and props for the productions.
- Client liaison staff who liaise with potential customers, test out programme ideas and give information and advice to programme makers.
- An engineering department that cares for, modifies and designs technical equipment.
- Production units that organise and shoot the programmes and videos.
- The finance and costing department that estimates the likely cost of future projects, controls operational budgets, pays bills and invoices customers.

Creating end-to-end processes – PVD produces several products and services that fulfil customer needs. Each of these, to different extents, involves several of the existing departments within the company. For example, preparing a 'pitch' (a sales presentation that includes estimates of the time and cost involved in potential projects) mainly needs the contributions of Client relations and the Finance and costing departments, but also needs smaller contributions from other departments. Figure 1.8 illustrates the contribution of each department to each product or service. (No particular sequence is implied by Figure 1.8.) The contributions of each department may not all occur in the same order. Currently, all the division's processes are clustered into conventional departments defined by the type of activity they perform, engineering, client relationship, etc. A radical redesign of the operation could involve regrouping activities and resources into five 'business' processes that fulfil each of the five defined customer needs. This is shown diagrammatically by the dotted lines in Figure 1.8. It would involve the physical movement of resources (people and facilities) out of the current functional processes into the new end-to-end business processes. This is an example of how processes can be designed in ways that do not necessarily reflect conventional functional groupings.

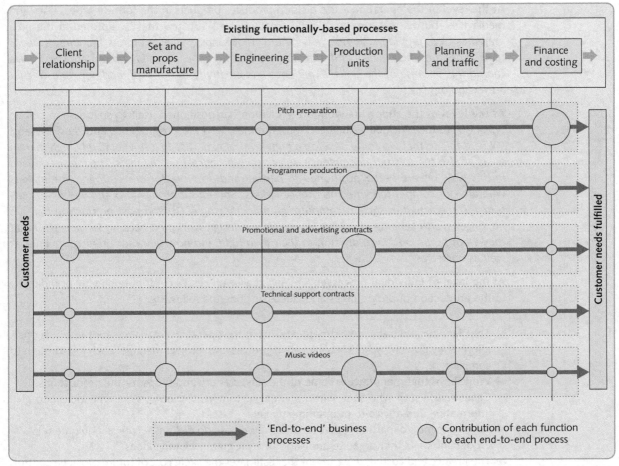

Existing functionally-based processes

Client relationship → Set and props manufacture → Engineering → Production units → Planning and traffic → Finance and costing

Pitch preparation

Programme production

Promotional and advertising contracts

Technical support contracts

Music videos

Customer needs

Customer needs fulfilled

→ 'End-to-end' business processes

○ Contribution of each function to each end-to-end process

Figure 1.8 **An example of how processes in the Programme and Video Division (PVD) could be reorganised around end-to-end business processes that fulfil defined customer needs**

DIAGNOSTIC QUESTION

Does operations and process management have a strategic impact?

Video

One of the biggest mistakes a business can make is to confuse 'operations' with 'operational'. Operational is the opposite of strategic; it means detailed, localised, short-term, day-to-day. 'Operations', on the other hand, is the set of resources that produce products and services. Operations can be treated both at an operational *and a strategic level*. We shall examine some views of operations strategy in the next chapter. For now, we treat a fundamental question for any operation – does the way we manage operations and processes have a strategic impact? If a business does not fully appreciate the strategic impact that effective operations and process management can have, at the very least, it is missing an opportunity. The IKEA and Virgin Atlantic examples at the beginning of this chapter are just two of many businesses that have harnessed their operations to create strategic impact.

Operations and process management can make or break a business. Although for most businesses, the operations function represents the bulk of its assets and the majority of its people, the true value of the operation is more than 'bulk'. It can 'make' the businesses in the sense that it gives the ability to compete through both the short-term ability to respond to customers and the long-term capabilities that will keep it ahead of its competitors. But if an operations function cannot produce its products and services effectively, it could 'break' the business by handicapping its performance no matter how it positions and sells itself in its markets.

Cost, revenue, risk, investment and capability

The strategic importance of operations and process management is being increasingly recognised. When compared with only a few years ago, it attracts far more attention and, according to some reports, accounts for the largest share of all the money spent by businesses on consultancy advice. This may be partly because the area has been neglected in the past, but it also denotes an acceptance that it can have both short-term and long-term impact. This can be seen in the impact that operations and process management can have on the businesses' cost, revenue, risk, investment and capabilities.

- It can reduce the **costs** of producing products and services by being efficient. The more productive the operation is at transforming inputs into outputs, the lower will be the cost of producing a unit of output. Cost is never totally unimportant for any business, but generally the higher the cost of a product or service when compared to the price it commands in the market, the more important cost reduction will be as an operations objective. Even so, cost reduction is almost always treated as an important contribution that operations can make to the success of any business.
- It can increase **revenue** by increasing customer satisfaction through quality, service and innovation. Existing customers are more likely to be retained and new customers are more likely to be attracted to products and services if they are error-free and appropriately designed, if the operation is fast and responsive in meeting their needs and keeping its delivery promises, and if an operation can be flexible, both in customising its products and services and introducing new ones. It is operations that directly influence the quality, speed, dependability and flexibility of the business, all of which have a major impact on a company's ability to maximise its revenue.
- It can reduce the **risk** of operational failure, because well-designed and run operations should be less likely to fail. All failures can eventually be traced back to some kind of failure within a process. Furthermore, a well-designed process, if it does fail, should be able to recover faster and with less disruption (this is called *resilience*).
- It can ensure **effective investment** (capital employed) to produce its products and services. Eventually all businesses in the commercial world are judged by the return that they produce for their investors. This is a function of profit (the difference between costs and revenues) and the amount of money invested in the business's operations resources. We have already established that effective and efficient operations can reduce costs and increase revenue, but what is sometimes overlooked is the operation's role in reducing the investment required per unit of output. It does this by increasing the effective capacity of the operation and by being innovative in how it uses its physical resources.

OPERATIONS PRINCIPLE

All operations should be expected to contribute to their business by controlling costs, increasing revenue, reducing risks, making investment more effective and growing long-term capabilities.

- It can **build capabilities** that will form the basis for *future* innovation by building a solid base of operations skills and knowledge within the business. Every time an operation produces a product or a service it has the opportunity to accumulate knowledge about how that product or service is best produced. This accumulation of knowledge should be used as a basis for learning and improvement. If so, in the long term, capabilities can be built that will allow the operation to respond to future market challenges. Conversely, if an operations function is simply seen as the mechanical and routine fulfilment of customer requests, then it is difficult to build the knowledge base that will allow future innovation.

> **EXAMPLE**   **The programme and Video Division (PVD) continued**
>
> The PVD described earlier should be able to identify all four ways in which its operations and processes can have a strategic impact. The division is expected to generate reasonable returns by controlling its costs and being able to command relatively high fees. *'Sure, we need to keep our costs down. We always review our budgets for bought-in materials and services. Just as important, we measure the efficiency of all our processes, and we expect annual improvements in process efficiency to compensate for any increases in input costs.'* (Reducing costs.) *'Our services are in demand by customers because we are good to work with,'* says the division's Managing Director. *'We have the technical resources to do a really great job and we always give good service. Projects are completed on time and within budget. More importantly, our clients know that we can work with them to ensure a high level of programme creativity. That is why we can command reasonably high prices.'* (Increasing revenue.) *'Also, we have a robust set of processes that minimise the chances of projects failing to achieve success.'* (Reducing risk.) The division also has to justify its annual spend on equipment to its main board. *'We try and keep up to date with the new technology that can really make an impact on our programme making, but we always have to demonstrate how it will improve profitability.'* (Effective investment.) *'We also try to adapt new technology and integrate it into our creative processes in some way so that gives us some kind of advantage over our competitors.'* (Build capabilities.)

Operations management in not-for-profit organisations

Terms such as *competitive advantage*, *markets* and *business* that are used in this book are usually associated with companies in the for-profit sector. Yet operations management is also relevant to organisations whose purpose is not primarily to earn profits. Managing operations in an animal welfare charities, hospitals, research organisations or government departments is essentially the same as in commercial organisations. However, the strategic objectives of not-for-profit organisations may be more complex and involve a mixture of political, economic, social or environmental objectives. Consequently, there may be a greater chance of operations decisions being made under conditions of conflicting objectives. So, for example, it is the operations staff in a children's welfare department who have to face the conflict between the cost of providing extra social workers and the risk of a child not receiving adequate protection.

DIAGNOSTIC QUESTION

Should all processes be managed in the same way?

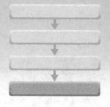

OPERATIONS PRINCIPLE

The way in which processes need to be managed is influenced by volume, variety, variation and visibility.

All processes differ in some way, so, to some extent, all processes will need to be managed differently. Some of the differences between processes are 'technical' in the sense that different products and services require different skills and technologies to produce them. However, processes also differ in terms of the nature of demand for their products or services. Four characteristics of demand in particular have a significant effect on how processes need to be managed:

Video

- the volume of the products and services produced
- the variety of the different products and services produced
- the variation in the demand for products and services
- the degree of visibility that customers have of the production of products and services.

The four Vs of processes

Volume

Animated
diagram

Processes with a high volume of output will have a high degree of repeatability, and because tasks are repeated frequently it often makes sense for staff to specialise in the tasks they perform. This allows the systemisation of activities, where standard procedures may be codified and set down in a manual with instructions on how each part of the job should be performed. Also, because tasks are systemised and repeated, it is often worthwhile developing specialised technology that gives higher processing efficiencies. By contrast, low-volume processes with less repetition cannot specialise to the same degree. Staff are likely to perform a wide range of tasks, and while this may be more rewarding, it is less open to systemisation. Nor is it likely that efficient, high-throughput technology could be used. The implications of this are that high-volume processes have more opportunities to produce products or services at low unit cost. So, for example, the volume and standardisation of large fast-food restaurant chains, such as McDonald's or KFC, enables them to produce with greater efficiency than a small, local cafeteria or diner.

Variety

Processes that produce a high variety of products and services must engage in a wide range of different activities, changing relatively frequently between each activity. It must also contain a wide range of skills and technology sufficiently 'general purpose' to cope with the range of activities and sufficiently flexible to change between them. A high level of variety may also imply a relatively wide range of inputs to the process and the additional complexity of matching customer requirements to appropriate products or services. So, high variety processes are invariably more complex and costly than low variety ones. For example, a taxi company is usually prepared to pick up and drive customers almost anywhere (at a price); they may even take you by the route of your choice. There are an infinite number of potential routes (products) that it offers. But, its cost per kilometre travelled will be higher than a less customised form of transport such as a bus service.

Variation

Processes are generally easier to manage when they only have to cope with predictably constant demand. Resources can be geared to a level that is just capable of meeting demand. All activities can be planned in advance. By contrast, when demand is variable and/or unpredictable, resources will have to be adjusted over time. Worse still, when demand is unpredictable, extra resources will have to be designed into the process to provide a 'capacity cushion' that can absorb unexpected demand. So, for example, processes that manufacture high fashion garments will have to cope with the general seasonality of the garment market together with the uncertainty of whether particular styles may or may not prove popular. Operations that make conventional business suits are likely to have less fluctuation in demand over time, and be less prone to unexpected fluctuations. Because processes with lower variation do not need any extra safety capacity and can be planned in advance, they will generally have lower costs than those with higher variation.

Visibility

Process visibility is a slightly more difficult concept to envisage. It indicates how much of the processes are 'experienced' directly by customers, or how much the process is 'exposed' to its customers. Generally processes that act directly on customers (such as retail processes or health care process) will have more of their activities visible to their customers than those that act on materials and information. However, even material and information transforming processes may provide a degree of visibility to the customers. For example, parcel distribution operations provide internet-based 'track and trace' facilities to enable their customers to have visibility of where their packages are at any time. Low-visibility processes, if they communi-cate with their customers at all, do so using less immediate channels such as the telephone or the internet. Much of the process can be more 'factory-like'. The time lag between customer request and response could be measured in days rather than the near immediate response expected from high-visibility processes. This lag allows the activities in a low-visibility process to be performed when it is convenient to the operation, so achieving high utilisation. Also, because the customer interface needs managing, staff in high-visibility processes need cus-tomer contact skills that shape the customer's perception of process performance. For all these reasons, high-visibility processes tend to have higher costs than low-visibility processes.

Many operations have both high- and low-visibility processes. This serves to emphasise the difference that the degree of visibility makes. For example, in an airport, some of its processes are relatively visible to its customers (check-in desks, information desks, restaurants, passport control, security staff etc.). These staff operate in a high-visibility 'front-office' environment. Other proc-esses in the airport have relatively little, if any, customer visibility (baggage handling processes, overnight freight operations, loading meals on to the aircraft, cleaning etc.). We rarely see these processes they perform the vital but low-visibility tasks, in the 'back-office' part of the operation.

The implications of the four Vs of processes

All four dimensions have implications for processing costs. Put simply, high volume, low vari-ety, low variation and low visibility all help to keep processing costs down. Conversely, low volume, high variety, high variation and high customer contact generally carry some kind of cost penalty for the process. This is why the volume dimension is drawn with its 'low' end at the left, unlike the other dimensions, to keep all the 'low cost' implications on the right. Figure 1.9 summarises the implications of such positioning.

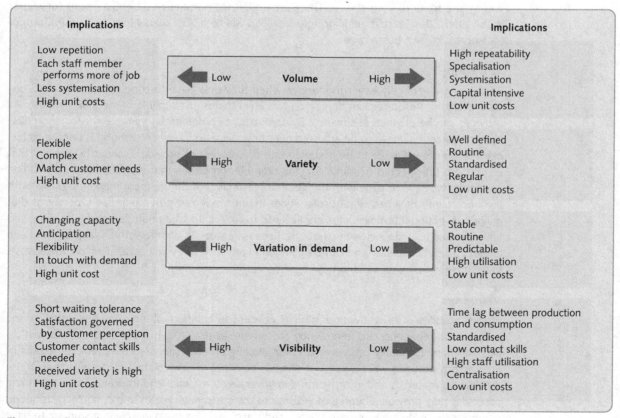

Figure 1.9 A typology of operations

Charting processes using the four Vs

In almost any operation, processes can be identified that have different positions on the four dimensions, and which therefore have different objectives and will need managing in different ways. To a large extent the position of a process on the four dimensions is deter-

OPERATIONS PRINCIPLE

Operations and processes can (other things being equal) reduce their costs by increasing volume, reducing variety, reducing variation and reducing visibility.

mined by the demand of the market it is serving. However, most processes have some discretion in moving themselves on the dimensions. Look at the different positions on the visibility dimension that retail banks have adopted. At one time, using branch tellers was the only way customers could contact a bank. Now access to the bank's services could be through (in decreasing order of visibility) a personal banker, who visits your home or office, a conversation with a branch manager, the teller at the window,

Practice
note

telephone contact through a call centre, internet banking services or an ATM cash machine. These other processes offer services that have been developed by banks to serve different market needs.

Figure 1.10 illustrates the different positions on the four Vs for some retail banking processes. Note that the personal banking/advice service is positioned at the high-cost end of the four Vs. For this reason, such services are often only offered to relatively wealthy customers that represent high profit opportunities for the bank. Note also that the more recent developments in retail banking, such as call centres, internet banking and ATMs, all represent a shift towards the low-cost end of the four Vs. New processes that exploit new technologies can often have a profound impact on the implications of each dimension. For example, internet banking, when compared with an ATM cash machine, offers a far higher variety of options for customers but, because the process is automated through its information technology, the cost of offering this variety is less than at a conventional branch or even a call centre.

A model of operations and process management

Managing operations and processes involves a whole range of separate decisions that will determine their overall purpose, structure and operating practices. These decisions can be grouped together in various ways. Look at other books on operations management and you will find many different ways of structuring operations decisions and therefore the subject as

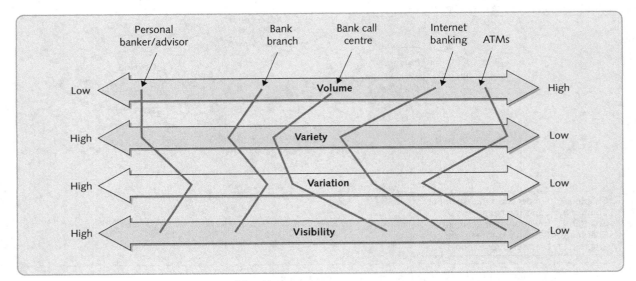

Figure 1.10 Four Vs analysis for some retail banking processes

a whole. Here we have chosen to classify activities into four broad groups, relating to four broad activities. Although there are some overlaps between these four categories, they more or less follow a sequence that corresponds to the life cycle of operations and processes.

- **Directing** the overall strategy of the operation. A general understanding of operations and processes and their strategic purpose, together with an appreciation of how strategic purpose is translated into reality (direct), is a prerequisite to the detailed design of operations and process.
- **Designing** the operation's products, services and processes. Design is the activity of determining the physical form, shape and composition of operations and processes together with the products and services that they produce.
- **Planning and control process delivery**. After being designed, the delivery of products and services from suppliers and through the total operation to customers must be planned and controlled.
- **Developing** process performance. Increasingly it is recognised that operations and process managers cannot simply routinely deliver products and services in the same way that they always have done. They have a responsibility to develop the capabilities of their processes to improve process performance.

Video

We can now combine two ideas to develop the model of operations and process management that will be used throughout this book. The first is the idea that *operations* and the *processes* that make up both the operations and other business functions are transformation systems that take in inputs and use process resources to transform them into outputs. The second idea is that the resources, both in an organisation's operations as a whole and in its individual processes, need to be managed in terms of how they are *directed*, how they are *designed*, how *delivery* is planned and controlled and how they are *developed* and improved. Figure 1.11 shows how

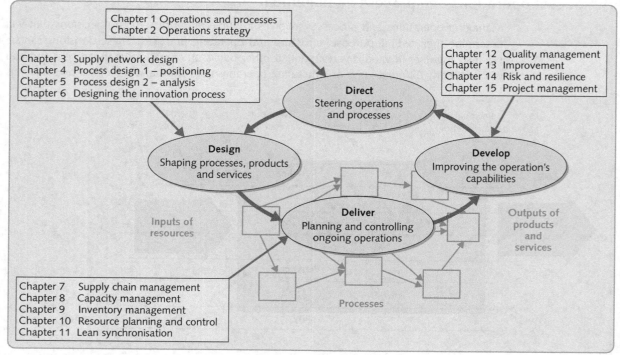

Figure 1.11 Operations and processes management: a general model

these two ideas go together. This book will use this model to examine the more important decisions that should be of interest to all managers of operations and processes.

Critical commentary

All chapters contain a short critical commentary on the main ideas covered in the chapter. Its purpose is not to undermine the issues discussed in the chapter, but to emphasise that, although we present a relatively orthodox view of operation, there are other perspectives.

● The central idea in this introductory chapter is that all organisations have operations (and other functions) that have processes that produce products and services, and that all these processes are essentially similar. However, some believe that by even trying to characterise organisations in this way (perhaps even by calling them 'processes') one loses or distorts their nature and depersonalises or takes the 'humanity' out of the way in which we think of the organisation. This point is often raised in not-for-profit organisations, especially by 'professional' staff. For example, the head of one European 'Medical Association' (a Doctors' Trade Union) criticised hospital authorities for expecting a 'sausage factory service based on productivity targets'. No matter how similar they appear on paper, it is argued, a hospital can never be viewed in the same as a factory. Even in commercial businesses, professionals, such as creative staff, often express discomfort at their expertise being described as a 'process'.

● To some extent these criticisms of taking such a process perspective are valid. How we describe organisations does say much about our underlying assumptions of what an 'organisation' is and how it is supposed to work. Notwithstanding the point we made earlier about how a purely process view can misleadingly imply that organisations are neat and controllable with unambiguous boundaries and lines of accountability, a process perspective can risk depicting the messy reality of organisations in a naïve manner. Yet, in our view it is a risk well worth taking.

SUMMARY CHECKLIST

This checklist comprises questions that can be usefully applied to any type of operations and reflect the major diagnostic questions used within the chapter.

- [ ] Is the operations function of the business clearly defined?
- [ ] Do operations managers realise that they are operations managers even if they are called by some other title?
- [ ] Do the non-operations functions within the business realise that they manage processes?
- [ ] Does everyone understand the inputs, activities and outputs of the processes of which they are part?
- [ ] Is the balance between products and services produced by the operations function well understood?
- [ ] Are future changes that may occur in the balance between products and services produced by the operation understood?
- [ ] What contribution are operations making towards reducing the cost of products and services?
- [ ] What contribution are operations making towards increasing the revenue from products and services?
- [ ] What contribution are operations making towards reducing the risks of failure and increasing the effectiveness of recovery?
- [ ] What contribution are operations making towards better use of capital employed?
- [ ] How are operations developing the capability for future innovation?
- [ ] Does the operation understand its position in the overall supply network?
- [ ] Does the operation contribute to the overall supply network?
- [ ] Are the individual processes that comprise the operations function defined and understood?
- [ ] Are individual processes aware of the internal customer and supplier concept?
- [ ] Do they use the internal customer and supplier concept to increase their contribution to the business as a whole?
- [ ] Do they use the ideas and principles of operations management to improve the performance of their processes?
- [ ] Has the concept of end-to-end business processes being examined and considered?
- [ ] Are the differences (in terms of volume, variety, variation and visibility) between processes understood?
- [ ] Are the volume, variety, variation and visibility characteristics of processes reflected in the way they are managed?

Design House Partnerships at Concept Design Services

'I can't believe how much we have changed in a relatively short time. From being an inward looking manufacturer, we became a customer focused "design and make" operation. Now we are an "integrated service provider". Most of our new business comes from the partnerships we have formed with design houses. In effect, we design products jointly with specialist design houses that have a well-known brand, and offer them a complete service of manufacturing and distribution. In many ways we are now a "business-to-business" company rather than a "business-to-consumer" company.' (Jim Thompson, CEO, Concept Design Services (CDS))

Concept Design Services (CDS) had become one of Europe's most profitable homeware businesses. It had moved in two stages from making precision plastic components, mainly in the aerospace sector, together with some cheap 'homeware' items such as buckets and dustpans, sold under the 'Focus' brand name, to making very high-quality (expensive) stylish homewares with a high 'design value' for well-known brands.

The first stage – from 'Focus' to 'Concept'

The initial move into higher margin homeware had been masterminded by Linda Fleet, CDS's Marketing Director. 'My previous experience in the decorative products industry had taught me the importance of fashion and product development, even in mundane products such as paint. Premium-priced colours and new textures would catch the popular imagination and would need supporting by promotion and editorial features in lifestyle magazines. The players who embraced this fashion element of the market were dramatically more profitable than those who simply provided standard ranges. Instinctively, I felt that this must also apply to homeware. We decided to develop a whole coordinated range of such items, and to open up a new distribution network for them to serve the more exclusive stores, kitchen equipment and specialty retailers. Within a year of launching our first new range of kitchen homeware under the 'Concept' brand name, we had over 3,000 retail outlets across Northern Europe with full point-of-sale display facilities and supported by press coverage and product placement on TV 'lifestyle'

Source: Yang Yu/Alamy Images

programmes. Within two years 'Concept' products were providing over 75 per cent of our revenue and 90 per cent of our profits.' (The margin on Concept products is many times higher than for the Focus range. During this period the Focus (basic) range continued to be produced, but as a drastically reduced range.)

The second stage – from 'Concept' to 'design house partnerships'

Linda was also the driving force behind the move to design house partnerships. 'It started as a simple design collaboration between our design team and an Italian "design house".' (Design houses are creative product designers who may, or may not, own a brand of their own, but rarely manufacture or distribute their products, relying on outsourcing to subcontractors.) 'It seemed a natural progression to them asking us to first manufacture and then distribute this and other of their designs. Over the next five years, we built up this business, so now we design (often jointly with the design house), manufacture and distribute products for several of the more prestigious European design houses. We think this sort of business is likely to grow. The design houses appreciate our ability to offer a full service. We can design products in conjunction with their own design staff and offer them a level of manufacturing expertise they can't get elsewhere. More significantly, we can offer a distribution service which is tailored to their needs. From the customer's point of view the distribution arrangements appear to belong to the design house itself. In fact they are based exclusively on our own call centre, warehouse and distribution resources.'

The most successful collaboration was with Villessi, the Italian designers. Generally it was CDS's design expertise which was attractive to 'design house' partners. Not only did CDS employ professionally respected designers, they had also acquired a reputation for being able to translate difficult technical designs into manufacturable and saleable products. Design house partnerships usually involved relatively long lead times but produced unique products with very high margins, nearly always carrying the design house's brand.

Manufacturing operations

All manufacturing was carried out in a facility located 20 km from Head Office. Its moulding area housed large injection-moulding machines, most with robotic material handling capabilities. Products and components passed to the packing hall, where they were assembled and inspected. The newer more complex products often had to move from moulding to assembly and then back again for further moulding. All products followed the same broad process route but with more products needing several progressive moulding and assembly stages, there was an increase in 'process flow recycling' which was adding complexity. One idea was to devote a separate cell to the newer and more complex products until they had 'bedded in'. This cell could also be used for testing new moulds. However, it would need investment in extra capacity that would not always be fully utilised. After manufacture, products were packed and stored in the adjacent distribution centre.

'When we moved into making the higher margin 'Concept' products, we disposed of most of our older, small injection-moulding machines. Having all larger machines allowed us to use large multi-cavity moulds. This increased productivity by allowing us to produce several products, or components, each machine cycle. It also allowed us to use high-quality and complex moulds which, although cumbersome and more difficult to change over, were very efficient and gave a very high-quality product. For example, with the same labour we could make three items per minute on the old machines, and 18 items per minute on the modern ones using multi-moulds. That's a 600 per cent increase in productivity. We also achieved high-dimensional accuracy, excellent surface finish and extreme consistency of colour. We could do this because of our expertise derived from years making aerospace products. Also, by standardising on single large machines, any mould could fit any machine. This was an ideal situation from a planning perspective, as we were often asked to make small runs of Concept products at short notice.' (Grant Williams, CDS Operations Manager)

Increasing volume and a desire to reduce cost had resulted in CDS subcontracting much (but not all) of its Focus products to other (usually smaller) moulding companies. 'We would never do it with any complex or design house partner products, but it should allow us to reduce the cost of making basic products while releasing capacity for higher margin ones. However there have been quite a few "teething problems". Coordinating the production schedules is currently a problem, as is agreeing quality standards. To some extent it's our own fault. We didn't realise that subcontracting was a skill in its own right. And although we have got over some of the problems, we still do not have a satisfactory relationship with all of our subcontractors.' (Grant Williams, CDS Operations Manager)

Planning and distribution services

The distribution services department of the company was regarded as being at the heart of the company's customer service drive. Its purpose was to integrate the efforts of design, manufacturing and sales by planning the flow of products from production, through the distribution centre, to the customer. Sandra White, the Planning Manager, reported to Linda Fleet and was responsible for the scheduling of all manufacturing and distribution, and for maintaining inventory levels for all the warehoused items. 'We try to stick to a preferred production sequence for each machine and mould so as to minimise set-up times by starting on a light colour, and progressing through a sequence to the darkest. We can change colours in 15 minutes, but because our moulds are large and technically complex, mould changes can take up to three hours. Good scheduling is important to maintain high plant utilisation. With a higher variety of complex products, batch sizes have reduced and it has brought down average utilisation. Often we can't stick to schedules. Short-term changes are inevitable in a fashion market. Certainly better forecasts would help . . . but even our own promotions are sometimes organised at such short notice that we often get caught with stockouts. New products in particular are difficult to forecast, especially when they are 'fashion' items and/or seasonal. Also, I have to schedule production time for new product mould trials; we normally allow 24 hours for the testing of each new mould received, and this has to be done on production machines. Even if we have urgent orders, the needs of the designers always have priority.' (Sandra White)

Customer orders for Concept and design house partnership products were taken by the company's sales call centre located next to the warehouse. The individual orders would then be dispatched using the company's own fleet of medium and small distribution vehicles for UK orders, but using carriers for the Continental European market. A standard delivery timetable was used and an 'express delivery' service was offered for those customers prepared to pay a small delivery premium. However, a recent study had shown that almost 40 per cent of express deliveries were initiated by the company rather than customers. Typically this would be to fulfil deliveries of orders containing products out of stock at the time of ordering. The express delivery service was not required for Focus products because almost all deliveries were to five large customers. The size of each order was usually very large, with deliveries to customers' own distribution depots. However, although the organisation of Focus delivery was relatively straightforward, the consequences of failure were large. Missing a delivery meant upsetting a large customer.

Challenges for CDS

Although the company was financially successful and very well regarded in the homeware industry, there were a number of issues and challenges that it knew it would have to address. The first was the role of the design department and its influence over new product development. New product development had become particularly important to CDS, especially since they had formed alliances with design houses. This had led to substantial growth in both the size and the influence of the design department, which reported to Linda Fleet. *'Building up and retaining design expertise will be the key to our future. Most of our growth is going to come from the business which will be bought in through the creativity and flair of our designers. Those who can combine creativity with an understanding of our partners' business and design needs can now bring in substantial contracts. The existing business is important of course, but growth will come directly from these peoples' capabilities.'* (Linda Fleet)

But not everyone was so sanguine about the rise of the Design department. *'It is undeniable that relationships between the designers and other parts of the company have been under strain recently. I suppose it is, to some extent, inevitable. After all, they really do need the freedom to design as they wish. I can understand it when they get frustrated at some of the constraints which we have to work under in the manufacturing or distribution parts of the business. They also should be able to expect a professional level of service from us. Yet the truth is that they make most of the problems themselves. They sometimes don't seem to understand the consequences or implications of their design decisions or the promises they make to the design houses. More seriously, they don't really understand that we could actually help them do their job better if they cooperated a bit more. In fact, I now see*

some of our design house partners' designers more than I do our own designers. The Villessi designers are always in my factory and we have developed some really good relationships.' (Grant Williams)

The second major issue concerned sales forecasting, and again there were two different views. Grant Williams was convinced that forecasts should be improved. *'Every Friday morning we devise a schedule of production and distribution for the following week. Yet, usually before Tuesday morning, it has had to be significantly changed because of unexpected orders coming in from our customers' weekend sales. This causes tremendous disruption to both manufacturing and distribution operations. If sales could be forecast more accurately we would achieve far higher utilisation, better customer service and, I believe, significant cost savings.'*

However, Linda Fleet saw things differently. *'Look, I do understand Grant's frustration, but after all, this is a fashion business. By definition it is impossible to forecast accurately. In terms of month-by-month sales volumes we are in fact pretty accurate, but trying to make a forecast for every week end every product is almost impossible to do accurately. Sorry, that's just the nature of the business we're in. In fact, although Grant complains about our lack of forecast accuracy, he always does a great job in responding to unexpected customer demand.'*

Jim Thompson, the Managing Director, summed up his view of the current situation. *'Particularly significant has been our alliances with the Italian and German design houses. In effect we are positioning ourselves as a complete service partner to the designers. We have a world-class design capability together with manufacturing, order processing, order taking and distribution services. These abilities allow us to develop genuinely equal partnerships which integrate us into the whole industry's activities.'*

Linda Fleet also saw an increasing role for collaborative arrangements. *'It may be that we are seeing a fundamental change in how we do business within our industry. We have always seen ourselves as primarily a company that satisfies consumer desires through the medium of providing good service to retailers. The new partnership arrangements put us more into the 'business-to-business' sector. I don't have any problem with this in principle, but I'm a little anxious as to how much it gets us into areas of business beyond our core expertise.'*

The final issue which was being debated within the company was longer term, and particularly important. *'The two big changes we have made in this company have both happened because we exploited a strength we already had within the company. Moving into Concept products was only possible because we brought our high-tech precision expertise that we had developed in the* aerospace sector into the homeware sector where none of our new competitors could match our manufacturing excellence. Then, when we moved into design house partnerships we did so because we had a set of designers who could command respect from the world-class design houses with whom we formed partnerships. So what is the next move for us? Do we expand globally? We are strong in Europe but nowhere else in the world. Do we extend our design scope into other markets, such as furniture? If so, that would take us into areas where we have no manufacturing expertise. We are great at plastic injection moulding, but if we tried any other manufacturing processes, we would be no better than, and probably worse than, other firms with more experience. So what's the future for us?' (Jim Thompson, CEO CDS)

QUESTIONS

1 Why is operations management important in CDS?

2 Draw a 'four Vs' profile for the company's products/services.

3 What would you recommend to the company if they asked you to advise them in improving their operations?

APPLYING THE PRINCIPLES

Hints

Some of these exercises can be answered by reading the chapter. Others will require some general knowledge of business activity and some might require an element of investigation. Hints on how they all can be answered are to be found in the eText at www.pearsoned.co.uk/slack.

1 Quentin Cakes make about 20,000 cakes per year in two sizes, both based on the same recipe. Sales peak at Christmas time when demand is about 50 per cent higher than in the more quiet summer period. Their customers (the stores who stock their products) order their cakes in advance through a simple internet-based ordering system. Knowing that they have some surplus capacity, one of their customers has approached them with two potential new orders.

(a) The *Custom Cake* option – this would involve making cakes in different sizes where consumers could specify a message or greeting to be 'iced' on top of the cake. The consumer would give the inscription to the store who would e-mail it through to the factory. The customer thought that demand would be around 1,000 cakes per year, mostly at celebration times such as Valentine's Day and Christmas.

(b) The *Individual Cake* option – this would involve Quentin Cakes introducing a new line of very small cakes intended for individual consumption. Demand for this individual-sized cake was forecast to be around 4,000 per year, with demand likely to be more evenly distributed throughout the year than their existing products.

The total revenue from both options is likely to be roughly the same and the company has only capacity to adopt one of the ideas. But which one should it be?

2 Described as having *'revolutionised the concept of sandwich making and eating'*, Pret A Manger opened their first shop in London in the mid 1980s. Now they have over 130 shops in UK, New York, Hong Kong and Tokyo. They say that their secret is to focus continually on quality, in all its activities. *'Many food retailers focus on extending the shelf life of their food, but that's of no interest to us. We maintain our edge by selling food that simply can't be beaten for freshness. At the end of the day, we give whatever we haven't sold to charity to help feed those who would otherwise go hungry.'* The first Pret A Manger shop had its own kitchen where fresh ingredients were delivered first thing every morning, and food was prepared throughout the day. Every Pret shop since has followed this model. The team members serving on the tills at lunchtime will have been making sandwiches in the kitchen that morning. They rejected the idea of a huge centralised sandwich factory even though it could significantly reduce costs. Pret also own and manage all their shops directly so that they can ensure consistently high standards. *'We are determined never to forget that our hardworking people make all the difference. They are our heart and soul. When they care, our business is sound. If they cease to care, our business goes down the drain. We work hard at building great teams. We take our reward schemes and career opportunities very seriously. We don't work nights (generally), we wear jeans, we party!'*

(a) Do you think Pret A Manger fully understand the importance of their operations management?

(b) What evidence is there for this?

(c) What kind of operations management activities at Pret A Manger might come under the four headings of direct, design, deliver and develop?

3   Visit a furniture store (other than IKEA). Observe how the shop operates, for example, where customers go, how staff interact with them, how big it is, how the shop has chosen to use its space, what variety of products it offers, and so on. Talk with the staff and managers if you can. Think about how the shop that you have visited is different from IKEA. Then consider the question:

● What implications do the differences between IKEA and the shop you visited have for their operations management?

4   Write down five services that you have 'consumed' in the last week. Try and make these as varied as possible. Examples could include public transport, a bank, any shop or supermarket, attendance at an education course, a cinema, a restaurant etc.

For each of these services, ask yourself the following questions:

(a) Did the service meet your expectations? If so, what did the management of the service have to do well in order to satisfy your expectations? If not, where did they fail? Why might they have failed?

(b) If you were in charge of managing the delivery of these services what would you do to improve the service?

(c) If they wanted to, how could the service be delivered at a lower cost so that the service could reduce its prices?

(d) How do you think that the service copes when something goes wrong (such as a piece of technology breaking down)?

(e) Which other organisations might supply the service with products and services? (In other words, they are your 'supplier', but who are *their* suppliers)?

(f) How do you think the service copes with fluctuation of demand over the day, week, month or year?

These questions are just some of the issues which the operations managers in these services have to deal with. Think about the other issues they will have to manage in order to deliver the service effectively.

5   Find a copy of a financial newspaper (*Financial Times, Wall Street Journal, Economist* etc.) and identify one company that is described in the paper that day. What do you think would be the main operations issues for that company?

Notes on chapter

1 Thanks to Mike Shulver and Paul Walley for this information. Further sources include 'IKEA plans an end to stressful shopping' (2006), *London Evening Standard*, 24 April.

2 Source: Virgin Atlantic website.

TAKING IT FURTHER

Chase, R.B., Aquilano, N.J. and Jacobs, F.R. (2010) *Production and Operations Management: Manufacturing and Services* (11th Edition), McGraw-Hill. *There are many good general textbooks on operations management. This was one of the first and is still one of the best, though written very much for an American audience.*

Hall, J.M. and Johnson, M.E. (2009) 'When should a process be art', *Harvard Business Review*, March. *An article that provides a good discussion of how to deal with more creative processes.*

Johnston, R. and Clark, E. (2008) *Service Operations Management*, Financial Times Prentice Hall. *What can we say! A great treatment of service operations from the same stable as this textbook.*

Schmenner, R.W., van Wassenhove, L., Ketokivi, M., Heyl, J. and Lusch, R.F. (2009) 'Too much theory, not enough understanding', *Journal of Operations Management*, Vol. 27, 339–343. *An academic treatment of one aspect of the operations management literature.*

Slack, N. and Lewis, M. (eds) (2005) *The Blackwell Encyclopedic Dictionary of Operations Management* (2nd Edition). Blackwell Business, Oxford. *For those who like technical descriptions and definitions.*

Sousa, R. and Voss, C.A. (2008) 'Contingency research in operations management practices', *Journal of Operations Management*, Vol. 26, 697–713. *Another academic treatment, this time, of why context matters.*

USEFUL WEBSITES

www.opsman.org *Definitions, links and opinions on operations and process management.*

www.iomnet.org *The Institute of Operations Management site. One of the main professional bodies for the subject.*

www.poms.org *A US academic society for production and operations management. Academic, but some useful material, including a link to an encyclopedia of operations management terms.*

www.sussex.ac.uk/users/dt31/TOMI/ *One of the longest established portals for the subject. Useful for academics and students alike.*

www.ft.com *Useful for researching topics and companies.*

Interactive
quiz

For further resources including examples, animated diagrams, self-test questions, Excel spreadsheets and video materials please explore the eText on the companion website at **www.pearsoned.co.uk/slack**.

2

Operations strategy

Introduction

In the long term, the major (and some would say, only) objective for operations and processes is to provide a business with some form of strategic advantage. That is why the management of a business's processes and operations and its intended overall strategy must be logically connected. Yet for many in business, the very idea of an 'operations strategy' is a contradiction in terms. After all, to be involved in the strategy process is the complete opposite of those day-to-day tasks and activities associated with being an operations manager. Nevertheless, it is also clear that operations can have a real strategic impact. Many *enduringly* remarkable enterprises, from Apple to Zara, use their operations resources to gain long-term strategic success. Such firms have found that it is the way they manage their operations that sets them apart from, and above, their competitors. Without a strong link with overall strategy, operations and processes will be without a coherent direction. And without direction they may finish up making internal decisions that either do not reflect strategy, or that conflict with each other, or both. So, although operations and process management is largely 'operational', it also has a strategic dimension that is vital if operations are to fulfil their potential to contribute to competitiveness. Figure 2.1 shows the position of the ideas described in this chapter in the general model of operations management.

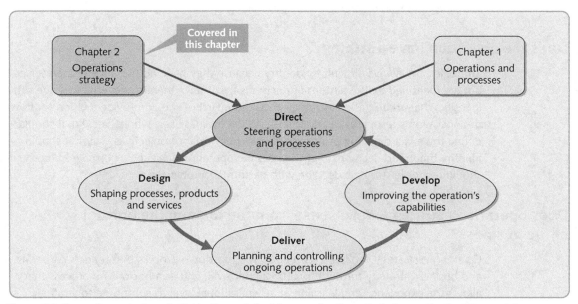

Figure 2.1 Operations strategy is the pattern of decisions and actions that shapes the long-term vision, objectives and capabilities of the operation and its contribution to overall strategy

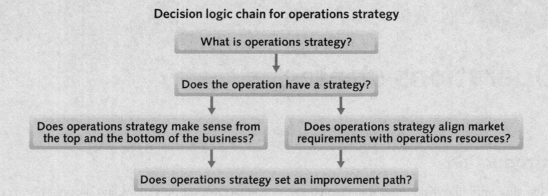

Decision logic chain for operations strategy

What is operations strategy?

Does the operation have a strategy?

Does operations strategy make sense from the top and the bottom of the business?

Does operations strategy align market requirements with operations resources?

Does operations strategy set an improvement path?

Each chapter is structured around a set of diagnostic questions. These questions suggest what you should ask in order to gain an understanding of the important issues of a topic, and, as a result, improve your decision making. An executive summary addressing these questions is provided below.

What is operations strategy?

Operations strategy is the pattern of decisions and actions that shapes the long-term vision, objectives and capabilities of the operation and its contribution to overall strategy. It is the way in which operations resources are developed over the long term to create sustainable competitive advantage for the business. Increasingly, many businesses are seeing their operations strategy as one of the best ways to differentiate themselves from competitors. Even in those companies that are marketing led (such as fast-moving consumer goods), an effective operations strategy can add value by allowing the exploitation of market positioning.

Does the operation have a strategy?

Strategies are always difficult to identify because they have no presence in themselves, but are identified by the pattern of decisions that they generate. Nevertheless one can identify what an operations strategy should do. First, it should provide a vision for how the operation's resources can contribute to the business as a whole. Second, it should define the exact meaning of the operation's performance objectives. Third, it should identify the broad decisions that will help the operation achieve its objectives. Finally, it should reconcile strategic decision with performance objectives.

Does operations strategy make sense from the top and the bottom of the business?

Operations strategy can been seen both as a top-down process that reflects corporate and business strategy through to a functional level, and as a bottom-up process that allows the experience and learning at an operational level to contribute to strategic thinking. Without both of these perspectives, operations strategy will be only partially effective. It should communicate both top to bottom *and* bottom to top throughout the hierarchical levels of the business.

Does operations strategy align market requirements with operations resources?

The most important short-term objective of operations strategy is to ensure that operations resources can satisfy market requirements. But this is not the only objective. In the longer term, operations strategy must build the capabilities within its resources that will allow the business to provide something to the market that its competitors find difficult to imitate or match. These two objectives are called the market requirements perspective and the operations resource capability perspective. The latter is very much influenced by the resource-based view (RBV) of the firm. The objective of operations strategy can be seen as achieving 'fit' between these two perspectives.

Does operations strategy set an improvement path?

The purpose of operations strategy is to improve the business's performance relative to its competitors' in the long term. It therefore must provide an indication of how this improvement is to take place. This is best addressed by considering the trade-offs between performance objectives in terms of the 'efficient frontier' model. This describes operations strategy as a combination of repositioning performance along an existing efficient frontier, and increasing overall operations effectiveness by overcoming trade-offs to expand the efficient frontier.

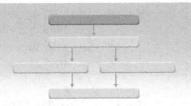

DIAGNOSTIC QUESTION

What is operations strategy?

Video

Operations strategy is the pattern of decisions and actions that shapes the long-term vision, objectives and capabilities of the operation and its contribution to the overall strategy of the business[1]. The term 'operations strategy' sounds at first like a contradiction. How can 'operations', a subject that is generally concerned with the day-to-day creation and delivery of goods and services, be strategic? 'Strategy' is usually regarded as the opposite of those day-to-day routine activities. But, as we indicated previously, 'operations' is not the same as 'operational'. 'Operations' are the resources that create products and services. 'Operational' is the opposite of strategic, meaning day-to-day and detailed.

Perhaps more significantly, many of the businesses that seem to be especially competitively successful, and who appear to be sustaining their success into the longer term, have a clear and often inventive operations strategy. Just look at some of the high-profile companies quoted in this book, or that feature in the business press. It is not just that their operations strategy provides these companies with adequate support; it is their operations strategy that is the pivotal reason for their competitive superiority. Just as revealing, when companies stumble, it is often because they have either taken their eye off the operations ball, or failed to appreciate its importance in the first place. More generally, all enterprises, *and all parts of the enterprise*, need to prevent strategic decisions being frustrated by poor operational implementation. And this idea leads us to the second purpose of this chapter (and indeed the book as a whole): to show how, by using the principles of operations strategy, *all* parts of any business and *all* functions of a business can contribute effectively to the overall success of the business. So the idea of 'operations strategy' has two different but related meanings. The first is concerned with the operations function itself, and how it can contribute to strategic success. The second is concerned with how *any* function can develop its process and resources and establish its strategic role.

Look at these two examples of businesses with operations strategies that are clear and explicit and have contributed to their competitive success.

EXAMPLE   Flextronics[2]

Behind every well-known brand name in consumer electronics, much of the high-tech manufacturing which forms the heart of the product is probably done by companies few of us have heard of. Companies such as Ericsson and IBM are increasingly using Electronic Manufacturing Services (EMS) companies which specialise in providing the outsourced design, engineering, manufacturing and logistics operations for big brand names. Flextronics is one of the leading

EMS providers in providing 'operational services' to technology companies. With over 70,000 employees spread throughout its facilities in 28 countries, it has a global presence that allows it the flexibility to serve customers in all the key markets throughout the world.

Flextronics manufacturing locations have to balance their customers' need for low costs (electronic goods are often sold in a fiercely competitive market) with their need for responsive and flexible service (electronics markets can also be volatile). Flextronics could have set up manufacturing plants close to its main customers in North America and Western Europe. This would certainly facilitate fast response and great service to customers; unfortunately these markets also tend to have high manufacturing costs. Flextronics' operations strategy must therefore achieve a balance between low costs and high levels of service. One way Flextronics achieves this is through its strategic location and supply network decisions, adopting what it calls its 'Industrial Park Strategy'. This involves finding locations which have relatively low manufacturing costs but are close to its major markets. It has established Industrial Parks in places such as Hungary, Poland, Brazil and Mexico (the Guadalajara Park in Mexico is shown in the illustration above). Flextronics own suppliers also are encouraged to locate within the Park to provide stability and further reduce response times.

EXAMPLE   ### Amazon[3]

As a publicly stated ambitious target it takes some beating. *'Amazon.com strives to be'*, it says, *'Earth's most customer-centric company.'* Founded by Jeff Bezos in 1995, the Amazon.com website started as a place to buy books, giving its customers what at the time was a unique customer experience. Bezos believed that only the internet could offer customers the convenience of browsing a selection of millions of book titles in a single sitting. During its first 30 days of

Source: AFP/Getty Images.

business, Amazon.com fulfilled orders for customers in 45 countries – all shipped from Bezos' Seattle-area garage. And that initial success has been followed by continued growth that is based on a clear strategy of technological innovation. Among its many technological innovations for customers, Amazon.com offers a personalised shopping experience for each customer, book discovery through 'Search Inside The Book', convenient checkout using '1-Click® Shopping', and community features like Listmania and Wish Lists that help customers discover new products and make informed buying decisions. In addition, Amazon.com operates retail websites and offers programs that enable other retailers and to individual sellers to sell products on their websites. Now, many prominent retailers work with Amazon Services to power their e-commerce offerings from end-to-end, including technology services, merchandising, customer service and order fulfilment.

In the mid-2000s, Bezos, speaking at a number of public events about the company's plans, made its future strategy clearer. Although Amazon was generally seen as an internet book retailer and then a more general internet retailer, Bezos was promoting Amazon's 'utility computing' services. These provided cheap access to online computer storage, allowed program developers to rent computing capacity on Amazon systems, and connected firms with other firms who perform specialist tasks that are difficult to automate. The problem with online retailing, said Bezos, is its seasonality. At peak times, such as Christmas, Amazon has far more computing capacity than it needs for the rest of the year. At low points it may be using as little as 10 per cent of its total capacity. Hiring out that spare capacity is an obvious way to bring in extra revenue. In addition, Amazon soon had developed a search engine, a video download business, a service ('Fulfilment By Amazon') that allowed other companies to use Amazon's logistics capability including the handling of returned items, and a service that provided access to Amazon's 'back-end' technology.

A couple of years later, Amazon announced its EC2 (Elastic Compute Cloud) service that provides resizable computing capacity 'in the cloud'[4]. It is designed, say Amazon, to make web-scale computing easier for developers: *'Amazon EC2's simple web service interface allows you to obtain and configure capacity with minimal friction. It provides you with complete control of your computing resources and lets you run on Amazon's proven computing environment. Amazon EC2 reduces the time required to obtain and boot new server instances to minutes, allowing you to quickly scale capacity, both up and down, as your computing requirements change. Amazon EC2 changes the economics of computing by allowing you to pay only for capacity that you actually use. Amazon EC2 provides developers with the tools to build failure resilient applications and isolate themselves from common failure scenarios.'* Don't worry if you can't follow the technicalities of Amazon's statement, it is aimed at IT professionals. The important point is that it is a business-to-business service based on the company's core competence of leveraging its processes and technology that can make retail operations ultra efficient.

However, Amazon's apparent redefinition of its strategy was immediately criticised by some observers. 'Why not,' they said, 'stick to what you know, focus on your core competence of internet retailing?' Bezos's response was clear. 'We *are* sticking to our core competence; this is what we've been doing for the last 11 years. The only thing that's changed is that we are exposing it for (the benefit of) others.' At least for Jeff Bezos, Amazon is not so much an internet retailer as a provider of internet-based technology and logistics services.

What do these two examples have in common?

Neither of these companies suffered from any lack of clarity regarding what they wanted to do in the market. They are clear about what they are offering their customers (and they document it explicitly on their websites). They are also both equally clear in spelling out their operations strategy. Flextronics is willing to relocate whole operations in its commitment to responsive but low-cost customer service. Amazon redefined its market to sell its core operations-based capability. Without this type of clear 'top-down' strategy it is difficult to achieve clarity in the way individual processes should be managed. Yet both these companies are also known for the way they have perfected the operational-level processes to the extent that their learned expertise contributes to strategy in a 'bottom-up' manner. Also, in both these cases the requirements of their markets are clearly reflected in their operations' performance objectives (responsiveness and cost for Flextronics, and closely shadowing a changing market with its own internal technological and process capabilities in the case of Amazon). Similarly, both businesses have defined the way in which they achieve these objectives by strategically directing their operations resources (through its technological and process capabilities with Amazon, and through their location and supply chain decisions in the case of Flextronics). In other words, both have reconciled their market requirements with what their operations resource capabilities. These are the issues that we shall address in this chapter.

DIAGNOSTIC QUESTION

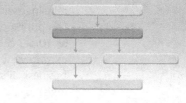

Does the operation have a strategy?

Video

There are some problems in asking this apparently simple question. In most operations management decisions you can see what you are dealing with. You can touch inventory, talk to people, programme machines, and so on. But strategy is different. You cannot see a strategy, feel it or touch it. Also, whereas the effects of most operations management decisions become evident relatively fast, it may be years before an operations strategy decision can be judged to be a success or not. Moreover, any 'strategy' is always more than a single decision. Operations strategy will be revealed in the total *pattern* of decisions that a business takes in developing its operations in the long term. Nevertheless, the question is an obvious starting point and one that must be addressed by all operations.

So, what should an operations strategy do? First, it should articulate a vision of how the businesses operations and processes can contribute to its overall strategy. This is something beyond the individual collection of decisions that will actually constitute the strategy. Second, it should translate market requirements into a message that will have some meaning within its operations. This means describing what customers want in terms of a clear and prioritised set of operations' *performance objectives*. Third, it should identify the broad decisions that will shape the operation's capabilities, and allow their long-term development so that they will provide the basis for the business's sustainable advantage. Finally, it should explain how its intended market requirements and its strategic operations decisions are to be reconciled.

An operations strategy should take significant stakeholders into account

All operations have stakeholders. They are the people and groups who have a legitimate interest in the operation's strategy. Some are internal (employees); others are external (customers, society or community groups, and a company's shareholders). External stakeholders may have a direct commercial relationship with the organisation, (suppliers and customers); others may not, (industry regulators). In not-for-profit operations, these stakeholder groups can overlap. So, voluntary workers in a charity may be employees, shareholders and customers all at once. However, in any kind of organisation, it is a responsibility of the operations function to understand the (often conflicting) objectives of its stakeholders and set it objectives accordingly. Yet, although all stakeholder groups, to different extents, will be interested in operations performance, they are likely to have very different views of which aspect of performance is important. Table 2.1 identifies typical stakeholder requirements. But stakeholder relationships are not just one way. It is also useful to consider what an individual organisation or business wants of the stakeholder groups themselves. Some of these requirements are illustrated in Table 2.1. The dilemma with using this wide range of stakeholders to judge performance is that organisations, particularly commercial companies, have to cope with the conflicting pressures of maximising profitability on one hand, with the expectation that they will manage in the interests of (all or part of) society in general with accountability and transparency. Even if a business wanted to reflect aspects of performance beyond its own immediate interests, how is it to do it?

> **OPERATIONS PRINCIPLE**
>
> *Operations strategy should take significant stakeholders into account.*

Corporate social responsibility (CSR) and the 'triple bottom line'

Strongly related to the stakeholder perspective of operations performance is that of corporate social responsibility (generally known as CSR). A direct link with the stakeholder concept is to be found in the definition used by Marks & Spencer, the UK-based retailer. *'Corporate Social Responsibility . . . is listening and responding to the needs of a company's stakeholders. This includes the requirements of sustainable development. We believe that building good relationships with employees, suppliers and wider society is the best guarantee of long-term success. This is the backbone of our approach to CSR.'* The issue of how broader social performance objectives can be included in operations management's activities is of increasing importance, both from an ethical and a commercial point of view. However, converting the CSR concept into operational reality presents considerable difficulty, although several attempts have been made. One such is the 'triple bottom line', an approach to value creation which attempts to integrate economic, environmental and

Table 2.1 Typical stakeholders' performance objectives

Stakeholder	What stakeholders want from the operation	What the operation wants from stakeholders
Shareholders	Return on investment Stability of earnings Liquidity of investment	Investment capital Long-term commitment
Directors/top management	Low/acceptable operating costs Secure revenue Well-targeted investment Low risk of failure Future innovation	Coherent, consistent, clear and achievable strategies Appropriate investment
Staff	Fair wages Good working conditions Safe work environment Personal and career development	Attendance Diligence/best efforts Honesty Engagement
Staff representative bodies (e.g. trade unions)	Conformance with national agreements Consultation	Understanding Fairness Assistance in problem solving
Suppliers (of materials, services, equipment etc.)	Early notice of requirements Long-term orders Fair price On-time payment	Integrity of delivery, quality and volume Innovation Responsiveness Progressive price reductions
Regulators (e.g. Financial regulators)	Conformance to regulations Feedback on effectiveness of regulations	Consistency of regulation Consistency of application of regulations Responsiveness to industry concerns
Government (local, national, regional)	Conformance to legal requirements Contribution to (local/national/regional) economy	Low/simple taxation Representation of local concerns Appropriate infrastructure
Lobby groups (e.g. environmental lobby groups)	Alignment of the organisation's activities with whatever the group are promoting	No unfair targeting Practical help in achieving aims (if the organisation wants to achieve them)
Society	Minimise negative effects from the operation (noise, traffic etc., and maximise positive effects (jobs, local sponsorship etc.)	Support for organisation's plans

social impacts. It first came to prominence in John Elkington's book, *Cannibals with Forks: the Triple Bottom Line of 21st Century Business*[5]. It advocated expanding the conventional financial reporting conventions to include ecological (sustainability) and social performance in addition to financial performance. So, for example, Holcim, the Swiss cement and aggregates group, have established a set of group-wide performance targets to achieve their triple bottom line business goals. But, before targets are met, the company aim to understand their current performance. They do this by establishing consistent measurement and reporting techniques, as well as implementing management systems to monitor progress toward their goals. Yet CSR-related performance measurement systems should not, say Holcim, be separate from the more conventional business systems. To work effectively, CSR performance systems are integrated into overall business processes and supported by appropriate training.

An operations strategy should articulate a vision for the operations contribution

The 'vision' for an operation is a clear statement of how operations intend to contribute value for the business. It is not a statement of what the operation wants to *achieve* (those are its objectives), but rather an idea of what it must *become* and what contribution it should make.

A common approach to summarising operations contribution is the Hayes and Wheelwright Four-Stage Model.[6] The model traces the progression of the operations function from what is the largely negative role of 'stage 1' operations to it becoming the central element of competitive strategy in excellent 'stage 4' operations. Figure 2.2 illustrates the four steps involved in moving from stage 1 to stage 4.

Stage 1: Internal neutrality

Video

This is the very poorest level of contribution by the operations function. The other functions regard it as holding them back from competing effectively. The operations function is inward looking and at best reactive with very little positive to contribute towards competitive success. Its goal is to be ignored. At least then it isn't holding the company back in any way. Certainly the rest of the organisation would not look to operations as the source of any originality, flair or competitive drive. Its vision is to be 'internally neutral', a position it attempts to achieve not by anything positive but by avoiding the bigger mistakes.

Stage 2: External neutrality

The first step of breaking out of stage 1 is for the operations function to begin comparing itself with similar companies or organisations in the outside market. This may not

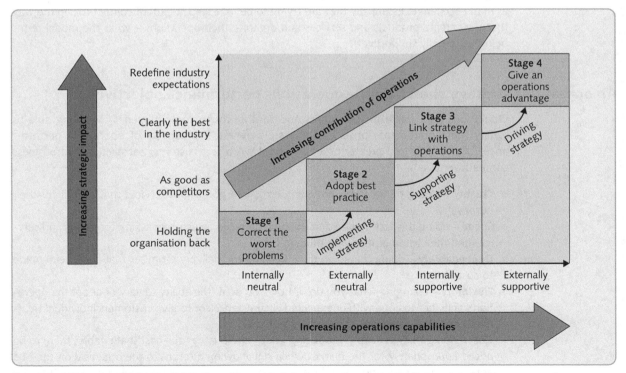

Figure 2.2 **Hayes and Wheelwright's Four-Stage Model of operations contribution sees operations as moving from implementation of strategy, through to supporting strategy, and finally driving strategy**

Practice
note

immediately take it to the 'first division' of companies in the market, but at least it is meas-uring itself against its competitors' performance and trying to be 'appropriate', by adopting 'best practice' from them. Its vision is to become 'up to speed' or 'externally neutral' with similar businesses in its industry by adopting 'best practice' ideas and norms of performance from others.

Stage 3: Internally supportive

Stage 3 operations have probably reached the 'first division' in their market. They may not be better than their competitors on every aspect of operations performance but they are broadly up with the best. Yet, the vision of stage 3 operations is to be clearly and unambiguously the very best in the market. They may try to achieve this by gaining a clear view of the company's competitive or strategic goals and developing 'appropriate' operations resources to Excel in the areas in which the company needs to compete effectively. The operation is trying to be 'inter-nally supportive' by providing a credible operations strategy.

Stage 4: Externally supportive

Stage 3 used to be taken as the limit of the operations function's contribution. Yet the model captures the growing importance of operations management by suggesting a further stage – stage 4. The difference between stages 3 and 4 is subtle, but important. A stage 4 company is one where the vision for the operations function is to provide *the* foundation for competitive success. Operations looks to the long term. It forecasts likely changes in markets and supply, and, over time, it develops the operations-based capabilities that will be required to compete in future market conditions. The operations function is becoming central to strategy-making. Stage 4 operations are creative and proactive. They are innovative and capable of adaptation as markets change. Essentially they are trying to be 'one step ahead' of competitors in the way that they create products and services and organise their operations – what the model terms being 'externally supportive'.

An operations strategy should define operations performance objectives

Operations adds value for customers and contributes to competitiveness by being able to satisfy the requirements of its customers. There are five aspects of operations perform-ance, all of which to a greater or lesser extent will affect customer satisfaction and business competitiveness.

- **Quality** – doing things right, providing error-free goods and services that are 'fit for their purpose'.
- **Speed** – doing this fast, minimising the time between a customer asking for goods and serv-ices and the customer receiving them in full.
- **Dependability** – doing things on time, keeping the delivery promises that have been made to customers.
- **Flexibility** – changing what you do or how you do it, the ability to vary or adapt the opera-tion's activities to cope with unexpected circumstances or to give customers individual treat-ment, or to introduce new products or services.
- **Cost** – doing things cheaply, producing goods and services at a cost that enables them to be priced appropriately for the market while still allowing a return to the organisation (or, in a not-for-profit organisation, that give good value to the tax payers or whoever is funding the operation).

The exact meaning of performance objectives is different in different operations

Different operations will have different views of what each of the performance objectives actually mean. Table 2.2 looks at how two operations, an insurance company and a steel plant, define each performance objective. For example, the insurance company sees quality as being at least as much about the manner in which their customers relate to their service as it does about the absence of technical errors. The steel plant, on the other hand, while not ignoring quality of service, primarily, emphasises product-related technical issues. Although, they are selecting from the same pool of factors which together constitute the generic performance objective, they will emphasise different elements.

> **OPERATIONS PRINCIPLE**
>
> *Operations performance objectives can be grouped together as quality, speed, dependability, flexibility and cost.*

Sometimes operations may choose to re-bundle elements using slightly different headings. For example, it is not uncommon in some service operations to refer to 'quality of service' as representing all the competitive factors we have listed under quality *and* speed *and* dependability (and sometimes aspects of flexibility). For example, information network operations use the term 'Quality of Service' (QoS) to describe their goal of providing guarantees on the ability of a network to deliver predictable results. This is often specified as including uptime (dependability), bandwidth provision (dependability and flexibility), latency or delay (speed of throughput), and error rate (quality). In practice, the issue is not so much one of universal definition but rather consistency within one, or a group of operations. At the very least it is important that individual companies have it clear in their own minds how each performance objective is to be defined.

> **OPERATIONS PRINCIPLE**
>
> *The interpretation of the five performance objectives will differ between different operations.*

Table 2.2 Aspects of performance objectives for two operations

Insurance company	Performance objectives	Steel plant
Aspects of each performance objective include . . .		*Aspects of each performance objective include . . .*
• Professionalism of staff • Friendliness of staff • Accuracy of information • Ability to change details in future	**Quality**	• Percentage of products conforming to their specification • Absolute specification of products • Usefulness of technical advice
• Time for call centre to respond • Prompt advice response • Fast quotation decisions • Fast response to claims	**Speed**	• Lead-time from enquiry to quotation • Lead-time from order to delivery • Lead-time for technical advice
• Reliability of original promise date • Customers kept informed	**Dependability**	• Percentage of deliveries 'on-time, in-full' • Customers kept informed of delivery dates
• Customisation of terms of insurance cover • Ability to cope with changes in circumstances, such as level of demand • Ability to handle wide variety of risks	**Flexibility**	• Range of sizes, gauges, coatings etc. possible • Rate of new product introduction • Ability to change quantity, composition and timing of an order
• Premium charged • Arrangement charges • 'No-claims' deals • 'Excess' charges	**Cost**	• Price of products • Price of technical advice • Discounts available • Payment terms

The relative priority of performance objectives differs between businesses

Not every operation will apply the same priorities to its performance objectives. Businesses that compete in different ways should want different things from their operations functions. In fact, there should be a clear logical connection between the competitive stance of a business and its operations objectives. So, a business that competes primarily on low prices and 'value for money' should be placing emphasis on operations objectives such as cost, productivity and efficiency; one that competes on a high degree of customisation of its services or products should be placing an emphasis on flexibility, and so on. Many successful companies understand the importance of making this connection between their message to customers and the operations performance objectives that they emphasise. For example:[7]

> **OPERATIONS PRINCIPLE**
>
> *The relative importance of the five performance objectives depends on how the business competes in its market.*

'Our management principle is the commitment to quality and reliability . . . to deliver safe and innovative products and services . . . and to improve the quality and reliability of our businesses.'
(Komatsu)

'The management team will . . . develop high quality, strongly differentiated consumer brands and service standards . . . use the benefits of the global nature and scale economies of the business to operate a highly efficient support infrastructure (with) . . . high quality and service standards which deliver an excellent guest experience . . .'
(InterContinental Hotels Group)

'A level of quality, durability and value that's truly superior in the market place . . . the principle that what is best for the customer is also best for the company . . . (our) . . . customers have learnt to expect a high level of service at all times – from initiating the order, to receiving help and advice, to speedy shipping and further follow-up where necessary . . . (our) . . . employees "go that extra mile". '
(Lands' End)

An operations strategy should identify the broad decisions that will help the operation achieve its objectives

Few businesses have the resources to pursue every single action that might improve their operations performance. So an operations strategy should indicate broadly how the operation might best achieve its performance objectives. For example, a business might specify that it will attempt to reduce its costs by aggressive outsourcing if its non-core business processes and by investing in more efficient technology. Or, it may declare that it intends to offer a more customised set of products or services through adopting a modular approach to its product or service design. The balance here is between a strategy that is overly restrictive in specifying how performance objectives are to be achieved, and one that is so open that it gives little guidance as to what ideas should be pursued.

There are several categorisations of operations strategy decisions. Any of them are valid if they capture the key decisions. Here we categorise operations strategy decisions in the same way we categorise operations management decisions; as applying to the activities of design, delivery and development. Table 2.3 illustrates some of the broad operations strategy decisions that fall within each category.

An operations strategy should reconcile strategic decisions to objectives

> **OPERATIONS PRINCIPLE**
>
> *An operation's strategy should articulate the relationship between operations objectives and the means of achieving them.*

We can now bring together two sets of ideas and, in doing so, we also bring together the two perspectives of (a) market requirements and (b) operations resources to form the two dimensions of a matrix. This *operations strategy* matrix is shown in Figure 2.3. It describes operations strategy as the intersection of a company's performance objectives and the strategic decisions that it makes. In fact there are several

Table 2.3 Some strategic decisions that may be addressed in an operations strategy

Strategic decisions concerned with the *design* of operations and processes	• How should the operation decide which products or services to develop and how to manage the development process? • Should the operation develop its products or services in-house or outsource the designs? • Should the operation outsource some of its activities, or take more activities in-house? • Should the operation expand by acquiring its suppliers or its customers? If so, which ones should it acquire? • How many geographically separate sites should the operation have? • Where should operations sites be located? • What activities and capacity should be allocated to each site? • What broad types of technology should the operation be using? • How should the operation be developing its people? • What role should the people who staff the operation play in its management?
Strategic decisions concerned with planning and controlling the *delivery* of products and services	• How should the operation forecast and monitor the demand for its products and services? • How should the operation adjust its activity levels in response to demand fluctuations? • How should the operation monitor and develop its relationship with its suppliers? • How much inventory should the operation have and where should it be located? • What approach and system should the operation use to plan its activities?
Strategic decisions concerned with the development of operations performance	• How should the operation's performance be measured and reported? • How should the operation ensure that its performance is reflected in its improvement priorities? • Who should be involved in the improvement process? • How fast should improvement in performance be? • How should the improvement process be managed? • How should the operation maintain its resources so as to prevent failure? • How should the operation ensure continuity if a failure occurs?

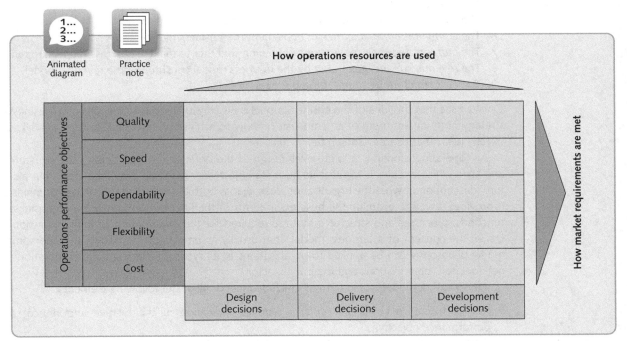

Figure 2.3 The operations strategy matrix defines operations strategy by the intersections of performance objectives and operations decisions

intersections between each performance objective and each decision area (however one wishes to define them). If a business thinks that it has an operations strategy, then it should have a coherent explanation for each of the cells in the matrix. That is, it should be able to explain and reconcile the intended links between each performance objective and each decision area. The process of reconciliation takes place between what is required from the operations function (performance objectives), and how the operation tries to achieve this through the set of choices made (and the capabilities that have been developed) in each decision area.

The concepts of the 'business model' and the 'operating model'

Two concepts have emerged over the last few years that are relevant to operations strategy (or at least the terms are new – one could argue that the ideas are far older). These are the concepts of the 'business model' and the 'operating model'.

Put simply, a 'business model' is the plan that is implemented by a company to generate revenue and make a profit. It includes the various parts and organisational functions of the business, as well as the revenues it generates and the expenses it incurs. In other words, what a company does and how they make money from doing it. More formally, it is 'a conceptual tool that contains a big set of elements and their relationships and allows [the expression of] the business logic of a specific firm. It is a description of the value a company offers to one or several segments of customers and of the architecture of the firm and its network of partners for creating, marketing and delivering this value and relationship capital, to generate profitable and sustainable revenue streams'[8].

One synthesis of literature[9] shows that business models have a number of common elements.

1. The *value proposition* of what is offered to the market.
2. The *target customer segments* addressed by the value proposition.
3. The communication and *distribution channels* to reach customers and offer the value proposition.
4. The *relationships* established with customers.
5. The *core capabilities* needed to make the business model possible.
6. The *configuration of activities* to implement the business model.
7. The *partners* and their motivations of coming together to make a business model happen.
8. The *revenue streams* generated by the business model constituting the revenue model.
9. The *cost structure* resulting of the business model.

One can see that this idea of the business model is broadly analogous to the idea of a 'business strategy', but implies more of an emphasis on *how* to achieve an intended strategy as well as exactly *what* that strategy should be.

An 'operating model' is a 'high-level design of the organisation that defines the structure and style which enables it to meet its business objectives'. It should provide a clear, 'big picture' description of what the organisation does, across both business and technology domains. It provides a way to examine the business in terms of the key relationships between business functions, processes and structures that are required for the organisation to fulfil its mission. Unlike the concept of a business model, that usually assumes a profit motive, the operating model philosophy can be applied to organisations of all types – including large corporations, not-for-profit organisations and the public sector.[10]

An operating model would normally include most or all of the following elements:

- Key performance indicators (KPIs) – with an indication of the relative importance of performance objectives.
- Core financial structure – Profit and Loss (P&L), new investments and cash flow.

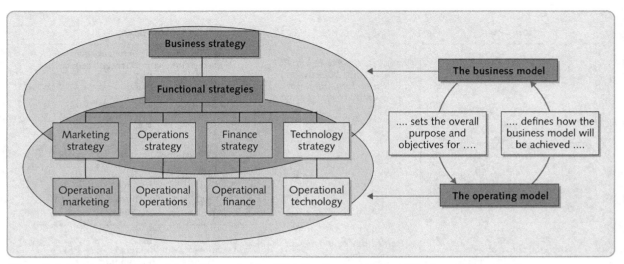

Figure 2.4 The relationship between the concepts of the 'business model' and the 'operating model'

- The nature of accountabilities for products, geographies, assets etc.
- The structure of the organisation – often expressed as capability areas rather than functional roles.
- Systems and technologies.
- Processes responsibilities and interactions.
- Key knowledge and competence.

Note two important characteristics of an operating model. First, it does not respect conventional functional boundaries as such. In some ways the concept of the operating model reflects the idea that we proposed in Chapter 1, namely that all managers are operations managers and all functions can be considered as operations because they comprise processes that deliver some kind of service. An operating model is like an operations strategy, but applied across all functions and domains of the organisation. Second, there are clear overlaps between the 'business model' and the 'operating model'. The main difference being that an operating model focuses more on how an overall business strategy is to be achieved. Operating models have an element of implied change or transformation of the organisation's resources and processes. Often the term 'target operating model' is used to describe the way the organisation should operate in the future if it is going to achieve its objectives and make a success of its business model. Figure 2.4 illustrates the relationship between business and operating models.

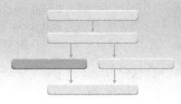

DIAGNOSTIC QUESTION

Does operations strategy make sense from the top and the bottom of the business?

Video

The traditional view of operations strategy is that it is one of several *functional strategies* that are governed by decisions taken at the top of the organisational tree. In this view, operations strategy, together with marketing, human resources and other functional strategies, take their lead exclusively from the needs of the business as a whole. This is often called a 'top-down' perspective on operations strategy. An alternative view is that operations strategies emerge

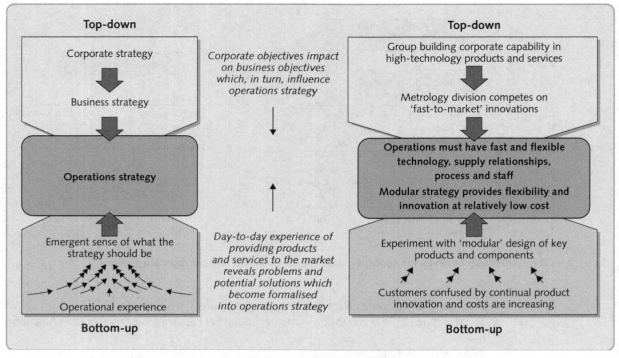

Figure 2.5 **Top-down and bottom-up perspectives of strategy for the metrology company**

over time from the operational level, as the business learns from the day-to-day experience of running processes (both operations and other processes). This is known as the 'emergent' or 'bottom-up' perspective on operations strategy. An operations strategy should reflect both of these perspectives. Any functional strategy, especially operations strategy, cannot afford to be in conflict with the business's overall strategy. Yet at the same time, any operation will be strongly influenced by its day-to-day experiences. Not only will operational issues set practical constraints on strategic direction, more significantly, day-to-day experiences can be exploited to provide an important contribution to strategic thinking. The left-hand side of Figure 2.5 illustrates this.

Top-down operations strategy should reflect the needs of the whole business

A top-down perspective often identifies three levels of strategy: corporate, business and functional. A corporate strategy should position the corporation in its global, economic, political and social environment. This will consist of decisions about what types of business the group wants to be in, what parts of the world it wants to operate in, how to allocate its cash between its various businesses, and so on. Each business unit within the corporate group will also need to put together its own business strategy which sets out its individual mission and objectives. This business strategy guides the business in relation to its customers, markets and competitors, and also defines its role within the corporate group of which it is a part. Similarly, within the business, functional strategies need to consider what part each function should play in contributing to the strategic objectives of the business. The operations, marketing, product/service development and other functions will all need to consider how best they should organise themselves to support the business's objectives.

> **OPERATIONS PRINCIPLE**
>
> *Operations strategies should reflect top-down corporate and/or business objectives.*

Bottom-up operations strategy should reflect operational reality

Although it is a convenient way of thinking about strategy, the top-down hierarchical model does not represent the way strategies are always formulated in practice. When any group is reviewing its corporate strategy, it will also take into account the circumstances, experiences and capabilities of the various businesses that form the group. Similarly, businesses, when reviewing their strategies, will consult the individual functions within the business about their constraints and capabilities. They may also incorporate the ideas which come from each function's day-to-day experience. In fact many strategic ideas emerge over time from operational experience rather than being originated exclusively at a senior level. Sometimes companies move in a particular strategic direction because the ongoing experience of providing products and services to customers at an operational level convinces them that it is the right thing to do. There may be no formal high-level decision making that examines alternative strategic options and chooses the one that provides the best way forward. Instead, a general consensus emerges from the operational experience. The 'high-level' strategic decision making, if it occurs at all, may simply confirm the consensus and provide the resources to make it happen effectively. This is sometimes called the concept of emergent strategies.[11] It sees strategies as often being formed in a relatively unstructured and fragmented manner to reflect the fact that the future is at least partially unknown and unpredictable.

> **OPERATIONS PRINCIPLE**
>
> *Operations strategy should reflect bottom-up experience of operational reality.*

This view of operations strategy reflects how things often happen, but at first glance it seems less useful in providing a guide for specific decision-making. Yet while emergent strategies are less easy to categorise, the principle governing a bottom-up perspective is clear: an operation's objectives and action should be shaped, at least partly, by the knowledge it gains from its day-to-day activities. The key virtues required for shaping strategy from the bottom up are an ability to learn from experience and a philosophy of continual and incremental improvement.

EXAMPLE

Flexibility in innovation

A metrology systems company develops integrated systems for large international clients in several industries. It is part of a group that includes several high-tech companies. It competes through a strategy of technical excellence and innovation together with an ability to advise and customise its systems to clients' needs. As part of this strategy it attempts to be the first in the market with every available new technical innovation. From a top-down perspective, its operations function, therefore, needs to be capable of coping with the changes which constant innovation will bring. It must develop processes that are flexible enough to develop and assemble novel components and systems. It must organise and train its staff to understand the way technology is developing so that they can put in place the necessary changes to the operation. It must develop relationships with its suppliers that will help them to respond quickly when supplying new components. Everything about the operation, its processes, staff, and its systems and procedures, must, in the short term, do nothing to inhibit and, in the long term, actively develop the company's competitive strategy of innovation.

However, over time, as its operations strategy develops, the business discovers that continual product and system innovation is having the effect of dramatically increasing its costs. And, although it does not compete on low prices, its rising costs were impacting profitability. Also there was some evidence that continual changes were confusing some customers. Partially in response to customer requests, the company's system designers started to work out a way of 'modularising' their system and product designs. This allowed one part of the system to be updated for those customers who valued the functionality the innovation could bring, without interfering with the overall design of the main body of the system. Over time, this approach becomes standard design practice within the company. Customers appreciated the extra customisation, and modularisation reduced operations costs. Note that this strategy emerged from the company's experience. No top-level board decision was ever taken to confirm this practice, but nevertheless it emerged as the way in which the company organises its design activity. The right-hand side of Figure 2.5 illustrates these top-down and bottom-up influences for the business.

DIAGNOSTIC QUESTION

Does operations strategy align market requirements with operations resources?

Video

Any operations strategy should reflect the intended market position of the business. Companies compete in different ways; some compete primarily on cost, others on the excellence of their products or services, others on high levels of customer service, and so on. The operations function must respond to this by providing the ability to perform in a manner that is appropriate for the intended market position. This is a market perspective on operations strategy. But, operations strategy must do more than simply meet the short-term needs of the market (important though this is). The processes and resources within operations also need to be developed in the long term to provide the business with a set of competencies or capabilities (we use the two words interchangeably). Capabilities in this context is the 'know-how' that is embedded within the business's resources and processes. These capabilities may be built up over time, as the result of the experiences of the operation, or they may be bought-in or acquired. If they are refined and integrated they can form the basis of the business's ability to offer unique and 'difficult to imitate' products and services to its customers. This idea of the basis of long-term competitive capabilities deriving from the operation's resources and processes is called the resource perspective on operations strategy.

Operations strategy should reflect market requirements

A particularly useful way of determining the relative importance of competitive factors is to distinguish between what have been termed 'order-winners' and 'qualifiers'. Figure 2.6 shows the difference between order-winning and qualifying objectives in terms of their utility, or worth, to the competitiveness of the organisation. The curves illustrate the relative amount of competitiveness (or attractiveness to customers) as the operation's performance varies.

> **OPERATIONS PRINCIPLE**
>
> *Operations strategy should reflect the requirements of the business's markets.*

- **Order-winners** are those things that directly and significantly contribute to winning business. They are regarded by customers as key reasons for purchasing the product or service. Raising performance in an order-winner will either result in more business or improve the chances of gaining more business. Order-winners show a steady and significant increase in their contribution to competitiveness as the operation gets better at providing them.
- **Qualifiers** may not be the major competitive determinants of success, but are important in another way. They are those aspects of competitiveness where the operation's performance has to be above a particular level just to be considered by the customer. Performance below this 'qualifying' level of performance may disqualify the operation from being considered by customers, but any further improvement above the qualifying level is unlikely to gain the company much competitive benefit. Qualifiers are those things that are generally expected by customers. Being great at them is unlikely to excite them, but being bad at them can disadvantage the competitive position of the operation.

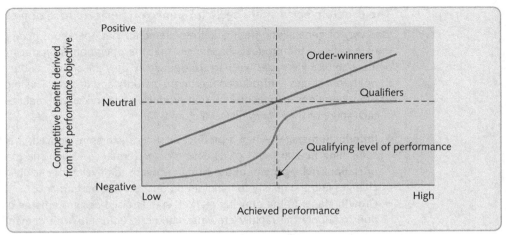

Figure 2.6 Order-winners and qualifiers. Order-winners gain more business the better you are. Qualifiers are the 'givens' of doing business

Different customer needs imply different objectives

If, as is likely, an operation produces goods or services for more than one customer group, it will need to determine the order-winners and qualifiers for each group. For example, Table 2.4 shows two 'product' groups in the banking industry. Here the distinction is drawn between the customers who are looking for banking services for their private and domestic needs and the corporate customers who need banking services for their (often large) businesses.

> **OPERATIONS PRINCIPLE**
>
> *Different customer needs imply different priorities of performance objectives.*

Table 2.4 Different banking services require different performance objectives

	Retail banking	Corporate banking
Products	Personal financial services, such as loans and credit cards	Special services for corporate customers
Customers	Individuals	Businesses
Product range	Medium but standardised, little need for special terms	Very wide range, many need to be customised
Design changes	Occasional	Continual
Delivery	Fast decisions	Dependable service
Quality	Means error-free transactions	Means close relationships
Volume per service type	Most service are high volume	Most services are low volume
Profit margins	Most are low to medium, some high	Medium to high
Order-winners	Price Accessibility Speed	Customisation Quality of service Reliability
Qualifiers	Quality Range	Speed Price
Performance objectives emphasised within the processes that produce each service	Cost Speed Quality	Flexibility Quality Dependability

The product/service life cycle influence on performance objectives

One way of generalising the market requirements that operations need to fulfil is to link it to the life cycle of the products or services that the operation is producing. The exact form of product/service life cycles will vary, but generally they are shown as the sales volume passing through four stages – introduction, growth, maturity and decline. The important implication of this for operations management is that products and services will require operations strategies in each stage of their life cycle (see Figure 2.7).

- **Introduction stage**. When a product or service is first introduced, it is likely to be offering something new in terms of its design or performance. Given the market uncertainty, the operations management of the company needs to develop the flexibility to cope with these changes and the quality to maintain product/service performance.
- **Growth stage**. In the growing market, standardised designs emerge that allows the operation to supply the rapidly growing market. Keeping up with demand through rapid and

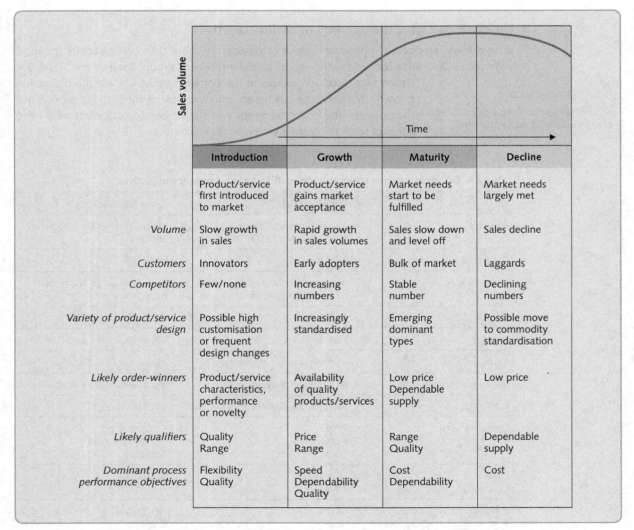

	Introduction	Growth	Maturity	Decline
	Product/service first introduced to market	Product/service gains market acceptance	Market needs start to be fulfilled	Market needs largely met
Volume	Slow growth in sales	Rapid growth in sales volumes	Sales slow down and level off	Sales decline
Customers	Innovators	Early adopters	Bulk of market	Laggards
Competitors	Few/none	Increasing numbers	Stable number	Declining numbers
Variety of product/service design	Possible high customisation or frequent design changes	Increasingly standardised	Emerging dominant types	Possible move to commodity standardisation
Likely order-winners	Product/service characteristics, performance or novelty	Availability of quality products/services	Low price Dependable supply	Low price
Likely qualifiers	Quality Range	Price Range	Range Quality	Dependable supply
Dominant process performance objectives	Flexibility Quality	Speed Dependability Quality	Cost Dependability	Cost

Figure 2.7 The effects of the product/service life cycle on the operation and its process performance objectives

dependable response and maintaining quality levels will help to keep market share as competition starts to increase.

- **Maturity stage**. Eventually demand starts to level off as the market becomes dominated by a few larger companies with standardised designs. Competition will probably emphasise price or value for money, so operations will be expected to get costs down in order to maintain profits, or to allow price cutting, or both. So, cost and productivity issues, together with dependable supply, are likely to be the operation's main concerns.
- **Decline stage**. After time, sales will decline. To the companies left there might be a residual market, but if capacity in the industry lags demand, the market will be dominated by price competition; therefore cost-cutting continues to be important.

Operations strategy should build operations capabilities

Building operations capabilities means understanding the existing resources and processes within the operation, starting with the simple questions, what do we have, and what can

> **OPERATIONS PRINCIPLE**
>
> *The long-term objective of operation strategy is to build operations-based capabilities.*

we do? However, trying to understand an operation by listing its resources alone is like trying to understand an automobile by listing its component parts. To understand an automobile we need to describe how the component parts form its internal mechanisms. Within the operation, the equivalents of these mechanisms are its *processes*. Yet, even a technical explanation of an automobile's mechanisms does not convey its style or

'personality'. Something more is needed to describe these. In the same way, an operation is not just the sum of its processes. It also has *intangible* resources. An operation's intangible resources include such things as:

- its relationship with suppliers and the reputation it has with its customers
- its knowledge of and experience in handling its process technologies
- the way its staff can work together in new product and service development
- the way it integrates all its processes into a mutually supporting whole.

These intangible resources may not be as evident within an operation, but they are important and often have real value. And both tangible and intangible resources and processes shape its capabilities. The central issue for operations management, therefore, is to ensure that its pattern of strategic decisions really does develop appropriate capabilities.

The resource-based view

The idea that building operations capabilities should be an important objective of operations strategy is closely linked with the popularity of an approach to business strategy called the resource-based view (RBV) of the firm.[12] This holds that businesses with an 'above average' strategic performance are likely to have gained their sustainable competitive advantage because of their core competences (or capabilities). This means that the way an organisation inherits, or acquires, or develops its operations resources will, over the long term, have a significant impact on its strategic success. The RBV differs in its approach from the more traditional view of strategy which sees companies as seeking to protect their competitive advantage through their control of the market. For example, by creating *barriers to entry* through product differentiation, or making it difficult for customers to switch to competitors, or controlling the access to distribution channels (a major barrier to entry in gasoline retailing, for example, where oil companies own their own retail stations). By contrast, the RBV sees firms being able to protect their competitive advantage through *barriers to imitation*, that is, by building up 'difficult-to-imitate' resources. Some of these 'difficult-to-imitate' resources are particularly important, and can be classified as 'strategic' if they exhibit the following properties:

- *They are scarce.* Scarce resources, such as specialised production facilities, experienced engineers, proprietary software, etc. can underpin competitive advantage.
- *They are imperfectly mobile.* Some resources are difficult to move out of a firm. For example, resources that were developed in-house, or are based on the experience of the company's staff, or are interconnected with the other resources in the firm, cannot be traded easily.
- *They are imperfectly imitable and imperfectly substitutable.* It is not enough only to have resources that are unique and immobile. If a competitor can copy these resources or, replace them with alternative resources, then their value will quickly deteriorate. The more the resources are connected with process knowledge embedded deep within the firm, the more difficult they are for competitors to understand and to copy.

Reconciling market requirements and operations resource capabilities

The market requirements and the operations resource perspectives on operations strategy represent two sides of a strategic equation that all operations managers have to reconcile. On one hand, the operation must be able to meet the requirements of the market. On the other hand, it also needs to develop operations capabilities that make it able to do the things that customers find valuable but competitors find difficult to imitate. And ideally, there should be a reasonable degree of alignment, or 'fit' between the requirements of the market and the capabilities of operations resources. Figure 2.8 illustrates the concept of fit diagrammatically. The vertical dimension represents the nature of market requirements either because they reflect the intrinsic needs of customers or because their expectations have been shaped by the firm's marketing activity. This includes such factors as the strength of the brand or reputation, the degree of differentiation or the extent of market promises. Movement along the dimension indicates a broadly enhanced level of market 'performance'. The horizontal scale represents the nature of the firm's operations resources and processes. This includes such things as the performance of the operation in terms of its ability to achieve competitive objectives, the efficiency with which it uses its resources, and the ability of the firm's resources to underpin its business processes. Movement along the dimension broadly indicates an enhanced level of 'operations capability'.

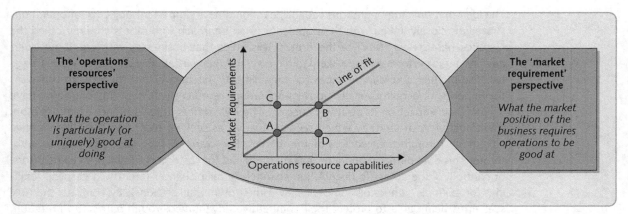

Figure 2.8 Operations strategy must attempt to achieve 'fit' between market requirements and operations resource capabilities

If market requirements and operations capability of an operation are aligned it would diagrammatically be positioned on the 'line of fit' in Figure 2.8. 'Fit' is to achieve an approximate balance between 'market requirements' and 'operations capability'. So when fit is achieved, firms' customers do not need, or expect, levels of operations capability that cannot be supplied. Nor does the operation have strengths that are either inappropriate for market needs or remain unexploited in the market.

An operation that has position A in Figure 2.8 has achieved 'fit' in so much as its operations capabilities are aligned with its market requirements, yet both are at a relatively low level. In other words, the market does not want much from the business, which is just as well because its operation is not capable of achieving much. An operation with position B has also achieved 'fit', but at a higher level. Other things being equal, this will be a more profitable position that position A. Positions C and D are out of alignment. Position C denotes an operation that does not have sufficient operations capability to satisfy what the market wants. Position D indicates an operation that has more operations capability than it is able to exploit in its markets. Generally, operations at C and D would wish to improve their operations capability (C), or reposition itself in its market (D) in order to get back into a position of fit.

DIAGNOSTIC QUESTION

Does operations strategy set an improvement path?

Video

An operations strategy is the starting point for operations improvement. It sets the direction in which the operation will change over time. It is implicit that the business will want operations to change for the better. Therefore, unless an operations strategy gives some idea as to how improvement will happen, it is not fulfilling its main purpose. This is best thought about in terms of how performance objectives, both in themselves and relative to each other, will change over time. To do this, we need to understand the concept of, and the arguments concerning, the trade-offs between performance objectives.

An operations strategy should guide the trade-offs between performance objectives

An operations strategy should address the relative priority of operation's performance objectives ('for us, speed of response is more important than cost efficiency, quality is more important than variety', and so on). To do this it must consider the possibility of improving its performance in one objective by sacrificing performance in another. So, for example, an operation might wish to improve its cost efficiencies by reducing the variety of products or services that it offers to its customers. Taken to its extreme, this 'trade-off' principle implies that improvement in one performance objective can *only* be gained at the expense of another. 'There is no such thing as a free lunch' could be taken as a summary of this approach to managing. Probably the best-known summary of the trade-off idea comes from Professor Wickham Skinner, the most influential of the originators of the strategic approach to operations, who said:[13]

> OPERATIONS PRINCIPLE
>
> *In the short term, operations cannot achieve outstanding performance in all its operations objectives.*

> . . . *most managers will readily admit that there are compromises or trade-offs to be made in designing an airplane or truck. In the case of an airplane, trade-offs would involve matters such*

as cruising speed, take-off and landing distances, initial cost, maintenance, fuel consumption, passenger comfort and cargo or passenger capacity. For instance, no one today can design a 500-passenger plane that can land on an aircraft carrier and also break the sound barrier. Much the same thing is true in . . . [operations].

But there is another view of the trade-offs between performance objectives. This sees the very idea of trade-offs as the enemy of operations improvement, and regards the acceptance that one type of performance can only be achieved at the expense of another as both limiting and unambitious. For any real improvement of total performance, it holds, the effect of trade-offs must be overcome in some way. In fact, overcoming trade-offs must be seen as the central objective of strategic operations improvement.

These two approaches to managing trade-offs result in two approaches to operations improvement. The first emphasises 'repositioning' performance objectives by trading-off improvements in some objectives for a reduction in performance in other. The other emphasises increasing the 'effectiveness' of the operation by overcoming trade-offs so that improvements in one or more aspects of performance can be achieved without any reduction in the performance of others. Most businesses at some time or other will adopt both approaches. This is best illustrated through the concept of the 'efficient frontier' of operations performance.

> **OPERATIONS PRINCIPLE**
>
> *In the long term, a key objective of operations strategy is to improve all aspects of operations performance.*

Trade-offs and the efficient frontier

Figure 2.9(a) shows the relative performance of several companies in the same industry in terms of their cost efficiency and the variety of products or services that they offer to their customers. Presumably all the operations would ideally like to be able to offer very high variety while still having very high levels of cost efficiency. However, the increased complexity that a high variety of product or service offerings brings will generally reduce the operation's ability to operate efficiently. Conversely, one way of improving cost efficiency is to severely limit the variety on offer to customers. The spread of results in Figure 2.9(a) is typical of an exercise

Animated diagram

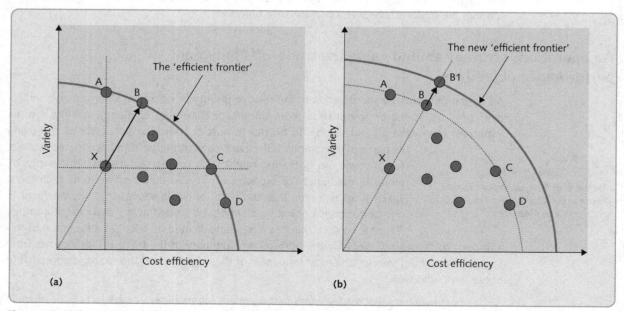

Figure 2.9 If the performance of a group of operations is compared, some will lie on the efficient frontier

such as this. Operations A, B, C, D all have chosen a different balance between variety and cost efficiency. But none is dominated by any other operation in the sense that another operation necessarily has 'superior' performance. Operation X however, has an inferior performance because operation A is able to offer higher variety at the same level of cost efficiency, and operation C offers the same variety but with better cost efficiency. The convex line on which operations A, B, C and D lie is known as the 'efficient frontier'. They may choose to position themselves differently (presumably because of different market strategies) but they cannot be criticised for being ineffective. Of course any of these operations that lie on the efficient frontier may come to believe that the balance they have chosen between variety and cost efficiency is inappropriate. In these circumstances they may choose to reposition themselves at some other point along the efficient frontier. By contrast, operation X has also chosen to balance variety and cost efficiency in a particular way but is not doing so effectively. Operation B has the same ratio between the two performance objectives but is achieving them more effectively. Operation X will generally have a strategy that emphasises increasing its effectiveness before considering any repositioning.

> **OPERATIONS PRINCIPLE**
>
> *Operations that lie on the 'efficient frontier' have performance levels that dominate those which do not.*

However, a strategy that emphasises increasing effectiveness is not confined to those operations that are dominated, such as operation X. Those with a position on the efficient frontier will generally also want to improve their operations effectiveness by overcoming the trade-off that is implicit in the efficient frontier curve. For example, suppose operation B in Figure 2.9(b) is the metrology company described earlier in this chapter. By adopting a modular product design strategy it improved both its variety and its cost efficiency simultaneously (and moved to position B1). What has happened is that operation B has adopted a particular operations practice (modular design) that has pushed out the efficient frontier. This distinction between positioning on the efficient frontier and increasing operations effectiveness to reach the frontier is an important one. Any operations strategy must make clear the extent to which it is expecting the operation to reposition itself in terms of its performance objectives and the extent to which it is expecting the operation to improve its effectiveness.

Improving operations effectiveness by using trade-offs

Improving the effectiveness of an operation by pushing out the efficient frontier requires different approaches depending on the original position of the operation on the frontier. For example, in Figure 2.10 operation P has an original position that offers a high level of variety at the expense of low cost efficiency. It has probably reached this position by adopting a series of operations practices that enable it to offer the variety even if these practices are intrinsically expensive. For example, it may have invested in general purpose technology and recruited employees with a wide range of skills. Improving variety even further may mean adopting even more extreme operations practices that emphasise variety. For instance, it may reorganise its processes so that each of its larger customers has a dedicated set of resources that understands the specific requirements of that customer and can organise itself to totally customise every product and service it produces. This will probably mean a further sacrifice of cost efficiency, but it allows an ever greater variety of products or services to be produced (P1). Similarly, operation Q may increase the effectiveness of its cost efficiency, by becoming even less able to offer any kind of variety (Q1). For both operations P and Q effectiveness is being improved through increasing the focus of the operation on one (or a very narrow set of) performance objectives and accepting an even further reduction in other aspects of performance.

The same principle of focus also applies to organisational units smaller than a whole operation. For example, individual processes may choose to position themselves on a highly focused set of performance objectives that match the market requirements of their own customers.

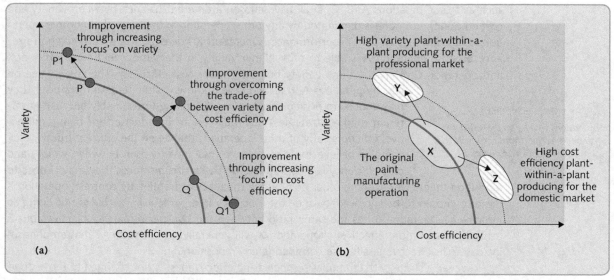

Figure 2.10 Operations 'focus' and the 'plant-within-a-plant' concept illustrated using the efficient frontier model

So, for example, a business that manufactures paint for interior decoration may serve two quite distinct markets. Some of its products are intended for domestic customers who are price sensitive but demand only a limited variety of colours and sizes. The other market is professional interior decorators who demand a very wide variety of colours and sizes but are less price sensitive. The business may choose to move from a position where all types of paint are made on the same processes (position X in Figure 2.10(b)) to one where it has two separate sets of processes (Y and Z); one that only makes paint for the domestic market and the other that only makes paint for the professional market. In effect, the business has segmented its operations processes to match the segmentation of the market. This is sometimes called the 'plant-within-a-plant' concept.

Improving operations effectiveness by overcoming trade-offs

This concept of highly focused operations is not universally seen as appropriate. Many companies attempt to give 'the best of both worlds' to their customers. At one time, for example, a high-quality, reliable and error-free automobile was inevitably an expensive automobile. Now, with few exceptions, we expect even budget-priced automobiles to be reliable and almost free of any defects. Auto manufacturers found that not only could they reduce the number of defects on their vehicles without necessarily incurring extra costs, but they could actually reduce costs by reducing errors in manufacture. If auto manufacturers had adopted a purely focused-based approach to improvement over the years, we may now only be able to purchase either very cheap, low-quality automobiles or very expensive, high-quality automobiles. So a permanent expansion of the efficient frontier is best achieved by overcoming trade-offs through improvements in operations practice.

> **OPERATIONS PRINCIPLE**
>
> *An operation's strategy improvement path can be described in terms of repositioning and/or overcoming its performance trade-offs.*

Even trade-offs that seem to be inevitable can be reduced to some extent. For example, one of the decisions that any supermarket manager has to make is how many checkout positions to open at any time. If too many checkouts are opened then there will be times when the checkout staff do not have any customers to serve and will be idle. The customers, however, will have excellent service in terms of little or no waiting time. Conversely, if too few checkouts are opened, the staff will be working all the time but customers will have to wait in long queues. There seems to be a direct trade-off between staff utilisation (and therefore cost) and customer waiting time (speed of service). Yet even the supermarket manager deciding how many checkouts to open can go some way to affecting the trade-off between customer waiting time and staff utilisation. The manager might, for example, allocate a number of 'core' staff to operate the checkouts but also arrange for those other staff who are performing other jobs in the supermarket to be trained and 'on-call' should demand suddenly increase. If the manager on duty sees a build-up of customers at the checkouts, these other staff could quickly be used to staff checkouts. By devising a flexible system of staff allocation, the manager can both improve customer service and keep staff utilisation high.

Critical commentary

Each chapter contains a short critical commentary on the main ideas covered in the chapter. Its purpose is not to undermine the issues discussed in the chapter, but to emphasise that, although we present a relatively orthodox view of operation, there are other perspectives.

● Starting any discussion of strategy from a stakeholder perspective is far from undisputed. Listen to Michael Jensen of Harvard Business School. '*At the economy-wide or social level, the issue is this: if we could dictate the criterion or objective function to be maximised by firms (and thus the performance criterion by which corporate executives choose among alternative policy options), what would it be? Or, to put the issue even more simply: how do we want the firms in our economy to measure their own performance? How do we want them to determine what is better versus worse?*' He also holds that using stakeholder perspectives gives undue weight to narrow special interests who want to use the organisation's resources for their own ends. The stakeholder perspective gives them a spurious legitimacy which '*undermines the foundations of value-seeking behaviour*'.[14]

● Similarly, the idea that operations strategy could ever become the driver of a business's overall strategy, and the associated concept of the resource-based view of the firm, are both problematic to some theorists. Business strategies, and functional strategies, were, for many years, seen as, first, market driven and, second, planned in a systematic and deliberative manner. So, it became almost axiomatic to see strategy as starting from a full understanding of market positioning. In fact, the main source of sustainable competitive advantage was seen as unequivocally associated with how a business positioned itself in its markets. Get the market proposition right and customers would respond by giving you business. Get it wrong and they would go to the competitors with a better offering. Strategy was seen as aligning the whole organisation to the market position that could achieve long-term profitable differentiation when compared to competitors. Functional strategies were simply a more detailed interpretation of this overall imperative. Furthermore, strategy must be something that could be planned and directed. If managers could not influence strategy, then how could business be anything other than a lottery?

● The idea that sustainable competitive advantage could come from the capabilities of one's resources was a clear threat to the established position. Furthermore, the idea that strategies emerged, sometimes haphazardly and unpredictably, over time rather than were deliberate decisions taken by senior managers was also seemingly counter-intuitive. Yet there is now considerable research evidence to support both these, once outrageous, propositions. The position we have taken in this chapter is one of blending some aspects of the traditional view with the more recent ideas. Nevertheless, it is important to understand that there are still different views on the very nature of strategic management.

SUMMARY CHECKLIST

This checklist comprises questions that can be usefully applied to any type of operations and reflect the major diagnostic questions used within the chapter.

- [ ] Does the operation have a fully articulated operations strategy?

- [ ] Does it include a vision for the role and contribution of the operations function?

- [ ] What position on the Hayes and Wheelwright stage 1 to 4 model are your operations?

- [ ] Are the operation's performance objectives fully articulated?

- [ ] Are the main strategic decisions that shape operations resources fully identified?

- [ ] Are the logical links established between what the market requires (in terms of performance objectives) and what capabilities an operations possesses (in terms of the major strategic decision areas)?

- [ ] What is the balance between top-down direction and bottom-up learning in formulating operations strategy?

- [ ] Is there a recognised process both for top-down and bottom-up communication on strategic issues?

- [ ] Are performance objectives understood in terms of whether they are order-winners or qualifiers?

- [ ] Have different parts of the operation (probably producing different products or services) their own relative priority of performance objectives that reflect their possibly different competitive positions?

- [ ] Is the idea of operations-based capabilities fully understood?

- [ ] What capabilities does the operation currently possess?

- [ ] Are these operations and/or resources scarce, imperfectly mobile, imperfectly imitable or imperfectly substitutable?

- [ ] If none of the above, are they really useful in terms of their strategic impact?

- [ ] Where would you put the operation in terms of Figure 2.8 that describes the broad fit between market requirements and operations resource capabilities?

- [ ] Have the key trade-offs for the operation been identified?

- [ ] What combination of repositioning in order to change the nature of trade-offs, and overcoming the trade-offs themselves, is going to be used to improve overall operations performance?

McDonald's: Half a Century of Growth[15]

It's loved and it's hated. It is a shining example of how good value food can be brought to a mass market. It is a symbol of everything that is wrong with 'industrialised', capitalist, bland, high-calorie and environmentally unfriendly commercialism. It is the best-known and most-loved fast food brand in the world with more than 32,000 restaurants in 117 countries, providing jobs for 1.7 million staff and feeding 60 million customers per day (yes, per day!). It is part of the homogenisation of individual national cultures, filling the world with bland, identical, 'cookie cutter', Americanised and soulless operations that dehumanise its staff by forcing them to follow rigid and over-defined procedures. But whether you see it as friend, foe, or a bit of both, McDonald's has revolutionised the food industry, affecting the lives both of the people who produce food and the people who eat it. It has also had its ups (mainly) and downs (occasionally). Yet, even in the toughest times it has always displayed remarkable resilience. Even after the economic turbulence of 2008, McDonald's reported an exceptional year of growth in 2009, posting sales increases and higher market share around the world – it was the sixth consecutive year of positive sales in every geographic region of their business.

Source: David Pearson/Alamy Images

Starting small

Central to the development of McDonald's is Ray Kroc, who by 1954 and at the age of 52 had been variously a piano player, a paper cup salesman and a multi-mixer salesman. He was surprised by a big order for eight multi-mixers from a restaurant in San Bernardino, California. When he visited the customer he found a small but successful restaurant run by two brothers Dick and Mac McDonald. They had opened their 'Bar-B-Que' restaurant 14 years earlier adopting the usual format at that time: customers would drive-in, choose from a large menu and be served by a 'car hop'. However, by the time Ray Kroc visited the brothers' operation it had changed to a self-service drive-in format with a limited menu of nine-items. He was amazed by the effectiveness of their operation. Focusing on a limited menu, including burgers, fries and beverages, had allowed them to analyse every step of the process of producing and serving their food. Ray Kroc was so overwhelmed by what he saw that he persuaded the brothers to adopt his vision of creating McDonald's restaurants all over the US, the first of which opened in Des Plaines, Illinois, in June 1955. However, later, Kroc and

the McDonald brothers quarrelled, and Kroc brought the brothers out. Now with exclusive rights to the McDonald's name, the restaurants spread, and in five years there were 200 restaurants through the US. After ten years the company went public, the share price doubling in the first month. But through this and later expansion, Kroc insisted on maintaining the same principles that he had seen in the original operation. 'If I had a brick for every time I've repeated the phrase 'Quality, Service, Cleanliness and Value', I think I'd probably be able to bridge the Atlantic Ocean with them.' (Ray Kroc)

Priority to the process

Ray Kroc had been attracted by the cleanliness, simplicity, efficiency and profitability of the McDonald brothers' operation. They had stripped fast food delivery down to its essence and eliminated needless effort to make a swift assembly line for a meal at reasonable prices. Kroc wanted to build a process that would become famous for food of consistently high quality using uniform methods of preparation. His burgers, buns, fries and beverages should taste just the same in Alaska as they did in Alabama. The answer was the 'Speedee Service System', a standardised process that prescribed exact preparation methods, specially designed equipment and strict product specifications. The emphasis on process standardisation meant that customers could be assured of identical levels of food and service quality every time they visited any store, anywhere. Operating procedures were specified in minute detail. In its first operations manual, which by 1991 had reached 750 pages, it prescribed specific cooking instructions such as temperatures, cooking times and portions to be followed rigorously. Similarly, operating procedures were defined to ensure the required customer experience, for example, no food items were to be held more than ten minutes in the transfer bin between being cooked and being served. Technology was also automated, and specially designed equipment helped to guarantee consistency using 'fool-proof' devices. For example, the ketchup was dispensed through a metered pump; specially designed 'clam shell' grills cooked both sides of each meat patty simultaneously for a pre-set time; and when it became clear that the metal tongs used by staff to fill French-fry containers were awkward to use efficiently, McDonald's engineers devised a simple V-shaped aluminium scoop that made the job faster and easier as well as presenting the fries in a more attractive alignment with their container.

For Kroc, the operating process was both his passion and the company's central philosophy. It was also the foundation of learning and improvement. The company's almost compulsive focus on process detail was not an end in itself. Rather it was to learn what contributed to consistent high-quality service in practice and what did not. Learning was always seen as important by McDonald's. In 1961, it founded 'Hamburger University', initially in the basement of a restaurant in Elk Grove Village, Illinois. It had a research and development laboratory to develop new cooking, freezing, storing and serving methods. Also franchisees and operators were trained in the analytical techniques necessary to run a successful McDonald's. It awarded degrees in 'Hamburgerology'. But learning was not just for headquarters. The company also formed a 'field service' unit to appraise and help its restaurants by sending field service consultants to review their performance on a number of 'dimensions' including cleanliness, queuing, food quality and customer service. As Ray Kroc, said, '*We take the hamburger business more seriously than anyone else. What sets McDonald's apart is the passion that we and our suppliers share around producing and delivering the highest-quality beef patties. Rigorous food safety and quality standards and practices are in place and executed at the highest levels every day.*'

No story illustrates the company's philosophy of learning and improvement better than its adoption of frozen fries. French-fried potatoes had always been important. Initially, the company tried observing the temperature levels and cooking methods that produced the best fries. The problem was that the temperature during the cooking process was very much influenced by the temperature of the

potatoes when they were placed into the cooking vat. So, unless the temperature of the potatoes before they were cooked were also controlled (not very practical) it was difficult to specify the exact time and temperature that would produce perfect fries. But McDonald's researchers have perseverance. They discovered that, irrespective of the temperature of the raw potatoes, fries were always at their best when the oil temperature in the cooking vat increased by three degrees above the low temperature point after they were put in the vat. So by monitoring the temperature of the vat, perfect fries could be produced every time. But that was not the end of the story. The ideal potato for fries was the Idaho Russet, which was seasonal and not available in the summer months, when an alternative (inferior) potato was used. One grower, who, at the time, supplied a fifth of McDonald's potatoes, suggested that he could put Idaho Russets into cold storage for supplying during the summer period. Notwithstanding investment in cold storage facilities, all the stored potatoes rotted. Not to be beaten, he offered another suggestion. Why don't McDonald's consider switching to frozen potatoes? This was no trivial decision and the company was initially cautious about meddling with such an important menu item. However there were other advantages in using frozen potatoes. Supplying fresh potatoes in perfect condition to McDonald's rapidly expanding chain was increasingly difficult. Frozen potatoes could actually increase the quality of the company's fries if a method of satisfactorily cooking them could be found. Once again McDonald's developers came to the rescue. They developed a method of air drying the raw fries, quick frying, and then freezing them. The supplier, who was a relatively small and local suppler when he first suggested storing Idaho Russets grew its business to supply around half of McDonald's US business.

Throughout their rapid expansion a significant danger facing McDonald's was losing control of their operating system. They avoided this, partly by always focusing on four areas – improving the product, establishing strong supplier relationships, creating (largely customised) equipment, and developing franchise holders. But it was also their strict control of the menu which provided a platform of stability. Although their competitors offered a relatively wide variety of menu items, McDonald's limited theirs to ten items. This allowed uniform standards to be established, which in turn encouraged specialisation. As one of McDonald's senior managers at the time stressed, '*It wasn't because we were smarter. The fact that we were selling just ten items [and] had a facility that was small, and used a limited number of suppliers created an ideal environment.*' Capacity growth (through additional stores) was also managed carefully. Well-utilised stores were important to franchise holders, so franchise opportunities were located only where they would not seriously undercut existing stores. Ray Kroc used the company plane to spot from the air the best locations and road junctions for new restaurant branches.

Securing supply

McDonald's says that it has been the strength of the alignment between the company, its franchisees and its suppliers (collectively referred to as the System) that has been the explanation for its success. Expanding the McDonald's chain, especially in the early years, meant persuading both franchisees and suppliers to buy into the company's vision. 'Working', as Ray Kroc put it, *'not for McDonald's, but for themselves, together with McDonald's.'* He promoted the slogan, *'In business for yourself, but not by yourself.'* But when they started suppliers proved problematic. McDonald's approached the major food suppliers, such as Kraft and Heinz, but without much success. Large and established suppliers were reluctant to conform to McDonald's requirements, preferring to focus on retail sales. It was the relatively small companies who were willing to risk supplying what seemed then to be a risky venture. Yet as McDonald's grew, so did its suppliers. Also, McDonald's relationship with its suppliers was seen as less adversarial than with some other customers. One supplier is quoted as saying, *'Other chains would walk away from you for half a cent. McDonald's was more concerned with getting quality. McDonald's always treated me with respect even when they became much bigger and didn't have to.'* Furthermore, suppliers were always seen as a source if innovation. For example, one of McDonald's meat suppliers, Keystone Foods, developed a novel quick-freezing process that captured the fresh taste and texture of beef patties. This meant that every patty could retain its consistent quality until it hit the grill. Keystone shared its technology with other McDonald's meat suppliers for McDonald's, and today the process is an industry standard. Yet, although innovative and close, supplier relationships are also rigorously controlled. Unlike some competitors who simply accepted what suppliers provided, complaining only when supplies were not up to standard, McDonald's routinely analysed its supplier's products.

Fostering franchisees

McDonald's revenues consist of sales by company-operated restaurants and fees from restaurants operated by franchisees. McDonald's view themselves primarily as a franchisor and believe franchising is . . . *'important to delivering great, locally-relevant customer experiences and driving profitability'*. However, they also believe that directly operating restaurants is essential to providing the company with real operations experience. In 2009, of the 32,478 restaurants in 117 countries, 26,216 were operated by franchisees and 6,262 were operated by the company.

Where McDonald's was different to other franchise operations was in their relationships. Some restaurant chains concentrated on recruiting franchisees that may then be ignored. McDonalds, on the other hand expected its franchisees to contribute their experiences for the benefit of all, Ray Kroc's original concept was that franchisees would make money before the company did, so he made sure that the revenues that went to McDonald's came from the success of the restaurants themselves rather from initial franchise fees.

Initiating innovation

Ideas for new menu items have often come from franchisees. For example, Lou Groen, a Cincinnati franchise holder had noticed that in Lent (a 40-day period when some Christians give up eating red meat on Fridays and instead eat only fish or no meat at all) some customers avoided the traditional hamburger. He went to Ray Kroc, with his idea for a 'Filet-o-Fish', a steamed bun with a shot of tartar sauce, a fish fillet, and cheese on the bottom bun. But Kroc wanted to push his own meatless sandwich, called the hula burger, a cold bun with a piece of pineapple and cheese. Groen and Kroc competed on a Lenten Friday to see whose sandwich would sell more. Kroc's hula burger failed, selling only six sandwiches all day while Groen sold 350 Filet-o-Fish. Similarly, the Egg McMuffin was introduced by franchisee Herb Peterson, who wanted to attract customers into his McDonalds stores all through the day, not just at lunch and dinner. He came up with idea for the signature McDonald's breakfast item because he was reputedly *'very partial to eggs Benedict and wanted to create something similar'*.

Other innovations came from the company itself. By the beginning of the 1980s, poultry was becoming more fashionable to eat and sales of beef were sagging. Fred Turner, then the Chairman of McDonald's had an idea for a new meal – a chicken finger-food without bones, about the size of a thumb. After six months of research, the food technicians and scientists managed to reconstitute shreds of white chicken meat into small portions which could be breaded, fried, frozen then reheated. Test-marketing the new product was positive, and in 1983 they were launched under the name Chicken McNuggets. These were so successful that within a month McDonald's became the second largest purchaser of chicken in the USA. By 1992, Americans were eating more chicken than beef.

Other innovations came as a reaction to market conditions. Criticised by nutritionists who worried about calorie-rich burgers and shareholders who were alarmed by flattening sales, McDonald's launching its biggest menu revolution in 30 years in 2003 when it entered the prepared salad market. They offered a choice of dressings for their grilled chicken salad with Caesar dressing (and croutons) or the lighter option of a drizzle of balsamic dressing. Likewise, recent moves towards coffee sales were prompted by the ever-growing trend set by big coffee shops like Starbucks. McCafé, a coffee-house-style food and drink chain, owned by McDonald's, had expanded to about 1,300 stores worldwide by 2011.

Problematic periods

The period from the early 1990s to the mid 2000s was difficult for parts of the McDonald's Empire. Although growth in many parts of the world continued, in some developed markets, the company's hitherto rapid growth stalled. Partly this was due to changes in food fashion, nutritional concerns and demographic changes. Partly it was because competitors were learning to either emulate McDonald's operating system, or focus on one aspect of the traditional 'quick service' offering, such as speed of service, range of menu items, (perceived) quality of food, or price. Burger King, promoted itself on its 'flame-grilled' quality. Wendy's offered a fuller service level. Taco Bell undercut McDonald's prices with their 'value pricing' promotions. Drive-through specialists such as Sonic speeded up service times. But it was not only competitors that were a threat to McDonald's growth. So called 'fast food' was developing a poor reputation in some quarters, and as its iconic brand, McDonald's was taking much of the heat. Similarly the company became a lightning rod for other questionable aspects of modern life that it was held to promote, from cultural imperialism, low-skilled jobs, abuse of animals, the use of hormone-enhanced beef, to an attack on traditional (French) values (in France). A French farmer called Jose Bové (who was briefly imprisoned) got other farmers to drive their tractors through, and wreck, a half-built McDonald's. When he was tried, 40,000 people rallied outside the courthouse.

The Chief Executive of McDonald's in the UK, Jill McDonald (yes, really!), said that some past difficulties were self-induced. They included a refusal to face criticisms and a reluctance to acknowledge the need for change. '*I think by the end of 1990s we were just not as close to the customer as we needed to be, we were given a hard time in the press and we lost our confidence. We needed to reconnect, and make changes that would disrupt people's view of McDonald's.*' Investing in its people also needed to be re-emphasised. '*We invest about £35m a year in training people. We have become much more of an educator than an employer of people*'. Nor does she accept the idea of 'McJobs' (meaning boring, poorly paid, often temporary jobs with few prospects). '*That whole McJob thing makes me so angry. It's snobbish. We are the biggest employer of young people in Britain. Many join us without qualifications. They want a better life, and getting qualifications is something they genuinely value.*'

Surviving strategies

Yet, in spite of its difficult period, the company has not only survived, but through the late 2000s has thrived. In 2009, McDonald's results showed that in the US, sales and market share both grew for the seventh consecutive year with new products such as McCafé premium coffees, the premium Angus Third Pounder, smoothies and frappes, together with more convenient locations, extended hours, efficient drive thru service and value-oriented promotions. In the UK, changes to the stores' decor have also helped stimulate growth. Jill McDonald's views are not untypical of other regions: '*We have probably changed more in the past four years than the past 30: more chicken, 100% breast meat, snack wraps, more coffee – lattes and cappuccinos, ethically sourced, not at rip-off prices. That really connected with customers. We sold 100m cups last year.*'

Senior managers put their recent growth down to the decision in 2003 to reinvent McDonald's by becoming 'better, not just bigger' and implementing its 'Plan to Win'. This focused on 'restaurant execution', with the goal of . . . 'improving the overall experience for our customers'. It provided a common framework for their global business yet allowed for local adaptation. Multiple improvement initiatives were based on its 'five key drivers of exceptional customer experiences' (People, Products, Place, Price and Promotion). But what of McDonald's famous standardisation? During its early growth no franchise holder could deviate from the 700+ page McDonald's operations manual known as 'the Bible'. Now things are different, at least partly because different regions have developed their own products. In India, the 'Maharaja Mac' is made of mutton, and the vegetarian options contain no meat or eggs. Similarly, McDonald's in Pakistan offers three spicy 'McMaza meals'. Even in the US things have changed. In at least one location in Indiana, there's now a McDonald's with a full service 'Diner' inside, where waitresses serve 100 combinations of food, on china – a far cry from Ray Kroc's vision of stripping out choice to save time and money.

QUESTIONS

1 How has the competitive situation that McDonald's faces changed since it was founded (in its current form) in the 1950s?

2 How have McDonald's operations activities, in terms of its design, delivery and development, influenced its operations performance objectives?

3 Draw an operations strategy matrix for McDonald's.

4 Search the internet site of Intel, the best known microchip manufacturer, and identify what appear to be its main elements in its operations strategy.

APPLYING THE PRINCIPLES

Hints

Some of these exercises can be answered by reading the chapter. Others will require some general knowledge of business activity and some might require an element of investigation. Hints on how they can all be answered are to be found in the eText at www.pearsoned.co.uk/slack.

1   The environmental services department of a city has two recycling services – newspaper collection (NC) and general recycling (GR). The NC service is a door-to-door collection service which, at a fixed time every week, collects old newspapers which householders have placed in reusable plastic bags at their gate. An empty bag is left for the householders to use for the next collection. The value of the newspapers collected is relatively small, the service is offered mainly for reasons of environmental responsibility. By contrast the GR service is more commercial. Companies and private individuals can request a collection of materials to be disposed of, either using the telephone or the internet. The GR service guarantees to collect the material within 24 hours unless the customer prefers to specify a more convenient time. Any kind of material can be collected and a charge is made depending on the volume of material. This service makes a small profit because the revenue both from customer charges and from some of the more valuable recycled materials exceeds the operation's running costs.

How would you describe the differences between the performance objectives of the two services?

2   *'It is about four years now since we specialised in the small-to-medium firms' market. Before that we also used to provide legal services for anyone who walked in the door. So now we have built up our legal skills in many areas of corporate and business law. However, within the firm, I think we could focus our activities even more. There seem to be two types of assignment that we are given. About 40 per cent of our work is relatively routine. Typically these assignments are to do with things like property purchase and debt collection. Both these activities involve a relatively standard set of steps which can be automated or carried out by staff without full legal qualifications. Of course, a fully qualified lawyer is needed to make some decisions, however most work is fairly routine. Customers expect us to be relatively inexpensive and fast in delivering the service. Nor do they expect us to make simple errors in our documentation; in fact if we did this too often we would lose business. Fortunately our customers know that they are buying a standard service and don't expect it to be customised in any way. The problem here is that specialist agencies have been emerging over the last few years and they are starting to undercut us on price. Yet I still feel that we can operate profitably in this market and anyway, we still need these capabilities to serve our other clients. The other 60 per cent of our work is for clients who require far more specialist services, such as assignments involving company merger deals or major company restructuring. These assignments are complex, large, take longer, and require significant legal skill and judgement. It is vital that clients respect and trust the advice we give them across a wide range of legal specialisms. Of course they assume that we will not be slow or unreliable in preparing advice, but mainly it's trust in our legal judgement which is important to the client. This is popular work with our lawyers. It is both interesting and very profitable.'*

'The help I need from you is in deciding whether to create two separate parts to our business; one to deal with routine services and the other to deal with specialist services. What I may do is appoint a senior "Operations Partner" to manage each part of the business, but if I do, what aspects of operations performance should they be aiming to Excel at?'

(Managing Partner, Branton Legal Services)

3   Revisit the descriptions of Flexitronics and Amazon at the beginning of the chapter. Think about the following issues:

(a)   What are the key performance objectives for Flexitronics and the retail (Amazon.com) part of Amazon?

(b)   What are the key design, delivery, and development decisions that will need to be taken by each business?

(c)   Why does the 'capabilities-based' strategy described by Jeff Bezos present such a challenge?

Notes on chapter

1 For a more thorough explanation, *see* Slack, N. and Lewis, M. (2001) *Operations Strategy*, Financial Times Prentice Hall.

2 Source: company website (www.flextronics.com) and press releases.

3 Sources include: 'Clouds under the hammer: processing capacity is becoming a tradable commodity' (2010), *The Economist* 11 March; 'Lifting the bonnet' (2006),*The Economist*, 7 October; company website.

4 Cloud computing is a general term for the provision of internet-based access to computing capacity so that shared resources, such as software, can be provided on-demand.

5 Elkington, J. (1998), *Cannibals with Forks: the Triple Bottom Line of 21st Century Business*, New Society Publishers.

6 Hayes, R.H. and Wheelwright, S.C. (1984) *Restoring our Competitive Edge*, John Wiley.

7 All quotes taken from each company's website.

8 Osterwalder, A., Pigneur, Y. and Tucci, C. (2005) 'Clarifying business models: origins, present and future of the concept, *CAIS*, Vol. 15, p. 751–75.

9 Osterwalder, A (2005) 'What is a business model?', http://business-model-design.blogspot.com/2005/11/what-is-business-model.html.

10 Based on the definitions developed by Cap Gemin.i.

11 Mintzberg, H. and Waters, J.A. (1995) 'Of strategies: deliberate and emergent', *Strategic Management Journal*, July/Sept.

12 For a full explanation of this concept see Slack, N. and Lewis, M. (2011) *Operations Strategy* (3rd Edition), Financial Times Prentice Hall.

13 A point made initially by Skinner in Skinner, W. (1985) *Manufacturing: The Formidable Competitive Weapon*, John Wiley.

14 From a speech by Michael Jensen of Harvard Business School.

15 Sources include: Kroc, R.A. (1977) *Grinding it Out: The Making of McDonald's*, St. Martin's Press; Love, J. (1995) *McDonald's: Behind the Golden Arches*, Random House Publishing Group; www.aboutmcdonalds.com (2009); Davidson, A. (2011) 'So Mrs McDonald, would you like fries with that?' *Sunday Times*, 13 February; McDonalds Annual Report (2009); Upton, D. (1992) *McDonald's Corporation Case Study*, Harvard Business School.

TAKING IT FURTHER

Johnson, G., Whittington R. and Scholes, K. (2011) *Exploring Strategy* (9th Edition), Financial Times Prentice Hall.

Boyer, K. and McDermot, C. (1999) 'Strategic consensus in operations strategy', *Journal of Operations Management*, Vol. 17, Issue 3, March. *Academic, but interesting.*

Hamel, G. and Prahalad, C.K. (1993) 'Strategy as stretch and leverage', *Harvard Business Review*, Vol. 71, Nos 2 and 3. *This article is typical of some of the (relatively) recent ideas influencing operations strategy.*

Hayes, R. (2006) 'Operations, strategy, and technology: pursuing the competitive edge', *Strategic Direction*, Vol. 22 Issue 7, Emerald Group Publishing Limited. *A summary of the subject from one of (if not the) leading academics in the area.*

Hayes, R.H. and Pisano, G.P. (1994) 'Beyond world class: the new manufacturing strategy', *Harvard Business Review*, Vol. 72, No 1. *Same as above.*

Hill, T. (2006) *Manufacturing Operations Strategy* (3rd Edn Texts and Cases), Palgrave Macmillan; *The descendant of the first non-US book to have a real impact in the area.*

Slack, N. and Lewis, M. (2011) *Operations Strategy (3rd Edn)*, Financial Times Prentice Hall. *What can we say – just brilliant!*

USEFUL WEBSITES

www.opsman.org *Definitions, links and opinions on operations and process management.*

www.cranfield,ac.uk/som *Look for the 'Best factory awards' link. Manufacturing, but interesting.*

www.worldbank.org *Global issues. Useful for international operations strategy research.*

www.weforum.org *Global issues, including some operations strategy ones.*

www.ft.com *Great for industry and company examples.*

Interactive
quiz

For further resources including examples, animated diagrams, self-test questions, Excel spreadsheets and video materials please explore the eText on the companion website at **www.pearsoned.co.uk/slack**.

7

Supply chain management

Introduction

An operation's ability to deliver products or services to customers is fundamentally influenced by how its supply chains are managed. Chapter 3 treated the strategic design of supply networks. This chapter considers the planning and control activity for the individual supply chains in the network. Supply chain management is the overarching operations management activity that dictates an operation's *delivery* performance because it controls the flow of products and services from suppliers right through to the end customer. That is why it is the first chapter dealing with the planning and control of delivery. But planning and controlling delivery is a much larger topic, and includes, capacity management (Chapter 8), inventory management (Chapter 9), resource planning and control (Chapter 10), and lean synchronisation (Chapter 11). Figure 7.1 illustrates the supply–demand linkage treated in this chapter.

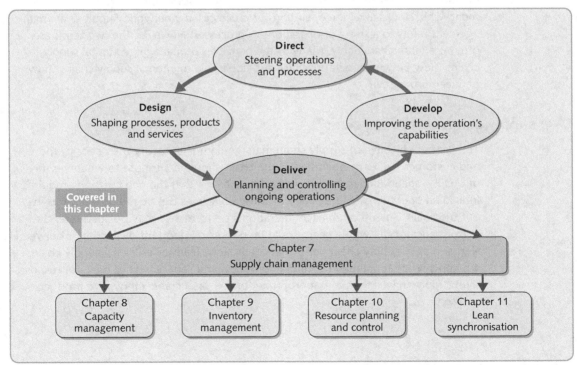

Figure 7.1 Supply chain management is the management of the relationships and flows between operations and processes; it is the topic that integrates all the issues concerning the delivery of products and services

EXECUTIVE SUMMARY

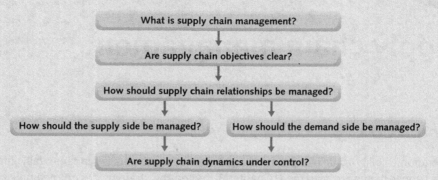

Decision logic chain for supply chain management

Each chapter is structured around a set of diagnostic questions. These questions suggest what you should ask in order to gain an understanding of the important issues of a topic, and, as a result, improve your decision making. An executive summary addressing these questions is provided below.

What is supply chain management?

Supply chain management is the management of relationships and flows between operations and processes. Technically, it is different from supply network management, which looks at all the operations or processes in a network. Supply chain management refers to a string of operations or processes. However, the two terms are often used interchangeably. Many of the principles of managing external supply chains (flow between operations) are also applicable to internal supply chains (flow between processes).

Are supply chain objectives clear?

The central objective of supply chain management is to satisfy the needs of the end customer. So, each operation in the chain should contribute to whatever mix of quality, speed, dependability, flexibility and cost that the end customer requires. Individual operations failure in any of these objectives can be multiplied throughout the chain. So, although each operation's performance may be adequate, the performance of the whole chain could be poor. An important distinction is between lean and agile supply chain performance. Broadly, lean (or efficient) supply chains are appropriate for stable 'functional' products and services, while agile (or responsive) supply chains are more appropriate for less predictable innovative products and services.

How should supply chain relationships be managed?

Supply chain relationships can be described on a spectrum from market-based, contractual, 'arms-length' relationships, through to close and long-term partnership relationships. Each has its advantages and disadvantages. Developing relationships involves assessing which relationship will provide the best potential for developing overall performance. However, the types of relationships adopted may be dictated by the structure of the market itself. If the number of potential suppliers is small, there are few opportunities to use market mechanisms to gain any kind of advantage.

How should the supply side managed?

Managing supply side relationships involves three main activities: selecting appropriate suppliers; planning and controlling on-going supply activity; supplier development. Supplier selection involves trading off different supplier attributes, often using scoring assessment methods. Managing ongoing supply involves clarifying supply expectations, often using service level agreements to manage the supply relationships. Supplier development can benefit both suppliers and customers, especially in partnership relationships. Very often barriers are the mismatches in perception between customers and suppliers.

How should the demand side managed?

This will depend partly on whether demand is dependent on some known factor and therefore predictable, or independent of any known factor and therefore less predictable. Approaches such as materials requirements planning (MRP) are used in the former case, while approaches such as inventory management are used in the latter case. The increasing outsourcing of physical distribution and the use of new tracking technologies, such as RFID, have brought efficiencies to the movement of physical goods and customer service. But customer service may be improved even more if suppliers take on responsibility for customer development, i.e. helping customers to help themselves.

Are supply chain dynamics under control?

Supply chains have a dynamic of their own that is often called the *bull-whip* effect. It means that relatively small changes at the demand end of the chain increasingly amplify into large disturbances as they move upstream. Three methods can be used to reduce this effect. Information sharing can prevent over-reaction to immediate stimuli and give a better view of the whole chain. Channel alignment through standardised planning and control methods allows for easier coordination of the whole chain. Improving the operational efficiency of each part of the chain prevents local errors multiplying to affect the whole chain.

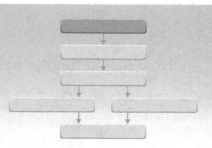

DIAGNOSTIC QUESTION

What is supply chain management?

Video

Supply chain management (SCM) is the management of the relationships and flows between the 'string' of operations and processes that produce value in the form of products and services to the ultimate consumer. It is a holistic approach to managing across the boundaries of companies and of processes. Technically, supply *chains* are different to supply *networks*. A supply network is *all* the operations that are linked together so as to provide goods and services through to end customers. In large supply networks there can be many hundreds of supply chains of linked operations passing through a single operation. The same distinction holds within operations. Internal supply network, and supply chain management concerns flow between processes or departments (see Figure 7.2). Confusingly, the terms supply network and supply chain management are often used interchangeably.

OPERATIONS PRINCIPLE

The supply chain concept applies to the internal relationships between processes as well as the external relationships between operations.

It is worth emphasising again that the supply chain concept applies to internal process networks as well as external supply networks. Many of the ideas discussed in the context of the 'operation-to-operation' supply chain, also apply to the 'process-to-process' internal supply chain. It is also worth noting that the 'flows' in supply chains are not restricted to the downstream flow of products and services from suppliers through to customers. Although the most obvious failure in supply chain management occurs when downstream flow fails to meet customer requirements, the root cause may be a failure in the upstream flow of information. Modern supply chain management is as much concerned with managing information

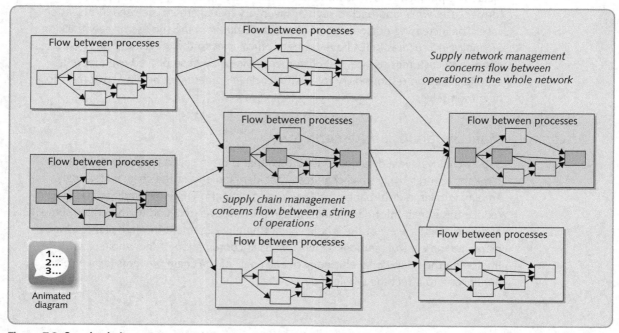

Figure 7.2 Supply chain management is concerned with managing the flow of materials and information between a string of operations that form the strands or 'chains' of a supply network

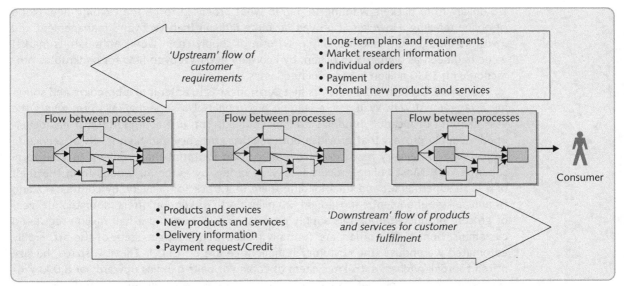

Figure 7.3 Supply chain management is concerned with the flow of information as well as the flow of products and services

flows (upstream and downstream) as it is with managing the flow of products and services (see Figure 7.3). In fact, the supply chain concept could be broadened further. There may not be any flow of physical items at all. Many 'flows' from suppliers to customers are non-tangible. Banks supply information about your cash (or lack of it). Media operations supply entertainment, education and information. Consultants supply advice, reassurance and knowledge. Police services supply a feeling of security, and so on.

OPERATIONS PRINCIPLE

The supply chain concept applies to non-physical flow between operations and processes as well as physical flows.

The following two examples of supply chain management illustrate some of the issues that are discussed in this chapter.

EXAMPLE   Ocado[1]

It was a proud moment for a business that many had forecast would never survive 12 months. In 2010, eight years after it was founded by three ex-Goldman Sachs bankers,

Source: Bloomberg/Getty Images

the Ocado Group scooped World E-tailer of the Year' award from Oracle World Retail. Tim Steiner, the Chief Executive Officer of Ocado, said: *'For a business that didn't deliver to its first customer until 2002, I'm immensely proud of where Ocado has got to in a few years. To now have our achievements recognised globally is a great accolade for all of our 4500-strong team. Ocado is now entering a big phase of growth, development and job creation with our recent announcements of new distribution facilities. We are very excited about the future and I am more convinced than ever that we offer a convenient, efficient and engaging alternative to the traditional supermarket.'*

By 2010, Ocado was the only dedicated online supermarket in the UK and the largest dedicated online supermarket by turnover in the world. What it had succeeded in doing in the UK was to reshape the final 'business-to-consumer' configuration of the traditional food supply chain. It had become one of the most successful online grocers in the world. But it was not the first. Back in 1999 an internet grocer called Webvan erupted on to the scene in California. It gained considerable publicity and more than a billion

US dollars from backers wanting to join in what promised to be the exciting new world of online retailing. However, it proved far more difficult than Webvan's management and investors thought to make a totally new form of supply chain work. Although its market value had been as high as $15 billion, by February 2001 Webvan filed for bankruptcy protection with $830 million in accumulated losses.

Yet Ocado has thrived. One of its first decisions was to enter into a branding and sourcing arrangement with Waitrose, a leading high-quality UK supermarket, from where the vast majority of Ocado's products are still sourced. But, just as important, it has developed a supply process that provides both relative efficiency and high levels of service (a typical Ocado delivery has a lower overall carbon footprint than walking to your local supermarket). Most online grocers fulfil web orders by gathering goods from the shelf of a local supermarket and then loading them in a truck for delivery. By contrast, Ocado from its distribution centre in Hatfield, 20 miles north of London offers 'doorstep' delivery of grocery products through its supply process, to over one-and-a-half million registered customers' homes. The orders are centrally picked from a single, state-of-the-art, highly automated warehouse (the customer fulfilment centre or 'CFC'). This is a space the size of ten football pitches, a 15-km system of conveyor belts handles upwards of 8,000 grocery containers an hour, which are then shipped to homes, mainly in the southern part of the UK. Ocado operates what it calls its 'hub and spoke' supply system; with its central CFC (hub) serving regional (spoke) distribution points. In contrast with traditional 'bricks-and-mortar' supermarkets (Ocado has no 'physical' shops), it delivers direct to customers from its distribution centre rather than from stores. The largely automated picking process, which was developed by its own software engineers, allows the company to pick and prepare groceries for delivery up to seven times faster than its rivals. Although as many as one million separate items are picked for individual customer orders every day, there are fewer than 80 mistakes.

Making its deliveries of more than 21,000 different products from a central location means it can carry more items than smaller local stores which are more likely to run out of stock. Also fresh or perishable items that are prepared centrally will have more 'shelf life'. Ocado's food waste, at 0.3 per cent of sales, is the lowest in the industry. The structural advantage of this supply arrangement means that 99 per cent of all orders are fulfilled accurately. Just as important as the physical distribution to the customers' door is the ease of use of the company's website (Ocado.com) and the convenience of booking a delivery slot. Ocado offer reliable one-hour, next day timeslots in an industry where two-hour timeslots prevail. This is made possible thanks, again, to the centralised model and world-class processes, systems and controls. The company say that its website is designed to be simple to use and intuitive. Smart lists personalised to each customer offer prompts and ideas so that the absence of any in-store inspiration becomes irrelevant. For a pre-registered customer, a weekly shop can be completed in less than five minutes. The site also has an extensive range of recipes including some as video and ideas such as craft activities and lunchbox fillers. Ocado makes a conscious effort to recruit people with customer service skills and then train them as drivers rather than vice versa. Drivers, known as Customer Service Team Members, are paid well above the industry norm and are empowered to process refunds and deal with customer concerns on the doorstep. This has led some commentators to label Ocado 'the new Amazon'. 'Not so,' say others. 'In some ways it's actually more complex than Amazon's operation. Amazon built a dominant brand in the US, the world's biggest market, by selling books and CDs, which essentially you just stick in an envelope and put a stamp on. That is not the same as having a highly automated warehouse with expensive machines and a huge fleet of delivery vans taking the goods to every house.'

Burberry links the catwalk with the consumer[2]

Back in 1914, Thomas Burberry began producing trench coats for use by soldiers during World War I. Since then Burberry has become one of the best known luxury brands in the world. The British heritage is important. Even now Burberry trench coats still have the traditional

'D-rings', initially designed to hold hand grenades, and the collars are still sewn on by hand in a factory in Castleford in the north of England. The journey from a slightly old-fashioned maker of traditional rainwear into a luxury brand dynamo was a marketing, design and branding success story. Yet the operations side of the business did not fully reflect the company's status as a global fashion brand. Not only was the Castleford factory inefficient, the company's supply chain was confusing, complex and chaotic. '*It was,*' said Andy Janowski, Burberry's Chief Operating Officer, '*still jumbled under the hood, beset by late shipments and an onerous process that required 432 different steps to get from sketch to customer.*'

Burberry's Chief Executive, Rose Marie Bravo, had led the transformation of the Burberry brand, but it was her successor, Angela Ahrendts, who decided to tackle the supply chain that was draining cash from the company's finances and, because it was slow and unresponsive, holding back the company's brand strength. But Burberry was not alone. Supply inefficiency was (and is) common in the luxury-fashion industry, where slow manufacturing and late deliveries were normal. One of the main problems was the traditional supply chain configuration in the high-fashion industry where most sales are achieved through a complex arrangement of wholesalers, franchisees or licensing partners. This resulted in a number of problems for luxury brands. Perhaps most significantly, each independent stage in the supply chain had to make its own profit, and although margins are relatively high in the luxury goods market, it still left a smaller share for Burberry. The other operations between Burberry and its end customer also made it difficult to respond to market changes and emerging trends. However the multi-stage supply chain does have some advantages. Wholesalers and retailers carry inventory which acts as a buffer between Burberry's production schedules and the fluctuations in the market. Conversely, viewed another way, inventory can cover up numerous forecasting and supply flaws, and keeping close to its market is exactly what a fashion label must be good at. So Burberry elected to become a more retail-focused business. It sold more merchandise directly to customers, both through the internet and its own expanding network of stores. These included buying out its long-time franchise partner in China to operate the 50 stores there directly.

The supply side of Burberry's supply chain has also been reorganised. It consolidated its manufacturing operations on the Castleford site, reorganising its production processes to enhance efficiency and responsiveness. It also trimmed its manufacturing suppliers from 300 to 90, cut its network of 26 warehouses to three global distribution hubs and reduced 31 logistic hauliers down to three, all of which required a significant investment in new information technology systems. One innovation was to connect its designers and manufacturers on Skype to save time collaborating on new designs. The changes were effective. The average cost of making a garment at Castleford decreased by between 10 and 15 per cent within two years. In addition, delivery reliability improved. Before, deliveries could be as much as three months late. Andy Janowski holds that it was the overhaul of the supply chain that made it possible for Burberry to do things that would have been impossible in the past. For example, Burberry launched its 'Runway to Reality' initiative, in which it streamed its semi-annual fashion show live on the internet and simultaneously sold the designs coming down the catwalk online.

What do these two examples have in common?

The first lesson from these two companies is that they both take supply chain management seriously. In fact, more than that, they both understand that, no matter how good individual operations or processes are, a business's overall performance is a function of the whole chain of which it is a part. That is why both of these companies put so much effort into managing the whole chain. This does not mean that both companies adopt the same, or even similar, approaches to supply chain management. Each has a slightly different set of priorities. Ocado does not so much *have* a supply chain, it *is* a supply chain in the sense that its entire purpose is supply. Moreover it is making a business of supply using a relatively new concept (internet-based customer ordering) where other businesses have failed. It therefore needs to keep its costs under strict control if it is to avoid the fate of its predecessors like Webvan. Burberry, on the other hand, needs a responsive supply chain so that its fashion ideas can have up-to-the-minute impact. It needs agility from its supply chain so that it can keep close to its market. So, although they are very different businesses with different supply chain objectives, the commonality between them is that both see the way they configure and manage their supply chains as a source of innovation. Both are doing something different from their competitors; both are innovating through their supply chain management; both have a clear idea of what they want to be and realise the importance of understanding customers as the starting point of successful supply chain management. Although the examples emphasise Ocado's downstream customer relationships and Burberry's total supply chain relationships, the common theme is the importance of investing in a supply perspective. In addition, both companies have invested in mechanisms for communicating along the supply chain and coordinating material and information flows. The rest of this chapter is structured around these three main issues: clarifying supply chain objectives; supply chain relationships, both with suppliers and with customers; and controlling and coordinating flow.

DIAGNOSTIC QUESTION

Are supply chain objectives clear?

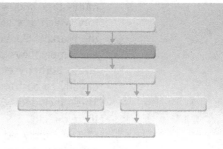

Video

All supply chain management shares one common, and central, objective – to satisfy the end customer. All stages in a chain must eventually include consideration of the final customer, no matter how far an individual operation is from the end customer. When a customer decides to make a purchase, he or she triggers action back along the whole chain. All the businesses in the supply chain pass on portions of that end customer's money to each other, each retaining a margin for the value it has added. Each operation in the chain should be satisfying its own customer, but also making sure that eventually the end customer is satisfied.

For a demonstration of how end customer perceptions of supply satisfaction can be very different from that of a single operation, examine the customer 'decision tree' in Figure 7.4. It charts the hypothetical progress of 100 customers requiring service (or products) from a business (for example, a printer requiring paper from an industrial paper stockist). Supply performance, as seen by the core operation (the warehouse), is represented by the shaded part of the diagram. It has received 20 orders, 18 of which were 'produced' (shipped to customers) as promised (on time, and in full). However, originally 100 customers may have requested service,

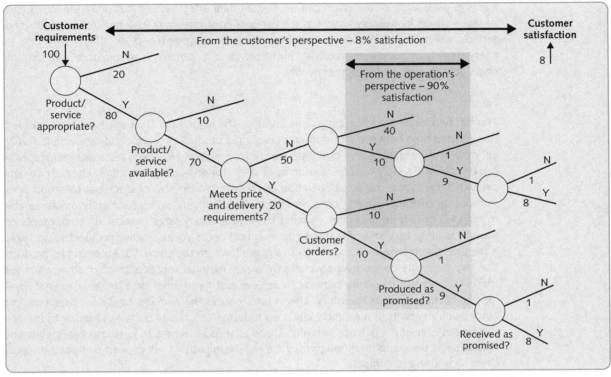

Figure 7.4 Taking a customer perspective of supply performance can lead to very different conclusions

> **OPERATIONS PRINCIPLE**
>
> *The performance of an operation in a supply chain does not necessarily reflect the performance of the whole supply chain.*

20 of who found the business did not have appropriate products (did not stock the right paper), 10 of whom could not be served because the products were not available (out of stock), 50 of whom were not satisfied with the price and/or delivery (of whom 10 placed an order notwithstanding). Of the 20 orders received, 18 were produced as promised (shipped) but two were not received as promised (delayed or damaged in transport). So what seems a 90 per cent supply performance is in fact an 8 per cent performance from the customer's perspective.

This is just one operation in a whole network. Include the cumulative effect of similar reductions in performance for all the operations in a chain, and the probability that the end customer is adequately served could become remote. The point here is not that all supply chains have unsatisfactory supply performances (although most supply chains have considerable potential for improvement). Rather it is that the performance both of the supply chain as a whole, and its constituent operations, should be judged in terms of how all end customer needs are satisfied.

Supply chain objectives

The objective of supply chain management is to meet the requirements of end customers by supplying appropriate products and services when they are needed at a competitive cost. Doing this requires the supply chain to achieve appropriate levels of the five operations performance objectives: quality, speed, dependability, flexibility and cost.

Quality

The quality of a product or service when it reaches the customer is a function of the quality performance of every operation in the chain that supplied it. The implication of this is that errors in each stage of the chain can multiply in their effect on end customer service (if each of seven stages in a supply chain has a 1 per cent error rate, only 93.2 per cent of products or services will be of good quality on reaching the end customer (i.e. 0.99). This is why, only by every stage taking some responsibility for its own *and its suppliers'* performance, can a supply chain achieve high end customer quality.

Speed

This has two meanings in a supply chain context. The first is how fast customers can be served, (the elapsed time between a customer requesting a product or service and receiving it in full), an important element in any business's ability to compete. However, fast customer response can be achieved simply by over-resourcing or over-stocking within the supply chain. For example, very large stocks in a retail operation can reduce the chances of stock-out to almost zero, so reducing customer waiting time virtually to zero. Similarly, an accounting firm may be able to respond quickly to customer demand by having a very large number of accountants on standby waiting for demand that may (or may not) occur. An alternative perspective on speed is the time taken for goods and services to move through the chain. So, for example, products that move quickly down a supply chain from raw material suppliers through to retailers will spend little time as inventory because to achieve fast throughput time, material cannot dwell for significant periods as inventory. This in turn reduces the working capital requirements and other inventory costs in the supply chain, so reducing the overall cost of delivering to the end customer. Achieving a balance between speed as responsiveness to customers' demands and speed as fast throughput (although they are not incompatible) will depend on how the supply chain is choosing to compete.

Dependability

Dependability in a supply chain context is similar to speed insomuch as one can almost guarantee 'on-time' delivery by keeping excessive resources, such as inventory, within the chain. However, dependability of throughput time is a much more desirable aim because it reduces uncertainty within the chain. If the individual operations in a chain do not deliver as promised on time, there will be a tendency for customers to over-order, or order early, in order to provide some kind of insurance against late delivery. The same argument applies if there is uncertainty regarding the *quantity* of products or services delivered. This is why delivery dependability is often measured as 'on time, in full' in supply chains.

Flexibility

In a supply chain context, this is usually taken to mean the chain's ability to cope with changes and disturbances. Very often this is referred to as supply chain agility. The concept of agility includes previously discussed issues such as focusing on the end customer and ensuring fast throughput and responsiveness to customer needs. But, in addition, agile supply chains are sufficiently flexible to cope with changes, either in the nature of customer demand or in the supply capabilities of operations within the chain.

Cost

In addition to the costs incurred within each operation to transform its inputs into outputs, the supply chain as a whole incurs additional costs that derive from each operation in a chain doing business with each other. These transaction costs may include such things as the costs of finding appropriate suppliers, setting up contractual agreements, monitoring supply performance, transporting products between operations, holding inventories, and so on. Many of the recent developments in supply chain management, such as partnership agreements or reducing the number of suppliers, are an attempt to minimise transaction costs.

Should supply chains be lean or agile?

Video

A distinction is often drawn between supply chains that are managed to emphasise supply chain efficiency (lean supply chains), and those that emphasise supply chain responsiveness and flexibility (agile supply chains). These two modes of managing supply chains are reflected in an idea proposed by Professor Marshall Fisher of Wharton Business School: that supply chains serving different markets should be managed in different ways. Even companies that have seemingly similar products or services, in fact, may compete in different ways with different products.[3] For example, shoe manufacturers may produce classics that change little over the years, as well as fashion shoes that last only one season. Chocolate manufacturers have stable lines that have been sold for 50 years, but also product 'specials' associated with an event or film release, the latter selling only for a matter of months. Hospitals have routine 'standardised' surgical procedures, such as cataract removal, but also have to provide emergency post-trauma surgery. Demand for the former products will be relatively stable and predictable, but demand for the latter will be far more uncertain. Also, the profit margin commanded by the innovative product will probably be higher than that of the more functional product. However, the price (and therefore the margin) of the innovative product may drop rapidly once it has become unfashionable in the market.

The supply chain policies that are seen to be appropriate for functional products and innovative products are termed efficient (or lean), and responsive (or agile) supply chain policies, respectively. Efficient supply chain policies include keeping inventories low, especially in the downstream parts of the network, so as to maintain fast throughput and reduce the amount of working capital tied up in the inventory. What inventory there is in the network is concentrated mainly in the manufacturing operation, where it can keep utilisation high and therefore manufacturing costs low. Information must flow quickly up and down the chain from retail outlets back up to the manufacturer so that schedules can be given the maximum amount of time to adjust efficiently. The chain is then managed to make sure that products flow as quickly as possible down the chain to replenish what few stocks are kept downstream.

> **OPERATIONS PRINCIPLE**
>
> *Supply chains with different end objectives need managing differently.*

> **OPERATIONS PRINCIPLE**
>
> *'Functional' products require lean supply chain management; 'innovative' products require agile supply chain management.*

By contrast, responsive supply chain policy stresses high service levels and responsive supply to the end customer. The inventory in the network will be deployed as closely as possible to the customer. In this way, the chain can still supply even when dramatic changes occur in customer demand. Fast throughput from the upstream parts of the chain will still be needed to replenish downstream stocks. But those downstream stocks are needed to ensure high levels of availability to end customers. Figure 7.5 illustrates how the different supply chain policies match the different market requirements implied by functional and innovative products.

The SCOR model[4]

The Supply Chain Operations Reference Model (SCOR) is a broad, but highly structured and systematic, framework to supply chain improvement that has been developed by the Supply Chain Council (SCC), a global non-profit consortium. The framework uses a methodology, and diagnostic and benchmarking tools that are increasingly widely accepted for evaluating and comparing supply chain activities and their performance. Just as important, the SCOR model allows its users to improve, and communicate supply chain management practices within and between all interested parties in their supply chain by using a standard language and a set of structured definitions. The SCC also provides a benchmarking database by which companies can compare their supply chain performance to others in their industries and training classes. Companies that have used the model include BP AstraZeneca, Shell, SAP AG, Siemens AG and Bayer.

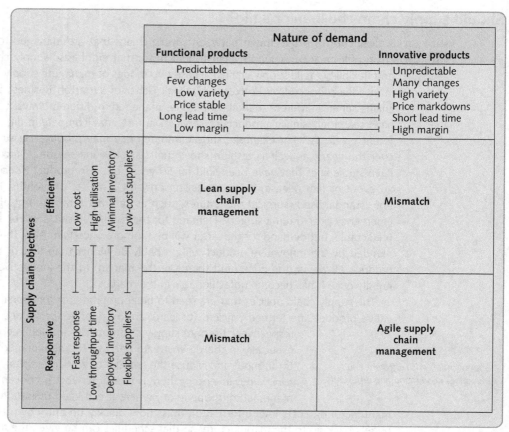

Figure 7.5 Matching the operations resources in the supply chain with market requirements

Source: Adapted from Fisher, M.C. (1997) 'What is the right supply chain for your product?' *Harvard Business Review*, March–April, pp 105–116.

The model uses three well-known individual techniques turned into an integrated approach. These are:

- business process modelling
- benchmarking performance
- best practice analysis.

Business process modelling

SCOR does not represent organisations or functions, but rather processes. Each basic 'link' in the supply chain is made up of five types of process, each process being a 'supplier–customer' relationship (see Figure 7.6).

- 'Source', is the procurement, delivery, receipt and transfer of raw material items, subassemblies, product and or services.
- 'Make, is the transformation process of adding value to products and services through mixing production operations processes.
- 'Deliver' processes perform all customer-facing order management and fulfilment activities including outbound logistics.
- 'Plan' processes manage each of these customer–supplier links and balance the activity of the supply chain. They are the supply and demand reconciliation process, which includes prioritisation when needed.

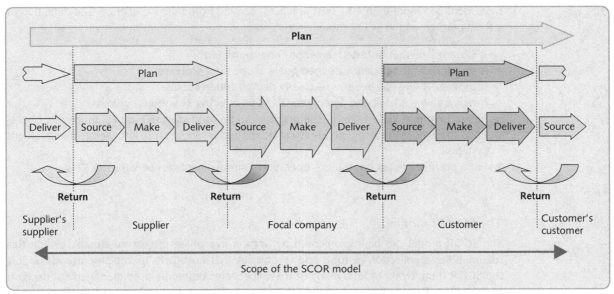

Figure 7.6 The structure of supply chains implicit in the SCOR model showing the relationship between Plan, Source, Make, Deliver and Return elements of the model

- 'Return' processes look after the reverse logistics flow of moving material back from end customers upstream in the supply chain because of product defects or post-delivery customer support.

All these processes are modelled at increasingly detailed levels (see Chapter 4 for a description of the different levels of process analysis). The first level (level 1) identifies the five processes and allows managers to set the scope of the business issues. The SCC advocates the idea that 'if it isn't broken, don't model it'. If no problem has been identified in a particular area, it will be of no significant help to map processes in any further level of detail. More detailed modelling (level 2) identifies which type of supply chain configuration the company operates, for example make-to-stock, make-to-order or engineer-to-order environment. Yet more detailed process modelling (level 3) is then done in terms of the company's ability to compete successfully in its chosen markets.

Benchmarking performance

Performance metrics in the SCOR model are also structured by level, as is process analysis. Level 1 metrics are the yardsticks by which an organisation can measure how successful it is in achieving its desired positioning within the competitive environment, as measured by the performance of a particular supply chain. These level 1 metrics are the Key Performance Indicators (KPIs) of the chain and are created from lower-level diagnostic metrics (called level 2 and level 3 metrics) which are calculated on the performance of lower level processes. Some metrics do not 'roll up' to level 1; these are intended to diagnose variations in performance against plan.

Best practice analysis

Best practice analysis follows the benchmarking activity that should have measured the performance of the supply chain processes and identified the main performance gaps. Best practice analysis identifies the activities that need to be performed to close the gaps. SCC members have identified more than 400 'best practices' derived from their experience. The definition of a 'best practice' in the SCOR model is one that:

- is current – neither untested (emerging) nor outdated
- is structured – it has clearly defined goals, scope, and processes
- is proven – there has been some clearly demonstrated success
- is repeatable – it has been demonstrated to be effective in various contexts
- has an unambiguous method – the practice can be connected to business processes, operations strategy, technology, supply relationships and information or knowledge management systems
- has a positive impact on results – operations improvement can be linked to KPIs.

The SCOR roadmap

The SCOR model can be implemented by using a five-phase project 'roadmap'. Within this roadmap lies a collection of tools and techniques that both help to implement and support the SCOR framework. In fact, many of these tools are commonly used management decision tools, such as Pareto charts, cause–effect diagrams, maps of material flow, brainstorming, etc. The roadmap has five stages as follows:

Phase 1: Discover. Involves supply-chain definition and prioritisation where a 'Project Charter' sets the scope for the project. This identifies logic groupings of supply chains within the scope of the project. The priorities, based on a weighted rating method, determine which supply chains should be dealt with first. This phase also identifies the resources that are required. identified and secured through business process owners/actors.

Phase 2: Analyse. Using data from benchmarking and competitive analysis, the appropriate level of performance metrics are identified, that will define the strategic requirements of each supply chain.

Phase 3: Material flow design. In this phase the project teams have their first go at creating a common understanding of how processes can be developed. The current state of processes are identified and an initial analysis attempts to see where there are opportunities for improvement.

Phase 4: Work and information flow design. The project teams collect and analyse the work involved in all relevant processes (plan, source, make, deliver and return) and map the productivity and yield of all transactions.

Phase 5: Implementation planning. This is the final preparation phase for communicating the findings of the project. Its purpose is to transfer the knowledge of the SCOR team(s) to individual implementation or deployment teams.

Benefits of the SCOR model

Claimed benefits from using the SCOR model include: improved process understanding and performance; improved supply chain performance; increased customer satisfaction and retention; a decrease in required capital; better profitability and return on investment; increased productivity. And, although most of these results could arguably be expected when any company starts focusing on business processes improvements, SCOR proponents argue that using the model gives an above average and supply focused improvement.

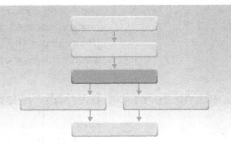

How should supply chain relationships be managed?

Video

The 'relationship' between operations in a supply chain is the basis on which the exchange of products, services, information and money is conducted. Managing supply chains is about managing relationships, because relationships influence the smooth flow between operations and processes. Different forms of relationship will be appropriate in different circumstances. An obvious but important factor in determining the importance of relationships to any operation is the extent to which they outsource their activities. In Chapter 3 we distinguished between non-vertically integrated operations that outsource almost all activities, and vertically integrated operations that outsource almost nothing. Only extremely vertically integrated businesses are able to ignore the question of how to manage customer–supplier relationships (because they do everything themselves). Initially, we can examine this question by describing two contrasting 'pure' arrangements – pure *contractual*, market-based, transactional relationships, and close, longer-term, pure *partnership* relationships. However, it is better to think of these as the two basic ingredients of any supply arrangement. Whatever arrangement with its suppliers a firm chooses to take; it can be described by the balance between contracts and partnerships.

Contract-based 'transactional' relationships

Contract-based, transactional relationships involve purchasing goods and services in a 'pure' market fashion, often seeking the 'best' supplier every time it is necessary to make a purchase. Each transaction effectively becomes a separate decision. The relationship may be short-term, with no guarantee of further trading between the parties once the goods or services are delivered and payment is made.[5] The *advantages* of contract-based 'transactional' relationships are usually seen as follows:

- They maintain competition between alternative suppliers. This promotes a constant drive between suppliers to provide best value.
- A supplier specialising in a small number of products or services, but supplying them to many customers, can gain natural economies of scale, enabling the supplier to offer the products and services at a lower price than if customers performed the activities themselves on a smaller scale.
- There is inherent flexibility in outsourced supplies. If demand changes, customers can simply change the number and type of suppliers, a faster and cheaper alternative to redirecting internal activities.
- Innovations can be exploited no matter where they originate. Specialist suppliers are more likely to come up with innovations that can be acquired faster and cheaper than developing them in-house.

There are, however, *disadvantages* in buying in a totally contractual manner:

- Suppliers owe little loyalty to customers. If supply is difficult, there is no guarantee of receiving supply.
- Choosing who to buy from takes time and effort. Gathering sufficient information and making decisions continually are, in themselves, activities that need to be resourced.

Short-term contractual relationships of this type may be appropriate when new companies are being considered as more regular suppliers, or when purchases are one-off or very irregular. (for example, the replacement of all the windows in a company's office block would typically involve this type of competitive-tendering market relationship).

Long-term 'partnership' relationships

Partnership relationships in supply chains are sometimes seen as a compromise between vertical integration on the one hand (owning the resources which supply you) and transactional relationships on the other. Partnership relationships are defined as:[6] '. . . *relatively enduring inter-firm cooperative agreements, involving flows and linkages that use resources and/ or governance structures from autonomous organisations, for the joint accomplishment of individual goals linked to the corporate mission of each sponsoring firm.*' This means that suppliers and customers are expected to cooperate, even to the extent of sharing skills and resources, to achieve joint benefits beyond those they could have achieved by acting alone. At the heart of the concept of partnership lies the issue of the *closeness* of the relationship. Partnerships are close relationships, the degree of which is influenced by a number of factors, as follows:

- *Sharing success* – both partners jointly benefit from the cooperation rather than manoeuvring to maximise their own individual contribution.
- *Long-term expectations* – relatively long-term commitments, but not necessarily permanent ones.
- *Multiple points of contact* – communication is not restricted to formal channels, but may take place between many individuals in both organisations.
- *Joint learning* – a relationship commitment to learn from each other's experience.
- *Few relationships* – a commitment on the part of both parties to limit the number of customers or suppliers with whom they do business.
- *Joint coordination of activities* – fewer relationships allow joint coordination of activities such as the flow of materials or service, payment, and so on.
- *Information transparency* – confidence is built through information exchange between the partners.
- *Joint problem solving* – jointly approaching problems can increase closeness over time.
- *Trust* – probably the key element in partnership relationships. In this context, trust means the willingness of one party to relate to the other on the understanding that the relationship will be beneficial to both, even though that cannot be guaranteed. Trust is widely held to be both the key issue in successful partnerships, but also, by far the most difficult element to develop and maintain.

Which type of relationship?

It is very unlikely that any business will find it sensible to engage exclusively in one type of relationship or another. Most businesses will have a portfolio of, possibly, widely differing relationships. Also, there are degrees to which any particular relationship can be managed on a transactional or partnership basis. The real question is: where, on the spectrum from transactional to partnership, should each relationship be positioned? And, while there is no simple formula for choosing the 'ideal' form of relationship in each case, there are some important factors that can sway the decision. The most obvious issue will concern how a business intends to compete in its marketplace. If price is the main competitive factor then the relationship could be determined by which approach offers the highest potential savings.

OPERATIONS PRINCIPLE

All supply chain relationships can be described by the balance between their 'contractual' and 'partnership' elements.

On one hand, market-based contractual relationships could minimise the actual price paid for purchased products and services, while partnerships could minimise the transaction costs of doing business. If a business is competing primarily on product or service innovation, the type of relationship may depend on where innovation is likely to happen. If innovation depends on close collaboration between supplier and customer, partnership relationships are needed. On the other hand, if suppliers are busily competing to out-do each other in terms of their innovations, and especially if the market is turbulent and fast growing (as with many software and internet-based industries), then it may be preferable to retain the freedom to change suppliers quickly using market mechanisms. However, if markets are very turbulent, partnership relationships may reduce the risks of being unable to secure supply.

The main differences between the two ends of this relationship spectrum concerns whether a customer sees advantage in long-term or short-term relationships. Contractual relationships can be either long or short term, but there is no guarantee of anything beyond the immediate contract. They are appropriate when short-term benefits are important. Many relationships and many businesses are best served by concentrating on the short term (especially if, without short-term success, there is no long term). Partnership relationships are by definition long-term. There is a commitment to work together over time to gain mutual advantage. The concept of mutuality is important here. A supplier does not become a 'partner' merely by being called one. True partnership implies mutual benefit, and often mutual sacrifice. Partnership means giving up some freedom of action in order to gain something more beneficial over the long term. If it is not in the culture of a business to give up some freedom of action, it is very unlikely to ever make a success of partnerships. Opportunities to develop relationships can be limited by the structure of the market itself. If the number of potential suppliers is small, there may be few opportunities to use market mechanisms to gain any kind of supply advantage and it would probably be sensible to develop a close relationship with at least one supplier. On the other hand, if there are many potential suppliers, and especially if it is easy to judge the capabilities of the suppliers, contractual relationships are likely to be best.

> **OPERATIONS PRINCIPLE**
>
> *True 'partnership' relationships involve mutual sacrifice as well as mutual benefit.*

DIAGNOSTIC QUESTION

How should the supply side be managed?

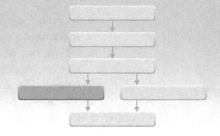

Video

The ability of any process or operation to produce outputs is dependent on the inputs it receives, so good supply management is a necessary (but not sufficient) condition for effective operations management in general. It involves three main activities: selecting appropriate suppliers; planning and controlling the ongoing supply activity; developing and improving suppliers' capabilities. All three activities are usually the responsibility of the purchasing or procurement function within the business. Purchasing should provide a vital link between the operation itself and its suppliers. They should understand the requirements of all the processes within their own operation and also the capabilities of the suppliers who could potentially provide products and services for the operation.

Supplier selection

Choosing appropriate suppliers should involve trading off alternative attributes. Rarely are potential suppliers so clearly superior to their competitors that the decision is self-evident. Most businesses find it best to adopt some kind of supplier 'scoring' or assessment procedure. This should be capable of rating alternative suppliers in terms of factors such as the following:

- range of products or services provided
- quality of products or services
- responsiveness
- dependability of supply
- delivery and volume flexibility
- total cost of being supplied
- ability to supply in the required quantity.

In addition, there are likely to be less quantifiable or longer-term factors that will need taking into consideration. These may include the following:

- potential for innovation
- ease of doing business
- willingness to share risk
- long-term commitment to supply
- ability to transfer knowledge as well as products and services.

Choosing suppliers should involve evaluating the relative importance of all these factors. So, for example, a business might choose a supplier who, although more expensive than alternative suppliers, has an excellent reputation for on time delivery, because that is more appropriate to the way the business competes itself, or because the high level of supply dependability allows the business to hold lower stock levels, which may even save costs overall. Other trade-offs may be more difficult to calculate. For example, a potential supplier may have high levels of technical capability, but may be financially weak, with a small but finite risk of going out of business. Other suppliers may have little track record of supplying the products or services required, but show the managerial talent and energy for potential customers to view developing a supply relationship as an investment in future capability. But to make sensible trade-offs it is important to assess four basic capabilities:

> **OPERATIONS PRINCIPLE**
> *Supplier selection should reflect overall supply chain objectives.*

- *Technical capability* – the product or service knowledge to supply to high levels of specification.
- *Operations capability* – the process knowledge to ensure consistent, responsive, dependable and reasonable cost supply.
- *Financial capability* – the financial strength to fund the business in the short and long terms.
- *Managerial capability* – the management talent and energy to develop supply potential in the future.

Single- or multi-sourcing

A closely linked decision is whether to source each individual product or service from one, or more than one, supplier (single-sourcing or multi-sourcing). Some of the advantages and disadvantages of single- and multi-sourcing are shown in Table 7.1.

It may seem as though companies who multi-source do so exclusively for their own short-term benefit. However, this is not always the case: multi-sourcing can have an altruistic motive, or at least one that brings benefits to both supplier and purchaser in the long term. For example, Robert Bosch GmbH, the German automotive components manufacturer and distributor,

Table 7.1 **Advantages and disadvantages of single- and multi-sourcing**

	Single-sourcing	*Multi-sourcing*
Advantages	Potentially better quality because of more supplier quality assurance possibilities	Purchaser can drive price down by competitive tendering
	Strong relationships that are more durable	Can switch sources in case of supply failure
	Greater dependency encourages more commitment and effort	Wide sources of knowledge and expertise to tap
	Better communication	
	Easier to cooperate on new product/service development	
	More economies of scale	
	Higher confidentiality	
Disadvantages	More vulnerable to disruption if a failure to supply occurs	Difficult to encourage commitment supplier
	Individual supplier more affected by volume fluctuations	Less easy to develop effective supplier quality assurance
	Supplier might exert upward pressure on prices if no alternative supplier is available	More effort needed to communicate
		Suppliers less likely to invest in new processes
		More difficult to obtain economies of scale

at one time required that sub-contractors do no more than 20 per cent of their total business with them.[7] This was to prevent suppliers becoming too dependent on them. The purchasing organisation could then change volumes up and down without pushing the supplier into bankruptcy. However, despite these perceived advantages, there has been a trend for purchasing functions to reduce their supplier base in terms of numbers of companies supplying any one part or service, mainly because it reduces the costs of transacting business.

Purchasing, the internet and e-commerce

For some years, electronic means have been used by businesses to confirm purchased orders and ensure payment to suppliers. The rapid development of the internet, however, opened up the potential for far more fundamental changes in purchasing behaviour. Partly this was as the result of supplier information made available through the internet. Previously, a purchaser of industrial components may have been predisposed to return to suppliers who had been used before. There was inertia in the purchasing process because of the costs of seeking out new suppliers. By making it easier to search for alternative suppliers, the internet changes the economics of the search process and offers the potential for wider searches. It also changed the economics of scale in purchasing. Purchasers requiring relatively low volumes find it easier to group together in order to create orders of sufficient size to warrant lower prices. In fact, the influence of the internet on purchasing behaviour is not confined to *e-commerce*. Usually e-commerce is taken to mean the trade that actually takes place over the internet. This is usually assumed to be a buyer visiting the seller's website, placing an order for parts and making a payment (also through the site). But the internet is also an important source of purchasing information. For every 1 per cent of business transacted directly via the internet, there may be 5 or 6 per cent of business that, at some point, involved it, probably with potential buyers using it to compare prices or obtain technical information.

One increasingly common use of internet technology in purchasing (or e-procurement as it is sometimes known) is for large companies, or groups of companies, to link their e-commerce systems into a common 'exchange'. In their more sophisticated form, such an exchange may be linked into the purchasing companies' own information systems (*see* the explanation of ERP in Chapter 10). Many of the large automotive, engineering and petrochemical companies, for example, have adopted such an approach. An early example of this was Dow Corning's 'Xiameter' service. Dow Corning was the global market leader in silicon, a material which has a wide range of industrial applications, from clothing and computers, to cosmetics construction. Traditionally its customers had paid top prices for pioneering technology and premium quality products, delivered with an emphasis on "solutions-based" service'. However, in the early 2000s some of its larger and more sophisticated customers wanted a different kind of supply arrangement. As one customer put it: *'I don't need these services. I know I can go and buy a tanker of this fluid at a lower price. I'll buy this but I just need low price and guaranteed delivery.'* This part of their market consisted of experienced purchasers of commonly used silicone materials who wanted the lowest price and an easy way of doing business with their supplier. Their solution was to offer a 'no-frills', limited availability service with low prices that could only be accessed on the web. This service would offer only regular products without any technical advice. They branded this service 'Xiameter' (rhymes with 'diameter'). It was limited to about 350 common silicone compounds (out of more than 7,500) ordered in high volumes. It would have a 'lean' management structure and would secure its supply from Dow Corning's manufacturing sites around the world. Customers could only place orders online (a novel approach at the time). Minimum order quantities were strictly applied. Delivery lead times were fixed by production scheduling. Standard payment terms were 30 days. All communication was via e-mail including automated order confirmation, shipping notices and invoices. E-mail enquiries had a one-day guaranteed response. Any customers deviating from these rules faced additional charges. Order cancellation fees were set at 5 per cent of the order's value. Expedited orders incurred a 10 per cent supplement and late payment carried an 18 per cent annual interest charge.

Managing ongoing supply

Managing supply relationships is not just a matter of choosing the right suppliers and then leaving them to get on with day-to-day supply. It is also about ensuring that suppliers are given the right information and encouragement to maintain smooth supply and that internal inconsistency does not negatively affect their ability to supply. A basic requirement is that some mechanism should be set up that ensures the two-way flow of information between customer and supplier. It is easy for both suppliers and customers simply to forget to inform each other of internal developments that could affect supply. Customers may see suppliers as having the responsibility for ensuring appropriate supply 'under any circumstances'. Or, suppliers themselves may be reluctant to inform customers of any potential problems with supply because they see it as risking the relationship. Yet, especially if customer and supplier see themselves as 'partners', the free flow of information, and a mutually supportive tolerance of occasional problems, is the best way to ensure smooth supply. Often day-to-day supplier relationships are damaged because of internal inconsistencies. For example, one part of a business may be asking a supplier for some special service beyond the strict nature of their agreement, while another part of the business is not paying suppliers on time.[8]

Service-level agreements

Some organisations bring a degree of formality to supplier relationships by encouraging (or requiring) all suppliers to agree service-level agreements (SLAs). SLAs are formal definitions of the dimensions of service and the relationship between suppliers and the organisation. The type of issues covered by such an agreement could include response times, the range of services, dependability of service supply, and so on. Boundaries of responsibility and appropriate performance measures could also be agreed. For example, an SLA between an information systems support unit and a research unit in the laboratories of a large pharmaceutical company could define such performance measures as:

- the types of information network services which may be provided as 'standard'
- the range of special information services which may be available at different periods of the day
- the minimum 'up time', i.e. the proportion of time the system will be available at different periods of the day
- the maximum response time and average response time to get the system fully operational should it fail
- the maximum response time to provide 'special' services, and so on.

Although SLAs are described here as mechanisms for governing the ongoing relationship between suppliers and customers, they often prove inadequate because they are seen as being useful in setting up the terms of the relationship, but then are only used to resolve disputes. For SLAs to work effectively, they must be treated as working documents that establish the details of ongoing relationships *in the light of experience*. Used properly, they are a repository of the knowledge that both sides have gathered through working together. Any SLA that stays unchanged over time is, at the very least, failing to encourage improvement in supply.

How can suppliers be developed?

In any relationship other than pure market-based transactional relationships, it is in a customer's long-term interests to take some responsibility for developing supplier capabilities. Helping a supplier to improve not only enhances the service (and hopefully price) from the supplier, it may also lead to greater supplier loyalty and long-term commitment. This is why some particularly successful businesses (including Japanese automotive manufacturers) invest in supplier development teams whose responsibility is to help suppliers to improve their own operations processes. Of course, committing the resources to help suppliers is only worthwhile if it improves the effectiveness of the supply chain as a whole. Nevertheless, the potential for such enlightened self-interest can be significant.

How customers and suppliers see each other[9]

One of the major barriers to supplier development is the mismatch between how customers and suppliers perceive both what is required and how the relationship is performing. Exploring potential mismatches is often a revealing exercise, both for customers and suppliers. Figure 7.7 illustrates this. It shows that gaps may exist between four sets of ideas. As a customer you (presumably) have an idea about what you really want from a supplier. This may, or may not, be formalised in the form of a service level agreement. But no SLA can capture everything about what is required. There may be a gap between how you as a customer interpret what is required and how the supplier interprets it. This is the *requirements perception gap*. Similarly, as a customer, you (again presumably) have a view on how your supplier is performing in terms of fulfilling your requirements. That may not coincide with how your supplier believes it is performing. This is the *fulfilment perception gap*. Both these gaps are a function of the effectiveness of the communication between supplier and customer. But there are also two other gaps. The gap between what you want from your supplier and how they are performing indicates the type of development that, as a customer, you should be giving to your supplier. Similarly, the gap between your supplier's perceptions of your needs

> **OPERATIONS PRINCIPLE**
>
> *Unsatisfactory supplier relationships can be caused by requirements and fulfilment perception gaps.*

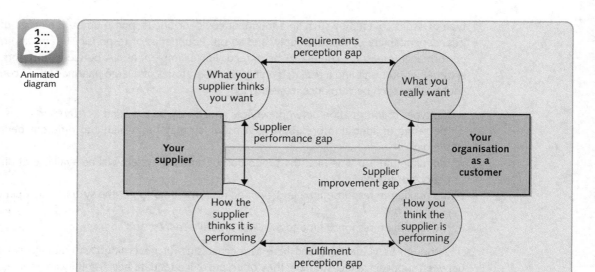

Figure 7.7 Explore the potential perception mismatches to understand supplier development needs

and its performance indicates how they should initially see themselves improving their own performance. Ultimately, of course, their responsibility for improvement should coincide with their customer's views of requirements and performance.

DIAGNOSTIC QUESTION

How should the demand side be managed?

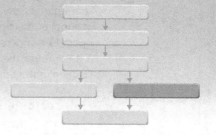

Video

The management of demand side relationships will depend partly on the nature of demand, in particular how uncertain it is. Knowing the exact demands that customers are going require allows a supplier to plan its own internal processes in a systematic manner. This type of demand is called 'dependent' demand; it is relatively predictable because it is dependent upon some factor which is itself predictable. For example, supplying tyres to an automobile factory involves examining the manufacturing schedules in the car plant and deriving the demand for tyres from these. If 200 cars are to be manufactured on a particular day, then it is simple to calculate that 1,000 tyres will be demanded by the car plant (each car has five tyres). Because of this, the tyres can be ordered from the tyre manufacturer to a delivery schedule which is closely in line with the demand for tyres from the plant. In fact, the demand for every part of the car plant will be derived from the assembly schedule for the finished cars. Manufacturing instructions and purchasing requests will all be dependent upon this figure. Managing internal process networks when external demand is dependent is largely a matter of calculating, in as precise a way as possible, the internal consequences of demand. MRP, treated in Chapter 10, is the best known dependent demand approach.

But not all operations have such predictable demand. Some operations are subject to independent demand. There is a random element in demand which is virtually independent of any obvious factors. They are required to supply demand without having any firm forward visibility of customer orders. A drive-in tyre replacement service will need to manage a stock of tyres. In that sense it is exactly the same task that faced the supplier of tyres to the car plant, but demand is very different. It cannot predict either the volume or the specific needs of customers. It must make decisions on how many and what type of tyres to stock, based on demand forecasts and in the light of the risks it is prepared to run of being out of stock. Managing internal process networks when external demand is independent involves making 'best guesses' concerning future demand, attempting to put the resources in place to satisfy this demand, and attempting to respond quickly if actual demand does not match the forecast. Inventory planning and control, treated in Chapter 9, is a typical approach.

Logistics services

Logistics means moving products to customers. Sometimes the term 'physical distribution management', or simply 'distribution', is used as being analogous to logistics. Logistics is now frequently outsourced to 'third party' logistics (or 3PL) providers, which vary in terms of the range and integration of their services. At the simplest level, the 'haulage' and 'storage' businesses either move goods around or they store them in warehouses. Clients take responsibility for all planning. Physical distribution companies bring haulage and storage together, collecting clients' products, putting them into storage facilities and delivering them to the end customer as required. 'Contract' logistics service providers tend to have more sophisticated clients with more complex operations. Total 'supply chain management' (or 4PL) providers offer to manage supply chains from end to end, often for several customers simultaneously. Doing this requires a much greater degree of analytical and modelling capability, business process reengineering and consultancy skills.

Logistics management and the internet

Internet-based communication has had a significant impact on physical distribution management. Information can be made available more readily along the distribution chain, so that transport companies, warehouses, suppliers and customers can share knowledge of where goods are in the chain (and sometimes where they are going next). This allows the operations within the chain to coordinate their activities more readily. It also gives the potential for some significant cost savings. For example, an important issue for transportation companies is back-loading. When the company is contracted to transport goods from A to B, its vehicles may have to return from B to A empty. Back-loading means finding a potential customer who wants their goods transported from B to A in the right time-frame. With the increase in information availability through the internet, the possibility of finding a back-load increases. Companies that can fill their vehicles on both the outward and return journeys will have significantly lower costs per distance travelled than those whose vehicles are empty for half the total journey. Similarly, internet-based technology that allows customers visibility of the progress of distribution can be used to enhance the perception of customer service. 'Track-and-trace' technologies, for example, allow package distribution companies to inform and reassure customers that their service is being delivered as promised.

Automatic identification technologies

Tracing the progress of items through a supply chain has involved the use of bar codes to record progress. During manufacture, bar codes are used to identify the number of products passing through a particular point in the process. In warehouses, bar codes are used to keep track of how many products are stored at particular locations. But bar codes have disadvantages. It is sometimes difficult to align the item so that the bar code can be read conveniently, items can only be scanned one by one, and the bar code only identifies the *type* of item not a specific item itself. That is, the code identifies that an item is, say, a can of one type of drink rather than one specific can. These drawbacks can be overcome through the use of 'automated identification' or Auto-ID. Usually this involves Radio Frequency Identification (RFID). Here an Electronic Product Code (ePC) that is a unique number, 96 bits long, is embedded in a memory chip or smart tag. These tags are put on individual items so that each item has its own unique identifying code. At various points during its manufacture, distribution, storage and sale each smart tag can be scanned by a wireless radio frequency 'reader'. This transmits the item's embedded identify code to a network such as the internet, describing, for example, when and where it was made, where it has been stored, etc. This information can then be fed into control systems. It is also controversial – see the Critical Commentary, later.

Customer development

Earlier in the chapter, Figure 7.7 illustrated some of the gaps in perception and performance that can occur between customers and suppliers. The purpose then was to demonstrate the nature of supplier development. The same approach can be used to analyse the nature of requirements and performance with customers. In this case the imperative is to understand customer perceptions, both of their requirements and their view of your performance, and feed these into your own performance improvement plans. What is less common, but can

OPERATIONS PRINCIPLE

Unsatisfactory customer relationships can be caused by requirement and fulfilment perception gaps.

be equally valuable, is to use these gaps (shown in Figure 7.8) to examine the question of whether customer requirements and perceptions of performance are either accurate or reasonable. For example, customers may be placing demands on suppliers without fully considering their consequences. It may be that slight modifications in what is demanded would not inconvenience customers and yet would provide significant benefits to suppliers that could then be passed on to customers. Similarly, customers may be incompetent at measuring supplier performance, in which case the benefits of excellent supplier service will not be recognised. So, just as customers have a responsibility to help develop their own supplier's performance, in their own as well as their supplier's interests, suppliers have a responsibility to develop their customer's understanding of how supply should be managed.

Animated diagram

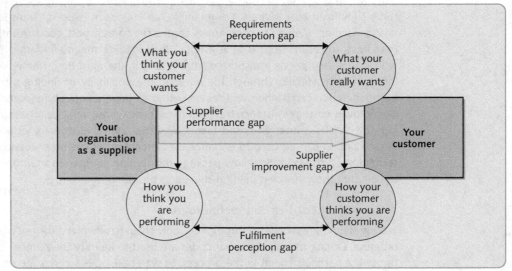

Figure 7.8 Explore the potential perception mismatches to understand customer development needs

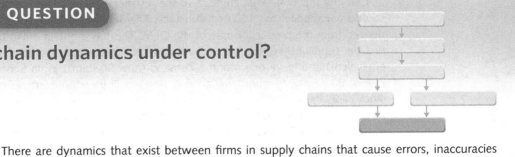

DIAGNOSTIC QUESTION

Are supply chain dynamics under control?

Video

There are dynamics that exist between firms in supply chains that cause errors, inaccuracies and volatility, and these increase for operations further upstream in the supply chain. This effect is known as the 'bull whip effect'[10], so called, because a small disturbance at one end of the chain causes increasingly large disturbances as it works its way towards the end. Its main cause is a perfectly understandable and rational desire by the different links in the supply chain to manage their levels of activity and inventory sensibly. To demonstrate this, examine the production rate and stock levels for the supply chain shown in Table 7.2. This is a four-stage supply chain where an original equipment manufacturer (OEM) is served by three tiers of suppliers. The demand from the OEM's market has been running at a rate of 100 items per period, but in period 2, demand reduces to 95 items per period. All stages in the supply chain work on the principle that they will keep in stock one period's demand. This is a simplification but not a gross one. Many operations gear their inventory levels to their demand rate. The column headed 'stock' for each level of supply shows the starting stock at the beginning of the period and the finish stock at the end of the period. At the beginning of period 2, the OEM has 100 units in stock (that being the rate of demand up to period 2). Demand in period 2 is 95 and so the OEM knows that it would need to produce sufficient items to finish up at the end of the period with 95 in stock (this being the new demand rate). To do this, it need only manufacture 90 items; these, together with five items taken out of the starting stock, will supply demand and leave a finished stock of 95 items. The beginning of period 3 finds the OEM with 95 items in stock. Demand is also 95 items and therefore its production rate to maintain a stock level of 95 will be 95 items per period. The original equipment manufacturer now operates at a steady rate of producing 95 items per period. Note, however, that a change in demand of only five items has produced a fluctuation of ten items in the OEM's production rate.

Table 7.2 Fluctuations of production levels along supply chain in response to small change in end customer demand

Period	Third-tier supplier Prodn.	Third-tier supplier Stock	Second-tier supplier Prodn.	Second-tier supplier Stock	First-tier supplier Prodn.	First-tier supplier Stock	Original equipment mfr. Prodn.	Original equipment mfr. Stock	Demand
1	100	100 / 100	100	100 / 100	100	100 / 100	100	100 / 100	100
2	20	100 / 60	60	100 / 80	80[b]	100[a] / 90[c]	90[d]	100 / 95	95
3	180	60 / 120	120	80 / 100	100	90 / 95	95	95 / 95	95
4	60	120 / 90	90	100 / 95	95	95 / 95	95	95 / 95	95
5	100	90 / 95	95	95 / 95	95	95 / 95	95	95 / 95	95
6	95	95 / 95	95	95 / 95	95	95 / 95	95	95 / 95	95

Starting stock (a) + production (b) = finishing stock (c) + demand, that is production in previous tier down (d): see explanation in text. All stages in the supply chain keep one period's inventory: c = d.

Carrying this same logic through to the first-tier supplier, at the beginning of period 2, the second-tier supplier has 100 items in stock. The demand which it has to supply in period 2 is derived from the production rate of the OEM. This has dropped down to 90 in period 2. The first-tier supplier therefore has to produce sufficient to supply the demand of 90 items (or the equivalent) and leave one month's demand (now 90 items) as its finish stock. A production rate of 80 items per month will achieve this. It will therefore start period 3 with an opening stock of 90 items, but the demand from the OEM has now risen to 95 items. It therefore has to produce sufficient to fulfil this demand of 95 items and leave 95 items in stock. To do this, it must produce 100 items in period 3. After period 3 the first-tier supplier then resumes a steady state, producing 95 items per month. Note again, however, that the fluctuation has been even greater than that in the OEM's production rate, decreasing to 80 items a period, increasing to 100 items a period, and then achieving a steady rate of 95 items a period.

> **OPERATIONS PRINCIPLE**
>
> *Demand fluctuations become progressively amplified as their effects work back up the supply chain.*

Extending the logic back to the third-tier supplier, it is clear that the further back up the supply chain an operation is placed, the more drastic are the fluctuations.

This relatively simple demonstration ignores any time lag in material and information flow between stages. In practice there will be such a lag, and this will make the fluctuations even more marked. Figure 7.9 shows the net result of all these effects in a typical supply chain. Note the increasing volatility further back in the chain.

Controlling supply chain dynamics

The first step in improving supply chain performance involves attempting to reduce the bull whip effect. This usually means coordinating the activities of the operations in the chain in several ways:[11]

Share information throughout the supply chain

> **OPERATIONS PRINCIPLE**
>
> *The bull whip effect can be reduced by information sharing, aligning planning and control decisions, improving flow efficiency, and better forecasting.*

One reason for the bull whip effect is that each operation in the chain reacts only to the orders placed by its *immediate* customer. They have little overview of what is happening throughout the chain. But if chain-wide information is shared throughout the chain, it is unlikely that such wild fluctuations will occur. With information transmitted throughout the chain, all the operations can monitor true demand, free of distortions. So, for example, information regarding supply problems, or shortages, can be transmitted

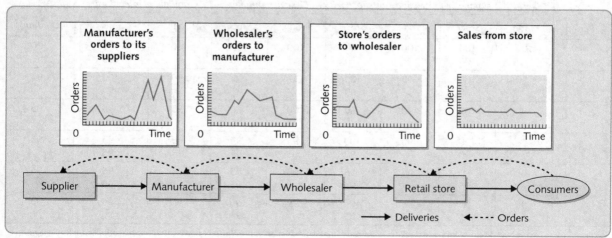

Figure 7.9 Typical supply chain dynamics

Animated
diagram

down the chain so that downstream customers can modify their schedules and sales plans accordingly. For example, the electronic point-of-sale (EPOS) systems, used by many retailers, make information on current demand downstream in the supply chain available to upstream operations. Sales data from checkouts or cash registers is consolidated and transmitted to the warehouses, transportation companies and supplier operations in the supply chain. This means that suppliers can be aware of the 'real' movements in the market.

Align all the channels of information and supply

Channel alignment means the adjustment of scheduling, material movements, stock levels, pricing and other sales strategies so as to bring all the operations in the chain into line with each other. This goes beyond the provision of information. It means that the systems and methods of planning and control decision making are harmonised through the chain. For example, even when using the same information, differences in forecasting methods or purchasing practices can lead to fluctuations in orders between operations in the chain. One way of avoiding this is to allow an upstream supplier to manage the inventories of its downstream customer. This is known as vendor-managed inventory (VMI). So, for example, a packaging supplier could take responsibility for the stocks of packaging materials held by a food manufacturing customer. In turn, the food manufacturer takes responsibility for the stocks of its products that are held in its customer's (the supermarket's) warehouses.

Increase operational efficiency throughout the chain

'Operational efficiency' in this context means the efforts that each operation in the chain makes to reduce its own complexity, the cost of doing business with other operations in the chain, and its throughput time. The cumulative effect of this is to simplify throughput in the whole chain. For example, imagine a chain of operations whose performance level is relatively poor: quality defects are frequent, the lead time to order products and services is long, delivery is unreliable and so on. The behaviour of the chain would be a continual sequence of errors and effort wasted in replanning to compensate for the errors. Poor quality would mean extra and unplanned orders being placed, and unreliable delivery and slow delivery lead times would mean high safety stocks. Just as important, most operations managers' time would be spent coping with the inefficiency. By contrast, a chain whose operations had high levels of operations performance would be more predictable and have faster throughput, both of which would help to minimise supply chain fluctuations.

Improve forecasts

Improved forecast accuracy also helps to reduce the bull whip effect. Bull whip is caused by the demand pattern, lead times, forecasting mechanisms and the replenishment decisions used to order product from production facilities or suppliers. Improving the accuracy of your forecasts directly reduces the inventory holding requirements that will achieve customer service level targets. Reducing lead-times means that you need to forecast less far into the future and thus lead times have a large impact on bull whip and inventory costs. The exact nature of how bull whip propagates in a supply chain is also dependent on the nature of the demand pattern. Negatively correlated demands require less inventory in the supply chain that positively correlated demand patters, for example. But bull whip is not unavoidable. By using sophisticated replenishment policies, designed using control engineering principles, many businesses have been able to eliminate bullwhip effects. Sometimes this comes at a cost. Extra inventory may be required in parts of the chain, or customer service levels reduce. But more often bullwhip avoidance creates a 'win-win'. It reduces inventory requirements and improves customer service.

Critical commentary

Each chapter contains a short critical commentary on the main ideas covered in the chapter. Its purpose is not to undermine the issues discussed in the chapter, but to emphasise that, although we present a relatively orthodox view of operation, there are other perspectives.

● This emphasis on understanding the end customer in a supply chain has led some authorities to object to the very term *supply* chain. Rather, they say, they should be referred to as *demand* chains. Their argument is based on the idea that the concept of 'supply' implies a 'push' mentality. Any emphasis on pushing goods through a supply chain should be avoided. It implies that customers should consume what suppliers see fit to produce. On the other hand, referring to 'demand chains' puts proper emphasis on the importance of seeing customers as pulling demand through the chain. Nevertheless, 'supply chain' is still the most commonly used term.

● Although the SCOR model is increasingly adopted, it has been criticised for under-emphasising people issues. The SCOR model assumes, but does not explicitly address, the human resource base skill set, notwithstanding the model's heavy reliance on supply chain knowledge to understand the model and methodology properly. Often external expertise is needed to support the process. This, along with the nature of the SCC membership also imply that the SCOR model may be appropriate only for relatively large companies that are more likely to have the necessary business capabilities to implement the model. Many small- to medium-sized companies may find difficulty in handle full-scale model implementation. Some critics would also argue that the model lacks a link to the financial plans of a company making it very difficult to highlight the benefits obtainable, as well as inhibiting senior management support.

● The use of technology in supply chain management is not always universally welcomed. Even e-procurement is seen by some as preventing closer partnership-type relationships that, in the long run, may be more beneficial. Similarly, track-and-trace technology is seen by some as a waste of time and money. '*What we need,*' they argue, '*is to know that we can trust the delivery to arrive on time; we do not need the capability to waste our time finding out where the delivery is.*' The idea of RFID also opens up many ethical issues. People see its potential and its dangers in very different ways. Take the following two statements:[12]

'We are on the brink of a revolution of "smart products" that will interconnect everyday objects, consumers and manufacturers in a dynamic cycle of world commerce. . . . The vision of the Auto-ID centre is to create a universal environment in which computers understand the world without help from human beings.'

'Supermarket cards and other retail surveillance devices are merely the opening volley of the marketers' war against consumers. If consumers fail to oppose these practices now our long-term prospects may look like something from a dystopian science fiction novel . . . though many Auto-ID proponents appear focused on inventory and supply chain efficiency, others are developing financial and consumer applications that, if adopted, will have chilling effects on consumers' ability to escape the oppressive surveillance of manufacturers, retailers, and marketers. Of course, government and law enforcement will be quick to use the technology to keep tabs on citizens as well.'

● It is this last issue which particularly scares some civil liberties activists. Keeping track of items within a supply chain is a relatively uncontentious issue. Keeping track of items when those items are identified with a particular individual going about their everyday lives, is far more problematic. So, beyond the check-out for every arguably beneficial application there is also potential for misuse. For example, smart tags could drastically reduce theft because items could automatically report when they are stolen; their tags serving as a homing device pinpoint their exact location. But, similar technology could be used to trace any citizen, honest or not.

SUMMARY CHECKLIST

This checklist comprises questions that can be usefully applied to any type of operations and reflect the major diagnostic questions used within the chapter.

- ☐ Is it understood that the performance of any one operation is partly a function of all the other operations in the supply chain?
- ☐ Are supply chain concepts applied internally as well as externally?
- ☐ Are supply chain objectives understood in the context of the whole chain rather than the single operation?
- ☐ Which product or service groups are 'functional' and which are 'innovative'?
- ☐ Which products or service groups need 'lean' and which need 'agile' supply chain management?
- ☐ Is the position on the 'transactional to partnership' spectrum understood for each customer and supplier relationship?
- ☐ Are customer and supplier relationships at an appropriate point on the transactional to partnership spectrum?
- ☐ Are 'partnership' relationships *really* partnerships or are they just called that?
- ☐ Are suppliers and potential suppliers rigorously assessed using some scoring procedure?
- ☐ Are the trade-offs inherent in supplier selection understood?
- ☐ Is the approach to single- or multi-sourcing appropriate?
- ☐ Is the purchasing activity making full use of internet-based mechanisms?
- ☐ Are service level agreements used? Do they develop over time?
- ☐ Is sufficient effort put into supplier development?
- ☐ Are actual and potential mismatches of perception in the supplier relationships explored?
- ☐ Is the difference between dependent and independent demand understood?
- ☐ Is the potential for outsourcing logistics services regularly explored?
- ☐ Could new technologies such as RFID have any benefit?
- ☐ Has the idea of customer development been explored?
- ☐ Have mechanisms for reducing the impact of the bull whip effect been explored?
- ☐ Has there been a risk assessment to assess supply chain vulnerability?

Supplying fast fashion[13]

Garment retailing has changed. No longer is there a standard look that all retailers adhere to for a whole season. Fashion is fast, complex and furious. Different trends overlap and fashion ideas that are not even on a store's radar screen can become 'must haves' within six months. Many retail businesses with their own brands, such as H&M and Zara, sell up-to-the-minute fashionability at low prices in stores that are clearly focused on one particular market. In the world of fast fashion, catwalk designs speed their way into high street stores at prices anyone can afford. The quality of the garment means that it may only last one season, but fast fashion customers don't want yesterday's trends. As *Newsweek* puts it, '. . . *being a "quicker picker-upper" is what made fashion retailers H&M and Zara successful. [They] thrive by practising the new science of "fast fashion", compressing product development cycles as much as six times.*' But the retail operations that customers see are only the end part of the supply chains that feeds them. And these have also changed.

At its simplest level, the fast fashion supply chain has four stages. First, the garments are designed, after which they are manufactured, they are then distributed to the retail outlets where they are displayed and sold in retail operations designed to reflect the business's brand values. In this short case study, we examine two fast fashion operations, Hennes and Mauritz (known as H&M) and Zara, together with United Colours of Benetton (UCB), a similar chain, but with a different market positioning.

United Colours of Benetton. Almost 50 years ago Luciano Benetton took the world of fashion by storm by selling the bright, casual sweaters designed by his sister across Europe (and later the rest of the world), promoted by controversial advertising. By 2005, the Benetton Group was present in 120 countries throughout the world. Selling casual garments, mainly under its United Colours of Benetton (UCB) and its more fashion-oriented Sisley brands, it produces 110 million garments a year, over 90 per cent of them in Europe. Its retail network of over 5,000 stores produces revenue of around €2 billion. Benetton products are seen as less 'high fashion' but of higher quality and durability, and with higher prices, than H&M and Zara.

H&M. Established in Sweden in 1947, H&M now sell clothes and cosmetics in over 1,000 stores in 20 countries

Source: KevinFoy/Alamy Images

around the world. The business concept is 'fashion and quality at the best price'. With more than 40,000 employees, and revenues of around SEK 60,000 million, its biggest market is Germany, followed by Sweden and the UK. H&M are seen by many as the originator of the fast fashion concept. Certainly they have years of experience at driving down the price of up-to-the-minute fashions. '*We ensure the best price,*' they say, '*by having few middlemen, buying large volumes, having extensive experience of the clothing industry, having a great knowledge of which goods should be bought from which markets, having efficient distribution systems, and being cost-conscious at every stage.*'

Zara. The first store opened almost by accident in 1975 when Amancio Ortega Gaona, a women's pyjama manufacturer, was left with a large cancelled order. The shop he opened was intended only as an outlet for cancelled orders. Now, Inditex, the holding group that includes the Zara brand, has over 1,300 stores in 39 countries with sales of over €3 billion. The Zara brand accounts for over 75 per cent of the group's total retail sales, and is still based in north-west Spain. By 2003 it had become the world's fastest growing volume garment retailer. The Inditex group also has several other branded chains including Pull and Bear, and Massimo Dutti. In total it employs almost 40,000 people in a business that is known for a high degree of vertical integration compared with most fast fashion companies. The company believes that it is their integration along the supply chain that allows them to respond to customer demand fast and flexibly while keeping stock to a minimum.

Design

All three businesses emphasise the importance of design in this market. Although not *haute couture*, capturing design trends is vital to success. Even the boundary between high and fast fashion is starting to blur. In 2004, H&M recruited high fashion designer Karl Lagerfeld, previous noted for his work with more exclusive brands. For H&M his designs were priced for value rather than exclusivity. *'Why do I work for H&M? Because I believe in inexpensive clothes, not 'cheap' clothes,'* said Lagerfeld. Yet most of H&M's products come from over 100 designers in Stockholm who work with a team of 50 pattern designers, around 100 buyers and a number of budget controllers. The department's task is to find the optimum balance between the three components comprising H&M's business concept – fashion, price and quality. Buying volumes and delivery dates are then decided.

Zara's design functions are organised in a different way to most similar companies. Conventionally, the design input comes from three *separate* functions: the designers themselves, market specialists, and buyers who place orders on to suppliers. At Zara the design stage is split into three product areas: women's, men's and children's garments. In each area, designers, market specialists and buyers are co-located in design halls that also contain small workshops for trying out prototype designs. The market specialists in all three design halls are in regular contact with Zara retail stores, discussing customer reaction to new designs. In this way, the retail stores are not the end of the whole supply chain but the beginning of the design stage of the chain. Zara's around 300 designers, whose average age is 26, produce approximately 40,000 items per year of which about 10,000 go into production.

Benetton also has around 300 designers, who not only design for all their brands, but also are engaged in researching new materials and clothing concepts. Since 2000, the company has moved to standardise their range globally. At one time more than 20 per cent of its ranges were customised to the specific needs of each country, now only between 5 and 10 per cent of garments are customised. This reduced the number of individual designs offered globally by over 30 per cent, strengthening the global brand image and reducing production costs.

Both H&M and Zara have moved away from the traditional industry practice of offering two 'collections' a year, for Spring/Summer and Autumn/Winter. Their 'seasonless cycle' involves the continual introduction of new products on a rolling basis throughout the year. This allows designers to learn from customers' reactions to their new products and incorporate them quickly into more new products. The most extreme version of this idea is practiced by Zara. A garment will be designed; a batch manufactured and 'pulsed' through the supply chain. Often the design is never repeated, it may be modified and another batch produced, but there are no 'continuing' designs as such. Even Benetton, have increased the proportion of what they call 'flash' collections, small collections that are put into its stores during the season.

Manufacturing

At one time Benetton focused its production on its Italian plants. Then it significantly increased its production outside Italy to take advantage of lower labour costs. Non-Italian operations include factories in North Africa, Eastern Europe and Asia. Yet each location operates in a very similar manner. A central, Benetton owned, operation performs some manufacturing operations (especially those requiring expensive technology) and coordinates the more labour intensive production activities that are performed by a network of smaller contractors (often owned and managed by ex-Benetton employees). These contractors may in turn sub-contract some of their activities. The company's central facility in Italy allocates production to each of the non-Italian networks, deciding what and how much each is to produce. There is some specialisation, for example, jackets are made in Eastern Europe while T-shirts are made in Spain. Benetton also has a controlling share in its main supplier of raw materials, to ensure fast supply to its factories. Benetton are also known for the practice of dying garments after assembly rather than using died thread or fabric. This postpones decisions about colours until late in the supply process so that there is a greater chance of producing what is needed by the market.

H&M does not have any factories of its own, but instead works with around 750 suppliers. Around half of production takes place in Europe and the rest mainly in Asia. It has 21 production offices around the world that between them are responsible for coordinating the suppliers who produce over half a billion items a year for H&M. The relationship between production offices and suppliers is vital, because it allows fabrics to be bought in early. The actual dyeing and cutting of the garments can then be decided at a later stage in the production The later an order can be placed on suppliers, the less the risk of buying the wrong thing. Average supply lead times vary from three weeks up to six months, depending on the nature of the goods. *'The most important thing,'* they say, *'is to find the optimal time to order each item. Short lead times are not always best. For some high-volume fashion basics, it is to our advantage to place orders far in advance. Trendier garments require considerably shorter lead times.'*

Zara's lead times are said to be the fastest in the industry, with a 'catwalk to rack' time as little as 15 days. According to one analyst, this is because they *'owned most of the manufacturing capability used to make their products, which they use as a means of exciting and stimulating customer demand.'* About half of Zara's products are produced in its network of 20 Spanish factories, which, like at Benetton, tend to concentrate on the more capital intensive operations such as cutting and dyeing. Sub-contractors are used for most labour intensive operations like sewing. Zara buy around 40 per cent of their fabric from its own wholly-owned subsidiary, most of which is in undyed form for dyeing after assembly. Most Zara factories and their sub-contractors work on a single shift system to retain some volume flexibility.

Distribution

Both Benetton and Zara have invested in highly automated warehouses, close to their main production centres that store, pack and assemble individual orders for their retail networks. These automated warehouses represent a major investment for both companies. In 2001, Zara caused some press comment by announcing that it would open a second automated warehouse even though, by its own calculations, it was only using about half its existing warehouse capacity. More recently, Benetton caused some controversy by announcing that it was exploring the use of RFID tags to track its garments.

At H&M, while the stock management is primarily handled internally, physical distribution is subcontracted. A large part of the flow of goods is routed from production site to the retail country via H&M's transit terminal in Hamburg. Upon arrival the goods are inspected and allocated to the stores or to the centralised store stock room. The centralised store stock room, within H&M referred to as 'Call-Off Warehouse' replenishes stores on item level according to what is selling.

Retail

All H&M stores (average size 1,300 square metres) are owned and solely run by H&M. The aim is to *'create a comfortable and inspiring atmosphere in the store that makes it simple for customers to find what they want and to feel at home'*. This is similar to Zara stores, although they tend to be smaller (average size 800 square metres). Perhaps the most remarkable characteristic of Zara stores is that garments rarely stay in the store for longer than two weeks. Because product designs are often not repeated and are produced in relatively small batches, the range of garments displayed in the store can change radically every two or three week. This encourages customers both to avoid delaying a purchase and to revisit the store frequently.

Since 2000 Benetton has been reshaping its retail operations. At one time the vast majority of Benetton retail outlets were small shops run by third parties. Now these small stores have been joined by several, Benetton owned and operated, larger stores (average size 1,500 to 3,000 square metres). These mega-stores can display the whole range of Benetton products and reinforce the Benetton shopping experience.

QUESTION

Compare and contrast the approaches taken by H&M, Benetton and Zara to managing their supply chain.

APPLYING THE PRINCIPLES

Hints

Some of these exercises can be answered by reading the chapter. Others will require some general knowledge of business activity and some might require an element of investigation. Hints on how they can all be answered are to be found in the eText at www.pearsoned.co.uk/slack.

1   If you were the owner of a small local retail shop, what criteria would you use to select suppliers for the goods that you wish to stock in your shop? Visit three shops that are local to you and ask the owners how they select their suppliers. In what way were their answers different from what you thought they might be?

2   What is your purchasing strategy? How do you approach buying the products and services that you need (or want)? Classify the types and products and services that you buy and record the criteria you use to purchase each category. Discuss these categories and criteria with others. Why are their views different?

3   Visit a C2C (consumer-to-consumer) auction site (for example eBay) and analyse the function of the site in terms of the way it facilitates transactions. What does such a site have to get right to be successful?

4   The example of the bull whip effect shown in Table 7.2 shows how a simple 5 per cent reduction in demand at the end of supply chain causes fluctuations that increase in severity the further back an operation is placed in the chain.

   (a) Using the same logic and the same rules (i.e. all operations keep one period's demand as inventory), what would the effect on the chain be if demand fluctuated period by period between 100 and 95? That is, period 1 had a demand of 100, period 2 had a demand of 95, period 3 had a demand of 100, period 4 had a demand of 95, and so on?

   (b) What happens if all operations in the supply chain decide to keep only half of each period's demand as inventory?

   (c) Find examples of how supply chains try to reduce this bull whip effect.

5   Visit the websites of some distribution and logistics companies. For example, you might start with some of the following: www.eddiestobart.co.uk, www.norbert-dentressangle.com, www.accenture.com (under 'services' look for supply chain management), www.logisticsonline.com.

   (a) What do you think are the market promises that these companies make to their clients and potential clients?

   (b) What are the operations capabilities they need to carry out these promises successfully?

Notes on chapter

1 Sources include: (2010) 'Ocado wins world e-tailer of the year: online supermarket scoops award at World Retail Awards in Berlin', Ocado press release (Jenny Davey).

2 Sonne, P. (2010) 'Off the catwalk: Burberry gets a makeover', *The Wall Street Journal*, 9 September.

3 Fisher, M.L. (1997), 'What is the right supply chain for your product', *Harvard Business Review*, March–April.

4 We are grateful to Carsten Dittrich for very significant help with this section.

5 Kapour, V. and Gupta, A. (1997), 'Aggressive sourcing: a free-market approach', *Sloan Management Review*, Fall.

6 Parkhe, A. (1993) 'Strategic alliance structuring', *Academy of Management Journal*, Vol 36, pp 794–829.

7 Source: Grad, C. (2000) 'A network of supplies to be woven into the web', *Financial Times*, 9 February.

8 Lee, L. and Dobler, D.W. (1977) *Purchasing and Materials Management*, McGraw-Hill.

9 Harland, C.M. (1996), 'Supply chain management relationships, chains and networks', *British Journal of Management*, Vol. 1, No. 7.

10 Lee, H.L., Padmanabhan, V. and Whang, S. (1997) 'The bull whip effect in supply chains', *Sloan Management Review*, Spring.

11 Thanks to Stephen Disney at Cardiff Business School, UK, for help with this section.

12 Sources: MIT Auto-ID website; Albercht, K. (2002), 'Supermarket cards: tip of the surveillance iceberg', *Denver University Law Review*, June.

13 All data from public sources and reflects period 2004–05.

TAKING IT FURTHER

Bolstorff, P. and Rosenbaum, R. (2008) *Supply Chain Excellence – A Handbook for Dramatic Improvement Using the SCOR Model* (2nd edn), American Management Association.

Bolstorff, P. (2004), 'Supply chain by the numbers', *Logistics Today*, July, 46–50.

Christopher, M. (2010) *Logistics and Supply Chain Management*, Financial Times Prentice Hall. *A comprehensive treatment on supply chain management from a distribution perspective by one of the gurus of supply chain management.*

Fisher, M.L. (1997) 'What is the right supply chain for your product?', *Harvard Business Review*, Vol. 75, No. 2. *A particularly influential article that explores the issue of how supply chains are not all the same.*

Harrison, A. and van Hoek, R. (2007) *Logistics Management and Strategy: Competing through the Supply Chain*, Financial Times Prentice Hall. *A short but readable book that explains may of the modern ideas in supply chain management including lean supply chains and agile supply chains.*

Hines, P. and Rich, N. (1997) 'The seven value stream mapping tools', *International Journal of Operations and Production Management*, Vol. 17, No. 1. *Another academic paper, but one that explores some practical techniques that can be used to understand supply chains.*

Parmigiania A., Klassenb R.D., Russoa M.V. (2011) 'Efficiency meets accountability: performance implications of supply chain configuration, control, and capabilities', *Journal of Operations Management*, Vol. 29, pp 212–223. *Excellent review and discussion of broad supply issues.*

Presutti Jr., William D. and Mawhinney, J.R. (2007), 'The supply chain finance link', *Supply Chain Management Review*, September, 32–38.

USEFUL WEBSITES

www.opsman.org *Definitions, links and opinions on operations and process management.*

http://www.cio.com/research/scm/edit/012202_scm *Site of CIO's Supply Chain Management Research Center. Topics include procurement and fulfilment, with case studies.*

http://www.stanford.edu/group/scforum/ *Stanford University's supply chain forum. Interesting debate.*

http://www.rfidc.com/ *Site of the RFID Centre that contains RFID demonstrations and articles to download.*

http://www.spychips.com/ *Vehemently anti-RFID site. If you want to understand the nature of some activist's concern over RFID, this site provides the arguments.*

http://www.cips.org/ *The Chartered Institute of Purchasing & Supply (CIPS) is an international organisation, serving the purchasing and supply profession and dedicated to promoting best practice. Some good links.*

http://www.supply-chain.org/cs/root/home *The Supply Chain Council homepage.*

Interactive quiz

For further resources including examples, animated diagrams, self-test questions, Excel spreadsheets and video materials please explore the eText on the companion website at **www.pearsoned.co.uk/slack.**

11

Lean synchronisation

Introduction

Lean synchronisation aims to meet demand instantaneously, with perfect quality and no waste. This involves supplying products and services in perfect synchronisation with the demand for them, using 'lean' or 'just-in-time' (JIT) principles. These principles were once a radical departure from traditional operations practice, but have now become orthodox in promoting the synchronisation of flow through processes, operations and supply networks (see Figure 11.1).

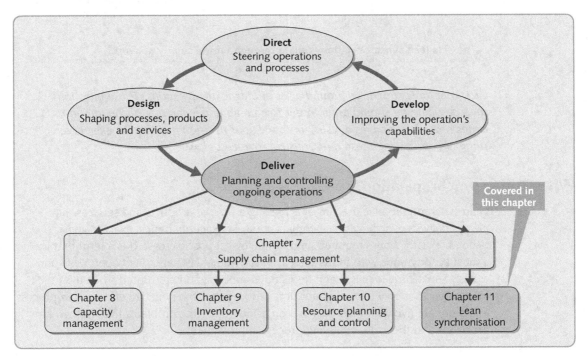

Figure 11.1 Lean synchronisation is the aim of achieving a flow of products and services that always delivers exactly what customers want, in exact quantities, exactly when needed, exactly where required, and at the lowest possible cost

EXECUTIVE SUMMARY

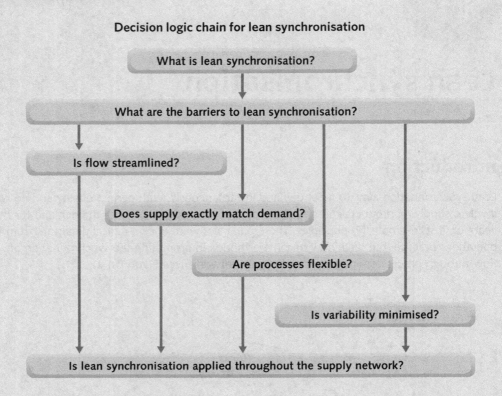

Decision logic chain for lean synchronisation

What is lean synchronisation?

What are the barriers to lean synchronisation?

Is flow streamlined?

Does supply exactly match demand?

Are processes flexible?

Is variability minimised?

Is lean synchronisation applied throughout the supply network?

Each chapter is structured around a set of diagnostic questions. These questions suggest what you should ask in order to gain an understanding of the important issues of a topic, and, as a result, improve your decision making. An executive summary addressing these questions is provided below.

What is lean synchronisation?

Lean synchronisation is the aim of achieving a flow of products and services that always delivers exactly what customers want, in exact quantities, exactly when needed, exactly where required, and at the lowest possible cost. It is a term that is almost synonymous with terms such as 'just-in-time' (JIT) and 'lean operations principles'. The central idea is that if items flow smoothly, uninterrupted by delays in inventories, not only is throughput time reduced, but the negative effects of in-process inventory are avoided. Inventory is seen as obscuring the problems that exist within processes and therefore inhibiting process improvement.

What are the barriers to lean synchronisation?

The aim of lean synchronisation can be inhibited in three ways. First is the failure to eliminate waste in all parts of the operation. The causes of waste are more extensive than is generally understood. The second is a failure to involve all the people within the operation in the shared task of smoothing flow and eliminating waste. Japanese proponents of lean synchronisation often use a set of 'basic working practices' to ensure involvement. Third is the failure to adopt continuous improvement principles. Because pure lean synchronisation is an aim rather than something that can be implemented quickly, it requires the continual application of incremental improvement steps to reach it.

Is flow streamlined?

Long process routes are wasteful and cause delay and inventory build up. Physically reconfiguring processes to reduce distance travelled and aid cooperation between staff can help to streamline flow. Similarly, ensuring flow visibility helps to make improvement to flow easier. Sometimes this can involve small-scale technologies that can reduce fluctuations in flow volume.

Does supply exactly match demand?

The aim of lean synchronisation is to meet demand exactly; neither too much nor too little and only when it is needed. Achieving this often means pull control principles. The most common method of doing this is the use of kanbans, simple signalling devices that prevent the accumulation of excess inventory.

Are processes flexible?

Responding exactly to demand only when it is need often requires a degree of flexibility in processes, both to cope with unexpected demand and to allow processes to change between different activities without excessive delay. This often means reducing changeover times in technologies.

Is variability minimised?

Variability in processes disrupts flow and prevents lean synchronisation. Variability includes quality variability and schedule variability. Statistical process control (SPC) principles are useful in reducing quality variability. The use of levelled scheduling and mixed modelling can be used to reduce flow variability and total productive maintenance (TPM) can reduce variability caused by breakdowns.

Is lean synchronisation applied throughout the network?

The same benefits of lean synchronisation that apply within operations can also apply between operations. Furthermore, the same principles that can be used to achieve lean synchronisation within operations can be used to achieve it between operations. This is more difficult, partly because of the complexity of flow and partly because supply networks are prone to the type of unexpected fluctuations that are easier to control within operations.

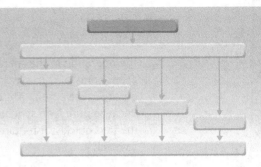

DIAGNOSTIC QUESTION

What is lean synchronisation?

Video

Synchronisation means that the flow of products and services always delivers exactly what customers want (perfect quality), in exact quantities (neither too much nor too little), exactly when needed (not too early or too late), and exactly where required (not to the wrong location). *Lean* synchronisation is to do all this at the lowest possible cost. It results in items flowing rapidly and smoothly through processes, operations and supply networks.

The benefits of synchronised flow

The best way to understand how lean synchronsation differs from more traditional approaches to managing flow is to contrast the two simple processes in Figure 11.2. The traditional approach assumes that each stage in the process will place its output in an inventory that 'buffers' that stage from the next one downstream in the process. The next stage down will then (eventually) take outputs from the inventory, process them, and pass them through to the next buffer inventory. These buffers are there to 'insulate each stage from its neighbours, making each stage relatively independent so that if, for example, stage A stops operating for some reason, stage B can continue, at least for a time. The larger the buffer inventory, the greater the degree of insulation between the stages. This insulation has to be paid for in terms

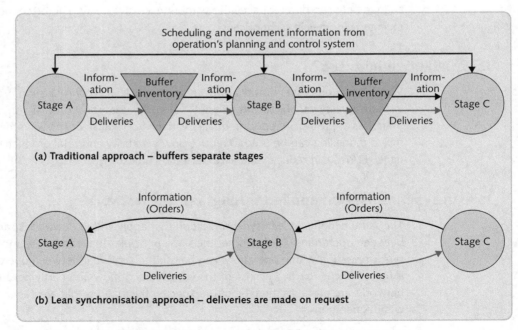

(a) Traditional approach – buffers separate stages

(b) Lean synchronisation approach – deliveries are made on request

Figure 11.2   (a) Traditional and (b) lean synchronised flow between stages

of inventory and slow throughput times because items will spend time waiting in the buffer inventories.

But, the main 'learning' argument against this traditional approach lies in the very conditions it seeks to promote, namely the insulation of the stages from one another. When a problem occurs at one stage, the problem will not immediately be apparent elsewhere in the system. The responsibility for solving the problem will be centred largely on the people within that stage, and the consequences of the problem will be prevented from spreading to the whole system. However, contrast this with the pure lean synchronised process illustrated in Figure 11.2. Here items are processed and then passed directly to the next stage 'just-in-time' for them to be processed further. Problems at any stage have a very different effect in such a system. Now if stage A stops processing, stage B will notice immediately and stage C very soon after. Stage A's problem is now quickly exposed to the whole process, which is immediately affected by the problem. This means that the responsibility for solving the problem is no longer confined to the staff at stage A. It is now shared by everyone, considerably improving the chances of the problem being solved, if only because it is now too important to be ignored. In other words, by preventing items accumulating between stages, the operation has increased the chances of the intrinsic efficiency of the plant being improved.

Non-synchronised approaches seek to encourage efficiency by protecting each part of the process from disruption. The lean synchronised approach takes the opposite view. Exposure of the system (although not suddenly, as in our simplified example) to problems can both make them more evident and change the 'motivation structure' of the whole system towards solving the problems. Lean synchronisation sees accumulations of inventory as a 'blanket of obscurity' that lies over the production system and prevents problems being noticed. This same argument can be applied when, instead of queues of material, or information (inventory), an operation has to deal with queues of customers. Table 11.1 shows how certain aspects of inventory are analogous to certain aspects of queues.

OPERATIONS PRINCIPLE

Buffer inventory used to insulate stages or processes localises the motivation to improve.

Table 11.1 Inventories of materials – information or customers have similar characteristics

	Inventory		
	Of material (queue of material)	*Of information (queue of information)*	*Of customers (queue of people)*
Cost	Ties up working capital	Less current information and so worth less	Wastes customers' time
Space	Needs storage space	Needs memory capacity	Needs waiting area
Quality	Defects hidden, possible damage	Defects hidden, possible data corruption	Gives negative perception
Decoupling	Makes stages independent	Makes stages independent	Promotes job specialisation/ fragmentation
Utilisation	Stages kept busy by work in progress	Stages kept busy by work in data queues	Servers kept busy by waiting customers
Coordination	Avoids need for synchronisation	Avoids need for straight-through processing	Avoids having to match supply and demand

Source: Adapted from Fitzsimmons, J.A. (1990) 'Making Continual Improvement: A Competitive Strategy for Service Firms' *in* Bowen, D.E., Chase, R.B., Cummings, T.G. and Associates (eds) *Service Management Effectiveness*, Jossey-Bass.

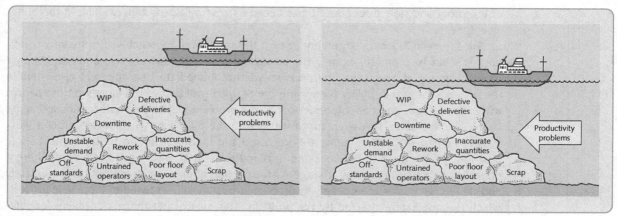

Figure 11.3 Reducing the level of inventory (water) allows operations management (the ship) to see the problems in the operation (the rocks) and work to reduce them

The river and rocks analogy

The idea of obscuring effects of inventory is often illustrated diagrammatically, as in Figure 11.3. The many problems of the operation are shown as rocks in a river bed that cannot be seen because of the depth of the water. The water in this analogy represents the inventory in the operation. Yet, even though the rocks cannot be seen, they slow the progress of the river's flow and cause turbulence. Gradually reducing the depth of the water (inventory) exposes the worst of the problems which can be resolved, after which the water is lowered further, exposing more problems, and so on. The same argument will also apply for the flow between whole processes, or whole operations. For example, stages A, B and C in Figure 11.2 could be a supplier operation, a manufacturer and a customer's operation, respectively.

Synchronisation, 'lean' and 'just-in-time'

Different terms are used to describe what here we call lean synchronisation. Our shortened definition – *'lean synchronisation aims to meet demand instantaneously, with perfect quality and no waste'* – could also be used to describe the general concept of 'lean', or 'just-in-time' (JIT). The concept of 'lean' stresses the elimination of waste, while 'just-in-time' emphasises the idea of producing items only when they are needed. But all three concepts overlap to a large degree, and no definition fully conveys the full implications for operations practice. Here we use the term lean synchronisation because it best describes the impact of these ideas on flow and delivery.

Two operations that have implemented lean synchronisation are briefly described below. One is the company that is generally credited with doing most to develop the whole concept; the other is a not-for-profit hospital that nevertheless has derived benefits from adopting some of the principles.

EXAMPLE   **Toyota[1]**

Seen as the leading practitioner and the main originator of the lean approach, the Toyota Motor Company has progressively synchronised all its processes simultaneously to give high quality, fast throughput and exceptional productivity. It has done this by developing a set of practices that has largely shaped what we now call 'lean' or 'just-in-time' but which Toyota calls the Toyota Production System (TPS). The TPS has two themes: 'just-in-time' and *jidoka*. Just-in-time is defined as the rapid and coordinated movement of parts throughout the production system and supply network to meet customer demand. It is operationalised by means of *heijunka* (levelling and smoothing the flow of items), *kanban* (signalling to the preceding process that more parts are needed) and *nagare* (laying out processes to achieve smoother flow of parts throughout the production process). *Jidoka* is described as 'humanising the interface

Source: Courtesy of Toyota Motor Manufacturing (UK) Ltd

between operator and machine'. Toyota's philosophy is that the machine is there to serve the operator's purpose. The operator should be left free to exercise his/her judgement. *Jidoka* is operationalised by means of fail-safeing (or machine *jidoka*), line-stop authority (or human *jidoka*), and visual control (at-a-glance status of production processes and visibility of process standards).

Toyota believe that both just-in-time and *jidoka* should be applied ruthlessly to the elimination of waste, where waste is defined as 'anything other than the minimum amount of equipment, items, parts and workers that are absolutely essential to production'. Fujio Cho of Toyota identified seven types of waste that must be eliminated from all operations processes. They are: waste from over production; waste from waiting time; transportation waste; inventory waste; processing waste; waste of motion; waste from product defects. Beyond this, authorities on Toyota claim that its strength lies in understanding the differences between the tools and practices used with Toyota operations and the overall philosophy of their approach to lean synchronisation. This is what some have called the apparent paradox of the Toyota production system, 'namely, that activities, connections and production flows in a Toyota factory are rigidly scripted, yet at the same time Toyota's operations are enormously flexible and adaptable. Activities and processes are constantly being challenged and pushed to a higher level of performance, enabling the company to continually innovate and improve'.

One influential study of Toyota identified four rules that guide the design, delivery, and development activities within the company.

1. All work shall be highly specified as to content, sequence, timing and outcome.
2. Every customer–supplier connection must be direct and there must be an unambiguous yes or no method of sending requests and receiving responses.
3. The route for every product and service must be simple and direct.
4. Any improvement must be made in accordance with the scientific method, under the guidance of a teacher, and at the lowest possible level in the organisation.

EXAMPLE

Lean hospitals[2]

In one of the increasing number of healthcare services to adopt lean principles, the Bolton Hospitals National Health Service Trust in the north of the UK, has reduced one of its hospital's mortality rate from one injury by more than a third. David Fillingham, Chief Executive of Bolton Hospitals NHS Trust said, *'We had far more people dying from fractured hips than should have been dying.'* Then the trust greatly reduced its mortality rate for fractured neck of femur by redesigning the patient's stay in hospital to reduce or remove the waits between 'useful activity'. The mortality rate fell from 22.9 per cent to 14.6 per cent, which is the equivalent of 14 more patients surviving every six months. At the same time, the average length of stay fell by a third from 34.6 days to 23.5 days.

Source: Upper Cut Images/Getty Images

The trust held five 'rapid improvement events', involving employees from across the organisation who spent several days examining processes and identifying alternative ways how to improve them. Some management consultants were also used but strictly in an advisory role. In addition third-party experts were brought in. These included staff from the Royal Air Force, who has been applying lean principles to running aircraft carriers. The value of these outsiders was not only their expertise. *'They asked all sorts of innocent, naïve questions,'* said Mr Fillingham, *'to which, often, no member of staff has an answer'*. Other lean-based improvement initiatives included examining the patient's whole experience from start to finish so that delays (some of which could prove fatal) could be removed on their journey to the operating theatre, radiology processes were speeded up and unnecessary paperwork was eliminated. Cutting the length of stay and reducing process complications should also start to reduce costs, although Mr Fillingham says that it could take several years for the savings to become substantial. Not only that, but staff are also said to be helped by the changes because they can spend more time helping patients rather than doing non-value added activities.

Meanwhile at Salisbury district hospital in the south of the UK, lean principles have reduced delays in waiting for the results of tests from the ultrasound department. Waiting lists have been reduced from 12 weeks to between two weeks and zero after an investigation showed that 67 per cent of demand was coming from just 5 per cent of possible ultrasound tests: abdominal, gynaecological and urological. So all work was streamed into routine 'green' streams and complex 'red' ones. This is like having different traffic lanes on a motorway dedi-cated to different types of traffic, with fast cars in one lane and slow trucks in another. Mixing both types of work is like mixing fast cars and slow-moving trucks in all lanes. The department then concentrated on doing the routine 'green' work more efficiently. For example, the initial date scan used to check the age of a foetus took only two minutes, so a series of five-minute slots were allocated just for these. *'The secret is to get the steady stream of high-volume, low-variety chugging down the ultrasound motorway,'* says Kate Hobson, who runs the depart-ment. Streaming routine work in this way has left more time to deal with the more complex jobs, yet staff are not overloaded. They are more likely to leave work on time and also believe that the department is doing a better job, all of which has improved morale says Kate Hobson. *'I think people feel their day is more structured now. It's not that madness, opening the doors and people coming at you.'* Nor has this more disciplined approach impaired the depart-ment's ability to treat really urgent jobs. In fact it has stopped leaving space in its schedule for emergencies – the, now standard, short waiting time is usually sufficient for urgent jobs.

What do these two examples have in common?

Here are two types of operation separated by product, culture, size, location, and their route to adopting lean synchronisation principles. Toyota took decades to develop a fully integrated and coherent philosophy to managing their operations and have become one of the world's leading and most profitable automotive companies as a result. The hospitals are far earlier in their path to lean synchronisation, yet they have adopted and adapted several ideas from the lean synchronisation philosophy and gained benefits. The exact interpretation of what 'lean' means in practice will differ (and 'lean' is something of a fashion in healthcare) but it still has the potential to improve their service delivery. That is because, notwithstanding the differ-ences between the two operations, the basic principles of lean synchronisation remain the same, namely aiming to achieve perfect synchronisation through smooth and even flow. But, lean synchronisation is an *aim*. It is not something that can simply be implemented overnight. Both these organisations have worked hard at overcoming the barriers to lean synchronisa-tion. These can be summarised as: the elimination of all waste; the involvement of everyone in the business; the adoption of a continuous improvement philosophy. The focus on eliminat-ing waste uses four important methods: streamlining flow; making sure that supply matches demand exactly; increasing process flexibility; reducing the effects of variability. And, although rooted in manufacturing, the techniques of lean or just-in-time philosophies are now being extended to service operations.

Before further discussion, it is important to be clear on the distinction between the *aim* (lean synchronisation), the *approach to overcoming the barriers* to achieving lean synchronisa-tion, the *methods of eliminating waste*, and the various *techniques* that can be used to help eliminate waste. The relationship between these elements is shown in Figure 11.4.

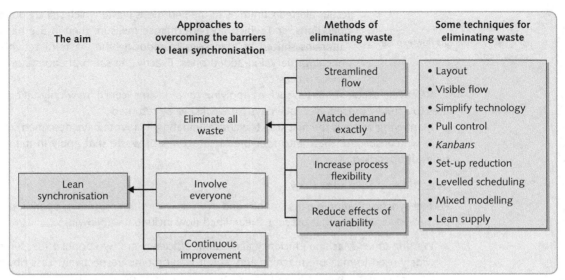

Figure 11.4 **Schematic of the issues covered in this chapter**

What are the barriers to lean synchronisation?

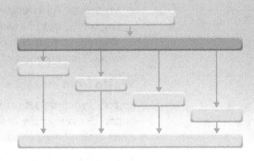

Video

The aim of pure lean synchronisation represents an ideal of smooth, uninterrupted flow without delay, waste or imperfection of any kind. The supply and demand between stages in each process, between processes in each operation, and between operations in each supply network, are all perfectly synchronised. It represents the ultimate in what customers are looking from an operation. But first one must identify the barriers to achieving this idea state. We group these under three headings:

- a failure to eliminate waste in all parts of the operation
- a failure to harness the contribution of all the people within the operation
- a failure to establish improvement as a continuous activity.

The waste elimination barrier

Practice note

Arguably the most significant part of the lean philosophy is its focus on the elimination of all forms of waste. Waste can be defined as any activity that does not add value. For example, a study by Cummins Worldwide Fortune 500, the engine company, showed that, at best, an engine was only being worked on for 15 per cent of the time it was in the factory.[3] At worst, this fell to 9 per cent, which meant that for 91 per cent of its time, the operation was adding cost to the engine, not adding value. Although already a relatively efficient manufacturer, the results alerted Cummins to the enormous waste which still lay dormant in its operations, and which no performance measure then in use had exposed. Cummins shifted its objectives to reducing the wasteful activities and to enriching the value-added ones. Exactly the same phenomenon applies in service processes.

Relatively simple requests, such as applying for a driving licence, may only take a few minutes to actually process, yet take days (or weeks) to be returned.

Identifying waste is the first step towards eliminating it. Toyota have described seven types. Here we consolidate these into four broad categories of waste that apply in many different types of operation.

Waste from irregular flow

Perfect synchronisation means smooth and even flow through processes, operations and supply networks. Barriers that prevent streamlined flow include the following:

- *Waiting time.* Machine efficiency and labour efficiency are two popular measures that are widely used to measure machine and labour waiting time, respectively. Less obvious is the time when items wait as inventory, there simply to keep operators busy.
- *Transport.* Moving items around the plant, together with double and triple handling, does not add value. Layout changes that bring processes closer together, improvements in transport methods and workplace organisation can all reduce waste.
- *Process inefficiencies.* The process itself may be a source of waste. Some operations may only exist because of poor component design, or poor maintenance, and so could be eliminated.
- *Inventory.* All inventory should become a target for elimination. However, it is only by tackling the causes of inventory, such as irregular flow, that it can be reduced.
- *Wasted motions.* An operator may look busy but sometimes no value is being added by the work. Simplification of work is a rich source of reduction in the waste of motion.

Waste from inexact supply

Perfect synchronisation supplies exactly what is wanted, exactly when it is needed. Any under- or over-supply and any early or late delivery will result in waste. Barriers to achieving an exact match between supply and demand include the following:

- *Over-production or under-production.* Supplying more than, or less than, is immediately needed by the next stage, process or operation. (This is the greatest source of waste according to Toyota).
- *Early or late delivery.* Items should only arrive exactly when they are needed. Early delivery is as wasteful as late delivery.
- *Inventory.* Again, all inventories should become a target for elimination. However, it is only by tackling the causes of inventory, such as inexact supply, that it can be reduced.

Waste from inflexible response

Customer needs can vary, in terms of what they want, how much they want, and when they want it. However, processes usually find it more convenient to change what they do relatively infrequently, because every change implies some kind of cost. That is why hospitals schedule specialist clinics only at particular times, and why machines often make a batch of similar products together. Yet responding to customer demands exactly and instantaneously requires a high degree of process flexibility. Symptoms of inadequate flexibility include the following:

- *Large batches.* Sending batch of items through a process inevitably increases inventory as the batch moves through the whole process.
- *Delays between activities.* The longer the time (and the cost) of changing over from one activity to another, the more difficult it is to synchronise flow to match customer demand instantaneously.

- *More variation in activity mix than in customer demand.* If the mix of activities in different time periods varies more than customer demand varies, then some 'batching' of activities must be taking place.

Waste from variability

Synchronisation implies exact levels of quality. If there is variability in quality levels then customers will not consider themselves as being adequately supplied. Variability therefore is an important barrier to achieving synchronised supply. Symptoms of poor variability include the following:

- *Poor reliability of equipment.* Unreliable equipment usually indicates a lack of conformance in quality levels. It also means that there will be irregularity in supplying customers. Either way, it prevents synchronisation of supply.
- *Defective products or services.* Waste caused by poor quality is significant in most operations. Service or product errors cause both customers and processes to waste time until they are corrected.

But capacity utilisation may be sacrificed in the short term

A paradox in the lean synchronisation concept is that adoption may mean some sacrifice of capacity utilisation. In organisations that place a high value on the utilisation of capacity this can prove particularly difficult to accept. But it is necessary. Return to the process shown in Figure 11.2. When stoppages occur in the traditional system, the buffers allow each stage to continue working and thus achieve high capacity utilisation. The high utilisation does not necessarily make the system as a whole produce more parts. Often the extra production goes into the large buffer inventories. In a synchronised lean process, any stoppage will affect the rest of the system, causing stoppages throughout the operation. This will necessarily lead to lower capacity utilisation, at least in the short term. However, there is no point in producing output just for its own sake. Unless the output is useful and enables the operation as a whole to produce saleable output, there is no point in producing it anyway. In fact, producing just to keep utilisation high is not only pointless, it is counter-productive, because the extra inventory produced merely serves to make improvements less likely. Figure 11.5 illustrates the two approaches to capacity utilisation.

> **OPERATIONS PRINCIPLE**
>
> *Focusing on lean synchronisation can initially reduce resource utilisation.*

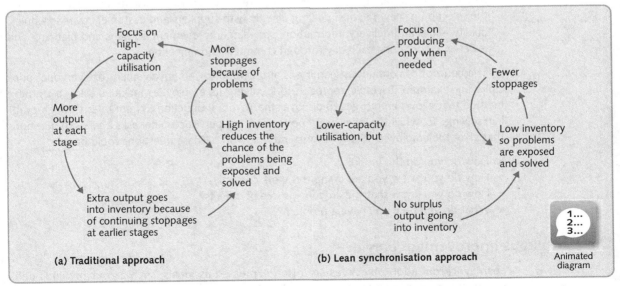

(a) Traditional approach

(b) Lean synchronisation approach

Animated diagram

Figure 11.5 **The different views of capacity utilisation in (a) traditional and (b) lean synchronisation approaches to planning and controlling flow**

The involvement barrier

An organisational culture that supports lean synchronisation must place a very significant emphasis on involving everyone in the organisation. This approach to people management (sometimes called the 'respect-for-people' system, after a rough translation from the Japanese) is seen by some as the most controversial aspect of the lean philosophy. It encourages (and often requires) team-based problem-solving, job enrichment, job rotation and multi-skilling. The intention is to encourage a high degree of personal responsibility, engagement and 'ownership' of the job. Some Japanese companies refer to the operationalising of the 'involvement of everyone' principle by adopting 'basic working practices'. They are held to be the basic preparation of the operation and its employees for implementing lean synchronisation. They include the following:

- **Discipline.** Work standards that are critical for the safety of staff, the environment and quality must be followed by everyone all the time.
- **Flexibility.** It should be possible to expand responsibilities to the extent of people's capabilities. This applies as much to managers as it does to shop-floor personnel. Barriers to flexibility, such as grading structures and restrictive practices, should be removed.
- **Equality.** Unfair and divisive personnel policies should be discarded. Many companies implement the egalitarian message through to company uniforms, consistent pay structures which do not differentiate between full-time staff and hourly-rated staff, and open-plan offices.
- **Autonomy.** Delegate responsibility to people involved in direct activities so that management's task becomes one of supporting processes. Delegation includes giving staff the responsibility for stopping processes in the event of problems, scheduling work, gathering performance monitoring data, and general problem solving.
- **Development of personnel.** Over time, the aim is to create more company members who can support the rigours of being competitive.
- **Quality of working life (QWL).** This may include, for example, involvement in decision-making, security of employment, enjoyment and working area facilities.
- **Creativity.** This is one of the indispensable elements of motivation. Creativity in this context means not just doing a job, but also improving how it is done, and building the improvement into the process.
- **Total people involvement.** Staff take on more responsibility to use their abilities to the benefit of the company as a whole. They are expected to participate in activities such as the selection of new recruits, dealing directly with suppliers and customers over schedules, quality issues and delivery information, spending improvement budgets and planning and reviewing work done each day through communication meetings.

The concept of continuous learning is also central to the 'involvement of everyone' principle. For example, Toyota's approach to involving its employees includes using a learning method that allows employees to discover the Toyota Production System rules through problem solving. So, while the job is being performed, a supervisor/trainer asks a series of questions that gives the employee deeper insights into the work[4]. These questions could be:

- How do you do this work?
- How do you know you are doing this work correctly?
- How do you know that the outcome is free of defects?
- What do you do if you have a problem?

The continuous improvement barrier

Lean synchronisation objectives are often expressed as ideals, such as our previous definition: 'to meet demand instantaneously with perfect quality and no waste'. While any operation's current performance may be far removed from such ideals, a fundamental lean belief is that it is possible to get closer to them over time. Without such beliefs to drive progress, lean proponents claim improvement is more likely to be transitory than continuous. This is why the concept of continuous improvement is such an important part of the lean philosophy. If its aims are set in terms of ideals which individual organisations may never fully achieve, then the emphasis must be on the way in which an organisation moves closer to the ideal state. The Japanese word that incorporates the idea of continuous improvement is *kaizen*. It is one of the main pillars of process improvement and is explained fully in Chapter 13.

Techniques to address the four sources of waste

Of the three barriers to achieving lean synchronisation (reduce waste, involve everyone and adopt continuous improvement), the last two are addressed further in Chapter 13. Therefore the rest of this chapter is devoted to what could be called the 'core' of lean synchronisation. These are a collection of 'just-in-time' tools and techniques that are the means of cutting out waste. Although many of these techniques are used to reduce waste generally within processes, operations, and supply networks, we will group the approaches to reducing waste under the four main headings: streamlining flow; matching demand exactly; increasing process flexibility; reducing the effects of variability.

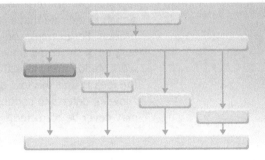

DIAGNOSTIC QUESTION

Is flow streamlined?

Video

The smooth flow of materials, information and people in the operation is a central idea of lean synchronisation. Long process routes provide opportunities for delay and inventory build-up, add no value, and slow down throughput time. So, the first contribution any operation can make to streamlining flow is to reconsider the basic layout of its processes. Primarily, reconfiguring the layout of a process to aid lean synchronisation involves moving it down the 'natural diagonal' of process design that was discussed in Chapter 4. Broadly speaking, this means moving from functional layouts towards cell-based layouts, or from cell-based layouts towards product layouts. Either way, it is necessary to move towards a layout that brings more systematisation and control to the process flow. At a more detailed level, typical layout techniques include: placing workstations close together so that inventory physically just cannot build up because there is no space for it to do so, and arranging workstations in such a way that all those who contribute to a common activity are in sight of each other and can provide mutual help, for example by facilitating movement between workstations to balance capacity.

OPERATIONS PRINCIPLE

Simple, transparent flow exposes sources of waste.

Examine the shape of process flow

The pattern that flow makes within or between processes is not a trivial issue. Processes that have adopted the practice of curving line arrangements into U-shaped or 'serpentine' arrangements can have a number of advantages (U shapes are usually used for shorter lines and serpentines for longer lines). One authority[5] sees the advantages of this type of flow patterns as *staffing flexibility and balance*, because the U shape enables one person to tend several jobs, *rework*, because it is easy to return faulty work to an earlier station, *free flow*, because long straight lines interfere with cross travel in the rest of the operation, and *teamwork*, because the shape encourages a team feeling.

Ensure visibility

Appropriate layout also includes the extent to which all movement is transparent to everyone within the process. High visibility of flow makes it easier to recognise potential improvements to flow. It also promotes quality within in a process because the more transparent the operation or process, the easier it is for all staff to share in its management and improvement. Problems are more easily detectable and information becomes simple, fast and visual. Visibility measures include the following:

- Clearly indicated process routes using signage.
- Performance measures clearly displayed in the workplace.
- Coloured lights used to indicate stoppages.
- An area is devoted to displaying samples of one's own and competitors' process outputs, together with samples of good and defective output.
- Visual control systems (e.g. *kanbans*, discussed later).

An important technique used to ensure flow visibility is the use of simple, but highly visual signals to indicate that a problem has occurred, together with operational authority to stop the process. For example, on an assembly line, if an employee detects some kind of quality problem, he or she could activate a signal that illuminates a light (called an 'andon' light) above the work station and stops the line. Although this may seem to reduce the efficiency of the line, the idea is that this loss of efficiency in the short term is less than the accumulated losses of allowing defects to continue on in the process. Unless problems are tackled immediately, they may never be corrected.

Use small-scale simple process technology

There may also be possibilities to encourage smooth streamlined flow through the use of small-scale technologies, that is, using several small units of process technology (for example, machines), rather than one large unit. Small machines have several advantages over large ones. First, they can process different products and services simultaneously. For example, in Figure 11.6 one large machine produces a batch of A, followed by a batch of B, and followed by a batch of C. However, if three smaller machines are used they can each produce A, B or C simultaneously. The system is also more robust. If one large machine breaks down, the whole system ceases to operate. If one of the three smaller machines breaks down, it is still operating at two-thirds effectiveness. Small machines are also easily moved, so that layout flexibility is enhanced, and the risks of making errors in investment decisions are reduced. However, investment in capacity may increase in total because parallel facilities are needed, so utilisation may be lower (see the earlier arguments).

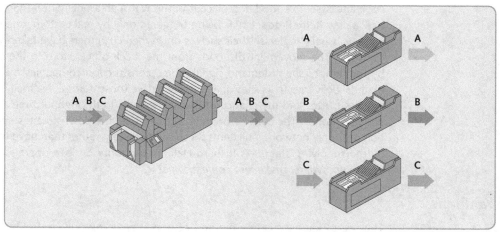

Figure 11.6 Using several small machines rather than one large one allows simultaneous processing, is more robust, and is more flexible

Does supply exactly match demand?

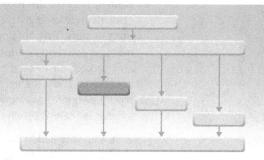

Video

The value of the supply of products or services is always time dependent. Something that is delivered early or late often has less value than something that is delivered exactly when it is needed. We can see many everyday examples of this. For example, parcel delivery companies charge more for guaranteed faster delivery. This is because our real need for the delivery is often for it to be as fast as possible. The closer to instantaneous delivery we can get the more value the delivery has for us and the more we are willing to pay for it. In fact delivery of information earlier than it is required can be even more harmful than late delivery because it results in information inventories that serve to confuse flow through the process. For example, an Australian tax office used to receive applications by mail, open the mail and send it through to the relevant department who, after processing it, sent it to the next department. This led to piles of unprocessed applications building up within its processes, causing problems in tracing applications, and losing them, sorting through and prioritising applications, and worst of all, long throughput times. Now they only open mail when the stages in front can process it. Each department requests more work only when they have processed previous work.

OPERATIONS PRINCIPLE

Delivering only and exactly what is needed and when it is needed, smoothes flow and exposes waste.

Pull control

The exact matching of supply and demand is often best served by using 'pull control' wherever possible (discussed in Chapter 10). At its simplest, consider how some fast-food restaurants cook and assemble food and place it in the warm area only when the customer-facing server has sold an item. Production is being triggered only by real customer demand. Similarly supermarkets usually replenish their shelves only when customers have taken sufficient products off the shelf. The movement of goods from the 'back office' store to the shelf is triggered only by the 'empty-shelf' demand signal. Some construction companies make it a rule to call for material deliveries to its sites only the day before those items are actually needed. This not only reduces clutter and the chance of theft, it speeds up throughput time and reduces confusion and inventories. The essence of pull control is to let the downstream stage in a process, operation or supply network, pull items through the system rather than have them 'pushed' to them by the supplying stage. As Richard Hall, an authority on lean operations put it, *'Don't send nothing nowhere, make 'em come and get it.'*[6]

Kanbans

Practice
note

The use of kanbans is one method of operationalising pull control. *Kanban* is the Japanese for card or signal. It is sometimes called the 'invisible conveyor' that controls the transfer of items between the stages of an operation. In its simplest form, it is a card used by a customer stage to instruct its supplier stage to send more items. Kanbans can also take other forms. In some Japanese companies, they are solid plastic markers or even coloured ping-pong balls. Whichever kind of kanban is being used, the principle is always the same; the receipt of a kanban triggers the movement, production or supply of one unit or a standard container of units. If two kanbans are received, this triggers the movement, production or supply of two units or standard containers of units, and so on. Kanbans are the only means by which movement, production or supply can be authorised. Some companies use 'kanban squares'. These are marked spaces on the shop floor or bench that are drawn to fit one or more work pieces or containers. Only the existence of an empty square triggers production at the stage that supplies the square. As one would expect, at Toyota the key control tool is its kanban system. The kanban is seen as serving three purposes:

- It is an instruction for the preceding process to send more.
- It is a visual control tool to show up areas of over-production and lack of synchronisation.
- It is a tool for *kaizen* ('continuous improvement'). Toyota's rules state that 'the number of kanbans should be reduced over time'.

DIAGNOSTIC QUESTION

Are processes flexible?

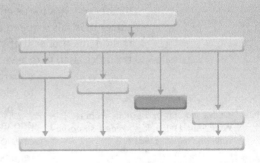

Video

Responding exactly and instantaneously to customer demand implies that operations resources need to be sufficiently flexible to change both what they do and how much they do of it without incurring high cost or long delays. In fact, flexible processes (often with flexible technologies) can significantly enhance smooth and synchronised flow. For example, new publishing technologies allow professors to assemble printed and e-learning course material customised to the needs of individual courses or even individual students. In this case flexibility is allowing customised, small batches to be delivered 'to order'. In another example, a firm of lawyers used to take ten days to prepare its bills for customers. This meant that customers were not asked to pay until ten days after the work had been done. Now they use a system that, everyday, updates each customer's account. So, when a bill is sent it includes all work up to the day before the billing date. The principle here is that process inflexibility also delays cash flow.

Reduce setup times

For many technologies, increasing process flexibility means reducing set-up times, defined as the time taken to change over the process from one activity to the next. Compare the time it takes you to change the tyre on your car with the time taken by a Formula 1 team. Set-up reduction can be achieved by a variety of methods such as cutting out time taken to search for tools and equipment, the pre-preparation of tasks which delay changeovers, and the constant practice of set-up routines. Set-up time reduction is also called single minute exchange of dies, (SMED), because this was the objective in some manufacturing operations. The other common approach to set-up time reduction is to convert work which was previously performed while the machine was stopped (called *internal* work) to work that is performed while the machine is running (called *external* work). There are three major methods of achieving the transfer of internal setup work to external work:[7]

- Pre-prepare equipment instead of having to do it while the process is stopped. Preferably, all adjustment should be carried out externally.
- Make equipment capable of performing all required tasks so that changeovers become a simple adjustment.
- Facilitate the change of equipment, for example by using simple devices such as roller conveyors.

Fast changeovers are particularly important for airlines because they can't make money from aircraft that are sitting idle on the ground. It is called 'running the aircraft hot' in the industry. For many smaller airlines, the biggest barrier to running hot is that their markets are not large enough to justify passenger flights during the day *and* night. So, in order to avoid aircraft being idle over night, they must be used in some other way. That was the motive behind Boeing's 737 'Quick Change' (QC) aircraft. With it, airlines have the flexibility to use it for passenger flights during the day and, with less than a one-hour changeover (set-up) time, use it as a cargo airplane throughout the night. Boeing engineers designed frames that hold entire rows of seats that could smoothly glide on and off the aircraft allowing 12 seats to be rolled into place at once. When used for cargo, the seats are simply rolled out and replaced by special cargo containers designed to fit the curve of the fuselage and prevent damage to the interior. Before reinstalling the seats the sidewalls are thoroughly cleaned so that, once the seats are in place, passengers cannot tell the difference between a QC aircraft and a normal 737. Airlines, like Aloha Airlines that serves Hawaii, particularly value the aircraft's flexibility. It allows them to provide frequent reliable services in both passenger and cargo markets. So the aircraft that has been carrying passengers around the islands during the day can be used to ship fresh supplies over night to the hotels that underpin the tourist industry.

Is variability minimised?

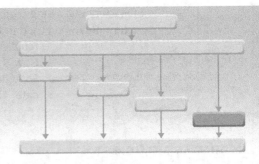

Video

One of the biggest causes of the variability that will disrupt flow and prevent lean synchronisation is variation in the quality of items. This is why a discussion of lean synchronisation should always include an evaluation of how quality conformance is ensured within processes. In particular, the principles of statistical process control (SPC) can be used to understand quality variability. Chapter 12 and its supplement on SPC examine this subject, so in this section we shall focus on other causes of variability. The first of these is variability in the mix of products and services moving through processes, operations or supply networks.

Level schedules as much as possible

Levelled scheduling (or *heijunka*) means keeping the mix and volume of flow between stages even over time. For example, instead of producing 500 parts in one batch, that would cover the needs for the next three months; levelled scheduling would require the process to make only one piece per hour regularly. Thus, the principle of levelled scheduling is very straightforward – however, the requirements to put it into practice are quite severe, although the benefits resulting from it can be substantial. The move from conventional to levelled scheduling is illustrated in Figure 11.7. Conventionally, if a mix of products were required in a time period (usually a month), a batch size would be calculated for each product and the batches produced in some sequence. Figure 11.7(a) shows three products that are produced in a 20-day time period in a production unit.

$$\text{Quantity of product A required} = 3000$$
$$\text{Quantity of product B required} = 1000$$
$$\text{Quantity of product C required} = 1000$$
$$\text{Batch size of product A} = 600$$
$$\text{Batch size of product B} = 200$$
$$\text{Batch size of product C} = 200$$

Starting at day 1, the unit commences producing product A. During day 3, the batch of 600 As is finished and dispatched to the next stage. The batch of Bs is started but is not finished until day 4. The remainder of day 4 is spent making the batch of Cs and both batches are dispatched at the end of that day. The cycle then repeats itself. The consequence of using large batches is, first, that relatively large amounts of inventory accumulate within and between the units, and second, that most days are different from one another in terms of what they are expected to produce (in more complex circumstances, no two days would be the same).

Now suppose that the flexibility of the unit could be increased to the point where the batch sizes for the products were reduced to a quarter of their previous levels without loss of capacity (see Figure 11.7b):

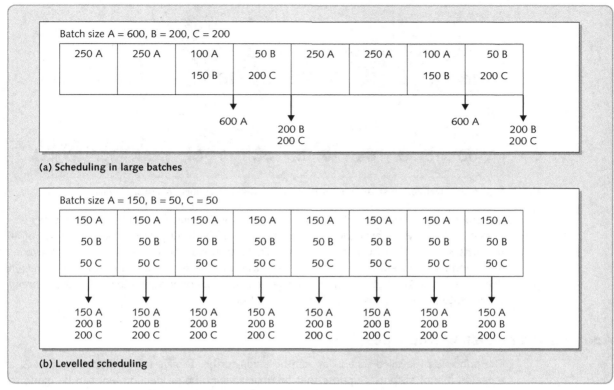

Figure 11.7   Levelled scheduling equalises the mix of products made each day

Batch size of product A = 150
Batch size of product B = 50
Batch size of product C = 50

A batch of each product can now be completed in a single day, at the end of which the three batches are dispatched to their next stage. Smaller batches of inventory are moving between each stage, which will reduce the overall level of work-in-progress in the operation. Just as significant, however, is the effect on the regularity and rhythm of production at the unit. Now every day in the month is the same in terms of what needs to be produced. This makes planning and control of each stage in the operation much easier. For example, if on day 1 of the month the daily batch of As was finished by 11.00 am, and all the batches were successfully completed in the day, then the following day the unit will know that, if it again completes all the As by 11.00 am, it is on schedule. When every day is different, the simple question, 'Are we on schedule to complete our production today?' requires some investigation before it can be answered. However, when every day is the same, everyone in the unit can tell whether production is on target by looking at the clock. Control becomes visible and transparent to all, and the advantages of regular, daily schedules can be passed to upstream suppliers.

Level delivery schedules

A similar concept to levelled scheduling can be applied to many transportation processes. For example, a chain of convenience stores may need to make deliveries of all the different types of products it sells every week. Traditionally it may have dispatched a truck loaded with one particular product around all its stores so that each store received the appropriate amount of

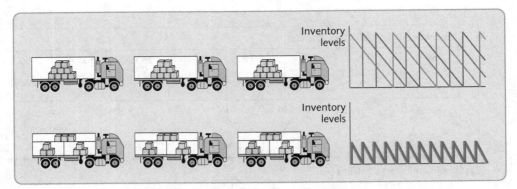

Figure 11.8 Delivering smaller quantities more often can reduce inventory levels

the product that would last them for one week. This is equivalent to the large batches discussed in the previous example. An alternative would be to dispatch smaller quantities of all products in a single truck more frequently. Then, each store would receive smaller deliveries more frequently, inventory levels would be lower and the system could respond to trends in demand more readily because more deliveries means more opportunity to change the quantity delivered to a store. This is illustrated in Figure 11.8.

Adopt mixed modelling where possible

The principle of levelled scheduling can be taken further to give mixed modelling, that is, a repeated mix of outputs. Suppose that the machines in the production unit can be made so flexible that they achieve the JIT ideal of a batch size of one. The sequence of individual products emerging from the unit could be reduced progressively as illustrated in Figure 11.9. This would produce a steady stream of each product flowing continuously from the unit. However, the sequence of products does not always fall as conveniently as in Figure 11.9. The unit production times for each product are not usually identical and the ratios of required volumes are less convenient. For example, if a process is required to produce products A, B and C in the ratio 8:5:4. It could produce 800 of A, followed by 500 of B, followed by 400 of A; or 80A, 50B, and 40C. But ideally, to sequence the products as smoothly as possible, it would produce in the order . . . BACABACABACABACAB . . . repeated . . . repeated . . . etc. Doing this achieves relatively smooth flow (but does rely on significant process flexibility).

Low	Degree of levelling	High
High	Setup times	Low
Low	System flexibility	High

Large batches, e.g.	Small batches, e.g.	Mixed modelling, e.g.
200 A 120 B 80 C	5 A 3 B 2 C	A A B A B C A B C A

Figure 11.9 Levelled scheduling and mixed modelling: mixed modelling becomes possible as the batch size approaches one

Adopt total productive maintenance (TPM)

Total productive maintenance aims to eliminate the variability in operations processes caused by the effect of breakdowns. This is achieved by involving everyone in the search for maintenance improvements. Process owners are encouraged to assume ownership of their machines and to undertake routine maintenance and simple repair tasks. By so doing, maintenance specialists can then be freed to develop higher-order skills for improved maintenance systems. TPM is treated in more detail in Chapter 14.

DIAGNOSTIC QUESTION

Is lean synchronisation applied throughout the supply network?

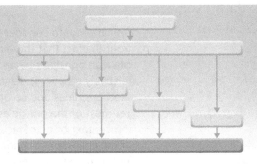

Video

Although most of the concepts and techniques discussed in this chapter are devoted to the management of stages *within* processes and processes *within* an operation, the same principles can apply to the whole supply chain. In this context, the stages in a process are the whole businesses, operations or processes between which products flow. And as any business starts to approach lean synchronisation it will eventually come up against the constraints imposed by the lack of lean synchronisation of the other operations in its supply chain. So, achieving further gains must involve trying to spread lean synchronisation practice outward to its partners in the chain. Ensuring lean synchronisation throughout an entire supply network is clearly a far more demanding task than doing the same within a single process. It is a complex task. And it becomes more complex as more of the supply chain embraces the lean philosophy. The nature of the interaction between whole operations is far more complex than between individual stages within a process. A far more complex mix of products and services is likely to be being provided and the whole network is likely to be subject to a less predictable set of potentially disruptive events. Making a supply chain adopt lean synchronisation means more than making each operation in the chain lean. A collection of localised lean operations rarely leads to an overall lean chain. Rather one needs to apply the lean synchronisation philosophy to the supply chain as a whole. Yet the advantages from truly lean chains can be significant.

> **OPERATIONS PRINCIPLE**
>
> *The advantages of lean synchronisation apply at the level of the process, the operation and the supply network.*

Essentially the principles of lean synchronisation are the same for a supply chain as they are for a process. Fast throughput throughout the whole supply network is still valuable and will save cost throughout the supply network. Lower levels of inventory will still make it easier to achieve lean synchronisation. Waste is just as evident (and even larger) at the level of the supply network and reducing waste is still a worthwhile task. Streamline flow, exact matching of supply and demand, enhanced flexibility, and minimising variability are all still tasks that will benefit the whole network. The principles of pull control can work between whole operations in the same way as they can between stages within a single process. In fact, the principles and the techniques of lean synchronisation are essentially the same no matter what level of analysis is being used. And because lean synchronisation is being implemented on a larger scale, the benefits will also be proportionally greater.

One of the weaknesses of lean synchronisation principles is that they are difficult to achieve when conditions are subject to unexpected disturbance (see the Critical Commentary at the end of this chapter). This is especially a problem with applying lean synchronisation principles in the context of the whole supply network. Whereas unexpected fluctuations and disturbances do occur within operations, local management has a reasonable degree of control that it can exert in order to reduce them. Outside the operation, within the supply network, fluctuations can also be controlled to some extent (see Chapter 7), but it is far more difficult to do so. Nevertheless, it is generally held that, although the task is more difficult and although it may take longer to achieve, the aim of lean synchronisation is just as valuable for the supply network as a whole as it is for an individual operation.

Lean service

Any attempt to consider how lean ideas apply throughout a whole supply chain must also confront the fact that these chains include service operations, often dealing in intangibles. So how can lean principles be applied in these parts of the chain? The idea of lean factory operations is relatively easy to understand. Waste is evident in over-stocked inventories, excess scrap, badly sited machines and so on. In services it is less obvious; inefficiencies are more difficult to see. Yet most of the principles and techniques of lean synchronisation, although often described in the context of manufacturing operations, are also applicable to service settings. In fact, some of the philosophical underpinning to lean synchronisation can also be seen as having its equivalent in the service sector. Take, for example, the role of inventory. The comparison between manufacturing systems that hold large stocks of inventory between stages and those that do not centres on the effect which inventory has on improvement and problem-solving. Exactly the same argument can be applied when, instead of queues of material (inventory), an operation has to deal with queues of information, or even customers.

With its customer focus, standardisation, continuous quality improvement, smooth flow, and efficiency, lean thinking has direct application in all operations, manufacturing or service. Bradley Staats and David Upton of Harvard Business School have studied how lean ideas can be applied in service operations[8]. They make three main points:

- In terms of operations and improvements, the service industries in general are a long way behind manufacturing.
- Not all lean manufacturing ideas translate from factory floor to office cubicle. For example, tools such as those that empower manufacturing workers to 'stop the line' when they encounter a problem is not directly replicable when there is no line to stop.
- Adopting lean operations principles alters the way a company learns through changes in problem-solving, coordination through connections, and pathways and standardisation.

Examples of lean service

Many of the examples of lean philosophy and lean techniques in service industries are directly analogous to those found in manufacturing industries because physical items are being moved or processed in some way. Consider the following examples:

- Supermarkets usually replenish their shelves only when customers have taken sufficient products off the shelf. The movement of goods from the 'back office' store to the shelf is triggered only by the 'empty-shelf' demand signal. *Principle – pull control*.
- An Australian tax office used to receive applications by mail, open the mail and send it through to the relevant department who, after processing it, sent it to the next department. Now they only open mail when the stages in front can process it. Each department requests

more work only when they have processed previous work. *Principle – don't let inventories build up, use pull control.*

- One construction company makes a rule of only calling for material deliveries to its sites the day before materials are needed. This reduces clutter and the chance of theft. *Principle – pull control reduces confusion.*
- Many fast-food restaurants cook and assemble food and place it in the warm area only when the customer-facing server has sold an item. *Principle – pull control reduces throughput time.*

Other examples of lean concepts and methods apply even when most of the service elements are intangible.

- Some websites allow customers to register for a reminder service that automatically e-mails reminders for action to be taken. For example, the day before a partner's birthday, in time to prepare for a meeting, etc. *Principle – the value of delivered information, like delivered items, can be time dependent. Too early and it deteriorates (you forget it), too late and it's useless (because it's too late).*
- A firm of lawyers used to take ten days to prepare its bills for customers. This meant that customers were not asked to pay until ten days after the work had been done. Now they use a system that, everyday, updates each customer's account. So, when a bill is sent it includes all work up to the day before the billing date. *Principle – process delays also delay cash flow, fast throughput improves cash flow.*
- New publishing technologies allow professors to assemble printed and e-learning course material customised to the needs of individual courses or even individual students. *Principle – flexibility allows customisation and small batch sizes delivered 'to order'.*

EXAMPLE   Pixar adopts lean[9]

It seems that lean principles (or some lean principles) can be applied even to the most unlikely of processes. None less likely than Pixar Animation Studios, the Academy Award-winning computer animation studio and makers of feature films that have resulted in an unprecedented streak of both critical and box office success including *Toy Story* (1, 2 and 3), *A Bug's*

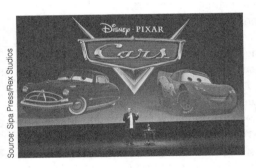

Source: Sipa Press/Rex Studios

Life, Monsters, Inc., Finding Nemo, The Incredibles, Ratatouille, WALL-E and *Up*. Since its incorporation, Pixar has been responsible for many important breakthroughs in the application of computer graphics (CG) for filmmaking. So, the company has attracted some of the world's finest technical, creative and production talent in the area. And such 'knowledge-based' talent is notoriously difficult to manage – certainly not the type of processes that are generally seen as being appropriate for lean synchronisation. Managing creativity involves a difficult trade-off, between encouraging the freedom to produce novel ideas, yet making sure that they work within an effective overall structure.

Nevertheless, Pixar did get the inspiration from Toyota and the way it uses lean production. In particular the way Toyota has encouraged continuous advice and criticism from its production line workers to improve its performance. Pixar realised that it could do the same with producing cartoon characters. Adopting constant feedback surfaces problems before they become crises, and provides creative teams with inspiration and challenge. Pixar also devotes a great deal of effort to persuading its creative staff to work together. In similar companies, people may collaborate on specific projects, but are less good at focusing on what's going on elsewhere in the business. Pixar, however, tries to cultivate a sense of collective responsibility. Staff even show unfinished work to one another in daily meetings, so get used to giving and receiving constructive criticism.

Lean supply chains are like an air traffic control systems[10]

The concept of the lean supply chain has been likened to an air traffic control system, in that it attempts to provide continuous 'real-time visibility and control' to all elements in the chain. This is the secret of how the world's busiest airports handle thousands of departures and arrivals daily. All aircraft are given an identification number that shows up on a radar map. Aircraft approaching an airport are detected by the radar and contacted using radio. The control tower precisely positions the aircraft in an approach pattern which it coordinates. The radar detects any small adjustments that are necessary, which are communicated to the aircraft. This real-time visibility and control can optimise airport throughput while maintaining extremely high safety and reliability.

Contrast this to how most supply chains are coordinated. Information is captured only periodically, probably once a day, and any adjustments to logistics, output levels at the various operations in the supply chain are adjusted, and plans rearranged. But imagine what would happen if this was how the airport operated, with only a 'radar snapshot' once a day. Coordinating aircraft with sufficient tolerance to arrange take-offs and landings every two minutes would be out of the question. Aircraft would be jeopardised, or alternatively, if aircraft were spaced further apart to maintain safety, throughput would be drastically reduced. Yet this is how most supply chains have traditionally operated. They use a daily 'snapshot' from their ERP systems (see Chapter 10 for an explanation of ERP). This limited visibility means operations must either space their work out to avoid 'collisions' (i.e. missed customer orders) thereby reducing output, or they must 'fly blind' thereby jeopardising reliability.

Lean and agile

One continuing debate on how lean principles can be applied across the supply chain concerns whether supply network should be lean or 'agile'. Professor Martin Christopher of Cranfield University defines agility as *'rapid strategic and operational adaptation to large scale, unpredictable changes in the business environment. Agility implies responsiveness from one end of the supply chain to the other. It focuses upon eliminating the barriers to quick response, be they organizational or technical.'* Other definitions stress that agility is the capability of operating profitably in a competitive environment of continually changing customer opportunities. The clue lies in how the word 'agile' is often defined; it implies being responsive, quick moving, flexible, nimble, active and constantly ready to change. But some proponents of operational agility go further than this. They see agility as also implying a rejection of a planning paradigm that makes any assumption of a predictable future. Like lean, it is more of a philosophy than an approach. Agile encourages a better match to what customers want by placing an emphasis on producing 'emergent' demand as opposed to rigid plans or schedules. Furthermore, rather than uncertainty and change being seen as things to be 'coped with' or preferably avoided, it should be embraced so that agility becomes changing faster than one's customer. Even less ambitious approaches to agility see it as more than simply organisational flexibility. It involves an organisational mastery of uncertainty and change, where people within the organisation, and their capacity to learn from change and their collective knowledge, are regarded as the organisation's greatest assets because they allow the operation to respond effectively to uncertainty and change. Continually inventing innovative business processes solutions to new market demands becomes a key operations objective.

All this seems very different to the underlying assumptions of the lean philosophy. Again, look at the word: lean means 'thin, having no superfluous fat, skinny, gaunt, undernourished'. Lean attempts to eliminate waste and provide value to the customer throughout the entire supply chain. It thrives on standardisation, stability, defined processes and repeatability – not at all the way agility has been described. Lean is also a well defined (although frequently misunderstood) concept. Agility, on the other hand, is a far newer and less 'operationalised' set of relatively strategic objectives. But some operational level distinctions can be inferred.

The type of principles needed to support a lean philosophy include such things as: simple processes; waste elimination; simple (if any) IT; the use of manual and robust planning and control as well as pull control and kanbans with overall MRP. Agile philosophies, by contrast, require: effective demand management to keep close to market needs; a focus on customer relationship management; responsive supply coordination, visibility across the extended supply chain; continuous rescheduling and quick response to changing demand; short planning cycles; integrated knowledge management; fully exploited e-commerce solutions.

So are lean and agile philosophies fundamentally opposed? Well, yes and no. Certainly they have differing emphases. Saying that lean equals synchronised, regular flow and low inventory, and agile equals responsiveness, flexibility and fast delivery, may be something of a simplification, but it more or less captures the distinction between the two. But because they have different objectives and approaches does not mean that they cannot co-exist. Nor does it mean that there is a 'lean versus agile' argument to be resolved. The two approaches may not be complimentary, as some consultants claim, but both do belong to the general collection of methodologies that are available to help companies meet the requirements of their markets. In the same way as it was wrong to think that JIT would replace MRP, so 'agile' is not a substitute for lean[11].

However, agile and lean are each more appropriate for differing market and product/service conditions. Put simply, if product/service variety or complexity is high, and demand predictability low then you have the conditions in which agile principles keep an operation ready to cope with instability in the business environment. Conversely, if product/service variety is low, and demand predictability high, then a lean approach can exploit the stable environment to achieve cost efficiency and dependability. So the two factors of product/service variety or complexity and demand uncertainty influence whether agile or lean principles should dominate. But what of the conditions where complexity and uncertainty are not related in this manner? Figure 11.10 illustrates how complexity and uncertainty affect the adoption of lean, agile, and other approaches to organising the flow in a supply chain.

- When complexity is low, and demand uncertainty is also low (operations that produce commodities), lean planning and control is appropriate.
- When is complexity is low, and demand uncertainty is high (operations that produce fashion-based products/services), agile planning and control is appropriate.
- When complexity is high, and demand uncertainty is also high (operations that produce 'super value' products/services) project or requirements planning and control (for example MRPII, see Chapter 10) is appropriate.
- When product/service complexity is high, and demand uncertainty is low (operations that produce 'consumer durable type products/services), a combination of agile and lean planning and control is appropriate.

This last category, shown as the bottom left quadrant in Figure 11.10 has been rather clumsily called 'leagile'. Leagile is based on the idea that both lean and agile practices can be employed within supply chains. It envisages an inventory decoupling point that is the separation between the responsive (and therefore agile) 'front end' of the supply chain that reacts fast and flexibly to customer demand, and the efficient (and therefore lean). This is not a new idea and in product-based supply chains involves 'making to *forecast*' before the decoupling point and 'making (or assembling, adapting or finishing) to *order*' after it. The idea has many similarities with the idea of 'mass customisation'. However, it is difficult to transpose the idea directly into supply chains that deal exclusively in non-tangible services.

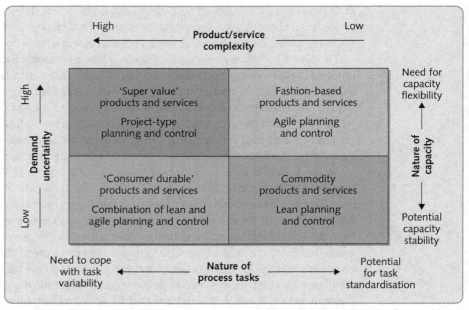

Figure 11.10 The degree of complexity of products/services and the uncertainty of demand influence the relative emphasis of lean or agile supply-chain principles

Critical commentary

Each chapter contains a short critical commentary on the main ideas covered in the chapter. Its purpose is not to undermine the issues discussed in the chapter, but to emphasise that, although we present a relatively orthodox view of operation, there are other perspectives.

● Lean synchronisation principles can be taken to an extreme. When just-in-time ideas first started to have an impact on operations practice in the West, some authorities advocated the reduction of between-process inventories to zero. While in the long term this provides the ultimate in motivation for operations managers to ensure the efficiency and reliability of each process stage, it does not admit the possibility of some processes always being intrinsically less than totally reliable. An alternative view is to allow inventories (albeit small ones) around process stages with higher than average uncertainty. This at least allows some protection for the rest of the system. The same ideas apply to just-in-time delivery between factories. The Toyota Motor Corp., often seen as the epitome of modern JIT, has suffered from its low inter-plant inventory policies. Both the Kobe earthquake and fires in supplier plants have caused production at Toyota's main factories to close down for several days because of a shortage of key parts. Even in the best-regulated manufacturing networks, one cannot always account for such events.

● One of the most counter-intuitive issues in lean synchronisation is the way it appears to downplay the idea of capacity under-utilisation. And it is true that, when moving towards lean synchronisation, fast throughput time and smooth flow *is* more important than the high utilisation which can result in inventory build-up. However, this criticism is not really valid in the long term. Consider the relationship between capacity utilisation and process throughput time (or inventory), shown in Figure 11.11. The improvement path envisaged by adopting lean synchronisation is shown as moving from the state that most businesses find themselves in (high utilisation but long throughput times) towards the lean synchronisation ideal (short throughput times). Although, inevitably, this means moving towards a position of lower capacity utilisation, lean synchronisation also stresses a reduction in all types of process variability. As this begins to become reality, the improvement path moves towards the point where throughput time is short and capacity utilisation high. It manages to do this because of the reduction in process variability.

● Not all commentators see lean synchronisation-influenced people-management practices as entirely positive. The JIT approach to people management can be viewed as patronising. It may be, to some extent, less autocratic than some Japanese management practice dating from earlier times. However, it is certainly not in line with some of the job design philosophies which place a high emphasis on contribution and commitment. Even in Japan, the JIT approach is not without its critics. Kamata wrote an autobiographical description of life as an employee at a Toyota plant called *Japan in the Passing Lane*.[12] His account speaks of 'the inhumanity and the unquestioning adherence' of working under such a system. Similar criticisms have been voiced by some trade union representatives.

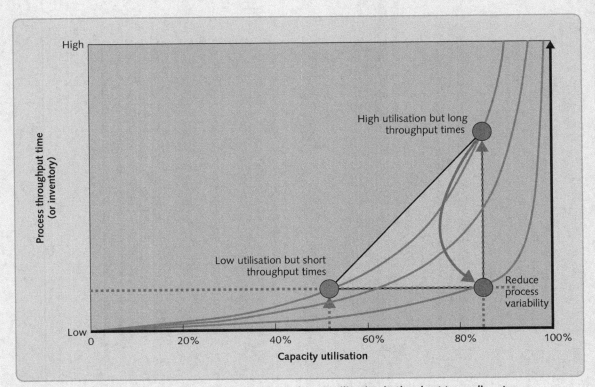

Figure 11.11 Developing processes can mean accepting lower utilisation in the short to medium term

Any textbook of this type has to segment the ideas and knowledge contained within its subject so as to treat them in such a way as to explain it, to communicate each set of ideas as clearly as possible. Yet doing this inevitably means imposing artificial boundaries between the various topics. No more so than in the case of lean synchronisation. There are some particularly evangelical proponents of the lean philosophy who object strongly to separating out the whole concept of lean into a separate chapter. The underlying ideas of lean, they say, have now comprehensively replaced those ideas described as 'traditional' at the beginning of this chapter. Rather, lean principles should be foundation for the whole of operations and process management. Lean principles have something to tell us about everything in the subject from quality management to inventory management, from job design to product design. And they are right of course. Nevertheless, the ideas behind lean synchronisation are both counter-intuitive and important enough to warrant separate treatment. Also lean in its pure form is not necessarily equally applicable to every situation (refer to the discussion about lean and agile). Hence the inclusion of this chapter that focuses on this topic. Remember though, lean synchronisation is one of those topics (like operations strategy, quality and improvement) that has a particularly strong influence over the whole subject.

SUMMARY CHECKLIST

This checklist comprises questions that can be usefully applied to any type of operations and reflect the major diagnostic questions used within the chapter.

☐ Are the benefits of attempting to achieve lean synchronisation well understood within the business?

☐ Notwithstanding that the idea derives from manufacturing operations, have the principles been considered for non-manufacturing processes within the business?

☐ Is the extent of waste within operations and processes fully understood?

☐ Can the flow of items through processes be made more regular?

☐ How much inventory of items is building up because of inexact supply?

☐ How much waste is caused because of inflexibility in the operation's processes?

☐ How much waste is caused because of variability (especially of quality) within the operation's processes?

☐ Are capacity utilisation performance measures likely to prove a barrier to achieving lean synchronisation?

☐ Does the culture of the organisation encourage the involvement in the improvement process of all people in the organisation?

☐ Are the ideas of continuous improvement understood?

☐ Are the ideas of continuous improvement used in practice?

☐ Are the various techniques used to promote lean synchronisation understood and practised?

☐ Is the concept of lean synchronisation applied throughout the supply network?

☐ Has the possibility of blending push (such as MRP) and pull (such as lean synchronisation) been considered?

Implementing lean at CWHT

by Nicola Burgess, Warwick University

In July 2011, the acting Chief Executive of Chaswick and Wallasey NHS Hospital Trust (CWHT) took the decision to implement lean thinking across the organisation. The idea was to bring the hospital into line with other hospitals in the UK where lean improvement initiatives were becoming increasingly widespread. In fact, the trust had started to experiment with lean principles two years earlier. The external consultants used for this initial work were not asked to bid for the new initiative. Despite their global reputation for world-class engineering it was felt that the previous lean work had been disjointed, fragmented and too focused on the need to optimise departments around targets. This time the trust wanted a much more coherent and joined up approach to lean implementation. This time they were thinking about 'transformation' into becoming a total *lean organisation*. All the consultants who were bidding for the contract emphasised building 'soft skills' training and 'project facilitation' that would equip the organisation with an internal change team capable of rolling out lean throughout the hospital. The internal change team was led by a 'Head of Lean' and several Lean Leaders, many of whom joined the team as part of a secondment from their clinical roles. The 'Lean team' comprised 11 staff employed on two-year contracts.

During the period September–December 2011, preparations for implementing lean throughout the trust took place led by the external consultants who had won the contract: 'Change M'. Eighteen projects were designed to take place across three streams of work to reflect a number of patient pathways throughout the organisation. The aim was to move staff out of their functional 'silos' and to help them see their role within the whole patient pathway rather than within a single function. Meanwhile, the lean facilitators underwent training in project facilitation and change management skills. The project roll-out was set to begin January 2012.

A new Chief Executive

In October 2011 a new Chief Executive Sir William Oberon was appointed to begin work in January. He had an impressive record, with Chief Executive roles at a number of hospitals, including a world-leading heart specialist hospital, and had overseen successful turnarounds in two of the worst performing hospitals in England. Following his appointment, Sir William immediately instructed

Source: Alex Segre/Alamy Images

consultants TOC-Health (with whom he had worked in the past) to enter CWHT in December 2011 and begin work straight away in the Accident and Emergency (A&E) department. A new Director of Operations also began in post in December 2011. This made the assignment difficult for TOC-Health. Adam Smith, Client Director of TOC-Health explained: *'It was a funny situation really. We arrived in the Trust before William had taken up his appointment and before the new Director of Operations. We had to introduce ourselves to the Lean Team. It was rather embarrassing and awkward, but William had said: "I want it done very quickly Adam". It's not usually the way we work.'*

TOC-Health had been employed with very clear responsibility to sort out problems in A&E. The Lean Team had been asked to steer clear of the work. At the time UK healthcare targets specified that 98 per cent of patients must be seen within four hours of arrival and so CWHT had implemented a new Clinical Decision Unit (CDU) to help expedite people out of A&E so as not to breach the target. Unfortunately, at the end of 2011, the Trust was still operating at around 95 per cent which meant that the trust would not obtain a good performance rating. In addition, the trust had a large number of patient outliers (patients in the wrong beds, on the wrong wards) and some financial overruns. In addition they were also struggling on other important targets. Speaking about Sir William's decision to take on the Chief Executive role, the Director of TOC-Health quoted Sir William's words: *'CWHT has this fantastic new building, it's just ridiculous it's not meeting it targets. The hospital is punching well below its weight – the size of the prize is huge!'*

Approaches to improvement

Talking about the approach of TOC-Health, their Director explained: *'The whole point about our approach is fast, focused breakthroughs in performance. You must identify the one true bottleneck and focus on fixing that. In our opinion, if you improve process by process you are chasing your tail, you're just never going to get there; it will take you so long that by the time you've improved, it will have changed anyway.'* It soon became clear that the two consultancy firms had very different approaches to the number of improvement projects that should run concurrently. TOC-Health was focused around the idea that an organisation should not have many disparate projects on the go simultaneously, rather they should focus on just one (the bottleneck). Change M, on the other hand were happy to let many projects take place in various parts of the organisation using what they called the Rapid Improvement Event (RIE) approach.

Meanwhile, although the Head of Lean had begun her projects on schedule, the instruction to keep away from A&E where TOC-Health was working meant her planned activities had to be rescheduled. Nor was she happy with the changes in responsibilities. *'I think we had a reasonably clear understanding of how lean would be implemented until we had a change of Chief Executive. I now feel we don't have a clear way forward to becoming a lean organisation. The emphasis has shifted to get some events done and get some money out; that isn't what lean is about.'* Similar concerns had been expressed about how to measure the success and benefits of the Lean Team. *'Again the emphasis has shifted. Originally it was about having a positive impact, getting people involved in lean, engaging and empowering them towards continuous improvement and following a set of key principles, but now it's changed to "save some money", and people are forgetting the cultural side of it.'*

The 'principles' that the Head of Lean was referring to had been adapted from the lessons learned from lean practitioners in healthcare.* The main principles were as follows:

1 Focus on the patient (not the organisation and its employees, suppliers, etc.) and design care around them in order to determine what real value represents.
2 Identify what represents value for the patient (along the whole value stream or patient pathway) and get rid of everything else.
3 Reduce the time required to go from start to finish along every pathway (which creates more value at less cost).

*Particularly a book called *On the Mend* by John Toussaint and Roger Gerard (www.onthemendbook.org)

4 Pursue principles 1, 2, and 3 endlessly through continuous improvement that engages everyone (doctors, nurses, technicians, managers, suppliers, and patients and their families) who 'touch' the patient pathways.

A new arrival

In February, and much to the Head of Lean's surprise, a third set of consultants was appointed to focus on the application of Work Study Method to operating theatres. *'I think the timescales have changed. Before, there was a recognition that we're in it for the long haul, it wasn't going to be a quick fix. I think now the driver is that "you will become a high performing trust come hell or high water and if what we need to do to get there is to bring a hundred management consultants in who've all got a different approach then that's what we'll do". My worry is that in the longer term we'll fall over again because actually all we've done is stick sticking plaster over again which is what we were doing before.'*

The impact of lean

Consultants and nurses in the trust were divided on the impact of lean. Those who had experienced Change M's rapid improvement events (RIEs) in their area tended to be enthusiastic about the benefits and the changes they had made. Small, but significant, changes could produce benefits including reduced confusion, increased staff morale and better patient flow. For example, improved prominence and clarity of signage stopped patients getting lost, and leaving clinicians to wait for them. A reduction in stock levels produced cost and space savings as well as reducing the amount of time spent looking for the correct items. In one store cupboard 25,000 pairs of surgical gloves were identified from 500 different suppliers. Another RIE blew the myth on the effectiveness of the Medical Records Department: *'It was amazing. We just exploded the myth that when you didn't get case notes in a clinical area it was medical records fault, but it hardly ever was. Consultants had notes in their cars, they had them at home, we had a thousand notes in the secretary's offices, and we wondered why we couldn't get case notes! Two people walked seven miles a day looking for them – they were all over the place. Now that was a good RIE because we did manage to sort out medical records and create some semblance of order in their lives.'*

Yet those who had no direct involvement in the lean activity are sceptical: *'We're not making cars, people are different and the processes that we put people through repeatedly are more complicated than the processes that you go through to make a car. These ideas may be OK in manufacturing, but all it has resulted in here are teams of expensive consultants crawling all over the hospital'* (Consultant Surgeon). But there were some converts according to the Head of Lean. *'A consultant (medical) came to me at the beginning of the week saying, "This is all a load of rubbish. There's no point in mapping the process, we all know what happens: the patient goes from there to there and this is the solution and this is what we need to do". During the middle of the improvement week, the Consultant said: "I never realised what actually does happen in reality." By the end of the week the Consultant's mindset has changed to: "Actually this has been great because I never understood, I only saw my bit of it".'*

Although frustrated by the confusion caused by using multiple consultants, the Head of Lean was optimistic. *'We are starting to see some quite significant, if limited, results. The real issue is getting everyone to change the way they behave. It is tackling doctors who are used to doing their own thing and having no performance measures. It is negotiating with suppliers familiar with a culture that allows them to offer new apparatus with little attention to cost or clinical benefits. It is gradually persuading nurses that constantly working around problems*

in the care delivery process will not make deep-seated problems go away. It is slowly educating administrators to accept that that you cannot simply run broken processes harder. Ultimately we have seen that lean can potentially work in healthcare. What we have yet to discover is a method for communicating the benefits and value of lean to others, and quantifying this value in a manner that is significant at an executive level of the organisation.'

QUESTIONS

1 What complexities and barriers to lean implementation are demonstrated in the case study?

2 How do the complexities and barriers identified above relate to your own organisation?

3 How might an organisation overcome these barriers?

APPLYING THE PRINCIPLES

Hints

Some of these exercises can be answered by reading the chapter. Others will require some general knowledge of business activity and some might require an element of investigation. Hints on how they can all be answered are to be found in the eText at **www.pearsoned.co.uk/slack**.

1 Re-examine the description of the Toyota production system at the beginning of the chapter.

(a) List all the different techniques and practices which Toyota adopts. Which of these would you call just-in-time philosophies and which are just-in-time techniques?

(b) How are operations objectives (quality, speed, dependability, flexibility, cost) influenced by the practices which Toyota adopts?

2 Consider this record of an ordinary flight.

'Breakfast was a little rushed but left the house at 6.15. Had to return a few minutes later, forgot my passport. Managed to find it and leave (again) by 6.30. Arrived at the airport 7.00, dropped Angela off with bags at terminal and went to the long-term car park. Eventually found a parking space after ten minutes. Waited eight minutes for the courtesy bus. Six-minute journey back to the terminal, we start queuing at the check-in counters by 7.24. Twenty-minute wait. Eventually get to check-in and find that we have been allocated seat at different ends of the plane. Staff helpful but takes eight minutes to sort it out. Wait in queue for security checks for ten minutes. Security decide I look suspicious and search bags for three minutes. Waiting in lounge by 8.05. Spend one hour five minutes in lounge reading computer magazine and looking at small plastic souvenirs. Hurrah, flight is called 9.10! Takes two minutes to rush to the gate and queue for further five minutes at gate. Through the gate and on to air bridge that is continuous queue going onto plane, takes four minutes but finally in seats by 9.21. Wait for plane to fill up with other passengers for 14 minutes. Plane starts to taxi to runway at 9.35. Plane queues to take-off for ten minutes. Plane takes off 9.45. Smooth flight to Amsterdam: 55 minutes. Stacked in queue of planes waiting to land for ten minutes. Touch down at Schiphol Airport 10.50. Taxi to terminal and wait 15 minutes to disembark. Disembark at 11.05 and walk to luggage collection (calling at lavatory on way); arrive luggage collection 11.15. Wait for luggage eight minutes. Through customs (not searched by Netherlands security who decide I look

trustworthy) and to taxi rank by 11.26. Wait for taxi four minutes. Into taxi by 11.30; 30-minute ride into Amsterdam. Arrive at hotel 12.00.'

(a) Analyse the journey in terms of value added time (actually going somewhere) and non-value added time (the time spent queueing, etc.).

(b) Visit the websites of two or three airlines and examine their business class and first class services to look for ideas that reduce the non-value-added time for customers who are willing to pay the premium.

(c) Next time you go on a journey, time each part of the journey and perform a similar analysis.

3   Examine the value-added versus non-value-added times for some other services. For example:

(a) Handing an assignment in for marking if you are currently studying for a qualification. What is the typical elapsed time between handing the assignment in and receiving it back with comments? How much of this elapsed time do you think is value-added time?

(b) Posting a letter (the elapsed time is between posting the letter in the box and it being delivered to the recipient).

(c) Taking a garment to be professionally dry cleaned.

4   Using an internet search engine, enter 'kanban', and capture who uses such devices for planning and control. Contrast the ways in which they are used.

5   Consider how set-up reduction principles can be used on the following:

(a) Changing a tyre at the side of the road (following a puncture).

(b) Cleaning out an aircraft and preparing it for the next flight between its inbound flight landing and disembarking its passengers, and the same aircraft being ready to take-off on its outbound flight.

(c) The time between the finish of one surgical procedure in a hospital's operating theatre, and the start of the next one.

(d) The 'pitstop' activities during a Formula One race (how does this compare to (a) above?).

6   In the chapter the example of Boeing's success in enabling aircraft to convert between passenger and cargo operations was described.

(a) If the changeover between 'passengers' and 'cargo' took two hours instead of one hour, how much impact do you think it would have on the usefulness of the aircraft?

(b) For an aircraft that carries passengers all the time, what is the equivalent of set-up reduction? And why might it be important?

Notes on chapter

1 Spears, S. and Bowen, H.K. (1999), 'Decoding the DNA of the Toyota production system', *Harvard Business Review*, October, pp 96–106.

2 Source: Mathieson, S.A. (2006), 'NHS should embrace lean times', *Guardian*, 8 June.

3 Lee, D.C. (1987) 'Set-up time reduction: making JIT work' in Voss, C.A. (ed), *Just-in-time Manufacture*, IFS/Springer-Verlag.

4 Spears, S. and Bowen, H.K. *op. cit.*

5 Harrison, A. (1992) *Just-in-time Manufacturing in Perspective*, Prentice Hall.

6 Hall R. (1983) *Zero Inventories*, McGraw Hill, New York.

7 Yamashina, H. 'Reducing set-up times makes your company flexible and more competitive', unpublished, quoted in Harrison A., *op. cit.*

8 Reported in Hanna, J. (2007), 'Bringing lean principles to service industries', *Harvard* Business Review, October.

9 Source: 'Planning for the sequel: how Pixar's leaders want to make their creative powerhouse outlast them' (2010), *The Economist* 17 June.

10 This great metaphor seems to have originated from the consultancy '2think': http://www.2think.biz/index.htm.

11 Kruse, G. (2002) 'IT enabled lean agility', *Control*, November.

12 Kamata, S. (1983) *Japan in the Passing Lane*, Allen and Unwin.

TAKING IT FURTHER

Bicheno, J. and Holweg, M. (2010) *The Lean Toolbox: The Essential Guide to Lean Transformation* (4th edn), PICSIE Books. *A practical guide from two of the European authorities on all matters lean.*

Holweg, M. (2007) 'The genealogy of lean production', *Journal of Operations Management Vol. 25, 420–437.*

Mann, D. (2010) *Creating a Lean Culture* (2nd edn), Productivity Press. *Treats the soft side of lean.*

Schonberger, R.J. (1996) *World Class Manufacturing: The Next Decade*, The Free Press. *One of the really influential authors who established JIT in the West. Now seen as over-simplistic but worth looking at to understand pure JIT.*

Spear, S. and Bowen, H.K. (1999) 'Decoding the DNA of the Toyota production system', *Harvard Business Review*, September–October. *Revisits the leading company as regards JIT practice and re-valuates the underlying philosophy behind the way it manages its operations. Recommended.*

Womack, J.P., Jones, D.T. and Roos, D. (1990) *The Machine that Changed the World*, Rawson Associates. *Arguably the most influential book on operations management practice of the last fifty years. Firmly rooted in the automotive sector but did much to establish JIT.*

Womack, J. P. and Jones, D. T. (2003) *Lean Thinking: Banish Waste and Create Wealth in Your Corporation*, Free Press. *Some of the lessons from 'The Machine that Changed the World' but applied in a broader context.*

USEFUL WEBSITES

www.opsman.org *Definitions, links and opinions on operations and process management.*

http://www.lean.org/ *Site of the Lean Enterprise Unit, set up by one of the founders of the lean thinking movement.*

http://www.iet.org/index.cfm *The site of the Institution Electrical Engineers (that includes Manufacturing engineers surprisingly) has material on this and related topics as well as other issues covered in this book.*

http://www.mfgeng.com *The manufacturing engineering site.*

Interactive quiz

For further resources including examples, animated diagrams, self-test questions, Excel spreadsheets and video materials please explore the eText on the companion website at **www.pearsoned.co.uk/slack**

13

Improvement

Introduction

All operations, no matter how well managed, are capable of improvement. In fact in recent years the emphasis has shifted markedly towards making improvement one of the main responsibilities of operations managers. And although the whole of this book is focused on improving the performance of individual processes, operations and whole supply networks, there are some issues that relate to the activity of improving itself. In any operation, whatever is improved, and how-ever it is done, the overall direction and approach to improvement needs to be addressed (see Figure 13.1).

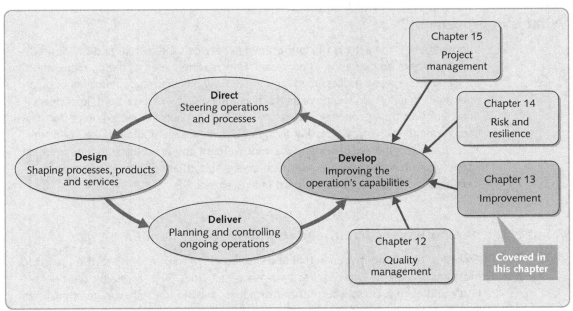

Figure 13.1 Improvement is the activity of closing the gap between the current and the desired performance of an operation or process

EXECUTIVE SUMMARY

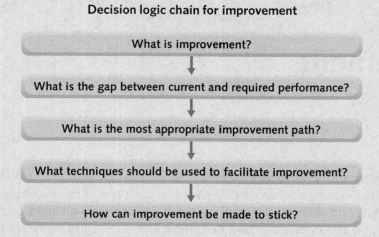

Decision logic chain for improvement

What is improvement?

What is the gap between current and required performance?

What is the most appropriate improvement path?

What techniques should be used to facilitate improvement?

How can improvement be made to stick?

Each chapter is structured around a set of diagnostic questions. These questions suggest what you should ask in order to gain an understanding of the important issues of a topic, and, as a result, improve your decision making. An executive summary addressing these questions is provided below.

What is improvement?

Improvement is the activity of closing the gap between the current and the desired performance of an operation or process. It is increasingly seen as the ultimate objective for all operations and process management activity. Furthermore, almost all popular operations initiatives in recent years, such as total quality management, lean operations, business process reengineering, and Six Sigma, have all focused on performance improvement. It involves assessing the gaps between current and required performance, balancing the use of continuous improvement and breakthrough improvement, adopting appropriate improvement techniques, and attempting to ensure that the momentum of improvement does not fade over time.

What is the gap between current and required performance?

Assessing the gap between actual and desired performance is the starting point for most improvement. This requires two sets of activities: first, assessing the operation's and each process's current performance; second, deciding on an appropriate level of target performance. The first activity will depend on how performance is measured within the operation. This involves deciding what aspects of performance to measure, which are the most important aspects of performance, and what detailed measures should be used to assess each factor. The balanced score card approach is an approach to performance measurement that is currently influential in many organisations. Setting targets for performance can be done in a number of ways. These include historically based targets, strategic targets that reflect strategic objectives, external performance targets that relate to external and/or competitor operations, and absolute performance targets based on the theoretical upper limit of performance. Benchmarking is an important input to this part of performance improvement.

What is the most appropriate improvement path?

Two improvement paths represent different philosophies of improvement, although both may be appropriate at different times. They are breakthrough improvement and continuous improvement. Breakthrough improvement focuses on major and dramatic changes that are intended to result in dramatic increases in performance. The business process reengineering approach is typical of breakthrough improvement. Continuous improvement focuses on small but never-ending improvements that become part of normal operations life. Its objective is to make improvement part of the culture of the organisation. Often continuous improvement involves the use of multi-stage improvement cycles for regular problem solving. The Six Sigma approach to improvement brings many existing ideas together and can be seen as a combination of continuous and breakthrough improvement.

What techniques should be used to facilitate improvement?

Almost all techniques in operations management contribute directly or indirectly to the performance improvement. However, some more general techniques have become popularly associated with improvement. These include scatter diagrams (correlation), cause–effect diagrams, Pareto analysis, and why–why analysis.

How can improvement be made to stick?

One of the biggest problems in improvement is to preserve improvement momentum over time. One factor that inhibits improvement becoming accepted as a regular part of operations activity is the emphasis on the fashionability of each new improvement approach. Most new improvement ideas contain some worthwhile elements but none will provide the ultimate answer. There must be some overall management of the improvement process that can absorb the best of each new idea. And, although authorities differ to some extent, most emphasise the importance of an improvement strategy, top management support and training.

What is improvement?

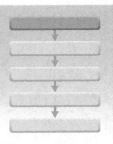

Video

Improvement comes from closing the gap between what you are and what you want to be. Or, in a specifically operations context, it comes from closing the gap between current and desired performance. Performance improvement is the ultimate objective of operations and process management. It has also become the subject of innumerable ideas that have been put forward as particularly effective methods of ensuring improvement. These include many that are described in this book, for example, total quality management (TQM), 'lean' operations, business process reengineering (BPR), Six Sigma, and so on. All of these, and other, ideas have something to contribute. What is important is that all managers develop an understanding of the underlying elements of improvement. The following two examples illustrate many of these.

> **OPERATIONS PRINCIPLE**
>
> *Performance improvement is the ultimate objective of operations and process management.*

EXAMPLE

Reinventing Singapore's libraries[1]

Is the traditional library still relevant in a world where information and entertainment is dominated by digital media? Borrowing from local libraries in most parts of the world has declined in recent years. Why? Libraries are often shut when people want to use them and when they are open they can be a dull with shelves full of old books, queues to borrow or return books, unhelpful or unapproachable staff who insist that users are quiet. Furthermore, libraries are increasingly under threat from the internet, an easy-to-use and efficient source of information. Yet some libraries are working hard to change this image. The National Library Board of Singapore (NLB) created and implemented a radical improvement plan to transform the library system in Singapore, designed to move its libraries from being merely a functional space to welcoming social spaces. Libraries have cafés, are located in shopping centres and are integrated into the community who see them as inviting havens to relax, meet people and share in the company of other book-lovers. So successful was the improvement initiative that there has been a significant increase in usage, and many libraries in other parts of the world have copied the Singapore model in their own countries.

Source: World of Asia/Alamy Images

One of the first steps in their improvement journey was to develop a set of 'service standards' covering five areas: customer service, printed collections, housekeeping, programmes, and staffing and administration. They cover such things as the running of programmes, opening times, shelving of books, the answering of telephones, and response time to e-mails. Audit teams monitor libraries against these service standards with awards for the best-performing libraries and individuals. Importantly, processes are continually being reviewed and improved. The NLB changed the librarys' performance evaluation process from one relying solely on supervisory discretion to a more objective system that also required input from peers and customers. Metrics and standards for operations and front-line customer service were established. Performance measurements, such as a 'complaints versus compliments' ratio, were introduced. Training was also seen as vital to improvement, with staff expected to undertake around 60 hours of training each year. For front-line staff this might include customer service courses on dealing with difficult customers or handling complaints.

After a while staff began to see little successes based on changes they had proposed. This improved their confidence and led to greater service improvement. NLB facilitated this with sessions they called 'ask stupid questions' (ASQ), where staff were free to ask 'stupid' questions. However, as one senior manager put it, '*In my view there are no stupid questions, there are only stupid answers*'. These initiatives were also supported by staff suggestion schemes, a performance bonus linking success to remuneration, training needs analysis and personal development based on individual training plans.

At a more structured level, some of the innovative improvements were the result of business process re-engineering (BPR). Their BPR methodology included several key phases:

- *Envisioning* – to reaffirm NLB's vision for its future operations and specific initiatives.
- *Core process identification* – to identify focus areas for BPR, set stretch performance targets and establish working groups for each focus area.
- *Process analysis* – to map out current business processes in full detail, collect data, perform model-based simulations, and diagnose critical issues within these processes.
- *Process redesign* – to develop new process designs with the intent to attain quantum improvements as defined by the stretch targets.
- *Blueprinting* – to consolidate all redesign recommendations and to discern organisation-wide issues such as technology infrastructure, human resources, organisation structure and customer services.
- *Implementation planning* – to develop a complete masterplan of implementation activities necessary to bring NLB from the current state towards the desired future state.

The BPR team, reporting to the Chief Executive, carried out a review of the core internal processes. The main objective was to develop a set of integrated designs and strategies for the NLB to manage its fast expanding network of libraries for the 21st century. Participants were required to identify, analyse and redesign the NLB's core business processes to remove redundancies and inneficiencies. The core processes included:

- *Time-to-market process* – the activities needed to bring book titles to the libraries, including title selection, acquisition, cataloguing, processing, transportation, packaging and shelf display.
- *Time-to-checkout process* – the activities between the time when a library user has an interest in a title and the time when the user leaves the library with the title checked out.
- *Time-to-shelf process* – the activities between the time when a library user turns up at a book return point and the time when the returned books are made available on the shelf for the next user.
- *Time-to-information process* – the activities between the time when a customer poses his information enquiry to the library and the time when the customer has received and accepted the information product.
- *Library planning, set-up and renewal process* – the activities in the planning, construction/renovation, moving-in and other logistics for setting up new libraries and upgrading existing ones.

Along with using a BPR approach, the NLB were keen to exploit technology fully. It was the first public library in the world to prototype radio-frequency identification (RFID) to create its Electronic Library Management System. RFID tags, or transponders contained in 'smart labels', receive and respond to radio-frequency queries from an RFID transceiver, which enables the remote and automatic retrieval, storing and sharing of information. Unlike barcodes, which need to be manually scanned, RFID simply broadcasts its presence and automatically sends data about the item to electronic readers. They have installed RFID tags in 10 million books making NLB one of the largest users of RFID tags in the world. Customers now have to spend little time queuing, as book issuing is automatic, as are book returns. Indeed, books can be returned to any book-drop at any library where RFID enables fast and easy sorting. Yet the NLB had to be very careful that they did not alienate or intimidate customers with their use of technology. Younger people are comfortable with the sort of technology that uses computers for returning, borrowing and searching for books, creating and checking accounts, and even paying fines. But some older customers needed help, so they enlisted a group of volunteers (including senior citizens) to get them familiar with the new technology.

But even with the stress on BPR methods and technology, NLB still stress the paramount importance of their staff's contribution. *'When there are challenges our staff respond and achieve wonderful results. That's because the organisation is very open to change. And that is the key thing; it's an attitude. Innovations are possible because everybody has the mindset that they would like to see things done differently. Improving all aspects of the library is an integral part of all my colleagues' jobs. Managers and librarians are expected to be involved in improvement projects, many of which are cross-functional, involving people from various functions working on specific issues raised by either staff or customers. We also often form small improvement teams. They will brainstorm for ideas, test out their suggestions and when they are successful we will have sessions where the teams from across the libraries will discuss and share what they have done. Where appropriate we will adopt the proven ideas or schemes for implementation in all our libraries. While this is seen as a normal and natural part of the job, we do reward staff for their ideas.'*

EXAMPLE   ### Improvement at Heineken[2]

Heineken International brews beer that is sold around the world and operates in over 170 countries with brands such as Heineken and Amstel. Its Zoeterwoude facility, a packaging plant that fills

bottles and cans in The Netherlands faced two challenges. First, it needed to improve its operations processes to reduce its costs. Second, it needed to improve the efficiency of its existing lines in order to increase their capacity, without which it would have to invest in a new packaging line. The goal of a 20 per cent improvement in operating efficiency was set because it was seen as challenging yet achievable. It was also decided to focus the improvement project around two themes: (a) obtaining accurate operational data on which improvement decisions could be based; (b) changing the culture of the operation to promote fast and effective decision-making. Before the improvement, project staff at the Zoeterwoude plant had approached problem-solving as an ad hoc activity, only to be done when circumstances made it unavoidable. By contrast, the improvement initiative taught the staff to use various problem-solving techniques such as cause–effect and Pareto diagrams (discussed later in this chapter).

'Until we started using these techniques,' says Wilbert Raaijmakers, Heineken Netherlands Brewery Director, *'there was little consent regarding what was causing any problems. There was poor communication between the various departments and job grades. For example, maintenance staff believed that production stops were caused by operating errors, while operators were of the opinion that poor maintenance was the cause.'* The use of better information, analysis and improvement techniques helped the staff to identify and treat the root causes of problems. With many potential improvements to make, staff teams were encouraged to set priorities that would reflect the overall improvement target. There was also widespread use of benchmarking performance against targets to gauge progress.

Improvement teams had been 'empowered, organised and motivated' before the improvement initiative, through the company's 'cultural change' programme. *'Its aim,'* according to Wilbert Raaijmakers, *'was to move away from a command-and-control situation and evolve towards a more team-oriented organisation.'* Fundamental to this was a programme to improve the skills and knowledge of individual operators through special training programmes. Nevertheless, the improvement initiative exposed a number of further challenges. For example, the improvement team discovered that people were more motivated to improve when the demand was high, but it was more difficult to motivate them when production pressures were lower. To overcome this, communication was improved so that staff were kept fully informed of future production levels and the upcoming schedule of training and maintenance activities that were planned during slumps in demand. The lesson being that it is difficult to convince people to change if they are not aware of the underlying reason for it. Even so, some staff much preferred to stick with their traditional methods, and some team leaders were more skilled at encouraging change than others. Many staff needed coaching, reassurance and formal training on how to take ownership of problems. But, at the end of 12 months, the improvement project had achieved its 20 per cent goal allowing the plant to increase the volume of its exports and cut its costs significantly. Yet Wilbert Raaijmakers still sees room for improvement: *'The optimisation of an organisation is a never-ending process. If you sit back and do the same thing tomorrow as you did today, you'll never make it. We must remain alert to the latest developments and stress the resulting information to its full potential.'*

What do these two examples have in common?

The improvement initiatives at these two operations, and the way they managed them, is typical of improvement projects. Both measured performance and placed information gathering at the centre of their improvement initiative. Both had a view of improvement targets that related directly to strategic objectives. Both made efforts to collect information that would allow decisions based on evidence rather than opinion. Heineken also made extensive use of simple improvement techniques that would both analyse problems and help to channel its staff's creativity at all levels. NLB used business process reengineering (BPR), exploited technology and focused on their customers' perceptions, needs and requirements. This included how customers, both old and young, could use the newer technologies. They both had to foster an environment that allowed all staff to contribute to its improvement, and both came to view improvement not as a 'one off', but rather as the start of a never-ending cycle of improvement. Most importantly, both had to decide how to organise the whole improvement initiative. Different organisations with different objectives may choose to implement improvement initiatives in a different way, but all will face a similar set of issues to these two operations, even if they choose to make different decisions.

DIAGNOSTIC QUESTION

What is the gap between current and required performance?

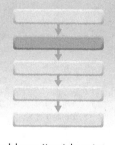

Video

The gap between how an operation or process is currently performing, and how it wishes to perform, is the key driver of any improvement initiative. The wider the gap, the more importance is likely to be given to improvement. But, in order to harness the gap as a driver of improvement, it must be addressed in some detail, both in terms of exactly what is failing to meet targets, and by how much. Answering these questions depends on the operation's ability to do three things: assess its current performance, derive a set of target levels of performance that the organisation can subscribe to, and compare current against target performance in a systematic and graphic manner that demonstrates to everyone the need for improvement.

Assessing current performance – performance measurement

> **OPERATIONS PRINCIPLE**
>
> *Performance measurement is a prerequisite for the assessment of operations performance.*

Some kind of *performance measurement* is a prerequisite for judging whether an operation is good, bad or indifferent, although this is not the only reason for investing in effective performance measurement. Without one, it would be impossible to exert any control over an operation on an ongoing basis. However, a performance measurement system that gives no help to ongoing improvement is only partially effective. Performance measurement, as we are treating it here, concerns three generic issues.

- What factors to include as performance measures?
- Which are the most important performance measures?
- What detailed measures to use?

What factors to include as performance measures?

An obvious starting point for deciding which performance measures to adopt is to use the five generic performance objectives: quality, speed, dependability, flexibility and cost. These can be broken down into more detailed measures, or they can be aggregated into 'composite' measures, such as 'customer satisfaction', 'overall service level' or 'operations agility'. These composite measures may be further aggregated by using measures such as 'achieve market objectives', 'achieve financial objectives', 'achieve operations objectives' or even 'achieve overall strategic objectives'. The more aggregated performance measures have greater strategic relevance insomuch as they help to draw a picture of the overall performance of the business, although by doing so they necessarily include many influences outside those that operations performance improvement would normally address. The more detailed performance measures are usually monitored more closely and more often, and although they provide a limited view of an operation's performance, they do provide a more descriptive and complete picture of what should be and what is happening within the operation. In practice, most organisations will choose to use performance targets from throughout the range. This idea is illustrated in Figure 13.2.

Choosing the important performance measures

One of the problems of devising a useful performance measurement system is trying to achieve some balance between having a few key measures on one hand (straightforward and simple, but may not reflect the full range of organisational objectives), or, on the other hand, having many detailed measures (complex and difficult to manage, but capable of conveying many nuances of performance). Broadly, a compromise is reached by making sure that there

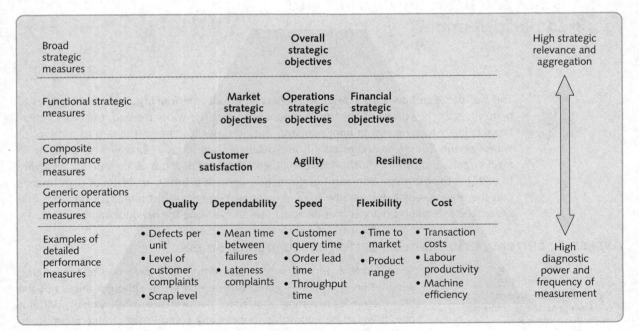

Figure 13.2 Performance measures can involve different levels of aggregation

is a clear link between the operation's overall strategy, the most important (or 'key') performance indicators (KPI's) that reflect strategic objectives, and the bundle of detailed measures that are used to 'flesh out' each key performance indicator. Obviously, unless strategy is well defined then it is difficult to 'target' a narrow range of key performance indicators.

What detailed measures to use?

The five performance objectives – quality, speed, dependability, flexibility and cost – are really composites of many smaller measures. For example, an operation's cost is derived from many factors which could include the purchasing efficiency of the operation, the efficiency with which it converts materials, the productivity of its staff, the ratio of direct to indirect staff, and so on. All of these measures individually give a partial view of the operation's cost performance, and many of them overlap in terms of the information they include. However, each of them does give a perspective on the cost performance of an operation that could be useful either to identify areas for improvement or to monitor the extent of improvement. If an organisation regards its 'cost' performance as unsatisfactory, disaggregating it into 'purchasing efficiency', 'operations efficiency', 'staff productivity', etc. might explain the root cause of the poor performance. Table 13.1 shows some of the partial measures which can be used to judge an operation's performance.

Table 13.1 Some typical partial measures of performance

Performance objective	Some typical measures
Quality	Number of defects per unit Level of customer complaints Scrap level Warranty claims Mean time between failures Customer satisfaction score
Speed	Customer query time Order lead time Frequency of delivery Actual *versus* theoretical throughput time Cycle time
Dependability	Percentage of orders delivered late Average lateness of orders Proportion of products in stock Mean deviation from promised arrival Schedule adherence
Flexibility	Time needed to develop new products/services Range of products/services Machine change-over time Average batch size Time to increase activity rate Average capacity/maximum capacity Time to change schedules
Cost	Minimum delivery time/average delivery time Variance against budget Utilisation of resources Labour productivity Added value Efficiency Cost per operation hour

The balanced scorecard approach

'The balanced scorecard retains traditional financial measures. But financial measures tell the story of past events, an adequate story for industrial age companies for which investments in long-term capabilities [and] customer relationships were not critical for success. These financial measures are inadequate, however, for guiding and evaluating the journey that information age companies must make to create future value through investment in customers, suppliers, employees, processes, technology, and innovation.'[3]

Generally, operations performance measures have been broadening in their scope. It is now generally accepted that the scope of measurement should, at some level, include external as well as internal, long-term as well as short-term, and 'soft' as well as 'hard' measures. The best-known manifestation of this trend is the 'balanced scorecard' approach taken by Kaplan and Norton[4]. As well as including financial measures of performance, in the same way as traditional performance measurement systems, the balanced scorecard approach also attempts to provide the important information that is required to allow the overall strategy of an organisation to be reflected adequately in specific performance measures. In addition to financial measures of performance, it also includes more operational measures of customer satisfaction, internal processes, innovation and other improvement activities. In doing so it measures the factors behind financial performance which are seen as the key drivers of future financial success. In particular, it is argued that a balanced range of measures enables managers to address the following questions (see Figure 13.3):

- How do we look to our shareholders (financial perspective)?
- What must we Excel at (internal process perspective)?
- How do our customers see us (the customer perspective)?
- How can we continue to improve and build capabilities (the learning and growth perspective)?

The balanced scorecard attempts to bring together the elements that reflect a business's strategic position, including product or service quality measures, product and service development times, customer complaints, labour productivity, and so on. At the same time it attempts to avoid performance reporting becoming unwieldy by restricting the number of measures and focusing especially on those seen to be essential. The advantages of the approach are that it presents an overall picture of the organisation's performance in a single report, and by

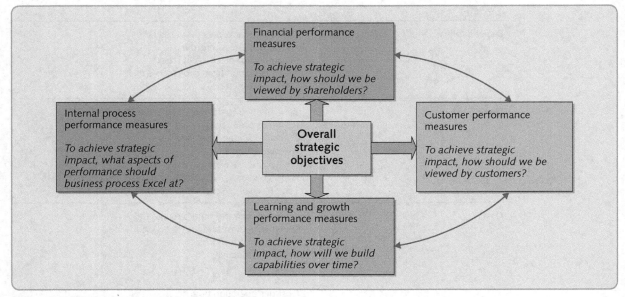

Figure 13.3 The measures used in the balanced scorecard

being comprehensive in the measures of performance it uses, encourages companies to take decisions in the interests of the whole organisation rather than sub-optimising around narrow measures. Developing a balanced scorecard is a complex process and is now the subject of considerable debate. One of the key questions that have to be considered is how specific measures of performance should be designed? Inadequately designed performance measures can result in dysfunctional behaviour, so teams of managers are often used to develop a scorecard which reflects their organisation's specific needs.

Setting target performance

A performance measure means relatively little until it is compared against some kind of target. Knowing that only one document in 500 is sent out to customers containing an error tells us relatively little unless we know whether this is better or worse than what we were achieving previously, and whether it is better or worse than what other similar operations (especially competitors) are achieving. Setting performance targets transforms performance measures into performance 'judgements'. Several approaches to setting targets can be used, including the following.

- *Historically-based targets* – targets that compare current against previous performance.
- *Strategic targets* – targets set to reflect the level of performance that is regarded as appropriate to achieve strategic objectives.
- *External performance-based targets* targets set to reflect the performance that is achieved by similar, or competitor, external operations.
- *Absolute performance targets* – targets based on the theoretical upper limit of performance.

One of the problems in setting targets is that different targets can give very different messages regarding the improvement being achieved. So, for example, in Figure 13.4, one of an operation's performance measures is 'delivery' (in this case defined as the proportion of orders delivered on time). The performance for one month has been measured at 83 per cent, but any judgement regarding performance will be dependent on the performance targets. Using a *historical* target, when compared to last year's performance of 60 per cent, this months' performance of 83 per cent is good. But, if the operation's *strategy* calls for a 95 per cent delivery performance, the actual performance of 83 per cent looks decidedly poor. The company may also be concerned with how they perform against *competitors'* performances. If competitors are currently averaging delivery performances of around 80 per cent, the company's

OPERATIONS PRINCIPLE

Performance measures only have meaning when compared against targets.

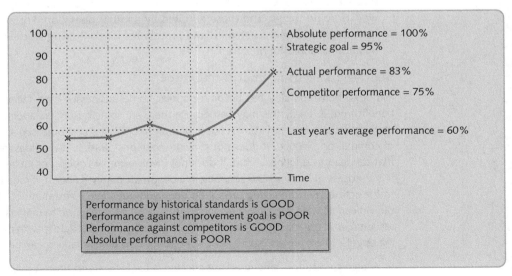

Performance by historical standards is GOOD
Performance against improvement goal is POOR
Performance against competitors is GOOD
Absolute performance is POOR

Figure 13.4 Different standards of comparison give different messages

performance looks rather good. Finally, the more ambitious managers within the company may wish to at least try and seek perfection. Why not, they argue, use an *absolute* performance standard of 100 per cent delivery on time? Against this standard the company's actual 83 per cent again looks disappointing.

Benchmarking

Benchmarking, is 'the process of learning from others' and involves comparing one's own performance or methods against other comparable operations. It is a broader issue than setting performance targets, and includes investigating other organisations' operations practice in order to derive ideas that could contribute to performance improvement. Its rationale is based on the idea that (a) problems in managing processes are almost certainly shared by processes elsewhere, and (b) that there is probably another operation somewhere that has developed a better way of doing things. For example, a bank might learn some things from a supermarket about how it could cope with demand fluctuations during the day. Benchmarking is essentially about stimulating creativity in improvement practice.

> **OPERATIONS PRINCIPLE**
> *Improvement is aided by contextualising processes and operations.*

Types of benchmarking

Practice note

There are many different types of benchmarking (which are not necessarily mutually exclusive), some of which are listed below:

- *Internal benchmarking* is a comparison between operations or parts of operations which are within the same total organisation. For example, a large motor vehicle manufacturer with several factories might choose to benchmark each factory against the others.
- *External benchmarking* is a comparison between an operation and other operations which are part of a different organisation.
- *Non-competitive benchmarking* is benchmarking against external organisations which do not compete directly in the same markets.
- *Competitive benchmarking* is a comparison directly between competitors in the same, or similar, markets.
- *Performance benchmarking* is a comparison between the levels of achieved performance in different operations. For example, an operation might compare its own performance in terms of some or all of our performance objectives – quality, speed, dependability, flexibility and cost – against other organisations' performance in the same dimensions.
- *Practice benchmarking* is a comparison between an organisation's operations practices, or way of doing things, and those adopted by another operation. For example, a large retail store might compare its systems and procedures for controlling stock levels with those used by another department store.

Benchmarking as an improvement tool

Although benchmarking has become popular, some businesses have failed to derive maximum benefit from it. Partly this may be because there are some misunderstandings as to what benchmarking actually entails. First, it is not a 'one-off' project. It is best practised as a continuous process of comparison. Second, it does not provide 'solutions'. Rather, it provides ideas and information that can lead to solutions. Third, it does not involve simply copying or imitating other operations. It is a process of learning and adapting in a pragmatic manner. Fourth, it means devoting resources to the activity. Benchmarking cannot be done without some investment, but this does not necessarily mean allocating exclusive responsibility to a set of highly paid managers. In fact, there can be advantages in organising staff at all levels to investigate and collate information from benchmarking targets. There are also some basic rules about how benchmarking can be organised.

- A prerequisite for benchmarking success is to understand thoroughly your own processes. Without this it is difficult to compare your processes against those of other companies.

- Look at the information that is available in the public domain. Published accounts, journals, conferences and professional associations can all provide information which is useful for benchmarking purposes.
- Do not discard information because it seems irrelevant. Small pieces of information only make sense in the context of other pieces of information that may emerge subsequently.
- Be sensitive in asking for information from other companies. Don't ask any questions that you would not like to be asked yourself.

Assess the gap between actual and target performance

A comparison of actual and target performance should guide the relative priorities for improvement. A significant aspect of performance is the relative importance of the various performance measures. Because some factor of performance is relatively poor does not mean that it should be improved immediately if current performance as a whole exceeds target performance. In fact, both the relative importance of the various performance measures, and their performance against targets, need to be brought together in order to prioritise for improvement. One way of doing this is through the importance–performance matrix.

The importance–performance matrix

Practice note

As its name implies, the importance–performance matrix positions each aspect of performance on a matrix according to its scores or ratings on how important each aspect of relative performance is, and what performance it is currently achieving. Figure 13.5 shows an importance–performance matrix divided into zones of improvement priority. The first zone boundary is the 'lower bound of acceptability' shown as line AB in Figure 13.5. This is the boundary between acceptable and unacceptable current performance. When some aspect of performance is rated as relatively unimportant, this boundary will be low. Most operations are prepared to tolerate lower performance for relatively unimportant performance factors. However, for performance factors that are rated more important, they will be markedly less sanguine at poor or mediocre levels of current performance. Below this minimum bound of acceptability (AB) there is clearly a need for improvement; above this line there is no immediate urgency for any improvement.

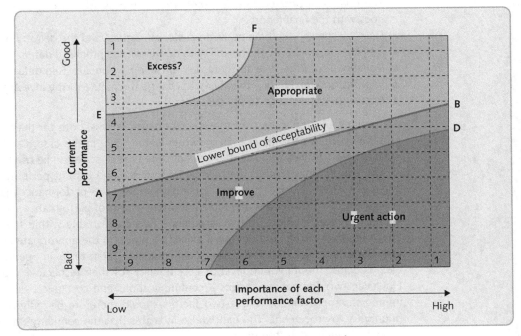

Figure 13.5 Priority zones in the importance–performance matrix

However, not all factors of performance that fall below the minimum line will be seen as having the same degree of improvement priority. A boundary approximately represented by line CD represents a distinction between an urgent priority zone and a less urgent improvement zone. Similarly, above the line AB, not all competitive factors are regarded as having the same priority. The line EF can be seen as the approximate boundary between performance levels which are regarded as 'good' or 'appropriate' on one hand and those regarded as 'too good' or 'excess' on the other. Segregating the matrix in this way results in four zones which imply very different priorities:

- *The 'appropriate' zone.* Performance factors in this area lie above the lower bound of acceptability and so should be considered satisfactory.
- *The 'improve' zone.* Lying below the lower bound of acceptability, any performance factors in this zone must be candidates for improvement.
- *The 'urgent-action' zone.* These performance factors are important to customers but current performance is unacceptable. They must be considered as candidates for immediate improvement.
- *The 'excess?' zone.* Performance factors in this area are 'high performing', but are not particularly important. The question must be asked, therefore, whether the resources devoted to achieving such a performance could be used better elsewhere.

EXAMPLE

EXL Laboratories

EXL Laboratories is a subsidiary of an electronics company. It carries out research and development as well as technical problem-solving work for a wide range of companies. It is particularly keen to improve the level of service that it gives to its customers. However, it needs to decide which aspect of its performance to improve first. It has devised a list of the most important aspects of its service:

- *The quality of its technical solutions* – the perceived appropriateness by customers.
- *The quality of its communications with customers* – the frequency and usefulness of information.
- *The quality of post-project documentation* – the usefulness of the documentation which goes with the final report.
- *Delivery speed* – the time between customer request and the delivery of the final report.
- *Delivery dependability* – the ability to deliver on the promised date.
- *Delivery flexibility* – the ability to deliver the report on a revised date.
- *Specification flexibility* – the ability to change the nature of the investigation.
- *Price* – the total charge to the customer.

EXL assigns a rating to each of these performance factors, both for their relative importance and their current performance, as shown in Figure 13.6. In this case, EXL have used a 1 to 9 scale, where 1 is 'very important' or 'good'. Any type of scale can be used.

EXL Laboratories plotted the relative importance and current performance ratings it had given to each of its performance factors on an importance–performance matrix. This is shown in Figure 13.7. It shows that the most important aspect of performance – the ability to deliver sound technical solutions to its customers – falls comfortably within the appropriate zone. Specification flexibility and delivery flexibility are also in the appropriate zone, although only just. Both delivery speed and delivery dependability seem to be in need of improvement as each is below the minimum level of acceptability for their respective importance positions. However, two competitive factors – communications and cost/price – are clearly in need of immediate improvement. These two factors should therefore be assigned the most urgent priority for improvement. The matrix also indicates that the company's documentation could almost be regarded as 'too good'.

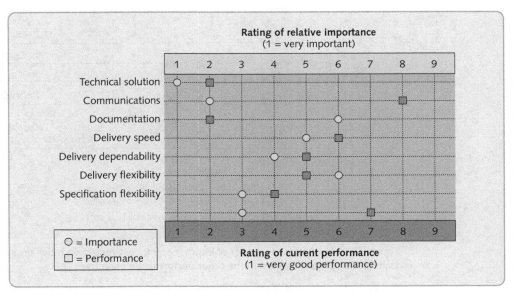

Figure 13.6 Ratings of relative 'importance' and 'current performance' at EXL Laboratories

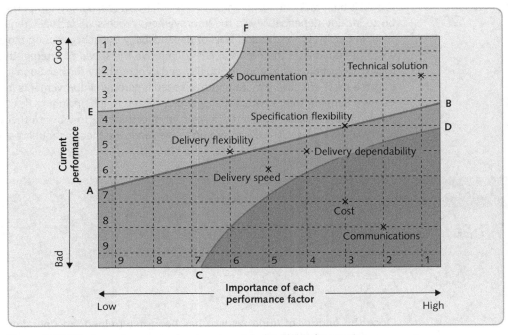

Figure 13.7 The importance–performance matrix for EXL Laboratories

The sandcone theory

As well as approaches that base improvement priority on an operation's specific circumstances, some authorities believe that there is also a generic 'best' sequence of improvement. The best-known theory is called *the sandcone theory*[5], so called because the sand is analogous to management effort and resources. Building a stable sandcone needs a stable foundation of quality upon which one can build layers of dependability, speed, flexibility and cost (see Figure 13.8). Building up improvement is thus a cumulative process, not a sequential one. Moving on to the

Animated
diagram

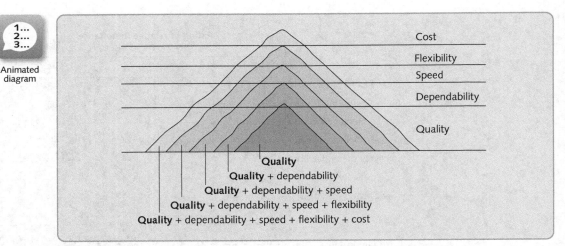

Quality
Quality + dependability
Quality + dependability + speed
Quality + dependability + speed + flexibility
Quality + dependability + speed + flexibility + cost

Figure 13.8 **The sandcone model of improvement: cost reduction relies on a cumulative foundation of improvement in the other performance objectives**

second priority for improvement does not mean dropping the first, and so on. According to the sandcone theory, the first priority should be *quality*, since this is a precondition to all lasting improvement. Only when the operation has reached a minimally acceptable level in quality should it then tackle the next issue, that of internal *dependability*. Importantly though, moving on to include dependability in the improvement process will actually require further improvement in quality. Once a critical level of dependability is reached, enough to provide some stability to the operation, the next stage is to improve the *speed* of internal throughput, but again only while continuing to improve quality and dependability further. Soon it will become evident that the most effective way to improve speed is through improvements in response *flexibility*, that is, changing things within the operation faster. Again, including flexibility in the improvement process should not divert attention from continuing to work further on quality, dependability and speed. Only now, according to the sandcone theory, should *cost* be tackled head on.

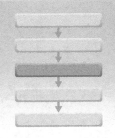

DIAGNOSTIC QUESTION

What is the most appropriate improvement path?

Video

Once the priority of improvement has been determined, an operation must consider the approach or path it wishes to take to reaching its improvement goals. Two paths represent different, and to some extent opposing, philosophies: *breakthrough improvement* and *continuous improvement*. Although they represent different philosophies of improvement, they are not mutually exclusive. Few operations cannot benefit from improving their operations performance on a continuous basis, and few operations would reject investing in a major improvement breakthrough leap in performance if it represented good value. For most operations, both approaches are relevant to some extent, although possibly at different points in time. But to understand how and when each approach is appropriate one must understand their underlying philosophies.

OPERATIONS PRINCIPLE

Breakthrough and continuous improvement are not mutually exclusive.

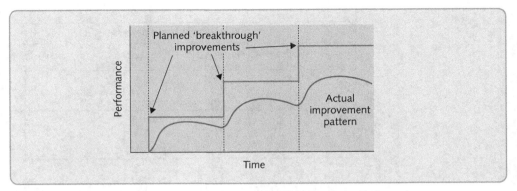

Figure 13.9 'Breakthrough' improvement may not provide the dramatic leaps in performance hoped for

Breakthrough improvement

Breakthrough (or 'innovation'-based) improvement assumes that the main vehicle of improvement is major and dramatic change in the way the operation works, for example, the total reorganisation of an operation's process structure, or the introduction of a fully integrated information system. The impact of these improvements represents a step change in practice (and hopefully performance). Such improvements can be expensive, often disrupting the ongoing workings of the operation, and frequently involving changes in the product/service or process technology. The bold line in Figure 13.9 illustrates the intended pattern of performance with several breakthrough improvements. The improvement pattern illustrated by the dotted line in Figure 13.9 is regarded by some as being more representative of what really occurs when operations rely on pure breakthrough improvement.

The business process re-engineering approach

Typical of the radical breakthrough way of tackling improvement is the business process re-engineering (BPR) approach. It is a blend of a number of ideas such as fast throughput, waste elimination through process flow charting, customer-focused operations, and so on. But it was the potential of information technologies to enable the fundamental redesign of processes that acted as the catalyst in bringing these ideas together. BPR has been defined as[6] *'the fundamental rethinking and radical redesign of business processes to achieve dramatic improvements in critical, contemporary measures of performance, such as cost, quality, service and speed.'*

Underlying the BPR approach is the belief that operations should be organised around the total process which adds value for customers, rather than the functions or activities which perform the various stages of the value-adding activity. The core of BPR is a redefinition of the processes within a total operation, to reflect the business processes that satisfy customer needs. Figure 13.10 illustrates this idea. The main principles of BPR have been summarised as follows:[7]

- Rethink business processes in a cross-functional manner which organises work around the natural flow of information (or materials or customers). This means organising around outcomes of a process rather than the tasks which go into it.
- Strive for dramatic improvements in the performance by radically rethinking and redesigning the process.
- Have those who use the output from a process perform the process. Check to see if all internal customers can be their own supplier rather than depending on another function in the business to supply them (which takes longer and separates out the stages in the process).

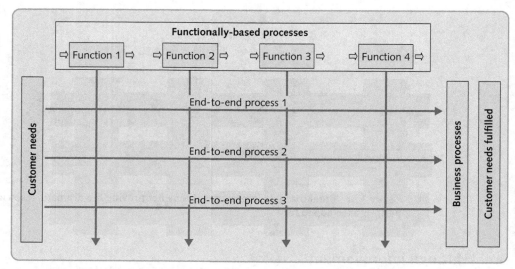

Figure 13.10 BPR advocates reorganising (re-engineering) processes to reflect the natural processes that fulfil customer needs

- Put decision points where the work is performed. Do not separate those who do the work from those who control and manage the work. Control and action are just one more type of supplier–customer relationship which can be merged.

Continuous improvement

Continuous improvement as the name implies, adopts an approach to improving performance which assumes a never-ending series of small incremental improvement steps. For example, modifying the way a product is fixed to a machine to reduce changeover time, or simplifying the question sequence when taking a hotel reservation. While there is no guarantee that such small steps towards better performance will be followed by other steps, the whole philosophy of continuous improvement attempts to ensure that they will be. It is also known as *kaizen*, defined by Masaaki Imai[8] (who has been one of the main proponents of continuous improvement) as follows: '*Kaizen means improvement. Moreover, it means improvement in personal life, home life, social life and work life. When applied to the work place, kaizen means continuing improvement involving everyone – managers and workers alike.*'

Continuous improvement is not concerned with promoting small improvements *per se*, but it does view small improvements as having one significant advantage over large ones – they can be followed relatively painlessly by others. It is not the *rate* of improvement which is important; it is the *momentum* of improvement. It does not matter if successive improvements are small; what does matter is that every month (or week, or quarter, or whatever period is appropriate) some kind of improvement has actually taken place. Continuous improvement does not always come naturally. There are specific abilities, behaviours and actions which need to be consciously developed if continuous improvement is to be sustained over the long term. Bessant and Caffyn[9] distinguish between what they call 'organisational abilities' (the ability to adopt a particular approach to continuous improvement), 'constituent behaviours' (the behaviour that staff adopt) and 'enablers' (the techniques used to progress the continuous improvement effort). They identify six generic organisational abilities, each with its own set of constituent behaviours. These are identified in Table 13.2. Examples of enablers are the improvement techniques described later in this chapter.

Table 13.2 Continuous improvement (CI) abilities and some associated behaviours[10]

Organisational ability	Constituent behaviours
Getting the CI habit Developing the ability to generate sustained involvement in CI	• People use formal problem-finding and solving cycle • People use simple tools and techniques • People use simple measurement to shape the improvement process • Individuals and/or groups initiate and carry through CI activities – they participate in the process • Ideas are responded to in a timely fashion – either implemented or otherwise dealt with • Managers support the CI process through allocation of resources • Managers recognise in formal ways the contribution of employees to CI • Managers lead by example, becoming actively involved in design and implementation of CI • Managers support experiment by not punishing mistakes, but instead encouraging learning from them
Focusing on CI Generating and sustaining the ability to link CI activities to the strategic goals of the company	• Individuals and groups use the organisation's strategic objectives to prioritise improvements • Everyone is able to explain what the operation's strategy and objectives are • Individuals and groups assess their proposed changes against the operation's objectives • Individuals and groups monitor/measure the results of their improvement activity • CI activities are an integral part of the individual's or group's work, not a parallel activity
Spreading the word Generating the ability to move CI activity across organisational boundaries	• People cooperate in cross-functional groups • People understand and share an holistic view (process understanding and ownership) • People are oriented towards internal and external customers in their CI activity • Specific CI projects with outside agencies (customers, suppliers, etc.) take place • Relevant CI activities involve representatives from different organisational levels
CI on the CI system Generating the ability to manage strategically the development of CI	• The CI system is continually monitored and developed • There is a cyclical planning process whereby the CI system is regularly reviewed and amended • There is periodic review of the CI system in relation to the organisation as a whole • Senior management make available sufficient resources (time, money, personnel) to support the development of the CI system • The CI system itself is designed to fit within the current structure and infrastructure • When a major organisational change is planned, its potential impact on the CI system is assessed
Walking the talk Generating the ability to articulate and demonstrate CI's values	• The 'management style' reflects commitment to CI values • When something goes wrong, people at all levels look for reasons why, rather than blame individuals • People at all levels demonstrate a shared belief in the value of small steps and that everyone can contribute, by themselves being actively involved in making and recognising incremental improvements

continued overleaf

Table 13.2 *(continued)*

Organisational ability	Constituent behaviours
Building the learning organisation Generating the ability to learn through CI activity	• Everyone learns from their experiences, both good and bad • Individuals seeks out opportunities for learning/personal development • Individuals and groups at all levels share their learning • The organisation captures and shares the learning of individuals and groups • Managers accept and act on all the learning that takes place • Organisational mechanisms are used to deploy what has been learned across the organisation

Improvement cycle models

An important element of continuous improvement is the idea that improvement can be represented by a never-ending process of repeatedly questioning and re-questioning the detailed working of a process. This is usually summarised by the idea of the *improvement cycle*, of which there are many, including some proprietary models owned by consultancy companies. Two of the more generally used models are: the PDCA cycle (sometimes called the Deming Cycle, named after the famous quality 'guru', W.E. Deming); the DMAIC cycle (made popular by the Six Sigma approach to improvement – see later).

> **OPERATIONS PRINCIPLE**
>
> *Continuous improvement necessarily implies a never-ending cycle of analysis and action.*

The PDCA cycle

The PDCA cycle model is shown in Figure 13.11(a). It starts with the P (for plan) stage, which involves an examination of the current method or the problem area being studied. This involves collecting and analysing data so as to formulate a plan of action which is intended to improve performance. (Some of the techniques used to collect and analyse data are explained later.) The next step is the D (for do) stage. This is the implementation stage during which the plan is tried out in the operation. This stage may itself involve a mini-PDCA cycle as the problems of implementation are resolved. Next comes the C (for check) stage where the new implemented solution is evaluated to see whether it has resulted in the expected improvement. Finally, at least for this cycle, comes the A (for act) stage. During this stage the change is consolidated or standardised if it has been successful. Alternatively, if the change has not been successful, the lessons learned from the 'trial' are formalised before the cycle starts again.

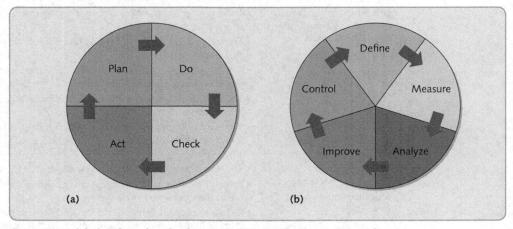

Figure 13.11 (a) the plan–do–check–act, or 'Deming' improvement cycle;
(b) the define–measure–analyse–improve–control, or DMAIC Six Sigma improvement cycle

The DMAIC cycle

In some ways this cycle is more intuitively obvious than the PDCA cycle insomuch as it follows a more 'experimental' approach. The DMAIC cycle starts with defining the problem or problems, partly to understand the scope of what needs to be done and partly to define exactly the requirements of the process improvement. Often at this stage a formal goal or target for the improvement is set. After definition comes the measurement stage, important because the Six Sigma approach emphasises the importance of working with hard evidence rather than opinion. It involves validating the problem (to make sure it is really worth solving), using data to refine the problem and measuring exactly what is happening. The analysis stage can be seen as an opportunity to develop hypotheses as to what the root causes of the problem really are. Such hypotheses are validated (or not) by the analysis and the main root causes of the problem identified. Once the causes of the problem are identified, work can begin on improving the process. Ideas are developed to remove the root causes of problems, solutions are tested and those solutions that seem to work are implemented, formalised and results measured. The improved process needs then to be continually monitored and controlled to check that the improved level of performance is being sustained. Then the cycle starts again, defining the problems that are preventing further improvement.

The last point in both cycles is the most important – *'the cycle starts again'*. It is only by accepting that in a continuous improvement philosophy these cycles quite literally never stop that improvement becomes part of every person's job.

The differences between breakthrough and continuous improvement

Breakthrough improvement places a high value on creative solutions, and encourages free thinking and individualism. It is a radical philosophy insomuch as it fosters an approach to improvement which does not accept many constraints on what is possible. 'Starting with a clean sheet of paper', 'going back to first principles' and 'completely rethinking the system' are all typical breakthrough improvement principles. Continuous improvement, on the other hand, is less ambitious, at least in the short term. It stresses adaptability, teamwork and attention to detail. It is not radical; rather it builds upon the wealth of accumulated experience within the operation itself, often relying primarily on the people who operate the system to improve it. One analogy used to explain this difference is the sprint versus the marathon. Breakthrough improvement is a series of explosive and impressive sprints. Continuous improvement, like marathon running, does not require the expertise and prowess required for sprinting, but it does require that the runner (or operations manager) keeps on going. Yet notwithstanding these differences, it is possible to use both approaches. Large and dramatic improvements can be implemented as and when they seem to promise significant improvement steps, but between such occasions the operation can continue making its quiet and less spectacular kaizen improvements. Table 13.3 lists some of the differences between the two approaches.

> **OPERATIONS PRINCIPLE**
>
> *Breakthrough improvement necessarily implies radical and/or extensive change.*

The Six Sigma approach to organising improvement

One approach to improvement that combines breakthrough and continuous philosophies is *Six Sigma*. Although technically the 'Six Sigma' name derives from statistical process control (SPC), and more specifically the concept of process capability, it has now come to mean a much broader approach to improvement. The following definition gives a sense of its modern usage: *'Six Sigma is a comprehensive and flexible system for achieving, sustaining and maximising business success. Six Sigma is uniquely driven by close understanding of customer needs, disciplined use of facts, data, and statistical analysis, and diligent attention to managing, improving, and reinventing business processes.'*[12]

Table 13.3 Some features of breakthrough and continuous improvement (based on Imai)[11]

	Breakthrough improvement	*Continuous improvement*
Effect	Short-term but dramatic	Long-term and long-lasting but undramatic
Pace	Big steps	Small steps
Time-frame	Intermittent and non-incremental	Continuous and incremental
Change	Abrupt and volatile	Gradual and constant
Involvement	Select a few 'champions'	Everybody
Approach	Individualism, individual ideas and efforts	Collectivism, group efforts, systems approach
Stimulus	Technological breakthroughs, new inventions, new theories	Conventional know-how and state of the art
Risks	Concentrated – 'all eggs in one basket'	Spread – many projects simultaneously
Practical requirements	Requires large investment but little effort to maintain	Requires little investment but great effort to maintain it
Effort orientations	Technology	People
Evaluation criteria	Results for profit	Process and effects for better results

The Six Sigma concept, therefore, includes many of the issues covered in this and other chapters of this book. For example, process design and redesign, balanced scorecard measures, continuous improvement, statistical process control, ongoing process planning and control, and so on. However, at the heart of Six Sigma lies an understanding of the negative effects of variation in all types of business process. This aversion to variation was first popularised by Motorola, the electronics company, who set its objective as 'total customer satisfaction' in the 1980s, then decided that true customer satisfaction would only be achieved when its products were delivered when promised, with no defects, with no early-life failures and no excessive failure in service. To achieve this, they initially focused on removing manufacturing defects, but soon realised that many problems were caused by latent defects, hidden within the design of its products. The only way to eliminate these defects was to make sure that design specifications were tight (i.e. narrow tolerances) and its processes very capable.

Motorola's Six Sigma quality concept was so named because it required that the natural variation of processes (±3 standard deviations) should be half their specification range. In other words, the specification range of any part of a product or service should be ±6 the standard deviation of the process. The Greek letter sigma (σ) is often used to indicate the standard deviation of a process, hence the Six Sigma label. The Six Sigma approach also used the measure of 'defects per million *opportunities*' (DPMO). This is the number of defects that the process will produce if there were one million opportunities to do so. So difficult processes with many opportunities for defects can be compared with simple processes with few opportunities for defects.

The Six Sigma approach also holds that improvement initiatives can only be successful if significant resources and training are devoted to their management. It recommends a specially trained cadre of practitioners, many of whom should be dedicated full time to improving processes as internal consultants. The terms that have become associated with this group of experts (and denote their level of expertise) are Master Black Belt, Black Belt and Green Belt.

- *Master Black Belts* are experts in the use of Six Sigma tools and techniques as well as how such techniques can be used and implemented. They are seen as teachers who can not only guide improvement projects, but also coach and mentor Black Belts and Green Belts. Given their responsibilities, it is expected that Master Black Belts are employed full time on their improvement activities.

- *Black Belts* take a direct hand in organising improvement teams, and will usually have undertaken a minimum of 20 to 25 days training and carried out at least one major improvement project. Black Belts are expected to develop their quantitative analytical skills and also act as coaches for Green Belt. Like Master Black Belts, they are dedicated full time to improvement, and although opinions vary, some organisations recommend one Black Belt for every 100 employees.
- *Green Belts* work within improvement teams, possibly as team leaders. They have less training than Black Belts – typically around 10 to 15 days. Green Belts are not full time positions. They have normal day-to-day process responsibilities but are expected to spend at least twenty per cent of their time on improvement projects.

Devoting such a large amount of training and time to improvement is a significant investment, especially for small companies. Nevertheless, Six Sigma proponents argue that the improvement activity is generally neglected in most operations and if it is to be taken seriously, it deserves the significant investment implied by the Six Sigma approach. Furthermore, they argue, if operated well, Six Sigma improvement projects run by experienced practitioners can save far more than their cost.

The Work-Out approach[13]

The idea of including all staff in the process of improvement has formed the core of many improvement approaches. One of the best known ways of this is the 'Work-Out' approach that originated in the US conglomerate GE. Jack Welch, the then boss of GE, reputedly developed the approach to recognise that employees were an important source of brainpower for new and creative ideas, and as a mechanism for *'creating an environment that pushes towards a relentless, endless companywide search for a better way to do everything we do'*. The Work-Out programme was seen as a way to reduce the bureaucracy often associated with improvement and of *'giving every employee, from managers to factory workers, an opportunity to influence and improve GE's day-to-day operations'*. According to Welch, Work-Out was meant to help people stop *'wrestling with the boundaries, the absurdities that grow in large organisations. We're all familiar with those absurdities: too many approvals, duplication, pomposity, waste. Work-Out in essence turned the company upside down, so that the workers told the bosses what to do. That forever changed the way people behaved at the company. Work-Out is also designed to reduce, and ultimately eliminate all of the waste hours and energy that organisations like GE typically expend in performing day-to-day operations.'* GE also used, what it called 'town meetings' of employees. And although proponents of Work-Out emphasise the need to modify the specifics of the approach to fit the context in which it is applied, there is a broad sequence of activities implied within the approach.

- Staff, other key stakeholders and their manager hold a meeting away from the operation (a so called 'off-siter').
- At this meeting the manager gives the group the responsibility to solve a problem or set of problems shared by the group but which are ultimately the manager's responsibility.
- The manager then leaves and the group spend time (maybe two or three days) working on developing solutions to the problems, sometimes using outside facilitators.
- At the end of the meeting, the responsible manager (and sometimes the manager's boss) rejoins the group to be presented with its recommendations.
- The manager can respond in three ways to each recommendation: 'yes', 'no', or 'I have to consider it more'. If it is the last response the manager must clarify what further issues must be considered and how and when the decision will be made.

Work-Out programmes are also expensive: outside facilitators, off-site facilities and the payroll costs of a sizeable group of people meeting away from work can be substantial, even without considering the potential disruption to everyday activities. But arguably the most important implications of adopting Work-Out are cultural. In its purest form Work-Out reinforces an underlying culture of fast (and some would claim, superficial) problem-solving. It also relies on full and near universal employee involvement and empowerment together with direct dialogue between managers and their subordinates. What distinguishes the Work-Out approach from the many other types of group-based problem solving is fast decision-making and the idea that managers must respond immediately and decisively to team suggestions. But some claim that it is intolerant of staff and managers who are not committed to its values. In fact, it is acknowledged in GE that resistance to the process or outcome is not tolerated and that obstructing the efforts of the workout process is 'a career-limiting move'.

DIAGNOSTIC QUESTION

What techniques should be used to facilitate improvement?

Video

All the techniques described in this book and its supplements can be regarded as 'improvement' techniques. However, some techniques are particularly useful for improving operations and processes generally. Here we select some techniques which either have not been described elsewhere or need to be re-introduced in their role of helping operations improvement particularly.

Scatter diagrams

Scatter diagrams provide a quick and simple method of identifying whether there is evidence of a connection between two sets of data: for example, the time at which you set off for work every morning and how long the journey to work takes. Plotting each journey on a graph which has departure time on one axis and journey time on the other could give an indication of whether departure time and journey time are related, and if so, how. Scatter diagrams can be treated in a far more sophisticated manner by quantifying how strong the relationship between the sets of data is. But, however sophisticated the approach, this type of graph only identifies the existence of a relationship, not necessarily the existence of a cause–effect relationship. If the scatter diagram shows a very strong connection between the sets of data, it is important evidence of a cause–effect relationship, but not proof positive. It could be coincidence!

OPERATIONS PRINCIPLE

Improvement is facilitated by relatively simple analytical techniques.

EXAMPLE   **Kaston Pyral Services Ltd (1)**

Kaston Pyral Services Ltd (KPS) installs and maintains environmental control, heating and air conditioning systems. It has set up an improvement team to suggest ways in which it might improve its levels of customer service. The improvement team had completed its first customer satisfaction survey. The survey asked customers to score the service they received from KPS in several ways. For example, it asked customers to score services on a scale of one to ten on promptness, friendliness, level of advice, etc. Scores were then summed to give a 'total satisfaction score' for each customer – the higher the score, the greater the satisfaction. The spread of satisfaction scores puzzled the team and they considered what factors might be causing

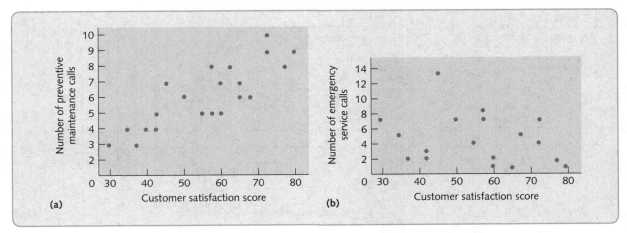

Figure 13.12 Scatter diagrams for customer satisfaction versus (a) number of preventive maintenance calls and (b) number of emergency service calls

such differences in the way their customers viewed them. Two factors were put forward to explain the differences:

1 the number of times in the past year the customer had received a preventive maintenance visit
2 the number of times the customer had called for emergency service.

All this data was collected and plotted on scatter diagrams as shown in Figure 13.12. Figure 13.12(a) shows that there seems to be a clear relationship between a customer's satisfaction score and the number of times the customer was visited for regular servicing. The scatter diagram in Figure 13.12(b) is less clear. Although all customers who had very high satisfaction scores had made very few emergency calls, so had some customers with low satisfaction scores. As a result of this analysis, the team decided to survey customers' views on its emergency service.

Cause–effect diagrams

Cause–effect diagrams are a particularly effective method of helping to search for the root causes of problems. They do this by asking what, when, where, how and why questions, but also add some possible 'answers' in an explicit way. They can also be used to identify areas where further data is needed. Cause–effect diagrams (which are also known as Ishikawa diagrams) have become extensively used in improvement programmes. This is because they provide a way of structuring group brainstorming sessions. Often the structure involves identifying possible causes under the (rather old fashioned) headings of: machinery, manpower, materials, methods and money. Yet in practice, any categorisation that comprehensively covers all relevant possible causes could be used.

EXAMPLE   **Kaston Pyral Services Ltd (2)**

The improvement team at KPS was working on a particular area which was proving a problem. Whenever service engineers were called out to perform emergency servicing for a customer, they took with them the spares and equipment which they thought would be necessary to repair the system. Although engineers could never be sure exactly what materials and equipment they would need for a job, they could guess what was likely to be needed and take a range of spares and equipment which would cover most eventualities. Too often, however, the engineers would find that they needed a spare that they had not brought with them. The cause–effect diagram for this particular problem, as drawn by the team, is shown in Figure 13.13.

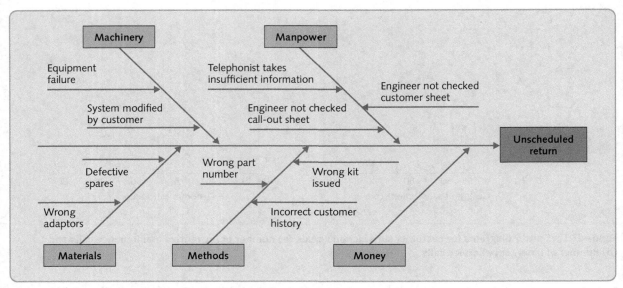

Figure 13.13 Cause–effect diagram of unscheduled returns at KPS

Pareto diagrams

In any improvement process, it is worthwhile distinguishing what is important and what is less so. The purpose of the Pareto diagram (that was first introduced in Chapter 9) is to distinguish between the 'vital few' issues and the 'trivial many'. It is a relatively straightforward technique which involves arranging items of information on the types of problem or causes of problem into their order of importance (usually measured by 'frequency of occurrence). This can be used to highlight areas where further decision-making will be useful. Pareto analysis is based on the phenomenon of relatively few causes explaining the majority of effects. For example, most revenue for any company is likely to come from relatively few of the company's customers. Similarly, relatively few of a doctor's patients will probably occupy most of his or her time.

EXAMPLE **Kaston Pyral Services Ltd (3)**

The KPS improvement team which was investigating unscheduled returns from emergency servicing (the issue which was described in the cause–effect diagram in Figure 13.13) examined all occasions over the previous 12 months on which an unscheduled return had been made. They categorised the reasons for unscheduled returns as follows:

1 The wrong part had been taken to a job because, although the information which the engineer received was sound, he or she had incorrectly predicted the nature of the fault.
2 The wrong part had been taken to the job because there was insufficient information given when the call was taken.
3 The wrong part had been taken to the job because the system had been modified in some way and not recorded on KPS's records.
4 The wrong part had been taken to the job because the part had been incorrectly issued to the engineer by stores.
5 No part had been taken because the relevant part was out of stock.
6 The wrong equipment had been taken for whatever reason.
7 Any other reason.

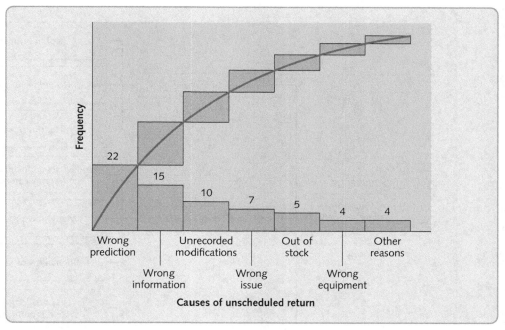

Figure 13.14 Pareto diagram for causes of unscheduled returns

The relative frequency of occurrence of these causes is shown in Figure 13.14. About a third of all unscheduled returns were due to the first category, and more than half the returns were accounted for by the first and second categories together. It was decided that the problem could best be tackled by concentrating on how to get more information to the engineers which would enable them to predict the causes of failure accurately.

Why–why analysis

Why–why analysis starts by stating the problem and asking *why* that problem has occurred. Once the major reasons for the problem occurring have been identified, each of the major reasons is taken in turn and again the question is asked *why* those reasons have occurred, and so on. This procedure is continued until either a cause seems sufficiently self-contained to be addressed by itself or no more answers to the question 'Why?' can be generated.

EXAMPLE   **Kaston Pyral Services Ltd (4)**

The major cause of unscheduled returns at KPS was the incorrect prediction of reasons for the customer's system failure. This is stated as the 'problem' in the why–why analysis in Figure 13.15. The question is then asked, 'Why was the failure wrongly predicted?' Three answers are proposed: first, that the engineers were not trained correctly; second, that they had insufficient knowledge of the particular product installed in the customer's location; third, that they had insufficient knowledge of the customer's particular system with its modifications. Each of these three reasons is taken in turn, and the questions are asked. 'Why is there a lack of training?', 'Why is there a lack of product knowledge?' and 'Why is there a lack of customer knowledge?' And so on.

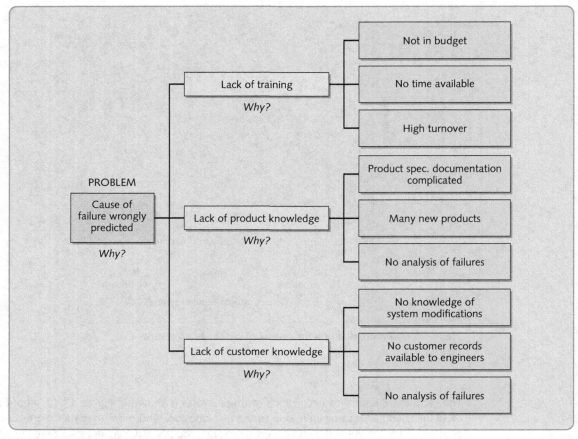

Figure 13.15 Why–why analysis for 'failure wrongly predicted'

How can improvement be made to stick?

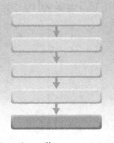

Video

Not all of the improvement initiatives, (often launched with high expectations), will go on to fulfil their potential. Even those improvement initiatives that are successfully implemented may lose impetus over time. Sometimes this is because of managers' view of the nature of improvement, at other times it is because managers fail to manage the improvement process adequately.

Avoid becoming a victim of improvement 'fashion'

OPERATIONS PRINCIPLE

The popularity of an improvement approach is not necessarily an indicator of its effectiveness.

Improvement has, to some extent, become a fashion industry with new ideas and concepts continually being introduced as offering a novel way to improve business performance. There is nothing intrinsically wrong with this. Fashion stimulates and refreshes through introducing novel ideas. Without it, things would stagnate. The problem lies not with new improvement ideas, but rather with some managers becoming a victim of the process, where some new idea will entirely displace whatever went before. Most new ideas have something to say, but jumping from one fad to another will not only generate a backlash against any new idea, but also destroy the ability to accumulate the experience that comes from experimenting with each one.

Avoiding becoming an improvement fashion victim is not easy. It requires that those directing the improvement process take responsibility for a number of issues.

- They must take responsibility for improvement as an ongoing activity, rather than becoming champions for only one specific improvement initiative.
- They must take responsibility for understanding the underlying ideas behind each new concept. Improvement is not 'following a recipe' or 'painting by numbers'. Unless one understands *why* improvement ideas are supposed to work, it is difficult to understand *how* they can be made to work properly.
- They must take responsibility for understanding the antecedents to a 'new' improvement idea, because it helps to understand it better and to judge how appropriate it may be for one's own operation.
- They must be prepared to adapt new idea so that they make sense within the context of their own operation. 'One size' rarely fits all.
- They must take responsibility for the (often significant) education and learning effort that will be needed if new ideas are to be intelligently exploited.
- Above all they must avoid the over-exaggeration and hype that many new ideas attract. Although it is sometimes tempting to exploit the motivational 'pull' of new ideas through slogans, posters and exhortations, carefully thought-out plans will always be superior in the long run, and will help avoid the inevitable backlash that follows 'over-selling' a single approach.

Managing the improvement process

There is no absolute prescription for the way improvement should be managed. Any improvement process should reflect the uniqueness of each operation's characteristics. What appear to be almost a guarantee of difficulty in managing improvement processes, are attempts to squeeze improvement into a standard mould. Nevertheless, there are some aspects of any improvement process that appear to influence its eventual success, and should at least be debated.

OPERATIONS PRINCIPLE

There is no one universal approach to improvement.

Should an improvement *strategy* be defined?

Without thinking through the overall purpose and long-term goals of the improvement process it is difficult for any operation to know where it is going. Specifically, an improvement strategy should have something to say about:

- the competitive priorities of the organisation, and how the improvement process is expected to contribute to achieving increased strategic impact
- the roles and responsibilities of the various parts of the organisation in the improvement process
- the resources that will be available for the improvement process
- the general approach to, and philosophy of, improvement in the organisation.

Yet, too rigid a strategy can become inappropriate if the business's competitive circumstances change, or as the operation learns through experience. But, the careful modification of improvement strategy in the light of experience is not the same as making dramatic changes in improvement strategy as new improvement fashions appear.

What degree of top-management support is required?

For most authorities, the answer is unambiguous – a significant amount. Without top-management support, improvement cannot succeed. It is the most crucial factor in almost all the studies of improvement process implementation. It also goes far beyond merely allocating senior resources to the process. 'Top-management support' usually means that senior personnel must:

- understand and believe in the link between improvement and the business overall strategic impact
- understand the practicalities of the improvement process and be able to communicate its principles and techniques to the rest of the organisation
- be able to participate in the total problem-solving process to improve performance
- formulate and maintain a clear idea of the operation's improvement philosophy.

Should the improvement process be formally supervised?

Some improvement processes fail because they develop an unwieldy 'bureaucracy' to run them. But any process needs to be managed, so all improvement processes will need some kind of group to design, plan and control its efforts. However, a worthwhile goal for many improvement processes is to make themselves 'self-governing' over time. In fact there are significant advantages in terms of people's commitment in giving them responsibility for managing the improvement process. However, even when improvement is driven primarily by self-managing improvement groups, there is a need for some sort of 'repository of knowledge' to ensure that the learning and experience accumulated from the improvement process is not lost.

To what extent should improvement be group-based?

No one can really know a process quite like the people who operate it. They have access to the informal as well as the formal information networks that contain the way processes really work. But, working alone, individuals cannot pool their experience or learn from one another. So improvement processes are almost always based on teams. The issue is how these teams should be formulated, which will depend on the circumstances of the operation, its context and its objectives. For example, *quality circles*, much used in Japan, encountered mixed success in the West. A very different type of team is the *task force*, or what some US companies call a 'tiger team'. Compared with quality circles, this type of group is far more management directed and focused. Most improvement teams are between these two extremes (see Figure 13.16).

How should success be recognised?

If improvement is so important, it should be recognised, with success, effort and initiative being formally rewarded. The paradox is that, if improvement is to become part of everyday operational life, then why should improvement effort be especially rewarded? One compromise is to devise a recognition and rewards system that responds to improvement initiatives early in the improvement process, but then merges into the operation's normal reward procedures. In this way people are rewarded not just for the efficient and effective running of their processes on an ongoing basis, but also for improving their processes. Then improvement will become an everyday responsibility of all people in the operation.

How much training is required?

Training has two purposes in the development of improvement processes. The first is to provide the necessary skills that will allow staff to solve process problems and implement improvements. The second is to provide an understanding of the appropriate interpersonal, group,

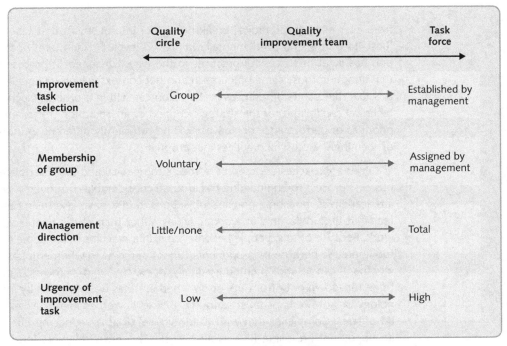

Figure 13.16 Different types of improvement groups have different characteristics

and organisational skills that are needed to 'lubricate' the improvement process. This second objective is more difficult than the first. Training and improvement techniques may take up significant time and effort, but none of this knowledge will be of much use if the organisational context for improvement mitigates against the techniques being used effectively. Although the nature of appropriate organisational development is beyond the scope of this book, it is worth noting both technique-based skills and organisational skills are enhanced if staff have a basic understanding of the core ideas and principles of operations and process management.

Critical commentary

Each chapter contains a short critical commentary on the main ideas covered in the chapter. Its purpose is not to undermine the issues discussed in the chapter, but to emphasise that, although we present a relatively orthodox view of operation, there are other perspectives.

● Many of the issues covered in this chapter are controversial, for different reasons. Some criticism concerns the effectiveness of improvement methods. For example, it can be argued that there is a fundamental flaw in the concept of benchmarking. Operations that rely on others to stimulate their creativity, especially those that are in search of 'best practice', are always limiting themselves to currently accepted methods of operating or currently accepted limits to performance. 'Best practice' is not 'best' in the sense that it cannot be bettered, it is only 'best' in the sense that it is the best one can currently find. And accepting what is currently defined as 'best' may prevent operations from ever making the radical breakthrough or improvement that takes the concept of 'best' to a new and fundamentally improved level. Furthermore, because one operation has a set of successful practices in the way it manages it process does not mean that adopting those same practices in another context will prove equally successful. It is possible that subtle differences in the resources within a process (such as staff skills or technical capabilities) or the strategic context of an operation (for example, the relative priorities of performance objectives) will be sufficiently different to make the adoption of seemingly successful practices inappropriate.

● Other approaches are seen by some as too radical and too insensitive. For example, business process re-engineering has aroused considerable controversy. Most of its critics are academics, but some practical objections to BPR have also been raised, such as the fear that BPR looks only at work activities rather than at the people who perform the work. Because of this, people become 'cogs in a machine'. Also some see BPR as being too imprecise because its proponents cannot agree as to whether it has to be radical or whether it can be implemented gradually, or exactly what a process is, or whether it has to be top-down or bottom-up, or on whether it has be supported by information technology or not. Perhaps most seriously, BPR is viewed as merely an excuse for getting rid of staff. Companies that wish to 'downsize' (that is, reduce numbers of staff within an operation) are using BPR as an excuse. This puts the short-term interests of the shareholders of the company above either their longer-term interests or the interests of the company's employees. Moreover, a combination of radical redesign together with downsizing can mean that the essential core of experience is lost from the operation. This leaves it vulnerable to any marked turbulence since it no longer has the knowledge and experience of how to cope with unexpected changes.

● Even the more gentle approach of continuous improvement is not universally welcomed. Notwithstanding its implications of empowerment and liberal attitude toward shop-floor staff, it is regarded by some worker representatives as merely a further example of management exploiting workers. Relatively established ideas such as TQM have been defined by its critics as 'management by stress'. Or, even more radically, 'TQM is like putting a vacuum cleaner next to a worker's brain and sucking out ideas. They don't want to rent your knowledge anymore, they want to own it – in the end that makes you totally replaceable.'

SUMMARY CHECKLIST

This checklist comprises questions that can be usefully applied to any type of operations and reflect the major diagnostic questions used within the chapter.

☐ Is the importance of performance improvement fully recognised within the operation?

☐ Do all operations and process managers see performance improvement as an integral part of their job?

☐ Is the gap between current and desired performance clearly articulated in all areas?

☐ Is the current performance measurement system seen as forming a basis for improvement?

☐ Does performance measurement focus on factors that reflect the operation's strategic objectives?

☐ Do performance measures allow likely problem areas to be diagnosed?

☐ Is some kind of balanced score card approach used that includes financial, internal, customer and learning perspectives?

☐ Is target performance set using an appropriate balance between historical, strategic, external and absolute performance targets?

☐ Are both performance and process methods benchmarked against similar operations and/or processes externally?

☐ Is benchmarking done on a regular basis and seen as an important contribution to improvement?

☐ Is some formal method of comparing actual and desired performance (such as the importance–performance matrix) used?

☐ To what extent does the operation have a predisposition towards breakthrough or continuous improvement?

☐ Have breakthrough improvement approaches such as business process re-engineering been evaluated?

☐ Are continuous improvement methods and problem-solving cycles used within the operation?

☐ If they are, has continuous improvement become a part of everyone's' job?

☐ Which 'abilities' and 'associated behaviours' (see Table 13.2) are evident within the operation?

☐ Has the Six Sigma approach to improvement been evaluated?

☐ Are the more common improvement techniques used to facilitate improvement within the operations?

☐ Does the operation show any signs of becoming a fashion victim of the latest improvement approach?

☐ Does the operation have a well thought-through approach to managing improvement?

Geneva Construction and Risk

'This is not going to be like last time. Then, we were adopting an improvement programme because we were told to. This time it's our idea and, if it's successful, it will be us that are telling the rest of the group how to do it.'
(Tyko Mattson, Six Sigma Champion, GCR)

Tyko Mattson was speaking as the newly appointed 'Champion' at Geneva Construction and Risk Insurance, who had been charged with *'steering the Six Sigma programme until it is firmly established as part of our ongoing practice'*. The previous improvement initiative that he was referring to dated back many years to when GCR's parent company, Wichita Mutual Insurance, had insisted on the adoption of totally quality management (TQM) in all its businesses. The TQM initiative had never been pronounced a failure and had managed to make some improvements, especially in customers' perception of the company's levels of service. However, the initiative had 'faded out' during the 1990s and, even though all departments still had to formally report on their improvement projects, their number and impact was now relatively minor.

Source: Digital Vision/Getty Images

History

The Geneva Construction Insurance Company was founded in 1922 to provide insurance for building contractors and construction companies, initially in German-speaking Europe and then, because of the emigration of some family members to the USA, in North America. The company had remained relatively small and had specialised in housing construction projects until the early 1950s when it had started to grow, partly because of geographical expansion and partly because it has moved into larger (sometimes very large) construction insurance in the industrial, oil, petrochemical and power plant construction areas. In 1983 it had been bought by the Wichita Mutual Group and had absorbed the group's existing construction insurance businesses.

By 2000 it had established itself as one of the leading providers of insurance for construction projects, especially complex, high-risk projects, where contractual and other legal issues, physical exposures and design uncertainty needed 'customised' insurance responses. Providing such insurance needed particular knowledge and skills from specialists, including construction underwriters, loss adjusters, engineers, international lawyers, and specialist risk consultants. Typically, the company would insure losses resulting

from contractor failure, related public liability issues, delays in project completion, associated litigation, other litigation (such as ongoing asbestos risks) and negligence issues.

The company's headquarters were in Geneva and housed all major departments including sales and marketing, underwriting, risk analysis, claims and settlement, financial control, general admin, specialist and general legal advice, and business research. There were also 37 local offices around the world, organised into four regional areas: North America; South America; Europe, Middle East and Africa; and Asia. These regional offices provided localised help and advice directly to clients and also to the 890 agents that GCR used worldwide.

The previous improvement initiative

When Wichita Mutual had insisted that CGR adopt a TQM initiative, it had gone as far as to specify exactly how it should do it and which consultants should be used to help establish the programme. Tyko Mattson shakes his head as he describes it. *'I was not with the company at that time but, looking back, it's amazing that it ever managed to do any good. You can't impose the structure of an improvement initiative from the top. It has to, at least partially, be shaped by the people who* are going to be involved in it. But everything had to be done according to the handbook. The cost of quality was measured for different departments according to the handbook. Everyone had to learn the improvement techniques that were described in the handbook. Everyone had be part of a quality circle that was organised according to the handbook. We even had to have annual award ceremonies where we gave out special 'certificates of merit' to those quality circles that had achieved the type of improvement that the handbook said they should.' The TQM initiative had been run by the 'Quality Committee', a group of eight people with representatives from all the major departments at head office. Initially, it had spent much of its time setting up the improvement groups and organising training in quality techniques. However, soon it had become swamped by the work needed to evaluate which improvement suggestions should be implemented. Soon the work load associated with assessing improvement ideas had become so great that the company decided to allocate small improvement budgets to each department on a quarterly basis that they could spend without reference to the Quality Committee. Projects requiring larger investment or that had a significant impact on other parts of the business still needed to be approved by the committee before they were implemented.

Department improvement budgets were still used within the business and improvement plans were still required from each department on an annual basis. However, the Quality Committee had stopped meeting by 1994 and the annual award ceremony had become a general communications meeting for all staff at the headquarters. 'Looking back,' said Tyko, 'the TQM initiative faded away for three reasons. First, people just got tired of it. It was always seen as something extra rather than part of normal business life, so it was always seen as taking time away from doing your normal job. Second, many of the supervisory and middle management levels never really bought into it, I guess because they felt threatened. Third, only a very few of the local offices around the world ever adopted the TQM philosophy. Sometimes this was because they did not want the extra effort. Sometimes, however, they would argue that improvement initiatives of this type may be OK for head office processes, but not for the more dynamic world of supporting clients in the field.'

The Six Sigma initiative

Early in 2005, Tyko Mattson, who for the last two years had been overseeing the outsourcing of some of GCR's claims processing to India, had attended a conference on 'Operations Excellence in Financial Services', and had heard several speakers detail the success they had achieved through using a Six Sigma approach to operations improvement. He had persuaded his immediate boss, Marie-Dominique Tomas, the Head of Claims for the company, to allow him to investigate its applicability to GCR. He had interviewed a number of other financial services who had implemented Six Sigma as well as a number of consultants and in September 2005 had submitted a report entitled, 'What is Six Sigma and how might it be applied in GRC?' Extracts from this are included in the Appendix (see below). Marie-Dominique Tomas was particularly concerned that they should avoid the mistakes of the TQM initiative. 'Looking back, it is almost embarrassing to see how naive we were. We really did think that it would change the whole way that we did business. And although it did produce some benefits, it absorbed a large amount of time at all levels in the organisation. This time we want something that will deliver results without costing too much or distracting us from focusing on business performance. That is why I like Six Sigma. It starts with clarifying business objectives and works from there.'

By late 2005, Tyko's report had been approved both by GCR and by Wichita Mutual's main board. Tyko had been given the challenge of carrying out the recommendations in his report, reporting directly to GCR's executive board. Marie-Dominique Tomas, was cautiously optimistic: 'It is quite a challenge for Tyko. Most of us on the executive board remember the TQM initiative and some are still sceptical concerning the value of such initiatives. However, Tyko's gradualist approach and his emphasis on the 'three pronged' attack on revenue, costs, and risk, impressed the board. We now have to see whether he can make it work.'

Appendix – Extract from *What is Six Sigma and how might it be applied in GCR?*

Six Sigma – pitfalls and benefits

Some pitfalls of Six Sigma

It is not simple to implement, and is resource hungry. The focus on measurement implies that the process data is available and reasonably robust. If this is not the case, it is possible to waste a lot of effort in obtaining process performance data. It may also over-complicate things if advanced techniques are used on simple problems.

It is easier to apply Six Sigma to repetitive processes – characterised by high volume, low variety and low visibility to customers. It is more difficult to apply Six Sigma to low-volume, higher-variety and high-visibility processes where standardisation is harder to achieve and the focus is on managing the variety.

Six Sigma is not a 'quick fix'. Companies that have implemented Six Sigma effectively have not treated it as just another new initiative but as an approach that requires the long-term systematic reduction of waste. Equally, it is not a panacea and should not be implemented as one.

Some benefits of Six Sigma

Companies have achieved significant benefits in reducing cost and improving customer service through implementing Six Sigma.

Six Sigma can reduce process variation, which will have a significant impact on operational risk. It is a tried-and-tested methodology, which combines the strongest parts of existing improvement methodologies. It lends itself to being customised to fit individual company's circumstances. For example, Mestech Assurance has extended their Six Sigma initiative to examine operational risk processes.

Six Sigma could leverage a number of current initiatives. The risk self-assessment methodology, Sarbanes Oxley, the process library, and our performance metrics work are all laying the foundations for better knowledge and measurement of process data.

Six Sigma – key conclusions for GCR

Six Sigma is a powerful improvement methodology. It is not all new but what it does do successfully is to combine some of the best parts of existing improvement methodologies, tools and techniques. Six Sigma has helped many companies achieve significant benefits. It could help GCR significantly improve risk management because it focuses on driving errors and exceptions out of processes.

Six Sigma has significant advantages over other process improvement methodologies. It engages senior management actively by establishing process ownership and linkage to strategic objectives. This is seen as integral to successful implementation in the literature and by all companies interviewed who had implemented it. It forces a rigorous approach to driving out variance in processes by analysing the root cause of defects and errors and measuring improvement. It is an 'umbrella' approach, combining all the best parts of other improvement approaches.

Implementing Six Sigma across GCR is not the right approach

Companies who are widely quoted as having achieved the most significant headline benefits from Six Sigma were already relatively mature in terms of process management.

Those companies, who understood their process capability, typically had achieved a degree of process standardisation and had an established process improvement culture.

Six Sigma requires significant investment in performance metrics and process knowledge. GCR is probably not yet sufficiently advanced. However, we are working towards a position where key process data are measured and known and this will provide a foundation for Six Sigma.

Why is targeted implementation recommended?

Full implementation is resource hungry. Dedicated resource and budget for implementation of improvements is required. Even if the approach is modified, resource and budget will still be needed, just to a lesser extent. However, the evidence is that the investment is well worth it and pays back relatively quickly.

There was strong evidence from companies interviewed that the best implementation approach was to pilot Six Sigma, and select failing processes for the pilot. In addition, previous internal piloting of implementations has been successful in GCR – we know this approach works within our culture.

Six Sigma would provide a platform for GSR to build on and evolve over time. It is a way of leveraging the ongoing work on processes and the risk methodology (being developed by the Operational Risk Group). This diagnostic tool could be blended into Six Sigma, giving GCR a powerful model to drive reduction in process variation and improve operational risk management.

Recommendations

It is recommended that GCR management implement a Six Sigma pilot. The characteristics of the pilot would be as follows:

- A tailored approach to Six Sigma that would fit GCR's objectives and operating environment. Implementing Six Sigma in its entirety would not be appropriate.

- The use of an external partner: GCR does not have sufficient internal Six Sigma, and external experience will be critical to tailoring the approach, and providing training.

- Establishing where GCR's sigma performance is now. Different tools and approaches will be required to advance from 2 to 3 Sigma than those required to move from 3 to 4 Sigma.

- Quantifying the potential benefits. Is the investment worth making? What would a 1 Sigma increase in performance vs. risk be worth to us?

- Keeping the methods simple, if simple will achieve our objectives. As a minimum for us that means Team Based Problem Solving and basic statistical techniques.

Next steps

1 Decide priority and confirm budget and resourcing for initial analysis to develop a Six Sigma risk improvement programme in 2006.

2 Select an external partner experienced in improvement and Six Sigma methodologies.

3 Assess GCR current state to confirm where to start in implementing Six Sigma.

4 Establish how much GCR is prepared to invest in Six Sigma and quantify the potential benefits.

5 Tailor Six Sigma to focus on risk management.

6 Identify potential pilot area(s) and criteria for assessing its suitability.

7 Develop a Six Sigma pilot plan.

8 Conduct and review the pilot programme.

QUESTIONS

1 How does the Six Sigma approach seem to differ from the TQM approach adopted by the company almost 20 years ago?

2 Is Six Sigma a better approach for this type of company?

3 Do you think Tyko can avoid the Six Sigma initiative suffering the same fate as the TQM initiative?

APPLYING THE PRINCIPLES

Hints

Some of these exercises can be answered by reading the chapter. Others will require some general knowledge of business activity and some might require an element of investigation. Hints on how they can all be answered are to be found in the eText at www.pearsoned.co.uk/slack.

1 Visit a library (for example, a university library) and consider how they could start a performance measurement programme which would enable it to judge the effectiveness with which it organises its operations. The library probably loans (if a university library) books to students on both a long-term and short-term basis, keeps an extensive stock of journals, will send off for specialist publications to specialist libraries and has an extensive online database facility. What measures of performance do you think it would be appropriate to use in this kind of operation and what type of performance standards should the library adopt?

2 (a) Devise a benchmarking programme that will benefit the course or programme that you are currently taking. In doing so, decide whether you are going to benchmark against other courses at the same institution, competitor courses at other institutions, or some other point of comparison. Also decide whether you are more interested in the performance of these other courses or the way they organise their processes, or both.

   (b) Identify the institutions and courses against which you are going to benchmark your own course.

   (c) Collect data on these other courses (visit them, send off for literature, or visit their website).

   (d) Compare your own course against these others and draw up a list of implications for the way your course could be improved.

3 Think back to the last product or service failure that caused you some degree of inconvenience. Draw a cause–effect diagram that identifies all the main causes of why the failure could have occurred. Try and identify the frequency with which such causes happen. This could be done by talking with the staff of the operation that provided the service. Draw a Pareto diagram that indicates the relatively frequency of each cause of failure. Suggest ways in which the operation could reduce the chances of failure.

4 (a) As a group, identify a 'high visibility' operation that you all are familiar with. This could be a type of quick service restaurant, record stores, public transport systems, libraries, etc.

(b) Once you have identified the broad class of operation, visit a number of them and use your experience as customers to identify the main performance factors that are of importance to you as customers, and how each store rates against each other in terms of their performance on these same factors.

(c) Draw an importance–performance diagram for one of the operations that indicates the priority they should be giving to improving their performance.

(d) Discuss the ways in which such an operation might improve its performance and try to discuss your findings with the staff of the operation.

Notes on chapter

1 Based on a case study written by Robert Johnston, Chai Kah Hin and Jochen Wirtz, National University of Singapore, and Christopher Lovelock, Yale University. Adapted by permission.

2 Source: The EFQM website: www.efqm.org.

3 See Kaplan, R.S. and Norton, D.P. (1996), *The Balanced Scorecard,* Harvard Business School Press, Boston.

4 Kaplan, R.S. and Norton, D.P. (1996) *op. cit.*

5 Ferdows, K. and de Meyer, A. (1990) 'Lasting Improvement in Manufacturing', *Journal of Operations Management,* Vol 9, No 2. However, research for this model is mixed. For example, Patricia Nemetz questions the validity of the mode, finding more support for the idea that the sequence of improvement is generally dictated by technological (operations resource) or market (requirements) pressures: Nemetz, P. (2002) 'A longitudinal study of strategic choice, multiple advantage, cumulative model and order winner/qualifier view of manufacturing strategy', *Journal of Business and Management,* January.

6 Hammer, M. and Champy, J. (1993) *Re-engineering the Corporation*, Nicholas Brealey Publishing.

7 Hammer, M. (1990) 'Re-engineering Work: Don't Automate, Obliterate', *Harvard Business Review*, Vol 68, No 4.

8 Imai, M. (1986) *Kaizen – The Key to Japan's Competitive Success*, McGraw-Hill.

9 Bessant, J. and Caffyn, S. (1997) 'High Involvement Innovation', *International Journal of Technology Management*, Vol 14, No 1.

10 Bessant, J. and Caffyn, S. (1997) *op. cit.*

11 Imai, M. (1986), *op. cit.*

12 Pande, P.S., Neuman, R.P., and Cavanagh, R.R. (2000) *The Six Sigma Way*, McGraw-Hill, New York.

13 For further details of this approach see Schaninger, W.S., Harris, S.G. and Niebuhr, R.L. (2000) 'Adapting General Electric's Workout for use in other organizations: a template', http://www.isixsigma.com; Quinn, J. (1994) 'What a workout!' *Sales & Marketing Management, Performance Supplement* November, 58–63; Stewart, T. (1991). 'GE keeps those ideas coming', *Fortune*, 124 (4), 40–45.

TAKING IT FURTHER

Chang, R.Y. (1995) *Continuous Process Improvement: A Practical Guide to Improving Processes for Measurable Results*, Cogan Page.

Leibfried, K.H.J. and McNair, C.J. (1992) *Benchmarking: A Tool for Continuous Improvement*, HarperCollins. *There are many books on benchmarking; this is a comprehensive and practical guide to the subject.*

Pande, P.S., Neuman, R.P. and Cavanagh, R. (2002) *Six Sigma Way Team Field Book: An Implementation Guide for Project Improvement Teams*, McGraw Hill. *Obviously based on the Six Sigma principle and related to the book by the same author team recommended in Chapter 12, this is an unashamedly practical guide to the Six Sigma approach.*

USEFUL WEBSITES

www.opsman.org   *Definitions, links and opinions on operations and process management.*

http://www.processimprovement.com/   *Commercial site but some content that could be useful.*

http://www.kaizen.com/   *Professional institute for kaizen. Gives some insight into practitioner views.*

http://www.ebenchmarking.com   *Benchmarking information.*

http://www.quality.nist.gov/   *American Quality Assurance Institute. Well established institution for all types of business quality assurance.*

http://www.balancedscorecard.org/   *Site of an American organisation with plenty of useful links.*

Interactive
quiz

For further resources including examples, animated diagrams, self-test questions, Excel spreadsheets and video materials please explore the eText on the companion website at **www.pearsoned.co.uk/slack**.

Section 5:

Management Science

Introduction to Modeling

Management science is the application of a scientific approach to solving management problems in order to help managers make better decisions. As implied by this definition, management science encompasses a number of mathematically oriented techniques that have either been developed within the field of management science or been adapted from other disciplines, such as the natural sciences, mathematics, statistics, and engineering. This text provides an introduction to the techniques that make up management science and demonstrates their applications to management problems.

Management science is a scientific approach to solving management problems.

Management science is a recognized and established discipline in business. The applications of management science techniques are widespread, and they have been frequently credited with increasing the efficiency and productivity of business firms. In various surveys of businesses, many indicate that they use management science techniques, and most rate the results to be very good. Management science (also referred to as *operations research, quantitative methods, quantitative analysis*, and *decision sciences*) is part of the fundamental curriculum of most programs in business.

Management science can be used in a variety of organizations to solve many different types of problems.

As you proceed through the various management science models and techniques contained in this text, you should remember several things. First, most of the examples presented in this text are for business organizations because businesses represent the main users of management science. However, management science techniques can be applied to solve problems in different types of organizations, including services, government, military, business and industry, and health care.

Second, in this text all of the modeling techniques and solution methods are mathematically based. In some instances the manual, mathematical solution approach is shown because it helps one understand how the modeling techniques are applied to different problems. However, a computer solution is possible for each of the modeling techniques in this text, and in many cases the computer solution is emphasized. The more detailed mathematical solution procedures for many of the modeling techniques are included as supplemental modules on the companion Web site for this text.

Management science encompasses a logical approach to problem solving.

Finally, as the various management science techniques are presented, keep in mind that management science is more than just a collection of techniques. Management science also involves the philosophy of approaching a problem in a logical manner (i.e., a scientific approach). The logical, consistent, and systematic approach to problem solving can be as useful (and valuable) as the knowledge of the mechanics of the mathematical techniques themselves. This understanding is especially important for those readers who do not always see the immediate benefit of studying mathematically oriented disciplines such as management science.

The Management Science Approach to Problem Solving

As indicated in the previous section, management science encompasses a logical, systematic approach to problem solving, which closely parallels what is known as the scientific method for attacking problems. This approach, as shown in Figure 1.1, follows a generally recognized and ordered series of steps: (1) observation, (2) definition of the problem, (3) model construction, (4) model solution, and (5) implementation of solution results. We will analyze each of these steps individually.

The steps of the scientific method are (1) observation, (2) problem definition, (3) model construction, (4) model solution, and (5) implementation.

Observation

The first step in the management science process is the identification of a problem that exists in the system (organization). The system must be continuously and closely observed so that problems can be identified as soon as they occur or are anticipated. Problems are not always the result of a crisis that must be reacted to but, instead, frequently involve an anticipatory or planning situation. The person who normally identifies a problem is the manager because managers work in places where problems might occur. However, problems can often be identified by a

FIGURE 1.1

The management science process

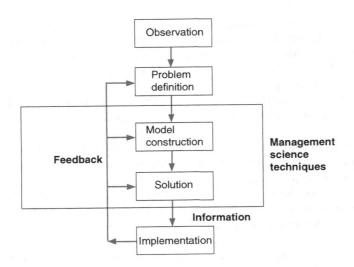

A *management scientist is a person skilled in the application of management science techniques.*

management scientist, a person skilled in the techniques of management science and trained to identify problems, who has been hired specifically to solve problems using management science techniques.

Definition of the Problem

Once it has been determined that a problem exists, the problem must be clearly and concisely *defined*. Improperly defining a problem can easily result in no solution or an inappropriate solution. Therefore, the limits of the problem and the degree to which it pervades other units of the organization must be included in the problem definition. Because the existence of a problem implies that the objectives of the firm are not being met in some way, the goals (or objectives) of the organization must also be clearly defined. A stated objective helps to focus attention on what the problem actually is.

Model Construction

A *model is an abstract mathematical representation of a problem situation.*

A management science model is an abstract representation of an existing problem situation. It can be in the form of a graph or chart, but most frequently a management science model consists of a set of mathematical relationships. These mathematical relationships are made up of numbers and symbols.

As an example, consider a business firm that sells a product. The product costs $5 to produce and sells for $20. A model that computes the total profit that will accrue from the items sold is

$$Z = \$20x - 5x$$

A *variable is a symbol used to represent an item that can take on any value.*

In this equation, x represents the number of units of the product that are sold, and Z represents the total profit that results from the sale of the product. The *symbols x and Z are variables*. The term variable is used because no set numeric value has been specified for these items. The number of units sold, x, and the profit, Z, can be any amount (within limits); they can vary. These two variables can be further distinguished. Z is a *dependent variable* because its value is dependent on the number of units sold; x is an *independent variable* because the number of units sold is *not* dependent on anything else (in this equation).

Parameters are known, constant values that are often coefficients of variables in equations.

The numbers $20 and $5 in the equation are referred to as parameters. Parameters are constant values that are generally coefficients of the variables (symbols) in an equation. Parameters

Data are pieces of information from the problem environment.

usually remain constant during the process of solving a specific problem. The parameter values are derived from data (i.e., pieces of information) from the problem environment. Sometimes the data are readily available and quite accurate. For example, presumably the selling price of $20 and product cost of $5 could be obtained from the firm's accounting department and would be very accurate. However, sometimes data are not as readily available to the manager or firm, and the parameters must be either estimated or based on a combination of the available data and estimates. In such cases, the model is only as accurate as the data used in constructing the model.

A model is a functional relationship that includes variables, parameters, and equations.

The equation as a whole is known as a functional relationship (also called *function and relationship*). The term is derived from the fact that profit, Z, is a *function* of the number of units sold, x, and the equation *relates* profit to units sold.

Because only one functional relationship exists in this example, it is also the *model*. In this case the relationship is a model of the determination of profit for the firm. However, this model does not really replicate a problem. Therefore, we will expand our example to create a problem situation.

Let us assume that the product is made from steel and that the business firm has 100 pounds of steel available. If it takes 4 pounds of steel to make each unit of the product, we can develop an additional mathematical relationship to represent steel usage:

$$4x = 100 \text{ lb. of steel}$$

This equation indicates that for every unit produced, 4 of the available 100 pounds of steel will be used. Now our model consists of two relationships:

$$Z = \$20x - 5x$$
$$4x = 100$$

We say that the profit equation in this new model is an *objective function*, and the resource equation is a *constraint*. In other words, the objective of the firm is to achieve as much profit, Z, as possible, but the firm is constrained from achieving an infinite profit by the limited amount of steel available. To signify this distinction between the two relationships in this model, we will add the following notations:

$$\text{maximize } Z = \$20x - 5x$$
$$\text{subject to}$$
$$4x = 100$$

This model now represents the manager's problem of determining the number of units to produce. You will recall that we defined the number of units to be produced as x. Thus, when we determine the value of x, it represents a potential (or recommended) *decision* for the manager. Therefore, x is also known as a *decision variable*. The next step in the management science process is to solve the model to determine the value of the decision variable.

Model Solution

A management science technique usually applies to a specific model type.

Once models have been constructed in management science, they are solved using the management science techniques presented in this text. A management science solution technique usually applies to a specific type of model. Thus, the model type and solution method are both part of the management science technique. We are able to say that *a model is solved* because the model represents a problem. When we refer to model solution, we also mean problem solution.

Throughout this text TIME OUT boxes introduce you to the individuals who developed the various techniques that are described in the chapters. This will provide a historical perspective on the development of the field of management science. In this first instance we will briefly outline the development of management science.

Although a number of the mathematical techniques that make up management science date to the turn of the twentieth century or before, the field of management science itself can trace its beginnings to military operations research (OR) groups formed during World War II in Great Britain circa 1939. These OR groups typically consisted of a team of about a dozen individuals from different fields of science, mathematics, and the military, brought together to find solutions to military-related problems. One of the most famous of these groups—called "Blackett's circus" after its leader, Nobel Laureate P. M. S. Blackett of the University of Manchester and a former naval officer—included three physiologists, two mathematical physicists, one astrophysicist, one general physicist, two mathematicians, an Army officer, and a surveyor. Blackett's group and the other OR teams made significant contributions in improving Britain's early-warning radar system (which was instrumental in their victory in the Battle of Britain), aircraft gunnery, antisubmarine warfare, civilian defense, convoy size determination, and bombing raids over Germany.

The successes achieved by the British OR groups were observed by two Americans working for the U.S. military, Dr. James B. Conant and Dr. Vannevar Bush, who recommended that OR teams be established in the U.S. branches of the military. Subsequently, both the Air Force and Navy created OR groups.

After World War II the contributions of the OR groups were considered so valuable that the Army, Air Force, and Navy set up various agencies to continue research of military problems. Two of the more famous agencies were the Navy's Operations Evaluation Group at MIT and Project RAND, established by the Air Force to study aerial warfare. Many of the individuals who developed operations research and management science techniques did so while working at one of these agencies after World War II or as a result of their work there.

As the war ended and the mathematical models and techniques that were kept secret during the war began to be released, there was a natural inclination to test their applicability to business problems. At the same time, various consulting firms were established to apply these techniques to industrial and business problems, and courses in the use of quantitative techniques for business management began to surface in American universities. In the early 1950s the use of these quantitative techniques to solve management problems became known as management science, and it was popularized by a book of that name by Stafford Beer of Great Britain.

For the example model developed in the previous section,

$$\text{maximize } Z = \$20x - 5x$$
$$\text{subject to}$$
$$4x = 100$$

the solution technique is simple algebra. Solving the constraint equation for x, we have

$$4x = 100$$
$$x = 100/4$$
$$x = 25 \text{ units}$$

Substituting the value of 25 for x into the profit function results in the total profit:

$$Z = \$20x - 5x$$
$$= 20(25) - 5(25)$$
$$= \$375$$

A management science solution can be either a recommended decision or information that helps a manager make a decision.

Thus, if the manager decides to produce 25 units of the product and all 25 units sell, the business firm will receive $375 in profit. Note, however, that the value of the decision variable does not constitute an actual decision; rather, it is *information* that serves as a recommendation or guideline, helping the manager make a decision.

Some management science techniques do not generate an answer or a recommended decision. Instead, they provide *descriptive results:* results that describe the system being modeled.

For example, suppose the business firm in our example desires to know the average number of units sold each month during a year. The monthly *data* (i.e., sales) for the past year are as follows:

Month	Sales	Month	Sales
January	30	July	35
February	40	August	50
March	25	September	60
April	60	October	40
May	30	November	35
June	25	December	50
		Total	480 units

Monthly sales average 40 units (480 ÷ 12). This result is not a decision; it is information that describes what is happening in the system. The results of the management science

Management Science Application

Room Pricing with Management Science at Marriott

Marriott International, Inc., headquartered in Bethesda, Maryland, has more than 140,000 employees working at more than 3,300 hotels in 70 countries. Its hotel franchises include Marriott, JW Marriott, The Ritz-Carlton, Renaissance, Residence Inn, Courtyard, TownePlace Suites, Fairfield Inn, and Springhill Suites. *Fortune* magazine ranks Marriott as the lodging industry's most admired company and one of the best companies to work for.

Marriott uses a revenue management system for individual hotel bookings. This system provides forecasts of customer demand and pricing controls, makes optimal inventory allocations, and interfaces with a reservation system that handles more than 75 million transactions each year. The system makes a demand forecast for each rate category and length of stay for each arrival day up to 90 days in advance, and it provides inventory allocations to the reservation system. This inventory of hotel rooms is then sold to individual customers through channels such as Marriott.com, the company's toll-free reservation number, the hotels directly, and global distribution systems.

One of the most significant revenue streams for Marriott is for group sales, which can contribute more than half of a full-service hotel's revenue. However, group business has challenging characteristics that introduce uncertainty and make modeling it difficult, including longer booking windows (as compared to those for individuals), price negotiation as part of the booking process, demand for blocks of rooms, and lack of demand data. For a group request, a hotel must know if it has sufficient rooms and determine a recommended rate. A key

© David Zanzinger/Alamy

challenge is estimating the value of the business the hotel is turning away if the room inventory is given to a group rather than being held for individual bookings.

To address the group booking process, Marriott developed a decision support system, Group Pricing Optimizer (GPO), that provides guidance to Marriott personnel on pricing hotel rooms for group customers. GPO uses various management science modeling techniques and tools, including simulation, forecasting, and optimization techniques, to recommend an optimal price rate. Marriott estimates that GPO provided an improvement in profit of over $120 million derived from $1.3 billion in group business in its first 2 years of use.

Source: Based on S. Hormby, J. Morrison, P. Dave, M. Myers, and T. Tenca, "Marriott International Increases Revenue by Implementing a Group Pricing Optimizer," *Interfaces* 40, no. 1 (January–February 2010): 47–57.

techniques in this text are examples of the two types shown in this section: (1) solutions/decisions and (2) descriptive results.

Implementation

Implementation is the actual use of a model once it has been developed.

The final step in the management science process for problem solving described in Figure 1.1 is implementation. Implementation is the actual use of the model once it has been developed or the solution to the problem the model was developed to solve. This is a critical but often overlooked step in the process. It is not always a given that once a model is developed or a solution found, it is automatically used. Frequently the person responsible for putting the model or solution to use is not the same person who developed the model, and thus the user may not fully understand how the model works or exactly what it is supposed to do. Individuals are also sometimes hesitant to change the normal way they do things or to try new things. In this situation the model and solution may get pushed to the side or ignored altogether if they are not carefully explained and their benefit fully demonstrated. If the management science model and solution are not implemented, then the effort and resources used in their development have been wasted.

Model Building: Break-Even Analysis

Break-even analysis is a modeling technique to determine the number of units to sell or produce that will result in zero profit.

In the previous section we gave a brief, general description of how management science models are formulated and solved, using a simple algebraic example. In this section we will continue to explore the process of building and solving management science models, using break-even analysis, also called *profit analysis*. Break-even analysis is a good topic to expand our discussion of model building and solution because it is straightforward, relatively familiar to most people, and not overly complex. In addition, it provides a convenient means to demonstrate the different ways management science models can be solved—mathematically (by hand), graphically, and with a computer.

The purpose of break-even analysis is to determine the number of units of a product (i.e., the volume) to sell or produce that will equate total revenue with total cost. The point where total revenue equals total cost is called the *break-even point*, and at this point profit is zero. The break-even point gives a manager a point of reference in determining how many units will be needed to ensure a profit.

Components of Break-Even Analysis

The three components of break-even analysis are volume, cost, and profit. *Volume* is the level of sales or production by a company. It can be expressed as the number of units (i.e., quantity) produced and sold, as the dollar volume of sales, or as a percentage of total capacity available.

Fixed costs are independent of volume and remain constant.

Two type of costs are typically incurred in the production of a product: fixed costs and variable costs. Fixed costs are generally independent of the volume of units produced and sold. That is, fixed costs remain constant, regardless of how many units of product are produced within a given range. Fixed costs can include such items as rent on plant and equipment, taxes, staff and management salaries, insurance, advertising, depreciation, heat and light, and plant maintenance. Taken together, these items result in total fixed costs.

Variable costs depend on the number of items produced.

Variable costs are determined on a per-unit basis. Thus, total variable costs depend on the number of units produced. Variable costs include such items as raw materials and resources, direct labor, packaging, material handling, and freight.

Total variable costs are a function of the *volume* and the *variable cost per unit*. This relationship can be expressed mathematically as

$$\text{total variable cost} = vc_v$$

where c_v = variable cost per unit and v = volume (number of units) sold.

Total cost (TC) equals the fixed cost (c_f) plus the variable cost per unit (c_v) multiplied by volume (v).

The **total cost** of an operation is computed by summing total fixed cost and total variable cost, as follows:

$$\text{total cost} = \text{total fixed cost} + \text{total variable cost}$$

or

$$TC = c_f + vc_v$$

where c_f = fixed cost.

As an example, consider Western Clothing Company, which produces denim jeans. The company incurs the following monthly costs to produce denim jeans:

$$\text{fixed cost} = c_f = \$10,000$$
$$\text{variable cost} = c_v = \$8 \text{ per pair}$$

If we arbitrarily let the monthly sales volume, v, equal 400 pairs of denim jeans, the total cost is

$$TC = c_f + vc_v = \$10,000 + (400)(8) = \$13,200$$

Profit is the difference between total revenue (volume multiplied by price) and total cost.

The third component in our break-even model is **profit**. Profit is the difference between *total revenue* and total cost. Total revenue is the volume multiplied by the price per unit,

$$\text{total revenue} = vp$$

where p = price per unit.

For our clothing company example, if denim jeans sell for $23 per pair and we sell 400 pairs per month, then the total monthly revenue is

$$\text{total revenue} = vp = (400)(23) = \$9,200$$

Now that we have developed relationships for total revenue and total cost, profit (Z) can be computed as follows:

$$\text{total profit} = \text{total revenue} - \text{total cost}$$
$$Z = vp - (c_f + vc_v)$$
$$= vp - c_f - vc_v$$

Computing the Break-Even Point

For our clothing company example, we have determined total revenue and total cost to be $9,200 and $13,200, respectively. With these values, there is no profit but, instead, a loss of $4,000:

$$\text{total profit} = \text{total revenue} - \text{total cost} = \$9,200 - 13,200 = -\$4,000$$

We can verify this result by using our total profit formula,

$$Z = vp - c_f - vc_v$$

and the values $v = 400$, $p = \$23$, $c_f = \$10,000$, and $c_v = \$8$:

$$Z = vp - c_f - vc_v$$
$$= \$(400)(23) - 10,000 - (400)(8)$$
$$= \$9,200 - 10,000 - 3,200$$
$$= -\$4,000$$

Obviously, the clothing company does not want to operate with a monthly loss of $4,000 because doing so might eventually result in bankruptcy. If we assume that price is static because of market conditions and that fixed costs and the variable cost per unit are not subject to change, then the only part of our model that can be varied is *volume*. Using the modeling terms we developed earlier in this chapter, price, fixed costs, and variable costs are parameters, whereas the volume, v, is a decision variable. In break-even analysis we want to compute the value of v that will result in zero profit.

At the **break-even point**, where total revenue equals total cost, the profit, Z, equals zero. Thus, if we let profit, Z, equal zero in our total profit equation and solve for v, we can determine the break-even volume:

$$Z = vp - c_f - vc_v$$
$$0 = v(23) - 10{,}000 - v(8)$$
$$0 = 23v - 10{,}000 - 8v$$
$$15v = 10{,}000$$
$$v = 666.7 \text{ pairs of jeans}$$

In other words, if the company produces and sells 666.7 pairs of jeans, the profit (and loss) will be zero and the company will *break even*. This gives the company a point of reference from which to determine how many pairs of jeans it needs to produce and sell in order to gain a profit (subject to any capacity limitations). For example, a sales volume of 800 pairs of denim jeans will result in the following monthly profit:

$$Z = vp - c_f - vc_v$$
$$= \$(800)(23) - 10{,}000 - (800)(8) = \$2{,}000$$

In general, the break-even volume can be determined using the following formula:

$$Z = vp - c_f - vc_v$$
$$0 = v(p - c_v) - c_f$$
$$v(p - c_v) = c_f$$
$$v = \frac{c_f}{p - c_v}$$

For our example,

$$v = \frac{c_f}{p - c_v}$$
$$= \frac{10{,}000}{23 - 8}$$
$$= 666.7 \text{ pairs of jeans}$$

Graphical Solution

It is possible to represent many of the management science models in this text graphically and use these graphical models to solve problems. Graphical models also have the advantage of providing a "picture" of the model that can sometimes help us understand the modeling process better than mathematics alone can. We can easily graph the break-even model for our Western Clothing Company example because the functions for total cost and total revenue are *linear*. That means we can graph each relationship as a straight line on a set of coordinates, as shown in Figure 1.2.

In Figure 1.2, the fixed cost, c_f, has a constant value of \$10,000, regardless of the volume. The total cost line, *TC*, represents the sum of variable cost and fixed cost. The total cost line increases because variable cost increases as the volume increases. The total revenue line also increases as volume increases, but at a faster rate than total cost. The point where these two lines intersect indicates that total revenue equals total cost. The volume, v, that corresponds to this point is the *break-even volume*. The break-even volume in Figure 1.2 is 666.7 pairs of denim jeans.

FIGURE 1.2

Break-even model

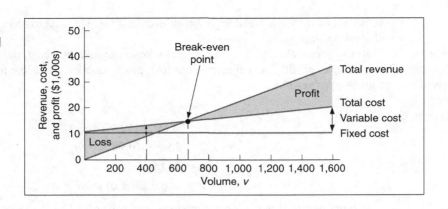

Sensitivity Analysis

We have now developed a general relationship for determining the break-even volume, which was the objective of our modeling process. This relationship enables us to see how the level of profit (and loss) is directly affected by changes in volume. However, when we developed this model, we assumed that our parameters, fixed and variable costs and price, were constant. In reality such parameters are frequently uncertain and can rarely be assumed to be constant, and changes in any of the parameters can affect the model solution. The study of changes on a management science model is called sensitivity analysis—that is, seeing how sensitive the model is to changes.

Sensitivity analysis sees how sensitive a management model is to changes.

Sensitivity analysis can be performed on all management science models in one form or another. In fact, sometimes companies develop models for the primary purpose of experimentation to see how the model will react to different changes the company is contemplating or that management might expect to occur in the future. As a demonstration of how sensitivity analysis works, we will look at the effects of some changes on our break-even model.

In general, an increase in price lowers the break-even point, all other things held constant.

The first thing we will analyze is price. As an example, we will increase the price for denim jeans from $23 to $30. As expected, this increases the total revenue, and it therefore reduces the break-even point from 666.7 pairs of jeans to 454.5 pairs of jeans:

$$v = \frac{c_f}{p - c_v}$$

$$= \frac{10,000}{30 - 8} = 454.5 \text{ pairs of denim jeans}$$

The effect of the price change on break-even volume is illustrated in Figure 1.3.

FIGURE 1.3

Break-even model with an increase in price

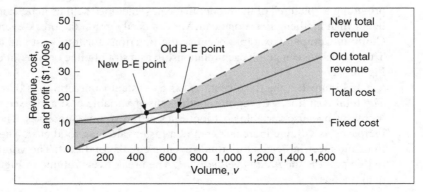

Although a decision to increase price looks inviting from a strictly analytical point of view, it must be remembered that the lower break-even volume and higher profit are *possible* but not guaranteed. A higher price can make it more difficult to sell the product. Thus, a change in price often must be accompanied by corresponding increases in costs, such as those for advertising, packaging, and possibly production (to enhance quality). However, even such direct changes as these may have little effect on product demand because price is often sensitive to numerous factors, such as the type of market, monopolistic elements, and product differentiation.

In general, an increase in variable costs will increase the break-even point, all other things held constant.

When we increased price, we mentioned the possibility of raising the quality of the product to offset a potential loss of sales due to the price increase. For example, suppose the stitching on the denim jeans is changed to make the jeans more attractive and stronger. This change results in an increase in variable costs of $4 per pair of jeans, thus raising the variable cost per unit, c_v, to $12 per pair. This change (in conjunction with our previous price change to $30) results in a new break-even volume:

$$v = \frac{c_f}{p - c_v}$$

$$= \frac{10,000}{30 - 12} = 555.5 \text{ pairs of denim jeans}$$

This new break-even volume and the change in the total cost line that occurs as a result of the variable cost change are shown in Figure 1.4.

FIGURE 1.4

Break-even model with an increase in variable cost

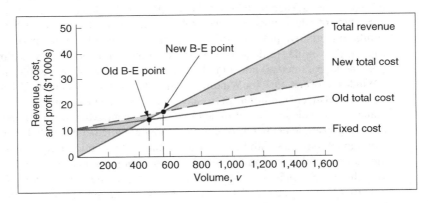

Next let's consider an increase in advertising expenditures to offset the potential loss in sales resulting from a price increase. An increase in advertising expenditures is an addition to fixed costs. For example, if the clothing company increases its monthly advertising budget by $3,000, then the total fixed cost, c_f, becomes $13,000. Using this fixed cost, as well as the increased variable cost per unit of $12 and the increased price of $30, we compute the break-even volume as follows:

$$v = \frac{c_f}{p - c_v}$$

$$= \frac{13,000}{30 - 12}$$

$$= 722.2 \text{ pairs of denim jeans}$$

In general, an increase in fixed costs will increase the break-even point, all other things held constant.

This new break-even volume, representing changes in price, fixed costs, and variable costs, is illustrated in Figure 1.5. Notice that the break-even volume is now higher than the original volume of 666.7 pairs of jeans, as a result of the increased costs necessary to offset the potential loss in sales. This indicates the necessity to analyze the effect of a change in one of the break-even

FIGURE 1.5

Break-even model with a change in fixed cost

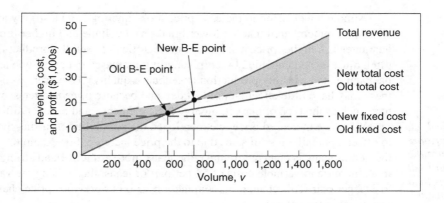

components on the whole break-even model. In other words, generally it is not sufficient to consider a change in one model component without considering the overall effect.

Computer Solution

Throughout the text we will demonstrate how to solve management science models on the computer by using Excel spreadsheets and QM for Windows, a general-purpose quantitative methods software package by Howard Weiss. QM for Windows has program modules to solve almost every type of management science problem you will encounter in this book. There are a number of similar quantitative methods software packages available on the market, with characteristics and capabilities similar to those of QM for Windows. In most cases you simply input problem data (i.e., model parameters) into a model template, click on a solve button, and the solution appears in a Windows format. QM for Windows is included on the companion Web site for this text.

Spreadsheets are not always easy to use, and you cannot conveniently solve every type of management science model by using a spreadsheet. Most of the time you must not only input the model parameters but also set up the model mathematics, including formulas, as well as your own model template with headings to display your solution output. However, spreadsheets provide a powerful reporting tool in which you can present your model and results in any format you choose. Spreadsheets such as Excel have become almost universally available to anyone who owns a computer. In addition, spreadsheets have become very popular as a teaching tool because they tend to guide the student through a modeling procedure, and they can be interesting and fun to use. However, because spreadsheets are somewhat more difficult to set up and apply than is QM for Windows, we will spend more time explaining their use to solve various types of problems in this text.

One of the difficult aspects of using spreadsheets to solve management science problems is setting up a spreadsheet with some of the more complex models and formulas. For the most complex models in the text we will show how to use Excel QM, a supplemental spreadsheet macro that is included on the companion Web site for this text. A *macro* is a template or an overlay that already has the model format with the necessary formulas set up on the spreadsheet so that the user only has to input the model parameters. We will demonstrate Excel QM in six chapters, including this chapter, Chapter 6 ("Linear Programming Transportation Models"), Chapter 12 ("Decision-Making Models"), Chapter 13 ("Waiting Line Models"), Chapter 15 ("Forecasting Models"), and Chapter 16 ("Inventory Models").

Later in this text, we will also demonstrate two spreadsheet add-ins, TreePlan and Crystal Ball, which are also included on the companion Web site for this text. TreePlan is a program for setting up and solving decision trees that we use in Chapter 12 ("Decision-Making Models"), whereas Crystal Ball is a simulation package that we use in Chapter 14 ("Simulation Models"). Also, in Chapter 8 ("Managing Projects with CPM/PERT Models") we will demonstrate Microsoft Project.

In this section, we will demonstrate how to use Excel, Excel QM, and QM for Windows, using our break-even model example for Western Clothing Company.

Excel Spreadsheets

To solve the break-even model using Excel, you must set up a spreadsheet with headings to identify your model parameters and variables and then input the appropriate mathematical formulas into the cells where you want to display your solution. Exhibit 1.1 shows the spreadsheet for the Western Clothing Company example. Setting up the different headings to describe the parameters and the solution is not difficult, but it does require that you know your way around Excel a little. Appendix B provides a brief tutorial titled "Setting Up and Editing a Spreadsheet" for solving management science problems.

EXHIBIT 1.1

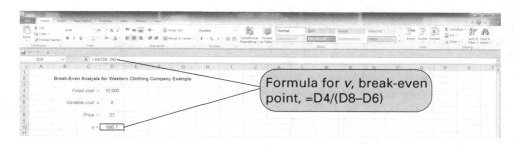

Formula for *v*, break-even point, =D4/(D8–D6)

Notice that cell D10 contains the break-even formula, which is displayed on the toolbar near the top of the screen. The fixed cost of $10,000 is typed in cell D4, the variable cost of $8 is in cell D6, and the price of $23 is in cell D8.

As we present more complex models and problems in the chapters to come, the spreadsheets we will develop to solve these problems will become more involved and will enable us to demonstrate different features of Excel and spreadsheet modeling.

The Excel QM Macro for Spreadsheets

Excel QM is included on the companion Web site for this text. You can install Excel QM onto your computer by following a brief series of steps displayed when the program is first accessed.

After Excel is started, Excel QM is normally accessed from the computer's program files, where it is usually loaded. When Excel QM is activated, "Add-Ins" will appear at the top of the spreadsheet (as indicated in Exhibit 1.2). Clicking on "Excel QM" or "Taylor" will pull down a

EXHIBIT 1.2

Click on "Add-Ins", then the menu of Excel QM modules

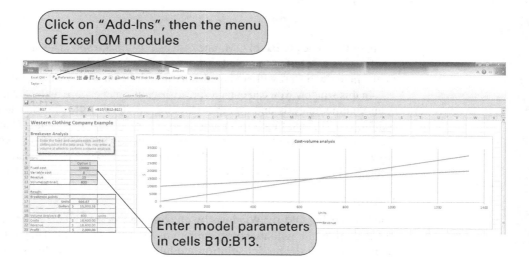

Enter model parameters in cells B10:B13.

Management Science Application

The Application of Management Science with Spreadsheets

Excel spreadsheets have become an increasingly important management science tool because of their ability to support numerous software add-ins for various management science techniques, their ability to effectively convey complex models to clients, their general availability on virtually every computer, their flexibility and ease of use, and the fact that they are inexpensive. As a result, spreadsheets are used for the application of management science techniques to a wide variety of different problems across many diverse organizations; following are just a few examples of these applications.

Used with permission from Microsoft

- Hewlett-Packard uses spreadsheets for a wide range of management science applications, including modeling supply-chain networks, forecasting, planning, procurement, inventory control, and product management.

- Procter & Gamble also uses spreadsheets for supply-chain management and specifically inventory control, to which it has attributed over $350 million in inventory reductions.

- Lockheed Martin Space Systems Company uses spreadsheets to apply mathematical programming techniques for project selection.

- The Centers for Disease Control and Prevention (CDC), use Excel spreadsheets to provide people at county health departments in the United States (who have minimal management science skills) with tools using queuing techniques to plan for dispensing medications and vaccines during emergencies, such as epidemics and terrorist attacks.

- A spreadsheet application for the Canadian Army allowed it to reduce annual over-budget expenditures for ammunition for its training programs from over $24 million to $1.3 million in a 2-year period.

- Hypo Real Estate Bank International in Stuttgart, Germany, uses an Excel-based simulation model to assess the potential impact of economic events on the default risk of its portfolio of over €40 billion in real estate loans around the world.

- Business students at the University of Toronto created an Excel spreadsheet model for assigning medical residents in radiology to on-call and emergency rotations at the University of Vermont's College of Medicine.

- The American Red Cross uses Excel spreadsheets to apply data envelopment analysis (DEA) and linear programming techniques for allocating resources and evaluating the performance of its 1,000 chapters.

These are just a few of the many applications of management science techniques worldwide using Excel spreadsheets.

Source: Based on L. LeBlanc and T. Grossman, "Introduction: The Use of Spreadsheet Software in the Application of Management Science and Operations Research," *Interfaces* 38, no. 4 (July–August 2008): 225–27.

menu of the topics in Excel QM, one of which is break-even analysis. Clicking on "Break-Even Analysis" will result in the window for spreadsheet initialization. Every Excel QM macro listed on the menu will start with a Spreadsheet Initialization window.

In this window, you can enter a spreadsheet title and choose under "Options" whether you also want volume analysis and a graph. Clicking on "OK" will result in the spreadsheet shown in Exhibit 1.2. The first step is to input the values for the Western Clothing Company example in cells B10 to B13, as shown in Exhibit 1.2. The spreadsheet shows the break-even volume in cell B17. However, notice that we have also chosen to perform some volume analysis by entering a hypothetical volume of 800 units in cell B13, which results in the volume analysis in cells B20 to B23.

QM for Windows

You begin using QM for Windows by clicking on the "Module" button on the toolbar at the top of the main window that appears when you start the program. This will pull down a window with a list of all the model solution modules available in QM for Windows. Clicking on the

"Break-even Analysis" module will access a new screen for typing in the problem title. Clicking again will access a screen with input cells for the model parameters—that is, fixed cost, variable cost, and price (or revenue). Next, clicking on the "Solve" button at the top of the screen will provide the solution to the Western Clothing Company example, as shown in Exhibit 1.3.

EXHIBIT 1.3

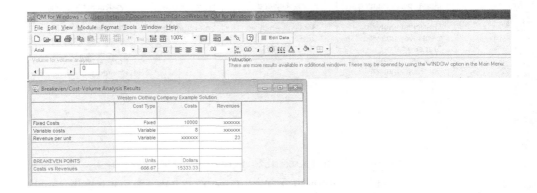

You can also get the graphical model and solution for this problem by clicking on "Window" at the top of the solution screen and selecting the menu item for a graph of the problem. The break-even graph for the Western Clothing example is shown in Exhibit 1.4.

EXHIBIT 1.4

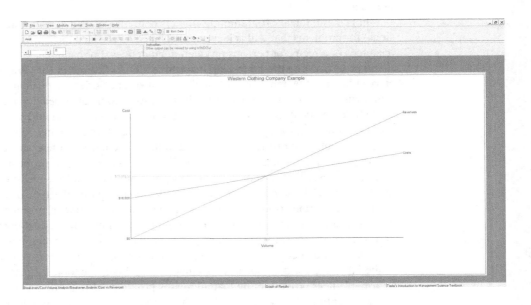

Management Science Modeling Techniques

This text focuses primarily on two of the five steps of the management science process described in Figure 1.1—model construction and solution. These are the two steps that use the management science techniques. In a textbook, it is difficult to show how an unstructured real-world problem is identified and defined because the problem must be written out. However, once a problem statement has been given, we can show how a model is constructed and a solution is derived. The techniques presented in this text can be loosely classified into four categories, as shown in Figure 1.6.

FIGURE 1.6

Classification of management science techniques

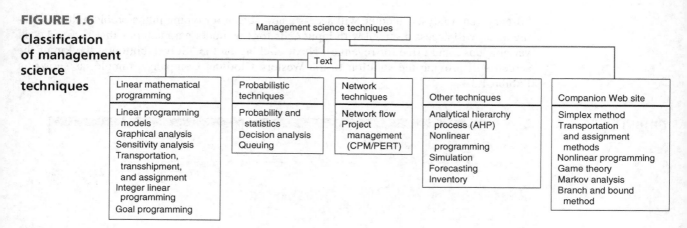

Linear Mathematical Programming Techniques

Chapters 2 through 6 and 9 present techniques that together make up *linear mathematical programming*. (The first example used to demonstrate model construction earlier in this chapter is a very rudimentary linear programming model.) The term *programming* used to identify this technique does not refer to computer programming but rather to a predetermined set of mathematical steps used to solve a problem. This particular class of techniques holds a predominant position in this text because it includes some of the more frequently used and popular techniques in management science.

In general, linear programming models help managers determine solutions (i.e., make decisions) for problems that will achieve some objective in which there are restrictions, such as limited resources or a recipe or perhaps production guidelines. For example, you could actually develop a linear programming model to help determine a breakfast menu for yourself that would meet dietary guidelines you may have set, such as number of calories, fat content, and vitamin level, while minimizing the cost of the breakfast. Manufacturing companies develop linear programming models to help decide how many units of different products they should produce to maximize their profit (or minimize their cost), given scarce resources such as capital, labor, and facilities.

Six chapters in this text are devoted to this topic because there are several variations of linear programming models that can be applied to specific types of problems. Chapter 4 is devoted entirely to describing example linear programming models for several different types of problem scenarios. Chapter 6, for example, focuses on one particular type of linear programming application for transportation, transshipment, and assignment problems. An example of a transportation problem is a manager trying to determine the lowest-cost routes to use to ship goods from several sources (such as plants or warehouses) to several destinations (such as retail stores), given that each source may have limited goods available and each destination may have limited demand for the goods. Also, Chapter 9 includes the topic of goal programming, which is a form of linear programming that addresses problems with more than one objective or goal.

As mentioned previously in this chapter, some of the more mathematical topics in the text are included as supplementary modules on the companion Web site for the text. Among the linear programming topics included on the companion Web site are modules on the simplex method; the transportation and assignment solution methods; and the branch and bound solution method for integer programming models. Also included on the companion Web site are modules on nonlinear programming, game theory, and Markov analysis.

Probabilistic Techniques

Probabilistic techniques are presented in Chapters 11 through 13. These techniques are distinguished from mathematical programming techniques in that the results are probabilistic. Mathematical programming techniques assume that all parameters in the models are known with *certainty*. Therefore, the solution results are assumed to be known with certainty, with no probability that other solutions might exist. A technique that assumes certainty in its solution is referred to as deterministic. In contrast, the results from a probabilistic technique *do* contain uncertainty, with some possibility that alternative solutions might exist. In the model solution presented earlier in this chapter, the result of the first example ($x = 25$ units to produce) is deterministic, whereas the result of the second example (estimating an average of 40 units sold each month) is probabilistic.

An example of a probabilistic technique is decision analysis, the subject of Chapter 12. In decision analysis, it is shown how to select among several different decision alternatives, given uncertain (i.e., probabilistic) future conditions. For example, a developer may want to decide whether to build a shopping mall, build an office complex, build condominiums, or not build anything at all, given future economic conditions that might be good, fair, or poor, each with a probability of occurrence. Chapter 13, on queuing analysis, presents probabilistic techniques for analyzing waiting lines that might occur, for example, at the grocery store, at a bank, or at a movie. The results of waiting line analysis are statistical averages showing, among other things, the average number of customers in line waiting to be served or the average time a customer might have to wait for service.

Network Techniques

Networks, the topic of Chapters 7 and 8, consist of models that are represented as diagrams rather than as strictly mathematical relationships. As such, these models offer a pictorial representation of the system under analysis. These models represent either probabilistic or deterministic systems.

For example, in shortest-route problems, one of the topics in Chapter 7 ("Shortest Route, Minimal Spanning Tree, and Maximal Flow Models"), a network diagram can be drawn to help a manager determine the shortest route among a number of different routes from a source to a destination. For example, you could use this technique to determine the shortest or quickest car route from St. Louis to Daytona Beach for a spring break vacation. In Chapter 8 ("Managing Projects with CPM/PERT Models"), a network is drawn that shows the relationships of all the tasks and activities for a project, such as building a house or developing a new computer system. This type of network can help a manager plan the best way to accomplish each of the tasks in the project so that it will take the shortest amount of time possible. You could use this type of technique to plan for a concert or an intramural volleyball tournament on your campus.

Other Techniques

Some topics in the text are not easily categorized; they may overlap several categories, or they may be unique. The analytical hierarchy process (AHP) in Chapter 9 is such a topic that is not easily classified. It is a mathematical technique for helping the decision maker choose between several alternative decisions, given more than one objective; however, it is not a form of linear programming, as is goal programming, the shared topic in Chapter 9, on multicriteria decision making. The structure of the mathematical models for nonlinear programming problems in Chapter 10 is similar to the linear programming problems in Chapters 2 through 6; however, the mathematical equations and functions in nonlinear programming can be nonlinear instead of linear, thus requiring the use of calculus to solve them. Simulation, the subject of Chapter 14, is probably the single most unique topic in the text. It has the capability to solve probabilistic and deterministic problems and is often the technique of last resort when no other management science technique will work. In simulation, a mathematical model is constructed (typically using a computer) that replicates a real-world system under analysis, and then that simulation model is used to solve problems in the "simulated" real-world system. For example, with simulation you could build a model to simulate the traffic patterns of vehicles at a busy intersection to determine how to set the traffic light signals.

Forecasting, the subject of Chapter 15, and inventory management, in Chapter 16, are topics traditionally considered to be part of the field of operations management. However, because they are both important business functions that also rely heavily on quantitative models for their analysis, they are typically considered important topics in the study of management science as well. Both topics also include probabilistic as well as deterministic aspects. In Chapter 15, we will look at several different quantitative models that help managers predict what the future demand for products and services will look like. In general, historical sales and demand data are used to build a mathematical function or formula that can be used to estimate product demand in the future. In Chapter 16, we will look at several different quantitative models that help organizations determine how much inventory to keep on hand in order to minimize inventory costs, which can be significant.

Business Usage of Management Science Techniques

Not all management science techniques are equally useful or equally used by business firms and other organizations. Some techniques are used quite frequently by business practitioners and managers; others are used less often. The most frequently used techniques are linear and integer programming, simulation, network analysis (including critical path method/project evaluation and review technique [CPM/PERT]), inventory control, decision analysis, and queuing theory, as well as probability and statistics. An attempt has been made in this text to provide a comprehensive treatment of all the topics generally considered within the field of management science, regardless of how frequently they are used. Although some topics may have limited direct applicability, their study can reveal informative and unique means of approaching a problem and can often enhance one's understanding of the decision-making process.

The variety and breadth of management science applications and of the potential for applying management science, not only in business and industry but also in government, health care, and service organizations, are extensive. Areas of application include project planning, capital budgeting, production planning, inventory analysis, scheduling, marketing planning, quality control, plant location, maintenance policy, personnel management, and product demand forecasting, among others. In this text the applicability of management science to a variety of problem areas is demonstrated via individual chapter examples and the problems that accompany each chapter.

A small portion of the thousands of applications of management science that occur each year are recorded in various academic and professional journals. Frequently, these journal articles are as complex as the applications themselves and are very difficult to read. However, one particular journal, *Interfaces*, is devoted specifically to the application of management science and is written not just for college professors but for business people, practitioners, and students as well. *Interfaces* is published by INFORMS (Institute for Operations Research and Management Sciences), an international professional organization whose members include college professors, businesspeople, scientists, students, and a variety of professional people interested in the practice and application of management science and operations research.

Interfaces regularly publishes articles that report on the application of management science to a wide variety of problems. The chapters that follow present examples of applications of management science from *Interfaces* and other professional journals. These applications are from a variety of U.S. and overseas companies and organizations in business, industry, services, and government. These examples, as presented here, do not detail the actual models and the model components. Instead, they briefly indicate the type of problem the company or organization faced, the objective of the solution approach developed to solve the problem, and the benefits derived from the model or technique (i.e., what was accomplished). The interested reader who desires more detailed information about these and other management science applications is

Management Science Application

Management Science in the Asian Airline Industry

Management science is a discipline that applies a series of advanced analytical methods to help companies make better choices. This involves tools taken from a series of disciplines, from statistics to operation research and project management, to name a few. One of the sectors that intensively use management science is the airline industry. This is understandable, given the challenges faced when managing a profitable airline.

This is especially true in Asia, where the sector has experienced a huge expansion in the last 20 years, due essentially to the economic rise of the countries in the region, China in particular. Already the best in the world in terms of service level, the airlines in Asia are now experiencing a sustained growth that is also leading the global recovery of the sector. According to some industry figures, nine of the top 20 airports in the world are currently in Asia; China alone accounts for 158 airports and is planning to build 86 more due to huge problems in accommodating incoming traffic.

Air China is the world's largest airline in terms of market capitalization ($20 billon), twice the size of Delta or Lufthansa. It is followed by Singapore Airlines, with $14 billion, and by Hong Kong–based Cathay Pacific, with $12 billion.

Managing an airline requires the combination of a series of methods, applied to internal and external tasks. First, there is the major issue of scheduling, which applies to three main areas of an airline's activity: fleet assignment, aircraft maintenance routing, and crew scheduling.

Fleet assignment mainly consists of deciding which kind of aircraft has to be assigned to a specific route, with the objective of maximizing the revenue.

Aircraft maintenance routing contains a specific routine of periodic maintenance of the aircraft. There are several kinds of maintenance an aircraft has to undertake to abide by local and international regulations, and a schedule has to be fixed in order to minimize the costs of each one. Finally, crew scheduling consists of deciding the personnel assignment of the crew to flights schedules. This is done for the pilots according to their qualification in flying certain types of aircraft and for the rest of the crew by respecting labor laws and staff constraints. Wages increase quickly for overtime and overnight stays, so these aspects have to be taken into account.

It has been shown that a full optimization of these three main areas of scheduling is computationally too complicated; therefore in practice, it is split into a series of subproblems, sometimes linked together in a sequential approach or, in other cases, using other linear programming approaches.

Although linear programming is generally the tool of choice for most of the scheduling activities, other branches of management science are also used. Airlines are among the heaviest users of network planning techniques (Chapter 8). This is easy to understand, because the business is centered around planning

© chungking - Fotolia.com

activities with the smallest slack possible in order to maximize profit, but still allow for delays without compromising the overall schedule. Market deregulation, which allowed the entrance of new players in previously protected national airspaces, made this kind of planning even more fundamental.

Another area of airline management that benefits greatly from the application of management science techniques is customer relations.

Customer relations essentially involve two sectors. The first is called revenue management, which is a complicated strategy, heavy in computer calculation, which uses forecasting models (Chapter 15) to ensure that different types of fares match different types of customers, independently of when they buy the ticket and, to a certain extent, of their destinations. This sometimes produces the paradox of short-haul tickets being more expensive than intercontinental flights, but it ensures that the airlines maximize their profit.

The second sector is the relation with the airports, especially the hubs. Although airport authorities are independent entities from airlines (even if a certain degree of co-participation is present in the case of big national airlines), companies can still do a lot to make a passenger's experience the best possible. In some cases, such as in Singapore and Hong Kong, passenger handling has been streamlined, and pressure at the airport check-in has been eased by introducing an online and in-town check-in.

Sources: N. Papadakos, "Integrated Airline Scheduling," *Computers & Operations Research* 36, no. 1 (2009): 176–95; Q. Xiangtong, J. Yang, and G. Yu, "Scheduling Problems in the Airline Industry," in J.Y-T. Leung (ed.), *Handbook of Scheduling: Algorithms, Models, and Performance Analysis* (Boca Raton, FL: Chapman & Hall/CRC, 2004); R. Gopalan and K. Talluri, "The Aircraft Maintenance Routing Problem," *Operations Research* 46, no. 2 (1998): 260–71; J. Abara, "Applying Integer Linear Programming to the Fleet Assignment Problem," *Interfaces* 19, no. 4 (1989): 20–8; S. Lavoie, M. Minoux, and E. Odier, "A New Approach for Crew Pairing Problems by Column Generation With Applications to Air Transport," *European Journal of Operational Research* 35 (1988): 45–58; "Asian Airline Industry to Spearhead Growth," (2010), accessed at http://www.theborneopost.com/2010/12/14/ /#ixzz1cxDNBdRD.

encouraged to go to the library and peruse *Interfaces* and the many other journals that contain articles on the application of management science.

Management Science Models in Decision Support Systems

Historically, management science models have been applied to the solution of specific types of problems; for example, a waiting line model is used to analyze a specific waiting line system at a store or bank. However, the evolution of computer and information technology has enabled the development of expansive computer systems that combine several management science models and solution techniques in order to address more complex, interrelated organizational problems. A **decision support system (DSS)** is a computer-based system that helps decision makers address complex problems that cut across different parts of an organization and operations.

A DSS is normally *interactive*, combining various databases and different management science models and solution techniques with a user interface that enables the decision maker to ask questions and receive answers. In its simplest form any computer-based software program that helps a decision maker make a decision can be referred to as a DSS. For example, an Excel spreadsheet like the one shown for break-even analysis in Exhibit 1.1 or the QM for Windows model shown in Exhibit 1.3 can realistically be called a DSS. Alternatively, enterprise-wide DSSs can encompass many different types of models and large data warehouses, and they can serve many decision makers in an organization. They can provide decision makers with interrelated information and analyses about almost anything in a company.

Figure 1.7 illustrates the basic structure of a DSS with a database component, a modeling component, and a user interface with the decision maker. As noted earlier, a DSS can be small and singular, with one analytical model linked to a database, or it can be very large and complex, linking many models and large databases. A DSS can be primarily a data-oriented system, or it can be a model-oriented system. A new type of DSS, called an *online analytical processing* system, or *OLAP*, focuses on the use of analytical techniques such as management science models and statistics for decision making. A desktop DSS for a single user can be a spreadsheet program such as Excel to develop specific solutions to individual problems. Exhibit 1.1 includes all the components of a DSS—cost, volume, and price data, a break-even model, and the opportunity for the user to manipulate the data and see the results (i.e., a user interface). Expert Choice is another example of a desktop DSS that uses the analytical hierarchy process (AHP) described in Chapter 9 to structure complex problems by establishing decision criteria, developing priorities, and ranking decision alternatives.

FIGURE 1.7
A decision support system

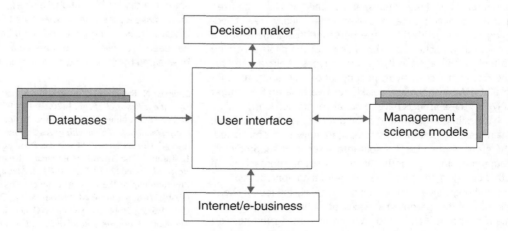

On the other end of the DSS spectrum, an *enterprise resource planning (ERP)* system is software that can connect the components and functions of an entire company. It can transform data, such as individual daily sales, directly into information that supports immediate decisions in other parts of the company, such as ordering, manufacturing, inventory, and distribution. A large-scale DSS such as an ERP system in a company might include a forecasting model (Chapter 15) to analyze sales data and help determine future product demand; an inventory model (Chapter 16) to determine how much inventory to keep on hand; a linear programming model (Chapters 2–5) to determine how much material to order and product to produce, and when to produce it; a transportation model (Chapter 6) to determine the most cost-effective method of distributing a product to customers; and a network flow model (Chapter 7) to determine the best delivery routes. All these different management science models and the data necessary to support them can be linked in a single enterprisewide DSS that can provide many decisions to many different decision makers.

In addition to helping managers answer specific questions and make decisions, a DSS may be most useful in answering What if? questions and performing sensitivity analysis. In other words, a DSS provides a computer-based laboratory to perform experiments. By linking various management science models together with different databases, a user can change a parameter in one model related to one company function and see what the effect will be in a model related to a different operation in the company. For example, by changing the data in a forecasting model, a manager could see the impact of a hypothetical change in product demand on the production schedule, as determined by a linear programming model.

Advances in information and computer technology have provided the opportunity to apply management science models to a broad array of complex organizational problems by linking different models to databases in a DSS. These advances have also made the application of management science models more readily available to individual users in the form of desktop DSSs that can help managers make better decisions relative to their day-to-day operations. In the future it will undoubtedly become even easier to apply management science to the solution of problems with the development of newer software, and management science will become even more important and pervasive as an aid to decision makers as managers are linked within companies with sophisticated computer systems and to other companies via the Internet.

Many companies now interface with new types of DSS over the Internet. In e-business applications, companies can link to other business units around the world through computer systems called *intranets*, with other companies through systems called *extranets*, and over the Internet. For example, electronic data interchange (EDI) and point-of-sale data (through bar codes) can provide companies with instantaneous records of business transactions and sales at retail stores that are immediately entered into a company's DSS to update inventory and production scheduling, using management science models. Internet transportation exchanges enable companies to arrange cost-effective transportation of their products at Web sites that match shipping loads with available trucks at the lowest cost and fastest delivery speed, using sophisticated management science models.

Summary

Management science is an art.

In the chapters that follow, the model construction and solutions that constitute each management science technique are presented in detail and illustrated with examples. In fact, the primary method of presenting the techniques is through examples. Thus, the text offers you a broad spectrum of knowledge of the mechanics of management science techniques and the types of problems to which these techniques are applied. However, the ultimate test of a management scientist or a manager who uses management science techniques is the ability to transfer textbook knowledge to the business world. In such instances there is an *art* to the application of management science, but it is an art predicated on practical experience and sound textbook knowledge. Providing the first of these necessities is beyond the scope of textbooks; providing the second is the objective of this text.

Problems

1. The Willow Furniture Company produces tables. The fixed monthly cost of production is $8,000, and the variable cost per table is $65. The tables sell for $180 apiece.
   a. For a monthly volume of 300 tables, determine the total cost, total revenue, and profit.
   b. Determine the monthly break-even volume for the Willow Furniture Company.

2. The Retread Tire Company recaps tires. The fixed annual cost of the recapping operation is $60,000. The variable cost of recapping a tire is $9. The company charges $25 to recap a tire.
   a. For an annual volume of 12,000 tires, determine the total cost, total revenue, and profit.
   b. Determine the annual break-even volume for the Retread Tire Company operation.

3. The Rolling Creek Textile Mill produces denim. The fixed monthly cost is $21,000, and the variable cost per yard of denim is $0.45. The mill sells a yard of denim for $1.30.
   a. For a monthly volume of 18,000 yards of denim, determine the total cost, total revenue, and profit.
   b. Determine the annual break-even volume for the Rolling Creek Textile Mill.

4. Evergreen Fertilizer Company produces fertilizer. The company's fixed monthly cost is $25,000, and its variable cost per pound of fertilizer is $0.15. Evergreen sells the fertilizer for $0.40 per pound. Determine the monthly break-even volume for the company.

5. Graphically illustrate the break-even volume for the Retread Tire Company determined in Problem 2.

6. Graphically illustrate the break-even volume for the Evergreen Fertilizer Company determined in Problem 4.

7. Andy Mendoza makes handcrafted dolls, which he sells at craft fairs. He is considering mass-producing the dolls to sell in stores. He estimates that the initial investment for plant and equipment will be $25,000, whereas labor, material, packaging, and shipping will be about $10 per doll. If the dolls are sold for $30 each, what sales volume is necessary for Andy to break even?

8. If the maximum operating capacity of the Retread Tire Company, as described in Problem 2, is 8,000 tires annually, determine the break-even volume as a percentage of that capacity.

9. If the maximum operating capacity of the Rolling Creek Textile Mill described in Problem 3 is 25,000 yards of denim per month, determine the break-even volume as a percentage of capacity.

10. If the maximum operating capacity of Evergreen Fertilizer Company described in Problem 4 is 120,000 pounds of fertilizer per month, determine the break-even volume as a percentage of capacity.

11. If the Retread Tire Company in Problem 2 changes its pricing for recapping a tire from $25 to $31, what effect will the change have on the break-even volume?

12. If Evergreen Fertilizer Company in Problem 4 changes the price of its fertilizer from $0.40 per pound to $0.60 per pound, what effect will the change have on the break-even volume?

13. If Evergreen Fertilizer Company changes its production process to add a weed killer to the fertilizer in order to increase sales, the variable cost per pound will increase from $0.15 to $0.22. What effect will this change have on the break-even volume computed in Problem 12?

14. If Evergreen Fertilizer Company increases its advertising expenditures by $14,000 per year, what effect will the increase have on the break-even volume computed in Problem 13?

15. Pastureland Dairy makes cheese, which it sells at local supermarkets. The fixed monthly cost of production is $4,000, and the variable cost per pound of cheese is $0.21. The cheese sells for $0.75 per pound; however, the dairy is considering raising the price to $0.95 per pound. The

dairy currently produces and sells 9,000 pounds of cheese per month, but if it raises its price per pound, sales will decrease to 5,700 pounds per month. Should the dairy raise the price?

16. For the doll-manufacturing enterprise described in Problem 7, Andy Mendoza has determined that $10,000 worth of advertising will increase sales volume by 400 dolls. Should he spend the extra amount for advertising?

17. Andy Mendoza in Problem 7 is concerned that the demand for his dolls will not exceed the break-even point. He believes he can reduce his initial investment by purchasing used sewing machines and fewer machines. This will reduce his initial investment from $25,000 to $17,000. However, it will also require his employees to work more slowly and perform more operations by hand, thus increasing variable cost from $10 to $14 per doll. Will these changes reduce his break-even point?

18. The General Store at State University is an auxiliary bookstore located near the dormitories that sells academic supplies, toiletries, sweatshirts and T-shirts, magazines, packaged food items, and canned soft drinks and fruit drinks. The manager of the store has noticed that several pizza delivery services near campus make frequent deliveries. The manager is therefore considering selling pizza at the store. She could buy premade frozen pizzas and heat them in an oven. The cost of the oven and freezer would be $27,000. The frozen pizzas cost $3.75 each to buy from a distributor and to prepare (including labor and a box). To be competitive with the local delivery services, the manager believes she should sell the pizzas for $8.95 apiece. The manager needs to write up a proposal for the university's director of auxiliary services.
   a. Determine how many pizzas would have to be sold to break even.
   b. If The General Store sells 20 pizzas per day, how many days would it take to break even?
   c. The manager of the store anticipates that once the local pizza delivery services start losing business, they will react by cutting prices. If after a month (30 days) the manager has to lower the price of a pizza to $7.95 to keep demand at 20 pizzas per day, as she expects, what will the new break-even point be, and how long will it take the store to break even?

19. Kim Davis has decided to purchase a cellular phone, but she is unsure about which rate plan to select. The "regular" plan charges a fixed fee of $55 per month for 1,000 minutes of airtime plus $0.33 per minute for any time over 1,000 minutes. The "executive" plan charges a fixed fee of $100 per month for 1,200 minutes of airtime plus $0.25 per minute over 1,200 minutes.
   a. If Kim expects to use the phone for 21 hours per month, which plan should she select?
   b. At what level of use would Kim be indifferent between the two plans?

20. Annie Russell, a student at Tech, plans to open a hot dog stand inside Tech's football stadium during home games. There are seven home games scheduled for the upcoming season. She must pay the Tech athletic department a vendor's fee of $3,000 for the season. Her stand and other equipment will cost her $4,500 for the season. She estimates that each hot dog she sells will cost her $0.35. She has talked to friends at other universities who sell hot dogs at games. Based on their information and the athletic department's forecast that each game will sell out, she anticipates that she will sell approximately 2,000 hot dogs during each game.
   a. What price should she charge for a hot dog in order to break even?
   b. What factors might occur during the season that would alter the volume sold and thus the break-even price Annie might charge?
   c. What price would you suggest that Annie charge for a hot dog to provide her with a reasonable profit while remaining competitive with other food vendors?

21. Hannah Byers and Kathleen Taylor are considering the possibility of teaching swimming to kids during the summer. A local swim club opens its pool at noon each day, so it is available to rent during the morning. The cost of renting the pool during the 10-week period for which Hannah and Kathleen would need it is $1,700. The pool would also charge Hannah and Kathleen an admission, towel service, and life guarding fee of $7 per pupil, and Hannah and Kathleen estimate

an additional $5 cost per student to hire several assistants. Hannah and Kathleen plan to charge $75 per student for the 10-week swimming class.

   a. How many pupils do Hannah and Kathleen need to enroll in their class to break even?

   b. If Hannah and Kathleen want to make a profit of $5,000 for the summer, how many pupils do they need to enroll?

   c. Hannah and Kathleen estimate that they might not be able to enroll more than 60 pupils. If they enroll this many pupils, how much would they need to charge per pupil in order to realize their profit goal of $5,000?

22. The College of Business at Tech is planning to begin an online MBA program. The initial start-up cost for computing equipment, facilities, course development, and staff recruitment and development is $350,000. The college plans to charge tuition of $18,000 per student per year. However, the university administration will charge the college $12,000 per student for the first 100 students enrolled each year for administrative costs and its share of the tuition payments.

   a. How many students does the college need to enroll in the first year to break even?

   b. If the college can enroll 75 students the first year, how much profit will it make?

   c. The college believes it can increase tuition to $24,000, but doing so would reduce enrollment to 35. Should the college consider doing this?

23. The Star Youth Soccer Club helps to support its 20 boys' and girls' teams financially, primarily through the payment of coaches. The club puts on a tournament each fall to help pay its expenses. The cost of putting on the tournament is $8,000, mainly for development, printing, and mailing of the tournament brochures. The tournament entry fee is $400 per team. For every team that enters, it costs the club about $75 to pay referees for the three-game minimum each team is guaranteed. If the club needs to clear $60,000 from the tournament, how many teams should it invite?

24. A group of developers is opening a health club near a new housing development. The health club—which will have exercise and workout equipment, basketball courts, swimming pools, an indoor walking/running track, and tennis courts—is one of the amenities the developers are building to attract new homebuyers. However, they want the health club to at least break even the first year or two. The annual fixed cost for the building, equipment, utilities, staff, and so on is $875,000, and annual variable costs are $200 per member for things like water, towels, laundry, soap, shampoo, and other member services. The membership fee is $225 per month. How many members will the club need to break even? If the club doubles its break-even membership after a year, what will its profit be?

25. The Tech Student Government Association (SGA) has several campus projects it undertakes each year and its primary source of funding to support these projects is a T-shirt sale in the fall for what is known as the "orange effect" football game (with orange being one of Tech's colors). The club's publicized (media) objective is for everyone in the stadium to wear orange. The club's financial goal is to make a profit of $150,000, but in order to have a significant number of fans buy the shirts and wear them to the game, it doesn't want to price the T-shirts much more than $6. The stadium seats 62,000 fans, and the SGA would like to sell approximately 45,000 orange T-shirts to achieve the desired orange effect, which it's relatively confident it can do. It will cost $100,000 to purchase, silk-screen print, and ship this many T-shirts. The SGA sells the shirts through three sources: online, the two Tech bookstores, and a local independent bookstore. While the bookstores don't expect to share in the profits from the sale of the shirts, they do expect for their direct costs to be covered, including labor, space, and other costs. The two Tech bookstores charge the SGA $0.35 per shirt, and the local independent store charges $0.50 per shirt. The cost per sale online (including handling, packaging, and shipping) is $2.30 per shirt. The SGA estimates that it will sell 50% of the shirts at the two Tech bookstores, 35% at the local bookstore, and 15% online. If the SGA sells the T-shirts for $6 and if it sells all the shirts it orders, will it make enough profit to achieve its financial goal? If not, at what price would the SGA need to sell the T-shirts, or how many would the SGA have to sell to achieve its financial goal?

26. The owners of Backstreets Italian Restaurant are considering starting a delivery service for pizza and their other Italian dishes in the small college town where they are located. They can purchase a used delivery van and have it painted with their name and logo for $21,500. They can hire part-time drivers who will work in the evenings from 5 P.M. to 10 P.M. for $8 per hour. The drivers are mostly college students who study at the restaurant when they are not making deliveries. During the day, there are so few deliveries that the regular employees can handle them. The owners estimate that the van will last 5 years (365 days per year) before it has to be replaced and that each delivery will cost about $1.35 in gas and other maintenance costs (including tires, oil, scheduled service, etc.). They also estimate that on average each delivery order will cost $15 for direct labor and ingredients to prepare and package, and will generate $34 in revenue.
    a. How many delivery orders must Backstreets make each month in order for the service to break even?
    b. The owners believe that if they have approximately the break-even number of deliveries during the week, they will at least double that number on Fridays, Saturdays, and Sundays. If that's the case, how much profit will they make, at a minimum, from their delivery service each month (4 weeks per month)?

27. Kathleen Taylor is a high school student who has been investigating the possibility of mowing lawns for a summer job. She has a couple of friends she thinks she could hire on an hourly basis per job. The equipment, including two new lawnmowers and weed-eaters, would cost her $500, and she estimates her cost per lawn, based on the time required to pay her friends to mow an average residential lawn (and not including her own labor) and gas for driving to the jobs and mowing, would be about $14.
    a. If she charges customers $30 per lawn, how many lawns would she need to mow to break even?
    b. Kathleen has 8 weeks available to mow lawns before school starts again, and she estimates that she can get enough customers to mow at least three lawns per day, 6 days per week. How much money can she expect to make over the summer?
    c. Kathleen believes she can get more business if she lowers her price per lawn. If she lowers her price to $25 per lawn and increases her number of jobs to four per day (which is about all she can handle anyway), should she make this decision?

28. The Weemow Lawn Service mows its customers' lawns and provides lawn maintenance starting in the spring, through the summer, and into the early fall. During the winter, the service doesn't operate, and Weemow's owners, Jeff and Julie Weems, find part-time jobs. They are considering the possibility of doing snow removal during the winter. A snowblower and a shovel would cost them $700. Since Jeff would do all the work, with occasional help from Julie, their cost per job would be about $3.
    a. If they charge $35 to clear a normal-size home driveway, how many jobs would they need to break even?
    b. Based on past winters, Jeff and Julie believe they can expect about six major snowfalls in the winter and would be able to work all day for the two days immediately following the snows, when people want their driveways cleared. If they are able to do about 10 snow removal jobs per day (and they believe they will have that much demand because of their existing customer base), how much money can they expect to make?
    c. Another possibility for Weemow is to remove snow from business parking lots. Weemow would need a small tractor with a snow plow, which costs $1,800, and would have to hire someone on an hourly basis to help, which with gas would cost about $28 per job. Jeff and Julie estimate that they could do four of these large jobs per day. If they charged $150 per job, would this be a better alternative than clearing individuals' driveways?
    d. If Weemow wanted to do both (b) and (c), Jeff and Julie would need to hire one more person to do the driveways, while Jeff worked with the other person on the parking lots. This would add $15 in cost per driveway job. Should they do this?

29. In the example used to demonstrate model construction in this chapter (p. 22), a firm sells a product, x, for \$20 that costs \$5 to make, it has 100 pounds of steel to make the product, and it takes 4 pounds of steel to make each unit. The model that was constructed is

$$\text{maximize } Z = 20x - 5x$$
$$\text{subject to}$$
$$4x = 100$$

Now suppose that there is a second product, y, that has a profit of \$10 and requires 2 pounds of steel to make, such that the model becomes

$$\text{maximize } Z = 15x + 10y$$
$$\text{subject to}$$
$$4x + 2y = 100$$

Can you determine a solution to this new model that will achieve the objective? Explain your answer.

30. Consider a model in which two products, x and y, are produced. There are 100 pounds of material and 80 hours of labor available. It requires 2 pounds of material and 1 hour of labor to produce a unit of x, and 4 pounds of material and 5 hours of labor to produce a unit of y. The profit for x is \$30 per unit, and the profit for y is \$50 per unit. If we want to know how many units of x and y to produce to maximize profit, the model is

$$\text{maximize } Z = 30x + 50y$$
$$\text{subject to}$$
$$2x + 4y = 100$$
$$x + 5y = 80$$

Determine the solution to this problem and explain your answer.

31. A textile company in China is deciding whether or not they should specialize in jeans or t-shirts in order to maximize profit. It can make 70 HKD with one pair of jeans and 50 HKD with a t-shirt. Each pair of jeans needs 3 hours of manufacturing time and 2 hours of dying, whereas for t-shirts, this time is 4 hours and 1 hour, respectively. The company has only 2,400 hours of manufacturing time and 1,000 hours of dying available daily.

   There are other constraints the company needs to consider before deciding the perfect allocation. It knows that the market cannot absorb more than 450 t-shirts per day. Also, for contractual reasons, it needs to have a daily output of at least 100 pairs of jeans.

   Determine:
   a. The liner programming model
   b. The optimal combination of t-shirt and jeans that maximizes the profit
   c. A graphical solution
   d. A computer solution

32. The Easy Drive Car Rental Agency needs 500 new cars in its Nashville operation and 300 new cars in Jacksonville, and it currently has 400 new cars in both Atlanta and Birmingham. It costs \$30 to move a car from Atlanta to Nashville, \$70 to move a car from Atlanta to Jacksonville, \$40 to move a car from Birmingham to Nashville, and \$60 to move a car from Birmingham to Jacksonville. The agency wants to determine how many cars should be transported from the agencies in Atlanta and Birmingham to the agencies in Nashville and Jacksonville in order to meet demand while minimizing the transport costs. Develop a mathematical model for this problem and use logic to determine a solution.

33. Ed Norris has developed a Web site for his used textbook business at State University. To sell advertising he needs to forecast the number of site visits he expects in the future. For the past 6 months he has had the following number of site visits:

Month	1	2	3	4	5	6
Site Visits	6,300	10,200	14,700	18,500	25,100	30,500

Determine a forecast for Ed to use for month 7 and explain the logic used to develop your forecast.

34. When Tracy McCoy wakes up on Saturday morning, she remembers that she promised the PTA she would make some cakes and/or homemade bread for its bake sale that afternoon. However, she does not have time to go to the store and get ingredients, and she has only a short time to bake things in her oven. Because cakes and breads require different baking temperatures, she cannot bake them simultaneously, and she has only 3 hours available to bake. A cake requires 3 cups of flour, and a loaf of bread requires 8 cups; Tracy has 20 cups of flour. A cake requires 45 minutes to bake, and a loaf of bread requires 30 minutes. The PTA will sell a cake for $10 and a loaf of bread for $6. Tracy wants to decide how many cakes and loaves of bread she should make. Identify all the possible solutions to this problem (i.e., combinations of cakes and loaves of bread Tracy has the time and flour to bake) and select the best one.

35. The local Food King grocery store has eight possible checkout stations with registers. On Saturday mornings customer traffic is relatively steady from 8 A.M. to noon. The store manager would like to determine how many checkout stations to staff during this time period. The manager knows from information provided by the store's national office that each minute past 3 minutes a customer must wait in line costs the store on average $50 in ill will and lost sales. Alternatively, each additional checkout station the store operates on Saturday morning costs the store $60 in salary and benefits. The following table shows the waiting time for the different staff levels.

How many registers should the store staff and why?

Registers Staffed	1	2	3	4	5	6	7	8
Waiting Time (min.)	20.0	14.0	9.0	4.0	1.7	1.0	0.5	0.1

36. A delivery company in Hong Kong (1) has to make a delivery in Zhuhai (9), and it has various options to reach its final destination.

The network diagram is presented below.
a. What is the shortest path the company can take?
b. What is the shortest possible distance it has to cover?

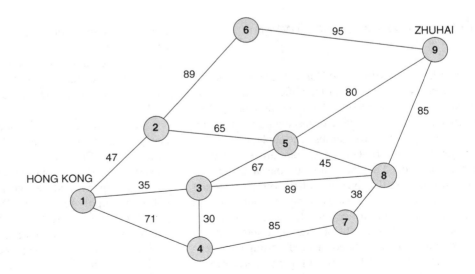

Case Problem

THE CLEAN CLOTHES CORNER LAUNDRY

When Molly Lai purchased the Clean Clothes Corner Laundry, she thought that because it was in a good location near several high-income neighborhoods, she would automatically generate good business if she improved the laundry's physical appearance. Thus, she initially invested a lot of her cash reserves in remodeling the exterior and interior of the laundry. However, she just about broke even in the year following her acquisition of the laundry, which she didn't feel was a sufficient return, given how hard she had worked. Molly didn't realize that the dry-cleaning business is very competitive and that success is based more on price and quality service, including quickness of service, than on the laundry's appearance.

In order to improve her service, Molly is considering purchasing new dry-cleaning equipment, including a pressing machine that could substantially increase the speed at which she can dry-clean clothes and improve their appearance. The new machinery costs $16,200 installed and can clean 40 clothes items per hour (or 320 items per day). Molly estimates her variable costs to be $0.25 per item dry-cleaned, which will not change if she purchases the new equipment. Her current fixed costs are $1,700 per month. She charges customers $1.10 per clothing item.

A. What is Molly's current monthly volume?
B. If Molly purchases the new equipment, how many additional items will she have to dry-clean each month to break even?
C. Molly estimates that with the new equipment she can increase her volume to 4,300 items per month. What monthly profit would she realize with that level of business during the next 3 years? After 3 years?
D. Molly believes that if she doesn't buy the new equipment but lowers her price to $0.99 per item, she will increase her business volume. If she lowers her price, what will her new break-even volume be? If her price reduction results in a monthly volume of 3,800 items, what will her monthly profit be?
E. Molly estimates that if she purchases the new equipment and lowers her price to $0.99 per item, her volume will increase to about 4,700 units per month. Based on the local market, that is the largest volume she can realistically expect. What should Molly do?

Case Problem

THE OCOBEE RIVER RAFTING COMPANY

Vicki Smith, Penny Miller, and Darryl Davis are students at State University. In the summer they often go rafting with other students down the Ocobee River in the nearby Blue Ridge Mountain foothills. The river has a number of minor rapids but is not generally dangerous. The students' rafts basically consist of large rubber tubes, sometimes joined together with ski rope. They have noticed that a number of students who come to the river don't have rubber rafts and often ask to borrow theirs, which can be very annoying. In discussing this nuisance, it occurred to Vicki, Penny, and Darryl that the problem might provide an opportunity to make some extra money. They considered starting a new enterprise, the Ocobee River Rafting Company, to sell rubber rafts at the river. They determined that their initial investment would be about $3,000 to rent a small parcel of land next to the river on which to make and sell the rafts; to purchase a tent to operate out of; and to buy some small equipment such as air pumps and a rope cutter. They estimated that the labor and material cost per raft will be about $12, including the purchase and shipping costs for the rubber tubes and rope. They plan to sell the rafts for $20 apiece, which they think is about the maximum price students will pay for a preassembled raft.

Soon after they determined these cost estimates, the newly formed company learned about another rafting company in North Carolina that was doing essentially what they planned to do. Vicki got in touch with one of the operators of that company, and he told her the company would be willing to supply rafts to the Ocobee River Rafting Company for an initial fixed fee of $9,000 plus $8 per raft, including shipping. (The Ocobee River Rafting Company would still have to rent the parcel of riverside land and tent for $1,000.) The rafts would already be inflated and assembled. This alternative appealed to Vicki, Penny, and Darryl because it would reduce the amount of time they would have to work pumping up the tubes and putting the rafts together, and it would increase time for their schoolwork.

Although the students prefer the alternative of purchasing the rafts from the North Carolina company, they are concerned about the large initial cost and worried about whether they will lose money. Of course, Vicki, Penny, and Darryl realize that their profit, if any, will be determined by how many rafts they sell. As such, they believe that they first need to determine how many rafts they must sell with each alternative in order to make a profit and which alternative would be best given different levels of demand. Furthermore, Penny has conducted a brief sample survey of people at the river and estimates that demand for rafts for the summer will be around 1,000 rafts.

Perform an analysis for the Ocobee River Rafting Company to determine which alternative would be best for different levels of demand. Indicate which alternative should be selected if demand is approximately 1,000 rafts and how much profit the company would make.

Case Problem

CONSTRUCTING A DOWNTOWN PARKING LOT IN DRAPER

The town of Draper, with a population of 20,000, sits adjacent to State University, which has an enrollment of 27,000 students. Downtown Draper merchants have long complained about the lack of parking available to their customers. This is one primary reason for the steady migration of downtown businesses to a mall several miles outside town. The local chamber of commerce has finally convinced the town council to consider the construction of a new multilevel indoor parking facility downtown. Kelly Mattingly, the town's public works director, has developed plans for a facility that would cost $4.5 million to construct. To pay for the project, the town would sell municipal bonds with a duration of 30 years at 8% interest. Kelly also estimates that five employees would be required to operate the lot on a daily basis, at a total annual cost of $140,000. It is estimated that each car that enters the lot would park for an average of 2.5 hours and pay an average fee of $3.20. Further, it is estimated that each car that parks in the lot would (on average) cost the town $0.60 in annual maintenance for cleaning and repairs to the facility. Most of the downtown businesses (which include a number of restaurants) are open 7 days per week.

A. Using break-even analysis, determine the number of cars that would have to park in the lot on an annual basis to pay off the project in the 30-year time frame.
B. From the results in (A), determine the approximate number of cars that would have to park in the lot on a daily basis. Does this seem to be a reasonable number to achieve, given the size of the town and college population?

Modeling with Linear Programming

Objectives of a business frequently are to maximize profit or minimize cost.

Many major decisions faced by a manager of a business focus on the best way to achieve the objectives of the firm, subject to the restrictions placed on the manager by the operating environment. These restrictions can take the form of limited resources, such as time, labor, energy, material, or money; or they can be in the form of restrictive guidelines, such as a recipe for making cereal or engineering specifications. One of the most frequent objectives of business firms is to gain the most profit possible or, in other words, to *maximize* profit. The objective of individual organizational units within a firm (such as a production or packaging department) is often to *minimize* cost. When a manager attempts to solve a general type of problem by seeking an objective that is subject to restrictions, the management science technique called linear programming is frequently used.

Linear programming is a model that consists of linear relationships representing a firm's decision(s), given an objective and resource constraints.

There are three steps in applying the linear programming technique. First, the problem must be identified as being solvable by linear programming. Second, the unstructured problem must be formulated as a mathematical model. Third, the model must be solved by using established mathematical techniques. The linear programming technique derives its name from the fact that the functional relationships in the mathematical model are *linear*, and the solution technique consists of predetermined mathematical steps—that is, a *program*. In this chapter, we will concern ourselves with the formulation of the mathematical model that represents the problem and then with solving this model by using a graph.

Model Formulation

Decision variables are mathematical symbols that represent levels of activity.

A linear programming model consists of certain common components and characteristics. The model components include decision variables, an objective function, and model constraints, which consist of decision variables and parameters. Decision variables are mathematical symbols that represent levels of activity by the firm. For example, an electrical manufacturing firm desires to produce x_1 radios, x_2 toasters, and x_3 clocks, where x_1, x_2, and x_3 are symbols representing unknown variable quantities of each item. The final values of x_1, x_2, and x_3, as determined by the firm, constitute a *decision* (e.g., the equation $x_1 = 100$ radios is a decision by the firm to produce 100 radios).

The objective function is a linear relationship that reflects the objective of an operation.

The objective function is a linear mathematical relationship that describes the objective of the firm in terms of the decision variables. The objective function always consists of either *maximizing* or *minimizing* some value (e.g., maximize the profit or minimize the cost of producing radios).

A model constraint is a linear relationship that represents a restriction on decision making.

The model constraints are also linear relationships of the decision variables; they represent the restrictions placed on the firm by the operating environment. The restrictions can be in the form of limited resources or restrictive guidelines. For example, only 40 hours of labor may be available to produce radios during production. The actual numeric values in the objective function and the constraints, such as the 40 hours of available labor, are parameters.

Parameters are numerical values that are included in the objective functions and constraints.

The next section presents an example of how a linear programming model is formulated. Although this example is simplified, it is realistic and represents the type of problem to which linear programming can be applied. In the example, the model components are distinctly identified and described. By carefully studying this example, you can become familiar with the process of formulating linear programming models.

A Maximization Model Example

Beaver Creek Pottery Company is a small crafts operation run by a Native American tribal council. The company employs skilled artisans to produce clay bowls and mugs with authentic Native American designs and colors. The two primary resources used by the company are special pottery clay and skilled labor. Given these limited resources, the company desires to know how many bowls and mugs to produce each day in order to maximize profit. This is generally referred to as a *product mix* problem type. This scenario is illustrated in Figure 2.1.

FIGURE 2.1

Beaver Creek Pottery Company

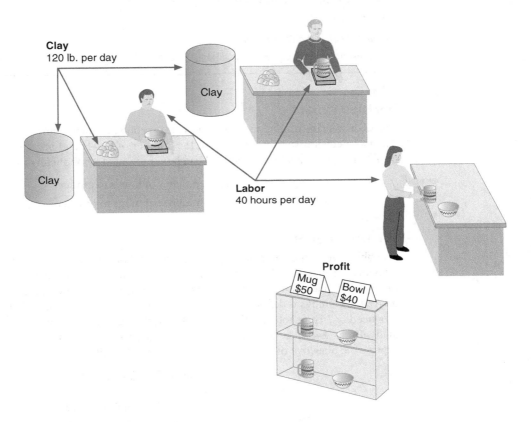

The two products have the following resource requirements for production and profit per item produced (i.e., the model parameters):

| Product | Resource Requirements | | |
	Labor (hr./unit)	Clay (lb./unit)	Profit ($/unit)
Bowl	1	4	40
Mug	2	3	50

There are 40 hours of labor and 120 pounds of clay available each day for production. We will formulate this problem as a linear programming model by defining each component of the

A linear programming model consists of decision variables, an objective function, and constraints.

model separately and then combining the components into a single model. The steps in this formulation process are summarized as follows:

Summary of LP Model Formulation Steps

Step 1: Define the decision variables
How many bowls and mugs to produce

Step 2: Define the objective function
Maximize profit

Step 3: Define the constraints
The resources (clay and labor) available

Decision Variables

The decision confronting management in this problem is how many bowls and mugs to produce. The two decision variables represent the number of bowls and mugs to be produced on a daily basis. The quantities to be produced can be represented symbolically as

$$x_1 = \text{number of bowls to produce}$$
$$x_2 = \text{number of mugs to produce}$$

The Objective Function

The objective of the company is to maximize total profit. The company's profit is the sum of the individual profits gained from each bowl and mug. Profit derived from bowls is determined by multiplying the unit profit of each bowl, \$40, by the number of bowls produced, x_1. Likewise, profit derived from mugs is derived from the unit profit of a mug, \$50, multiplied by the number of mugs produced, x_2. Thus, total profit, which we will define symbolically as Z, can be expressed mathematically as $\$40x_1 + \$50x_2$. By placing the term *maximize* in front of the profit function, we express the objective of the firm—to maximize total profit:

$$\text{maximize } Z = \$40x_1 + 50x_2$$
where
$$Z = \text{total profit per day}$$
$$\$40x_1 = \text{profit from bowls}$$
$$\$50x_2 = \text{profit from mugs}$$

Model Constraints

In this problem, two resources are used for production—labor and clay—both of which are limited. Production of bowls and mugs requires both labor and clay. For each bowl produced, 1 hour of labor is required. Therefore, the labor used for the production of bowls is $1x_1$ hours. Similarly, each mug requires 2 hours of labor; thus, the labor used to produce mugs every day is $2x_2$ hours. The total labor used by the company is the sum of the individual amounts of labor used for each product:

$$1x_1 + 2x_2$$

However, the amount of labor represented by $1x_1 + 2x_2$ is limited to 40 hours per day; thus, the complete labor constraint is

$$1x_1 + 2x_2 \leq 40 \text{ hr.}$$

The "less than or equal to" ($\le$) inequality is employed instead of an equality ($=$) because the 40 hours of labor is a maximum limitation that *can be used*, not an amount that *must be used*. This constraint allows the company some flexibility; the company is not restricted to using exactly 40 hours but can use whatever amount is necessary to maximize profit, up to and including 40 hours. This means that it is possible to have idle, or excess, capacity (i.e., some of the 40 hours may not be used).

The constraint for clay is formulated in the same way as the labor constraint. Because each bowl requires 4 pounds of clay, the amount of clay used daily for the production of bowls is $4x_1$ pounds; and because each mug requires 3 pounds of clay, the amount of clay used daily for mugs is $3x_2$. Given that the amount of clay available for production each day is 120 pounds, the material constraint can be formulated as

$$4x_1 + 3x_2 \le 120 \text{ lb.}$$

A final restriction is that the number of bowls and mugs produced must be either zero or a positive value because it is impossible to produce negative items. These restrictions are referred to as nonnegativity constraints and are expressed mathematically as

Nonnegativity constraints restrict the decision variables to zero or positive values.

$$x_1 \ge 0, \, x_2 \ge 0$$

The complete linear programming model for this problem can now be summarized as follows:

$$\text{maximize } Z = \$40x_1 + 50x_2$$
$$\text{subject to}$$
$$1x_1 + 2x_2 \le 40$$
$$4x_1 + 3x_2 \le 120$$
$$x_1, \, x_2 \ge 0$$

The solution of this model will result in numeric values for x_1 and x_2 that will maximize total profit, Z. As *one possible* solution, consider $x_1 = 5$ bowls and $x_2 = 10$ mugs. First, we will substitute this hypothetical solution into each of the constraints in order to make sure that the solution does not require more resources than the constraints show are available:

$$1(5) + 2(10) \le 40$$
$$25 \le 40$$

and

$$4(5) + 3(10) \le 120$$
$$50 \le 120$$

A feasible solution does not violate any of the constraints.

Because neither of the constraints is violated by this hypothetical solution, we say the solution is feasible (i.e., possible). Substituting these solution values in the objective function gives $Z = 40(5) + 50(10) = \$700$. However, for the time being, we do not have any way of knowing whether $700 is the *maximum* profit.

Now consider a solution of $x_1 = 10$ bowls and $x_2 = 20$ mugs. This solution results in a profit of

$$Z = \$40(10) + 50(20)$$
$$= 400 + 1{,}000$$
$$= \$1{,}400$$

An infeasible problem violates at least one of the constraints.

Although this is certainly a better solution in terms of profit, it is infeasible (i.e., not possible) because it violates the resource constraint for labor:

$$1(10) + 2(20) \le 40$$
$$50 \not\le 40$$

Management Science Application

Allocating Seat Capacity on Indian Railways Using Linear Programming

Indian Railways, with more than 1,600 trains, serves more than 7 million passengers each day. Its reservation system books passengers in three coach classes: reserved air-conditioned, reserved non-air conditioned, and unreserved non-air-conditioned. A train can make multiple stops from its origin to its destination, and thus passengers can book many combinations of tickets from a train's origin to its destination or to and/or from intermediate stations. Because passengers can depart the train or board en route, multiple passengers can occupy a single seat during a train's journey from origin to destination. This also means that a seat might be vacant for some segments of the trip and thus will not earn any revenue. If there are an abnormally high number of reservations for intermediate trips, then there might be a high number of partially vacant seats, which might deny subsequent passengers the ability to book complete origin-to-destination trips. This results in suboptimal utilization of a train's capacity. However, in many cases, passenger demand is not high at the train's origin station, and the highest passenger demand occurs en route, at intermediate stations. As a result, the railway has traditionally allocated various seat quotas to intermediate stations and limited the seats allocated for end-to-end trips, in order to maximize capacity utilization and the number of confirmed seat reservations and reduce the number of passengers wait-listed at intermediate stations.

© Neil McAllister/Alamy

In this application, a linear programming model was formulated, with an objective of minimizing the total seats required to fill all possible seat demand (in a specific coach class) between any two major stations, subject to constraints for station-to-station quotas based on historical seat demand. In a test case of 17 trains in the Western Railway zone (based in Mumbai) of Indian Railways, revenue was increased between 2.6% and 29.3%, and the number of passengers carried increased from 8.4% to 29%.

Source: Based on R. Gopalakrishnan and N. Rangaraj, "Capacity Management on Long-Distance Passenger Trains of Indian Railways," *Interfaces* 40, no. 4 (July–August 2010): 291–302.

The solution to this problem must maximize profit without violating the constraints. The solution that achieves this objective is $x_1 = 24$ bowls and $x_2 = 8$ mugs, with a corresponding profit of $1,360. The determination of this solution is shown using the graphical solution approach in the following section.

Graphical Solutions of Linear Programming Models

Graphical solutions are limited to linear programming problems with only two decision variables.

Following the formulation of a mathematical model, the next stage in the application of linear programming to a decision-making problem is to find the solution of the model. A common solution approach is to solve algebraically the set of mathematical relationships that form the model either manually or using a computer program, thus determining the values for the decision variables. However, because the relationships are *linear*, some models and solutions can be illustrated *graphically*.

The graphical method is realistically limited to models with only two decision variables, which can be represented on a graph of two dimensions. Models with three decision variables can be graphed in three dimensions, but the process is quite cumbersome, and models of four or more decision variables cannot be graphed at all.

The graphical method provides a picture of how a solution is obtained for a linear programming problem.

Although the graphical method is limited as a solution approach, it is very useful at this point in our presentation of linear programming in that it gives a picture of how a solution is derived. Graphs can provide a clearer understanding of how the computer and mathematical solution approaches presented in subsequent chapters work and, thus, a better understanding of the solutions.

Graphical Solution of a Maximization Model

The product mix model will be used to demonstrate the graphical interpretation of a linear programming problem. Recall that the problem describes Beaver Creek Pottery Company's attempt to decide how many bowls and mugs to produce daily, given limited amounts of labor and clay. The complete linear programming model was formulated as

$$\text{maximize } Z = \$40x_1 + 50x_2$$

subject to

$$x_1 + 2x_2 \leq 40 \text{ hr. of labor}$$
$$4x_1 + 3x_2 \leq 120 \text{ lb. of clay}$$
$$x_1, x_2 \geq 0$$

where

$$x_1 = \text{number of bowls produced}$$
$$x_2 = \text{number of mugs produced}$$

Figure 2.2 is a set of coordinates for the decision variables x_1 and x_2, on which the graph of our model will be drawn. Note that only the positive quadrant is drawn (i.e., the quadrant where x_1 and x_2 will always be positive) because of the nonnegativity constraints, $x_1 \geq 0$ and $x_2 \geq 0$.

FIGURE 2.2

Coordinates for graphical analysis

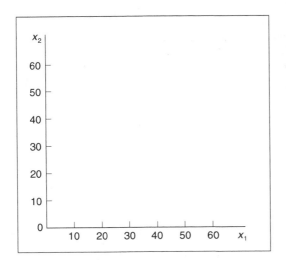

Constraint lines are plotted as equations.

The first step in drawing the graph of the model is to plot the constraints on the graph. This is done by treating both constraints as equations (or straight lines) and plotting each line on the graph. Let's consider the labor constraint line first:

$$x_1 + 2x_2 = 40$$

A simple procedure for plotting this line is to determine two points that are on the line and then draw a straight line through the points. One point can be found by letting $x_1 = 0$ and solving for x_2:

$$(0) + 2x_2 = 40$$
$$x_2 = 20$$

Thus, one point is at the coordinates $x_1 = 0$ and $x_2 = 20$. A second point can be found by letting $x_2 = 0$ and solving for x_1:

$$x_1 + 2(0) = 40$$
$$x_1 = 40$$

Now we have a second point, $x_1 = 40$, $x_2 = 0$. The line on the graph representing this equation is drawn by connecting these two points, as shown in Figure 2.3. However, this is only the graph of the constraint *line* and does not reflect the entire constraint, which also includes the values that are less than or equal to ($\leq$) this line. The *area* representing the entire constraint is shown in Figure 2.4.

FIGURE 2.3

Graph of the labor constraint line

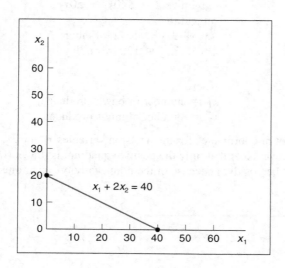

FIGURE 2.4

The labor constraint area

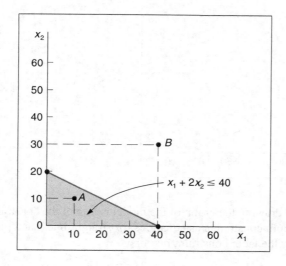

To test the correctness of the constraint area, we check any two points—one inside the constraint area and one outside. For example, check point A in Figure 2.4, which is at the intersection of $x_1 = 10$ and $x_2 = 10$. Substituting these values into the following labor constraint,

$$10 + 2(10) \leq 40$$
$$30 \leq 40 \text{ hr.}$$

shows that point A is indeed within the constraint area, as these values for x_1 and x_2 yield a quantity that does not exceed the limit of 40 hours. Next, we check point B at $x_1 = 40$ and $x_2 = 30$:

$$40 + 2(30) \leq 40$$
$$100 \nleq 40 \text{ hr.}$$

Point B is obviously outside the constraint area because the values for x_1 and x_2 yield a quantity (100) that exceeds the limit of 40 hours.

We draw the line for the clay constraint the same way as the one for the labor constraint— by finding two points on the constraint line and connecting them with a straight line. First, let $x_1 = 0$ and solve for x_2:

$$4(0) + 3x_2 = 120$$
$$x_2 = 40$$

Performing this operation results in a point, $x_1 = 0, x_2 = 40$. Next, we let $x_2 = 0$ and then solve for x_1:

$$4x_1 + 3(0) = 120$$
$$x_1 = 30$$

This operation yields a second point, $x_1 = 30, x_2 = 0$. Plotting these points on the graph and connecting them with a line gives the constraint line and area for clay, as shown in Figure 2.5.

FIGURE 2.5

The constraint area for clay

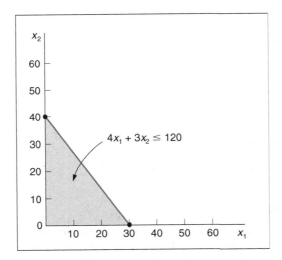

Combining the two individual graphs for both labor and clay (Figures 2.4 and 2.5) produces a graph of the model constraints, as shown in Figure 2.6. The shaded area in Figure 2.6 is the area that is common to both model constraints. Therefore, this is the only area on the graph that contains points (i.e., values for x_1 and x_2) that will satisfy both constraints simultaneously. For example, consider the points R, S, and T in Figure 2.7. Point R satisfies both constraints; thus, we say it is a *feasible* solution point. Point S satisfies the clay constraint ($4x_1 + 3x_2 \leq 120$) but exceeds the labor constraint; thus, it is infeasible. Point T satisfies neither constraint; thus, it is also infeasible.

The feasible solution area is an area on the graph that is bounded by the constraint equations.

The shaded area in Figure 2.7 is referred to as the *feasible solution area* because all the points in this area satisfy both constraints. Some point within this feasible solution area will result in *maximum profit* for Beaver Creek Pottery Company. The next step in the graphical solution approach is to locate this point.

FIGURE 2.6

Graph of both model constraints

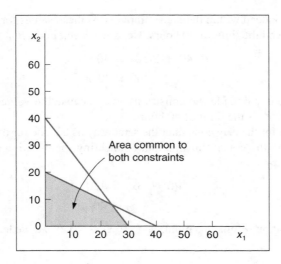

FIGURE 2.7

The feasible solution area constraints

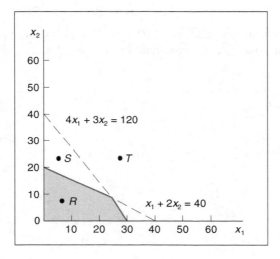

The Optimal Solution Point

The second step in the graphical solution method is to locate the point in the feasible solution area that will result in the greatest total profit. To begin the solution analysis, we first plot the objective function line for an *arbitrarily* selected level of profit. For example, if we say profit, Z, is $800, the objective function is

$$\$800 = 40x_1 + 50x_2$$

Plotting this line just as we plotted the constraint lines results in the graph shown in Figure 2.8. Every point on this line is in the feasible solution area and will result in a profit of $800 (i.e., every combination of x_1 and x_2 on this line will give a Z value of $800). However, let us see whether an even greater profit will still provide a feasible solution. For example, consider profits of $1,200 and $1,600, as shown in Figure 2.9.

A portion of the objective function line for a profit of $1,200 is outside the feasible solution area, but part of the line remains within the feasible area. Therefore, this profit line indicates that there are feasible solution points that give a profit greater than $800. Now let us increase profit again, to $1,600. This profit line, also shown in Figure 2.9, is completely outside the feasible solution area. The fact that no points on this line are feasible indicates that a profit of $1,600 is not possible.

FIGURE 2.8

Objective
function line
for Z = $800

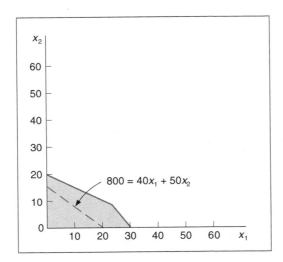

FIGURE 2.9

Alternative objec-
tive function lines
for profits, Z, of
$800, $1,200, and
$1,600

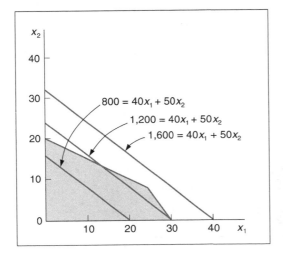

Because a profit of $1,600 is too great for the constraint limitations, as shown in Figure 2.9, the question of the maximum profit value remains. We can see from Figure 2.9 that profit increases as the objective function line moves away from the origin (i.e., the point $x_1 = 0$, $x_2 = 0$). Given this characteristic, the maximum profit will be attained at the point where the objective function line is farthest from the origin *and* is still touching a point in the feasible solution area. This point is shown as point B in Figure 2.10.

To find point B, we place a straightedge parallel to the objective function line $\$800 = 40x_1 + 50x_2$ in Figure 2.10 and move it outward from the origin as far as we can without losing contact with the feasible solution area. Point B is referred to as the optimal (i.e., best) solution.

*The optimal solution
is the best feasible
solution.*

The Solution Values

The third step in the graphical solution approach is to solve for the values of x_1 and x_2 once the optimal solution point has been found. It is possible to determine the x_1 and x_2 coordinates of point B in Figure 2.10 directly from the graph, as shown in Figure 2.11. The graphical coordinates corresponding to point B in Figure 2.11 are $x_1 = 24$ and $x_2 = 8$. This is the optimal solution for the decision

FIGURE 2.10

Identification of optimal solution point

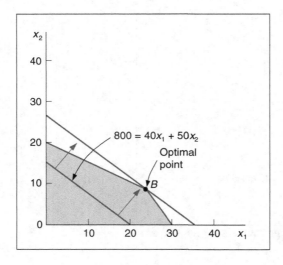

FIGURE 2.11

Optimal solution coordinates

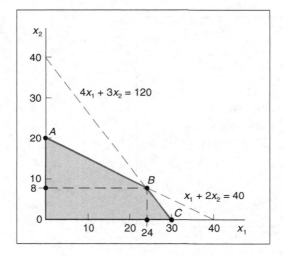

variables in the problem. However, unless an absolutely accurate graph is drawn, it is frequently difficult to determine the correct solution directly from the graph. A more exact approach is to determine the solution values mathematically once the optimal point on the graph has been determined. The mathematical approach for determining the solution is described in the following pages. First, however, we will consider a few characteristics of the solution.

The optimal solution point is the last point the objective function touches as it leaves the feasible solution area.

In Figure 2.10, as the objective function was increased, the last point it touched in the feasible solution area was on the boundary of the feasible solution area. The solution point is always on this boundary because the boundary contains the points farthest from the origin (i.e., the points corresponding to the greatest profit). This characteristic of linear programming problems reduces the number of possible solution points considerably, from all points in the solution area to just those points on the boundary. However, the number of possible solution points is reduced even more by another characteristic of linear programming problems.

Extreme points are corner points on the boundary of the feasible solution area.

The solution point will be on the boundary of the feasible solution area and at one of the *corners* of the boundary where two constraint lines intersect. (The graphical axes, you will recall, are also constraints because $x_1 \geq 0$ and $x_2 \geq 0$.) These corners (points A, B, and C in Figure 2.11) are protrusions, or *extremes*, in the feasible solution area; they are called **extreme points**. It has been proven mathematically that the optimal solution in a linear programming model will always occur at an extreme point. Therefore, in our sample problem the possible solution points are limited to the three extreme points, *A, B,* and *C*. The optimal extreme point is the extreme point the objective function touches last as it leaves the feasible solution area, as shown in Figure 2.10.

From the graph shown in Figure 2.10, we know that the optimal solution point is *B*. Because point *B* is formed by the intersection of two constraint lines, as shown in Figure 2.11, these two lines are *equal* at point *B*. Thus, the values of x_1 and x_2 at that intersection can be found by solving the two equations *simultaneously*.

Constraint equations are solved simultaneously at the optimal extreme point to determine the variable solution values.

First, we convert both equations to functions of x_1:

$$x_1 + 2x_2 = 40$$
$$x_1 = 40 - 2x_2$$

and

$$4x_1 + 3x_2 = 120$$
$$4x_1 = 120 - 3x_2$$
$$x_1 = 30 - (3x_2/4)$$

Now, we let x_1 in the first equation equal x_1 in the second equation,

$$40 - 2x_2 = 30 - (3x_2/4)$$

and solve for x_2:

$$5x_2/4 = 10$$
$$x_2 = 8$$

Substituting $x_2 = 8$ into either one of the original equations gives a value for x_1:

$$x_1 = 40 - 2x_2$$
$$x_1 = 40 - 2(8)$$
$$= 24$$

Thus, the optimal solution at point *B* in Figure 2.11 is $x_1 = 24$ and $x_2 = 8$. Substituting these values into the objective function gives the maximum profit,

$$Z = \$40x_1 + 50x_2$$
$$Z = \$40(24) + 50(8)$$
$$= \$1,360$$

In terms of the original problem, the solution indicates that if the pottery company produces 24 bowls and 8 mugs, it will receive $1,360, the maximum daily profit possible (given the resource constraints).

Given that the optimal solution will be at one of the extreme corner points, *A, B,* or *C*, we can also find the solution by testing each of the three points to see which results in the greatest profit, rather than by graphing the objective function and seeing which point it last touches as it moves out of the feasible solution area. Figure 2.12 shows the solution values for all three points, *A, B,* and *C*, and the amount of profit, *Z*, at each point.

As indicated in the discussion of Figure 2.10, point *B* is the optimal solution point because it is the last point the objective function touches before it leaves the solution area. In other words, the objective function determines which extreme point is optimal. This is because the objective function designates the profit that will accrue from each combination of x_1 and x_2 values at the extreme points. If the objective function had had different coefficients (i.e., different x_1 and x_2 profit values), one of the extreme points other than *B* might have been optimal.

FIGURE 2.12

Solutions at all corner points

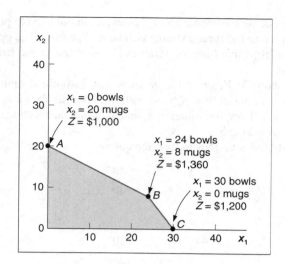

Let's assume for a moment that the profit for a bowl is $70 instead of $40, and the profit for a mug is $20 instead of $50. These values result in a new objective function, $Z = \$70x_1 + 20x_2$. If the model constraints for labor or clay are not changed, the feasible solution area remains the same, as shown in Figure 2.13. However, the location of the objective function in Figure 2.13 is different from that of the original objective function in Figure 2.10. The reason for this change is that the new profit coefficients give the linear objective function a new *slope*.

FIGURE 2.13

The optimal solution with
$Z = 70x_1 + 20x_2$

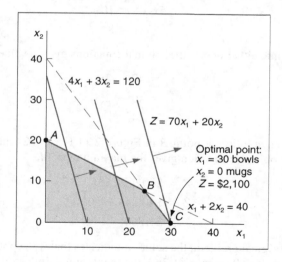

The slope is computed as the "rise" over the "run."

The slope can be determined by transforming the objective function into the general equation for a straight line, $y = a + bx$, where y is the dependent variable, a is the y intercept, b is the slope, and x is the independent variable. For our sample objective function, x_2 is the dependent variable corresponding to y (i.e., it is on the vertical axis), and x_1 is the independent variable. Thus, the objective function can be transformed into the general equation of a line as follows:

$$Z = 70x_1 + 20x_2$$
$$20x_2 = Z - 70x_1$$
$$x_2 = \frac{Z}{20} - \frac{7}{2}x_1$$
$$\uparrow \qquad \uparrow \qquad \uparrow$$
$$y \qquad a \qquad b$$

This transformation identifies the slope of the new objective function as $-7/2$ (the minus sign indicates that the line slopes downward). In contrast, the slope of the original objective function was $-4/5$.

If we move this new objective function out through the feasible solution area, the last extreme point it touches is point C. Simultaneously solving the constraint lines at point C results in the following solution:

$$x_1 = 30$$
$$4x_1 + 3x_2 = 120$$

and

$$x_2 = 40 - (4x_1/3)$$
$$x_2 = 40 - 4(30)/3$$
$$x_2 = 0$$

Thus, the optimal solution at point C in Figure 2.13 is $x_1 = 30$ bowls, $x_2 = 0$ mugs, and $Z = \$2,100$ profit. Altering the objective function coefficients results in a new solution.

This brief example of the effects of altering the objective function highlights two useful points. First, the optimal extreme point is determined by the objective function, and an extreme point on one axis of the graph is as likely to be the optimal solution as is an extreme point on a different axis. Second, the solution is sensitive to the values of the coefficients in the objective function. If the objective function coefficients are changed, as in our example, the solution may change. Likewise, if the constraint coefficients are changed, the solution space and solution points may change also. This information can be of consequence to the decision maker trying to determine how much of a product to produce. Sensitivity analysis—the use of linear programming to evaluate the effects of changes in model parameters—is discussed in Chapter 3.

Sensitivity analysis is used to analyze changes in model parameters.

It should be noted that some problems do not have a single extreme point solution. For example, when the objective function line parallels one of the constraint lines, an entire line segment is bounded by two adjacent corner points that are optimal; there is no single extreme point on the objective function line. In this situation there are multiple optimal solutions. This and other irregular types of solution outcomes in linear programming are discussed at the end of this chapter.

Multiple optimal solutions can occur when the objective function is parallel to a constraint line.

Slack Variables

Once the optimal solution was found at point B in Figure 2.12, simultaneous equations were solved to determine the values of x_1 and x_2. Recall that the solution occurs at an extreme point where constraint equation lines intersect with each other or with the axis. Thus, the model constraints are considered as *equations* ($=$) rather than $\leq$ or $\geq$ inequalities.

A slack variable is added to a $\leq$ constraint to convert it to an equation ($=$).

There is a standard procedure for transforming $\leq$ inequality constraints into equations. This transformation is achieved by adding a new variable, called a slack variable, to each constraint. For the pottery company example, the model constraints are

A slack variable represents unused resources.

$$x_1 + 2x_2 \leq 40 \text{ hr. of labor}$$
$$4x_1 + 3x_2 \leq 120 \text{ lb. of clay}$$

The addition of a unique slack variable, s_1, to the labor constraint and s_2 to the constraint for clay results in the following equations:

$$x_1 + 2x_2 + s_1 = 40 \text{ hr. of labor}$$
$$4x_1 + 3x_2 + s_2 = 120 \text{ lb. of clay}$$

The slack variables in these equations, s_1 and s_2, will take on any value necessary to make the left-hand side of the equation equal to the right-hand side. For example, consider a hypothetical solution of $x_1 = 5$ and $x_2 = 10$. Substituting these values into the foregoing equations yields

$$x_1 + 2x_2 + s_1 = 40 \text{ hr. of labor}$$
$$5 + 2(10) + s_1 = 40 \text{ hr. of labor}$$
$$s_1 = 15 \text{ hr. of labor}$$

and

$$4x_1 + 3x_2 + s_2 = 120 \text{ lb. of clay}$$
$$4(5) + 3(10) + s_2 = 120 \text{ lb. of clay}$$
$$s_2 = 70 \text{ lb. of clay}$$

In this example, $x_1 = 5$ bowls and $x_2 = 10$ mugs represent a solution that does not make use of the total available amount of labor and clay. In the labor constraint, 5 bowls and 10 mugs require only 25 hours of labor. This leaves 15 hours that are not used. Thus, s_1 represents the amount of *unused* labor, or slack.

In the clay constraint, 5 bowls and 10 mugs require only 50 pounds of clay. This leaves 70 pounds of clay unused. Thus, s_2 represents the amount of *unused* clay. In general, slack variables represent the amount of *unused resources*.

The ultimate instance of unused resources occurs at the origin, where $x_1 = 0$ and $x_2 = 0$. Substituting these values into the equations yields

$$x_1 + 2x_2 + s_1 = 40$$
$$0 + 2(0) + s_1 = 40$$
$$s_1 = 40 \text{ hr. of labor}$$

and

$$4x_1 + 3x_2 + s_2 = 120$$
$$4(0) + 3(0) + s_2 = 120$$
$$s_2 = 120 \text{ lb. of clay}$$

Because no production takes place at the origin, all the resources are unused; thus, the slack variables equal the total available amounts of each resource: $s_1 = 40$ hours of labor and $s_2 = 120$ pounds of clay.

What is the effect of these new slack variables on the objective function? The objective function for our example represents the profit gained from the production of bowls and mugs,

$$Z = \$40x_1 + \$50x_2$$

A slack variable contributes nothing to the objective function value.

The coefficient $40 is the contribution to profit of each bowl; $50 is the contribution to profit of each mug. What, then, do the slack variables s_1 and s_2 contribute? They contribute *nothing* to profit because they represent unused resources. Profit is made only after the resources are put to use in making bowls and mugs. Using slack variables, we can write the objective function as

$$\text{maximize } Z = \$40x_1 + \$50x_2 + 0s_1 + 0s_2$$

As in the case of decision variables (x_1 and x_2), slack variables can have only nonnegative values because negative resources are not possible. Therefore, for this model formulation $x_1, x_2, s_1,$ and $s_2 \geq 0$.

The complete linear programming model can be written in what is referred to as *standard form* with slack variables as follows:

$$\text{maximize } Z = \$40x_1 + \$50x_2 + 0s_1 + 0s_2$$

subject to

$$x_1 + 2x_2 + s_1 = 40$$
$$4x_1 + 3x_2 + s_2 = 120$$
$$x_1, \ x_2, \ s_1, \ s_2 \geq 0$$

The solution values, including the slack at each solution point, are summarized as follows:

Solution Summary with Slack			
Point	Solution Values	Z	Slack
A	$x_1 = 0$ bowls, $x_2 = 20$ mugs	$1,000	$s_1 = 0$ hr.; $s_2 = 60$ lb.
B	$x_1 = 24$ bowls, $x_2 = 8$ mugs	$1,360	$s_1 = 0$ hr.; $s_2 = 0$ lb.
C	$x_1 = 30$ bowls, $x_2 = 0$ mugs	$1,200	$s_1 = 10$ hr.; $s_2 = 0$ lb.

Figure 2.14 shows the graphical solution of this example, with slack variables included at each solution point.

FIGURE 2.14

Solutions at points A, B, and C with slack

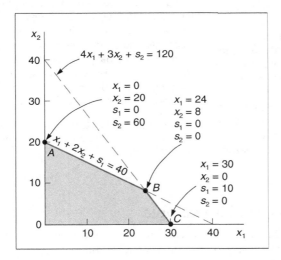

Summary of the Graphical Solution Steps

The steps for solving a graphical linear programming model are summarized here:

1. Plot the model constraints as equations on the graph; then, considering the inequalities of the constraints, indicate the feasible solution area.
2. Plot the objective function; then, move this line out from the origin to locate the optimal solution point.
3. Solve simultaneous equations at the solution point to find the optimal solution values.

Or

2. Solve simultaneous equations at each corner point to find the solution values at each point.
3. Substitute these values into the objective function to find the set of values that results in the maximum Z value.

Management Science Application

Improving Customer Service at Amazon.com

Amazon.com started as an Internet book retailer in 1995 and 10 years later was a Fortune 500 company with annual sales of more than $7 billion. Amazon.com is now an Internet retailer that offers new and used products in a variety of categories including music and video, consumer electronics, food, clothing, furniture, and appliances. From 2001 through 2003 Amazon.com achieved the highest score ever recorded in any service industry by the American Customer Satisfaction Index. The company's success is partly a result of its strong customer service operations. Customer service is provided through features on the Web site or via telephone or e-mail. Customer service representatives are available at internally or externally managed contact centers 24 hours a day. Because of its sales growth and the seasonality of its sales (which generally decline in the summer), Amazon must make accurate decisions about the capacity of its contact centers, including the number of customer service representatives to hire and train at its internally managed centers, and the volume of voice calls and e-mails to allocate to external service providers (referred to as *cosourcers*). The service times for calls and e-mails are categorized depending on the product type, the customer type, and the purchase type. Amazon's objective is to process calls and e-mails at target service levels for different categories; for voice calls the target is that a specific percentage of callers wait no more than a specific time, and for e-mails the target is that a percentage of them receive a response within some time period. Amazon uses a linear programming model to optimize its capacity decisions at its customer service contact centers. The approach provides a minimum-cost capacity plan that provides the number of representatives to hire and train at Amazon's

DYLAN MARTINEZ/Reuters/Landov

own centers and the volume of contacts to allocate to each cosourcer each week for a given planning horizon. Objective function costs include the number of normal and overtime hours, the number of new representatives hired and transferred, and the cost of contracting with cosourcers. There are several categories of constraints related to the number of voice calls and e-mails and for normal and overtime hours at both the internally managed contact centers and at cosourcers. For a 1-year (52-week) planning horizon the linear programming model consists of approximately 134,000 constraints and almost 16,000 variables.

Source: Based on M. Keblis and M. Chen, "Improving Customer Service Operations at Amazon.com," *Interfaces* 36, no. 5 (September–October 2006): 433–45.

A Minimization Model Example

As mentioned at the beginning of this chapter, there are two types of linear programming problems: maximization problems (like the Beaver Creek Pottery Company example) and minimization problems. A minimization problem is formulated the same basic way as a maximization problem, except for a few minor differences. The following sample problem will demonstrate the formulation of a minimization model.

A farmer is preparing to plant a crop in the spring and needs to fertilize a field. There are two brands of fertilizer to choose from, Super-gro and Crop-quick. Each brand yields a specific amount of nitrogen and phosphate per bag, as follows:

	Chemical Contribution	
Brand	Nitrogen (lb./bag)	Phosphate (lb./bag)
Super-gro	2	4
Crop-quick	4	3

The farmer's field requires at least 16 pounds of nitrogen and at least 24 pounds of phosphate. Super-gro costs $6 per bag, and Crop-quick costs $3. The farmer wants to know how many bags of each brand to purchase in order to minimize the total cost of fertilizing. This scenario is illustrated in Figure 2.15.

The steps in the linear programming model formulation process are summarized as follows:

Summary of LP Model Formulation Steps

Step 1: Define the decision variables

How many bags of Super-gro and Crop-quick to buy

Step 2: Define the objective function

Minimize cost

Step 3: Define the constraints

The field requirements for nitrogen and phosphate

FIGURE 2.15
Fertilizing farmer's field

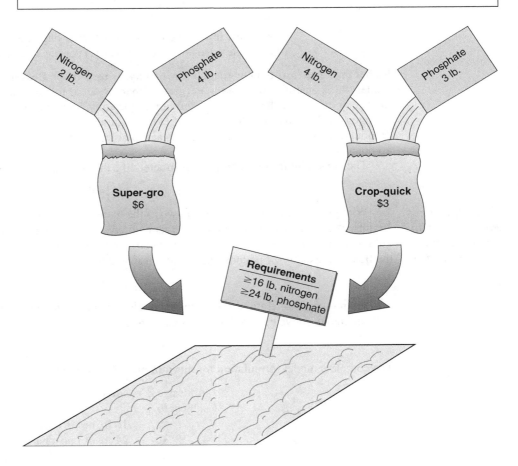

Decision Variables

This problem contains two decision variables, representing the number of bags of each brand of fertilizer to purchase:

$$x_1 = \text{bags of Super-gro}$$
$$x_2 = \text{bags of Crop-quick}$$

The Objective Function

The farmer's objective is to minimize the total cost of fertilizing. The total cost is the sum of the individual costs of each type of fertilizer purchased. The objective function that represents total cost is expressed as

$$\text{minimize } Z = \$6x_1 + 3x_2$$

where

$\$6x_1$ = cost of bags of Super-gro
$\$3x_2$ = cost of bags of Crop-quick

Model Constraints

The requirements for nitrogen and phosphate represent the constraints of the model. Each bag of fertilizer contributes a number of pounds of nitrogen and phosphate to the field. The constraint for nitrogen is

$$2x_1 + 4x_2 \geq 16 \text{ lb.}$$

where

$2x_1$ = the nitrogen contribution (lb.) per bag of Super-gro
$4x_2$ = the nitrogen contribution (lb.) per bag of Crop-quick

Rather than a $\leq$ (less than or equal to) inequality, as used in the Beaver Creek Pottery Company model, this constraint requires a $\geq$ (greater than or equal to) inequality. This is because the nitrogen content for the field is a minimum requirement specifying that at least 16 pounds of nitrogen be deposited on the farmer's field. If a minimum cost solution results in more than 16 pounds of nitrogen on the field, that is acceptable; however, the amount cannot be less than 16 pounds.

The constraint for phosphate is constructed like the constraint for nitrogen:

$$4x_1 + 3x_2 \geq 24 \text{ lb.}$$

The three types of linear programming constraints are $\leq$, $=$, and $\geq$. With this example, we have shown two of the three types of linear programming model constraints, $\leq$ and $\geq$. The third type is an exact equality, $=$. This type specifies that a constraint requirement must be exact. For example, if the farmer had said that the phosphate requirement for the field was exactly 24 pounds, the constraint would have been

$$4x_1 + 3x_2 = 24 \text{ lb.}$$

As in our maximization model, there are also nonnegativity constraints in this problem to indicate that negative bags of fertilizer cannot be purchased:

$$x_1, x_2 \geq 0$$

The complete model formulation for this minimization problem is

$$\text{minimize } Z = \$6x_1 + 3x_2$$
subject to
$$2x_1 + 4x_2 \geq 16 \text{ lb. of nitrogen}$$
$$4x_1 + 3x_2 \geq 24 \text{ lb. of phosphate}$$
$$x_1, x_2 \geq 0$$

Graphical Solution of a Minimization Model

We follow the same basic steps in the graphical solution of a minimization model as in a maximization model. The fertilizer example will be used to demonstrate the graphical solution of a minimization model.

The first step is to graph the equations of the two model constraints, as shown in Figure 2.16. Next, the feasible solution area is chosen, to reflect the $\geq$ inequalities in the constraints, as shown in Figure 2.17.

FIGURE 2.16

Constraint lines for fertilizer model

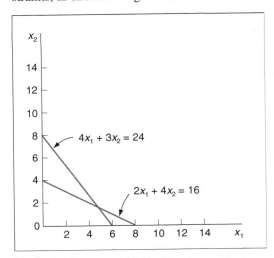

FIGURE 2.17

Feasible solution area

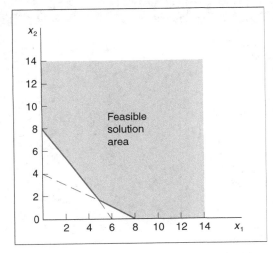

The optimal solution of a minimization problem is at the extreme point closest to the origin.

After the feasible solution area has been determined, the second step in the graphical solution approach is to locate the optimal point. Recall that in a maximization problem, the optimal solution is on the boundary of the feasible solution area that contains the point(s) farthest from the origin. The optimal solution point in a minimization problem is also on the boundary of the feasible solution area; however, the boundary contains the point(s) *closest* to the origin (zero being the lowest cost possible).

As in a maximization problem, the optimal solution is located at one of the extreme points of the boundary. In this case, the corner points represent extremities in the boundary of the feasible solution area that are *closest* to the origin. Figure 2.18 shows the three corner points—*A, B,* and *C*—and the objective function line.

As the objective function edges *toward* the origin, the last point it touches in the feasible solution area is *A*. In other words, point *A* is the closest the objective function can get to the origin without encompassing infeasible points. Thus, it corresponds to the lowest cost that can be attained.

The final step in the graphical solution approach is to solve for the values of x_1 and x_2 at point *A*. Because point *A* is on the x_2 axis, $x_1 = 0$; thus,

$$4(0) + 3x_2 = 24$$
$$x_2 = 8$$

FIGURE 2.18

The optimal solution point

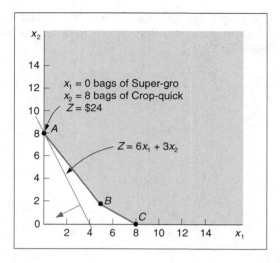

Management Science Application

Finance, Investment, and Linear Programming Solutions: Evidence from Dubai and Kuwait

The current economic and financial crisis, which began in 2008, has seriously affected economies all over the world, and the Middle East is no exception.

In particular, Dubai has been experiencing a free fall in its stock exchange share prices and a high level of failures and business closures. The once-blooming property market has been particularly affected, with some of the main projects put on hold or closed permanently.

It is well known that one of the most problematic issues in financial crises is credit and debt entanglements coupled with a high volume of business failures, which makes their lawful resolutions in court a difficult and time-consuming process. Legal and operational costs can be high as well, generally resulting in a procedural nightmare.

This is one of the fields in which the application of linear programming (LP) procedures and methods can be particularly useful. By identifying important variables and working together on the constraints, it is possible to determine the best possible combination for reducing handling costs of market failures. Thanks to existing software, such as LINDO and AMPL, even situations with thousands of variable and constraints can be easily modeled and solved.

This is not the first time LP has been used to address financial settlement problems. Previously in the Middle East, in August 1982, the "Souk al-Manakh stock market crash" occurred in Kuwait; the crash was named after the unofficial but very active local stock market. To solve the huge problem of settling all business failures caused by the crash, the

© Patrik Dietrich - Fotolia.com

Kuwaiti government decided to develop a linear programming model. The main needs addressed by the model were to help the court to identify insolvent operators and to determine what amount insolvent traders could pay, identified by asset kinds and creditors. The model worked admirably, avoiding, according to some estimates, approximately $10 billion in court costs and attorney fees, and significantly reducing the average lawsuit handling time. It also reduced the overall number of bankruptcies, with a net benefit for the Kuwaiti economy and for the region's recovery.

Sources: A. Eliman, M. Girgis, S. Kotob, "A Solution to Post Crash Debt Entanglements in Kuwait's al-Manakh Stock Market," *Interfaces* 27, no. 1 (January–February 1997): 89–106; "A Very Special Recession," *Time Magazine* (November 28, 1983); "Global Financial Crisis Takes Toll on UAE," accessed at http://news.xinhuanet.com/english/2008-12/02/content_10445926.htm.

Given that the optimal solution is $x_1 = 0$, $x_2 = 8$, the minimum cost, Z, is

$$Z = \$6x_1 + \$3x_2$$
$$Z = 6(0) + 3(8)$$
$$= \$24$$

This means the farmer should not purchase any Super-gro but, instead, should purchase eight bags of Crop-quick, at a total cost of $24.

Surplus Variables

Greater-than or equal-to constraints cannot be converted to equations by adding slack variables, as with $\leq$ constraints. Recall our fertilizer model, formulated as

$$\text{minimize } Z = \$6x_1 + \$3x_2$$
$$\text{subject to}$$
$$2x_1 + 4x_2 \geq 16 \text{ lb. of nitrogen}$$
$$4x_1 + 3x_2 \geq 24 \text{ lb. of phosphate}$$
$$x_1, x_2 \geq 0$$

where

$x_1 =$ bags of Super-gro fertilizer
$x_2 =$ bags of Crop-quick fertilizer
$Z =$ farmer's total cost (\$) of purchasing fertilizer

A surplus variable is subtracted from a $\geq$ constraint to convert it to an equation ($=$).

A surplus variable represents an excess above a constraint requirement level.

Because this problem has $\geq$ constraints as opposed to the $\leq$ constraints of the Beaver Creek Pottery Company maximization example, the constraints are converted to equations a little differently.

Instead of adding a slack variable as we did with a $\geq$ constraint, we subtract a **surplus variable**. Whereas a slack variable is added and reflects unused resources, a surplus variable is subtracted and reflects the excess above a minimum resource requirement level. Like a slack variable, a surplus variable is represented symbolically by s_1 and must be nonnegative.

For the nitrogen constraint, the subtraction of a surplus variable gives

$$2x_1 + 4x_2 - s_1 = 16$$

The surplus variable s_1 transforms the nitrogen constraint into an equation.

As an example, consider the hypothetical solution

$$x_1 = 0$$
$$x_2 = 10$$

Substituting these values into the previous equation yields

$$2(0) + 4(10) - s_1 = 16$$
$$- s_1 = 16 - 40$$
$$s_1 = 24 \text{ lb. of nitrogen}$$

In this equation, s_1 can be interpreted as the *extra* amount of nitrogen above the minimum requirement of 16 pounds that would be obtained by purchasing 10 bags of Crop-quick fertilizer.

In a similar manner, the constraint for phosphate is converted to an equation by subtracting a surplus variable, s_2:

$$4x_1 + 3x_2 - s_2 = 24$$

As is the case with slack variables, surplus variables contribute nothing to the overall cost of a model. For example, putting additional nitrogen or phosphate on the field will not affect the farmer's cost; the only thing affecting cost is the number of bags of fertilizer purchased. As such the standard form of this linear programming model is summarized as

$$\text{minimize } Z = \$6x_1 + 3x_2 + 0s_1 + 0s_2$$

subject to

$$2x_1 + 4x_2 - s_1 = 16$$
$$4x_1 + 3x_2 - s_2 = 24$$
$$x_1, x_2, s_1, s_2 \geq 0$$

Figure 2.19 shows the graphical solutions for our example, with surplus variables included at each solution point.

FIGURE 2.19

Graph of the fertilizer example

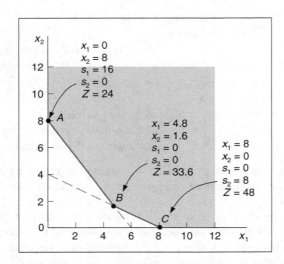

Irregular Types of Linear Programming Problems

For some linear programming models, the general rules do not always apply.

The basic forms of typical maximization and minimization problems have been shown in this chapter. However, there are several special types of atypical linear programming problems. Although these special cases do not occur frequently, they will be described so that you can recognize them when they arise. These special types include problems with more than one optimal solution, infeasible problems, and problems with unbounded solutions.

Multiple Optimal Solutions

Consider the Beaver Creek Pottery Company example, with the objective function changed from $Z = 40x_1 + 50x_2$ to $Z = 40x_1 + 30x_2$:

$$\text{maximize } Z = 40x_1 + 30x_2$$

subject to

$$x_1 + 2x_2 \leq 40 \text{ hr. of labor}$$
$$4x_1 + 3x_2 \leq 120 \text{ lb. of clay}$$
$$x_1, x_2 \geq 0$$

where

$x_1 =$ bowls produced

$x_2 =$ mugs produced

The graph of this model is shown in Figure 2.20. The slight change in the objective function makes it now *parallel* to the constraint line, $4x_1 + 3x_2 = 120$. Both lines now have the same slope of $-4/3$. Therefore, as the objective function edge moves outward from the origin, it touches the whole line segment BC rather than a single extreme corner point before it leaves the feasible solution area. This means that every point along this line segment is optimal (i.e., each point results in the same profit of $Z = \$1,200$). The endpoints of this line segment, B and C, are typically referred to as the **alternate optimal solutions**. It is understood that these points represent the endpoints of a range of optimal solutions.

Alternate optimal solutions are at the endpoints of the constraint line segment that the objective function parallels.

FIGURE 2.20

Graph of the Beaver Creek Pottery Company example with multiple optimal solutions

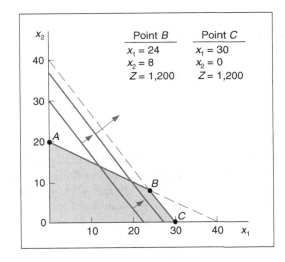

The pottery company, therefore, has several options in deciding on the number of bowls and mugs to produce. Multiple optimal solutions can benefit the decision maker because the number of decision options is enlarged. The multiple optimal solutions (along the line segment BC in Figure 2.20) allow the decision maker greater flexibility. For example, in the case of Beaver Creek Pottery Company, it may be easier to sell bowls than mugs; thus, the solution at point C, where only bowls are produced, would be more desirable than the solution at point B, where a mix of bowls and mugs is produced.

Multiple optimal solutions provide greater flexibility to the decision maker.

An Infeasible Problem

An infeasible problem has no feasible solution area; every possible solution point violates one or more constraints.

In some cases, a linear programming problem has no feasible solution area; thus, there is no solution to the problem. An example of an infeasible problem is formulated next and depicted graphically in Figure 2.21:

$$\text{maximize } Z = 5x_1 + 3x_2$$
$$\text{subject to}$$
$$4x_1 + 2x_2 \leq 8$$
$$x_1 \geq 4$$
$$x_2 \geq 6$$
$$x_1, x_2 \geq 0$$

Point A in Figure 2.21 satisfies only the constraint $4x_1 + 2x_2 \leq 8$, whereas point C satisfies only the constraints $x_1 \geq 4$ and $x_2 \geq 6$. Point B satisfies none of the constraints. The three constraints do not overlap to form a feasible solution area. Because no point satisfies all three constraints simultaneously, there is no solution to the problem. Infeasible problems do not typically occur, but when they do, they are usually a result of errors in defining the problem or in formulating the linear programming model.

FIGURE 2.21

Graph of an infeasible problem

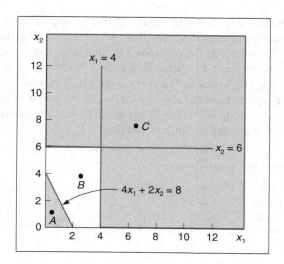

*In an **unbounded** problem the objective function can increase indefinitely without reaching a maximum value.*

An Unbounded Problem

In some problems, the feasible solution area formed by the model constraints is not closed. In these cases it is possible for the objective function to increase indefinitely without ever reaching a maximum value because it never reaches the boundary of the feasible solution area.

An example of this type of problem is formulated next and shown graphically in Figure 2.22:

$$\text{maximize } Z = 4x_1 + 2x_2$$
$$\text{subject to}$$
$$x_1 \geq 4$$
$$x_2 \leq 2$$
$$x_1, x_2 \geq 0$$

FIGURE 2.22

An unbounded problem

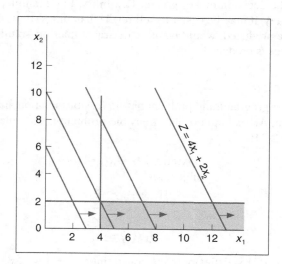

The solution space is not completely closed in.

In Figure 2.22, the objective function is shown to increase without bound; thus, a solution is never reached.

Unlimited profits are not possible in the real world; an unbounded solution, like an infeasible solution, typically reflects an error in defining the problem or in formulating the model.

Characteristics of Linear Programming Problems

The components of a linear programming model are an objective function, decision variables, and constraints.

Now that we have had the opportunity to construct several linear programming models, let's review the characteristics that identify a linear programming problem.

A linear programming problem requires a choice between alternative courses of action (i.e., a decision). The decision is represented in the model by decision variables. A typical choice task for a business firm is deciding how much of several different products to produce, as in the Beaver Creek Pottery Company example presented earlier in this chapter. Identifying the choice task and defining the decision variables is usually the first step in the formulation process because it is quite difficult to construct the objective function and constraints without first identifying the decision variables.

The problem encompasses an objective that the decision maker wants to achieve. The two most frequently encountered objectives for a business are maximizing profit and minimizing cost.

A third characteristic of a linear programming problem is that restrictions exist, making unlimited achievement of the objective function impossible. In a business firm these restrictions often take the form of limited resources, such as labor or material; however, the sample models in this chapter exhibit a variety of problem restrictions. These restrictions, as well as the objective, must be definable by mathematical functional relationships that are linear. Defining these relationships is typically the most difficult part of the formulation process.

Properties of Linear Programming Models

In addition to encompassing only linear relationships, a linear programming model also has several other implicit properties, which have been exhibited consistently throughout the examples in this chapter. The term *linear* not only means that the functions in the models are graphed as a straight line; it also means that the relationships exhibit proportionality. In other words, the rate of change, or slope, of the function is constant; therefore, changes of a given size in the value of a decision variable will result in exactly the same relative changes in the functional value.

Proportionality means the slope of a constraint or objective function line is constant.

Linear programming also requires that the objective function terms and the constraint terms be additive. For example, in the Beaver Creek Pottery Company model, the total profit (Z) must equal the sum of profits earned from making bowls ($\$40x_1$) and mugs ($\$50x_2$). Also, the total resources used must equal the sum of the resources used for each activity in a constraint (e.g., labor).

The terms in the objective function or constraints are additive.

Another property of linear programming models is that the solution values (of the decision variables) cannot be restricted to integer values; the decision variables can take on any fractional value. Thus, the variables are said to be *continuous* or divisible, as opposed to *integer* or *discrete*. For example, although decision variables representing bowls or mugs or airplanes or automobiles should realistically have integer (whole number) solutions, the solution methods for linear programming will not necessarily provide such solutions. This is a property that will be discussed further as solution methods are presented in subsequent chapters.

The values of decision variables are continuous or divisible.

All model parameters are assumed to be known with certainty.

The final property of linear programming models is that the values of all the model parameters are assumed to be constant and known with certainty. In real situations, however, model parameters are frequently uncertain because they reflect the future as well as the present, and future conditions are rarely known with certainty.

To summarize, a linear programming model has the following general properties: linearity, proportionality, additivity, divisibility, and certainty. As various linear programming solution methods are presented throughout this book, these properties will become more obvious, and their impact on problem solution will be discussed in greater detail.

Summary

The two example problems in this chapter were formulated as linear programming models in order to demonstrate the modeling process. These problems were similar in that they concerned achieving some objective subject to a set of restrictions or requirements. Linear programming models exhibit certain common characteristics:

- An objective function to be maximized or minimized
- A set of constraints
- Decision variables for measuring the level of activity
- Linearity among all constraint relationships and the objective function

The graphical approach to the solution of linear programming problems is not a very efficient means of solving problems. For one thing, drawing accurate graphs is tedious. Moreover, the graphical approach is limited to models with only two decision variables. However, the analysis of the graphical approach provides valuable insight into linear programming problems and their solutions.

In the graphical approach, once the feasible solution area and the optimal solution point have been determined from the graph, simultaneous equations are solved to determine the values of x_1 and x_2 at the solution point. In Chapter 3, we will show how linear programming solutions can be obtained using computer programs.

Example Problem Solutions

As a prelude to the problems, this section presents example solutions to two linear programming problems.

Problem Statement

Moore's Meatpacking Company produces a hot dog mixture in 1,000-pound batches. The mixture contains two ingredients—chicken and beef. The cost per pound of each of these ingredients is as follows:

Ingredient	Cost/lb.
Chicken	$3
Beef	$5

Each batch has the following recipe requirements:

a. At least 500 pounds of chicken
b. At least 200 pounds of beef

The ratio of chicken to beef must be at least 2 to 1. The company wants to know the optimal mixture of ingredients that will minimize cost. Formulate a linear programming model for this problem.

Solution

Step 1: Identify Decision Variables

Recall that the problem should not be "swallowed whole." Identify each part of the model separately, starting with the decision variables:

$$x_1 = \text{lb. of chicken}$$
$$x_2 = \text{lb. of beef}$$

Step 2: Formulate the Objective Function

$$\text{minimize } Z = \$3x_1 + \$5x_2$$
where
$$Z = \text{cost per 1,000-lb batch}$$
$$\$3x_1 = \text{cost of chicken}$$
$$\$5x_2 = \text{cost of beef}$$

Step 3: Establish Model Constraints

The constraints of this problem are embodied in the recipe restrictions and (not to be overlooked) the fact that each batch must consist of 1,000 pounds of mixture:

$$x_1 + x_2 = 1,000 \text{ lb.}$$
$$x_1 \geq 500 \text{ lb. of chicken}$$
$$x_2 \geq 200 \text{ lb. of beef}$$
$$x_1/x_2 \geq 2/1 \text{ or } x_1 - 2x_2 \geq 0$$

and

$$x_1, x_2 \geq 0$$

The Model

$$\text{minimize } Z = \$3x_1 + \$5x_2$$
subject to
$$x_1 + x_2 = 1,000$$
$$x_1 \geq 500$$
$$x_2 \geq 200$$
$$x_1 - 2x_2 \geq 0$$
$$x_1, x_2 \geq 0$$

Problem Statement

Solve the following linear programming model graphically:

$$\text{maximize } Z = 4x_1 + 5x_2$$
subject to
$$x_1 + 2x_2 \leq 10$$
$$6x_1 + 6x_2 \leq 36$$
$$x_1 \leq 4$$
$$x_1, x_2 \geq 0$$

Solution

Step 1: Plot the Constraint Lines as Equations

A simple method for plotting constraint lines is to set one of the constraint variables equal t[o] zero and solve for the other variable to establish a point on one of the axes. The three constrai[n] lines are graphed in the following figure:

The constraint equations

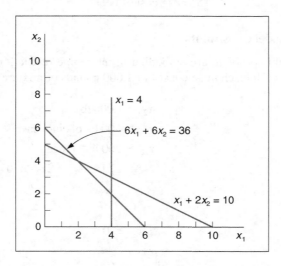

Step 2: Determine the Feasible Solution Area

The feasible solution area is determined by identifying the space that jointly satisfies the [s] conditions of all three constraints, as shown in the following figure:

The feasible solution space and extreme points

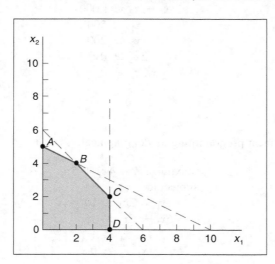

Step 3: Determine the Solution Points

The solution at point A can be determined by noting that the constraint line intersects the x_2 axis at 5; thus, $x_2 = 5$, $x_1 = 0$, and $Z = 25$. The solution at point D on the other axis can be determined similarly; the constraint intersects the axis at $x_1 = 4$, $x_2 = 0$, and $Z = 16$.

The values at points B and C must be found by solving simultaneous equations. Note that point B is formed by the intersection of the lines $x_1 + 2x_2 = 10$ and $6x_1 + 6x_2 = 36$. First, convert both of these equations to functions of x_1:

$$x_1 + 2x_2 = 10$$
$$x_1 = 10 - 2x_2$$

and

$$6x_1 + 6x_2 = 36$$
$$6x_1 = 36 - 6x_2$$
$$x_1 = 6 - x_2$$

Now, set the equations equal and solve for x_2:

$$10 - 2x_2 = 6 - x_2$$
$$-x_2 = -4$$
$$x_2 = 4$$

Substituting $x_2 = 4$ into either of the two equations gives a value for x_1:

$$x_1 = 6 - x_2$$
$$x_1 = 6 - (4)$$
$$x_1 = 2$$

Thus, at point B, $x_1 = 2$, $x_2 = 4$, and $Z = 28$.

At point C, $x_1 = 4$. Substituting $x_1 = 4$ into the equation $x_1 = 6 - x_2$ gives a value for x_2:

$$4 = 6 - x_2$$
$$x_2 = 2$$

Thus, $x_1 = 4$, $x_2 = 2$, and $Z = 26$.

Step 4: Determine the Optimal Solution

The optimal solution is at point B, where $x_1 = 2$, $x_2 = 4$, and $Z = 28$. The optimal solution and solutions at the other extreme points are summarized in the following figure:

Optimal solution point

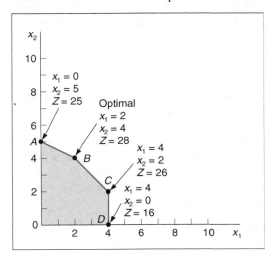

Problems

1. In Problem 34 in Chapter 1, when Tracy McCoy wakes up Saturday morning, she remembers that she promised the PTA she would make some cakes and/or homemade bread for its bake sale that afternoon. However, she does not have time to go to the store to get ingredients, and she has only a short time to bake things in her oven. Because cakes and breads require different baking temperatures, she cannot bake them simultaneously, and she has only 3 hours available to bake. A cake requires 3 cups of flour, and a loaf of bread requires 8 cups; Tracy has 20 cups of flour. A cake requires 45 minutes to bake, and a loaf of bread requires 30 minutes. The PTA will sell a cake for $10 and a loaf of bread for $6. Tracy wants to decide how many cakes and loaves of bread she should make.
   a. Formulate a linear programming model for this problem.
   b. Solve this model by using graphical analysis.

2. A company produces two products that are processed on two assembly lines. Assembly line 1 has 100 available hours, and assembly line 2 has 42 available hours. Each product requires 10 hours of processing time on line 1, while on line 2 product 1 requires 7 hours and product 2 requires 3 hours. The profit for product 1 is $6 per unit, and the profit for product 2 is $4 per unit.
   a. Formulate a linear programming model for this problem.
   b. Solve this model by using graphical analysis.

3. The Munchies Cereal Company makes a cereal from several ingredients. Two of the ingredients, oats and rice, provide vitamins A and B. The company wants to know how many ounces of oats and rice it should include in each box of cereal to meet the minimum requirements of 48 milligrams of vitamin A and 12 milligrams of vitamin B while minimizing cost. An ounce of oats contributes 8 milligrams of vitamin A and 1 milligram of vitamin B, whereas an ounce of rice contributes 6 milligrams of A and 2 milligrams of B. An ounce of oats costs $0.05, and an ounce of rice costs $0.03.
   a. Formulate a linear programming model for this problem.
   b. Solve this model by using graphical analysis.

4. What would be the effect on the optimal solution in Problem 3 if the cost of rice increased from $0.03 per ounce to $0.06 per ounce?

5. The Kalo Fertilizer Company makes a fertilizer using two chemicals that provide nitrogen, phosphate, and potassium. A pound of ingredient 1 contributes 10 ounces of nitrogen and 6 ounces of phosphate, while a pound of ingredient 2 contributes 2 ounces of nitrogen, 6 ounces of phosphate, and 1 ounce of potassium. Ingredient 1 costs $3 per pound, and ingredient 2 costs $5 per pound. The company wants to know how many pounds of each chemical ingredient to put into a bag of fertilizer to meet the minimum requirements of 20 ounces of nitrogen, 36 ounces of phosphate, and 2 ounces of potassium while minimizing cost.
   a. Formulate a linear programming model for this problem.
   b. Solve this model by using graphical analysis.

6. The Pinewood Furniture Company produces chairs and tables from two resources—labor and wood. The company has 80 hours of labor and 36 board-ft. of wood available each day. Demand for chairs is limited to 6 per day. Each chair requires 8 hours of labor and 2 board-ft. of wood, whereas a table requires 10 hours of labor and 6 board-ft. of wood. The profit derived from each chair is $400 and from each table, $100. The company wants to determine the number of chairs and tables to produce each day in order to maximize profit.
   a. Formulate a linear programming model for this problem.
   b. Solve this model by using graphical analysis.

7. In Problem 6, how much labor and wood will be unused if the optimal numbers of chairs and tables are produced?

8. In Problem 6, explain the effect on the optimal solution of changing the profit on a table from $100 to $500.

9. The Crumb and Custard Bakery makes coffee cakes and Danish pastries in large pans. The main ingredients are flour and sugar. There are 25 pounds of flour and 16 pounds of sugar available, and the demand for coffee cakes is 5. Five pounds of flour and 2 pounds of sugar are required to make a pan of coffee cakes, and 5 pounds of flour and 4 pounds of sugar are required to make a pan of Danish. A pan of coffee cakes has a profit of $1, and a pan of Danish has a profit of $5. Determine the number of pans of cakes and Danish to produce each day so that profit will be maximized.
   a. Formulate a linear programming model for this problem.
   b. Solve this model by using graphical analysis.

10. In Problem 9, how much flour and sugar will be left unused if the optimal numbers of cakes and Danish are baked?

11. Solve the following linear programming model graphically:

$$\text{maximize } Z = 3x_1 + 6x_2$$
$$\text{subject to}$$
$$3x_1 + 2x_2 \leq 18$$
$$x_1 + x_2 \geq 5$$
$$x_1 \leq 4$$
$$x_1, x_2 \geq 0$$

12. The Elixer Drug Company produces a drug from two ingredients. Each ingredient contains the same three antibiotics, in different proportions. One gram of ingredient 1 contributes 3 units, and 1 gram of ingredient 2 contributes 1 unit of antibiotic 1; the drug requires 6 units. At least 4 units of antibiotic 2 are required, and the ingredients contribute 1 unit each per gram. At least 12 units of antibiotic 3 are required; a gram of ingredient 1 contributes 2 units, and a gram of ingredient 2 contributes 6 units. The cost for a gram of ingredient 1 is $80, and the cost for a gram of ingredient 2 is $50. The company wants to formulate a linear programming model to determine the number of grams of each ingredient that must go into the drug in order to meet the antibiotic requirements at the minimum cost.
   a. Formulate a linear programming model for this problem.
   b. Solve this model by using graphical analysis.

13. A jewelry store makes necklaces and bracelets from gold and platinum. The store has 18 ounces of gold and 20 ounces of platinum. Each necklace requires 3 ounces of gold and 2 ounces of platinum, whereas each bracelet requires 2 ounces of gold and 4 ounces of platinum. The demand for bracelets is no more than four. A necklace earns $300 in profit and a bracelet, $400. The store wants to determine the number of necklaces and bracelets to make in order to maximize profit.
   a. Formulate a linear programming model for this problem.
   b. Solve this model by using graphical analysis.

14. In Problem 13, explain the effect on the optimal solution of increasing the profit on a bracelet from $400 to $600. What will be the effect of changing the platinum requirement for a necklace from 2 ounces to 3 ounces?

15. In Problem 13:
   a. The maximum demand for bracelets is four. If the store produces the optimal number of bracelets and necklaces, will the maximum demand for bracelets be met? If not, by how much will it be missed?
   b. What profit for a necklace would result in no bracelets being produced, and what would be the optimal solution for this profit?

16. A clothier makes coats and slacks. The two resources required are wool cloth and labor. The clothier has 150 square yards of wool and 200 hours of labor available. Each coat requires

3 square yards of wool and 10 hours of labor, whereas each pair of slacks requires 5 square yards of wool and 4 hours of labor. The profit for a coat is $50, and the profit for slacks is $40. The clothier wants to determine the number of coats and pairs of slacks to make so that profit will be maximized.

a. Formulate a linear programming model for this problem.

b. Solve this model by using graphical analysis.

17. In Problem 16, what would be the effect on the optimal solution if the available labor were increased from 200 to 240 hours?

18. The Weemow Lawn Service wants to start doing snow removal in the winter when there are no lawns to maintain. Jeff and Julie Weems, who own the service, are trying to determine how much equipment they need to purchase, based on the various job types they have. They plan to work themselves and hire some local college students on a per-job basis. Based on historical weather data, they estimate that there will be six major snowfalls next winter. Virtually all customers want their snow removed no more than 2 days after the snow stops falling. Working 10 hours per day (into the night), Jeff and Julie can remove the snow from a normal driveway in about 1 hour, and it takes about 4 hours to remove the snow from a business parking lot and sidewalk. The variable cost (mainly for labor and gas) per job is $12 for a driveway and $47 for a parking lot. Using their lawn service customer base as a guideline, they believe they will have demand of no more than 40 homeowners and 25 businesses. They plan to charge $35 for a home driveway and $120 for a business parking lot, which is slightly less than the going rate. They want to know how many jobs of each type will maximize their profit.

a. Formulate a linear programming model for this problem.

b. Solve this model graphically.

19. In Problem 18:

a. If Jeff and Julie pay $3,700 for snow removal equipment, will they make any money?

b. If Jeff and Julie reduce their prices to $30 for a driveway and $100 for a parking lot, they will increase demand to 55 for driveways and 32 for businesses. Will this affect their possible profit?

c. Alternatively, hiring additional people on a per-job basis will increase Jeff and Julie's variable cost to $16 for a driveway and $53 for a parking lot, but it will lower the time it takes to clear a driveway to 40 minutes and a parking lot to 3 hours. Will this affect their profit?

d. If Jeff and Julie combine the two alternatives suggested in (b) and (c), will this affect their profit?

20. Solve the following linear programming model graphically:

$$\text{maximize } Z = 1.5x_1 + x_2$$
$$\text{subject to}$$
$$x_1 \leq 4$$
$$x_2 \leq 6$$
$$x_1 + x_2 \leq 5$$
$$x_1, x_2 \geq 0$$

21. Transform the model in Problem 20 into standard form and indicate the value of the slack variables at each corner point solution.

22. Solve the following linear programming model graphically:

$$\text{maximize } Z = 5x_1 + 8x_2$$
$$\text{subject to}$$
$$3x_1 + 5x_2 \leq 50$$
$$2x_1 + 4x_2 \leq 40$$
$$x_1 \leq 8$$
$$x_2 \leq 10$$
$$x_1, x_2 \geq 0$$

23. Transform the model in Problem 22 into standard form and indicate the value of the slack variables at each corner point solution.

24. Solve the following linear programming model graphically:

$$\text{maximize } Z = 6.5x_1 + 10x_2$$
$$\text{subject to}$$
$$2x_1 + 4x_2 \leq 40$$
$$x_1 + x_2 \leq 15$$
$$x_1 \geq 8$$
$$x_1, x_2 \geq 0$$

25. In Problem 24, if the constraint $x_1 \geq 8$ is changed to $x_1 \leq 8$, what effect does this have on the feasible solution space and the optimal solution?

26. Universal Claims Processors processes insurance claims for large national insurance companies. Most claim processing is done by a large pool of computer operators, some of whom are permanent and some of whom are temporary. A permanent operator can process 16 claims per day, whereas a temporary operator can process 12 per day, and on average the company processes at least 450 claims each day. The company has 40 computer workstations. A permanent operator generates about 0.5 claim with errors each day, whereas a temporary operator averages about 1.4 defective claims per day. The company wants to limit claims with errors to 25 per day. A permanent operator is paid $64 per day, and a temporary operator is paid $42 per day. The company wants to determine the number of permanent and temporary operators to hire in order to minimize costs.
    a. Formulate a linear programming model for this problem.
    b. Solve this model by using graphical analysis.

27. In Problem 26, explain the effect on the optimal solution of changing the daily pay for a permanent claims processor from $64 to $54. Explain the effect of changing the daily pay for a temporary claims processor from $42 to $36.

28. In Problem 26, what would be the effect on the optimal solution if Universal Claims Processors decided not to try to limit the number of defective claims each day?

29. In Problem 26, explain the effect on the optimal solution if the minimum number of claims the firm processes each day increased from 450 to at least 650.

30. Solve the following linear programming model graphically:

$$\text{minimize } Z = 8x_1 + 6x_2$$
$$\text{subject to}$$
$$4x_1 + 2x_2 \geq 20$$
$$-6x_1 + 4x_2 \leq 12$$
$$x_1 + x_2 \geq 6$$
$$x_1, x_2 \geq 0$$

31. Solve the following linear programming model graphically:

$$\text{minimize } Z = 3x_1 + 6x_2$$
$$\text{subject to}$$
$$3x_1 + 2x_2 \leq 18$$
$$x_1 + x_2 \geq 5$$
$$x_1 \leq 4$$
$$x_2 \leq 7$$
$$x_2/x_1 \leq 7/8$$
$$x_1, x_2 \geq 0$$

32. In Problem 31, what would be the effect on the solution if the constraint $x_2 \leq 7$ were changed to $x_2 \geq 7$?

33. Solve the following linear programming model graphically:

$$\text{minimize } Z = 5x_1 + x_2$$
subject to
$$3x_1 + 4x_2 = 24$$
$$x_1 \leq 6$$
$$x_1 + 3x_2 \leq 12$$
$$x_1, x_2 \geq 0$$

34. Solve the following linear programming model graphically:

$$\text{maximize } Z = 3x_1 + 2x_2$$
subject to
$$2x_1 + 4x_2 \leq 22$$
$$-x_1 + 4x_2 \leq 10$$
$$4x_1 - 2x_2 \leq 14$$
$$x_1 - 3x_2 \leq 1$$
$$x_1, x_2 \geq 0$$

35. Solve the following linear programming model graphically:

$$\text{minimize } Z = 8x_1 + 2x_2$$
subject to
$$2x_1 - 6x_2 \leq 12$$
$$5x_1 + 4x_2 \geq 40$$
$$x_1 + 2x_2 \geq 12$$
$$x_2 \leq 6$$
$$x_1, x_2 \geq 0$$

36. Gillian's Restaurant has an ice-cream counter where it sells two main products, ice cream and frozen yogurt, each in a variety of flavors. The restaurant makes one order for ice cream and yogurt each week, and the store has enough freezer space for 115 gallons total of both products. A gallon of frozen yogurt costs $0.75 and a gallon of ice cream costs $0.93, and the restaurant budgets $90 each week for these products. The manager estimates that each week the restaurant sells at least twice as much ice cream as frozen yogurt. Profit per gallon of ice cream is $4.15 and profit per gallon of yogurt is $3.60.
    a. Formulate a linear programming model for this problem.
    b. Solve this model by using graphical analysis.

37. In Problem 36, how much additional profit would the restaurant realize each week if it increased its freezer capacity to accommodate 20 extra gallons total of ice cream and yogurt?

38. Copperfield Mining Company owns two mines, each of which produces three grades of ore—high, medium, and low. The company has a contract to supply a smelting company with at least 12 tons of high-grade ore, 8 tons of medium-grade ore, and 24 tons of low-grade ore. Each mine produces a certain amount of each type of ore during each hour that it operates. Mine 1 produces 6 tons of high-grade ore, 2 tons of medium-grade ore, and 4 tons of low-grade ore per hour. Mine 2 produces 2, 2, and 12 tons, respectively, of high-, medium-, and low-grade ore per hour. It costs Copperfield $200 per hour to mine each ton of ore from mine 1, and it costs $160 per hour to mine each ton of ore from mine 2. The company wants to determine the number of hours it needs to operate each mine so that its contractual obligations can be met at the lowest cost.
    a. Formulate a linear programming model for this problem.
    b. Solve this model by using graphical analysis.

39. A canning company produces two sizes of cans—regular and large. The cans are produced in 10,000-can lots. The cans are processed through a stamping operation and a coating operation. The company has 30 days available for both stamping and coating. A lot of regular-size cans requires 2 days to stamp and 4 days to coat, whereas a lot of large cans requires 4 days to stamp and 2 days to coat. A lot of regular-size cans earns $800 profit, and a lot of large-size cans earns $900 profit. In order to fulfill its obligations under a shipping contract, the company must produce at least nine lots. The company wants to determine the number of lots to produce of each size can (x_1 and x_2) in order to maximize profit.
    a. Formulate a linear programming model for this problem.
    b. Solve this model by using graphical analysis.

40. A manufacturing firm produces two products. Each product must undergo an assembly process and a finishing process. It is then transferred to the warehouse, which has space for only a limited number of items. The firm has 80 hours available for assembly and 112 hours for finishing, and it can store a maximum of 10 units in the warehouse. Each unit of product 1 has a profit of $30 and requires 4 hours to assemble and 14 hours to finish. Each unit of product 2 has a profit of $70 and requires 10 hours to assemble and 8 hours to finish. The firm wants to determine the quantity of each product to produce in order to maximize profit.
    a. Formulate a linear programming model for this problem.
    b. Solve this model by using graphical analysis.

41. Assume that the objective function in Problem 40 has been changed from $Z = 30x_1 + 70x_2$ to $Z = 90x_1 + 70x_2$. Determine the slope of each objective function and discuss what effect these slopes have on the optimal solution.

42. The Valley Wine Company produces two kinds of wine—Valley Nectar and Valley Red. The wines are produced from 64 tons of grapes the company has acquired this season. A 1,000-gallon batch of Nectar requires 4 tons of grapes, and a batch of Red requires 8 tons. However, production is limited by the availability of only 50 cubic yards of storage space for aging and 120 hours of processing time. A batch of each type of wine requires 5 cubic yards of storage space. The processing time for a batch of Nectar is 15 hours, and the processing time for a batch of Red is 8 hours. Demand for each type of wine is limited to seven batches. The profit for a batch of Nectar is $9,000, and the profit for a batch of Red is $12,000. The company wants to determine the number of 1,000-gallon batches of Nectar (x_1) and Red (x_2) to produce in order to maximize profit.
    a. Formulate a linear programming model for this problem.
    b. Solve this model by using graphical analysis.

43. In Problem 42:
    a. How much processing time will be left unused at the optimal solution?
    b. What would be the effect on the optimal solution of increasing the available storage space from 50 to 60 cubic yards?

44. Kroeger supermarket sells its own brand of canned peas as well as several national brands. The store makes a profit of $0.28 per can for its own peas and a profit of $0.19 for any of the national brands. The store has 6 square feet of shelf space available for canned peas, and each can of peas takes up 9 square inches of that space. Point-of-sale records show that each week the store never sells more than half as many cans of its own brand as it does of the national brands. The store wants to know how many cans of its own brand of peas and how many cans of the national brands to stock each week on the allocated shelf space in order to maximize profit.
    a. Formulate a linear programming model for this problem.
    b. Solve this model by using graphical analysis.

45. In Problem 44, if Kroeger discounts the price of its own brand of peas, the store will sell at least 1.5 times as much of the national brands as its own brand, but its profit margin on its own brand will be reduced to $0.23 per can. What effect will the discount have on the optimal solution?

46. Shirtstop makes T-shirts with logos and sells them in its chain of retail stores. It contracts wi two different plants—one in Puerto Rico and one in The Bahamas. The shirts from the plant Puerto Rico cost $0.46 apiece, and 9% of them are defective and can't be sold. The shirts fro The Bahamas cost only $0.35 each, but they have an 18% defective rate. Shirtstop needs 3,5(shirts. To retain its relationship with the two plants, it wants to order at least 1,000 shirts fro each. It would also like at least 88% of the shirts it receives to be salable.
    a. Formulate a linear programming model for this problem.
    b. Solve this model by using graphical analysis.

47. In Problem 46:
    a. Suppose Shirtstop decided it wanted to minimize the defective shirts while keeping costs belo $2,000. Reformulate the problem with these changes and solve graphically.
    b. How many fewer defective items were achieved with the model in (a) than with the model Problem 46?

48. Angela and Bob Ray keep a large garden in which they grow cabbage, tomatoes, and onio to make two kinds of relish—chow-chow and tomato. The chow-chow is made primarily cabbage, whereas the tomato relish has more tomatoes than does the chow-chow. Both re ishes include onions, and negligible amounts of bell peppers and spices. A jar of chow-cho contains 8 ounces of cabbage, 3 ounces of tomatoes, and 3 ounces of onions, whereas a jar tomato relish contains 6 ounces of tomatoes, 6 ounces of cabbage, and 2 ounces of onion The Rays grow 120 pounds of cabbage, 90 pounds of tomatoes, and 45 pounds of onio each summer. The Rays can produce no more than 24 dozen jars of relish. They make $2.2 in profit from a jar of chow-chow and $1.95 in profit from a jar of tomato relish. The Ra want to know how many jars of each kind of relish to produce to generate the most profit.
    a. Formulate a linear programming model for this problem.
    b. Solve this model graphically.

49. In Problem 48, the Rays have checked their sales records for the past 5 years and have four that they sell at least 50% more chow-chow than tomato relish. How will this additional info mation affect their model and solution?

50. A California grower has a 50-acre farm on which to plant strawberries and tomatoes. Th grower has available 300 hours of labor per week and 800 tons of fertilizer, and he has co tracted for shipping space for a maximum of 26 acres' worth of strawberries and 37 acre worth of tomatoes. An acre of strawberries requires 10 hours of labor and 8 tons of fertilize whereas an acre of tomatoes requires 3 hours of labor and 20 tons of fertilizer. The profit fro an acre of strawberries is $400, and the profit from an acre of tomatoes is $300. The farm wants to know the number of acres of strawberries and tomatoes to plant to maximize profit.
    a. Formulate a linear programming model for this problem.
    b. Solve this model by using graphical analysis.

51. In Problem 50, if the amount of fertilizer required for each acre of strawberries were determine to be 20 tons instead of 8 tons, what would be the effect on the optimal solution?

52. The admissions office at Tech wants to determine how many in-state and how many out-of-state st dents to accept for next fall's entering freshman class. Tuition for an in-state student is $7,600 per ye whereas out-of-state tuition is $22,500 per year. A total of 12,800 in-state and 8,100 out-of-sta freshmen have applied for next fall, and Tech does not want to accept more than 3,500 student However, because Tech is a state institution, the state mandates that it can accept no more tha 40% out-of-state students. From past experience the admissions office knows that 12% in-state students and 24% of out-of-state students will drop out during their first year. Tec wants to maximize total tuition while limiting the total attrition to 600 first-year students.
    a. Formulate a linear programming model for this problem.
    b. Solve this model by using graphical analysis.

53. The Robinsons are planning a wedding and reception for their daughter, Rachel. Some of the most expensive items served at the reception and dinner are wine and beer. The Robinsons are planning on 200 guests at the reception, and they estimate that they need at least four servings (i.e., a glass of wine or bottle of beer) for each guest in order to be sure they won't run out. A bottle of wine contains five glasses. They also estimate that 50% more guests will prefer wine to beer. A bottle of wine costs $8, and a bottle of beer costs $0.75. The Robinsons have budgeted $1,200 for wine and beer. Finally, the Robinsons want to minimize their waste (i.e., unused wine and beer). The caterer has advised them that typically 5% of the wine and 10% of the beer will be left over. How many bottles of wine and beer should the Robinsons order?
    a. Formulate a linear programming model for this problem.
    b. Solve this model graphically.

54. Suppose that in Problem 53, it turns out that twice as many guests prefer wine as beer. Will the Robinsons have enough wine with the amount they ordered in the Problem 53 solution? How much waste will there be with the solution in Problem 53?

55. Xara Stores in the United States imports the designer-inspired clothes it sells from suppliers in China and Brazil. Xara estimates that it will have 45 orders in a year, and it must arrange to transport orders (in less-than-full containers) by container ship with shippers in Hong Kong and Buenos Aires. The shippers Xara uses have a travel time of 32 days from Buenos Aires and 14 days from Hong Kong, and Xara wants its orders to have an average travel time of no more than 21 days. About 10% of the annual orders from the shipper in Hong Kong are damaged, and the shipper in Buenos Aires damages about 4% of all orders annually. Xara wants to receive no more than 6 damaged orders each year. Xara does not want to be dependent on suppliers from just one country, so it wants to receive at least 25% of its orders from each country. It costs $3,700 per order from China and $5,100 per order to ship from Brazil. Xara wants to know how many orders it should ship from each port in order to minimize shipping costs.
    a. Formulate a linear programming model for this problem.
    b. Solve this model by using graphical analysis.

56. In Problem 55, the Chinese shipper would like to gain more shipping orders from Xara because it's a prestigious company and would enhance the shipper's reputation. It has therefore made the following proposals to Xara:
    a. Would Xara give the Chinese shipper more orders if it reduced its shipping costs to $2,500 per shipment?
    b. Would Xara give the Chinese shipper more orders if it reduced its damaged orders to 5%.
    c. Would Xara give the shipper more of its orders if it reduced its travel time to 28 days?

57. Janet Lopez is establishing an investment portfolio that will include stock and bond funds. She has $720,000 to invest, and she does not want the portfolio to include more than 65% stocks. The average annual return for the stock fund she plans to invest in is 18%, whereas the average annual return for the bond fund is 6%. She further estimates that the most she could lose in the next year in the stock fund is 22%, whereas the most she could lose in the bond fund is 5%. To reduce her risk, she wants to limit her potential maximum losses to $100,000.
    a. Formulate a linear programming model for this problem.
    b. Solve this model by using graphical analysis.

58. Professor Smith teaches two sections of business statistics, which combined will result in 120 final exams to be graded. Professor Smith has two graduate assistants, Brad and Sarah, who will grade the final exams. There is a 3-day period between the time the exam is administered and when final grades must be posted. During this period Brad has 12 hours available and Sarah has 10 hours available to grade the exams. It takes Brad an average of 7.2 minutes to grade an exam, and it takes Sarah 12 minutes to grade an exam; however, Brad's exams will have errors that will

require Professor Smith to ultimately regrade 10% of the exams, while only 6% of Sarah'
exams will require regrading. Professor Smith wants to know how many exams to assign to eacl
graduate assistant to grade in order to minimize the number of exams to regrade.

 a. Formulate a linear programming model for this problem.

 b. Solve this model by using graphical analysis.

59. In Problem 58, if Professor Smith could hire Brad or Sarah to work 1 additional hour, whicl
should she choose? What would be the effect of hiring the selected graduate assistant for 1 addi
tional hour?

60. Starbright Coffee Shop at the Galleria Mall serves two coffee blends it brews on a daily basis
Pomona and Coastal. Each is a blend of three high-quality coffees from Colombia, Kenya, an
Indonesia. The coffee shop has 6 pounds of each of these coffees available each day. Each poun
of coffee will produce sixteen 16-ounce cups of coffee. The shop has enough brewing capacit
to brew 30 gallons of these two coffee blends each day. Pomona is a blend of 20% Colombian
35% Kenyan, and 45% Indonesian, while Coastal is a blend of 60% Colombian, 10% Kenyan
and 30% Indonesian. The shop sells 1.5 times more Pomona than Coastal each day. Pomon
sells for $2.05 per cup, and Coastal sells for $1.85 per cup. The manager wants to know hov
many cups of each blend to sell each day in order to maximize sales.

 a. Formulate a linear programming model for this problem.

 b. Solve this model by using graphical analysis.

61. In Problem 60:

 a. If Starbright Coffee Shop could get 1 more pound of coffee, which one should it be? Wha
would be the effect on sales of getting 1 more pound of this coffee? Would it benefit the sho
to increase its brewing capacity from 30 gallons to 40 gallons?

 b. If the shop spent $20 per day on advertising that would increase the relative demand fc
Pomona to twice that of Coastal, should it be done?

62. Solve the following linear programming model graphically and explain the solution result:

$$\text{minimize } Z = \$3,000x_1 + 1,000x_2$$
$$\text{subject to}$$
$$60x_1 + 20x_2 \geq 1,200$$
$$10x_1 + 10x_2 \geq 400$$
$$40x_1 + 160x_2 \geq 2,400$$
$$x_1, x_2 \geq 0$$

63. Solve the following linear programming model graphically and explain the solution result:

$$\text{maximize } Z = 60x_1 + 90x_2$$
$$\text{subject to}$$
$$60x_1 + 30x_2 \leq 1,500$$
$$100x_1 + 100x_2 \geq 6,000$$
$$x_2 \geq 30$$
$$x_1, x_2 \geq 0$$

64. Solve the following linear programming model graphically and explain the solution result:

$$\text{maximize } Z = 110x_1 + 75x_2$$
$$\text{subject to}$$
$$2x_1 + x_2 \geq 40$$
$$-6x_1 + 8x_2 \leq 120$$
$$70x_1 + 105x_2 \geq 2,100$$
$$x_1, x_2 \geq 0$$

Case Problem

MINIMISING COSTS FOR EMPLOYEES' SCHEDULE SHIFT AT DRAGONAIR

The Hong Kong–based airline DragonAir has decided to expand its network in China, and it will need to hire additional staff to cover the additional shifts necessary for these new routes. Therefore, a linear programming model has been set up to estimate and minimize the additional costs. This has to be done not only by minimizing the costs, but also by abiding by Hong Kong labor laws concerning maximum working hours and allowed night shifts. Each crew can only work for 8 hours and 5 days a week.

These are the allowed shifts:

Shift 1: 6:00 A.M. to 2:00 P.M.
Shift 2: 8:00 A.M. to 4:00 P.M.
Shift 3: Noon to 8:00 P.M.
Shift 4: 4:00 P.M. to midnight
Shift 5: Midnight to 6:00 A.M.

Also, different needs of staff are forecasted for each of the hours, as can be seen in the analytical table opposite. Finally, some shifts are better paid than others to encourage staff to work them (e.g., the night shift).

Table of Allocation/Cost

Time period	Shift 1	Shift 2	Shift 3	Shift 4	Shift 5	Crew Needed
	1	2	3	4	5	
6:00–8:00 A.M.	X					48
8:00–10:00 A.M.	X	X				79
10:00 A.M.–noon	X	X				60
Noon–2:00 P.M.	X	X	X			88
2:00–4:00 P.M.		X	X			64
4:00–6:00 P.M.			X	X		89
6:00–8:00 P.M.			X	X		70
8:00–10:00 P.M.				X		43
10:00 P.M.–midnight				X	X	55
Midnight–6:00 A.M.					X	16
Daily cost/crew	170	180	156	180	205	

Using the information in the table:

a. Formulate the linear programming model in order to minimize the cost for manning the new routes.
b. Solve the problem by using Excel Solver or another software.

Case Problem

"THE POSSIBILITY" RESTAURANT

Angela Fox and Zooey Caulfield were food and nutrition majors at State University, as well as close friends and roommates. Upon graduation Angela and Zooey decided to open a French restaurant in Draperton, the small town where the university was located. There were no other French restaurants in Draperton, and the possibility of doing something new and somewhat risky intrigued the two friends. They purchased an old Victorian home just off Main Street for their new restaurant, which they named "The Possibility."

Angela and Zooey knew in advance that at least initially they could not offer a full, varied menu of dishes. They had no idea what their local customers' tastes in French cuisine would be, so they decided to serve only two full-course meals each night, one with beef and the other with fish. Their chef, Pierre, was confident he could make each dish

so exciting and unique that two meals would be sufficient, at least until they could assess which menu items were most popular. Pierre indicated that with each meal he could experiment with different appetizers, soups, salads, vegetable dishes, and desserts until they were able to identify a full selection of menu items.

The next problem for Angela and Zooey was to determine how many meals to prepare for each night so they could shop for ingredients and set up the work schedule. They could not afford too much waste. They estimated that they would sell a maximum of 60 meals each night. Each fish dinner, including all accompaniments, requires 15 minutes to prepare, and each beef dinner takes twice as long. There is a total of 20 hours of kitchen staff labor available each day. Angela and Zooey believe that because of the health consciousness of their potential clientele, they will sell at least three fish dinners for every two beef dinners. However, they also believe that at least 10% of their customers will order beef dinners. The profit from each fish dinner will be approximately $12, and the profit from a beef dinner will be about $16.

Formulate a linear programming model for Angela and Zooey that will help them estimate the number of meals they should prepare each night and solve this model graphically.

If Angela and Zooey increased the menu price on the fish dinner so that the profit for both dinners was the same, what effect would that have on their solution? Suppose Angela and Zooey reconsidered the demand for beef dinners and decided that at least 20% of their customers would purchase beef dinners. What effect would this have on their meal preparation plan?

Case Problem

ANNABELLE INVESTS IN THE MARKET

Annabelle Sizemore has cashed in some treasury bonds and a life insurance policy that her parents had accumulated over the years for her. She has also saved some money in certificates of deposit and savings bonds during the 10 years since she graduated from college. As a result, she has $120,000 available to invest. Given the recent rise in the stock market, she feels that she should invest all of this amount there. She has researched the market and has decided that she wants to invest in an index fund tied to S&P stocks and in an Internet stock fund. However, she is very concerned about the volatility of Internet stocks. Therefore, she wants to balance her risk to some degree.

She has decided to select an index fund from Shield Securities and an Internet stock fund from Madison Funds, Inc. She has also decided that the proportion of the dollar amount she invests in the index fund relative to the Internet fund should be at least one-third but that she should not invest more than twice the amount in the Internet fund that she invests in the index fund. The price per share of the index fund is $175, whereas the price per share of the Internet fund is $208. The average annual return during the last 3 years for

the index fund has been 17%, and for the Internet stock fund it has been 28%. She anticipates that both mutual funds will realize the same average returns for the coming year that they have in the recent past; however, at the end of the year she is likely to reevaluate her investment strategy anyway. Thus, she wants to develop an investment strategy that will maximize her return for the coming year.

Formulate a linear programming model for Annabelle that will indicate how much money she should invest in each fund and solve this model by using the graphical method.

Suppose Annabelle decides to change her risk-balancing formula by eliminating the restriction that the proportion of the amount she invests in the index fund to the amount that she invests in the Internet fund must be at least one-third. What will the effect be on her solution? Suppose instead that she eliminates the restriction that the proportion of money she invests in the Internet fund relative to the stock fund not exceed a ratio of 2 to 1. How will this affect her solution?

If Annabelle can get $1 more to invest, how will that affect her solution? $2 more? $3 more? What can you say about her return on her investment strategy, given these successive changes?

Decision-Making Models

In the previous chapters dealing with linear programming, models were formulated and solved in order to aid the manager in making a decision. The solutions to the models were represented by values for *decision* variables. However, these linear programming models were all formulated under the assumption that certainty existed. In other words, it was assumed that all the model coefficients, constraint values, and solution values were known with certainty and did not vary.

The two categories of decision situations are probabilities that can be assigned to future occurrences and probabilities that cannot be assigned.

In actual practice, however, many decision-making situations occur under conditions of *uncertainty*. For example, the demand for a product may be not 100 units next week, but 50 or 200 units, depending on the state of the market (which is uncertain). Several decision-making techniques are available to aid the decision maker in dealing with this type of decision situation in which there is uncertainty.

See Web site Module E for a chapter on "Game Theory" and Module F for a chapter on "Markov Analysis."

Decision situations can be categorized into two classes: situations in which probabilities *cannot* be assigned to future occurrences and situations in which probabilities *can* be assigned. In this chapter, we will discuss each of these classes of decision situations separately and demonstrate the decision-making criterion most commonly associated with each. Decision situations in which there are two or more decision makers who are in competition with each other are the subject of *game theory*, a topic included on the companion Web site that accompanies this text.

Components of Decision Making

A decision-making situation includes several components—the decisions themselves *and* the actual events that may occur in the future, known as states of nature. At the time a decision is made, the decision maker is uncertain which states of nature will occur in the future and has no control over them.

A state of nature is an actual event that may occur in the future.

Suppose a distribution company is considering purchasing a computer to increase the number of orders it can process and thus increase its business. If economic conditions remain good, the company will realize a large increase in profit; however, if the economy takes a downturn, the company will lose money. In this decision situation, the possible decisions are to purchase the computer and to not purchase the computer. The states of nature are *good* economic conditions and *bad* economic conditions. The state of nature that occurs will determine the outcome of the decision, and it is obvious that the decision maker has no control over which state will occur.

Using a payoff table is a means of organizing a decision situation, including the payoffs from different decisions, given the various states of nature.

As another example, consider a concessions vendor who must decide whether to stock coffee for the concession stands at a football game in November. If the weather is cold, most of the coffee will be sold, but if the weather is warm, very little coffee will be sold. The decision is to order or not to order coffee, and the states of nature are warm and cold weather.

To facilitate the analysis of these types of decision situations so that the best decisions result, they are organized into payoff tables. In general, a payoff table is a means of organizing and illustrating the payoffs from the different decisions, given the various states of nature in a decision problem. A payoff table is constructed as shown in Table 12.1.

TABLE 12.1
Payoff table

Decision	State of Nature	
	a	*b*
1	Payoff 1*a*	Payoff 1*b*
2	Payoff 2*a*	Payoff 2*b*

Each decision, 1 or 2, in Table 12.1 will result in an outcome, or *payoff*, for the particular state of nature that will occur in the future. Payoffs are typically expressed in terms of profit revenues, or cost (although they can be expressed in terms of a variety of values). For example, if decision 1 is to purchase a computer and state of nature a is good economic conditions, payoff $1a$ could be $100,000 in profit.

It is often possible to assign probabilities to the states of nature to aid the decision maker in selecting the decision that has the best outcome. However, in some cases the decision maker is not able to assign probabilities, and it is this type of decision-making situation that we will address first.

Decision Making Without Probabilities

The following example will illustrate the development of a payoff table without probabilities. An investor is to purchase one of three types of real estate, as illustrated in Figure 12.1. The investor must decide among an apartment building, an office building, and a warehouse. The future states of nature that will determine how much profit the investor will make are good

FIGURE 12.1

Decision situation with real estate investment alternatives

economic conditions and poor economic conditions. The profits that will result from each decision in the event of each state of nature are shown in Table 12.2.

TABLE 12.2

Payoff table for the real estate investments

	State of Nature	
Decision (purchase)	Good Economic Conditions	Poor Economic Conditions
Apartment building	$ 50,000	$ 30,000
Office building	100,000	−40,000
Warehouse	30,000	10,000

Decision-Making Criteria

Once the decision situation has been organized into a payoff table, several criteria are available for making the actual decision. These decision criteria, which will be presented in this section, include maximax, maximin, minimax regret, Hurwicz, and equal likelihood. On occasion these criteria will result in the same decision; however, often they will yield different decisions. The decision maker must select the criterion or combination of criteria that best suits his or her needs.

The Maximax Criterion

The maximax criterion results in the maximum of the maximum payoffs.

With the maximax criterion, the decision maker selects the decision that will result in the maximum of the maximum payoffs. (In fact, this is how this criterion derives its name—a maximum of a maximum.) The maximax criterion is very optimistic. The decision maker assumes that the most favorable state of nature for each decision alternative will occur. Thus, for example, using this criterion, the investor would optimistically assume that good economic conditions will prevail in the future.

The maximax criterion is applied in Table 12.3. The decision maker first selects the maximum payoff for each decision. Notice that all three maximum payoffs occur under good economic conditions. Of the three maximum payoffs—$50,000, $100,000, and $30,000—the maximum is $100,000; thus, the corresponding decision is to purchase the office building.

TABLE 12.3

Payoff table illustrating a maximax decision

	State of Nature	
Decision (purchase)	Good Economic Conditions	Poor Economic Conditions
Apartment building	$ 50,000	$ 30,000
Office building	100,000	−40,000
Warehouse	30,000	10,000

Maximum payoff

Although the decision to purchase an office building will result in the largest payoff ($100,000), such a decision completely ignores the possibility of a potential loss of $40,000. The decision maker who uses the maximax criterion assumes a very optimistic future with respect to the state of nature.

Before the next criterion is presented, it should be pointed out that the maximax decision rule as presented here deals with *profit*. However, if the payoff table consisted of costs, the opposite selection would be indicated: the minimum of the minimum costs, or a *minimin* criterion. For the subsequent decision criteria we encounter, the same logic in the case of costs can be used.

The Maximin Criterion

The maximin criterion results in the maximum of the minimum payoff.

In contrast with the maximax criterion, which is very optimistic, the maximin criterion is pessimistic. With the maximin criterion, the decision maker selects the decision that will reflect the *maximum* of the *minimum* payoffs. For each decision alternative, the decision maker assumes that the minimum payoff will occur. Of these minimum payoffs, the maximum is selected. The maximin criterion for our investment example is demonstrated in Table 12.4.

TABLE 12.4

Payoff table illustrating a maximin decision

Decision (purchase)	State of Nature	
	Good Economic Conditions	Poor Economic Conditions
Apartment building	$ 50,000	$ 30,000
Office building	100,000	−40,000
Warehouse	30,000	10,000

Maximum payoff

The minimum payoffs for our example are $30,000, −$40,000, and $10,000. The maximum of these three payoffs is $30,000; thus, the decision arrived at by using the maximin criterion would be to purchase the apartment building. This decision is relatively conservative because the alternatives considered include only the worst outcomes that could occur. The decision to purchase the office building as determined by the maximax criterion includes the possibility of a large loss (−$40,000). The worst that can occur from the decision to purchase the apartment building, however, is *a gain of $30,000*. On the other hand, the largest possible gain from purchasing the apartment building is much less than that of purchasing the office building (i.e., $50,000 vs. $100,000).

If Table 12.4 contained costs instead of profits as the payoffs, the conservative approach would be to select the maximum cost for each decision. Then the decision that resulted in the minimum, the minimax, of these costs would be selected.

The Minimax Regret Criterion

Regret is the difference between the payoff from the best decision and all other decision payoffs.

In our example, suppose the investor decided to purchase the warehouse, only to discover that economic conditions in the future were better than expected. Naturally, the investor would be disappointed that she had not purchased the office building because it would have resulted in the largest payoff ($100,000) under good economic conditions. In fact, the investor would *regret* the decision to purchase the warehouse, and the *degree of regret would be $70,000*, the difference between the payoff for the investor's choice and the best choice.

The minimax regret criterion minimizes the maximum regret.

This brief example demonstrates the principle underlying the decision criterion known as minimax regret criterion. With this decision criterion, the decision maker attempts to avoid regret by selecting the decision alternative that minimizes the maximum regret.

To use the minimax regret criterion, a decision maker first selects the maximum payoff under each state of nature. For our example, the maximum payoff under good economic conditions is $100,000, and the maximum payoff under poor economic conditions is $30,000. All other payoffs under the respective states of nature are subtracted from these amounts, as follows:

Good Economic Conditions	*Poor Economic Conditions*
$100,000 − 50,000 = $50,000	$30,000 − 30,000 = $0
$100,000 − 100,000 = $0	$30,000 − (−40,000) = $70,000
$100,000 − 30,000 = $70,000	$30,000 − 10,000 = $20,000

These values represent the regret that the decision maker would experience if a decision were made that resulted in less than the maximum payoff. The values are summarized in a modified version of the payoff table known as a *regret table*, shown in Table 12.5. (Such a table is sometimes referred to as an *opportunity loss table*, in which case the term *opportunity loss* is synonymous with *regret*.)

TABLE 12.5

Regret table

Decision (purchase)	State of Nature	
	Good Economic Conditions	Poor Economic Conditions
Apartment building	$50,000	$ 0
Office building	0	70,000
Warehouse	70,000	20,000

To make the decision according to the minimax regret criterion, the maximum regret for *each decision* must be determined. The decision corresponding to the minimum of these regret values is then selected. This process is illustrated in Table 12.6.

TABLE 12.6

Regret table illustrating the minimax regret decision

Decision (purchase)	State of Nature	
	Good Economic Conditions	Poor Economic Conditions
Apartment building	$50,000	$ 0
Office building	0	70,000
Warehouse	70,000	20,000

The minimax regret value

According to the minimax regret criterion, the decision should be to purchase the apartment building rather than the office building or the warehouse. This particular decision is based on the philosophy that the investor will experience the least amount of regret by purchasing the apartment building. In other words, if the investor purchased either the office building or the warehouse, $70,000 worth of regret could result; however, the purchase of the apartment building will result in, at most, $50,000 in regret.

The Hurwicz Criterion

The Hurwicz criterion is a compromise between the maximax and maximin criteria.

The coefficient of optimism, α, is a measure of the decision maker's optimism.

The Hurwicz criterion multiplies the best payoff by α, the coefficient of optimism, and the worst payoff by $1 - \alpha$, for each decision, and the best result is selected.

The Hurwicz criterion strikes a compromise between the maximax and maximin criteria. The principle underlying this decision criterion is that the decision maker is neither totally optimistic (as the maximax criterion assumes) nor totally pessimistic (as the maximin criterion assumes). With the Hurwicz criterion, the decision payoffs are weighted by a coefficient of optimism, a measure of the decision maker's optimism. The coefficient of optimism, which we will define as α, is between zero and one (i.e., $0 \leq \alpha \leq 1.0$). If $\alpha = 1.0$, then the decision maker is said to be completely optimistic; if $\alpha = 0$, then the decision maker is completely pessimistic. (Given this definition, if α is the coefficient of optimism, $1 - \alpha$ is the *coefficient of pessimism*.)

The Hurwicz criterion requires that for each decision alternative, the maximum payoff be multiplied by α and the minimum payoff be multiplied by $1 - \alpha$. For our investment example, if α equals .4 (i.e., the investor is slightly pessimistic), $1 - \alpha = .6$, and the following values will result:

Decision	Values
Apartment building	$ 50,000(.4) + 30,000(.6) = $38,000
Office building	$100,000(.4) − 40,000(.6) = $16,000
Warehouse	$ 30,000(.4) + 10,000(.6) = $18,000

The Hurwicz criterion specifies selection of the decision alternative corresponding to the maximum weighted value, which is $38,000 for this example. Thus, the decision would be to purchase the apartment building.

It should be pointed out that when $\alpha = 0$, the Hurwicz criterion is actually the maximin criterion; when $\alpha = 1.0$, it is the maximax criterion. A limitation of the Hurwicz criterion is the fact that α must be determined by the decision maker. It can be quite difficult for a decision maker to accurately determine his or her degree of optimism. Regardless of how the decision maker determines α, it is still a completely *subjective* measure of the decision maker's degree of optimism. Therefore, the Hurwicz criterion is a completely subjective decision-making criterion.

The Equal Likelihood Criterion

The equal likelihood, or LaPlace, criterion multiplies the decision payoff for each state of nature by an equal weight.

When the maximax criterion is applied to a decision situation, the decision maker implicitly assumes that the most favorable state of nature for each decision will occur. Alternatively, when the maximin criterion is applied, the least favorable states of nature are assumed. The equal likelihood, or LaPlace, criterion weights each state of nature equally, thus assuming that the states of nature are equally likely to occur.

Because there are two states of nature in our example, we assign a weight of .50 to each one. Next, we multiply these weights by each payoff for each decision:

Decision	Values
Apartment building	$\$50,000(.50) + 30,000(.50) = \$40,000$
Office building	$\$100,000(.50) - 40,000(.50) = \$30,000$
Warehouse	$\$30,000(.50) + 10,000(.50) = \$20,000$

As with the Hurwicz criterion, we select the decision that has the maximum of these weighted values. Because $40,000 is the highest weighted value, the investor's decision would be to purchase the apartment building.

In applying the equal likelihood criterion, we are assuming a 50% chance, or .50 probability, that either state of nature will occur. Using this same basic logic, it is possible to weight the states of nature differently (i.e., unequally) in many decision problems. In other words, different probabilities can be assigned to each state of nature, indicating that one state is more likely to occur than another. The application of different probabilities to the states of nature is the principle behind the decision criteria to be presented in the section on expected value.

Summary of Criteria Results

The decisions indicated by the decision criteria examined so far can be summarized as follows:

Criterion	Decision (Purchase)
Maximax	Office building
Maximin	Apartment building
Minimax regret	Apartment building
Hurwicz	Apartment building
Equal likelihood	Apartment building

A dominant decision is one that has a better payoff than another decision under each state of nature.

The decision to purchase the apartment building was designated most often by the various decision criteria. Notice that the decision to purchase the warehouse was never indicated by any criterion. This is because the payoffs for an apartment building, under either set of future economic conditions, are always better than the payoffs for a warehouse. Thus, given any situation with these two alternatives (and any other choice, such as purchasing the office building), the decision to purchase an apartment building will always be made over the decision to purchase a warehouse. In fact, the warehouse decision alternative could have been eliminated from consideration under each of our criteria. The alternative of purchasing a warehouse is said to be dominated by the alternative of purchasing an apartment building. In general, dominated decision alternatives can be removed from the payoff table and not considered when the various decision-making criteria are applied. This reduces the complexity of the decision analysis somewhat. However, in our discussions throughout this chapter of the application of decision criteria, we will leave the dominated alternative in the payoff table for demonstration purposes.

The use of several decision criteria often results in a mix of decisions, with no one decision being selected more than the others. The criterion or collection of criteria used and the resulting decision depend on the characteristics and philosophy of the decision maker. For example, the extremely optimistic decision maker might eschew the majority of the foregoing results and make the decision to purchase the office building because the maximax criterion most closely reflects his or her personal decision-making philosophy.

Solution of Decision-Making Problems Without Probabilities with QM for Windows

QM for Windows includes a module to solve decision analysis problems. QM for Windows will be used to illustrate the use of the maximax, maximin, minimax regret, equal likelihood, and Hurwicz criteria for the real estate problem considered in this section. The problem data are input very easily. A summary of the input and solution output for the maximax, maximin, and Hurwicz criteria is shown in Exhibit 12.1. The decision with the equal likelihood criterion can be determined by using an alpha value for the Hurwicz criterion equal to the equal likelihood weight, which is .5 for our real estate investment example. The solution output with alpha equal to .5 is shown in Exhibit 12.2. The decision with the minimax regret criterion is shown in Exhibit 12.3.

EXHIBIT 12.1

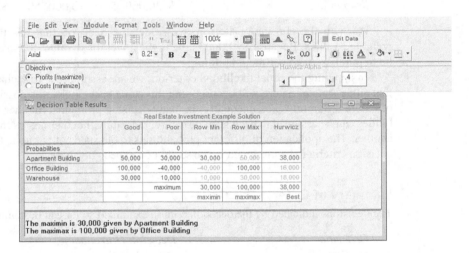

EXHIBIT 12.2

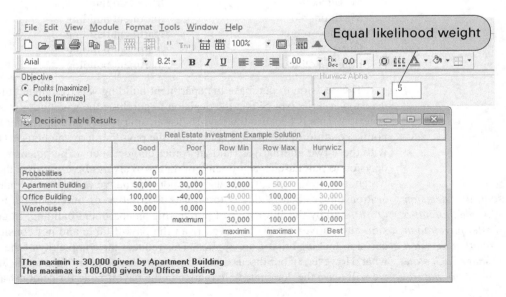

EXHIBIT 12.3

Regret or Opportunity Loss				
Real Estate Investment Example Solution				
	Good Regret	Poor Regret	Maximum Regret	Expected Regret
Probabilities	0	0		
Apartment Building	50,000	0	50,000	0
Office Building	0	70,000	70,000	0
Warehouse	70,000	20,000	70,000	0
Minimax regret			50,000	

Solution of Decision-Making Problems Without Probabilities with Excel

Excel can also be used to solve decision analysis problems using the decision-making criteria presented in this section. Exhibit 12.4 illustrates the application of the maximax, minimax, minimax regret, Hurwicz, and equal likelihood criteria for our real estate investment
example.

EXHIBIT 12.4

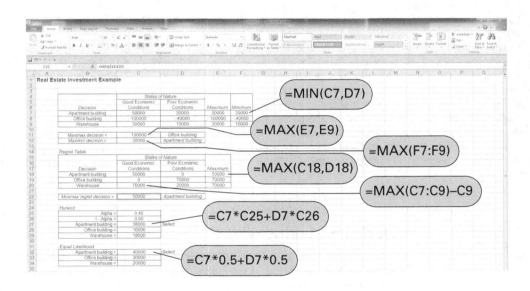

In cell E7, the formula **=MAX(C7,D7)** selects the maximum payoff outcome for the decision to purchase the apartment building. Next, in cell C11 the maximum of the maximum payoffs is determined with the formula **=MAX(E7:E9)**. The maximin decision is determined
similarly.

In the regret table in Exhibit 12.4, in cell C18, the formula **=MAX(C7:C9) – C7** computes
the regret for the apartment building decision under good economic conditions, and then the
maximum regret for the apartment building is determined in cell E18, using the formula
=MAX(C18,D18). The minimax regret value is determined in cell C22 with the formula
=MIN(E18:E20).

The Hurwicz and equal likelihood decisions are determined using their respective formulas
in cells **C27:C29** and **C32:C34**.

Management Science Application

Planning for Terrorist Attacks and Epidemics in Los Angeles County with Decision Analysis

The Centers for Disease Control and Prevention (CDC) has asked all state and local health departments in the United States to develop plans to provide vaccines and antibiotics (referred to as *prophylaxis*) to the general population in the event of a bioterrorism attack or natural epidemic. Outbreaks of diseases such as smallpox and influenza are very contagious, while diseases such as anthrax have a very short incubation period, resulting in deaths within 48 hours. Therefore, any preventive agents need to be distributed within 48 hours. Distributing prophylaxis to a locality such as Los Angeles County, with almost 10 million legal residents, 1 million tourists on any given day, and several million illegal residents, is a complex task.

The CDC requires that points of dispensing (PODs) be used as the primary means for distributing prophylaxis drugs. POD plans are funded by the CDC and have been tested and proven effective in many places. However, an area as large as Los Angeles would require 167 geographically dispersed PODs staffed with 48,000 individuals, who would need to be gathered at staging points, trained, and sent to the POD sites within a few hours—with security maintained all the while. A city such as Los Angeles will require supplemental modes of dispensing vaccines and antibiotics beyond just PODs.

In this management science application, researchers used multicriteria decision analysis to assess alternative modes for dispensing prophylaxis. Alternative distribution modes that have been previously tested on a limited basis or used during the normal flu season include delivery by the U.S. Postal Service

AP Photo/Marcio Jose Sanchez

(USPS), dispensing through local pharmacies, and use of drive-through PODs. Value measures for each alternative dispensing mode include speed of distribution, staffing requirements, and a subjective assessment of security requirements, which were subsequently used to calculate a total measure of effectiveness for each alternative. The decision analysis indicated that delivery by the USPS and the use of pharmacies were the two best alternatives to supplement the PODs, and the drive-through alternative, although popularly thought to be the best, was the worst. Both of the preferred alternatives had a 100% staffing reduction and were much faster dispensing modes than the traditional POD.

Source: Based on A. Richter and S. Khan, "Pilot Model: Judging Alternate Modes of Dispensing Prophylaxis in Los Angeles County," *Interfaces* 39, no. 3 (May–June 2009): 238–40.

Decision Making with Probabilities

The decision-making criteria just presented were based on the assumption that no information regarding the likelihood of the states of nature was available. Thus, no *probabilities of occurrence* were assigned to the states of nature, except in the case of the equal likelihood criterion. In that case, by assuming that each state of nature was equally likely and assigning a weight of .50 to each state of nature in our example, we were implicitly assigning a probability of .50 to the occurrence of each state of nature.

It is often possible for the decision maker to know enough about the future states of nature to assign probabilities to their occurrence. Given that probabilities can be assigned, several decision criteria are available to aid the decision maker. We will consider two of these criteria: *expected value* and *expected opportunity loss* (although several others, including the *maximum likelihood criterion*, are available).

Expected value is computed by multiplying each decision outcome under each state of nature by the probability of its occurrence.

Expected Value

To apply the concept of **expected value** as a decision-making criterion, the decision maker must first estimate the probability of occurrence of each state of nature. Once these estimates have been made, the expected value for each decision alternative can be computed. The expected value is computed by multiplying each outcome (of a decision) by the probability of its occurrence and then summing these products. The expected value of a random variable x, written symbolically as $EV(x)$, is computed as follows:

$$EV(x) = \sum_{i=1}^{n} x_i P(x_i)$$

where
n = number of values of the random variable x

Using our real estate investment example, let us suppose that, based on several economic forecasts, the investor is able to estimate a .60 probability that good economic conditions will prevail and a .40 probability that poor economic conditions will prevail. This new information is shown in Table 12.7.

TABLE 12.7
Payoff table with probabilities for states of nature

Decision (purchase)	State of Nature	
	Good Economic Conditions .60	Poor Economic Conditions .40
Apartment building	$ 50,000	$30,000
Office building	100,000	−40,000
Warehouse	30,000	10,000

The expected value (EV) for each decision is computed as follows:

$$EV(\text{apartment}) = \$50,000(.60) + 30,000(.40) = \$42,000$$
$$EV(\text{office}) = \$100,000(.60) - 40,000(.40) = \$44,000$$
$$EV(\text{warehouse}) = \$30,000(.60) + 10,000(.40) = \$22,000$$

The best decision is the one with the greatest expected value. Because the greatest expected value is $44,000, the best decision is to purchase the office building. This does not mean that $44,000 will result if the investor purchases the office building; rather, it is assumed that one of the payoff values will result (either $100,000 or −$40,000). The expected value means that if this decision situation occurred a large number of times, an *average* payoff of $44,000 would result. Alternatively, if the payoffs were in terms of costs, the best decision would be the one with the lowest expected value.

Expected Opportunity Loss

Expected opportunity loss is the expected value of the regret for each decision.

A decision criterion closely related to expected value is expected opportunity loss. To use this criterion, we multiply the probabilities by the regret (i.e., opportunity loss) for each decision outcome rather than multiplying the decision outcomes by the probabilities of their occurrence, as we did for expected monetary value.

The concept of regret was introduced in our discussion of the minimax regret criterion. The regret values for each decision outcome in our example were shown in Table 12.6. These values are repeated in Table 12.8, with the addition of the probabilities of occurrence for each state of nature.

TABLE 12.8
Regret (opportunity loss) table with probabilities for states of nature

Decision (purchase)	State of Nature	
	Good Economic Conditions .60	Poor Economic Conditions .40
Apartment building	$50,000	$ 0
Office building	0	70,000
Warehouse	70,000	20,000

The expected opportunity loss (*EOL*) for each decision is computed as follows:

$$EOL(\text{apartment}) = \$50{,}000(.60) + 0(.40) = \$30{,}000$$
$$EOL(\text{office}) = \$0(.60) + 70{,}000(.40) = \$28{,}000$$
$$EOL(\text{warehouse}) = \$70{,}000(.60) + 20{,}000(.40) = \$50{,}000$$

As with the minimax regret criterion, the best decision results from minimizing the regret, or, in this case, minimizing the *expected* regret or opportunity loss. Because $28,000 is the minimum expected regret, the decision is to purchase the office building.

Notice that the decisions recommended by the expected value and expected opportunity loss criteria were the same—to purchase the office building. This is not a coincidence because these two methods always result in the same decision. Thus, it is repetitious to apply both methods to a decision situation when one of the two will suffice.

The expected value and expected opportunity loss criteria result in the same decision.

In addition, note that the decisions from the expected value and expected opportunity loss criteria are totally dependent on the probability estimates determined by the decision maker. Thus, if inaccurate probabilities are used, erroneous decisions will result. It is therefore important that the decision maker be as accurate as possible in determining the probability of each state of nature.

Solution of Expected Value Problems with QM for Windows

QM for Windows not only solves decision analysis problems without probabilities but also has the capability to solve problems using the expected value criterion. A summary of the input data and the solution output for our real estate example is shown in Exhibit 12.5. Notice that the expected value results are included in the third column of this solution screen.

EXHIBIT 12.5

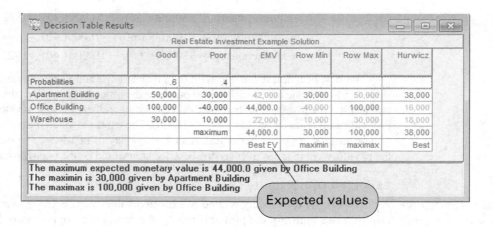

Solution of Expected Value Problems with Excel and Excel QM

This type of expected value problem can also be solved by using an Excel spreadsheet. Exhibit 12.6 shows our real estate investment example set up in a spreadsheet format. Cells E7, E8, and E9

EXHIBIT 12.6

include the expected value formulas for this example. The expected value formula for the first decision, purchasing the apartment building, is embedded in cell E7 and is shown on the formula bar at the top of the spreadsheet.

Excel QM is a set of spreadsheet macros that is included on the companion Web site that accompanies this text, and it has a macro to solve decision analysis problems. Once activated, clicking on "Decision Analysis" will result in a Spreadsheet Initialization window. After entering several problem parameters, including the number of decisions and states of nature, and then clicking on "OK," the spreadsheet shown in Exhibit 12.7 will result. Initially, this spreadsheet contains example values in cells **B8:C11**. Exhibit 12.7 shows the spreadsheet with our problem data already typed in. The results are computed automatically as the data are entered, using the cell formulas already embedded in the macro.

EXHIBIT 12.7

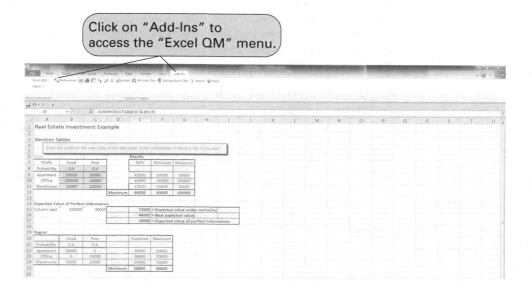

Expected Value of Perfect Information

It is often possible to purchase additional information regarding future events and thus make a better decision. For example, a real estate investor could hire an economic forecaster to perform an analysis of the economy to more accurately determine which economic condition will occur in the future. However, the investor (or any decision maker) would be foolish to pay more for this information than he or she stands to gain in extra profit from having the information. That is, the information has some maximum value that represents the limit of what the decision maker would be willing to spend. This value of information can be computed as an expected value—hence its name, the expected value of perfect information (also referred to as EVPI).

The expected value of perfect information (EVPI) is the maximum amount a decision maker would pay for additional information.

To compute the expected value of perfect information, we first look at the decisions under each state of nature. If we could obtain information that assured us which state of nature was going to occur (i.e., perfect information), we could select the best decision for that state of nature. For example, in our real estate investment example, if we know for sure that good economic conditions will prevail, then we will decide to purchase the office building. Similarly, if we know for sure that poor economic conditions will occur, then we will decide to purchase the apartment building. These hypothetical "perfect" decisions are summarized in Table 12.9.

TABLE 12.9

Payoff table with decisions, given perfect information

| | State of Nature | |
Decision (purchase)	Good Economic Conditions .60	Poor Economic Conditions .40
Apartment building	$ 50,000	$30,000
Office building	100,000	−40,000
Warehouse	30,000	10,000

The probabilities of each state of nature (i.e., .60 and .40) tell us that good economic conditions will prevail 60% of the time and poor economic conditions will prevail 40% of the time (if this decision situation is repeated many times). In other words, even though perfect information enables the investor to make the right decision, each state of nature will occur only a certain portion of the time. Thus, each of the decision outcomes obtained using perfect information must be weighted by its respective probability:

$$\$100,000(.60) + 30,000(.40) = \$72,000$$

The amount $72,000 is the expected value of the decision, *given* perfect information, not the expected value *of* perfect information. The expected value of perfect information is the maximum amount that would be paid to gain information that would result in a decision better than the one made without perfect information. Recall that the expected value decision without perfect information was to purchase an office building, and the expected value was computed as

$$EV(\text{office}) = \$100,000(.60) - 40,000(.40) = \$44,000$$

EVPI equals the expected value, given perfect information, minus the expected value without perfect information.

The expected value of perfect information is computed by subtracting the expected value without perfect information ($44,000) from the expected value given perfect information ($72,000):

$$EVPI = \$72,000 - 44,000 = \$28,000$$

The expected value of perfect information, $28,000, is the maximum amount that the investor would pay to purchase perfect information from some other source, such as an economic forecaster. Of course, perfect information is rare and usually unobtainable. Typically, the decision maker would be willing to pay some amount less than $28,000, depending on how accurate (i.e., close to perfection) the decision maker believed the information was.

The expected value of perfect information equals the expected opportunity loss for the best decision.

It is interesting to note that the expected value of perfect information, $28,000 for our example, is the same as the *expected opportunity loss (EOL)* for the decision selected, using this later criterion:

$$EOL(\text{office}) = \$0(.60) + 70,000(.40) = \$28,000$$

This will always be the case, and logically so, because regret reflects the *difference between the best decision under a state of nature and the decision actually made*. This is actually the same thing determined by the expected value of perfect information.

Excel QM for decision analysis computes the expected value of perfect information, as shown in cell E17 at the bottom of the spreadsheet in Exhibit 12.7. The expected value of perfect information can also be determined by using Excel. Exhibit 12.8 shows the EVPI for our

A decision tree is a diagram consisting of square decision nodes, circle probability nodes, and branches representing decision alternatives.

real estate investment example.

Decision Trees

Another useful technique for analyzing a decision situation is using a decision tree. A decision tree is a graphical diagram consisting of nodes and branches. In a decision tree, the user computes the expected value of each outcome and makes a decision based on these expected values.

EXHIBIT 12.8

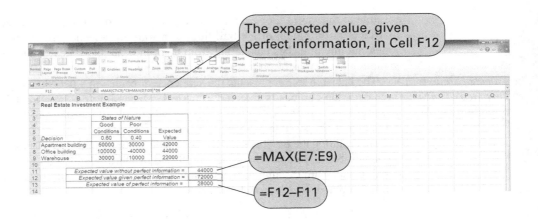

The expected value, given perfect information, in Cell F12

=MAX(E7:E9)

=F12–F11

The primary benefit of a decision tree is that it provides an illustration (or picture) of the decision-making process. This makes it easier to correctly compute the necessary expected values and to understand the process of making the decision.

We will use our example of the real estate investor to demonstrate the fundamentals of decision tree analysis. The various decisions, probabilities, and outcomes of this example, initially presented in Table 12.7, are repeated in Table 12.10. The decision tree for this example is shown in Figure 12.2.

The circles (●) and the square (■) in Figure 12.2 are referred to as *nodes*. The square is a decision node, and the *branches* emanating from a decision node reflect the alternative decisions

TABLE 12.10

Payoff table for real estate investment example

	State of Nature	
Decision (purchase)	Good Economic Conditions .60	Poor Economic Conditions .40
Apartment building	$ 50,000	$30,000
Office building	100,000	−40,000
Warehouse	30,000	10,000

FIGURE 12.2

Decision tree for real estate investment example

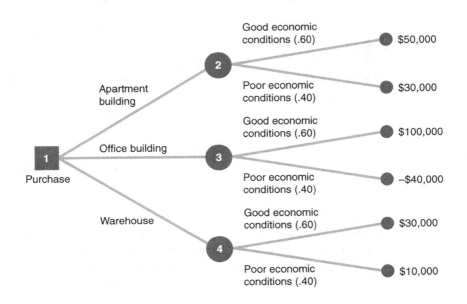

possible at that point. For example, in Figure 12.2, node 1 signifies a decision to purchase an apartment building, an office building, or a warehouse. The circles are probability, or event, nodes, and the branches emanating from them indicate the states of nature that can occur: good economic conditions or poor economic conditions.

The expected value is computed at each probability node.

The decision tree represents the sequence of events in a decision situation. First, one of the three decision choices is selected at node 1. Depending on the branch selected, the decision maker arrives at probability node 2, 3, or 4, where one of the states of nature will prevail, resulting in one of six possible payoffs.

Determining the best decision by using a decision tree involves computing the expected value at each probability node. This is accomplished by starting with the final outcomes (payoffs) and working backward through the decision tree toward node 1. First, the expected value of the payoffs is computed at each probability node:

$$EV(\text{node } 2) = .60(\$50,000) + .40(\$30,000) = \$42,000$$
$$EV(\text{node } 3) = .60(\$100,000) + .40(-\$40,000) = \$44,000$$
$$EV(\text{node } 4) = .60(\$30,000) + .40(\$10,000) = \$22,000$$

Branches with the greatest expected value are selected.

These values are now shown as the *expected* payoffs from each of the three branches emanating from node 1 in Figure 12.3. Each of these three expected values at nodes 2, 3, and 4 is the outcome of a possible decision that can occur at node 1. Moving toward node 1, we select the branch that comes from the probability node with the highest expected payoff. In Figure 12.3, the branch corresponding to the highest payoff, $44,000, is from node 1 to node 3. This branch represents the decision to purchase the office building. The decision to purchase the office building, with an expected payoff of $44,000, is the same result we achieved earlier by using the expected value criterion. In fact, when only one decision is to be made (i.e., there is not a series of decisions), the decision tree will always yield the same decision and expected payoff as the expected value criterion. As a result, in these decision situations a decision tree is not very useful. However, when a sequence or series of decisions is required, a decision tree can be very useful.

FIGURE 12.3

Decision tree with expected value at probability nodes

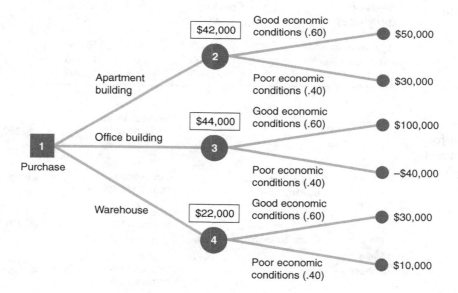

Decision Trees with Excel QM

Both QM for Windows and Excel QM have modules for performing decision tree analysis. However, Excel QM has the capability to actually construct a decision tree, whereas QM for Windows does not; it only performs the tree computations at the nodes. We will therefore demonstrate how to use Excel QM to perform decision tree analysis using our real estate investment example.

After opening Excel QM, click on "Add-Ins" then on "Taylor," and from the drop down menu select "Decision Analysis," then click on "Decision Trees." A window like the one in Exhibit 12.9 will appear, with only node "1" in cell A10. A window titled Decision Tree Creation will also be on your screen; this is the primary tool for developing the decision tree. The "Decision Tree Creation" window automatically will show "1" as the "Selected node" and the "Number of branches to add" as "2," so the first step is to increase this to "3" and then click on "Add 3 DECISIONS from node 1." This will result in the three new branches connected to nodes 2, 3 and 4, as shown in Exhibit 12.9.

EXHIBIT 12.9

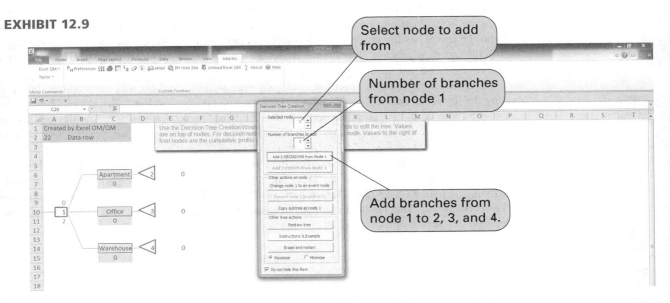

Next, we use the Decision Tree Creation window to add 2 new "Event" branches from nodes 2, 3, and 4. The resulting new window is shown in Exhibit 12.10. Notice that six new

EXHIBIT 12.10

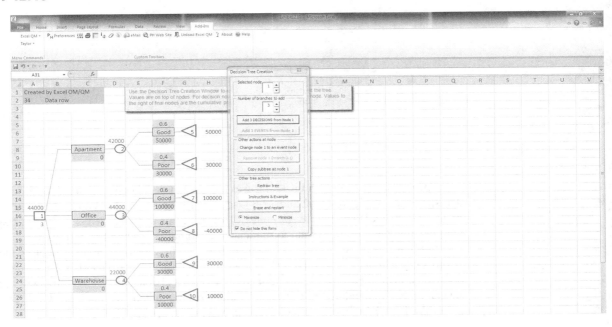

branches have been created. The cells next to node 5 are initially empty, and we enter "0.6" into cell F5 and "50,000" in cell F7. When we enter "0.6" in cell F5, "0.4" automatically appears in cell F9. We repeat this process for the next 4 new event branches to re-create the decision tree in Figure 12.3. Notice that the maximum expected value of $44,000 is shown in cell A15, just above node 1, and in cell D15, above node 3, indicating that the office building is the best decision.

Decision Trees with Excel and TreePlan (www.treeplan.com)

TreePlan is an Excel add-in program developed by Michael Middleton that can be obtained from Decision Tool Works to construct and solve decision trees in an Excel spreadsheet format. Although Excel has the graphical and computational capability to develop decision trees, it is a difficult and slow process. TreePlan is basically a decision tree template that greatly simplifies the process of setting up a decision tree in Excel.

The first step in using TreePlan is to gain access to it. The best way to go about this is to copy the TreePlan add-in file, TreePlan.xla, from the companion Web site accompanying this text onto your hard drive and then add it to the "Add-Ins" menu that you access at the top of your spreadsheet screen. Once you have added TreePlan to the "Add-Ins" menu, you can invoke it by clicking on the "Decision Trees" menu item.

We will demonstrate how to use TreePlan with our real estate investment example shown in Figure 12.3. The first step in using TreePlan is to generate a new tree on which to begin work. Exhibit 12.11 shows a new tree that we generated by invoking the "Add-ins" menu and clicking on "Decision Trees." This results in a menu from which we click on "New Tree," which creates the decision tree shown in Exhibit 12.11.

EXHIBIT 12.11

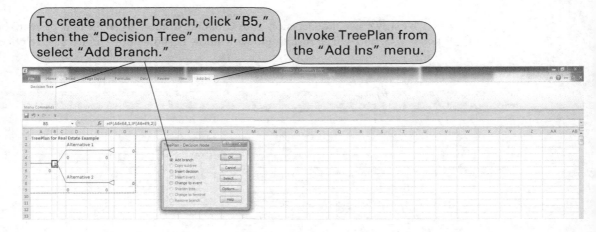

The decision tree in Exhibit 12.11 uses the normal nodal convention we used in creating the decision trees in Figures 12.2 and 12.3—squares for decision nodes and circles for probability nodes (which TreePlan calls *event nodes*). However, this decision tree is only a starting point or template that we need to expand to replicate our example decision tree in Figure 12.3.

In Figure 12.3, three branches emanate from the first decision node, reflecting the three investment decisions in our example. To create a third branch using TreePlan, click on the decision node in cell B5 in Exhibit 12.11 and then click on "Decision Tree". A window will appear, with several options, including "Add Branch". Select this menu item and click on "OK." This will create a third branch on our decision tree, as shown in Exhibit 12.12.

EXHIBIT 12.12

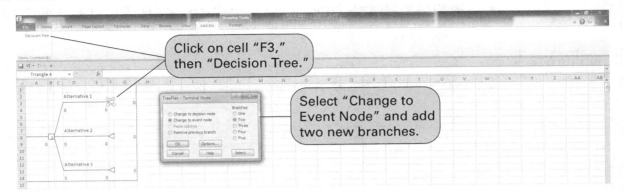

Click on cell "F3," then "Decision Tree."

Select "Change to Event Node" and add two new branches.

Next, we need to expand our decision tree in Exhibit 12.12 by adding probability (event) nodes (2, 3, and 4 in Figure 12.3) and branches from these nodes for our example. To add a new node, click on the end node in cell F3 in Exhibit 12.12 and then "Decision Tree." From the menu window that appears, select "Change to Event Node" and then select "Two" Branches from the same window and click on "OK." This process must be repeated two more times for the other two end nodes to create our three probability (event) nodes. The resulting decision tree is shown in Exhibit 12.13, with the new probability nodes at cells F5, F15, and F25 and with accompanying branches.

EXHIBIT 12.13

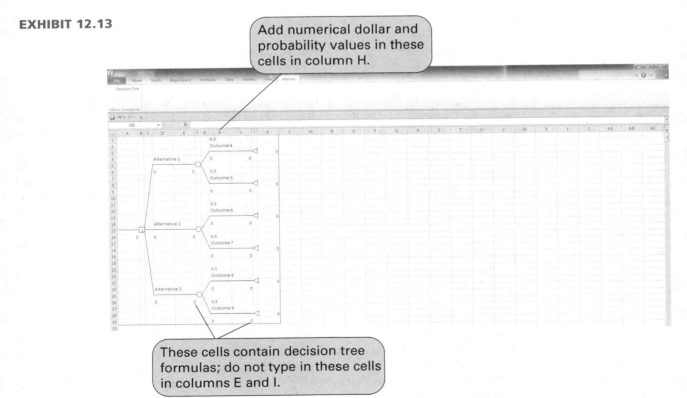

Add numerical dollar and probability values in these cells in column H.

These cells contain decision tree formulas; do not type in these cells in columns E and I.

The next step is to edit the decision tree labels and add the numeric data from our example. Generic descriptive labels are shown above each branch in Exhibit 12.13—for example, "Alternative 1" in cell D4 and "Outcome 4" in cell H2. We edit the labels the same way we would edit any spreadsheet. For example, if we click on cell D4, we can type in "Apartment

Building" in place of "Decision 1," reflecting the decision corresponding to this branch in our example, as shown in Figure 12.3. We can change the other labels on the other branches the same way. The decision tree with the edited labels corresponding to our example is shown in Exhibit 12.14.

EXHIBIT 12.14

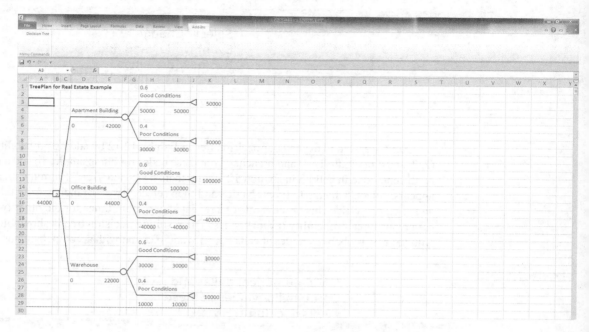

Looking back to Exhibit 12.13 for a moment, focus on the two 0 values below each branch—for example, in cells D6 and E6 and in cells H9 and I4. The first 0 cell is where we type in the numeric value (i.e., $ amount) for that branch. For our example, we would type in 50,000 in cell H4, 30,000 in H9, 100,000 in H14, and so on. These values are shown on the decision tree in Exhibit 12.14. Likewise, we would type in the probabilities for the branches in the cells just above the branch—H1, H6, H11, and so on. For example, we would type in 0.60 in cell H1 and 0.40 in cell H6. These probabilities are also shown in Exhibit 12.14. However, we need to be very careful not to type anything into the second 0 branch cell—for example, E6, I4, I9, E16, I14, I19, and so on. These cells automatically contain the decision tree formulas that compute the expected values at each node and select the best decision branches, so we do not want to type anything in these cells that would eliminate these formulas.

The expected value for this decision tree and our example, $44,000, is shown in cell A16 in Exhibit 12.14.

Sequential Decision Trees

A sequential decision tree illustrates a situation requiring a series of decisions.

As noted earlier, when a decision situation requires only a single decision, an expected value payoff table will yield the same result as a decision tree. However, a payoff table is usually limited to a single decision situation, as in our real estate investment example. If a decision situation requires a series of decisions, then a payoff table cannot be created, and a decision tree becomes the best method for decision analysis.

To demonstrate the use of a decision tree for a sequence of decisions, we will alter our real estate investment example to encompass a 10-year period during which several decisions must be made. In this new example, the *first decision* facing the investor is whether to purchase an apartment building or land. If the investor purchases the apartment building, two states of nature are possible: Either the population of the town will grow (with a probability of .60) or the population will

Management Science Application

Evaluating Electric Generator Maintenance Schedules Using Decision Tree Analysis

Electric utility companies plan annual outage periods for preventive maintenance on generators. The outages are typically part of 5- to-20-year master schedules. However, at Entergy Electric Systems these scheduled outages were traditionally based on averages that did not reflect short-term fluctuations in demand due to breakdowns and bad weather conditions. The master schedule had to be reviewed each week by outage planners who relied on their experience to determine whether the schedule needed to be changed. A user-friendly software system was developed to assist planners at Entergy Electric Systems in making changes in their schedule. The system is based on decision tree analysis.

Each week in the master schedule is represented by a decision tree that is based on changes in customer demand, unexpected generator breakdowns, and delays in returning generators from planned outages. The numeric outcome of the decision tree is the average reserve margin of megawatts (MW) for a specific week. This value enables planners to determine whether customer demand will be met and whether the maintenance schedule planned for the week is acceptable. The planner's objective is to avoid negative power reserves by making changes in the generators' maintenance schedule. The branches of the decision tree, their probabilities of occurrence, and the branch MW values are based on historical data. The system has enabled Entergy Electric Systems to isolate

© Corbis Flirt/Alamy

high-risk weeks and to develop timely maintenance schedules on short notice. The new computerized system has reduced the maintenance schedules review time for as many as 260 weeks from several days to less than an hour.

Source: Based on H. A. Taha and H. M. Wolf, "Evaluation of Generator Maintenance Schedules at Entergy Electric Systems," *Interfaces* 26, no. 4 (July–August 1996): 56–65.

not grow (with a probability of .40). Either state of nature will result in a payoff. On the other hand, if the investor chooses to purchase land, 3 years in the future another decision will have to be made regarding the development of the land. The decision tree for this example, shown in Figure 12.4, contains all the pertinent data, including decisions, states of nature, probabilities, and payoffs.

At decision node 1 in Figure 12.4, the decision choices are to purchase an apartment building or to purchase land. Notice that the cost of each venture ($800,000 and $200,000, respectively) is shown in parentheses. If the apartment building is purchased, two states of nature are possible at probability node 2: The town may exhibit population growth, with a probability of .60, or there may be no population growth or a decline, with a probability of .40. If the population grows, the investor will achieve a payoff of $2,000,000 over a 10-year period. (Note that this whole decision situation encompasses a 10-year time span.) However, if no population growth occurs, a payoff of only $225,000 will result.

If the decision is to purchase land, two states of nature are possible at probability node 3. These two states of nature and their probabilities are identical to those at node 2; however, the payoffs are different. If population growth occurs *for a 3-year period*, no payoff will occur, but the investor will make another decision at node 4 regarding development of the land. At that point, either apartments will be built, at a cost of $800,000, or the land will be sold, with a payoff of $450,000. Notice that the decision situation at node 4 can occur only if population growth occurs first. If no population growth occurs at node 3, there is no payoff, and another decision situation becomes necessary at node 5: The land can be developed commercially at a cost of $600,000, or the land can be sold for

FIGURE 12.4

Sequential decision tree

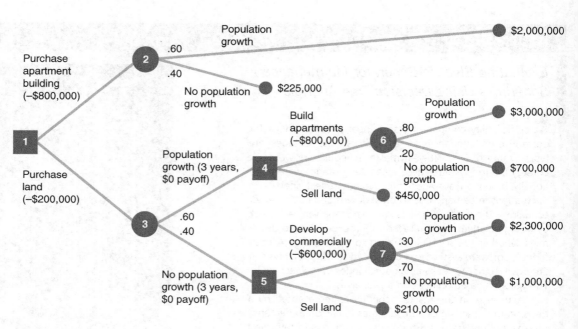

$210,000. (Notice that the sale of the land results in less profit if there is no population growth than if there is population growth.)

If the decision at decision node 4 is to build apartments, two states of nature are possible: The population may grow, with a conditional probability of .80, or there may be no population growth, with a conditional probability of .20. The probability of population growth is higher (and the probability of no growth is lower) than before because there has already been population growth for the first 3 years, as shown by the branch from node 3 to node 4. The payoffs for these two states of nature at the end of the 10-year period are $3,000,000 and $700,000, respectively, as shown in Figure 12.4.

If the investor decides to develop the land commercially at node 5, then two states of nature can occur: Population growth can occur, with a probability of .30 and an eventual payoff of $2,300,000, or no population growth can occur, with a probability of .70 and a payoff of $1,000,000. The probability of population growth is low (i.e., .30) because there has already been no population growth, as shown by the branch from node 3 to node 5.

This decision situation encompasses several sequential decisions that can be analyzed by using the decision tree approach outlined in our earlier (simpler) example. As before, we start at the end of the decision tree and work backward toward a decision at node 1.

First, we must compute the expected values at nodes 6 and 7:

$$EV(\text{node 6}) = .80(\$3,000,000) + .20(\$700,000) = \$2,540,000$$
$$EV(\text{node 7}) = .30(\$2,300,000) + .70(\$1,000,000) = \$1,390,000$$

These expected values (and all other nodal values) are shown in boxes in Figure 12.5.

At decision nodes 4 and 5, we must make a decision. As with a normal payoff table, we make the decision that results in the greatest expected value. At node 4 we have a choice between two values: $1,740,000, the value derived by subtracting the cost of building an apartment building ($800,000) from the expected payoff of $2,540,000, *or* $450,000, the expected value of selling the land computed with a probability of 1.0. The decision is to build the apartment building, and the value at node 4 is $1,740,000 ($2,540,000 − 800,000).

This same process is repeated at node 5. The decisions at node 5 result in payoffs of $790,000 (i.e., $1,390,000 − 600,000 = $790,000) and $210,000. Because the value $790,000 is higher, the decision is to develop the land commercially.

FIGURE 12.5

Sequential
decision tree
with nodal
expected
values

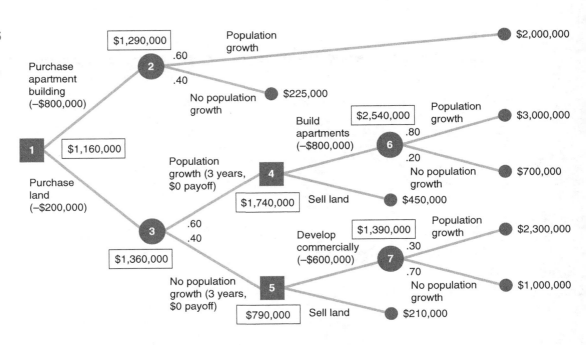

Next, we must compute the expected values at nodes 2 and 3:

$$EV(\text{node } 2) = .60(\$2,000,000) + .40(\$225,000) = \$1,290,000$$
$$EV(\text{node } 3) = .60(\$1,740,000) + .40(\$790,000) = \$1,360,000$$

(Note that the expected value for node 3 is computed from the decision values previously determined at nodes 4 and 5.)

Now we must make the final decision for node 1. As before, we select the decision with the greatest expected value *after the cost of each decision is subtracted out*:

$$\text{apartment building: } \$1,290,000 - 800,000 = \$490,000$$
$$\text{land: } \$1,360,000 - 200,000 = \$1,160,000$$

Because the highest *net* expected value is $1,160,000, the decision is to purchase land, and the payoff of the decision is $1,160,000.

This example demonstrates the usefulness of decision trees for decision analysis. A decision tree allows the decision maker to see the logic of decision making because it provides a picture of the decision process. Decision trees can be used for decision problems more complex than the preceding example without too much difficulty.

Sequential Decision Tree Analysis with Excel QM

We have already demonstrated the capability of Excel QM to build decision trees (Exhibits 12.9 and 12.10). For the sequential decision tree example described in the preceding section and illustrated in Figures 12.4 and 12.5, the Excel QM decision tree is shown in Exhibit 12.15. Notice that the expected value for the decision tree (i.e., the investment decision), $1,160,000, is shown in cell A17. You might notice that the node numbers are a little different in Exhibit 12.15 from Figure 12.3; the reason is that Excel QM assigns node numbers sequentially for every node, while the decision tree drawn in Figure 12.3 did not assign node numbers to end nodes.

Sequential Decision Tree Analysis with Excel and TreePlan

The sequential decision tree example shown in Figure 12.5, developed and solved by using TreePlan, is shown in Exhibit 12.16. Although this TreePlan decision tree is larger than the one we previously developed in Exhibit 12.14, it was accomplished in exactly the same way.

EXHIBIT 12.15

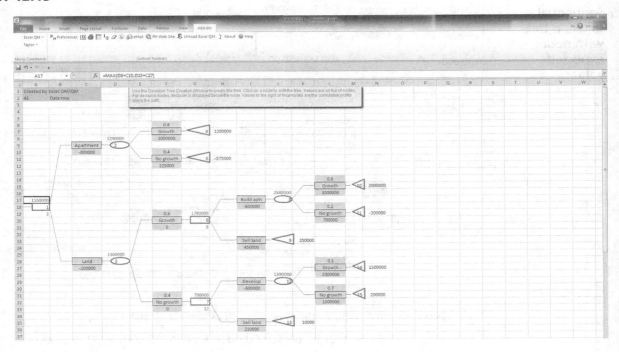

EXHIBIT 12.16

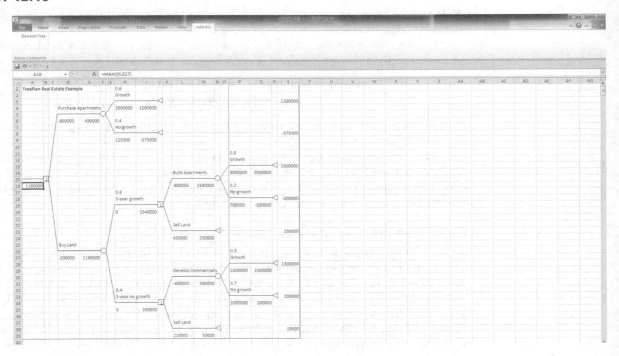

Decision Analysis with Additional Information

Earlier in this chapter, we discussed the concept of the expected value of perfect information. We noted that if perfect information could be obtained regarding which state of nature would occur in the future, the decision maker could obviously make better decisions. Although perfect information

In Bayesian analysis, additional information is used to alter the marginal probability of the occurrence of an event.

about the future is rare, it is often possible to gain some amount of additional (imperfect) information that will improve decisions.

In this section, we will present a process for using additional information in the decision-making process by applying Bayesian analysis. We will demonstrate this process using the real estate investment example employed throughout this chapter. Let's review this example briefly: A real estate investor is considering three alternative investments, which will occur under one of the two possible economic conditions (states of nature) shown in Table 12.11.

TABLE 12.11

Payoff table for the real estate investment example

Decision (purchase)	State of Nature	
	Good Economic Conditions .60	Poor Economic Conditions .40
Apartment building	$ 50,000	$30,000
Office building	100,000	−40,000
Warehouse	30,000	10,000

Recall that, using the expected value criterion, we found the best decision to be the purchase of the office building, with an expected value of $44,000. We also computed the expected value of perfect information to be $28,000. Therefore, the investor would be willing to pay up to $28,000 for information about the states of nature, depending on how close to perfect the information was.

Now suppose that the investor has decided to hire a professional economic analyst who will provide additional information about future economic conditions. The analyst is constantly researching the economy, and the results of this research are what the investor will be purchasing.

The economic analyst will provide the investor with a report predicting one of two outcomes. The report will be either positive, indicating that good economic conditions are most likely to prevail in the future, or negative, indicating that poor economic conditions will probably occur. Based on the analyst's past record in forecasting future economic conditions, the investor has determined conditional probabilities of the different report outcomes, given the occurrence of each state of nature in the future. We will use the following notations to express these conditional probabilities:

A conditional probability is the probability that an event will occur, given that another event has already occurred.

g = good economic conditions

p = poor economic conditions

P = positive economic report

N = negative economic report

The conditional probability of each report outcome, given the occurrence of each state of nature, follows:

$$P(P|g) = .80$$
$$P(N|g) = .20$$
$$P(P|p) = .10$$
$$P(N|p) = .90$$

For example, if the future economic conditions are, in fact, good (g), the probability that a positive report (P) will have been given by the analyst, $P(P|g)$, is .80. The other three conditional probabilities can be interpreted similarly. Notice that these probabilities indicate that the analyst is a relatively accurate forecaster of future economic conditions.

The investor now has quite a bit of probabilistic information available—not only the conditional probabilities of the report but also the *prior probabilities* that each state of nature will occur. These prior probabilities that good or poor economic conditions will occur in the future are

$$P(g) = .60$$
$$P(p) = .40$$

Given the conditional probabilities, the prior probabilities can be revised to form **posterior probabilities** by means of Bayes' rule. If we know the conditional probability that a positive report was presented, given that good economic conditions prevail, $P(P \mid g)$, the posterior probability of good economic conditions, given a positive report, $P(g \mid P)$, can be determined using Bayes' rule, as follows:

$$P(g \mid P) = \frac{P(P \mid g)P(g)}{P(P \mid g)P(g) + P(P \mid p)P(p)}$$
$$= \frac{(.80)(.60)}{(.80)(.60) + (.10)(.40)}$$
$$= .923$$

The prior probability that good economic conditions will occur in the future is .60. However, by obtaining the additional information of a positive report from the analyst, the investor can revise the prior probability of good conditions to a .923 probability that good economic conditions will occur. The remaining posterior (revised) probabilities are

$$P(g \mid N) = .250$$
$$P(p \mid P) = .077$$
$$P(p \mid N) = .750$$

Decision Trees with Posterior Probabilities

The original decision tree analysis of the real estate investment example is shown in Figures 12.2 and 12.3. Using these decision trees, we determined that the appropriate decision was the purchase of an office building, with an expected value of $44,000. However, if the investor hires an economic analyst, the decision regarding which piece of real estate to invest in will not be made until after the analyst presents the report. This creates an additional stage in the decision-making process, which is shown in the decision tree in Figure 12.6. This decision tree differs in two respects from the decision trees in Figures 12.2 and 12.3. The first difference is that there are two new branches at the beginning of the decision tree that represent the two report outcomes. Notice, however, that given either report outcome, the decision alternatives, the possible states of nature, and the payoffs are the same as those in Figures 12.2 and 12.3.

The second difference is that the probabilities of each state of nature are no longer the prior probabilities given in Figure 12.2; instead, they are the revised posterior probabilities computed in the previous section, using Bayes' rule. If the economic analyst issues a positive report, then the upper branch in Figure 12.6 (from node 1 to node 2) will be taken. If an apartment building is purchased (the branch from node 2 to node 4), the probability of good economic conditions is .923, whereas the probability of poor conditions is .077. These are the revised posterior probabilities of the economic conditions, given a positive report. However, before we can perform an expected value analysis using this decision tree, one more piece of probabilistic information must be determined—the initial branch probabilities of positive and negative economic reports.

The probability of a positive report, $P(P)$, and of a negative report, $P(N)$, can be determined according to the following logic. The probability that two dependent events, A and B, will both occur is

$$P(AB) = P(A \mid B)P(B)$$

FIGURE 12.6

Decision tree with posterior probabilities

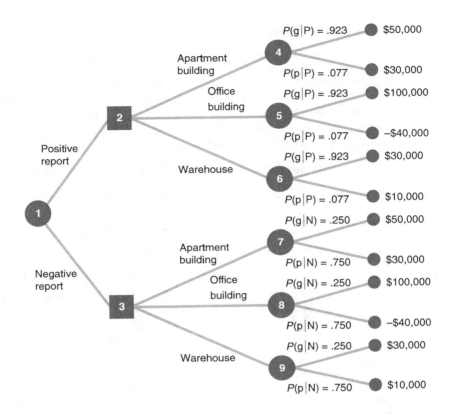

If event A is a positive report and event B is good economic conditions, then according to the preceding formula,

$$P(Pg) = P(P\,|\,g)P(g)$$

We can also determine the probability of a positive report and poor economic conditions the same way:

$$P(Pp) = P(P\,|\,p)P(p)$$

Next, we consider the two probabilities $P(Pg)$ and $P(Pp)$, also called *joint probabilities*. These are, respectively, the probability of a positive report and good economic conditions and the probability of a positive report and poor economic conditions. These two sets of occurrences are **mutually exclusive** because both good and poor economic conditions cannot occur simultaneously in the immediate future. Conditions will be either good or poor, but not both. To determine the probability of a positive report, we add the mutually exclusive probabilities of a positive report with good economic conditions and a positive report with poor economic conditions, as follows:

Events are mutually exclusive if only one can occur at a time.

$$P(P) = P(Pg) + P(Pp)$$

Now, if we substitute into this formula the relationships for $P(Pg)$ and $P(Pp)$ determined earlier, we have

$$P(P) = P(P\,|\,g)P(g) + P(P\,|\,p)P(p)$$

You might notice that the right-hand side of this equation is the denominator of the Bayesian formula we used to compute $P(g\,|\,P)$ in the previous section. Using the conditional and prior probabilities that have already been established, we can determine that the probability of a positive report is

$$P(P) = P(P\,|\,g)P(g) + P(P\,|\,p)P(p) = (.80)(.60) + (.10)(.40) = .52$$

Similarly, the probability of a negative report is

$$P(N) = P(N|g)P(g) + P(N|p)P(p) = (.20)(.60) + (.90)(.40) = .48$$

$P(P)$ and $P(N)$ are also referred to as *marginal probabilities*.

Now we have all the information needed to perform a decision tree analysis. The decision tree analysis for our example is shown in Figure 12.7. To see how the decision tree analysis is conducted, consider the result at node 4 first. The value $48,460 is the expected value of the purchase of an apartment building, given both states of nature. This expected value is computed as follows:

$$EV(\text{apartment building}) = \$50,000(.923) + 30,000(.077) = \$48,460$$

The expected values at nodes 5, 6, 7, 8, and 9 are computed similarly.

FIGURE 12.7

Decision tree analysis for real estate investment example

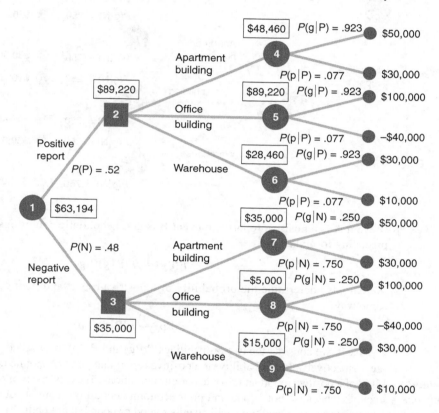

The investor will actually make the decision about the investment at nodes 2 and 3. It is assumed that the investor will make the best decision in each case. Thus, the decision at node 2 will be to purchase an office building, with an expected value of $89,220; the decision at node 3 will be to purchase an apartment building, with an expected value of $35,000. These two results at nodes 2 and 3 are referred to as *decision strategies*. They represent a plan of decisions to be made, given either a positive or a negative report from the economic analyst.

The final step in the decision tree analysis is to compute the expected value of the decision strategy, given that an economic analysis is performed. This expected value, shown as $63,194 at node 1 in Figure 12.7, is computed as follows:

$$EV(\text{strategy}) = \$89,220(.52) + 35,000(.48)$$
$$= \$63,194$$

This amount, $63,194, is the expected value of the investor's decision strategy, given that a report forecasting future economic condition is generated by the economic analyst.

Computing Posterior Probabilities with Tables

One of the difficulties that can occur with decision analysis with additional information is that as the size of the problem increases (i.e., as we add more decision alternatives and states of nature), the application of Bayes' rule to compute the posterior probabilities becomes more complex. In such cases, the posterior probabilities can be computed by using tables. This tabular approach will be demonstrated with our real estate investment example. The table for computing posterior probabilities for a positive report and $P(\text{P})$ is initially set up as shown in Table 12.12.

TABLE 12.12

Computation of posterior probabilities

(1) State of Nature	(2) Prior Probability	(3) Conditional Probability	(4) Prior Probability × Conditional Probability: (2) × (3)	(5) Posterior Probability: (4) ÷ ∑(4)
Good conditions	$P(\text{g}) = .60$	$P(\text{P}|\text{g}) = .80$	$P(\text{Pg}) = .48$	$P(\text{g}|\text{P}) = \dfrac{.48}{.52} = .923$
Poor conditions	$P(\text{p}) = .40$	$P(\text{P}|\text{p}) = .10$	$P(\text{Pp}) = .04$ $\sum = P(\text{P}) = .52$	$P(\text{p}|\text{P}) = \dfrac{.04}{.52} = .077$

The posterior probabilities for either state of nature (good or poor economic conditions), given a negative report, are computed similarly.

No matter how large the decision analysis, the steps of this tabular approach can be followed the same way as in this relatively small problem. This approach is more systematic than the direct application of Bayes' "rule," making it easier to compute the posterior probabilities for larger problems.

Computing Posterior Probabilities with Excel

The posterior probabilities computed in Table 12.12 can also be computed by using Excel. Exhibit 12.17 shows Table 12.12 set up in an Excel spreadsheet format, as well as the table for computing $P(\text{N})$.

EXHIBIT 12.17

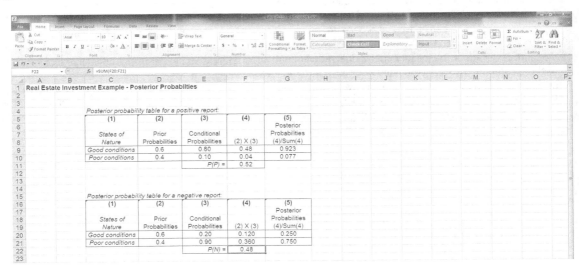

The Expected Value of Sample Information

Recall that we computed the expected value of our real estate investment example to be $44,000 when we did not have any additional information. After obtaining the additional information provided by the economic analyst, we computed an expected value of $63,194, using the decision tree in Figure 12.7. The difference between these two expected values is called the **expected value of sample information (EVSI)**, and it is computed as follows:

$$EVSI = EV_{\text{with information}} - EV_{\text{without information}}$$

For our example, the expected value of sample information is

$$EVSI = \$63,194 - 44,000 = \$19,194$$

The expected value of sample information (EVSI) is the difference between the expected value with and without additional information.

Management Science Application

The Use of Decision Analysis to Determine the Optimal Size of the South African National Defense Force

It is common knowledge that the armed forces need to be commensurate with the kind and level of external threat they face. This usually helps significantly in determining the characteristics and size of the armed forces in all countries. However, when a formal, conventional threat is clearly missing, this apparently simple task becomes a difficult one, especially in a situation of scarce resources in need of optimal allocation.

This was the situation faced in the mid-1990s by the South African National Defense Force (SANDF), which decided to set up, together with a team from Deloitte & Touche, a joint strategic management process (JSMP) to address this issue.

The JSMP used a series of tools for this purpose. The first and most fundamental component was a risk model, which could simulate different defensive scenarios based on an assessment of their probability. This was then coupled with a budgeting plan based on a zero-based approach to insert a cost constraint in the model. Finally, and after designing a growth model to take care of the military operational requirement, all of these components were combined and run in a mixed integer linear programming optimizing model, which maximizes defense value and reduces risks for a given budget.

The results were certainly encouraging. The model had a substantial influence on SANDF's strategic choices, allowing for a

© Andre Maritz | Dreamstime.com

perfect reshaping of the armed forces in terms of their operational components and staffing. In addition, and even more importantly, the project resulted in important savings on the approved force design (size and shape) of more than 22%, with a considerable reduction in budgeted costs. Finally, evidence suggested that further savings were also possible after a punctual implementation of the mixed-integer problems (MIP) solutions.

Source: I. Gryffenberg, J. Lausberg, W. Smit, and S. Uys, "Guns or Butter: Decision Support for Determining the Size and Shape of the South African National Defense Force," *Interfaces* 27, no. 1 (January–February 1997): 7–28.

This means that the real estate investor would be willing to pay the economic analyst up to $19,194 for an economic report that forecasted future economic conditions.

After we computed the expected value of the investment without additional information, we computed the expected value of perfect information, which equaled $28,000. However, the expected value of the sample information was only $19,194. This is a logical result because it is rare that absolutely perfect information can be determined. Because the additional information that is obtained is less than perfect, it will be worth less to the decision maker. We can determine how close to perfect our sample information is by computing the efficiency of sample information as follows:

The efficiency of sample information is the ratio of the expected value of sample information to the expected value of perfect information.

$$\text{efficiency} = EVSI \div EVPI = \$19{,}194 / 28{,}000 = .69$$

Thus, the analyst's economic report is viewed by the investor to be 69% as efficient as perfect information. In general, a high efficiency rating indicates that the information is very good, or close to being perfect information, and a low rating indicates that the additional information is not very good. For our example, the efficiency of .69 is relatively high; thus, it is doubtful that the investor would seek additional information from an alternative source. (However, this is usually dependent on how much money the decision maker has available to purchase information.) If the efficiency had been lower, however, the investor might seek additional information elsewhere.

Utility

All the decision-making criteria presented so far in this chapter have been based on monetary value. In other words, decisions have been based on the potential dollar payoffs of the alternatives. However, there are certain decision situations in which individuals do not make decisions based on the expected dollar gain or loss.

For example, consider an individual who purchases automobile insurance. The decisions are to purchase and to not purchase, and the states of nature are *an accident* and *no accident*. The payoff table for this decision situation, including probabilities, is shown in Table 12.13.

TABLE 12.13

Payoff table for auto insurance example

	State of Nature	
Decision	No Accident .992	Accident .008
Purchase insurance	$500	$ 500
Do not purchase insurance	0	10,000

The dollar outcomes in Table 12.13 are the *costs* associated with each outcome. The insurance costs $500 whether there is an accident or no accident. If the insurance is not purchased and there is no accident, then there is no cost at all. However, if an accident does occur, the individual will incur a cost of $10,000.

The expected cost (*EC*) for each decision is

$$EC(\text{insurance}) = .992(\$500) + .008(\$500) = \$500$$

$$EC(\text{no insurance}) = .992(\$0) + .008(\$10{,}000) = \$80$$

Because the *lower* expected cost is $80, the decision *should be* not to purchase insurance. However, people almost always purchase insurance (even when they are not legally required to do so). This is true of all types of insurance, such as accident, life, or fire.

People who forgo a high expected value to avoid a disaster with a low probability are risk averters.

Why do people shun the greater *expected* dollar outcome in this type of situation? The answer is that people want to avoid a ruinous or painful situation. When faced with a relatively small dollar cost versus a disaster, people typically pay the small cost to avert the disaster. People who display this characteristic are referred to as risk averters because they avoid risky situations.

Alternatively, people who go to the track to wager on horse races, travel to Atlantic City to play roulette, or speculate in the commodities market decide to take risks even though the greatest *expected value* would occur if they simply held on to the money. These people shun the greater expected value accruing from a sure thing (keeping their money) in order to take a chance on receiving a "bonanza." Such people are referred to as risk takers.

People who take a chance on a bonanza with a very low probability of occurrence in lieu of a sure thing are risk takers.

For both risk averters and risk takers (as well as those who are indifferent to risk), the decision criterion is something other than the expected dollar outcome. This alternative criterion is known as utility. Utility is a measure of the satisfaction derived from money. In our examples of risk averters and risk takers presented earlier, the utility derived from their decisions *exceeded* the expected dollar value. For example, the utility to the average decision maker of having insurance is much greater than the utility of not having insurance.

Utility is a measure of personal satisfaction derived from money.

As another example, consider two people, each of whom is offered $100,000 to perform some particularly difficult and strenuous task. One individual has an annual income of $10,000; the other individual is a multimillionaire. It is reasonable to assume that the average person with an annual income of only $10,000 would leap at the opportunity to earn $100,000, whereas the multimillionaire would reject the offer. Obviously, $100,000 has more *utility* (i.e., value) for one individual than for the other.

In general, the same incremental amount of money does not have the same intrinsic value to every person. For individuals with a great deal of wealth, more money does not usually have as much intrinsic value as it does for individuals who have little money. In other words, although the dollar value is the same, the value as measured by utility is different, depending on how much wealth a person has. Thus, utility in this case is a measure of the pleasure or satisfaction an individual would receive from an incremental increase in wealth.

Utiles are units of subjective measures of utility.

In some decision situations, decision makers attempt to assign a subjective value to utility. This value is typically measured in terms of units called utiles. For example, the $100,000 offered to the two individuals may have a utility value of 100 utiles to the person with a low income and 0 utiles to the multimillionaire.

In our automobile insurance example, the *expected utility* of purchasing insurance could be 1,000 utiles, and the expected utility of not purchasing insurance only 1 utile. These utility values are completely reversed from the *expected monetary values* computed from Table 12.13, which explains the decision to purchase insurance.

As might be expected, it is usually very difficult to measure utility and the number of utiles derived from a decision outcome. The process is a very subjective one in which the decision maker's psychological preferences must be determined. Thus, although the concept of utility is realistic and often portrays actual decision-making criteria more accurately than does expected monetary value, its application is difficult and, as such, somewhat limited.

Summary

The purpose of this chapter was to demonstrate the concepts and fundamentals of decision making when uncertainty exists. Within this context, several decision-making criteria were presented. The maximax, maximin, minimax regret, equal likelihood, and Hurwicz decision criteria were demonstrated for cases in which probabilities could not be attached to the occurrence of outcomes. The expected value criterion and decision trees were discussed for cases in which probabilities could be assigned to the states of nature of a decision situation.

All the decision criteria presented in this chapter were demonstrated by rather simplified examples; actual decision-making situations are usually more complex. Nevertheless, the process of analyzing decisions presented in this chapter is the logical method that most decision makers follow to make a decision.

Example Problem Solution

The following example will illustrate the solution procedure for a decision analysis problem.

Problem Statement

T. Bone Puckett, a corporate raider, has acquired a textile company and is contemplating the future of one of its major plants, located in South Carolina. Three alternative decisions are being considered: (1) expand the plant and produce lightweight, durable materials for possible sales to the military, a market with little foreign competition; (2) maintain the status quo at the plant, continuing production of textile goods that are subject to heavy foreign competition; or (3) sell the plant now. If one of the first two alternatives is chosen, the plant will still be sold at the end of a year. The amount of profit that could be earned by selling the plant in a year depends on foreign market conditions, including the status of a trade embargo bill in Congress. The following payoff table describes this decision situation:

	State of Nature	
Decision	Good Foreign Competitive Conditions	Poor Foreign Competitive Conditions
Expand	$ 800,000	$ 500,000
Maintain status quo	1,300,000	−150,000
Sell now	320,000	320,000

A. Determine the best decision by using the following decision criteria:
   1. Maximax
   2. Maximin
   3. Minimax regret
   4. Hurwicz ($\alpha = .3$)
   5. Equal likelihood
B. Assume that it is now possible to estimate a probability of .70 that good foreign competitive conditions will exist and a probability of .30 that poor conditions will exist. Determine the best decision by using expected value and expected opportunity loss.
C. Compute the expected value of perfect information.
D. Develop a decision tree, with expected values at the probability nodes.
E. T. Bone Puckett has hired a consulting firm to provide a report on future political and market situations. The report will be positive (P) or negative (N), indicating either a good (g) or poor (p) future foreign competitive situation. The conditional probability of each report outcome, given each state of nature, is

$$P(P\,|\,g) = .70$$
$$P(N\,|\,g) = .30$$
$$P(P\,|\,p) = .20$$
$$P(N\,|\,p) = .80$$

Determine the posterior probabilities by using Bayes' rule.

F. Perform a decision tree analysis by using the posterior probability obtained in (E).

Solution

Step 1 (part A): Determine Decisions Without Probabilities

Maximax:

Expand	$ 800,000	
Status quo	1,300,000	← Maximum
Sell	320,000	

Decision: Maintain status quo.

Maximin:

Expand	$ 500,000	← Maximum
Status quo	−150,000	
Sell	320,000	

Decision: Expand.

Minimax regret:

Expand	$500,000	← Minimum
Status quo	650,000	
Sell	980,000	

Decision: Expand.

Hurwicz ($\alpha = .3$):

Expand	$800,000(.3) + 500,000(.7) = \$590,000$
Status quo	$1,300,000(.3) - 150,000(.7) = \$285,000$
Sell	$320,000(.3) + 320,000(.7) = \$320,000$

Decision: Expand.

Equal likelihood:

Expand	$800,000(.50) + 500,000(.50) = \$650,000$
Status quo	$1,300,000(.50) - 150,000(.50) = \$575,000$
Sell	$320,000(.50) + 320,000(.50) = \$320,000$

Decision: Expand.

Step 2 (part B): Determine Decisions with *EV* and *EOL*

Expected value:

Expand	$800,000(.70) + 500,000(.30) = \$710,000$
Status quo	$1,300,000(.70) - 150,000(.30) = \$865,000$
Sell	$320,000(.70) + 320,000(.30) = \$320,000$

Decision: Maintain status quo.

Expected opportunity loss:

Expand	$500,000(.70) + 0(.30) = \$350,000$
Status quo	$0(.70) + 650,000(.30) = \$195,000$
Sell	$980,000(.70) + 180,000(.30) = \$740,000$

Decision: Maintain status quo.

Step 3 (part C): Compute *EVPI*

expected value given perfect information $= 1,300,000(.70) + 500,000(.30)$
$$= \$1,060,000$$

expected value without perfect information $= \$1,300,000(.70) - 150,000(.30)$
$$= \$865,000$$

$$EVPI = \$1,060,000 - 865,000 = \$195,000$$

Step 4 (part D): Develop a Decision Tree

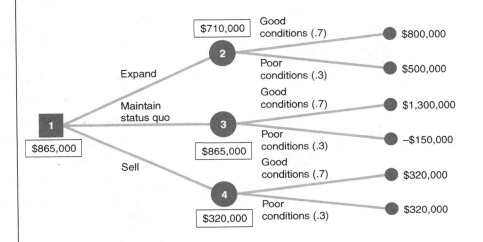

Step 5 (part E): Determine Posterior Probabilities

$$P(g|P) = \frac{P(P|g)P(g)}{P(P|g)P(g) + P(P|p)P(p)}$$

$$= \frac{(.70)(.70)}{(.70)(.70) + (.20)(.30)}$$

$$= .891$$

$$P(p|P) = .109$$

$$P(g|N) = \frac{P(N|g)P(g)}{P(N|g)P(g) + P(N|p)P(p)}$$

$$= \frac{(.30)(.70)}{(.30)(.70) + (.80)(.30)}$$

$$= .467$$

$$P(p|N) = .533$$

Step 6 (part F): Perform Decision Tree Analysis with Posterior Probabilities

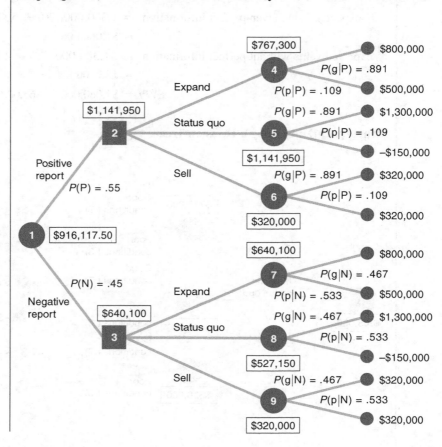

Problems

1. A farmer in the Cotswolds, United Kingdom, is considering either leasing additional land to grow wheat or placing the money in a bank savings account. If weather conditions are good, the extra land will be a good opportunity to make money; however, if the weather conditions are bad, the farmer will lose money. However, if the money is placed in the bank, the weather will have no effect on the rate, and the farmer is guaranteed a return. The return for each investment decision is given in the table here below.

$	State of Nature	
	Good	Bad
Lease land	100,000	−60,000
Savings account	20,000	20,000

Select the best decision, according to the following criteria:
a. Maximax
b. Maximin

2. The owner of the Burger Doodle Restaurant is considering two ways to expand operations: open a drive-up window or serve breakfast. The increase in profits resulting from these proposed expansions depends on whether a competitor opens a franchise down the street. The possible profits

from each expansion in operations, given both future competitive situations, are shown in the following payoff table:

	Competitor	
Decision	Open	Not Open
Drive-up window	$-6,000	$20,000
Breakfast	4,000	8,000

Select the best decision, using the following decision criteria.
a. Maximax
b. Maximin

3. A young graduate has been offered two positions in different companies. One position is relatively secured with a decent wage, but in the case of a recession, the company, to avoid redundancies, would ask employees to lessen their wage. The other company offers less money but would change its wage system in case of a recession by lowering the base salary and implementing a bonus scheme for the best performing employees. The graduate, knowing the difficult economic times, must make a decision according to the different states of nature.

	State of Nature	
$	Good	Recession
Company A (no bonus)	25,000	22,000
Company B (bonus)	24,000	30,000

Select the best decision, using the following decision criteria.
a. Minimax regret
b. Hurwicz ($\alpha = .3$)
c. Equal likelihood

4. Brooke Bentley, a student in business administration, is trying to decide which management science course to take next quarter—I, II, or III. "Steamboat" Fulton, "Death" Ray, and "Sadistic" Scott are the three management science professors who teach the courses. Brooke does not know who will teach what course. Brooke can expect a different grade in each of the courses, depending on who teaches it next quarter, as shown in the following payoff table:

	Professor		
Course	Fulton	Ray	Scott
I	B	D	D
II	C	B	F
III	F	A	C

Determine the best course to take next quarter, using the following criteria.
a. Maximax
b. Maximin

5. A farmer in Holland must decide which crop to plant next season: wheat, corn, or barley. The return on each will be determined by weather conditions. The profit the farmer will realize from each crop, given the weather conditions, is shown in the following table:

	State of Nature	
$	Good	Bad
Wheat	100,000	32,000
Corn	60,000	40,000
Barley	80,000	20,000

Determine the best crop to plant according to the following decision criteria.
a. Maximax
b. Maximin
c. Minimax regret
d. Hurwicz ($\alpha = .4$)
e. Equal likelihood

6. A company must decide now which of three products to make next year to plan and order proper materials. The cost per unit of producing each product will be determined by whether a new union labor contract passes or fails. The cost per unit for each product, given each contract result, is shown in the following payoff table:

	Contract Outcome	
Product	Pass	Fail
1	$7.50	$6.00
2	4.00	7.00
3	6.50	3.00

Determine which product should be produced, using the following decision criteria.
a. Minimin
b. Minimax

7. The owner of the Columbia Construction Company must decide between building a housing development, constructing a shopping center, and leasing all the company's equipment to another company. The profit that will result from each alternative will be determined by whether material costs remain stable or increase. The profit from each alternative, given the two possibilities for material costs, is shown in the following payoff table:

	Material Costs	
Decision	Stable	Increase
Houses	$70,000	$30,000
Shopping center	105,000	20,000
Leasing	40,000	40,000

Determine the best decision, using the following decision criteria.
a. Maximax
b. Maximin
c. Minimax regret
d. Hurwicz ($\alpha = .2$)
e. Equal likelihood

8. A couple in Britain is deciding to invest in one of the following hospitality businesses according to the exchange rate of the neighboring countries: bed and breakfast, restaurant, or hotel. According to the type of business and the affluence of local or foreign visitors, the investments will have different returns. If fewer foreigners come to the country due to a low exchange rate, they will be able to offset this to the local population, hence the importance of the choice given low, medium, and high exchange rates in favor of foreign visitors. The profits the couple will realize from each business, given the exchange rate conditions, are shown in the following table:

	State of Nature		
$	Low	Medium	High
Bed and Breakfast	10,000	22,000	30,000
Restaurant	40,000	35,000	20,000
Hotel	30,000	50,000	23,000

Determine the best investment according to the following decision criteria.
a. Maximax
b. Maximin
c. Minimax regret
d. Equal likelihood

9. An oil exploration company has to decide between three sites in which to invest in its next drilling project. The decision to drill in a region is determined by oil prices and the cost of setting up the drill. If oil prices are high, it is worth drilling in remote locations, whereas if prices are low, it is better to minimize the investment to guarantee profits. The table below summarizes the different profits given oil prices.

	State of Nature		
Million $	Low	Medium	High
North Sea	3,000	2,000	1,000
Brazil offshore	300	2,500	5,000
Russia	1,500	4,000	2,200

Determine the best investment according to the following decision criteria.
a. Maximax
b. Maximin
c. Minimax regret
d. Equal likelihood

10. Ann Tyler has come into an inheritance from her grandparents. She is attempting to decide among several investment alternatives. The return after 1 year is primarily dependent on the interest rate during the next year. The rate is currently 7%, and Ann anticipates that it will stay the same or go up or down by at most two points. The various investment alternatives plus their returns ($10,000s), given the interest rate changes, are shown in the following table:

	Interest Rate				
Investment	5%	6%	7%	8%	9%
Money market fund	2	3.1	4	4.3	5
Stock growth fund	−3	−2	2.5	4	6
Bond fund	6	5	3	3	2
Government fund	4	3.6	3.2	3	2.8
Risk fund	−9	−4.5	1.2	8.3	14.7
Savings bonds	3	3	3.2	3.4	3.5

Determine the best investment, using the following decision criteria.

a. Maximax

b. Maximin

c. Equal likelihood

11. The Tech football coaching staff has six basic offensive plays it runs every game. Tech has an upcoming game against State on Saturday, and the Tech coaches know that State employs five different defenses. The coaches have estimated the number of yards Tech will gain with each play against each defense, as shown in the following payoff table:

Play	Defense				
	54	63	Wide Tackle	Nickel	Blitz
Off tackle	3	−2	9	7	−1
Option	−1	8	−2	9	12
Toss sweep	6	16	−5	3	14
Draw	−2	4	3	10	−3
Pass	8	20	12	−7	−8
Screen	−5	−2	8	3	16

a. If the coaches employ an offensive game plan, they will use the maximax criterion. What will be their best play?

b. If the coaches employ a defensive plan, they will use the maximin criterion. What will be their best play?

c. What will be their best offensive play if State is equally likely to use any of its five defenses?

12. Microcomp is a U.S.-based manufacturer of personal computers. It is planning to build a new manufacturing and distribution facility in either South Korea, China, Taiwan, the Philippines, or Mexico. It will take approximately 5 years to build the necessary infrastructure (roads, etc.), construct the new facility, and put it into operation. The eventual cost of the facility will differ between countries and will even vary within countries depending on the financial, labor, and political climate, including monetary exchange rates. The company has estimated the facility cost (in $1,000,000s) in each country under three different future economic and political climates, as follows:

Country	Economic/Political Climate		
	Decline	Same	Improve
South Korea	21.7	19.1	15.2
China	19.0	18.5	17.6
Taiwan	19.2	17.1	14.9
Philippines	22.5	16.8	13.8
Mexico	25.0	21.2	12.5

Determine the best decision, using the following decision criteria.

a. Minimin

b. Minimax

c. Hurwicz ($\alpha = .4$)

d. Equal likelihood

13. Place-Plus, a real estate development firm, is considering several alternative development projects. These include building and leasing an office park, purchasing a parcel of land and building an office building to rent, buying and leasing a warehouse, building a strip mall, and building and selling condominiums. The financial success of these projects depends on interest rate movement in the next 5 years. The various development projects and their 5-year financial return (in $1,000,000s) given that interest rates will decline, remain stable, or increase, are shown in the following payoff table:

	Interest Rate		
Project	Decline	Stable	Increase
Office park	$0.5	$1.7	$4.5
Office building	1.5	1.9	2.5
Warehouse	1.7	1.4	1.0
Mall	0.7	2.4	3.6
Condominiums	3.2	1.5	0.6

Determine the best investment, using the following decision criteria.

a. Maximax

b. Maximin

c. Equal likelihood

d. Hurwicz ($\alpha = .3$)

14. The Oakland Bombers professional basketball team just missed making the playoffs last season and believes it needs to sign only one very good free agent to make the playoffs next season. The team is considering four players: Barry Byrd, Rayneal O'Neil, Marvin Johnson, and Michael Gordan. Each player differs according to position, ability, and attractiveness to fans. The payoffs (in $1,000,000s) to the team for each player, based on the contract, profits from attendance, and team product sales for several different season outcomes, are provided in the following table:

	Season Outcome		
Player	Loser	Competitive	Makes Playoffs
Byrd	$-3.2	$ 1.3	4.4
O'Neil	−5.1	1.8	6.3
Johnson	−2.7	0.7	5.8
Gordan	−6.3	−1.6	9.6

Determine the best decision, using the following decision criteria.

a. Maximax

b. Maximin

c. Hurwicz ($\alpha = .60$)

d. Equal likelihood

15. A machine shop owner is attempting to decide whether to purchase a new drill press, a lathe, or a grinder. The return from each will be determined by whether the company succeeds in getting

a government military contract. The profit or loss from each purchase and the probabilities associated with each contract outcome are shown in the following payoff table:

Purchase	Contract .40	No Contract .60
Drill press	$40,000	$−8,000
Lathe	20,000	4,000
Grinder	12,000	10,000

Compute the expected value for each purchase and select the best one.

16. A concessions manager at the Tech versus A&M football game must decide whether to have the vendors sell sun visors or umbrellas. There is a 30% chance of rain, a 15% chance of overcast skies, and a 55% chance of sunshine, according to the weather forecast in College Junction, where the game is to be held. The manager estimates that the following profits will result from each decision, given each set of weather conditions:

Decision	Weather Conditions		
	Rain .30	Overcast .15	Sunshine .55
Sun visors	$−500	$ −200	$1,500
Umbrellas	2,000	0	−900

a. Compute the expected value for each decision and select the best one.
b. Develop the opportunity loss table and compute the expected opportunity loss for each decision.

17. Allen Abbott has a wide-curving, uphill driveway leading to his garage. When there is a heavy snow, Allen hires a local carpenter, who shovels snow on the side in the winter, to shovel his driveway. The snow shoveler charges $30 to shovel the driveway. Following is a probability distribution of the number of heavy snows each winter:

Heavy Snows	Probability
1	.13
2	.18
3	.26
4	.23
5	.10
6	.07
7	.03
	1.00

Allen is considering purchasing a new self-propelled snowblower for $625 that would allow him, his wife, or his children to clear the driveway after a snow. Discuss what you think Allen's decision should be and why.

18. The Miramar Company is going to introduce one of three new products: a widget, a hummer, or a nimnot. The market conditions (favorable, stable, or unfavorable) will determine the profit or loss the company realizes, as shown in the following payoff table:

	Market Conditions		
Product	Favorable .2	Stable .7	Unfavorable .1
Widget	$120,000	$70,000	$ −30,000
Hummer	60,000	40,000	20,000
Nimnot	35,000	30,000	30,000

a. Compute the expected value for each decision and select the best one.

b. Develop the opportunity loss table and compute the expected opportunity loss for each product.

c. Determine how much the firm would be willing to pay to a market research firm to gain better information about future market conditions.

19. The financial success of the Downhill Ski Resort in the Blue Ridge Mountains is dependent on the amount of snowfall during the winter months. If the snowfall averages more than 40 inches, the resort will be successful; if the snowfall is between 20 and 40 inches, the resort will receive a moderate financial return; and if snowfall averages less than 20 inches, the resort will suffer a financial loss. The financial return and probability, given each level of snowfall, follow:

Snowfall Level (in.)	Financial Return
> 40, .4	$ 120,000
20–40, .2	40,000
< 20, .4	−40,000

A large hotel chain has offered to lease the resort for the winter for $40,000. Compute the expected value to determine whether the resort should operate or lease. Explain your answer.

20. An investor must decide between two alternative investments—stocks and bonds. The return for each investment, given two future economic conditions, is shown in the following payoff table:

	Economic Conditions	
Investment	Good	Bad
Stocks	$10,000	$−4,000
Bonds	7,000	2,000

What probability for each economic condition would make the investor indifferent to the choice between stocks and bonds?

21. In Problem 10, Ann Tyler, with the help of a financial newsletter and some library research, has been able to assign probabilities to each of the possible interest rates during the next year, as follows:

Interest Rate (%)	Probability
5	.2
6	.3
7	.3
8	.1
9	.1

Using expected value, determine her best investment decision.

22. In Problem 11, the Tech coaches have reviewed game films and have determined the following probabilities that State will use each of its defenses:

Defense	Probability
54	.40
63	.10
Wide tackle	.20
Nickel	.20
Blitz	.10

a. Using expected value, rank Tech's plays from best to worst.
b. During the actual game, a situation arises in which Tech has a third down and 10 yards to go, and the coaches are 60% certain State will blitz, with a 10% chance of any of the other four defenses. What play should Tech run? Is it likely the team will make the first down?

23. A global economist hired by Microcomp, the U.S.-based computer manufacturer in Problem 12, estimates that the probability that the economic and political climate overseas and in Mexico will decline during the next 5 years is .40, the probability that it will remain approximately the same is .50, and the probability that it will improve is .10. Determine the best country to construct the new facility in and the expected value of perfect information.

24. In Problem 13, the Place-Plus real estate development firm has hired an economist to assign a probability to each direction interest rates may take over the next 5 years. The economist has determined that there is a .50 probability that interest rates will decline, a .40 probability that rates will remain stable, and a .10 probability that rates will increase.
a. Using expected value, determine the best project.
b. Determine the expected value of perfect information.

25. Two friends have decided to invest in a dealership in Britain. They have the choice between a quality German car manufacturer, a luxury British manufacturer, and a high-volume French manufacturer. According to the economic climate, customers will favor a certain type of car. The following table shows the expected profits, given economic conditions.

	State of Nature	
$	Good	Bad
Probability	.3	.7
German	30,000	8,000
British	20,000	−10,000
French	6,000	15,000

Make a decision according to EV (Expected Value) computation value, and calculate the EVPI (Expected Value of Perfect Information).

26. The Steak and Chop Butcher Shop purchases steak from a local meatpacking house. The meat is purchased on Monday at $2.00 per pound, and the shop sells the steak for $3.00 per pound. Any steak left over at the end of the week is sold to a local zoo for $.50 per pound. The possible demands for steak and the probability of each are shown in the following table:

Demand (lb.)	Probability
20	.10
21	.20
22	.30
23	.30
24	.10
	1.00

The shop must decide how much steak to order in a week. Construct a payoff table for this decision situation and determine the amount of steak that should be ordered, using expected value.

27. The Loebuck Grocery must decide how many cases of milk to stock each week to meet demand. The probability distribution of demand during a week is shown in the following table:

Demand (cases)	Probability
15	.20
16	.25
17	.40
18	.15
	1.00

Each case costs the grocer $10 and sells for $12. Unsold cases are sold to a local farmer (who mixes the milk with feed for livestock) for $2 per case. If there is a shortage, the grocer considers the cost of customer ill will and lost profit to be $4 per case. The grocer must decide how many cases of milk to order each week.

a. Construct the payoff table for this decision situation.

b. Compute the expected value of each alternative amount of milk that could be stocked and select the best decision.

c. Construct the opportunity loss table and determine the best decision.

d. Compute the expected value of perfect information.

28. The manager of the greeting card section of Mazey's department store is considering her order for a particular line of Christmas cards. The cost of each box of cards is $3; each box will be sold for $5 during the Christmas season. After Christmas, the cards will be sold for $2 a box. The card section manager believes that all leftover cards can be sold at that price. The estimated demand during the Christmas season for the line of Christmas cards, with associated probabilities, is as follows:

Demand (boxes)	Probability
25	.10
26	.15
27	.30
28	.20
29	.15
30	.10

a. Develop the payoff table for this decision situation.

b. Compute the expected value for each alternative and identify the best decision.

c. Compute the expected value of perfect information.

29. The Palm Garden Greenhouse specializes in raising carnations that are sold to florists. Carnations are sold for $3.00 per dozen; the cost of growing the carnations and distributing them to the florists is $2.00 per dozen. Any carnations left at the end of the day are sold to local restaurants and hotels for $0.75 per dozen. The estimated cost of customer ill will if demand is not met is $1.00 per dozen. The expected daily demand (in dozens) for the carnations is as follows:

Daily Demand	Probability
20	.05
22	.10
24	.25
26	.30
28	.20
30	.10
	1.00

a. Develop the payoff table for this decision situation.
b. Compute the expected value of each alternative number of (dozens of) carnations that could be stocked and select the best decision.
c. Construct the opportunity loss table and determine the best decision.
d. Compute the expected value of perfect information.

30. Assume that the probabilities of demand in Problem 28 are no longer valid; the decision situation is now one without probabilities. Determine the best number of boxes of cards to stock, using the following decision criteria.
a. Maximin
b. Maximax
c. Hurwicz ($\alpha = .4$)
d. Minimax regret

31. Federated Electronics, Ltd., manufactures display screens and monitors for computers and televisions, which it sells to companies around the world. It wants to construct a new warehouse and distribution center in Asia to serve emerging markets there. It has identified potential sites in the port cities Shanghai, Singapore, Pusan, Kaohsiung, and Hong Kong, and it has estimated the possible revenues for each (minus construction costs, which are higher in some cities, such as Hong Kong). At each site the projected revenues are primarily based on two factors—the economic conditions at the port, including the projected traffic, infrastructure, labor rates and availability, and expansion and modernization; and the future government situation, which inclues the political stability, fees, tariffs, duties, and trade regulations. Following is a payoff table that shows the projected revenues (in $billions) for 6 years, given the four possible combinations for positive and negative port and government conditions:

Port	Government Conditions			
	Port Negative/ Government Negative	Port Negative/ Government Positive	Port Positive/ Government Negative	Port Positive/ Government Positive
Shanghai	−0.271	$0.437	$0.523	$1.08
Singapore	−0.164	0.329	0.441	0.873
Pusan	0.119	0.526	0.337	0.732
Kaoshiung	−0.235	0.522	0.226	1.116
Hong Kong	−0.317	0.256	0.285	1.653

Determine the port city Federated should select for its new distribution center using the following decision criteria.

a. Maximax
b. Maximin
c. Equal likelihood
d. Hurwicz ($\alpha = .55$)

32. In Problem 31, Federated Electronics, Ltd., has hired a Washington, DC–based global trade research firm to assess the probabilities of each combination of port and government conditions for the five ports. The research firm probability estimates for the five ports are as follows:

	Government Conditions			
Port	Port Negative/ Government Negative	Port Negative/ Government Positive	Port Positive/ Government Negative	Port Positive/ Government Positive
Shanghai	0.09	0.27	0.32	0.32
Singapore	0.05	0.22	0.22	0.51
Pusan	0.08	0.36	0.27	0.29
Kaoshiung	0.11	0.12	0.46	0.31
Hong Kong	0.10	0.23	0.30	0.37

a. Using expected value, determine the best port to construct the distribution center.
b. Using any decision criteria, determine the port you think would be the best location for the distribution center and justify your answer.

33. In Problem 14, the Bombers' management has determined the following probabilities of the occurrence of each future season outcome for each player:

	Probability		
Player	Loser	Competitive	Makes Playoffs
Byrd	.15	.55	.30
O'Neil	.18	.26	.56
Johnson	.21	.32	.47
Gordan	.30	.25	.45

Compute the expected value for each player and indicate which player the team should try to sign.

34. The director of career advising at Orange Community College wants to use decision analysis to provide information to help students decide which 2-year degree program they should pursue. The director has set up the following payoff table for six of the most popular and successful degree programs at OCC that shows the estimated 5-year gross income ($) from each degree for four future economic conditions:

	Economic Conditions			
Degree Program	Recession	Average	Good	Robust
Graphic design	145,000	175,000	220,000	260,000
Nursing	150,000	180,000	205,000	215,000
Real estate	115,000	165,000	220,000	320,000
Medical technology	130,000	180,000	210,000	280,000
Culinary technology	115,000	145,000	235,000	305,000
Computer information technology	125,000	150,000	190,000	250,000

Determine the best degree program in terms of projected income, using the following decision criteria:
a. Maximax
b. Maximin
c. Equal likelihood
d. Hurwicz ($\alpha = .50$)

35. In Problem 34, the director of career advising at Orange Community College has paid a small fee to a local investment firm to indicate a probability for each future economic condition over the next 5 years. The firm estimates that there is a .20 probability of a recession, a .40 probability that the economy will be average, a .30 probability that the economy will be good, and a .10 probability that it will be robust. Using expected value determine the best degree program in terms of projected income. If you were the director of career advising, which degree program would you recommend?

36. The Blue Sox American League baseball team is going to enter the free-agent market over the winter to sign a new starting pitcher. They are considering five prospects who will enter the free-agent market. All five pitchers are in their mid-20s, have been in the major leagues for approximately 5 years, and have been relatively successful. The team's general manager has compiled a lot of information about the pitchers from scouting reports and their playing histories since high school. He has developed a chart projecting how many wins each pitcher will likely have during the next 10 years given three possible future states of nature: the pitchers will be relatively injury free, they will have a normal career with injuries, or they will have excessive injuries, as shown in the following payoff table:

	Physical Condition		
Pitcher	No injuries	Normal	Excessive Injuries
Jose Diaz	153	122	76
Jerry Damon	173	135	46
Frank Thompson	133	115	88
Derek Rodriguez	105	101	95
Ken Griffin	127	98	75

Determine the best pitcher to sign, using the following decision criteria:
a. Maximax
b. Maximin
c. Equal likelihood
d. Hurwicz ($\alpha = .35$)

37. In Problem 36, the Blue Sox general manager has asked a superscout to assign a probability to each of the three states of nature for the pitchers during the next 10 years. The scout estimates there is a .10 probability that these pitchers at this stage of their careers will have no injuries, a .60 probability that they will have a career with the normal number of injuries, and a .30 probability that they will have excessive injuries.
a. Using expected value, determine the best pitcher to sign.
b. Given the following 10-year contract price for each pitcher (in $millions), which would you recommend signing?

Jose Diaz	$ 97.3
Jerry Damon	$121.5
Frank Thompson	$ 73.5
Derek Rodriguez	$103.4
Ken Griffin	$ 85.7

c. Suppose that the general manager asked the superscout to determine the probabilities of each state of nature for each individual pitcher, and the results were as follows:

Pitcher	Physical Condition		
	No injuries	Normal	Excessive Injuries
Jose Diaz	0.30	0.45	0.25
Jerry Damon	0.13	0.47	0.40
Frank Thompson	0.45	0.35	0.20
Derek Rodriguez	0.50	0.40	0.10
Ken Griffin	0.15	0.60	0.25

Determine the expected number of wins for each pitcher, and combined with the contract price in part b, indicate which pitcher you would recommend signing.

38. Construct a decision tree for the decision situation described in Problem 25 and indicate the best decision.

39. Given the following sequential decision tree, determine which is the optimal investment, A or B:

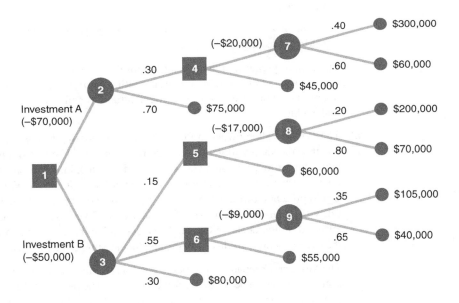

40. The management of First American Bank was concerned about the potential loss that might occur in the event of a physical catastrophe such as a power failure or a fire. The bank estimated that the loss from one of these incidents could be as much as $100 million, including losses due to interrupted service and customer relations. One project the bank is considering is the installation of an emergency power generator at its operations headquarters. The cost of the emergency generator is $800,000, and if it is installed, no losses from this type of incident will be incurred. However, if the generator is not installed, there is a 10% chance that a power outage will occur during the next year. If there is an outage, there is a .05 probability that the resulting losses will be very large, or approximately $80 million in lost earnings. Alternatively, it is estimated that there is a .95 probability of only slight losses of around $1 million. Using decision tree analysis, determine whether the bank should install the new power generator.

41. The Americo Oil Company is considering making a bid for a shale oil development contract to be awarded by the federal government. The company has decided to bid $112 million. The company estimates that it has a 60% chance of winning the contract with this bid. If the firm wins the contract, it can choose one of three methods for getting the oil from the shale. It can develop a new method for oil extraction, use an existing (inefficient) process, or subcontract the processing to a number of smaller companies once the shale has been excavated. The results from these alternatives are as follows:

Develop new process:

Outcomes	Probability	Profit ($1,000,000s)
Great success	.30	$ 600
Moderate success	.60	300
Failure	.10	−100

Use present process:

Outcomes	Probability	Profit ($1,000,000s)
Great success	.50	$ 300
Moderate success	.30	200
Failure	.20	−40

Subcontract:

Outcome	Probability	Profit ($1,000,000s)
Moderate success	1.00	250

The cost of preparing the contract proposal is $2 million. If the company does not make a bid, it will invest in an alternative venture with a guaranteed profit of $30 million. Construct a sequential decision tree for this decision situation and determine whether the company should make a bid.

42. The machine shop owner in Problem 15 is considering hiring a military consultant to ascertain whether the shop will get the government contract. The consultant is a former military officer who uses various personal contacts to find out such information. By talking to other shop owners who have hired the consultant, the owner has estimated a .70 probability that the consultant would present a favorable report, given that the contract is awarded to the shop, and a .80 probability that the consultant would present an unfavorable report, given that the contract is not awarded. Using decision tree analysis, determine the decision strategy the owner should follow, the expected value of this strategy, and the maximum fee the owner should pay the consultant.

43. The Miramar Company in Problem 18 is considering contracting with a market research firm to do a survey to determine future market conditions. The results of the survey will indicate either positive or negative market conditions. There is a .60 probability of a positive report, given favorable conditions; a .30 probability of a positive report, given stable conditions; and a .10 probability of a positive report, given unfavorable conditions. There is a .90 probability of a negative report, given unfavorable conditions; a .70 probability, given stable conditions; and a .40 probability, given favorable conditions. Using decision tree analysis *and* posterior probability tables, determine the decision strategy the company should follow, the expected value of the strategy, and the maximum amount the company should pay the market research firm for the survey results.

44. The two friends from Question 25 are still uncertain about the decision they should make. They decide to run further analysis in order to make their choice. The table in Question 15 presents the profits of each dealership, given the economic conditions.

Using the table, determine the best investment according to the following decision criteria.
a. Maximax
b. Maximin
c. Minimax regret
d. Hurwicz ($\alpha = .4$) $\alpha = 0.4$
e. Equal likelihood

45. Jeffrey Mogul is a Hollywood film producer, and he is currently evaluating a script by a new screenwriter and director, Betty Jo Thurston. Jeffrey knows that the probability of a film by a new director being a success is about .10 and that the probability it will flop is .90. The studio accounting department estimates that if this film is a hit, it will make $25 million in profit, whereas if it is a box office failure, it will lose $8 million. Jeffrey would like to hire noted film critic Dick Roper to read the script and assess its chances of success. Roper is generally able to correctly predict a successful film 70% of the time and correctly predict an unsuccessful film 80% of the time. Roper wants a fee of $1 million. Determine whether Roper should be hired, the strategy Mogul should follow if Roper is hired, and the expected value.

46. A European oil company has to decide whether to optimize its existing wells in the North Sea or to invest in the Arctic, which is rentable only with high oil prices. Choosing the North Sea will cost the company $1,000,000, with 60% chance that oil prices will rise. The expected profit is $3,000,000. If oil prices fall, the expected profit will be $200,000.

   The other decision is to explore in the Arctic for $2,000,000. There is 60% chance oil prices will go up. The company can either decide to drill for $7,000,000 or abandon the project or develop shale drilling in another location for $5,000,000 with an expected profit of $6,000,000. If the company continues in the Arctic, there is 80% chance oil prices will go up, with an expected profit of $10,000,000. If oil prices fall, the loss will be $3,000,000.

   To finish the tree, the "explore in Arctic" decision node has also a 40% chance that oil prices will fall. If they fall, the company can drill in the Arctic for $7,000,000. If prices rise (80% chance), the expected profit will be $10,000,000. If prices fall, the loss will be $3,000,000. Finally developing shale drilling somewhere else will cost $5,000,000, with a profit of $6,000,000.

   Construct a sequential decision tree with the best choice for the company.

47. Jay Seago is suing the manufacturer of his car for $3.5 million because of a defect that he believes caused him to have an accident. The accident kept him out of work for a year. The company has offered him a settlement of $700,000, of which Jay would receive $600,000 after attorneys' fees. His attorney has advised him that he has a 50% chance of winning his case. If he loses, he will incur attorneys' fees and court costs of $75,000. If he wins, he is not guaranteed his full requested settlement. His attorney believes that there is a 50% chance he could receive the full settlement, in which case Jay would realize $2 million after his attorney takes her cut, and a 50% chance that the jury will award him a lesser amount of $1 million, of which Jay would get $500,000.

   Using decision tree analysis, decide whether Jay should proceed with his lawsuit against the manufacturer.

48. Tech has three health care plans for its faculty and staff to choose from, as follows:

   Plan 1—monthly cost of $32, with a $500 deductible; the participants pay the first $500 of medical costs for the year; the insurer pays 90% of all remaining expenses.

   Plan 2—monthly cost of $5 but a deductible of $1,200, with the insurer paying 90% of medical expenses after the insurer pays the first $1,200 in a year.

   Plan 3—monthly cost of $24, with no deductible; the participants pay 30% of all expenses, with the remainder paid by the insurer.

Tracy McCoy, an administrative assistant in the management science department, estimates that her annual medical expenses are defined by the following probability distribution:

Annual Medical Expenses	Probability
$ 100	.15
500	.30
1,500	.35
3,000	.10
5,000	.05
10,000	.05

Determine which medical plan Tracy should select.

49. The Valley Wine Company purchases grapes from one of two nearby growers each season to produce a particular red wine. It purchases enough grapes to produce 3,000 bottles of the wine. Each grower supplies a certain portion of poor-quality grapes, resulting in a percentage of bottles being used as fillers for cheaper table wines, according to the following probability distribution:

	Probability of Percentage Defective	
Defective (%)	Grower A	Grower B
2	.15	.30
4	.20	.30
6	.25	.20
8	.30	.10
10	.10	.10

The two growers charge different prices for their grapes and, because of differences in taste, the company charges different prices for its wine, depending on which grapes it uses. Following is the annual profit from the wine produced from each grower's grapes for each percentage defective:

	Profit	
Defective (%)	Grower A	Grower B
2	$44,200	$42,600
4	40,200	40,300
6	36,200	38,000
8	32,200	35,700
10	28,200	33,400

Use decision tree analysis to determine from which grower the company should purchase grapes.

50. Kroft Food Products is attempting to decide whether it should introduce a new line of salad dressings called Special Choices. The company can test market the salad dressings in selected geographic areas or bypass the test market and introduce the product nationally. The cost of the test market is $150,000. If the company conducts the test market, it must wait to see the results before deciding whether to introduce the salad dressings nationally. The probability of a positive test market result is estimated to be 0.6. Alternatively, the company can decide not to conduct

the test market and go ahead and make the decision to introduce the dressings or not. If the salad dressings are introduced nationally and are a success, the company estimates that it will realize an annual profit of $1.6 million, whereas if the dressings fail, it will incur a loss of $700,000. The company believes the probability of success for the salad dressings is 0.50 if they are introduced without the test market. If the company does conduct the test market and it is positive, then the probability of successfully introducing the salad dressings increases to 0.8. If the test market is negative and the company introduces the salad dressings anyway, the probability of success drops to 0.30.

Using decision tree analysis, determine whether the company should conduct the test market.

51. In Problem 50, determine the expected value of sample information (EVSI) (i.e., the test market value) and the expected value of perfect information (EVPI).

52. Ellie Daniels has $200,000 and is considering three mutual funds for investment—a global fund, an index fund, and an Internet stock fund. During the first year of investment, Ellie estimates that there is a .70 probability that the market will go up and a .30 probability that the market will go down. Following are the returns on her $200,000 investment at the end of the year under each market condition:

Fund	Market Conditions	
	Up	Down
Global	$25,000	$ −8,000
Index	35,000	5,000
Internet	60,000	−35,000

At the end of the first year, Ellie will either reinvest the entire amount plus the return or sell and take the profit or loss. If she reinvests, she estimates that there is a .60 probability the market will go up and a .40 probability the market will go down. If Ellie reinvests in the global fund after it has gone up, her return on her initial $200,000 investment plus her $25,000 return after 1 year will be $45,000. If the market goes down, her loss will be $15,000. If she reinvests after the market has gone down, her return will be $34,000, and her loss will be $17,000. If Ellie reinvests in the index fund after the market has gone up, after 2 years her return will be $65,000 if the market continues upward, but only $5,000 if the market goes down. Her return will be $55,000 if she reinvests and the market reverses itself and goes up after initially going down, and it will be $5,000 if the market continues to go down. If Ellie invests in the Internet fund, she will make $60,000 if the market goes up, but she will lose $35,000 if it goes down. If she reinvests as the market continues upward, she will make an additional $100,000; but if the market reverses and goes down, she will lose $70,000. If she reinvests after the market has initially gone down, she will make $65,000, but if the market continues to go down, she will lose an additional $75,000.

Using decision tree analysis, determine which fund Ellie should invest in and its expected value.

53. Blue Ridge Power and Light is an electric utility company with a large fleet of vehicles, including automobiles, light trucks, and construction equipment. The company is evaluating four alternative strategies for maintaining its vehicles at the lowest cost: (1) do no preventive maintenance at all and repair vehicle components when they fail; (2) take oil samples at regular intervals and perform whatever preventive maintenance is indicated by the oil analysis; (3) change the vehicle oil on a regular basis and perform repairs when needed; (4) change the oil at regular intervals, take oil samples regularly, and perform maintenance repairs as indicated by the sample analysis.

For autos and light trucks, strategy 1 (no preventive maintenance) costs nothing to implement and results in two possible outcomes: There is a .10 probability that a defective component will occur, requiring emergency maintenance at a cost of $1,200, or there is a .90 probability that no defects will occur and no maintenance will be necessary.

Strategy 2 (take oil samples) costs $20 to implement (i.e., take a sample), and there is a .10 probability that there will be a defective part and .90 probability that there will not be a defect. If there is actually a defective part, there is a .70 probability that the sample will correctly identify it, resulting in preventive maintenance at a cost of $500. However, there is a .30 probability that the sample will not identify the defect and indicate that everything is okay, resulting in emergency maintenance later at a cost of $1,200. On the other hand, if there are actually no defects, there is a .20 probability that the sample will erroneously indicate that there is a defect, resulting in unnecessary maintenance at a cost of $250. There is an .80 probability that the sample will correctly indicate that there are no defects, resulting in no maintenance and no costs.

Strategy 3 (changing the oil regularly) costs $14.80 to implement and has two outcomes: a .04 probability of a defective component, which will require emergency maintenance at a cost of $1,200, and a .96 probability that no defects will occur, resulting in no maintenance and no cost.

Strategy 4 (changing the oil and sampling) costs $34.80 to implement and results in the same probabilities of defects and no defects as strategy 3. If there is a defective component, there is a .70 probability that the sample will detect it and $500 in preventive maintenance costs will be incurred. Alternatively, there is a .30 probability that the sample will not detect the defect, resulting in emergency maintenance at a cost of $1,200. If there is no defect, there is a .20 probability that the sample will indicate that there is a defect, resulting in an unnecessary maintenance cost of $250, and there is an .80 probability that the sample will correctly indicate no defects, resulting in no cost.

Develop a decision strategy for Blue Ridge Power and Light and indicate the expected value of this strategy.[1]

54. In Problem 53, the decision analysis is for automobiles and light trucks. Blue Ridge Power and Light would like to reformulate the problem for its heavy construction equipment. Emergency maintenance is much more expensive for heavy equipment, costing $15,000. Required preventive maintenance costs $2,000, and unnecessary maintenance costs $1,200. The cost of an oil change is $100, and the cost of taking an oil sample and analyzing it is $30. All the probabilities remain the same. Determine the strategy Blue Ridge Power and Light should use for its heavy equipment.

55. In Problem 14, the management of the Oakland Bombers is considering hiring superscout Jerry McGuire to evaluate the team's chances for the coming season. McGuire will evaluate the team, assuming that it will sign one of the four free agents. The team's management has determined the probability that the team will have a losing record with any of the free agents to be .21 by averaging the probabilities of losing for the four free agents in Problem 33. The probability that the team will have a competitive season but not make the playoffs is developed similarly, and it is .35. The probability that the team will make the playoffs is .44. The probability that McGuire will correctly predict that the team will have a losing season is .75, whereas the probability that he will predict a competitive season, given that it has a losing season, is .15, and the probability that he will incorrectly predict a playoff season, given that the team has a losing season, is .10. The probability that he will successfully predict a competitive season is .80, whereas the probability that he will incorrectly predict a losing season, given that the team is competitive, is .10, and the probability that he will incorrectly predict a playoff season, given the team has a competitive season, is .10. The probability that he will correctly predict a playoff season is .85, whereas the probability that he will incorrectly predict a losing season, given that the team

[1]This problem is based on J. Mellichamp, D. Miller, and O.-J. Kwon, "The Southern Company Uses a Probability Model for Cost Justification of Oil Sample Analysis," *Interfaces* 23, no. 3 (May–June 1993): 118–24.

makes the playoffs, is .05, and the probability that he will predict a competitive season, given the team makes the playoffs, is .10. Using decision tree analysis and posterior probabilities, determine the decision strategy the team should follow, the expected value of the strategy, and the maximum amount the team should pay for Jerry McGuire's predictions.

56. The Place-Plus real estate development firm in Problem 24 is dissatisfied with the economist's estimate of the probabilities of future interest rate movement, so it is considering having a financial consulting firm provide a report on future interest rates. The consulting firm is able to cite a track record which shows that 80% of the time when interest rates declined, it had predicted they would, whereas 10% of the time when interest rates declined, the firm had predicted they would remain stable and 10% of the time it had predicted they would increase. The firm has been correct 70% of the time when rates have remained stable, whereas 10% of the time it has incorrectly predicted that rates would decrease, and 20% of the time it has incorrectly predicted that rates would increase. The firm has correctly predicted that interest rates would increase 90% of the time and incorrectly predicted rates would decrease 2% and remain stable 8% of the time. Assuming that the consulting firm could supply an accurate report, determine how much Place-Plus should be willing to pay the consulting firm and how efficient the information will be.

57. A young couple has $5,000 to invest in either savings bonds or a real estate deal. The expected return on each investment, given good and bad economic conditions, is shown in the following payoff table:

	Economic Conditions	
	Good	Bad
Investment	.6	.4
Savings bonds	$ 1,000	$ 1,000
Real estate	10,000	−2,000

The expected value of investing in savings bonds is $1,000, and the expected value of the real estate investment is $5,200. However, the couple decides to invest in savings bonds. Explain the couple's decision in terms of the utility they might associate with each investment.

58. An entrepreneur in plastic binding has detected a drop in his factory productivity. His main machine, the binder, is old and is the main cause of the productivity decline. The machine still works, but its inconsistency forces the quality manager to reject more and more products. The decision the entrepreneur has to make is whether to invest in a new machine, repair the existing machine, or do nothing. He is worried because the market is showing signs of decline. He has estimated a 60% chance the market will rise and a 40% chance it will decline. He wants to make sure that if he makes an investment, the increase in production will be absorbed by the market. If the market rises and he invests in a new machine, his expected profit will be $500,000, but if the market falls, he will lose $300,000. If he repairs his existing machine, profit will be $300,000 if the market rises and $100,000 if it falls. Finally, if he does nothing, he will lose $200,000 if the market rises but will make $100,000 if it falls.

    Using a decision tree analysis, help the entrepreneur in his decision-making process.

59. Labran Jones has played for the Cleveland professional basketball team for the past eight seasons and has established himself as one of the top players in the league. He has recently become a free agent, meaning he can sign a new contract with Cleveland or sign a contract with any other team in the league. Cleveland has never seriously contended for a championship, and Labran is strongly considering moving to Miami, where he would have a better chance at a

championship, or to New York, which is a bigger media market and would give him more financial opportunities and endorsements. All three teams are offering Labran a 6-year contract, but because of a salary cap rule, Miami can only offer Labran $110 million, while New York is offering $120 million and Cleveland $125 million. Odds makers give Miami a 70% chance of winning the championship with Labran, while they give Cleveland a 40% chance and New York only a 10% chance. If Labran wins a championship, he will almost certainly finish his career with the team he wins it with. If that team is New York, he will sign a new contract after 6 years that with endorsements and financial deals is estimated to be worth around $500 million by the end of his career. However, if New York doesn't win a championship during his 6 years, he will either stay with New York for a career total of $200 million, or sign a new 4-year contract with a new team. If he signs with a new team, he assumes he will sign with a team good enough to give him a 50–50 chance of winning a championship but, because of his likely diminished abilities, he will have eventual earnings of only around $120 million if he wins a championship with his new team. However, if he doesn't win a championship, his eventual earnings would only be about $65 million. If he signs with Miami and Miami wins the championship, he will stay with the team and have eventual long-term earnings of $375 million, but if Miami doesn't win a championship, he will either stay with Miami for earnings of about $90 million or sign with a new team, with the same expected outcomes if he signs with a new team after playing in New York. If he re-signs with Cleveland and Cleveland wins a championship, his eventual earnings are expected to be $300 million by the end of his playing career, but if Cleveland doesn't win, he can stay with the team and expect eventual possible earnings of around $145 million or sign with a new team with the same expected outcomes if he signs with a new team after playing in New York and Miami. Using decision tree analysis, determine which team Labran should sign a new contract with and the expected value of his decision.

Case Problem

STEELEY ASSOCIATES VERSUS CONCORD FALLS

Steeley Associates, Inc., a property development firm, purchased an old house near the town square in Concord Falls, where State University is located. The old house was built in the mid-1800s, and Steeley Associates restored it. For almost a decade, Steeley has leased it to the university for academic office space. The house is located on a wide lawn and has become a town landmark.

However, in 2008, the lease with the university expired, and Steeley Associates decided to build high-density student apartments on the site, using all the open space. The community was outraged and objected to the town council. The legal counsel for the town spoke with a representative from Steeley and hinted that if Steeley requested a permit, the town would probably reject it. Steeley had reviewed the town building code and felt confident that its plan was within the guidelines, but that did not necessarily mean that it could win a lawsuit against the town to force the town to grant a permit.

The principals at Steeley Associates held a series of meetings to review their alternatives. They decided that they had three options: They could request the permit, they could sell the property, or they could request a permit for a low-density office building, which the town had indicated it would not fight. Regarding the last two options, if Steeley sells the house and property, it thinks it can get $900,000. If it builds a new office building, its return will depend on town business growth in the future. It feels that there is a 70% chance of future growth, in which case Steeley will see a return of $1.3 million (over a 10-year planning horizon); if no growth (or erosion) occurs, it will make only $200,000.

If Steeley requests a permit for the apartments, a host of good and bad outcomes are possible. The immediate good outcome is approval of its permit, which it estimates will result in a return of $3 million. However, Steeley gives that result only a 10% chance that it will occur. Alternatively, Steeley thinks there is a 90% chance that the town will reject its application, which will result in another set of decisions.

Steeley can sell the property at that point. However, the rejection of the permit will undoubtedly decrease the value to potential buyers, and Steeley estimates that it will get only $700,000. Alternatively, it can construct the office building and face the same potential outcomes it did earlier, namely, a 30% chance of no town growth and a $200,000 return or a 70% chance of growth with a return of $1.3 million. A third option is to sue the town. On the surface, Steeley's case looks good, but the town building code is vague, and a sympathetic judge could throw out its suit. Whether or not it wins, Steeley estimates its possible legal fees to be $300,000, and it feels it has only a 40% chance of winning. However, if Steeley does win, it estimates that the award will be approximately $1 million, and it will also get its $3 million return for building the apartments. Steeley also estimates that there is a 10% chance that the suit could linger on in the courts for such a long time that any future return would be negated during its planning horizon, and it would incur an additional $200,000 in legal fees.

If Steeley loses the suit, it will then be faced with the same options of selling the property or constructing an office building. However, if the suit is carried this far into the future, it feels that the selling price it can ask will be somewhat dependent on the town's growth prospects at that time, which it feels it can estimate at only 50–50. If the town is in a growth mode that far in the future, Steeley thinks that $900,000 is a conservative estimate of the potential sale price, whereas if the town is not growing, it thinks $500,000 is a more likely estimate. Finally, if Steeley constructs the office building, it feels that the chance of town growth is 50%, in which case the return will be only $1.2 million. If no growth occurs, it conservatively estimates only a $100,000 return.

A. Perform a decision tree analysis of Steeley Associates's decision situation, using expected value, and indicate the appropriate decision with these criteria.
B. Indicate the decision you would make and explain your reasons.

Case Problem

Salvaging Wrecks in Subic bay, Philippines

Subic Bay, near Manila, Philippines, was the largest American facility in the Pacific before being shut down in 1991. Reminiscent of the Spanish period in the nineteen century, it is an area of outstanding beauty, and after its closure for military purposes, it has been popular among scuba divers, especially for wreck diving.

One day, a group of dive shops in Subic Bay decide to evaluate the possibility of salvaging one of the deep wrecks (a recent one and therefore still in good condition) and bringing it to shallow water to use as a training vessel for scuba diving students. However, to do this, they have to get permission from the national and local authorities and this decision is likely to be informed by the value of the wreck.

The dive shops have done some preliminary enquiries and have been informally told that if the chosen wreck is evaluated at a substantial value, the authorization would be withheld, whereas if the value is low, authorization would be granted.

However, in order for an evaluation to be done in the first place, they have been asked to submit a bid. If the bid is too low, no evaluation mechanism will be set up, because it will be considered not worth the hassle. The dive shops have an alternative, which would be to sink a boat, but they have calculated the price of buying a boat with the desired characteristics and sinking it to be around $15,000.

The shops know they could get an evaluation for $10,000, but this might lead the authorities to consider the wreck important and not give the authorization. With less than $3,000, they will most likely not get the evaluation in the first place.

Based on this scenario, draw a decision tree for the dive shops' available choices.

Sources: Subic Bay Metropolitan Authority website, accessed on October 1, 2011 at http://www.sbma.com/; D. Bell, D. (1984), "Bidding for the SS Kuniang," *Interface* 14 (1984): 17–23; R. T. Clemen, and T. Reilly, *Making Hard Decision* (Mason, OH: South-Western Cengage Edition, 2001).

Case Problem

THE CAROLINA COUGARS

The Carolina Cougars is a major league baseball expansion team beginning its third year of operation. The team had losing records in each of its first 2 years and finished near the bottom of its division. However, the team was young and generally competitive. The team's general manager, Frank Lane, and manager, Biff Diamond, believe that with a few additional good players, the Cougars can become a contender for the division title and perhaps even for the pennant. They have prepared several proposals for free-agent acquisitions to present to the team's owner, Bruce Wayne.

Under one proposal the team would sign several good available free agents, including two pitchers, a good fielding shortstop, and two power-hitting outfielders for $52 million in bonuses and annual salary. The second proposal is less ambitious, costing $20 million to sign a relief pitcher, a solid, good-hitting infielder, and one power-hitting outfielder. The final proposal would be to stand pat with the current team and continue to develop.

General Manager Lane wants to lay out a possible season scenario for the owner so he can assess the long-run ramifications of each decision strategy. Because the only thing the owner understands is money, Frank wants this analysis to be quantitative, indicating the money to be made or lost from each strategy. To help develop this analysis, Frank has hired his kids, Penny and Nathan, both management science graduates from Tech.

Penny and Nathan analyzed league data for the previous five seasons for attendance trends, logo sales (i.e., clothing, souvenirs, hats, etc.), player sales and trades, and revenues. In addition, they interviewed several other owners, general managers, and league officials. They also analyzed the free agents that the team was considering signing.

Based on their analysis, Penny and Nathan feel that if the Cougars do not invest in any free agents, the team will have a 25% chance of contending for the division title and a 75% chance of being out of contention most of the season. If the team is a contender, there is a .70 probability that attendance will increase as the season progresses and the team will have high attendance levels (between 1.5 million

and 2.0 million) with profits of $170 million from ticket sales, concessions, advertising sales, TV and radio sales, and logo sales. They estimate a .25 probability that the team's attendance will be mediocre (between 1.0 million and 1.5 million) with profits of $115 million and a .05 probability that the team will suffer low attendance (less than 1.0 million) with profit of $90 million. If the team is not a contender, Penny and Nathan estimate that there is .05 probability of high attendance with profits of $95 million, a .20 probability of medium attendance with profits of $55 million, and a .75 probability of low attendance with profits of $30 million.

If the team marginally invests in free agents at a cost of $20 million, there is a 50–50 chance it will be a contender. If it is a contender, then later in the season it can either stand pat with its existing roster or buy or trade for players that could improve the team's chances of winning the division. If the team stands pat, there is a .75 probability that attendance will be high and profits will be $195 million. There is a .20 probability that attendance will be mediocre with profits of $160 million and a .05 probability of low attendance and profits of $120 million. Alternatively, if the team decides to buy or trade for players, it will cost $8 million, and the probability of high attendance with profits of $200 million will be .80. The probability of mediocre attendance with $170 million in profits will be .15, and there will be a .05 probability of low attendance, with profits of $125 million.

If the team is not in contention, then it will either stand pat or sell some of its players, earning approximately $8 million in profit. If the team stands pat, there is a .12 probability of high attendance, with profits of $110 million; a .28 probability of mediocre attendance, with profits of $65 million; and a .60 probability of low attendance, with profits of $40 million. If the team sells players, the fans will likely lose interest at an even faster rate, and the probability of high attendance with profits of $100 million will drop to .08, the probability of mediocre attendance with profits of $60 million will be .22, and the probability of low attendance with profits of $35 million will be .70.

The most ambitious free-agent strategy will increase the team's chances of being a contender to 65%. This strategy will also excite the fans most during the off-season and boost ticket sales and advertising and logo sales early in the year. If the team does contend for the division title, then later in the season it will have to decide whether to invest in more players. If the Cougars stand pat, the probability of high attendance with profits of $210 million will be .80, the probability of mediocre attendance with profits of $170 million will be .15, and the probability of low attendance with profits of $125 million will be .05. If the team buys players at a cost of $10 million, then the probability of having high attendance with profits of $220 million will increase to .83, the probability of mediocre attendance with profits of $175 million will be .12, and the probability of low attendance with profits of $130 million will be .05.

If the team is not in contention, it will either sell some players' contracts later in the season for profits of around $12 million or stand pat. If it stays with its roster, the probability of high attendance with profits of $110 million will be .15, the probability of mediocre attendance with profits of $70 million will be .30, and the probability of low attendance with profits of $50 million will be .55. If the team sells players late in the season, there will be a .10 probability of high attendance with profits of $105 million, a .30 probability of mediocre attendance with profits of $65 million, and a .60 probability of low attendance with profits of $45 million.

Assist Penny and Nathan in determining the best strategy to follow and its expected value.

Case Problem

EVALUATING R&D PROJECTS AT WESTCOM SYSTEMS PRODUCTS COMPANY

WestCom Systems Products Company develops computer systems and software products for commercial sale. Each year it considers and evaluates a number of different R&D projects to undertake. It develops a road map for each project, in the form of a standardized decision tree that identifies the different decision points in the R&D process from the initial decision to invest in a project's development through the actual commercialization of the final product.

The first decision point in the R&D process is whether to fund a proposed project for 1 year. If the decision is no, then there is no resulting cost; if the decision is yes, then the project proceeds at an incremental cost to the company. The company establishes specific short-term, early technical milestones for its projects after 1 year. If the early milestones are achieved, the project proceeds to the next phase of project development; if the milestones are not achieved, the project is abandoned. In its planning process, the company develops probability estimates of achieving and not achieving the early milestones. If the early milestones are achieved, the project is funded for further development during an extended time frame specific to a project. At the

end of this time frame, a project is evaluated according to a second set of (later) technical milestones. Again, the company attaches probability estimates for achieving and not achieving these later milestones. If the later milestones are not achieved, the project is abandoned.

If the later milestones are achieved, technical uncertainties and problems have been overcome, and the company next assesses the project's ability to meet its strategic business objectives. At this stage, the company wants to know if the eventual product coincides with the company's competencies and whether there appears to be an eventual, clear market for the product. It invests in a product "prelaunch" to ascertain the answers to these questions. The outcomes of the prelaunch are that either there is a strategic fit or there is not, and the company assigns probability estimates to each of these two possible outcomes. If there is not a strategic fit at this point, the project is abandoned and the company loses its investment in the prelaunch process. If it is determined that there is a strategic fit, then three possible decisions result: (1) The company can invest in the product's launch, and a successful or unsuccessful outcome will result, each with an estimated probability of occurrence; (2) the company can delay the product's launch and at a later date decide whether to launch or abandon; and (3) if it launches later, the outcomes are success or failure, each with an estimated probability of occurrence.

Also, if the product launch is delayed, there is always a likelihood that the technology will become obsolete or dated in the near future, which tends to reduce the expected return.

The following table provides the various costs, event probabilities, and investment outcomes for five projects the company is considering:

Decision Outcomes/Event	Project				
	1	2	3	4	5
Fund—1 year	$ 200,000	$ 350,000	$ 170,000	$ 230,000	$ 400,000
P(Early milestones—yes)	.70	.67	.82	.60	.75
P(Early milestones—no)	.30	.33	.18	.40	.25
Long-term funding	$ 650,000	780,000	450,000	300,000	450,000
P(Late milestones—yes)	.60	.56	.65	.70	.72
P(Late milestones—no)	.40	.44	.35	.30	.28
Prelaunch funding	$ 300,000	450,000	400,000	500,000	270,000
P(Strategic fit—yes)	.80	.75	.83	.67	.65
P(Strategic fit—no)	.20	.25	.17	.33	.35
P(Invest—success)	.60	.65	.70	.75	.80
P(Invest—failure)	.40	.35	.30	.25	.20
P(Delay—success)	.80	.70	.65	.80	.85
P(Delay—failure)	.20	.30	.35	.20	.15
Invest—success	$ 7,300,000	8,000,000	4,500,000	5,200,000	3,800,000
Invest—failure	−2,000,000	−3,500,000	−1,500,000	−2,100,000	−900,000
Delay—success	4,500,000	6,000,000	3,300,000	2,500,000	2,700,000
Delay—failure	−1,300,000	−4,000,000	−800,000	−1,100,000	−900,000

Determine the expected value for each project and then rank the projects accordingly for the company to consider.

This case is based on R. K. Perdue, W. J. McAllister, P. V. King, and B. G. Berkey, "Valuation of R and D Projects Using Options Pricing and Decision Analysis Models," *Interfaces* 29, no. 6 (November–December 1999): 57–74.

Inventory Models

Inventory analysis is one of the most popular topics in management science. One reason is that almost all types of business organizations have inventory. Although we tend to think of inventory only in terms of stock on a store shelf, it can take on a variety of forms, such as partially finished products at different stages of a manufacturing process, raw materials, resources, labor, or cash. In addition, the purpose of inventory is not always simply to meet customer demand. For example, companies frequently stock large inventories of raw materials as a hedge against strikes. Whatever form inventory takes or whatever its purpose, it often represents a significant cost to a business firm. It is estimated that the average annual cost of manufactured goods inventory in the United States is approximately 30% of the total value of the inventory. Thus, if a company has $10.0 million worth of products in inventory, the cost of holding the inventory (including insurance, obsolescence, depreciation, interest, opportunity costs, storage costs, etc.) would be approximately $3.0 million. If the amount of inventory could be reduced by half to $5.0 million, then $1.5 million would be saved in inventory costs, a significant cost reduction.

In this chapter we describe the classic economic order quantity models, which represent the most basic and fundamental form of inventory analysis. These models provide a means for determining how much to order (the order quantity) and when to place an order so that inventory-related costs are minimized. The underlying assumption of these models is that demand is known with certainty and is constant. In addition, we will describe models for determining the order size and reorder points (when to place an order) when demand is uncertain.

Elements of Inventory Management

Inventory is a stock of items kept on hand to meet demand.

Inventory is defined as a stock of items kept on hand by an organization to use to meet customer demand. Virtually every type of organization maintains some form of inventory. A department store carries inventories of all the retail items it sells; a nursery has inventories of different plants, trees, and flowers; a rental car agency has inventories of cars; and a major league baseball team maintains an inventory of players on its minor league teams. Even a family household will maintain inventories of food, clothing, medical supplies, personal hygiene products, and so on.

The Role of Inventory

A company or an organization keeps stocks of inventory for a variety of important reasons. The most prominent is holding finished goods inventories to meet customer demand for a product, especially in a retail operation. However, customer demand can also be in the form of a secretary going to a storage closet to get a printer cartridge or paper, or a carpenter getting a board or nail from a storage shed. A level of inventory is normally maintained that will meet anticipated or expected customer demand. However, because demand is usually not known with certainty, additional amounts of inventory, called safety, or *buffer*, stocks, are often kept on hand to meet unexpected variations in excess of expected demand.

Safety stocks are additional inventory to compensate for demand uncertainty.

Additional stocks of inventories are sometimes built up to meet seasonal or cyclical demand. Companies will produce items when demand is low to meet high seasonal demand for which their production capacity is insufficient. For example, toy manufacturers produce large inventories during the summer and fall to meet anticipated demand during the Christmas season. Doing so enables them to maintain a relatively smooth production flow throughout the year. They would not normally have the production capacity or logistical support to produce enough to meet all of the Christmas demand during that season. Correspondingly, retailers might find it necessary to keep large stocks of inventory on their shelves to meet peak seasonal demand, such as at Christmas, or for display purposes to attract buyers.

A company will often purchase large amounts of inventory to take advantage of price discounts, as a hedge against anticipated future price increases, or because it can get a lower price by purchasing in volume. For example, Walmart has long been known to purchase an entire manufacturer's stock of soap powder or other retail items because it can get a very low price, which it subsequently passes on to its customers. Companies will often purchase large stocks of items when a supplier liquidates to get a low price. In some cases, large orders will be made simply because the cost of an order may be very high, and it is more cost-effective to have higher inventories than to make a lot of orders.

Many companies find it necessary to maintain in-process inventories at different stages in a manufacturing process to provide independence between operations and to avoid work stoppages or delays. Inventories of raw materials and purchased parts are kept on hand so that the production process will not be delayed as a result of missed or late deliveries or shortages from a supplier. Work-in-process inventories are kept between stages in the manufacturing process so that production can continue smoothly if there are temporary machine breakdowns or other work stoppages. Similarly, a stock of finished parts or products allows customer demand to be met in the event of a work stoppage or problem with the production process.

Demand

A crucial component and the basic starting point for the management of inventory is customer demand. Inventory exists for the purpose of meeting the demand of customers. Customers can be inside the organization, such as a machine operator waiting for a part or a partially completed product to work on, or outside the organization, such as an individual purchasing groceries or a new stereo. As such, an essential determinant of effective inventory management is an accurate forecast of demand. For this reason the topics of forecasting (Chapter 15) and inventory management are directly interrelated.

Dependent demand items are used internally to produce a final product.

In general, the demand for items in inventory is classified as dependent or independent. Dependent demand items are typically component parts, or materials, used in the process of producing a final product. For example, if an automobile company plans to produce 1,000 new cars, it will need 5,000 wheels and tires (including spares). In this case the demand for wheels is dependent on the production of cars; that is, the demand for one item is a function of demand for another item.

Independent demand items are final products demanded by an external customer.

Alternatively, cars are an example of an independent demand item. In general, independent demand items are final or finished products that are not a function of, or dependent upon, internal production activity. Independent demand is usually external, and, thus, beyond the direct control of the organization. In this chapter we will focus on the management of inventory for independent demand items.

Inventory Costs

Inventory costs include carrying, ordering, and shortage costs.

There are three basic costs associated with inventory: carrying (or holding) costs, ordering costs, and shortage costs. Carrying costs are the costs of holding items in storage. These vary with the level of inventory and occasionally with the length of time an item is held; that is, the greater the level of inventory over time, the higher the carrying cost(s). Carrying costs can include the cost of losing the use of funds tied up in inventory; direct storage costs, such as rent, heating, cooling, lighting, security, refrigeration, record keeping, and logistics; interest on loans used to purchase inventory; depreciation; obsolescence as markets for products in inventory diminish; product deterioration and spoilage; breakage; taxes; and pilferage.

Carrying costs are the costs of holding inventory in storage.

Carrying costs are normally specified in one of two ways. The most general form is to assign total carrying costs, determined by summing all the individual costs mentioned previously, on a per-unit basis per time period, such as a month or a year. In this form, carrying costs would commonly be expressed as a per-unit dollar amount on an annual basis (for example, $10 per year). Alternatively, carrying costs are sometimes expressed as a percentage of the value of an item or as a percentage of average inventory value. It is generally estimated that carrying costs range from 10% to 40% of the value of a manufactured item.

Ordering costs are the cost of replenishing inventory.

Ordering costs are the costs associated with replenishing the stock of inventory being held. These are normally expressed as a dollar amount per order and are independent of the order size. Thus, ordering costs vary with the number of orders made (i.e., as the number of

Management Science Application

Evaluating Inventory Costs at Hewlett-Packard

Hewlett-Packard, with annual revenues exceeding $90 billion and 150,000 employees worldwide, is the *Fortune 500* 11th-ranked company. Although demand for PCs increased by five-fold in the 1990s, becoming a veritable household product, many PC companies struggled to remain profitable. By the end of the 1990s HP was struggling to make a profit in the increasingly competitive global PC market because of price cuts throughout the decade. Because prices were not really controllable, inventory costs became especially critical in the PC profit equation. Rapid technological advancements render new PC products obsolete in a few months, and, in general, it's believed that the value of a PC decreases at the rate of 1% per week. Consequently, holding any excess inventory is very costly.

HANDOUT/Newscom

In the late 1990s, to return its PC business to more sustainable profitability, HP undertook an extensive evaluation of its inventory costs. It discovered that inventory-related costs were the main determinants of overall PC cost, and, in fact, in 1 year alone inventory-related costs equaled the PC business's total operating margin. Further, HP determined that the traditional inventory carrying (or holding) costs (which encompass capital costs plus storage, taxes, insurance, breakage, etc.) accounted for less than 10% of the total inventory-related costs. HP identified four additional inventory costs in their PC business that were a major factor in overall supply chain costs. The single biggest inventory cost was determined to be the "component devaluation cost." This is the penalty cost HP incurred when the price dropped for excess components and parts (for example, CPUs, memory, and chips) being held in inventory. HP held inventories of parts and components in factories, in distribution centers, and in transit and incurred a devaluation cost at all these points in its supply chain whenever a price reduction occurred. Another inventory cost is the "price protection cost," which occurs when the retail price of a product drops after it has already been shipped to the sales outlet. HP had to reimburse its sales partners for the difference in price for any unsold units so its partners wouldn't incur a loss. Given how fast PC products lose their value, excess inventory can result in large protection costs. A third inventory-related cost in the PC business is the "product return cost." This is the cost of a full refund HP paid its distributors when unsold products were returned; essentially it is a 100% price protection cost.

In some cases sales partners and distributors returned excess unsold inventory valued at more than 10% of a product's revenue. The fourth inventory cost is "obsolescence cost," which is the cost of writing-off unsold products in inventory after the life of the product ends. Because PC products' life cycles are so short, there is the potential for large costs if excessive inventories are held. Related costs include price discounts for products that are about to be discontinued and the marketing costs to quickly reduce inventory. The Mobile Computing Division (which manufactures notebooks) was the first HP PC business unit to focus on all these inventory-related costs in redesigning its supply chain. The original supply chain consisted of a central manufacturing facility with local product configuration occurring at regional sites. (In this configuration about 40% of the total supply chain cost was related to inventory.) In the redesigned supply chain there is a central manufacturing facility, and products are air freighted directly to customers around the world. Positive results were immediate; in a 2-year period inventory-related costs dropped from almost 19% of total revenue to less than 4%, and the notebook division became profitable. As a result, all other HP PC operations began using these inventory costs to evaluate and redesign their supply chains.

Source: Based on "Inventory Driven Costs," by G. Callioni, X. de Montgros, R. Slagmulder, L. N. Van Wassenove, and L. Wright. *Harvard Business Review*, March 2005.

orders increases, the ordering cost increases). Costs incurred each time an order is made can include requisition costs, purchase orders, transportation and shipping, receiving, inspection, handling and placing in storage, and accounting and auditing.

Ordering costs generally react inversely to carrying costs. As the size of orders increases, fewer orders are required, thus reducing annual ordering costs. However, ordering larger amounts results in higher inventory levels and higher carrying costs. In general, as the order size increases, annual ordering costs decrease and annual carrying costs increase.

Shortage costs, also referred to as *stockout costs*, occur when customer demand cannot be met because of insufficient inventory on hand. If these shortages result in a permanent loss of sales for items demanded but not provided, shortage costs include the loss of profits. Shortages can also cause customer dissatisfaction and a loss of goodwill that can result in a permanent loss of customers and future sales. In some instances the inability to meet customer demand or lateness in meeting demand results in specified penalties in the form of price discounts or rebates. When demand is internal, a shortage can cause work stoppages in the production process and create delays, resulting in downtime costs and the cost of lost production (including indirect and direct production costs).

Costs resulting from immediate or future lost sales because demand could not be met are more difficult to determine than carrying or ordering costs. As a result, shortage costs are frequently subjective estimates and many times no more than educated guesses.

Shortages occur because it is costly to carry inventory in stock. As a result, shortage costs have an inverse relationship to carrying costs; as the amount of inventory on hand increases, the carrying cost increases, while shortage costs decrease.

The objective of **inventory management** is to employ an inventory control system that will indicate how much should be ordered and when orders should take place to minimize the sum of the three inventory costs described here.

Shortage costs are incurred when customer demand cannot be met.

The purpose of inventory management is to determine how much and when to order.

Inventory Control Systems

An inventory system is a structure for controlling the level of inventory by determining how much to order (the level of replenishment) and when to order. There are two basic types of inventory systems: a *continuous* (or *fixed–order quantity*) *system* and a *periodic* (or *fixed–time period*) *system*. The primary difference between the two systems is that in a continuous system, an order is placed for the same constant amount whenever the inventory on hand decreases to a certain level, whereas in a periodic system, an order is placed for a variable amount after an established passage of time.

Continuous Inventory Systems

In a continuous inventory system, a constant amount is ordered when inventory declines to a predetermined level.

In a *continuous inventory system*, alternatively referred to as a *perpetual system* or a *fixed–order quantity system*, a continual record of the inventory level for every item is maintained. Whenever the inventory on hand decreases to a predetermined level, referred to as the *reorder point*, a new order is placed to replenish the stock of inventory. The order that is placed is for a "fixed" amount that minimizes the total inventory carrying, ordering, and shortage costs. This fixed order quantity is called the *economic order quantity*; its determination will be discussed in greater detail in a later section.

A positive feature of a continuous system is that the inventory level is closely and continuously monitored so that management always knows the inventory status. This is especially advantageous for critical inventory items such as replacement parts or raw materials and supplies. However, the cost of maintaining a continual record of the amount of inventory on hand can also be a disadvantage of this type of system.

A simple example of a continuous inventory system is a ledger-style checkbook that many of us use on a daily basis. Our checkbook comes with 300 checks; after the 200th check has been used (and there are 100 left), there is an order form for a new batch of checks that has been inserted by the printer. This form, when turned in at the bank, initiates an order for a new batch of 300 checks from the printer. Many office inventory systems use "reorder" cards that are placed within stacks of stationery or at the bottom of a case of pens or paper clips to signal when a new order should be placed. If you look behind the items on a hanging rack in a Kmart store, you will see a card indicating that it is time to place an order for this item, for an amount indicated on the card.

A more sophisticated example of a continuous inventory system is a computerized checkout system with a laser scanner, used by many supermarkets and retail stores. In this system a laser scanner reads the Universal Product Code (UPC), or bar code, off the product package, and the transaction is instantly recorded and the inventory level updated. Such a system is not only quick and accurate, but it also provides management with continuously updated information on the status of inventory levels. Although not as publicly visible as supermarket systems, many manufacturing companies, suppliers, and distributors also use bar code systems and handheld laser scanners to inventory materials, supplies, equipment, in-process parts, and finished goods.

Because continuous inventory systems are much more common than periodic systems, models that determine fixed order quantities and the time to order will receive most of our attention in this chapter.

Periodic Inventory Systems

In a periodic inventory system, an order is placed for a variable amount after a fixed passage of time.

In a periodic inventory system, also referred to as a *fixed–time period system* or *periodic review system*, the inventory on hand is counted at specific time intervals—for example, every week or at the end of each month. After the amount of inventory in stock is determined, an order is placed for an amount that will bring inventory back up to a desired level. In this system the inventory level is not monitored at all during the time interval between orders, so it has the advantage of requiring little or no record keeping. However, it has the disadvantage of less direct control. This typically results in larger inventory levels for a periodic inventory system than in a continuous system, to guard against unexpected stockouts early in the fixed period. Such a system also requires that a new order quantity be determined each time a periodic order is made.

Periodic inventory systems are often found at a college or university bookstore. Textbooks are normally ordered according to a periodic system, wherein a count of textbooks in stock (for every course) is made after the first few weeks or month during the semester or quarter. An order for new textbooks for the next semester is then made according to estimated course enrollments for the next term (i.e., demand) and the number remaining in stock. Smaller retail stores, drugstores, grocery stores, and offices often use periodic systems; the stock level is checked every week or month, often by a vendor, to see how much (if anything) should be ordered.

Economic Order Quantity Models

You will recall that in a continuous or fixed–order quantity system, when inventory reaches a specific level, referred to as the *reorder point*, a fixed amount is ordered. The most widely used and traditional means for determining how much to order in a continuous system is the economic order quantity (EOQ) model, also referred to as the economic lot size model.

EOQ is a continuous inventory system.

The function of the EOQ model is to determine the optimal order size that minimizes total inventory costs. There are several variations of the EOQ model, depending on the assumptions made about the inventory system. In this and following sections we will describe three model versions: the basic EOQ model, the EOQ model with noninstantaneous receipt, and the EOQ model with shortages.

The Basic EOQ Model

The simplest form of the economic order quantity model on which all other model versions are based is called the basic EOQ model. It is essentially a single formula for determining the optimal order size that minimizes the sum of carrying costs and ordering costs. The model formula is derived under a set of simplifying and restrictive assumptions, as follows:

- Demand is known with certainty and is relatively constant over time.
- No shortages are allowed.
- Lead time for the receipt of orders is constant.
- The order quantity is received all at once.

The graph in Figure 16.1 reflects these basic model assumptions.

FIGURE 16.1

The inventory order cycle

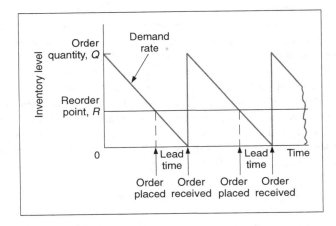

Figure 16.1 describes the continuous inventory order cycle system inherent in the EOQ model. An order quantity, Q, is received and is used up over time at a constant rate. When the inventory level decreases to the reorder point, R, a new order is placed, and a period of time, referred to as the *lead time*, is required for delivery. The order is received all at once, just at the moment when demand depletes the entire stock of inventory (and the inventory level reaches zero), thus allowing no shortages. This cycle is continuously repeated for the same order quantity, reorder point, and lead time.

As we mentioned earlier, Q is the order size that minimizes the sum of carrying costs and holding costs. These two costs react inversely to each other in response to an increase in the order size. As the order size increases, fewer orders are required, causing the ordering cost to decline, whereas the average amount of inventory on hand increases, resulting in an increase in carrying costs. Thus, in effect, the optimal order quantity represents a compromise between these two conflicting costs.

Carrying Cost

Carrying cost is usually expressed on a per-unit basis for some period of time (although it is sometimes given as a percentage of average inventory). Traditionally, the carrying cost is referred to on an annual basis (i.e., per year).

The total carrying cost is determined by the amount of inventory on hand during the year. The amount of inventory available during the year is illustrated in Figure 16.2.

In Figure 16.2, Q represents the size of the order needed to replenish inventory, which is what a manager wants to determine. The line connecting Q to time, t, in our graph represents the rate at which inventory is depleted, or *demand*, during the time period, t. Demand is assumed to be *known with certainty* and is thus constant, which explains why the line representing demand

FIGURE 16.2
Inventory usage

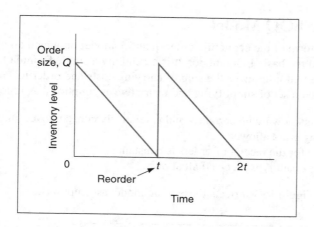

is straight. Also, notice that inventory never goes below zero; shortages do not exist. In addition, when the inventory level does reach zero, it is assumed that an order arrives immediately after an infinitely small passage of time, a condition referred to as **instantaneous receipt**. This is a simplifying assumption that we will maintain for the moment.

Referring to Figure 16.2, we can see that the amount of inventory is Q, the size of the order, for an infinitely small period of time because Q is always being depleted by demand. Similarly, the amount of inventory is zero for an infinitely small period of time because the only time there is no inventory is at the specific time t. Thus, the amount of inventory available is somewhere between these two extremes. A logical deduction is that the amount of inventory available is the *average inventory* level, defined as

$$\text{average inventory} = \frac{Q}{2}$$

To verify this relationship, we can specify any number of points—values of Q—over the entire time period, t, and divide by the number of points. For example, if $Q = 5,000$, the six points designated from 5,000 to 0, as shown in Figure 16.3, are summed and divided by 6:

$$\text{average inventory} = \frac{5,000 + 4,000 + 3,000 + 2,000 + 1,000 + 0}{6}$$

$$= 2,500$$

FIGURE 16.3
Levels of Q

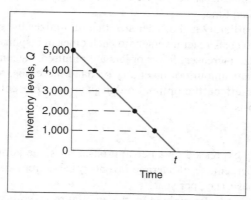

Alternatively, we can sum just the two extreme points (which also encompass the range of time, t) and divide by 2. This also equals 2,500. This computation is the same, in principle, as adding Q and 0 and dividing by 2, which equals $Q/2$. This relationship for average inventory is maintained, regardless of the size of the order, Q, or the frequency of orders (i.e., the time period, t). Thus, the average inventory on an *annual basis* is also $Q/2$, as shown in Figure 16.4.

FIGURE 16.4

Annual average inventory

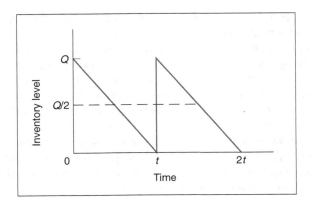

Now that we know that the amount of inventory available *on an annual basis* is the average inventory, $Q/2$, we can determine the total annual carrying cost by multiplying the average number of units in inventory by the carrying cost per unit per year, C_c:

$$\text{annual carrying cost} = C_c \frac{Q}{2}$$

Ordering Cost

The total annual ordering cost is computed by multiplying the cost per order, designated as C_o, by the number of orders per year. Because annual demand is assumed to be known and constant, the number of orders will be D/Q, where Q is the order size:

$$\text{annual ordering cost} = C_o \frac{D}{Q}$$

The only variable in this equation is Q; both C_o and D are constant parameters. In other words, demand is known with certainty. Thus, the relative magnitude of the ordering cost is dependent upon the order size.

Total Inventory Cost

The total annual inventory cost is simply the sum of the ordering and carrying costs:

$$TC = C_o \frac{D}{Q} + C_c \frac{Q}{2}$$

These cost functions are shown in Figure 16.5. Notice the inverse relationship between ordering cost and carrying cost, resulting in a convex total cost curve.

FIGURE 16.5

The EOQ cost model

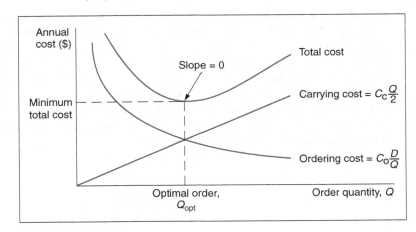

Observe the general upward trend of the total carrying cost curve. As the order size Q (shown on the horizontal axis) increases, the total carrying cost (shown on the vertical axis) increases. This is logical because larger orders will result in more units carried in inventory. Next, observe the ordering cost curve in Figure 16.5. As the order size, Q, increases, the ordering cost *decreases* (just the opposite of what occurred with the carrying cost). This is logical, because an increase in the size of the orders will result in fewer orders being placed each year. Because one cost increases as the other decreases, the result of summing the two costs is a convex total cost curve.

The optimal value of Q corresponds to the lowest point on the total cost curve.

The optimal order quantity occurs at the point in Figure 16.5 where the total cost curve is at a minimum, which also coincides exactly with the point where the ordering cost curve intersects with the carrying cost curve. This enables us to determine the optimal value of Q by equating the two cost functions and solving for Q, as follows:

$$C_o \frac{D}{Q} = C_c \frac{Q}{2}$$

$$Q^2 = \frac{2 C_o D}{C_c}$$

$$Q_{opt} = \sqrt{\frac{2 C_o D}{C_c}}$$

Alternatively, the optimal value of Q can be determined by differentiating the total cost curve with respect to Q, setting the resulting function equal to zero (the slope at the minimum point on the total cost curve), and solving for Q, as follows:

$$TC = C_o \frac{D}{Q} + C_c \frac{Q}{2}$$

$$\frac{\delta TC}{\delta Q} = -\frac{C_o D}{Q^2} + \frac{C_c}{2}$$

$$0 = -\frac{C_o D}{Q^2} + \frac{C_c}{2}$$

$$Q_{opt} = \sqrt{\frac{2 C_o D}{C_c}}$$

The total minimum cost is determined by substituting the value for the optimal order size, Q_{opt}, into the total cost equation:

$$TC_{min} = C_o \frac{D}{Q_{opt}} + C_o \frac{Q_{opt}}{2}$$

We will use the following example to demonstrate how the optimal value of Q is computed. The I-75 Carpet Discount Store in north Georgia stocks carpet in its warehouse and sells it through an adjoining showroom. The store keeps several brands and styles of carpet in stock; however, its biggest seller is Super Shag carpet. The store wants to determine the optimal order size and total inventory cost for this brand of carpet, given an estimated annual demand of 10,000 yards of carpet, an annual carrying cost of $0.75 per yard, and an ordering cost of $150. The store would also like to know the number of orders that will be made annually and the time between orders (i.e., the order cycle), given that the store is open every day except Sunday, Thanksgiving Day, and Christmas Day (that is not on a Sunday).

We can summarize the model parameters as follows:

$$C_c = \$0.75$$
$$C_o = \$150$$
$$D = 10,000 \text{ yd.}$$

The optimal order size is computed as follows:

$$Q_{opt} = \sqrt{\frac{2C_oD}{C_c}}$$

$$= \sqrt{\frac{2(150)(10,000)}{(0.75)}}$$

$$Q_{opt} = 2,000 \text{ yd.}$$

The total annual inventory cost is determined by substituting Q_{opt} into the total cost formula, as follows:

$$TC_{min} = C_o\frac{D}{Q_{opt}} + C_c\frac{Q_{opt}}{2}$$

$$= (150)\frac{10,000}{2,000} + (0.75)\frac{(2,000)}{2}$$

$$= \$750 + 750$$

$$TC_{min} = \$1,500$$

The number of orders per year is computed as follows:

$$\text{number of orders per year} = \frac{D}{Q_{opt}} = \frac{10,000}{2,000} = 5$$

Given that the store is open 311 days annually (365 days minus 52 Sundays, plus Thanksgiving and Christmas), the order cycle is determined as follows:

$$\text{order cycle time} = \frac{311 \text{ days}}{D/Q_{opt}} = \frac{311}{5} = 62.2 \text{ store days}$$

The EOQ model is robust; because Q is a square root, errors in the estimation of D, C_c, and C_o are dampened.

It should be noted that the optimal order quantity determined in this example, and in general, is an approximate value because it is based on estimates of carrying and ordering costs as well as uncertain demand (although all these parameters are treated as known, certain values in the EOQ model). Thus, in practice it is acceptable to round off the Q values to the nearest whole number. The precision of a decimal place generally is neither necessary nor appropriate. In addition, because the optimal order quantity is computed from a square root, errors or variations in the cost parameters and demand tend to be dampened. For instance, if the order cost had actually been a third higher, or $200, the resulting optimal order size would have varied by about 15% (i.e., 2,390 yards instead of 2,000 yards). In addition, variations in both inventory costs will tend to offset each other because they have an inverse relationship. As a result, the EOQ model is relatively robust, or resilient to errors in the cost estimates and demand, which has tended to enhance its popularity.

EOQ Analysis Over Time

One aspect of inventory analysis that can be confusing is the time frame encompassed by the analysis. Therefore, we will digress for just a moment to discuss this aspect of EOQ analysis.

Recall that previously we developed the EOQ model "regardless of order size, Q, and time, t." Now we will verify this condition. We will do so by developing our EOQ model on a *monthly basis*. First, demand is equal to 833.3 yards per month (which we determined by dividing the annual demand of 10,000 yards by 12 months). Next, by dividing the annual carrying cost, C_c, of $0.75 by 12, we get the monthly (per-unit) carrying cost: $C_c = \$0.0625$. (The ordering cost of $150 is not related to time.) We thus have the values

$$D = 833.3 \text{ yd. per month}$$

$$C_c = \$0.0625 \text{ per yd. per month}$$

$$C_o = \$150 \text{ per order}$$

which we can substitute into our EOQ formula:

$$Q_{\text{opt}} = \sqrt{\frac{2C_o D}{C_c}}$$

$$= \sqrt{\frac{2(150)(833.3)}{(0.0625)}} = 2,000 \text{ yd.}$$

This is the same optimal order size that we determined on an annual basis. Now we will compute total monthly inventory cost:

$$\text{total monthly inventory cost} = C_c \frac{Q_{\text{opt}}}{2} + C_o \frac{D}{Q_{\text{opt}}}$$

$$= (\$0.0625) \frac{(2,000)}{2} + (\$150) \frac{(833.3)}{(2,000)}$$

$$= \$125 \text{ per month}$$

To convert this monthly total cost to an annual cost, we multiply it by 12 (months):

$$\text{total annual inventory cost} = (\$125)(12) = \$1,500$$

This brief example demonstrates that regardless of the time period encompassed by EOQ analysis, the economic order quantity (Q_{opt}) is the same.

The EOQ Model with Noninstantaneous Receipt

The noninstantaneous receipt model relaxes the assumption that Q is received all at once.

A variation of the basic EOQ model is achieved when the assumption that orders are received all at once is relaxed. This version of the EOQ model is known as the **noninstantaneous receipt model**, also referred to as the *gradual usage*, or *production lot size, model*. In this EOQ variation, the order quantity is received gradually over time and the inventory level is depleted at the same time it is being replenished. This is a situation most commonly found when the inventory user is also the producer, as, for example, in a manufacturing operation where a part is produced to use in a larger assembly. This situation can also occur when orders are delivered gradually over time or the retailer and producer of a product are one and the same. The noninstantaneous receipt model is illustrated graphically in Figure 16.6, which highlights the difference between this variation and the basic EOQ model.

FIGURE 16.6

The EOQ model with noninstantaneous order receipt

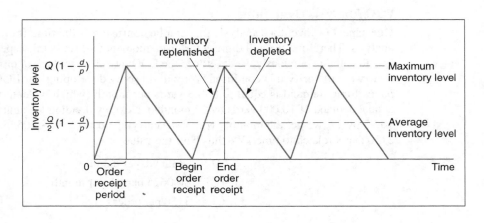

The ordering cost component of the basic EOQ model does not change as a result of the gradual replenishment of the inventory level because it is dependent only on the number of annual orders. However, the carrying cost component is not the same for this model variation because average inventory is different. In the basic EOQ model, average inventory was half the maximum inventory level, or $Q/2$, but in this variation, the maximum inventory level is not simply Q; it is an amount somewhat lower than Q, adjusted for the fact that the order quantity is depleted during the order receipt period.

To determine the average inventory level, we define the following parameters that are unique to this model:

p = daily rate at which the order is received over time, also known as the *production rate*

d = the daily rate at which inventory is demanded

The demand rate cannot exceed the production rate because we are still assuming that no shortages are possible, and if $d = p$, then there is no order size because items are used as fast as they are produced. Thus, for this model, the production rate must exceed the demand rate, or $p > d$.

Figure 16.6 shows that the time required to receive an order is the order quantity divided by the rate at which the order is received, or Q/p. For example, if the order size is 100 units and the production rate, p, is 20 units per day, the order will be received in 5 days. The amount of inventory that will be depleted or used up during this time period is determined by multiplying by the demand rate, or $(Q/p)d$. For example, if it takes 5 days to receive the order and during this time inventory is depleted at the rate of 2 units per day, then a total of 10 units is used. As a result, the maximum amount of inventory that is on hand is the order size minus the amount depleted during the receipt period, computed as follows and shown earlier in Figure 16.6:

$$\text{maximum inventory level} = Q - \frac{Q}{p}d$$

$$= Q\left(1 - \frac{d}{p}\right)$$

Because this is the maximum inventory level, the average inventory level is determined by dividing this amount by 2, as follows:

$$\text{average inventory level} = \frac{1}{2}\left[Q\left(1 - \frac{d}{p}\right)\right]$$

$$= \frac{Q}{2}\left(1 - \frac{d}{p}\right)$$

The total carrying cost, using this function for average inventory, is

$$\text{total carrying cost} = C_c\frac{Q}{2}\left(1 - \frac{d}{p}\right)$$

Thus, the total annual inventory cost is determined according to the following formula:

$$TC = C_o\frac{D}{Q} + C_c\frac{Q}{2}\left(1 - \frac{d}{p}\right)$$

The total inventory cost is a function of two other costs, just as in our previous EOQ model. Thus, the minimum inventory cost occurs when the total cost curve is lowest and where the carrying cost curve and ordering cost curve intersect (see Figure 16.5). Therefore, to find optimal Q_{opt}, we equate total carrying cost with total ordering cost:

$$C_c \frac{Q}{2}\left(1 - \frac{d}{p}\right) = C_o \frac{D}{Q}$$

$$C_c \frac{Q^2}{2}\left(1 - \frac{d}{p}\right) = C_o D$$

$$Q_{opt} = \sqrt{\frac{2C_o D}{C_c(1 - d/p)}}$$

For our previous example we will now assume that the I-75 Carpet Discount Store has its own manufacturing facility, in which it produces Super Shag carpet. We will further assume that the ordering cost, C_o, is the cost of setting up the production process to make Super Shag carpet. Recall that $C_c = \$0.75$ per yard and $D = 10,000$ yards per year. The manufacturing facility operates the same days the store is open (i.e., 311 days) and produces 150 yards of the carpet per day. The optimal order size, the total inventory cost, the length of time to receive an order, the number of orders per year, and the maximum inventory level are computed as follows:

$$C_o = \$150$$
$$C_c = \$0.75 \text{ per unit}$$
$$D = 10,000 \text{ yd.}$$
$$d = \frac{10,000}{311} = 32.2 \text{ yd. per day}$$
$$p = 150 \text{ yd. per day}$$

The optimal order size is determined as follows:

$$Q_{opt} = \sqrt{\frac{2C_o D}{C_c\left(1 - \frac{d}{p}\right)}}$$

$$= \sqrt{\frac{2(150)(10,000)}{0.75\left(1 - \frac{32.2}{150}\right)}}$$

$$Q_{opt} = 2,256.8 \text{ yd.}$$

This value is substituted into the following formula to determine total minimum annual inventory cost:

$$TC_{min} = C_o \frac{D}{Q} + C_c \frac{Q}{2}\left(1 - \frac{d}{p}\right)$$

$$= (150)\frac{(10,000)}{(2,256.8)} + (0.75)\frac{(2,256.8)}{2}\left(1 - \frac{32.2}{150}\right)$$

$$= \$1,329$$

The length of time to receive an order for this type of manufacturing operation is commonly called the length of the *production run*. It is computed as follows:

$$\text{production run length} = \frac{Q}{p} = \frac{2,256.8}{150} = 15.05 \text{ days}$$

The number of orders per year is actually the number of production runs that will be made, computed as follows:

$$\text{number of production runs} = \frac{D}{Q}$$
$$= \frac{10,000}{2,256.8}$$
$$= 4.43 \text{ runs}$$

Finally, the maximum inventory level is computed as follows:

$$\text{maximum inventory level} = Q\left(1 - \frac{d}{p}\right)$$
$$= 2,256.8\left(1 - \frac{32.2}{150}\right)$$
$$= 1,755 \text{ yd.}$$

The EOQ Model with Shortages

The EOQ model with shortages relaxes the assumption that shortages cannot exist.

One of the assumptions of our basic EOQ model is that shortages and back ordering are not allowed. The third model variation that we will describe, the EOQ model with shortages, relaxes this assumption. However, it will be assumed that all demand not met because of inventory shortage can be back-ordered and delivered to the customer later. Thus, all demand is eventually met. The EOQ model with shortages is illustrated in Figure 16.7.

FIGURE 16.7

The EOQ model with shortages

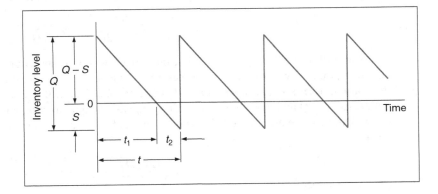

Because back-ordered demand, or shortages, S, are filled when inventory is replenished, the maximum inventory level does not reach Q, but instead a level equal to $Q - S$. It can be seen from Figure 16.7 that the amount of inventory on hand ($Q - S$) decreases as the amount of the shortage increases, and vice versa. Therefore, the cost associated with shortages, which we described earlier in this chapter as primarily the cost of lost sales and lost customer goodwill, has an inverse relationship to carrying costs. As the order size, Q, increases, the carrying cost increases and the shortage cost declines. This relationship between carrying and shortage cost as well as ordering cost is shown in Figure 16.8.

We will forgo the lengthy derivation of the individual cost components of the EOQ model with shortages, which requires the application of plane geometry to the graph in Figure 16.8.

FIGURE 16.8

Cost model with shortages

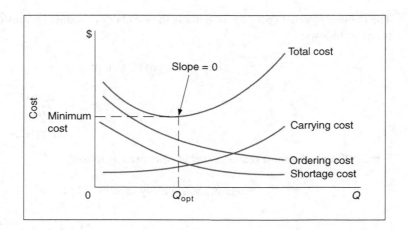

The individual cost functions are provided as follows, where S equals the shortage level and C_s equals the annual per-unit cost of shortages:

$$\text{total shortage cost} = C_s \frac{S^2}{2Q}$$

$$\text{total carrying cost} = C_c \frac{(Q - S)^2}{2Q}$$

$$\text{total ordering cost} = C_o \frac{D}{Q}$$

Combining these individual cost components results in the total inventory cost formula:

$$TC = C_s \frac{S^2}{2Q} + C_c \frac{(Q - S)^2}{2Q} + C_o \frac{D}{Q}$$

You will notice in Figure 16.8 that the three cost component curves do not intersect at a common point, as was the case in the basic EOQ model. As a result, the only way to determine the optimal order size *and the optimal shortage level, S,* is to differentiate the total cost function with respect to Q and S, set the two resulting equations equal to zero, and solve them simultaneously. Doing so results in the following formulas for the optimal order quantity and shortage level:

$$Q_{opt} = \sqrt{\frac{2C_o D}{C_c}\left(\frac{C_s + C_c}{C_s}\right)}$$

$$S_{opt} = Q_{opt}\left(\frac{C_c}{C_c + C_s}\right)$$

For example, we will now assume that the I-75 Carpet Discount Store allows shortages and the shortage cost, C_s, is \$2 per yard per year. All other costs and demand remain the same ($C_c = \$0.75$, $C_o = \$150$, and $D = 10,000$ yd.). The optimal order size and shortage level and total minimum annual inventory cost are computed as follows:

$$C_o = \$150$$
$$C_c = \$0.75 \text{ per yd.}$$
$$C_s = \$2 \text{ per yd.}$$
$$D = 10,000 \text{ yd.}$$

$$Q_{opt} = \sqrt{\frac{2C_oD}{C_c}\left(\frac{C_s + C_c}{C_s}\right)}$$

$$= \sqrt{\frac{2(150)(10,000)}{0.75}\left(\frac{2 + 0.75}{2}\right)}$$

$$= 2,345.2 \text{ yd.}$$

$$S_{opt} = Q_{opt}\left(\frac{C_c}{C_c + C_s}\right)$$

$$= 2,345.2\left(\frac{0.75}{2 + 0.75}\right)$$

$$= 639.6 \text{ yd.}$$

$$TC_{min} = \frac{C_sS^2}{2Q} + \frac{C_c(Q - S)^2}{2Q} + C_o\frac{D}{Q}$$

$$= \frac{(2)(639.6)^2}{2(2,345.2)} + \frac{(0.75)(1,705.6)^2}{2(2,345.2)} + \frac{(150)(10,000)}{2,345.2}$$

$$= \$174.44 + 465.16 + 639.60$$

$$= \$1,279.20$$

Several additional parameters of the EOQ model with shortages can be computed for this example, as follows:

$$\text{number of orders} = \frac{D}{Q} = \frac{10,000}{2,345.2} = 4.26 \text{ orders per year}$$

$$\text{maximum inventory level} = Q - S = 2,345.2 - 639.6 = 1,705.6 \text{ yd.}$$

The time between orders, identified as t in Figure 16.7, is computed as follows:

$$t = \frac{\text{days per year}}{\text{number of orders}} = \frac{311}{4.26} = 73.0 \text{ days between orders}$$

The time during which inventory is on hand, t_1 in Figure 16.7, and the time during which there is a shortage, t_2 in Figure 16.7, during each order cycle can be computed using the following formulas:

$$t_1 = \frac{Q - S}{D}$$

$$= \frac{2,345.2 - 639.6}{10,000}$$

$$= 0.171 \text{ year, or } 53.2 \text{ days}$$

$$t_2 = \frac{S}{D}$$

$$= \frac{639.6}{10,000}$$

$$= 0.064 \text{ year, or } 19.9 \text{ days}$$

Management Science Application

Determining Inventory Ordering Policy at Dell

Dell Inc., the world's largest computer-systems company, bypasses retailers and sells directly to customers via phone or the Internet. After an order is processed, it is sent to one of its assembly plants in Austin, Texas, where the product is built, tested, and packaged within 8 hours.

Dell carries very little components inventory itself. Technology changes occur so fast that holding inventory can be a huge liability; some components lose 0.5% to 2.0% of their value per week. In addition, many of Dell's suppliers are located in Southeast Asia, and their shipping times to Austin range from 7 days for air transport to 30 days for water and ground transport. To compensate for these factors, Dell's suppliers keep inventory in small warehouses called "revolvers" (for revolving inventory), which are a few miles from Dell's assembly plants. Dell keeps very little inventory at its own plants, so it withdraws inventory from the revolvers every few hours, and most of Dell's suppliers deliver to their revolvers three times per week.

The cost of carrying inventory by Dell's suppliers is ultimately reflected in the final price of a computer. Thus, in order to maintain a competitive price advantage in the market, Dell strives to help its suppliers reduce inventory costs. Dell has a vendor-managed inventory (VMI) arrangement with its suppliers, who decide how much to order and when to send their orders to the revolvers. Dell's suppliers order in batches (to offset ordering costs), using a continuous ordering system with a

© Richard Levine/Alamy

batch order size, Q, and a reorder point, R, where R is the sum of the inventory on order and a safety stock. The order size estimate, based on long-term data and forecasts, is held constant. Dell sets target inventory levels for its suppliers—typically 10 days of inventory—and keeps track of how much suppliers deviate from these targets and reports this information back to suppliers so that they can make adjustments accordingly.

Source: Based on R. Kapuscinski, R. Zhang, P. Carbonneau, R. Moore, and B. Reeves, "Inventory Decisions in Dell's Supply Chain," *Interfaces* 34, no. 3 (May–June 2004): 191–205.

EOQ Analysis with QM for Windows

QM for Windows has modules for all the EOQ models we have presented, including the basic model, the noninstantaneous receipt model, and the model with shortages. To demonstrate the capabilities of this program, we will use our basic EOQ example, for which the solution output summary is shown in Exhibit 16.1.

EXHIBIT 16.1

Inventory Results				
I-75 Carpet Discount Store Solution				
Parameter	Value		Parameter	Value
Demand rate(D)	10,000		Optimal order quantity (Q*)	2,000
Setup/Ordering cost(S)	150		Maximum Inventory Level (Imax)	2,000
Holding cost(H)	.75		Average inventory	1,000
Unit cost	0		Orders per period(year)	5
			Annual Setup cost	750
			Annual Holding cost	750
			Unit costs (PD)	0
			Total Cost	1,500

EOQ Analysis with Excel and Excel QM

Exhibit 16.2 shows an Excel spreadsheet set up to perform EOQ analysis for our noninstantaneous receipt model example. The parameters of the model have been input in cells **D3:D8**, and all the formulas for optimal Q, total cost, and so on have been embedded in cells **D10:D14**. Notice that the formula for computing optimal Q in cell D10 is shown on the formula bar at the top of the screen.

EXHIBIT 16.2

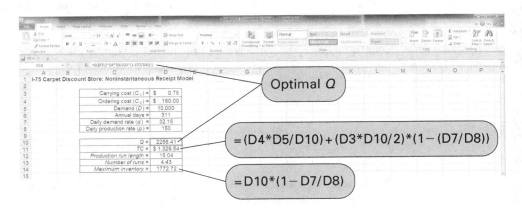

In Chapter 1, we introduced Excel QM, a set of spreadsheet macros that we also used in several other chapters. Excel QM includes a set of spreadsheet macros for "Inventory" that includes EOQ analysis. After Excel QM is activated, the "Excel QM" menu is accessed by clicking on "Add-Ins" on the menu bar at the top of the spreadsheet. Clicking on "Inventory" from this menu results in a Spreadsheet Initialization window, in which you enter the problem title and the form of holding (or carrying) cost. Clicking on "OK" will result in the spreadsheet shown in Exhibit 16.3. Initially, this spreadsheet will have example values in the data cells **B8:B13**. Thus, the first step in using this macro is to type in cells **B8:B13** the data for the noninstantaneous receipt model for our I-75 Carpet Discount Store problem. The model results are computed automatically in cells **B16:B26** from formulas already embedded in the spreadsheet.

EXHIBIT 16.3

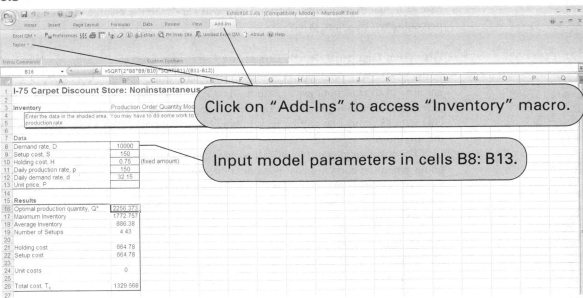

Quantity Discounts

It is often possible for a customer to receive a price discount on an item if a predetermined number of units are ordered. For example, occasionally in the back of a magazine you might see an advertisement for a firm that will produce a coffee mug (or hat) with a company or organizational logo on it, and the price will be $5 per mug if you purchase 100, $4 per mug if you purchase 200, or $3 per mug if you purchase 500 or more. Many manufacturing companies receive price discounts for ordering materials and supplies in high volume, and retail stores receive price discounts for ordering merchandise in large quantities.

Determining whether an order size with a discount is more cost-effective than optimal Q.

The basic EOQ model can be used to determine the optimal order size with quantity discounts; however, the application of the model is slightly altered. The total inventory cost function must now include the purchase price for the order, as follows:

$$TC = C_o \frac{D}{Q} + C_c \frac{Q}{2} + PD$$

where
P = per unit price of the item
D = annual demand

Purchase price was not considered as part of our basic EOQ formulation earlier because it had no real impact on the optimal order size. PD in the foregoing formula is a constant value that would not alter the basic shape of the total cost curve (i.e., the minimum point on the cost curve would still be at the same location, corresponding to the same value of Q). Thus, the optimal order size will be the same, no matter what the purchase price. However, when a discount price is available, it is associated with a specific order size that may be different from the optimal order size, and the customer must evaluate the trade-off between possibly higher carrying costs with the discount quantity versus EOQ cost. As a result, the purchase price does influence the order size decision when a discount is available.

Quantity discounts are evaluated with constant C_c and as a percentage of price.

Quantity discounts can be evaluated using the basic EOQ model under two different scenarios—with constant carrying costs and with carrying costs as a percentage of the purchase price. It is not uncommon for carrying costs to be determined as a percentage of purchase price, although it was not considered as such in our previous basic EOQ model. Carrying cost very well could have been a percentage of purchase price, but it was reflected as a constant value, C_c, in the basic EOQ model because the purchase price was not part of the EOQ formula. However, in the case of a quantity discount, carrying cost will vary with the change in price if it is computed as a percentage of purchase price.

Quantity Discounts with Constant Carrying Costs

In the EOQ cost model with constant carrying costs, the optimal order size, Q_{opt}, is the same, regardless of the discount price. Although total cost decreases with each discount in price because ordering and carrying cost are constant, the optimal order size, Q_{opt}, does not change. The total cost with Q_{opt} must be compared with any lower total cost with a discount price to see which is the minimum.

The following example will illustrate the evaluation of an EOQ model with a quantity discount when the carrying cost is a constant value. Comptek Computers wants to reduce a large stock of personal computers it is discontinuing. It has offered the University Bookstore at Tech a quantity discount pricing schedule if the store will purchase the personal computers in volume, as follows:

Quantity	Price
1–49	$1,400
50–89	1,100
90+	900

The annual carrying cost for the bookstore for a computer is $190, the ordering cost is $2,500, and annual demand for this particular model is estimated to be 200 units. The bookstore wants to determine whether it should take advantage of this discount or order the basic EOQ order size.

First, determine both the optimal order size and the total cost by using the basic EOQ model:

$$C_o = \$2,500$$
$$C_c = \$190 \text{ per unit}$$
$$D = 200$$
$$Q_{opt} = \sqrt{\frac{2C_o D}{C_c}}$$
$$= \sqrt{\frac{2(2,500)(200)}{190}}$$
$$Q_{opt} = 72.5$$

This order size is eligible for the first discount of $1,100; therefore, this price is used to compute total cost, as follows:

$$TC = \frac{C_o D}{Q_{opt}} + C_c \frac{Q_{opt}}{2} + PD$$
$$= \frac{(2,500)(200)}{(72.5)} + (190)\frac{(72.5)}{2} + (1,100)(200)$$
$$TC_{min} = \$233,784$$

Because there is a discount for an order size larger than 72.5, this total cost of $233,784 must be compared with total cost with an order size of 90 and a price of $900, as follows:

$$TC = \frac{C_o D}{Q} + C_c \frac{Q}{2} + PD$$
$$= \frac{(2,500)(200)}{(90)} + \frac{(190)(90)}{2} + (900)(200)$$
$$= \$194,105$$

Because this total cost is lower ($194,105 < $233,784), the maximum discount price should be taken and 90 units ordered.

Quantity Discounts with Constant Carrying Costs as a Percentage of Price

The difference between the model in the previous section and the quantity discount model with carrying cost as a percentage of price is that there is a different optimal order size, Q_{opt}, for each price discount. This requires that the optimal order size with a discount be determined a little differently from the case for a constant carrying cost.

The optimal order size and total cost are determined by using the basic EOQ model for the case with no quantity discount. This total cost value is then compared with the various discount quantity order sizes to determine the minimum cost order size. However, once this minimum cost order size is determined, it must be compared with the EOQ-determined order size for the specific discount price because the EOQ order size, Q_{opt}, will change for every discount level.

Reconsider our previous example, except now assume that the annual carrying cost for a computer at the University Bookstore is 15% of the purchase price. Using the same discount pricing schedule, determine the optimal order size.

The annual carrying cost is determined as follows:

Quantity	Price	Carrying Cost
1–49	$1,400	1,400(.15) = $210
50–89	1,100	1,100(.15) = 165
90+	900	900(.15) = 135

$$C_o = \$2,500$$
$$D = 200 \text{ computers per year}$$

First, compute the optimal order size for the purchase price without a discount and with $C_c = \$210$, as follows:

$$Q_{opt} = \sqrt{\frac{2C_oD}{C_c}}$$

$$= \sqrt{\frac{2(2,500)(200)}{210}}$$

$$Q_{opt} = 69$$

Because this order size exceeds 49 units, it is not feasible for this price, and a lower total cost will automatically be achieved with the first price discount of $1,100. However, the optimal order size will be different for this price discount because carrying cost is no longer constant. Thus, the new order size is computed as follows:

$$Q_{opt} = \sqrt{\frac{2(2,500)(200)}{165}} = 77.8$$

This order size is the true optimum for this price discount instead of the 50 units required to receive the discount price; thus, it will result in the minimum total cost, computed as follows:

$$TC = \frac{C_oD}{Q} + C_c\frac{Q}{2} + PD$$

$$= \frac{(2,500)(200)}{77.8} + 165\frac{(77.8)}{2} + (1,100)(200)$$

$$= \$232,845$$

This cost must still be compared with the total cost for lowest discount price ($900) and order quantity (90 units), computed as follows:

$$TC = \frac{(2,500)(200)}{90} + \frac{(135)(90)}{2} + (900)(200)$$

$$= \$191,630$$

Because this total cost is lower ($191,630 < $232,845), the maximum discount price should be taken and 90 units ordered. However, as before, we still must check to see whether there is a new optimal order size for this discount that will result in an even lower cost. The optimal order size with $C_c = \$135$ is computed as follows:

$$Q_{opt} = \sqrt{\frac{2(2,500)(200)}{135}} = 86.1$$

Because this order size is less than the 90 units required to receive the discount, it is not feasible; thus, the optimal order size is 90 units.

Management Science Application

Quantity Discount Orders at Mars

Mars is one of the world's largest privately owned companies, with over $14 billion in annual sales. It has grown from making and selling buttercream candies door-to-door to a global business spanning 100 countries that includes food, pet care, beverage vending, and electronic payment systems. It produces such well-known products as Mars candies, M&M's, Snickers, and Uncle Ben's rice.

Mars relies on a small number of suppliers for each of the huge number of materials it uses in its products. One way that Mars purchases materials from its suppliers is through online electronic auctions, in which Mars buyers negotiate bids for orders from suppliers. The most important purchases are those of high value and large volume, for which the suppliers provide quantity discounts. The suppliers provide a pricing schedule that includes quantity ranges associated with each price level. Such quantity-discount auctions are tailored (by online brokers) for industries in which volume discounts are common, such as bulk chemicals and agricultural commodities.

A Mars buyer selects the bids that minimize total purchasing costs, subject to several rules: There must be a minimum and maximum number of suppliers so that Mars is not dependent on too few suppliers nor loses quality control by having too

© Eric Carr/Alamy

many; there must be a maximum amount purchased from each supplier to limit the influence of any one supplier; and a minimum amount must be ordered to avoid economically inefficient orders (i.e., less than a full truckload).

Source: Based on G. Hohner, J. Rich, E. Ng, A. Davenport, J. Kalagnanam, H. Lee, and C. An, "Combinatorial and Quantity-Discount Procurement Auctions Benefit Mars, Incorporated and Its Suppliers," *Interfaces* 33, no. 1 (January–February 2003): 23–35.

Quantity Discount Model Solution with QM for Windows

QM for Windows has the capability to perform EOQ analysis with quantity discounts when carrying costs are constant. Exhibit 16.4 shows the solution summary for our University Bookstore example.

EXHIBIT 16.4

Inventory Results

University Bookstore Example Solution

Parameter	Value				Parameter	Value
Demand rate(D)	200	xxxxxxx	xxxxxxx		Optimal order quantity (Q*)	90
Setup/Ordering cost(S)	2,500	xxxxxxx	xxxxxxx		Maximum Inventory Level	90
Holding cost(H)	190	xxxxxxx	xxxxxxx		Average inventory	45
					Orders per period(year)	2.22
	From	To	Price		Annual Setup cost	5,555.56
1	1	49	1,400		Annual Holding cost	8,550
2	50	89	1,100			
3	90	999,999	900		Unit costs (PD)	180,000
					Total Cost	194,105.6

Quantity Discount Model Solution with Excel

It is also possible to use Excel to solve the quantity discount model with constant carrying costs. Exhibit 16.5 shows the Excel solution screen for the University Bookstore example. Notice that the selection of the appropriate order size, Q, that results in the minimum total cost for each discount range is determined by the formulas embedded in cells E8, E9, and E10. For example, the formula for the first quantity discount range, 1–49, is embedded in cell E8 and shown on the formula bar at

EXHIBIT 16.5

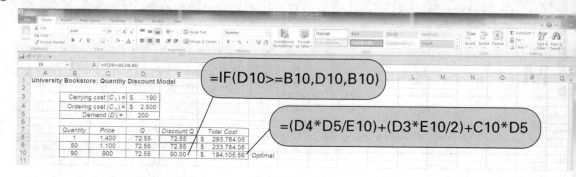

=IF(D10>=B10,D10,B10)

=(D4*D5/E10)+(D3*E10/2)+C10*D5

the top of the screen, $= IF(D8>=B8,D8,B8)$. This means that if the discount order size in cell D8 (i.e., $Q = 72.55$) is greater than or equal to the quantity in cell B8 (i.e., 1), the quantity in cell D8 (72.55) is selected; otherwise, the amount in cell B8 is selected. The formulas in cells E9 and E10 are constructed similarly. The result is that the order quantity for the final discount range, $Q = 90$, is selected.

Reorder Point

The reorder point is the level of inventory at which a new order is placed.

In our presentation of the basic EOQ model in the previous section, we addressed one of the two primary questions related to inventory management: *How much should be ordered?* In this section we will discuss the other aspect of inventory management: *When to order?* The determinant of when to order in a continuous inventory system is the **reorder point**, the inventory level at which a new order is placed.

The concept of lead time is illustrated graphically in Figure 16.9. Notice that the order must be made prior to the time when the level of inventory falls to zero. Because demand is consuming the inventory while the order is being shipped, the order must be made while there is enough inventory in stock to meet demand during the lead-time period. This level of inventory is referred to as the *reorder point* and is so designated in Figure 16.9.

FIGURE 16.9

Reorder point and lead time

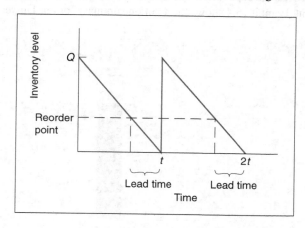

The reorder point for our basic EOQ model with constant demand and a constant lead time to receive an order is relatively straightforward. It is simply equal to the amount demanded during the lead-time period, computed using the following formula:

$$R = dL$$

where
$d =$ demand rate per time period (e.g., daily)
$L =$ lead time

Consider the I-75 Carpet Discount Store example described previously. The store is open 311 days per year. If annual demand is 10,000 yards of Super Shag carpet and the lead time to receive an order is 10 days, the reorder point for carpet is determined as follows:

$$R = dL$$
$$= \left(\frac{10,000}{311}\right)(10)$$
$$= 321.54 \text{ yd.}$$

Thus, when the inventory level falls to approximately 321 yards of carpet, a new order is placed. Notice that the reorder point is not related to the optimal order quantity or any of the inventory costs.

Safety Stocks

In our previous example for determining the reorder point, an order is made when the inventory level reaches the reorder point. During the lead time, the remaining inventory in stock is depleted as a constant demand rate, such that the new order quantity arrives at exactly the same moment as the inventory level reaches zero in Figure 16.9. Realistically, however, demand—and to a lesser extent lead time—is uncertain. The inventory level might be depleted at a slower or faster rate during lead time. This is depicted in Figure 16.10 for uncertain demand and a constant lead time.

FIGURE 16.10

Inventory model with uncertain demand

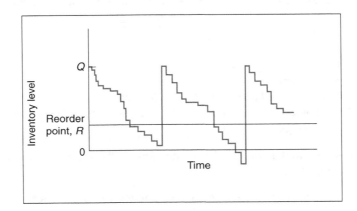

Notice in the second order cycle that a stockout occurs when demand exceeds the available inventory in stock. As a hedge against stockouts when demand is uncertain, a safety (or buffer) stock of inventory is frequently added to the demand during lead time. The addition of a safety stock is shown in Figure 16.11.

FIGURE 16.11

Inventory model with safety stock

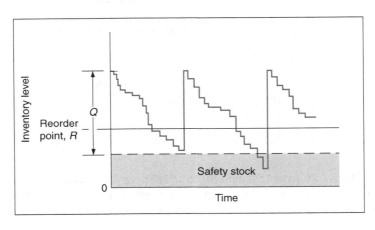

Determining Safety Stock by Using Service Levels

The service level is the probability that the inventory available during the lead time will meet demand.

There are several approaches to determining the amount of the safety stock needed. One of the most popular methods is to establish a safety stock that will meet a specified service level. The service level is the probability that the amount of inventory on hand during the lead time is sufficient to meet expected demand (i.e., the probability that a stockout will not occur). The word *service* is used because the higher the probability that inventory will be on hand, the more likely that customer demand will be met (i.e., the customer can be served). For example, a service level of 90% means that there is a .90 probability that demand will be met during the lead time period and a .10 probability that a stockout will occur. The specification of the service level is typically a policy decision based on a number of factors, including costs for the "extra" safety stock and present and future lost sales if customer demand cannot be met.

Reorder Point with Variable Demand

To compute the reorder point with a safety stock that will meet a specific service level, we will assume that the individual demands during each day of lead time are uncertain and independent and can be described by a normal probability distribution. The average demand for the lead-time period is the sum of the average daily demands for the days of the lead time, which is also the product of the average daily demand multiplied by the lead time. Likewise, the variance of the distribution is the sum of the daily variances for the number of days in the lead-time period. Using these parameters, the reorder point to meet a specific service level can be computed as follows:

$$R = \bar{d}L + Z\sigma_d\sqrt{L}$$

where

$\bar{d}$ = average daily demand
L = lead time
σ_d = the standard deviation of daily demand
Z = number of standard deviations corresponding to the service level probability
$Z\sigma_d\sqrt{L}$ = safety stock

The term $\sigma_d\sqrt{L}$ in this formula for reorder point is the square root of the sum of the daily variances during lead time:

$$\text{variance} = (\text{daily variances}) \times (\text{number of days of lead time}) = \sigma_d^2 L$$
$$\text{standard deviation} = \sqrt{\sigma_d^2 L} = \sigma_d\sqrt{L}$$

The reorder point relative to the service level is shown in Figure 16.12. The service level is the shaded area, or probability, to the left of the reorder point, R.

FIGURE 16.12

Reorder point for a service level

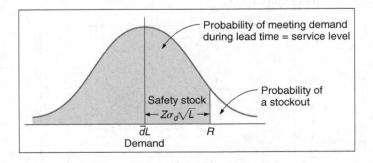

The I-75 Carpet Discount Store sells Super Shag carpet. The average daily customer demand for the carpet stocked by the store is normally distributed, with a mean daily demand of 30 yards and a standard deviation of 5 yards of carpet per day. The lead time for receiving a new order of carpet is 10 days. The store wants a reorder point and safety stock for a service level of 95%, with the probability of a stockout equal to 5%:

$$\bar{d} = 30 \text{ yd. per day}, \ L = 10 \text{ days}, \ \sigma_d = 5 \text{ yd. per day}$$

For a 95% service level, the value of Z (from Table A.1 in Appendix A) is 1.65. The reorder point is computed as follows:

$$R = \bar{d}L + Z\sigma_d\sqrt{L} = 30(10) + (1.65)(5)(\sqrt{10}) = 300 + 26.1 = 326.1 \text{ yd.}$$

The safety stock is the second term in the reorder point formula:

$$\text{safety stock} = Z\sigma_d\sqrt{L} = (1.65)(5)(\sqrt{10}) = 26.1 \text{ yd.}$$

Determining the Reorder Point Using Excel

Excel can be used to determine the reorder point with variable demand. Exhibit 16.6 shows an Excel spreadsheet set up to compute the reorder point for our I-75 Carpet Discount Store example. Notice that the formula for computing the reorder point in cell E7 is shown on the formula bar at the top of the spreadsheet.

EXHIBIT 16.6

Reorder Point with Variable Lead Time

In the model in the previous section for determining the reorder point, we assumed a variable demand rate and a constant lead time. In the case where demand is constant and the lead time varies, we can use a similar formula, as follows:

$$R = d\bar{L} + Zd\sigma_L$$

where
d = constant daily demand
$\bar{L}$ = average lead time
σ_L = standard deviation of lead time
$d\sigma_L$ = standard deviation of demand during lead time
$Zd\sigma_L$ = safety stock

For our previous example of the I-75 Carpet Discount Store, we will now assume that daily demand for Super Shag carpet is a constant 30 yards. Lead time is normally distributed, with a mean of 10 days and a standard deviation of 3 days. The reorder point and safety stock corresponding to a 95% service level are computed as follows:

$$d = 30 \text{ yd. per day}$$
$$\bar{L} = 10 \text{ days}$$
$$\sigma_L = 3 \text{ days}$$
$$Z = 1.65 \text{ for a 95\% service level}$$
$$R = d\bar{L} + Zd\sigma_L = (30)(10) + (1.65)(30)(3) = 300 + 148.5 = 448.5 \text{ yd.}$$

Management Science Application

Establishing Inventory Safety Stocks at Kellogg's

Kellogg's is the world's largest cereal producer and a leading maker of convenience foods. The company started with a single product, Kellogg's Corn Flakes, in 1906, and over the years has developed a product line of other cereals, including Rice Krispies and Corn Pops, as well as convenience foods, such as Pop-Tarts and Nutri-Grain cereal bars. Kellogg's operates five plants in the United States and Canada and seven distribution centers, and it contracts with 15 co-packers to produce or pack some Kellogg's products. Kellogg's must coordinate the production, packaging, inventory, and distribution of roughly 80 cereal products alone at these various facilities.

Kellogg's uses a model called the Kellogg Planning System (KPS) to plan its weekly production, inventory, and distribution decisions. The data used in the model are subject to much uncertainty, and the greatest uncertainty is in product demand. Demand in the first few weeks of a planning horizon is based on customer orders and is fairly accurate; however, demand in the third and fourth weeks may be significantly different from marketing forecasts. However, Kellogg's primary goal is to meet

© Richard Levine/Alamy

customer demand, and in order to achieve this goal, Kellogg's employs safety stocks as a buffer against uncertain demand. The safety stock for a product at a specific production facility in week t is the sum of demands for weeks t and $t + 1$. However, for a product that is being promoted in an advertising campaign, the safety stock is the sum of forecasted demand for a 4-week horizon or longer. KPS has saved Kellogg's many millions of dollars since the mid-1990s. The tactical version of KPS recently helped the company consolidate production capacity, with estimated projected savings of almost $40 million.

Source: Based on G. Brown, J. Keegan, B. Vigus, and K. Wood, "The Kellogg Company Optimizes Production, Inventory, and Distribution," *Interfaces* 31, no. 6 (November–December 2001): 1–15.

Reorder Point with Variable Demand and Lead Time

The final reorder point case we will consider is the case in which both demand and lead time are variables. The reorder point formula for this model is as follows:

$$R = \bar{d}\,\bar{L} + Z\sqrt{\sigma_d^2\bar{L} + \sigma_L^2\bar{d}^2}$$

where

$$\bar{d} = \text{average daily demand}$$
$$\bar{L} = \text{average lead time}$$
$$\sqrt{\sigma_d^2\bar{L} + \sigma_L^2\bar{d}^2} = \text{standard deviation of demand during lead time}$$
$$Z\sqrt{\sigma_d^2\bar{L} + \sigma_L^2\bar{d}^2} = \text{safety stock}$$

Again we will consider the I-75 Carpet Discount Store example, used previously. In this case, daily demand is normally distributed, with a mean of 30 yards and a standard deviation of 5 yards. Lead time is also assumed to be normally distributed, with a mean of 10 days and a standard deviation of 3 days. The reorder point and safety stock for a 95% service level are computed as follows:

$$\bar{d} = 30 \text{ yd./day}$$
$$\sigma_d = 5 \text{ yd./day}$$
$$\bar{L} = 10 \text{ days}$$
$$\sigma_L = 3 \text{ days}$$
$$Z = 1.65 \text{ for a } 95\% \text{ service level}$$
$$R = \bar{d}\,\bar{L} + Z\sqrt{\sigma_d^2\bar{L} + \sigma_L^2\bar{d}^2}$$
$$= (30)(10) + (1.65)\sqrt{(5)^2(10) + (3)^2(30)^2}$$
$$= 300 + 150.8$$
$$R = 450.8 \text{ yd.}$$

Thus, the reorder point is 450.8 yards, with a safety stock of 150.8 yards. Notice that this reorder point encompasses the largest safety stock of our three reorder point examples, which would be anticipated, given the increased variability resulting from variable demand and lead time.

Order Quantity for a Periodic Inventory System

A periodic inventory system uses variable order sizes at fixed time intervals.

Previously we defined a continuous, or fixed–order quantity, inventory system as one in which the order quantity was constant and the time between orders varied. So far, this type of inventory system has been the primary focus of our discussion. The less common **periodic**, or *fixed–time period*, **inventory system** is one in which the time between orders is constant and the order size varies. A drugstore is one example of a business that sometimes uses a fixed-period inventory system. Drugstores stock a number of personal hygiene and health-related products, such as shampoo, toothpaste, soap, bandages, cough medicine, and aspirin. Normally, the vendors that provide these items to the store will make periodic visits—for example, every few weeks or every month—and count the stock of inventory on hand for their products. If the inventory is exhausted or at some predetermined reorder point, a new order will be placed for an amount that will bring the inventory level back up to the desired level. The drugstore managers will generally not monitor the inventory level between vendor visits but instead rely on the vendor to take inventory at the time of the scheduled visit.

A periodic inventory system normally requires a larger safety stock.

A limitation of this type of inventory system is that inventory can be exhausted early in the time period between visits, resulting in a stockout that will not be remedied until the next scheduled order. Alternatively, in a fixed–order quantity system, when inventory reaches a reorder point, an order is made that minimizes the time during which a stockout might exist. As a result of this drawback, a larger safety stock is normally required for the fixed-interval system.

Order Quantity with Variable Demand

If the demand rate and lead time are constant, then the fixed-period model will have a fixed order quantity that will be made at specified time intervals, which is the same as the fixed quantity (EOQ) model under similar conditions. However, as we have already explained, the fixed-period model reacts significantly differently from the fixed–order quantity model when demand is a variable.

The order size for a fixed-period model, given variable daily demand that is normally distributed, is determined by the following formula:

$$Q = \bar{d}(t_b + L) + Z\sigma_d\sqrt{t_b + L} - I$$

where

$$\bar{d} = \text{average demand rate}$$
$$t_b = \text{the fixed time between orders}$$
$$L = \text{lead time}$$
$$\sigma_d = \text{standard deviation of demand}$$
$$Z\sigma_d\sqrt{t_b + L} = \text{safety stock}$$
$$I = \text{inventory in stock}$$

The first term in the preceding formula, $\bar{d}(t_b + L)$, is the average demand during the order cycle time plus the lead time. It reflects the amount of inventory that will be needed to protect against shortages during the entire time from this order to the next and the lead time, until the order is received. The second term, $Z\sigma_d\sqrt{t_b + L}$, is the safety stock for a specific service level, determined in much the same way as previously described for a reorder point. The final term, I, is the amount of inventory on hand when the inventory level is checked and an order is made. We will demonstrate the computation of Q with an example.

The Corner Drug Store stocks a popular brand of sunscreen. The average demand for the sunscreen is 6 bottles per day, with a standard deviation of 1.2 bottles. A vendor for the sunscreen producer checks the drugstore stock every 60 days, and during a particular visit the drugstore had 8 bottles in stock. The lead time to receive an order is 5 days. The order size for this order period that will enable the drugstore to maintain a 95% service level is computed as follows:

$$\bar{d} = 6 \text{ bottles per day}$$
$$\sigma_d = 1.2 \text{ bottles}$$
$$t_b = 60 \text{ days}$$
$$L = 5 \text{ days}$$
$$I = 8 \text{ bottles}$$
$$Z = 1.65 \text{ for } 95\% \text{ service level}$$
$$Q = \bar{d}(t_b + L) + Z\sigma_d\sqrt{t_b + L} - I$$
$$= (6)(60 + 5) + (1.65)(1.2)\sqrt{60 + 5} - 8$$
$$= 398 \text{ bottles}$$

Determining the Order Quantity for the Fixed-Period Model with Excel

Exhibit 16.7 shows an Excel spreadsheet set up to compute the order quantity for the fixed-period model with variable demand for our Corner Drug Store example. Notice that the formula for the order quantity in cell D10 is shown on the formula bar at the top of the spreadsheet.

EXHIBIT 16.7

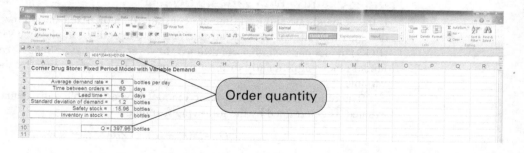

Summary

In this chapter the classical economic order quantity model was presented. The basic form of the EOQ model we discussed included simplifying assumptions regarding order receipt, no shortages, and constant demand known with certainty. By relaxing some of these assumptions, we were able to create increasingly complex but realistic models. These EOQ variations included the reorder point model, the noninstantaneous receipt model, the model with shortages, and models with safety stocks. The techniques for inventory analysis presented in this chapter are not widely used to analyze other types of problems. Conversely, however, many of the techniques presented in this text are used for inventory analysis (in addition to the methods presented in these chapters). The wide use of management science techniques for inventory analysis attests to the importance of inventory to all types of organizations.

Example Problem Solutions

The following example will demonstrate EOQ analysis for the classical model and the model with shortages and back ordering.

Problem Statement

Electronic Village stocks and sells a particular brand of personal computer. It costs the store $450 each time it places an order with the manufacturer for the personal computers. The annual cost of carrying the PCs in inventory is $170. The store manager estimates the annual demand for the PCs will be 1,200 units.

    a. Determine the optimal order quantity and the total minimum inventory cost.

    b. Assume that shortages are allowed and that the shortage cost is $600 per unit per year. Compute the optimal order quantity and the total minimum inventory cost.

Solution

Step 1: (part a): Determine the Optimal Order Quantity

$$D = 1,200 \text{ personal computers}$$
$$C_c = \$170$$
$$C_o = \$450$$

$$Q = \sqrt{\frac{2C_oD}{C_c}}$$
$$= \sqrt{\frac{2(450)(1,200)}{170}}$$
$$= 79.7 \text{ personal computers}$$

$$\text{total cost} = C_c\frac{Q}{2} + C_o\frac{D}{Q}$$
$$= 170\left(\frac{79.7}{2}\right) + 450\left(\frac{1,200}{79.7}\right)$$
$$= \$13,549.91$$

Step 2: (part b): Compute the EOQ with Shortages

$$C_s = \$600$$

$$Q = \sqrt{\frac{2C_oD}{C_c}\left(\frac{C_s + C_c}{C_s}\right)}$$
$$= \sqrt{\frac{2(450)(1,200)}{170}\left(\frac{600 + 170}{600}\right)}$$
$$= 90.3 \text{ personal computers}$$

$$S = Q\left(\frac{C_c}{C_c + C_s}\right)$$
$$= 90.3\left(\frac{170}{170 + 600}\right)$$
$$= 19.9 \text{ personal computers}$$

$$\text{total cost} = \frac{C_sS^2}{2Q} + C_c\frac{(Q - S)^2}{2Q} + \frac{C_oD}{Q}$$
$$= \frac{(600)(19.9)^2}{2(90.3)} + 170\frac{(90.3 - 19.9)^2}{2(90.3)} + 450\left(\frac{1,200}{90.3}\right)$$
$$= \$1,315.65 + 4,665.27 + 5,980.07$$
$$= \$11,960.98$$

Problem Statement

A computer products store stocks color graphics monitors, and the daily demand is normally distributed, with a mean of 1.6 monitors and a standard deviation of 0.4 monitor. The lead time to receive an order from the manufacturer is 15 days. Determine the reorder point that will achieve a 98% service level.

Solution

Step 1: Identify Parameters

$$\overline{d} = 1.6 \text{ monitors per day}$$
$$L = 15 \text{ days}$$
$$\sigma_d = 0.4 \text{ monitor per day}$$
$$Z = 2.05 \text{ (for a 98\% service level)}$$

Step 2: Solve for R

$$R = \overline{d}L + Z\sigma_d\sqrt{L} = (1.6)(15) + (2.05)(0.4)\sqrt{15} = 24 + 3.18 = 27.18 \text{ monitors}$$

Problems

1. Hayes Electronics stocks and sells a particular brand of personal computer. It costs the firm $450 each time it places an order with the manufacturer for the personal computers. The cost of carrying one PC in inventory for a year is $170. The store manager estimates that total annual demand for the computers will be 1,200 units, with a constant demand rate throughout the year. Orders are received within minutes after placement from a local warehouse maintained by the manufacturer. The store policy is never to have stockouts of the PCs. The store is open for business every day of the year except Christmas Day. Determine the following:
   a. The optimal order quantity per order
   b. The minimum total annual inventory costs
   c. The optimal number of orders per year
   d. The optimal time between orders (in working days)

2. Hayes Electronics in Problem 1 assumed with certainty that the ordering cost is $450 per order and the inventory carrying cost is $170 per unit per year. However, the inventory model parameters are frequently only estimates that are subject to some degree of uncertainty. Consider four cases of variation in the model parameters: (a) Both ordering cost and carrying cost are 10% less than originally estimated, (b) both ordering cost and carrying cost are 10% higher than originally estimated, (c) ordering cost is 10% higher and carrying cost is 10% lower than originally estimated, and (d) ordering cost is 10% lower and carrying cost is 10% higher than originally estimated. Determine the optimal order quantity and total inventory cost for each of the four cases. Prepare a table with values from all four cases and compare the sensitivity of the model solution to changes in parameter values.

3. A firm is faced with the attractive situation in which it can obtain immediate delivery of an item it stocks for retail sale. The firm has therefore not bothered to order the item in any systematic way. Recently, however, profits have been squeezed due to increasing competitive pressures, and the firm has retained a management consultant to study its inventory management. The consultant has determined that the various costs associated with making an order for the item stocked are approximately $30 per order. She has also determined that the costs of carrying the item in inventory amount to approximately $20 per unit per year (primarily direct storage costs and foregone profit on investment in inventory). Demand for the item is reasonably constant over time,

and the forecast is for 19,200 units per year. When an order is placed for the item, the entire order is immediately delivered to the firm by the supplier. The firm operates 6 days a week plus a few Sundays, or approximately 320 days per year. Determine the following:

a. The optimal order quantity per order
b. The total annual inventory costs
c. The optimal number of orders to place per year
d. The number of operating days between orders, based on the optimal number of orders

4. The Western Jeans Company purchases denim from Cumberland Textile Mills. The Western Jeans Company uses 35,000 yards of denim per year to make jeans. The cost of ordering denim from the textile company is $500 per order. It costs Western $0.35 per yard annually to hold a yard of denim in inventory. Determine the optimal number of yards of denim the Western Jeans Company should order, the minimum total annual inventory cost, the optimal number of orders per year, and the optimal time between orders.

5. The Metropolitan Book Company purchases paper from the Atlantic Paper Company. Metropolitan produces magazines and paperbacks that require 1,215,000 pounds of paper per year. The cost per order for the company is $1,200; the cost of holding 1 pound of paper in inventory is $0.08 per year. Determine the following:

a. The economic order quantity
b. The minimum total annual cost
c. The optimal number of orders per year
d. The optimal time between orders

6. The Simple Simon Bakery produces fruit pies for freezing and subsequent sale. The bakery, which operates 5 days per week, 52 weeks per year, can produce pies at the rate of 64 pies per day. The bakery sets up the pie production operation and produces until a predetermined number (Q) of pies has been produced. When not producing pies, the bakery uses its personnel and facilities for producing other bakery items. The setup cost for a production run of fruit pies is $500. The cost of holding frozen pies in storage is $5 per pie per year. The annual demand for frozen fruit pies, which is constant over time, is 5,000 pies. Determine the following:

a. The optimal production run quantity (Q)
b. The total annual inventory costs
c. The optimal number of production runs per year
d. The optimal cycle time (time between run starts)
e. The run length, in working days

7. The Pedal Pusher Bicycle Shop operates 7 days per week, closing only on Christmas Day. The shop pays $300 for a particular bicycle purchased from the manufacturer. The annual holding cost per bicycle is estimated to be 25% of the dollar value of inventory. The shop sells an average of 25 bikes per week. Frequently, the dealer does not have a bike in stock when a customer purchases it, and the bike is back-ordered. The dealer estimates his shortage cost per unit back-ordered, on an annual basis, to be $250 due to lost future sales (and profits). The ordering cost for each order is $100. Determine the optimal order quantity and shortage level and the total minimum cost.

8. The Petroco Company uses a highly toxic chemical in one of its manufacturing processes. It must have the product delivered by special cargo trucks designed for safe shipment of chemicals. As such, ordering (and delivery) costs are relatively high, at $2,600 per order. The chemical product is packaged in 1-gallon plastic containers. The cost of holding the chemical in storage is $50 per gallon per year. The annual demand for the chemical, which is constant over time, is 2,000 gallons per year. The lead time from time of order placement until receipt is 10 days. The company operates 310 working days per year. Compute the optimal order quantity, the total minimum inventory cost, and the reorder point.

9. The Big Buy Supermarket stocks Munchies Cereal. Demand for Munchies is 4,000 boxes per year (365 days). It costs the store $60 per order of Munchies, and it costs $0.80 per box per year to keep the cereal in stock. Once an order for Munchies is placed, it takes 4 days to receive the order from a food distributor. Determine the following:
   a. The optimal order size
   b. The minimum total annual inventory cost
   c. The reorder point

10. The Wood Valley Dairy makes cheese to supply to stores in its area. The dairy can make 250 pounds of cheese per day (365 days per year), and the demand at area stores is 180 pounds per day. Each time the dairy makes cheese, it costs $125 to set up the production process. The annual cost of carrying a pound of cheese in a refrigerated storage area is $12. Determine the optimal order size and the minimum total annual inventory cost.

11. The Rainwater Brewery produces Rainwater Light Beer, which it stores in barrels in its warehouse and supplies to its distributors on demand. The demand for Rainwater is 1,500 barrels of beer per day (365 days per year). The brewery can produce 2,000 barrels of Rainwater per day. It costs $6,500 to set up a production run for Rainwater. Once it is brewed, the beer is stored in a refrigerated warehouse at an annual cost of $50 per barrel. Determine the economic order quantity and the minimum total annual inventory cost.

12. The purchasing manager for the Atlantic Steel Company must determine a policy for ordering coal to operate 12 converters. Each converter requires exactly 5 tons of coal per day to operate, and the firm operates 360 days per year. The purchasing manager has determined that the ordering cost is $80 per order and the cost of holding coal is 20% of the average dollar value of inventory held. The purchasing manager has negotiated a contract to obtain the coal for $12 per ton for the coming year.
   a. Determine the optimal quantity of coal to receive in each order.
   b. Determine the total inventory-related costs associated with the optimal ordering policy (do not include the cost of the coal).
   c. If 5 days of lead time are required to receive an order of coal, how much coal should be on hand when an order is placed?

13. In Problem 1 in Chapter 15, the Saki motorcycle dealer in Minneapolis–St. Paul orders the Saki Super TXII motorcycle it sells from the manufacturer in Japan. Using the 3-month moving average forecast of demand for January as the monthly forecast for the next year, an annual carrying cost of $375, an ordering cost of $3,200, and a lead time for receiving an order of 1 month, determine the optimal order size, the minimum total annual inventory cost, the optimal time between orders, the number of orders, and the reorder point.

14. In Problem 2 in Chapter 15, Carpet City orders Soft Shag carpet from its own mill. Using the 3-month moving average forecast of demand for month 9 as the monthly forecasts for all of next year, a production rate at the mill of 1,200 yards per day (with the mill operating 260 days per year), an annual carrying cost of $0.63, a $425 cost for setting up a production run and delivering the carpet to the store, and a lead time for receiving an order of 7 days, determine the optimal order size, the minimum total annual inventory cost, and the reorder point (given that Carpet City is open 360 days per year).

15. In Problem 30 in Chapter 15, the supplier receives shipments of partially completed laptops from its manufacturing facility in Southeast Asia, which has maximum production rate of 200 units per day. Using the forecast of annual demand developed in that problem, an annual carrying cost of $115.75 (which includes an average obsolescence cost), a shipping cost from Asia of $6,500 per shipment, and a lead time for receiving an order of 25 days, determine the optimal order size, the minimum total annual inventory cost, the maximum inventory level, and the reorder point (given that the Bell assembly operation operates 365 days per year).

16. Craftwood Furniture Company is a U.S.–based furniture manufacturer that offshored all of its actual manufacturing operations to China about a decade ago. It set up a distribution center in Hong Kong, from which the company ships its items to the United States on container ships. The company learned early on that it could not rely on local Chinese freight forwarders to arrange for sufficient containers for the company's shipments, so it contracted to purchase containers from a Taiwanese manufacturer and then sell them to shipping companies at the U.S. ports the containers are shipped to. Craftwood needs 715 containers each year. It costs $265 to hold a container at its distribution center, and it costs $6,000 to process and receive an order for the containers. The cost of not having sufficient containers and delaying a shipment is $14,000 per container. Determine the optimal order size, minimum total annual inventory cost, and maximum shortage level.

17. The Pacific Lumber Company and Mill processes 10,000 logs annually, operating 250 days per year. Immediately upon receiving an order, the logging company's supplier begins delivery to the lumber mill, at a rate of 60 logs per day. The lumber mill has determined that the ordering cost is $1,600 per order and the cost of carrying logs in inventory before they are processed is $15 per log on an annual basis. Determine the following:
    a. The optimal order size
    b. The total inventory cost associated with the optimal order quantity
    c. The number of operating days between orders
    d. The number of operating days required to receive an order

18. The Roadking Tire Store sells a brand of tires called the Roadrunner. The annual demand from the store's customers for Roadrunner tires is 3,700. The cost to order tires from the tire manufacturer is $420 per order. The annual carrying cost is $1.75 per tire. The store allows shortages, and the annual shortage cost per tire is $4. Determine the optimal order size, maximum shortage level, and minimum total annual inventory cost.

19. The Laurel Creek Lawn Shop sells Fastgro Fertilizer. The annual demand for the fertilizer is 270,000 pounds. The cost to order the fertilizer from the Fastgro Company is $105 per order. The annual carrying cost is $0.25 per pound. The store operates with shortages, and the annual shortage cost is $0.70 per pound. Compute the optimal order size, minimum total annual inventory cost, and maximum shortage level.

20. Videoworld is a discount store that sells color televisions. The annual demand for color television sets is 400. The cost per order from the manufacturer is $650. The carrying cost is $45 per set each year. The store has an inventory policy that allows shortages. The shortage cost per set is estimated at $60. Determine the following:
    a. The optimal order size
    b. The maximum shortage level
    c. The minimum total annual inventory cost

21. The University Bookstore at Tech stocks the required textbook for Management Science 2405. The demand for this text is 1,200 copies per year. The cost of placing an order is $350, and the annual carrying cost is $2.75 per book. If a student requests the book and it is not in stock, the student will likely go to the privately owned Tech Bookstore. It is likely that the student will not buy books at the University Bookstore in the future; thus the shortage cost to the University Bookstore is estimated to be $45 per book. Determine the optimal order size, the maximum shortage level, and the total inventory cost.

22. The A-to-Z Office Supply Company is open from 8:00 A.M. to 6:00 P.M., and it receives 200 calls per day for delivery orders. It costs A-to-Z $20 to send out its trucks to make deliveries. The company estimates that each minute a customer spends waiting for an order costs A-to-Z $0.20 in lost sales.

a. How frequently should A-to-Z send out its delivery trucks each day? Indicate the total daily cost of deliveries.

b. If a truck could carry only six orders, how often would deliveries be made, and what would be the cost?

23. The Union Street Microbrewery makes 1220 Union beer, which it bottles and sells in its adjoining restaurant and by the case. It costs $1,700 to set up, brew, and bottle a batch of the beer. The annual cost to store the beer in inventory is $1.25 per bottle. The annual demand for the beer is 18,000 bottles, and the brewery has the capacity to produce 30,000 bottles annually.

a. Determine the optimal order quantity, the total annual inventory cost, the number of production runs per year, and the maximum inventory level.

b. If the microbrewery has only enough storage space to hold a maximum of 2,500 bottles of beer in inventory, how will that affect total inventory costs?

24. Eurotronics is a European manufacturer of electronic components. During the course of a year, it requires container cargo space on ships leaving Hamburg bound for the United States, Mexico, South America, and Canada. Annually, the company needs 160,000 cubic feet of cargo space. The cost of reserving cargo space is $7,000, and the cost of holding cargo space is $0.80 per cubic foot. Determine how much storage space Eurotronics should optimally order, the total cost, and how many times per year it should place orders to reserve space.

25. The Summer Outdoor Furniture Company produces wooden lawn chairs. The annual demand from its store customers is 17,400 chairs per year. The transport and handling costs are $2,600 each time a shipment of chairs is delivered to stores from its warehouse. The annual carrying cost is $3.75 per chair.

a. Determine the optimal order quantity and minimum total annual cost.

b. The company is thinking about relocating its warehouse closer to its customers, which would reduce transport and handling costs to $1,900 per order but increase carrying costs to $4.50 per chair per year. Should the company relocate based on inventory costs?

26. The Spruce Creek Vegetable Farm produces organically grown greenhouse tomatoes that are sold to area grocery stores. The annual demand for Spruce Creek's tomatoes is 270,000 pounds. The farm is able to produce 305,000 pounds annually. The cost to transport the tomatoes from the farm to the stores is $620 per load. The annual carrying cost is $0.12 per pound.

a. Compute the optimal order size, the maximum inventory level, and the total minimum cost.

b. If Spruce Creek can increase production capacity to 360,000 tomatoes per year, will it reduce total inventory cost?

27. The Uptown Kiln is an importer of ceramics from overseas. It has arranged to purchase a particular type of ceramic pottery from a Korean artisan. The artisan makes the pottery in 120-unit batches and will ship only that exact number of units. The transportation and handling cost of a shipment is $7,600 (not including the unit cost). The Uptown Kiln estimates its annual demand to be 900 units. What storage and handling cost per unit does it need to achieve in order to minimize its inventory cost?

28. The I-75 Carpet Discount Store has an annual demand of 10,000 yards of Super Shag carpet. The annual carrying cost for a yard of this carpet is $0.75, and the ordering cost is $150. The carpet manufacturer normally charges the store $8 per yard for the carpet; however, the manufacturer has offered a discount price of $6.50 per yard if the store will order 5,000 yards. How much should the store order, and what will be the total annual inventory cost for that order quantity?

29. The Fifth Quarter Bar buys Old World draft beer by the barrel from a local distributor. The bar has an annual demand of 900 barrels, which it purchases at a price of $205 per barrel. The annual carrying cost is 12% of the price, and the cost per order is $160. The distributor has offered

the bar a reduced price of $190 per barrel if it will order a minimum of 300 barrels. Should the bar take the discount?

30. The bookstore at State University purchases from a vendor sweatshirts emblazoned with the school name and logo. The vendor sells the sweatshirts to the store for $38 apiece. The cost to the bookstore for placing an order is $120, and the carrying cost is 25% of the average annual inventory value. The bookstore manager estimates that 1,700 sweatshirts will be sold during the year. The vendor has offered the bookstore the following volume discount schedule:

Order Size	Discount %
1–299	0
300–499	2
500–799	4
800+	5

The bookstore manager wants to determine the bookstore's optimal order quantity, given the foregoing quantity discount information.

31. Determine the optimal order quantity of sweatshirts and total annual cost in Problem 30 if the carrying cost is a constant $8 per sweatshirt per year.

32. The office manager for the Gotham Life Insurance Company orders letterhead stationery from an office products firm in boxes of 500 sheets. The company uses 6,500 boxes per year. Annual carrying costs are $3 per box, and ordering costs are $28. The following discount price schedule is provided by the office supply company:

Order Quantity (boxes)	Price per Box
200–999	$16
1,000–2,999	14
3,000–5,999	13
6,000+	12

Determine the optimal order quantity and the total annual inventory cost.

33. Determine the optimal order quantity and total annual inventory cost for boxes of stationery in Problem 32 if the carrying cost is 20% of the price of a box of stationery.

34. The 23,000-seat City Coliseum houses the local professional ice hockey, basketball, indoor soccer, and arena football teams, as well as various trade shows, wrestling and boxing matches, tractor pulls, and circuses. Coliseum vending annually sells large quantities of soft drinks and beer in plastic cups, with the name of the coliseum and the various team logos on them. The local container cup manufacturer that supplies the cups in boxes of 100 has offered coliseum management the following discount price schedule for cups:

Order Quantity (boxes)	Price per Box
2,000–6,999	$47
7,000–11,999	43
12,000–19,999	41
20,000+	38

The annual demand for cups is 2.3 million, the annual carrying cost per box of cups is $1.90, and the ordering cost is $320. Determine the optimal order quantity and total annual inventory cost.

35. Community Hospital orders latex sanitary gloves from a hospital supply firm. The hospital expects to use 40,000 pairs of gloves per year. The cost to order and to have the gloves delivered is $180. The annual carrying cost is $0.18 per pair of gloves. The hospital supply firm offers the following quantity discount pricing schedule:

Quantity	Price
0–9,999	$0.34
10,000–19,999	0.32
20,000–29,999	0.30
30,000–39,999	0.28
40,000–49,999	0.26
50,000+	0.24

Determine the optimal order size for the hospital.

36. Tracy McCoy is the office administrator for the department of management science at Tech. The faculty uses a lot of printer paper, and although Tracy is constantly reordering, paper frequently runs out. She orders the paper from the university central stores. Several faculty members have determined that the lead time to receive an order is normally distributed, with a mean of 2 days and a standard deviation of 0.5 day. The faculty has also determined that daily demand for the paper is normally distributed, with a mean of 2 packages and a standard deviation of 0.8 package. What reorder point should Tracy use in order not to run out 99% of the time?

37. Determine the optimal order quantity and total annual inventory cost for cups in Problem 34 if the carrying cost is 5% of the price of a box of cups.

38. The amount of denim used daily by the Western Jeans Company in its manufacturing process to make jeans is normally distributed, with an average of 3,000 yards of denim and a standard deviation of 600 yards. The lead time required to receive an order of denim from the textile mill is a constant 6 days. Determine the safety stock and reorder point if the Western Jeans Company wants to limit the probability of a stockout and work stoppage to 5%.

39. In Problem 38, what level of service would a safety stock of 2,000 yards provide?

40. The Atlantic Paper Company produces paper from wood pulp ordered from a lumber products firm. The paper company's daily demand for wood pulp is a constant 8,000 pounds. Lead time is normally distributed, with an average of 7 days and a standard deviation of 1.6 days. Determine the reorder point if the paper company wants to limit the probability of a stockout and work stoppage to 2%.

41. The Uptown Bar and Grill serves Rainwater draft beer to its customers. The daily demand for beer is normally distributed, with an average of 18 gallons and a standard deviation of 4 gallons. The lead time required to receive an order of beer from the local distributor is normally distributed, with a mean of 3 days and a standard deviation of 0.8 day. Determine the safety stock and reorder point if the restaurant wants to maintain a 90% service level. What would be the increase in the safety stock if a 95% service level were desired?

42. In Problem 41, the manager of the Uptown Bar and Grill has negotiated with the beer distributor for the lead time to receive orders to be a constant 3 days. What effect does this have on the reorder point developed in Problem 41 for a 90% service level?

43. The daily demand for Sunlight paint at the Rainbow Paint Store in East Ridge is normally distributed, with a mean of 26 gallons and a standard deviation of 10 gallons. The lead time for receiving an order of paint from the Sunlight distributor is 9 days. Because this is the only paint store in East Ridge, the manager is interested in maintaining only a 75% service level. What reorder point should be used to meet this service level? The manager subsequently has learned that a new paint store will open soon in East Ridge, which has prompted her to increase the service level to 95%. What reorder point will maintain this service level?

44. PM Computers assembles personal computers from generic components. It purchases its color monitors from a manufacturer in Taiwan; thus, there is a long and uncertain lead time for receiving orders. Lead time is normally distributed, with a mean of 25 days and a standard deviation of 10 days. Daily demand is also normally distributed, with a mean of 2.5 monitors and a standard deviation of 1.2 monitors. Determine the safety stock and reorder point corresponding to a 90% service level.

45. PM Computers in Problem 44 is considering purchasing monitors from an American manufacturer that would guarantee a lead time of 8 days, instead of the Taiwanese company. Determine the new reorder point, given this lead time, and identify the factors that would enter into the decision to change manufacturers.

46. The Corner Drug Store fills prescriptions for a popular children's antibiotic, amoxicillin. The daily demand for amoxicillin is normally distributed, with a mean of 200 ounces and a standard deviation of 80 ounces. The vendor for the pharmaceutical firm that supplies the drug calls the drugstore pharmacist every 30 days to check the inventory of amoxicillin. During a call, the druggist indicated that the store had 60 ounces of the antibiotic in stock. The lead time to receive an order is 4 days. Determine the order size that will enable the drugstore to maintain a 95% service level.

47. The Fast Service Food Mart stocks frozen pizzas in a refrigerated display case. The average daily demand for the pizzas is normally distributed, with a mean of 8 pizzas and a standard deviation of 2.5 pizzas. A vendor for a packaged food distributor checks the market's inventory of frozen foods every 10 days, and during a particular visit, there were no pizzas in stock. The lead time to receive an order is 3 days. Determine the order size for this order period that will result in a 99% service level. During the vendor's following visit, there were 5 frozen pizzas in stock. What is the order size for the next order period?

48. The Impanema Restaurant stocks a red Brazilian table wine it purchases from a wine merchant in a nearby city. The daily demand for the wine at the restaurant is normally distributed, with a mean of 18 bottles and a standard deviation of 4 bottles. The wine merchant sends a representative to check the restaurant's wine cellar every 30 days, and during a recent visit, there were 25 bottles in stock. The lead time to receive an order is 2 days. The restaurant manager has requested an order size that will enable him to limit the probability of a stockout to 2%. Determine the order size.

49. The concession stand at the Blacksburg High School stadium sells slices of pizza during soccer games. Concession stand sales are a primary source of revenue for high school athletic programs, so the athletic director wants to sell as much food as possible. However, any pizza not sold is given away to the players, coaches, and referees, or it is thrown away. The athletic director wants to determine a reorder point that will meet, not exceed, the demand for pizza. Pizza sales are normally distributed, with a mean of 6 pizzas per hour and a standard deviation of 2.5 pizzas. The pizzas are ordered from Pizza Town restaurant, and the mean delivery time is 30 minutes, with a standard deviation of 8 minutes.
    a. Currently, the concession stand places an order when it has 1 pizza left. What level of service does this result in?
    b. What should the reorder point be to have a 98% service level?

Case Problem

THE NORTHWOODS GENERAL STORE

The Northwoods General Store in Vermont sells a variety of outdoor clothing items and equipment and several food products at its modern but rustic-looking retail store. Its food products include salmon and maple syrup. The store also runs a lucrative catalog operation. One of its most popular products is maple syrup, which is sold in metal half-gallon cans with a picture of the store on the front.

Maple syrup was one of the first products the store produced and sold, and it continues to do so. Setting up the syrup-making equipment to produce a batch of syrup costs $450. Storing the syrup for sales throughout the year is a tricky process because the syrup must be kept in a temperature-controlled facility. The annual cost of

carrying a gallon of the syrup is $15. Based on past sales data, the store has forecasted a demand of 7,500 gallons of maple syrup for the coming year. The store can produce approximately 100 gallons of syrup per day during the maple syrup season, which runs from February through May.

Because of the short season when the store can actually get sap out of trees, it obviously must produce enough during this 4-month season to meet demand for the whole year. Specifically, store management would like a production and inventory schedule that minimizes costs and indicates when during the year they need to start operating the syrup-making facility full time on a daily basis to meet demand for the remaining 8 months.

Develop a syrup production and inventory schedule for the Northwoods General Store.

Case Problem

THE TEXANS STADIUM STORE

The Fort Worth Texans have won three Super Bowls in the past 5 years, including two in a row the past 2 years. As a result, sportswear such as hats, sweatshirts, sweatpants, and jackets with the Texans logo are particularly popular in Texas. The Texans operate a stadium store outside the football stadium where they play. It is near a busy highway, so the store has heavy customer traffic throughout the year, not just on game days. In addition, the stadium holds high school or college football and soccer games almost every week in the fall, and it holds baseball games in the spring and summer. The most popular single item the stadium store sells is a blue and silver baseball cap with the Texans logo embroidered on it in a special and very attractive manner. The cap has an elastic headband inside it, which automatically conforms to different head sizes. However, the store has had a difficult time keeping the cap in stock, especially during the time between the placement and receipt of an order. Often customers come to the store just for the hat; when it is not in stock, customers are visibly upset, and the store management believes they tend to go to competing stores to purchase their Texans clothing. To rectify this problem, the store manager, Jenny Jones, would like to develop an inventory control policy that would ensure that

customers would be able to purchase the cap 99% of the time they asked for it. Jenny has accumulated the following demand data for the cap for a 30-week period:

Week	Demand	Week	Demand	Week	Demand
1	38	11	28	21	52
2	51	12	41	22	38
3	25	13	37	23	49
4	60	14	44	24	46
5	35	15	45	25	47

Week	Demand	Week	Demand	Week	Demand
6	42	16	56	26	41
7	29	17	62	27	39
8	46	18	53	28	50
9	55	19	46	29	28
10	19	20	41	30	34

(Demand includes actual sales plus a record of the times a cap has been requested but not available and an estimate of the number of times a customer wanted a cap when it was not available but did not ask for it.)

The store purchases the hats from a small manufacturing company in Jamaica. The shipments from Jamaica are somewhat erratic, with a lead time anywhere between

10 days and 1 month. The following lead time data (in days) were accumulated during approximately a 1-year period:

Order	Lead Time	Order	Lead Time
1	12	11	14
2	16	12	16
3	25	13	23
4	18	14	18
5	10	15	21
6	30	16	19
7	24	17	17
8	19	18	16
9	17	19	22
10	15	20	18

In the past, Jenny placed an order whenever the stock got down to 150 caps. To what level of service does this reorder point correspond? What would the reorder point and safety stock need to be to attain the desired service level? Discuss how Jenny might determine the order size for caps and what additional, if any, information would be needed to determine the order size.

Case Problem

THE A-TO-Z OFFICE SUPPLY COMPANY

Christine Yamaguchi is the manager of the A-to-Z Office Supply Company in Charlotte. The company attempts to gain an advantage over its competitors by providing quality customer service, which includes prompt delivery of orders by truck or van and always being able to meet customer demand from its stock. In order to achieve this degree of customer service, A-to-Z must stock a large volume of items on a daily basis at a central warehouse and at three retail stores in the city and suburbs. Christine maintains these inventory levels by borrowing cash on a daily basis from the First Piedmont Bank. She estimates that for the coming fiscal year, the company's demand for cash to pay for inventory will be $17,000 per day for 305 working days. Any money she borrows during the year must be repaid with interest by the end of the year. The annual interest rate currently charged by the bank is 9%. Any

time Christine takes out a loan to purchase inventory, the bank charges the company a loan origination fee of $1,200 plus 2¼ points (2.25% of the amount borrowed).

Christine often uses EOQ analysis to determine optimal amounts of inventory to order for different office supplies. Now she is wondering if she can use the same type of analysis to determine an optimal borrowing policy. Determine the amount of the loan Christine should secure from the bank, the total annual cost of the company's borrowing policy, and the number of loans the company should obtain during the year. Also determine the level of cash on hand at which the company should apply for a new loan, given that it takes 15 days for a loan to be processed by the bank.

Suppose the bank offers Christine a discount, as follows: On any loan amount equal to or greater than $500,000, the bank will lower the number of points charged on the loan origination fee from 2.25% to 2.00%. What would the company's optimal loan amount be?

Case Problem

DIAMANT FOODS COMPANY

Diamant Foods Company produces a variety of food products, including a line of candies. One of its most popular candy items is Divine Diamonds, a bag of a dozen individually wrapped diamond-shaped candies made primarily from a blend of dark and milk chocolates, macadamia nuts, and a blend of heavy cream fillings. The

item is relatively expensive, so Diamant Foods produces it only for its eastern market, encompassing urban areas such as New York, Atlanta, Philadelphia, and Boston. The item is not sold in grocery or discount stores but mainly in specialty shops and specialty groceries, candy stores, and department stores. Diamant Foods supplies the candy to a single food distributor, which has several warehouses on the East Coast. The candy is shipped in cases of 60 bags of the candy per case. Diamonds sell well, despite the fact that they are expensive, at $9.85 per bag (wholesale). Diamant uses high-quality, fresh ingredients and does not store large stocks of the candy in inventory for very long periods of time.

Diamant's distributor believes that demand for the candy follows a seasonal pattern. It has collected demand data (i.e., cases sold) for Diamonds from its warehouses and the stores it supplies for the past 3 years, as follows:

Month	Demand (cases)		
	Year 1	Year 2	Year 3
January	192	212	228
February	210	223	231
March	205	216	226
April	260	252	293
May	228	235	246
June	172	220	229
July	160	209	217
August	147	231	226
September	256	263	302
October	342	370	411
November	251	260	279
December	273	277	293

The distributor must hold the candy inventory in climate-controlled warehouses and be careful in handling it. The annual carrying cost is $116 per case. Diamonds must be shipped a long distance from the manufacturer to the distributor, and in order to keep the candy as fresh as possible, trucks must be air-conditioned, shipments must be direct, and shipments are often less than a truckload. As a result, the ordering cost is $4,700.

Diamant Foods makes Diamonds from three primary ingredients it orders from different suppliers: dark and milk chocolate, macadamia nuts, and a special heavy cream filling. Except for its unique shape, a Diamond is almost like a chocolate truffle. Each Diamond weighs 1.2 ounces and requires 0.70 ounce of blended chocolates, 0.50 ounce of macadamia nuts, and 0.40 ounce of filling to produce (including spillage and waste). Diamant Foods orders chocolate, nuts, and filling from its suppliers by the pound. The annual ordering cost is $5,700 for chocolate, and the annual carrying cost is $0.45 per pound. The ordering cost for macadamia nuts is $6,300, and the annual carrying cost is $0.63 per pound. The ordering cost for filling is $4,500, and the annual carrying cost is $0.55 per pound.

Each of the suppliers offers the candy manufacturer a quantity discount price schedule for the ingredients, as follows:

Chocolate		Macadamia Nuts		Filling	
Price	Quantity (lb.)	Price	Quantity (lb.)	Price	Quantity (lb.)
$3.05	0–50,000	$6.50	0–30,000	$1.50	0–40,000
2.90	50,001–100,000	6.25	30,001–70,000	1.35	40,001–80,000
2.75	100,001–150,000	5.95	70,001+	1.25	80,001+
2.60	150,001+				

Determine the inventory order quantity for Diamant's distributor. Compare the optimal order quantity with a seasonally adjusted forecast for demand. Does the order quantity seem adequate to meet the seasonal demand pattern for Diamonds (i.e., is it likely that shortages or excessive inventories will occur)? Can you identify the causes of the seasonal demand pattern for Diamonds? Determine the inventory order quantity for each of the three primary ingredients that Diamant Foods orders from its suppliers.

Index